T0205598

Communications
in Computer and Information Science 1716

Editorial Board Members

Joaquim Filipe 📵
Polytechnic Institute of Setúbal, Setúbal, Portugal

Ashish Ghosh
Indian Statistical Institute, Kolkata, India

Raquel Oliveira Prates 📵
Federal University of Minas Gerais (UFMG), Belo Horizonte, Brazil

Lizhu Zhou
Tsinghua University, Beijing, China

More information about this series at https://link.springer.com/bookseries/7899

Edward Szczerbicki · Krystian Wojtkiewicz ·
Sinh Van Nguyen · Marcin Pietranik ·
Marek Krótkiewicz (Eds.)

Recent Challenges in Intelligent Information and Database Systems

14th Asian Conference, ACIIDS 2022
Ho Chi Minh City, Vietnam, November 28–30, 2022
Proceedings

 Springer

Editors
Edward Szczerbicki ⓘ
University of Newcastle Australia
Newcastle, NSW, Australia

Sinh Van Nguyen ⓘ
International University - VNU-HCM
Ho Chi Minh City, Vietnam

Marek Krótkiewicz ⓘ
Wrocław University of Science
and Technology
Wrocław, Poland

Krystian Wojtkiewicz ⓘ
Wrocław University of Science
and Technology
Wrocław, Poland

Marcin Pietranik ⓘ
Wrocław University of Science
and Technology
Wrocław, Poland

ISSN 1865-0929   ISSN 1865-0937 (electronic)
Communications in Computer and Information Science
ISBN 978-981-19-8233-0   ISBN 978-981-19-8234-7 (eBook)
https://doi.org/10.1007/978-981-19-8234-7

© The Editor(s) (if applicable) and The Author(s), under exclusive license
to Springer Nature Singapore Pte Ltd. 2022
This work is subject to copyright. All rights are reserved by the Publisher, whether the whole or part of the material is concerned, specifically the rights of translation, reprinting, reuse of illustrations, recitation, broadcasting, reproduction on microfilms or in any other physical way, and transmission or information storage and retrieval, electronic adaptation, computer software, or by similar or dissimilar methodology now known or hereafter developed.
The use of general descriptive names, registered names, trademarks, service marks, etc. in this publication does not imply, even in the absence of a specific statement, that such names are exempt from the relevant protective laws and regulations and therefore free for general use.
The publisher, the authors, and the editors are safe to assume that the advice and information in this book are believed to be true and accurate at the date of publication. Neither the publisher nor the authors or the editors give a warranty, expressed or implied, with respect to the material contained herein or for any errors or omissions that may have been made. The publisher remains neutral with regard to jurisdictional claims in published maps and institutional affiliations.

This Springer imprint is published by the registered company Springer Nature Singapore Pte Ltd.
The registered company address is: 152 Beach Road, #21-01/04 Gateway East, Singapore 189721, Singapore

Preface

ACIIDS 2022 was the 14th event in a series of international scientific conferences on research and applications in the field of intelligent information and database systems. The aim of ACIIDS 2022 was to provide an international forum for research workers with scientific backgrounds in the technology of intelligent information and database systems and its various applications. The ACIIDS 2022 conference was co-organized by the International University - Vietnam National University HCMC (Vietnam) and the Wrocław University of Science and Technology (Poland) in cooperation with the IEEE SMC Technical Committee on Computational Collective Intelligence, the European Research Center for Information Systems (ERCIS), Al-Farabi Kazakh National University (Kazakhstan), the University of Newcastle (Australia), Yeungnam University (South Korea), Quang Binh University (Vietnam), Leiden University (The Netherlands), Universiti Teknologi Malaysia (Malaysia), Nguyen Tat Thanh University (Vietnam), BINUS University (Indonesia), the Committee on Informatics of the Polish Academy of Sciences (Poland) and Vietnam National University, Hanoi (Vietnam). ACIIDS 2022 was scheduled to be held in Almaty, Kazakhstan, during June 6–9, 2022. However, due to the unstable political situation, the conference was moved to Ho Chi Minh City, Vietnam, and was conducted as a hybrid event during 28–30 November 2022.

The ACIIDS conference series is already well established. The 12th and 13th events were planned to take place in Phuket (Thailand). However, the global COVID-19 pandemic resulted in both editions of the conference being held online in virtual space. We were, therefore, pleased to be able to hold ACIIDS 2022 in person, whilst still providing an option for people participate online.

This volume contains 58 peer-reviewed papers selected for poster presentation from 406 submissions, with each submission receiving at least three reviews in a single blind process. Papers included in this volume cover the following topics: data mining and machine learning methods, advanced data mining techniques and applications, intelligent and contextual systems, natural language processing, network systems and applications, computational imaging and vision, decision support and control systems, and data modeling and processing for Industry 4.0.

The accepted and presented papers focus on new trends and challenges facing the intelligent information and database systems community. The presenters showed how research work could stimulate novel and innovative applications. We hope that you found these results useful and inspiring for future research.

We would like to express our sincere thanks to the honorary chairs for their support: Arkadiusz Wójs (Rector of Wrocław University of Science and Technology, Poland) and Zhanseit Tuymebayev (Rector of Al-Farabi Kazakh National University, Kazakhstan). We would like to thank the keynote speakers for their world-class plenary speeches: Tzung-Pei Hong from the National University of Kaohsiung (Taiwan), Michał Woźniak from the Wrocław University of Science and Technology (Poland), Minh-Triet Tran from the University of Science and the John von Neumann Institute, VNU-HCM (Vietnam), and Minh Le Nguyen from the Japan Advanced Institute of Science and Technology (Japan).

We cordially thank our main sponsors: International University - Vietnam National University HCMC, Hitachi Vantara Vietnam Co., Ltd, Polish Ministry of Education and Science, and Wrocław University of Science and Technology (Poland), as well as all of the aforementioned cooperating universities and organizations. Our special thanks are also due to Springer for publishing the proceedings and to all the other sponsors for their kind support.

We are grateful to the Special Session Chairs, Organizing Chairs, Publicity Chairs, Liaison Chairs, and Local Organizing Committee for their work towards the conference. We sincerely thank all the members of the international Program Committee for their valuable efforts in the review process, which helped us to select the highest quality papers for the conference. We cordially thank all the authors and the other conference participants for their valuable contributions. The conference would not have been possible without their support. Thanks are also due to the many experts who contributed to the event being a success.

November 2022

Edward Szczerbicki
Krystian Wojtkiewicz
Sinh Van Nguyen
Marcin Pietranik
Marek Krótkiewicz

Organization

Honorary Chairs

Arkadiusz Wójs
Wrocław University of Science and Technology, Poland

Zhanseit Tuymebayev
Al-Farabi Kazakh National University, Kazakhstan

Conference Chairs

Tien Khoa Tran
International University - Vietnam National University HCMC, Vietnam

Ngoc Thanh Nguyen
Wrocław University of Science and Technology, Poland

Ualsher Tukeyev
Al-Farabi Kazakh National University, Kazakhstan

Program Chairs

Tzung-Pei Hong
National University of Kaohsiung, Taiwan

Edward Szczerbicki
University of Newcastle, Australia

Bogdan Trawiński
Wrocław University of Science and Technology, Poland

Steering Committee

Ngoc Thanh Nguyen (Chair)
Wrocław University of Science and Technology, Poland

Longbing Cao
University of Science and Technology Sydney, Australia

Suphamit Chittayasothorn
King Mongkut's Institute of Technology Ladkrabang, Thailand

Ford Lumban Gaol
Bina Nusantara University, Indonesia

Tu Bao Ho
Japan Advanced Institute of Science and Technology, Japan

Tzung-Pei Hong
National University of Kaohsiung, Taiwan

Dosam Hwang
Yeungnam University, South Korea

Bela Stantic
Griffith University, Australia

Geun-Sik Jo
Inha University, South Korea

Hoai An Le-Thi	University of Lorraine, France
Toyoaki Nishida	Kyoto University, Japan
Leszek Rutkowski	Częstochowa University of Technology, Poland
Ali Selamat	Universiti Teknologi Malaysia, Malaysia

Special Session Chairs

Van Sinh Nguyen	International University - Vietnam National University HCMC, Vietnam
Krystian Wojtkiewicz	Wrocław University of Science and Technology, Poland
Bogumiła Hnatkowska	Wrocław University of Science and Technology, Poland
Madina Mansurova	Al-Farabi Kazakh National University, Kazakhstan

Doctoral Track Chairs

Marek Krótkiewicz	Wrocław University of Science and Technology, Poland
Marcin Pietranik	Wrocław University of Science and Technology, Poland
Thi Thuy Loan Nguyen	International University - Vietnam National University HCMC, Vietnam
Paweł Sitek	Kielce University of Technology, Poland

Liaison Chairs

Ford Lumban Gaol	Bina Nusantara University, Indonesia
Quang-Thuy Ha	VNU-University of Engineering and Technology, Vietnam
Mong-Fong Horng	National Kaohsiung University of Applied Sciences, Taiwan
Dosam Hwang	Yeungnam University, South Korea
Le Minh Nguyen	Japan Advanced Institute of Science and Technology, Japan
Ali Selamat	Universiti Teknologi Malaysia, Malaysia

Organizing Chairs

| Van Sinh Nguyen | International University - Vietnam National University HCMC, Vietnam |
| Krystian Wojtkiewicz | Wrocław University of Science and Technology, Poland |

Publicity Chairs

Thanh Tung Tran — International University - Vietnam National University HCMC, Vietnam

Marek Kopel — Wrocław University of Science and Technology, Poland

Marek Krótkiewicz — Wrocław University of Science and Technology, Poland

Webmaster

Marek Kopel — Wroclaw University of Science and Technology, Poland

Local Organizing Committee

Le Van Canh — International University - Vietnam National University HCMC, Vietnam

Le Hai Duong — International University - Vietnam National University HCMC, Vietnam

Le Duy Tan — International University - Vietnam National University HCMC, Vietnam

Marcin Jodłowiec — Wrocław University of Science and Technology, Poland

Patient Zihisire Muke — Wrocław University of Science and Technology, Poland

Thanh-Ngo Nguyen — Wrocław University of Science and Technology, Poland

Rafał Palak — Wrocław University of Science and Technology, Poland

Keynote Speakers

Tzung-Pei Hong — National University of Kaohsiung, Taiwan

Michał Woźniak — Wrocław University of Science and Technology, Poland

Minh-Triet Tran — University of Science and John von Neumann Institute, VNU-HCM, Vietnam

Minh Le Nguyen — Japan Advanced Institute of Science and Technology, Japan

Special Sessions Organizers

ACMLT 2022: Special Session on Awareness Computing Based on Machine Learning

Yung-Fa Huang	Chaoyang University of Technology, Taiwan
Rung Ching Chen	Chaoyang University of Technology, Taiwan

ADMTA 2022: Special Session on Advanced Data Mining Techniques and Applications

Chun-Hao Chen	Tamkang University, Taiwan
Bay Vo	Ho Chi Minh City University of Technology, Vietnam
Tzung-Pei Hong	National University of Kaohsiung, Taiwan

AIIS 2022: Special Session on Artificial Intelligence in Information Security

Shynar Mussiraliyeva	Al-Farabi Kazakh National University, Kazakhstan
Batyrkhan Omarov	Al-Farabi Kazakh National University, Kazakhstan

BMLLC 2022: Special Session on Bio-modeling and Machine Learning in Prediction of Metastasis in Lung Cancer

Andrzej Swierniak	Silesian University of Technology, Poland
Rafal Suwinski	Institute of Oncology, Poland

BTAS 2022: Special Session on Blockchain Technology and Applications for Sustainability

Chien-wen Shen	National Central University, Taiwan
Ping-yu Hsu	National Central University, Taiwan

CIV 2022: Special Session on Computational Imaging and Vision

Manish Khare	Dhirubhai Ambani Institute of Information and Communication Technology, India
Prashant Srivastava	NIIT University, India
Om Prakash	HNB Garwal University, India
Jeonghwan Gwak	Korea National University of Transportation, South Korea

DMPI-APP 2022: Special Session on Data Modelling and Processing Air Pollution Prevention

Marek Krótkiewicz	Wrocław University of Science and Technology, Poland
Krystian Wojtkiewicz	Wrocław University of Science and Technology, Poland
Hoai Phuong Ha	UiT The Arctic University of Norway, Norway
Jean-Marie Lepioufle	Norwegian Institute for Air Research, Norway

DMSN 2022: Special Session on Data Management in Sensor Networks

Khouloud Salameh	American University of Ras Al Khaimah, UAE
Yannis Manolopoulos	Open University of Cyprus, Cyprus
Richard Chbeir	Université de Pau et des Pays de l'Adour (UPPA), France

ICxS 2022: Special Session on Intelligent and Contextual Systems

Maciej Huk	Wrocław University of Science and Technology, Poland
Keun Ho Ryu	Ton Duc Thang University, Vietnam
Rashmi Dutta Baruah	Indian Institute of Technology Guwahati, India
Tetsuji Kuboyama	Gekushuin University, Japan
Goutam Chakraborty	Iwate Prefectural University, Japan
Seo-Young Noh	Chungbuk National University, South Korea
Chao-Chun Chen	National Cheng Kung University, Taiwan

IPROSE 2022: Special Session on Intelligent Problem Solving for Smart Real World

Doina Logofătu	Frankfurt University of Applied Sciences, Germany
Costin Bădică	University of Craiova, Romania
Florin Leon	Gheorghe Asachi Technical University of Iaşi, Romania
Mirjana Ivanovic	University of Novi Sad, Serbia

ISCEC 2022: Special Session on Intelligent Supply Chains and e-Commerce

Arkadiusz Kawas	Łukasiewicz Research Network – The Institute of Logistics and Warehousing, Poland
Bartłomiej Pierański	Poznan University of Economics and Business, Poland

ISMSFuN 2022: Special Session on Intelligent Solutions for Management and Securing Future Networks

Grzegorz Kołaczek	Wrocław University of Science and Technology, Poland
Łukasz Falas	Wrocław University of Science and Technology, Poland
Patryk Schauer	Wrocław University of Science and Technology, Poland
Krzysztof Gierłowski	Gdańsk University of Technology, Poland

LPAIA 2022: Special Session on Learning Patterns/Methods in Current AI Applications

Urszula Boryczka	University of Silesia, Poland
Piotr Porwik	University of Silesia, Poland

LRLSTP 2022: Special Session on Low Resource Languages Speech and Text Processing

Ualsher Tukeyev	Al-Farabi Kazakh National University, Kazakhstan
Orken Mamyrbayev	Al-Farabi Kazakh National University, Kazakhstan

MISSI 2022: Satellite Workshop on Multimedia and Network Information Systems

Kazimierz Choroś	Wrocław University of Science and Technology, Poland
Marek Kopel	Wrocław University of Science and Technology, Poland
Mikołaj Leszczuk	AGH University of Science and Technology, Poland
Maria Trocan	Institut Supérieur d'Electronique de Paris, France

MLLSCP 2022: Special Session on Machine Learning in Large-Scale and Complex Problems

Jan Kozak	University of Economics in Katowice, Poland
Przemysław Juszczuk	University of Economics in Katowice, Poland
Barbara Probierz	University of Economics in Katowice, Poland

MLND 2022: Special Session on Machine Learning Prediction of Neurodegenerative Diseases

Andrzej W. Przybyszewski	Polish-Japanese Academy of Information Technology, Poland
Jerzy P. Nowacki	Polish-Japanese Academy of Information Technology, Poland

MMAML 2022: Special Session on Multiple Model Approach to Machine Learning

Tomasz Kajdanowicz	Wrocław University of Science and Technology, Poland
Edwin Lughofer	Johannes Kepler University Linz, Austria
Bogdan Trawiński	Wrocław University of Science and Technology, Poland

PPiBDA 2022: Special Session on Privacy Protection in Big Data Approaches

Abdul Razaque	International Information Technology University, Kazakhstan
Saleem Hariri	University of Arizona, USA
Munif Alotaibi	Shaqra University, Saudi Arabia
Fathi Amsaad	Eastern Michigan University, USA
Bandar Alotaibi	University of Tabuk, Saudi Arabia

SIOTBDTA 2022: Special Session on Smart IoT and Big Data Technologies and Applications

Octavian Postolache	ISCTE-University Institute of Lisbon, Portugal
Madina Mansurova	Al-Farabi Kazakh National University, Kazakhstan

Senior Program Committee

Ajith Abraham	Machine Intelligence Research Labs, USA
Jesus Alcala-Fdez	University of Granada, Spain
Lionel Amodeo	University of Technology of Troyes, France
Ahmad Taher Azar	Prince Sultan University, Saudi Arabia
Thomas Bäck	Leiden University, Netherlands
Costin Badica	University of Craiova, Romania
Ramazan Bayindir	Gazi University, Turkey
Abdelhamid Bouchachia	Bournemouth University, UK
David Camacho	Universidad Autonoma de Madrid, Spain
Leopoldo Eduardo Cardenas-Barron	Tecnologico de Monterrey, Mexico

Oscar Castillo	Tijuana Institute of Technology, Mexico
Nitesh Chawla	University of Notre Dame, USA
Rung-Ching Chen	Chaoyang University of Technology, Taiwan
Shyi-Ming Chen	National Taiwan University of Science and Technology, Taiwan
Simon Fong	University of Macau, Macau SAR
Hamido Fujita	Iwate Prefectural University, Japan
Mohamed Gaber	Birmingham City University, UK
Marina L. Gavrilova	University of Calgary, Canada
Danicla Godoy	ISISTAN Research Institute, Argentina
Fernando Gomide	University of Campinas, Brazil
Manuel Grana	University of the Basque Country, Spain
Claudio Gutierrez	Universidad de Chile, Chile
Francisco Herrera	University of Granada, Spain
Tzung-Pei Hong	National University of Kaohsiung, Taiwan
Dosam Hwang	Yeungnam University, South Korea
Mirjana Ivanovic	University of Novi Sad, Serbia
Janusz Jeżewski	Institute of Medical Technology and Equipment ITAM, Poland
Piotr Jedrzejowicz	Gdynia Maritime University, Poland
Kang-Hyun Jo	University of Ulsan, South Korea
Jason J. Jung	Chung-Ang University, South Korea
Janusz Kacprzyk	Systems Research Institute, Polish Academy of Sciences, Poland
Nikola Kasabov	Auckland University of Technology, New Zealand
Muhammad Khurram Khan	King Saud University, Saudi Arabia
Frank Klawonn	Ostfalia University of Applied Sciences, Germany
Joanna Kolodziej	Cracow University of Technology, Poland
Józef Korbicz	University of Zielona Gora, Poland
Ryszard Kowalczyk	Swinburne University of Technology, Australia
Bartosz Krawczyk	Virginia Commonwealth University, USA
Ondrej Krejcar	University of Hradec Králové, Czech Republic
Adam Krzyzak	Concordia University, Canada
Mark Last	Ben-Gurion University of the Negev, Israel
Hoai An Le Thi	University of Lorraine, France
Kun Chang Lee	Sungkyunkwan University, South Korea
Edwin Lughofer	Johannes Kepler University Linz, Austria
Nezam Mahdavi-Amiri	Sharif University of Technology, Iran
Yannis Manolopoulos	Open University of Cyprus, Cyprus
Klaus-Robert Müller	Technical University of Berlin, Germany
Saeid Nahavandi	Deakin University, Australia

Grzegorz J. Nalepa	AGH University of Science and Technology, Poland
Ngoc-Thanh Nguyen	Wrocław University of Science and Technology, Poland
Dusit Niyato	Nanyang Technological University, Singapore
Yusuke Nojima	Osaka Prefecture University, Japan
Manuel Núñez	Universidad Complutense de Madrid, Spain
Jeng-Shyang Pan	Fujian University of Technology, China
Marcin Paprzycki	Systems Research Institute, Polish Academy of Sciences, Poland
Bernhard Pfahringer	University of Waikato, New Zealand
Hoang Pham	Rutgers University, USA
Tao Pham Dinh	INSA Rouen, France
Radu-Emil Precup	Politehnica University of Timisoara, Romania
Leszek Rutkowski	Częstochowa University of Technology, Poland
Juergen Schmidhuber	Swiss AI Lab IDSIA, Switzerland
Björn Schuller	University of Passau, Germany
Ali Selamat	Universiti Teknologi Malaysia, Malaysia
Andrzej Skowron	Warsaw University, Poland
Jerzy Stefanowski	Poznań University of Technology, Poland
Edward Szczerbicki	University of Newcastle, Australia
Ryszard Tadeusiewicz	AGH University of Science and Technology, Poland
Muhammad Atif Tahir	National University of Computing and Emerging Sciences, Pakistan
Bay Vo	Ho Chi Minh City University of Technology, Vietnam
Gottfried Vossen	University of Münster, Germany
Dinh Duc Anh Vu	Vietnam National University HCMC, Vietnam
Lipo Wang	Nanyang Technological University, Singapore
Junzo Watada	Waseda University, Japan
Michał Woźniak	Wrocław University of Science and Technology, Poland
Farouk Yalaoui	University of Technology of Troyes, France
Sławomir Zadrożny	Systems Research Institute, Polish Academy of Sciences, Poland
Zhi-Hua Zhou	Nanjing University, China

Program Committee

Muhammad Abulaish	South Asian University, India
Bashar Al-Shboul	University of Jordan, Jordan
Toni Anwar	Universiti Teknologi Petronas, Malaysia

Taha Arbaoui	University of Technology of Troyes, France
Mehmet Emin Aydin	University of the West of England, UK
Amelia Badica	University of Craiova, Romania
Kambiz Badie	ICT Research Institute, Iran
Hassan Badir	École Nationale des Sciences Appliquées de Tanger, Morocco
Zbigniew Banaszak	Warsaw University of Technology, Poland
Dariusz Barbucha	Gdynia Maritime University, Poland
Maumita Bhattacharya	Charles Sturt University, Australia
Leon Bobrowski	Białystok University of Technology, Poland
Bülent Bolat	Yildiz Technical University, Turkey
Mariusz Boryczka	University of Silesia, Poland
Urszula Boryczka	University of Silesia, Poland
Zouhaier Brahmia	University of Sfax, Tunisia
Stephane Bressan	National University of Singapore, Singapore
Peter Brida	University of Žilina, Slovakia
Piotr Bródka	Wroclaw University of Science and Technology, Poland
Grażyna Brzykcy	Poznan University of Technology, Poland
Robert Burduk	Wrocław University of Science and Technology, Poland
Aleksander Byrski	AGH University of Science and Technology, Poland
Dariusz Ceglarek	WSB University in Poznań, Poland
Somchai Chatvichienchai	University of Nagasaki, Japan
Chun-Hao Chen	Tamkang University, Taiwan
Leszek J. Chmielewski	Warsaw University of Life Sciences, Poland
Kazimierz Choroś	Wrocław University of Science and Technology, Poland
Kun-Ta Chuang	National Cheng Kung University, Taiwan
Dorian Cojocaru	University of Craiova, Romania
Jose Alfredo Ferreira Costa	Federal University of Rio Grande do Norte (UFRN), Brazil
Ireneusz Czarnowski	Gdynia Maritime University, Poland
Piotr Czekalski	Silesian University of Technology, Poland
Theophile Dagba	University of Abomey-Calavi, Benin
Tien V. Do	Budapest University of Technology and Economics, Hungary
Rafał Doroz	University of Silesia, Poland
El-Sayed M. El-Alfy	King Fahd University of Petroleum and Minerals, Saudi Arabia
Keiichi Endo	Ehime University, Japan

Sebastian Ernst   AGH University of Science and Technology,
                           Poland
Nadia Essoussi   University of Carthage, Tunisia
Usef Faghihi   Université du Québec à Trois-Rivières, Canada
Dariusz Frejlichowski   West Pomeranian University of Technology,
                           Szczecin, Poland
Blanka Frydrychova Klimova   University of Hradec Králové, Czech Republic
Janusz Getta   University of Wollongong, Australia
Daniela Gifu   Alexandru Ioan Cuza University of Iaşi, Romania
Gergo Gombos   Eötvös Loránd University, Hungary
Manuel Grana   University of the Basque Country, Spain
Janis Grundspenkis   Riga Technical University, Latvia
Dawit Haile   Addis Ababa University, Ethiopia
Marcin Hernes   Wrocław University of Business and Economics,
                           Poland
Koichi Hirata   Kyushu Institute of Technology, Japan
Bogumiła Hnatkowska   Wrocław University of Science and Technology,
                           Poland
Bao An Mai Hoang   Vietnam National University HCMC, Vietnam
Huu Hanh Hoang   Posts and Telecommunications Institute of
                           Technology, Vietnam
Van-Dung Hoang   Quang Binh University, Vietnam
Jeongkyu Hong   Yeungnam University, South Korea
Yung-Fa Huang   Chaoyang University of Technology, Taiwan
Maciej Huk   Wrocław University of Science and Technology,
                           Poland
Kha Tu Huynh   Vietnam National University HCMC, Vietnam
Sanjay Jain   National University of Singapore, Singapore
Khalid Jebari   LCS Rabat, Morocco
Joanna Jędrzejowicz   University of Gdańsk, Poland
Przemysław Juszczuk   University of Economics in Katowice, Poland
Krzysztof Juszczyszyn   Wrocław University of Science and Technology,
                           Poland
Mehmet Karaata   Kuwait University, Kuwait
Rafał Kern   Wrocław University of Science and Technology,
                           Poland
Zaheer Khan   University of the West of England, UK
Marek Kisiel-Dorohinicki   AGH University of Science and Technology,
                           Poland
Attila Kiss   Eötvös Loránd University, Hungary
Shinya Kobayashi   Ehime University, Japan
Grzegorz Kołaczek   Wrocław University of Science and Technology,
                           Poland

Marek Kopel	Wrocław University of Science and Technology, Poland
Jan Kozak	University of Economics in Katowice, Poland
Adrianna Kozierkiewicz	Wrocław University of Science and Technology, Poland
Dalia Kriksciuniene	Vilnius University, Lithuania
Dariusz Król	Wrocław University of Science and Technology, Poland
Marek Krótkiewicz	Wrocław University of Science and Technology, Poland
Marzena Kryszkiewicz	Warsaw University of Technology, Poland
Jan Kubicek	VSB -Technical University of Ostrava, Czech Republic
Tetsuji Kuboyama	Gakushuin University, Japan
Elżbieta Kukla	Wrocław University of Science and Technology, Poland
Marek Kulbacki	Polish-Japanese Academy of Information Technology, Poland
Kazuhiro Kuwabara	Ritsumeikan University, Japan
Annabel Latham	Manchester Metropolitan University, UK
Tu Nga Le	Vietnam National University HCMC, Vietnam
Yue-Shi Lee	Ming Chuan University, Taiwan
Florin Leon	Gheorghe Asachi Technical University of Iasi, Romania
Chunshien Li	National Central University, Taiwan
Horst Lichter	RWTH Aachen University, Germany
Tony Lindgren	Stockholm University, Sweden
Igor Litvinchev	Nuevo Leon State University, Mexico
Doina Logofatu	Frankfurt University of Applied Sciences, Germany
Lech Madeyski	Wrocław University of Science and Technology, Poland
Bernadetta Maleszka	Wrocław University of Science and Technology, Poland
Marcin Maleszka	Wrocław University of Science and Technology, Poland
Tamás Matuszka	Eötvös Loránd University, Hungary
Michael Mayo	University of Waikato, New Zealand
Héctor Menéndez	University College London, UK
Mercedes Merayo	Universidad Complutense de Madrid, Spain
Jacek Mercik	WSB University in Wrocław, Poland
Radosław Michalski	Wrocław University of Science and Technology, Poland

Peter Mikulecky	University of Hradec Králové, Czech Republic
Miroslava Mikusova	University of Žilina, Slovakia
Marek Milosz	Lublin University of Technology, Poland
Jolanta Mizera-Pietraszko	Opole University, Poland
Dariusz Mrozek	Silesian University of Technology, Poland
Leo Mrsic	IN2data Data Science Company, Croatia
Agnieszka Mykowiecka	Institute of Computer Science, Polish Academy of Sciences, Poland
Pawel Myszkowski	Wrocław University of Science and Technology, Poland
Huu-Tuan Nguyen	Vietnam Maritime University, Vietnam
Le Minh Nguyen	Japan Advanced Institute of Science and Technology, Japan
Loan T. T. Nguyen	Vietnam National University HCMC, Vietnam
Quang-Vu Nguyen	Korea-Vietnam Friendship Information Technology College, Vietnam
Thai-Nghe Nguyen	Cantho University, Vietnam
Thi Thanh Sang Nguyen	Vietnam National University HCMC, Vietnam
Van Sinh Nguyen	Vietnam National University HCMC, Vietnam
Agnieszka Nowak-Brzezińska	University of Silesia, Poland
Alberto Núñez	Universidad Complutense de Madrid, Spain
Tarkko Oksala	Aalto University, Finland
Mieczysław Owoc	Wrocław University of Business and Economics
Panos Patros	University of Waikato, New Zealand
Maciej Piasecki	Wrocław University of Science and Technology, Poland
Bartłomiej Pierański	Poznan University of Economics and Business, Poland
Dariusz Pierzchała	Military University of Technology, Poland
Marcin Pietranik	Wrocław University of Science and Technology, Poland
Elias Pimenidis	University of the West of England, UK
Jaroslav Pokorný	Charles University in Prague, Czech Republic
Nikolaos Polatidis	University of Brighton, UK
Elvira Popescu	University of Craiova, Romania
Piotr Porwik	University of Silesia in Katowice, Poland
Petra Poulova	University of Hradec Králové, Czech Republic
Małgorzata Przybyła-Kasperek	University of Silesia, Poland
Paulo Quaresma	Universidade de Evora, Portugal
David Ramsey	Wrocław University of Science and Technology, Poland
Mohammad Rashedur Rahman	North South University, Bangladesh
Ewa Ratajczak-Ropel	Gdynia Maritime University, Poland

Sebastian A. Rios	University of Chile, Chile
Keun Ho Ryu	Chungbuk National University, South Korea
Daniel Sanchez	University of Granada, Spain
Rafał Scherer	Częstochowa University of Technology, Poland
Donghwa Shin	Yeungnam University, South Korea
Andrzej Sieminski	Wrocław University of Science and Technology, Poland
Dragan Simic	University of Novi Sad, Serbia
Bharat Singh	Universiti Teknologi PETRONAS, Malaysia
Paweł Sitck	Kielce University of Technology, Poland
Krzysztof Slot	Łódź University of Technology, Poland
Adam Słowik	Koszalin University of Technology, Poland
Vladimir Sobeslav	University of Hradec Králové, Czech Republic
Kamran Soomro	University of the West of England, UK
Zenon A. Sosnowski	Białystok University of Technology, Poland
Bela Stantic	Griffith University, Australia
Stanimir Stoyanov	University of Plovdiv "Paisii Hilendarski", Bulgaria
Ja-Hwung Su	Cheng Shiu University, Taiwan
Libuse Svobodova	University of Hradec Králové, Czech Republic
Jerzy Swiątek	Wrocław University of Science and Technology, Poland
Andrzej Swierniak	Silesian University of Technology, Poland
Julian Szymański	Gdańsk University of Technology, Poland
Yasufumi Takama	Tokyo Metropolitan University, Japan
Zbigniew Telec	Wrocław University of Science and Technology, Poland
Dilhan Thilakarathne	Vrije Universiteit Amsterdam, Netherlands
Satoshi Tojo	Japan Advanced Institute of Science and Technology, Japan
Diana Trandabat	Alexandru Ioan Cuza University of Iaşi, Romania
Bogdan Trawiński	Wrocław University of Science and Technology, Poland
Maria Trocan	Institut Superieur d'Electronique de Paris, France
Krzysztof Trojanowski	Cardinal Stefan Wyszyński University in Warsaw, Poland
Ualsher Tukeyev	Al-Farabi Kazakh National University, Kazakhstan
Olgierd Unold	Wrocław University of Science and Technology, Poland
Jørgen Villadsen	Technical University of Denmark, Denmark
Thi Luu Phuong Vo	Vietnam National University HCMC, Vietnam
Wahyono Wahyono	Universitas Gadjah Mada, Indonesia

Paweł Weichbroth   Gdańsk University of Technology, Poland
Izabela Wierzbowska   Gdynia Maritime University, Poland
Krystian Wojtkiewicz   Wrocław University of Science and Technology,
                                   Poland
Xin-She Yang   Middlesex University London, UK
Tulay Yildirim   Yildiz Technical University, Turkey
Drago Zagar   University of Osijek, Croatia
Danuta Zakrzewska   Łódź University of Technology, Poland
Constantin-Bala Zamfirescu   Lucian Blaga University of Sibiu, Romania
Katerina Zdravkova   Ss. Cyril and Methodius University in Skopje,
                                   Macedonia
Vesna Zeljkovic   Lincoln University, USA
Aleksander Zgrzywa   Wroclaw University of Science and Technology,
                                   Poland
Jianlei Zhang   Nankai University, China
Zhongwei Zhang   University of Southern Queensland, Australia
Adam Ziębiński   Silesian University of Technology, Poland

Contents

G-Fake: Tell Me How It is Shared and I Shall Tell You If It is Fake

Nawfal Abbassi Saber[1(✉)], Rachid Guerraoui[2], Anne-Marie Kermarrec[2], and Alexandre Maurer[1]

[1] UM6P, Ben Guerir, Morocco
nawfal.abbassi@um6p.ma
[2] EPFL, Lausanne, Switzerland

Abstract. The propagation of fake news is an increasingly serious concern in social platforms, and designing methods to automatically detect them and limit their spread is an important research challenge. Most existing methods rely on inspecting the content of news to decide on their veracity, but this information is not always available.

In this paper, we present G-Fake (Graph-Fake), the first fake-news detection method that is entirely network-based. G-Fake only relies on the sharing history of news items. It does not assume any information on the content of these items (e.g. text or pictures), nor on the trustworthiness of users. In fact, G-Fake does not even require access to the underlying social graph, nor to the interactions between users. Our experimental evaluation conducted on real-world data shows that G-Fake can limit the spread of fake news in the earliest stages of propagation with an accuracy of 96.8%.

Keywords: Fake news detection · Graph embedding · Influence graph

1 Introduction

Social networks have become the first information exchange platforms, gathering billions of active users. On these platforms, information is often shared without any control. In many cases, anyone can share and propagate anything, including false information. In particular, individuals with bad intentions, typically organized within effective groups, use social networks to spread fake news. For instance, Twitter was subject to this kind of manipulations to influence the 2016 US presidential election [4].

The use of a human workforce to fact-check the news and counter the propagation of fake ones is generally inefficient, and does not scale to the immense volume of content currently shared on these platforms. Clearly, this calls for automatic methods to solve this problem.

Although automatic fake news detectors raise the risk of censorship, these systems can be used to assist humans in charge of detecting false information. In practice, without taking the final decision, they can be used to simplify the

© The Author(s), under exclusive license to Springer Nature Singapore Pte Ltd. 2022
E. Szczerbicki et al. (Eds.): ACIIDS 2022, CCIS 1716, pp. 1–13, 2022.
https://doi.org/10.1007/978-981-19-8234-7_1

work of human moderators by asking them to verify suspected news items. In particular, they may enable them to detect viral fake news items before they spread too much. They can also help to build an alert system that quickly makes moderators aware of the spread of (potentially harmful) viral fake news.

Several recent approaches modeled fake-news detection as a data-science problem. Most of these approaches rely on the content of shared news items. They typically use natural language processing to classify news items based on their text content and implement filters. Although powerful, this technique has two major limitations. First, it is not always applicable, as some items have other formats than text. Second, it is possible to train generative models to bypass these filters.

Besides analyzing the content of news items, a complementary approach consists in exploiting the underlying social graph, i.e., the graph of friendships or followers. However, such a graph is not always accessible. Furthermore, explicit relationships are not always real: a user can be friends with another user, or follow her, without being influenced by her. On the other hand, there might be mutual influences between two disconnected users.

In this paper, we explore a novel approach that does not require access to the content of news items, nor to the underlying social graph. More specifically, we propose *G-Fake*, a novel protocol that constructs an *influence graph* from the history of shared news items, and exploits this graph to effectively detect fake news early in the dissemination process, without requiring the access to any content. Roughly speaking, G-Fake reveals hidden characteristics of the users of a social network, and uses this network to dynamically gather information on *how* a news item is shared, to determine how likely this item is to be fake. More importantly, G-Fake does not classify a news item as possibly fake based on the specific user who initiated it, but rather on the sharing patterns collected from the users involved in the dissemination. We explain this difference later in the paper.

G-Fake assumes a realistic view of the environment. It only accesses the history of *sharing actions*. This can of course be achieved by the social network owner, but also by third parties (external observers) that have access to very limited data. G-Fake is itself composed of three sub-protocols, each interesting in its own right. The first protocol is a fast and lightweight *social influence graph construction* method. The second is a deep-learning-based *graph-embedding* method that derives rich representations of users, reflecting their sharing patterns. The third protocol is a *content-agnostic, network-based* approach for fake-news detection.

The three sub-protocols correspond to the following steps: (1) We construct an approximation of the social graph, based on the sharing history; (2) We use this graph as an input for an unsupervised learning scheme, that identifies relevant representations (characteristics) for each user and embeds them in a multidimensional space; (3) We exploit these representations to train a fake-news classifier, by addressing the following question: given that a news item X has been shared by those particular users (with specific characteristics), how likely is X to be real/fake? Once this classifier is trained, it can be applied to news items on which we have very little sharing information ("how they are shared"), and no content information. We demonstrate the power of this approach in our experiments.

We evaluate G-Fake using a real-world dataset, FakeNewsNet [27], that contains 21,595 labeled news items with more than 1.7 million tweets and more than 500k users. We split the dataset into two equivalent subsets (training set and test set). We build the influence graph using the training set, learn embeddings using the resulting graph, and finally train a news classifier using the same training set. Since the dataset is unbalanced, we do not only rely on accuracy to evaluate the performance of the classifier: we also use precision, recall and F1-score by class, to determine the extent to which the model is capable of detecting fake news. Using only the first 30 sharing actions (for each news item), G-Fake is able to achieve excellent results: 96.8% in accuracy, 85.5% in F1-score and 92.0% in precision for the fake-news class, but also 98.2% in F1-score and 97.5% in precision for the real-news class.

To sum up, we go over three information transformation and extraction blocks, as illustrated in Fig. 1: influence graph construction, users and news embedding, then classifier training. Each block takes input data, transforms it to extract more information, and forwards it to the next block, until a prediction is made. The Fig. 1a illustrates the training phase. The first block builds an influence graph. The second block learns representations of users. The third block calculates news embedding as an aggregation of users' embeddings. Finally, the last block trains a supervised model, and learns to classify news items as "fake" or "not fake". On the other hand, the Fig. 1b illustrates the inference phase. To infer the trustworthiness of unknown news items, we take their sharing history as an input, then calculate users representations using the previously learned embeddings. After that, we calculate the news embedding using the same formula in the training phase. Finally, using the trained classifier, we run a prediction on the news embedding to classify the news item.

The rest of the paper is organized as follows. We discuss related work in Sect. 2. We present our approach in Sect. 3. We present our experimental results on real-world data in Sect. 4, and conclude in Sect. 5.

2   Related Work

Three main ways to perform automatic fake-news detection can be distinguished. *Content*-based methods are the most common, and rely principally on the analysis of the content of news items (e.g. text and pictures). *Reputation*- and *credibility*-based methods are less common. They exploit the history of user engagement w.r.t. fake news, and try to estimate the credibility of news items based on the reputation of users who choose to share or not share them. Finally, *network*-based methods try to leverage social-graph properties and the diffusion process of news items to classify them. Many approaches are hybrid, i.e. they combine content-based methods with network- or credibility-based methods.

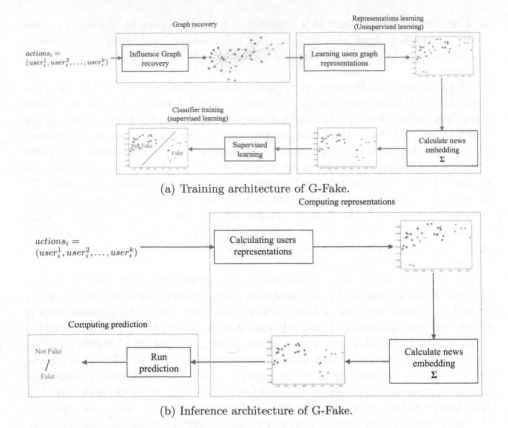

(a) Training architecture of G-Fake.

(b) Inference architecture of G-Fake.

Fig. 1. Architecture of G-Fake.

We first discuss content-based methods. The idea in [5, 23] consists in using a list of handcrafted linguistic features extracted from news text to train a classifier. In [10], the bag-of-words technique and the naive Bayes classifier are used to train text-based fake-news classifiers. In [8], TF-IDF (term frequency - inverse document frequency) was applied to automatically extract textual features, and then train classification models to predict misleading text. The idea in [39] is to extract rich-content features from different levels (lexicon-level, syntax-level, semantic-level, and discourse-level) to train machine learning classification models. Deep neural networks (RNN) were used in [38] to learn latent features of textual content from both the creator and the subject of the news item, and then classify them. In [18], LSTM (Long Short Term Memory networks) were used to capture hierarchical discourse-level structures to build classifiers. This suggests that real and fake news present substantial differences in the hierarchical discourse-level structures. A more sophisticated architecture of neural networks was used in [22] to learn representations of the content of messages and their propagation tree. NLP techniques, like sentiment analysis and Part-of-

Speech (POS) tagging, were also used in [14] for automatic feature extraction to train classifiers. In [24], style features are combined with feature-selection-based analysis to distinguish hyper-partisan news from mainstream news. A fake-news classification dataset and an investigation of the use of supervised learning for fake-news detection were presented in [32]. In the same vein, [28] proposed a richer dataset that includes, not only the textual content, but also the social context of each news item. It also investigates the use of supervised learning and its potential applications. An unsupervised approach that does not require labeled data was presented in [36], to classify news items by leveraging the analysis of feelings and engagement. An approach based on deep neural networks was implemented to learn classification models from news text and user-reaction history, like retweets and likes. More advanced neural-networks architectures and mechanisms, like LSTM and attention, were used in [21] to extract features from the text of tweets and information in user profiles. In [33], multi-modal deep learning architectures were used to learn representation jointly from text and images. The correlation between the content of user profiles and fake/real news was investigated in [28].

Compared to content-based techniques, methods based on reputation and credibility remain less explored. In [12], a credibility-propagation approach similar to PageRank was proposed to establish event credibility. In [16], a credibility network was proposed using opinion mining to detect supporting and opposing tweets, and combined with graph optimization such that (a) each supporting node has similar credibility values and (b) opposing nodes have opposite credibility values. In [3], a Bayesian approach was proposed to assess the trustworthiness of news items, using the estimation of each user's inclination to share fake news (in a content-agnostic way). However, this approach assumes a team of fact-checkers (checking the most viral news items) to evaluate the trustworthiness of each user. Other algorithms from the domain of peer-to-peer (P2P) networks can be borrowed to estimate the trust score of users in the social network. Indeed, users can propagate corrupted files in P2P overlay networks, similarly to fake news in social media. Trying to solve this problem in P2P systems has lead to a wide variety of algorithms [1,17,20].

Recently, network-based methods attracted a lot of interest. The information encapsulated in the social graph of social networks appears to be very useful for predicting fake news. Besides extracting content features, in [35], a so-called graph kernel was used with SVM (Support Vector Machine) to classify news items using their propagation trees. In [30], the spread of stories was leveraged on Twitter to compare the speed of propagation of false and real news items. It was shown that fake news spreads further and faster than real news. In [13], a full access to the social graph was assumed to detect existing echo-chambers and to represent users. The technique also used content representation extracted with bag-of-words techniques. Like previous works, [29] used both network properties and content to predict fake news (assuming an access to the social graph) by learning users representations with non-negative matrix factorization. In [39], access to the friendship graph was also assumed, but instead of automatically learning users' latent representations, a list of handcrafted graph-features extractions was applied. On the other hand, [26] did not assume access to the social graph, but used co-shares to build users' social graph, and applied SVD (Singular Value Decomposition) to extract users' features. Besides content linguistic features, temporal and structural diffusion properties of news items were used to calculate handcrafted features and to train classifiers [19]. [15,31,37] formulate fake-news detection as a reliable sensing problem, where individuals are considered as sensors making observations about the world. They use expectation maximization to estimate the probability of correctness of those observations, by leveraging the social graph and the source claim graph.

3   G-Fake

Our goal is to quickly assess the credibility of a news item that starts spreading in a social network, e.g., during the first sharing actions. Such an early detection scheme enables to avoid the viral dissemination of fake news items, by stopping them before they spread exponentially. We do not assume access to the content of the news item, only to the identifiers of users sharing it.

A sharing action is described by the identifier of its author. The observer, i.e., the entity trying to limit the dissemination of fake news, can be the social network owner or a third party. The owner of a social network has usually access to the sharing actions and to the connections between users, but a third party can only observe the sharing actions. Our goal is to use *only* these actions to detect fake news.

In other words, the data (1) we consider is simply the history of sharing actions of news items and their labels (2). Sharing actions (3) are represented by a list of user identifiers, ordered by time of sharing. Labels are binary variables "fake"/"not fake". For experiments, we use the FakeNewsNet [27] dataset, containing 21,595 labeled news items and a list of tweets representing the sharing actions for each item.

$$data = \{item_1, item_2, \ldots, item_N\} \tag{1}$$

$$item_i = (actions_i, label_i) \tag{2}$$

$$actions_i = (user_i^1, user_i^2, \ldots, user_i^K) \tag{3}$$

The goal of G-Fake is to use a set of actions (tweeting, in the context of Twitter) related to some news items, to classify the latter as fake or not fake. The users' IDs are converted to some n-dimensional vectors (4) that encapsulate the information that is meaningful and useful for the prediction. This vector is called *embedding* (E). The representation of a news item is an aggregation G (5) of the embeddings of users sharing it.

$$E(user) \in \mathcal{R}^n \tag{4}$$

$$E(actions_i) = G(E(user_i^1), E(user_i^2), \ldots, E(user_i^K)) \tag{5}$$

Using those embeddings (5) as input, a classifier C_θ (that outputs the probability of the item being fake) is trained with the objective of minimizing the binary cross-entropy loss (6).

$$x_i = E(actions_i)$$

$$y_i = \begin{cases} 1, & \text{if } label_i = Fake \\ 0, & \text{otherwise} \end{cases}$$

$$\hat{y}_i = C_\theta(x_i)$$
$$C_\theta(x_i) = \Pr(label_i = Fake \mid actions_i)$$

$$Cost = \frac{1}{m} \sum_{i=1}^{m} -(y_i \log(\hat{y}_i) + (1 - y_i) \log(1 - \hat{y}_i)) \tag{6}$$

G-Fake involves three main steps, as illustrated in Fig. 1.

The first one is the construction of a social influence graph (based on the history of sharing actions). The second consists in learning users' embeddings using the social influence graph, and aggregate them to derive news embeddings. The third part consists in training a machine learning model to classify news items (fake or not fake), using the previously learned representations.

The network inference problem, where one tries to recover the edges of an unknown graph from the observations of cascades propagating over this graph, has gained the attention of many researchers in the last few years. Many solutions consider different types of graph and a variety of cascades models [9,25]. Most of these are computationally expensive, and are typically only tested on small networks. As the problem at hand involves a lot of data and large graphs (tens of thousands of nodes and hundreds of thousands of edges), it is practically impossible, when using those models, to keep updating them regularly when new data is obtained.

We propose a simpler way of constructing the social influence graph, that achieves very good results at a much lower cost. The intuition here is that we do not need to recover the entire and exact graph topology in the context of fake news detection. In fact, we rather exploit the sharing patterns of the users with respect to fake news dissemination. We build our social graph of influence based on the idea that users that often share the same news items are more likely to be connected and influenced by each other. More precisely, we assume that two nodes (users) are connected if they have shared the same news item in successive rounds. We then define the weight of an edge between two nodes as the number of previous co-shares.

Despite the fact that our social influence graph is approximate and might not be the exact social graph on which fake news are disseminated, this is enough for G-Fake to learn relevant features from the graph and to successfully detect fake news, which is confirmed by our experimental results.

In the following, we call the users "nodes". We define the following events, for all i and j:

$A_{i,j}$: node i infected node j, that is: j shared a news item because it was previously shared by i;

$B_{i,j}^k$: nodes i and j appeared in the sharing history of the same news item k;

$C_{i,j}$: nodes i and j are connected in the influence graph.

Assuming that L nodes shared $item_k$ before node j:

$$P(A_{i,j}|B_{i,j}^k) = \frac{1}{L}$$

One occurrence of event $A_{i,j}$, given an event $B_{i,j}^k$ (for any k), is sufficient to conclude that nodes i and j are connected.

$P(\overline{A_{i,j}}|B_{i,j})$ is the probability for j not to be infected by node i, for any M news items:

$$P(\overline{A_{i,j}}|B_{i,j}) = \left(1 - \frac{1}{L}\right)^M$$

$$P(C_{i,j}|B_{i,j}) = 1 - \left(1 - \frac{1}{L}\right)^M$$

This probability is higher for small values of L, and also for large numbers of observations M. The more i and j co-appear, the more likely they are to be connected. Hence, the idea to use M as weight to recover the influence graph.

Having approximately built the influence graph, we then use graph-embedding models to learn high-quality representations that capture a large number of connectivity patterns and semantic features.

A news item embedding is determined by aggregating its sharers' embedding. In our experiments, we use the mean value over different embedding dimensions, but other methods can be used [2,6]. Averaging over users' representations dimensions is simple and fast, and provides satisfying results.

Once the news embeddings are available, several machine learning algorithms could be used to train the news classifier. Here, we use the simple logistic regression algorithm to capture the quality of representations learned using our method. However, note that training more sophisticated classifiers will very likely lead to even better results.

4   Experiments

In this section, we demonstrate the effectiveness of G-Fake on a real-world dataset. We first introduce this dataset, then evaluate the quality of users' features (i.e. what we call "embedding"), learned using the unsupervised machine learning algorithm Node2Vec. Then, we assess the performance of G-Fake along two metrics: the effectiveness of the social network inference algorithm, and the effectiveness of the nodes (users) embedding algorithm.

In our experiments, we used the FakeNewsNet dataset [27]. This is the only publicly available dataset that provides a list of fake news items with the social context, e.g., the users who shared it. It is composed of 21,595 labeled news items, and more than 1.7 million tweets from 535,367 users.

We split the dataset into two sets of equal size: a training set and a test set. To obtain well-separated sets, we had to sacrifice some data points to avoid overlapping in time: all news items of the training set should be shared before those of the test set. The best splits we could obtain have the following size: 6236 news items for the training set, and 6234 for the test set. The resulting influence graph contains more than 6.5 million edges. To reduce the simulation time, we filtered edges with weights lower than 6, which brings the number of edges to 196,327. The filtering also means that we only keep connections (edges) with the highest likelihood. We set the size of the embedding vectors to 30 dimensions.

In addition to accuracy, we use three other metrics to evaluate G-Fake: recall, precision and F1-score. Because the dataset used to evaluate our approach is imbalanced, trained models can overfit the large class and underfit the smaller class. Thus, accuracy alone is not sufficient: the model can learn to classify everything in only one class, and still reach high accuracy.

We evaluate our methodology on two levels. First, we evaluate the use of Node2Vec as a graph-embedding technique. We compare it with several other well-known graph-embedding techniques. Then, we evaluate the influence graph recovery (IGR)[1]. We compare our IGR approach (that we call "Light IGR") with the Netrate algorithm [25]. In the experiments, we report results using the first 30 sharing actions. This number is optimal: as shown in Fig. 2b, the F1-score does not increase significantly beyond 30. We also compare G-Fake with a content-based approach using the title of news items. For this comparison, we use BERT [7], a state-of-the-art model showing very good performance on many NLP tasks.

For graph embedding, we consider four algorithms: N2V (Node2Vec), Bi-spectral embedding (BiSpectral), SVD (Singular Value Decomposition) and GSVD (Generalized Singular Value Decomposition). Node2Vec is a well known graph-embedding algorithm based on deep learning. It is tested to evaluate the relevance of deep-learning models for this kind of tasks.

For Node2Vec, we use the official implementation [11]. For the other embedding algorithms, we use the Scikit-Network library, which contains a large variety of graph-embedding techniques.

Figure 2a depicts the evaluation metrics used: F1-score, recall, precision and accuracy. Since the dataset is unbalanced, it contains much more real news items than fake news items. Thus, we report F1-score, recall and precision by class, to avoid being biased by the score of the real-news class. Accuracy values are very close because the dataset is unbalanced: it is sufficient to overfit on the dominating class to obtain a high accuracy. On the other hand, the other metrics (per class) are a good indication of overfitting to a class and ignoring the other. F1-score can be interpreted as a weighted average of precision and recall, which is useful when trying to maximize both.

---

[1] The method used to construct the social influence graph.

10   N. Abbassi Saber et al.

GE	IGR	All Accuracy	Real F1-score	Fake F1-score	Real Precision	Fake Precision	Real Recall	Fake Recall
BiSpectral	Light IGR	0.949	0.972	0.738	0.977	0.702	0.966	0.779
	Netrate	0.904	0.949	0.215	**0.993**	0.129	0.909	0.688
GSVD	Light IGR	0.943	0.969	0.683	0.980	0.618	0.958	0.778
	Netrate	0.949	0.971	0.779	0.961	0.845	0.982	0.727
N2V	Light IGR	0.965	0.980	0.839	0.973	0.892	**0.988**	0.792
	Netrate	**0.966**	**0.981**	**0.845**	0.973	**0.899**	**0.988**	**0.798**
SVD	Light IGR	0.943	0.968	0.680	0.981	0.603	0.956	0.787
	Netrate	0.937	0.965	0.649	0.978	0.574	0.953	0.753

(a) Evaluation metrics values

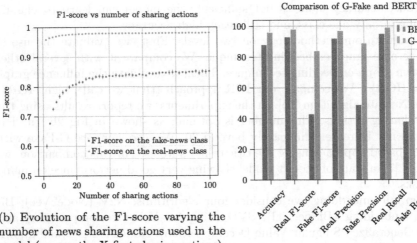

(b) Evolution of the F1-score varying the number of news sharing actions used in the model (we use the X first sharing actions). The value 30 seems to be optimal.

(c) Evaluation metrics values for G-Fake and BERT.

Fig. 2. Experimental results

In terms of F1-score, Node2Vec with both IGR algorithms clearly outperforms other GE algorithms (especially for the fake news class), followed by GSVD using Netrate, and BiSpectral using Light IGR. Node2Vec is better than GSVD by 4%, and better than BiSpectral by 9%. Even for real news, Node2Vec is better than the other algorithms.

The roots of differences in performance are detailed in terms of precision and recall. However, the price for Node2Vec's performance is execution time: it is slower than other algorithms (but still fast for a deep-learning-based technique).

For any GE algorithm, and compared to Netrate, our Light IGR method performed similarly most of the time. However, learning the influence graph using Netrate takes more than 72 h on a server with 80 cores, since it solves a convex optimization problem for every single node in the graph. In comparison, Light IGR takes less than 1 h on a 4-core laptop to reconstruct the influence graph, and therefore appears to be significantly more practical and more scalable.

Finally, we compare G-Fake with a content-based approach. We chose a pre-trained version of BERT, using the Transformers library [34], and trained on the title of news items. The results are presented in Fig. 2c. This suggests that the sharing patterns of news items are a better predictor of their reliability than their title, even when a state-of-the-art model is used for comparison.

5 Concluding Remarks

In this paper, we proposed and evaluated G-Fake, a novel content-agnostic approach to detect fake news. Despite the limited access to data, we were able to achieve high performance in detecting fake news, and demonstrated that unsupervised learning is useful in extracting rich and meaningful user representations from social graphs.

More generally, our results strongly suggest that content-agnostic and privacy-preserving machine learning is feasible, in particular for automatic fake-news detection. Our findings open the way for third parties to efficiently fight against fake-news propagation. This work could be extended to an end-to-end machine learning model, that would embed sharing cascades and use them to make predictions for different kinds of applications.

Given the importance of fake-news detection, one might ask why a solution like ours has not been experimented and implemented in the past. We argue that there are two reasons for this. First, advances in graph embedding using machine learning approaches, as used in G-Fake, are quite recent. Second, the way we use graph embedding is novel: we go through an indirect aggregation phase which, we believe, is non-trivial.

It is important to notice that our G-Fake approach has some limitations. It relies on the sharing history, which is not immediate to get for new users. Also, when a new user joins our network, this changes the embedding of other users. Finding an effective way to integrate newcomers is an interesting open problem to complement our approach.

References

1. Aberer, K., et al.: Managing trust in a peer-2-peer information system. In: Proceedings of the Tenth International Conference on Information and Knowledge Management. CIKM '01, New York, NY, USA, pp. 310–317 (2001)
2. Arora, S., et al.: A simple but tough-to-beat baseline for sentence embeddings (2016)
3. Balmau, O., et al.: Limiting the spread of fake news on social media platforms by evaluating users' trustworthiness (2018)

4. Bovet, A., et al.: Influence of fake news in twitter during the 2016 us presidential election. Nat. Commun. **10**(1), 1–14 (2019)
5. Castillo, C., et al.: Information credibility on Twitter. In: Proceedings of the 20th International Conference Companion on World Wide Web, WWW 2011, pp. 675–684 (2011)
6. Conneau, A., et al.: Supervised learning of universal sentence representations from natural language inference data. CoRR abs/1705.02364 (2017)
7. Devlin, J., et al.: BERT: pre-training of deep bidirectional transformers for language understanding. CoRR abs/1810.04805 (2018)
8. Gilda, S.: Evaluating machine learning algorithms for fake news detection. In: IEEE Student Conference on Research and Development: Inspiring Technology for Humanity, SCOReD 2017 - Proceedings 2018-January, pp. 110–115 (2018)
9. Gomez-Rodriguez, M., et al.: Inferring networks of diffusion and influence. ACM Trans. Knowl. Discov. Data **5**(4), 1–37 (2012)
10. Granik, M., et al.: Fake news detection using naive Bayes classifier. In: 2017 IEEE 1st Ukraine Conference on Electrical and Computer Engineering, UKRCON 2017 - Proceedings (2017)
11. Grover, A., et al.: node2vec: scalable feature learning for networks. In: Proceedings of the 22nd ACM SIGKDD International Conference on Knowledge Discovery and Data Mining (2016)
12. Gupta, M., et al.: Evaluating event credibility on twitter. In: Proceedings of the 12th SIAM International Conference on Data Mining, SDM 2012, pp. 153–164 (2012)
13. Gupta, S., et al.: CIMT detect: a community infused matrix-tensor coupled factorization based method for fake news detection. In: Proceedings of the 2018 IEEE/ACM International Conference on Advances in Social Networks Analysis and Mining, ASONAM 2018, pp. 278–281 (2018)
14. Hassan, N., et al.: Toward automated fact-checking: Detecting check-worthy factual claims by claimbuster. In: Proceedings of the ACM SIGKDD International Conference on Knowledge Discovery and Data Mining **Part F1296**, pp. 1803–1812 (2017)
15. Huang, C., et al.: Towards time-sensitive truth discovery in social sensing applications. In: 2015 IEEE 12th International Conference on Mobile Ad Hoc and Sensor Systems, pp. 154–162 (2015)
16. Jin, Z., et al.: News verification by exploiting conflicting social viewpoints in microblogs. In: 30th AAAI Conference on Artificial Intelligence, AAAI 2016 pp. 2972–2978 (2016)
17. Kamvar, S.D., et al.: The eigentrust algorithm for reputation management in p2p networks. In: Proceedings of the 12th International Conference on World Wide Web. WWW 2003, New York, NY, USA, pp. 640–651 (2003)
18. Karimi, H., et al.: Learning Hierarchical Discourse-level Structure for Fake News Detection, pp. 3432–3442 (2019)
19. Kwon, S., et al.: Prominent features of rumor propagation in online social media. In: Proceedings - IEEE International Conference on Data Mining, ICDM, pp. 1103–1108 (2013)
20. Xiong, L., et al.: Peertrust: supporting reputation-based trust for peer-to-peer electronic communities. IEEE Trans. Knowl. Data Eng. **16**(7), 843–857 (2004)
21. Long, Y., et al.: Fake news detection through multi-perspective speaker profiles. In: Proceedings of the Eighth International Joint Conference on Natural Language Processing, vol. 2, no. 8, pp. 252–256 (2017)

22. Ma, J., et al.: Rumor detection on twitter with tree-structured recursive neural networks. In: ACL 2018–56th Annual Meeting of the Association for Computational Linguistics, Proceedings of the Conference (Long Papers), vol. 1, pp. 1980–1989 (2018)
23. Pérez-Rosas, V., et al.: Automatic detection of fake news, 3391–3401 (2017)
24. Potthast, M., et al.: A stylometric inquiry into hyperpartisan and fake news. In: ACL 2018–56th Annual Meeting of the Association for Computational Linguistics, Proceedings of the Conference (Long Papers), vol. 1, pp. 231–240 (2018)
25. Rodriguez, M.G., et al.: Uncovering the temporal dynamics of diffusion networks. arXiv preprint arXiv:1105.0697 (2011)
26. Ruchansky, N., et al.: CSI: A hybrid deep model for fake news detection. In: International Conference on Information and Knowledge Management, Proceedings **Part F1318**, pp. 797–806 (2017)
27. Shu, K., et al.: Fakenewsnet: A data repository with news content, social context and dynamic information for studying fake news on social media. arXiv preprint arXiv:1809.01286 (2018)
28. Shu, K., et al.: FakeNewsNet: A Data Repository with News Content, Social Context and Spatialtemporal Information for Studying Fake News on Social Media (2018)
29. Shu, K., et al.: Beyond news contents: the role of social context for fake news detection. In: WSDM 2019 - Proceedings of the 12th ACM International Conference on Web Search and Data Mining (i), pp. 312–320 (2019)
30. Vosoughi, S., et al.: News On-line. Science **1151**(March), 1146–1151 (2018)
31. Wang, D., et al.: Using humans as sensors: an estimation-theoretic perspective. In: Proceedings of the 13th International Symposium on Information Processing in Sensor Networks. IPSN 2014, pp. 35–46 (2014)
32. Wang, W.Y.: "Liar, liar pants on fire": a new benchmark dataset for fake news detection. In: ACL 2017–55th Annual Meeting of the Association for Computational Linguistics, Proceedings of the Conference (Long Papers), vol. 2, pp. 422–426 (2017)
33. Wang, Y., et al.: EANN: event adversarial neural networks for multi-modal fake news detection. In: Proceedings of the ACM SIGKDD International Conference on Knowledge Discovery and Data Mining, pp. 849–857 (2018)
34. Wolf, T., et al.: Transformers: State-of-the-art natural language processing. In: Proceedings of the 2020 Conference on Empirical Methods in Natural Language Processing: System Demonstrations, pp. 38–45. Online (Oct 2020)
35. Wu, K., et al.: False rumors detection on Sina Weibo by propagation structures. In: Proceedings - International Conference on Data Engineering 2015-May, pp. 651–662 (2015)
36. Yang, S., et al.: Unsupervised fake news detection on social media: a generative approach. In: Proceedings of the AAAI Conference on Artificial Intelligence, vol. 33, pp. 5644–5651 (2019)
37. Yao, S., et al.: On source dependency models for reliable social sensing: algorithms and fundamental error bounds. In: Proceedings - 2016 IEEE 36th International Conference on Distributed Computing Systems, ICDCS 2016. Proceedings - International Conference on Distributed Computing Systems, United States, pp. 467–476, August 2016
38. Zhang, J., et al.: FAKEDETECTOR: effective fake news detection with deep diffusive neural network, December 2018
39. Zhou, X., et al.: Fake news early detection: a theory-driven model. Digital Threats Res. Pract. **1**(1), 1–24 (2019)

LDA+: An Extended LDA Model for Topic Hierarchy and Discovery

Amani Drissi[1]([✉])[iD], Ahmed Khemiri[1][iD], Salma Sassi[2,3][iD], Anis Tissaoui[2,3][iD], Richard Chbeir[2,3][iD], and Abderrazek Jemai[4][iD]

[1] FST, University of Manar, SERCOM, Tunis, Tunisia
drissiamani19@gmail.com
[2] FSJEGJ, University of Jendouba, 8189, VPNC Lab., Avcnue U.M.A, 8189, Jendouba, Tunisia
{salma.sassi,anis.tissaoui}@fsjegj.rnu.tn, rchbeir@acm.org
[3] Univ Pau & Pays Adour, E2S UPPA, LIUPPA, EA3000 Anglet, France
[4] INSAT, University of Carthage, SERCOM, Tunis, Tunisia
Abderrazak.Jemai@insat.rnu.tn

Abstract. The success of topic modeling algorithms depends on their ability to analyze, index and classify large text corpora. These algorithms could be classified into two groups where the first one is oriented to classify textual corpus according to their dominant topics such as LDA, LSA and PLSA which are the most known techniques. The second group is dedicated to extract the relationships among the generated topics like HLDA, PAM and CTM. However, each algorithm among these groups is dedicated to a single task and there is no technique that makes it possible to carry out several analyses on textual corpus at the same time. In order to cope with this problem, we propose here a new technique based on LDA topic modeling to automatically classify a large text corpora according to their relevant topics, discover new topics (sub-topics) based on the extracted ones and hierarchy the generated topics in order to analyse data more deeply. Experiments have been conducted to measure the performance of our solution compared to the existing techniques. The results obtained are more than satisfactory.

Keywords: LDA · Topic modeling · Hierarchical topic model · Topic generation · Topic discovering

1 Introduction

In recent years, there has been an exponential growth in the number of complex documents and texts that require a deeper understanding of machine learning methods to be able to accurately classify texts in many applications [6]. So, it requires using new techniques or tools that deals with automatically organizing, searching and indexing a large collection of textual documents, in order to have a better way of managing the explosion of electronic document archives [11].

Topic modeling has garnered a lot of attention and demonstrated a good performance in a wide variety of tasks thanks to their ability to provide a practical

© The Author(s), under exclusive license to Springer Nature Singapore Pte Ltd. 2022
E. Szczerbicki et al. (Eds.): ACIIDS 2022, CCIS 1716, pp. 14–26, 2022.
https://doi.org/10.1007/978-981-19-8234-7_2

way to analyze large corpus and find abstract topics within a large collection of documents, as well as it can discover the mixture of latent topics that varies from one document to another in a given corpus.

Many topic modeling techniques could be used to classify corpus documents according to their relevant topics such as Latent Semantic Analysis (LSA) [29] which is helpful in uncovering the most important topics in the used corpus and classifying each document according to his relevant topic, Probabilistic Latent Semantic Analysis (PLSA) [27] which differs from LSA in the ability to calculate the probability distribution of each topic in the corpus documents collection, Latent Dirichlet Allocation (LDA) [26] which is constructed around the idea that a document is represented as a mixture of topics and each topic is a mixture of words with different probabilities. As a result, LDA is able to classify a document on more than one topic, but with different probability. However, LSA, PLSA and LDA are very useful techniques to identify the corpus topics and classify each document based on his relevant topic (or topics in the case of LDA). To semantically analyse a large text corpora in depth, researchers have devoted many efforts to automatically explore the semantic relationships among topics which is beneficial for many applications such as the category hierarchy in Web pages [17] and research topic hierarchy in academia community [12]. As a consequence, the hierarchical topic models have attracted much attention, because being able not only to identify topics, but also to organize them into hierarchies in order to discover how they are related to each others or how they are extended or depended to each other [20] such as the Hierarchical LDA (HLDA) [25] that especially helps to hierarchy the generated corpus topics, but this algorithm is not deterministic and do not able to extract the probability distribution of each topic in the used documents. The Pachinko Allocation Model (PAM) [23] which is able just to extract the probability distribution of each subtopic in the topic and hierarchy them, this technique performs better with a correlated documents topics. And the Correlated Topic Model (CTM) [21] which performs better with a corpus of correlated domains. The output of this technique is a correlated topic matrix.

However, the existing topic modeling techniques are dedicated to a single task and there is no technique that makes it possible to carry out several analyses on textual corpus at the same time. So, in order to overcome these challenges, we provide in this paper a new approach consisting of automatic large text corpora classification based on the LDA [3] topic model which provides a powerful tool for discovering and exploiting the hidden topics structure in large text archives and it can easily used as a module in more complicated models for more complex goals. Our approach named LDA+ and it is able to (i) automatically classify documents from a heterogeneous corpus according to their dominant topics, (ii) automatically discover new topics (sub-topics) from the extracted ones in order to analyse the data more deeply, and (iii) automatically hierarchy the generated topics which facilitate the data analysis and interpretation tasks.

To achieve our objectives, three main challenges have been addressed in our study:

1. How to automatically extract relevant topics from a heterogeneous corpus and evaluate the generated classification?
2. How to re-stabilize our model to guarantee a better performance even with the change of the domain or the corpus size?
3. How to automatically generate and discover new topics as well as the hierarchy between them?

The rest of the paper is organized as follows: We study in Sect. 2 the well-known topic models algorithms and we illustrate a comparative study between these techniques. Next, we explain in Sect. 3 the methodology of our approach. Section 4 describes the experiments conducted to validate our approach. It also shows the comparison of our results with some existing topic modeling methods based on the same data set. Finally, Sect. 5 concludes the paper and discusses some future work.

2   Related Works

The LSA, PLSA and LDA topic models can only find topics in a flat structure, but fail to discover the hierarchical relationship among topics [7]. [1,5] evaluate two topic model algorithms: LSA and LDA with the same data set and the same metrics to conclude the performance of LDA rather than LSA for topic modeling using a large collection of data. However, [5] mentions that the Latent semantic analysis is a powerful technique, especially for word ambiguity detection in information retrieval task [8,14,28] rather than extract topics from a large corpus.

Although it has been shown in existing work [13] that LDA is better than PLSA by studying the property of topic models more directly, and using topic features in low-dimensional in their experiments. [13] observe that LDA consistently outperforms PLSA on both data sets, indicating that (1) PLSA may suffer from the over-fitting problem; and (2) LDA is more effective when used as a latent semantic structure.

An alternative model that not only represents the topic correlations, but also learns them, is the Correlated Topic Model (CTM) [21]. Thus, in CTM topics are not independent, however, note that only pairwise correlations are modeled, and the number of parameters in the covariance matrix grows as the square of the number of topics [22].

Traditional topic modeling has been widely studied and popularly employed in expertise and information systems. Nonetheless, these topic model categories cannot discover structural relations among topics, thus losing the chance to explore the data more deeply. Hierarchical topic modeling has the capability of learning topics, as well as discovering the hierarchical topic structure of text data. The task of hierarchical topic modeling is to learn a topic hierarchy from text corpora, in which the topics are organized according to the semantic generality of each topic [7].

Table 1. Comparative study

Criterion/Existing study	Challenge 1			Challenge 2		Challenge 3	
	C1	C2	C3	C4	C5	C6	C7
LSA	Small	Yes	a	No	No	No	–
PLSA	Small	Yes	a	No	No	No	–
LDA	Large	No	a + b	Yes	No	No	–
CTM	Large	Yes	d	Yes	No	No	2
PAM	Large	Yes	c	Yes	No	No	2
HLDA	Large	No	c	Yes	No	No	N
Our proposed LDA+	Large	No	a + b + c	Yes	Yes	Yes	N

In order to compare the existing approaches and to overcome the challenges described previously, we define here 7 criteria with respect to the defined challenges:

Challenge 1. How to automatically extract relevant topics from a heterogeneous corpus and evaluate the generated classification?

- **Criterion 1 (C1): Corpus size**: this criterion helps us to determine if the used method performs well with a small or large corpus. It can be ("Small"/"Large").
- **Criterion 2 (C2): Over-fitting risk**, indicates the ability of a method to distinguish between topics which are independent or strongly related, it could be ("Yes"/"No").
- **Criterion 3 (C3): Output task**, indicates the output task of each used method which could be ("Documents/Topics matrix": (a), "Topics/Terms matrix": (b), "Topics hierarchy": (c) and "Correlated topics matrix": (d)).

Challenge 2. How to re-stabilize our model to guarantee a better performance even with the change of the domain or the corpus size?

- **Criterion 4 (C4): Auto-classification ability** measures the ability of a topic modeling technique to classify new documents according to the existing topics. It could be ("Yes"/"No")
- **Criterion 5 (C5): Auto-parameters stabilization**, indicates the ability of a method to re-stabilize its parameters with no human intervention, it could be ("Yes"/"No").

Challenge 3. How to automatically generate and discover new topics as well as the hierarchy between them?

- **Criterion 6 (C6): New topic discovery**, measures the ability of a method to automatically discover and generate new topics rather the existing ones (Sub-topics). New topic discovery criterion can be ("Yes"/"No").

- **Criterion 7 (C7): Hierarchy level** determines the level of the generated hierarchy. The above criterion was determined after an experimental process using the same metrics.

Our comparative study shown that the LSA and PLSA topic models perform better with a small corpus and both of them suffer from the over-fitting risk. The LDA, HLDA, PAM and CTM topic models performs better using a large textual corpus. The Table 1 shows that CTM and PAM models suffer from the over-fitting risk which could be explained by their performance to model a correlated topics only. About the third criterion, the out-put task of both LSA and PLSA is a "Documents/Topics matrix". The out-put of LDA model are "Documents/Topics matrix" and "Topics/Termes matrix". For CTM the out-put task is a "Correlated topics matrix" and the out-put of both PAM and HLDA is a "Topics hierarchy". Concerning LDA+ the originality of our approach reside in providing several out-put tasks in the same time: "Documents/Topics matrix", "Topics/Termes matrix" and "Topics hierarchy". The fourth criterion shown the limit of LSA and PLSA topic models to automatically classify a new document according to an existing classification. For the fifth criterion, we note that all existing approaches need a user intervention to manually configure them.

The sixth criterion indicates the ability of a model to automatically discover a new topic from the extracted ones to facilitate corpus data analysis in depth. Table 1 shows that none of existing studies is able to discover and generate new topics rather the existing ones. The last criterion gives an idea about the hierarchy level generated for each model. The LSA, PLSA and LDA models are able to extract topics only in a flat structure. The CTM and PAM models are able to extract and hierarchy the corpus topics into only two levels which are respectively topics level and sub-topics level.

3   Methodology

The proposed architecture (Fig. 1) consists of two phases: **(1)** Text preprocessing and **(2)** Topic analysis. We detail them in what follows:

3.1   Text Preprocessing (1)

Preprocessing is an important task and critical step in Natural Language Processing (NLP), it acts a significant role [9] for transferring text from human language to machine-readable format and it affects substantially the results of the experiments. The preprocessing stage is important to structure the unstructured text and keep the keywords which are useful to represent the category of text topics [24]. Natural language text can contain many words with no specific meaning, such as prepositions, pronouns, etc. So, after a text is obtained the preprocessing process consists of two steps: **(i)** Text cleaning and **(ii)** Reconfiguration [4].

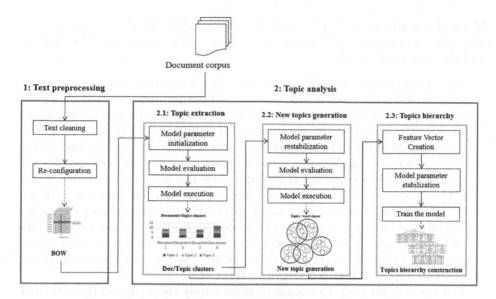

Fig. 1. LDA+ framework.

The text cleaning step consists of: **(i)** Normalization: this step is important in order to shrink the size of the vocabulary by converting the characters to lowercase, deleting numbers, symbols and removing punctuation. **(ii)** Tokenization: in this step, the given text splitting into sentences and each sentence were split into tokens (Words). **(iii)** Lemmatization: this step is supported by providing the Part-Of-Speech (POS). And **(iv)** Big-grams extraction: this task consists of combining multi-word terms into single tokens, such as data-mining, webpage and machine-Learning. The Re-configuration step: it is helpful to convert text data to an appropriate format, this task is necessary for an automated process. To establish this step we generated a Bag Of Words matrix representation where each document in our corpus represents a vector of tokens and the tokens represent the document terms.

3.2 Topic Analysis (2)

The topic analysis task consists of three steps which are respectively: (i) Topic extraction, (ii) New topic generation and (iii) Topics hierarchy.

Topic Extraction: This phase consists of four steps which are respectively: The model parameter initialization, the model evaluation, the model execution and the document cluster.

- The model parameter initialization: the objective of this step is to automatically stabilize the LDA model. The stabilization process is based on **alpha** which represents a document topic density and **beta** which represents a topic word density as well as **the topic number**. The standard LDA is configured manually. Therefore, the user needs to test a set of alpha, beta and topics number combinations in order to use the most optimum combination of these parameters. The originality of our approach lies in the automation of the LDA configuration by choosing the most optimum combination relative to the used corpus, to ensure high model performance because, to have a stable and efficient model. It is necessary to choose the optimal combination of alpha and beta values by taking into consideration the optimal number of topics according to the used corpus, this step was explained in more details in our previous approach named Learn2Construct [2].
- The model evaluation: To evaluate quantitatively the quality of the extracted topics we used Topic coherence metrics, which are described in more details in Evaluation Metrics (Sect. 4). In [19] the authors verified that perplexity does not always conform with human judgements, and cannot correctly measure whether a topic is semantically coherent or not. By comparison, [16] showed that Topic Coherence is consistent with human interpretation [7].
- The model execution: in this step we execute the LDA using the optimal alpha, beta and topic numbers values according to our corpus based on the coherence metrics.
- The document cluster: this step consists in generating and viewing the document/topic clusters.

New Topics Generation: In this phase, the input data is not a textual corpus, but a bag of the extracted topics. The LDA topic models can only find topics within a flat structure, but are not able to discover the sub-topics or the hierarchical relationships among topics. The originality of our approach resides in discovering and generating new topics from existing ones, which allows to discover the sub-topics of each extracted topic and analyze the data in greater depth. This phase consists of:

- Model parameter re-stabilization: as we have changed the input data so we need to re-stabilize the LDA model by finding the new optimum combination of alpha, beta and topics number.
- Model evaluation: the performance of our model is related to the best selection of the optimum parameter. In the reason to guarantee the out-performance of our approach we evaluate our model based on coherence measure.
- Model execution: in this step, we execute our model based on the new optimum selected parameter. The output of this phase was the sub-topics of the extracted ones.

Topics Hierarchy: After extracting and discovering topics, we integrate in our approach, a new unsupervised machine learning technique named the hierarchical clustering algorithm [10], which is the well known and the most used technique in the literature in order to hierarchy our corpus topics. So, we combined LDA model with hierarchical clustering in the objective to extract, discover and visualize our corpus topics in a hierarchical form.

- Feature vectors creation: used to represent numeric data of an object in easily analyzable way, this step was important for data processing.
- Model parameter stabilization: after using this technique we tried to configure the model parameter.
- Train the model: the role of this state, is to automatically hierarchy the extracted and the discovered topics. As a result, our corpus topics were represented through a dendogram, at varying levels of granularity. This hierarchical representation is created in top-down strategy.

4 Experiments

Our experiments aimed at comparing well-known topic modeling techniques such as LSA, PLSA, LDA, CTM, HLDA, PAM and our approach (LDA+) in order to evaluate the quality of the extracted and discovered topics as well as the performance of each method with a different corpus size.

We implement and experiment these techniques on the same dataset and with the same parameters setting. We evaluate the results using the coherence measures and run-times. In what follows the used tools and dataset, after, we detail the evaluation process and results.

4.1 Environment

As a programming language, we use Python. For the natural language processing we used NLTK[1] (Natural Language Toolkit), this library is used for tokenization, lemmatization and stop words removal. Regarding topic modeling, we use Gensim[2], a Python library for topic modelling, document indexing and similarity retrieval with large corpora. We use Scikit-Learn[3], a free software machine learning library for python programming language for the other topic models. To train our models, we use a laptop on Intel core (TM) i7-6500U 2.59 GHz of CPU with 8 GB of RAM and 64 GB of disk.

4.2 Evaluation Metrics

Topic Coherence measures score a single topic by measuring the degree of semantic similarity between high scoring words in the topic. These measurements help distinguish between topics that are semantically interpretable topics and topics

---

[1] https://www.nltk.org/.

[2] https://pypi.org/project/gensim/.

[3] https://scikit-learn.org/.

that are artifacts of statistical inference. In our evaluations, we consider two coherence measures [15]: **(1) The UCI measure** [18] and **(2) The UMass measure** [16]. Both measures compute the coherence of a topic as the sum of pairwise distributional similarity scores over the set of topic words, V. We generalize this as

$$Coherence(V) = \sum_{(V_i, \ V_j) \in V} Score_{(V_i, \ V_j, \ e)} \tag{1}$$

where V is a set of word describing the topic, Vi and Vj are two words included in the topic V and e indicates a smoothing factor which guarantees that score returns real numbers. (We will be exploring the effect of the choice of e; the original authors used e = 1.)

The UCI metric defines a word pair's score to be the pointwise mutual information (PMI) between two words, i.e.

$$Score_{(V_i, \ V_j, \ e)} = \log \frac{P(V_i, \ V_j) + e}{P(V_i)P(V_j)} \tag{2}$$

where V is a topic and i, j are tow words in topic V. The word probabilities are computed by counting words co-occurrence frequencies in a sliding window over an external corpus, such as Wikipedia. To some degree, this metric can be thought of as an external comparison to known semantic evaluations.

The UMass metric defines the score to be based on document co-occurrence:

$$Score_{(V_i, \ V_j, \ e)} = \log \frac{D(V_i, \ V_j) + e}{D(V_j)} \tag{3}$$

where D (Vi, Vj) counts the number of documents containing words i and j and D(Vi) counts the number of documents containing the word i. Significantly, the UMass metric computes these counts over the original corpus used to train the topic models, rather than an external corpus. This metric is more intrinsic in nature. It attempts to confirm that the models learned data known to be in the corpus.

4.3 Experimental Protocol

We have generated a set of documents from Pub-med[4], these documents are divided into three corpora with different size (corpus 1, corpus 2 and corpus 3). The corpus 1, contains 10 documents with 43895 terms. The corpus 2, contains 250 documents including 1092603 terms, corpus 3 contains 500 Pub-med documents with 2715871 terms. These corpora are used to generate topics using some existing topic modeling techniques such as LDA [26], LSA [29], PLSA [27], CTM [21], PAM [23], HLDA [25] and our approach LDA+ in order to compare the quality of the extracted topics and to evaluate the influence of the corpus size on the performance of each method.

---

[4] https://pubmed.ncbi.nlm.nih.gov/.

We build the different models by considering a sequence of topics values that starts with 2 up to 50 not only different numbers of topics in order to guarantee better performance of each used method. For each model and for each number of topics, we collect the UCI score, the UMass score and the runtime. The obtained results are presented in what follow.

The figure (Fig. 2) shows the results of the comparison study between the mentioned techniques by considering the runtime score, which is a very important criterion especially for the information retrieval systems because it helps to measure the performance of each method based on the model execution time. The values of this measurement are calculated in seconds and represents the time needed for model learning in order to extract or hierarchy the corpus topics. The figure (Fig. 2) shows that LSA, LDA and LDA+ dominate HLDA, PLSA, PAM and CTM in term of runtime. This score represents the time spent by each model in the processing phase in order to classify the corpus documents. The second part of our evaluation deals with the comparison results between the evaluated methods based on UMass measure using corpus 1 and corpus 3 which helps to evaluate the performance of each model based on an internal corpus (Fig. 3).

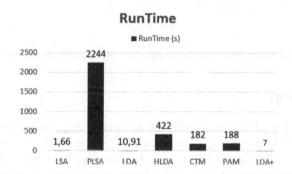

Fig. 2. Comparison results between topic models based on runtime

The results shown in (Fig. 3) justify the performance of LDA+ regards the other methods. For corpus 1, HLDA outscores LSA, PLSA, LDA, LDA+, CTM and PAM. For corpus 3, (Fig. 3) shown the out-performance of our approach as well as the LDA, HLDA and CTM cmpared to the other methods when the corpus size changing. These results demonstrate that the corpus size negatively influence LSA, PLSA, and PAM.

For the UCI score, we used UMLS[5] as an external corpus, this corpus was constructed with 2000 concepts. In this step we tried to match the most represented topic terms generated from each used technique with the identified concepts in UMLS in order to measure the performance of each topic model to correctly identify topics as well as their significant terms based on an external corpus. (Fig. 4) shown that LDA+ absolutely outperforms LSA, PLSA, PAM, CTM and HLDA and LDA.

---

[5] https://www.nlm.nih.gov/research/umls/index.html.

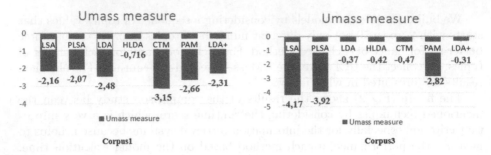

Fig. 3. Comparison results between topic models based on UMass using corpus 1 and corpus3

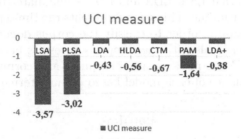

Fig. 4. Comparison results between topic models based on UCI

5   Conclusion

Topic modeling has attracted significant attention and demonstrated good performance in a wide variety of tasks thanks to their ability to analyse a large corpus and determine the corpus topics. In this paper, we presented a comparative study between some topic model techniques. Next, we proposed a novel topic model LDA+ that can generate topics from multiple domain corpora, discover new topics from the extracted ones and learn the topic hierarchy for the target corpus with a high performance. The obtained results are evaluated with topic coherence metrics as well as runtime factor.

As future work, we plan to evaluate the topic hierarchies based on a reference model and study the influence of preprocessing tasks on the performance of topic modeling algorithms.

References

1. Slimane, B., Mounsif, M., Ghada, I.D.: Topic modeling: comparison of LSA and LDA on scientific publications. In: DSDE 2021, 18–20 February, Barcelona, Spain (2021)
2. Khemiri, A., Drissi, A., Tissaoui, A., Sassi, S., Chbier, R.: Learn2Construct: an automatic ontology construction based on LDA from texual data. In: MEDES 2021, Proceedings of the 13th International Conference on Management of Digital Ecosystems, November 2021, pp. 49–56 (2021)

3. Liu, Z., Lin, Y., Sun, M.: Representation Learning for Natural Language Processing. Springer, Singapore (2020). ISBN 978-981-15-5573-2 (eBook) https://doi.org/10.1007/978-981-15-5573-2

4. Shaymaa, H.M., Al-augby, S.: LSA and LDA topic modeling classification: comparison study on E-books. Indonesian J. Electr. Eng. Comput. Sci. **19**(1), 353–362 (2020)

5. Kherwa, P., Bansal, P.: Topic modeling: a comprehensive review. EAI Endorsed Trans. Scalable Inf. Syst. **7**(24), e2 (2020)

6. Kowsari, K., Meimandi, K.J., Heidarysafa, M., Mendu, S., Barnes, L., Brown, D.: Text classification algorithms: a survey. Information (2019). https://www.mdpi.com/2078-2489/10/4/150

7. Yueshen, X., Jianwei, Y., Jianbin, H., Yuyu, Y.: Hierarchical topic modeling with automatic knowledge mining. Expert Syst. Appl. **103**, 106–117 (2018)

8. Rashid, J., Shah, S.M.A., Irtaza, A.: An efficient topic modeling approach for text mining and information retrieval through k-means clustering. Mehran Univ. Res. J. Eng. Technol. **39**(1), 213–222 (2020). https://doi.org/10.22581/muet1982.2001.20. p-ISSN: 0254–7821, e-ISSN: 2413–7219

9. Rajasundari, T., Subathra, P., Kumar, P.: Performance analysis of topic modeling algorithms for news articles. J. Adv. Res. Dyn. Control Syst. **2017**(11), 175–183 (2017)

10. Maimon, O., Rokach, L.: Clustering methods. In: Maimon, O., Rokach, L. (eds.)Data Mining and Knowledge Discovery Handbook, pp. 321–352. Springer, Boston (2006). https://doi.org/10.1007/0-387-25465-X_15

11. Rubayyi, A., Khalid, A.: A survey of topic modeling in text mining. Int. J. Adv. Comput. Sci. Appl. **6**(1), 147–153 (2015)

12. Paisley, J., Wang, C., Blei, D.M., Jordan, M.I.: Nested hierarchical Dirichlet processes. IEEE Trans. Pattern Anal. Mach. Intell. (PAMI) **37**(2), 256–270 (2015)

13. Yue, L., Qiaozhu, M., ChengXiang, Z.: Investigating task performance of probabilistic topic models: an empirical study of PLSA and LDA. Inf. Retrieval **V14**, 178–203 (2012)

14. Bullinaria, J.A., Levy, J.P.: Extracting semantic representations from word co-occurrence statistics: stoplists, stemming, and SVD. Behavior Res. Methods **44**, 890–907 (2012)

15. Keith, S., Philip, K., David, A., David, B.: Exploring Topic Coherence over many models and many topics. In: Proceedings of the 2012 Joint Conference on Empirical Methods in Natural Language Processing and Computational Natural Language Learning, pp. 952–961 (2012)

16. David, M., Hanna, M. W., Edmund, T., Miriam, L., Andrew, M.: Optimizing semantic coherence in topic models. In: Proceedings of the Conference on Empirical Methods in Natural Language Processing (Edinburgh, United Kingdom), USA, pp. 262–272. Association for Computational Linguistics (2011)

17. Ming, Z.-Y., Wang, K., Chua, T.-S.: Prototype hierarchy based clustering for the categorization and navigation of web collections. In: Proceedings of ACM SIGIR, pp. 2–9 (2010)

18. Newman, D., Noh, Y., Talley, E., Karimi, S., Baldwin, T.: 2010: evaluating topic models for digital libraries. In: Proceedings of the 10th Annual Joint Conference on Digital Libraries, JCDL 2010, New York, NY, USA, pp. 215–224. ACM (2010)

19. Chang, J., Boyd-Graber, J. L., Gerrish, S., Wang, C., Blei, D.M.: Reading tea leaves: how humans interpret topic models. In: Advances in Neural Information Processing Systems (NIPS), pp. 288–296 (2009)

20. Mimno, D., Li, W., McCallum, A.: Mixtures of hierarchical topics with pachinko allocation. In: Appearing in Proceedings of the 24th International Conference on Machine Learning, Corvallis, OR (2007). Copyright 2007 by the author(s)/owner(s) (2007)
21. Blei, D., Lafferty, J.D.: A correlated topic model of science. In: AAS 2007, pp. 17–35 (2007)
22. Li, W., McCallum, A.: Pachinko allocation: DAG-structured mixture models of topic correlations. In: Appearing in Proceedings of the 23rd International Conference on Machine Learning, Pittsburgh, PA (2006). Copyright 2006 by the author(s)/owner(s)
23. Li, W., McCallum, A.: Pachinko allocation: DAG-structured mixture models of topic correlations. In: ICML (2006)
24. Gonçalves, T., Quaresma, P.: Evaluating preprocessing techniques in a text classification problem. São Leopoldo, RS, Bras. SBC-Sociedade Brasilleira De Computacao, pp. 841–850 (2005)
25. Blei, D., Griffiths, T., Jordan, M., Tenenbaum, J.: Hierarchical topic models and the nested Chinese restaurant process. In: NIPS (2004)
26. Blei, D.M., Ng, A.Y., Jordan, M.I.: Latent dirichlet allocation. J. Mach. Learn. Res. **3**, 993–1022 (2003)
27. Hofmann, T.: Probabilistic latent semantic analysis. In: Uncertainty in Artificial Intelligence (1999)
28. Landauer, T.K., Dumais, S.T.: A solution to Plato's problem: the latent semantic analysis theory of acquisition, induction, and representation of knowledge. Psychol. Rev. **104**, 211 (1997)
29. Peter, W.: FOLTZ, 1996: latent semantic analysis for text-based research, Springer. Behav. Res. Methods Instrum. Comput. **28**(2), 197–202 (1996)

Schema Formalism for Semantic Summary Based on Labeled Graph from Heterogeneous Data

Amal Beldi[1]([⊠]), Salma Sassi[2], Richard Chbeir[3], and Abderrazak Jemai[1,4]

[1] Faculty of Mathematical Physical and Natural Sciences of Tunis,
SERCOM Laboratory, Tunis El Manar University, 1068 Tunis, Tunisia
`amal.beldi@fst.utm.tn`
[2] Faculty of Law Economics and Management of Jendouba, VPNC Laboratory,
Jendouba University, 8189 Jendouba, Tunisia
`salma.sassi@fsjegj.rnu.tn`
[3] University Pau & Pays Adour, LIUPPA, 64600 Anglet, France
`richard.chbeir@univ-pau.fr`
[4] Polytechnic School of Tunisia, SERCOM Laboratory, INSAT, Carthage University,
1080 Tunis, Tunisia

Abstract. Graphs are used in various applications and to model real world objects. To understand the underlying characteristics of large graphs, graph summarization becomes a hot topic aiming to facilitate the identification of structure and meaning in data. The problem of graph summarization has been studied in the literature and many approaches for static contexts are proposed to summarize the graph in terms of its communities. These approaches typically produce groupings of nodes which satisfy or approximate some optimization function. Nevertheless, they fail to characterize the subgraphs and do not summarize both the structure and the content in the same approach. Existing approaches are only suitable for a static context, and do not offer direct dynamic counterparts. This means that there is no framework that provides summarization of mixed-source and information with the goal of creating a dynamic, syntactic, and semantic data summary. In this paper, the main contribution relies on summarizing data into a single graph model for heterogeneous sources. It's a schema-driven approach based on labeled graph. Our approach allows also to link the graph model to the relevant domain knowledge to find relevant concepts to provide meaningful and concise summary. After extracting relevant domain, we provide a personalized visualization model capable of summarize graphically both the structure and the content of the data from databases, devices, and sensors to reduce cognitive barriers related to the complexity of the information and its interpretation. We illustrate this approach through a case study on the use of E-health domain.

Keywords: Graph formalism · Heterogenous data · Real time ·
Interoperability · Structure summarization · Based content
summarization · Aggregation · Compression

© The Author(s), under exclusive license to Springer Nature Singapore Pte Ltd. 2022
E. Szczerbicki et al. (Eds.): ACIIDS 2022, CCIS 1716, pp. 27–44, 2022.
https://doi.org/10.1007/978-981-19-8234-7_3

1 Introduction

Graph data management provides better support for highly interconnected datasets [1]. Most big data applications including social networks [2], bioinformatics [3] and astronomy [4] are examples of large-scale interconnected graphs. Such data can be more easily expressed using entities of a graph (nodes and edges). Querying and reasoning about the interconnections between entities in such graph dataset can lead to interesting and deep insights into a variety of phenomena. However, due to sheer volume, complexity, and temporal characteristics, building a concise representation (i.e., summary) helps to understand these datasets as well as to formulate queries in a meaningful way. In this context, graph summarization becomes a hot topic in the database research community in recent years. It facilitates the identification of structure and meaning in data. A summary is a concise representation of the original graph, whose objectives can greatly vary from reducing the number of bits needed for encoding the original graph, to more complex database-style operations that summarize graphs where the resolution could be scaled-up or scaled-down interactively [5]. With the advent of dynamic graphs and streams, there is a demand for analyzing the time-evolving properties of such graphs, and once again graph synopsis construction has found increasing interests [6]. Given its advantages, graph summarization has a wide range of application including interactive and exploratory analysis [7], approximate query processing [8], visualization [9], data-driven Visual graph query interface construction [10] and distributed Graph Systems [11] among others. The problem of graph summarization has been studied in the fields of graph mining and data management. Many approaches for static contexts such as modularity-based community detection [12], spectral clustering [13], graph-cut algorithms [14] exist to summarize the graph in terms of its communities, but lack explicit ordering [15]. These approaches typically produce groupings of nodes which only satisfy or approximate some optimization function. They also fail to characterize the subgraphs and do not summarize both the structure and the content in the same approach. Existing approaches also do not offer characterization of the outputs. The lack of explicit ordering in the groupings leaves a user with limited time and no insights on where to begin understanding his data. Furthermore, existing approaches are only suitable for a static context, and do not offer direct dynamic counterparts. Some algorithms like [14] do work in a dynamic setting, but focus only on finding static patterns that appear over multiple time steps. This means that there is no framework that provides summarization of mixed-source and information with the goal of creating a syntactic and semantic data summary. Given the above problems, the proposed paper focus on how we can best describe in one summary both structure and content and thus not just generate succinct summaries for the mixed-sources, but also understand its corresponding interactions and relationships with the past. Thus, towards building a semantic and dynamic summary, the following challenges emerge.

- **Challenge 1**: How to provide multi-sources-based summary, due to multi-modality of data (e.g., text, video, and image) that can be encoded in different formats ?
- **Challenge 2**: How to provide user oriented semantic based summary, due to the difficulty of retrieving information according to user 'needs?
- **Challenge 3**: How to incorporate the dynamic nature of real data in computation and perform analysis efficiently? Our work aims to generate a concise semantic summary of heterogeneous sources to better understand their underlying characteristics.

The main contribution of this study relies on summarizing data into a single graph model for heterogeneous sources. It's a schema-driven approach based on labeled graph. Our approach allows also to link the graph model to the relevant domain knowledge to find relevant concepts to provide meaningful and concise summary. So, we propose a summary-driven formalism based on labeled graphs, which provides interesting data summary conserving better data integrity. Also, this formalism allows more structured summary of the data stored within a graph database. The rest of this paper is organized as follows. Section 2 provides a Literature review describing and discussing related works on graph summarization. Section 3 describes the overall of our approach. In Sect. 4, we describe a schema-driven approach for summarization of the LPG graph, based on our proposed formalism. Section 5 described the summarization model-based content and Sect. 7 provides the implementation of our approach, the conducted experimentation, results, and discussions. Section 8 concludes this study and provides several perspectives.

2   Related Works

2.1   Summarization Approaches

- **Static plain graph approach**: most works in static graph summarization focuses on graph structure without side information or labels. At a high level, the problem of summarization, aggregation or coarsening of static is described as simplification-based summarization methods streamline the original graph by removing less "important" nodes or edges, resulting in a sparsified graph [27]. A representative work on node simplification-based summarization techniques is OntoVis [20], representing a visual analytical tool that relies on node filtering for the purpose of understanding large, heterogeneous social networks in which nodes and links. Toivonen et al. [16] focus on compressing graphs with edge weights, proposing to merge nodes with similar relationships to other entities (structurally equivalent nodes. SPINE, an alternative to CSI [17], sparsifies social networks to only keep the edges that "explain" the information propagation those that maximize the likelihood of the observed data. In the visualization domain, Dunne and Shneiderman [18] introduce motif simplification to enhance network visualization.

- **Static labled graph approach**: We have reviewed summarization methods that use the structural properties of static graphs without additional information like node and edge attributes. The main challenge in summarizing labeled graphs is the efficient combination of two different types of data: structural connections and attributes [29]. Currently, most existing works focus on node attributes alone, although other types of side information are certainly of interest in summarization. The first and most famous frequent-subgraph-based summarization scheme is SUBDUE [22] employing a greedy beam search to iteratively replace the most frequent subgraph in a labeled graph. The S-Node representation [23] is a novel two-level lossless graph compression scheme optimizing specifically Web graphs. SNAP and k-SNAP are two popular database-style approaches [19] rely on (attribute and relationship-compatibility), which guarantees that nodes in all groups are homogeneous in terms of attributes, and are also adjacent to nodes in the same groups for all types of relationships. Song and al [21] proposes a lossy graph summarization framework as a collection of d-summaries, which intuitively are supergraphs that group similar entities.
- **Dynamic graph approach**: analyzing large and complex data is challenging by itself, so adding the dimension of time makes the analysis even more challenging and time-consuming. For this reason, the temporal graph mining literature is rich, mostly focusing on laws and patterns of graph evolution. Summarization techniques for time-evolving networks have not been studied to the same extent as those for static networks, possibly because of the new challenges introduced by the dimension of time. The methods are sensitive to the choice of time granularity, which is often chosen arbitrarily: depending on the application, granularity can be set to minutes, hours, days, weeks, months, years, or some other unit that makes sense in a given setting. This category's only representative is TCM [6] and TimeCrunch [24], which succinctly describe a large dynamic graph with a set of important temporal structures. (Qu et al. 2014) [30] is a stream of time-ordered interactions, represented as undirected edges between labeled nodes. NetCondense [25] is a node-grouping approach that maintains specific properties of the original time-varying graph, like diffusive properties important in marketing and influence dynamics, governed by its maximum eigen value.

2.2   Discussion and Limitations

In order to compare the existing approaches and to overcome the challenges described previously, we define here 7 criteria with respect to the defined challenges:

Challenge 1: How to provide multi-sources-based summary, due to multimodality of data (e.g., text, video, and image) that can be encoded in different formats?

- **Type of input Data (C1)**: this criterion refers to the input data which could be: structured data such as already defined knowledge models include existing ontologies and database schema/graph (ii) Semi-structured data designates the use of some mixed structured data with free text such as Web pages, Wikipedia sources, dictionaries, and XML documents, and (iii) Unstructured data is related to any plain text content, video, signal. etc.

- **Data type (C2)**: this criterion describe the type of data incorporate (text, xml, numeric, video, image).
- **Representation standard (C3)**: this criterion describes if the approach incorporates standard((i.e. information based standard, document based standard or Hybrid standard) (e.g., Yes or No).

Challenge 2: How to provide user oriented semantic based summary, due to the difficulty of retrieving information according to user 'needs?

- **Summarization technique (C4)**: this criterion refers to the techniques deployed to summarize ehr which could be: grouping, compression, analysis, pattern- mining, classification, visualization.
- **Summarization approach (C5)**: this criterion refers to the target of the summarization approach abstractive, extractive, informative or inducative.
- **Medical knowledge based summarization(C6)**: this criterion describe the medical knowledge that system incorporate (e.g., Yes or No).

Challenge 3: How to incorporate the dynamic nature of real data in computation and perform analysis efficiently?

- **Output type (C7)**: this criterion concerns the type of displayed summarized data which is a combination of: numerical data, textual data, document, graph.
- **Context-aware criterion (C8)**: defines two types of context-aware:(i) Partial, used to demonstrate if an existing system uses concepts about the deployed context of the devices (e.g., time, location, and trajectory) or concepts about the static data and (ii) Total, used to determine if an existing system uses both of deployed context of devices and other static data context.
- **User oriented summarization (C9)**: this criterion represent that the approach oriented user (e.g., yes or No).

Our comparison highlights that the evolution of the summary is still an open challenge. So, we observe that most of existing studies [16–18,20] do not consider real data in their analysis and do not consider the context on creating the summary and they rely only on the time property. Thus, existing systems [6,25,26] are still unable to contextually interpret and reason on the transferred knowledge among real data, and consequently cannot synthetize data in order to provide accurate desired results. All existing systems focus on one objective, while none of them provide in the same framework various functionalities despite its importance in supporting users' preferences to find the data according to various needs. All objectives should be an integral part of a summarization-based system. Most of the above studies [19,20,28,29] can only satisfy a certain aspect of users' needs. Finally, another important part of this study is the output type of summarized data. They do not propose dedicated tools that make the summary accessible to the user nor provide them with appropriate perceptions of their needs. Users are more and more concerned about security, confidentiality, understanding their data, and the accuracy and completeness of their data. In this study, the main approach that we address the aforementioned problems by proposing an appropriate approach able to model heterogeneous sources based in a single graph based on a schema-driven approach, providing a personalized summary model capable of synthesize graphically the content based and finally summarizing the structure of the graph in order to reduce its size and minimize its complexity and keep the important nodes and relations (Table 1).

Table 1. Qualitative Comparison of static, static labeled dynamic plain Graph Summarization Approach

Existing study/Criterion	Challenge 1			Challenge 2				Challenge 3	
	C1	C2	C3	C4	C5	C6	C7	C8	C9
Category 1: Dynamic graph									
(Adhikariet al. 2017)	Structured	Weighted, Directed, Unidirected	Yes	Structure	Influence	Grouping	Supergraph	Partial Time	Yes
(Tan et al.,2016)	Structured	Weighted, Directed, Undirected	Yes	structure	Query efficiency	Grouping	Supergraph	Partial time	Yes
(Shah et al., 2015)	Structured	Unweighted, Directed, Undirected	Yes	Structure	Visualization	Compression	List of temporal structure	Partial time	Yes
(Qu et al., 2014)	Structured	Unweighted, Undirected	Yes	Structure	Influence	Influence	Subgraph	Partial time	Yes
Category 2: Static graph									
(Maccioni et al.,2016)	Structured	Unweigted, Directd, Undirected	No	Structure	Query efficiency	Grouping	Sparsified graph	No	No
(Dunne et al., 2013)	Structured	Unweighted, Undirected	No	Structure	Visualization	Grouping	Supergraph	No	No
(Toivonen et al. 2011)	Structured	Weighted, Directed, Undirected	No	Structure	Compression	Grouping	Supergraph	No	No
(Mathioudakis et al., 2011)	Strctured	Weighted, Directed	No	Structure	Influence	Influence	Sparsified graph	No	No
Category 3: Static labeled graph									
(Song et al. 2016)	Structured	Unweighted, Undirected	No	Structure	Query efficiency	Grouping	Supergraph	No	No
(Mehmood et al. 2013)	Structured	Unweighted, Directed	No	Structure	Influence	Influence	Supergraph	No	No
(Toiven et al. 2011)	Structured	Weighted, Undirected, Directed	No	Structure	Grouping	Compression	Super graph	No	No
(Shein et al. 2006)	Structured	Unweighted, Undirected	No	Structure	Simplification	Visualization	Sparsified graph	No	No
Proposed approach	Structured, Unstructured	Unweighted, Undirected	Yes	Structure, Content	Summarization	Aggregation, Mathematics operations	Graph summary	Yes	Yes

3   Contribution

The proposed approach aims to summarize data into a single graph model for heterogonous sources. It's a a schema-driven approach based on labeled graph. It allows also to link the graph model to the relevant domain knowledge to find relevant concepts in order to provide meaningful and concise summary. Last but not least, it provides a personalized visualization model capable to summarize graphically both the structure and the content of the data from databases, devices and sensors to reduce cognitive barriers related to the complexity of the information and its interpretation. To achieve this goal, our framework architecture is composed of four main modules as shown in Fig. 1:

A) **Data Pre-Processing module**: consists of processing and indexing data in order to summarize them. Every incoming data is processed and transformed according to two-steps: data cleaning and data semantization. This module is composed of:

a) **Data Cleaning**: consists of preprocessing data and involves transforming raw data into an understandable format. It consists of data extraction from multiple and heterogeneous sources. Then, data cleaning is applied which is the most important task in building any analysis model. This includes outliers quantizing and handling missing values.

b) **Data Semantization**: integrates semantics into preprocessed data by normalizing them based on an existing domain knowledge. Based on the heterogeneity characteristics of data, we propose an integrated framework composed of three processes:

   i) **Modeling unstructured data**: we use here NLP tools to identify data and to convert them into their appropriate data types.

   ii) **Mapping data with domain knowledge**: we combine here structured data with the previous process (unstructured data) output before mapping them with knowledge domain metadata for better normalization.

   iii) **Integrating Data**: we integrate the different normalized data into a generic framework that supports direct generation of the data in a common format.

B) **Data Graph generation module**: it consists of transforming input data and generating aggregated items into a graph-based data model. We introduce here a new Data Graph Model (DGM) representing important structured and unstructured data in a domain. We define the DGM graph to efficiently represent a domain data and the relationship between them. The GDM model will be detailed in Sect. 4.

C) **Data Summarization module**: defines the data summarization model-based graph, which is the core module of our framework. It allows to transform input data and generates the summary. So, it aims, firstly, at modeling through a data graph schema the most appropriate data that must be summarized. Secondly, summarizing data using a driven schema approach based on structure and content. The data summarization model-based graph will be detailed in next section. This module is composed by two sub-module:

a) **Based content module:** This sub-module provides a user-centered summarization model depending on the user preferences. Our goal behind this proposed graph summarization-based content is to provide data model adjusted based user preferences and needs. For this end, we define, a new node to allow users personalizing the content according to the analysis needs and preferences. We allow creating a calcul to one or many Data Nodes from the graph data GD to calculate a mathematic function from any number of incoming numeric values. Then the resulting score is placed in a new Data Node. The node result is related to the data nodes sources through a calculation Node, a condition Node, and a logic Node. The proposed graph summarization-based content will be detailed in Sect. 5.

b) **Based structure module:** Summarization model based structure consists of summarizing the graph in terms of its topology in order to reduce the size and minimize the complexity of the graph and keep the important nodes and relations. It is called structural summarization. In order to summarize the graph structurally, we define new "Super-DataNode" and "Super-Edge" nodes. Our goal is to generate a summary network by grouping similar data nodes and finding hierarchical "Super-DataNode" (representing collection of data nodes) and "Super-Edges" (representing similarities between groups of Data Nodes). Once the graph GD constructed, the summarization process begins. The goal is to generate a smaller network: GDs = (DNs, DRs, Ls, Ts, As, Vs) from the original network GD = (DN, DR, , L, T, A, V) such that data nodes representing similar/relevant nodes in GD are grouped into a single node (a "super-DataNode") in GDs. We call GDs = (DNs, DRs, Ls, Ts, As, Vs) a "summary network," where super-DataNodes (SuperDNs) are the groups of related data nodes and super-Edges (SuperE) represent the average similarity between group of data nodes represented by the two end points. We obtain GDs via a series of "Assign" relations. The Assign Relation assigns data nodes to their super-nodes. This relation partitions the original network DG and groups each partition to form a Super-DataNode in the summary network GDS. We define three types of assign relation:

   i) **Data Nodes aggregation relation** consists of summarizing the graph by aggregating the same data node types into super nodes.

   ii) **Relation aggregation relation** consists of summarizing the graph by aggregating the same relationship types into super relations.

   iii) **Compression relation** consists of defining graph summary from the input. By Minimizing the number of bits needed to describe the input graph via its summary

D) **Data Post-Processing module**: is responsible of the visual representation of data. It provides visual and interactive communication and includes the techniques to graphically present data so as to summarize and understand the meaning of data. Also, it allows to rapidly find insights in data.

The domain description module provides users (and mainly experts) the domain knowledge description to enable meaningful domain interoperability. This description provides the organizational and functional interoperability, the semantic interoperability using domain terminology, and the device data annotation using an existing IoT ontology.

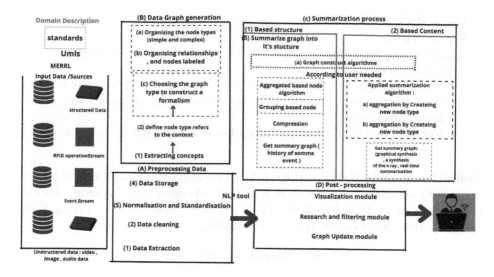

Fig. 1. Architecture of our proposed system

4   A Graph Data Model

An aggregation process is performed on the transformed input data and generates the aggregated value. Indeed, given a set of data items, a graph-based data
model of aggregated items is iteratively built. The graph root is an aggregated
item that represents the whole data set. Each aggregated item consists of one or
more children which can be the original data items (leaves) or aggregated items
(nodes). We introduce here a new Data Graph Model (DGM). The main goal
behind DGM is to build and manipulate a common synthesis of a large amount
of data to facilitate and perform the summarization process.

4.1   Data Graph Formalism

The Data Graph Model (DGM) represents important structured and unstructured data in a domain. We define the DGM graph to efficiently represent a
domain data and the relationship between them.

Definition 1: Data Node A Data Node (DN) represents the information contained in a data structure. The data node contains a value of structured or unstructured data. Nodes are represented by a single parent node. A Data Node (DN) is
described by an identification, a name, and a type. We define here a data node
which can be simple node or complex node. A data node is defined as follow:

$$DN: (IdN, NameN, Val, ValType, TypeN)$$

where

- IdN: is the node identifier
- NameN: is the node name

36   A. Beldi et al.

- Val: is the a value for each node attribute
- ValType: is the type of the value of each node attribute
- TypeN: is the type of node which can be simple Node or complex node We distinguish two types of Data Node:
  - Simple Data Node (SDN) is the most elementary unit. It can only be of the following ones: textual node, numerical node, Boolean node, image node, video node.
  - Complex Node (CDN) is composed of one or many simple and/or complex nodes.

Definition 2: Data Relationship: A Data Relationship (DR) connects two or many data nodes in the graph G. It is a directed edge consisting of an ordered pair of data nodes. It is characterized by a set of attributes, a role, a Data Node Source, a Data Node Destination. A relationship is defined as follow:

$$DR\ (IdR,\ NameR,\ nS,\ nD,\ Label)$$

where

- IdDR: is the relation identifier
- NameDR is the relation's name
- dnS: is the node source of the relation ri
- dnD: is the node destination of the relation ri Label: is a word or a set of words used to describe the relation

Definition 3: Data Graph Model: We denote a graph GD as (DN, DR, L, T, A, V, ft, fa, fv, fr,) where N is the set of nodes, and R is a set of relationships.

Each Ri $\subseteq$ N * N representing the set of edges of a particular type. Nodes in a graph have a set of associated attributes, which is denoted as A Each node has a value for each attribute. These attributes are used to describe the features of the objects that the nodes represent.

$$GD = (DN,\ DR,\ ,\ L,\ T,\ A,\ V,\ ft,\ fa,\ fv,\ fr)$$

where:

- DN: is a set of (nodes) ni, denoting model Nodes Simple nodes and Complex Nodes.
- DR: is a set of relationships,
- L: is a set of edge labels li designating each a node or a relationship
- T: is a set of types of ti
- A: is a set of attributes ai
- V: is a set of values vi
- ft: N$\rightarrow$ T is a function associating each node ni to its type (ft(ni))
- fa: N$\rightarrow$A is a function associating each node ni to a set of attributes (fa(ni))
- fv: A$\rightarrow$V is a function associating each type of attribute ai A to a possible value (fv(ai))
- fR: is a function defined on R, assigning a label from L to each edge in R

- fSr: R→ N is a function associating for each relation ri to its node source ((fSr(ri)))
- fD: R→ N is a function associating for each relation ri to its node destination ((fD (ri)))

Algorithm 1: Data Graph Formalism

Input: heterogeneous data: image, document, text, numeric
Output: DG
1 begin;
2 Construct data node;
3 Construct simple node and complex node:DN;
4 Construct relation types:DR;
5 Attribute the properties for node types:A;
6 Value of nodes: is a set of values vi ;
7 Attribute label for nodes (L);
8 for i ← 0 to the number of different data type do ;
9 if (the content of data is one type) then ;
10 type T = simple data node: SDN;
11 else complex data node: CDN;
12 end if;
13 end for;
14 For j ← 0 to the number of nodes N do;
15 fl:Defined label L;
16 ft: Defined type T;
17 fv: Defined value,V;
18 End for;
19 Return DG ;
20 end

The algorithm Graph Formalism Algorithm 1 describes how to build our Data Graph DG into it simple nodes, complex nodes and relations.

5   Summarization-Based Content Model

We Provide a user-centered summarization model depending on the user preferences. Our goal behind this proposed graph summarization-based content is to provide data model adjusted based user preferences and needs. For this end, we define, a new node to allow users personalizing the content according to the analysis needs and preferences. We can create a calcul to one or many Data Nodes from the graph data GD to calculate a mathematic function from any number of incoming numeric values. The node result is related to the data nodes sources through a calculation Node.

Definition 1: Calculation Node. A calculation Node performs calculations on a single value. The following Calculation Nodes represent basic mathematical calculation: add, subtract, multiply, divide, exponent, remainder, average, count, last, Max, Min, Sum. A Calculation Node is defined as follows:

CalculNodeV (FirstV, CalculSymb, SecondVal, DisplayList)

where:

- FirstVal: is the first input value that will be used in the calculation
- CalculSymb: the symbol that corresponds with the mathematical calculation that is performed by the node.
- SecondVal: is the second input value that will be used in the calculation
- DisplayList: determines the label that appears on the node in the policy model

A Data node result is generated contain respectively, The max value of diabetes for the first collection and the max value diabetes for the second collection. After That, we apply an Average Node to calculate the average value of the max values. Also we can integrate other nodes type proposed such as

- **Definition 2: Logic node:** And and Or that you can use in a policy model to specify whether or not policy execution should continue based on the results of the incoming logic paths. Specifically: The And node evaluates whether or not all incoming logic paths result in a value of true passed to the And node. The Or node evaluates whether or not at least one incoming logic path results in a value of true passed to the Or node.
- **Definition 3: Conditional node:** We define this type to apply a variety of conditions, calculations, and logic to the values represented by data nodes.
- **Definition 4: Comparison node:** To compare two values using the comparison operator that corresponds to the name of the node. The following comparison nodes are available: Equal, Not Equal, Greater Than, Greater Than or Equal, Less Than. In our work the based content summarization process focused in the numeric node, formalized by these different steps.

Algorithm 2: Based content summarization

Input: Data Graph

Output: summary result: GDs, supernodes , graphical, list

1 based content summarization applied;
2 For i = 1 to n ;
3 if typeDN=(numeric node);
4 applied operation node according to user needs;
5 case 1 : CalculNodeV (FirstV, CalculSymb, SecondVal, Displayresult);
6 case 2: ComparisonNode (FirstV, operatorSymb, SecondVal, Displayresult);
7 $\forall$ DGi, DGsj $\in$ G, i = j, DGi $\cap$ DGsj $\neq$ $\varnothing$;
8 Return result;
9 end

---

6   Summarization Based Structure Model

In this model is to summarize the graph in terms of its topology, the objective of which is to reduce the size and minimize the complexity of the graph and keep the important nodes and relations. We note it structural summarization. Graph structure is prominently used in summarization technique (compression, grouping, simplification, visualization). In order to summarize the graph structurally, we define new Super-Data-Node and Super Edge. Our goal is to generate a summary network by grouping similar data nodes and finding hierarchical "Super-Data-Node" and "Super-Edges" . Once the graph GD constructed, the summarization process begins. The goal is to generate a smaller graph GDs = (DNs, DRs, Ls, Ts, As, Vs) from the original graph

GD = (DN, DR, , L, T, A, V) such that data nodes representing similar/relevant nodes in GD are grouped into a single node (a "super- node") in GDs.

Algorithm 3: Structured summarization

Input: Data Graph
Output: Data graph summary DGs
1 Structured summarization applied;
2 For i= 1 to n;
3 regrouping nodes that have same types;
4 if DN=textual node, DN=numeric node or DN=image node;
5 Regrouping nodes in the supernode;
6 DGs = DNs1, DNs2,..DNsk;
7 if $\forall$ DGi $\in$ DG, DNs (DGi) $\cap$ DNs (DGs) and DGi $\neq \emptyset$;
8 $\forall$ DGi, DGsj$\in$ DG, i = j, DGi $\cap$ DGsj $\neq \varnothing$;
9 Return supernode of SDN types regrouping;
10 end

---

7   Experimentation and Results

In this section we provide an experimental study of our proposed approach and analysis of the proposed algorithms and operational nodes. We have developed a prototype of our methodology implemented in NEO4J visualization and Python database. Graphs GD are stored using the following formalism proposed and described in Sect. 4.1.

7.1   Datasets and Experimental Setup

Our scenario is described by various essential steps for our approach, the first step consists of loading heterogeneous information containing a patient's medical file in several formats (Word doc, PDF doc, xlsx, image, video, audio) that represented our heterogeneous database. The second step is the building of a data graph that describes how to model heterogeneous data into graph: each node follows the formalism proposed (data node, data relationship, calculation node, logic node, condition node) and each node type has its own color (exp image node refers the red color shows in Fig. 2 textual node refers the green color Fig. 3. The summarization process, in this context we have proposed two types of tha graph summary. The first one a based content which is interested in summarizing the digital measurements (temperature, blood measure, glucose level) coming from the 3 sensors. The result of this type of synthesis shows us either the maximum value, the minimum value, the average of these measurements during the period mentioned (1 month) Fig. 5 or a curve which interprets the variations of the measurements Fig. 6. The second type of summarization is interested in complex nodes, we start with an extraction and a cleaning is explained that a PDF document will be extracted in cleaned pages (texts apart and images apart) afterwards each text will be accompanied by an annotation (node annotation) which comes from mapping with the UMLS dictionary to facilitate the diagnosis and decision-making of doctor.

For structural summarization it's an aggregation operation and compression algorithm, node based attribute or relationship. The result of summary graph visualization containing only linked nodes (an attribute that expresses user need such as a particular disease or to Summarize medical prescriptions of X-ray interpretation Fig. 3 figured in textual node (in green color) or image node in (red color) to summarize only X-ray. Or an aggregation of images (ultrasounds by date) presented with pink color Or aggregation to display a summary graph mentioned the last nodes visualised (patient history) Fig. 4.

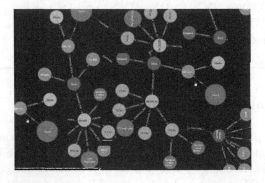

Fig. 2. Electronic health record model represented by data graph (Color figure online)

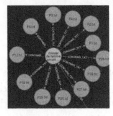

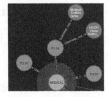

Fig. 3. Structured summarization (based on aggregation node (same type of node)) (Color figure online)

Fig. 4. Structured summarization (based on aggregation by attribute) (Color figure online)

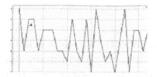

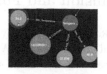

Fig. 5. Based content summarization visualized in graphical node

Fig. 6. Based content summarization using calculation node (max, min, avg) (Color figure online)

7.2 Evaluation

For our benchmarking, we used formalism graph data (GD) for medical database. Moreover, we known that for graph summarization based on content there are not yet evaluation metrics to use in the literature. We have proposed two metrics the running time and the loss of information to evaluate our approach. First step for the content summarization we associate this evaluation: In Fig. 7, we depict the impact of the variation of the number of node and relationships on the summarizing algorithms. We compared our algorithm in term based content summarization to other ones based structure in the literature. We choice the approach proposed in the literature [19] using execution time metric. We considered the execution time of our algorithm always remains low and this guarantees its applicability to large graph (nodes, relationships) and that shows good performance for our approach. In Fig. 8 we compare our algorithms from aggregation nodes, aggregation relationships with algorithm of approach [19] using a loss of information metric. We noted that our approach is more efficient (yellow curve and orange curve) keep a large percentage of content graph (nodes and relationships).

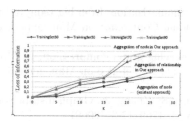

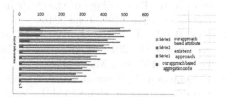

Fig. 7. Relative improvement on runtime between based content summary (our approach) vs structured summarization approach (Color figure online)

Fig. 8. Relative improvement on loss of information between graph summary aggregated (node, relationship) in our approach vs based ksnap graph summary (Color figure online)

8 Conclusion and Future Work

In this work, we study utility-driven graph summarization in-depth and made several novel contributions. We present a new, lossless graph summary, the first one structured based and the second one content based. Moreover we introduced our approach by the formalism proposed of data graph into heterogeneous data in the input. We proposed four main operations to the summarization process. We design a scalable, lossy summarization algorithm in our experimentation, based on two principal metrics the running time and the non-loss of information. Finally, the problem of graph summarization has been extensively addressed for existing graph data models, such as static, labeled, and weighted graphs that mentioned in our related works. Furthermore, our interesting future direction would be to investigate quality metrics for summaries and evaluation benchmarks for structured graph summary and based content. Also to ameliorate summarization process with integration of all operation node types proposed.

References

1. Boldi, P., Rosa, M., Santini, M., Vigna, S.: Layered label propagation: a multiresolution coordinate-free ordering for compressing social networks. In: Proceedings of the 20th International Conference on World Wide Web, pp. 587–596, March 2011
2. Cudré-Mauroux, P., Elnikety, S.: Graph data management systems for new application domains. Proc. VLDB Endowment 4(12), 1510–1511 (2011)
3. Hooper, S.D., Bork, P.: Medusa: a simple tool for interaction graph analysis. Bioinformatics 21(24), 4432–4433 (2005)
4. Barceló, P., Pérez, J., Reutter, J.L.: Relative expressiveness of nested regular expressions. AMW 12, 180–195 (2012)
5. Tian, Y., Hankins, R.A., Patel, J.M.: Efficient aggregation for graph summarization. In: Proceedings of the 2008 ACM SIGMOD International Conference on Management of Data, pp. 567–580, June 2008
6. Tang, N., Chen, Q., Mitra, P.: Graph stream summarization: from big bang to big crunch. In: Proceedings of the 2016 International Conference on Management of Data, pp. 1481–1496, June 2016
7. Fan, W., Li, J., Wang, X., Wu, Y.: Query preserving graph compression. In: Proceedings of the 2012 ACM SIGMOD International Conference on Management of Data, pp. 157–168, May 2012
8. Feigenbaum, J., Kannan, S., McGregor, A., Suri, S., Zhang, J.: Graph distances in the data-stream model. SIAM J. Comput. 38(5), 1709–1727 (2009)
9. Han, W., et al.: Chronos: a graph engine for temporal graph analysis. In: Proceedings of the Ninth European Conference on Computer Systems, pp. 1–14, April 2014
10. Kang, U., Faloutsos, C.: Beyond 'caveman communities': hubs and spokes for graph compression and mining. In: 2011 IEEE 11th International Conference on Data Mining, pp. 300–309. IEEE, December 2011

11. Kang, U., Tong, H., Sun, J., Lin, C.Y., Faloutsos, C.: GBASE: a scalable and general graph management system. In: Proceedings of the 17th ACM SIGKDD International Conference on Knowledge Discovery and Data Mining, pp. 1091–1099, August 2011

12. Huang, J., Abadi, D.J., Ren, K.: Scalable SPARQL querying of large RDF graphs. Proc. VLDB Endowment 4(11), 1123–1134 (2011)

13. Khan, K.U., Nawaz, W., Lee, Y.K.: Set-based unified approach for summarization of a multi-attributed graph. World Wide Web 20(3), 543–570 (2017)

14. Shah, N., Koutra, D., Zou, T., Gallagher, B., Faloutsos, C.: Timecrunch: interpretable dynamic graph summarization. In: Proceedings of the 21th ACM SIGKDD International Conference on Knowledge Discovery and Data Mining, pp. 1055–1064, August 2015

15. Akoglu, L., Tong, H., Koutra, D.: Graph based anomaly detection and description: a survey. Data Min. Knowl. Discovery 29(3), 626–688 (2015)

16. Toivonen, H., Zhou, F., Hartikainen, A., Hinkka, A.: Compression of weighted graphs. In: Proceedings of the 17th ACM SIGKDD International Conference on Knowledge Discovery and Data Mining, pp. 965–973, August 2011

17. Mathioudakis, M., Bonchi, F., Castillo, C., Gionis, A., Ukkonen, A.: Sparsification of influence networks. In: Proceedings of the 17th ACM SIGKDD International Conference on Knowledge Discovery and Data Mining, pp. 529–537, August 2011

18. Dunne, C., Shneiderman, B.: Motif simplification: improving network visualization readability with fan, connector, and clique glyphs. In: Proceedings of the SIGCHI Conference on Human Factors in Computing Systems, pp. 3247–3256, April 2013

19. Tian, Y., Patel, J.M.: Tale: a tool for approximate large graph matching. In: 2008 IEEE 24th International Conference on Data Engineering, pp. 963–972. IEEE, April 2008

20. Shen, Z., Ma, K.L., Eliassi-Rad, T.: Visual analysis of large heterogeneous social networks by semantic and structural abstraction. IEEE Trans. Visual Comput. Graphics 12(6), 1427–1439 (2006)

21. Lebanoff, L., Song, K., Liu, F.: Adapting the neural encoder-decoder framework from single to multi-document summarization. arXiv preprint arXiv:1808.06218 (2018)

22. Cook, D.J., Holder, L.B.: Graph-based data mining. IEEE Intell. Syst. Their Appl. 15(2), 32–41 (2000)

23. Raghavan, S., Garcia-Molina, H.: Representing web graphs. In: Proceedings 19th International Conference on Data Engineering (Cat. No. 03CH37405), pp. 405–416. IEEE, March 2003

24. Zhang, N., Tian, Y., Patel, J.M.: Discovery-driven graph summarization. In: 2010 IEEE 26th International Conference on Data Engineering (ICDE 2010), pp. 880–891. IEEE, March 2010

25. Adhikari, B., Zhang, Y., Amiri, S.E., Bharadwaj, A., Prakash, B.A.: Propagation-based temporal network summarization. IEEE Trans. Knowl. Data Eng. 30(4), 729–742 (2017)

26. Tan, J., Wan, X., Xiao, J.: Abstractive document summarization with a graph-based attentional neural model. In: Proceedings of the 55th Annual Meeting of the Association for Computational Linguistics (Volume 1: Long Papers), pp. 1171–1181, July 2017

27. Maccioni, A., Abadi, D.J.: Scalable pattern matching over compressed graphs via dedensification. In: Proceedings of the 22nd ACM SIGKDD International Conference on Knowledge Discovery and Data Mining, August 2016

28. Shi, L., Tong, H., Tang, J., Lin, C.: Vegas: visual influence graph summarization on citation networks. IEEE Trans. Knowl. Data Eng. **27**(12), 3417–3431 (2015)
29. Fan, W., Li, J., Wang, X., Wu, Y.: Query preserving graph compression. In: Proceedings of the 2012 ACM SIGMOD International Conference on Management of Data, pp. 157–168, May 2012
30. Qu, Q., Liu, S., Jensen, C. S., Zhu, F., Faloutsos, C.: Interestingness-driven diffusion process summarization in dynamic networks. In: Joint European Conference on Machine Learning and Knowledge Discovery in Databases, September 2014

Individual Source Camera Identification with Convolutional Neural Networks

Jarosław Bernacki[1]($\boxtimes$) (ID), Kelton A.P. Costa[2] (ID), and Rafał Scherer[1] (ID)

[1] Department of Intelligent Computer Systems, Częstochowa University
of Technology, al. Armii Krajowej 36, 42-200 Częstochowa, Poland
{jaroslaw.bernacki,rafal.scherer}@pcz.pl
[2] Department of Computing, São Paulo State University, São Paulo, Brazil
kelton.costa@unesp.br

Abstract. In this paper we consider the issue of digital camera identification which matches the area of digital forensics. This problem is well-known in the literature and many algorithms based on camera's fingerprint have been proposed. However, one may find that there is a little number of methods providing a fast and accurate digital camera identification. This problem is especially observed in terms of today's digital cameras, producing images of big sizes. In this paper we discuss several existing approaches based on convolutional neural networks (CNN). We try to find out whether it is possible to speed up the process of learning the networks by the images. One of the findings include replacing the ReLU with SELU activation function. We experimentally show that using SELU speeds up significantly the process of learning. We also compare the identification accuracy of all considered methods. The experiments are held on extensive image dataset, consisting of many images coming from modern cameras.

Keywords: Security · Image processing · Imaging sensor identification · Camera identification · Digital forensics

1 Introduction

Digital forensics is a field that has attracted much attention in recent years. One of the most popular topics in digital forensics is the identification of imaging sensors that are present in digital cameras. Nowadays, digital cameras are widely accessible and affordable, which makes them very popular. Smartphones and mobile devices are even more popular. Today's smartphones are equipped with built-in digital cameras what encourages people to take photos and share them on social media networks. However, the possibility of establishing whether an image was taken by a given camera may expose users' privacy to a serious threat. Hence, a number of papers in recent years are dedicated to the study of imaging device artifacts that may be used for digital camera identification.

Digital camera identification can be realized in two approaches: individual source camera identification (ISCI) and source model camera identification

© The Author(s), under exclusive license to Springer Nature Singapore Pte Ltd. 2022
E. Szczerbicki et al. (Eds.): ACIIDS 2022, CCIS 1716, pp. 45–55, 2022.
https://doi.org/10.1007/978-981-19-8234-7_4

(SCMI). The ISCI is capable of distinguishing a certain camera model among cameras of both the same and different camera models. On the other hand, the SCMI distinguishes a certain camera model among the different models but is not able to distinguish an individual copy of the camera among other cameras of the same model. For instance, if we have the following cameras: Canon EOS R (0), Canon EOS R (1), ..., Canon EOS R (n), Nikon D780 (0), Nikon D780 (1), Sony A1 (0), Sony A1 (1), the ISCI will distinguish all cameras as different. The SCMI would distinguish only the general models, i.e., Canon EOS R, Nikon D780, and Sony A1. Therefore, it is the limitation of the SCMI approach. This motivates to development of such methods and algorithms for camera identification that would work in terms of the ISCI aspect.

The state-of-the-art algorithm for the ISCI aspect was proposed by Lukás et al.'s [14]. This algorithm used a so-called photo response non-uniformity (PRNU) that is present in images and allows for camera identification. The PRNU $\mathbf{N}$ may be calculated in the following manner: $\mathbf{N} = \mathbf{I} - F(\mathbf{I})$, where $\mathbf{I}$ is an input image and F is a denoising filter. The PRNU serves as a unique camera's fingerprint. Many studies [1,8,9] confirmed high efficacy of camera identification in such way. However, this approach shows some weaknesses. The greatest disadvantage is the representation of the camera's fingerprint, which is represented as a matrix in the original images' dimensions. This may be problematic in the aspect of storing a large number of PRNUs in some forensic centers, which motivates us to develop a method that would minimize this problem.

Our main goal is to find such a convolutional neural network (CNN) structure that will make it possible a fast learning process. We will show that using different activation functions may speed up the process of learning. We are interested that CNN should ensure the identification accuracy for at least 90% per device.

The paper is organized as follows. The next section discusses previous and related works. In Sect. 3 we recall existing algorithms and methods for individual source camera identification. In Sect. 4 we present the analysis of considered methods. The final section concludes this work.

2   Previous and Related Work

In [22] there is presented an algorithm for camera's fingerprint compact representation. For this purpose, a random projection matrix whose dimensions will be matched to the camera's fingerprint matrix in terms of matrices multiplication must be generated. The random projected matrix is then multiplied with the camera's fingerprint matrix, what produces a new matrix. Such a new matrix serves as a compact camera's fingerprint representation and is much lower than the original fingerprint. The accuracy of this method is similar to the use of original fingerprints, which makes the considered method useful. However, such an approach requires generating random matrix and matrix multiplication, which may not be computationally optimal. A linear discriminant analysis used to extract more discriminant sensor pattern noise (SPN) features is discussed [11]. The compact representation of the SPN is featured as vector. In [13] a patch-level camera identification with the convolutional neural networks (CNN) is described. The advantage of the method is also image tampering detection. In [6] a generative adversarial network (GAN) for compromising the PRNUs is presented. Considered GAN produces synthetic images which are injected with other cameras' traces. Experiments confirmed that GAN-generated images may successfully deceive state-of-the-art algorithms for camera identification. In [10], a Hierarchy Clustering method for the camera's fingerprint identification is discussed. Such a novel approach allows for the classification without training image datasets. In [19] there is proposed a method for clustering the cameras' fingerprints. The images are distinguished by applying various denoising algorithms. In [2], a fuzzy min-max neural network is considered for the identification of the camera's digital fingerprint (PRNU). The PRNU patterns are represented as Hu's invariants and then passed into a neural network for training and classification. The experimental evaluation confirmed the accuracy of the proposed method. In [18] a PRNU-based method for camera identification is described. This is realized with the use of a convolutional neural network that is adopted to eliminate scenes in the images which obscure the noise used to calculate the PRNU. Experiments confirmed that considered methods achieve high accuracy. In [23], a dual-tree complex wavelet transform (DTCWT) method to extract the PRNU from the images is depicted. The method is usable both for PRNU-based camera identification and also may be used for the detection of image tampering localization. CNNs for digital camera identification are also proposed in [15] and [9].

In [16], a technique using a convolutional neural network (CNN) for fooling the camera's PRNU is described. The CNN works as a generator that changes the original cameras' images containing the PRNU into PRNU-less images in order to make it impossible to identify a camera. Another works matching the issue of camera's identification are presented in [5,17,20]. A comprehensive analysis of different techniques for camera identification, including EXIF metadata analysis, lens aberration, CFA and demosaicing, sensor imperfections, image statistics, and convolutional neural networks, is presented in [4]. The robustness of camera identification methods based on deep neural networks (DNN) are discussed in [3, 12].

3   State-of-the-art Algorithms and Methods for Individual Source Camera Identification

Let us briefly recall state-of-the-art algorithms and methods that may be used for an individual source camera identification.

Lukás et al.'s algorithm. The Lukás et al.'s algorithm [14] is based on the calculation of the noise residual $\mathbf{N}$ in the manner as described in Eq. 1.

$$\mathbf{N} = \mathbf{I} - F(\mathbf{I}) \tag{1}$$

The F is a denoising filter, the **N** stands for a noise residual of one image **I**. Thus, this procedure should be repeated for a certain number of images from a camera (authors propose using at least 45 images). Images are denoised using a wavelet-based denoising filter F. The camera's noise residual is finally calculated as an average of a particular number of noise residuals. Images are processed in their original resolution.

Proposed CNN. We propose a shallow convolutional neural network that may be used for an individual source camera identification. Its structure is the following:

1. A first convolutional layer with 8 filters of size $3 \times 3 \times 3$ and stride 1 with a max-pooling layer with kernel size 2 and stride 2, ReLU as activation function;
2. The second convolutional layer with 8 filters of size $3 \times 3 \times 8$ and stride 1 with a max-pooling layer with kernel size 2 and stride 2, ReLU as activation function;
3. The third convolutional layer with 16 filters of size $3 \times 3 \times 8$ and stride 1 with a max-pooling layer with kernel size 2 and stride 2, ReLU as activation function;
4. Fully connected layers for classification.

Bondi et al.'s CNN. Bondi et al.'s [1] proposed a deep model architecture based on a convolutional neural network (CNN). The network structure is the following:

1. A first convolutional layer with 32 filters of size $4 \times 4 \times 3$ and stride 1 with a max-pooling layer with kernel size 2 and stride 2, ReLU as activation function;
2. The second convolutional layer with 48 filters of size $5 \times 5 \times 32$ and stride 1 with a max-pooling layer with kernel size 2 and stride 2, ReLU as activation function;
3. The third convolutional layer with 64 filters of size $5 \times 5 \times 48$ and stride 1 with a max-pooling layer with kernel size 2 and stride 2, ReLU as activation function;
4. The fourth convolutional layer with 128 filters of size $5 \times 5 \times 64$ and stride 1 gives as output a vector with 128 elements;
5. An inner product layer with 128 output neurons is followed by a ReLU layer to produce a 128 dimensional feature vector;
6. The final $128 \times N$ inner product layer, where N is the number of training classes, is followed by a soft-max layer for loss computation.

Other parameters are listed in the paper [1].

Tuama et al.'s CNN. Tuama et al.'s [21] described a convolutional neural network with the following structure:

1. A high pass filter with 5×5 kernel for image preprocessing producing filtered images;
2. A first convolutional layer of kernel 3×3 with stride 2 producing 64 feature maps of size 126×126 pixels with ReLU as an activation method;

3. A second convolutional layer of kernel 3×3 with stride 2 producing 64 feature maps of size 63×63 pixels with ReLU as an activation method;
4. A third convolutional layer of kernel 3×3 with stride 2 producing 32 feature maps of size 63×63 pixels with ReLU as an activation method;
5. A max-pooling layer of kernel 3×3 with stride 2 producing 32 feature maps of size 31×31 pixels;
6. Three fully connected layers followed by a soft-max layer for final classification.

The other hyper-parameters are listed in the authors' paper.

All the CNNs are trained with noise residuals calculated with the denoising formula discussed in Lukás et al.'s algorithm [14] $\mathbf{I} - F(\mathbf{I})$, where $\mathbf{I}$ is the input image and F denotes a denoising filter.

4 Experimental Evaluation

We conduct two experiments. The first includes a comparison of classification accuracy of Lukás et al.'s, proposed CNN, Bondi et al.'s and Tuama et al.'s CNNs. The second experiment contains a comparison of CNNs with various hyper-parameters and the impact on the train accuracy.

We use a set of 17 modern cameras[1] The used cameras include Canon EOS 1D X Mark II (C1), Canon EOS 5D Mark IV (C2), Canon EOS M5 (C3), Canon EOS M50 (C4), Canon EOS R (C5), Canon EOS R6 (C6), Canon EOS RP (C7), Fujifilm X-T200 (F1), Nikon D5 (N1), Nikon D6 (N2), Nikon D500 (N3), Nikon D780 (N4), Nikon D850 (N5), Nikon Z6 II (N6), Nikon Z7 II (N7), Sony A1 (S1), Sony A9 (S2). At least 40 images per each camera are used for learning.

As evaluation, we use standard *accuracy* (ACC), *true positive rate* (TPR) and *false positive rate* (FPR) measures, defined as:

$$ACC = \frac{TP + TN}{TP + TN + FP + FN} \ , \ TPR = \frac{TP}{TP + FN} \ , \ FPR = \frac{FP}{FP + TN}$$

where TP/TN denotes "true positive/true negative"; FP/FN stands for "false positive/false negative". TP denotes number of cases correctly classified to a specific class; TN are instances that are correctly rejected. FP denotes cases incorrectly classified to the specific class; FN are cases incorrectly rejected.

Experiments are held on personal computer equipped with Intel Core i5-10400@2.9 GHz CPU with 20 gigabytes of RAM and nVidia GeForce RTX 3060 GPU with 12 gigabytes of video memory. Scripts for CNNs are implemented in Python under the Keras framework.

---

[1] To be published soon, draft of the web page: https://kisi.pcz.pl/imagine/.

4.1   Experiment I – Results of Classification

We present confusion matrices of cameras' classification. Results are presented as Tables 1, 2, 3 and 4. All discussed algorithms and methods are run with their original parameters.

Table 1. Confusion matrix of identification accuracy (Lukás et al.'s algorithm). The ACC = 92%. The symbol * represents values smaller than 5 [%]

	C1	C2	C3	C4	C5	C6	C7	F1	N1	N2	N3	N4	N5	N6	N7	S1	S2
C1	91.0	*	*	*	*	*	*	*	*	*	*	*	*	*	*	*	*
C2	*	91.0	*	*	*	*	*	*	*	*	*	*	*	*	*	*	*
C3	*	*	92.0	*	*	*	*	*	*	*	*	*	*	*	*	*	*
C4	*	*	*	94.0	*	*	*	*	*	*	*	*	*	*	*	*	*
C5	*	*	*	*	92.0	*	*	*	*	*	*	*	*	*	*	*	*
C6	*	*	*	*	*	91.0	*	*	*	*	*	*	*	*	*	*	*
C7	*	*	*	*	*	*	95.0	*	*	*	*	*	*	*	*	*	*
F1	*	*	*	*	*	*	*	95.0	*	*	*	*	*	*	*	*	*
N1	*	*	*	*	*	*	*	*	91.0	*	*	*	*	*	*	*	*
N2	*	*	*	*	*	*	*	*	*	91.0	*	*	*	*	*	*	*
N3	*	*	*	*	*	*	*	*	*	*	92.0	*	*	*	*	*	*
N4	*	*	*	*	*	*	*	*	*	*	*	92.0	*	*	*	*	*
N5	*	*	*	*	*	*	*	*	*	*	*	*	91.0	*	*	*	*
N6	*	*	*	*	*	*	*	*	*	*	*	*	*	92.0	*	*	*
N7	*	*	*	*	*	*	*	*	*	*	*	*	*	*	93.0	*	*
S1	*	*	*	*	*	*	*	*	*	*	*	*	*	*	*	91.0	*
S2	*	*	*	*	*	*	*	*	*	*	*	*	*	*	*	*	92.0

The results clearly indicate that all methods ensure very high identification accuracy. In all cases, the overall identification accuracy obtains 92%; the particular TPRs are not lower than 90% for each camera. What is interesting, Lukás et al.'s algorithm achieves almost the same results compared to CNN-based methods. This clearly confirms that all methods ensure a reliable individual source camera identification. In the case of the discussed CNNs, the results are very similar to each other both in terms of identification accuracy and speed of learning. All the CNNs require a similar number of training epochs to obtain the desired level of identification accuracy.

4.2   Experiment II – Comparison of Activation Functions

The inspiration for our experiments was the work presented by Obregon et al. [7], where the analysis of different network parameters was conducted. We have analyzed the usage of different activation functions for each convolutional layers. Analyzed functions include the ReLU, Leaky ReLU and SELU activation

Table 2. Confusion matrix of identification accuracy (proposed CNN). The ACC = 92%. The symbol * represents values smaller than 5 [%]

	C1	C2	C3	C4	C5	C6	C7	F1	N1	N2	N3	N4	N5	N6	N7	S1	S2
C1	92.0	*	*	*	*	*	*	*	*	*	*	*	*	*	*	*	*
C2	*	91.0	*	*	*	*	*	*	*	*	*	*	*	*	*	*	*
C3	*	*	93.0	*	*	*	*	*	*	*	*	*	*	*	*	*	*
C4	*	*	*	91.0	*	*	*	*	*	*	*	*	*	*	*	*	*
C5	*	*	*	*	92.0	*	*	*	*	*	*	*	*	*	*	*	*
C6	*	*	*	*	*	93.0	*	*	*	*	*	*	*	*	*	*	*
C7	*	*	*	*	*	*	92.0	*	*	*	*	*	*	*	*	*	*
F1	*	*	*	*	*	*	*	91.0	*	*	*	*	*	*	*	*	*
N1	*	*	*	*	*	*	*	*	90.0	*	*	*	*	*	*	*	*
N2	*	*	*	*	*	*	*	*	*	91.0	*	*	*	*	*	*	*
N3	*	*	*	*	*	*	*	*	*	*	92.0	*	*	*	*	*	*
N4	*	*	*	*	*	*	*	*	*	*	*	91.0	*	*	*	*	*
N5	*	*	*	*	*	*	*	*	*	*	*	*	92.0	*	*	*	*
N6	*	*	*	*	*	*	*	*	*	*	*	*	*	92.0	*	*	*
N7	*	*	*	*	*	*	*	*	*	*	*	*	*	*	91.0	*	*
S1	*	*	*	*	*	*	*	*	*	*	*	*	*	*	*	91.0	*
S2	*	*	*	*	*	*	*	*	*	*	*	*	*	*	*	*	93.0

Table 3. Confusion matrix of identification accuracy (Bondi et al.'s CNN). The ACC = 92%. The symbol * represents values smaller than 5 [%]

	C1	C2	C3	C4	C5	C6	C7	F1	N1	N2	N3	N4	N5	N6	N7	S1	S2
C1	93.0	*	*	*	*	*	*	*	*	*	*	*	*	*	*	*	*
C2	*	92.0	*	*	*	*	*	*	*	*	*	*	*	*	*	*	*
C3	*	*	89.0	*	*	*	*	*	*	*	*	*	*	*	*	*	*
C4	*	*	*	91.0	*	*	*	*	*	*	*	*	*	*	*	*	*
C5	*	*	*	*	91.0	*	*	*	*	*	*	*	*	*	*	*	*
C6	*	*	*	*	*	92.0	*	*	*	*	*	*	*	*	*	*	*
C7	*	*	*	*	*	*	91.0	*	*	*	*	*	*	*	*	*	*
F1	*	*	*	*	*	*	*	94.0	*	*	*	*	*	*	*	*	*
N1	*	*	*	*	*	*	*	*	91.0	*	*	*	*	*	*	*	*
N2	*	*	*	*	*	*	*	*	*	92.0	*	*	*	*	*	*	*
N3	*	*	*	*	*	*	*	*	*	*	92.0	*	*	*	*	*	*
N4	*	*	*	*	*	*	*	*	*	*	*	93.0	*	*	*	*	*
N5	*	*	*	*	*	*	*	*	*	*	*	*	91.0	*	*	*	*
N6	*	*	*	*	*	*	*	*	*	*	*	*	*	92.0	*	*	*
N7	*	*	*	*	*	*	*	*	*	*	*	*	*	*	92.0	*	*
S1	*	*	*	*	*	*	*	*	*	*	*	*	*	*	*	92.0	*
S2	*	*	*	*	*	*	*	*	*	*	*	*	*	*	*	*	92.0

Table 4. Confusion matrix of identification accuracy (Tuama et al.'s CNN). The ACC = 92%. The symbol * represents values smaller than 5 [%]

	C1	C2	C3	C4	C5	C6	C7	F1	N1	N2	N3	N4	N5	N6	N7	S1	S2
C1	94.0	*	*	*	*	*	*	*	*	*	*	*	*	*	*	*	*
C2	*	90.0	*	*	*	*	*	*	*	*	*	*	*	*	*	*	*
C3	*	*	91.0	*	*	*	*	*	*	*	*	*	*	*	*	*	*
C4	*	*	*	92.0	*	*	*	*	*	*	*	*	*	*	*	*	*
C5	*	*	*	*	91.0	*	*	*	*	*	*	*	*	*	*	*	*
C6	*	*	*	*	*	92.0	*	*	*	*	*	*	*	*	*	*	*
C7	*	*	*	*	*	*	93.0	*	*	*	*	*	*	*	*	*	*
F1	*	*	*	*	*	*	*	92.0	*	*	*	*	*	*	*	*	*
N1	*	*	*	*	*	*	*	*	91.0	*	*	*	*	*	*	*	*
N2	*	*	*	*	*	*	*	*	*	92.0	*	*	*	*	*	*	*
N3	*	*	*	*	*	*	*	*	*	*	91.0	*	*	*	*	*	*
N4	*	*	*	*	*	*	*	*	*	*	*	93.0	*	*	*	*	*
N5	*	*	*	*	*	*	*	*	*	*	*	*	93.0	*	*	*	*
N6	*	*	*	*	*	*	*	*	*	*	*	*	*	91.0	*	*	*
N7	*	*	*	*	*	*	*	*	*	*	*	*	*	*	92.0	*	*
S1	*	*	*	*	*	*	*	*	*	*	*	*	*	*	*	92.0	*
S2	*	*	*	*	*	*	*	*	*	*	*	*	*	*	*	*	91.0

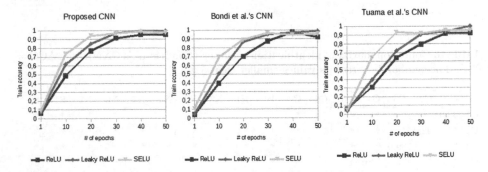

Fig. 1. Train accuracy (50 epochs) of the considered CNNs – ReLU vs. Leaky ReLU vs. SELU activation functions

functions. Since the ReLU, Leaky ReLU and SELU activation functions are well-known, we are not going to recall them. Let us note that the discussed CNNs use ReLU as the activation function. Instead, we propose to use the Leaky ReLU and SELU functions. We have analyzed the train accuracy using all three activation functions. The results can be seen in Fig. 1.

The results clearly indicate that using the SELU activation function allows for much faster learning than ReLU or Leaky ReLU functions. Training already of 10 epochs for all considered CNNs gives 80% train accuracy, while training for 20 epochs obtains 90% of train accuracy. The Leaky ReLU function needs at least 10 epochs more for the same results, while the ReLU achieves the lowest results, demanding even two times more of training epochs than the SELU function. Therefore, achieving at least 90% of train accuracy for ReLU activation function requires learning all the networks for at least 35 epochs.

Due to paper limitations, we are not able to present detailed results of the impact of training the CNNs with all the considered activation functions for camera's identification accuracy. We can only say that training the networks with all the considered activation functions allows for identification accuracy for at least 95%, but in case of training with SELU function, we can obtain such result with much lower number of training epochs. The TPRs for nearly all considered CNNs are at least 90% after training already of $15 - 20$ epochs with SELU function, while obtaining such result with Leaky ReLU and ReLU requires $30 - 35$ and at least 45 epochs, respectively.

5   Conclusion

In this paper, we have discussed the issue of individual source camera identification based on images. We have analyzed several approaches for digital camera identification in terms of identification accuracy and speed of learning. Experiments conducted on an extensive image dataset confirmed that modern algorithms obtain very high identification accuracy. We have also shown that in the case of convolutional deep learning methods, different activation functions have a huge impact on the speed of network learning. Experiments clearly confirmed that using the SELU activation function significantly speeds up the process of network learning. The Leaky ReLU activation function obtains visibly lower learning speed, while the very common ReLU is the slowest.

Future works will concern further experiments on the considered issue. In particular, we are interested in developing a fast method for individual source camera identification. We expect that convolutional autoencoders might be useful for this purpose. We also consider a scenario for camera identification-based anomaly detection.

Acknowledgements. The project financed under the program of the Polish Minister of Science and Higher Education under the name "Regional Initiative of Excellence" in the years 2019–2022 project number 020/RID/2018/19, the amount of financing 12,000,000.00 PLN.

References

1. Bondi, L., Baroffio, L., Guera, D., Bestagini, P., Delp, E.J., Tubaro, S.: First steps toward camera model identification with convolutional neural networks. IEEE Signal Process. Lett. **24**(3), 259–263 (2017). https://doi.org/10.1109/LSP.2016.2641006
2. Borole, M., Kolhe, S.R.: A feature-based approach for digital camera identification using photo-response non-uniformity noise. Int. J. Comput. Vis. Robot. **11**(4), 374–384 (2021). https://doi.org/10.1504/IJCVR.2021.116559

3. Bruno, A., Cattaneo, G., Capasso, P.: On the reliability of the PNU for source camera identification tasks. CoRR abs/2008.12700 (2020). https://arxiv.org/abs/2008.12700
4. Chen, L., Li, A., Yu, L.: Forensic technology for source camera identification. In: Sun, X., Wang, J., Bertino, E. (eds.) Artificial Intelligence and Security, pp. 466–477. Springer, Singapore (2020)
5. Chowdhury, D.P., Bakshi, S., Sa, P.K., Majhi, B.: Wavelet energy feature based source camera identification for ear biometric images. Pattern Recognit. Lett. **130**, 139–147 (2020). https://doi.org/10.1016/j.patrec.2018.10.009
6. Cozzolino, D., Thies, J., Rössler, A., Nießner, M., Verdoliva, L.: SpoC: spoofing camera fingerprints. In: IEEE Conference on Computer Vision and Pattern Recognition Workshops, CVPR Workshops 2021, virtual, June 19–25, 2021, pp. 990–1000. Computer Vision Foundation/IEEE (2021). https://doi.org/10.1109/CVPRW53098.2021.00110
7. Freire-Obregón, D., Narducci, F., Barra, S., Santana, M.C.: Deep learning for source camera identification on mobile devices. Pattern Recogn. Lett. **126**, 86–91 (2019). https://doi.org/10.1016/j.patrec.2018.01.005
8. Galdi, C., Nappi, M., Dugelay, J.: Combining hardwaremetry and biometry for human authentication via smartphones. In: Image Analysis and Processing - ICIAP 2015–18th International Conference, Genoa, Italy, September 7–11, 2015, Proceedings, Part II, pp. 406–416 (2015)
9. Kirchner, M., Johnson, C.: SPN-CNN: boosting sensor-based source camera attribution with deep learning. CoRR abs/2002.02927 (2020). https://arxiv.org/abs/2002.02927
10. Lai, Z., Wang, Y., Sun, W., Zhang, P.: Automatic source camera identification technique based-on hierarchy clustering method. In: Sun, X., Zhang, X., Xia, Z., Bertino, E. (eds.) ICAIS 2021. LNCS, vol. 12737, pp. 715–723. Springer, Cham (2021). https://doi.org/10.1007/978-3-030-78612-0_58
11. Li, R., Li, C., Guan, Y.: Inference of a compact representation of sensor fingerprint for source camera identification. Pattern Recogn. **74**, 556–567 (2018). https://doi.org/10.1016/j.patcog.2017.09.027
12. Lin, H., Wo, Y., Wu, Y., Meng, K., Han, G.: Robust source camera identification against adversarial attacks. Comput. Secur. **100**, 102079 (2021). https://doi.org/10.1016/j.cose.2020.102079
13. Liu, Y., Zou, Z., Yang, Y., Law, B.N., Bharath, A.A.: Efficient source camera identification with diversity-enhanced patch selection and deep residual prediction. Sensors **21**(14), 4701 (2021). https://doi.org/10.3390/s21144701
14. Lukás, J., Fridrich, J.J., Goljan, M.: Digital camera identification from sensor pattern noise. IEEE Trans. Info. Forensics Secur. **1**(2), 205–214 (2006). https://doi.org/10.1109/TIFS.2006.873602
15. Mandelli, S., Cozzolino, D., Bestagini, P., Verdoliva, L., Tubaro, S.: CNN-based fast source device identification. IEEE Signal Process. Lett. **27**, 1285–1289 (2020). https://doi.org/10.1109/LSP.2020.3008855
16. Picetti, F., Mandelli, S., Bestagini, P., Lipari, V., Tubaro, S.: DIPPAS: a deep image prior PRNU anonymization scheme. CoRR abs/2012.03581 (2020). https://arxiv.org/abs/2012.03581
17. Quintanar-Reséndiz, A.L., Rodríguez-Santos, F., Pichardo-Méndez, J.L., Delgado-Gutiérrez, G., Ramírez, O.J., Vázquez-Medina, R.: Capture device identification from digital images using Kullback-Leibler divergence. Multimed. Tools Appl. **80**(13), 19513–19538 (2021). https://doi.org/10.1007/s11042-021-10653-1

18. Rafi, A.M., Tonmoy, T.I., Kamal, U., Wu, Q.M.J., Hasan, M.K.: RemNet: remnant convolutional neural network for camera model identification. Neural Comput. Appl. **33**(8), 3655–3670 (2020). https://doi.org/10.1007/s00521-020-05220-y
19. Salazar, D.A., Ramirez-Rodriguez, A.E., Nakano, M., Cedillo-Hernandez, M., Perez-Meana, H.: Evaluation of denoising algorithms for source camera linking. In: Roman-Rangel, E., Kuri-Morales, Á.F., Martínez-Trinidad, J.F., Carrasco-Ochoa, J.A., Olvera-López, J.A. (eds.) MCPR 2021. LNCS, vol. 12725, pp. 282–291. Springer, Cham (2021). https://doi.org/10.1007/978-3-030-77004-4_27
20. Sarkar, B.N., Barman, S., Naskar, R.: Blind source camera identification of online social network images using adaptive thresholding technique. In: Bhattacharjee, D., Kole, D.K., Dey, N., Basu, S., Plewczynski, D. (eds.) Proceedings of International Conference on Frontiers in Computing and Systems. AISC, vol. 1255, pp. 637–648. Springer, Singapore (2021). https://doi.org/10.1007/978-981-15-7834-2_59
21. Tuama, A., Comby, F., Chaumont, M.: Camera model identification with the use of deep convolutional neural networks. In: IEEE International Workshop on Information Forensics and Security, WIFS 2016, Abu Dhabi, United Arab Emirates, December 4–7, 2016, pp. 1–6. IEEE (2016). https://doi.org/10.1109/WIFS.2016.7823908
22. Valsesia, D., Coluccia, G., Bianchi, T., Magli, E.: Compressed fingerprint matching and camera identification via random projections. IEEE Trans. Inf. Forensics Secur. **10**(7), 1472–1485 (2015). https://doi.org/10.1109/TIFS.2015.2415461
23. Zeng, H., Wan, Y., Deng, K., Peng, A.: Source camera identification with dual-tree complex wavelet transform. IEEE Access **8**, 18874–18883 (2020). https://doi.org/10.1109/ACCESS.2020.2968855

Exploring the Effect of Vehicle Appearance and Motion for Natural Language-Based Vehicle Retrieval

Quang-Huy Can[1], Hong-Quan Nguyen[2], Thi-Ngoc-Diep Do[1], Hoai Phan[3], Thuy-Binh Nguyen[4], Thi Thanh Thuy Pham[3(✉)], Thanh-Hai Tran[1], and Thi-Lan Le[1]

[1] School of Electrical and Electronics Engineering,
Hanoi University of Science and Technology, Hanoi, Vietnam
[2] Faculty of Information Technology, Viet-Hung Industrial University, Hanoi, Vietnam
[3] Faculty of Information Security, Academy of People Security, Hanoi, Vietnam
thanh-thuy.pham@mica.edu.vn
[4] Faculty of Electrical-Electronic Engineering,
University of Transport and Communications, Hanoi, Vietnam

Abstract. Vehicle searching from videos by textual descriptions is one of the most important tasks in traffic management towards smart cities. This paper proposes a method for retrieval of vehicles using a natural language-based query. Our method consists of two main components of textual extractor based on Bi-LSTM and visual extractor using ResNet-50 model. Both components extract hidden features from different modalities and then match them in a common space. This end-to-end process tries to build a textual-visual alignment model that will be utilized for the search phase. Our particularities in this framework are two-fold. In the video stream, we evaluate in detail the role of vehicle appearance compared to its motion. In the textual stream, we apply back-translation systems to enrich the textual dataset for the training phase. Experiments are conducted on AI City Challenging, showing the efficiency of each contribution in the overall framework. It confirms that not only appearance but additional motion cues are promising for vehicle retrieval, which provides the results of MRR, Rank@5 and Rank@10 are 0.2333, 0.3587 and 0.4837, respectively.

Keywords: Vehicle retrieval · Nature language · Appearance · Motion

1   Introduction

Vehicle searching from videos by textual descriptions has emerged recently thanks to its widely applications in different real situations [1]. In comparison with image-based or example-based object search and retrieval, natural language-based methods provide more intuitive manner for users to express their

© The Author(s), under exclusive license to Springer Nature Singapore Pte Ltd. 2022
E. Szczerbicki et al. (Eds.): ACIIDS 2022, CCIS 1716, pp. 56–68, 2022.
https://doi.org/10.1007/978-981-19-8234-7_5

queries in their own natural language as well as make object search feasible in the situations where examples are not available. A common approach to performing natural language-based object retrieval is to embed the images and descriptions into shared feature space and then rank the object images based on the cross-modal similarities. In natural language-based object search, person search has recently attracted more attention. Recent years have witnessed a numerous methods proposed for person search [1]. As results, several datasets and demos have been developed for person search through natural languages [2,3]. Since last year, natural language-based vehicle search has been introduced for the first time in the 5th AI City Challenge [4]. In order to leverage the research on this topic, a dataset named CityFlow-NL [5] has been released. Of course, different methods proposed for person search can be applied for vehicle search through natural language descriptions. However, vehicle search has its own characteristics and challenges and the straightforward using of the existing methods for person search may results poor search performance. In person search, appearance information is the most important cue to distinguish the person ID, because one can be distinguished from other by clothing, hair styles,...which belongs to the person's appearance. However, in vehicle searching, the vehicle's appearance information (vehicle color or shapes) is not diverse enough to distinguish one from others. Furthermore, the available datasets and existing works for person search use one or two images for each person, so motion aspect is not considered in person search but in vehicle search, motion information could become the most relevant cue to distinguish one vehicle from the others.

In this work, we explore the vehicle motion information in addition to vehicle appearance information for the vehicle searching problem based on textual descriptions. An appearance alignment model is proposed to learning the common space of the visual and textual features extracted from these information cues. In order to improve the model performance, the pre-processing steps for vehicle images and textual descriptions are implemented. The vehicle images are cropped from the video frames of the tracks, and the feature extraction is carried out on these to eliminate the redundant background information. The textual descriptions are translated from English to French and vice versa in order to enrich the vocabulary size of the word embedding dictionary.

The extensive experiments have been conducted on test set of 2022 AI City challenge. Experimental results show that thanks to the proposed visual-textual alignment framework, the vehicle retrieval performance obtained by using a combination of the appearance and motion cues is very promising with the values of MRR, Rank@5 and Rank@10 are 0.2333, 0.3587 and 0.4837 respectively. However, it still exists a large margin between the performance of the proposed method with others participated teams in AI City challenge.

The remaining of the paper is organized as follows. Section 2 aims at presenting relevant works for natural language-based object search in general and vehicle search in particular. Section 3 is dedicated to the proposed framework for vehicle search through natural language. Ablation study and experimental results on AI City Challenge are described in Sect. 4. Section 5 concludes the paper while pointing out some directions for future works.

2 Related Work

This section briefly discusses some remarkable researches on natural language-based video retrieval problem of which vehicle searching in video based on natural language descriptions is a particular case. In addition, the related works in textual data augmentation by back-translation are also discussed.

2.1 Natural Language-Based Video Retrieval

The main goal of nature language-based video retrieval is to find the most relevant video corresponding to a given language description from a gallery of candidate videos. The main approach to this problem includes the steps of (1) designing a language model to encode a natural language description [6], (2) developing a deep learned network for video representation [7], and (3) learning a common semantic space on which the features of the two different modalities are projected.

For language representation, there were some earlier studies on textual feature extraction such as Word2vec [8]. However, the drawback of these techniques is that they cannot capture the sequential property in a description sentence. To handle this issue, LSTM [9] - a deep learning model - was introduced. By using LSTM network, the relationship between words in a sentence is exploited. Recently, transformer architecture [10] has shown outstanding performance for language representation through applying a self-attention mechanism. This transformer architecture is considered as the base for building the popular language modeling network BERT [11]. For video representation, several deep neural networks are proposed to extract visual information. Simonyan et al. [12] made an effort to design a two-stream network which exploits both spatial and temporal information for action recognition problem. From this, Carreira et al. [13] integrated 3D convolutions into a two-stream network to improve the performance of the temporal structure network, called as C3D network. Recently, transformer architecture has been applied not only to extract textual cues but also to capture visual information. BERT [11] pre-training model is applied to S3D features in VideoBERT. [14]. In order to estimate the similarity between textual and visual features, most of the current works have tried to jointly embed these features into the same semantic space [15–17].

Furthermore, several studies also exploit additional information, such as motion or audio for video understanding [18,19]. In vehicle retrieval problem, the vehicle's movement trajectory is also valuable information to distinguish vehicles participating in road traffic. Park et al. [18] exploited the information of motion trajectories based on the position of a target vehicle and velocity vector to estimate vehicle's movement direction. Bain et al. [19] adopted background and trajectory modeling to preserve environment and motion information as a motion image. Background is considered as useful information to indicate the sequential property between sequence frames in a video. These characteristics help to enrich features for video representation as well as improve the video retrieval accuracy.

2.2   Data Augmentation Through Back-Translation

An early method for data augmentation was back translation: translating text from one language to another and then back from the translation to the original language. The back-translation leverages the semantic variances encoded in translation data sets to produce new augmentation. In [20], to augment the data for translation task, authors treat pairs of monolingual data with automatic back-translations as additional parallel training data. This obtains substantial improvements on the task of machine translation between English and German. [21] also creates a bigger training corpus for translation system from existing parallel corpus. One translation system in reverse direction was trained and then used to translate the data from the target side of existing parallel corpus backward into the source side. The new training corpus gathered both original parallel corpus and the new synthetic source side with target side.

In the task of natural language-based video retrieval, the size of the description text is relatively smaller than in other natural NLP tasks. Therefore, textual data augmentation can help to increase the semantic variances of the descriptions and improve the textual feature extraction quality.

3   Proposed Framework

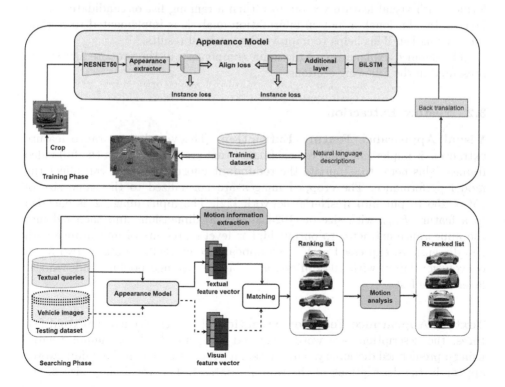

Fig. 1. The proposed framework for natural language-based vehicle retrieval.

3.1 Overall Framework

The proposed overall framework is shown in Fig. 1. It contains two phases of training and searching. In the training phase, an appearance model is trained to align language descriptions and visual vehicle tracks. In appearance model, only appearance information of vehicles in textual descriptions and images is exploited. For example the descriptions or visual presentation of color or type of vehicles (SUV, Sedan, Minvan..) belongs to appearance information. The appearance model training is done by two crucial steps of (1) appearance feature extraction for both branches of image and text; (2) visual-textual alignment. In (1), visual appearance feature extraction is done on the cropped vehicle images from the video frames using ResNet50 model and appearance extractor. The textual appearance features are extracted from the descriptions by using Bidirectional long short-term memory (BiLSTM) network and additional layer. However, in order to increase the size of textual dataset and improve the model performance, data augmentation by back-translation is implemented for the original textual descriptions. In (2) a combination of cross-modal alignment loss and instance loss for each model of vision and text is utilized for joint training of image and text.

In the searching phase, the trained appearance model is used for feature extraction of vehicle images and the textual descriptions in the testing dataset. For each feature vector of an input textual query, the matching phase is performed with visual feature vectors to return a ranking list of candidate vehicle images. In additional, a motion information analysis is implemented to re-rank the ranking list. This helps to improve the retrieval results.

The detailed explanation of the main components in the proposed system is presented in the following sections.

3.2 Feature Extraction

Visual Appearance Feature Extraction. The visual appearance feature extraction is implemented on vehicle images that are cropped from the full video frames. This helps to eliminate the redundant information that can affect the model performance. The cropped images are normalized to the same size of 256×256 to put into ResNet50 network [22]. The input image I is encoded to a feature F_{img} with size of $(1024 \times 24 \times 8)$ dimensions and then fed into the appearance extractor to output higher level represents of appearance with 256 dimensions, expressed as V. The appearance extractor contains two 3×3 convolution layers with 2048 filters, an adaptive average pooling and a linear layer in the last.

Textual Appearance Feature Extraction. In order to extract textual features, the descriptions are word tokenized and embedded to one-hot vectors using a pre-defined dictionary. This dictionary is built based on the unique words appear in the descriptions of the training dataset. The vocabulary size of the dictionary is 847 words and 731 words with and without data augmentation, respectively.

Each one-hot vector is then fed into BiLSTM network to extract feature vector $\boldsymbol{F}_{\text{txt}}$ of $(1024 \times 1 \times 1)$.

$$\boldsymbol{F}_{\text{txt}} = BiLSTM(one - hot - encoder(sentences)) \tag{1}$$

Finally, a linear additional layer maps the output of BiLSTM to the feature vector t_a of 256 dimentions. W, bias is weight and bias of linear layer:

$$t_a = W \bigotimes F_{\text{txt}} + bias \tag{2}$$

Visual-Textual Alignment. After extracting features from vehicle images and description sentences, we perform model training on image-text feature pairs in end-to-end manner as inspired by [16]. The goal of visual-textual alignment training is to build a common embedding space for cross-mapping between image and text attribute features. In order to learn this mapping, contrast learning method with triplet loss is utilized. In addition, the instance loss is also used for discriminative learning in each appearance model of vision and text.

- Triplet loss: In this work, a logistic form of triplet loss function is used for learning the alignment between the appearance visual features and the textual features. For contrast learning, the positive samples (a pair of descriptions and images belongs to the same class) and the negative samples (the remaining pairs of other classes) are exploited. The input for contrast learning are expressed as $(\boldsymbol{v}_g^i, \boldsymbol{t}_g^+, \boldsymbol{t}_g^-)$ and $(\boldsymbol{t}_g^i, \boldsymbol{v}_g^+, \boldsymbol{v}_g^-)$, where $\boldsymbol{i}$ indicates identity index of a class. $\boldsymbol{v}_g^i$ and $\boldsymbol{t}_g^i$ define as the anchors. $\boldsymbol{v}^+$, $\boldsymbol{t}^+$ denotes visual feature and textual feature in a positive pair while $\boldsymbol{v}^-$, $\boldsymbol{t}^-$ are features in a negative pair. The score function for matching images and descriptions is cosine similarity, $cos\theta = \frac{\vec{v} \cdot \vec{t}}{\|\vec{v}\| \, \|\vec{t}\|}$. The logistic triplet loss function is formulated as follows:

$$L_{align} = \frac{1}{N} \sum_{i=1}^{N} \{log\,[1 + P] + log\,[1 + Q]\} \tag{3}$$

where $P = e^{-\tau_p(cos\theta_i^+ - \alpha)}$ and $Q = e^{\tau_n(cos\theta_i^- - \beta)}$. $cos\theta_i^+$ and $cos\theta_i^-$ are cosine similarity of a positive pair and a negative pair, respectively. τ_p and τ_n are hyper-parameters that control the slope of gradient (in our work, $\tau_p = 40$ and $\tau_n = 10$). α defines as the lower bound for positive score and β defines as the upper bound for negative score, ($\alpha = 0.6$ and $\beta = 0.4$).
- Instance loss: The triple loss only focuses on cross modal alignment and ignores the relationship in each modal of vision and text. Inspired of [23], in this work, instance loss (L_{img} for visual model, L_{img} for textual model) is applied to explicitly deal with the relationship within each modal:

$$L_{img} = -\frac{1}{B} \sum_{i=1}^{B} \sum_{k=1}^{C} y_{i,k} log \frac{e^{z_{i,k}^{img}}}{\sum_{j=1}^{C} e^{z_{i,j}^{img}}} \tag{4}$$

with

$$z_i^{img} = W_{img} \bigotimes v_i + b_{img} \quad (\forall i = 1, 2, 3...B) \tag{5}$$

$$L_{txt} = -\frac{1}{B} \sum_{i=1}^{B} \sum_{k=1}^{C} y_{i,k} log \frac{e^{z_{i,k}^{txt}}}{\sum_{j=1}^{C} e^{z_{i,j}^{txt}}} \tag{6}$$

with

$$z_i^{txt} = W_{txt} \bigotimes v_i + b_{txt} \quad (\forall i = 1, 2, 3...B) \tag{7}$$

where B is the batch size, C is the number of classes, v_i and t_i are textual and visual feature vectors with size of $(1, C)$. y_i is a $(1, C)$ one-hot vector which represents the ground truth vector of ith image or description of a batch. $W_{img}, b_{img}, W_{txt}, b_{txt}$ define projection weights and bias for feature vectors of image or text before through instance loss.

The final loss for training cross appearance model is expressed as follows:

$$L_{joint} = L_{img} + L_{txt} + L_{align} \tag{8}$$

3.3 Movement Analysis

The purpose of motion analysis stage is to extract motion information from the textual descriptions to improve the ranking results from the appearance model.

– Motion information extraction: From the observation of the descriptions in training dataset, we built a set of six motion classes: "Straight", "Left", "Right", "Stop", "Slow" and "Other". Table 1 shows the number of track in each motion class from training dataset.

Table 1. The number of tracks for each motion class.

Labels	Straight	Left	Right	Stop	Slow	Other
Number	1808	156	155	20	4	12

The motion information of vehicles is extracted from two sources of the descriptions and the vehicle trajectory. For the first one, the verb phrases are extracted from the description by a built-in NLP tool. They are classified to the corresponding motion classes based on a pre-defined set of keywords. For example, given a description "A black sedan makes a right turn at the intersection.", a verb phrase "makes a right turn" is obtained from the NLP tool. It is classified to "Right" class because of the presence of the keyword "right turn". For the second one, inspired by [18], we convert track positions into GPS values. Based on the GPS coordinates, the velocity and the turn angle of the vehicle are computed as follows:

$$\theta = \arcsin \left(\frac{\left\| \vec{V}_{\text{in}} \times \vec{V}_{\text{out}} \right\|}{\left\| \vec{V}_{\text{in}} \right\| \cdot \left\| \vec{V}_{\text{out}} \right\|} \cdot n \right), n \in \{1, -1\} \qquad (9)$$

where $\vec{V}_{\text{in}}$ is input velocity vector; $\vec{V}_{\text{out}}$ is output velocity vector; and θ is the angle change after vehicle makes a turn. n represents the direction of the vehicle's turn (1 is right, −1 is left). In order to decide the turn direction of the vehicle, two thresholds are set for left turn and right turn. If the angle θ is greater than the right turn threshold then the class of vehicle's motion is "Right". Similarly, the angle θ is lower than left turn threshold, the class of this motion is "Left". When the angle θ is in range of left turn threshold and right turn threshold, the corresponding motion is classified as "Straight". For "Stop" and "Slow", two velocity thresholds are set in a similar way as the turn direction.

– Re-ranking the results of appearance model: As shown in Fig. 1, for each query we have a list of tracks ranked by the appearance model, in which the higher the order track is the more similar it is to the query description. The result list from the appearance model then goes through the motion analysis phase for re-ranking. In this phase, the vehicle motion is classified based on both the query description and the trajectory of tracks in input list. If the class of query and the class of track's trajectory is not matched, the track's ranking will be decreased.

4 Experiment and Results

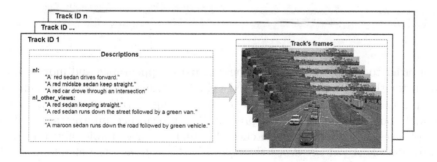

Fig. 2. Vehicle track and its corresponding descriptions in the dataset.

4.1   Dataset and Evaluation Metric

Experimental Dataset. The dataset for natural language-based vehicle track retrieval is set by using the CityFlow Benchmark dataset of multi-camera and multi-vehicle tracking images [24] with natural language descriptions are annotated for 2,498 tracks of vehicles. Each track is described by at least three unique natural language descriptions. In this work, 2,155 unique vehicle tracks with their corresponding query sets of at least three descriptions for each are used for the training phase, and 184 tracks of vehicles and corresponding query sets for testing phase. Figure 2 illustrates an example of a track ID and the corresponding natural language descriptions for vehicles from one or other views.

From the original dataset, a new augmented text dataset was built using the back translation technique. In [7], two ways of data augmentations were applied including back translation. To increase the number of descriptions in English, the authors proposed to translate them into Chinese and then translate back to English. However, the result using back translation was not reported. Further, selecting of a target language like Chinese can cause the low-quality of translations due to the differences between two languages. In our experiments, two translation systems were selected to make the translation from English to French (the Google Translate API) and the back translation from French to English (the Systran translation system). Using the same translation system for both forward and backward translations can bring out very little variation or even unchanged sentences. However, using two different translation systems can create a back translation results different from the original one because of two different dictionaries. Furthermore, the quality of back translation is still high due to the high quality of these two famous translation systems. Table 2 shows some examples of back translation using the same translation system and two different translation systems.

Table 2. Examples of back translation for vehicle descriptions.

EN	EN-FR	EN-GoogleAPI-FR-GoogleAPI-EN	EN-GoogleAPI-FR-Systran-EN
"A red car drove through an intersection."	"Une voiture rouge à traversé une intersection."	"A red car drove through an intersection."	"A red car crossed an intersection."
"A white car is going straight."	"Une voiture blanche va tout droit."	"A white car is going straight."	"A white car goes straight ahead."
"Black Chevy SUV driving straight through the intersection."	"Black Chevy SUV conduisant directement à travers l'intersection."	"Black Chevy SUV driving straight through the intersection."	"Black Chevy SUV driving directly through the intersection."

In order to compare the effectiveness of using appearance and motion information for the natural language-based vehicle retrieval problem, the noun and verb phrases are chunked from the textual using NLTK (Natural Language Toolkit) tool. The noun phrases present the appearance information and the verb phrases indicate the motion cues of vehicles. For example, given an input description of *"A red car drove through an intersection."*, the chunking results are two noun phrases ['*A red car*', '*an intersection*'] and one verb phrase ['*drove through an intersection*']. The feature vectors extracted from these phrases are then matched with the visual features of vehicles to find out the most relevant candidates.

Evaluation Metric. To evaluate the performance of vehicle, Mean Reciprocal Rank (MRR) [25] is employed as the main evaluation metric. MRR is defined as follows:

$$\text{MRR} = \frac{1}{Q} \sum_{i=1}^{Q} \frac{1}{\text{rank}_i} \tag{10}$$

where Q is the number of queries and $rank_i$ is the position of the highest-ranked answer of the ith query. MRR is as large as possible and maximum is 1 when all the correct search results for Q queries are returned at rank 1. Otherwise, the MRR can be zero when all the results of the queries are incorrect. Besides, the value of recalls at rank 5, 10 named Rank@5, Rank@10 are also reported. It is similar to MRR, the larger the two metrics are, the better the method is.

4.2   Experimental Results

In order to evaluate the performance of the proposed system, three different experimental scenarios are set in this work. The obtained results for these are shown in Table 3.

Table 3. Results obtained with different models on the whole test set of 2022 AI Challenge Task 2.

Models	MRR	Rank@5	Rank@10
Appearance (1 image + 2 descriptions)	0.1848	0.2717	0.4620
Appearance (4 images + 5 descriptions)	0.2272	0.3315	0.5109
Appearance noun phrase with augmented descriptions	0.1668	0.2663	0.3804
Appearance with augmented descriptions	0.2195	0.3098	0.4728
Appearance + Motion with augmented descriptions	0.2333	0.3587	0.4837

In the first scenario, the impact of the number of vehicle images and the descriptions on the quality of the ranking accuracy is evaluated. Two options with different amounts of vehicle images and descriptions are chosen for evaluation including (1) one image and two descriptions, and (2) four images and five descriptions. The experimental results show that the more images and descriptions used for vehicle representation, the higher accuracy obtained. The MRR, Rank@5 and Rank@10 obtained for the case of one image and two descriptions are 0.1848, 0.2717, 0.4620, while those for the option of four images and five descriptions are 0.2272, 0.3315 and 0.5109 respectively.

The second scenario aims at assessing the role of textual data augmentation through back translation and the appearance cues expressed through noun phrases for vehicle searching based on textual descriptions. Some previous works on person search [16, 26] shown that noun phases play a significant role in person description and then suggested to employ only noun phases for person retrieval.

However for vehicle retrieval, besides appearance, motion could be an important cue to distinguish the vehicles, especially in case the vehicles have the same appearance. This confirms by our experimental results. In comparison with the case of using the whole description and augmented textual data (Appearance with augmented descriptions), the case of using appearance noun phrase with augmented descriptions gains lower results at MRR, Rank@5, Rank@10 (0.1668 compared to 0.2195 at MRR, 0.2663 against 0.3098 at Rank@5, and 0.3804 versus 0.4728 at Rank@10).

Finally, in the third scenario, when using motion analysis as the post processing step on the retrieved list, we obtain a light improvement with the gains of 0.0138, 0.0489 and 0.0109 for MRR, Rank@5 and Rank@10 respectively.

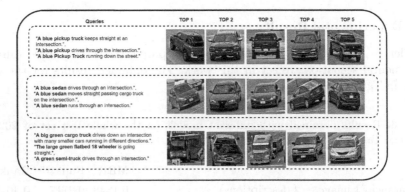

Fig. 3. Examples of five top results in the retrieved list obtained by the proposed method. Relevant results are marked in red. (Color figure online)

We have submitted our results to 2022 AI Challenge Task 2. The proposed method is ranked 13th out of 94 participating teams. Although the ranking accuracy of the proposed method is still low in comparison with other teams at MRR and Rank@5, the margin between the proposed method and others methods at Rank@10 is relatively small. MRR of the method ranked 10th is 0.2832 while that of our method is 0.233. The performance of other lower ranked methods of 14th and 15th) drops dramatically with the values of MRR are 0.0389 and 0.0216 respectively. This indicates that this task is very challenging. Therefore, in this case, appearance model could not fully represent the vehicle of interest. Motion aspect should be more exploited and integrated in our method.

Figure 3 illustrates some vehicle searching results obtained from the proposed method. Relevant results are marked in the red bounding box. It can be seen from Fig. 3 that all five first results for the two first queries have the appearance matches the query description.

5 Conclusions and Future Works

This work presents the proposed framework for vehicle search based on natural language descriptions. The deep learning models of ResNet50 and BiLSTM are applied for visual and textual feature extraction respectively. Based on this, joint training strategy is applied by combining both instance loss of each model and triple loss. In addition, vocabulary enrichment for textual embedding is done by translating back and forth vehicle descriptions from English to French. The experiments are carried out in the test set of AI City Challenge. The achieved experimental results show that the proposed method can exploit effectively the vehicle appearance and motion information for vehicle searching by textual descriptions. The obtained results are promising but it still exists a large margin between the performance of the proposed method with others teams participated in AI City challenge. In the future, more attention will be done for motion aspect of vehicles by exploring the camera locations and directions.

Acknowledgement. This research is funded by the Vietnam MPS under grant number BCN. 2020. T01. 04.

References

1. Islam, K.: Person search: new paradigm of person re-identification: a survey and outlook of recent works. Image Vis. Comput. **101**, 103970 (2020)
2. Li, S., Xiao, T., Li, H., Zhou, B., Yue, D., Wang, X.: Person search with natural language description. In: 2017 IEEE Conference on Computer Vision and Pattern Recognition (CVPR), Los Alamitos, CA, USA, IEEE Computer Society, July 2017, pp. 5187–5196 (2017)
3. Pham, T.T.T., et. al.: Towards a large-scale person search by Vietnamese natural language: dataset and methods. Multimedia Tools. Appl. **81**, 1–32 (2022). https://doi.org/10.1007/s11042-022-12138-1
4. Naphade, M., et al.: The 5th AI city challenge. In: The IEEE Conference on Computer Vision and Pattern Recognition (CVPR) Workshops (2021)
5. Feng, Q., Ablavsky, V., Sclaroff, S.: CityFlow-NL: tracking and retrieval of vehicles at city scale by natural language descriptions. CoRR abs/2101.04741 (2021)
6. Yu, Y., Ko, H., Choi, J., Kim, G.: End-to-end concept word detection for video captioning, retrieval, and question answering. In: Proceedings of the IEEE Conference on Computer Vision and Pattern Recognition, pp. 3165–3173 (2017)
7. Bai, S., et al.: Connecting language and vision for natural language-based vehicle retrieval. In: Proceedings of the IEEE/CVF Conference on Computer Vision and Pattern Recognition, pp. 4034–4043 (2021)
8. Mikolov, T., Chen, K., Corrado, G., Dean, J.: Efficient estimation of word representations in vector space. arXiv preprint arXiv:1301.3781 (2013)
9. Hochreiter, S., Schmidhuber, J.: Long short-term memory. Neural Comput. **9**(8), 1735–1780 (1997)
10. Vaswani, A., et al.: Attention is all you need. In: Advances in Neural Information Processing Systems, vol. 30 (2017)
11. Devlin, J., Chang, M.W., Lee, K., Toutanova, K.: BERT: pre-training of deep bidirectional transformers for language understanding. arXiv preprint arXiv:1810.04805 (2018)

12. Simonyan, K., Zisserman, A.: Two-stream convolutional networks for action recognition in videos. In: Advances in Neural Information Processing Systems, vol. 27 (2014)
13. Carreira, J., Zisserman, A.: Quo Vadis, action recognition? a new model and the kinetics dataset. In: Proceedings of the IEEE Conference on Computer Vision and Pattern Recognition, pp. 6299–6308(2017)
14. Sun, C., Myers, A., Vondrick, C., Murphy, K., Schmid, C.: VideoBERT: a joint model for video and language representation learning. In: Proceedings of the IEEE/CVF International Conference on Computer Vision, pp. 7464–7473 (2019)
15. Faghri, F., Fleet, D.J., Kiros, J.R., Fidler, S.: VSE++: improving visual-semantic embeddings with hard negatives. arXiv preprint arXiv:1707.05612 (2017)
16. Wang, Z., Fang, Z., Wang, J., Yang, Y.: Visual-textual attributes alignment in person search by natural language. In: Vedaldi, A., Bischof, H., Brox, T., Frahm, J.-M. (eds.) ECCV 2020. LNCS, vol. 12357, pp. 402–420. Springer, Cham (2020). https://doi.org/10.1007/978-3-030-58610-2_24
17. Dzabraev, M., Kalashnikov, M., Komkov, S., Petiushko, A.: MDMMT: multidomain multimodal transformer for video retrieval. In: Proceedings of the IEEE/CVF Conference on Computer Vision and Pattern Recognition, pp. 3354–3363 (2021)
18. Park, E.J., Kim, H., Jeong, S., Kang, B., Kwon, Y.: Keyword-based vehicle retrieval. In: Proceedings of the IEEE/CVF Conference on Computer Vision and Pattern Recognition (CVPR) Workshops, pp. 4220–4227 (2021)
19. Bain, M., Nagrani, A., Varol, G., Zisserman, A.: Frozen in time: a joint video and image encoder for end-to-end retrieval. In: Proceedings of the IEEE/CVF International Conference on Computer Vision, pp. 1728–1738 (2021)
20. Sennrich, R., Haddow, B., Birch, A.: Improving neural machine translation models with monolingual data. arXiv preprint arXiv:1511.06709 (2015)
21. Hoang, V.C.D., Koehn, P., Haffari, G., Cohn, T.: Iterative back-translation for neural machine translation. In: Proceedings of the 2nd Workshop on Neural Machine Translation and Generation, pp. 18–24 (2018)
22. He, K., Zhang, X., Ren, S., Sun, J.: Deep residual learning for image recognition. In: Proceedings of the IEEE Conference on Computer Vision and Pattern Recognition, pp. 770–778 (2016)
23. Zheng, Z., Zheng, L., Garrett, M., Yang, Y., Xu, M., Shen, Y.D.: Dual-path convolutional image-text embeddings with instance loss. ACM Trans. Multimedia Comput. Commun. Appl. (TOMM) **16**(2), 1–23 (2020)
24. Tang, Z., et al.: A city-scale benchmark for multi-target multi-camera vehicle tracking and re-identification. In: Proceedings of the IEEE/CVF Conference on Computer Vision and Pattern Recognition, pp. 8797–8806 (2019)
25. Voorhees, E.M., Tice, D.M.: The TREC-8 question answering track. In: Proceedings of the Second International Conference on Language Resources and Evaluation (LREC 2000), Athens, Greece, European Language Resources Association (ELRA) (2000)
26. Pham, T.T.T., et al.: Person search by natural language description in Vietnamese using pre-trained visual-textual attributes alignment model. In: 2021 13th International Conference on Knowledge and Systems Engineering (KSE), pp. 1–6. IEEE (2021)

Shapley Additive Explanations for Text Classification and Sentiment Analysis of Internet Movie Database

Christine Dewi[1,2], Bing-Jun Tsai[1], and Rung-Ching Chen[1,1(✉)]

[1] Department of Information Management, Chaoyang University of Technology Taichung, Taiwan, Republic of China
`christine.dewi@uksw.edu`, `s11014617@gm.cyut.edu.tw`, `crching@cyut.edu.tw`
[2] Faculty of Information Technology, Satya Wacana Christian University, Salatiga, Indonesia

Abstract. The application of Artificial Intelligence (AI) is increasing in areas like sentiment analysis and natural language processing (NLP). Automatic sentiment analysis provides a guide to capture the user emotions and classify the reviews into positive or negative. One of the challenges of using general lexicon analysis is its insensitivity to all domains. There arises a need for the interpretability of the output predicted from the AI sentiment analysis models. This paper developed a Shapley Additive Explanations for Text Classification (SHAP) based model to classify the user opinion texts into negative or positive labels. Our sentiment analysis model is evaluated on the Internet Movie Database (IMDB) datasets which have rich vocabulary and coherence of the textual data. Results showed that the model predicted 89% of the user reviews correctly. This model is very flexible for extending it to the unlabeled data.

Keywords: Natural language processing · Sentiment analysis · Shapley additive explanations (SHAP) · Bidirectional encoder representations from transformers (BERT)

1 Introduction

Sentiment analysis (SA) is a rapidly expanding field of research due to the massive growth of digital information. In the field of artificial intelligence (AI), SA is a crucial tool for extracting emotional information from massive amounts of data [1]. Sentiment analysis is a branch of text analysis that seeks to glean from unstructured written language the subjective viewpoints and attitudes of people toward things and their qualities [2]. Notably, transformer models like bidirectional encoder representations from transformers (BERT) [3] and its refinement RoBERTa [4] have achieved state-of-the-art performance in various sentiment analysis tasks. Using a vast amount of unlabeled data, these deep learning algorithms profit from unsupervised representation learning in order to gain remarkable general language knowledge [5, 6].

© The Author(s), under exclusive license to Springer Nature Singapore Pte Ltd. 2022
E. Szczerbicki et al. (Eds.): ACIIDS 2022, CCIS 1716, pp. 69–80, 2022.
https://doi.org/10.1007/978-981-19-8234-7_6

SA is largely used in the industrial environment to gather and analyze customer feedback. SA and natural language processing (NLP) are inseparable [7–9]. NLP is analyzing these natural texts to create things that the machine can understand for SA. In the Internet Movie Database (IMDB) dataset, there are equal numbers of 25,000 train and 25,000 test reviews, for a total of 50,000 total reviews. Whether a film review is positive or negative, users must try to deduce the author's intent from the context in which it was written. The sentiment of a movie review is usually associated with a different rating, which can be used for classification dilemmas. It can be used as a reference instrument for movie preference [10].

Shapley Additive Explanations (SHAP) is a highly valuable technique for dealing with one of the most difficulties associated with machine learning models: interpretability and explain ability. It can be utilized both during the development stage and during the verification step. SHAP can aid in the creation of an ML model by detecting outliers and missing values, segmenting data, selecting variables, and doing variable interaction analysis [11–13]. In the validation governance stage, SHAP provides a clear means of explaining the interactions and consequences of the components, it can aid in finding the cause of a decline in performance, and it can enable the validator to recommend changes that may be able to remedy the difficulties.

The following are the significant contributions of this work: (1). The study is based on the IMDB dataset, which comprises movie reviews and the positive or negative labels that are connected with them. (2). The goal of our study experiment is to do the text classification and sentiment analysis by Shapley Additive Explanations (SHAP).

There are 5 parts in this research. Presented in Sect. 2 is another relevant work. The third section describes the research process. The research findings are discussed in Sect. 4. Conclusions and future research projects are summarized in Sect. 5 of the paper.

2 Related Work

2.1 Sentiment Analysis (SA) and BERT

Internet users' online text data has been used by researchers to develop a variety of recommendation algorithms during the past few years [14, 15]. Three different Sentimental Analysis Algorithms are popular among the research community. Sentiment Analysis Based on Sentiment Lexicon, Machine Learning and Deep Learning. Taboada *et al.* [16] proposed an approach to extract the sentiments from text using a semantic orientation calculator and assign positive or negative labels based on the polar-ity and strength. Bandhakavi *et al.* [17] proposed a generative unigram mixture model to extract the emotions of weekly labelled data using the word emotion association. *Feng* et al. [18] constructed a random walk two-layer graph, which integrated emoticon and user sentiments in the microblog to extract the sentiment lexicons.

Lexicons based algorithms can achieve greater benefit to certain languages like English and Chinese and it requires high manual maintenance costs [19]. Therefore, Machine Learning (ML) methods are more popular among researchers, uses computational intelligence to extract sentiments from the texts. Huq et al. [21] used Support Vector Machine (SVM) and k-Nearest Neighbours (KNN) algorithms to analyze the sentiment from Twitter blogs. Furthermore, Long et al. [22] classified stock forum posts using SVM. ML methods majorly depend on the feature selection process while Deep

Learning methods can automatically extract from neural network structures and learn from the errors. Hyun et al. [23] proposed a model named a target-dependent convolutional neural network (TCNN). TCNN uses attention mechanisms to learn from the surrounding words to understand the emotional polarity of the sentences. Chen et al. [24] proposed a neural network-based sequence model to classify sentences using the divide-and-conquer method.

BERT is a transformers model that is faster and more efficient than distilBERT, and it was pretrained on the same corpus in a self-supervised manner [25–27]. This means that it was pretrained on solely the raw texts, with no human labeling them in any manner (which is why it may use a large amount of publically available data), with an automatic method to produce inputs and labels from those texts, utilizing the BERT base model as a training set for the model. Our work implement *tokenizer_name = "distilbert-base-uncased"* and *model_name = "distilbert-base-uncased-finetuned-sst-2-english"* [28].

2.2 Text to Text Analysis by Shapley Additive Explanations (SHAP)

SHAP is the state-of-the-art Machine Learning explain ability, and it is available for free. Developed by Lundberg and Lee in 2017 [29, 30], this method provides a great approach to reverse-engineer the output of any prediction algorithm. The purpose of SHAP is to provide an explanation for the prediction of an instance x by calculating the contribution of each characteristic to the prediction of the instance x.

Text-to-Text Visualization displays the text that was entered into the model on the left side and the text that was output from it on the right side (in the default layout) [31, 32]. When we hover over the tokens on the right (output) side, the importance of each input token is exaggerated above it, and this is indicated by the token's background color. Specifically, red sections correspond to textual elements that, when included in the model, enhance the output, whereas blue regions relate to textual elements that lower the output, when included in the model [30]. The explanation for a specific output token can be anchored by clicking on the specific output token in question (it can be un-anchored by clicking again).

3 Methodology

3.1 Research Workflow

This section will describe our research workflow, as shown in Fig. 1. SHAP Values dissect a prediction to reveal the relative importance of its various components. How much each player contributed to the success of a collaborative game can be determined using this method. To put it another way, each SHAP value measures how much of a role each feature in our model plays in our prediction.

3.2 Internet Movie Database (IMDB)

The IMDB dataset is a binary sentiment classification dataset comprised of movie reviews extracted from the internet movie database [27, 33]. There is a lot of polarization in the dataset training documents. Moreover, there is a one-to-one correspondence

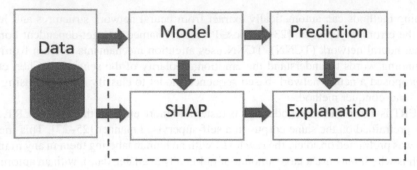

Fig. 1. SHAP model explanation architecture.

between negative and positive when we label the data. All documents in the collection need to be used, including training, test, and unlabeled data, to create a vector for the document in question [34]. Table 1 contains several samples drawn from the IMDB dataset. In our experiment, we use 100 data of IMDB and implement SHAP for text classification and sentiment analysis.

Table 1. Examples of movie reviews for each class.

No	Review	Sentiment
1	*I remember this film; it was the first film i had watched at the cinema the picture was dark in places i was very nervous it was back in 74/75 my Dad took me my brother & sister to Newbury cinema in Newbury Berkshire England. I recall the tigers and the lots of snow in the film also the appearance of Grizzly Adams actor Dan Haggery i think one of the tigers gets shot and dies. If anyone knows where to find this on DVD etc. please let me know. The cinema now has been turned in a fitness club which is a very big shame as the nearest cinema now is 20 miles away, would love to hear from others who have seen this film or any other like it*	Positive
2	*The cast played Shakespeare. < br/> < br/ > Shakespeare lost. < br /> I appreciate that this is trying to bring Shakespeare to the masses, but why ruin something so good. < br/ > < br/ > Is it because 'The Scottish Play' is my favorite Shakespeare? I do not know. What I do know is that a certain Rev Bowdler (hence bowdlerization) tried to do something similar in the Victorian era. < br/ > < br/ > n other words, you cannot improve perfection. < br/> < br/> I have no more to write but as I have to write at least ten lines of text (and English composition was never my forte I will just have to keep going and say that this movie, as the saying goes, just does not cut it*	Negative

4   Experiment and Result

4.1   Experiment Results

Sentiment analysis by SHAP explained in Table 2. Our work implements 100 data from IMDB dataset and uses full analysis. In Table 2 review number 1 achieve 0.000165096 negative score and 0.999835 positive score. Based on the result of review number 1 belongs to positive and it is match with the IMDB Sentiment positive result yes. Our experiments label "yes" if the sentiment analysis by SHAP matches the IMDB sentiment dataset. On the other hand, if it is different, we label it with "no". For example, in review number 12 achieve 0.825068 negative score and 0.174932 positive score. Further, from the results of the analysis using SHAP review number 12 is negative and this is different from the sentiment of the IMDB dataset, so we label it with "no".

Table 2. Sentiment Analysis by SHAP.

Review No	SHAP			IMDB Sentiment	Result
	Negative score	Positive score	Sentiment		
1	0.000165095	0.999835	Positive	Positive	Yes
2	0.000204888	0.999795	Positive	Positive	Yes
3	0.000226608	0.999773	Positive	Positive	Yes
4	0.000231536	0.999768	Positive	Positive	Yes
5	0.000238009	0.999762	Positive	Positive	Yes
6	0.000289527	0.999711	Positive	Positive	Yes
7	0.00030916	0.999691	Positive	Positive	Yes
8	0.000331213	0.999669	Positive	Positive	Yes
9	0.000455403	0.999545	Positive	Positive	Yes
10	0.000515331	0.999485	Positive	Positive	Yes
11	0.507588	0.492412	Negative	Positive	No
12	0.825068	0.174932	Negative	Positive	No
13	0.825068	0.174932	Negative	Negative	Yes
14	0.825068	0.174932	Negative	Positive	No
15	0.878919	0.121081	Negative	Positive	No
16	0.896451	0.103549	Negative	Positive	No
17	0.934477	0.0655226	Negative	Negative	Yes
18	0.957786	0.0422139	Negative	Negative	Yes
19	0.960905	0.0390946	Negative	Negative	Yes
20	0.961433	0.0385668	Negative	Positive	No

The statistic performance of SHAP describe in Table 3. From the 100 data of IMDB dataset the sentiment analysis by SHAP got 89% accuracy. The total of positive data is

31 and Negative 58 for class "Yes". In other hand, class "No" have 4 sentiments positive and 7 sentiments negative.

Table 3. Statistic performance of SHAP.

Data	Yes %	No %	Total
Positive	31	4	35
Negative	58	7	65
Total	89	11	100

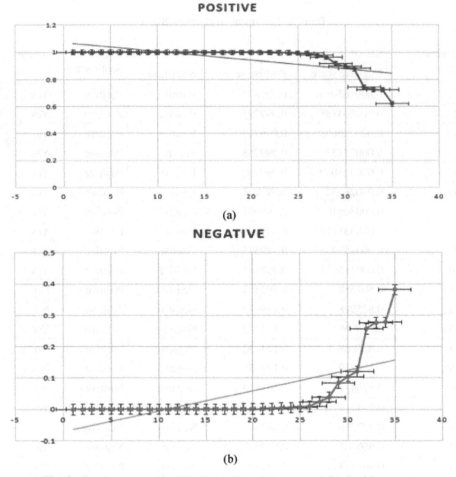

(a)

(b)

Fig. 2. Sentiment score by SHAP. (a). Negative score and (b). Positive score.

Figure 2 depicts the positive and negative scores of SHAP. The maximum score for negative sentiment is 0.381245 and the minimum score is 0.000165. While the maximum value of positive SHAP sentiment is 0.999 and the minimum value is 0.618.

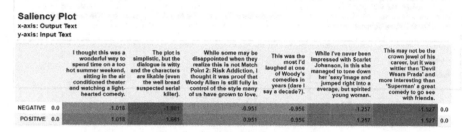

Fig. 3. Saliency Plot by SHAP.

Figure 3 describe the saliency plot by SHAP. Positive contributions to feelings are represented by darker pinks, while negative contributions are represented by darker blues. This allows us to gain a better knowledge of what goes on under the hood and not just accept projections at face value. The color scaling for all token (input and output) are consistent and the brightest red is assigned to the maximum SHAP value of input tokens for any output token. Figures 4 explain the input and output heatmap for positive text and Fig. 5 describes the input and output for negative text. The importance values returned for text models are often hierarchical and follow the structure of the text, just like the single output plots described in Fig. 4 and Fig. 5.

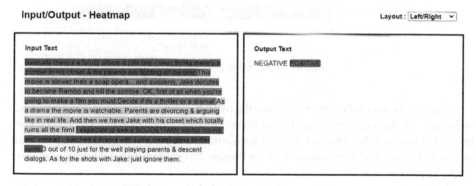

Fig. 4. Input/output- heat map for negative text.

Input/Output - Heatmap   Layout : Top/Bottom ⌄

Input Text

Basically there's a family where a little boy (Jake) thinks there's a zombie in his closet & his parents are fighting all the time. This movie is slower than a soap opera... and suddenly, Jake decides to become Rambo and kill the zombie. OK, first of all when you're going to make a film you must Decide if its a thriller or a drama! As a drama the movie is watchable. Parents are divorcing & arguing like in real life. And then we have Jake with his closet which totally ruins all the film! I expected to see a BOOGEYMAN similar movie, and instead i watched a drama with some meaningless thriller spots. 3 out of 10 just for the well playing parents & descent dialogs. As for the shots with Jake: just ignore them.

Output Text

NEGATIVE POSITIVE

Fig. 5. Input/output- heat map for positive text.

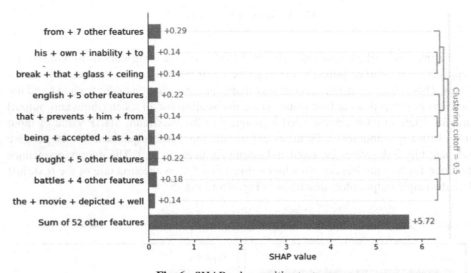

Fig. 6. SHAP value positive text.

There are times when users want to see the overall impact of tokens on a large number of instances but using the text plot to plot several instance-level explanations can be very useful information. SHAP can explain the meaning of the text and give a value as seen in Fig. 6 and Fig. 7. Figure 6 show the SHAP value for positive text and for negative text could be seen on Fig. 7.

Some greats benefits of the explanation by SHAP are as follows: (1). At the global level, the SHAP values together contribute to the interpretation and understanding of the model. Specifically, they demonstrate how much each predictor contributes to the target variable, either favorably or negatively [35, 36]. It permits a fairly intuitive interpretation of the model structure and is generalizable across a wide range of modeling approaches. (2) At the local level, each observation receives its own set of SHAP values, which are then combined (one for each predictor). Transparency is substantially increased as a result of this, as contributions to predictions are shown on a case-by-case basis, something that standard variable significance algorithms are unable to achieve. Having

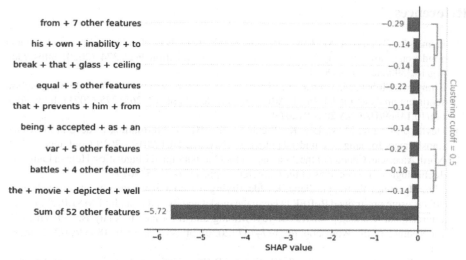

Fig. 7. SHAP value negative text.

the ability to explain each granular forecast opens the door to the application of machine learning algorithms in credit decision, where banks are compelled to explain why a certain credit decision was made. Additionally, local interpretability can be used to aid in the segmentation and detection of outliers.

There is some limitation of SHAP as follows: (1) An expected value is inferred by SHAP using data from the surrounding environment. Using the complete dataset is computationally prohibitive for huge datasets, therefore we must make do with approximations. The correctness of the explanation will be affected by this. (2) Predictions are explained by SHAP by comparing them to the training dataset's expected value. Rather of using the complete training set, it may be more useful to estimate the expected value based on a subset of the data.

5 Conclusions

In this paper, we introduced SHAP based movie sentiment analysis model for user comments. The model learns the word representation and gives insight into the captured sentiments, classifying the comments into positive and negative categories based on the text analysis. IMDB dataset is used for evaluating the model. The reviews are labelled with a positive/negative rating. A total of 100 samples with 35 positives and 65 negative ratings are evaluated using the model. The model correctly predicted 31 positive and 58 negative ratings. The user comments largely influenced the text perturbations and correlated well with our model analysis. The end goal is to develop a digital movie advisor platform. In the future, this model can be extended to characterize a wide variety of text data, thus can be applied in various areas of sentiment analysis.

Acknowledgment. This paper is supported by the Ministry of Science and Technology, Taiwan. The Nos are MOST-107–2221-E-324 -018 -MY2 and MOST-109–2622-E-324-004, Taiwan.

References

1. Kumar, S., Gahalawat, M., Roy, P.P., Dogra, D.P., Kim, B.G.: Exploring impact of age and gender on sentiment analysis using machine learning. Electron. **9**(2), 374, (2020). https://doi.org/10.3390/electronics9020374
2. Chiny, M., Chihab, M., Chihab, Y., Bencharef, O.: LSTM, VADER and TF-IDF based hybrid sentiment analysis model. Int. J. Adv. Comput. Sci. Appl. **12**, 265–275 (2021). https://doi.org/10.14569/IJACSA.2021.0120730
3. Devlin, J., Chang, M.W., Lee, K., Toutanova, K.: BERT: Pre-training of deep bidirectional transformers for language understanding. In: NAACL HLT 2019 - 2019 Conference of the North American Chapter of the Association for Computational Linguistics: Human Language Technologies - Proceedings of the Conference, pp. 4171–4186 (2019)
4. Zhu, M., Song, Y., Jin, G., Jiang, K.: Identifying personal experience tweets of medication effects using pre-trained RoBERTa language model and its updating. In: EMNLP 2020 - 11th International Workshop on Health Text Mining and Information Analysis, LOUHI 2020, Proceedings of the Workshop, pp. 127–137 (2020). https://doi.org/10.18653/v1/2020.louhi-1.14
5. Chen, R.-C., Dewi, C., Huang, S.-W., Caraka, R.E.: Selecting critical features for data classification based on machine learning methods. J. Big Data **7**(1), 1–26 (2020). https://doi.org/10.1186/s40537-020-00327-4
6. Dewi, C., Chen, R.-C., Yu, H., Jiang, X.: Robust detection method for improving small traffic sign recognition based on spatial pyramid pooling. J. Ambient. Intell. Humaniz. Comput. , 1–18 (2021). https://doi.org/10.1007/s12652-021-03584-0
7. Chatterjee, S., Chakrabarti, K., Garain, A., Schwenker, F., Sarkar, R.: Jumrv1: A sentiment analysis dataset for movie recommendation. Appl. Sci. **11**(20), 9381, (2021). https://doi.org/10.3390/app11209381
8. Lauriola, I., Lavelli, A., Aiolli, F.: An introduction to deep learning in natural language processing: models, techniques, and tools. Neurocomputing. **470**, 443–456 (2022). https://doi.org/10.1016/j.neucom.2021.05.103
9. Zhou, M., Duan, N., Liu, S., Shum, H.Y.: Progress in neural NLP: modeling, learning, and reasoning. Engineering **6**(3), 275–290 (2020). https://doi.org/10.1016/j.eng.2019.12.014
10. Chen, R.-C., Dewi, C., Zhang, W.-W., Liu, J.-M.: Integrating gesture control board and image recognition for gesture recognition based on deep learning. Int. J. Appl. Sci. Eng. **17**, 237–248 (2020)
11. Wang, D., Thunéll, S., Lindberg, U., Jiang, L., Trygg, J., Tysklind, M.: Towards better process management in wastewater treatment plants: process analytics based on SHAP values for tree-based machine learning methods. J. Environ. Manage. **301**, 113941 (2022). https://doi.org/10.1016/j.jenvman.2021.113941
12. Dewi, C., Chen, R.-C., Tai, S.-K.: Evaluation of robust spatial pyramid pooling based on convolutional neural network for traffic sign recognition system. Electronics **9**, 889 (2020). https://doi.org/10.3390/electronics9060889
13. Dewi, C., Chen, R.-C., Jiang, X., Yu, H.: Deep convolutional neural network for enhancing traffic sign recognition developed on Yolo V4. Multimed. Tools Appl. 1–25 (2022). https://doi.org/10.1007/s11042-022-12962-5
14. Kokalj, E., Škrlj, B., Lavrač, N., Pollak, S., Robnik-Šikonja, M.: BERT meets shapley: extending SHAP explanations to transformer-based classifiers. In: EACL Hackashop on News Media Content Analysis and Automated Report Generation, Hackashop 2021 at 16th conference of the European Chapter of the Association for Computational Linguistics, EACL 2021 – Proceedings, pp. 16–21 (2021)

15. Dewi, C., Chen, R.-C.: Human activity recognition based on evolution of features selection and random forest. In: 2019 IEEE International Conference on Systems, Man and Cybernetics (SMC), pp. 2496–2501 (2019)
16. Taboada, M., Brooke, J., Tofiloski, M., Voll, K., Stede, M.: Lexicon-based methods for sentiment analysis draft draft draft! Comput. Linguist. **37**(2), 267–307 (2011)
17. Bandhakavi, A., Wiratunga, N., Padmanabhan, D., Massie, S.: Lexicon based feature extraction for emotion text classification. Pattern Recognit. Lett. **93**, 133–142 (2017). https://doi.org/10.1016/j.patrec.2016.12.009
18. Feng, S., Song, K., Wang, D., Yu, G.: A word-emoticon mutual reinforcement ranking model for building sentiment lexicon from massive collection of microblogs. World Wide Web **18**(4), 949–967 (2014). https://doi.org/10.1007/s11280-014-0289-x
19. Al-Ayyoub, M., Khamaiseh, A.A., Jararweh, Y., Al-Kabi, M.N.: A comprehensive survey of arabic sentiment analysis. Inf. Process. Manag. **56**(2), 320–342 (2019). https://doi.org/10.1016/j.ipm.2018.07.006
20. Dewi, C., Chen, R.-C.: Random forest and support vector machine on features selection for regression analysis. Int. J. Innov. Comput. Inf. Control. **15**, 2027–2038 (2019)
21. Rezwanul, M., Ali, A., Rahman, A.: Sentiment analysis on twitter data using KNN and SVM. Int. J. Adv. Comput. Sci. Appl. **8**(6), (2017). https://doi.org/10.14569/ijacsa.2017.080603
22. Long, W., Tang, Y.-R., Tian, Y.-J.: Investor sentiment identification based on the universum SVM. Neural Comput. Appl. **30**(2), 661–670 (2016). https://doi.org/10.1007/s00521-016-2684-y
23. Hyun, D., Park, C., Yang, M.C., Song, I., Lee, J.T., Yu, H.: Target-aware convolutional neural network for target-level sentiment analysis. Inf. Sci. (Ny). **491**, 166–178 (2019). https://doi.org/10.1016/j.ins.2019.03.076
24. Chen, T., Xu, R., He, Y., Wang, X.: Improving sentiment analysis via sentence type classification using BiLSTM-CRF and CNN. Expert Syst. Appl. **72**, 221–230 (2017). https://doi.org/10.1016/j.eswa.2016.10.065
25. Reimers, N., Gurevych, I.: Sentence-BERT: Sentence embeddings using siamese BERT-networks. In: EMNLP-IJCNLP 2019 - 2019 Conference on Empirical Methods in Natural Language Processing and 9th International Joint Conference on Natural Language Processing, Proceedings of the Conference (2020). https://doi.org/10.18653/v1/d19-1410
26. Gao, Z., Feng, A., Song, X., Wu, X.: Target-dependent sentiment classification with BERT. IEEE Access. **7**, 154290–154299 (2019). https://doi.org/10.1109/ACCESS.2019.2946594
27. Dewi, C., Chen, R.-C., Liu, Y.-T., Tai, S.-K.: Synthetic Data generation using DCGAN for improved traffic sign recognition. Neural Comput. Appl. , 1–16 (2021). https://doi.org/10.1007/s00521-021-05982-z
28. Subies, G.G., Sánchez, D.B., Vaca, A.: Bert and shap for humor analysis based on human annotation. In: CEUR Workshop Proceedings (2021)
29. Lundberg, S.M., Lee, S.I.: A unified approach to interpreting model predictions. In: Advances in Neural Information Processing Systems, pp. 4766–4775 (2017)
30. Aas, K., Jullum, M., Løland, A.: Explaining individual predictions when features are dependent: More accurate approximations to Shapley values. Artif. Intell. **298**, 103502 (2021). https://doi.org/10.1016/j.artint.2021.103502
31. Dewi, C., Chen, R.-C.: Combination of resnet and spatial pyramid pooling for musical instrument identification. Cybern. Inf. Technol. **22**, 104 (2022)
32. Dewi, C., Chen, R.-C., Yu, H.: Weight analysis for various prohibitory sign detection and recognition using deep learning. Multimedia Tools Appl. **79**(43–44), 32897–32915 (2020). https://doi.org/10.1007/s11042-020-09509-x
33. Lakshmipathi, N.: IMDB Dataset of 50K Movie Reviews
34. Dewi, C., Chen, R., Liu, Y., Yu, H.: Various generative adversarial networks model for synthetic prohibitory sign image generation. Appl. Sci. **11**, 2913 (2021)

35. De Groote, W., Van Hoecke, S., Crevecoeur, G.: Prediction of follower jumps in cam-follower mechanisms: The benefit of using physics-inspired features in recurrent neural networks. Mech. Syst. Sign. Process. **166**, 108453 (2022). https://doi.org/10.1016/j.ymssp.2021.108453

36. Dewi, C., Chen, R.C., Liu, Y.T., Jiang, X., Hartomo, K.D.: Yolo V4 for advanced traffic sign recognition with synthetic training data generated by various GAN. IEEE Access. **9**, 97228–97242 (2021). https://doi.org/10.1109/ACCESS.2021.3094201

Explaining Predictive Scheduling in Cloud

Muhammad Fahimullah[1]([✉]), Rohit Gupta[2], Shohreh Ahvar[1],
and Maria Trocan[1]

[1] Institut Supérieur d'Électronique de Paris ISEP, Paris, France
muhammad.fahimullah@ext.isep.fr, {shohreh.ahvar,maria.trocan}@isep.fr
[2] MorningStar India Pvt. Ltd., Mumbai, India

Abstract. The importance of cloud computing has been rapidly growing due to the increasing number of users' requests for diverse sets of resources. Although clouds have rich resources to handle these incoming requests, under or over-provisioning of resources can lead to failure. Therefore, it is important to provision cloud resources appropriately. Machine-learning based techniques have been proven to be effective in the management of resources along with maintaining a Service Level Agreement (SLA). These techniques require complete data to produce better prediction results. In practice, it may happen that the data is incomplete and data with more missing attribute values can negatively affect the outcome of the predictions. Therefore, interpolation of missing attribute values is crucial for better predictions. However, the existing methods for interpolation of missing attribute values are heavy in terms of computation. This paper first predicts resource usage in terms of CPU by applying the lightGBM model to a real dataset. Furthermore, using the explanations of SHapley Additive exPlanations (SHAP) in combination with the K-Nearest Neighbor (KNN) to interpolate missing values in the dataset for CPU usage prediction. The experimental results show that SHAP explanations can be helpful for cloud providers in the selection of important features for interpolation of missing values. This SHAP-based interpolation results in lower computational time along with acceptable accuracy in comparison with KNN-based interpolation.

Keywords: Resource prediction · Light Gradient Boosting Machine (LightGBM) · SHapley Additive exPlanations (SHAP) · K-Nearest Neighbor (KNN)

1 Introduction

Cloud computing has received considerable attention due to advancements in technology and dramatic increase in the demand for resources. Many companies provide virtualized resources on a pay-as-you-go basis, which can be accessed over the internet [1]. Furthermore, for many cloud providers, effective utilization and predicting resource demands, especially CPU usage is a complex task due to unpredictable workload fluctuations. A lot of literature can be found to predict

© The Author(s), under exclusive license to Springer Nature Singapore Pte Ltd. 2022
E. Szczerbicki et al. (Eds.): ACIIDS 2022, CCIS 1716, pp. 81–91, 2022.
https://doi.org/10.1007/978-981-19-8234-7_7

the effective utilization of resources for various purposes. As an example, clustering algorithms have been used for effective Virtual Machine (VM) scheduling to save energy [2] and reduce cost. Classical time series and machine learning techniques were also used to optimize resource provisioning [3]. The ability to upscale or downscale the computing resources helps in optimizing the needs of the users. However, getting the full benefit of the scaling feature and correctly scaling, depends on the incoming request of the users [4]. Furthermore, companies need to know the usage of cloud capacity, as inappropriate provisioning of resources can cause serious risks. Under-provisioning of resources can result in low performance and overprovisioning of resources such as CPU and memory can result in an extensive amount of cost [3,5]. Furthermore, predicting optimal resource provisioning depends on providing the complete data to the model. As for missing attribute values, more than 15 % can negatively affect the outcome of the predictions [6].

Therefore, for the predictions, it is essential to have complete data. However, it is difficult to have it in practice [7,8]. Therefore, interpolation of missing values is required to achieve better prediction results. In this work, we considered the publicly available dataset from Delft University of technology GWA-T-12 Bitbrains (tudelft.nl) that provides the performance matrices of VMs. Furthermore, to tackle with missing attribute values problem for prediction, we consulted SHAP explanations and K-Nearest Neighbor (KNN) for interpolation of missing values. The contribution of this work can be summarized as follows.

- Using SHAP for model explanation and extracting important features
- Using KNN and SHAP explanations for interpolation of missing values and using it for prediction
- Applying KNN and SHAP combination method for completing a real dataset feeding Light Gradient Boosting Machine (LightGBM) model for predicting CPU resource

This paper is organized as follows, in Sect. 2 the related work to resource provisioning, SHAP, and missing values interpolations are analyzed. Furthermore, Sect. 3 provides details on the experimental process of LightGBM and model explanation using SHAP. Section 4 demonstrates the experimental results of using KNN for interpolation in combination with SHAP explanations. Finally, Sect. 5 contains the conclusion and future work.

2   Related Work

Under or overprovisioning resources is one of the critical issues. Provisioning fewer resources than required contributes to poor latency and low performance and overprovisioning results in high costs for both cloud providers and cloud customers [5]. The work in [9], investigates resource usage for the VMs using different machine learning techniques to optimize energy consumption. The authors in [3] considered the resource allocation as a time series problem by predicting the CPU usage, memory usage as well as disk read and write time using classical and machine learning techniques. The proposed approach can help to reduce over-provisioning of resources. Many studies provided static resource allocation and placement methods. Under static placement, an initial placement of a VM holds throughout the lifetime of the VM. This kind of placement leads to near-optimal placement, when detailed information about the job, processor characteristics, and network's topology characteristics are known in advance [10]. However, a Data Center (DC) configuration often changes over time (e.g., some VMs leave the DC). Therefore, it is not sufficient to make good initial placement choices by only using a static consolidation approach. To design efficient service provisioning, different types of uncertainties associated with cloud computing should be considered [10]. If there is enough data, it may be possible to provide predictive models for parameters that cause uncertainty in cloud computing. Due to confidentiality, few cloud platform providers are willing to publish their resource utilization data. However, Alibaba released its cloud resource usage data and several analytical reports on their data have been done [11]. In addition, new algorithms and models were proposed using the released data [12].

Furthermore, the explanations of complex machine learning models can help in identifying important features of the model. In addition, it can also be helpful in eliminating the typical trade-off between interpretability and accuracy [13]. SHAP is one of the methods used in literature for complex model explanations from local and global perspectives. As an example, authors in [14] provided the comparative study using different machine learning techniques in predicting the end-to-end response latency in the microservice domain. In addition, the authors consulted SHAP to explain black-box models such as Random Forest and Convolutional Neural Network (CNN) to get important features based on SHAP values and also the impact of features on workload prediction output. The proposed study can be helpful to practitioners in selecting the most important features for resource management. Furthermore, [13] used LightGBM for predicting the workload of serverless cloud computing along with SHAP for explaining their model. The predictive approach of workload and SHAP explanation for CPU usage provided in the paper can be used as a decision support system for the management of serverless computing.

However, to achieve better and more realistic prediction results, it is also important to have a complete set of data. However, in practice, it is difficult to have it and the data missing rate greater than 15 % have a negative impact on the outcome [6]. Several methods have been proposed in the literature for interpolation of missing values for improving accuracy or computational time or both. For instance, the work in [15], used KNN for interpolation of missing values throughout 2.5,5,10 and 20% of the data, considering evaluation metrics such as accuracy and computational time. Furthermore, the work showed its improved performance by validating the proposed idea in the domain of quality predictions. Similarly, the work in [8], performed comparative analyses of different machine learning-based interpolation techniques. The study suggests that the Classification and Regression Tree (CART) is a good choice for interpolating missing values. However, it is worth mentioning that an increase in data size (i.e., an increase in the dataset's number of rows or attributes) has a direct influence on the computational time of the interpolation process [16]. Therefore, in addition to metrics of accuracy, the computational time of the techniques is also one of the important metrics to consider when the missing values are interpolated. Performing interpolation with fewer attributes may significantly reduce the computational time of interpolating method. However, the selection of appropriate attributes for interpolation of missing values is still one of the issues.

To address the aforementioned issues of dealing with missing values, we consulted KNN with the help of SHAP explanations that provides us an overview of the most important attributes for CPU usage prediction considering the complete dataset. Furthermore, we evaluated this idea by applying predictive resource usage using the machine learning technique.

3   Experimental Methodology

The flow of the experiments is shown in Fig. 1. The numbers on the arrows represent the flow of events. The experiments are divided into two parts. First, the dataset is trained on the LightGBM model. Secondly, SHAP explanations are considered in combination with KNN for interpolation of null values.

3.1   Dataset Background

We used a publicly available dataset from Delft University of technology GWA-T-12 Bitbrains (tudelft.nl) that provides the performance matrices of VM such as CPU cores, CPU capacity provisioned, CPU usage, memory provisioned (memory requested), memory usage, disk read throughput, disk write throughput, network received throughput and network transmitted throughput. We considered only the Rnd traces of the dataset which is 500 VMs.

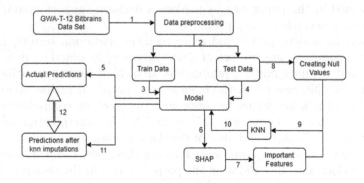

Fig. 1. Workflow of experiment

3.2   Light Gradient Boosting Machine (LightGBM)

The model we used for prediction is LightGBM. It is based on GBDT model framework [13]. It is widely used in literature for the prediction of resources in cloud computing [17,18] due to its lightweight boosting nature. For our work, we considered CPU usage as the target variable (dependent) to be predicted and other variables as an independent. Independent variables in this work include CPU cores, memory usage [KB], disk read throughput [KB/s], disk write throughput [KB/s], network received throughput [KB/s], network transmitted throughput [KB/s]. In the first step, we removed all the null entries from the dataset. Next, we split the data into training and testing with the ratio of 90% and 10%. In the third and fourth steps, we used LightGBM to train and test our data. Root Mean Square Error (RMSE) of 805.15 and an accuracy of 93.96% were obtained in the experiments. Some parts of the prediction results are shown in Table 1. In the next section, we used SHAP for obtaining the LightGBM model explanation and getting an insight into the features impact on the output.

Table 1. Test data prediction vs actual CPU usage sample

Actual CPU Usage	Predictions
3437.199100	3137.943705
169.866641	158.887996
35.467031	148.972001
0.000000	50.825364
0.000000	2.395781
0.000000	1.963156
109.237311	367.000206
0.000000	8.122719
178.533262	168.943388
3045.466343	4302.655889
64.371990	114.830104
20.799994	10.903816
64.133324	107.477695
173.333308	158.659754
6.933331	5.029626
5.199999	23.321325
3590.997323	3561.321011
181.411956	155.772485
13.86666	6.948473

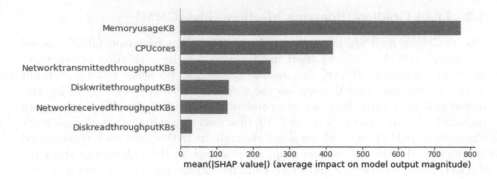

Fig. 2. Features importance based on SHAP

3.3 SHapley Additive exPlanations (SHAP)

In this work, we consulted SHAP [19] to get an insight into LightGBM. SHAP is based on a game-theoretical concept of Shapely values. SHAP can be used for both local and global explanations of black-box models. With the help of SHAP, we can examine the contribution of each feature in our model predictions. Therefore, we used SHAP for the explanation of the model to extract the most important features and to get the contribution of each feature in predictions. The interpretation of SHAP cannot only be used to understand each feature's importance but can be also helpful in reducing the efforts in the interpolation of null values to achieve better resource provisioning accuracy with low computational time.

In Fig. 2, we used the SHAP bar chart to provide a global explanation and mean SHAP values for each feature. The x-axis is the mean SHAP value and the y-axis represents the features. The feature with a large mean SHAP value contributes more to the model prediction compared to the bottom ones. The most significant feature is listed in descending order as shown in Fig. 2. For example, memory usage has a high SHAP mean value, thus indicating a high influence or contribution to the predictions. Similarly, the CPU core and network transmitted throughput have high SHAP mean scores as well and are also important contributors to the predictions. The influence of a feature on the output can be both positive and negative and depends on the SHAP value of the feature contributing toward the prediction as shown in Fig. 3. Furthermore, for other features such as network received throughput and disk write and read throughput, the mean SHAP values are comparatively low indicating lower influences of these features in the predictions.

Furthermore, Fig. 3 represents the impact of SHAP values on the model output. The x-axis shows the distribution of Shapley value and the y-axis represents the features and the impact of the feature on the model predictions. The blue points in the figure represent low feature values and the red points represent high feature values. Let's consider the scenario of memory usage impact on the model output. The memory usage with a low feature value as shown in Fig. 3 results

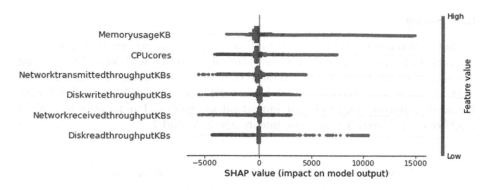

Fig. 3. SHAP Values impact on LightGBM model output

mostly in a lower SHAP value and indicates less contribution to the prediction of CPU usage and the feature with a high value indicates more contribution to prediction. However, it is not always the case that a feature with a high value has a positive and a feature with a low value has a negative contribution toward the prediction. For instance, if we consider the SHAP explanations of disk- write throughput and network transmitted throughput as shown in Fig. 3, the higher the value of these features, the lower they contribute to CPU usage prediction score and the lower the values of the features, the higher they contribute. The feature importance is shown in Fig. 2 and the impact of SHAP values in Fig. 3, can be helpful in the selection of features for interpolation of missing values for better predictions and reducing computational time.

Table 2. Experimental results

Actual		RMSE: 805.15 Test Data Accuracy: 0.9306								
Percentage of Null values		10%			30%			60%		
K-nearest neighbors		K=3	K=5	K=7	K=3	K=5	K=7	K=3	K=5	K=7
KNN	RMSE:	851.33	856.07	869.78	966.59	952.73	975.49	1042.74	1022.83	1074.18
	Accuracy:	0.9324	0.9317	0.9295	0.9129	0.9154	0.91136	0.8987	0.9025	0.8925
	Computational time:	1h 9min 26s	1h 16min 41s	1h 14min 14s	3h 15min 58s	3h 19min 58s	3h 14min 20s	4h 7min 54s	4h 20min 11s	4h 38min 24s
KNN with Most Important Attribute	RMSE:	907.00	901.40	906.34	1044.82	1095.30	1129.89	1189.38	1169.75	1189.46
	Accuracy:	0.9233	0.9243	0.9234	0.8983	0.8882	0.8810	0.8748	0.8725	0.8682
	Computational time:	1h 5min 1s	1h 11min 59s	1h 17min 52s	2h 46min 8s	3h 1min 14s	3h 3min 6s	4h 39s	4h 13min 21s	4h 15min 57s
KNN with Mult-lple Attributes	RMSE:	874.38	893.33	898.37	1017.24	1037.77	1039.21	1116.30	1136.53	1156.82
	Accuracy:	0.9287	0.9256	0.9248	0.9036	0.8996	0.8994	0.8839	0.8796	0.8753
	Computational time:	1h 10min 12s	1h 14min 41s	1h 38min 32s	2h 52min 55s	3h 16min 33s	3h 26min 33s	4h 5min 9s	4h 19min 16s	4h 30min 12s
KNN with Least Important Attribute	RMSE:	958.88	922.17	953.40	1175.37	1211.14	1195.62	1330.29	1394.31	1404.14
	Accuracy:	0.9143	0.9207	0.9153	0.8713	0.8633	0.8668	0.8351	0.8189	0.8115
	Computational time:	1h 5min	1h 7min 21s	1h 9min 54s	3h 23s	3h 4min 58s	3h 10min 5s	3h 58min 33s	4h 10min 20s	4h 12min 50s

4 Missing Values Interpolation

This section consists of a setup for creating null datasets. Furthermore, using KNN for interpolation of missing values and lastly comparing the results of interpolations. The flow of events can be seen in Fig. 1.

4.1   Setup

To have incomplete data for interpolation purposes, we created three test datasets with missing values over the interval of 10, 30, and 50%. The missing values were created only in one attribute (i.e., network transmitted throughput). Next, datasets were used to examine the performance of KNN and KNN with the most important and the least important attributes. The number of nearest neighbors considered for the experiments are 3, 5, and 7.

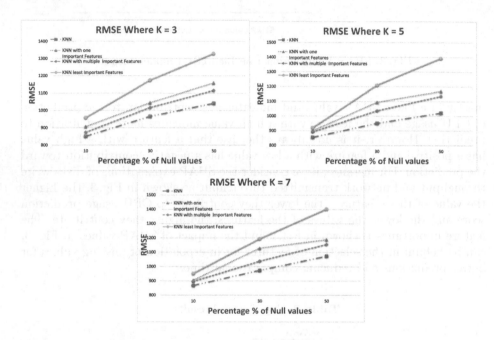

Fig. 4. RMSE with varying k-nearest neighbours

4.2   Tested Methods

One of the methods to compare is KNN which is used to interpolate the missing values of all three test datasets. The experimental results of KNN imputer with different intervals of missing values along with the variations in some neighbors are shown in Table 2. KNN imputer considers all attributes in the selection of k-nearest neighbors. The filled datasets are then used for the predictions and evaluated in terms of RMSE, accuracy, and computational time.

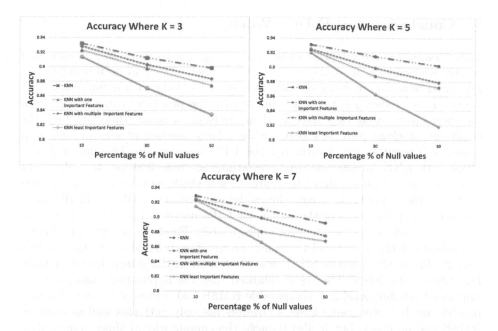

Fig. 5. Accuracy with varying k-nearest neighbours

In addition, we also considered KNN for interpolation of missing values in all three datasets but with a reduced number of attributes (i.e., the most important attribute, more than one important attribute, and the least important attribute). Finally, the selection of attributes for interpolation is performed based on SHAP explanations in the last test. These interpolated datasets are used for predictions and evaluated in terms of RMSE, accuracy, and computational time. The results are shown in Table 2.

4.3   Comparison

The RMSE and accuracy of test datasets with missing values interpolated using the KNN method with one important feature is very much comparable to the actual predictions of the complete dataset as shown in Figs. 4 and 5. The x-axis in the figures represents datasets with the percentage of missing values (i.e., 10, 30, and 50%) and the y-axis represents RMSE and the accuracy score. Similarly, RMSE and accuracy of the datasets interpolated using KNN with multiple attributes are close to actual prediction RMSE and accuracy. However, predictions with datasets that are interpolated only with the least important attribute lead to poor performance compared to others as shown in Figs. 4 and 5. The results in Table 2 show that interpolation of missing values with one or fewer features compared to a complete set of features, leads to less computational time compared to interpolation considering all attributes.

5   Conclusion and Future Work

Many companies are adopting cloud computing due to increasing demands of computational, storage, and other resources which alone can be too expensive. For cloud providers meeting the demands of users along with maintaining SLA is one of the challenging tasks. In this regard, the providers can get help from the data history that they have in their decisions making. However, here the challenge for cloud providers is to tackle a large number of missing values in datasets. Therefore, we investigated the CPU resource provisioning challenge along with KNN imputation, with variations in some features to reduce the extensive computational time. To address these challenges, we used LightGBM for the prediction of CPU usage. The model was tested on GWA-T-12 Bitbrains dataset. The predictions of the model for CPU usage can leverage the practitioners in provisioning the resource appropriately. Furthermore, we used SHAP to understand the model and the contribution of each attribute to the model's output. The explanation of SHAP was then used in the interpolation of missing values using KNN. The results showed that the imputations using limited important attributes achieve comparable RMSE and accuracy to that of actual predictions. However, using fewer attributes not only performs well in terms of RMSE and accuracy, but it also reduces the computational time compared to normal KNN considering all attributes.

Although this study showed that explanation of SHAP can be helpful in the selection of attributes for KNN, a more detailed study is required for using the SHAP explanations not only with KNN but other interpolation methods such as Classification and Regression Tree (CART), multilayer perceptron neural network (MLP), naive Bayes, and Support Vector Machine (SVM).

References

1. Shaw, R., Howley, E., Barrett, E.: Applying reinforcement learning towards automating energy efficient virtual machine consolidation in cloud data centers. Inf. Syst. **107**, 101722 (2021)
2. Saxena, S., Khan, M., Singh, R., Noorwali, A.: Proactive virtual machine scheduling to optimize the energy consumption of computational cloud. Int. J. Adv. Comput. Sci. Appl. **12**, 10 (2021)
3. Sarikaa, S., Niranjana, S., Sri Vishnu Deepika, K.: Time Series Forecasting of Cloud Resource Usage. In: 2021 IEEE 6th International Conference On Computing, Communication And Automation (ICCCA), pp. 372–382 (2021)
4. Shahidinejad, A., Ghobaei-Arani, M., Masdari, M.: Resource provisioning using workload clustering in cloud computing environment: a hybrid approach. Cluster Comput. **24**, 319–342 (2021)
5. Goodarzy, S., Nazari, M., Han, R., Keller, E., Rozner, E.: Resource management in cloud computing using machine learning: a survey. In: 2020 19th IEEE International Conference On Machine Learning And Applications (ICMLA), pp. 811–816 (2020)

6. Acuna, E., Rodriguez, C.: The treatment of missing values and its effect on classifier accuracy. In: Banks, D., McMorris, F.R., Arabie, P., Gaul, W. (eds.) Classification, Clustering, And Data Mining Applications, pp. 639–647. Springer, Berlin (2004). https://doi.org/10.1007/978-3-642-17103-1_60
7. Grzymala-Busse, J., Grzymala-Busse, W.: Handling missing attribute values. Data Mining And Knowledge Discovery Handbook, pp. 33–51 (2009)
8. Tsai, C., Hu, Y.: Empirical comparison of supervised learning techniques for missing value imputation. Knowl. Inf. Syst. **64**, 1–29 (2022)
9. Khan, T., Tian, W., Ilager, S., Buyya, R.: Workload forecasting and energy state estimation in cloud data centres: ML-centric approach. Future Gener. Comput. Syst. **128**, 320–332 (2022)
10. Tchernykh, A., Schwiegelshohn, U., Alexandrov, V., Talbi, E.: Towards understanding uncertainty in cloud computing resource provisioning. Procedia Comput. Sci. **51**, 1772–1781 (2015)
11. Deng, L., Ren, Y.-L., Xu, F., He, H., Li, C.: Resource utilization analysis of Alibaba cloud. In: Huang, D.-S., Bevilacqua, V., Premaratne, P., Gupta, P. (eds.) ICIC 2018. LNCS, vol. 10954, pp. 183–194. Springer, Cham (2018). https://doi.org/10.1007/978-3-319-95930-6_18
12. Perennou, L., Callau-Zori, M., Lefebvre, S.: Understanding scheduler workload on non-hyperscale cloud platform. In: 19th ACM International Middleware Conference, pp. 23–24 (2018)
13. Wei, J., Gao, M.: Workload Prediction of Serverless Computing. In: 2021 5th International Conference On Deep Learning Technologies (ICDLT), pp. 93–99 (2021)
14. Mohamed, H., El-Gayar, O.: End-to-end latency prediction of microservices workflow on Kubernetes: a comparative evaluation of machine learning models and resource metrics. In: Proceedings Of The 54th Hawaii International Conference On System Sciences, p. 1717 (2021)
15. Huang, J., et al.: Cross-validation based K nearest neighbor imputation for software quality datasets: an empirical study. J. Syst. Softw. **132**, 226–252 (2017)
16. Lin, W., Tsai, C.: Missing value imputation: a review and analysis of the literature (2006–2017). Artif. Intell. Rev. **53**, 1487–1509 (2020)
17. Zhi-xin, G., Teng-fei, B., Yang-tao, L., Yi-bing, W.: Dam deformation prediction model based on Bayesian optimization and LightGBM. J. Yangtze River Sci. Res. Inst. **38**, 46–50 (2021)
18. Hao, J., Wang, J., OuYang, Z.: Performance prediction and fine-grained resource provision of virtual machines via LightGBM. In: International Conference On Data Mining And Big Data, pp. 261–272 (2021)
19. Lundberg, S., Lee, S.: A unified approach to interpreting model predictions. In: Proceedings Of The 31st International Conference On Neural Information Processing Systems, pp. 4768–4777 (2017)

Exploring Word Embedding for Arabic Sentiment Analysis

Sana Gayed[1,2]([⊠]), Souheyl Mallat[2], and Mounir Zrigui[2]

[1] Higher Institute of Computer Science and Communication Techniques ISITCom, University of Sousse, Hammam Sousse 4011, Sousse, Tunisia
sana.gaied@gmail.com
[2] Research Laboratory in Algebra, Numbers Theory and Intelligent Systems RLANTIS, University of Monastir, 5019 Monastir, Tunisia
souheyl.mallat@gmail.com, mounir.zrigui@fsm.rnu.tn

Abstract. In Natural Language Processing (NLP), the manual features (part-of-speech tagging, stemming…) might not be helpful sometimes to deciding the feeling expressed in a sentence. That More properties need to be considered. Word embeddings which are the key component for learning the text features, has just started to appear in Arabic sentiment analysis. On the other hand, Deep Neural Networks were widely used recently for this task, especially for the English language. In this paper, we focus on the Tunisian dialect sentiment analysis used on social media using a Convolutional Neural Networks and Bidirectional Long Short-Term Memory. The results show that our models on the publicly available TUNIZI dataset achieved superior performances than the other models applied for the same dataset.

Keywords: Sentiment analysis · Tunisian romanized alphabet comments · Word embeddings · Deep learning · Sentiment classification

1 Introduction

Today, with the proliferation of reviews, recommendations and other forms of expression due to the emergence of the participatory web, sentiment analysis has become one of the essential research areas whose application is clearly visible in many domains (politics, health, tourism…).

Sentiment analysis, also called opinion mining, is the field of study that analyzes people's opinions, sentiments, evaluations, appraisals, attitudes, and emotions towards entities such as products, services, organizations, individuals, issues, events, topics, and their attributes [1].

Most of studies in sentiment analysis have been applied on English and some other Latin languages successfully [2–4]. However, very few studies have focused on sentiment analysis in Arabic [5], due to its complexity and rich morphology, which makes the sentiment analysis a challenging process. The growing number of Arab Internet users and the exponential growth of Arabic content online pushed the attention of many researchers to this task.

© The Author(s), under exclusive license to Springer Nature Singapore Pte Ltd. 2022
E. Szczerbicki et al. (Eds.): ACIIDS 2022, CCIS 1716, pp. 92–101, 2022.
https://doi.org/10.1007/978-981-19-8234-7_8

Arabic has three main varieties: Classical Arabic, which is the language of the Quran (holy book of Islam), Modern Standard Arabic (MSA, Modern Standard Arabic) and Dialectical Arabic. MSA is the most eloquent variety of the Arabic language used in writing and in most official speech. Dialectical Arabic refers to all the oral varieties spoken in everyday communication. These vary from one Arab country to another and from one region to another of the same country [6, 7]. Moreover, Arabic can be written in both scripts, Arabic and Arabizi (was defined as the newly emerged Arabic variant written using the Arabic numeral system and roman script characters [8]).

A newly advanced techniques in Natural Language Processing (NLP), distributed representations of words, that depict text as Vector Space Model (VSM) has emerged. This process is called word embedding.

In this article, we try to improve sentiment classification results. We perform a Tunisian dialect used on social media using the word embedding: fastText. This representation is used as inputs to DNN classifiers, namely CNN and BiLSTM classifiers. We study the case of binary classification.

The rest of the paper is organized as follows. Section 2 describes related work. Section 3 introduces word embedding and the different architectures. Section 4 presents the proposed methodology, results and discussion. Conclusion is presented in Sect. 5.

2   Related Work

In machine learning, features are the input data for the learning algorithm. However, it is not always possible to know what the features are or might be.

In NLP, the manual features might include Part-Of-Speech tagging (POS), stemming, lemmatization. Majority of such work make use of lexicon and morphology-based features. For example, in [9], they used both morphology-based and lexical features for subjectivity and sentiment classification of Arabic. Labelled emotion words have been used for improving both subjectivity and sentiment in Standard Arabic [10].

On the other hand, the representation learning type of work has just started to appear in Arabic sentiment analysis, where word embeddings are the key component for learning the text features. Sentiment classifiers are trained on the generated embeddings to determine the text polarity.

Variety of architectures are used to build the embeddings, containing Continuous Bag Of Words (CBOW), skip-gram [11], and Global Vectors (GloVe) [12]. For instance, Convolutional Neural Network (CNN) has been used for a sentiment classification task to evaluate the quality of embeddings generated from 3.4 billion words [13]. Intrinsic and extrinsic evaluations have been investigated for building vectorized space representations for Arabic text in [14]. In addition, and to outperform state of the art hand-crafted features on Arabic MPQA[1] subjectivity dataset, CBOW model with a simple binary logistic regression classifier have been used [15].

---

[1] Multi-Perspective Question Answering corpus.

2.1   Sentiment Analysis for Tunisian Arabic Scripts

In [16], a lexicon-based sentiment analysis system was used to classify the sentiment of Tunisian tweets. A Tunisian morphological analyzer developed to produce a linguistic features. The author used 800 Arabic script tweets (TAC dataset) and achieved an accuracy of 72.1%.

A supervised sentiment analysis system was presented in [17] for Tunisian Arabic script tweets. The support vector machine achieved the best results for binary classification with an accuracy of 71.09% and an F-measure of 63%. Different bag-of-word schemes used as features, binary and multiclass classifications were conducted on a Tunisian Election dataset (TEC) of 3,043 positive/negative tweets combining MSA and Tunisian dialect.

In [18], a study is conducted on the impact on the Tunisian sentiment classification performance when it is combined with other Arabic based preprocessing tasks (Named Entity Tagging, stopwords removal…). A lexicon-based approach and the support vector machine model were used to evaluate the performances on two datasets; TEC (Tunisian Election dataset) and TSAC (Tunisian Sentiment Analysis Corpus).

In [19], authors evaluate, three deep learning methods (Convolutional Neural Network (CNN), long short-term memory (LSTM), and bidirectional long-short-term-memory (BiLSTM)) on a corpus containing comments posted on the official Facebook pages of Tunisian supermarkets to conduct to an automatic sentiment analysis. In their evaluation, authors wanted to show that the gathered features could lead to very encouraging performances through the use of CNN and BiLSTM neural networks.

A robustly optimized BERT approach was used to establish sentiment classification from the Tunisian corpus in [20] due to the urgent need to sentiment analysis by marketing and business firms, government organizations, and society as a whole. Authors proposed a Tunisian Robustly optimized BERT approach model called TunRoBERTa which outperformed Multilingual-BERT, CNN, CNN combined with LSTM and RoBERTa. Their proposed model was pretrained on seven unlabeled Tunisian datasets publicly available.

In [21], to produce document embeddings of Tunisian Arabic and Tunisian Romanized alphabet comments, authors used the doc2vec algorithm. The generated embeddings were fed to train a Multi-Layer Perceptron (MLP) classifier where both the achieved accuracy and F-measure values were 78% on the TSAC (Tunisian Sentiment Analysis Corpus) dataset. This last dataset combines 7,366 positive/negative Tunisian Arabic and Tunisian Romanized alphabet Facebook comments.

In [22], syntax-ignorant n-gram embeddings representation composed and learned using an unordered composition function and a shallow neural model was proposed, it helps to relieve hard work due to the hand-crafted features. The proposed model, called Tw-StAR, was evaluated to predict the sentiment on five Arabic dialect datasets including the TSAC dataset.

We observe that, word embeddings are used for learning the text features. This type of work, the representation learning, has just started to appear in Arabic sentiment analysis. Therefore, fastext word embedding will be used.

Table 1. The dataset we used in our sentiment classification [35].

Dataset	TUNIZI
# Words	82384
#UniqueWords	30635
#Comments	9210
#NegativeComments	4838
#PositiveComments	4372
#Train	8616
# Test	1295

3 Word Embedding

Word embedding refers to a set of machine learning techniques that aim to represent the words or sentences of a text by vectors of real numbers, described in a vector model (or Vector Space Model). These new representations of textual data have made it possible to improve the performance of automatic language processing methods (or Natural Language Processing) [23, 24], such as Sentiment Analysis.

Word2Vec is a powerful tool developed by Google in 2013 [25, 26]. Word2Vec[2] tool was the main implementation where CBOW and Skip-Gram models were first introduced. Later, other implementations of word2vec have appeared in several packages (such as gensim[3] and SpaCy[4]). In the CBOW model, the distributed representations of context (or surrounding words) are combined to predict the word in the middle. While in the Skip-Gram model, the distributed representation of the input word is used to predict the context. The word vector representations proved to be efficient and successful technique in the applications of NLP among them Sentiment Analysis.

An extension for word2vec algorithms has been proposed and implemented in a library called fastText[5].

fastText extends the functionality of word2vec in two ways:

1. It let learning word vectors directly during a supervised sentence classification task [27].
2. By assigning distinct vectors for each word, it extends the capability of Skip-Gram model to account for the morphology of words [28].

Measuring the quality of the embeddings from these architectures is an ongoing research.

---

[2] https://github.com/tmikolov/word2vec.
[3] https://radimrehurek.com/gensim/models/word2vec.html.
[4] https://spacy.io/docs/usage/word-vectors-similarities.
[5] https://github.com/facebookresearch/fastText.

4 Proposed Methodology, Results and Discussion

4.1 Feature and Dataset Used

We were used fastText as an initial representation in our work to evaluate TUNIZI [29], the Tunisian Romanized sentiment analysis dataset. TUNIZI dataset, is stated in Table 1.

fastText model: We use fastText embedding model and apply it to generate one embedding for each word of a given comment in the TUNIZI dataset.

fastText proposes two main models: Continuous Bag of Words (CBOW) and Skip-Gram. CBOW model predicts a center word given the surrounding context words. Skip-Gram is the opposite of CBOW; it predicts the probability for each word to appear in the surrounding context of an input word. We use CBOW (Fig. 1) to learn the embeddings; since it is simpler and computationally efficient [30].

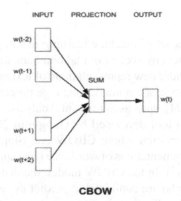

Fig. 1. CBOW architecture [31].

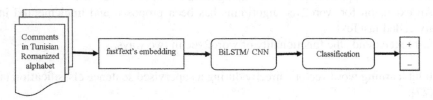

Fig. 2. Proposed methodology.

4.2 Approach

CNN and BiLSTM deep neural network classifiers were used:

– Convolutional Neural Network (CNN) is traditionally used in the application of image processing, and is good at capturing the patterns. Kim [32] demonstrated the efficient use of CNN for Natural Language Processing (NLP) on various benchmark tasks.

- Bidirectional Long Short-Term Memory (BiLSTM) is a class of RNN models. BiL-STMs are used for sequential processing of the data and are efficient at capturing long-range dependencies [33, 34].

Our work consists of experimented these two classifiers; a Convolutional Neural Network (CNN) with a number of filters equal to 100 and a BiLSTM. As shown in the proposed methodology in Fig. 2, our model takes advantage of fastText as initial representation to train the classifiers (BiLSTM or CNN) on the generated embeddings.

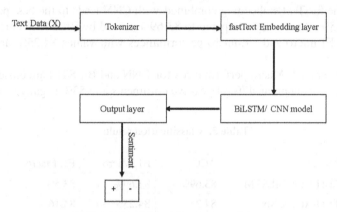

Fig. 3. Architecture of our model.

Table 2. The hyperparameters used.

Embedding	Classifier	Number of filters	Number of epochs	Batch size
fastText	BiLSTM	–	3	16
	CNN	100	3	16

The hyperparameters used during the training of our models (number of filters, number of epochs and batch size for each embedding and classifier) are described above in Table 2.

4.3 Results

Experiments were carried out on Tunisian Romanized alphabet dataset introduced as "TUNIZI" in [35], presented in Table 1. The dataset includes more than 9k Tunisian social media comments written only using Latin script was presented in [29]. The dataset was annotated by Tunisian native speakers who described the comments as positive or negative. The dataset is balanced, containing 47% of positive comments and 53% negative comments. And it is divided randomly for train and test.

We need performance metrics to evaluate how well our models do. In sentiment analysis area, accuracy and F-score are usually the most used.

- Accuracy (ACC.) capture information on how many correct predictions for positive and negative occurred as well as incorrect predictions.
- F-score provides a measure of the overall quality of a classification model as it combines the precision and recall through a weighted harmonic mean.

Two variants of F-score were used in our experiments. F1. Micro; the micro-averaging biased by class frequency and F1. Macro; the macro-averaging taking all classes as equally important.

Table 3 shows the results of the proposed models on the TUNIZI dataset. We can notice that the fastText embedding combined with CNN leads to the best performance with an 84.25% of accuracy compared to 83.69% scored by BiLSTM. This is also the case for the F1.micro and F1.macro performances with values 84.25% and 84.16%, respectively.

F1. Micro and F1. Macro performances for CNN and BiLSTM are close due to the balanced dataset containing 47% of positive comments and 53% negative comments.

Table 3. Classification results.

Model	ACC	F1. Micro	F1. Macro
fastText + BiLSTM	83.69%	83.69%	83.5%
fastText + CNN	84.25%	84.25%	84.16%

4.4 Discussion

In order to test the quality of the fastText-based CBOW, we compare his performance on a polarity sentiment classification task to the results achieved by other models from literature on the same set of dataset [36]. In all experiments, two classifiers where trained and tested on the mentioned dataset. The proposed models outperformed the other models (cited in Table 4) on the relevant dataset.

As shown in Table 3, our results showed that CNN trained with fastText outperformed BiLSTM trained with this same representation. These results are maybe due to the size of the dataset used where CNN, generally, proved to be an effective approach on small datasets.

Compared to other models applied on the tackled dataset, our fastText models based CBOW outperformed other models. This is one of the main strength in our models, which demonstrate their capacity for handling this type of Dialectal Arabic emerged in social media. As we can see in Table 5, with the proposed approaches, the performed accuracy, the micro averaging and the macro averaging outperformed the baselines performances.

fastText embedding model takes into consideration the structure of words, which makes it suitable for morphologically rich languages such as Arabic language. Our findings validate this observation. In general, the performance of the model depends on the corpus size and vocabulary coverage. A larger corpus might result in higher performance gains.

Table 4. Other models classification results.

Model	ACC	F1.micro	F1.macro
Word2vec + CNN	67.2%	67.2%	67.1%
FrWaC + CNN	70.2%	70.2%	69%
M-BERT + BiLSTM	76.3%	76.3%	74.3%
M-BERT + CNN	78.3%	78.3%	78.1

Table 5. ACC., F1.micro and F1.macro scores results on the sentiment classification task.

Model	ACC	F1. Micro	F1. Macro
Word2vec + CNN	67,2%	67,2%	67,1%
FrWaC + CNN	70,2%	70,2%	69%
M-BERT + BiLSTM	76,3%	76,3%	74,3%
M-BERT + CNN	78,3%	78,3%	78,1%
fastText + BiLSTM	**83.69%**	**83.69%**	**83.5%**
fastText + CNN	**84.25%**	**84.25%**	**84.16%**

5   Conclusion

We achieved a good results on the TUNIZI dataset. This last helped us to better understand the nature of the Tunisian dialect.

We have experimented, in our work, fastText embedding based CBOW with deep neural networks (CNN and BiLSTM), without the use of any preprocessing step. Our work try to solve the task of sentiment analysis applied on a Tunisian dialect used on social media. Our findings of CNN trained with fastText embedding achieved better results than BiLSTM with this same representation.

In order to test the quality of our models, we compare their performances on a polarity sentiment classification task to the results achieved by other models from literature on the same set of dataset. We run fastText with the cited parameters. However, these parameters may not be optimal and one can try several settings to achieve better results.

References

1. Liu, B.: Sentiment Analysis and Opinion Mining. Morgan & Claypool Publishers (2012)
2. Guellil, I., Boukhalfa, K.: Social big data mining: a survey focused on opinion mining and sentiments analysis. In: 12th International Symposium on Programming and Systems (ISPS), pp. 1–10. IEEE (2015)
3. Guellil, I., Faical, A.: Bilingual lexicon for algerian arabic dialect treatment in social media. In: WiNLP: Women & Underrepresented Minorities in Natural Language Processing. ACL (2017)

4. Guellil, I., Azouaou, F., Valitutti, A. (2019): English vs arabic sentiment analysis: A survey presenting 100 work studies, resources and tools. In: 16th International Conference on Computer Systems and Applications, pp. 1–8. IEEE (2019)
5. Abdellaoui, H., Zrigui, M.: Using tweets and Emojis to build TEAD: an Arabic dataset for sentiment analysis. Computación y Sistemas **22**(3), (2018)
6. Sghaier, MA., Zrigui, M. : Rule-based machine translation from Tunisian dialect to modern standard Arabic. In: 24th International Conference on Knowledge-Based and Intelligent Information & Engineering Systems, pp. 310–319. Elsevier, a virtual conference (2020)
7. Sghaier, MA., Zrigui, M.: Tunisian dialect-modern standard Arabic Bilingual Lexicon. In: 14th IEEE/ACS International Conference on Computer Systems and Applications, AICCSA, pp. 973–979. IEEE, Hammamet, Tunisia (2017)
8. Mulki, H., Haddad, H., Babaoglu, I.: Modern trends in Arabic sentiment analysis: a survey. Traitement Automatique des Langues **58**(3), 15–39 (2018)
9. Abdul-Mageed, M., Diab, M.T., Korayem, M.: Subjectivity and sentiment analysis of modern standard Arabic. In: HLT 2011Proceedings of the 49th Annual Meeting of the Association for Computational Linguistics: Human Language Technologies, pp. 587–591. Association for Computational Linguistics, Columbia University (2011)
10. Abdul-Mageed, M., Diab, M. T.: Awatif: a multi-genre corpus for modern standard Arabic subjectivity and sentiment analysis. In: LREC 2012, pp. 3907–3914
11. Pennington, J., Socher, R., Manning, C. D.: GloVe: global vectors for word representation. In: EMNLP, pp. 1532–1543 (2014)
12. Dahou, A., Xiong, S., Zhou, J., Haddoud, M.H., Duan, P.: Word embeddings and convolutional neural network for arabic sentiment classification. In: Coling, pp. 2418–2427. (2016)
13. Zahran, M.A., Magooda, A., Mahgoub, A.Y., Raafat, H.M., Rashwan, M., Atyia, A.: Word representations in vector space and their applications for Arabic. In: CICLing, vol. 1, pp. 430–443 (2015)
14. Altowayan, A., Tao, L.: Word embeddings for Arabic sentiment analysis. In: Big Data (Big Data), 2016 IEEE International Conference, pp. 3820–3825. IEEE (2016)
15. Karmani, N.: Tunisian Arabic Customer's Reviews Processing and Analysis for an Internet Supervision System. Doctoral dissertation (2017)
16. Sayadi, K., Liwicki, M., Ingold, R., Bui, M.: Tunisian dialect and modern standard Arabic dataset for sentiment analysis: Tunisian election context. In: 2nd International Conference on Arabic Computational Linguistics. Turkey, pp. 35–53 (2016)
17. Mulki, H., Haddad, H., Bechikh Ali, C., Babaoglu, I.: Tunisian dialect sentiment analysis: a natural language processing-based approach. Computaci´on y Sistemas **22**(4), 1223–1232 (2018)
18. Medhaffar, S. Bougares, F., Estève, Y., Hadrich-Belguith, L.: Sentiment analysis of Tunisian dialects: linguistic ressources and experiments. In: 3rd Arabic Natural Language Processing Workshop, pp. 55–61. Association for Computational Linguistics, Valencia, Spain (2017)
19. Masmoudi, A., Hamdi, J., Hadrich Belguith, L.: Deep learning for sentiment analysis of tunisian dialect. Computación y Sistemas **25**(1), 129–148 (2021)
20. Antit, C., Mechti, S., Faiz, R.: TunRoBERTa: a Tunisian robustly optimized BERT approach model for sentiment analysis. In: 2nd International Conference on Industry 4.0 and Artificial Intelligence (ICIAI), pp. 227–231 (2021)
21. Mulki, H., Haddad, H., Gridach, M., Babaoglu, I.: Syntax-ignorant n-gram embeddings for sentiment analysis of Arabic Dialects. In: 4th Arabic Natural Language Processing Workshop, pp. 30–39. Association for Computational Linguistics, Florence, Italy (2019)
22. Zahran, M.A., Magooda, A., Mahgoub, A.Y., Raafat, H.M., Rashwan, M., Atyia, A.: Word representations in vector space and their applications for Arabic. CICLing **1**, 430–443 (2015)
23. Mahmoud, A., Zrigui, M.: Semantic similarity analysis for corpus development and paraphrase detection in Arabic. Int. Arab J. Inf. Technol. **18**(1), 1–7 (2021)

24. Mahmoud, A., Zrigui, M.: Arabic semantic textual similarity identification based on convolutional gated recurrent units. In: International Conference on Innovations in Intelligent Systems and Applications (INISTA), pp. 1–7. IEEE, Kocaeli, Turkey (2021)
25. AMikolov, T., Chen, K., Corrado, G., Dean, J.: Efficient estimation of word representations in vector space. In: Proceedings of Workshop at International Conference on Learning Representations (2013)
26. Mikolov, T., Sutskever, I., Chen, K., Corrado, G.S., Dean, J.: Distributed representations of words and phrases and their compositionality. In: Advances in Neural Information Processing Systems, pp. 3111–3119 (2013)
27. Joulin, A., Grave, E., Bojanowski, P., Mikolov, T.: Bag of Tricks for Efficient Text Classification. arXiv.org (2016)
28. Bojanowski, P., Grave, E., Joulin, A., Mikolov, T.: Enriching word vectors with subword information. arXiv, (2016)
29. TUNIZI dataset. https://github.com/chaymafourati/TUNIZI-Sentiment-Analysis-Tunisian-Arabizi-Dataset. Accessed 07 Mar 2022
30. Baroni, M., Dinu, G., Kruszewski, G.: Don't count, predict! a systematic comparison of context-counting vs. context-predicting semantic vectors. In: ACL, vol. 1 (2014)
31. kdnuggets. https://www.kdnuggets.com/2018/04/implementing-deep-learning-methods-feature-engineering-text-data-cbow.html. Accessed 18 July 2022
32. Kim, Y.: Convolutional neural networks for sentence classification. In Proceedings of the Conference on Empirical Methods in Natural Language Processing (EMNLP), pp. 1746–1751. (2014)
33. Haffar, N., Ayadi, R., Hkiri, E., Zrigui, M.: Temporal ordering of events via deepneural networks. In 16th International Conference on Document Analysis and Recognition (ICDAR), pp. 762–777. Lausanne, Switzerland (2021)
34. Haffar, N., Hkiri, E., Zrigui, M.: Using bidirectional LSTM and shortest dependency path for classifying arabic temporal relations. In 24th International Conference Knowledge-Based and Intelligent Information & Engineering Systems (KES), pp. 370–379. Elsevier, a virtual conference (2020)
35. Fourati, C., Messaoudi, A., Haddad, H.: TUNIZI: a Tunisian Arabizi sentiment analysis Dataset. arXiv (2020)
36. Messaoudi, A., Haddad, H., Ben HajHmida, M., Fourati, C., Ben Hamida, A.: Learning Word Representations for Tunisian Sentiment Analysis. arXiv, (2020)

Improving Autoencoders Performance for Hyperspectral Unmixing Using Clustering

Bartosz Grabowski[1]([✉])(iD), Przemysław Głomb[1](iD), Kamil Książek[1,2](iD), and Krisztián Buza[3](iD)

[1] Institute of Theoretical and Applied Informatics, Polish Academy of Sciences, 44-100 Gliwice, Poland
{bgrabowski,przemg,kksiazek}@iitis.pl, kamil.ksiazek@polsl.pl
[2] Department of Data Sciences and Engineering, Silesian University of Technology, 44-100 Gliwice, Poland
[3] Department of Mathematics-Informatics, Sapientia Hungarian University of Transylvania, Târgu Mureș, Romania

Abstract. Hyperspectral cameras acquire images containing information across the electromagnetic spectrum, which convey useful information about the scene. To enable effective analysis of such data, spectral unmixing is often used. It is an important task in hyperspectral imaging, allowing one to obtain the information about spectral endmembers which make up each hyperspectral pixel. This task, traditionally solved with dedicated statistical methods, has recently been explored with deep learning methods. One of the methods well-suited to this task are autoencoders. These neural networks are initialized using multiple random weights, and their initialization often has a significant impact on their efficiency. Because of that, to improve the initialization of autoencoders for the spectral unmixing task, we propose to use the pre-training scheme consisting of clustering-based artificial labeling. We test the approach on two popular hyperspectral datasets, i.e. Samson and Jasper Ridge. Our experiment delivers promising results, improving autoencoders effectiveness in the case of Samson dataset, i.e. for 25-class labeling endmembers' and abundances' errors improve by 0.045 and 0.008, respectively. The worse results in the case of Jasper Ridge dataset (improvement of the endmembers' error by 0.001, and worsening of the abundances' error by 0.006 for 25-classes labeling) show that more research is required to understand when the proposed approach improves the results of the spectral unmixing. The auxiliary experiments that we also conduct allow us to partially answer that question.

Keywords: Autoencoders · Hyperspectral unmixing · Clustering · Transfer learning

1 Introduction

Hyperspectral cameras are used to gather images that contain information throughout the electromagnetic spectrum. Because of that, they convey rich information about the imaged scene. Due to conditions such as low spatial resolution, these cameras obtain

© The Author(s), under exclusive license to Springer Nature Singapore Pte Ltd. 2022
E. Szczerbicki et al. (Eds.): ACIIDS 2022, CCIS 1716, pp. 102–121, 2022.
https://doi.org/10.1007/978-981-19-8234-7_9

pictures with single pixels containing a mixture of spectra of multiple substances. To obtain the spectra of the original substances present in the scene, one is required to use hyperspectral unmixing methods. Those methods recover each substance spectrum, as well as coefficients specifying the amount of each substance in the given pixel. More precisely, spectral unmixing methods decompose a set of pixels' spectra into a collection of source spectra, or endmembers, along with abundances' values specifying each endmember's contribution.

Among the classical hyperspectral unmixing methods, one can point to N-FINDR [20] and VCA [13] as examples of pure pixel methods, which assume each endmember present fully in at least one pixel, or SISAL [2], which is an example of a method without pure pixel assumption. Recently, deep learning methods gained popularity as an alternative to classical approaches [1]. Among those, autoencoders are one of the possible solutions. They are a type of artificial neural network composed of two parts: encoder – transforming input data to other, usually lower dimensional space – and decoder – receiving as input the output of the encoder and trying to reconstruct the original signal as best as possible. This design of autoencoders can be used to perform hyperspectral unmixing [9, 15, 18].

Artificial neural networks, of which autoencoders are one example, require assigning multiple randomly determined parameters, called weights of the model. The initialization of these weights can have a significant impact on training of the model, as, e.g. [11] shows. One possible solution relies on the usage of transfer learning to minimize the problem. Instead of finding the way to initialize the weights in an efficient way from scratch, it improves the original weights using auxiliary dataset to pre-train the model.

One type of transfer learning that can be utilized was proposed by [12]. It does not require additional labeled dataset, but instead uses the original data. It does so by creating artificial labels to pre-train the model. These labels are created using a simple clustering algorithm, which divides the image into rectangular regions determining the borders of artificial classes. Although simple, this pre-training method improves the results across different datasets and neural network architectures. In some cases, the overall accuracy increases considerably, i.e. the greatest improvement is an increase of over 21 and 13 percentage points for Indian Pines and Pavia University datasets, respectively. This method can also be understood as a self-supervised learning approach, where the pretext task is used to pre-train the model and prepare it for the target task.

In this work, we explore the transfer learning approach to enhance the efficiency of autoencoders in the problem of spectral unmixing. We test our solution on the problem of hyperspectral unmixing, because it is an important step in hyperspectral image processing, for which autoencoders are an effective solution. We utilize the clustering algorithm to generate artificial labels for the unlabeled dataset. We then use these labels to pre-train the autoencoder on the classification task. Last, we use the pre-trained model to perform unmixing on the original, unlabeled dataset. We test our pipeline using two different hyperspectral datasets, as well as four different weight initialization methods. In the case of one of the datasets, the results show that the proposed approach improves the unmixing quality. In the case of the second dataset, the proposed approach does not bring about improvement. Given that with the subsequent experiments, we partially answer the question why this is the case.

In summary, the contributions of our work are the following:

1. We propose a way to improve the quality of hyperspectral unmixing in the case of autoencoder neural network, i.e. we utilize self-supervised learning approach, in which classification pretext task based on artificial labels is used to pre-train the model, making the subsequent unmixing easier to perform.
2. We test our approach using two different hyperspectral datasets and four different weight initialization methods.
3. In situations where our approach does not bring about any improvement over the baseline, we conduct additional experiments to find out why this is so.

The paper is structured as follows. Section 1.1 presents the related work. Section 2 describes the proposed pipeline in detail, while Sect. 3 summarizes the experiment proving the effectiveness of our method and discusses the results. Lastly, Sect. 4 briefly describes the paper.

1.1 Related Work

Different methods for hyperspectral unmixing were reviewed in [3]. Authors introduce geometrical, statistical, and sparse regression-based approaches. Among the methods examined, there are, e.g. SISAL [2] and N-FINDR [20] algorithms. In [8], the authors used constrained non-negative matrix factorization for hyperspectral unmixing. In their method, they utilized three aspects of the data: both spectra and abundances are nonnegative; the piecewise smoothness of material's spectra and abundances spatial distribution; the abundances distribution for each material is nearly sparse. Yet another example of the unmixing method was proposed in [14], where authors modeled the abundance fractions as a mixture of Dirichlet densities. The proposed method is designed to work with linear but highly mixed hyperspectral data. The mentioned methods, though effective, are costly in terms of the effort of experts to develop them. On the other hand, deep learning methods, an example of which is an autoencoder utilized in our work, are known to be very versatile, as long as enough data is present to train them.

Autoencoders are a type of deep learning method that is especially suited to solving the hyperspectral unmixing task. Numerous works utilized them in such a way. In [9], the authors compared the pixel-based deep convolutional autoencoders, which utilize only spectral information, with the cube-based approach, which uses spectral-spatial information. The latter approach provided better performance. In contrast to this work, we utilize a deep autoencoder without convolutional layers, focusing on simplicity at the expense of possible improvement in the effectiveness of the method. In [18], the stacked autoencoders are used together with variational autoencoders to create an unmixing method that can work well in the case of datasets that contain outliers as well as have low signal-to-noise ratio. Another usage of convolutional autoencoders for hyperspectral unmixing is presented in [15], which introduces a spectral-spatial variant of the method. By not using pooling or upsampling layers, it is possible to obtain abundance maps directly from a hidden convolutional layer. The authors of [16] proposed to use spectral information divergence (SID) objective function instead of MSE when using autoencoders for spectral unmixing, as in contrast to MSE this function is not sensitive to the absolute magnitude of the endmembers. In [21], the authors used an autoencoder network to solve the nonlinear spectral unmixing task. They used a 3D convolutional neural network-based model to jointly capture the spatial-spectral information about the scene. Yet another solution to non-linear spectral unmixing is proposed by [19], where two deep autoencoders are trained under the multi-task learning framework. In comparison to that, we utilize a self-supervised learning scheme, where the pretext task is first used to pre-train the network, followed by fine-tuning using the target task.

The problem of nonoptimal weights initialization in the case of deep learning models was observed in multiple studies. Many different solutions have been proposed to deal with this problem. As an example, in [6] authors propose a weight initialization method that maintains the activations' as well as gradients' variance as one moves up or down the layers of the network. Focusing on autoencoders, one can point to [11], where the authors conducted experiments showing that the stability of autoencoder training in the case of hyperspectral unmixing depends on initial weights. In [7, 10], Restricted Boltzmann Machines (RBMs) were used to pre-train the autoencoders. Autoencoders were also used as a means to initialize weights of other deep learning methods, e.g. [17], where stacked deep convolutional autoencoders were used to pre-train deep convolutional neural networks in the problem of emotion recognition from facial expressions.

In this work, we utilize the autoencoders used in the work [11], as their unique architecture is well-suited for the spectral unmixing task. Unlike the aforementioned work, however, we also use the pre-training method from [12] to pre-train the models. This method is chosen because of its simplicity without loss of efficiency.

2   Method

We propose the pipeline consisting of autoencoder used for spectral unmixing, which is pre-trained on the classification task using artificial labels generated using clustering, and then used to perform the target task of spectral unmixing. First, the artificial classes are created. These classes are used to train the encoder part of the autoencoder using subsidiary classification task. Then, the pre-trained encoder is put back into autoencoder, and the whole network is used to perform the spectral unmixing task. By pre-training the model utilizing the same dataset as for the unmixing task, we allow the network to learn useful task-independent data representation.

The visualisation of the pipeline is presented in Fig. 1. In the following subsections, the specific parts of the pipeline, more specifically the autoencoder A and the clustering algorithm C, are described in detail. The Linear Mixing Model is also introduced. Last, a step-by-step description of the pipeline is included.

2.1   Linear Mixing Model

In this work, we assume the Linear Mixing Model of the hyperspectral images' pixels. Given the matrix of hyperspectral image pixels $X = [x_1, \ldots, x_N] \in \mathbb{R}^{B \times N}$, where B is the number of hyperspectral bands, N is the number of pixels, and each pixel is represented as a column vector of the matrix X, any given pixel can be described in the following way

$$x_i = Ea_i + r_i, \tag{1}$$

where $E = [e_1, \ldots, e_M] \in \mathbb{R}^{B \times M}$ is a matrix of M endmembers, $a_i \in \mathbb{R}^M$ is a vector of abundances, and $r_i \in \mathbb{R}^B$ is a vector representing noise. Furthermore, the above equation can be rewritten in the following form

$$X = EA + R, \tag{2}$$

where $A = [a_1, \ldots, a_N] \in \mathbb{R}^{M \times N}$ and $R = [r_1, \ldots, r_N] \in \mathbb{R}^{B \times N}$. Two conditions on abundances are assumed to preserve their physical meaning:

1. Non-negativity constraint, that is $\forall a_j \in a_i \ a_j \geq 0$.
2. Sum-to-one constraint, that is $\sum_j a_j = 1, a_j \in a_i$.

2.2 Autoencoder

The autoencoder is composed of two parts. The encoder E transforms the example input data H into the latent space H', that is, $H' = E(H)$. Then the decoder D takes as input the output of the encoder and further transforms it into the output H'' of the autoencoder network, i.e. $H'' = D(H')$. Therefore, the autoencoder network can be described by the following equation

$$H'' = D(E(H)), \tag{3}$$

where H'' is the output of the network. The task of the autoencoder is to return H'' as similar to input H as possible. The intermediate output H' can be considered as the coding of the original data, often using a space with a lower dimension than the original. This makes it so that the autoencoder must reconstruct the input H using its compressed representation.

The autoencoder's unique architecture allows it to be applied in the task of spectral unmixing. In that case, the code vector can represent the abundances vector, while the decoder layer's weights represent the endmembers of the input pixels. Because of that, the decoder should have a single layer, which realises the mixing step corresponding to the process of image formation.

In this work, we consider a simple autoencoder architecture introduced in [11], denoted *Basic* by the authors. The encoder layer is composed of two linear layers with the Rectifier Linear (ReL) activation function, having $N_E M$ and M neurons, respectively, where M denotes the number of endmembers (which must be known in advance), while N_E is a hyperparameter of the network. After the encoder, the sum-to-one constraint is enforced, i.e. we take the sum of all the activations of the last layer of the encoder, and divide each activation by this sum. Last, the data is processed by the single decoder layer. See Fig. 2 for visualisation of the architecture.

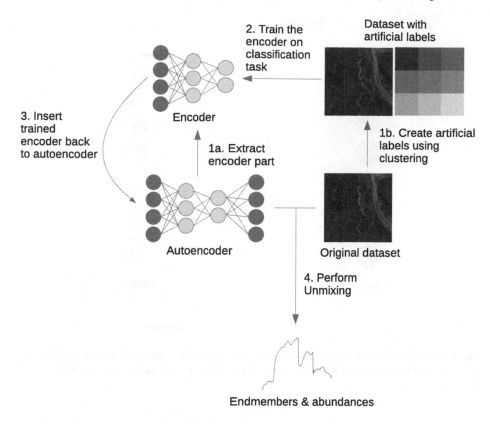

Fig. 1. Visualization of the pipeline proposed in this work. First, we extract encoder from autoencoder (1a) and create artificial labels (1b). Next, we train encoder on those labels (2). After training, the trained encoder is put back into autoencoder (3). Lastly, the spectral unmixing is performed using the pre-trained autoencoder (4).

2.3 Grid Clustering

We utilize the clustering algorithm to generate artificial labels from unlabeled data. More specifically, given dataset D, we derive dataset D' using clustering algorithm C. This new dataset is composed of the same hyperspectral pixels as the original dataset D, but contains the artificial labels represented by the N_C clusters returned by the clustering algorithm.

The spatial clustering algorithm that we use was originally introduced in [12]. We summarize the algorithm as follows: For a given hyperspectral scene, it is divided into N_C rectangles, where N_C is a hyperparameter of the method. The pixels contained in a given rectangle belong to the same cluster and are given the same artificial label. This simple labeling technique allows us to prepare the original dataset for the pre-training of the autoencoder. See Figs. 3b and 3d for example visualisations of the artificial ground truth.

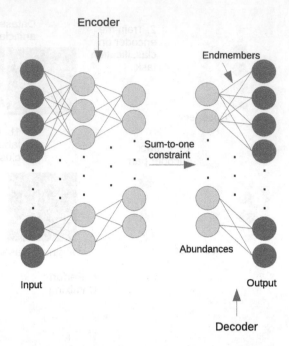

Fig. 2. Visualisation of the autoencoder *Basic* from [11], which is also used in our work. Sum-to-one constraint is enforced to make the output vector of the encoder sum to one (see Sect. 2.2 for details).

The chosen clustering method, though simple, utilizes the often present characteristic of the hyperspectral image, which is the local homogeneity of the spectra of pixels. In other words, we assume that the adjacent pixels are more similar than those further apart (and form the same 'class', thus fulfilling 'cluster assumption' [4]). These pixels are allocated to the same class by the algorithm. Furthermore, in contrast to the classical transfer learning approach, no expert knowledge is required to acquire the labels. This enables pre-training of the model without often costly ground-truth information.

2.4   Step-by-Step Pipeline Description

The proposed pipeline consists of the autoencoder A, the clustering algorithm C, and the unlabeled dataset D. It can be described as follows:

1. The randomly initialized encoder part E of the autoencoder A is acquired.
2. The classification layer of size N_C is added at the end of the encoder E, creating the neural network E'.

3. Additionally, the clustering algorithm C is used to create artificial labels for the considered dataset D, creating the new dataset D'.
4. The neural network E' is trained on the classification task using dataset D'. This is a pretext task, used to pre-train the encoder part of the network to improve its performance on the target task.
5. After training, the pre-trained encoder layers are put back into autoencoder A while the classification layer is removed.
6. The pre-trained autoencoder A is utilized to perform the unmixing task on the original dataset D. This is a target task.

3   Experiments and Results

3.1   Datasets

In this work, we used two popular hyperspectral datasets: Samson and Jasper Ridge [22]. Both datasets are briefly summarized below. All described changes to the datasets are considered standard in the community and were taken 'as is' to allow better comparison with other works.

The **Samson** dataset was originally composed of 952×952 pixels, but a subregion of 95×95 pixels was chosen to make the data more manageable. It contains 156 spectral channels covering the spectral range $401-889$ nm with the spectral resolution high up to 3.13 nm. Three endmembers are present in the image: soil, tree, and water. See Fig. 3a for a false-color visualisation of the dataset.

The **Jasper Ridge** dataset is a 512×614 scene, from which 100×100 subscene is taken. It contains 224 spectral channels covering the spectral range $380-2500$ nm with the spectral resolution up to 9.46 nm. Some of the spectral channels ($1-3$, $108-112$, $154-166$, $220-224$) are removed, leaving 198 channels. Four endmembers are present in this dataset: road, soil, water, and tree. See Fig. 3c for a false-color visualization of the dataset.

In the case of both of the datasets, the sample values were divided by the global maximum of a given dataset. In other words, for a given sample x from dataset D, we have $x := \frac{x}{m_D}$, where $m_D = \max_{y \in D'} y$, and D' is a flattened version of the dataset D.

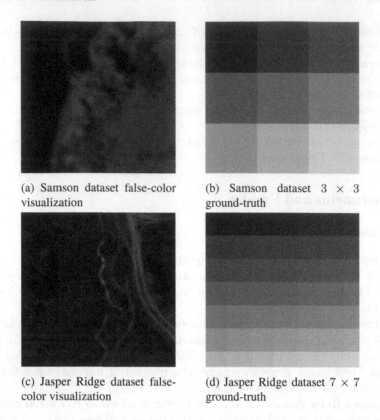

(a) Samson dataset false-color visualization

(b) Samson dataset 3 × 3 ground-truth

(c) Jasper Ridge dataset false-color visualization

(d) Jasper Ridge dataset 7 × 7 ground-truth

Fig. 3. False-color visualizations of bands 105, 50 and 18 for Samson dataset and bands 33, 15 and 4 for Jasper Ridge dataset, along with example artificial ground-truth generated using clustering.

3.2 Parameters

In our experiments, the *Basic* architecture from [11] was used, with $N_E = 10$ (see Sect. 2.2). The following parameters were used to train the model:

- Adam optimization algorithm;
- Number of epochs equal to 50 for both pre-training and fine-tuning stages;
- Cross Entropy loss function in the case of pre-training, and MSE loss function for fine-tuning;
- Batch size equal to 4 and 20 for the Samson and Jasper Ridge datasets, respectively;
- Learning rate equal to 10^{-4} and 10^{-3} for Samson and Jasper Ridge datasets, respectively.

These parameters are identical to those used in [11], from which the architecture used in this work was taken. We chose the same parameters for the pre-training as those used in the case of spectral unmixing. The source code necessary to replicate the experiments is publicly available on the GitHub repository.[1]

3.3 Synthetic Data Experiment

The synthetic dataset experiment was conducted to test the proposed approach in the controlled environment.[2] The dataset was prepared using the scheme presented in [5], but with the endmembers of the Samson dataset. The endmembers abundance maps for the experiment are presented in Fig. 4.

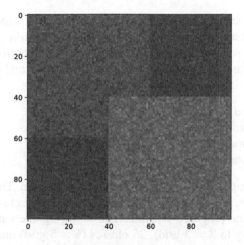

Fig. 4. Abundances map for the synthetic dataset. Red, green and blue colors represent abundances values for the water, tree and soil endmembers from the Samson dataset, respectively. Different intensity of the given color in each pixel represents the abundance fraction of the corresponding endmember. (Color figure online)

The synthetic dataset prepared for this experiment is composed of three different regions that form rectangles in the different parts of the image. This arrangement of the pixels is especially beneficial to the clustering method used to create artificial labels for pre-training, which allows us to test our approach when the assumptions regarding the dataset are met.

In this experiment, the *Basic* architecture was used, initialized using Xavier Glorot normal (XGN) initialization method and with parameters for Samson dataset from 3.2. This model was trained 15 times with and without pre-training (using 2×2 grid, which fits into the structure of the dataset), and Table 1 presents the results of the experiment. We can see that the pre-training improves the model performance.

---

[1] The source code is available at the following link: https://github.com/iitis/ClusteringAE.

[2] Please note that this experiment was added during the review process, after the main experiment described later. It was placed earlier in the paper to make the presentation easier for the reader.

Table 1. Results of the synthetic dataset experiment. For each metric, the mean and standard deviation for 15 runs of the experiment were reported.

Metrics	Baseline [11]	Grid 2 × 2
Endmembers error (SAD)	0.600 ± 0.13	0.493 ± 0.13
Abundances error (RMSE)	0.258 ± 0.10	0.248 ± 0.08
Reconstruction error (RMSE)	0.078 ± 0.01	0.074 ± 0.01

3.4 Experiment Scheme

In this section, the scheme of the experiment is presented. The experiment was carried out by pre-training the encoder part of the autoencoder using artificial labels like in [12]. Using the pre-trained weights, the autoencoder was trained to perform unmixing.

The experiment was performed using two datasets: Samson and Jasper Ridge. Moreover, the following weight initialization methods were used:

- Kaiming He normal (KHN),
- Kaiming He uniform (KHU),
- Xavier Glorot normal (XGN),
- Xavier Glorot uniform (XGU).

The experiment is composed of 50 runs per weight initialization. The number of classes for the artificial labels, which is a hyperparameter of the used clustering method, was varied to better test the proposed pipeline. The following alternatives were tested: 9 classes (corresponding to 3×3 grid), 25 classes (5×5 grid) and 49 classes (7×7 grid). This hyperparameter was thoroughly evaluated in the original work and one of the chosen values, i.e. 5×5 grid, provided the best results. Furthermore, statistical tests were utilized to verify whether the differences between baseline model initializations and grid pre-training experiments are statistically significant. For each pair of experiments, we performed a two-sided Wilcoxon signed-rank test at significance level $\alpha = 0.05$.

The following three measures were used in the experiment: mean reconstruction error (comparing inputs and outputs of the autoencoder) and mean abundances error (comparing ground-truth and predicted abundance values) using the RMSE measure, as well as mean endmembers error (comparing ground-truth and predicted endmembers) using Spectral Angle Distance (SAD) measure. To match predicted endmembers to ground-truth ones, we have chosen the permutation of predicted endmembers with the smallest distance to ground truth endmembers. These are the same measures (with the addition of reconstruction error) as those used in [11], which allows for better comparison with the proposed approach. Please note that the differences in metrics values reported in [11] and *baseline* values in our work are the result of different experiment schemes, i.e., different number of iterations between the experiments, as well as reporting averaged weight initialization results or results for each weight initialization separately.

3.5 Results

The results of the experiment are presented in the tables below.[3] Table 2 presents the results for the Samson dataset, while Table 3 presents the results for the Jasper Ridge dataset. The symbol of a filled square means that the difference between baseline runs from [11] and pre-training enhanced runs is statistically significant, while a white square represents the opposite case.

It can be noticed that for the Samson dataset in all but two cases (endmembers error for grid 3×3 and abundances error for grid 7×7) our approach is better than the baseline. In the case of the Jasper Ridge dataset, the improvements were not statistically significant. Moreover, in the case of reconstruction error and, in part, abundances error, the pre-training scheme resulted in higher errors. It is worth noting, however, that when considering only endmembers error and abundances error, in many cases the proposed approach resulted in better performance than the baseline even for Jasper Ridge dataset, though the resulting improvement was not statistically significant. On the other hand, the measure for which the usage of the proposed pre-training scheme resulted in worse performance, is a reconstruction error, and it can be regarded as less important than the other two when considering the spectral unmixing task. This is because the final objective of our autoencoder application is the extraction of endmember and abundance data, of which the performance is measured by endmembers error and abundances error. Reconstruction error is used to guide the optimization and can be a diagnostic measure of the output but is not directly measuring the endmembers and abundances quality.

It is also worth noting that in most cases, whether or not the proposed approach improved the baseline did not change across different grid shapes, proving the robustness of the method.

Table 2. Results of the experiment for the Samson dataset. For each metric, the mean and standard deviation for 200 runs of the experiment were reported.

Metrics	Baseline [11]	Grid 3×3	Grid 5×5	Grid 7×7
Endmembers error (SAD)	0.850 ± 0.24	0.835 ± 0.24 □	0.805 ± 0.26 ■	0.802 ± 0.27 ■
Abundances error (RMSE)	0.354 ± 0.04	0.345 ± 0.04 ■	0.346 ± 0.04 ■	0.347 ± 0.04 □
Reconstruction error (RMSE)	0.047 ± 0.05	0.041 ± 0.04 ■	0.042 ± 0.04 ■	0.043 ± 0.04 ■

Table 3. Results of the experiment for the Jasper Ridge dataset. For each metric, the mean and standard deviation for 200 runs of the experiment were reported.

Metrics	Baseline [11]	Grid 3×3	Grid 5×5	Grid 7×7
Endmembers error (SAD)	0.927 ± 0.12	0.921 ± 0.17 □	0.926 ± 0.16 □	0.914 ± 0.20 □
Abundances error (RMSE)	0.285 ± 0.04	0.284 ± 0.04 □	0.291 ± 0.04 □	0.289 ± 0.04 □
Reconstruction error (RMSE)	0.024 ± 0.04	0.047 ± 0.06 ■	0.046 ± 0.06 ■	0.048 ± 0.06 ■

---

[3] During the publication process, it was discovered that abundances error values for the baseline model were incorrectly reported due to the wrong order of the abundances values in the prepared dataset. This was fixed in the final version of the paper and does not affect the conclusions of this work.

3.6 Discussion

In this section, we explore the experiment introduced above more specifically. First, we look at detailed results for different weights initialization methods (4–11).

When considering the Samson dataset (4–7), we can see that including pre-training generally improves the results across different weight initializations and different grid shapes. There are, however, exceptions, e.g. reconstruction error in the case of KHN initialization and 3×3 and 5×5 grid shapes, or endmembers error in the case of KHU initialization and 3×3 grid shape.

In the case of Jasper Ridge dataset (8–11), the usage of pre-training most often leads to higher errors, with few exceptions e.g. endmembers error in the case of XGN weight initialization.

In summary, we can observe that the results for different datasets and across different weight initializations keep the trends that were observed in the main experiment (pre-training generally works for Samson dataset, but does not work in the case of Jasper Ridge dataset).

Table 4. Results of the grid clustering experiment for Samson dataset and KHN initialization.

Metrics	Baseline [11]	Grid 3×3	Grid 5×5	Grid 7×7
Endmembers error (SAD)	1.176 ± 0.12	1.116 ± 0.14	1.115 ± 0.14	1.117 ± 0.16
Abundances error (RMSE)	0.365 ± 0.03	0.352 ± 0.03	0.353 ± 0.03	0.361 ± 0.03
Reconstruction error (RMSE)	0.047 ± 0.04	0.053 ± 0.05	0.054 ± 0.04	0.046 ± 0.04

Table 5. Results of the grid clustering experiment for Samson dataset and KHU initialization.

Metrics	Baseline [11]	Grid 3×3	Grid 5×5	Grid 7×7
Endmembers error (SAD)	0.758 ± 0.19	0.778 ± 0.17	0.716 ± 0.20	0.736 ± 0.18
Abundances error (RMSE)	0.357 ± 0.03	0.346 ± 0.04	0.346 ± 0.04	0.344 ± 0.04
Reconstruction error (RMSE)	0.053 ± 0.05	0.042 ± 0.05	0.042 ± 0.05	0.036 ± 0.04

We have also looked at the classification maps obtained from the pre-training phase of the algorithm. Across all datasets and grid shapes, most classification maps look similar to ground truth, and few of them are empty (defined as maps for which only one class was predicted for every pixel). These empty maps may be a result of low quality model training, resulting from e.g. bad weights initialization. See Fig. 5 for the example prediction.

Table 6. Results of the grid clustering experiment for Samson dataset and XGN initialization.

Metrics	Baseline [11]	Grid 3×3	Grid 5×5	Grid 7×7
Endmembers error (SAD)	0.744 ± 0.14	0.726 ± 0.20	0.676 ± 0.20	0.727 ± 0.22
Abundances error (RMSE)	0.349 ± 0.04	0.343 ± 0.05	0.349 ± 0.04	0.339 ± 0.05
Reconstruction error (RMSE)	0.036 ± 0.04	0.038 ± 0.04	0.036 ± 0.04	0.039 ± 0.04

Table 7. Results of the grid clustering experiment for Samson dataset and XGU initialization.

Metrics	Baseline [11]	Grid 3 × 3	Grid 5 × 5	Grid 7 × 7
Endmembers error (SAD)	0.723 ± 0.12	0.718 ± 0.17	0.713 ± 0.21	0.628 ± 0.19
Abundances error (RMSE)	0.344 ± 0.05	0.337 ± 0.05	0.337 ± 0.04	0.343 ± 0.04
Reconstruction error (RMSE)	0.052 ± 0.05	0.030 ± 0.04	0.036 ± 0.04	0.049 ± 0.05

Table 8. Results of the grid clustering experiment for Jasper dataset and KHN initialization.

Metrics	Baseline [11]	Grid 3 × 3	Grid 5 × 5	Grid 7 × 7
Endmembers error (SAD)	1.033 ± 0.11	1.102 ± 0.13	1.099 ± 0.12	1.122 ± 0.11
Abundances error (RMSE)	0.300 ± 0.02	0.311 ± 0.03	0.313 ± 0.02	0.312 ± 0.03
Reconstruction error (RMSE)	0.021 ± 0.03	0.053 ± 0.06	0.049 ± 0.06	0.053 ± 0.06

Table 9. Results of the grid clustering experiment for Jasper dataset and KHU initialization.

Metrics	Baseline [11]	Grid 3 × 3	Grid 5 × 5	Grid 7 × 7
Endmembers error (SAD)	0.881 ± 0.10	0.885 ± 0.11	0.909 ± 0.09	0.923 ± 0.14
Abundances error (RMSE)	0.276 ± 0.04	0.272 ± 0.05	0.276 ± 0.05	0.272 ± 0.05
Reconstruction error (RMSE)	0.037 ± 0.05	0.045 ± 0.05	0.042 ± 0.05	0.041 + 0.05

Table 10. Results of the grid clustering experiment for Jasper dataset and XGN initialization.

Metrics	Baseline [11]	Grid 3 × 3	Grid 5 × 5	Grid 7 × 7
Endmembers error (SAD)	0.894 ± 0.11	0.862 ± 0.13	0.845 ± 0.14	0.805 + 0.19
Abundances error (RMSE)	0.285 ± 0.04	0.269 ± 0.04	0.286 ± 0.05	0.291 ± 0.04
Reconstruction error (RMSE)	0.020 ± 0.03	0.039 ± 0.05	0.044 ± 0.06	0.050 ± 0.06

Table 11. Results of the grid clustering experiment for Jasper dataset and XGU initialization.

Metrics	Baseline [11]	Grid 3 × 3	Grid 5 × 5	Grid 7 × 7
Endmembers error (SAD)	0.899 ± 0.11	0.834 ± 0.17	0.852 ± 0.15	0.808 ± 0.16
Abundances error (RMSE)	0.281 ± 0.04	0.283 ± 0.04	0.289 ± 0.05	0.280 ± 0.05
Reconstruction error (RMSE)	0.019 ± 0.03	0.050 ± 0.06	0.050 ± 0.06	0.048 ± 0.06

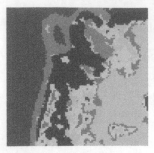 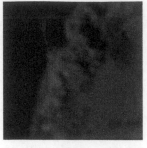 

(a) Example prediction visual-   (b) False-color visualisation of   (c) Artificial ground-truth vi-
isation   the Samson dataset   sualisation

Fig. 5. Example Samson classification map. As one can see, the prediction returned by the model is similar to false-color visualisation of the dataset, even though the model was trained using simple ground-truth shown on the right.

Specifically, the number of empty maps is slightly lower in the case of Samson dataset (8.5% for grid shape 3×3, and 9% in the case of grid shapes 5×5 and 7×7) when compared to Jasper Ridge dataset (11.5% for grid shape 3×3 and 10.5% in the case of grid shapes 5×5 and 7×7), which may explain the worse results for the second dataset.

Detailed Error Analysis Although the results presented in the previous section allow for evaluation of the proposed approach, their averaged nature may hide performance features; thus, we have performed a detailed error analysis with collected per-pixel error statistics. We have investigated the following six cases: Samson, KHN, 7×7; Samson, KHU, 3×3; Samson, XGN, 5×5; Samson, XGU, 3×3; Jasper, KHN, 3×3; Jasper, XGU, 5×5. The objective of the selection was to pick samples across all experimental variables, i.e., dataset (Samson/Jasper), initialization type (KHN/KHU/XGN/XGU); grid size (3/5/7) and grid method error relative to the baseline (smaller, comparable, larger). Since each case has $n = 50$ models, this analysis included $n = 300$ different models. For each case and the model within this case, we have collected per-pixel results of the RMSE of the baseline $e_i^b = \text{RMSE}(\boldsymbol{x}_i - \boldsymbol{x}_i^b)$, where $\boldsymbol{x}_i^b$ is a reconstruction of a pixel i from the image with the baseline method, and the grid $e_i^g = \text{RMSE}(\boldsymbol{x}_i - \boldsymbol{x}_i^g)$ approach defined in a similar fashion. Additionally, we have defined the error difference as $\delta_i = e_i^b - e_i^g$. A positive value of $\delta_i > 0$ means that pixel i is better represented with the grid model, while a negative $\delta_i < 0$ means that the baseline model performed better for that pixel. We have chosen to focus on the reconstruction error because the results for the Samson and Jasper Ridge datasets were very different when considering this measure, which prompted us to analyze it in more depth.

Our proposed way of investigating evaluates the scatterplots of (e_i^b, δ_i) i.e. the relation of error difference to the baseline model error. Upon inspecting the scatterplots for individual models from the selected cases, we have noticed that there is a limited number of patterns repeated across analysed results (see Fig. 6). In almost all cases ($n_a = 296$ of $n = 300$ considered) the application of a grid method has a single ten-

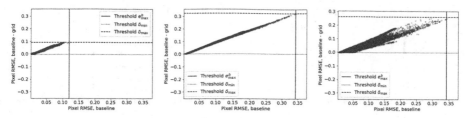

(a) Grid model improves baseline within small range of RMSE values.

(b) Grid model improves baseline within large range of RMSE values.

(c) Grid model improves baseline within large range of RMSE values, higher variance is observed.

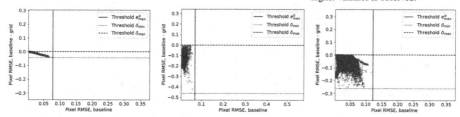

(d) Grid model worsens the performance of baseline.

(e) Grid model performs worse than baseline with small range of RMSE values.

(f) Grid model performs worse than baseline with small range of RMSE values, larger variance.

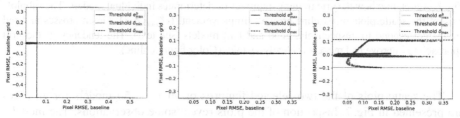

(g) Similar results for grid and baseline within small range of RMSE values.

(h) Similar results for grid and baseline within large range of RMSE values.

(i) A rare case ($n_r = 4$ across $n = 300$ observed models) where some pixels are improved, some worsened.

Fig. 6. Per pixel error patterns. Each individual subfigure presents a scatterplot for a single pair of models (corresponding to two reconstructions of a single image), baseline pixel RMSE vs. baseline - grid RMSE. Feature threshold values $e_{\max}^b$, $\delta_{\min}$ and $\delta_{\max}$ are superimposed (see text). The patterns presented here represent $n = 300$ models selected for analysis.

dency for a whole model: it either consistently improves all pixels, or worsens, or no change is observed. Only in rare cases ($n = 4$) parts of the pixels are improved and others are worsened. Since the tendency to improve or worsen is consistent and the number of patterns is limited, we propose to represent each model with the following features computed from descriptive statistics. For any single model, we define a set of thresholds as features of a single model $e_{\max}^b = \max_i e_i^b$, $\delta_{\min} = \min_i \delta_i$ and $\delta_{\max} = \max_i \delta_i$. We further narrow the set of features to $(e_{\max}^b, \delta_M)$ with the latter defined as

$$
\delta_M = \begin{cases} \delta_{\max} & \text{if } |\delta_{\max}| > |\delta_{\min}| \\ \delta_{\min} & \text{otherwise.} \end{cases} \tag{4}
$$

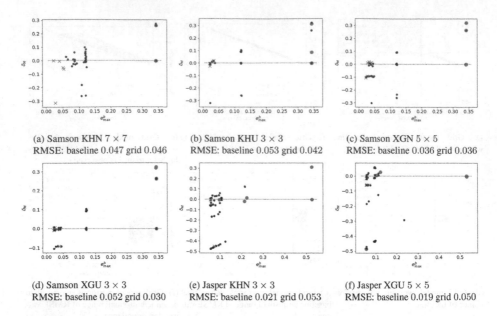

(a) Samson KHN 7 × 7
RMSE: baseline 0.047 grid 0.046

(b) Samson KHU 3 × 3
RMSE: baseline 0.053 grid 0.042

(c) Samson XGN 5 × 5
RMSE: baseline 0.036 grid 0.036

(d) Samson XGU 3 × 3
RMSE: baseline 0.052 grid 0.030

(e) Jasper KHN 3 × 3
RMSE: baseline 0.021 grid 0.053

(f) Jasper XGU 5 × 5
RMSE: baseline 0.019 grid 0.050

Fig. 7. A look into how the grid training improves or deteriorates individual models. The subplots present the scatterplots of baseline error vs. improvement, $(e^b_{\max}, \delta_M)$. Green crosses and red circles correspond to, respectively, good and bad models (see text). The tendency of the grid approach to improve bad models is clearly visible. (Color figure online)

The scatterplots of the two selected features of all $n = 50$ models for all cases are presented in Fig. 7. Inspection of the plots reveal some observations. The models' performance values tend to form clusters, with both error and error difference values far from being uniformly distributed. The fact that clusters are present in all cases suggests that this may be a feature of the architecture used, which may have a limited number of convergence points. It is interesting to note that for every case – irrespective of whether the baseline is on average better or worse than the proposed approach – some models are improved with the grid training. In particular, some of the worst models (right side of the plots in Fig. 7) are improved by a high value. To explore this further, we have identified in the previous experiments [11] the best ('good') and worst preforming ('bad') models and superimposed the labels of those models on the plots as green crosses and red circles, respectively. Almost all of the 'bad' models improved and in only one case did the performance significantly deteriorate. However, good models in terms of error are negatively affected by the grid approach. This suggests that grid training is interrelated to regular training; it can be of help when the latter is not performing well, but it can hamper its progress in the good case. However, at the simplest, one could train a model in both ways and select the better in terms of the chosen error measure.

Analysis of the result for the Jasper data shows that the grid approach improves some models and deteriorates others; however, the balance of improved and deteriorated models is in favour of the baseline approach. One possible explanation is that for smaller number of bad-performing baseline models, there is less room for the positive improvement effect from the grid method, visible on the Samson dataset. However, those few bad models present are improved at seemingly the same rate as for the other dataset.

4 Conclusions

In this work, we have investigated the usage of unsupervised pre-training method in the case of autoencoders and the spectral unmixing task. We conducted the experiment using two different hyperspectral datasets and four different weight initialization methods. Moreover, we used a known artificial labels generation algorithm based on clustering.

The results of our experiments are mixed. In the case of the Samson dataset, the proposed pre-training resulted in lower errors when compared to baseline results. However, when considering the Jasper Ridge dataset, our approach did not result in statistically significant improvement, and in some cases even higher errors were obtained compared to the baseline.

In summary, the investigated approach has potential to be a useful tool for improving the effectiveness of autoencoders in the task of spectral unmixing, but more research needs to be done to learn under what conditions the method can bring improvements. Our analysis of the classification maps, where we observed that more empty maps were present in the case of Jasper Ridge dataset, can be considered a first step in that direction.

During the review process of this paper, more clustering methods, as well as more datasets, were requested. Given the time and space constraints, the decision was made to extend the paper by adding a synthetic dataset experiment (see Sect. 3.3). The selected clustering technique was chosen because of its simplicity and because its single hyperparameter, which is the number of clusters, was thoroughly evaluated in the original work. In the future, more datasets can be evaluated, as well as more clustering algorithms.

Acknowledgements. B.G. acknowledges funding from the budget funds for science in the years 2018–2022, as a scientific project "Application of transfer learning methods in the problem of hyperspectral images classification using convolutional neural networks" under the "Diamond Grant" program, no. DI2017 013847. K.K. acknowledges funding from the European Union through the European Social Fund (grant POWR.03.02.00-00-I029). We would like to thank the anonymous reviewers for their suggestions and comments.

References

1. Bhatt, J.S., Joshi, M.V.: Deep learning in hyperspectral unmixing: a review. In: IGARSS 2020–2020 IEEE International Geoscience and Remote Sensing Symposium, pp. 2189–2192 (2020). https://doi.org/10.1109/IGARSS39084.2020.9324546
2. Bioucas-Dias, J.M.: A variable splitting augmented Lagrangian approach to linear spectral unmixing. In: 2009 First Workshop on Hyperspectral Image and Signal Processing: Evolution in Remote Sensing, pp. 1–4 (2009)

3. Bioucas-Dias, J.M., et al.: Hyperspectral unmixing overview: geometrical, statistical, and sparse regression-based approaches. IEEE J. Selected Topics Appl. Earth Observ. Remote Sens. **5**(2), 354–379 (2012). https://doi.org/10.1109/JSTARS.2012.2194696

4. Chapelle, O., Schlkopf, B., Zien, A.: Semi-supervised learning. In: IEEE Transactions on Neural Networks, vol. 20 (2006)

5. Dobigeon, N., Moussaoui, S., Coulon, M., Tourneret, J.Y., Hero, A.O.: Joint Bayesian endmember extraction and linear unmixing for hyperspectral imagery. IEEE Trans. Signal Process. **57**(11), 4355–4368 (2009). https://doi.org/10.1109/TSP.2009.2025797

6. Glorot, X., Bengio, Y.: Understanding the difficulty of training deep feedforward neural networks. In: Teh, Y.W., Titterington, M. (eds.) Proceedings of the Thirteenth International Conference on Artificial Intelligence and Statistics. Proceedings of Machine Learning Research, vol. 9, pp. 249–256. PMLR, Chia Laguna Resort, Sardinia, Italy (2010). https://proceedings. mlr.press/v9/glorot10a.html

7. Hinton, G.E., Salakhutdinov, R.R.: Reducing the dimensionality of data with neural networks. Science **313**(5786), 504–507 (2006)

8. Jia, S., Qian, Y.: Constrained nonnegative matrix factorization for hyperspectral unmixing. IEEE Trans. Geosci. Remote Sens. **47**(1), 161–173 (2009). https://doi.org/10.1109/TGRS. 2008.2002882

9. Khajehrayeni, F., Ghassemian, H.: Hyperspectral unmixing using deep convolutional autoencoders in a supervised scenario. IEEE J. Selected Topics Appl. Earth Observ. Remote Sens. **13**, 567–576 (2020). https://doi.org/10.1109/JSTARS.2020.2966512

10. Krizhevsky, A., Hinton, G.E.: Using very deep autoencoders for content-based image retrieval. In: ESANN, vol. 1, p. 2. Citeseer (2011)

11. Książek, K., Głomb, P., Romaszewski, M., Cholewa, M., Grabowski, B.: Stable training of autoencoders for hyperspectral unmixing (2021)

12. Masarczyk, W., Głomb, P., Grabowski, B., Ostaszewski, M.: Effective training of deep convolutional neural networks for hyperspectral image classification through artificial labeling. Remote Sens. **12**(16) (2020). https://doi.org/10.3390/rs12162653, https://www.mdpi.com/ 2072-4292/12/16/2653

13. Nascimento, J., Dias, J.: Vertex component analysis: a fast algorithm to unmix hyperspectral data. IEEE Trans. Geosci. Remote Sens. **43**(4), 898–910 (2005). https://doi.org/10.1109/ TGRS.2005.844293

14. Nascimento, J.M.P., Bioucas-Dias, J.M.: Hyperspectral unmixing based on mixtures of dirichlet components. IEEE Trans. Geosci. Remote Sens. **50**(3), 863–878 (2012). https:// doi.org/10.1109/TGRS.2011.2163941

15. Palsson, B., Ulfarsson, M.O., Sveinsson, J.R.: Convolutional autoencoder for spectral-spatial hyperspectral unmixing. IEEE Trans. Geosci. Remote Sens. **59**(1), 535–549 (2021). https:// doi.org/10.1109/TGRS.2020.2992743

16. Palsson, F., Sigurdsson, J., Sveinsson, J.R., Ulfarsson, M.O.: Neural network hyperspectral unmixing with spectral information divergence objective. In: 2017 IEEE International Geoscience and Remote Sensing Symposium (IGARSS), pp. 755–758 (2017). https://doi.org/10. 1109/IGARSS.2017.8127062

17. Ruiz-Garcia, A., Elshaw, M., Altahhan, A., Palade, V.: Stacked deep convolutional autoencoders for emotion recognition from facial expressions. In: 2017 International Joint Conference on Neural Networks (IJCNN), pp. 1586–1593 (2017). https://doi.org/10.1109/ IJCNN.2017.7966040

18. Su, Y., Li, J., Plaza, A., Marinoni, A., Gamba, P., Chakravortty, S.: Daen: deep autoencoder networks for hyperspectral unmixing. IEEE Trans. Geosci. Remote Sens. **57**(7), 4309–4321 (2019). https://doi.org/10.1109/TGRS.2018.2890633

19. Su, Y., Xu, X., Li, J., Qi, H., Gamba, P., Plaza, A.: Deep autoencoders with multitask learning for bilinear hyperspectral unmixing. IEEE Trans. Geosci. Remote Sens. **59**(10), 8615–8629 (2021). https://doi.org/10.1109/TGRS.2020.3041157
20. Winter, M.E.: N-FINDR: an algorithm for fast autonomous spectral end-member determination in hyperspectral data. In: Descour, M.R., Shen, S.S. (eds.) Imaging Spectrometry V, vol. 3753, pp. 266–275. International Society for Optics and Photonics, SPIE (1999). https://doi.org/10.1117/12.366289
21. Zhao, M., Wang, M., Chen, J., Rahardja, S.: Hyperspectral unmixing for additive nonlinear models with a 3-D-CNN autoencoder network. IEEE Trans. Geosci. Remote Sens., pp. 1–15 (2021). https://doi.org/10.1109/TGRS.2021.3098745
22. Zhu, F.: Hyperspectral unmixing: Ground truth labeling, datasets, benchmark performances and survey. Computer Vision and Pattern Recognition (2017)

Data-Driven Resilient Supply Management Supported by Demand Forecasting

Marek Grzegorowski[1]([✉])(iD), Andrzej Janusz[1,2](iD), Jarosław Litwin[2], and Łukasz Marcinowski[3]

[1] Institute of Informatics, University of Warsaw, Banacha 2, Warsaw 02-097, Poland
M.Grzegorowski@mimuw.edu.pl
[2] QED Software Sp. z o.o., Warsaw, Poland
{andrzej.janusz,jaroslaw.litwin}@qed.pl
[3] FitFood Sp. z o. o., Cracow, Poland
l.marcinowski@fitfoodpoland.pl

Abstract. The article discusses several challenges related to resilient supply management and demand forecasting. Both of those topics are of great importance for food retailers and producers who aim at reducing the risk of lost sales opportunities and food waste. In the investigated case study of FitBoxY.com, due to the overestimated demand and too large deliveries, historically, even 30% of the products were overdue. The developed ML framework integrated with the supply management system enabled optimization of business costs and reduced food waste from overestimated demand. The experimental evaluation showed that, with the developed solution, it is possible to improve demand forecasting by nearly 50% compared to estimates proposed by human operators.

Keywords: Time series · ML · Data-driven supply management · FMCG

1 Introduction

Providing reliable forecasts of the future demand for fast-moving consumer goods (FMCG) is a big challenge, especially for retailers and producers in the food market. Here, the demand misestimation may lead to lost sales opportunities and extra costs related to food waste [11]. A special case requiring even more attention is sales through vending machines, where the limited capacity of refrigerators causes additional difficulties in optimal supply management (SM) [2]. In this regard, researchers indicate an opportunity to build data-driven SM systems [14]. However, the correct analysis of data from a dispersed points-of-sale (PoS) network causes many difficulties, for instance, related to distributed data sources and their integration or challenges connected to a small number of historical purchase transactions of a particular product in an analyzed PoS.

Research co-funded by Polish National Centre for Research and Development (NCBiR) grant no. POIR.01.01.01-00-0963/19-00 and by Polish National Science Centre (NCN) grant no. 2018/31/N/ST6/00610.

© The Author(s), under exclusive license to Springer Nature Singapore Pte Ltd. 2022
E. Szczerbicki et al. (Eds.): ACIIDS 2022, CCIS 1716, pp. 122–134, 2022.
https://doi.org/10.1007/978-981-19-8234-7_10

Predicting demand may be modeled as the regression of the historically observed sales in the investigated location. Several approaches are often adapted to dealing with this task, including simple statistical methods, multivariate machine learning models, or obtaining near-optimal results with optimization metaheuristics [7, 10]. Another essential element of data-driven supply management systems is a concise and understandable data representation [5, 6]. Recently, entrepreneurs have also considered applying prescriptive analytics to support decision-making [4]. For such systems to make reliable recommendations, it is critical to employ effective mechanisms of demand forecasting.

In the article, we discuss the possibility of integrating the supply management system with a machine learning (ML) framework that allows for predicting the demand for a distributed sales network. The prediction of future sales over a specific period of time basing on historical data can be treated as a standard problem in the field of time series analysis. However, due to the specificity of the FMCG data in the food industry, where products have a short life cycle and are often substituted, this problem is very challenging. In a discussed case study of FitBoxY.com, out of over 200 different products, only 10% are sold regularly over a long period. As an effect, we observe a very big number of relatively short and scattered time series of sales (as a single time series, we consider the sales history of a given product in one PoS). Fitting a prediction model for such data is difficult for many state-of-the-art ML methods. It is, therefore, necessary to properly select and adjust utilized algorithms so that they could effectively predict the sale of new products with a short sales history, thus effectively coping with the so-called cold-start problem [8]. This effect is additionally exacerbated by the replacement of components and sensors or rotation of the physical refrigerators between locations. From the customers' perspective, such changes are imperceptible, although the machine learning algorithms may lose the continuity of impacted time series, significantly reducing the amount of historical data used for fitting predictive models.

We deployed the developed framework and confirmed its effectiveness with the analysis of real data collected from the FitBoxY.com. This technological start-up delivers healthy meals to the dispersed network of vending machines of own construction deployed in many office buildings. FitBoxY offers meals prepared with high-quality ingredients and packed under a protective atmosphere, avoiding chemical preservatives. The consequences of such a decision are a slightly higher price and a short expiry date of two weeks. Thus, accurately adjusting supply for the actual demand is critical, otherwise resulting in increased food waste and financial loss [11]. In the article, we present the results of predictions with several univariate auto-regressive methods, as well as multivariate machine learning models operating on multidimensional representations. Data constitute time series extracted from historical daily sales of products, separately for each PoS. However, for each of the investigated approaches (univariate vs. multivariate), the evaluated methods expected different representations.

The rest of the paper is organized as follows. Section 2 describes the problem of food waste in retail and the related task of supply management and demand estimation based on sales prediction with Industry 4.0 technologies like the Internet of Things (IoT) or machine learning (ML). Section 3 presents a general architecture of the solution. In Sect. 4, we outline the developed ML framework, including the description of the data preprocessing and feature extraction. Section 5 presents the case study of demand/sales forecasting, the data, and a comprehensive analysis of the results. In Sect. 6, we conclude the paper.

2   Related Works

Food production is a complex process under high uncertainty resulting in differences between the planned supply and actual demand. These cause additional costs for the company, related to unnecessary food waste due to the short shelf-life of many products and the surplus production, as well as negative environmental impact. Machine learning methods, like the random forest or boosting models, are often applied to address this challenge, reporting promising results [3,11]. With the emergence of IoT and Industry 4.0 [1], food production and retail can be benefited since by adapting to these concepts, companies may enhance the sustainability of production and effectiveness of order-to-cash processes [13]. The ongoing progress of intelligent industrialization is even more rapid due to cost-effective cloud computing and recent advances in Big Data analytics [7].

The idea of data-driven businesses strengthens the interest in unmanned retail, among which the concepts of unmanned shops or distributed smart vending machines lead the way [17]. Vending is a very fragmented and competitive market with thousands of small and medium enterprises per country, mainly because margins are relatively low. Therefore, any possibility to take advantage of the most recent technologies to minimize the total cost of ownership and operations is of growing interest [7]. From our perspective, it is particularly interesting how to fully embrace IoT and ML to optimize the operational processes related to production and delivery planning [3]. The main challenge is the formation of such an assortment for each vending machine, the realization of which will bring maximum profit and minimize the food waste at the same time [15].

Accurate demand forecasting is a great challenge for dispersed sales networks, especially considering the short shelf-life of food [11]. We model this problem by solving a well-known machine learning task, namely: the regression of demand in each investigated location - a special case of time series forecasting. Algorithms commonly applied in this context are often categorized into two main groups. Univariate methods fit parameters of a model independently for each time series in the data, such as ARIMA or BATS [7]. Those methods try to learn patterns and dependencies occurring in the historical data, and utilize them to make predictions about future time series behavior [12].

The second group of time series forecasting algorithms consists of multivariate methods [18]. In this approach, ML models are trained on data from multiple time series (or a single multi-dimensional series) to exploit the possible correlations between them. In practice, such an approach often helps in solving the cold-start problem [8]. In this context, it is worth paying special attention

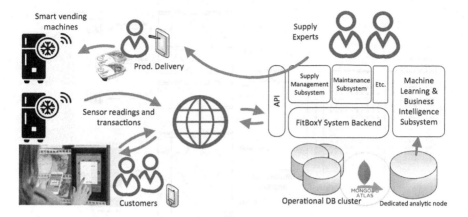

Fig. 1. Solution architecture.

to eXtreme Gradient Boosting (XGBoost) of regression trees is a widely used machine learning technique to model time series [5,20].

3 Integrating Supply Chain Management with ML

In Fig. 1, we present a high-level architecture of the developed solution. On the left side of the diagram, there are vending machines, each equipped with a number of sensors that monitor the condition of the equipment and a tablet integrated with the point-of-payment to carry out purchase transactions. Data from machines' sensors and transactions are collected by a dedicated integration API and stored in the database, where sensor readings and transactions are supplemented with other data-sources like hardware and application logs and information about deliveries.

The core of the system is related to Supply Management, and several other subsystems supporting the operational work as well as additional tablet applications. For instance, using the tablet app on the occasion of delivery, the supplier checks and updates the condition of the refrigerator, the available stock of products and their expiry dates, marking discrepancies and inconsistencies in the system, verifies the condition and quality of products, and replenishes with new items in accordance with the prepared delivery plan.

The visualization layer constitutes two reporting systems. The first, MongoCharts, is a business intelligence (BI) mechanism built into the Mongo Atlas cloud service that allows us to report on the current situation. A more advanced solution is AWS QuickSight - a BI service by our cloud provider. In the latter, the historical data presented in reports are combined with the ML models' predictions prepared with the developed ML framework (cf. Sect. 4). This allows us to visualize the historical, current, and expected future sales on one chart by supplementing it with the estimated sales in the next two weeks' horizon in a highly interpretable and easy-to-understand way.

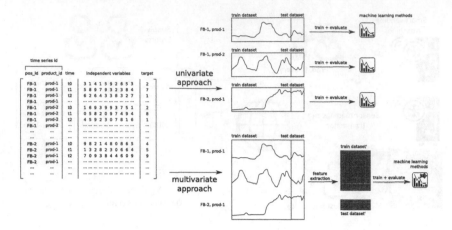

Fig. 2. Machine learning framework for applying uni- and multivariate methods.

4 Machine Learning Framework

In Fig. 2, we present the developed machine learning framework, which provides highly reliable and resilient demand forecasts. We achieve this goal by extensive feature extraction, leading toward two significantly different data representations, and using several state-of-the-art machine learning algorithms.

On the left side of Fig. 2, there is a tabular representation of time series data, i.e., each series is identified by a bi-factor identifier (composed of *pos_id* and *product_id*) and consists of a number of rows in the table corresponding to its length. Many ML algorithms can be trained on data derived from univariate time series and used as forecast models [16]. To make it possible, it is usually necessary to divide series into overlapping time windows. Each window from historical data is treated as a training instance, with a target corresponding to a shifted (future) value (or several consecutive values) of the series, and the values in the window are regarded as its attributes. Additionally, for each time window, we may construct auxiliary features that can better reflect the most relevant characteristics of the series.

The approach in which an independent ML model is trained for each time series can be naturally extended to a multivariate case, in which all available data is used to construct a single model. One of the biggest advantages of such a solution is the ability to deal with the cold-start problem, i.e., the model can make predictions for completely new time series. This situation is quite common in the considered application area – typically, a few new points-of-sale are opened every month, and new products are introduced at regular basis. However, in order to facilitate training of such models, it is necessary to extend the set of features describing individual time windows with characteristics that allow grouping similar time series. For training and applying the multivariate methods, the additional feature extraction is performed (see Fig. 2).

Many univariate time series forecasting models, such as ARIMA or BATS, do not require any additional feature extraction. Those models can be trained solely on raw historical time series values and make predictions without a need for any additional data. However, even such models may benefit from using extra features as external regressors. In our experiments, when we train the ARIMA model, we use additional information extracted from the transaction and delivery data. In particular, we add date-related information, e.g., one-hot encoded day of a week, month and quarter number, as well as long-term seasonal information, such as the values from the previous year. In the future, we also plan to add information about special calendar events, such as public holidays.

On the other hand, classical ML algorithms that we apply to univariate time series, i.e., k-NN, random forest [19], require a richer representation of data in order to fit the model. Since we use those algorithms to build a separate model for each time series, the features that we extract are mostly focusing on describing relevant characteristics of the series. We divide the historical data for each series into overlapping time windows, and we extract features such as lagged series values, running means, standard deviations, lagged differences of consecutive values, as well as min-max values. Moreover, we add the date-related and seasonal features that we were using as the external regressors for ARIMA.

The most extensive feature extraction was performed for the ML algorithms that we use to create a single model from data regarding all available time series. In this case, we use all the features that we defined for the purpose of ML models working on univariate time series data. We also construct several additional features using indicators commonly applied in the field of technical analysis of financial time series data. For instance, we compute the rate-of-change indicator values with one and seven day lags. In addition to the features describing behaviour of individual time series, we include selected characteristics of the corresponding products and product categories, e.g., an encoded ID, a number of different products in the category, and a product average price.

The representation of time series derived from the PoS transactions can be further combined with the data from the delivery sub-system, as well as the PoS and product meta-data. For example, we join the product nutrition data and information about the number of delivered products with the features extracted for the considered ML algorithms. We also add information about global or PoS-specific sales of a given product group and information about the availability of other products in the PoS. As a result, we obtain a high dimensional vector representation of each time window of series from our data. This representation is suitable for training various ML models.

4.1 Evaluated Machine Learning Algorithms

The last know value is a reasonably good naive approach for short-term regression problems, usually used as a baseline forecast. Therefore, we considered a *naive* prediction model - that refers to the observed demand (i.e., qty of purchased products) during the week preceding the evaluated period. Another popular approach in the FMCG market is the *last year* sales. The main reason behind this is related to the seasonality in the consumer market.

ARIMA (autoregressive integrated moving average) is widely applicable in the field of time series forecasting - known to be robust and efficient in short-term time series forecasting, e.g., appeared to be successful in predicting AWS cloud spot machine prices [7]. The *BATS* model is enhancing ARIMA with exponential smoothing and Box-Cox transformation for dealing with non-linear data and is capable of modeling complex seasonality.

A popular memory-based algorithm that is often used for both uni- and multivariate time series forecasting is *knn* [12]. In this approach, to create a forecast for a given time window, k most similar time windows from the historical data are found, and their targets are averaged. Another used model is random forest [18] (*rf*), which is an ensemble of decision trees that interpolate random bootstrap samples of training data [19]. When making predictions, outputs of individual trees are averaged with weights corresponding to their performance estimated using out-of-bag portions of training data.

Two examples of ML models that, in our experiments, were trained on combined data from all time series are *glmn* (elastic net regression) [9], and XGBoost (*xgbt*) [5,20]. The first one is a generalized linear model that combines the L_1 (lasso) and L_2 (ridge) penalties in the regularization term. The second is a regularized gradient boosting method that uses decision trees as the base predictors.

5   Experimental Study

5.1   Data Set

Before we can construct any prediction model, we need to come up with an appropriate representation of available data. In our case, the data needs to be transformed from a relational representation describing individual events extracted form several Supply Chain Management (SCM) sub-systems, to a representation that reflects relevant characteristics and variability of time series corresponding to combinations of points-of-sale and products. In Table 1, we present the most relevant data sources from the point of view of the investigated tasks.

Table 1. Structure of the four main data sources.

Point-of-sell sensors	Transaction and delivery sub-systems	Point-of-sell metadata	Product descriptions
- Temperature - Connectivity status - Tray-weight	- Sold products no. - Delivered products no. - Unsold products no	- Location (city, address) - Est. number of employees in surrounding offices - Company name	- Product categories - Ingredients - Nutrition data

The time series were constructed based on historical transactions of FitBoxY products offered at each vending machine (aggregated daily). If there were no transactions related to a particular product in a PoS (vending machine or location depending on data set) during a selected day, data were padded with zero. High product rotation and a relatively narrow stack at each PoS cause that many time series contain a large number of zero values. If we consider all types of products at any given time, the average daily sales for a product at a PoS is 0.0831, whereas the averaged standard deviation of sales equals 0.3990866. For this reason, we present the prediction results for all series (marked as *all data*) and for a more interesting subset of series filtered due to the low standard deviation, i.e., without those series with many zeros (marked as *filtered*). In data after filtration, the mean value and the standard deviation (averaged for all series) are equal to 0.3207494 and 0.7338199, respectively.

Furthermore, we constructed two additional dimensions basing on two different PoS interpretations. The first was based on identifiable vending machines basing on serial number of equipment. In such a case, if a given machine was replaced in a location, there is a new time series in data. We mark this data as *Vending Machines* in Tables 2 and 3. The second interpretation assumes prediction of demand in each office location basing, e.g., on address data, company name, floor, etc. We mark this data as *Office Locations*. If in a particular location are operating two vending machines, in the case of *Vending Machines* data, we have two separate time series, whereas for *Office Locations*, only one.

The analyzed data are limited to the period starting May 2017 (the very beginning of the FitBoxY operations) and ending early 2020. Avoiding the COVID-19 pandemic period was necessary for the proper evaluation of univariate models, for which long gaps in series (e.g., due to lock-downs) would enforce data imputation, resulting in high uncertainty of predictions. Furthermore, this data better reflect the expected post-pandemic reality. Hence, the test data refer to the last 14 weeks before lock-downs, i.e., November 16, 2019–March 1, 2020.

5.2   Results

Experimental analysis was performed independently on all 4 data sets (cf. Sect. 5.1) and selected machine learning algorithms as described below. For every bi-weekly test period, starting from 2019-11-16 to 2019-11-30 and ending on 2020-02-15 to 2020-02-29, the models were trained on the entire historical data (i.e., prior to the test period). Thereafter, daily sales prediction was performed for each time series for the consecutive 14 days included in the given test window. Then, the sliding time window was moved one week forward, the training period was extended (i.e., when performing sales prediction for the next 14 days starting on, e.g., 2020-02-02, the training period covered all data prior to this date), and the above procedure was applied iteratively for the remaining test windows.

Table 2 presents the evaluation results of the daily sales prediction calculated with root mean square error (RMSE), micro-averaged for all the examined periods and time series. There are two different prediction horizons examined.

Table 2. RMSE of daily demand predictions in one- and two-weeks horizons.

Model	Horizon (days)	Vending machines		Office locations	
		(all data)	(filtered)	(all data)	(filtered)
naive	7	0.1657	0.6214	0.2073	0.6233
last year	7	0.3689	0.6763	0.4181	0.6977
ARIMA	7	0.1788	0.6153	0.2240	0.6173
BATS	7	0.1743	0.6099	0.2176	0.6124
knn	7	0.1747	0.6162	0.2172	0.6184
rf	7	0.1998	0.6256	0.2595	0.6280
xgbt	7	0.1638	**0.5796**	0.2004	0.5980
glmn	7	**0.1609**	0.5820	**0.2003**	**0.5864**
naive	14	0.1824	0.6796	0.2284	0.6759
last year	14	0.4102	0.7348	0.4630	0.7547
ARIMA	14	0.1939	0.6683	0.2443	0.6667
BATS	14	0.1907	0.6677	0.2391	0.6657
knn	14	0.1898	0.6723	0.2372	0.6635
rf	14	0.2146	0.6800	0.2820	0.6729
xgbt	14	0.1770	**0.6333**	0.2193	**0.6212**
glmn	14	**0.1751**	0.6374	**0.2189**	0.6258

The first of 14 days corresponds to the shelf-life of products. The second of 7 days match the median time between deliveries. We also distinguish between the results of the analysis of all series and those after excluding time series containing (almost) only zeros.

In the case of time series related to vending machines, the best performance was achieved by the elastic net regression [9] ('glmn') and XGBoost [20] ('xgbt') models. Taking into account only filtered time series, the lowest RMSE error at the level of 0.6333 was achieved by the 'xgbt' model. Another performed experiment was on the time series corresponding to the office locations, without distinguishing between devices. Therefore, some of the time series were merged, e.g., in offices where 2 or 3 vendings were operating simultaneously. It is worth noting that due to this change, the mean value of all series in the test period increased significantly from 0.0831 to 0.1020, the standard deviation changed similarly, from 0.3991 to 0.4471. Naturally, this increased the difficulty of the prediction problem for all data resulting in an increased RMSE of all models in this test scenario. In the case of filtered locations, the mean and standard deviation only slightly increased, i.e., $0.3207 \rightarrow 0.3282$ and $0.7338 \rightarrow 0.7542$, respectively. However, the additional information from merging time series (resulting in an extended history of the series) allowed the models to fit the data better and somehow compensated for the increased difficulty of the prediction problem. As a result, the RMSE of the models remained roughly the same. The results are presented in Table 2.

In Table 3, we present the evaluation of the weekly sales prediction quality. Apart from RMSE, we show the mean absolute percentage error (MAPE).

Table 3. RMSE and MAPE of weekly demand predictions.

Model	Horizon (days)	Vending machines		Office locations	
		RMSE	MAPE	RMSE	MAPE
naive	7	2.3452	101.67	2.1918	83.56
last year	7	2.7675	104.93	2.8550	106.32
ARIMA	7	2.1012	86.46	2.0440	75.53
BATS	7	2.1423	88.71	2.0768	77.05
knn	7	2.2776	85.87	2.1444	70.96
rf	7	2.0659	77.25	1.9914	67.69
xgbt	7	**1.9889**	**75.62**	**1.8086**	**52.75**
glmn	7	2.0352	80.08	1.8627	60.13

As in the case of the daily sales regression, the xgbt model achieved the best results. When predicting the sales time series for each vending machine and product, it achieves an RMSE error of 1.9889 and a MAPE error of 75.05. For the time series corresponding to office locations, the results of weekly predictions changed significantly. The RMSE of most models has improved slightly. Combined with a relatively minor change in the series characteristics during the test period (i.e., comparing to vending machine data the mean value slightly increased $2.2452 \rightarrow 2.2974$, same as standard deviation: $2.4035 \rightarrow 2.5413$), it resulted in a significant improvement in MAPE. In the case of the most effective model xgbt, it was $75.62\% \rightarrow 52.75\%$). Figure 3 shows how the error measured with MAPE varied between the test periods for all evaluated methods. It also shows that the predictions made using xgbt were consistently outperforming other algorithms.

Let us recall that as a result of incorrect expert-based estimates of the demand and too large deliveries, historically, in some months up to 30% of the products have expired. To give a proper context for the results achieved, it is worth noting that the average MAPE for demand predicted by domain experts responsible for delivery planning is 106%. As presented in Table 3, it was possible to reduce the percentage error twice as compared to the prediction prepared by experts. Experts' predictions are calculated basing on historical deliveries, and more precisely, are based on the number of products of a given type in refrigerators at a given office location immediately after delivery. In this case, to make results comparable to the experts' delivery plans, we only evaluate the weekly predictions. Moreover, the days when the ML models perform prediction are also adjusted. Namely, the predictions for a given PoS (and product) are made only for the delivery days from the corresponding test windows (mind that the delivery days may differ between locations).

A detailed analysis of errors performed for the most effective model (xgbt) shows that in each of the test periods it is possible to identify a group of time series (PoS-product pairs), for which the error obtained is relatively low. In particular, considering MAPE lower than 15%, this relates to about 5% of filtered time series, whereas for MAPE lower than 30% about 13%. However, the time

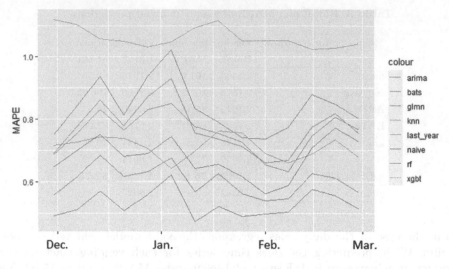

Fig. 3. Office locations

series for which the MAPE is low varies between the different test periods. For none of the tested PoS and product pairs, the MAPE error was lower than 15% during four consecutive test periods. In particular, all the time series with low prediction errors were associated with different locations. However, it was possible to identify a few products that appeared particularly frequently in the time series with a relatively low prediction error (i.e., MAPE < 30%). In particular, *Pad Thai Chicken (Lift: 3.01)*, *Sesame Beef (Lift: 2.93)*, *Thai with curry and coriander (Lift: 1.84)*, Tomato soup with basil (Lift: 1.72), and Chickpea curry soup (Lift: 1.59). The first three emphasized products appear particularly often in the time series with MAPE lower than 15%. The first two of which are relatively popular, as well. For those, the studied dependence is also the strongest, i.e., the lift of the rule *"product name"* → *"low MAPE"* is around 3.0.

In the case of time series for which we observed MAPE < 15%, the average sales volumes were significantly lower (by about 0.5 of the product) than the average sales for all series (with non-zero sales - i.e., filtered). A t-test confirmed that this difference is statistically significant with a p-value lower than 10^{-4}. However, for products with MAPE < 30%, we could not reject the same null hypothesis. Hence, we may conclude there is no statistical difference between the average sales for those products and all products.

6   Summary

The focus of our solution is on the optimization of business costs and the reduction of food waste resulting from overestimated demand at points-of-sale. We achieve this goal by embedding machine learning algorithms into the developed solution architecture. We highlighted challenges related to the specific nature of the data that we collect. In particular, we explained the need for feature extraction to handle the cold start of new products and new locations of points-of-sale. The presented experimental evaluation of several forecasting algorithms showed that by using our approach it is possible to significantly improve (by nearly 50%) over the demand estimates proposed by human operators.

The combination of IoT-driven, low-cost vending machines, data-driven supply management, and the resilient ML framework allows for optimizing costs associated with running a chain of unmanned points-of-sale. Our solution addresses the issue of food waste and the overwhelming amount of garbage produced in the world. This fact places our solution in the frame of the primary mission of modern businesses that opt to be profitable, yet responsible and sustainable.

Acknowledgment. This research was co-financed by Polish National Centre for Research and Development (NCBiR) grant no. POIR.01.01.01-00-0963/19-00 and by Polish National Science Centre (NCN) grant no. 2018/31/N/ST6/00610.

References

1. Bakhtari, A.R., Waris, M.M., Mannan, B., Sanin, C., Szczerbicki, E.: Assessing Industry 4.0 features using SWOT analysis. In: Sitek, P., Pietranik, M., Krótkiewicz, M., Srinilta, C. (eds.) ACIIDS 2020. CCIS, vol. 1178, pp. 216–225. Springer, Singapore (2020). https://doi.org/10.1007/978-981-15-3380-8_19

2. Ding, X., Chen, C., Li, C., Lim, A.: Product demand estimation for vending machines using video surveillance data: a group-lasso method. Transp. Res. Part E: Logist. Transp Rev. **150**, 102335 (2021). https://doi.org/10.1016/j.tre.2021.102335

3. Garre, A., Ruiz, M.C., Hontoria, E.: Application of machine learning to support production planning of a food industry in the context of waste generation under uncertainty. Oper. Res. Perspect. **7**, 100147 (2020). https://doi.org/10.1016/j.orp.2020.100147

4. Grzegorowski, M., Janusz, A., Lazewski, S., Swiechowski, M., Jankowska, M.: Prescriptive analytics for optimization of fMCG delivery plans. In: Proceedings of IPMU 2022 (2022)

5. Grzegorowski, M., Litwin, J., Wnuk, M., Pabis, M., Marcinowski, L.: Survival-based feature extraction - application in supply management for dispersed vending machines. IEEE Trans. Industr. Inf. (2022). https://doi.org/10.1109/TII.2022.3178547

6. Grzegorowski, M., Ślęzak, D.: On resilient feature selection: computational foundations of r-C-reducts. Inf. Sci. **499**, 25–44 (2019). https://doi.org/10.1016/j.ins.2019.05.041

7. Grzegorowski, M., Zdravevski, E., Janusz, A., Lameski, P., Apanowicz, C., Ślęzak, D.: Cost optimization for big data workloads based on dynamic scheduling and cluster-size tuning. Big Data Res. **25**, 100203 (2021). https://doi.org/10.1016/j.bdr.2021.100203

8. Janusz, A., Grzegorowski, M., Michalak, M., Wróbel, Ł, Sikora, M., Ślęzak, D.: Predicting seismic events in coal mines based on underground sensor measurements. Eng. Appl. Artif. Intell. **64**, 83–94 (2017)

9. Johnsen, T.K., Gao, J.Z.: Elastic net to forecast covid-19 cases. In: 2020 International Conference on Innovation and Intelligence for Informatics, Computing and Technologies (3ICT), pp. 1–6 (2020). https://doi.org/10.1109/3ICT51146.2020.9311968

10. Kardas, B., Piwowarczyk, M., Telec, Z., Trawiński, B., Zihisire Muke, P., Nguyen, L.T.T.: A method for building heterogeneous ensembles of regression models based on a genetic algorithm. In: Nguyen, N.T., Hoang, B.H., Huynh, C.P., Hwang, D., Trawiński, B., Vossen, G. (eds.) ICCCI 2020. LNCS (LNAI), vol. 12496, pp. 357–372. Springer, Cham (2020). https://doi.org/10.1007/978-3-030-63007-2_28

11. Malefors, C., Secondi, L., Marchetti, S., Eriksson, M.: Food waste reduction and economic savings in times of crisis: the potential of machine learning methods to plan guest attendance in swedish public catering during the covid-19 pandemic. Socio-Economic Planning Sciences, pp. 101041 (2021). https://doi.org/10.1016/j.seps.2021.101041

12. Martínez, F., Frías, M.P., Pérez, M.D., Rivera, A.J.: A methodology for applying k-nearest neighbor to time series forecasting. Artif. Intell. Rev. **52**(3), 2019–2037 (2017). https://doi.org/10.1007/s10462-017-9593-z

13. Misra, N.N., Dixit, Y., Al-Mallahi, A., Bhullar, M.S., Upadhyay, R., Martynenko, A.: IoT, big data and artificial intelligence in agriculture and food industry. IEEE Internet Things J. (2020). https://doi.org/10.1109/JIOT.2020.2998584

14. Pereira, M.M., Frazzon, E.M.: A data-driven approach to adaptive synchronization of demand and supply in omni-channel retail supply chains. Int. J. Inf. Manage. **57**, 102165 (2021). https://doi.org/10.1016/j.ijinfomgt.2020.102165

15. Semenov, V.P., Chernokulsky, V.V., Razmochaeva, N.V.: Research of artificial intelligence in the retail management problems. In: 2017 IEEE II International Conference on Control in Technical Systems (CTS), pp. 333–336 (2017). https://doi.org/10.1109/CTSYS.2017.8109560

16. Sewell, M.V.: Application of machine learning to financial time series analysis. Ph.D. thesis, University College London, UK (2017)

17. Solano, A., Duro, N., Dormido, R., González, P.: Smart vending machines in the era of internet of things. Futur. Gener. Comput. Syst. **76**, 215–220 (2017). https://doi.org/10.1016/j.future.2016.10.029

18. Tyralis, H., Papacharalampous, G.: Variable selection in time series forecasting using random forests. Algorithms **10**(4) (2017). https://doi.org/10.3390/a10040114

19. Wyner, A.J., Olson, M., Bleich, J., Mease, D.: Explaining the success of adaboost and random forests as interpolating classifiers. J. Mach. Learn. Res. **18**(1), 1558–1590 (2017)

20. Zhai, N., Yao, P., Zhou, X.: Multivariate time series forecast in industrial process based on XGBoost and GRU. In: 2020 IEEE 9th Joint International Information Technology and Artificial Intelligence Conference (ITAIC), vol. 9, pp. 1397–1400 (2020). https://doi.org/10.1109/ITAIC49862.2020.9338878

Machine Learning-Based Recommender System for Tweeting Factory in Industry 5.0 Paradigm

Dariusz Gasior[1,2(✉)] [ID], Slawomir Lasota[1], and Tomasz Kajdanowisz[1,2] [ID]

[1] DSR, Wrocław, Poland
{dariusz.gasior,tomasz.kajdanowicz}@pwr.edu.pl,
slawomir.lasota@dsr.com.pl
[2] Faculty of Information and Communication Technologies,
Wrocław University of Science and Technology, Wrocław, Poland

Abstract. This paper introduces the concept of the decision-making support system for operators of machines deployed at production sites. The architecture and basic concepts are discussed. It is indicated how the proposed solution fulfills the requirements concerning Industry 5.0 paradigm. The system also utilizes the idea of the Tweeting Factory [16] paradigm, making it easy to apply in various industry branches.

Keywords: Optimisation · Machine learning · Production

1 Introduction

To meet the Industry 5.0 [1] assumptions, the modern factories should support human operators as much as possible, taking into account their personal needs and individuality. That is why the decision-support tools acting as recommender systems seem to be one of the best solutions for such a case [2]. Having the whole production process digitalized, we may collect real-time data to provide an appropriate response for current situations. Optimizing the production process ensures a higher income for manufacturers and makes the factories more environment-friendly by reducing resource consumption (energy and materials). In this paper, we describe the production process optimization tool, which uses a recommendation engine to provide the best possible configuration of the production plant for the particular human operator. The purpose of the paper is to present the idea of the system. Thus formal details are omitted.

2 Related Works

There are many approaches to optimizing the production processes. However, most of the introduced production optimization methods apply only to the particular sectors of the industry. For example, in [3] the optimization of batik

© The Author(s), under exclusive license to Springer Nature Singapore Pte Ltd. 2022
E. Szczerbicki et al. (Eds.): ACIIDS 2022, CCIS 1716, pp. 135–146, 2022.
https://doi.org/10.1007/978-981-19-8234-7_11

production is given, and in [4] the oil and gas production is under consideration. In [5] the application of the Kalman filter and the common optimization algorithms (i.a. steepest ascent and stochastic gradient) are proposed. Nevertheless, such an approach may only be applied to the cases when the input signals may be changed during the process. In [6] authors propose to make a simulation model and perform optimization using a genetic algorithm using this proxy model.

Recently, much attention was also paid to applying machine learning methods in this area [7,8].

In [9] the artificial neural networks (ANN) and support vector machine (SVM) were used to predict the product quality in the milling process. To improve the production outcomes different optimization methods are applied including a genetic algorithm (GA), particle swarm optimization (PSO), and simulated annealing (SA). Similar approaches have been applied to optimize the gear hobbing process [10].

In [11] Authors have proposed a second-order regression model to predict the values of quality criteria in electrical discharge machining. Then they used an artificial bee colony algorithm to optimize the process parameters.

For optimizing the welding process, extreme machine learning together with the PSO algorithm has been proposed in [12].

In [13] the machine learning methods like the random forest, AdaBoost, XGBoost, and neural networks are proposed to make a digital twin for the petrochemical plant. This model is used to find the optimal parameters of the real process.

It must also be stressed that the human operator's role is not considered in all the cases above.

Contrary to the previous works, our approach is developed as a more universal one. It is possible since we use key performance indicators (KPI) like Overall Equipment Effectiveness (OEE), Quality (QBR), Effectiveness (E), and Availability (A) to evaluate the system. These indicators are widely used in the industry, and they are not sector-dependent. Moreover, taking into account Industry 5.0 requirements, our solution is also human-aware. The latter is achieved twofold. First, we take into account that the optimal process parameters may vary depending on the worker. And second, our solution is a recommendation system, thus the process parameters which are calculated and proposed by our tool will not be applied unless the operator understands and accepts them.

3   Problem Description

3.1   Production Plant as an Input-Output Decision-Making Object

Let us consider the single production plant, which is usually constituted by a single machine. For example, we can indicate press which is used to make car body shell elements. The operation of the plant may be described with some parameters, which may be divided into three groups: inputs, disturbances, and outputs, as it is depicted in Fig. 1.

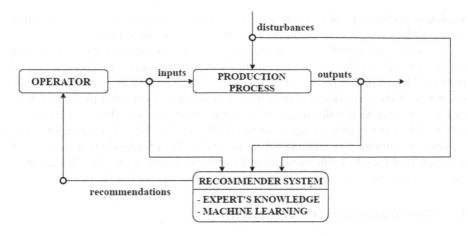

Fig. 1. The idea of the production process is supported by the recommender system.

Inputs. As inputs (or input signals), we consider all the parameters set to achieve a particular effect, usually concerning the plant's output. Usually, these parameters are placed on the machine by the human operator. The chosen values must fulfill specific requirements, which typically are due to the recipes given by the experts. Nevertheless, the recipes do not define strict values. Instead, the intervals of acceptable values are proposed. Moreover, the operator's decision affects the production's final effects, which are reflected by outputs. For the given example, we may treat the press configuration parameters such as the number of strokes per minute, the speed of the feeder, etc.

Disturbances. As disturbances, we consider all the parameters which affect the production plant and cannot be set or changed by the operator. They include environmental parameters such as air temperature, air humidity, etc., but also the parameters describing the quality of the material. Some of these parameters can be directly measured (with appropriate sensors), and some of them cannot be measured. Instead, we have some knowledge about their possible values.

Outputs. As outputs (or output signals) we consider all the parameters which depend on the inputs and/or disturbances. Examples of such parameters are the number of good quality products, the number of scraps, the total time of production, etc. All these parameters may be used to describe the performance of the production plant. Usually, the performance is measured in terms of the so-called KPI (Key Performance Indicator) [14]. Some KPIs are defined as direct values of outputs (e.g., number of good products), while the complex indices are used to reflect the production performance better. The most common is OEE (Overall Equipment Effectiveness) [15].

3.2 Problem Statement

From this perspective, we may treat the problem of choosing the proper configuration of the production plant as an optimal decision-making problem, which consists of finding such feasible values of the input parameters that the particular values of the disturbances optimize the production performance.

It is clear and worth stressing that appropriate decisions have a significant impact not only on the producer's income but also on many environment-related aspects. The higher values of KPIs, the less electric energy is consumed and the less waste of the material. Nevertheless, solving such a complex problem by the human operator is usually impossible. Thus, they base on their experience or feelings. However, it often leads to weak results. That is why developing decision-support systems for machine operators is crucial. We proposed the process optimization tool based on the recommender system, which allows for dealing with such problems effectively.

4   Recommendation Algorithm

The recommender algorithm should consider the whole system state, including machines and tools, materials, environment, and the human operator. The last element of the system is vital to make the proper recommendation.

The recommender algorithm addresses two problems:

(a) detecting and signaling the situation when the settings exceed the acceptable ranges (such a situation may take place as a result of a fault or human error),
(b) identifying situations when the change of settings may lead to an improvement in the operation of the production system.

In the case described in point (a), the recommendation mechanism is based on a rule-based system that enables inference about incorrect values of the input parameters of production. On the other hand, the second case (b) refers to the optimization module, which, using machine learning models built on historical data, tries to find alternative settings for the production process that could potentially improve its performance measured by the OEE indicator.

In other words, the system is composed of a rule-based module that allows for inference of the correctness of the production process. Based on data from sensors, the correctness of the settings made by employees is verified. In particular, exceedances of the acceptable ranges of input parameters are detected. This module is also designed to run an optimizer that will suggest setting adjustments to improve key performance indicators, particularly OEE. To achieve this, the recommendation module performs the following tasks:

(a) based on historical data, using machine learning techniques, a predictive model is built, allowing to assess of how changes in production settings will affect KPIs (such as A, E, or Q, and consequently on OEE),
(b) using the predictive model as a fitness function, the settings are optimized in the acceptable ranges to maximize the efficiency measured with selected KPIs.

The idea of this approach is given in Fig. 2.

The recommendation algorithm is implemented as a part of the process optimization tool.

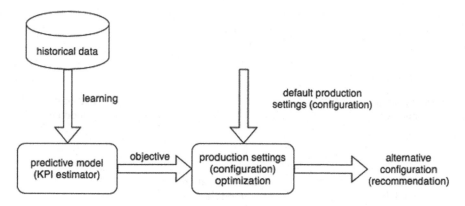

Fig. 2. The concept of the recommendation framework.

5   Architecture of the Recommender System

As it was stated in previous Sections, the production process optimization tool is designed to increase production efficiency measured by the key OEE indicator, which consists of primary KPIs such as availability, efficiency, and quality, through appropriate decision making or supporting operators' decisions. For this purpose, data on technology (from relevant IT subsystems) and the course of the production itself (from relevant automation subsystems, including sensors, actuators, and PLCs) are collected. The collected data is archived in a specially designed database. Historical data gathered in this way is used to create a current predictive model that allows estimating the possibility of improving the OEE indicator by adjusting settings. The calculated values of the input parameters of the predictive process are provided to machine operators in the form of recommendations, and the system allows for tracking the effects of their introduction on an ongoing basis. The tool integrates with the production process within the production system.

The tools consist of several interrelated modules responsible for implementing the above-described recommendation process, as shown in Fig. 3.

5.1   Data Collection Module (Acquisition)

This system element is responsible for collecting data directly from the production line, integrated automation elements (such as PLCs, sensors, and actuators), and the company's IT systems.

The element is also built based on a specially programmed PLC controller that can be configured using a web application (PlcConfigurator Web App). This part is responsible for broadcasting information about changes: process parameter values - the so-called signals (telemetry data), including input quantities, i.e., settings, as well as disturbances and output signals); system state changes, including configuration changes (adding a new tool, a new sensor, etc.).

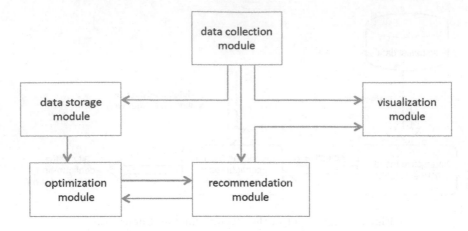

Fig. 3. The conceptual architecture of the proposed system.

Information from this module goes to the archiving module, can be tracked on an ongoing basis on appropriate operator panels, and are also the basis for determining recommendations. They are sent in the form of structured messages - the so-called tweets, a foundation for communication in Tweeting Factory [16]. The logic of this module's operation is shown in Fig. 4.

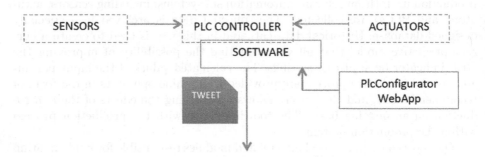

Fig. 4. The architecture of the data collection module.

5.2   Data Storage (Archiving) Module

All changes in the production process that are subject to optimization are stored in a specially prepared database. It includes elements describing the state of the production system, values of measured parameters, information on the current method of data collection, process performance results - KPI values, recommendations generated by the system, and their predicted consequences (predicted values of key performance indicators).

The main objective of this module is to achieve the correct receipt and processing of all tweets from all modules of the tool. An essential element of the processing part is the proper recognition of the state of the production system and the assignment of appropriate telemetry data to it. Based on the tweet's data, the tool automatically recognizes whether there has been a change in the system state. The logic of the module's operation is presented in Fig. 5.

Fig. 5. The logic of the data storage module.

5.3   Recommendation and Optimisation Module

The main task of these two modules is to detect situations when the settings made by the operator are correct and when a change in the production process settings can improve its efficiency measured based on the OEE indicator.

To complete these tasks, the recommendation algorithm described in Sect. 4 is implemented.

5.4   Visualisation Module

The task of the visualization module is to provide an overview of the production system if it works with the correct settings (values of input quantities) and present derived recommendations. These values can (in the initial phase) be approved by the operator and are presented to him in the form of a list of recommendations for production process parameters adjustments. User reaction is then logged (in particular, acceptance or rejection of suggestions for settings proposed by the tool). An essential element here is processing the generic recommendation generated by the recommendation module into a form that is understandable for the user and delivering it in a format that allows for further tracking.

When the effectiveness of the recommendation reaches a satisfactory effectiveness threshold, the system is switched to the autonomous mode, and the module automatically programs the PLC controller and sets the appropriate values of the input parameters of the production process by the recommendation. In this mode, its operation remains only supervised by the operator, who can turn off the automatic mode for a given recommendation and return to the manual mode at any time.

Systematic and evolutionary activation of the automatic mode for individual recommendations after they achieve a sufficiently high credibility index, as a result, will lead to the creation of a self-regulating - autonomous system. Achieving such a level of maturity of interactions between the recommendation system, technological lines, and machines will limit human involvement, which will result in the fact that one operator can operate more than one machine.

Thus, the recommendation should be constantly monitored to properly change the mode of interaction between the tool and the production process (from requiring approval to automatic).

5.5   Recommendation Monitoring

Recommendations regarding the settings of the production process are monitored on an ongoing basis. In particular, it is checked how often the operators accept the indicated suggestions, and the compliance of the estimated production efficiency with the measured one is also checked. The automatic mode is turned on if the effectiveness of determining the recommendations at a given level is achieved. Then the settings go directly to the actuators via the PLC controller. In the case when the effectiveness of the automatically made settings drops below the given threshold (the operator cancels the settings too often or the predicted OEE value differs too much from the actual one), the system returns to the mode in which it is necessary to approve the recommended settings manually.

6   Experiments

6.1   Applied Methods

In order to build a predictive model for the KPIs (which we refer to as the KPI estimator) we proposed the following approaches: gradient boosting [17], strochastic gradient descent [18], neural networks [19], Monte Carlo Dropout (MC Dropout) [20] and Bayesian Neural Networks [21].

For optimization step we proposed greedy algorithm (hill climbing) [22], Bayesian optimization [23] and the gradient method [24].

6.2   Experiment Methodolody

To verify the proposed methods, we conducted experiments for 4 production processes. For each production process, the historical data has been divided into three sets: a training set, a validation set, and a test set. The first set was used to train the predictive model (KPI estimator). The second set was used to choose the best methods and their parameters. The last set was utilized for final evaluation.

The first set always had a little more than 3000 examples, while the two others had exactly 300 examples.

The experiment has been performed in two stages. First, we tried to determine the best KPI estimator. At this stage, we used the root mean square error (RMSE) to evaluate the proposed methods. We considered two cases: with one common predictive model for all production processes which was learned with all the training data merged and with individual predictive models for each process. We use the "grouped" prefix to indicate the cases in which the latter approach has been applied. The validation set has been used to determine RMSE. Each experiment has been repeated 5 times.

Then, during the second stage, we tried to find the best optimization method using the estimator that was chosen in the previous stage.

To evaluate the optimization methods the following metrics have been applied:

- effectiveness (based on the KPI estimator) - a fraction of the recommended alternative production configurations which were better than the default one,
- performance - time needed to determine the one alternative production configuration,
- correctness - the ratio of the production configuration which violated constraints.

6.3   Results

As it is seen in Fig. 6 for all production processes, the best results were obtained for the approaches based on the Gradient Boosting method with individual models for each production process. Thus, we have chosen this method for the next stage.

As you can see in Fig. 7, when we take into account the effectiveness of the optimization algorithms, the gradient method turned out to be the best. Nevertheless, all the considered algorithms achieved very good results. Only for the 4th process, the hill climbing (greedy method) has given noticeably worse results than the two others.

However, as it can be seen in Fig 8, when we consider the performance time, the gradient method and the greedy algorithm outperforms the bayesian optimization.

All the proposed algorithms have always found the feasible solution, so the correctness of the methods were 100%.

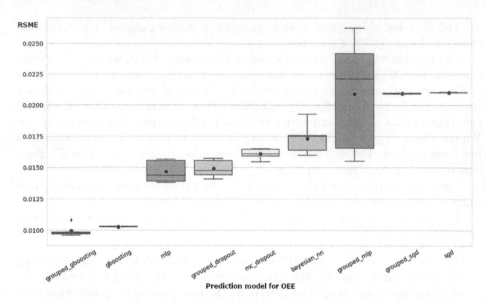

Fig. 6. Box plot of RMSE for the examined predictive models

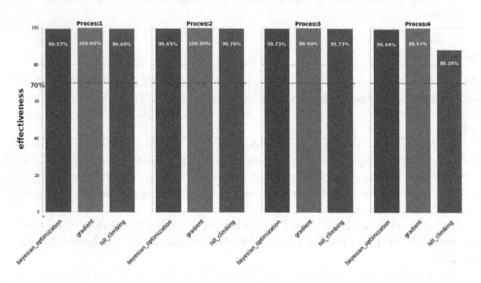

Fig. 7. The effectiveness of different optimization methods and individual processes

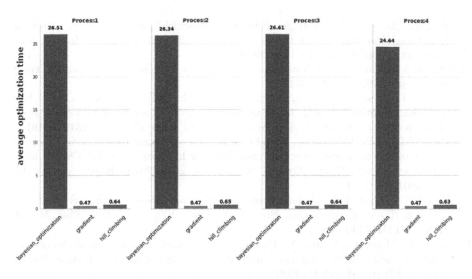

Fig. 8. The performance of different optimization methods and individual processes

7 Final Remarks

The idea of the recommender system, which supports machine operators' decision-making process, has been presented. The described system has been implemented, and the trial runs for two companies will be accomplished soon. However, the obtained initial results are auspicious.

Acknowledgements. The publication was partially supported by National Centre for Research and Development within the grant no. POIR.01.01.01–00-0900/19 "(PMSA) Production Management Smart Advisor." The system is the subject of patent application no. P.441016 in Poland.

References

1. Maddikunta, P., et al.: Industry 5.0: a survey on enabling technologies and potential applications. J. Indus. Inf. Integr. **26**, 100257 (2022)
2. Jafari, N., Azarian, M., Yu, H.: Moving from industry 4.0 to industry 5.0: what are the implications for smart logistics? Logistics **6**(2), 26 (2022)
3. Soesanti, I., Syahputra, R.: Batik production process optimization using particle swarm optimization method. J. Theor. Appl. Inf. Technol. **86**(2), 272 (2016)
4. Beggs, H. D. : Production optimization using nodal analysis (1991)
5. Wang, C., Li, G., Reynolds, A.C.: Production optimization in closed-loop reservoir management. SPE J. **14**(03), 506–523 (2009)
6. Zangl, G., Graf, T., Al-Kinani, A. : Proxy modeling in production optimization. Paper presented at the SPE Europec/EAGE Annual Conference and Exhibition, Vienna, Austria (2006)

7. Weichert, D., Link, P., Stoll, A., Rüping, S., Ihlenfeldt, S., Wrobel, S.: A review of machine learning for the optimization of production processes. Int. J. Adv. Manufact. Technol. **104** (5), 1889–1902 (2019)
8. Dogan, A., Birant, D.: Machine learning and data mining in manufacturing. Expert Syst. Appl. **166**, 114060 (2021)
9. Coppel, R., Abellan-Nebot, J.V., Siller, H.R., Rodriguez, C.A., Guedea, F.: Adaptive control optimization in micro-milling of hardened steels-evaluation of optimization approaches. Int. J. Adv. Manuf. Technol. **84**(9–12), 2219–2238 (2016)
10. Cao, W.D., Yan, C.P., Ding, L., Ma, Y.F.: A continuous optimization decision making of process parameters in high-speed gear hobbing using IBPNN/DE algorithm. Int. J. Adv. Manuf. Technol. **85**(9), 2657–2667 (2015). https://doi.org/10.1007/s00170-015-8114-y
11. Rao, R.V., Pawar, P.J.: Modelling and optimization of process parameters of wire electrical discharge machining. Proc. Inst. Mech. Eng. Part B: J. Eng. Manuf. **223**(11), 1431–1440 (2009)
12. Rong, Y., Zhang, G., Chang, Y., Huang, Y.: Integrated optimization model of laser brazing by extreme learning machine and genetic algorithm. Int. J. Adv. Manuf. Technol. **87**(9), 2943–2950 (2006)
13. Min, Q., Lu, Y., Liu, Z., Su, C., Wang, B.: Machine learning based digital twin framework for production optimization in petrochemical industry. Int. J. Inf. Manage. **49**, 502–519 (2019)
14. Varisco, M., Johnsson, C., Mejvik, J., Schiraldi, M.M., Zhu, L.: KPIs for Manufacturing Operations Management: driving the ISO22400 standard towards practical applicability. IFAC-PapersOnLine **51**(11), 7–12 (2018)
15. Ng Corrales, L.D.C., Lambán, M.P., Hernandez Korner, M.E., Royo, J.: Overall equipment effectiveness: systematic literature review and overview of different approaches. Appl. Sci. **10**(18), 6469 (2020)
16. Lennartson, B., Bengtsson, K., Wigström, O., Riazi, S.: Modeling and optimization of hybrid systems for the tweeting factory. IEEE Trans. Autom. Sci. Eng. **13**(1), 191–205 (2015)
17. Natekin, A., Knoll, A.: Gradient boosting machines, a tutorial. Frontiers Neurorobot. **7**, 21 (2013)
18. Amari, S.I.: Backpropagation and stochastic gradient descent method. Neurocomputing **5**(4–5), 185–196 (1993)
19. Dongare, A.D., Kharde, R.R., Kachare, A.D.: Introduction to artificial neural network. Int. J. Eng. Innov. Technol. (IJEIT) **2**(1), 189–194 (2012)
20. Gal, Y., Ghahramani, Z.: Dropout as a Bayesian approximation: representing model uncertainty in deep learning. In: International Conference on Machine Learning, pp. 1050–1059 (2016)
21. Kononenko, I.: Bayesian neural networks. Biol. Cybern. **61**(5), 361–370 (1989)
22. Vince, A.: A framework for the greedy algorithm. Discret. Appl. Math. **121**(1–3), 247–260 (2002)
23. Frazier, P.I.: Bayesian optimization. In: Recent advances in optimization and modeling of contemporary problems, Informs, pp. 255–278 (2018)
24. Boyd, S., Vandenberghe, L.: Convex optimization. Cambridge University Press (2004)

Automated Late Fusion of Low Level Descriptors for Feature Extraction and Texture Classification Using Data Augmentation

Mohamed Hazgui[1]([✉]) [iD], Haythem Ghazouani[1,2] [iD], and Walid Barhoumi[1,2] [iD]

[1] Université de Tunis El Manar, Institut Supérieur d'Informatique, Research Team on Intelligent Systems in Imaging and Artificial Vision (SIIVA), LR16ES06 Laboratoire de recherche en Informatique, Modélisation et Traitement de l'Information et de la Connaissance (LIMTIC), 2 Rue Abou Rayhane Bayrouni, 2080 Ariana, Tunisia
`mohamed.hazgui@fst.utm.tn`, `haythem.ghazouani@enicar.u-carthage.tn`,
`walid.barhoumi@enicarthage.rnu.tn`
[2] Université de Carthage, Ecole Nationale d'Ingénieurs de Carthage,
45 Rue des Entrepreneurs, 2035 Tunis-Carthage, Tunisia

Abstract. Feature extraction is an important task for texture image classification. Many descriptors have been proposed in the literature in order to describe textured images locally as well as globally. Researchers' interpretations differ on the effectiveness of these descriptors depending on the field of application, but no one can deny their complementarity. However, fusing different descriptors is not always easy, notably because of their different types (local vs. global, dense vs. sparse ...) and the heterogeneity of the generated features. In this work, we propose to use genetic programming to generate and fuse two different texture classifiers based respectively on HOG and uniform LBP descriptors. Indeed, the proposed method includes a late fusion and data augmentation process in order to combine the classifier's results while using small set of training data. The suggested method benefits from the different information captured by both descriptors while being robust to rotation changes. The performance of the proposed method has been validated on four challenging datasets including different variations. Results show that the proposed method significantly outperforms other low-level methods as well as GP-based methods intended for texture description and classification.

Keywords: Texture classification · Descriptors · Feature extraction · Genetic programming · Late fusion

1 Introduction

Image classification is a fundamental task in computer vision and pattern recognition. It consists of categorizing images into predefined groups based on their content and can be applied to a wide range of applications such as pedestrian

© The Author(s), under exclusive license to Springer Nature Singapore Pte Ltd. 2022
E. Szczerbicki et al. (Eds.): ACIIDS 2022, CCIS 1716, pp. 147–162, 2022.
https://doi.org/10.1007/978-981-19-8234-7_12

detection, face recognition and medical imaging [3, 4, 13, 16]. However, describing data accurately can be very challenging due to the different variations an image can undergo. In fact, the success in performing a good classification depends on the quality of the extracted features. Indeed, the extraction of representative information is a crucial step within the framework of image classification. Overall, there are two types of features that can be extracted from an image, i.e. global features and local features. The former (global features) refer to image patterns that can describe an image as a whole and do not discriminate between background and foreground. The latter (local features) aim to identify image patterns that are distinct from their adjacent neighborhood. Local features are the most used in object and image recognition tasks due to their ability to detect intra-class variation. Texture is one of the most used local features. It is a very complex pattern that can hold representative information about an image. Therefore, texture extraction and classification has always attracted attention and many state-of-the-art methods have been developed in order to analyze and describe textured images efficiently. They include well-known descriptors such as Local Binary Patterns (LBP) [26], Histogram of Oriented Gradients (HOG) [8], Scale Invariant Feature Transform (SIFT) [24] and Grey-Level Cooccurrence Matrix (GLCM) [17]. LBP and its variants such as uLBP are mostly used for texture description due to their ability to extract features locally. HOG in the other hand, is used for edge and shape description and works by generating histograms that describe gradient orientations in an image or a patch. Some studies tried to adapt HOG in order to perform texture description and classification [10]. Indeed, even if HOG is usually used on an image as a whole, it can also be adapted to work on local patches. However, these methods are designed for specific tasks and therefore, depend on domain knowledge which can be costly.

In order to reduce human intervention, many studies focused on Evolutionary Computation (EC) and particularly Genetic Programming (GP) [18]. Indeed, GP is based on an evolutionary trial and error process. Thus, it is known to be very efficient when it comes to finding the best solution among a set of possible outcomes. GP-based methods showed promising results when applied on feature extraction and image classification tasks. However they have always dealt with texture as a local feature ignoring the fact that it can also be described in a global way. In fact, considering one type of feature can result in a loss of performance when dealing with complex texture classification tasks. Indeed, images can be subject to many transformations such as rotation, scale and illumination. These changes result in a loss of information that can impact the feature extraction process. Thus, considering different types of features is important in order to perform an accurate classification. Indeed, features like local patterns are effective for finding similar images in the same class while edges and corners are more important for capturing distinctive information from objects in an image. In addition, even if descriptors as HOG and LBP are often used when dealing with image processing tasks, they are used separately in the most cases. Some methods tried to fuse both but encountered difficulties dealing with their output since they work differently [6]. This work tries to deal with these issues by taking advantage of image descriptors that capture information differently to perform feature extraction and classification. The developed method benefits from GP in order to evolve different types of classifiers that are combined lately using a data augmentation and fusion process. This allows the proposed method to train using a limited number of instances. The whole process is fully automated, since it does not require human intervention and can deal with challenging transformations such as scale, rotation and illumination.

The remainder of this paper is structured as follows. A brief review about the related work is presented in Sect. 2. The proposed method is discussed in Sect. 3. The validation datasets, parameter settings and results are investigated in Sect. 4. The conclusion and some ideas for future work are discussed in Sect. 5.

2   Related Work

A brief review on methods that tried to combine different types of features using GP-based methods designed for feature extraction and classification is provided in this section. Since GP can reduce human intervention and increase performance in many image-related tasks, many studies tried to benefit from its adaptability in order to develop effective methods for texture extraction and classification.

In [1], El Sahaf proposed a two-tier tree-based architecture for texture classification. The method used different statistical and mathematical operators in order to perform binary image classification on different datasets. It showed good results dealing with different image classification tasks but did not handle well image transformations. In [2], El Sahaf et al. combined LBP with GP in order to develop an image descriptor that can generate a prominent set of features used lately for classification. This method showed good results on challenging datasets but did not handle well transformations such as rotation. Inspired from the previously mentioned studies, Lensen et al. [23] developed an image classifier that combines HOG and GP in order to perform feature extraction and image classification simultaneously. The suggested method took advantage of Al Sahaf's two tier architecture and added a construction tier in order to generate a reliable set of feature and thus, improve classification results. In [14], authors proposed a GP-based descriptor that deals with scale and rotation changes in a different way. Their method extracts statistical information on edge pixels' arrangement and orientation in a specific local region. The idea is to automatically train a GP descriptor by applying elementary operations on a proposed operator (namely local edge signature) elements at a set of keypoints. However, all these methods considered only one type of feature i.e. global or local. In [6], Bi et al. developed a GP-based method that combines different descriptors in order to extract discriminative image features for both image description and classification. This method showed good results and a good adaptation level when tested on different datasets including texture. In [15] Ghazouani et al. tried to combine SIFT and LBP descriptors with a GP-based descriptor in order to perform feature extraction. This method showed good results and invariance against scale and rotation changes. In [18], Hazgui et al. assessed the method's robustness using a limited number of instances proving its ability to perform well even when compared with recent CNN methods. However, their work only relied on one way of capturing features and needed an external classifier resulting in an accuracy drop for some cases. Indeed, some classifiers are better suited than others depending on the generated features and tested datasets. Lately in [19], Hazgui et al. presented an early fusion GP-based method of HOG and LBP in order to perform texture classification using a small number of instances. This method showed good robustness on image transformations such as rotation, illumination and scale. The three aforementioned methods [6,15,19] managed to combine different types of descriptors proving the importance of combining different ways of capturing information in order to perform image description and classification. They also operated automatically, meaning that they managed to reduce human intervention. However, in order to adapt to the GP architecture, they only relied on an early fusion process that modifies the descriptors output and did not investigate the effects of a late fusion process that can combine different types of features without loosing information generated by one or another.

To summarize, most of the GP-based methods are designed to work on a reduced search space reducing computational cost. Even if they show good results proving they can deal with various image transformations, most mentioned methods benefit only from one type of feature (i.e. local patterns, edges, corners ...). Some GP-methods dealt with this problem by combining different descriptors that can prove complementary for feature extraction. However they mostly use early fusion techniques requiring the modification of output vectors in addition of complex feature selection approaches to perform classification. Differently, this work proposes a GP-based method for fully automated texture feature extraction and image classification. The proposed method takes advantage of different types of features using a late fusion process in order to combine uniform LBP and HOG descriptors. It works on detected patches of an image that are thereafter fed to a GP process in order to extract high level features. A robust image classifier that can handle transformations such as rotation, scale and illumination is then evolved The reduction of the search space leads automatically to a reduction of the computational cost. It also includes a data augmentation process that allows the evolved program to work effectively even when trained on a limited number of instances. In the next section, the suggested method will be detailed.

3   Proposed Method

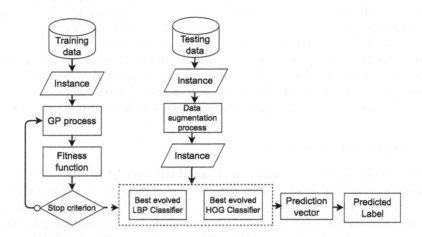

Fig. 1. Flowchart of the proposed method for classifying texture images.

The proposed method runs through a number of steps in order to perform feature extraction and classification simultaneously. This section discusses the workflow of every step. It also describes the structure of the tree-based program evolved by the GP process. The function set, terminal set as well as the late fusion and data augmentation processes are also discussed herein.

3.1   Overview of the Texture Classification Process

Fig. 1 shows the overall flowchart of the proposed method. First, the training data is fed to the GP process in order to generate a set of classifiers. The best performing programs are assessed using the fitness function. The evaluation process used in our case is the proportion of correctly classified instances to the total number of instances. Indeed, accuracy is an evaluation metric that is usually used to assess a classifier's performance. It measures the ability of a method to predict labels correctly and thus, its ability to generalize on actual unseen data. Accuracy is calculated by dividing the number of correctly predicted labels by the total number of instances as shown in Eq. (1) where TP = True positive, FP = False positive, TN = True negative and FN = False negative.

$$Accuracy = \frac{TP + TN}{TP + TN + FP + FN}, \tag{1}$$

Therefore, an ideal program will have an ideal fitness value of n corresponding to the total number of training instances. The minimum value is 0 representing the worst possible outcome (if the program does not classify any image correctly). When the stop criterion is met, the best evolved LBP-based classifier as well as the best HOG-based classifier are returned automatically in order to start the testing phase. The GP classifier, which is based on a tree structure is discussed in the next subsection. During the test phase, the remaining instances are used in order to predict a class label. Every instance is rotated three times. A vector including eight values corresponding to the prediction for every instance is generated by both classifiers. A voting process is then performed in order to select the majority predicted class. If the number of negative and positive predictions are equal , the decision of the best performing classifier during the training phase is kept. All the details concerning the classification method used by the GP programs as well as the late fusion approach are discussed later.

3.2   Program Architecture

The program structure is an extension of the HLGP (HOG-LBP GP) [19] method and benefits from the same multi-layer GP-Tree architecture. Indeed, the proposed structure can achieve patch detection, feature extraction/construction as well as classification simultaneously. Figure 2 shows an example of an evolved program where the operators are the internal nodes and the terminals are the leaf nodes. The tree represents a binary classifier and is evaluated in a bottom-up manner producing a single value as output. If the value is lower than 0, the instance is associated to the negative class and if it is greater, it is considered as a positive class. Since the program is inspired from HLGP, it also includes three layers: the Patch Detection layer, the Texture Feature Extraction layer and the Classification layer. The bottom layer (Patch Detection) includes three functions that can extract rectangular regions from an image working directly on raw pixel data. It takes three values as input i.e. a two dimensional array representing pixel values of the input image, a pair of coordinates (x, y) of the upper left corner pixel of a region and the size of a rectangular patch formed by a pair of values (width, height). The GP program is designed to optimize these parameters automatically in order to generate the optimal set of features used lately for classification. The middle layer (Texture Feature Extraction) allows the program to perform feature extraction efficiently. The main contribution compared to HLGP is the descriptor node that allows the program to use different

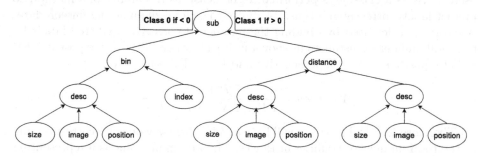

Fig. 2. Structure of the proposed GP structure for classifying texture images.

descriptors independently. In fact, this function replaces the HOG and uLBP descriptors. In every GP process, this node takes an image as input and generates a histogram as output. The histogram is composed of 8 bins for HOG and 10 bins for uniform LBP. Indeed, the first descriptor produces an 8 bin histogram capturing gradient orientations of an image. The latter, however, generates a feature vector composed of $p + 2$ patterns where p is the number of considered neighboring pixels (8 in our case).

In every learning phase, a set of programs using the uLBP node and another set with the HOG node are generated. At the end of the evolutionary process, one classifier of each type is returned. Other functions included in this layer are the "index" and "bin" nodes that can be combined to extract a particular value of a feature vector using its position in the histogram. The "distance" node calculates the euclidean distance between two generated histograms, $\vec{X}$ and $\vec{Y}$. Once the extraction and construction processes performed, the values are fed to the upper layer for classification. This layer assigns a class label to the input image after comparing the generated value with a predefined threshold. In our case, a threshold of 0 is chosen in order to discriminate instances from different categories. Indeed, since the program is performing binary classification, samples with a negative output are assigned to the negative class while samples with a positive output are assigned to the other class. It includes the four arithmetic operators "sub" $(-)$, "add" $(+)$, "mul" $(\times)$ and "div" $(/)$. They take two arguments as input and return a single output which can be fed as input to the parent node. The "div" operator is protected to avoid the "division by zero" problem, by returning zero whenever the denominator is equal to zero. With this architecture, every evolved program can detect important patches without the need to process images in a pixel by pixel procedure. Indeed, *position* and *size* nodes allow the GP-tree to only select prominent regions where informative features are detected. Lately, the"descriptor" node allows the program to extract different types of features such as local patterns, edges and corners generating a low dimensional vector. Finally, only important information is kept using the *bin* and *index* functions in order to perform classification. An in-depth analysis of the proposed HOG and uLBP fusion is provided in the next subsection.

3.3   Data Augmentation and Late Fusion Process

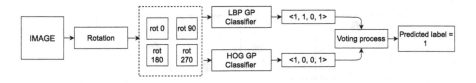

Fig. 3. Flowchart of the proposed data augmentation and late fusion process.

The proposed fusion process takes advantage of both uLBP and HOG descriptors in order to predict class labels accurately. Indeed, the adopted process combines the benefits of different features which can improve performance. The main difference from the early fusion mechanism used in HLGP is that this process uses every evolved descriptor independently as shown in Fig. 3. Since HOG and LBP capture information differently, it is always hard to generate a unique feature vector. In addition, when the early fusion process is performed in order to combine both descriptors, dimensionality problems always arise. Indeed, since LBP generates vectors composed of 256 bins, it is impossible to select the most informative features using only the *index* function implemented in our GP architecture. To overcome this problem, the proposed GP process returns two classifiers. The first one uses HOG as a descriptor while the second is based on uLBP. Indeed, Uniform LBP generates a relatively low dimensional feature vector composed only of ten bins. It is also robust to image transformations and can capture additional patterns. In the prediction phase, a data augmentation process is performed. During this process, every instance is rotated three times by a 90° angle. The number of rotations was chosen using a trial and errorexperiment where different numbers were tested. Results show that the best accuracy is recorded when the image is rotated three times. This is mainly due to the fact that the program has the possibility to access a maximum number of regions in an image. Increasing the number further does not improve results and can only bias the voting process and increase the computational time. Different experiments have been conducted where a number of rotation angles were used to find the optimal set for the augmentation task. In the first and second experiments, only two angles were used i.e. (0°,45°) and (0°,90°). In the third, fourth and fifth experiments, the number of rotation angles was increased by one for every experiment: three values for E3 i.e. (0°, 90°, 180°), four for E4 (0°, 90°, 180°, 270°), five for E5 (0°, 45°, 90°, 180°, 225°).

The generated images are then fed to every classifier for prediction. Rotated images can include additional information for GP since detected patches change location with every rotation as shown in Fig. 4. The output is a vector composed of eight bins representing the value of each prediction. As mentioned earlier, positive labels are associated to 1 while negative ones are associated to 0. Finally a voting process is started, where the majoritylabel is selected as the classifier's prediction. If the number of positive and negative values are equal, the prediction from the classifier with the best learning rate during the training phase is selected.

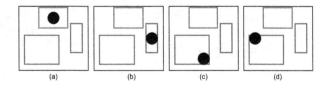

Fig. 4. Illustration of image rotations: (a) 0°, (b) 90°, (c) 180°, (d) 270° .

To summarize briefly, the proposed method combines a set of functions and arithmetic operators in order to automatically evolve a program that takes an image as input and predicts its label accurately. In fact, it evolves two classifiers. The first captures information about edges and corners while the second benefits from local patterns. This ensures robustness against scale, illumination and rotation. One difficult task is the need of labeled data in order to improve a classifier's performance. For this purpose, a data augmentation and voting process is introduced. Such a process achieves two objectives: the first is the combination of two different descriptors without the need to concatenate their output or to include a complex selection approach, and the second is the ability to use a limited number of instances for training. Indeed, the problem of a limited number of instances is always faced when dealing with texture classification tasks, notably within the framework of medical imaging and remote sensing. Generating new instances decreases the program's dependency on a large amount of data.

4   Experimental Study

Realized experiments are highlighted in this section. Details about used datasets, performance metrics, parameter settings and results are discussed.

4.1   Datasets and Parameter Settings

The performance of the proposed method is evaluated using four collections of images. These collections were carefully chosen from different challenging datasets specially intended for texture-related applications. They include various image transformations such as illumination, scale and rotation. Since the proposed method aims at dealing with binary image classification, every group is formed by selecting two classes with high similarity from the original dataset as shown in Fig. 5. Each collection is then split into a training and a test set where 15 images are used for training while the rest are used as unseen data. The main objective behind using only 15 instances from every class is to investigate the robustness of the proposed method when dealing with a low number of training samples. Textures 1 and 2 are composed of instances from the KTH-TIPS database [25]. It is an extension of the CuReT database [9] and is composed of 10 classes of 81 instances each. Images from this dataset are of dimensions 200×200 and vary in illumination and scale. Texture 3 is composed of instances of KTH-TIPS2a which is composed of 11 classes divided into four subclasses of 108 samples each that also vary in illumination and scale. Texture 4 is composed of samples chosen from the DTD database [7]. It includes 5640 texture images divided into 47 classes inspired by human perception. There are 120 images for each category with sizes ranging between 300×300 pixels and 640×640 pixels. Thus, the instances from DTD are cropped and normalized before processing.

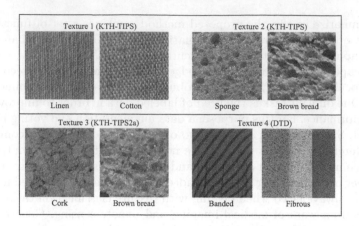

Fig. 5. Samples from the four investigated datasets used for binary classification.

Finding the best hyperparameters for a genetic process is always a difficult task. In order to solve this problem, we used an optimization algorithm known as Grid Search [22]. This tuning technique aims at finding the optimal combination of parameters from a given set of different parameters. First, a group of parameters is initialized in order to evaluate the performance of a generated classifier with different combinations of values. A number of experiments are then performed where a classifier's accuracy is assessed using different values from the search space. The optimal numbers for crossover rate, mutation rate, tree depth, population size and tournament size are finally extracted from the best performing classifier. The "Tournament" selection type was used in order to maintain the genetic diversity. Using the Grid Search algorithm we tested 256 hyperparameter combinations of Crossover/Mutation values, tournament size, tree depth and population size. The optimal parameters used during the GP process are as follows: the program tree depth varies between 4 and 6. The population size is set to 200 with a mutation rate of 20% and a crossover rate of 80%. The maximum number of generations is set to 50 in order to reduce the computation time while avoiding fast convergence. For each dataset, the test is run 10 times independently with a new population of programs. After 50 generations, the best program is tested on unseen data to evaluate its performance. Since the proposed method is evaluated using 15 instances for every class, the maximum fitness value is 30. Indeed, selecting an optimal number of iterations is usually a trial and error process. For our case, different settings have been tested and results proved that a higher number than 50 does not improve the learning rate further. It is also worth noting that the experiments have been executed on a PC with Ubuntu 20.04 LTS as operating system, an Intel i5-10400F CPU @ 4.30 GHz as a processor and 16G of memory. The measured time in our experiments being the CPU time and not the wall-clock time.

Table 1. Comparison of uLBP+HOG-GP with low-level methods.

	DT [29]	GNB [28]	1NN [21]	MLP [12]	RF [27]	SVM [31]
Texture 1 (uLBP+HOG-GP 88.5 ± 3.1)						
GLCM [17]	58.3 +	87.1 +	79.5 +	77.8 +	77.9 =	80.3 +
HIST	76.9 +	87.1 +	75.8 +	76.3 +	83.3 +	78.0 +
HOG [8]	82.5 +	75.7 +	78.0 +	83.7 +	86.1 +	84.0 +
LBP [26]	66.5 +	67.4 +	56.0 +	58.3 +	69.3 +	59.0 +
uLBP [26]	41.6 +	50.7 +	53.0 +	51.5 +	52.2 +	52.2 +
Texture 2 (uLBP+HOG-GP 90.1 ± 6.4)						
GLCM [17]	79.4 +	68.1 +	65.9 +	74.9 +	76.1 +	75.7 +
HIST	80.3 +	84.0 +	86.3 +	84.3 +	83.3 +	72.7 +
HOG [8]	73.5 +	88.6 +	84.8 +	81.4 +	80.5 +	90.0 +
LBP [26]	82.5 +	81.8 +	97.7 +	69.7 +	90.8 +	97.7 +
uLBP [26]	93.9 +	86.3 +	98.4 −	79.6 +	98.4 −	**98.5 −**
Texture 3 (uLBP+HOG-GP 93.4 ± 5.4)						
GLCM [17]	80.9 +	85.2 +	61.51 +	54.5 +	86.3 +	59.1 +
HIST	74.7 +	66.6 +	76.3 +	67.5 +	76.2 +	71.7 +
HOG [8]	44.8 +	49.2 +	48.1 +	45.1 +	48.7 +	50.9 +
LBP [26]	69.6 +	61.7 +	55.8 +	49.1 +	69.6 +	89.8 =
uLBP [26]	68.7 +	50.4 +	58.0 +	48.6 +	53.7 +	78.9 +
Texture 4 (uLBP+HOG-GP 91.4 ± 1.7)						
GLCM [17]	87.1 +	85.7 +	84.2 +	90.8 +	87.2 +	85.7 +
HIST	75.3 +	63.3 +	60.0 +	64.6 +	76.4 +	75.2 +
HOG [26]	85.2 +	81.4 +	90.0 +	87.7		86.0 +	90.0 +
LBP [26]	82.3 +	88.1 +	83.8 +	86.1 +	87.9 +	85.7 +
uLBP [26]	80.3 +	81.9 +	84.2 +	83.3 +	84.5 +	85.7 +

4.2 Results and Discussion

In order to examine its performance, the proposed method is compared to ten GP-based and 30 non-GP methods. The 30 non-GP methods were implemented using the Scikit-learn Python package and are based on six commonly used machine learning classifiers combined with five existing image feature extraction methods. In each experiment, image features are extracted by a descriptor and used to train a classifier. The five feature extraction methods are the Grey level co-occurrence matrix (GLCM) [17], Histogram of Oriented Gradients (HOG) [8], Local Binary Patterns [26], uniform Local Binary Patterns (uLBP) [26] and Histogram (HIST) which is composed of 256 histogram features based on pixel intensities of the gray-scale image. These descriptors were combined with six state of the art classifiers i.e. Decision Tree (DT) [29], Gaussian Naive Bayes [28], k-neighrest Neighbors (KNN) [21], Multi Layer Perceptron (MLP) [12],

Random Forest [27] and non linear Support Vector Machine (SVM) with an RBF kernel [31]. It is worth noting that MLP includes 50 neurons in the hidden layer combined with a logistic sigmoid activation function and an adaptive learning rate. Results are presented in Table 2 as average accuracies and the best result for every dataset is shown in bold. The methods with a better standard deviation then the proposed methods are highlighted with positive signs .In 23 of the 30 experiments, uLBP+HOG-GP outperforms the other classification methods significantly. Indeed, using a limited number of instances can result in a great drop of performance for conventional methods. The difference reaches more than 40% in some cases such as MLP combined with HOG on Texture 3 dataset. The proposed method is only outperformed on the Texture 2 dataset by uLBP combined with DT, 1NN, RF and SVM as well as LBP combined with 1NN, RF and SVM. This is explained by the high concentration of local features in Texture 2 instances. Indeed, LBP is good at extracting local maximas and can perform well when applied on texture images with a big number of features in a certain region. It is also worth mentioning that since our method is composed of an extraction layer in addition to the classification one, it can perform well even when applied on different datasets. Indeed, the proposed method's performance on the four datasets is stable and the difference doesn't exceed 6% while other methods can show a big drop of performance such as uLBP combined with SVM (40% accuracy drop between Texture 1 and Texture 2).

Table 2. Comparison of uLBP+HOG-GP with other GP methods (Methods designated with * use different training protocol).

Dataset	Texture 1		Texture 2		Texture 3		Texture 4	
Method	Train	Test ± std	Train	Test ± std	Train	Test ± std	Train	Test ± std
Conventional GP [11]	100.0	74.3 ± 5.6	96.4	68.1 ± 7.8	98.8	56.5 ± 4.4	100.0	78.3 ± 4.6
2TGP [1]	80.0	47.3 ± 4.2	96.6	77.5 ± 4.6	83.3	51.8 ± 5.0	86.6	60.9 ± 3.7
Hist+GP	96.6	58.6 ± 8.5	96.5	66.1 ± 12.9	93.3	47.9 ± 15.2	96.6	79.5 ± 6.2
MLGP [5]	100.0	75.0 ± 6.1	93.3	78.0 ± 5.1	100.0	57.6 ± 7.4	100.0	71.4 ± 7.2
GP-GLF+ 1NN* [6]	100.0	**91.2 ± 3.5**	95.6	88.5 ± 5.2	99.1	**97.8 ± 0.7**	100.0	89.8 ± 3.4
LBP+GP	70.0	40.8 ± 15.1	77.0	50.6 ± 12.5	66.6	40.2 ± 13.2	75.6	50.4 ± 10.7
uLBP+GP	96.6	86.6 ± 4.5	100.0	88.4 ± 7.8	100.0	90.3 ± 3.4	100.0	88.0 ± 4.2
GP-HOG [23]	82.9	67.7 ± 7.5	71.6	65.2 ± 4.7	93.3	75.5 ± 6.2	86.6	76.4 ± 3.2
HOG-LBP + GP	77.6	50.2 ± 9.1	68.3	38.6 ± 16.6	84.1	67.0 ± 6.7	58.3	30.2 ± 18.2
HLGP [19]	82.6	75.2 ± 3.7	94.1	86.9 ± 6.9	94.1	82.1 ± 3.7	100.0	87.2 ± 2.5
uLBP+HOG-GP	100.0	88.5 ± 3.1	94.7	**90.1 ± 6.4**	100.0	93.4 ± 5.4	100.0	**91.4 ± 1.7**

Table 2 shows the accuracy of the proposed method compared to other GP-based methods intended for feature extraction and texture image classification. The methods are Conventional GP [11], 2TGP [1], a combination between traditional histograms + GP [5], MLGP [5], GP-GLF combined with 1NN classifier

[6], LBP and uLBP with GP, GP-HOG [23], a combination of HOG and LBP descriptors fed to a GP architecture (HOG-LBP + GP) [18] and HLGP [18]. The performance of GP-GLF was assessed using a different evaluation protocol since is uses 75% of instances for training while testing only on 25% of unseen data. Indeed, GP-GLF needs to train a classifier with a tra-train set representing 50% of overall data in order to evolve an image descriptor. All other methods were implemented using the DEAP python package and use only 15 instances for training. Results show that apart of GP-GLF that achieved 91.2% accuracy on Texture 1 and 97.8% of accuracy on Texture 4 datasets, the proposed method outperforms all mentioned methods. In fact, the difference reaches more than 40% with some classifiers such as LBP+GP. This can be explained by the ability of the GP architecture to construct and combine different high level features. In fact, the late fusion process allows the proposed method to detect intra-class and inter-class variations efficiently since it considers many types of features for classification. In addition, the data augmentation phase provides information from different regions as the image rotates. In order to assess the impact of the late fusion process, we also implemented HOG, uLBP and a traditional concatenation between HOG and LBP with our GP architecture (named HOG-LBP+GP). They are used to compare the late fusion of uniform LBP and HOG with the performance of each descriptor, independently or combined, using an early fusion process. Results show that the traditional LBP or the combination of HOG and LBP achieves low performance when fed to the same GP architecture as HLGP. This is probably due to the high dimensional feature vectors generated by the two descriptors. The early fusion process used by HLGP achieves better performance reaching 87.2% on Texture 4 dataset but is still outperformed by uLBP-HOG late fusion method which achieves 89.3%.

Since CNN methods are very popular in image classification tasks, we compared our method with two well-known CNN architectures namely Resnet [20] and VGG [30]. The two mentioned methods can perform feature extraction and image classification efficiently. However, in order to adapt VGG to binary classification, we first froze its base then modified its head to include a binary output layer with a sigmoid activation function that generates values between 0 and 1. We also performed the same steps on Resnet and modified its head to include a global average pooling layer, three dense layers (two with 1024 neurons and one including 512 neurons) combined with Relu activation function and a last output layer with a sigmoid activation function. All mentioned methods are implemented using Keras framework and compared using Texture 2 dataset. The experiment is performed using a different number of instances for training and testing. This configuration aims at assessing the robustness of every method. Indeed, we performed tests using three sets of data distributions: 15 instances for training and 66 as unseen data (20%/80%); 40 for training and 41 as unseen data (50%/50%); 66 for training and 15 as unseen data (80%/20%). All the results are presented in Fig. 6. The proposed method outperforms CNN methods when trained with 15 instances reaching an accuracy of 90.1% while VGG and Resnet achieve only 75.0% and 62.3%, respectively. However, CNN methods outperform the proposed method when trained on 50% of the instances proving the dependency of CNN

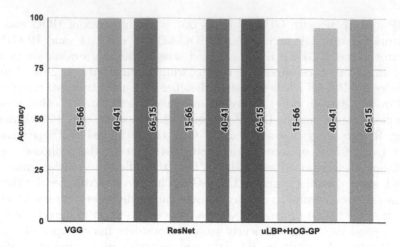

Fig. 6. Comparison with CNN methods for texture classification on the Texture 2 dataset using different number of instances for training and test.

methods on large data to perform well. Indeed, uLBP+HOG-GP achieves 95.2% accuracy when trained with 40 instances of the Texture 2 dataset. Finally, all methods achieve 100% accuracy when trained on 80% of data. It is worth noting that CNN methods always reach 100% of accuracy during the learning phase. However, accuracy drops drastically when tested on unseen data which proves that the models over-fit. Besides, it is worth noting that our method is tested 10 times using different evolved classifiers and the average accuracy is then used as a metric while CNN methods are tested only once on unseen data.

5   Conclusion

In this paper, we propose a genetic programming-based method that combines different descriptors for the purpose of texture image classification. The proposed method can operate automatically without human intervention and simultaneously perform feature extraction and classification using HOG and LBP. The main contribution of this work is the data augmentation and fusion process that combines both descriptors in order to capture texture information efficiently. In addition, the proposed method can evolve a robust classifier that can handle image transformations with a limited number of instances. To examine its performance, extensive experiments have been performed on many challenging datasets including variations such as illumination, scale and rotation. The proposed method has been compared to other state of the art methods and results show that it outperforms or achieves similar performance in most cases. Comparison with early fusion techniques shows also that the included fusion approach can prove more efficient. As future work, we plan to investigate the combination of other descriptors such as SIFT. Another important path is to adapt the GP-tree architecture in order to handle multiclass problems.

References

1. Al-Sahaf, H., Song, A., Neshatian, K., Zhang, M.: Extracting image features for classification by two-tier genetic programming. In: 2012 IEEE Congress on Evolutionary Computation. IEEE (2012). https://doi.org/10.1109/cec.2012.6256412
2. Al-Sahaf, H., Zhang, M., Johnston, M.: Binary image classification using genetic programming based on local binary patterns. In: 2013 28th International Conference on Image and Vision Computing New Zealand (IVCNZ 2013). IEEE (2013). https://doi.org/10.1109/ivcnz.2013.6727019
3. Bejaoui, H., Ghazouani, H., Barhoumi, W.: Fully automated facial expression recognition using 3D morphable model and mesh-local binary pattern. In: Blanc-Talon, J., Penne, R., Philips, W., Popescu, D., Scheunders, P. (eds.) ACIVS 2017. LNCS, vol. 10617, pp. 39–50. Springer, Cham (2017). https://doi.org/10.1007/978-3-319-70353-4_4
4. Bejaoui, H., Ghazouani, H., Barhoumi, W.: Sparse coding-based representation of LBP difference for 3D/4D facial expression recognition. Multimedia Tools Appl. **78**(16), 22773–22796 (2019). https://doi.org/10.1007/s11042-019-7632-2
5. Bi, Y., Xue, B., Zhang, M.: An automatic feature extraction approach to image classification using genetic programming. In: Sim, K., Kaufmann, P. (eds.) EvoApplications 2018. LNCS, vol. 10784, pp. 421–438. Springer, Cham (2018). https://doi.org/10.1007/978-3-319-77538-8_29
6. Bi, Y., Zhang, M., Xue, B.: Genetic programming for automatic global and local feature extraction to image classification. In: 2018 IEEE Congress on Evolutionary Computation (CEC), pp. 1–8 (2018)
7. Cimpoi, M., Maji, S., Kokkinos, I., Mohamed, S., Vedaldi, A.: Describing textures in the wild. In: Proceedings of the IEEE Conference on Computer Vision and Pattern Recognition, pp. 3606–3613 (2014)
8. Dalal, N., Triggs, B.: Histograms of oriented gradients for human detection. In: 2005 IEEE computer society conference on computer vision and pattern recognition (CVPR2005), vol. 1, pp. 886–893. IEEE (2005)
9. Dana, K.J., van Ginneken, B., Nayar, S.K., Koenderink, J.J.: Reflectance and texture of real-world surfaces. ACM Trans. Graph. **18**(1), 1–34 (1999). https://doi.org/10.1145/300776.300778
10. Demir, H.: Classification of texture images based on the histogram of oriented gradients using support vector machines. Istanbul Univ.-J. Electr. Electron. Eng. **18**(1), 90–94 (2018)
11. Evans, B., Al-Sahaf, H., Xue, B., Zhang, M.: Evolutionary deep learning: A genetic programming approach to image classification. In: 2018 IEEE Congress on Evolutionary Computation (CEC), pp. 1–6 (2018). https://doi.org/10.1109/CEC.2018.8477933
12. Gardner, M.W., Dorling, S.: Artificial neural networks (the multilayer perceptron)-a review of applications in the atmospheric sciences. Atmos. Environ. **32**(14–15), 2627–2636 (1998)
13. Ghazouani, H.: A genetic programming-based feature selection and fusion for facial expression recognition. Appl. Soft Comput. **103**, 107173 (2021)
14. Ghazouani, H., Barhoumi, W.: Genetic programming-based learning of texture classification descriptors from local edge signature. Expert Syst. Appl. **161**, 113667 (2020)
15. Ghazouani, H., Barhoumi, W., Antit, Y.: A genetic programming method for scale-invariant texture classification. In: Engineering Applications of Neural Networks Conference, pp. 593–604 (2020)

16. Ghourabi, A., Ghazouani, H., Barhoumi, W.: Driver drowsiness detection based on joint monitoring of yawning, blinking and nodding. In: International Conference on Intelligent Computer Communication and Processing, pp. 407–414 (2020)
17. Haralick, R.M., Shanmugam, K., Dinstein, I.H.: Textural features for image classification. IEEE Trans. Syst. Man Cybern. **6**, 610–621 (1973)
18. Hazgui, M., Ghazouani, H., Barhoumi, W.: Evolutionary-based generation of rotation and scale invariant texture descriptors from sift keypoints. Evolving Systems, pp. 1–13 (2021)
19. Hazgui, M., Ghazouani, H., Barhoumi, W.: Genetic programming-based fusion of HOG and LBP features for fully automated texture classification. Vis. Comput. **38**, 1–20 (2021). https://doi.org/10.1007/s00371-020-02028-8
20. He, K., Zhang, X., Ren, S., Sun, J.: Deep residual learning for image recognition. In: Proceedings of the IEEE Conference on Computer Vision and Pattern Recognition, pp. 770–778 (2016)
21. Keller, J.M., Gray, M.R., Givens, J.A.: A fuzzy k-nearest neighbor algorithm. IEEE Trans. Syst. Man Cybern. **4**, 580–585 (1985)
22. LaValle, S.M., Branicky, M.S., Lindemann, S.R.: On the relationship between classical grid search and probabilistic roadmaps. Int. J. Robot. Res. **23**(7–8), 673–692 (2004)
23. Lensen, A., Al-Sahaf, H., Zhang, M., Xue, B.: Genetic programming for region detection, feature extraction, feature construction and classification in image data. In: Heywood, M.I., McDermott, J., Castelli, M., Costa, E., Sim, K. (eds.) EuroGP 2016. LNCS, vol. 9594, pp. 51–67. Springer, Cham (2016). https://doi.org/10.1007/978-3-319-30668-1_4
24. Lowe, D.G.: Distinctive image features from scale-invariant keypoints. Int. J. Comput. Vision **60**(2), 91–110 (2004)
25. Mallikarjuna, P., Targhi, A., Fritz, M., Hayman, E., Caputo, B., Eklundh, J.O.: The kth-tips2 database (2004). http://www.nada.kth.se/cvap/databases/kth-tips/
26. Ojala, T., Pietikainen, M., Maenpaa, T.: Multiresolution gray-scale and rotation invariant texture classification with local binary patterns. IEEE Trans. Pattern Anal. Mach. Intell. **24**(7), 971–987 (2002)
27. Pal, M.: Random forest classifier for remote sensing classification. Int. J. Remote Sens. **26**(1), 217–222 (2005)
28. Rish, I., et al.: An empirical study of the Naive Bayes classifier. In: IJCAI 2001 Workshop on Empirical Methods in Artificial Intelligence, vol. 3, pp. 41–46 (2001)
29. Safavian, S.R., Landgrebe, D.: A survey of decision tree classifier methodology. IEEE Trans. Syst. Man Cybern. **21**(3), 660–674 (1991)
30. Simonyan, K., Zisserman, A.: Very deep convolutional networks for large-scale image recognition. arXiv preprint arXiv:1409.1556 (2014)
31. Suykens, J., Vandewalle, J.: Neural Process. Lett. **9**(3), 293–300 (1999). https://doi.org/10.1023/a:1018628609742

Door-to-Door Sampling Service with Drone

Tran Thi Hue[1,2]($\boxtimes$), Nguyen Quang Anh[2], Tran Van Thanh[2],
Pham Phu Manh[2], Huynh Thi Thanh Binh[2], and Nguyen Khanh Phuong[2]

[1] Banking Academy of Vietnam, Hanoi, Vietnam
[2] School of Information and Communication Technology,
Hanoi University of Science and Technology, Hanoi, Vietnam
huett@hvnh.edu.vn, anh.nq183476@sis.hust.edu.vn,
{binhht,phuongnk}@soict.hust.edu.vn

Abstract. Minimizing customer waiting time during service is the key to success of door-to-door service companies. The paper thus introduces the problem of addressing the integration of a drone into the existing sampling service system in which a set of technicians go to customers' locations to get samples and bring them back to the laboratory. We propose mathematical modeling and two meta-heuristics to solve the problem. Experiments are conducted to compare the MILP solutions with those obtained from meta-heuristics. The numerical results demonstrate the significant gain when implementing the proposed drone integration compared to the conventional technician-alone sampling service system.

Keywords: Drone · Healthcare · Routing · Synchronization

1 Introduction

In the past decade, technological advances in robotics have significantly promoted applications of drones in many fields of life, such as logistics, healthcare, disaster management, agriculture, and surveillance. In particular, the use of drones in last-mile delivery has witnessed a remarkable growth of interest in research due to the tremendous popularity of e-commerce. Drones could be used to transport packages of different sizes and limited weight in postal service. In this context, deploying drones with trucks could improve not only the service time and quality but also the operating costs and thus contribute to safeguarding the environment [9]. Moreover, drones also have been used to deliver health-related items. As of December 2021, Zipline, an American medical product delivery company, announced that they had made 225,000 drone deliveries containing more than 5 million units of vaccines and other medical products, reducing delivery emissions by 98% compared to traditional methods [1]. Drones also have been tested to transport health equipment such as surgical robots [10] and defibrillators [2] to remote areas. To our knowledge, most of the existing academic literature focuses on the use of a drone or a fleet of drones solely

© The Author(s), under exclusive license to Springer Nature Singapore Pte Ltd. 2022
E. Szczerbicki et al. (Eds.): ACIIDS 2022, CCIS 1716, pp. 163–175, 2022.
https://doi.org/10.1007/978-981-19-8234-7_13

for medical transportation rather than how to integrate them into traditional methods. The goal of this paper is to contribute to the investigation of possible integration. Hence it requires synchronization between vehicles, making the problem much more challenging.

We formally introduce and define the *Door-to-door sampling service with drone (DD-SSD)* addressing the integration of a drone into the existing sampling service system in which a set of technicians go to customers' locations to get samples and bring them back to the laboratory. The first mathematical model and meta-heuristic algorithms for the DD-SSD are our second contribution. Computational results are discussed to qualify search strategies on the quality of the meta-heuristics and the management of the Door-to-door sampling service system.

The remainder of the paper is organized as follows. Section 2 and 3 contain a detailed problem description and mathematical formulation. Section 4 provides the literature review. The details of the proposed methodologies are described in Sect. 5. Computational results are then reported and analyzed in Sect. 6, while conclusions are considered in Sect. 7.

2 Problem Definition

The sampling service system in the DD-SSD is composed of a laboratory where a set of technicians and a drone are based. A number of locations where customers are required to get samples are available. The route planning consists of two parts: (1) each technician only performs one trip that departs from the laboratory, gets samples from one or several customers, then goes back to the laboratory either with or without taken samples; (2) while the drone does either one trip or a sequence of trips, each trip starts from the laboratory to visit one or several technicians at customer locations to get samples and bring them back to the laboratory, and must not be longer than the maximum flight time L due to limited battery endurance. Thus, samples could be brought to the laboratory by either technicians or drone. The following assumptions are relevant: 1) Once arriving at a customer's location, technicians must take the sample from customers immediately (without any delay), then they may wait for the drone to arrive if needed. Neither technician nor drone may revisit any customers; 2) When a drone sortie involves a rendezvous with a technician, this must take place at the location of a customer serviced by the technician; the drone cannot reconnect with the technician at some intermediate location; 3) The drone is always assumed to be fully recharged when leaving the laboratory and remain in constant flight while on a sortie. Thus, the drone cannot temporarily land while en route to conserve battery power if the drone arrives before the technician; 4) The required times for the technician to collect a sample from a customer, give samples to the drone, and the time to recharge the drone at the laboratory are negligible.

All the technicians must leave the laboratory from time 0, and the last sample must be brought to the laboratory at the latest time L'. The waiting time to be tested for each customer's sample is the difference between its arrival time at the laboratory and the time at which the sample is taken. The aim of the problem is to minimize the total waiting time of all customers' samples.

3   Mathematical Modelling

Let $\mathcal{C} = \{1, 2, .., c\}$ represent the set of all customers and let $\mathcal{C}_1 \subset \mathcal{C}$ denote the subset of customers that the drone from laboratory can reach. Although a single physical laboratory location exists, we notationally assign it to two unique node numbers, such that technicians/drone depart from the laboratory at node 0 and return to the laboratory at node $c + 1$. Thus, $N = \{0, 1, ..., c + 1\}$ represents the set of all nodes in the network. To further facilitate the network structure of the problem, let $N_1 = \{0, 1, .., c\}$ represent the set of nodes from which a technician may depart, and let $N_2 = \{1, 2, ..., c + 1\}$ represent the set of nodes to which a technician may visit during a trip.

Table 1. Notations are used in the mathematical model of the DD-SSD

Parameters	
τ_{ij}	Travel time from node i to node j by technician
τ'_{ij}	Travel time from node i to node j by drone
L	Flight time range limit of drone
L'	Time range limit of task
Sets	
$\mathcal{R}$	Set of drone trips
$\mathcal{K}$	Set of technicians
Indexes	
i, j	Customers and laboratory (0 and c+1 indicate starting and ending laboratory, respectively)
r, r'	Drone trip indexes
k	Index of technician
Variables	
x^k_{ij}	Binary variable; 1 if k^{th} technician moves from node $i \in N_1$ to node $j \in N_2$; otherwise 0
v^r_{ij}	Binary variable; 1 if r^{th} drone's trip moves from node $i \in C_1 \cup \{0\}$ to node $j \in C_1 \cup \{c+1\}$; otherwise 0
$f^{k,r}_{ij}$	Binary variable; 1 if k^{th} technician meets drone at node $i \in C_1$ in drone's r^{th} trip to give all samples to the drone, and the technician continues his trip to node $j \in N_2$; otherwise 0
$g^{k,r}_{ij}$	Binary variable; 1 if k^{th} technician meets drone at node $j \in C_1$ in drone's r^{th} trip to give all samples to drone, that contain sample of node $i \in C$; otherwise 0
v^r_i	Cumulative flying time at node $i \in C_1 \cup \{c+1\}$ for the rth drone's trip after leaving the laboratory
s^k_i	Cumulative number of samples at node $i \in N_2$ that the kth technician has on hand after his leaving from laboratory or his last meeting with the drone
t_i	The time at which a technician leaves node $i \in N$, $t_0 = 0$
t'_i	The time at which a drone's trip leaves node $i \in N$
T_i	The time at which the customer $i \in N$ has just been sampled
A^r	The time at which r^{th} drone's trip completes its task, i.e. the arrival time at laboratory
B^k	The time at which k^{th} technician completes his task, i.e. the arrival time at laboratory
C^r_i	The time from the time sample of customer i is taken to the time it's brought to the laboratory at the rth drone's trip, if sample of customer i is not brought at the rth drone's trip, then this value is 0
D^k_i	The time from the time sample of customer i is taken to the time it is brought to the laboratory at the kth technician, if the sample of customer i is not brought at the kth technician, then this value is 0

We use the notations summarized in Table 1 to formulate the problem as a MILP model mathematically. The term *node* refers to a customer's location or the laboratory. The DD-SSD can be formulated as

$$\text{Minimize}\left\{\sum_{i \in \mathcal{C}} \sum_{r \in \mathcal{R}} C^r_i + \sum_{i \in \mathcal{C}} \sum_{k \in \mathcal{K}} D^k_i\right\} \tag{1}$$

$$\text{S.t. } A^r = t_i' + \tau_{i,c+1} \text{ if } y_{i,c+1}^r = 1 \quad \forall i \in \mathcal{C}_1, r \in \mathcal{R} \tag{2}$$

$$B^k = t_i + \tau_{i,c+1} \text{ if } x_{i,c+1}^k = 1 \quad \forall i \in N_1, k \in \mathcal{K} \tag{3}$$

$$\sum_{j \in N_2} x_{0j}^k = \sum_{i \in N_1} x_{i,c+1}^k \quad \forall k \in \mathcal{K} \tag{4}$$

$$\sum_{j \in N_2} x_{0j}^k \leq 1 \quad \forall k \in \mathcal{K} \tag{5}$$

$$\sum_{j \in \mathcal{C}1} y_{0j}^r \leq 1 \quad \forall r \in \mathcal{R} \tag{6}$$

$$\sum_{j \in \mathcal{C}_1} y_{0j}^r = \sum_{i \in \mathcal{C}_1} y_{i,c+1}^r \quad \forall r \in \mathcal{R} \tag{7}$$

$$\sum_{j \in N_2} x_{ij}^k = \sum_{j \in N_1} x_{ji}^k \quad \forall i \in \mathcal{C}, k \in \mathcal{K} \tag{8}$$

$$\sum_{j \neq i, j \in N_2} \sum_{k \in \mathcal{K}} x_{ij}^k = 1 \quad \forall i \in \mathcal{C}, \tag{9}$$

$$v_{c+1}^r \leq L \quad \forall r \in \mathcal{R}, \tag{10}$$

$$v_j^r = v_i^r + (t_j' - t_i') \text{ if } y_{ij}^r = 1 \quad \forall i,j \in \mathcal{C}_1, r \in \mathcal{R}, \tag{11}$$

$$v_j^r \geq \tau_{0j}' \text{ if } y_{0j}^r = 1 \quad \forall j \in \mathcal{C}_1, r \in \mathcal{R}, \tag{12}$$

$$v_{c+1}^r = v_j^r + \tau_{j,c+1}' \text{ if } y_{j,c+1}^r = 1 \quad \forall j \in \mathcal{C}_1, r \in \mathcal{R}, \tag{13}$$

$$\sum_{j \in \mathcal{C}_1} y_{0j}^r \geq \sum_{j \in \mathcal{C}_1} y_{0j}^{r+1} \quad \forall r \in \mathcal{R}, \tag{14}$$

$$\sum_{j \neq i, j \in \mathcal{C}_1 \cup 0} y_{ji}^r = \sum_{j \neq i, j \in \mathcal{C}_1 \cup c+1} y_{ij}^r \quad \forall i \in \mathcal{C}_1, r \in \mathcal{R} \tag{15}$$

$$\sum_{r \in \mathcal{R}} \sum_{j \neq i, j \in \mathcal{C}_1 \cup c+1} y_{ij}^r \leq 1 \quad \forall i \in \mathcal{C}_1, \tag{16}$$

$$\sum_{k \in \mathcal{K}} \sum_{j \in N_2} f_{ij}^{k,r} = \sum_{z \in \mathcal{C}_1 \cup \{0\}} y_{zi}^r \quad \forall i \in \mathcal{C}_1 \tag{17}$$

$$f_{ij}^{k,r} \leq x_{ij}^k \quad \forall i \in \mathcal{C}_1, j \in N_2 \tag{18}$$

$$s_j^k = 1 \text{ if } \sum_{r \in \mathcal{R}} \sum_{i \in \mathcal{C}_1} f_{ij}^{k,r} = 1 \quad \forall j \in \mathcal{C}, k \in \mathcal{K} \tag{19}$$

$$s_{c+1}^k = s_i^k \text{ if } x_{i,c+1}^k - \sum_{r \in \mathcal{R}} f_{i,c+1}^{k,r} = 1 \quad \forall i \in \mathcal{C}, \forall k \in \mathcal{K} \tag{20}$$

$$s_j^k = s_i^k + 1 \text{ if } x_{ij}^k - \sum_{r \in \mathcal{R}} f_{ij}^{k,r} = 1 \quad \forall i, j \in \mathcal{C}, k \in \mathcal{K} \tag{21}$$

$$s_{c+1}^k = 0 \text{ if } \sum_{r \in \mathcal{R}} \sum_{i \in \mathcal{C}_1} f_{i,c+1}^{k,r} = 1 \quad k \in \mathcal{K} \tag{22}$$

$$t_i' \geq T_i \quad \forall i \in \mathcal{C}_1 \tag{23}$$

$$t_i \geq t_z + \tau_{zi} \text{ if } \sum_{k \in \mathcal{K}} x_{zi}^k = 1 \quad \forall i \in \mathcal{C}, z \in N_1 \tag{24}$$

$$t_j \geq t_i \text{ if } y_{0i}^r = 1 \text{ and } y_{0j}^{r+1} = 1 \quad \forall i, j \in \mathcal{C}, r \in \mathcal{R} \tag{25}$$

$$t_j' \geq t_i' + \tau_{ij}' \text{ if } \sum_{r \in \mathcal{R}} y_{ij}^r = 1 \quad \forall i, j \in \mathcal{C}_1 \tag{26}$$

$$t_j' \geq \tau_{0j}' \text{ if } y_{0j}^1 = 1 \quad \forall j \in \mathcal{C}_1 \tag{27}$$

$$t_j' \geq A^{r-1} + \tau_{0j}' \text{ if } y_{0j}^r = 1 \quad \forall j \in \mathcal{C}_1, r \in \mathcal{R} \setminus \{1\} \tag{28}$$

$$T_j = t_i + \tau_{ij} \text{ if } \sum_{k \in \mathcal{K}} x_{ij}^k = 1 \quad \forall j \subset \mathcal{C}, i \in N_1 \tag{29}$$

$$\sum_{r \in \mathcal{R}} \sum_{k \in \mathcal{K}} \sum_{j \in \mathcal{C}_1} g_{ij}^{k,r} \leq 1 \quad \forall i \in \mathcal{C} \tag{30}$$

$$t_j \geq t_i \text{ if } \sum_{r \in \mathcal{R}} \sum_{k \in \mathcal{K}} g_{ij}^{k,r} = 1 \quad \forall i \in \mathcal{C}, j \in \mathcal{C}_1 \tag{31}$$

$$\sum_{r \in \mathcal{R}} \sum_{j \in \mathcal{C}_1} g_{ij}^{k,r} \leq \sum_{j \in N_2} x_{ij}^k \quad \forall i \in \mathcal{C}, k \in \mathcal{K} \tag{32}$$

$$\sum_{j \in N_2} f_{ij}^{k,r} \geq g_{zi}^{k,r} \text{ if } \sum_{j \in N_2} x_{zj}^k = 1 \quad \forall k \in \mathcal{K}, r \in \mathcal{R}, i \in \mathcal{C}_1, z \in \mathcal{C} \tag{33}$$

$$\sum_{i \in \mathcal{C}} g_{ij}^{k,r} = s_j^k \text{ if } \sum_{i \in N_2} f_{ji}^{k,r} = 1 \quad \forall r \in \mathcal{R}, k \in \mathcal{K} \tag{34}$$

$$\sum_{i \in \mathcal{C}} g_{ij}^{k,r} = 0 \text{ if } \sum_{i \in N_2} f_{ji}^{k,r} = 0 \quad \forall r \in \mathcal{R}, k \in \mathcal{K} \tag{35}$$

$$C_i^r = 0 \text{ if } \sum_{j \in \mathcal{C}_1} \sum_{k \in \mathcal{K}} g_{ij}^{k,r} = 0 \tag{36}$$

$$C_i^r = A^r - T_i \text{ if } \sum_{j \in \mathcal{C}_1} \sum_{k \in \mathcal{K}} g_{ij}^{k,r} = 1 \tag{37}$$

$$D_i^k = 0 \text{ if } \sum_{j \in \mathcal{C}_1} \sum_{r \in \mathcal{R}} g_{ij}^{k,r} = 1 \tag{38}$$

$$D_i^k = B^k - T_i \text{ if } \sum_{j \in N_2} x_{ij}^k - \sum_{j \in \mathcal{C}_1} \sum_{r \in \mathcal{R}} g_{ij}^{k,r} = 1 \tag{39}$$

$$B'^k = B^k \text{ if } \exists D_i^k > 0 \quad \forall k \in \mathcal{K} \tag{40}$$

$$B'^k \le L' \quad \forall k \in \mathcal{K} \tag{41}$$

$$t_i' + \tau_{i,c+1}' \le L' \text{ if } \sum_{r \in \mathcal{R}} y_{i,c+1}^r = 1 \tag{42}$$

The objective function (1) minimizes the total waiting time of all customers' samples. Constraints (2)–(3) are used respectively to calculate the arrival time at the laboratory of each rth drone's trip and k^{th} technician. Constraints (4)–(7) guarantee respectively technicians and a drone that leave laboratory must return to the laboratory when completing their trips. Constraints (8)–(9) ensure each customer is serviced exactly once by technicians. Constraints (10)–(13) guarantee the feasibility of the drone flying duration. Constraints (14) ensure the correct sequence of assignment trips to the drone. Constraints (15)–(16) respectively state that if a drone arrives at a customer, it must leave this customer, and each customer is visited by the drone at most once. Constraints (17)–(18) will ensure the synchronization between drone and technicians. Constraints (19)–(22) calculate the cumulative number of samples the technician has on hand at each node $j \in N_2$. Constraint (23) states that the drone is only allowed to leave a node after the technician has taken the sample at that node. Constraints (24)–(25) keep track of the technician's arrival time at every node. They add the technician travel time to the previous node when the technician travels from one node to another. Similarly, constraints (26)–(28) state that if the drone leaves node i to travel directly to some node j, then its arrival time at j must incorporate the drone's travel time from i to j. Constraints (29) calculate the time at which each customer j has just been sampled. Constraints (30) guarantee that the sample of a node is only taken at most once by the drone. Constraints (31) ensure the time synchronization between technician and drone in case the drone comes to get samples from him. Constraints (32) ensure that if a node sample is taken by a drone that meets k^{th} technician, the kth technician must visit that node. Constraints (33) ensure the synchronization between drone and technician at the node where a technician gives the drone samples to bring to the laboratory. Constraints (34)–(35) ensure the number of samples a technician brings when meeting the drone is equal to all the samples of the nodes it has visited since its last encounter. Constraints (36)–(37) combined to calculate the time from when a customer sample i is taken to when it is delivered to the laboratory during the trip of rth drone. Similarly, constraints (38)–(39) combined to calculate the time from when a customer sample i is taken to when it is delivered to the laboratory during the trip of kth technician. Further, as the objective function only counts technicians with samples brought back to the laboratory, then constraints (40) guarantee that if k^{th} technician gets at least one sample back to the laboratory, then $B'^k = B^k$, i.e., equals to the arrival time of the kth technician at the laboratory. Constraints (41)–(42) guarantee task completion time limit.

4   Literature Review

The literature on the use of drones in routing problems for postal service could be classified into three categories: a drone or several drones performing the delivery, two fleets of drones and trucks operating separately, a hybrid fleet of drones and trucks working together for delivery. The DD-SSD shares the hybrid setting with the third category. Yet, there are also differences in conditions and settings between them. When considering the hybrid mode, research avenues include two major variants: 1) only drones perform the delivery (see [6,11]), 2) both drones and trucks perform the delivery, some examples are [4,12]; each drone must coordinate with a truck after each trip for recharging or reloading in both variants. However, most of the works described in the literature assume a single delivery per trip for the drones and each drone coordinates with a fixed truck (see the survey of [9]). While in the DD-SSD, a drone might need to coordinate with more than one technician during each trip if it could help to reduce the waiting time of samples. Consequently, it requires more synchronization between vehicles during each drone trip, making the problem much more difficult to solve.

The use of drones in the sector of healthcare, health-related services, and disaster relief for last-mile distribution also has attracted significant attention from researchers (see the surveys of [5,13]). However, most works focus on using a drone or a fleet of drones solely for transportation, rather than how to integrate them into traditional methods. Only the contribution of Scott et al. considers the hybrid mode between truck and drone for delivery [15]. They study the problem where a customer set is divided into several clusters, and each cluster is served in turn. A truck goes to a location called drone nest in each cluster and stays there to serve as mobile depot for the drone to reload and to deliver to customers in that cluster. The drone performs only one delivery on each trip. This problem eventually does not require synchronization between vehicles as in the DD-SSD.

5   Solution Methodology

The DD-SSD is NP-hard as it includes the NP-hard Vehicle Routing Problem [7]. The complexity of the DD-SSD calls for heuristic solution approaches when realistically-sized instances are contemplated. In this section presents two methodologies: bi-level genetic algorithm (GA) and tabu search algorithm (TS) proposed to solve the DD-SSD problem.

5.1   Bi-level Genetic Algorithm

Individual Representation. Each solution to the problem is encoded into two chromosomes: the *Technician* chromosome representing the routes of technicians and the *Drone* chromosome encode the drone trips. The *Technician* chromosome is the concatenation of all the routes of technicians. Each route is an ordered sequence of customers. A number larger than the number of customers is added at the end of each route in the *Technician* chromosome to decode the routes. This number is different for each route. Figure 1a illustrates the *Technician* chromosome of a solution with ten customers and three technicians. In this illustration, the sequence of customers served by the 1st technician is 1, 2, 4. The *Drone* chromosome is a binary vector of $2\|\mathcal{C}\|$ bits. Starting from the left, every two bits corresponds to one customer so that the first bit equals 1 if the drone meets the technician at that customer and 0 otherwise. In contrast, the second bit equals 1 if the drone flies back to the laboratory after meeting the technician at that customer and 0 otherwise. Figure 1b illustrates a corresponding *Drone* chromosome of *Technician* chromosome in Fig. 1a, where the drone performs three trips. Figure 1c displays the corresponding solution with routes of three technicians by solid lines and three drone trips by dashed lines. The number on each dashed line shows the index of the trip that the drone is performing. Given the routes of technicians, *Drone* chromosome could be built as follows: 1) sort customers in ascending order of time serviced by technicians (for example, in this illustration, the ordered sequence is 1, 6, 10, 8, 3, 5, 2, 7, 9, 4); 2) produce two bits in *Drone* chromosome for each customer of this sequence in turn.

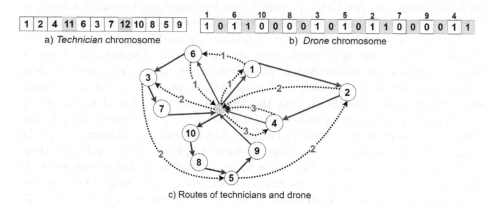

a) *Technician* chromosome   b) *Drone* chromosome

c) Routes of technicians and drone

Fig. 1. Representation of an individual.

The proposed bi-level GA is based on the composition of the dual GA. The goal of the first-level GA is to work on the population of *Technician* chromosomes to improve the technicians' routes, while the second-level GA aims to work on the population of *Drone* chromosomes to find the corresponding optimal drone's trips for each *Technician* chromosome transferred from the first level.

First-level GA. Initial population is generated randomly. At each generation, a mating pool of n individuals is formed by using binary tournament selection. Then, each time offspring are required during the course of GA, two individuals in the mating pool are selected randomly and passed to the PMX-based crossover operator. These two individuals are then deleted from the mating pool. Offspring are selected for mutation through a low probability p. Mutation selects two points randomly in the *Technician* chromosome, then reverses the gene sequence between these selected points.

Second-level GA. Given a *Technician* chromosome T transferred from the first level, a random population consisting of n corresponding *Drone* chromosomes is generated. Each *Drone* chromosome D in this population and the *Technician* chromosome T eventually form a solution to the problem. The fitness of this solution is used to evaluate chromosome D. The fitness of a solution z is calculated according to the weighted fitness function $f(z) = c(z) + p(z)$ where $c(z)$ is the value of the problem's objective function, $p(z)$ is a penalty value and equals to

$$p(z) = c(z) \sum_{k=1}^{||\mathcal{K}||} max(0, (b-a)(W_k - L')/L' + a), \qquad (43)$$

where W_k is the working time of the kth technician. At each generation, a mating pool of n individuals is formed by using binary tournament selection. The uniform crossover operator is then applied to every two individuals in the mating pool to create offspring. The mutation which selects one bit in the chromosome randomly and flips it will be applied to offspring with probability q. The best individual in the population will be used as the drone's trip for the *Technician* chromosome T, and the fitness of the corresponding solution will be used to evaluate the Technician chromosome T in the first level.

An elitist approach is used for generation replacement at both levels, keeping S_E best different parents and all best children so that the population size equals to n.

5.2   Tabu Search Algorithm

The overall structure of the proposed Tabu search algorithm is given in Algorithm 1. An initial feasible solution z is generated using a greedy method to minimize the total waiting time to be brought back to the laboratory of all customers' samples. At each iteration of the TS, one neighborhood is selected probabilistically based on the current value of r, then the selected neighborhood is explored, and the best move is chosen (lines 4–5). This move must not be tabu, unless it improves the current best solution z_{best}. The search is terminated when the maximum number of iterations IT_{max} is reached or after IT_{imp} iterations without improvement on the best solution (line 10).

Algorithm 1. Tabu search

1: Generate an initial feasible solution z
2: $z_{best} \leftarrow z$
3: **repeat**
4:     A neighborhood is selected based on the value of r
5:     Find the best solution z' (the one with minimum fitness) in the selected neighborhood of z and is not tabu or satisfies its aspiration criteria
6:     **if** z' is better than z_{best} **then**
7:         $z_{best} \leftarrow z'$
8:     **end if**
9:     $z \leftarrow z'$
10: **until** the stopping condition is met
11: return z_{best}

Search Space. Solutions in TS are evaluated according to the weighted fitness function $f(z) = c(z) + \alpha_1 d(z) + \alpha_2 w(z)$ where $c(z)$ is the value of problem's objective function, and $d(z)$, $w(z)$ are respectively the total violation of limited drone's flight endurance L and maximum working time L', while α_1, α_2 are penalty parameters adjusted dynamically during the search. The updating scheme is based on the idea of [3].

Neighborhoods. We use two types of neighborhoods:

– The routing neighborhoods try to improve technicians' routes by using different intra-route and inter-route neighborhoods: 1) Relocation neighborhood: For every two customers x and y, the customer x is taken from its current position and inserted after y; 2)Exchange neighborhood: two customers x and y are swapped on the route(s) of technicians; 3) 2-opt neighborhood [8]: apply on two customers x and y either on the same or different technicians' routes. These neighborhoods could also change trips of drone in case the positions of customers visited by both technician and drone have been moved by them.
– The sampling neighborhoods try to improve the sample assignments to the drone's trips by using: 1) Deletion neighborhood: remove a customer from a drone's trip; 2) Insertion neighborhood: for every customer x within drone's flying range from laboratory and not visited yet by the drone, find the best place to insert it into a drone's trip so that each drone's trip visits a technician exactly once.

Tabu List and Tabu Duration. We keep a separate tabu list for each type of move. The same type of move could not be applied again to the same customers while tabu. A tabu status is assigned to each tabu list element for θ iterations, where θ is randomly selected from a uniform interval which is $[a_1, a_2]$ for routing neighborhood or $[a_3, a_4]$ for sampling neighborhood.

Neighborhood Selection Strategy. The algorithm explores one neighborhood at each iteration. At the beginning of the search, both sampling and routing neighborhoods are given the same probability of being selected, which allows the TS to freely explore the solution space. Given that the number of customers reached by the drone is less than the number of customers in the problem, and the routes of drone depend on the routes of technicians, the algorithm should perform more routing than sampling moves to ensure adequate optimization of routes. Consequently, after the initial phase, the probability of selecting sampling neighborhoods becomes lower than the probability of selecting routing neighborhoods. We assign to these two neighborhoods probabilities of $1/(2+3r)$ and $r/(2+3r)$, respectively. The equal initial probabilities are then obtained by setting $r = 1$. After a number of iterations IT_r without improvement of the best solution, r is added an amount of Δr, where Δr is a user-defined parameter.

6 Experiments

Our algorithms are implemented in Python version 3.9.12. Experiments were run on an Intel Core i9-12900K 3.20 GHz. The instance set was introduced by Sacramento et al. in [14] consists of 80 instances, ranging from 6 to 100 customers. The laboratory is located at $[0,0]$ in all instances. Customers in each instance are generated following the uniform distribution $U(-d/2, d/2)$ in a grid size $d \times d$, ranging between 5×5 and 40×40. The instance set and results can be accessed via https://github.com/huetran1611/DD-SSD-problem. The user-defined parameters for bi-level GA (n, p, q, S_E, a, b) and TS $(\Delta r, IT_r, a_1, a_2, a_3, a_4, IT_{max}, IT_{imp})$ were set to (50, 0.1, 0.2, 25, 0.2, 1) and (0.4, 5, 5, 10, 3, 5, $1.2 * L' * log(||\mathcal{C}||/||\mathcal{K}||)$, 30), respectively. The GA of each level is run for 50 generations to adequately compare with the running time of the TS.

6.1 Numerical Results and Analyses

We have tested the MILP formulation proposed in Sect. 3 by running GUROBI solver for 10 h. Although it is able to obtain the optimal solutions within only 30 min on 6-customer problems, it could not obtain optimal solutions on 10-customer problems. Table 2 displays the comparative performance between proposed algorithms that run 10 times for each instance. Average best results, standard deviations, and computation time in seconds of both GA and TS algorithms are reported on six groups of problem instances. The rightmost column *GAP to GA(%)* displays the average gaps to the best GA solutions of the solutions obtained by the TS. Both GA and TS could obtain optimal solutions to all 6-customer problems. TS produces high-quality solutions, with an average improvement gap of 16.38% compared to GA, while requires 126% less computation time. One could see that the bi-level GA uses a decomposition approach that first found the routing of technicians. The obtained routes were then used as the input for finding the drone trips. However, these two sets of routing decisions for technicians and drone are not independent. Combining them into one formulation as proposed in TS thus yielded better results.

Table 2. Performance comparison between algorithms

Number of customers	GUROBI		Bi-level GA			Tabu search			
	Best avg.	Sol. status	Best avg.	Std.	Time(s)	Best avg.	Std.	Time (s)	GAP to GA(%)
6	35.33	Optimal	35.33	0.1	68	35.33	0.01	0.5	0.0
10	71.91	Feasible	67.18	1.83	356	65.07	0.01	3	−3.14
12	79.38	Feasible	70.62	0.77	498	70.62	0.05	4	0.0
20	–	Unknown	120.58	3.15	723	116.04	0.05	27	−3.77
50	–	Unknown	1129.86	56.37	1374	697.91	0.06	486	−38.23
100	–	Unknown	3293.88	152.71	2851	1543.4	0.21	2076	−53.14
Avg	–	–	786.24	35.82	979	421.40	0.065	432.75	−16.38

6.2   The Benefits of Integrating Drone

To evaluate the value of the integration of a drone into the system, we considered three scenarios: 1) $\mathcal{K}$, using $||\mathcal{K}||$ technicians; 2) $\mathcal{K}+1$, using $||\mathcal{K}||+1$ technicians; 3) drone+$\mathcal{K}$, using one drone and $||\mathcal{K}||$ technicians. Table 3 compares the average best results for all instances over ten runs of these scenarios. The average best objective value of the integrated scenario drone+$\mathcal{K}$, i.e., the DD-SSD problem, is given in column *Best*. The *GAP(%)* columns display the gaps for the average best objective values obtained by two other scenarios concerning drone+$\mathcal{K}$. Table 3 indicates that the drone integration provides the best solutions, with an impressive gain in performance. Without integration, but using an additional technician instead of using a drone, the obtained solution of $\mathcal{K}+1$ scenario is still significantly worse than that of the integration scenario, with an average increase in the objective value of 80.96%. Moreover, for instances having all customers within the flying range of the drone, the proposed drone+$\mathcal{K}$ integration scenario provides superior solutions, with an average improvement gap of 98.50% and 171.58% compared to $\mathcal{K}+1$ and $\mathcal{K}$ scenarios, respectively.

Table 3. Comparison of with and without drone

Number of customers	Drone+$\mathcal{K}$ Best	$\mathcal{K}$ GAP(%)	$\mathcal{K}+1$ GAP (%)
6	35.33	264.81	104.65
10	65.07	301.86	118.81
12	70.62	88.57	59.15
20	116.04	116.88	84.38
50	697.91	92.89	70.12
100	1543.40	59.27	48.65
Average	421.40	154.05	80.96

7   Conclusion

We introduced the DD-SSD problem by addressing the integration of a drone into the existing sampling service system. A mathematical modelling and two meta-heuristics were proposed to solve the problem. Experimental results clearly illustrated the superior performance of the proposed drone integration compared to the conventional technician-alone sampling service system.

Acknowledgement. This research is supported by the Asahi Glass Foundation under the project code AGF.2022–05.

References

1. Zipline receives the 2021 U.S. secretary of state's award for corporate excellence in health security. SUAS News (2021). https://www.suasnews.com/2021/12/zipline-receives-the-2021-u-s-secretary-of-states-award-for-corporate-excellence-in-health-security/
2. Andreas, C., et al.: Time to delivery of an automated external defibrillator using a drone for simulated out-of-hospital cardiac arrests vs emergency medical services. JAMA **317**(22), 2332–2334 (2017)
3. Cordeau, J.F., Laporte, G., Mercier, A.: A unified Tabu Search heuristic for vehicle routing problems with time windows. J. Oper. Res. Soc. **52**, 928–936 (2001)
4. Dell'Amico, M., Montemanni, R., Novellani, S.: Drone-assisted deliveries: new formulations for the flying sidekick traveling salesman problem. Optim. Lett. **15**(5), 1617–1648 (2021)
5. Hiebert, B., Nouvet, E., Jeyabalan, V., Donelle, L.: The application of drones in healthcare and health-related services in north America: a scoping review. Drones **4**(3), 30 (2020)
6. Karak, A., Abdelghany, K.: The hybrid vehicle-drone routing problem for pick-up and delivery services. Transp. Res. Part C: Emerg. Technol. **102**, 427–449 (2019)
7. Lenstra, J.K., Kan, A.H.G.R.: Complexity of vehicle routing and scheduling problems. Networks **11**(2), 221–227 (1981)
8. Lin, S., Kernighan, B.W.: An effective heuristic algorithm for the traveling-salesman problem. Oper. Res. **21**(2), 498–516 (1973)
9. Macrina, G., Di Puglia Pugliese, L., Guerriero, F., Laporte, G.: Drone-aided routing: a literature review. Transp. Res. Part C: Emerg. Technol. **120**, 102762 (2020)
10. Lum, M.J.H., et al.: Telesurgery via unmanned aerial vehicle (UAV) with a field deployable surgical robot. Stud. Health Technol. Inform. **125**, 313–315 (2007)
11. Poikonen, S., Golden, B.: Multi-visit drone routing problem. Comput. Oper. Res. **113**, 104802 (2020)
12. Raj, R., Murray, C.: The multiple flying sidekicks traveling salesman problem with variable drone speeds. Transp. Res. Part C: Emerg. Technol. **120**, 102813 (2020)
13. Rejeb, A., Rejeb, K., Simske, S., Treiblmaier, H.: Humanitarian drones: a review and research agenda. Internet Things **16**, 100434 (2021)
14. Sacramento, D., Pisinger, D., Ropke, S.: An adaptive large neighborhood search metaheuristic for the vehicle routing problem with drones. Transp. Res. Part C: Emerg. Technol. **102**, 289–315 (2019)
15. Scott, J., Scott, C.: Drone delivery models for healthcare. In: Proceedings of the 50th Hawaii International Conference on System Sciences (2017)

Error Investigation of Pre-trained BERTology Models on Vietnamese Natural Language Inference

Tin Van Huynh[1,2(✉)], Huy Quoc To[1,2], Kiet Van Nguyen[1,2],
and Ngan Luu-Thuy Nguyen[1,2]

[1] Faculty of Information Science and Engineering, University of Information Technology,
Ho Chi Minh, Vietnam
{tinhv,huytq,kietnv,ngannlt}@uit.edu.vn
[2] Vietnam National University, Ho Chi Minh City, Vietnam

Abstract. Natural Language Inference tasks have emerged in recent years and attracted significant attention from the natural language processing research community. There has been much success in this task with many quality datasets in English and Chinese for research and demonstrating the impressive performance of machine learning models. Pre-trained models play a crucial role, which is reflected in their superior performance compared to other models. However, they are still far from perfect and have many obstacles to the characteristics of the data. Especially in Vietnamese, we have just seen the emergence of the ViNLI benchmark dataset to serve the research community. In this paper, we experiment and analyze how the characteristics in the ViNLI benchmark dataset affect the performance of the pre-trained BETology-based models. In addition, the data parameters of ViNLI are also measured and analyzed on the accuracy of these models to see if it has any impact on the accuracy of the model.

Keywords: Natural language inference · Error analysis

1 Introduction

The original NLI task, known as Recognizing textual entailment [8,9], required the machine learning model to capture the semantics of a given pair of premise and hypothesis sentences. This semantic relationship can fall into cases like Entailment, Contradiction, or Neutral. In recent years, the Natural Language Inference task has achieved significant success, which plays a crucial role because it affects many NLP tasks such as machine reading comprehension [18] and question answering [4]. The remarkable point in this task is that the presence of many high-quality large datasets in many different languages ranging from rich-resource languages such as English [2,20,26] and Chinese [15] to poor-resource languages such as Korean [14], Indonesian [17], and Persian [1]. As a low-resource language, Vietnamese still has many limitations for outstanding research in this NLI task. However, recently the research community has witnessed the launch of the ViNLI dataset, which was developed by Huynh et al. [16] for Vietnamese. This dataset has yielded some positive research results, so it is hoped to promote more and better research outcomes in the future.

© The Author(s), under exclusive license to Springer Nature Singapore Pte Ltd. 2022
E. Szczerbicki et al. (Eds.): ACIIDS 2022, CCIS 1716, pp. 176–188, 2022.
https://doi.org/10.1007/978-981-19-8234-7_14

It can be seen that there is an interplay between datasets and machine learning models. In other words, datasets play an essential role in the evaluation of machine models, and machine learning models are increasingly thriving to improve accuracy on NLI tasks dramatically. In particular, the appearance of transformer architecture [24] is a leap forward for developing various tasks in NLP, including NLI task. After that, the BERTology model [10] is becoming a trend thanks to its transformer-based architecture. However, we still do not fully understand why BERT has such good performance, which is also a problem for that many researchers are trying to find an explanation.

In this paper, we try to investigate the behavior of the pre-trained BERT language model and variant models of BERT through the lens of the Vietmanses NLI task. Vietnamese is an interesting language, but not much research has been done. From the current research results from the ViNLI dataset [16], we focused on setting up experiments in this paper. We deeply analyzed the features contained in ViNLI to see what affects the pre-trained model performance. This study can help us better understand pre-trained models as well as the ViNLI dataset. We hope these analyses point to potential future studies to improve the Vietnamese NLI task outcomes further.

2 Related Work

In recent years, many NLI datasets have been built for studying the effectiveness of machine learning models such as deep learning and transfer learning. Many large benchmark datasets have been introduced related to human natural language inference. Specifically, the dataset named SNLI [2] introduced in 2015 is a large manually labeled dataset from Stanford University. Then, a series of other datasets appeared, such as STS-B [3], QQP [5], introduced in 2017 and 2018 for English. In 2018, a large dataset for this language was also published for research as MultiNLI [26] with 433K pairs. In addition, datasets for various languages have emerged in the NLP Research communities, including FarsTail [1] for Persian, KorNLI & KorSTS [14] for Korean, IndoNLI [17] for Indonesian, and OCNLI [15] for Chinese. Regarding the multilingual dataset, the XNLI dataset [7] was released in 2018 with more than 112K pairs for 15 languages. In Vietnamese, we have a ViNLI dataset introduced by Huynh et al. [16] to promote NLI research in Vietnamese.

Natural language inference research is growing rapidly due to the explosion of high-quality large datasets and deep learning models. Besides machine learning models based on neural networks such as RNN [11], Bi-LSTM [12] have achieved good performance on this task, the transformer-based core model plays a vital role. BERT was published by Devlin et al. [10]. Its architecture includes a variable number of Transformer encoder layers and self-attention heads. With this architecture, BERT achieves many state-of-the-art results for several Natural Language Understanding tasks on different datasets such as GLUE benchmark [25], SQuAD [22], and SWAG [28]. With the NLI task, pre-trained transformer models on many languages such as multilingual BERT [10], XLM-R [6], SBERT [23] give surprising results on the datasets MultiNLI [26], XNLI [7], QQP [5], STS-B [3]. PhoBERT [19] is a monolingual pre-trained model developed only for Vietnamese that is also giving positive results on many NLP tasks such as text classification, natural language inference, or named entity recognition.

3   Dataset

The ViNLI benchmark [16] is used for evaluating the accuracy of pre-trained models. The statistics on the dataset are shown in Table 1. ViNLI is an open-domain dataset built on Vietnamese news text. This dataset is quite large for Vietnamese at the moment, with 30,376 pairs of premise-hypothesis sentences manually annotated by humans. The special thing about ViNLI compared to other datasets is that it has an additional label Other instead of three labels Entailment, Contradiction, and Neutral like other datasets. The authors added the Other label to distinguish it from the Neural label.

Table 1. The number of premises-hypothesis pairs in the ViNLI dataset.

Label	Quantity			
	Train	Dev	Test	Total
Entailment	6,094	739	750	7,583
Contradiction	6,094	764	737	7,595
Neutral	6,094	752	777	7,623
Other	6,094	754	727	7,575
Total	**24,376**	**3,009**	**2,991**	**30,376**

4   Experiments and Results

This section presents experiments with multilingual pre-trained models on the ViNLI dataset. Following the prior work [2, 16], we use the accuracy measures and F1-score to evaluate the performance of those models.

4.1   Data Preparation

The ViNLI benchmark dataset is used for experiments on pre-trained models. However, according to the experimental results of Huynh et al. [16], the accuracy of the best model giving accurate results on the Other label is very high, above 98%, so we focus on the analysis of the dataset with three labels Contradiction, Entailment, and Neutral. Therefore, before installing the experiment, we remove the pairs of sentences labeled Other from the train, dev, and test set.

4.2   Experiment Settings

Besides experiments with pre-trained models, including multilingual BERT [10], PhoBERT [19], XLM-R [6] established on ViNLI by Huynh et al. [16], we also carry out the experiment on a model Another pre-trained model is SBERT [23]. The SBERT model is pre-trained in many different languages, including Vietnamese. We use these pre-trained models provided to HugggingFace's library in our experiments. The parameters in the SBERT model are we set up as follows: learning_rate = 1e−05, batch_size = 16, max_length = 256, in addition, we set epoch = 10.

4.3   Experimental Results

The experimental results are shown in Table 2. Compared with the experimental results of Huynh et al. [16], it can be seen that the performance of the SBERT model is the lowest with the accuracy on the dev and test sets of 59.29% and 58.17%, respectively. Besides, the experimental results on SBERT have a rather large gap compared with other pre-trained models, especially when compared with the XLM-R_large model. This difference in accuracy is more than 23% on both the dev set and test set.

Table 2. Machine performances on the development and test sets of ViNLI dataset. Results of mBERT, PhoBERT, and XLM-R are from Huynh et al. [16]

Model	Dev		Test	
	Acc	F1	Acc	F1
SBERT$_{Base}$	57.83	57.85	57.33	57.32
SBERT$_{Large}$	59.29	59.03	58.17	57.69
mBERT	67.41	67.46	64.84	64.83
PhoBERT$_{Base}$	75.07	75.08	72.87	72.79
PhoBERT$_{Large}$	**77.33**	**77.34**	**75.93**	**75.87**
XLM-R$_{Base}$	72.02	71.99	71.59	71.51
XLM-R$_{Large}$	**83.02**	**82.98**	**81.36**	**81.31**

5   Result Analysis

In this section, we carry out an analysis of the results of these pre-trained models, which aims to explore how the characteristics of the ViNLI dataset affect the performance of these pre-trained models. The issues in ViNLI that we are interested in analyzing include the influence of the annotation rule, word overlap, sentence length on performance, ability to capture annotation artifacts of pre-trained models, and error analysis by confusion matrixes.

5.1   Effects of Annotation Rules

According to Huynh et al. [16], to build the ViNLI dataset, annotators have to follow an annotation guideline. In the guidelines, they present suggested rules for annotators to writing a hypothesis corresponding to a premise sentence. To analyze how the characteristics of the ViNLI construction method affect the results of the pre-trained models, we investigate how the rules of creating hypothesis sentences for entailment and contradiction labels affect the performance of models. The rules list for creating the hypothesis sentences of the label entailment and contradiction is shown in Table 3 and Table 4. We selected 200 premise-hypothesis pairs of the entailment label and 200 premise-hypothesis pairs of the contradiction label in the test set for analysis. From these 400 pairs of sentences, we annotate the creating hypothesis sentence rules for these pairs of sentences following guidelines of Huynh et al. [16]. The percentages of each rule generating the hypothesis of the label entailment and contradiction are shown in Table 3 and Table 4, respectively.

In terms of entailment rules, we found that annotators tended to use the "replace words with synonyms" rule the most, with 56%. Besides, rules like "Add or remove modifiers that do not radically alter the meaning of the sentence" and "Change active sentences into passive sentences and vice versa" also account for a significant percentage of the annotators' writing style, with 54% and 35%, respectively. In contrast, rules like "Turn adjectives into relative clauses", "Create conditional sentences", or "Turn the object into relative clauses" are the least used by annotators to create the entailment hypothesis, with only from 1% to less than 4%.

We observe that the accuracy results of the pre-trained models on the entailment rules in Table 3 are interesting, with many similarities and differences between the models. All four models, SBERT, mBERT, PhoBERT, and XLM-R have the worst performance on pairs of sentences generated from the rule "Turn adjectives into relative clauses" even the mBERT model does not correctly predict any pairs, while the other three models correctly predicted half of those pairs of sentences. In addition, the rule "Create conditional sentences" is also a rule that makes it difficult for mBERT, PhoBERT, and XLM-R models with lower accuracy compared to the accuracy of other rules. SBERT model has the highest accuracy on two rules, "Replace words with synonyms" and "Create conditional sentences" with over 66%. Furthermore, the PhoBERT model has the best performance on the pairs of entailment sentences generated from the rule "Add or remove modifiers that do not radically alter the meaning of the sentence" with 86.11%. Both the mBERT and XLM- R models have the highest accuracy on the rule "Turn the object into relative clauses" with 85.71% and 100%, respectively.

Table 3. Statistics of rules generate entailment sentences and the accuracy of pre-trained models on these rules.

No.	Rule	Occurrence percentage (%)	Accuracy (%)			
			SBERT	mBERT	phoBERT	XLM-R
1	Change active sentences into passive sentences and vice versa	35.0	60.00	65.71	81.43	91.43
2	Replace words with synonyms	**56.0**	**66.96**	62.50	82.14	91.07
3	Add or remove modifiers that do not radically alter the meaning of the sentence	54.0	62.96	63.89	**86.11**	92.59
4	Replace Named Entities with a word that stands for the class	13.5	59.26	62.96	85.18	92.59
5	Turn nouns into relative clauses	4.0	62.50	37.50	75.00	75.00
6	Turn the object into relative clauses	3.5	57.14	**85.71**	71.43	**100.00**
7	Turn adjectives into relative clauses	**1.0**	**50.00**	**0.00**	**50.00**	**50.00**
8	Replace quantifiers with others that have a similar meaning	11.5	56.52	60.87	78.26	91.30
9	Create a presupposition sentence	12.5	56.00	64.00	80.00	80.00
10	Create conditional sentences	**1.5**	**66.67**	33.33	66.67	66.67
11	Other	11	**50.00**	63.63	68.18	81.81

Regarding contradiction rules, Annotators frequently use the "Replace words with antonyms" rule to generate most hypothesis sentences with over 36%, around five times as high as the "Opposite of time" rule, which has the lowest percentage. In addition, the percentage of contradiction hypothesis generated from "Opposite of quantity" and "Opposite of time" rules is quite low. Table 4 shows that four pre-trained models have the best predictive ability on pairs of "Use negative words" rule with high accuracy, especially mBERT and XLM-R models achieve nearly 90%. In particular, the XLM-R model does not have difficulty with pairs of sentences belonging to "Other" rules with absolute accuracy up to 100%, while the number of these pairs of sentences in the dataset is the lowest. The analysis results also show that the SBERT model has the worst performance on the hypothesis sentences generated from the "Replace words with antonyms" rule with only 32.87%. In contrast, the predictive ability of the PhoBERT and XLM-R model on this rule is quite high relative to 82.19% and 87.67%. Besides, The mBERT model has the lowest accuracy on sentence pairs from the rule "Wrong reasoning about an event". PhoBERT's accuracy is the lowest on the "Opposite of time" rule with around 50%.

Table 4. Statistics of rules generate contradiction sentences and the accuracy of pre-trained models on these rules.

No.	Rule	Occurrence percentage (%)	Accuracy (%)			
			SBERT	mBERT	phoBERT	XLM-R
1	Use negative words (no, not, never, nothing, hardly, etc.)	19.5	**76.92**	**89.74**	84.61	89.74
2	Replace words with antonyms	**36.5**	**32.87**	61.64	82.19	87.67
3	Opposite of quantity	9.0	72.22	66.67	83.33	**72.22**
4	Opposite of time	7.0	64.28	64.29	**50.00**	78.57
5	Create a sentence that has the opposite meaning of a presupposition	23.5	51.06	57.45	70.21	**72.34**
6	Wrong reasoning about an object (House, car, river, sea, person, etc.)	19.5	46.15	66.67	66.67	74.36
7	Wrong reasoning about an event	20.5	46.34	**51.22**	65.84	80.49
8	Other	2.5	40.00	60.00	80.00	**100.00**

We also analyze how annotators combine multiple rules to write hypothesis statements that affect the performance of pre-trained models. The ratio of the number of rules have in a hypothesis is shown in Table 5, along with the performance of the pre-trained models. In general, the number of rules used to generate the entailment hypothesis sentences is equally distributed over 1, 2, and more than 2 rules. In addition, most contradiction hypothesis sentences are written using a rule with 63% and a lower percentage of 37% for cases generated from more than 1 rule. We observe on the entailment label that while mBERT has the best accuracy on the entailment hypothesis sentences with only 1 rule, accuracy decreases as the number of rules increases. In contrast, the performance of the XLM-R model increases as the number of rules used to generate the entailment hypothesis sentences increases. Besides, both SBERT and PhoBERT models have the best predictive ability on entailment hypothesis sentences with 2 rules and maintain stability with 1 or more than 2 rules. For the number of rules in the contradiction hypothesis, all four pre-trained models have better predictability when the hypothesis is generated from multiple rules.

Table 5. The effect of the number of rules in the entailment and contradiction hypothesis sentence on the performance of the pre-trained models.

Label	Number of rule	Occurrence percentage (%)	Accuracy (%)			
			SBERT	mBERT	phoBERT	XLM-R
Entailment	1 rule	30.5	60.66	**72.13**	80.33	81.96
	2 rules	39.5	**64.55**	63.29	**83.54**	88.61
	More than 2 rules	30.0	60.00	58.33	80.00	**93.33**
Contradiction	1 rule	63.0	41.27	61.11	69.84	77.78
	More than 1 rules	37.0	**58.11**	**78.38**	78.38	83.78

5.2 Effects of Word Overlap

To analyze whether word overlap between premise and hypothesis sentences in ViNLI affects the performance of pre-trained models? We calculate the word overlap of premise-hypothesis pairs on the test set according to three different metrics, including Jaccard, The Longest Common Subsequence (LCS), and new token rate similar [17]. And then, we analyze the accuracy of the models according to these measures.

First, we use Jaccard to measure the degree of unordered word overlap by token level; The resulting accuracy of models by Jaccard is shown in Fig. 1a. It can be seen that the XLM-R model has the best performance on all Jaccard ranges. The accuracy of the SBERT model is quite low when Jaccard is less than 40%, and then slightly increases with Jaccard in a range of from 42% to more than 80%. All three models, mBERT, PhoBERT, and XLM-R have the worst performance when the Jaccard between the premise and the hypothesis is less than 20%, and performance increases dramatically as the Jaccard increases. However, the accuracy of the PhoBERT model decreases significantly when the Jaccard between premise and hypothesis sentences is more than 80%.

Second, we use LCS to measure the degree of word overlap in order between the premise and the hypothesis sentences by character. The accuracy of the models according to the LCS is indicated in Fig. 1b. We found that the XLM-R model has the highest performance and is relatively stable on most levels of LCS compared to the other models. While the PhoBERT model has low performance on premise-hypothesis pairs with LCS less than 20 characters, the mBERT model has difficulty when sentence pairs have LCS less than 20 characters and higher than 60 characters.

Third, we also analyze the results of the models according to the ratio of new words in the hypothesis sentence compared to the premise sentence. The analysis results are shown in Fig. 1c. Most of the performance of pre-trained models decreases remarkably as the new word rate increase from 0 to more than 80%.

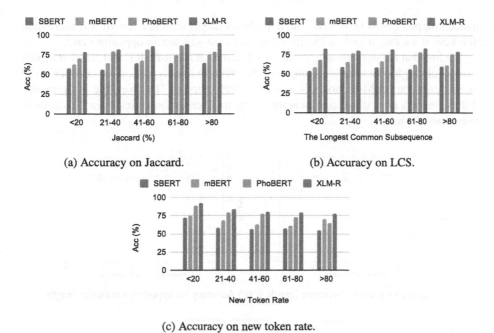

(a) Accuracy on Jaccard.

(b) Accuracy on LCS.

(c) Accuracy on new token rate.

Fig. 1. The effect of word overlap on the accuracy of pre-trained models.

From these analysis results, it can be seen that the degree of word overlap between the premise and the hypothesis sentences significantly influences the accuracy of the pre-trained models.

5.3 Effect of Sentence Length

The issue we are also interested in analyzing in this section is the effect of the length of inference sentences pair on the performance of pre-trained models. Models' accuracy on the test set concerning the length of the premise sentence, the length of the hypothesis sentence, and the total length of the premise sentence and the hypothesis sentence by token are shown in Figs. 2a, 2b, and 2c, respectively. We found that the accuracy of most models increases significantly as the length of the premise sentences rises from 1–10 tokens to 21–30 tokens. While the accuracy of the PhoBERT and mBERT models continues to increase slightly as the premise sentence length rises to more than 50 tokens, the XLM-R and SBERT models decrease slightly.

Regarding the hypothesis sentence length, the mBERT and XLM-R model's accuracy decreases significantly when the hypothesis sentence length increases from 1 to 40 tokens, followed by a gradual escalation when the hypothesis sentence length is more than 40 tokens. Looking at the 2b figure, we find that the performance of the PhoBERT and SBERT model when the same when the hypothesis sentence length is in the range of 1 to 40 tokens. While SBERT's performance continued to surge above 80% when the length of the hypothesis sentence increased from 41–50 Tokens before its performance dropped below 60% when the hypothesis length sentence length was more than 50 tokens if we take a look at PhoBERT models, we will see an opposite trend.

We find that the performance of the SBERT, mBERT, PhoBERT, and XLM-R model is relatively high when the total length of the premise and hypothesis is between 1–20 tokens; even the XLM-R model is almost entirely correct. However, the performance of these models goes down significantly as this total length increases from 20 tokens to more than 100 tokens.

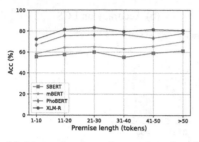
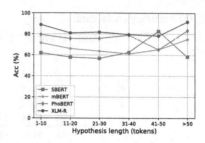

(a) Accuracy on premise sentence length.   (b) Accuracy on hypothesis sentence length.

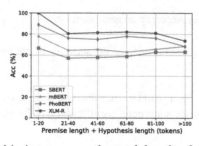

(c) Accuracy on the total length of the premise and hypothesis sentences.

Fig. 2. The effect of length of premise and hypothesis sentences on pre-trained models.

5.4   Hypothesis only Model Analysis

Inspired by the research of [21], we investigate whether the annotation artifacts leave any clues on the hypothesis sentence that help language inference models correctly predict the label. The models' performance is trained with only hypotheses illustrated in Table 6. We observe that the XLM-R and PhoBERT models have pretty impressive results when the accuracy on the Test set with 56.63% and 57.68%, respectively. Besides, we calculate Pointwise Mutual Information (PMI) [13] to observe which words in the hypothesis sentences can distinguish labels from each other. PMI results for the top 5 words of each label are shown in Table 7. With the entailment label, we found it quite interesting that the word *"không"* is actually a word that represents this class.

Table 6. Hypothesis-only baselines for ViNLI.

Model	Dev		Test	
	Acc	F1	Acc	F1
SBERT	50.51	50.48	49.91	49.88
mBERT	52.82	52.72	53.48	53.35
PhoBERT	56.14	56.12	57.68	57.59
XLM-R	57.87	57.67	56.63	56.43

This is entirely different from the OCNLI [15] and IndoNLI [17] datasets, where negative lexical dominate in hypothesis sentences of contradiction label. In addition, the word *"có"* and *"một"* can be a sign to discriminate the neutral class from other classes. However, the PMI results also show that some words can represent multiple classes, such as *"và"* and *"trong"*. There's not too influential in terms of the lexical difference between classes. Therefore, pre-trained models are made difficult by the ViNLI dataset if only trying to rely on hypothesis sentences to predict.

Table 7. Top 5 (word, label) pairs PMI for different labels of ViNLI.

Word		Label	PMI	Percentage
và	*and*	E	0.18	17.17
các	*some*	E	0.22	15.13
của	*of/object's*	E	0.28	27.51
trong	*in/inside*	E	0.35	18.94
không	*no/not*	E	0.35	9.81
của	*of/object's*	C	0.19	24.26
là	*to be*	C	0.21	16.19
trong	*in/inside*	C	0.22	15.73
và	*and*	C	0.23	18.45
các	*some/several*	C	0.30	17.17
một	*one/a/an*	N	0.27	10.49
là	*to be*	N	0.31	18.79
và	*and*	N	0.32	21.13
có	*has/have*	N	0.33	18.83
trong	*in/inside*	N	0.33	18.45

5.5   Error Analysis by Confusion Matrixes

Figure 3 illustrates the confusion matrix of the four pre-trained models the development set, including SBERT, mBERT, PhoBERT, and XLM-R. While the SBERT, mBERT, and PhoBERT models erroneously predict a significant number of sentence pairs with the CONTRADICTION label to the NEUTRAL label, many contradictory sentence pairs are mistakenly predicted by the XLM-R model as the label ENTAILMENT. In addition, the rate of EMTAILMENT sentence pairs being mispredicted to the CON-TRADICTION label and the NEUTRAL label was quite similar for each model except for the mBERT model, which had more false predictions to the CONTRADICTION label than to the NEUTRAL label. With sentence pairs of the NEUTRAL label, the XLM-R model has the best prediction ability on this label. Meanwhile, the mBERT model gives a significantly incorrect prediction from the NEUTRAL label to the CON-TRADICTION label.

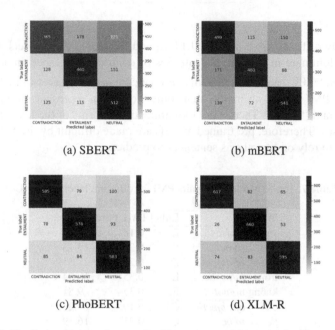

(a) SBERT   (b) mBERT

(c) PhoBERT   (d) XLM-R

Fig. 3. Confusion matrix of pre-trained language models on the development set.

6   Conclusion and Future Work

To analyze the performance of pre-trained models on the Vietnamese NLI task, we experimented with the SBERT model on the ViNLI dataset and in-depth analysis of other pre-trained models experimented by Huynh et al. [16]. There are many interesting findings relating between data characteristics and the accuracy of models. In particular, most models have relatively low accuracy on the sentences entailment hypothesis generated from the rules "Turn adjectives into relative clauses" and "Create conditional sentences". The contradiction hypothesis generated from the "Use negative words" rule is straightforward for the models to predict correctly. In addition, when multiple rules are combined to create a contradiction hypothesis, the prediction models are more accurate. Word overlap or premise and hypothesis length also significantly affect the model's performance. Pre-trained models are able to make predictions thanks to the clues of the annotation artifacts, although the accuracy is not too high.

In the future, we will also learn techniques to improve the accuracy of the models, such as data enhancement techniques. Besides, we will explore other transformer models like mT5 [27] which is a pre-trained text-to-text transformer in many languages.

Acknowledgement. This research is funded by Vietnam National University HoChiMinh City (VNU-HCM) under grant number DS2022-26-01. Tin Van Huynh was funded by Vingroup JSC and supported by the Master, PhD Scholarship Programme of Vingroup Innovation Foundation (VINIF), Institute of Big Data, code VINIF.2021.ThS.49.

References

1. Amirkhani, H., et al.: FarsTail: a Persian natural language inference dataset. arXiv preprint arXiv:2009.08820 (2020)
2. Bowman, S., Angeli, G., Potts, C., Manning, C.D.: A large annotated corpus for learning natural language inference. In: Proceedings of the 2015 Conference on Empirical Methods in Natural Language Processing, pp. 632–642 (2015)
3. Cer, D., Diab, M., Agirre, E., Lopez-Gazpio, I., Specia, L.:. SemEval-2017 task 1: semantic textual similarity-multilingual and cross-lingual focused evaluation. arXiv preprint arXiv:1708.00055 (2017)
4. Chen, J., Choi, E., Durrett, G.: Can NLI models verify QA systems' predictions? In: Findings of the Association for Computational Linguistics, EMNLP 2021, pp. 3841–3854 (2021)
5. Chen, Z., Zhang, H., Zhang, X., Zhao, L.: Quora question pairs (2018). https://www.kaggle.com/c/quora-question-pairs
6. Conneau, A., et al.: Unsupervised cross-lingual representation learning at scale (2019). arXiv preprint arXiv:1911.02116
7. Conneau, A., et al.: XNLI: evaluating cross-lingual sentence representations. In: Proceedings of the 2018 Conference on Empirical Methods in Natural Language Processing, pp. 2475–2485 (2018)
8. Cooper, R., et al.: Using the framework (1996)
9. Dagan, I., Glickman, O., Magnini, B.: The PASCAL recognising textual entailment challenge. In: Quiñonero-Candela, J., Dagan, I., Magnini, B., d'Alché-Buc, F. (eds.) MLCW 2005. LNCS (LNAI), vol. 3944, pp. 177–190. Springer, Heidelberg (2006). https://doi.org/10.1007/11736790_9
10. Devlin, J., Chang, M.-W., Lee, K., Toutanova, K.: BERT: pre-training of deep bidirectional transformers for language understanding. arXiv preprint arXiv:1810.04805 (2018)
11. Elman, J.L.: Finding structure in time. Cogn. Sci. **14**(2), 179–211 (1990)
12. Ghaeini, R.: Dependent reading bidirectional LSTM for natural language inference. arXiv preprint arXiv:1802.05577 (2018)
13. Gururangan, S., Swayamdipta, S., Levy, O., Schwartz, R., Bowman, S.R., Smith, N.A.: Annotation artifacts in natural language inference data. arXiv preprint arXiv:1803.02324 (2018)
14. Ham, J., Choe, Y.J., Park, K., Choi, I., Soh, H.: KorNLI and korSTS: new benchmark datasets for Korean natural language understanding. arXiv preprint arXiv:2004.03289 (2020)
15. Hu, H., Richardson, K., Xu, L., Li, L., Kübler, S., Moss, L.S.: OCNLI: original Chinese natural language inference. In: Findings of the Association for Computational Linguistics, EMNLP 2020, pp. 3512–3526 (2020)

16. Van Huynh, T., Van Nguyen, K., Nguyen, N.L.-T.: ViNLI: a Vietnamese corpus for studies on open-domain natural language inference. In: Proceedings of the 29th International Conference on Computational Linguistics (Accepted) (2022)
17. Mahendra, R., Aji, A.F., Louvan, S., Rahman, F., Vania, C.: IndoNLI: a natural language inference dataset for Indonesian. arXiv preprint arXiv:2110.14566 (2021)
18. Mishra, A., Patel, D., Vijayakumar, A., Li, X., Kapanipathi, P., Talamadupula, K.: Reading comprehension as natural language inference: a semantic analysis. In: Proceedings of the Ninth Joint Conference on Lexical and Computational Semantics, pp. 12–19 (2020)
19. Nguyen, D.Q., Nguyen, A.T.: PhoBERT: pre-trained language models for Vietnamese. In: Findings of the Association for Computational Linguistics: EMNLP 2020, 1037–1042 (2020)
20. Nie, Y., Williams, A., Dinan, E., Bansal, M., Weston, J., Kiela, D.: Adversarial NLI: a new benchmark for natural language understanding. In: Proceedings of the 58th Annual Meeting of the Association for Computational Linguistics, pp. 4885–4901 (2020)
21. Poliak, A., Naradowsky, J., Haldar, A., Rudinger, R., Van Durme, B.: Hypothesis only baselines in natural language inference. arXiv preprint arXiv:1805.01042 (2018)
22. Rajpurkar, P., Zhang, J., Lopyrev, K., Liang, P.: SQuAD: 100,000+ questions for machine comprehension of text. In: Proceedings of the 2016 Conference on Empirical Methods in Natural Language Processing, pp. 2383–2392 (2016)
23. Reimers, N., Gurevych, I.: Sentence-BERT: sentence embeddings using Siamese BERT-networks. arXiv preprint arXiv:1908.10084 (2019)
24. Vaswani, A., et al.: Attention is all you need. In: Advances in Neural Information Processing Systems, vol. 30 (2017)
25. Wang, A., Singh, A., Michael, J., Hill, F., Levy, O., Bowman, S.: GLUE: a multi-task benchmark and analysis platform for natural language understanding. In: Proceedings of the 2018 EMNLP Workshop BlackboxNLP: Analyzing and Interpreting Neural Networks for NLP, pp. 353–355 (2018)
26. Williams, A., Nangia, N., Bowman, S.R.: A broad-coverage challenge corpus for sentence understanding through inference. arXiv preprint arXiv:1704.05426 (2017)
27. Xue, L., et al.: mT5: a massively multilingual pre-trained text-to-text transformer. In: NAACL-HLT (2021)
28. Zellers, R., Bisk, Y., Schwartz, R., Choi, Y.: A large-scale adversarial dataset for grounded commonsense inference. In: EMNLP, Swag (2018)

Supervised Learning Use to Acquire Knowledge from 2D Analytic Geometry Problems

Anca-Elena Iordan[(✉)] [iD]

Department of Computer Science, Technical University of Cluj-Napoca,
Cluj-Napoca, Romania
anca.iordan@cs.utcluj.ro

Abstract. Understanding 2D analytic geometry problems described in natural language is an important and difficult open research task. In this paper it explores the theme of identifying geometric elements in unstructured documents and their classification. The proposed solution is based on the automatic recognition of geometric elements, achieved with the help of supervised learning. The chosen system is based on a model resulting from an automatic learning, in a supervised manner, made with the help of the support vector machine. A significant point for increasing the performance level is to provide a training data set as balanced as possible, a target attained with the help of the subsampling technique. The originality retrieves in the preprocessing phase of the data, both in the case of identifying the geometric elements characteristics, and in the case of finding a solution for balancing the data set used.

Keywords: Natural language processing · 2D analytic geometry · Machine learning · Support vector machine · Python

1 Introduction

Currently there are several software systems used in the automatic solution of geometry problems [1–3], but they receive the hypothesis and the conclusion in a specific format. Improving them would mean that the automatic solution would start from the statement of the geometry problem in natural language. Automatic identification of geometric elements from geometry problems expressed in natural language is a well-known challenge in the field of natural language processing [4]. When this task is applied to the field of geometry it becomes more complicated due to the terms used. In this paper are represented the steps towards an automatic identification of geometric elements found in problems of 2D analytic geometry in English.

The approach is based on an automatic identification of geometric elements using machine learning techniques [5,6] that involve supervised learning using the classifier based on vector support. The algorithm provided by it is based on a linear separation of clusters, the variant used being the multiclass type. The

© The Author(s), under exclusive license to Springer Nature Singapore Pte Ltd. 2022
E. Szczerbicki et al. (Eds.): ACIIDS 2022, CCIS 1716, pp. 189–200, 2022.
https://doi.org/10.1007/978-981-19-8234-7_15

solution requires annotated data in order to perform the training stage of the classifier, in which it learns the connection between the concept and the category to which it is assigned. In this phase, rules are created for mapping objects on the given labels, resulting in a model used to identify and classify new data. Although the problem addresses the use of a classifier as a central element, the most intense work focuses on providing an appropriate input to this method, which would allow a more precise delimitation of the desired entities. Thus, the following three objectives are outlined: the creation of a data preprocessing module, the training and testing of the proposed solution and the construction of a data postprocessing module to facilitate the analysis of the obtained performance. The preparation of the input data, necessary for the classifier, requires the most intense intellectual effort.

Thus, the objectives of the preprocessing [7] stage consist in identifying potential concepts from geometry problems, finding suitable features for them, calculating the values of the characteristics, and building the feature vector, necessary to be provided as input to the classification algorithm. The training and testing stages also involve the analysis of the advantages and disadvantages of choosing a learning algorithm. The type of problem proposed for solution, the important factors to be respected by the software and the necessary resources must be taken into account. Therefore, this stage has as objectives: identification of the algorithm according to the proposed problem, training of the system, followed by its testing.

After the training and testing stages, the results obtained after the test are interpreted. For this purpose, a module is created that automatically calculates different metrics needed for performance analysis, followed by the actual analysis, which aims to validate the system. If the results obtained are not the desired ones, this stage sends again to the first phase of collecting the features, where solutions must be identified for the problems that have arisen along the way.

Therefore, the general objectives of this research topic can be considered the three phases: data preparation, use of the classifier for training and testing, and then analysis and validation of the system. However, various challenges have arisen throughout the development process, the resolution of which has been of major importance in achieving final performance. Experiments show that the existence of a balanced data set is a key factor and an important step for achieving the best possible performance of the system based on supervised learning.

2   Related Works

2D analytic problems understanding represented in natural language is a important phase for multifarious automatic solvers [8,9]. Implementation of automated solutions for resolving 2D analytic geometry problems is a difficult research task since it is a difficult technology in developing intelligent educative software to lead learning [10].

Using a neural network design, in paper [11] it was introduced a two-step memory network used in process of deep semantic parsing. This model is language independent and optimized for low-resource domains, using a solver which can query the model about entities during the solving step that attenuates the problem of unaccomplished recalls.

Other approach, presented in [12], use a supervised learning model based on relation extraction for comprehension of geometry problems. The purpose was to create a cluster of relations to emblematize the given geometry problem. Supervised investigations into the collection of tested problems presented that the suggested model can obtain geometric relationships at raised F1 scores. In paper [13] was presented an adaptive filtering technique for extracting geometric information. The filtering method will permit improve d and adapted the queries of the user.

The idea analysed in [14] is to consider the relationships between algebra, geometry, computation, and proof. The relationships between two approaches, the attempts that have been made and the remaining impediments are debate. First approach uses first-order proofs in geometry, and the second follows Descartes back-translation from algebra to geometry. On the theoretical part, it is delivered a new first-order theory of vector geometry, adequate for formalizing geometry and algebra and the relationships between them.

For widely used educational software GeoGebra, in work [15] is related on a new command that affords the automatic discovery of loci of points in schemes defined by implicit conditions. This approach automates the dummy locus dragging' in dynamic geometry with great success. This improvement makes the cycle conjecturing-checking-proving accessible for geometry users.

The approach consider in work [16] consists in dealing automatically with iniquitous geometric statements which purpose is to discover complementary hypotheses for the statements to become true. It is proposed a reasonable protocol for automatic discovery and some algorithmic criterion, as well as the significance for the protocol success/failure.

In the research study [17] was provided the addition of a novel characteristic to an existent transition-based AMR parser that builds AMR graphs from statement of geometry problems presented in English language. The novel characteristic includes in clear embedding of the coreference detecting in the parser. The purpose of research study [18] was to realise a parsing system structured in two important elements: the parsing element and the learning element. A parser which uses transitions was introduced for the parsing element. The realisation of this element requires the implementation of a method for obtaining the actions sequence needed to acquire a UCCA graph.

In work [19] is presented a method which firstly engenders vector equations ground on done geometric relations concerning a geometric figure and, afterwards, converts the vector equations in a system of homogeneous linear equations. After calculating the determinants of the coefficient matrices corresponding to the system of equations, the elimination procedure is applied to get a great number of geometric relationships. The authors tested this method on more than 200 geometric problems and obtained that the geometric relationships discovered automatically are of obvious geometric significance.

In paper [20] is realized the arithmetic formalization of Euclidean plane geometry for the Coq proof assistant. For a concrete formalization, the authors present a formal proof of the nine-point circle theorem using the Gröbner basis method derived from Tarski's system of geometry. Furthermore, is proved that, given two points, an equilateral triangle based on these two points can be constructed in Euclidean Hilbert planes.

As it ensues from these enumerate studies, in research for comprehension of 2D analytic geometry problems was done outstanding progress. However, this area represents still an open research problem.

3 Solution Analysis

In order to extract the hypothesis and the conclusion from the statement of a geometry problem expressed in natural language, it is necessary to define a formalized structure for identifying the geometric concepts. Thus, the geometric elements can be categorized into four major clusters:

- Abstract geometric elements such as: point, line, segment, ellipse, hyperbola, parabola, circle, conic.
- Relational geometric elements such as: intersection(line, conic), tangent-line(conic, point), normal-line(conic, point).
- Quantitative geometric elements: length(segment), area(ellipse), measure(angle).
- Logical geometric elements: parallel(line, line), tangent(conic, line), collinear(point, point, point), perpendicular(line, line).

To enlighten the process of obtaining the geometric concepts and their classification in the four major clusters previously presented, a machine learning strategy [21] will be used, supervised, more exactly the classifier based on support vectors. SVM grants overfitting protectorship, which does not rely on the number of characteristics specified to the classifier, thus it has the prospective to handle a very extensive characteristic space.

SVM is based on finding a linear separator between classes and thus becomes the perfect candidate to achieve the classification of geometric concepts. The use of a classifier for supervised learning requires the creation of a feature vector, which will constitute the input of the classifier, on the basis of which it will be possible to construct the rules for mapping the entries on the labelled clusters. The entry of the system will be the documents with statements of 2D analytic geometry problems in English.

These documents will be parsed, and their text will be preprocessed in order to perform functions for calculating some proposed features. Candidate concepts will be extracted and for each one a feature vector will be calculated, and the resulting vectors will be sent as input to the classification algorithm. Each entry will be labelled with the class to which it belongs, namely abstract, relational, quantitative, or logical geometric element. The learning algorithm will result in a model, which will be used in classification.

A set of geometric problems will constitute the test set, for which the feature vectors will be recalculated. This new set of vectors will be sent as input, along with the learning model, for a classification algorithm. The result of this algorithm is represented by the classified geometric elements, extracted from a new data set, the test, on which no previous analysis was performed Fig. 1.

The personal contribution addresses the introduction of lexical and syntactic features of words and the proposal of the subsampling technique, based on the parts of speech and labels resulting from superficial syntactic parsing, in order to improve the results, balancing the data set. Another feature introduced is the superficial syntactic parsing, which provides syntactic details related to the structure of the sentence, used to obtain more information than from the speech part of a word. However, maximum system performance is achieved when the chunking technique is used to subsample the input data.

During the development of the system, a problem was encountered related to the report between the terms that did not represent interest and the geometric notions existing in the collections of geometry problems. Being large enough to influence the classification in a negative way, the classifier became bias towards the majority cluster, which represented the negative examples, and the system tended to classify the geometric elements as being of this type. To solve the problem, the undersampling technique was used, which aims to reduce the majority cluster. The support vector classifier was chosen, which offers the advantage of avoiding the overfitting problem [22], regardless of the number of features used. "Overfitting" is a system modelling error that occurs when a function is mapped too precisely on a data set, and thus its behaviour when entering new data will not be desired, failing to classify correctly.

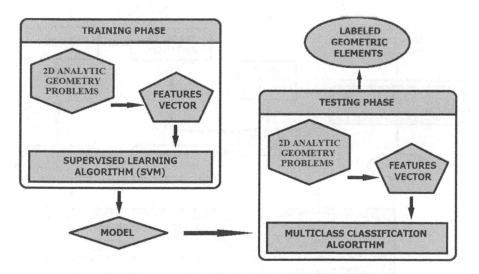

Fig. 1. Pattern for the identification of geometric elements.

4 Solution Design

4.1 Software Architecture

The architecture shown in Fig. 2 includes both the system training process and the testing phase, in which it is proved that the developed project achieves the proposed performances in a real environment. It can be seen that both processes use unstructured data sets. The documents used do not overlap, there is a number of geometry problems for the analysis and training of the system and a number of reports used for testing, of which the system has no prior knowledge, to see how it behaves when receiving new data and how well it generalizes. Having as input the geometry problems, the system will take each document in turn and extract different terms. With the generated terms, we move on to the next stage of preprocessing, in which for each of these terms the proposed features are calculated.

Natural language processing techniques are used: sentence-level text division, sentence-level sentence division, lemmatization, speech part identification, superficial syntactic parsing, to calculate word-level, syntactic, lexical, and contextual characteristics. At the end of this stage, it will have generated the feature vectors necessary for the classifier to be able to generate the rules for mapping the entries on the given labels in case of training. The training of the classifier has as input the feature vectors and the label given to each term from the set of possible clusters: abstract geometric elements, relational geometric elements, quantitative geometric elements, logical geometric elements, or none. "None" is the cluster of negative examples, meaning the candidate concepts that turn out not to be geometric concepts.

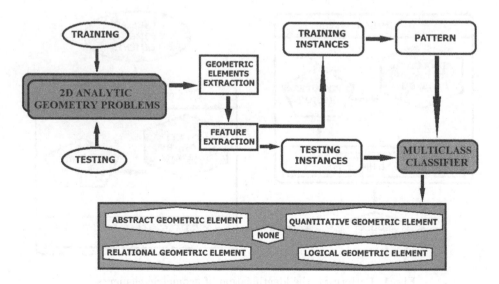

Fig. 2. Software architecture.

The result of the training is a model which, together with the feature vectors calculated for the training data set, will be the input for the classification algorithm. This algorithm is of the multiclass type, because five clusters are considered for the categorization of the input instances, previously exposed. Following classification, the set of terms from the test data annotated with the corresponding cluster will be obtained.

4.2 Preprocessing

The data preprocessing module is the most important component of the system. Documents are provided in the form of raw data, which often needs to be transformed to bring the text into a representation that computing machines can understand and process. Basically, 75% of the work focuses on analysis, followed by creating a system solution and building the preprocessing module. It includes both the part of taking over the unstructured files and the part of extracting the terms, the calculation of the feature vectors for each of them and their labelling with the corresponding class, necessary in the training process. Also, a sub-process is performed to eliminate the noise found in the documents with the statements of geometry problems. Noise is represented by different characters which appear incorrectly in the documents. So, it is needed a process of converting unstructured data into a format that can be read by computing machines, more precisely, a process of transforming text into a suitable representation for learning algorithms.

Candidate concepts are terms that have the potential to be geometric concepts before the classification process. When we extract information automatically, in the preprocessing phase, we extract both geometric concepts and negative examples and only after classification and annotation is the categorization of these terms. To achieve this sub-module, take over each document containing the statements of the 2D analytic geometry problems and use the partitioning techniques at the sentence level and at the word level specific to natural language processing. Because a sentence can contain many general words that are not of interest in the field of geometry, they are filtered before taking them for the calculation of feature vectors, thus avoiding an intensive calculation of the features of terms that have no chance to geometric elements.

After identifying the candidate concepts follows the process of calculating their features and building the feature vectors that will be provided as input to the learning and classification algorithms. In Machine Learning, the feature vector is an n-size vector that contains numeric features that describe certain objects. Numerical representation of objects facilitates computational processing and analysis. In the developed project, the feature vectors will be used as inputs for the multi-class classifier with support vectors. They will have a sparse matrix representation, meaning only those features that have a value other than zero or non-zero will be noted, accompanied by the corresponding index, which uniquely identifies a specific feature. We can say that unstructured documents can be encoded in vectors that contain numerical values, these being necessary for the action of categorizing the text.

4.3   Training and Testing

The training of the system consists in choosing a training algorithm and providing the feature vectors, coming from the preprocessing module, as input of this algorithm. The training will result in a model of the system. The system will create some rules for mapping objects to the corresponding given clusters. The training will be performed using an algorithm implemented in Python programming language. The testing of the system is based on the model resulting in the training phase. When testing, the classification algorithm is used. It must identify new concepts from an unseen set of documents. The test reflects how well the system will perform in the real world. In the case of both the drive flow and the test flow, the file with the unstructured text and the corresponding annotation file are taken in parallel to create the feature vectors.

The difference is that training requires both objects and their labels in order to create mapping rules. In testing, however, the category is used only at the end to be able to compare the label placed by the classifier with it, in order to analyse the results. Therefore, although in the preprocessing phase the expected label is taken over, in case of implementation, it will not influence the classifier, but will be used only in the next post-processing module, in which different formulas are calculated for analysing the system performance.

4.4   Postprocessing

The postprocessing module aims to calculate some formulas in order to analyse the performance of the built system. It uses the test file and the labels of the objects used in the test file as input. The proposed formulas for analysis are Precision, Recall and F-score. In order to calculate them more easily, we used the confusion matrix. The chosen formulas can be easily calculated once the confusion matrix has been generated. To obtain their values we need three terms, which can be easily derived from the confusion matrix: correctly identified clusters (TP), clusters identified as correct, but they are incorrect (FP), and identification clusters as incorrect, but they are correct (FN). TP is determined by taking for each custer x, the corresponding diagonal value is taken from the confusion matrix. FP is calculated from the confusion matrix, for each class x, as the sum of the values of the corresponding column, without the value on the diagonal. FN represents, for each cluster x, the sum of the values of the corresponding row, without the value on the diagonal in the confusion matrix. With these terms Precision and Recall can be calculated very easily, and the F-score is derived from them. Precision tells us the percentage of identification clulsters correctly reported to the total number of clusters labelled as correct. Recall gives us information about the number of correctly identified custers relative to the total examples corresponding to that custer. F-score represents the harmonic average of the two previously explained.

5   Testing and Validation

The software is tested using unstructured documents that are notice for the primary time. Validation is acquired by inspection of the results of some computation formulas usually used in classification problems. The metrics analysed for validation were Precision, Recall and F-score. These metrics were computed for every clusters. Precision tells us what percentage of the instances that the classifier labelled as correct are correct, being a measure of accuracy. Recall tells us what percentage of the correct courts the classifier labelled as correct, being a measure of completeness. F-score represents the harmonic mean between Precision and Recall, being also known as F measure in the literature.

Precision and Recall are calculated based on the court values true-positives, false-positives and false-negatives:

$$Precision = \frac{TP}{TP + FP} \tag{1}$$

$$Recall = \frac{TP}{TP + FN} \tag{2}$$

$$F - score = \frac{2 \cdot P \cdot R}{P + R} \tag{3}$$

The Recall metric plays a very important role in the field of geometry and aims to maximize it. This takes into account the false-negative elements, in other words, those terms that were to be classified as geometric concepts, but the classifier did not evaluate them properly. This anomaly becomes a problem in the field of geometry because the exclusion of some geometric concepts can be crucial in solving that problem. It is preferable to have a lower precision, in which to take concepts as geometric elements, even if they are not, than to omit them. The classifier chosen for training and testing is called L2-regularized L2-loss support vector classification. The algorithm allows the setting of three parameters: error cost, completion tolerance and weight of clusters. The cost of the wrong classification is the measure of the error allowed in the classification. If its value increases, a more precise model is created, but which risks not generalizing well. Termination tolerance is the number of iterations in an optimization.

The weight of the clusters provides information about the importance of that cluster, so the higher it is, the better the classifier will tend to identify that cluster. Following an analysis, it was chosen to set the cost to 1 and the termination tolerance to 0.001. Also, because the custer containing the negative examples is not of much interest, we reduced its weight to 0.2, the other clusters having a weight of 1. In this way, the meaning of terms that do not represent any kind of geometric concepts is reduced. The excellent results obtained by the developed geometric software acquired a mean F-score identical with 0.8452, if it takes into account the rank of negative examples, which demonstrated to be the optim classified. The mean F-score computed precisely for geometric concepts has a valuable of 0.7961. If this weighted metric is computed, the valuables are acquired: 0.9107, if the "none" cluster is taken into account and 0.8017 if just the geometric concepts are analyzed.

The first analysis of the data was performed to verify whether the binary features, generated with the help of the word lemma, with the completion of the training set, bring or not improvements to the system, taking into account that they could introduce the phenomenon of over-learning. A initial appraisal was made after the subsampling of preponderante cluster (none) based on the investigation of the speech side used in the geometric concepts. The outcomes are shown in Table 1.

Table 1. Subsampling based on speech part analysis.

	Precision	Recall
Abstract geometric element	72.82	64.97
Relational geometric element	72.03	63.29
Quantitative geometric element	69.92	62.65
Logical geometric element	67.42	61.23

For the succeeding betterment, subsampling was suggested based on labels resulting from superficial syntactic parsing. The concept of prior sampling is observed too in this situation. The outcomes are presented in Table 2. This subsampling established a huge advantage to the performance, the increases being also at the step of a few percent for each cluster. In two situation, the Recall metric become bigger than the Precision metric, which affordes appreciable input for software validation.

For a higher survey of results, in Table 3 are presented the F-score values for every cluster used in the classification: abstract geometric element, relational geometric element, quantitative geometric element, logical geometric element and negative examples (none). It can be observed that the best results, within the categories of interest, meaning that the geometric ones, were obtained in the case of the cluster Abstract geometric element, being followed by the clusters Relational geometric element and qualitative geometric element, and, finally, by the geometric element cluster logical.

Table 2. Subsampling based on superficial parsing.

	Precision	Recall
Abstract geometric element	81.17	81.92
Relational geometric element	79.72	75.16
Quantitative geometric element	77.03	77.06
Logical geometric element	75.36	73.56

Table 3. System performances reported by F-score.

	F-score
Abstract geometric element	79.63
Relational geometric element	77.95
Quantitative geometric element	74.79
Logical geometric element	73.79
None	88.92

6 Conclusions

In this research work was covered the subject of identifying geometric concepts and classifying them in four clusters: abstract geometric components, relational geometric components, quantitative geometric components, and logical geometric components. The chosen approach consists in automatic recognition of elements, reached with the assistance of supervised learning. The first stage to software design was to examine the available experimental proof for this work, in order to better comprehend the component function in procedure of solving. It has been presented that a fundamental point for growing the performance level is to deliver a collection of training data as balanced as possible, a scope reached through subsampling strategy.

An approach which use machine learning has been chosen since the available software, achieved on the foundation of rules and dictionaries, do not have a adequately satisfying effect, encountering in their process varied issues bound to the restraints imposed by the dimension of the information source or the hard rules.

References

1. Iordan, A., Panoiu, M., Baciu, I., Cuntan, C.D.: Design of an intelligent system for the automatic demonstration of geometry theorems. In: International Conference on Telecommunications and Informatics, Catania, Italy, pp. 221–226 (2010)
2. Mosese, N., Ogbonnaya, U.I.: GeoGebra and students' learning achievement in trigonometric functions graphs representations and interpretations. Cypriot J. Educ. Sci. **16**(2), 827–846 (2021)
3. Iordan, A., Panoiu, M., Muscalagiu, I., Rob, R.: Realization of an interactive informatical system for the quadric surfaces study. In: Proceedings of 13th International Conference on Computers, Rhodes, Greece, pp. 205–210 (2009)
4. Balyan, R., McCarthy, K.S., McNamara, D.S.: Applying natural language processing and hierarchical machine learning approaches to text difficulty classification. Int. J. Artif. Intell. Educ. **30**(3), 337–370 (2020). https://doi.org/10.1007/s40593-020-00201-7
5. Covaciu, F., Pisla, A., Iordan, A.E.: Development of a virtual reality simulator for an intelligent robotic system used in ankle rehabilitation. Sensors **21**(4), 1537 (2021)

6. Muscalagiu, I., Iordan, A., Muscalagiu, D., Panoiu, M.: Implementation and evaluation model with synchronization for the asynchronous search techniques. In: Proceedings of 13th International Conference on Computers, Rhodes, Greece, pp. 211–216 (2009)
7. Nguyen, H., Huynh, T., Hoang, S., Pha, V., Zelinka, I.: Language-oriented sentiment analysis based on the grammar structure and improved self-attention network. In: 15th International Conference on Evaluation of Novel Approaches to Software Engineering, Prague, Czech Republic, pp. 339–346 (2020)
8. Seo, M., Hajishirzi, H., Farhadi, A., Etzioni, O., Malcolm, C.: Solving geometry problems: combining text and diagram interpretation. In: Proceedings of the Empirical Methods in Natural Language Processing, Lisbon, Portugal, pp. 1466–1476 (2015)
9. Wang, K., Su, Z.: Automated geometry theorem proving for human readable proofs. In: Proceedings of the International Conference on Artificial Intelligence, Buenos Aires, Argentina, pp. 1193–1199 (2015)
10. Aleven, V., Roll, I., McLaren, B., Koedinger, K.: Help helps, but only so much: research on help with intelligent tutoring systems. Int. J. Artif. Intell. Educ. **26**, 205–223 (2016)
11. Jayasinghe, I., Ranathunga, S.: Two-step memory networks for deep semantic parsing of geometry word problems. In: Chatzigeorgiou, A., et al. (eds.) SOFSEM 2020. LNCS, vol. 12011, pp. 676–685. Springer, Cham (2020). https://doi.org/10.1007/978-3-030-38919-2_57
12. Gan, W., Yu, X., Wang, M.: Automatic understanding and formalization of plane geometry proving problems in natural language: a supervised approach. Int. J. Artif. Intell. Tools **28**(4), 1940003 (2019)
13. Quaresma, P., Santos, V., Graziani, P., Baeta, N.: Taxonomies of geometric problems. J. Symb. Comput. **97**, 31–55 (2020)
14. Beeson, M.: Proof and computation in geometry. In: Ida, T., Fleuriot, J. (eds.) ADG 2012. LNCS (LNAI), vol. 7993, pp. 1–30. Springer, Heidelberg (2013). https://doi.org/10.1007/978-3-642-40672-0_1
15. Abanades, M., Botana, F., Kovacs, Z., Recio, T., Solyom-Gecse, C.: Development of automatic reasoning tools in GeoGebra. ACM Commun. Comput. Algebra **50**(3), 85–88 (2016)
16. Dalzotto, G., Recio, T.: On protocols for the automated discovery of theorems in elementary geometry. J. Autom. Reason. **43**(2), 203–236 (2009)
17. Iordan, A.E.: Automatic comprehension of geometry problems using AMR parser. In: 33rd International Conference on Software Engineering and Knowledge Engineering, Pittsburg, USA, pp. 628–631 (2021)
18. Iordan, A.E.: Usage of stacked long short-term memory for recognition of 3D analytic geometry elements. In: 14th International Conference on Agents and Artificial Intelligence, Lisbon, Portugal, pp. 745–752 (2022)
19. Peng, X., Chen, Q., Zhang, J., Chen, M.: Automated discovery of geometric theorems based on vector equations. J. Autom. Reason. **65**(6), 711–726 (2021). https://doi.org/10.1007/s10817-021-09591-2
20. Boutry, P., Braun, G., Narboux, J.: Formalization of the arithmetization of Euclidean plane geometry and applications. J. Symb. Comput. **90**, 149–168 (2019)
21. Covaciu, F., Iordan, A.E.: Control of a drone in virtual reality using MEMS sensor technology and machine learning. Micromachines **13**, 521 (2022)
22. Poon, H., Yap, W., Tee, Y., Lee, W., Goi, B.: Hierarchical gated recurrent network with adversarial and virtual adversarial training on text classification. Neural Netw. **119**, 299–312 (2019)

Forecasting Cryptocurrency Price Fluctuations with Granger Causality Analysis

David L. John and Bela Stantic[✉]

School of Information and Communication Technology, Griffith University,
Brisbane, Australia
david.john2@griffithuni.edu.au, b.stantic@griffith.edu.au

Abstract. Forecasting various economic indicators has been a primary interest in economics and has attracted the attention of many researchers. Granger causality analysis has become quite popular in the econometrics literature and it aims to determine whether one time series is useful in forecasting another. In this work through the use of Granger causality analysis we investigate whether Twitter sentiment, expressed in large scale collections of daily tweets, can be correlated or even predictive of future prices of cryptocurrencies. The proposed framework considers tweets that mention the cryptocurrency "Dogecoin" and analyses the textual content of each of these tweets using a modified version of the lexicon-based sentiment polarity analysis method, VADER. The generated, Twitter sentiment time series is then compared to a time series of the closing prices of Dogecoin for each day. Granger causality analysis showed a unidirectional relationship between Twitter sentiment and cryptocurrency prices for day lags ranging from 2 to 4 days (with a 3-day lag having the lowest statistical significance value). This was also accompanied by a Pearson correlation coefficient of $r = 0.6940$ and a clear visual correlation between the two time series (with this 3-day lag). Findings indicate that Twitter sentiment is directly correlated and can be predictive of the future prices of cryptocurrencies.

Keywords: Granger causality · Sentiment analysis ·
Cryptocurrencies · Social media

1 Introduction

Statistical analysis is a vital research tool used by businesses, researchers, governments and other organizations to draw valid predictions about the future. This involves investigating patterns, trends and relationships using quantitative data, in an effort to improve data organisation and future projections. Prevailing methods of statistical analyses include the fundamental determination of the mean, standard deviation sample size, regression analysis, and hypothesis testing [4,9].

© The Author(s), under exclusive license to Springer Nature Singapore Pte Ltd. 2022
E. Szczerbicki et al. (Eds.): ACIIDS 2022, CCIS 1716, pp. 201–213, 2022.
https://doi.org/10.1007/978-981-19-8234-7_16

An innovative and unique analysis technique for the prediction of future values of a time series, was introduced by the econometrician Sir Clive Granger [11]. At the time, Granger was investigating the, relatively new concept of cross spectrum analysis and examining relationships between two different time series and how they can be related. Following the work of Norbert Wiener (a mathematician and philosopher), Granger formulated a new approach to causality relationships with the advantage of it having predictive power when applied to time series data. This became known as "Granger causality" [13].

Granger causality analysis has been applied to a plethora of studies which aim to identify a predictive or causative relationship between two time series. These studies have largely been confined to the field of economics and used to relate variables such as financial development, tourism development and economic growth [2,15,16]. Other works use this technique to relate various economic indicators to predict stock market fluctuations [3,6,18]. These works have all claimed a strong correlation between many of these variables and some have demonstrated, by using Granger causality analysis, that many of these variables can be accurately predicted, highlighting the power of Granger causality as an effective analysis technique.

This study investigates whether Granger causality analysis can be used to predict equity markets. In particular, a time series of public sentiment, expressed as the quantification of a large scale collection of daily tweets is used to predict the price of the cryptocurrency Dogecoin. This work endeavours to answer the question "Can Granger causality be used to predict future prices of Dogecoin using Twitter sentiment analysis?"

2   Background and Literature Review

Given the potential complexity involved with the types of applications described above, there are many challenges that need to be considered with Granger causality analysis. Two important parameters when performing Granger causality are: the size of the time window considered for analysis; and, the order of the autoregressive model i.e. how many past values of a time series should be considered to make accurate predictions of the future time series values (see Fig. 2).

As can be seen in Fig. 1, a relatively shorter or longer time window can be used for Granger causality analysis and there are advantages and disadvantages for each of these choices. If a longer time window is used, the autoregressive model will be more accurate, as there will be more data to fit the model, and so will give a better model estimation. Alternatively, there will also be a worse temporal precision as this window is incorporating data from a longer time period. For the shorter time window, the opposite is true: there will be better temporal precision but it will be more difficult to estimate the autoregressive model and so will give a poorer model estimation. In order to choose an optimal time window, the type of data that is being analysed needs to be considered. Stationary time periods can be considered for this time window. For example, in neuroscience a common time period used is the full width at half maximum (FWHM) for a wavelet,

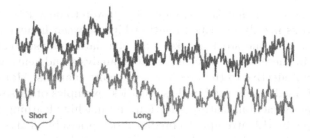

Fig. 1. Graphical representation of using shorter or longer time windows in Granger causality analysis

or for typical cognitive electrophysiology, values around 100 ms can be used. In general, for all other types of data sources, the best way to determine this time window is to try various values on test data which give a desirable outcome or, use values that have been previously used in the literature in the field of study.

As can be seen in Fig. 2, a relatively higher or lower model order can be used for Granger causality analysis and here there are also advantages and disadvantages for each of these choices. If a higher model order is considered, the model will be more sensitive to a longer period of history and so will give more information to produce an accurate model. However, there are more parameters for the autoregressive model to estimate which may lead to a poorer model estimation and additionally, will also lead to a longer computation time. Alternatively, for a lower model order, the opposite is true: there will be a better model estimation as there are fewer parameters for the model to estimate and will have a faster computation time; and, this order will be less sensitive to the previous values as it only covers a limited period of history. In order to choose an optimal model order for Granger causality analysis, similar approaches can be taken as for choosing an optimal time window. Granger causality analysis has been mostly used in the field of economics. From analysing the relationship between financial development and economic growth [2,15,16], to stock market

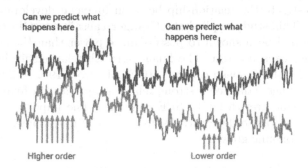

Fig. 2. Graphical representation of using higher or lower model orders in Granger causality analysis

prediction [3, 6, 18], this analysis technique has proven to be a useful and effective tool. These works mainly identified relationships between financial news media or social media and the stock market and the data analysis techniques that are employed in these works (specifically text analysis and sentiment analysis) prove to be very effective to the prediction of equity markets. Many methods of analysing news media were used in these studies, examples of these include: text mining, feature extraction, feature selection and machine learning methods.

One example by [12] attempts to predict stock prices by analysing corporate announcements. The authors used a four-step approach, in order to process the extremely large amount of textual information, which comprised of: in feature extraction; in feature selection; in feature representation; and machine learning. This robust, four-step approach allows selecting semantically relevant features and therefore reduces the problem of over- fitting when applying the machine learning algorithm. It is found that when feedback-based feature selection is combined with 2-word combinations, instead of just singular words, accuracies of up to 76% are achieved in predicting the stock market and additionally, it is then demonstrated that this approach is highly profitable for trading in practice.

Various other works have implemented Granger causality analysis (and Granger non-causality[1] analysis proposed by [6]) to further improve the prediction accuracy equity markets using investor sentiment based on financial news media and social media data [3, 6, 18].

Several uses of Granger causality in other areas of economics have also been carried out. A particularly effective use of Granger causality analysis was carried out by [2] to test the causal relationship between, economic growth and tourism development. Annual data from the World Bank across 12 Mediterranean countries from 1995 to 2012 was employed in this analysis. Granger causality analysis showed a bidirectional causality relationship between tourism development and economic growth meaning that increases tourism development can in turn increase economic growth, and economic growth can in turn increase tourism development. The identification of this relationship, led the authors to suggest that to achieve high economic growth, policy-makers should place a high priority on developing the tourism sector in these countries.

Another impactful application of Granger causality analysis was carried out by [15] to investigate the relationship between financial development and economic growth. This study applied the Granger causality test in the frequency domain, which had been shown to possess more power than the standard time domain Granger causality test. The finance-growth relationship in 19 Central, East, and Southeast European countries (CESEE) from 1991 to 2017 was investigated. The findings indicated a strong relationship between financial development and economic growth for CESEE countries. The importance of Granger causality analysis, was to demonstrate that financial development is important for improving economic growth.

---

[1] Granger non-causality requires that past information of one time series does not alter the conditional distribution of another time series i.e. where Granger causality fails to reject the null hypothesis.

[16] employed Granger causality to investigate the relationship between domestic demand, exports and economic growth in China. This is carried out using time-series data obtained from the Penn World Tables for the period of 1978 to 2002. The findings showed the presence of dynamic, bidirectional Granger causality relationships among all variables highlighting that both domestic demand and exports are important for economic growth, and conversely that economic growth has an impact on domestic demand and exports. Given the dynamic relationship among these variables, Granger causality analysis was able to demonstrate that successful and sustained economic growth requires growth in both exports and domestic demand.

3   Methodology

A collection of public tweets posted from worldwide are extracted through the use of the public Twitter API, using code developed in the Big Data and Smart Analytics lab at Griffith University. A collection of 5,331,040 public tweets were extracted and recorded between 5 May, 2021 and 31 May, 2021. The tweets contained only references to the cryptocurrency Dogecoin; this filtering included tweets which had mention of "dogecoin", "dogearmy", "dogecoinRise", "dogeEurope" or "dogecoins". Given the recent excitement on Twitter around this specific cryptocurrency, this was deemed the most appropriate equity to investigate the effects of Twitter sentiment [1]. In order to quantify the sentiment in these tweets, it was relied on a comprehensive lexicon rule-based model for general sentiment analysis of short messages VADER (for Valence Aware Dictionary for sEntiment Reasoning) [14]. The sentiment of each post was calculated using propriety methodology from the Big Data and Smart Analytics lab at Griffith University, which also takes into consideration length of the posts and is built on top of VADER [5].

The closing prices of Dogecoin for each day in the same period (between 5 May, 2021 and 31 May, 2021) were extracted from Yahoo! Finance[2] by using webscraping techniques. This method was developed and relied on the initial code provided at GitHub[3].

In order to compare the time series of average sentiment and the closing prices of Dogecoin for each day, a common scale for comparison is required. Thus, the Dogecoin prices and sentiment values are normalised to z-scores on the basis of a local mean and standard deviation within a sliding window of $2k$ days before and after a particular date. The z-score of a time series Y_t, denoted as $\mathbb{Z}_{X_t}$ is given by Eq. 1.

$$\mathbb{Z}_{X_t} = \frac{X_t - \overline{x}(X_{t\pm k})}{\sigma(X_{t\pm k})} \tag{1}$$

where $\overline{x}(X_{t\pm k})$ and $\sigma(X_{t\pm k})$ are the mean and standard deviation within the period of $[t - k, t + k]$. Normalising the values in this way results in each time

---

[2] https://finance.yahoo.com/quote/DOGE-USD/history.
[3] https://github.com/Gunjan933/stock-market-scraper.

series oscillating around a mean of 0 which can then be expressed on a scale of 1 standard deviation. After normalisation, analysis of the relationship between Twitter sentiment and Dogecoin prices can be carried out.

Granger causality [11] is then used to find the correlation between social media sentiment and Dogecoin. The sentiment and Dogecoin prices are converted to z-scores for a k value of 1 in Eq. 1.

The reason that Granger causality analysis was used rather than more powerful machine learning techniques, such as Deep learning which have given excellent results in previous works, is because the desired outcome of this analysis is simply a confirmation on whether Twitter sentiment is correlated to Dogecoin price to a statistical significance. To gain the full benefits of machine learning methods required costly and timely annotation, while our intention was essentially a 'yes' or 'no' answer which is exactly what Granger causality analysis was able to provide.

We plan to harness Granger causality analysis, a statistical hypothesis test, to investigate whether one variable can be used to forecast another variable. The technique describes that for a time series X_t to be causal of a time series Y_t, values of X_t should help in improving the forecast of Y_t. Therefore, systematic changes in the lagged values of X_t should exhibit a statistically significant relation with the present values of Y_t. This is shown graphically in Fig. 3 [17]. This analysis technique is closely related to the concept of cause-and-effect although, contrary to what the name suggests, it is not actually testing a causative relationship but rather testing correlation or prediction [7]. It is important to note here that correlation does not necessarily mean a causation relationship is present. Granger causality analysis is used for, not testing actual causation, but instead for evaluating if values from a time series contain predictive information about another time series. If this relationship is found to be present, it is said that one time series 'Granger-causes' another.

Therefore, Granger causality is fundamentally about investigating the flow of information between time series and whether two time series have directed functional interactions. For this reason, some prefer to refer to Granger causality as 'Granger prediction' [7], thus avoiding the mention of the term 'causality' given that causation is not actually being tested.

Quantitatively, a time series X_t, for a time t, is considered to Granger-cause a time series Y_t, for a time t, if the past values of X_t predict the future values of Y_t with statistical significance. This relation can be shown through a series of t-tests and F-tests on the lagged values of X_t (and with lagged values of Y_t also included). This will show whether the lagged values of X_t provide statistically significant information about the present (and also future) values of Y_t. The null hypothesis for the Granger causality test of: "X_t does not Granger-cause Y_t" is not rejected if and only if no lagged values of the explanatory time series, X_t, have been retained in the regression after the application of t-statistic and F-statistic. Otherwise, the null hypothesis is rejected in favour of the alternative, and it is concluded that the time series X_t does Granger-cause the time series Y_t and therefore the future values of Y_t are dependent on the past and present

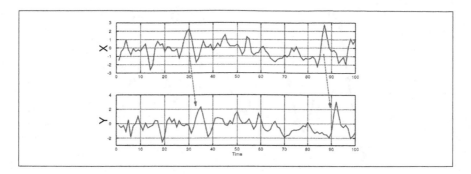

Fig. 3. Graphical representation of a time series X_t being shown to Granger-cause a time series Y_t [8]

values of variable X_t. In order to reject the null hypothesis, a probability value (p) needs to be less than an assigned α level (typically $p < 0.05$ or $p < 0.10$), and then the null hypothesis is rejected at that level. It is also important to note that it can be tested whether X_t Granger-causes Y_t *or* whether Y_t Granger-causes X_t. If one of these is true, this is called unidirectional Granger causality and if both are true, this is called a bidirectional Granger causality. To test the null hypothesis, the time series X_t and Y_t are to be first represented by an autoregressive model.

3.1   Autoregressive Models

The autoregressive model, which is a representation of a type of random process that can be used to describe certain processes that vary with time [10], is applied to the two time series: average sentiment; and Dogecoin prices. These models state that the output variable depends linearly on its own previous values and on a stochastic (random error) term, meaning the model is in the form of a recurrence relation. Examples of univariate autoregressive models can be shown in the following equations (Eq. 2) and Fig. 4.

$$X_t = a_1 X_{t-1} + a_2 X_{t-2} + \ldots + a_n X_{t-n} + e_t$$

$$Y_t = a_1 Y_{t-1} + a_2 Y_{t-2} + \ldots + a_n Y_{t-n} + e_t$$

$$Y_t = \sum_{n=1}^{N} a_n Y_{t-n} + e_t \tag{2}$$

where a_n are the coefficients of Y_{t-n} and e_t is the univariate autoregression error term. In the case of Granger causality, the analysis relies on one time series being able to predict another, meaning that one time series will be linearly dependent on both its own previous values and the values of another time series. This is

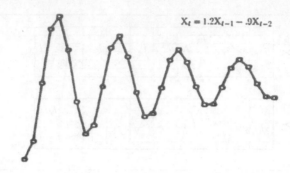

Fig. 4. Example of a univariate autoregressive model

described in the form of a bivariate autoregressive model which is described by
the following equations and shown graphically in Fig. 5.

$$Y_t = a_1 Y_{t-1} + \ldots + a_n Y_{t-n} + a_1 X_{t-1} + \ldots + a_n X_{t-n} + \epsilon_t$$

$$Y_t = \sum_{n=1}^{N} a_n Y_{t-n} + \sum_{n=1}^{N} b_n X_{t-n} + \epsilon_t \qquad (3)$$

where a_n and b_n are the Y_{t-n} and X_{t-n} coefficients respectively, and ϵ_t is the
bivariate autoregression error term. From these two autoregressive models, it can
be seen that if Eq. 2 is equal to Eq. 3, then $b_n = 0 \forall n$, so Y_t has no effect on X_t,
therefore Y_t does not Granger-cause X_t and $e_t = \epsilon_t$. Alternatively, if $b_n \neq 0$ for
at least one value of n, then Y_t does influence X_t, therefore Y_t Granger-causes
X_t and given that the Y_t terms add value to the model, then it is expected that
$\epsilon_t < e_t$. Therefore the variance of ϵ_t will also be smaller than the variance of
e_t. This is the key insight that leads to the quantification of Granger causality
which can be shown in Eq. 4.

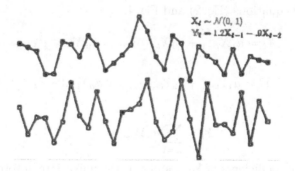

Fig. 5. Example of a bivariate autoregressive model

$$GC = \log(\frac{Var[e]}{Var[\epsilon]})\qquad(4)$$

"GC" is referred to as the Granger gain where the larger the GC value, the more accurate the bivariate model is in predicting the variable Y_t. Between two time series, patterns of synchronisation are expected to change over time and so, Granger causality analysis should not just be computed once over an entire time series but instead many times in a series of small, sliding windows. Here an output of Granger causality estimates, or directed synchronisation which in terms of Granger gain, can be found as is shown in Fig. 6. As mentioned in the introduction, determining the size of the time window considered for analysis and, the order of the autoregressive model (value of N from Eq. 3), are two important parameters to consider when performing Granger causality analysis.

Fig. 6. Bivariate autoregressive model

4   Results and Discussion

Figure 7 shows how the quantified Twitter sentiment varies with time (N.B Twitter sentiment values have been converted to z-scores via Eq. 1). These data values represent the average daily z-score for the 5,331,040 tweets captured from 5 May to 31 May, 2021. The data show large and significant (>2 standard deviations) daily changes in Twitter sentiment across this time period. Assuming this time series Granger-causes Dogecoin price values (across the same time period), price fluctuations mirroring the Twitter sentiment fluctuations would therefore expect to be seen. To test this assumption, Granger causality analysis was applied to the two time series. As discussed earlier two important parameters need to be considered when performing Granger causality analysis. These are: the size of the time window considered for analysis; and, the order of the autoregressive model (value of N from Eq. 3). Based on previous literature [3,6,18], analysis between sentiment and price is considered over daily intervals over the period of at least 1 month and so for this reason, the sentiment values are averaged for each day and the closing prices of Dogecoin is used.

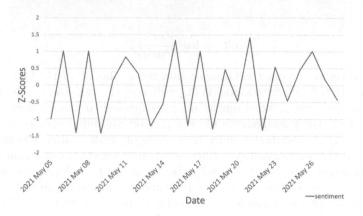

Fig. 7. Z-scores of daily average Twitter sentiment values

To test whether the sentiment time series predicts changes in Dogecoin values, the variance explained by two autoregressive models (as shown in Eqs. 2 and 3) was compared. The first model (employing Eq. 2) used only n lagged values of Y_t, i.e. $(Y_{t-1}, ..., Y_{t-n})$ for prediction, while the second model (implementing Eq. 3) used the n lagged values of both Y_t and the sentiment time series denoted $Y_{t-1}, ..., Y_{t-n}$. Granger causality was carried out using both models for the period of time between 5 May, 2021 and 31 May. As noted above, the Twitter sentiment time series is considered to Granger-cause the price of Dogecoin if and only if and the Twitter sentiment time series adds value to the model.

Table 1. Statistical significance (p-values) of Granger causality correlation between Twitter sentiment and Dogecoin prices from 5 May, 2021 to 31 May, 2021

Lag	1 day	2 days	3 days	4 days	5 days
P-value	0.3822	**0.0208****	**0.0063****	**0.0819***	0.32411

Based on the results of the Granger causality analysis, shown in Table 1, the null hypothesis that the Twitter sentiment time series did not predict the price of Dogecoin is rejected. This means that the coefficients of the Twitter sentiment time series X_t in Eq. 3, $b_{1,2,...,n} \neq 0$ with a high level of confidence.

A statistically significant, unidirectional Granger causality relation for Twitter sentiment and Dogecoin prices was found for lags ranging from 2 to 4 days (where $p < 0.05$ or $p < 0.10$). This means that changes in sentiment, according the results and fundamentals of Granger causality, prompt changes in the price of Dogecoin 2 to 4 days later. This can also be seen by a visual comparison of the two time series. Figure 8 shows a plot of normalised z-scores for both Twitter sentiment and Dogecoin price where the latter time series has been shifted back in time by three days (as a 3-day lag has the lowest p-value). Visual inspection

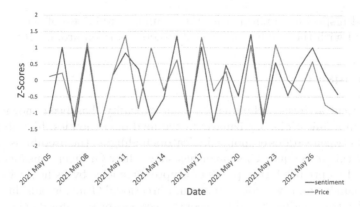

Fig. 8. Overlap of day-to-day difference of Dogecoin prices and daily average Twitter sentiment values which has been lagged 3 days

of the data show that both time series frequently overlap and trend in the same direction at many time points. This is also reflected in a Pearson correlation coefficient for these two data sets (with a 3-day lag) of $r = 0.6940$. This value, as well as the statistically significant results of Granger causality analysis accompanied by clear visual correlation between the two time series, all provide strong evidence that changes in the past values of Twitter sentiment (at time t) predicts a similar rise or fall in the price of Dogecoin three days later (at $t+3$). Therefore, Twitter sentiment about Dogecoin, as calculated by a method developed in the Big Data and Smart Analytics lab at Griffith University, has predictive value with regards to the price of Dogecoin. The only significant case in which the sentiment time series fails to track changes in the price of Dogecoin in Fig. 8, is on 13 May which correlates to the price of Dogecoin on 16 May (given the 3-day lag). This finding also is aligned with correlation of purchase volume of the Dogecoin and number of relevant tweets, as it can be seen in Fig. 9, where

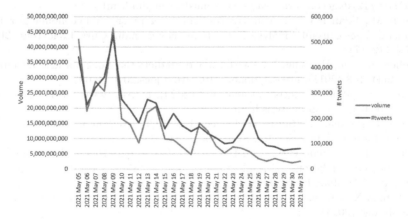

Fig. 9. Correlation between volume of purchase and number of Tweets.

even visual inspection confirms that the volume of purchase of the Dogecoin is well aligned with the number of relevant tweets apart on around 16th of May.

5   Conclusion

The statistical analysis technique, Granger causality, has been shown to have many useful applications particularly in the field of economics. Identifying relationships between various economic indicators highlights the usefulness and effectiveness of this technique. This paper has shown how Granger causality analysis can be used to predict future prices of cryptocurrencies by using Twitter sentiment data analytics. It was found that a unidirectional Granger causality relation between Twitter sentiment and Dogecoin prices was present for day lags ranging from 2 to 4 days (with a 3-day lag having the lowest p-value). This demonstrates that changes in polarity sentiment of relevant Twitter posts (as calculated by modified VADER), prompt changes in the price of cryptocurrencies 2 to 4 days later to a high statistical significance. This was also accompanied by a Pearson correlation coefficient of $r = 0.6940$ and a clear visual correlation between the two time series (with a 3-day lag).

A possible future work that can improve upon the results of this paper, is to consider the influence of the number of followers each Twitter user has. It stands to reason that the more followers a user has, the more influence over the general public they should have. Therefore, it can be incorporated into the analysis that the sentiment scores of each tweet by a user, affects the average sentiment value for each day in proportion to the number of follows that user has.

References

1. AliciaAdamczyk: What's behind dogecoin's price surge and why seemingly unrelated brands are capitalizing on its popularity (2021). https://www.cnbc.com/2021/05/12/dogecoin-price-surge-elon-musk-slim-jim.html
2. Bilen, M., Yilanci, V., Eryüzlü, H.: Tourism development and economic growth: a panel granger causality analysis in the frequency domain. Curr. Issue Tour. **20**(1), 27–32 (2017)
3. Bollen, J., Mao, H., Zeng, X.: Twitter mood predicts the stock market. J. Comput. Sci. **2**(1), 1–8 (2011). https://doi.org/10.1016/j.jocs.2010.12.007
4. Brooks, C.: What is statistical analysis? (2020). https://www.businessnewsdaily.com/6000-statistical-analysis.html
5. Chen, J., Becken, S., Stantic, B.: Lexicon based Chinese language sentiment analysis method. Comput. Sci. Inf. Syst. **16**(2), 639–655 (2019)
6. Chuang, C.C., Kuan, C.M., Lin, H.Y.: Causality in quantiles and dynamic stock return-volume relations. J. Bank. Financ. **33**(7), 1351–1360 (2009). https://doi.org/10.1016/j.jbankfin.2009.02.013
7. Cohen, M.X.: Analyzing Neural Time Series Data: Theory and Practice. MIT press, Cambridge (2014)
8. Wikimedia Commons: File:GrangerCausalityIllustration.svg (2014). https://commons.wikimedia.org/wiki/File:GrangerCausalityIllustration.svg

9. Dillard, J.: 5 most important methods for statistical data analysis (2015). https:// www.bigskyassociates.com/blog/bid/356764/5-Most-Important-Methods-For-Statistical-Data-Analysis

10. Encyclopedia: International encyclopedia of the social sciences (2021). https:// www.encyclopedia.com/social-sciences/applied-and-social-sciences-magazines/ autoregressive-models

11. Granger, C.W.: Investigating causal relations by econometric models and cross-spectral methods. J. Econom. Soc. **37**, 424–438 (1969)

12. Hagenau, M., Liebmann, M., Neumann, D.: Automated news reading: stock price prediction based on financial news using context-capturing features. Decis. Support Syst. **55**(3), 685–697 (2013). https://doi.org/10.1016/j.dss.2013.02.006

13. Hendry, D., Teräsvirta, T.: Sir Clive William John Granger 1934–2009. Biogr. Mem. Fellows Br. Acad. **12**, 451–469 (2013)

14. Hutto, C., Gilbert, E.: VADER: a parsimonious rule-based model for sentiment analysis of social media text. In: Proceedings of the International AAAI Conference on Web and Social Media, vol. 8, pp. 216–225 (2014)

15. Skare, M., Porada-Rochoń, M.: Financial and economic development link in transitional economies: a spectral granger causality analysis 1991–2017. Oecon. Copernic. **10**(1), 7–35 (2019)

16. Tsen, W.H.: Exports, domestic demand, and economic growth in China: Granger causality analysis. Rev. Dev. Econ. **14**(3), 625–639 (2010)

17. Wei, W.: Granger causality test (2016). https://www.sciencedirect.com/topics/ social-sciences/granger-causality-test

18. You, W., Guo, Y., Peng, C.: Twitter's daily happiness sentiment and the predictability of stock returns. Financ. Res. Lett. **23**, 58–64 (2017). https://doi.org/ 10.1016/j.frl.2017.07.018

Using Brain-Computer Interface (BCI) and Artificial Intelligence for EEG Signal Analysis

Jakub Kurczak[ID], Katarzyna Białas[✉][ID], Rafal Chalupnik[✉][ID],
and Michał Kedziora[✉][ID]

Wroclaw University of Science and Technology, Wroclaw, Poland
{katarzyna.bialas,rafal.chalupnik,michal.kedziora}@pwr.edu.pl

Abstract. The goal of this paper is to use a brain-computer interface (BCI) and artificial intelligence for EEG signal analysis. This includes answering the question whether it is possible to create a classifier that could correctly recognize emotions from EEG data recorded by simple and cheap equipment. In the paper, we compared the created classifier with the one that was taught on high-quality EEG data, which was recorded with the help of professional-grade equipment. Two experiments were planned. In both experiments, models had to classify three emotions based on EEG data: positive, negative, and neutral. In the first one, a classifier was trained on data from every person in a group and then tested on the data from the same group of people. In the second test, a classifier was trained on data from a group of people and then tested on a person from outside of this group. From the results of the conducted experiments, an appropriate set of conclusions were drawn. It is possible to create a classifier on a lower grade dataset. The best classifier made on the Mindwave dataset had a prediction accuracy of 89%. The classifier made on the lower grade dataset presented worse results than the classifier made on high-grade dataset. The difference in prediction accuracy between both classifiers is 10%. Classifiers tested on one set of people could not accurately predict the emotions of people outside of this group. The conclusions were consistent with related works results.

Keywords: Machine learning · Brain-computer interface · EEG

1 Introduction

EEG data can be provided by a plethora of devices, but most of them are very expensive [7,12,19]. It is to be expected as for many decades those devices were only used by medical professionals that needed very precise readings to accurately interpret data [10,22]. There is a need for an EEG recording device that has different characteristics, with more emphasis on the comfort of a subject that data is being read and with a cheaper price. Some devices fulfill these

© The Author(s), under exclusive license to Springer Nature Singapore Pte Ltd. 2022
E. Szczerbicki et al. (Eds.): ACIIDS 2022, CCIS 1716, pp. 214–226, 2022.
https://doi.org/10.1007/978-981-19-8234-7_17

requirements, most notably Neurosky Mindwave Mobile 2 [2,15]. But the data acquired from those cheaper devices might be less accurate [3,21].

The problem is to classify emotions based only on EEG data from easily acquirable, cheap, and widely used devices, instead of professional-grade gear. The study wants to answer several questions. Is it possible to create an emotion classifier, taught on data from cheap and amateur grade devices, what accuracy is achievable with this kind of classifier, how this classifier would compare to the one taught on high-quality dataset and can this model classify emotions only on the people it was taught in, or also people outside of this group?

In this paper, we want to answer the question whether it is possible to create a classifier that could correctly recognise emotions from EEG data recorded by simple and cheap equipment. This study also tries to compare this classifier with the one that was taught on high-quality EEG data, which was recorded with the help of professional-grade equipment.

The scope of this paper includes researching if it is possible to create an emotion classifier from EEG data extracted by a cheap device. Research also includes comparing classifiers trained on data from a cheap and simple device to classifiers trained on data from professional-grade dataset. For the professional dataset, we used the SEED dataset [14]. The dataset provided by NeuroSky Mindwave Mobile 2, as it is a cheaper device, was used as the lower-quality dataset. To reduce outside factors in our experiments, we presented stimuli in VR environment [18]. In a process of creating the classifier, three machine learning algorithms were used: KNN [5], feed-forward neural network and xgboost. Necessary data manipulation, training and testing, and result visualisations were done in the KNIME environment.

The remainder of this paper is structured as follows. The related work section reviews the literature and the state of the science related to the issues in this paper. In the next sections, the experiments are conducted. The experiment's purpose is to answer the question raised in this paper. From the results of the performed experiments, the conclusions are drawn in the last section of this paper.

2 Related Works

Detecting emotions using EEG was part of several research papers [4,9]. Article [14] presents a range of methods of feature extraction and classifiers. In this work, classifiers are divided into four categories: adaptive classifiers, matrix and tensor classifiers, transfer learning methods, and deep learning. There were also few methods outside these categories, notably shrinkage LDA and random forest classifier. The review concluded that adaptive classifiers almost always outperform static ones. Transfer learning methods are solid but the results vary. The most notable revelation was that, contrary to their success in other fields, deep learning methods have not demonstrated convincing and consistent improvements over state-of-the-art BCI methods. In paper [17] it was decided to use the emotion model which assumed a division into two groups: positive and negative [8].

Duan et al. [7] describe in a brief manner how the SEED dataset was constructed and what methods were used for feature extraction. The dataset includes two folders, one with raw EEG data and the other with processed data. Data was created with tests made on 15 subjects, age 22–24, that watched 15 movie clips. Each movie clip had associated emotions: negative, neutral, or positive. The test was performed on each subject three times with one week gap between tests. A model trained on this data, using only gamma frequency bands and an SVM classifier, can achieve an average accuracy of over 80%.

Thomas et al. [20] tried to prove the superiority of deep learning methods against traditional classifiers in EEG emotion classification. Researchers compared the accuracy of k-NN, SVM, CNN, and RNN with different feature extraction methods each. Results stated that CNN was the best with an accuracy of over 69%. The best traditional classifier was SVM with accuracy reaching 66%. The paper reaches the conclusion that deep learning methods rely less on feature extraction and present better overall performance than traditional classifiers.

Acharya et al. [1] describe the whole process of creating an emotion recognition model which includes making a dataset with a Mindwave 2 device. For data extraction, researchers created tests that included watching short movie clips. While wearing an EEG device, subjects were rating the aforementioned clips based on emotional response. The dataset includes 25 participants. Then, using multitree genetic programming with hybrid crossover, they created a classifier. With the created model, researchers achieved a staggering average accuracy of 88,42%.

Islam et al. [11] focus on developing an improved emotion recognition method with lower computation complexity and lower memory requirements without harm to performance. Researchers used the Convolutional Neural Network model for this purpose. They ignored theta brain waves as they have no significant influence on emotion recognition. Pearson's Correlation Coefficients featured images were considered for lower computation complexity and shorter operation time. The dataset includes a widely recognised dataset [12], which consists of EEG data labelled by 16 classes of emotions extracted from 32 participants. The accuracy of the proposed model for two-class valence and arousal is 78.22 % and 74.92 %, respectively. The paper concludes that more research and studies are essential in channel reduction, significant feature extraction, and deep network optimization in the future.

Liu et al. [13] propose new EEG emotion recognition framework. The framework, also known as EEG emotion Transformer (EEt), is built solely on self-attention. Researchers approach considers different contributions of different brain regions. The results presented in the paper show that a novel attention mechanism is able to improve the performance of emotion recognition in substantial ways. The framework consists of a sequential process that includes spatial electrodes position encoding, query-key-value mechanism, a few variants of attention mask learning, and multihead attention recalibration. Variants of attention mask learning include spatial attention, temporal attention, and spatial-temporal attention. This paper is particularly interesting in the way that it also uses a SEED dataset. The authors also worked on the creation of the SEED dataset itself, so their insight is very valuable.

Nawaz et al. [16] compare different extraction methods for EEG emotion recognition. The research was conducted on a dataset created by authors. The participants watched a short video clip that lasted one minute, during this time their EEG data was recorded. The model was three-dimensional. It consists of arousal, valence, and dominance. Several features were extracted from EEG signals. Power, entropy, fractal dimension statistical features and wavelets were extracted. The performance of the two feature selection methods was compared. The methods in question were PCA and relief-based algorithms. The results successfully demonstrated that with time-domain statistical characteristics of brain activity, it is possible to accurately predict different emotional states. It was also noticed that the three-dimensional emotion model was able to classify more emotions correctly than two-dimensional models.

3   Methodology

3.1   SEED Dataset

The SEED dataset is a high-grade dataset containing the EEG data. It was made by professionals from Brain-like Computing and Machine Intelligence Laboratory. Fifteen Chinese subjects participated in the experiments. Seven were male and eight were female. Each one of them took part in fifteen experiments. This whole batch of experiments was performed three times with intervals of seven days. Each person was presented with one of fifteen movie clips. Each clip had an assigned emotion(positive, negative, or neutral). The experiment unravels as follows: first, the 5-second hint was presented, then the movie clip was run, after that there was a short time for self-assessment and finally a 15 s resting time. During the experiments, subjects wore a special cap with 62 electrodes that measured brain activity [7]. The data was downsampled 200 Hz. A bandpass frequency filter from 0–75 Hz was than applied. Each subject file contains 16 arrays [6].

After getting access to the dataset through signing the licence agreement, the first step was choosing which part of the dataset will be used to make and train the classifier. After a thorough analysis, based on [7], logarithm of the average energy was chosen as a feature. To smooth the feature sequence, a moving average filter and linear dynamic system approach was used. It was noticed in [7] that the gamma signal bands correlate the strongest with emotional states. To simplify the computation, only features extracted from this band were used.

The data in SEED is presented in Matlab format. KNIME tool cannot read Matlab files, so conversion was necessary. Using a script, the data was extracted and converted into KNIME friendly CSV format.

In Table 1 we can see the sample data from SEED. Data is only from the gamma band. Columns from 1 to 62 refer to every one of the 62 electrodes that read brain activity during experiments. The last column refers to the emotion

Table 1. SEED dataset sample data (signal values per electrode)

1	2	3–61	62	Emotion
17.0531496910497	16.9866119359967	...	17.0257136806472	1
17.0531489385011	16.9861504356074	...	17.0250670452974	1
17.0527118747201	16.9853196391752	...	17.0243238547558	1
17.0524334280674	16.9854521285061	...	17.0239780450747	1
17.0521882207095	16.9858486400008	...	17.0239646840165	1
17.0517848381601	16.9863930097864	...	17.0246125228582	1
17.0506914592963	16.9866435169556	...	17.0257080858799	1
17.0492260921542	16.9864957441349	...	17.0267220579013	1
17.0478158990942	16.9861789779306	...	17.0278380702489	1
17.0465052162931	16.9863454194049	...	17.0292444407483	1
17.0446712113643	16.9861661065863	...	17.0307421066455	1
17.0430956897851	16.9863038162729	...	17.0317525246404	1
17.0416310204758	16.986428031102	...	17.0328722172074	1
17.040106802649	16.9867780050028	...	17.0342528644602	1
17.0378853862119	16.9861419751149	...	17.0357974333552	1
17.0360773492364	16.9857778241823	...	17.0375857155769	1
17.0337487852744	16.9846046738701	...	17.0393553292537	1
17.0302467596382	16.9825428404962	...	17.0400468144698	1
17.0271944100193	16.9814703706846	...	17.0400432311804	1

that the stimuli were intended to cause. Value of 1 refers to positive emotion, the value of 0 refers to neutral emotion and −1 refers to negative emotion.

3.2 Mindwave Dataset

Four clips, each representing different emotions, were presented to participants. Each person was watching the aforementioned clips in Oculus Quest 2 VR headset to reduce the involvement of outside factors. [18] Clips presented four emotions - one positive, two negative, and one neutral. Due to the data being unbalanced, the SMOTE algorithm was used to artificially generate more entries for classes with a lower number of records.

The Neurosky Mindwave Mobile 2 makes feature extraction by itself. It interprets EEG data assets of lower and higher pairs of particular frequencies with their relative strength of the signal. MindWave Mobile 2 exposes low and high values for every EEG band, except for delta and theta, which have singular values.

Because the brain takes a few seconds to react to the stimuli and after a while subjects are adjusted to the emotions, the first and last 10 s of each session were cut down. It leaves us with only data where brain activity most likely presents the felt emotion.

Another problem with EEG data from the Mindwave device is that even when isolating the subjects in the VR environment with a use of Oculus Quest 2 VR headset, the data presents itself as fairly noisy. It could potentially lower the classifier accuracy, so to battle this issue it was decided to smooth out data. As there are numerous ways to smooth the signal, it was decided to use the moving average algorithm.

In Table 2 we can see a sample of data from Mindwave. In the columns from lAlpha to hGamma, the prefix 'l' refers to low as low signal strength. Prefix 'h' refers to high as high signal strength. The label describes the emotion associated with reading. Value of 1 refers to positive emotion, the value of 0 refers to neutral emotion and −1 refers to negative emotion.

Table 2. Mindwave dataset sample data

delta	theta	lAlpha	hAlpha	lBeta	hBeta	lGamma	hGamma	Label
0	0	0	0	0	0	0	0	−1
1	0	0	0	0	0	1	0	−1
24	1	1	1	1	1	0	0	−1
155163	87541	108997	28806	34217	23522	32936	25780	−1
565232	125340	32626	17317	6748	53199	13642	9383	−1
451010	120392	5329	8883	6227	19384	16247	4198	−1
88429	20202	7522	18521	23869	8580	5210	8337	−1
361508	101702	17742	5937	21252	10405	5428	4773	−1
189648	94703	11474	35967	10584	15694	10695	2659	−1
691541	165778	2436	16261	7602	16793	15070	4174	−1
162676	46391	17540	23601	14806	8672	6880	4592	−1
122984	17823	2194	4271	6038	1191	1316	721	−1
32288	12024	4684	15758	9144	5483	4651	2449	−1
133299	26418	12080	1937	1903	2322	1564	353	−1
490348	50068	2276	6084	12100	30093	6477	1314	−1
35197	88189	14151	14643	14271	13395	4433	949	−1
23721	9756	8217	12768	13154	9007	3565	999	−1
1318766	314857	484025	161725	37852	41069	106014	12966	−1
51636	65204	14007	2181	1139	1938	7283	1305	−1

3.3   Models Taught and Tested on the Same Group of People

The goal of this experiment is to determine if it is possible to create a good model that could accurately classify emotions based on EEG data. We want to also compare this model performance to a model trained on a professional dataset (SEED) to examine if data quality contributes to model quality.

We search for a model with the best class prediction accuracy. We start with simple machine learning algorithms, tune them in until they present the best possible score. If the score is satisfactory, the test is stopped. If the score is not satisfactory, next, more advanced machine learning algorithm is chosen to conduct more research. The training and testing datasets contain records from every person from whom the EEG data was collected. When dividing the data into test and training sets, the class balance was preserved in each set.

Training and Testing Classifier Based on SEED Dataset. The tests started simple. Given the popularity of KNN in EGG data analysis [7], it was the first choice for research. It also has low computational complexity, which is helpful for testing small adjustments to the k value to get the best score. The first step included reading all data. After that, the data was partitioned with class ratios similar in both divisions. Next, the training dataset was normalized and the test dataset got applied normalization. Then KNN with k equal to 550 was trained and tested. Machine learning algorithm known as KNN gave an accuracy of 82,3%. It is a very good score, especially for such a simple algorithm.

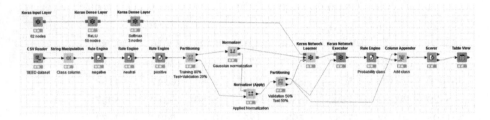

Fig. 1. Feed forward neural network workflow in KNIME

Given the popularity of neural networks in various fields [14,20], it was considered as the next contender for improving accuracy. The first step included reading data from the SEED dataset. The next step was to create new columns for each class in each row. The next step included partitioning the dataset into training and testing datasets with class balance in each dataset in mind. After that, the training dataset was normalized and the test dataset got normalization applied. Test dataset was split in half, with the class balanced preserved, into a test set and validation set. Then, the model was trained and tested. As said in [14], a neural network usually lacks consistency, but in this case, it presented good results. Feedforward neural network with one hidden layer with 50 nodes and ReLU function gave an accuracy of 98,5%. More than 16% improvement over KNN.

Training and Testing Classifier Based on the Dataset Created with Neurosky MindWave 2. The KNN algorithm was used first to create a usable model for emotion classification. Firstly, the data from a single movie clip was adjusted - the first and last 10 s were removed. Next, the data were smoothed with a moving average algorithm. After that, the data were divided into sets of training and testing sets with preserving each set balance in mind. The following step included normalizing the data with Gaussian normalization. After that node, we trained and tested the classifier. The value of k in KNN was chosen by trial and error. The results were satisfactory. The trained model resulted in class prediction accuracy reaching 78,1%. Over 10% drop compared to the same model taught by SEED dataset, but still acceptable.

The data was similarly prepared for the KNN experiment. Data was trimmed and after that, it was smoothed with a moving average algorithm. Next, it were divided into sets of training and testing sets while keeping each set balanced. The following step included normalizing the data with Gaussian normalization. The neural network presented the most disappointing results. Keras Network Learner was properly tuned to create the best possible model but still presented lacklustre performance. The class prediction accuracy topped at 55%. It is a considerable loss considering not only the SEED counterpart but also the KNN model presented earlier. As stated in [14], the neural networks are unreliable in EEG emotion classification. This statement was confirmed by our study.

In search of better results, the use of the XGBoost Tree algorithm was decided. The data was prepared in a similar fashion to previous experiments. The model performed really well, reaching 89%. This result renders our model really usable.

3.4   Models Taught and Tested on Different Groups of People

The goal of this research part is to determine if models trained on a subset of individuals could predict other people (whose data was not used in the model training) emotions based on EEG data.

Every model was trained on data from 14 people and then tested on data from subjects outside of this group. Therefore, in test 1, data from the person described as Subject_1 was used as a test set and data from everyone else (i.e., data from subjects from 2 to 15) was used as the training set. Tests were conducted on the SEED dataset and the MindWave dataset. Machine learning models used for the tests were: KNN, feed-forward neural network and XGBoost tree. These particular algorithms were used as they showed satisfactory performance on previous tests.

Training and Testing Classifiers Based on SEED Dataset. The same approach as in previous tests with SEED dataset was used. After a thorough analysis, based on the logarithm of average energy [7] was chosen as a feature. To smooth the feature sequence, a moving average filter and linear dynamic system approach was used. It was noticed that the gamma signal band correlates the strongest with emotional states. To simplify the dataset, only features extracted from this band were used.

As can be seen in Fig. 2, given the simplest machine learning algorithm, which in our case is k nearest neighbours, the class prediction accuracy ranges between

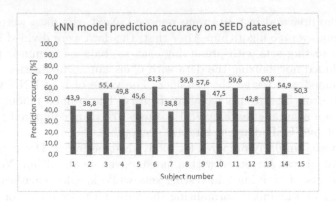

Fig. 2. Results for kNN model for SEED dataset

38,8% and 61,3%. With a median of 50,3% and disparities between the best and worst prediction of over 20% the results are far from ideal. The best prediction was from data from subjects six, thirteen, eleven, and eight. The worst prediction was from data from subjects two, seven, twelve, and one. In comparison to kNN scores, the feed-forward neural network presented a better best prediction of 69,7%, but also a lower worst prediction of 30,8%. Even the median is worse at 48,9%. The best prediction was from data from subjects eleven and six. The worst prediction presented data from subjects seven, twelve, and two.

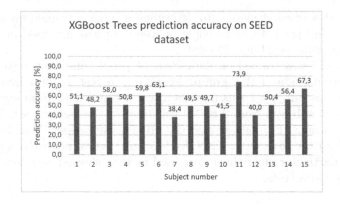

Fig. 3. Results for XGBoost Tree model for SEED dataset

As can be seen in Fig. 3, the XGBoost Tree sports the best single score of 74%, but similarly to the previous machine learning algorithm, with accuracy the disparity between the best and worse score has risen. With the lowest score of 38,4%, the disparity equals around 35,6%. Finally, the median rose to 50,8%. The best prediction was with data from subjects eleven, fifteen, and six. The worst prediction presented data from subjects seven, twelve, and ten.

As the test results presented, it was not possible to teach models with data from one group of people and accurately predict emotions for another subject. It was not omitted that data from some subjects presented better scores than others. Test data from subjects eleven and six was always in the top four scores. Test data from subjects seven and twelve in every test presented worse scores than data from other subjects. This means that those people have the most average EEG patterns for each emotion or that those people have the most things in common with other subjects.

Training and Testing Classifiers Based on Mindwave Dataset. The same approach as in previous tests with the Mindwave dataset was used. Every available feature from Mindwave was utilized. After trimming down the start and end of each test case to 10 s, the data only needs to be smoothed by the moving average algorithm.

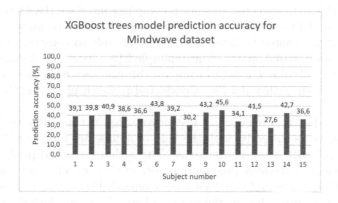

Fig. 4. Results for XGBoost Tree model for Mindwave dataset

As can be seen in Fig. 4, in opposition to the first batch of research, the XGBOOST Tree class prediction accuracy is very disappointing. Accuracy ranges between 27,6% and 45,6%. The median score reaches 39,2% which is just slightly better than the median score from the KNN model. Overall, the best scores present training data from subjects ten, six, and nine. On the other hand, the worst data is presented by training data from subjects eight, thirteen, and eleven.

No matter the algorithm used for teaching, none of the available models presented results that could be considered a success. Every model failed to accurately predict emotion based on data from EEG, but as with tests with the SEED dataset, there are a few interesting observations to be made. Subjects six and fourteen, whose data was used for testing, consistently scored the highest. The same is true for the worst scores, which consistently were taken by training data from subjects eleven and thirteen.

3.5 Summary

It was proved that it is possible to create a proper model with data from a very simple device. The best model learned on the Mindwave dataset had worse class prediction accuracy than the best model learned on the SEED dataset. The difference was not that big, roughly 10%. The biggest surprise was inconsistencies in the neural network model. It performed really well for the SEED dataset, but it performed worse in the MindWave dataset. Of course, the data from MindWave was lower quality and the feature extraction process was simple, but in [20] researchers point out that those are the conditions where neural networks performed the best. On the other hand, this outcome confirms the conclusion from [14] which states that neural networks are inconsistent in their results in emotion classification based on EEG data.

4 Conclusions and Future Work

The goal of this paper was to use a brain-computer interface (BCI) and artificial intelligence for EEG signal analysis. The study also tries to answer two questions. Firstly, we wanted to determine if it is possible to construct an accurate emotion classifier, based on data from a simple EEG device like Neurosky Mindwave Mobile 2. We also wanted to compare this classifier with the one that was thought on a high-quality dataset. Conducted research presented the following discoveries.

In the first batch of research, it was proven that it is possible to distinguish the three emotions correctly, with the help of a classifier based on data from a dataset created with a low-grade device. The highest recorded prediction accuracy of the created classifier presented a score of 89%, which is satisfactory that it solves a three-class problem. With such remarkable accuracy, it is only fair to conclude that even though the methodology of the conducted examination and the equipment used to perform the examination was inferior to ones from the SEED dataset, we can distinguish emotions within the use of the prepared dataset.

As was expected, the SEED dataset presented overall better results. The difference of 9% between the best score of the SEED model and the best score of the Mindwave model is not insignificant. The reasons for that are many. The team behind the SEED dataset spared much more time on feature extraction. Probably the stimuli also might have been chosen better in the SEED dataset. Of course, the much more precise equipment used for acquiring EEG data was also a significant factor. It is not unreasonable to expect that the dataset prepared for the research performs better than the SEED dataset. Both the SEED dataset and Mindwave dataset presented very good performance when we were trying to predict emotions on the same subjects that we were training the models on. However, when we tried a different, more challenging approach, it all fell apart. When we tried to predict the emotions of the person that whom the EEG data was not trained, we reached the accuracy higher than 70% only once. No matter the training dataset and no matter the machine learning algorithm, the prediction models presented scores from which the only logical conclusion is that, with the used features and machine learning models, we can not predict emotions from subjects that were not part of the teaching process of the classification model. The regularity was noticed in some subjects, on whom classification models were tested. The same group of people consistently presented scores that were better than others. This regularity was noticed on both datasets used to experiment. It may hint that those subjects' EEG data had the most in common with the group of subjects that the models were taught on. We have not had information about particular subject characteristics or distinct psychological and physiological features, so further research in this regard might be beneficial in the future.

References

1. Acharya, D., Billimoria, A., Srivastava, N., Goel, S., Bhardwaj, A.: Emotion recognition using fourier transform and genetic programming. Appl. Acoust. **164**, 107260 (2020). https://doi.org/10.1016/j.apacoust.2020.107260
2. Bialas, K., Kedziora, M.: Analiza mozliwosci sterowania aplikacja mobilna za pomoca interfejsu mozg-komputer. In: XII Ogolnokrajowa Konferencja Naukowa Młodzi Naukowcy w Polsce Badania i Rozwój (jesien 2020) (2020)
3. Chalupnik, R., Bialas, K., Jozwiak, I., Kedziora, M.: Acquiring and processing data using simplified EEG-based brain-computer interface for the purpose of detecting emotions. In: ACHI 2021: The Fourteenth International Conference on Advances in Computer-Human Interactions, Nice, France (2021)
4. Chalupnik, R., Bialas, K., Majewska, Z., Kedziora, M.: Using simplified EEG-based brain computer interface and decision tree classifier for emotions detection. In: Barolli, L., Hussain, F., Enokido, T. (eds.) AINA 2022. LNNS, vol. 450, pp. 306–316. Springer, Cham (2022). https://doi.org/10.1007/978-3-030-99587-4_26
5. Chuang, J., Nguyen, H., Wang, C., Johnson, B.: I think, therefore i am: usability and security of authentication using brainwaves. In: Adams, A.A., Brenner, M., Smith, M. (eds.) FC 2013. LNCS, vol. 7862, pp. 1–16. Springer, Heidelberg (2013). https://doi.org/10.1007/978-3-642-41320-9_1
6. SEED Dataset: Stimuli and Experiment (2021). https://bcmi.sjtu.edu.cn/home/seed/seed.html
7. Duan, R.N., Zhu, J.Y., Lu, B.L.: Differential entropy feature for EEG-based emotion classification. In: 2013 6th International IEEE/EMBS Conference on Neural Engineering (NER), pp. 81–84. IEEE (2013)
8. Ekman, P., Cordaro, D.: What is meant by calling emotions basic. Emot. Rev. **3**(4), 364–370 (2011)
9. Fatlawi, H.K., Kiss, A.: An adaptive classification model for predicting epileptic seizures using cloud computing service architecture. Appl. Sci. **12**(7), 3408 (2022)
10. He, H., Tan, Y., Ying, J., Zhang, W.: Strengthen EEG-based emotion recognition using firefly integrated optimization algorithm. Appl. Soft Comput. **94**, 106426 (2020)
11. Islam, M.R., et al.: EEG channel correlation based model for emotion recognition. Comput. Biol. Med. **136**, 104757 (2021). https://doi.org/10.1016/j.compbiomed.2021.104757

12. Koelstra, S., et al.: DEAP: a database for emotion analysis; using physiological signals. IEEE Trans. Affect. Comput. **3**(1), 18–31 (2012). https://doi.org/10.1109/T-AFFC.2011.15

13. Liu, J., Zhang, L., Wu, H., Zhao, H.: Transformers for EEG emotion recognition. CoRR abs/2110.06553 (2021). https://arxiv.org/abs/2110.06553

14. Lotte, F., et al.: A review of classification algorithms for EEG-based brain-computer interfaces: a 10 year update. J. Neural Eng. **15**(3), 031005 (2018). https://doi.org/10.1088/1741-2552/aab2f2

15. Mindwave: Technical Specs (2015). https://store.neurosky.com/pages/mindwave

16. Nawaz, R., Cheah, K.H., Nisar, H., Yap, V.V.: Comparison of different feature extraction methods for EEG-based emotion recognition. Biocybern. Biomed. Eng. **40**(3), 910–926 (2020). https://doi.org/10.1016/j.bbe.2020.04.005

17. Nie, D., Wang, X., Shi, L.C., Lu, B.L.: EEG-based emotion recognition during watching movies. In: EEG-Based Emotion Recognition During Watching Movies, pp. 667–670 (2011). https://doi.org/10.1109/NER.2011.5910636

18. Ryś, M.: Using the brain-computer interface (BCI) in a virtual-reality (VR) environment to acquire and analyze the EEG signal. Master's thesis, Wroclaw University of Science and Technology (2021)

19. Saganowski, S., et al.: Emotion recognition using wearables: a systematic literature review-work-in-progress. In: 2020 IEEE International Conference on Pervasive Computing and Communications Workshops (PerCom Workshops), pp. 1–6. IEEE (2020)

20. Thomas, J., Maszczyk, T., Sinha, N., Kluge, T., Dauwels, J.: Deep learning-based classification for brain-computer interfaces. In: 2017 IEEE International Conference on Systems, Man, and Cybernetics (SMC), pp. 234–239. IEEE (2017)

21. Wei, C., Chen, L.L., Song, Z.Z., Lou, X.G., Li, D.D.: EEG-based emotion recognition using simple recurrent units network and ensemble learning. Biomed. Signal Process. Control **58**, 101756 (2020)

22. Yin, Y., Zheng, X., Hu, B., Zhang, Y., Cui, X.: EEG emotion recognition using fusion model of graph convolutional neural networks and LSTM. Appl. Soft Comput. **100**, 106954 (2021)

Predicting Metastasis-Free Survival Using Clinical Data in Non-small Cell Lung Cancer

Emilia Kozłowska[1]([envelope]) [iD], Monika Giglok[2] [iD], Iwona Dębosz-Suwińska[3] [iD],
Rafał Suwiński[2] [iD], and Andrzej Świerniak[1]([envelope]) [iD]

[1] Department of Systems Biology and Engineering, Silesian University of Technology,
Akademicka 16, 44-100 Gliwice, Poland
{emilia.kozlowska,andrzej.swierniak}@polsl.pl
[2] The 2nd Radiotherapy and Chemotherapy Clinic, M. Sklodowska-Curie National Research
Institute of Oncology, Gliwice Branch, Gliwice, Poland
[3] Department of Radiotherapy, M. Sklodowska-Curie National Research Institute of Oncology,
Gliwice Branch, Gliwice, Poland

Abstract. Lung cancer is the most common and the deadliest type of cancer with
5-year overall survival equal to 15%. One of the main reasons for the high mortality
of lung cancer is the development of local and distant metastases. Lung cancer
patients mostly die because of distant metastases rather than the primary tumor.
Thus, here we tackle the problem of predicting when a patient relapse with a
distant metastatic tumor. This information is relevant not only to assess a patient's
prognosis but also to guide the first-line treatment. Here, we applied clinical data
from over 400 patients to predict the time to metastatic relapse which is also
called metastasis-free survival (MFS). Using Cox regression, we have got a fairly
good prediction with a c-index = 0.63 for a model with three clinical covariates.
In addition, we created also a nomogram that could be applied to predicting the
probability of metastases in newly diagnosed patients. In conclusion, solely based
on clinical data, it is possible to predict the time to metastasis.

Keywords: Non-small cell lung cancer · Metastases · Survival analysis

1 Introduction

Lung cancer is the most frequent type of cancer diagnosed in Poland and worldwide [1].
There are two main types of lung cancer small-cell (SCLC) and non-small cell (NSCLC),
where NSCLC constitutes 85% of all lung cancer cases. This type of cancer is also the
deadliest one in Poland with 5-year overall survival equal to 15% [2].

The treatment of lung cancer involves surgical resection, chemotherapy, radiotherapy,
and their combinations. For decades, chemotherapy combined with radiotherapy was
standard care in lung cancer treatment. More recently, immunotherapy and targeted
treatment (for example EGFR inhibitors) are also administered to lung cancer patients
[3].

It is known that lung cancer death is caused not by the primary tumor but rather
metastases, i.e., a tumor that spreads to distant locations. The most common sites of lung

© The Author(s), under exclusive license to Springer Nature Singapore Pte Ltd. 2022
E. Szczerbicki et al. (Eds.): ACIIDS 2022, CCIS 1716, pp. 227–237, 2022.
https://doi.org/10.1007/978-981-19-8234-7_18

cancer metastases are bone, brain, and liver which lead to shorter survival. Therefore, increased knowledge of metastatic patterns is crucial in the treatment of patients.

There are known two routes of metastasis dissemination of lung cancer – through lymphatic or blood vessels [4]. Lung cancers spread through lymphatic vessels is [5] easier and thus these tumors will first set regional lymph nodes metastases before dissemination to distant sites. It is known that the most important factor predicting the outcome in patients with lung cancer is whether the tumor has spread through blood or lymphatic vessels.

Previously [5], we have built the stochastic model of metastasis dissemination of NSCLC. We have developed a computational platform including machine learning and a mechanistic mathematical model to find the optimal protocol for the administration of platinum-doublet chemotherapy in a palliative setting. The platform has been applied to advanced metastatic non-small cell lung cancer (NSCLC). A simpler version of this model was used in [6] where we have found that chemotherapy combined with angiotherapy could delay the emergence of distant metastases. Unfortunately, this conclusion does not take into account the clinical limitations of such therapy.

Here, we approach a different clinical problem – predicting the risk of distant metastases dissemination. It is a clinically crucial problem as based on this information, clinicians are able to create a more efficient treatment plan.

We developed a clinical data signature that could be applied for the prediction if lung cancer patient will metastasize. We have got the performance of the signature measured as the concordance index equal to 0.63.

We concluded that it is possible to predict with fair accuracy the risk of metastasis based solely on clinical data. We have found that based on administered dose of radiotherapy, platelet level at the diagnosis as well as the fact if the tumor spread to lymph nodes it is possible to estimate the time to metastatic relapse.

2   Materials and Methods

2.1   Patients' Cohort

A retrospective cohort of over 900 patients with a lung cancer diagnosis was collected from the National Research Institute of Oncology (NRIO), Gliwice Branch in Poland. From the cohort, patients with non-small cell lung cancer were extracted. Next, from the cohort, the patients with missing values in any of the 15 covariates (See Fig. 1) were further excluded. In addition, patients with already metastatic tumors at the diagnosis were also excluded. It gives us a cohort of 465 patients included in the analysis.

Those patients were treated with radiotherapy, chemotherapy, chemoradiotherapy (combination of radiotherapy and chemotherapy), or were treated only with palliative intent. Interestingly, a similar number of patients had tumor burden at the diagnosis equal to T2 (early-stage patients) and T4 (advanced-stage patients). In addition, 73% of patients in the cohort have a squamous histopathological subtype of non-small cell lung cancer as expected based on epidemiological data.

Statistical data related to the analyzed patients' cohort are presented in Table 1. All patients gave informed consent, and the data collection was approved by the ethical committee at the NRIO.

Table 1. Patient's cohort characteristics. T, N, M – TNM classification, where T – primary tumor burden, N – lymph nodes tumor burden, M – the presence of distant metastases. Zubrod score – Eastern Cooperative Oncology Group (EOCG) patient's performance score, n – number of patients.

		n = 465
Sex	Female	136(30%)
	Male	329(70%)
Age		62(24–84)
T	T0	5(1%)
	T1	34(7%)
	T2	156(34%)
	T3	103(22%)
	T4	160(34%)
	Tx	17(2%)
N	N0	77(17%)
	N1	42(9%)
	N2	218(47)
	N3	116(25%)
	Nx	12(3%)
M	M0	465(100%)
	M1	0(0%)
Zubrod score	0	128(28%)
	1	300(65%)
	2	32(7%)
	3	5(1%)
Treatment	CT	36(8%)
	CT_RT	309(66%)
	No treatment	7(2%)
	RT	113(24%)
Subtype	Adenocarcinoma	93(20%)
	Large-Cell	18(4%)
	Other	13(3%)
	Squamous	341(73%)

2.2 Statistical Methods

We applied the R environment for all statistical analyses as well as data processing. More precisely, we applied a survival package for building Kaplan-Meier estimator and Cox regression. Nomogram was drawn using the RMS R package.

We computed metastasis-free survival as follows. In the case that the patient had metastasis diagnosed after the diagnosis, MFS is computed as a time interval from diagnosis to the time when the metastases are diagnosed. In other case, MFS is censored and is equal to the time of patient death/the last follow-up.

3 Results

3.1 Exploratory Data Analysis

In the first step, we performed exploratory data analysis to better understand the collected cohort of patients. We created histograms for continuous clinical covariates and bar plots for categorical ones.

All continuous variables, except the total dose of radiotherapy (which is bimodal), are monomodal given with normal or log-normal distribution. The bimodality of the total dose of radiotherapy is expected, as patients got different doses based on the treatment type (if radiotherapy is combined with chemotherapy or not).

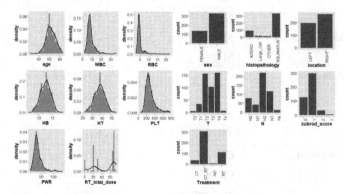

Fig. 1. Histograms (bar plots) for continuous (categorical) covariates.

Based on the bar plots from categorical variables, we can see that most of the patients are males. The most frequent subtype of diagnosed lung cancer is squamous lung cancer. We can also see that most of the patients are at a pretty advanced stage as 1/3 of patients have T in TNM classification equal T4, in addition to N that is most often equal to N2. It means that the cohort contains those patients that are surgically non-resectable.

3.2 Fifty Percent of Patients Have MFS Below Two years and a Half

Next, we performed a Kaplan-Meier analysis to estimate the survival function of metastasis-free survival.

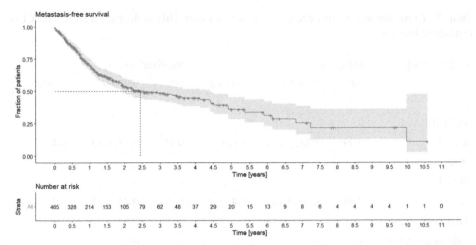

Fig. 2. Kaplan-Meier estimator of the MFS together with risk table for all patients in the cohort (all strata).

Based on Fig. 2, we can see that the median metastasis-free survival is about 2.5 years. During the first two years, the fraction of patients decreases exponentially and after that, we observe a much smaller decrease in MFS.

3.3   Cox Regression Identified Three Clinical Features that Could Predict MFS

We performed both univariate and multivariate Cox regression (see Table 2). The goal of this analysis is to find those clinical covariates that affect the MFS the most, i.e., to compute the hazard ratio for each covariate.

Based on univariate analysis, the following covariates affect the MFS:

N2 or N3 in TNM classification, treatment administered to the patient, level of WBC, hemoglobin, erythrocyte sedimentation rate (ESR), platelet at the diagnosis as well as the total dose of radiotherapy administered to the patients.

Based on multivariate analysis, however, the most affecting covariates are: a histopathological subtype of the lung cancer, tumor location (left/right lung), treatment modalities, as well as WBC and hemoglobin level at the diagnosis.

Next, we performed covariate selection as follows. For each covariate separately, we have built the Cox regression model and evaluated its performance using Harrell's concordance index (c-index). Each of fifteen models was built and the performance was checked using 1,000 bootstrapping samples. The mean value of the c-index from 1,000 bootstraps is then extracted and plotted (Fig. 3, left plot). Based on this analysis, the most predictive power has the following four covariates: the total dose of radiotherapy, platelet level at diagnosis, N from TNM classification, and WBC level at diagnosis.

The natural next step is multivariate Cox analysis performed in such a way that we can select the optimal number of the covariates that could form the best clinical data signature for predicting the risk of metastasis. Thus, we iteratively were adding covariates from the best to the worst (in terms of predictive power obtained from univariate Cox

232   E. Kozłowska et al.

Table 2. Univariate and multivariate Cox regression results. HR1 is the hazard ratio, 95% CI is confidence interval.

Characteristic	Univariate			Multivariate		
	HR	95% CI	p-value	HR	95% CI	p-value
Sex						
FEMALE	–	–		–	–	
MALE	0.99	0.81, 1.21	>0.9	0.91	0.73, 1.13	0.4
Age						
HIGH	–	–		–	–	
LOW	0.93	0.77, 1.11	0.4	1.01	0.82, 1.25	>0.9
Histopathology						
Adenocarcinoma	–	–		–	–	
Large-Cell	0.78	0.47, 1.30	0.3	0.76	0.43, 1.35	0.4
Other	1.76	0.98, 3.16	0.057	1.90	1.04, 3.46	0.035
Squamous	1.19	0.94, 1.50	0.14	1.27	0.99, 1.62	0.060
Location						
LEFT	–	–		–	–	
RIGHT	0.86	0.72, 1.04	0.12	0.77	0.62, 0.94	0.011
T						
T0	–	–		–	–	
T1	1.56	0.61, 3.99	0.4	0.73	0.27, 1.96	0.5
T2	1.59	0.65, 3.88	0.3	1.04	0.41, 2.64	>0.9
T3	1.79	0.73, 4.40	0.2	0.91	0.35, 2.33	0.8
T4	2.20	0.90, 5.38	0.082	1.06	0.41, 2.72	>0.9
Tx	1.81	0.57, 5.71	0.3	0.58	0.17, 1.94	0.4
N						
N0	–	–		–	–	
N1	1.43	0.97, 2.09	0.067	1.41	0.93, 2.13	0.10
N2	1.41	1.08, 1.84	0.011	1.42	1.05, 1.91	0.022
N3	1.87	1.39, 2.52	<0.001	1.76	1.26, 2.46	<0.001
Nx	1.59	0.86, 2.94	0.14	1.82	0.93, 3.58	0.083
Zubrod score						
0	–	–		–	–	
1	1.47	1.20, 1.82	<0.001	1.36	1.08, 1.71	0.008

(*continued*)

Table 2. (*continued*)

Characteristic	Univariate			Multivariate		
	HR	95% CI	p-value	HR	95% CI	p-value
2	2.44	1.65, 3.61	<0.001	1.73	1.13, 2.65	0.011
3	7.67	3.10, 19.0	<0.001	4.58	1.76, 11.9	0.002
Treatment modalities						
Cx	–	–		–	–	
Cx-Rx	0.55	0.39, 0.78	<0.001	0.61	0.40, 0.91	0.015
No treatment	0.25	0.11, 0.57	<0.001	0.33	0.14, 0.78	0.012
Rx	0.78	0.53, 1.14	0.2	0.69	0.45, 1.05	0.086
WBC						
HIGH	–	–		–	–	
LOW	0.67	0.56, 0.81	<0.001	0.75	0.60, 0.94	0.014
RBC						
HIGH	–	–		–	–	
LOW	1.19	0.99, 1.43	0.065	0.83	0.64, 1.09	0.2
HB						
HIGH	–	–		–	–	
LOW	1.52	1.26, 1.83	<0.001	1.45	1.01, 2.09	0.046
HT						
HIGH	–	–		–	–	
LOW	1.35	1.12, 1.63	0.001	1.05	0.72, 1.53	0.8
PLT						
HIGH	–	–		–	–	
LOW	0.66	0.55, 0.79	<0.001	0.83	0.65, 1.06	0.13
PWR						
HIGH	–	–		–	–	
LOW	0.96	0.80, 1.16	0.7	1.11	0.87, 1.42	0.4
The total dose of radiotherapy						
HIGH	–	–		–	–	
LOW	1.72	1.43, 2.06	<0.001	1.56	1.21, 2.00	<0.001

regression) to the Cox regression model. The resulting plot is shown in Fig. 3 on the right.

As we can see, signature with three covariates gives the best outcome in terms of c-index.

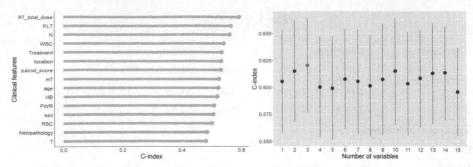

Fig. 3. Cox regression model for all covariates: univariate (left plot) and multivariate (right plot)

3.4   Cox Regression with Regularization

Next, we performed Cox regression with regularization using the glmnet R package. The goal of the regularization is to reduce the effect of those variables which do not add predictive power to the model and thus avoid overfitting. We applied elastic net regularization. The comparison of classical Cox regression with regularized Cox regression is shown in Fig. 4. As we can see, regularized Cox regression gives a bit better predictive power. However, the improvement of prediction with regularized Cox is not statistically relevant according to Welch's two-sample t-test (p-value < 0.001).

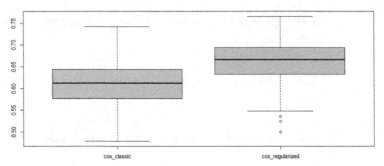

Fig. 4. Comparing the performance of Cox regression with regularized Cox regression in terms of c-index.

3.5   The Final Model Predicting Risk of Metastasis Based on Clinical Data

In the last step, we have built the Cox model using chosen covariates from the plot on the right in Fig. 3. Thus, the hazard function of the chosen model has the following form:

$$HF = \lambda_0 \cdot ex(\beta_1 \cdot RT_{totaldose} + \beta_2 \cdot PLT + \beta_3 \cdot N) \qquad (1)$$

where λ_0 is a baseline hazard, and $\beta_1, \beta_2, \beta_3$ are coefficients which values are estimated during the model fitting.

Lastly, we created the nomogram of our model as depicted in Fig. 5 to show graphically Cox regression model. The first is drawn points axis which is computed based on β values from the Cox regression model. Next, for each value of covariates, the number of points is assigned. For example, N3 has the highest number of points – one hundred. After all covariates, the total number of points is displayed together with the probability of metastatic relapse that could be converted to MFS through Kaplan-Meier estimator.

The nomogram is applied as follows. For each covariate, the number of points is calculated. Next, the points are summed. Lastly, for the given total number of points, the probability of metastatic relapse is read from the bottom axis. For example, let's consider a patient who was not treated with radiotherapy (RT_total_dose = 0 Gy), has a platelet level at the diagnosis equal to 100k/μl, and cancer did not spread to the lymph nodes (N = N0). In the first step, to compute the probability of developing metastasis, we need to read the number of points assigned to each clinical feature. Thus, we need to draw a vertical line from the scale of the given clinical feature to the scale representing the number of points. From the nomogram, we can read the following number of points. For the total dose of radiotherapy (0 Gy), platelet level at diagnosis (10 k/μl), and no lymph nodes metastases (N0) the number of points is 78,12, and 0. Next, we need to calculate the total number of points, which is equal to 90. Lastly, by drawing the vertical line from the total number of points to the probability of metastasis, we can read that the considered patient has a 42% probability to develop distant metastases.

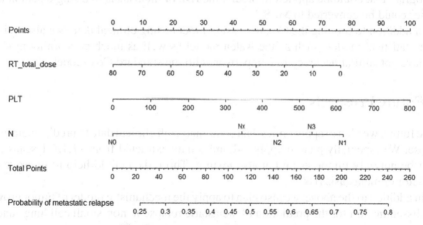

Fig. 5. Nomogram of the Cox model.

4   Discussion

Lung cancer is the most common cancer death worldwide [7] since this cancer type is diagnosed at a late stage because of lack of specific symptoms as well as a high probability of dissemination to distant organs, i.e., probability of metastasis. Thus, novel treatment modalities such as novel targeted treatment are searched to combat this type of cancer.

Here, we tackled the problem of metastases. Currently, it is difficult to predict which lung cancer patient will develop metastasis and when. This information is crucial for planning the treatment for a given patient to make anticancer treatment more personalized.

There is already an available predictive model for pre-operative prediction of lymph node metastases [8] as well as many models of prediction of survival of patients with brain metastases [9]. There exists also a model for predicting time-to-metastasis in early-stage non-small cell lung cancer [10]. However, to our best knowledge, there is no predictive model based solely on clinical features that could predict the risk of metastasis in a wide range of patients with NSCLC. Thus, to fill the gap, we developed model-based clinical data from over 400 NSCLC patients for the prediction of MFS.

We trained iteratively many Cox regression models to find the best combination of clinical covariates. We have found that a model with three covariates is able fairly accurate to predict the risk of metastasis. Next, based on those features, we created a nomogram that could be applied to predict the risk of metastasis in a single patient that further could be converted to MFS.

In addition to training the Cox regression model using clinical data, we also trained other statistical models such as the Aalen model as well as machine learning models. We have got similar accuracy in comparison with the standard Cox model.

5   Future Prospects

In the future, we plan to apply omics data combined with clinical data to predict metastatic relapse. We especially plan to apply radiomics data extracted from PET/CT scans that describe not only tumor shape but also texture. Those data could help to improve the predictor of metastasis risk.

In addition to the above, we also plan to apply the mechanistic model of tumor growth and dissemination for the prediction of metastatic relapse in non-small cell lung cancer.

Acknowledgments. We would like to acknowledge the financial support of the National Science Center, Poland - grant number 2020/37/B/ST6/01959 and EMBO short fellowship.

The work was partially carried out during a research visit at Inria (Marseille, France). We thank the leader of the visiting laboratory – Sebastien Benzekry for fruitful discussion and valuable comments.

References

1. Gridelli, C., Rossi, A., Carbone, D.P., et al.: Non-small-cell lung cancer. Nat. Rev. Dis. Primers **1**(1), 1–16 (2015). https://doi.org/10.1038/nrdp.2015.9

2. Adamek, M., Biernat, W., Chorostowska-Wynimko, J., et al.: Lung cancer in Poland. J. Thorac. Oncol. **15**, 1271–1276 (2020). https://doi.org/10.1016/J.JTHO.2020.03.035
3. Jones, G.S., Baldwin, D.R.: Recent advances in the management of lung cancer. Clin. Med. **18**, s41 (2018). https://doi.org/10.7861/CLINMEDICINE.18-2S-S41
4. Popper, H.H.: Progression and metastasis of lung cancer. Cancer Metastasis Rev. **35**(1), 75–91 (2016). https://doi.org/10.1007/s10555-016-9618-0
5. Kozłowska, E., Suwiński, R., Giglok, M., et al.: Mathematical model predicts response to chemotherapy in advanced non-resectable non-small cell lung cancer patients treated with platinum-based doublet. PLoS Comput. Biol. **16** (2020). https://doi.org/10.1371/journal.pcbi.1008234
6. Kozłowska, E., Świerniak, A.: The stochastic mathematical model predicts angio-therapy could delay the emergence of metastases in lung cancer. In: Pijanowska, D.G., Zieliński, K., Liebert, A., Kacprzyk, J. (eds.) Biocybernetics and Biomedical Engineering – Current Trends and Challenges. LNNS, vol. 293, pp. 64–73. Springer, Cham (2022). https://doi.org/10.1007/978-3-030-83704-4_7
7. Siegel, R.L., Miller, K.D., Fuchs, H.E., Jemal, A.: Cancer statistics. CA: Cancer J. Clin. **71**, 7–33 (2021). https://doi.org/10.3322/caac.21654
8. Zhang, C., Song, Q., Zhang, L., Wu, X.: Development of a nomogram for preoperative prediction of lymph node metastasis in non-small cell lung cancer: a SEER-based study. J. Thorac. Dis. **12**, 3651–3662 (2020). https://doi.org/10.21037/JTD-20-601
9. Shan, Q., Shi, J., Wang, X., et al.: A new nomogram and risk classification system for predicting survival in small cell lung cancer patients diagnosed with brain metastasis: a large population-based study. BMC Cancer **21**(1), 1–8 (2021). https://doi.org/10.1186/S12885-021-08384-5
10. Qi, Y., Wu, S., Tao, L., et al.: Development of nomograms for predicting lymph node metastasis and distant metastasis in newly diagnosed T1-2 non-small cell lung cancer: a population-based analysis. Front. Oncol. **11** (2021). https://doi.org/10.3389/FONC.2021.683282

Impact of Design Decisions on Performance of Embarrassingly Parallel .NET Database Application

Piotr Karwaczyński[1]([⊠]), Marcin Sitko[1], Sylwia Pietras[1], Bogdan Marczuk[1],
Jan Kwiatkowski[2]([⊠]) [iD], and Marius Fraś[2]([⊠]) [iD]

[1] Sygnity S.A., Strzegomska 140a, 54-429 Wrocław, Poland
{pkarwaczynski,msitko,spietras,bmarczuk}@sygnity.pl
[2] Wrocław University of Science and Technology, Wybrzeże Wyspiańskiego 27,
50-370 Wrocław, Poland
{jan.kwiatkowski,mariusz.fras}@pwr.edu.pl

Abstract. The implementation of parallel applications is always a challenge. It embraces many distinctive design decisions that are to be taken. The paper presents issues of parallel processing with use of .NET applications and popular database management systems. In the paper, three design dilemmas are addressed: how efficient is the auto-parallelism implemented in the .NET TPL library, how do popular DBMSes differ in serving parallel requests, and what is the optimal size of data chunks in the data parallelism scheme. All of them are analyzed in the context of the typical and practical business case originated from IT solutions which are dedicated for the energy market participants.

The paper presents the results of experiments conducted in a controlled, on-premises environment. The experiments allowed to compare the performance of the TPL auto-parallelism with a wide range of manually-set numbers of worker threads. They also helped to evaluate 4 DBMSes: Oracle, MySQL, PostgreSQL, and MSSQL in the scenario of serving parallel queries. Finally, they showed the impact of data chunk sizes on the overall performance.

Keywords: Parallel programming · TPL · Performance of processing · Data parallelism

1 Introduction

Meter Data Management (MDM) systems supporting storage and management of data delivered by smart metering systems play the key role in the energy industry utilizing "digital" solutions [1]. MDM provides a number of services that can be demanding for CPU and I/O operations. An example of such service is *reading of profile data* of energy consumption.

Nowadays, in the Polish liberalized energy market, the Distribution System Operator (DSO) IT infrastructure is used to process and disseminate information about electric energy consumption and production. The *reading of profile data* is carried out by each

© The Author(s), under exclusive license to Springer Nature Singapore Pte Ltd. 2022
E. Szczerbicki et al. (Eds.): ACIIDS 2022, CCIS 1716, pp. 238–250, 2022.
https://doi.org/10.1007/978-981-19-8234-7_19

of the national DSOs and is aimed at making the data available to other energy market entities (energy sellers, balance responsible parties), mostly for the purposes of balancing demand and supply for energy. In the coming years, the process of reading and sharing daily profile data will be standardized nationwide by launching CSIRE data hub and implementing the CSIRE Information Exchange Standards (IES) [2].

A typical pattern for data processing in MDM, including the *reading of profile data* service, is to perform the same operation on each element of a large collection of measurement data. The operation (if it is not trivial) can be CPU-bound or (as data usually is stored in a database in a separate network location) might be I/O-bound, or both.

At Sygnity company, the MDM solution that consists of a number of services based on the Microsoft .NET technology has been developed. It usually operates as part of the Distribution System Operator's IT infrastructure. The system can use a number of popular relational database management systems (DBMS): Oracle, MSSQL, PostgreSQL, and MySQL. To make the code independent of a DBMS, the solution benefits from the Entity Framework (EF) [3] technology that maps database objects onto domain objects. Energy consumption profiles are collected from millions of measurement points in Poland. In order to improve performance of the developed system, the parallel processing of data is used with the objective to distribute the load between computing units of a multi-core CPU of the application server. The applied .NET 5 framework includes the Task Parallel Library (TPL) [4] that provides useful parallel processing abstractions like Parallel. ForEach loop or Tasks.

One of a few key design issues was to control the number of threads allocated to a parallel algorithm. In the TPL, auto-parallelism (automatic parallelization of the code) is implemented – it automatically picks a number of parallel threads and partitions the computations in a loop. It is surprising that neither the TPL vendor nor the community of its users has carried out an exhaustive quantitative analysis showing how efficient is the auto-parallelism implemented in TPL.

The second issue was the choice of a relational DBMS. Obviously, a lot of criteria impact such a decision including those related to parallelism. Furthermore, the size of data chunks determines the number of executed iterations in parallel. On one extreme, no fragmentation means sequential execution. On the other side, too tiny data chunks impose large communication overheads.

The paper presents research on these issues expressed as three research questions:

- Q1: How efficient is the auto-parallelism implemented in TPL?
- Q2: How do popular DBMSes differ in serving parallel requests?
- Q3: What is the impact of the size of data chunks on the performance of tested service?

In the Sect. 2, previous works related to the issues considered in the paper are presented. The tested *reading of profile data* service as well as the performed experiments are described in the Sect. 3. The Sect. 4 presents the obtained results. Finally, in the Sect. 5 final remarks including planned future work are given.

2 Related Works

The Task Parallel Library was introduced in .NET Framework 4.0 in 2010. It is a well-established and convenient way of achieving parallelism in a C# code. It is able to dynamically scale the degree of concurrency in order to use available computing units efficiently. However, there are few publications analyzing its performance and none evaluating its auto-parallelism methods.

The quantitative comparison of TPL implementations in versions 4.0 and 4.5 of the .NET Framework is presented in the Microsoft whitepaper [5]. It does not help us as it focuses on performance differences between two versions of the library. Interesting insights on speedup achieved through parallelization of code for computing π using TPL and OpenMP are given in [6]. The authors show that even for the embarrassingly parallel problem the libraries do not achieve linear speedup. The problem considered in that paper varies from ours as it completely focuses on pure calculations. In [7] the authors use calculation-intensive factorization of a sparse matrix as a benchmark for parallel libraries implemented in C, C++, C#, and Java. They show the relation between speedup and the number of threads as well as speedup with 48 threads on different granularity (matrix/submatrix sizes). The latter relation is similar to our quest for optimal size of data chunks and shows that the granularity matters indeed. Luo et al. [8] explore performance of task-based parallel programming using TPL by comparison of the performance of sequential and parallel implementations of two applications: matrix multiplication and image blender. The authors point that the actual number of threads to use is dynamically calculated by the library, but do not analyze how accurate these dynamic calculations are. TPL performance is measured in [9] to compare the library with another concurrent computation model – the actor model. The authors run tests with different numbers of threads (2, 5, 10, 16, 32 and 64) but the results were published as averages. Consequently, it was impossible to compare our and their trends.

Benchmarking database performance for OLTP (short-running transactions with very selective data access) or OLAP (long-running queries scanning large portions of data) scenarios is widely used in IT industry. The experiments we performed were not intended to compete with any standard benchmarks like those from the TPC Council [10] nor contribute any new tests like authors did in e.g. [11]. Instead, we were curious to what extent the choice of the DBMS impacts the overall performance of the business scenario in which many concurrent, high-volume reads are performed, as in our MDM.

The comparisons of such DBMSes as we have selected for our experiments can be found in [12] and [13]. The authors investigate some specific aspects influencing their performance. In the first article, DBMSes are used as the part of a web application. Similarly to our approach, accessing data is achieved through the object-relational mapping library. The another article focuses on the containerization of DBMSes. Regarding DBMS performance measurements, its results suggest that the DBMS performance strongly depends on the specific test scenario. Unfortunately, both articles do not analyze concurrent queries, contrary to our case.

In [14], the aspect of handling concurrent transactions is evaluated for selected workloads and test scenarios. It does not fully address the Q2 question as it provides insights for MySQL only. Handling concurrency in selected databases is also addressed in [15]. Its authors focus on testing the implementations of isolation levels. To some extent, this aspect may influence our results, however it is not directly aligned with our research questions.

3 The Research Experiment

The research was focused on two areas:

1. The exploration of effectiveness of the TPL auto-parallelism mechanism. As the effectiveness it is assumed the performance of TPS-steered operations (quantity/rate) compared to the performance with manual settings.
2. Investigation of the impact of data chunk sizes on the performance of the tested parallel operations.

For both experiments research was performed using four database management systems: 1) Oracle 21c Enterprise Edition, 2) MSSQL Server 2019 Developer Edition, 3) PostgreSQL 14, and 4) MySQL Community Server 8.0.27 for Linux. As we could not provide comparable competencies to tune configurations of the installed DBMSes, they were tested with the default configurations.

The experiments were performed on two Dell PowerEdge R740 servers located in the Sygnity server room in Wrocław:

- Application server (*spectra-app*): Intel Xeon Gold 6226R 2.9 GHz, 16C/32T; 128 GB RDIMM; 2 x 480 GB SSD; 4x1 Gbps Ethernet; Windows Server 2022 Std,
- Database server (*spectra-db*): Intel Xeon Gold 6226R 2.9 GHz, 16C/32T; 64 GB RDIMM; 2 x 960 GB SSD; 4x1 Gbps Ethernet; Oracle Linux Server rel. 8.4.

Both servers were connected directly (point-to-point) by Ethernet 3x1Gbps network, with RTT below 1ms. The fourth port of the network card was used to connect each of the servers to the private corporate LAN network.

The tested operation was specified by the *reading of profile data* business case that consists in reading the daily *profiles* of electricity consumption with a 15-min resolution from the measurement database of a DSO for the purpose of their validation, transformation, and transfer to the appropriate recipient. Consumption profiles are recorded in relation to uniquely identifiable Energy Collection Points (PPE). A single PPE is a point in the power grid or the recipient's address where energy products are measured (including consumed or produced electricity) by appropriate devices (meters). The *reading of profile data* service was chosen due to the following features:

- it significantly strains computational resources in production deployments,
- it is very susceptible to parallelization,
- it belongs to the set of basic functionalities of the MDM system.

The test application was implemented using the Microsoft .NET 5 framework and C# 9.0. The core part of parallelized computation consists of reading the configuration data of PPE, reading the profile data, and finally processing this data, all that included in the `Parallel.ForEach` loop from the TPL library.

3.1 The Evaluation of the Auto-parallelism Implemented in TPL

In the first experiment, the efficiency of TPL auto-parallelism method was measured and compared to eight degrees of parallelization manually set to: 1, 2, 4, 8, 16, 32, 64, and 128 threads. The tests were performed for each of the four considered DBMSes. Each test measurement (a sample) was repeated 10 times which sums up to a total of 360 measurements.

In a single test, daily consumption profiles for 20.000 PPE (1,92 million of data records) were partitioned into separate chunks consisting of 128 PPE and then read and processed in parallel. The measured reading times were converted into the reading rates expressed in millions of data record reads per second.

3.2 Selection of the Optimal Size of Data Chunks

In the second experiment, processing was performed by using different sizes of data chunks in order to measure their impact on the performance of the parallel application. To this end, the daily consumption profiles for 100.000 PPE (96 data records per PPE, i.e. 9,6 million in total) were partitioned into separate data chunks, then read and processed in parallel. The analyzed sizes of data chunks expressed in a number of PPE were: 16, 32, 64, 128, 256, 512, 1024, 2048, 4096, 8192, 16384, 32768, 65536, 131072.

The tests were performed for each of the 4 considered DBMSes, with the TPL auto-parallelism method enabled. Each test measurement (a sample) was repeated 10 times, what sums up to a total of 560 measurements. The measured reading times were converted into the reading rates expressed in millions of data record reads per second.

4 The Experiment Results

4.1 Evaluation of the Auto-parallelism Implemented in TPL

In the Fig. 1 the variability of rate of performing tested operations for 8 manually-set numbers of threads and for the TPL auto-parallelism are compared. The results are presented using a combination of confidence intervals and box-plot diagrams.

The Shapiro-Wilk test showed that for 29 tests with a probability of 95% there is no reason to reject the hypothesis of the normal distribution of samples. Thus, a normal distribution in their populations can be assumed. Consequently, the confidence intervals (CIs) were computed for these populations with a 95% confidence level, using standard deviations of the samples. For 7 samples *p-value* was below the threshold and in the Fig. 1 the variation in these samples is presented in a form of box-plot diagrams through quartiles and outliers (Oracle: 128 threads; MySQL: 16 and 32 threads; PostgreSQL: 64 threads; and MSSQL: 1, 2, and 8 threads).

The results allow to observe some regularities – among others the following:

– for each DBMS, when the experiment is conducted in one thread, the spread of the observed reading rates is relatively small,

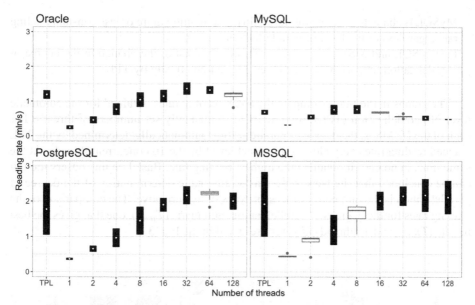

Fig. 1. The variability of data read rates for the numbers of threads set manually and by the TPL.

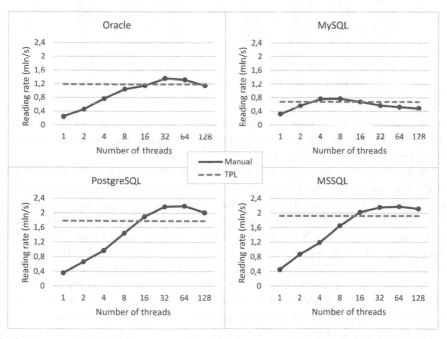

Fig. 2. The comparison of the mean reading rates for a manually set number of threads (Manual) to the mean rate obtained for the automatic level of parallelization (TPL).

- MySQL is characterized by low variability, maintaining more or less constant reading rate regardless of the level of parallelization,
- PostgreSQL and MSSQL seem to react the strongest to the change in the degree of parallelization, in particular for the level set automatically by TPL.

The graphs in the Fig. 2 compare the mean reading rates obtained for the automatic level of parallelization (TPL) to the rates for a manually-set numbers of threads. For each of the DBMSes, the degree of parallelization automatically determined by the TPL reached reading rates very close to those achieved by the 16 concurrent threads. At the same time, in no case it obtained the highest reading rate. Based on this observation, it can be concluded that the basic criterion for automatic determination of the degree of parallelization is the number of processor cores or its derivative. The comparison of the reading rates for the degrees of parallelization: automatic (T_{auto}), one that gives the best results (T_{best}), and 16 threads (T_{16}) is presented in the Fig. 3.

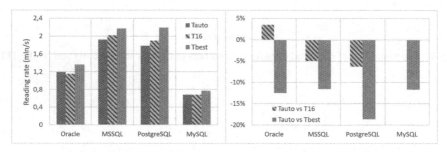

Fig. 3. The comparison of the reading rates: T_{auto}, T_{16}, and T_{best}.

It was also verified whether the similarities of the automatic degree of parallelization with the level of 16 threads can be statistically confirmed. The distributions of their reading rates are presented in the Fig. 4.

The graphs clearly show that the reading rates for Oracle and MySQL for 16 threads and the automatic TPL selection are very similar. For the remaining cases, the distributions seem to differ more. To check if these differences are statistically significant, the Kolmogorov-Smirnov test was used – a non-parametric test that allows to verify whether there are statistically significant differences between the observations in individual groups. The null hypothesis (H_0) says that the reading rates for 16 threads and the number of threads selected by the TPL come from populations with the same distributions, so the differences observed in these distributions are statistically insignificant. High *p-values* for each DBMS, as presented in Table 1, indicate that there is no reason to reject the null hypothesis. Concluding, the test results support our claims.

The *spectra-app* and *spectra-db* servers are built on processors with 16 cores using Hyper-Threading (HT), hence each core can behave like two logical processors sharing its cache and execution unit. In 3 out of 4 scenarios, the best reading rates were reached if the degree of parallelization was close to the number of logical cores. Based on these observations it may be concluded that TPL probably does not take HT into account!

Table 1. The Kolmogorov-Smirnov test results.

DBMS	*p-value*	Reject H_0?
Oracle	0,168	No
MySQL	0,787	No
PostgreSQL	0,418	No
MSSQL	0,787	No

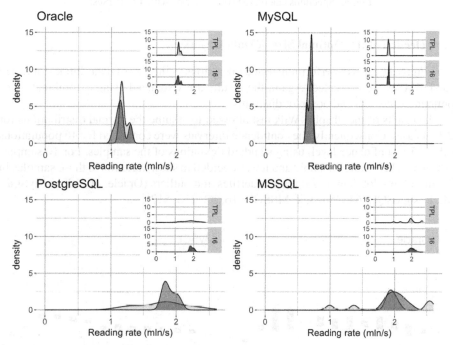

Fig. 4. Distributions of the reading rates obtained for the automatic degree of parallelization and 16 threads.

Finally, using reading rates the execution speedup was calculated. The Fig. 5 presents speedup $S_p = t_1/t_p$ (where: t_1 – time of sequential execution, t_p – time of p-threaded execution) vs the number of threads.

The calculated speedups are similar for all DBMSes except MySQL, which makes the least use of parallelization. For the 3 DBMSes, in the conditions of available resources (network bandwidth, processing units), the speedup increases very well, gaining the maximum near the number of logical cores. The subpar result for MySQL suggests some problem with its default configuration impacting parallel processing.

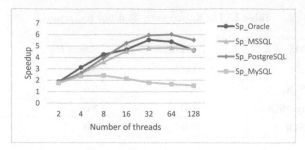

Fig. 5. Speedups calculated for scenarios with 4 DBMSes.

4.2 Selection of the Optimal Size of Data Chunks

In the Fig. 6 the rates of performing tested operations vs the size of data chunks for tested four DBMSes are presented. Again, the results are visualized using a combination of confidence intervals and box-plot diagrams.

The results of the Shapiro-Wilk test allowed to assume the normal distributions for 82% of cases. Consequently, the confidence intervals were computed for 46 populations with a 95% confidence level, using standard deviations of the samples. For 10 samples *p-value* was below the threshold and it was decided to show variation in these samples in a form of box-plot diagrams through quartiles and outliers (Oracle: 4k, 128k; MySQL: 64k; PostgreSQL: 64, 256, 32k; MSSQL: 16, 32, 256, 512).

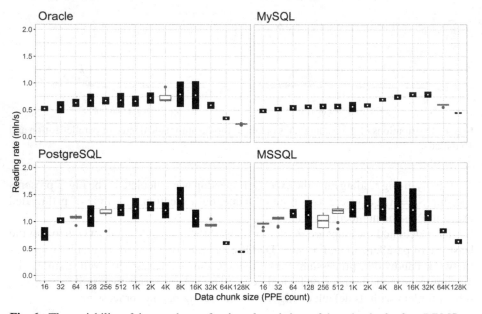

Fig. 6. The variability of data read rates for the selected sizes of data chunks for four DBMSes.

Visual analysis of the graphs shows that:

- for each DBMS, when the experiment is carried out in few threads due to the large data chunk size, the spread of the observed reading rates is very small,
- MySQL is characterized by the lowest and stable variability, regardless of the data chunk size,
- the highest variability is observed for MSSQL, with the largest number of outliers,
- for Oracle and MSSQL, the best reading rates are achieved for such tests that are characterized by the largest variability.

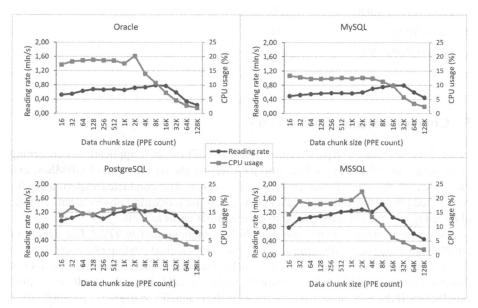

Fig. 7. Data reading rate and CPU usage depending on the size of the data chunk and DBMS.

The observations give the rationale of using such a data chunk size that each thread from the pool with a suboptimal size for a given execution environment has exactly one task to be performed. With such distribution of work, maximum read rates with an average load on the CPU were obtained (see the Fig. 7). Smaller sizes of data packets result in an increased CPU load and, at the same time, a lower data reading rate. The smaller the size of the package, and thus the greater the total number of packages, the greater the time spent on communication between the application and database servers. On the other hand, larger sizes of packages result in a significant reduction of the reading rate due to the limitation of the possibility of parallel execution of the task. In the extreme case, when the data package size is not smaller than the entire data pool, the task is performed by one thread.

The Fig. 7 also shows the similarity of the reading rates for the DBMS pairs: PostgreSQL and MSSQL as well as Oracle and MySQL. The similarity is clearly visible for the chunk sizes allowing a large number of threads to run concurrently (16-4096 PPE). The average differences in the reading rate for the indicated range of data chunk sizes are presented in the Table 2. Similarities in the results for the same pairs also occurred in the former experiment. We note this observation as a curiosity and do not plan any further work to explain its causes.

Table 2. Average differences in reading rates for selected DBMS pairs (16-4096 PPE range).

Pairs of DBMSes	Average difference in reading rates (million/s)
Oracle vs MySQL	0,08
MSSQL vs PostgreSQL	0,06
Oracle vs MSSQL	0,47
MySQL vs PostgreSQL	0,57

5   Conclusions and Future Work

In the work the research on parallel processing of .NET database applications concerning three issues, i.e. efficiency of TPL auto-parallelism, the impact of used DBMSes, and the choice of the size of data chunks, is presented. The conducted experiments for considered processing (business case) provided some interesting observations, and the obtained results may be generalized to other similar cases as well.

Firstly, *how efficient is the auto-parallelism implemented in TPL?* The degree of parallelization automatically determined by the TPL reached reading rates very close to those achieved by the manually set number of concurrent threads equaled the number of processor cores. Even if it did not obtain the highest reading rates, the results were quite satisfactory. If the performance is a top priority, the manually set degree of parallelization backed with a few experiments would be a better choice. However, if the target application runtime environment is unknown or may be subject to changes, opting for the TPL auto-parallelism method will be a rational approach, setting the degree of parallelization several percent worse than optimal.

Secondly, *how do popular DBMSes differ in serving parallel requests?* The reading rates were the highest and very similar for MSSQL and PostgreSQL. Oracle coped slightly worse, especially for more threads. MySQL seemed to make the least use of parallelization and got the poorest results. However, MySQL was characterized by low variability, maintaining more or less constant reading rates regardless of the level of parallelization. The highest variability in reading rates under tested degrees of parallelization experienced MSSQL and PostgreSQL. It was observed that the higher the reading rate, the wider the confidence intervals for the reading rate means.

Thirdly, *what is the optimal size of data chunks?* If the optimal number of threads for a given problem and an execution environment is known, then it is rational to consider such distribution of data among threads where each thread does exactly one iteration. Obviously, it can be done under the assumption that the resources (network, memory) allow for such an approach. Looking at the relation between the CPU usage and the reading rate in a function of the number of threads, some interesting observation may be noticed: the peak CPU usage appears before the peak reading rate. So abstracting from the reading rates, using the right data chunk size reduces the CPU need.

The next steps of the research are already in-progress and they include extending our auto-parallelism studies on auto-scaling of public cloud PaaS services and posing the Q2 question in relation to analogous DBMSes operating as managed services in the public clouds (GCP, AWS, OCI, Azure). It is expected that such experiments conducted in the clouds will also provide insights on the cost aspects of using these services.

Acknowledgments. Part of this work has been funded by the European Regional Development Fund under the Smart Growth Operational Programme (contract number POIR.01.01.01-00-0112/21-00), www.sygnity.pl/dotacje/.

References

1. Sumic, Z., Harrison, K.: Magic Quadrant for Meter Data Management Products. Market report, Gartner (2018)
2. CSIRE Information Exchange Standards. https://www.pse.pl/web/psc-cng/oire/information-exchange-standards-ies. Accessed 12 Apr 2022
3. Entity Framework Documentation. https://docs.microsoft.com/en-us/ef. Accessed 24 Jan 2022
4. Task Parallel Library (TPL) Documentation. https://docs.microsoft.com/en-us/dotnet/standard/parallel-programming/task-parallel-library-tpl. Accessed 24 Jan 2022
5. Hoag, F.E.: TPL Performance Improvements in .NET 4.5. Technical report, Microsoft (2011)
6. Vištica, M., Haseljić, H., Maksumić, A., Nosović, N.: Comparison of speedups for computing π using .NET TPL and OpenMP parallelization technologies. In: X International Symposium on Telecommunications (BIHTEL), pp. 1–4 (2014). https://doi.org/10.1109/BIHTEL.2014.6987657
7. Kaldéren, G.A., From, A.: A comparative analysis between parallel models in C/C++ and C#/Java. KTH BSc Thesis (2013). http://urn.kb.se/resolve?urn=urn:nbn:se:kth:diva-128606
8. Luo, Z., Zheng, Q., Hei, X., Giacaman, N.: Parallel programming based on Microsoft .NET TPL. In: Proceedings of the 2nd International Conference on Computer Science and Electronics Engineering (ICCSEE 2013) (2013). https://doi.org/10.2991/iccsee.2013.129
9. Zmaranda, D., Pop-Fele, L.-L., Győrödi, R., Győrödi, C.: Actor Model versus TPL for applications development. In: Proceedings of the 16th International Conference on Engineering of Modern Electric Systems (EMES) (2021). https://doi.org/10.1109/EMES52337.2021.9484154
10. TPC Council. https://www.tpc.org. Accessed 24 Jan 2022
11. Funke, F., Kemper, A., Neumann, T.: Benchmarking hybrid OLTP&OLAP database systems. In: Härder, T., Lehner, W., Mitschang, B., Schöning, H., Schwarz, H. (eds.) Datenbanksysteme für Business, Technologie und Web (BTW), pp. 390–409. Gesellschaft für Informatik e.V., Bonn (2011)
12. Lachewicz, K.: Performance analysis of selected database systems: MySQL, MS SQL, PostgerSQL in the context of web applications. J. Comput. Sci. Inst. **14**, 94–100 (2020). https://doi.org/10.35784/jcsi.1583

250   P. Karwaczyński et al.

13. Kleweka, R., Truskowski, W., Skublewska-Paszkowska, M.: Comparison of MySQL, MSSQL, PostgreSQL, Oracle databases performance, including virtualization. J. Comput. Sci. Inst. **16**, 279–284. https://doi.org/10.35784/jcsi.2026
14. Difallah, D.E., Pavlo, A., Curino, C., Cudre-Mauroux, P.: OLTP-Bench: an extensible testbed for benchmarking relational databases. Proc. VLDB Endow. **7**(4), 277–288 (2013). https://doi.org/10.14778/2732240.2732246
15. Liarokapis, D., O'Neil, E., O'Neil, P.: Testing concurrency in databases still matters. In: International Conference on Information Technologies (InfoTech), pp. 1–6 (2020). https://doi.org/10.1109/InfoTech49733.2020.9211014

Machine Learning to Diagnose Neurodegenerative Multiple Sclerosis Disease

Jin Si Lam[1], Md Rakibul Hasan[2]($\boxtimes$) [iD], Khandaker Asif Ahmed[3] [iD], and Md Zakir Hossain[1,3]($\boxtimes$) [iD]

[1] Australian National University, Canberra, Australia
{jinsi.lam,zakir.hossain}@anu.edu.au
[2] BRAC University, Dhaka, Bangladesh
rakibul.hasan@bracu.ac.bd
[3] Commonwealth Scientific and Industrial Research Organisation, Canberra, Australia
{khandakerasif.ahmed,zakir.hossain}@csiro.au

Abstract. Multiple sclerosis (MS) is a progressive neurodegenerative disease with a wide range of symptoms, making it difficult to diagnose and monitor. Current diagnosis methods are invasive and time-consuming. The use of smartphone monitoring is convenient, non-invasive, and can provide a reliable data source. Our study utilises an open-source dataset, namely—"Floodlight"—that uses smartphones to monitor the daily activities of MS patients. We evaluate whether the Floodlight data can be used in training a machine learning (ML) algorithm for MS diagnosis. After necessary data cleaning, we statistically measured the significance of different tests. Preliminary results show that individual test metrics are helpful for training ML algorithms. Accordingly, we use the selected tests in support vector machine (SVM) and rough set (RS) algorithms. Experimenting with several variations of the ML models, we achieve as high as 69% MS diagnosis accuracy. Since we experiment with SVMs and RSs on individual test metrics, we further report the relative significance of those tests and corresponding ML models suitable for the Floodlight dataset. Our model will serve as a baseline for developing ML-based prognostication tools for MS disease.

Keywords: Multiple sclerosis · Diagnosis · Machine learning · Support vector machine · Floodlight

1 Introduction

Multiple sclerosis (MS) is a chronic autoimmune and neurodegenerative disease characterised by progressive destruction of the myelin sheath, which insulates nerve cells [2,5]. Damage to nerves of the central nervous system can lead to severe physical and cognitive disability. Symptoms are widely varied and can include blindness, muscle weakness, fatigue, neurological deterioration, and many more [6]. As the disease progresses, these symptoms generally become more severe.

© The Author(s), under exclusive license to Springer Nature Singapore Pte Ltd. 2022
E. Szczerbicki et al. (Eds.): ACIIDS 2022, CCIS 1716, pp. 251–262, 2022.
https://doi.org/10.1007/978-981-19-8234-7_20

Currently, the precise cause behind MS is still unknown. The wide range of symptoms and unpredictable progression of the disease create further difficulties for diagnosis [4]. Diagnosis of MS is not straightforward and relies on a combination of tests such as blood tests, lumbar puncture, or magnetic resonance imaging (MRI) for lesions [5]. Some of these tests are intrusive but, even then, do not return definitive results.

Although early diagnosis is crucial for treatment, multiple criteria must be met before MS can be diagnosed confidently. For example, one major criterion is that the patient experience two discrete neurological episodes of time and space dissemination [10]. This way of diagnosis is problematic since it requires the patient's MS to be severe enough for this to occur. The expression of this symptom also varies significantly among individuals. These symptoms and episodes may also be unable to be monitored between clinical visits. Another significant criterion is the detection of a lesion via MRI [3]. Again, this requires the disease to have progressed far enough to have a lesion already. Furthermore, detecting lesions is often time-consuming and prone to human error. For these reasons, researchers are using machine learning (ML) algorithms to help with diagnosis [13].

Most current studies that use ML for MS diagnosis utilise MRI scans. In this area, ongoing research is extensive with several available datasets from various clinical settings and prior studies. Numerous methods of data processing and implementations of ML have been explored in this area [18].

Some studies investigate datasets aside from MRIs. Kaur et al. have explored the use of ML to analyse the gaits of MS patients [9]. However, their study is centred around monitoring disease progression, not the diagnosis. It also had a small sample size of 20 MS patients weighted towards older adults, and thus it requires more data to be generalised on different environments. Another study by Pinto et al. used the standard expanded disability status scale (EDSS) and ML to predict the progression of MS [16]. Therefore, existing non-MRI literatures investigated MS prognosis but lacked the diagnosis.

Floodlight Open is a study that uses a smartphone app to collect data from participants over time [14]. The app records information relevant to monitoring MS progression in a noninvasive, consistent, and convenient manner. In this sense, the use of the Floodlight data is unique and advantageous compared to clinical tests since clinical tests may be invasive and cannot monitor patients in-between multiple visits. The app supports several tests that the participants can actively perform daily, such as drawing shapes, pinching, and answering questions. Movements of participants are also passively monitored throughout the day.

Existing studies that use the Floodlight Open data evaluate the extent to which the smartphone app and the Floodlight tests can effectively track MS progression [19]. These studies confirm that smartphone monitoring is an effective way to assess MS progression continuously [12]. Woelfe et al. conducted a study with 264 participants over multiple weeks and found that repetitions of tests can lead to improvements of results due to practice [19]. Our study focuses on using the Floodlight data for diagnosis instead of disease progression monitoring.

We apply ML on the Floodlight data to determine whether these tests are helpful to diagnose MS. Firstly, we analyse the data to understand how it relates to MS diagnosis. Furthermore, we train ML algorithms with the data for predicting MS. This way of predicting MS may add a valuable noninvasive tool for MS diagnosis. An individual should be able to take the Floodlight app tests and input the results into the ML model. The ML model should then return the likelihood of that individual having MS in terms of a percentage score. Among different ML models, support vector machine (SVM) and rough set (RS) showed great potential for different classification tasks.

We utilise SVM and RS algorithms to split data into two groups—individuals with MS or without MS. Data belong to a plot on an n-dimensional space where n is the number of variables related to the groups. The variables are the results from the Floodlight tests as well as background information such as age, sex, and height. A line is drawn between the data points, separating two groups. This line defines which group new data points will fall into, which allows for predictions on whether an individual has MS or not. Compared to other ML algorithms such as random forest or decision tree, SVM is intrinsically suited to two-class problems and draws the line to maximise the margin between the two groups [1]. Hence we chose SVM to diagnose MS from Floodlight data. On the other hand, RS theory uses two sets to approximate the lower and upper bounds of an original set of data [11]. Unlike SVM, which ultimately sorts data into the defined categories (MS or no MS), RS makes it possible to identify borderline cases that do not fit into either lower or upper sets. This potential for "fuzziness" is useful in a medical context because of borderline cases. In a scenario where the SVM algorithm may classify a borderline case as not having MS, the RS algorithm may be able to flag it for further observation.

This paper is structured as follows. Section 2 explains the methodologies with a flow diagram of steps involved in this work. Necessary discussions with the results achieved from data analysis and ML implementation are reported in Sect. 3. The limitations of this study are explained in Sect. 4. Finally, we summarised our works with potential future scopes in Sect. 5.

2 Method

Figure 1 depicts the step-by-step processes we followed in this study, which are explained in the following subsections.

2.1 Understanding the Data

The Floodlight data is open source and available for download on the website[1]. A unique identifier (ID) is provided for each participant, so it is possible

---

[1] https://floodlightopen.com/.

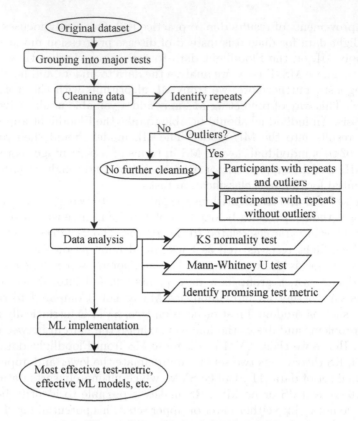

Fig. 1. Steps involved in this work.

to track which tests have been taken and how many times. Background information, including age, weight, sex, height, country of residence, and whether the participant has MS or not, is recorded. While accessing the database, there were 568,600 data points and 2505 unique participants: 1150 participants were without MS, and 1355 participants were diagnosed with MS. The participants (Floodlight app users) self-reported whether they had MS or not. These numbers vary among different test metrics (test metrics refer to different test categories for the users), as detailed in Table 1. Even with this preliminary information, it is possible to identify potential correlations and risk factors associated with certain backgrounds.

Ideal input data for training any ML algorithm is data that very accurately reflects reality. As mentioned previously, MS has varying degrees of severity. To accurately represent this, a continuous spectrum where a higher number indicates more severe MS and a lower number indicates less severe MS would be required. However, the Floodlight data does not reflect this, as participants are only given the option of stating whether they have MS or not. This binary choice leads to some limitations for training the ML algorithm. Due to this lack

Table 1. Number of participants for each test metric.

Test metric	MS	No MS	Total
Mean hausdorff distance	1229	969	2198
Top to bottom hausdorff distance	1223	961	2184
Bottom to top hausdorff distance	1223	960	2183
Circle hausdorff distance	1223	960	2183
Square hausdorff distance	1223	960	2183
Figure 8 hausdorff distance	1223	960	2183
Number of U turns	1024	774	1798
Average turn speed	1024	774	1798
Number of pinches	1230	981	2211
Daily mobility metric	1104	868	1972
1–5 mood scale	1297	1077	2374
IPS correct responses baseline	1242	994	2236
IPS average response time baseline	1242	994	2236

of data, the fuzzy aspect of the RS algorithm was not utilised, and patients were strictly sorted into the MS or no MS to easily compare with SVM performance.

An important distinction needs to be made here. For any given participant, there are two crucial theoretical numbers: how likely the participant has MS versus how severe the participant's MS is. Because the provided data only contains information on whether the patient has MS or not, the ML model will only be able to return the possibility of the participant having MS (and not its severity). However, this possibility will most likely reflect the severity of the participant's MS. For example, if a patient with severe MS takes the Floodlight app tests, this should be reflected in the results. Upon input into the ML model, the model should return that the participant is highly likely to have MS. In contrast, if a patient with mild MS takes the tests, the ML model will probably return that the participant is less likely to have MS compared to the more severe case. In a heuristic sense, the returned likelihood of a patient having MS may reflect the severity of their MS.

2.2 Data Cleaning

The original data source contains a variable called "test name," which describes eight major tests types. These types correspond to actual tests that the participants can perform in the Floodlight app. Each of these tests has one or more corresponding test metrics. This metric is an integer on a continuous scale describing how the participant performed on that test. Each metric has a different range and meaning.

Furthermore, a single test may return multiple test metrics. For example, in the information processing speed (IPS) test, participants are asked to answer a number of questions rapidly. Consequently, two test metrics are returned: the number of correct responses and the average time per response. In the first case, a higher test metric (more correct responses) is a better result, indicating that the participant is less likely to have MS or has less severe MS symptoms. Conversely, for the average response time metric, if the participant has a higher test metric (they take a longer time to respond to each question), the participant is more likely to have MS or has more severe MS symptoms.

Accordingly, we developed a new dataset for each of the eight major test types from the original data for ease of analysis. Within the new dataset, we further split the data into corresponding test metrics described in Table 2.

Table 2. Floodlight test types.

Test name	Test metric	Patient's condition at Higher score
Drawing shapes	Number of correct shapes	Better
	Hausdorff distance difference from correct shape	Worse
Pinching test	Number of pinches	Better
U-turn test	Number of U-turns	Better
Daily mood questions	Mood on a scale from 1–5	Better
Sway path and stability	Movement	Worse
Number of steps in 2 min	Number of steps taken	Better
Information processing speed (IPS)	Number of correct responses	Better
	Average time per response	Worse
Monitoring of daily mobility[a]	Daily movement	Better

[a]Passively monitored throughout day.

Within each of these test-metric subgroups, null values, zero values, outliers, and other potentially incorrect values were identified and separated. These data points could then be included or excluded. Repeating entries from the same individuals were also handled systematically. If a person repeats a test multiple times, the data for that person should be more accurate; however, it should not lead to the individual being weighted more than others. Thus, repeats from each individual were averaged into a single data point for input into the ML algorithm.

Accordingly, the data within each test-metric was further divided into participants with no repeats and participants with repeats. For participants with only one data point (no repeats), the test metrics' value was assumed to be correct as there is no point of comparison to verify whether the result is abnormal for that participant.

Participants with repeats were separated into two groups. A filter was applied that identified individual participants with potentially incorrect values.

Test metrics were plotted for each individual, and it was determined whether they contained any outliers within their own results. The outliers were calculated using the interquartile range (1.5× above or below). The results of the unfiltered participants (no self-contained outliers) were averaged into a single data point.

These three groups—individuals with no repeats, with consistent repeats, and with repeats that have outliers—may be used in combination or individually for inputting into the ML algorithm.

2.3   Preparation of ML Algorithm

For initial screening of which tests have the potential to perform better as input into the ML Algorithm, the Kolmogorov-Smirnov and Mann-Whitney U tests were performed on the cleaned data.

We made two groups for input into the ML algorithm: one group by removing the individuals with outliers, and another by treating them similarly to individuals without outliers (data points of the individual were averaged). Within these two groups, it was also possible to choose whether to use only the test metric (an integer) as the input data or include other variables such as age, height, weight, etc. This gives four groups that can be input into the SVM and RS algorithms: only test metrics without outliers, only test metrics with outliers, all variables without outliers, and all variables with outliers.

The data from the filtered test metrics were then fed into the ML algorithms imported from the python scikit-learn library [15] for SVM and the fuzzy-rough-learn library [11] for RS. There are different options for SVM kernel: linear, sigmoid, Gaussian, or polynomial. Each of the four data groups for each test-metric can be input into these different kernels. Accordingly, we tested 16 SVM and 4 RS variations for each test metric.

We split the data points of each test-metric in an 80/20 ratio: 80% for the training set and 20% for the test set. We used accuracy as our evaluation metric.

3   Results and Discussion

3.1   Exploratory Data Analysis

We analysed the data to identify test metrics that can train the ML algorithm. Ideally, useful test metrics would significantly differ in values when comparing MS patients versus non-MS patients.

Firstly, the data were tested for normality using the Kolmogorov-Smirnov test [7]. We found that most of the Floodlight tests were not normally distributed. For this reason, the nonparametric Mann-Whitney U test [8] was conducted to determine if the differences between MS positive and MS negative test metrics were statistically significant; the results are reported in Table 3 and Fig. 2. For visual ease of comparison, Fig. 2 shows the negative log of the Mann-Whitney U test p values, with the red line showing the $-\log_{10}(0.05)$ threshold.

Table 3. Significance of difference between MS and non-MS patient test metrics.

Test metric	Mann-Whitney U test p value
Number of correct shapes	8.46×10^{-2}
Mean hausdorff distance	6.78×10^{-3}
Top to bottom hausdorff distance	3.44×10^{-2}
Bottom to top hausdorff distance	2.99×10^{-3}
Circle hausdorff distance	1.40×10^{-2}
Square hausdorff distance	6.53×10^{-4}
Figure 8 hausdorff distance	4.85×10^{-5}
Spiral hausdorff distance	4.50×10^{-1}
Number of U turns	7.06×10^{-4}
Average turn speed	2.08×10^{-3}
Number of pinches	3.17×10^{-2}
Daily mobility metric	7.95×10^{-10}
Number of steps taken[a]	6.38×10^{-6}
Sway path[a]	9.06×10^{-1}
1–5 mood scale	4.06×10^{-29}
IPS correct responses baseline	8.95×10^{-15}
IPS average response time baseline	4.15×10^{-27}
IPS correct responses[a]	3.12×10^{-3}
IPS average response time[a]	3.90×10^{-14}

[a]Test metric result did not reflect expected meaning.

It can be seen that several Floodlight tests have promising p values, indicating that the difference between MS and non-MS patients has the potential to be recognised by an ML algorithm. The most statistically-significant differences are the baseline IPS tests, the mood test, and the daily mobility metric. However, three Floodlight tests—the number of correct shapes, spiral Hausdorff distance, and sway path—showed high p values (> 0.05) and so were not used in the ML implementation.

However, some of these results contradict what the test-metric values are expected to reflect. For example, as shown previously in Table 2, if a patient takes more steps in the 2-minute walk test, this should indicate that they are in a better condition and are less likely to have MS. However, the average number of steps by non-MS patients is actually lower than the non-MS patients in the Floodlight dataset. Therefore, these specific Floodlight tests did not reflect the expected meaning and were thus discarded from inputting into the ML algorithm.

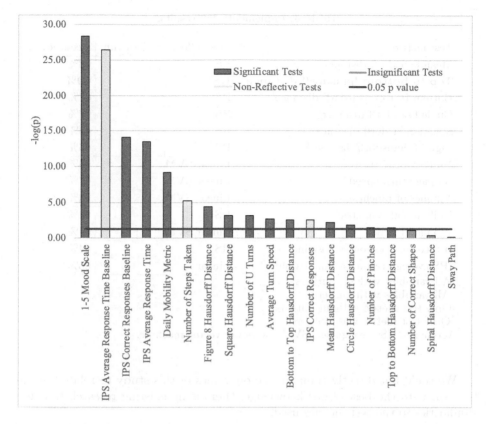

Fig. 2. Tests which have a significant difference between MS and non-MS patients according to the Mann-Whitney U Test.

3.2 ML Results

Table 4 shows the highest accuracy that we achieved for each test metric with corresponding SVM kernel or RS algorithm.

It can be seen that the top to bottom Hausdorff distance had the highest accuracy of 69%, followed by mean Hausdorff distance, square Hausdorff distance, and daily mobility metric, all having an accuracy of 68%.

Regarding the performance of RS compared to SVM, the highest, 2nd, 3rd, 4th, and 5th highest performances were achieved using the RS algorithm. Among SVM kernels, the linear kernel performed the best. In most Hausdorff distance test metrics, the Sigmoid and Gaussian kernels had very similar performances but were poor in comparison to the linear kernel.

Among different data subgroups of whether to consider outliers and all variables, all variables with outliers often gave the best accuracy (Table 4). Therefore, it implies that outliers removal is potentially unnecessary, and patients' background information, such as age, height, weight, etc., positively influences ML-based MS diagnosis.

Table 4. Implementation results.

Test metric	Most effective algorithm	Accuracy
Mean hausdorff distance[b]	RS	68%
Top to bottom hausdorff distance[b]	**RS**	**69%**
Bottom to top hausdorff distance[b]	RS	67%
Circle hausdorff distance[a]	RS	67%
Square hausdorff distance[a]	RS	68%
Figure 8 hausdorff distance[a]	RS	65%
Number of U turns[b]	Linear SVM	63%
Average turn speed[b]	Linear SVM	67%
Number of pinches[b]	Linear SVM	64%
Daily mobility metric[a]	RS	68%
1–5 mood scale[b]	Linear SVM	64%
IPS correct responses baseline[a]	RS	64%
IPS average response time baseline[b]	Linear	65%

[a] All variables without outliers.
[b] All variables with outliers.
[c] Only test metric without outliers.
[d] Only test metric with outliers.
Acronyms: RS – rough set, SVM – support vector machine.

We could not directly compare the outcomes of this study to related literature since, to the best of our knowledge, there is no existing research that has similarities to the test metrics used.

4   Limitation

As mentioned previously, the severity of a patient's MS is not recorded in the provided Floodlight dataset. This led to the ML algorithm only being able to return true or false as a prediction for whether the patient had MS. This scenario means that a patient with very severe MS and another with very mild MS would both output true with no way to distinguish between the two in terms of certainty. If it were possible to obtain data on the severity of each participant's MS, for example, through an EDSS score, it might be possible to distinguish between these two cases, especially using the RS algorithm.

It is worthwhile to note that the current accuracies are achieved using only single test metric within the dataset. For example, the 69% accurate prediction is achieved using data only from the top to bottom Hausdorff distance and nothing else. Thus, combining all Floodlight tests will most likely increase prediction accuracy.

Even though MRI-based studies to detect neural damage or demyelinating changes in the brain are proven as gold-standard to detect MS, we aimed to develop a cost-efficient ML model based on physiological signals, which will pave the way for future MS prognostication. Physical and physiological signals have shown great potential for monitoring mental health [17], and our study also prove their potential for MS detection.

5   Conclusion and Future Work

This study has investigated the potential of utilising the tests from the Floodlight smartphone app for diagnosing MS. We found that multiple test metrics could provide information that may distinguish between MS and non-MS patients. First, the Floodlight data were cleaned from repetitions and outliers. After applying two statistical tests—Kolmogorov-Smirnov and Mann-Whitney U test—we acquired statistically significant data that we used in SVM and RS algorithms. Experimenting with four different SVM kernels and RS algorithm on each of the selected tests individually, we achieved a maximum of 69% accuracy by a RS model in diagnosing MS patients using only a single test metric. We report top to bottom Hausdorff distance as the most effective Floodlight test metric. This research throw light on using smartphone monitoring data in ML-based MS diagnosis. Future research might focus on further refinements, such as implementing other ML algorithms like multilayer perceptron or decision trees, with further tuning on hyperparameters using algorithms like grid search method. Also, given a data set with information on the degree of severity of MS, it may be possible to extend the application of RS "fuzziness." Moreover, since this study has focused on investigating each test-metric separately, we may look into using multiple combinations or all of them in conjunction.

References

1. Abdullah, D.M., Abdulazeez, A.M.: Machine learning applications based on SVM classification a review. Qubahan Acad. J. **1**(2), 81–90 (2021). https://doi.org/10.48161/qaj.v1n2a50
2. Chaudhuri, A.: Multiple sclerosis is primarily a neurodegenerative disease. J. Neural Trans. **120**(10), 1463–1466 (2013). https://doi.org/10.1007/s00702-013-1080-3
3. Eshaghi, A., et al.: Identifying multiple sclerosis subtypes using unsupervised machine learning and MRI data. Nature Commun. **12**(2078), 1–12 (2021). https://doi.org/10.1038/s41467-021-22265-2
4. Gelfand, J.M.: Chapter 12 - multiple sclerosis: diagnosis, differential diagnosis, and clinical presentation. In: Goodin, D.S. (ed.) Multiple Sclerosis and Related Disorders, Handbook of Clinical Neurology, vol. 122, pp. 269–290. Elsevier (2014). https://doi.org/10.1016/B978-0-444-52001-2.00011-X
5. Ghasemi, N., Razavi, S., Nikzad, E.: Multiple sclerosis: pathogenesis, symptoms, diagnoses and cell-based therapy. Cell J. (Yakhteh) **19**(1), 1–10 (2017). https://doi.org/10.22074/cellj.2016.4867
6. Goldenberg, M.M.: Multiple sclerosis review. P & T **37**(3), 175–184 (2012)

7. Gupta, A., Mishra, P., Pandey, C., Singh, U., Sahu, C., Keshri, A.: Descriptive statistics and normality tests for statistical data. Ann. Cardiac Anaesthesia **22**(1), 67–72 (2019). https://doi.org/10.4103/aca.aca_157_18

8. Hart, A.: Mann-whitney test is not just a test of medians: differences in spread can be important. BMJ **323**(7309), 391–393 (2001). https://doi.org/10.1136/bmj.323.7309.391

9. Kaur, R., Chen, Z., Motl, R., Hernandez, M.E., Sowers, R.: Predicting multiple sclerosis from gait dynamics using an instrumented treadmill: a machine learning approach. IEEE Trans. Biomed. Eng. **68**(9), 2666–2677 (2021). https://doi.org/10.1109/tbme.2020.3048142

10. Leary, S.M.: Multiple sclerosis: diagnosis and the management of acute relapses. Postgraduate Med. J. **81**(955), 302–308 (2005). https://doi.org/10.1136/pgmj.2004.029413

11. Lenz, O.U., Peralta, D., Cornelis, C.: *fuzzy-rough-learn* 0.1: a python library for machine learning with fuzzy rough sets. In: Bello, R., Miao, D., Falcon, R., Nakata, M., Rosete, A., Ciucci, D. (eds.) IJCRS 2020. LNCS (LNAI), vol. 12179, pp. 491–499. Springer, Cham (2020). https://doi.org/10.1007/978-3-030-52705-1_36

12. Midaglia, L., et al.: Adherence and satisfaction of smartphone- and smartwatch-based remote active testing and passive monitoring in people with multiple sclerosis: nonrandomized interventional feasibility study. J. Med. Internet Res. **21**(8), e14863 (2019). https://doi.org/10.2196/14863

13. Moazami, F., Lefevre-Utile, A., Papaloukas, C., Soumelis, V.: Machine learning approaches in study of multiple sclerosis disease through magnetic resonance images. Front. Immunol. **12** (2021). https://doi.org/10.3389/fimmu.2021.700582

14. Montalban, X., et al.: A smartphone sensor-based digital outcome assessment of multiple sclerosis. Multiple Sclerosis J. **28**(4), 654–664 (2022). https://doi.org/10.1177/13524585211028561

15. Pedregosa, F., et al.: Scikit-learn: machine learning in python. J. Mach. Learn. Res. **12**, 2825–2830 (2011)

16. Pinto, M.F., et al.: Prediction of disease progression and outcomes in multiple sclerosis with machine learning. Sci. Rep. **10**(21038) (2020). https://doi.org/10.1038/s41598-020-78212-6

17. Rostov, M., Hossain, M.Z., Rahman, J.S.: Robotic emotion monitoring for mental health applications: preliminary outcomes of a survey. In: Ardito, C., et al. (eds.) INTERACT 2021. LNCS, vol. 12936, pp. 481–485. Springer, Cham (2021). https://doi.org/10.1007/978-3-030-85607-6_62

18. Shoeibi, A., et al.: Applications of deep learning techniques for automated multiple sclerosis detection using magnetic resonance imaging: A review. Comput. Biol. Med. **136**, 104697 (2021). https://doi.org/10.1016/j.compbiomed.2021.104697

19. Woelfle, T., Pless, S., Wiencierz, A., Kappos, L., Naegelin, Y., Lorscheider, J.: Practice effects of mobile tests of cognition, dexterity, and mobility on patients with multiple sclerosis: Data analysis of a smartphone-based observational study. J. Med. Internet Res. **23**(11), e30394 (2021). https://doi.org/10.2196/30394

A Novel Integrating Approach Between Graph Neural Network and Complex Representation for Link Prediction in Knowledge Graph

Thanh Le[1,2]($\boxtimes$) (iD), Loc Tran[1,2] (iD), and Bac Le[1,2] (iD)

[1] Faculty of Information Technology, University of Science,
Ho Chi Minh City, Vietnam
{lnthanh,lhbac}@fit.hcmus.edu.vn, txloc18@clc.fitus.edu.vn
[2] Vietnam National University, Ho Chi Minh City, Vietnam

Abstract. Deep learning brings high results in many problems, including Link Prediction on Knowledge Graphs (KGs). Although there are many techniques to implement deep learning into KGs, Graph Neural Networks (GNNs) have recently emerged as a promising direction for representing the structure of KGs as input for a decoder. With this structural information, GNNs can help to retain more information from the original graph than conventional embeddings like TransE, TransH, RESCAL. As a result, the learning model achieves higher accuracy in predicting missing links between entities in the KG. Meanwhile, several studies have successfully demonstrated the intrinsic properties of the embedding process in complex space while keeping many binary relations (symmetric and asymmetric). Thus, this paper proposes deploying GNNs into complex space to increase the model's predictive capability. Another issue with GNNs is that they are susceptible to over-squashing when a large amount of information propagating between nodes is compressed down to a fixed representation space. As a result, we utilize a dynamic attention mechanism to minimize the adverse effects of these factors, and experiments on benchmark datasets have indicated that our proposal achieves a significant improvement compared to baseline models on almost all standard metrics.

Keywords: Knowledge graph embedding · Link prediction · Graph convolutional networks · Dynamic graph attention networks

1 Introduction

Knowledge Graphs (KGs) are becoming a widely used term in the field of artificial intelligence. Some of its outstanding applications are in a number of areas such as medicine [1] and e-commerce [11]. Among the KG-related challenges, we are putting our efforts into tackling the link prediction (LP) problem, whose objective is discovering the missed links in KG to accomplish itself. In fact, data

© The Author(s), under exclusive license to Springer Nature Singapore Pte Ltd. 2022
E. Szczerbicki et al. (Eds.): ACIIDS 2022, CCIS 1716, pp. 263–275, 2022.
https://doi.org/10.1007/978-981-19-8234-7_21

in the KG is regularly gathered from various sources, including manually. Moreover, identifying the relations between data aids in order to complete KGs. Furthermore, we could forecast potential relations between entities in the future. Although numerous rule-based and probability-based methods for addressing this problem were initially proposed, these models suffer the exploding computational cost when performing on large KGs. As a result, the embedding approaches emerged and gained widespread attention in recent years because of their above mentioned characteristics.

Currently, KGE is classified into two categories: Translational and Semantic matching models. At the Translational-based models, the models projecting entities and relations into vector or matrix representation with simplicity, scalable characteristics, TransE [3] and its extensions such as TransH [19], TransR [12], and TransD [8] are the top striking models of translational research. The semantic-matching models include bilinear models and neural network-based models. Bilinear methods such as the RESCAL model [14], DistMult [21], and ComplEx [17] can mine the intrinsic properties of KGs by using tensor decomposition, characterized by the less time-consuming and effective computation except for RESCAL. In neural network-based models, researchers apply the success of Convolutional neural networks (CNNs) in KGs and archive potential results such as ConvE [7], ConvKB [13], but it suffers to time-consuming, increases model complexity and other related CNN's problems. Another variant of CNNs is Graph Convolutional Networks [9], levering the same convolutional operation but performing on graph data while considering graph features during the embedding phase. Some recent models such as RGCN [15], GATv2 [4], VR-GCN [22], and TransGCN [5] - an associated model between GCN and Translational model, on the graph neural networks branches. Furthermore, incorporating additional information into the embedding process, such as literals, textual descriptions, entity, and relation types, has been shown to yield higher quality embedding and is especially effective in many downstream tasks such as triple classification, entity classification, and link prediction [20].

Although the Translational models are outstanding by its qualities, it has flaws when modeling the complex relations and TransE's extensions ignore two important characteristics including heterogeneity and imbalance [6]. In the semantic-matching models, neural networks-based models significantly contribute to and improve the performance of link prediction tasks, but the connectivity information between entities and neighbors is neglected. To solve this problem, GCNs emerged as the prisoner of applying graph structure information to its embedding space to perform more semantic calculations. Specifically, they create entity embeddings that aggregate local information in neighborhoods. However, GCNs mainly solve problems in real space, which is the main weakness leading to marginal performance growth in recent years. Thus, we propose implementing GCNs in complex space and conducting experiments to demonstrate the effectiveness of this approach in this paper. Moreover, the ComplEx model is employed as a decoder to utilize the graph features in the complex space because of its simplicity and scalability over large graphs. Specifically, ComplEx has low complexity while still representing interactions and entities in complex spaces because it uses only the Hermitian dot product. Moreover, the reason we integrate the GCNs and GATv2 [4] to tackle the challenge of GNNs, which is detail reported in Sect. 3.

In conclusion, our contributions are summarized:

- Proposing an end-to-end framework ComplEx-GNN for learning entity and relation embedding characteristics in complex space.
- Constructing an association between GCN and Dynamic Graph Attention (GATv2) layer as an encoder to mapping entities, exploiting graph information and alleviating the bottleneck problem.
- Leveraging ComplEx as a decoder to simulate the interacting between entities and relations in complex space.

The remaining paper includes five sections. In Sect. 2, we discuss some related works and the typical models in each branch of KGE. We focus on presenting the main idea of the ComplEx-GNN framework in detail in Sect. 3. Section 4 contains experimental results in detail on FB15K-237 and WN18RR. Section 5 summarises our contributions and recommends future research directions.

2   Related Work

Models for KGE problems can be categorized into two types: translational models and semantic-matching models. Translational-based models were regarded as the pioneers of KGC by their simplicity, clarity, and high interpretability. The scoring function and representation space distinguish these approaches. Specifically, they utilize relations as translation operators in translation-based models. In the embedded space, the head entity $\mathbf{h}$ is expected to approximate the tail entity $\mathbf{t}$ via the translation $\mathbf{r}$, then the scoring function is computed based on the deviation of the predicted entities from the actual entities in the triple.

Semantic-based models include bilinear and neural network-based models, which leverage the similarity measures as the scoring functions for the triples. Bilinear models are based on matrix decomposition by using tensors to represent relational data $Y \in \{0, 1\}^{N \times R \times R}$ where N is the number of entities, R is the number of relations, Y is state of the connection between entities (yes or no). Moreover, these approaches are distinguished based on structural conditions on tensors with the capability of modeling binary relations. Furthermore, Bilinear models consider link prediction tasks as tensor decomposition problems. Meanwhile, neural networks-based models consist of many different layers to mine the fundamental relations between entities and relations with self-feedback and fast convergence. In addition, current models also integrate some additional information such as context information, entity type, and path information to be exploited deep semantic information.

2.1   Translational Based Models

TransE model [3] was developed based on the idea of the energy-based model, which is the cornerstone for later translational-based approaches because of its efficient, less parameter, and scalable characteristics. TransE is considered the backbone of the embedding space. Moreover, Bordes et al. also mentioned that KGs have many hierarchical relations, and the translation is a natural transformation. Thus, they represent each relation as a translation in the embedding space such that the tail entity is close to the head entity in the embedding space $(\mathbf{h} + \mathbf{r} \approx \mathbf{t})$. Each entity or relation is represented by a single embedding vector. However, the model is only suitable for $1-1$ relations. And it has flaws when representing $1-n$, $n-1$, and $n-n$ relations. To address these issues, TransH [19], motivated by TransE, interprets the interaction by shifting operations into hyperplanes and introducing a relation-specific mechanism. In this way, it allows entities to take different roles in each relation type. Each relation, as a hyperplane, is determined by two vectors including the norm vector $(\mathbf{w_r})$ and the translation vector $(\mathbf{d_r})$. Although the latter comparative researches such as TransR [12], TransD [8] conducted in that direction gained considerable improvements compared to TransE, the complexity also increased quite a bit.

2.2   Semantic-Matching Models

Bilinear models such RESCAL [14], DistMult [21], and ComplEx [17] employ similarity measures as scoring functions to assess the plausibility of triplets. RESCAL also applies tensor decomposition to obtain the implicit semantic by integrating a two-way interaction of relations and entities to measure the probability of forming triplets. DistMult represents entities and relations as diagonal matrices and modifies the scoring function to Eq. 1. Although it has less parameters and reduces memory parameters from $O(Ne_d + N_r k^2)$ $(d = k)$ to $O(Ne_d + N_r k)$ $(d = k)$ [19] compared to RESCAL, it only handles symmetric relations [18]. Meanwhile, ComplEx increases the ability to cope with asymmetric relations by utilizing the complex value to embed interactions and entities into complex space $\mathbb{C}^d$. We realize that by combining tensor decomposition with graph features, the ComplEx model could extract deeper semantic information from the embedding phase. Besides that, some investigations, such as ComplEx-Literal [10] and DistMult-Literal [10], have focused on exploiting additional information to enhance the overall performance of downstream tasks as link prediction. Despite the fact that the additional information is applied during the embedding phase, this information has not been fully exploited, and it does not bring significant improvement results.

$$f_r(\mathbf{h}, \mathbf{r}) = \mathbf{h}^T diag(\mathbf{r})\mathbf{t} \mid \mathbf{r} \in \mathbf{R}^d \qquad (1)$$

where d is the dimensionality of embedding space.

Neural networks-based models such as ConvE [7], ConvKB [13] are the representative models on this branch. ConvE uses a 2D reshaping operator to define the scoring function while using the convolutional and fully connected layers to model the interactions between entities and relations. ConvKB is inspired by a similar idea as ConvE by leveraging the success of a convolutional operator in computer vision but achieves a better result than ConvE. In particular, this approach uses the concatenate operator instead of the reshape operator to define the scoring function while keeping the transitional features and observing the global relationship among entities. Another variant of using the convolutional operator but performing on unstructured data is Graph Convolutional Networks. GCNs are applied in KGs such as RGCN [15], VR-GCN [22] and TransGCN [5], which aggregate the local informations of target entities by propagating the information between its neighbors. RGCN models the relational data by introducing relations-specific transformations for each relation type. Furthermore, RGCN uses parameter sharing techniques including basis and block diagonal-decomposition in regularization to tackle the sparsity problem and memory requirements of GCN on large KGs. Although RGCN leverages the benefit of different relation types in entity representation, it does not consider the representations of relations that contain rich semantic information. To address this problem, VR-GCN takes into account relations and entities to generate both embedding, allowing the relations to involve the multi-relational networks while keeping the translational properties. TransGCN operates on the same idea as VR-GCN because it considers entities and relations embedded in a unified framework, but TransGCN is supposed that each relation as a transformation operator transforms the head entity to the tail entity. When compared to R-GCN, TransGCN can transform a heterogeneous neighborhood in a KG into a homogeneous neighborhood with fewer parameters and directly perform link prediction without the support of external encoders such as DistMult in RGCN [2].

3   The Proposed Model

In this section, we demonstrate our model ComplEx-GNN. The encoder integrates a GCN layer and GATv2. It aims to aggregate the necessary information from a neighbor as specified by relations, then reproduce it into features representation for each entity including the real and the imaginary components. The decoder ComplEx focuses on representing entities and relations embedding in complex space, then calculates the possibility of forming triplets by leveraging the scoring function of the ComplEx model [17].

Our proposed framework including the encoder and decoder demonstrated in Fig. 1. For the encoder, entities and relations are embedded into the complex space to create two main components including real component and imaginary component for each entity and relation. The Graph Aggregation Layer takes the entities embedding as input, which consists GCN and GATv2 layers. We utilize GCN layer as the first layer to propagate information between neighbors because of its scalable on large KGs and can operate on local graph neighbors. Next, we expand the interaction between entities and assess neighbors contributions by

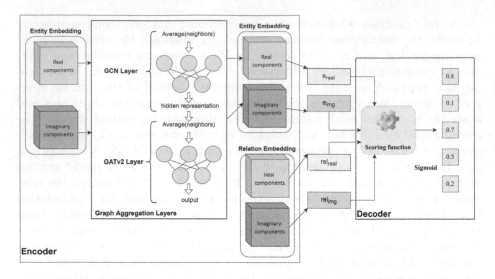

Fig. 1. An overview of our proposed model ComplEx-GNN

adding a Graph Attention Layer (GAL) to assign the different weight for the importance of neighbor's features in the entity's neighborhood. However, GAL could only compute the static attention layer for architecture including only one layer; if it exceeds $(n > 1)$, the dynamic attention can not be computed, detail in [4]. Thus, we use its upgraded version - Dynamic Graph Attention Networks (GATv2) in our framework. GATv2 could also assign the weight for neighbor, while reducing the amount of information passed through an activation function, and alleviate the bottleneck problem of GNN because of exponential growing information into fixed-size vectors [2]. After obtaining the entities embedding from Graph Aggregation Layers, we take the entities and relations embedding matrices as input to the decoder. For the decoder, $\mathbf{e}_{real}$, $\mathbf{e}_{img}$, $\mathbf{rel}_{real}$, and $\mathbf{rel}_{img}$ are passed into the scoring function. We utilize the ComplEx scoring function as the scoring function, because it is the standard approach applying the complex representation without any additional information, while their representation space could describe the symmetric and asymmetric relations more accurately than other approaches. Next, a sigmoid function is applied to get the prediction results.

3.1   Graph Aggregation Layers

A knowledge graph $G(E, R)$, where $E = \{e_1, e_2, ..., e_M\}$ denotes the set of M entities, $R = \{r_1, r_2, ..., r_N\}$ denoting the set of N relations, $(i, j) \in R$ denotes a connection between two entities i and j , and (h, r, t) denoting a triplet with h representing the head entity, r representing relations, and t representing the tail entity.

We utilize the complex representation and GNN layer to perform aggregating graph features in our approach. First, entities and relations are embedded into the complex space. Thus each embedding consists of a real component and an imaginary component. We denote $\mathbf{H}_{real}^{(0)}$ and $\mathbf{H}_{img}^{(0)}$ are the set of real and imaginary components of entities E; $\mathbf{R}_{real}^{(0)}$ and $\mathbf{R}_{img}^{(0)}$ are the set of real and imaginary components of relations R as follows:

$$\mathbf{H}_{real}^{(0)} = \{\mathbf{h_{r1}}, \mathbf{h_{r2}}, ..., \mathbf{h_{rN}}\}; \qquad \mathbf{H}_{img}^{(0)} = \{\mathbf{h_{i1}}, \mathbf{h_{i2}}, ..., \mathbf{h_{iN}}\} \qquad (2)$$

$$\mathbf{R}_{real}^{(0)} = \{\mathbf{r_{r1}}, \mathbf{r_{r2}}, ..., \mathbf{r_{rN}}\}; \qquad \mathbf{R}_{img}^{(0)} = \{\mathbf{r_{i1}}, \mathbf{r_{i2}}, ..., \mathbf{r_{iN}}\} \qquad (3)$$

where $\mathbf{h_{rj}}$ and $\mathbf{h_{ij}}$ are the real and imaginary components of entity j^{th}, $\mathbf{r_{rj}}$ and $\mathbf{r_{ij}}$ are the real and imaginary components of relation j^{th}.

Then, we collect neighbors' information in $\mathbf{H}_{real}^{(0)}$ and $\mathbf{H}_{img}^{(0)}$ by using the GCN and GATv2 layers. GCN is operated on graph structure as the KGs structure, so we applied GCN to propagating information around one-hop neighbors, which helps to exploit the structural information of KGs at the first layer. In our work, the first layer takes the input matrix $\mathbf{H}^{(0)}$, and generates a feature representation for the second layer. The output matrix $\mathbf{H}^{(1)}$ is calculated as follows:

$$\mathbf{H}^{(j+1)} = \sigma(\mathbf{W}^{(j)}\mathbf{H}^{(j)}\mathbf{A'}) \qquad (4)$$

where σ is an activation function, $\mathbf{W}^{(0)}$ is weight matrix at the first layer, $\mathbf{A'}$ is the normalized adjacency matrix. To construct the normalized adjacency matrix $\mathbf{A'}$, we first construct the adjacency matrix $\mathbf{A}$ representing connections between entities. In addition, to consider the features of each entity itself, we create a matrix $\widehat{\mathbf{A}}$ by adding $\mathbf{A}$ with its identity matrix as follows:

$$\widehat{\mathbf{A}} = \mathbf{A} + \mathbf{I_A} \qquad (5)$$

where $\mathbf{I_A}$ is the identity matrix of size $N \times N$. Next, $\widehat{\mathbf{A}}$ is normalized to form matrix $\mathbf{A'}$ as follows:

$$\mathbf{A'} = \mathbf{D}^{-1/2} \, \widehat{\mathbf{A}} \, \mathbf{D}^{-1/2} \qquad (6)$$

where $\mathbf{D}$ is the degree matrix.

After obtaining two components of feature's representation for each entity $\mathbf{H}_{real}^{(1)}$ and $\mathbf{H}_{img}^{(1)}$. In the GCN layer, we continue to expand these representations by performing an additional one-hop aggregation to assess the importance coefficients for each neighbor in the Dynamic graph attention layer. To do that, the attention scores are calculated as follows:

$$e_{ij} = e(\mathbf{h'_i}, \mathbf{h'_j}) = a^T \text{LeakyRELU}(\mathbf{W}.[\mathbf{h'_i}||\mathbf{h'_j}]) \qquad (7)$$

Next, these scores are normalized by Softmax function to make them easily compare as follows:

$$\alpha_{ij} = \text{Softmax}(e_{ij}) = \frac{\exp(e_{ij})}{\sum_{k \in N_i} \exp(e_{ik})} \qquad (8)$$

where α_{ij} is the normalized attention score between entity i^{th} and j^{th}.

Finally, this attention score is leveraged to calculate the final output $\mathbf{H}_{real}^{(2)}$ and $\mathbf{H}_{img}^{(2)}$ as follows:

$$\mathbf{H}^{(2)} = \sigma(\sum_{j \in N_i} \alpha_{ij} \mathbf{W}_j) \tag{9}$$

3.2 The Scoring Function

To measure the plausibility of triplet, we employ the ComplEx's scoring function by Eq. 11, which can model more accurately the symmetric and symmetric in each triplet. By obtaining the entity representation from $\mathbf{H}_{real}^{(2)}$, $\mathbf{H}_{img}^{(2)}$, and the relation embedding in complex space, we can easily compute the score of triplets. Moreover, we also apply the Sigmoid function to the score before assessing the result with the truth labels. The probability of forming triplet (h, r, t) as follows:

$$P(Y_{(h,r,t)} = 1) = \sigma(\ \phi(h,r,t)\ ) \tag{10}$$

where σ is the Sigmoid function, ϕ is the scoring function can be computed as Eq. 11, $Y \in \{-1, 1\}$ represent a binary value of a relation between head and tail entity.

$$\phi(h,r,t) = \langle Re(\mathbf{w_r}), Re(\mathbf{h_h''}), Re(\mathbf{h_t''})\rangle + \langle Re(\mathbf{w_r}), Im(\mathbf{h_h''}), Im(\mathbf{h_t''})\rangle$$
$$+ \langle Im(\mathbf{w_r}), Re(\mathbf{h_h''}), Im(\mathbf{h_t''})\rangle - \langle Im(\mathbf{w_r}), Im(\mathbf{h_h''}), Re(\mathbf{h_t''})\rangle \tag{11}$$

where $\mathbf{h_h''}, \mathbf{h_t''} \in \mathbf{H}^{(2)}, \mathbf{w_r} \in \mathbf{W}$.

Generally, our proposed model (ComplEx-GNN) considers the graph connectivity, relation type, and complex representation into the complex space. The graph aggregation layers allow learning the graph features while retaining the learning model's essential features. Additionally, we refer to the ComplEx model as the encoder and decoder for our framework. It helps to encode the entities and relation into complex values and then estimate triplets' plausibility by the scoring function. We also observe that our model acquired remarkable improvement over the ComplEx model without additional information.

4 Experiments and Result Analysis

4.1 Datasets and Evaluation Protocol

We use two widely used datasets to evaluate the link prediction task, including **FB15-237** [16] and **WN18RR** [7]. Table 1 illustrates statistics about two datasets. We also use two common benchmarks including Hit@k, and mean reciprocal rank (MRR), to evaluate the performance of the link prediction task.

Table 1. Statistics of FB15k-237 and WN18RR datasets.

Dataset	Entities	Relations	Training triples	Validation triples
FB15k-237	14541	237	272115	17535
WN18RR	40943	11	86835	3034

4.2 Hyperparameters

The hyperparameters include {learning rate, embedding dim, hidden dim, dropout rate}. Through experiment, the following hyperparameters gave the best result on FB15k-237: {0.001, 300, 400, 0.3}; on WN18RR: {0.003, 200, 400, 0.4} and the other configuration based on the framework of ConvE. We use PyTorch version 1.9.1 and run on NVIDIA Tesla V100-DGXS-32 GB. The training time on WN18RR and FB15k-237 is about 1–2 min, respectively.

4.3 Results

Table 2. Link prediction results on FB15k-237 and WN18RR

Model	FB15k-237				WN18RR			
	MRR	Hit@1	Hit@3	Hit@10	MRR	Hit@1	Hit@3	Hit@10
TransE-GCN [5]	0.315	0.229	**0.388**	0.477	0.233	0.203	0.338	0.508
DistMult [19]	0.241	0.155	0.263	0.419	0.43	0.39	0.44	0.49
ComplEx [17]	0.247	0.158	0.275	0.428	0.44	0.41	0.46	0.51
RGCN [15]	0.248	0.153	0.258	0.417	0.402	0.345	0.437	0.494
VR-GCN [22]	0.248	0.159	0.272	0.432	–	–	–	–
ConvE-Literal [10]	0.303	0.219	0.33	0.471	-	-	-	-
Complex-Literal [10]	0.305	0.222	0.336	0.466	–	–	-	–
ComplEx-GNN (our)	**0.328**	**0.238**	0.361	**0.509**	**0.451**	**0.415**	**0.462**	**0.522**

To illustrate the efficiency of our model, we compare our works with some standard models on the bilinear group such as DistMult and Complex, while comparing with models using additional information like ComplEx-Literal and ConvE-Literal to compare the power of structural information with additional information. Furthermore, our result is also compared with some pioneer GCN models employing both embeddings of entities and relations such as VR-GCN, TransE-GCN, and R-GCN to demonstrate the benefits of complex values in complex space. Table 2 illustrates our comparisons on FB15k-237, and WN18RR datasets. Summarizes the results of eight different baseline models including our models on FB15k-237 and WN18RR in terms of MRR - Mean reciprocal rank, Hits@1, Hits@3, and Hits@10.

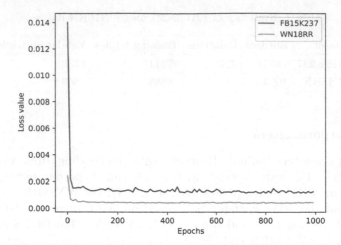

Fig. 2. The loss values of ComplEx-GNN models in FB15k-237 and WN18RR

In Table 2, our model achieved the best performance except for Hits@3. In detail, ComplEx-GNN model outperforms ComplEx Hits@10 by 5.9% and Complex Hits@3 by 7%. Furthermore, the Hits@1 in our model are 23.8%, which is 8% higher than the Complex model's 15.8%. Additionally, our approach improved the average rank of accurate triples by about 8.1% in MRR. The results confirmed the efficiency of the graph aggregation layer mentioned in Sect. 3. Meanwhile, when compared to the VR-GCN and RGCN models, our model achieved an improvement of more than 7% in all metrics. For the TransE-GCN model, ComplEx-GNN is higher around 1.3% on MRR, and 3.2% on Hits@10.

On WN18RR, the results of ConvE-Literal, ComplEx-Literal, and VR-GCN are empty due to the missing experiments on the original paper. In general, we obtain the best results on WN18RR. Compared with ComplEx, ComplEx-GNN enhances Hits@1 by 0.5% and MRR by 1.1%. For the Distmult, our model improves by around 2%-3% in all of metrics. Moreover, compared to the TransE-GCN model, ComplEx-GNN improves by 21.8% on MRR, 21.2% on Hits@1, 12.4% on Hit@3, and 1.4% on Hits@10. Meanwhile, our model achieves a marked increase of about 4.9% on MRR, 7% on Hits@1 and 2.5% on others metrics. This proves that our model retained the advantage property of the complex representations and enhancing the quality of embeddings to obtain improved results.

Next, we evaluate the convergence process of the model on both datasets. Figure 2 shows the loss proportion during the training phase of our model on FB15k-237 and WN18RR after every 10 epochs. Overall, the figure for WN18RR was consistently lower than that of FB15k-237. Additionally, after decreasing to 0.13% in FB15k-237 and 0.05% in WN18RR at the first 100 epochs, the WN18RR's loss percentage plateaued at 0.04%, and the figure for FB15k-237 witnessed a wild oscillation ranging from 0.13% to 0.16% in the remaining train-

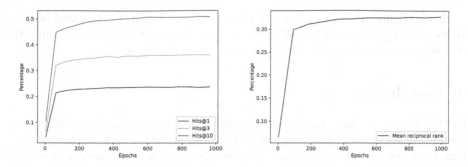

Fig. 3. The metric convergence research of ComplEx-GNN on FB15k-237

ing process, respectively. In addition, convergence proceeds quickly at the first 100 epochs on WN18RR, which is unstable on the remaining dataset. To save training time, we should use around the first 300 epochs on the WN18RR and about 1000 epochs for FB15k-237.

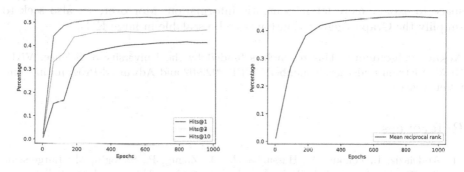

Fig. 4. The metric convergence research of ComplEx-GNN on WN18RR

Moreover, we also analyze the metrics' convergence to determine the possible epoch to train the model optimally. Figure 3 shows the Hit@n, mean rank, and mean reciprocal rank of ComplEx-GNN on FB15k-237 dataset. At first glance, on Hit@k's chart, the percentage saw an upward coverage tendency at the first 64 epochs, then having a mild fluctuation from 23.1% to 23.6% on Hits@1, 33.4% to 35.9% on Hits@3 and 49.4% to 50.6% on Hits@10, respectively. Meanwhile, a similar trend was experienced on MRR's chart ranging 32.1% to 32.8%, approximately. Figure 4 shows our experiments on WN18RR, the statistics for Hits@k(1, 3, 10) climbed substantially, reaching 37.6% on Hits@1, 45.6% on Hits@3, and 51.1% on Hits@10 at the first 304 epochs, before continuing to follow this tendency but less critically. Meanwhile, the MRR rapidly increased to 43.1% before fluctuating with a variation of around 1.6%. The charts shows that the convergence proceed of Hits@k is slightly slower than MRR on both two dataset.

In conclusion, the convergence of our model shows that it is fast and requires at least 300 epochs for WN18RR and 1000 epochs for FB15k-237. Although the stable process on WN18RR, the poor result on that dataset.

5 Conclusion

In this paper, we have proposed ComplEx-GNN model based on integrating graph neural networks and complex representation for the link prediction problem. First, we embedded entities and relations into complex space, then utilized the graph features by the Graph Aggregation Layers. By the way, the graph connectivity and relation types can be included in the learning process. The ComplEx's scoring function is applied to take advantage of the complex space, which could handle symmetric and asymmetric relations and enhance the model's expressivity. The gap between our model with ComplEx and LiteralE and GNN models proves the importance of structural information, indicating the power of complex space in representing entities and relations. Although obtaining the better result, the training time is significant and performs poorly on WN18RR.

In future work, we intend to embed graph features into the hypercomplex space to exploit more latent semantic information. Moreover, we also seek to simplify the Graph Aggregation Layer to be scalable in large KGs.

Acknowledgements. This research is funded by the University of Science, VNU-HCM, Vietnam under grant number CNTT 2022-02 and Advanced Program in Computer Science.

References

1. Abdelaziz, I., Fokoue, A., Hassanzadeh, O., Zhang, P., Sadoghi, M.: Large-scale structural and textual similarity-based mining of knowledge graph to predict drug-drug interactions. J. Web Semant. **44**, 104–117 (2017)
2. Alon, U., Yahav, E.: On the bottleneck of graph neural networks and its practical implications. arXiv preprint arXiv:2006.05205 (2020)
3. Bordes, A., Usunier, N., Garcia-Duran, A., Weston, J., Yakhnenko, O.: Translating embeddings for modeling multi-relational data. In: Advances in Neural Information Processing Systems, vol. 26 (2013)
4. Brody, S., Alon, U., Yahav, E.: How attentive are graph attention networks? arXiv preprint arXiv:2105.14491 (2021)
5. Cai, L., Yan, B., Mai, G., Janowicz, K., Zhu, R.: TransGCN: coupling transformation assumptions with graph convolutional networks for link prediction. In: Proceedings of the 10th International Conference on Knowledge Capture, pp. 131–138 (2019)
6. Dai, Y., Wang, S., Xiong, N.N., Guo, W.: A survey on knowledge graph embedding: approaches, applications and benchmarks. Electronics **9**(5), 750 (2020)
7. Dettmers, T., Minervini, P., Stenetorp, P., Riedel, S.: Convolutional 2D knowledge graph embeddings. In: Thirty-Second AAAI Conference on Artificial Intelligence (2018)

8. Ji, G., He, S., Xu, L., Liu, K., Zhao, J.: Knowledge graph embedding via dynamic mapping matrix. In: Proceedings of the 53rd Annual Meeting of the Association for Computational Linguistics and the 7th International Joint Conference on Natural Language Processing (Volume 1: Long Papers), pp. 687–696 (2015)
9. Kipf, T.N., Welling, M.: Semi-supervised classification with graph convolutional networks. arXiv preprint arXiv:1609.02907 (2016)
10. Kristiadi, A., Khan, M.A., Lukovnikov, D., Lehmann, J., Fischer, A.: Incorporating literals into knowledge graph embeddings. In: Ghidini, C., et al. (eds.) ISWC 2019. LNCS, vol. 11778, pp. 347–363. Springer, Cham (2019). https://doi.org/10.1007/978-3-030-30793-6_20
11. Li, F.L., et al.: Alime assist: an intelligent assistant for creating an innovative e-commerce experience. In: Proceedings of the 2017 ACM on Conference on Information and Knowledge Management, pp. 2495–2498 (2017)
12. Lin, Y., Liu, Z., Sun, M., Liu, Y., Zhu, X.: Learning entity and relation embeddings for knowledge graph completion. In: Twenty-Ninth AAAI Conference on Artificial Intelligence (2015)
13. Nguyen, D.Q., Nguyen, T.D., Nguyen, D.Q., Phung, D.: A novel embedding model for knowledge base completion based on convolutional neural network. arXiv preprint arXiv:1712.02121 (2017)
14. Nickel, M., Tresp, V., Kriegel, H.P.: A three-way model for collective learning on multi-relational data. In: ICML (2011)
15. Schlichtkrull, M., Kipf, T.N., Bloem, P., van den Berg, R., Titov, I., Welling, M.: Modeling relational data with graph convolutional networks. In: Gangemi, A., et al. (eds.) ESWC 2018. LNCS, vol. 10843, pp. 593–607. Springer, Cham (2018). https://doi.org/10.1007/978-3-319-93417-4_38
16. Toutanova, K., Chen, D., Pantel, P., Poon, H., Choudhury, P., Gamon, M.: Representing text for joint embedding of text and knowledge bases. In: Proceedings of the 2015 Conference on Empirical Methods in Natural Language Processing, pp. 1499–1509 (2015)
17. Trouillon, T., Welbl, J., Riedel, S., Gaussier, É., Bouchard, G.: Complex embeddings for simple link prediction. In: International Conference on Machine Learning, pp. 2071–2080. PMLR (2016)
18. Wang, Q., Mao, Z., Wang, B., Guo, L.: Knowledge graph embedding: a survey of approaches and applications. IEEE Trans. Knowl. Data Eng. **29**(12), 2724–2743 (2017)
19. Wang, Z., Zhang, J., Feng, J., Chen, Z.: Knowledge graph embedding by translating on hyperplanes. In: Proceedings of the AAAI Conference on Artificial Intelligence, vol. 28 (2014)
20. Xie, R., Liu, Z., Jia, J., Luan, H., Sun, M.: Representation learning of knowledge graphs with entity descriptions. In: Proceedings of the AAAI Conference on Artificial Intelligence, vol. 30 (2016)
21. Yang, B., Yih, W.T., He, X., Gao, J., Deng, L.: Embedding entities and relations for learning and inference in knowledge bases. arXiv preprint arXiv:1412.6575 (2014)
22. Ye, R., Li, X., Fang, Y., Zang, H., Wang, M.: A vectorized relational graph convolutional network for multi-relational network alignment. In: IJCAI, pp. 4135–4141 (2019)

Expandable-Convolutional-Block Neural Inference with Spatial-Fused Multi-resolution Features and Terse Convolution for IoT-Based Intelligent Automated Systems

Pei-Ju Li[1]([✉]), Lin-Yi Jiang[1], Ting-Yu Hu[1], Ding-Chau Wang[2],
Gwo-Jiun Horng[3], Yu-Chuan Lin[1], Min-Hsiung Hung[4], and Chao-Chun Chen[1]

[1] IMIS/CSIE, NCKU, Tainan City, Taiwan
{P96104154,P98101500,P98101021,chaochun}@gs.ncku.edu.tw,
duke@imrc.ncku.edu.tw
[2] MIS, Southern Taiwan University of Science and Technology, Tainan City, Taiwan
dcwang@stust.edu.tw
[3] CSIE, Southern Taiwan University of Science and Technology, Tainan City, Taiwan
grojium@stust.edu.tw
[4] CSIE, PCCU, Taipei City, Taiwan
hmx4@faculty.pccu.edu.tw

Abstract. We proposed two model compression methods by adjusting the structure of the deep network model, aiming to provide a small-sized model and realize the application requirement of edge computing. Edge Device has weak computing power and small storage capacity. The key idea of our proposed scheme is to minimize the computational cost of Expandableconvolutional-block neural network (ECB-Net) [7] to compress model size and optimize the model performance of ECB-Net. In order to achieve this, it is necessary to combine two model compression methods that adjust the ECB-Net network structure, including replacing Transpose Convolution in SIC-Block with SPP-Layer and replacing FC-Layer with TC-Layer. The experimental results reveal that the proposed scheme does have effective model compression capabilities and indeed prediction accuracy.

Keywords: Deep learning · Intelligent agriculture · Farming automation · System robustness · Transpose convolution

1 Introduction

With the development and popularization of deep learning image recognition technology, many applications require high availability networks with minimum

This work was supported by Ministry of Science and Technology (MOST) of Taiwan under Grants 111-2221-E-006-202, 110-2221-E-034-009-MY2. This work was financially supported by the "Intelligent Manufacturing Research Center" (iMRC) in NCKU from The Featured Areas Research Center Program within the framework of the Higher Education Sprout Project by the Ministry of Education in Taiwan.

© The Author(s), under exclusive license to Springer Nature Singapore Pte Ltd. 2022
E. Szczerbicki et al. (Eds.): ACIIDS 2022, CCIS 1716, pp. 276–286, 2022.
https://doi.org/10.1007/978-981-19-8234-7_22

delay to process large amounts of data, gradually extending the application requirements of edge computing [4, 8]. Edge computing is mainly to reduce the cost of network bandwidth required by traditional cloud computing and to provide real-time service. It is no longer like traditional cloud computing that is limited by network bandwidth speed and affects system performance. At present, many studies have proposed that the lightweight networks use Edge Device effectively filter invalid data to minimize the energy consumption of data transmission for in-depth discussion [1]. Edge Device has weak computing power and small storage capacity. Therefore, it is impossible to deploy complex model with excessive calculation or capacity in Edge Device. Many lightweight models sacrifice part of the prediction accuracy in exchange for low calculation and parameters, allowing the model to be deployed on Edge Devices. In our past research, we proposed Expandableconvolutional-block neural network (ECB-Net) [7], ECB-Net can meet the real-time requirements of the system and can select the best image classification model structure according to the computing power of Edge Device. Figure 1 shows the scenario diagram of ECB-Net applied in pig farm image collection. ECB-Net is mainly used in pig farm standing image collection. The filtering function of pig standing and non-standing images is realized through the AIOT device installed on the pig farm. This allows non-standing images to be filtered at the local side end without occupying network bandwidth and reducing the power consumption of edge devices. In this research, we use Convolutional Neural Networks to extract the features of the image, and use transposed convolution to reduce the dimensionality of the data so that the model can unlimitedly cascade. Then, the image features input into the Fully Connected Layer (FC-Layer) for image classification, and finally the network will output the category of the image. The function of image classification is a common application requirement in edge computing. Traditional methods mostly use CNN+FC-Layer to achieve classification tasks. However, in the application scenario of edge computing, the multi-layer CNN and transposed convolution network easily increase the model calculation, which makes the computing time of the model unable to meet the application requirements. When using FC-Layer for classification tasks, it is easy to generate many parameters, which makes the capacity of the model too large, and it is not easy to deploy in edge device. Take ECB-Net as an example, the computational cost of ECB-Net is too high (affected by SIC-Block and FC-Layer, the model calculation and parameters are too high, detail will be explained in Sect. 3.1), resulting in too long execution time to meet application requirements, and large model size, which makes it difficult to deploy on Edge Device.

In this research, we propose to replace the transpose convolution in SIC Block with SPP Layer to simultaneously achieve the purpose of reducing the model calculation and improving the model accuracy. At the same time, this research uses TC-Layer to replace FC-Layer to achieve the goal of reducing the model parameters.

The contributions of this research are explained as follows:

– We introduced two model compression technologies, SPP Layer and TC-Layer in ECB-Net, which can reduce the model calculation and size. This method is also suitable for other deep network models that need to be transplanted to edge computing devices. The two methods proposed in this paper can be the basic tools for adjusting the compressed deep network model.

- This paper proposes a lightweight model for classification of pig standing images to achieve the goal of filtering non-standing images, reducing the energy consumption of data transmission and ease of deployment. In the traditional classification model, there are too many parameters in FC-Layer. This study uses TC-Layer to effectively replace FC-Layer to reduce model parameters and model size by the characteristic of Shared Weight in the convolution operation. In this way, the model is easier to deploy on edge computing devices to run. In this paper, we propose an optimization method of SIC-Block in ECB-Net. When the image is transferred between SIC-Blocks, this method can extract the multi-scale features of the image and increase the quality of features. By retaining the important features of the original image, the model classification accuracy can be increased.

- SIC-Block is extensible in ECB-Net. Therefore, multi-scale features cannot be retained during the process of transmission, which will reduce the quality of the features. Finally, it will lead to a reduction of the model classification accuracy. This paper uses SPP-Layer to enable ECB-Net to maintain good feature quality and have good prediction accuracy regardless of the number of extended SIC-Blocks.

In this work, based on the design of ECB-Net, we combined SPP and TC-Layer to design a method of compressing model calculation and parameters, minimizing the computational cost of ECB-Net.

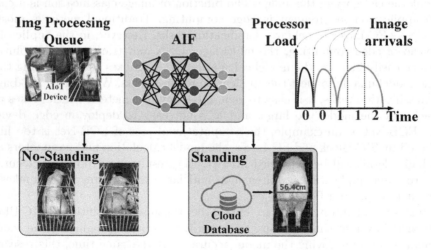

Fig. 1. Illustration of continuous livestock surveillance with the AIF module in IoT devices. Farm workers can understand the livestock health status by the shape measurement capacity anytime and any where via the AIoT and cloud technologies.

2   Backgrounds

2.1   Convolutional Neural Networks

With the development of Convolutional Neural Network architecture [6], computer has excellent performance in specific recognition, such as plant recognition, fire detection, etc. The main task of Convolutional Neural Network in image classification is to accept the input image and its defined category labels for learning. This way is just like the way humans learn from birth to the present. However, the way computer sees images is different from what human see. What the computer sees is the pixel array of the image, not the image. The length and width of the image and the pixel value in the channel will assign a value from 0 to 255 to the computer and describe the intensity of the pixel at each point from this value. CNN learns by automatically extracting pixel features from the image, and learns features through dozens or hundreds of Hidden Layers that can increase model learning ability and complexity. The operating mode of the image classification model is not to feed back all the pixel values of the image, but to segment the image pixels into multiple and multi-layered blocks, which are called Feature Map, and then the neural network model will analyze the features. CNN represents a huge breakthrough in the field of image recognition. It is often used to analyze visual images and is applied to various fields to solve problems, such as the photo tag in Facebook and the self-driving car. The way of the image classification model learns is to use a 2-dimensional convolutional layer to convolute the input self-defining labels and image features, which means that the model network is very suitable for processing 2-dimensional images.

3   Proposed Model Compression Scheme

3.1   Overall Architecture

Figure 2 shows the architecture diagram of the $ECB - Net[UncompSPP + TCLayer]$ we proposed, which mainly includes two model compression methods. The first model compression method is to replace Transpose Convolution with SPP-Layer in SIC-Block, which is mainly used to provide multi-size features to improve the prediction accuracy of the model and reduce the execution time of the model. The second model compression method is to replace FC-Layer with TC-Layer, which is mainly used to reduce parameters and size of the model. In this way, the model is easier to deploy in edge computing device. The compression method and technical details of the entire model will be introduced in the following subsections.

Table 1 shows flops and parameters of each layer of ECB-Net. It can be seen from the table that the cost of flops is mainly in SIC-Block. The flops of each SIC-Block is 0.58G, which accounts for $\frac{0.58}{1.8} \approx 32\%$ of the total flops. In 3-SIC-block ECB-Net, there are three SIC-Blocks, which account for 96% of flops in this network. One block in SIC Block uses two convolutions and two transposed

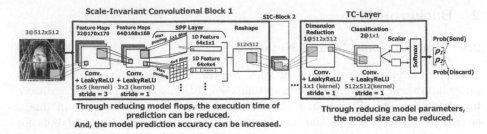

Fig. 2. Structure of the proposed $ECB - Net[UncompSPP + TCLayer]$, consisting of three components: SIC-blocks and TC-layer.

convolutions. In other words, when a Block increases, four computational structures that require a lot of flops need to be added. Massive flops will cause the problem of too long execution time when the edge computing device is running model. In this case, user needs to spend a high cost to upgrade the edge computing device to obtain good computing performance and complete tasks within the required time. It can be seen from the table that parameters of the model is mainly concentrated in FC-Layer, and the flops of FC-Layer is $39.32M$, which accounts for $\frac{39.32}{39.38} \approx 99\%$ of parameters in this network. The large number of parameters increase the model size, which makes it difficult to deploy edge computing device with small storage capacity. In edge computing device, the storage capacity of the device is proportional to the cost. The larger the storage capacity of the model has, the higher the cost of deployment needs.

Table 1. Unit analysis for an uncompressed 3-SIC-block ECB-Net.

Unit	# of Parameters	# of Multiplications
SIC-Block 1	20.92K	**0.58G**
SIC-Block 2	20.92K	**0.58G**
SIC-Block 3	20.92K	**0.58G**
MAP-Layer	≈ 0	≈ 0
FC-Layer	**39.32M**	39.32M
Total	39.38M	1.8G

In this work, in order to solve the problem of excessive flops and parameters of the ECB-Net model, this paper proposes two compression methods, replacing Transpose Convolution with SPP-Layer and replacing FC-Layer with TC-Layer, to reduce the flops and parameters of the model. By doing so, the execution time and model size required by ECB-Net in edge computing device can be reduced. The model can achieve better performance in edge computing device. The design of two model compression methods will be explained in Subsects. 3.2 and 3.3.

3.2　SPP Layer

The main feature of SPP-Layer [3]. is flexible input scale. The pooling of SPP Layer uses multiple Max pooling windows for feature extraction. Figure 3 shows the schematic diagram of the SPP-Layer structure proposed in this paper. SPP-Layer can extract features at different scales. In this way, important features of the original image can be preserved and passed to the next block to continue extraction. SPP Layer is used to output fixed length 1D context feature values (context 1, 2, 3...). Through the fixed-size Bin and the corresponding Max pooling window, each filter output of the Convolution layer collects the most important features at different resolutions, and each resolution outputs a 1D feature vector. In the original ECB-Net, transpose convolution realizes that the output size of each SIC-Block structure is the same, so that the model can be transferred between multiple SIC-Blocks. However, this method requires high flops, and it is not easy to retain the important features of the input image. Therefore, this paper uses SPP-Layer instead of transpose convolution to perform image size scaling tasks. At the same time, the important features of the picture are maintained without causing distortion of the data. The output result of SPP Layer can be resized into a 2D feature vector of the same size, and output to the next Block and continue to be superimposed. In the end, the goal of keeping the input and output sizes of SIC-Block the same can be accomplished.

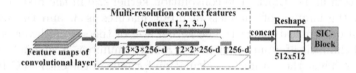

Fig. 3. SPP-Layer structure of ECB-Net

3.3　TC Layer

Common image classification models use fully connected layers to complete classification task. The characteristic of fully connected layer is that neurons in each layer are connected to all neurons in the previous layer, and the weight of each connection layer is retained, which will lead to excessive model parameters. A large number of parameters make edge computing devices need to occupy a large size of storage space when deploying models to perform prediction tasks. At the same time, this problem also easily leads to overfitting during model training. The output classified results in ECB-Net [7] are two categories of pig standing and pig non-standing images. Each fully connected layer (FC-Layer) we defined includes one input layer, one hidden layer and one output layer. FC-Layer parameter calculation formula can be written as:

$$|FC_1| \cdot |FC_2| + |FC_2| \cdot |FC_3| \tag{1}$$

Among them, the number of neurons in the input layer is the size of the input image multiplied by the number of channels ($128 \cdot 128 \cdot 3 = 49152$); the number of neurons in the hidden layer is defined here as 800; the number of neurons in the output layer indicates the number of classification categories is 2. Therefore, the amount of parameters required for ECB-Net is $49152 \cdot 800 + 800 \cdot 2 \approx 39.32M$. In this topic, in order to develop a lightweight pig image pose classification model structure, the image classification by convolution is realized with a small number of weight parameters, which greatly reduces the amount of model parameters. Shared weights means that the convolution operation is performed on the same filter, which means that the whole image will share these weights. Using the concept of convolution sharing weights, the parameter amount of convolution is calculated by multiplying the number of parameters of each convolution kernel by the number of common convolution kernels. Therefore, the parameter calculation formula of TC-Block can be written as the following formula, where K^l represents the size of the convolution kernel in the convolutional layer of l layer, n_{in}^l represents the number of channels of input features in l layer, and n_{out}^l represents the number of channels of output features in l layer:

$$\sum_{l=1}^{D} K^l \cdot K^l \cdot n_{in}^l \cdot n_{out}^l \tag{2}$$

Figure 4 shows the convolution structure diagram of TC-Layer in $ECB-Net_{[SPP+TC-Layer]}$. The classification network is implemented with two layers of convolution in TC-Block. The convolution kernel size in the first convolution layer is 1, the number of channels of input features is 3, and the number of channels of output features is 1; The kernel size of the second layer is 512, the number of channels of input features is 1, and the number of channels of output features is 2. Thus, the parameter calculation formula of the entire TC-Block can be written as: $(1 \cdot 1 \cdot 3 \cdot 1) + (512 \cdot 512 \cdot 1 \cdot 2) \approx 0.52M$ After ECB-Net is compressed by TC-Block, the number of parameters is greatly reduced to $1\% (\frac{0.52M}{39.32M} \approx 1\%)$ of the original. In this paper, by realizing a convolutional layer with a small number of weight parameters, we compress the amount of model parameters and avoid overfitting of the model. By doing so, deploying in a new animal husbandry system with a low cost and maintaining a high classification accuracy are be achieved.

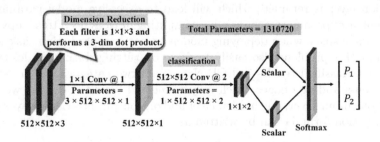

Fig. 4. TC-Layer structure of ECB-Net

4   Case Study

4.1   System Deployment and Experimental Settings

We deployed the $ECB - Net_{[SPP+TC-Layer]}$ proposed in this paper on the Raspberry Pi 4 of the AIOT device. Raspberry Pi 4 (RPi4) has a 1.5 GHz quad-core processor and 4 GB RAM. The system prototype was developed using the frameworks mainly used in deep learning research, including Python 3.5 and PyTorch 1.6.0. The data set used in this paper was collected by cameras deployed by our team in pregnant pig houses on a livestock farm in southern Taiwan. The collected pig data set contains 14,654 images, of which pigs are standing in 1,662 images. The ratio of training/validation/test data is 80%: 10%: 10%. Due to space constraints, this article only conducts experimental research on the overall performance of the model, which is the priority of the prediction accuracy, model execution time, model storage capacity, etc., which are prioritized by the deployment of the model in edge computing device. In the experiment, we will compare the model performance indicators of $ECB - Net_{[SPP+TC-Layer]}$ and other famous lightweight models on the test set. The experiment used three well-known lightweight models published in recent years, including MobileNet [5], GhostNet [2] and ShuffleNet [9].

4.2   Expr. 1: Comparisons of Model Accuracy

This experiment shows the comparison of accuracy with each model in the pig standing image data set. In the application environment of this paper, the goal of ECB-Net is to filter non-standing images of pigs. Therefore, the model performance indicators of this research work should be the number of true negatives (TN) correctly judged as non-standing images and the number of false negatives (FN) incorrectly judged as non-standing images in the data set. TN and FN will determine the number of non-standing images of pigs that our application can accurately filter. Thus, we choose to use Accuracy to measure the predictive performance of the classification model. The calculation formula of Accuracy is expressed as:

$$Accuracy = \frac{TP+TN}{TP+TN+FP+FN} \qquad (3)$$

Accuracy incorporates TN and FN into the calculation at the same time. If the Accuracy of the model is high, it means that the model has a good data pruning effect in this application scenario and can achieve good results in the image classification task of pigs standing. Figure 4 shows the comparison of accuracy between $ECB - Net_{[SPP+TC-Layer]}$ which constructed based on SPP-Layer and TC-Layer proposed in this paper, $ECB - Net_{[Uncompressed]}$ and the other lightweight model . The experimental result shows that $ECB - Net_{[SPP+TC-Layer]}$ has higher prediction accuracy than the original $ECB - Net_{[Uncompressed]}$. At the same time, the accuracy of $ECB - Net_{[SPP+TC-Layer]}$ is also higher than other lightweight models (Fig. 5).

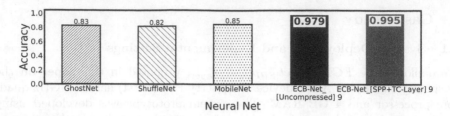

Fig. 5. Comparisons of accuracy of compressed and uncompressed ECB-Nets with best training models fitting RPi4 resources

4.3   Expr. 2: Comparisons of Model Parameters

This experiment shows the comparison of the parameters of each model. In the application scenario of edge computing, the smaller the model size is, the easier the model can be deployed on the edge computing device without the need to expand the storage capacity of the device. In other words, small model size means that the deployment cost of the model is low. Figure 6 shows the comparison of parameters between $ECB - Net_{[SPP+TC-Layer]}$, $ECB - Net_{[Uncompressed]}$ and other lightweight models. It can be seen from Fig. 6 that our model has lower parameters and model size than other models. This experiment proves that the two compression methods proposed in the paper can reduce flops and the model size, and have better result than other common lightweight models.

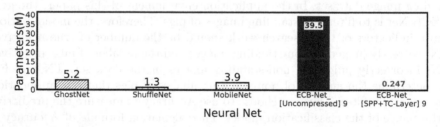

Fig. 6. Comparisons of parameters of compressed and uncompressed ECB-Nets with best training models fitting RPi4 resources

4.4   Expr. 3: Comparisons of Model Execution Time

This experiment shows the comparison of execution time of each model to perform a single image classification task. Figure 7 shows the comparison of execution time for single image prediction task between $ECB - Net_{[SPP+TC-Layer]}$, $ECB - Net_{[Uncompressed]}$ and other lightweight models. It can be seen from Fig. 7 that $ECB - Net_{[SPP+TC-Layer]}$ is compared to the original $ECB - Net_{[Uncompressed]}$ has lower execution time with model. Moreover, compared with other lightweight models, $ECB - Net_{[SPP+TC-Layer]}$ still retains the flexibility of $ECB - Net_{[Uncompressed]}$ to control execution time of the model according to the computing power of the device. In the image classification task of standing pigs, $ECB - Net_{[SPP+TC-Layer]}$ can still scale SIC-Block. By doing so, the model has the highest model prediction accuracy within the limited time of application.

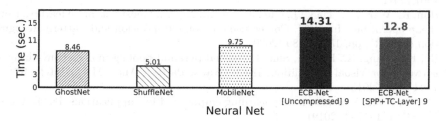

Fig. 7. Comparisons of execution time of compressed and uncompressed ECB-Nets with best training models fitting RPi4 resources

5 Conclusions and Future Work

In this paper, we propose a new compression technology of ECB-Net to optimize the model performance of ECB-Net. This technology allows the model to have higher execution efficiency and lower deployment costs, and it can be more easily deployed to small livestock farms. This paper proposes a new structure of $ECB - Net_{[SPP+TC-Layer]}$ to achieve the goal of reducing model execution time (flops) and model storage capacity (parameters). The experimental result shows that $ECB - Net_{[SPP+TC-Layer]}$ has lower model execution time and smaller storage capacity, and the model is easier to deploy on Edge Device. Besides, the accuracy is higher than the original ECB-Net. Through the compression method, which can output the important image features at different resolutions by SPP-Layer, proposed in this paper,the model prediction accuracy is increased. Meanwhile, the model flops and prediction time are reduced. Finally, according to the experimental results, it is proved that the SPP-Layer model compression method proposed in this paper can effectively reduce flops and prediction time. This paper proposes to replace FC-Layer with TC-Layer to perform classification tasks. With shared weights of the CNN characteristic, this method solved the problem of large model size caused by mass parameters of full connected layer.

The point of our future work is to promote the application of this model compression method to other application scenarios with model compression requirement, and to provide user with an optimized compression scheme. In the future, application developer with model compression need will be provided with a model compression selection strategy. In this way, developer can quickly select the most suitable model compression algorithm according to the strategy to achieve the purpose of model compression.

References

1. Chollet, F.: Xception: deep learning with depthwise separable convolutions. In: 2017 IEEE Conference on Computer Vision and Pattern Recognition (CVPR), pp. 1800–1807 (2017)
2. Han, K., Wang, Y., Tian, Q., Guo, J., Xu, C., Xu, C.: GhostNet: more features from cheap operations. In: IEEE Conference on Computer Vision and Pattern Recognition (CVPR), pp. 1580–1589 (2020)
3. He, K., Zhang, X., Ren, S., Sun, J.: Spatial pyramid pooling in deep convolutional networks for visual recognition. IEEE Trans. Pattern Anal. Mach. Intell. **37**(9), 1904–1916 (2015)
4. Ma, X., et al.: A survey on deep learning empowered IoT applications. IEEE Access **7**, 181721–181732 (2019)
5. Sandler, M., Howard, A., Zhu, M., Zhmoginov, A., Chen, L.C.: MobileNetV2: inverted residuals and linear bottlenecks. In: IEEE Conference on Computer Vision and Pattern Recognition (CVPR), pp. 4510–4520 (2018)
6. Shin, H.C., et al.: Deep convolutional neural networks for computer-aided detection: CNN architectures, dataset characteristics and transfer learning. IEEE Trans. Med. Imaging **35**(5), 1285–1298 (2016)
7. Su, W.T., Jiang, L.Y., Tang-Hsuan, O., Lin, Y.C., Hung, M.H., Chen, C.C.: Aiot-cloud-integrated smart livestock surveillance via assembling deep networks with considering robustness and semantics availability. IEEE Robot. Autom. Lett. **6**(4), 6140–6147 (2021)
8. Wang, F., Zhang, M., Wang, X., Ma, X., Liu, J.: Deep learning for edge computing applications: a state-of-the-art survey. IEEE Access **8**, 58322–58336 (2020). https://doi.org/10.1109/ACCESS.2020.2982411
9. Zhang, X., Zhou, X., Lin, M., Sun, J.: ShuffleNet: an extremely efficient convolutional neural network for mobile devices. In: IEEE Conference on Computer Vision and Pattern Recognition (CVPR), pp. 6848–6856 (2018)

Traffic Management in Smart City

M. E. Mansurova⑩, B. A. Belgibaev⑩, D. S. Zhamangarin⑩,
and N. A. Zholdas⁽✉⁾⑩

Al-Farabi Kazakh National University, 71 al-Farabi Ave., Almaty, Republic of Kazakhstan
{Madina.Mansurova,Zholdas.Nurassyl}@kaznu.edu.kz,
bbelgibaev@list.ru

Abstract. The article discusses new smart technologies for monitoring and controlling road traffic in the city of Almaty. It is shown that the megapolis has specific features in automating the processes of controlling the movement of vehicles. They are connected with the polycentricity of the city and a number of mutually intersecting traffic flows in the central part of Almaty. The algorithms and applications presented in the article for the AnyLogic PLE environment open up practical opportunities to predict, based on an event-probabilistic simulation model of traffic, the dynamics of the development of congestion processes with a few hours ahead of time.

Keywords: Smart technologies in motor transport · Simulation event-probabilistic model · Smart traffic light · IoT device

1 Introduction

The use of intelligent control systems in the automotive industry and the global practice of developing modern digital information exchange technologies have significantly altered the scientific, technological, and practical approaches to the organization of optimal traffic in densely populated cities. The mathematical models of traffic flow management that are currently in use are deterministic in nature, allowing for the empirical formulation of conflicting initial and boundary conditions that are related to determining the type of flow and the capacity of the transport artery at maximum load. This leads to insufficient capacity in the "rush hours" of one of the vehicle lanes with a significant underutilization of oncoming traffic lanes. For individual passenger cars and taxis, geodata collection systems will be used in the city with the help of GPS positioning of cars equipped with receiving and transmitting devices based on Lo@RA (Long Rang) series chips. The range of this GPS controller is up to 30 km in open terrain and up to 3 km on hilly and wooded terrain.

Collecting data on the location of certain groups of vehicles in the server equipment allows to find hidden patterns of the dynamics of traffic flows at certain intervals. The use of artificial intelligence, machine learning (ML) and big data (Big Data) is an important little-studied area of modern research in the field of traffic management.

© The Author(s), under exclusive license to Springer Nature Singapore Pte Ltd. 2022
E. Szczerbicki et al. (Eds.): ACIIDS 2022, CCIS 1716, pp. 287–298, 2022.
https://doi.org/10.1007/978-981-19-8234-7_23

Another novel and interesting field of information technology use in the practice of traffic management is the development of new mobile neurophysical traffic light controllers as a collective adaptive IoT device.

There are several densely populated residential neighborhoods and suburbs in the city of Almaty, the population of which works in the central part of Almaty [1]. This leads to the emergence of congestion during peak hours for mutually intersecting traffic flows. Finding effective methods to reduce the load on the city's road network is an urgent task of modern intelligent automated control systems.

2   Problem Statement

System analysis using simulation and simulation modeling in AnyLogic, VMware Workstation Pro, TIA Portal V13, Logo! Soft Comfort environments has shown that the dynamic change in the time phases of traffic light objects, as collective intelligent IoT devices, allows to change and actively manage the dynamics of traffic flows on the most loaded sections of highways [2].

The local application of simulation modeling in the AnyLogic environment allows for the landscape linking of highways to the expected flow of cars on the main highways at the entrance/exit to densely populated cities. In the AnyLogic environment, modern advanced experimental studies of the dynamics of traffic flows depending on the time of day are carried out interactively and traffic light cyclograms are selected semi-empirically. The disadvantage of this system is the complexity of its integration into the traffic control system [3, 4].

In the development environments of VMware Workstation Pro, TIA Portal V13, Logo! Soft Comfort there are developments on the creation of adaptive self-adjusting digital traffic light controllers based on Siemens microcontrollers in a network version [5]. There are few examples of creating traffic light controllers as IoT devices in the technical literature and practice.

The creation of collective intelligent traffic light controllers integrated with the Scada system of the automated traffic control system using advanced simulation of processes in the AnyLogic environment with data transmission algorithms is a new direction in the digitalization of traffic in Kazakhstan.

The symbiosis of the two approaches creates conditions for the fruitful modernization of existing analog traffic control systems. The phased introduction of smart traffic lights as IoT devices will make it possible to design and implement a modern intelligent computer network of smart traffic light objects that will be able to monitor the traffic situation in dynamics and will automate the adoption of optimal decisions by dispatchers of the central traffic control panel of the metropolis.

In the cities of Russia, Almaty and Nur-Sultan, experimental and survey work is being carried out on the introduction of smart traffic lights [6]. Creating a local smart traffic light that works autonomously without taking into account the general traffic situation can theoretically improve the throughput on this section of the road. The complexity of taking into account all traffic parameters on urban highways during peak hours creates prerequisites and stimulates research on simulation modeling of traffic lights as the main automatic regulators of the capacity of city highways, in combination with the multiparametric conditions of the significantly uncertain task of optimizing car traffic on the urban road network.

A high degree of uncertainty does not allow the use of deterministic theories of traffic flow management and increases the role of heuristic (intelligent) methods for solving problems of increasing traffic in cities with heavy traffic [7].

The creation of local systems, their gradual coordination among themselves over computer networks is also being considered and implemented by IT firms and electrical companies. For example, ROSIM ITS Technology Co., Ltd (China) has developed a compact set of road equipment to create an adaptive smart intersection with a set of induction sensors. Figure 1 shows a general view of the traffic management and monitoring complex at the intersection.

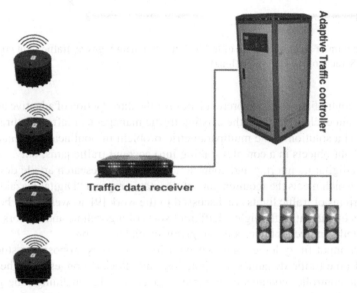

Traffic data receiver

Fig. 1. Adaptive microcontroller traffic control system at the intersection by ROSIM ITS Technology Co., Ltd (China).

High-tech digital equipment implements modern wireless vehicle detection. The ready-made software and hardware allow to implement the tasks of dynamic control and operational monitoring of the flow of cars. The functionality of the complex can calculate the intensity of traffic flow. The vehicle detection sensor on a secondary road allows to turn on the red light on an intense main road. Adaptive permitting green light turns on as the flow of cars increases. The diagram of his work is shown in Fig. 2.

Data collection on the dynamic characteristics of the traffic flow is carried out using modern digital technologies. This adaptive system has found wide application in a number of developed foreign countries, such as India, Turkey, France, USA, Philippines, Italy, Germany, Uruguay, Colombia, Spain, Australia, Canada and Romania, etc. In Kazakhstan, Russian hybrid small-sized traffic light controllers of the MDK type with fixed switching phases of control light signals are widely used.

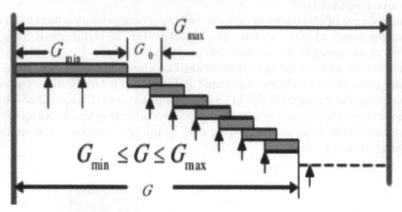

Fig. 2. Diagram of adaptive control of traffic-saturated main highway traffic light controllers by ROSIM ITS Technology Co., Ltd (China).

These contradictions create prerequisites for the introduction of adaptive automation of traffic light cyclograms with the existing traffic management infrastructure. It is possible to find a solution to the multiparametric problem of nonlinear automated control of traffic light objects in a complex, taking into account traffic jams, only on the basis of modern digital monitoring and control. The presented research article develops this direction, which meets the requirements of the state program "Digital Kazakhstan" [8].

The origins of traffic lights are discussed in the work [9], as well as the benefits and drawbacks of current traffic lights. Different sorts of algorithms and sensors employed in such intelligent technologies are also given special attention.

A three-input fuzzy logic controller with IoT sensors is proposed in study [10] to adapt real-time traffic dynamics at a junction and alleviate congestion. The proposed fuzzy logic controller contains three inputs: queue length, remaining time green, and peak hours, as well as one output parameter, time extension, which is influenced by the three input parameters.

3   The Proposed Method and Experimental Results

This implies that systematic investigation of intricate traffic processes and the creation of cutting-edge traffic management technology are required in order to address a variety of transport issues. An important link in improving the traffic light traffic control system are algorithms for quantization of the green light response time of traffic lights installed at busy intersections of the city of Almaty. The use of inductive and ultrasonic detectors for the formation of congestion phenomena on the highways of the city allows to collect important information to create algorithms for controlling the "smart intersection".

A receiving and transmitting radio device must be installed on every automobile in the new approach to traffic control in contrast to the methods now in use. To reach congested areas of the urban road network, the radio signal's range of transmission and reception should be sufficient. As a result, the vehicle and its driver are now part of a sophisticated, multifaceted, real-time automated traffic control system. In addition to being centralized, traffic management optimization algorithms can also be local for a specific stretch of road or a big urban region.

The basic concept behind microdistricts and important intersections is to decentralize and diversify urban networks and traffic corridors. This means that in Smart City neighborhoods, a smart intersection is a small-scale but essential connection in a decentralized transport management system. Figure 3 shows the adjusted master plan for the development of the transport network of the city of Almaty.

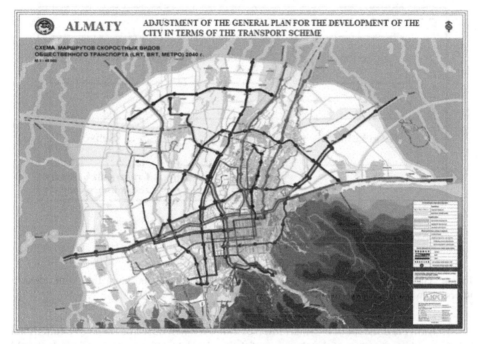

Fig. 3. Master plan for the development of the transport infrastructure of the city of Almaty.

Smart traffic lights, as an element of the intersection, should be studied and implemented as the main controller of an automated control system. Moreover, the intellectualization of traffic light objects should be carried out so that the existing traffic light equipment would undergo minimal changes. Let's look at what basic functionality modern traffic light objects have.

Firstly, intersection management based on a rigid schedule: here, traffic at each intersection is analyzed as a mathematical continuum model known as the "machine planning problem", where traffic flows are represented as a set of machine packages or sequences of queues of such vehicle packages. Control signals change the traffic light phase schedule to extend or switch the traffic light phase between different lanes of traffic at the intersection [11].

Secondly, adjacent traffic lights work in coordination based on the reference schedule of the main system-forming (root) traffic light: from it, the phase change schedule is transmitted to adjacent adjacent intersections and serves as input data for these intersections when optimizing traffic control. The data return mechanism was created in order to cope with uncoordinated situations by drivers and take into account changes in the schedules of the reference traffic light [12].

Below is a functional diagram of the hardware and software complex of several local traffic light objects as elementary regulators of the district automated traffic control system (Fig. 4).

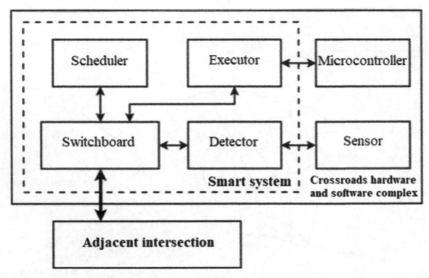

Fig. 4. The functional diagram of the "smart intersection" and its interaction with adjacent intersections.

To form the concept of a "Smart Intersection", we will describe the above functional scheme and the purpose of the elements of the projected traffic control system. It should be noted that the ultimate goal of the developed automated system of optimal traffic management of urban (multipolar) road networks in real time is a very difficult problem for the administrations of large cities. The first most important argument is the assertion that the method of decentralized traffic flow management at intersections and the regional diversification of subsystems of an automated traffic management system has no alternative.

3.1   Functional Scheme of Traffic Control

The most popular road controller RC 2 in Kazakhstan (manufactured in Russia) is built on a modular architecture using a modern element base, has support for all major communication channels: GSM, Ethernet and fiber-optic communication lines.

The main feature of this road controller is the presence of a remote-control panel, which allows only manual control of a traffic light object. RC 2 does not have a special interface device with microcontrollers and graphical reprogrammable interfaces for displaying current traffic information. The proposed program codes for this controller are "closed" and do not allow them to be reprogrammed to meet the requirements of Smart City.

The proposed design technical solution makes it possible to raise the level of traffic management in the country to Industry 4.0 technologies. The information process of controlling a traffic light object is a cyclic, pulse-time algorithm with a coordinated change in the state of the output information of the traffic light, depending on the traffic situation.

Figure 5 graphically shows the functionality of the joint work of traffic lights at a cruciform intersection.

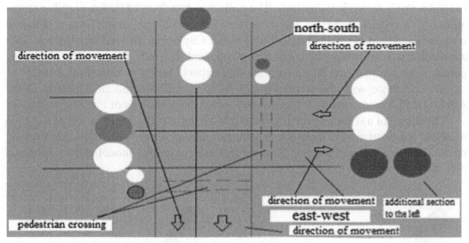

Fig. 5. Functional scheme of traffic lights at the cruciform intersection of Abai Avenue / Tlendiev Street.

Abai Avenue in Almaty is one of the busiest 6-lane highways in the city. The capacity of the avenue is 220 thousand cars per day. The distribution of the load on the avenue is uneven by day of the week and time of day. The maximum load on Abai Avenue falls on working days from west to east from 8 o'clock to 10 o'clock in the morning and in the opposite direction from 17 o'clock to 20 o'clock. A feature of the Abai / Tlendiev intersection is the low capacity of the leftmost row in the direction when turning from west to north. The mode of operation of traffic lights is programmed for all days as follows:

– along Abai Avenue from west to east, 90 s are given to the green light, from east to west -70 s. The leftmost row is reserved for turning left. The additional section is lit for 20 s;
– along Tlendiev Avenue, traffic from south to north on this section is one-way and the green light is on for only 20 s.

As a result, during the evening rush hours, a 10-point traffic jam is formed along Abai Avenue almost along the entire length of this highway. Traffic optimization is hampered by the presence of two bus lanes, which reduce the capacity of Abai Avenue. Manual regulation in this direction is not applied, although this highway is central and cuts the city in half.

In fact, this avenue is a "watershed" for the flows of cars moving from north to south. Assumptions about the streets of "dams" are spreading in the city, which do not allow traffic jams to form on the upper central streets.

A heuristic and contemplative approach to traffic management (TF) leads to an inadequate increase in congestion and traffic jams in the city and its suburbs from the costs of building bridges, interchanges.

The scientific foundations of the TF in Almaty require experimental studies using the LO@RA WAN network technology. The collected data from LO@RA mobile sensors allows for a system analysis of the array of dislocation of cars in the form of a closed information and mathematical model of a Smart City using artificial intelligence. This approach has a streaming and economic component. It is advantageous for the traffic police of the city to create their own computer network and save money resources.

In accordance with the technology of building traffic simulation models in the AnyLogic PLE environment, it is necessary to use the primitives of the *Traffic library*.

The design of a section of the road network begins with the construction of the main route and the creation of an intersection at the points of closure of the routes. After setting up and drawing the road profile, the graphical diagram of the model and its animated presentation looks like this (Fig. 6):

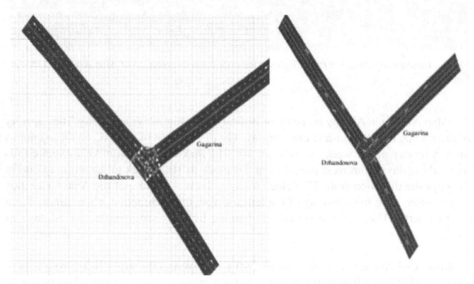

Fig. 6. Traffic management of the intersection of Dzhandosov and Gagarin streets with the traffic lights turned off.

As can be seen from Fig. 7, with a traffic intensity of up to 600 cars per hour, congestion is not observed at this intersection. Even with the traffic lights turned off, cars pass through the intersection in an organized manner. A more complex model with traffic lights and high traffic intensity requires changing the settings in the model construction.

To do this, firstly, we will set up traffic lights. The technology of setting traffic lights and operating phases of control signals is intuitive in this programming environment.

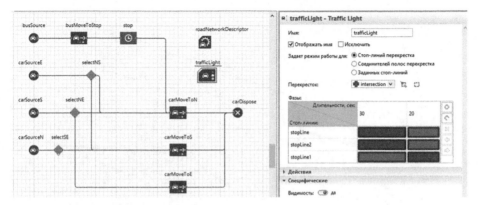

Fig. 7. Discrete-event traffic control code at the Dzhandosov-Gagarin intersection.

The simulation experiments showed the dependence of the appearance of congestion processes on the intensity of traffic on Gagarin Street (Fig. 8).

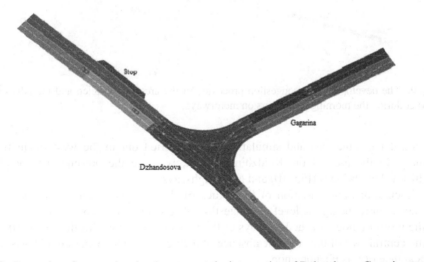

Fig. 8. Dynamics of congestion development at the intersection of Dzhandosov-Gagarin streets.

As can be seen, the increase in traffic intensity along Gagarin Street from 1000 to 1200 cars per hour leads to the emergence of congestion processes that develop into congestion after 4 cycles of traffic lights.

The given modeling technology was used to build simulation models of the development of the traffic situation in the area of Kaskelen and the Altyn Orda market, the main congestion processes are manifested up to Sain Avenue, the reason for this phenomenon is quite simple. Throughout this section, there is only an influx of vehicles moving in a westerly direction in the morning (see Fig. 9).

Fig. 9. The development of congestion processes in the area of Kaskelen and the Altyn Orda market during the morning peak hours on motorways.

Similar calculations and simulations were carried out in the western district of Almaty. In the area of the Kuldzhinsky tract, we note the presence of completed multi-level car bridges (Fig. 10) and good highways.

Calculations and variation of the values of the sources of cars show their weak influence on reducing the level of congestion. The main reason for this is the same as in the morning hours of the highways of the western direction. All the cars tried to go to the central part of the city. The absence of a ring multi-lane bypass road leads to the appearance of this phenomenon.

The organization of commuter trains from Uzun-Agach, Kaskelen and Talgar, Issyk cannot solve the problem of congestion, since the bulk of cars performs a logistical function, often in opposite parts of the city.

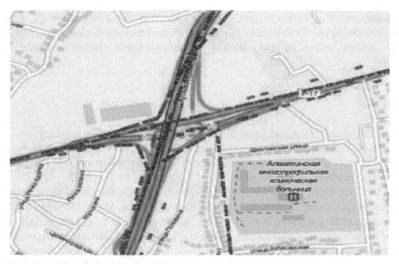

Fig. 10. The development of congestion processes on multilevel auto links in the area of the Kuldzhinsky tract.

4 Conclusion

1. It is shown that the replacement of the analog actuator in the traffic light controller RC 2 with a modern microcontroller with artificial intelligence elements allows to obtain a number of important additional functionality, such as: accounting for astronomical, weekly and daytime illumination of highways and their workload on days of the week.
2. The improvement of the RC 2 traffic light controller to an IoT device also enables an interactive way to control traffic lights and road signs from a mobile or stationary LED screen.
3. The calculation schemes and formulas obtained in the AnyLogic environment for optimizing the cyclograms of the operation of the "smart" traffic light, allowing the monitoring mode to predict and prevent effectively manage the flows of vehicles, resolve conflict and emergency situations.
4. It is shown that simulation modeling in the AnyLogic PLE environment is a promising direction for the development of algorithms for time forecasting the development of congestion processes and traffic regulation in large cities of the country.
5. Simulation experiments, taking into account the improved algorithms for changing the phases of traffic lights, allow to dynamically control the traffic situation at complex intersections.
6. The calculated data indicate the need to take administrative measures to reduce oncoming traffic flows that perform a logistical function for the wholesale markets of the country's megacities.

Acknowledgment. This work was carried out and sponsored within the framework of the scientific project AR09261344 "Development of methods for automatic extraction of geospatial objects from heterogeneous sources for information support of geographic information systems".

References

1. Almaty Sustainable Transport Strategy for 2013–2023. http://almatyinvest.kz/
2. Levin, B.K., Izyumsky, A.A., Maltsev, T.A., Bondarchuk, H.A.: To the study of the dynamic model of driver behavior in the traffic flow. In: Progress of Vehicles and systems 2002: Thesis report. International Conference of VSTU- Volgograd, pp. 89–97 (2002)
3. Cai, C., Wong, C.K., Heydecker, B.G.: Adaptive traffic signal control using approximate dynamic programming. Transp. Res. Part C: Emerg. Technol. **17**(5), 456–474 (2017)
4. Mansurova, M.E., Belgibaev, B.A., Ixanov, S., Karimsakova, D.T., Zhamangarin, D.S.: Interaction of adjacent smart traffic lights during traffic jams at an intersection. Appl. Math. Inf. Sci. **15**(3), 67–80 (2021)
5. Mansurova, M.E., Akhmetov, B.S., Zhamangarin, D.S., Smilov, N.K.: RK Patent No. 5097 for the utility model "Mobile intelligent road sign" dated 12.03.2021
6. Timofeeva, O.P., Malysheva, E.M., Sokolova, Yu.V.: Designing an intelligent traffic light control system based on a neural network. Mod. Probl. Sci. Educ. **6** (2014). http://www.science-education.ru/ru/article/view?id=16496. (Date of application: 10.12.2021)
7. Purtov, A.M.: Development of a geoinformation system for the analysis of road transport networks. SibADI Bull. **1**(29), 89–95 (2013)
8. On the approval of the State Program "Digital Kazakhstan". https://adilet.zan.kz/rus/docs/P1700000827
9. Palša, J., Vokorokos, L., Chovancová, E. and Chovanec, M.: Smart cities and the importance of smart traffic lights, pp. 587–592 (2019). https://doi.org/10.1109/ICETA48886.2019.9040086
10. Bhatia, M., Aggarwal, A., Kumar, N.: Smart traffic light system to control traffic congestion. PalArch's J. Archaeol. Egypt/Egyptol. PJAEE **17**(9), 7093–7109 (2020)
11. Al-Khateeb, K.A., Johari, J.A., Al-Khateeb, W.F.: Dynamic traffic light sequence algorithm using RFID. J. Comput. Sci. **4**, 517–524 (2018)
12. Zhao, N., Yuan, J., Xu, H.: Survey on intelligent transportation system. Comput. Sci. **41**(11), 7–11 (2014)

Identifying Non-intuitive Relationships Within Returns Data of a Furniture Online-Shop Using Temporal Data Mining

Katherina Meißner$^{(\boxtimes)}$, Anthony Boyd Stevenson , and Julia Rieck

Institute for Business Administration and Information Systems, University of Hildesheim, Universitätsplatz 1, 31141 Hildesheim, Germany
{meissner,stevenson,rieck}@bwl.uni-hildesheim.de

Abstract. Along with the growth in online retailing, there is a simultaneous increase in the number of returned products that have to be processed. These returns depend on various and often changing conditions, such as the product presentation in an online-shop, the quality of the product or of the logistics partner. Measures for improving the returns process and reducing the corresponding costs can thus not only be implemented on the basis of a static analysis. Rather, the temporal context of return characteristics should be studied for latent relationships that may have been previously neglected for managing the returns process. For providing insights into such non-intuitive relationships, we propose a data mining framework combining frequent itemset mining, time series clustering, forecasting, and scoring in order to detect returns characteristics with an interesting temporal behavior.

Keywords: Temporal data mining · Returns · E-Commerce

1 Introduction

Nowadays, it is common for many people to buy online. Not only clothes, shoes or household electronics are purchased in online-shops, but also furniture, cosmetics, and food. In 2020, the growth rates of global e-commerce reached their peak at 25.7%. This can be attributed to the closure of the stationary retail due to the Corona pandemic [11]. According to [14], the online furniture market recorded a growth rate of 19.0% in 2020. For the years 2019 to 2024, the average annual growth rate is expected to settle at around 16.0%. This high level prompts a closer look at the online furniture market.

In online retail, customers cannot physically inspect the goods before purchase, as opposed to buying on site. In the case of furniture (e. g., sofas, cupboards, beds or cushions), this problem is intensified by the fact that only the presentation in a furniture store illustrates to the customer the effect in his own

© The Author(s), under exclusive license to Springer Nature Singapore Pte Ltd. 2022
E. Szczerbicki et al. (Eds.): ACIIDS 2022, CCIS 1716, pp. 299–312, 2022.
https://doi.org/10.1007/978-981-19-8234-7_24

household. This can lead to a product purchased online being returned to the retailer, which is aggravating for both the retailer and the customer. The retailer incurs costs for shipping and taking back the product, while the customer is irritated by the unsatisfactory order. Returns that are sent back because of their characteristics, such as color, quality or size, are classified as product-related returns. Price-related returns occur when the customer has identified falling prices after ordering. Logistics-related returns are due to errors during picking or delivery. Besides the aforementioned reasons, complaints arise when purchased goods are returned within the statutory warranty period of two years due to a defect.

As a result of the high number of returns and due to economic, ecological-social, and legislative reasons, retailers are intensively concerned with returns. In this context, a distinction can basically be made between two fields [20]. On the one hand, measures can be introduced with the aim of ensuring that purchased goods are not returned and that returns are thus actively avoided (preventive returns management). If all preventive measures have failed, measures must be taken to ensure that incoming returns are processed, prepared, and accounted for in the best possible way (reactive returns management).

In the following, interesting and non-intuitive relationships in the furniture industry shall be identified, which can be used for the selection of reactive returns management measures. Only with the knowledge of, e. g., the number and frequency of returned products, the respective product characteristics, and the knowledge of changes in returns behavior can online retailers adjust the returns process in the warehouse. In particular, personnel and operating resources can be deployed as needed to reduce cycle times and achieve a high reuse rate. In Sect. 2, the considered data analysis problem from the online furniture market is described in detail. In addition, related literature in the field of data analytics is presented to illustrate the need for a temporal data mining procedure. Section 3 introduces a framework with several carefully coordinated analysis steps as a methodological approach to identify interesting relationships within returns data. A case study of a German furniture online retailer is presented in Sect. 4 to explain the individual phases of the framework including the selected parameters and to discuss the results. Finally, the paper ends with an outlook in Sect. 5.

2   Dataset, Goal of Analysis, and Related Work

In the online furniture market, small household products (such as table decorations), but also large and heavy products (such as sofas) are returned. While household products can be returned in a package and sent by post, the sofa must be picked up by freight. In the second case, high costs for transport as well as for personnel resources in the warehouse have to be considered in particular. In order to sustainably improve the returns process, we want to automatically uncover non-intuitive relationships in the returns data with the help of a comprehensive data mining framework. Intuitive relationships are known business influential features such as a product which breaks during the delivery process and is then immediately returned. These features are usually already documented and analyzed by the company. Thus, non-intuitive relationships are defined as features or feature combinations that are not already known to the company. Moreover, these relationships are not stable over time and might exhibit trends or fluctuations that make them worth tracking for possible business impacts. Only with an *exploratory* approach can these relationships be detected, since manual detection is not possible due to the high number of possible feature combinations. The *goal* of our research is to derive measures for improving the processes in reactive returns management for the non-intuitive relationships. High costs can be saved and there is a large potential for optimization, that remains hidden when only known relationships are taken into account.

In our analysis, we look at the *dataset* of our German cooperation partner with an international customer base who is active in the furniture e-commerce. The data on returns from 2014 to mid-2021 is available to us. Figure 1 shows the monthly returns rates, relating the number of returns to the number of sales, of our cooperation partner. Note that the returns rate fluctuates around the value of 10 % between 2014 and 2016, and 14 % between the years 2018 and 2021. Thus, the sharp increase in online sales during the Corona pandemic is also reflected in the number of returns, as the returns rate is quite stable over time.

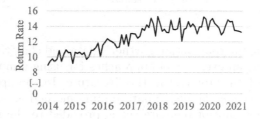

Fig. 1. Monthly returns rate

In the considered returns data, attributes are reported that are of interest for our analysis and the data mining framework. Each attribute consists of multiple values, e. g., the attribute "Country" has the values 'DE', 'CH' or 'US'. An individual value is often referred to as a *feature* or *item*, which also contains the attribute information to correctly specify the value. Thus, "Country = DE" is a specific feature or item. The attributes used in our study (see Table 1 for a listing with description and example value) were selected in consultation with the cooperation partner's returns department based on their applicability for describing individual returns and deriving insights for improving the reactive returns management process. Particularly, for the attributes "DaysOrderAnd-Shipping" and "DaysShippingAndReturn", reasonable time intervals were chosen. Based on the 14-day right of withdrawal in Germany, the intervals '0–14 days', 'within 6 months' and 'greater than 6 months' were selected.

Table 1. Dataset description

Attribute	Description	Example value
ReturnQuantity	One or more products returned	Single Return
DaysOrderAndShipping	Range of days between both dates	0–14
DaysShippingAndReturn	Range of days between both dates	15–20
Country	Country from which the return was sent	CH
Channel	Channel through which the product was purchased	Online Shop (CH)
Logistics	Logistics partner	Swiss Post
LogisticType	Parcel or freight returned	Parcel
Manufacturer	Manufacturer of returned product	Fritz Hansen
PriceCategory	Price category of returned product	10–100
ProductPriceType	Distinction between retail price and discount	Retail price
CommodityGroupSegm	Commodity group at highest level	Lighting technology
CommodityGroupMaster	Commodity group at a lower level	Lights
CommodityGroupMain	Commodity group at a lower level	Table lamps
CommodityGroupSub	Commodity group at lowest level	Table lamp
Color	Color of returned product	White
Weight	Weight of returned product in kg	1
CubicMeter	Product size in m^3	0.004
LeftoverQuantity	Quantity of products from order the customer kept	0
BackToStock	Can returned products be restocked?	True
SendReplacement	Was replacement sent for returned product?	False
IsFailedShipment	Was product returned because of failed shipment?	False
ReturnReason	Reason for return	Dislike
ReturnType	How was the article returned?	Company postage

After presenting the cooperation partner's data and clarifying the goal of the analysis, we provide an overview of approaches for using temporal data mining that have already been proposed in the literature. In the approach described by Böttcher [7] as *change mining*, a data mining method is applied repeatedly, whereby a new time slice of the data set is provided to the model each time. This makes it possible to discover changes within the data structure as they are reflected in the model parameters. Even before the formal introduction of change mining, [16] already applied association rules mining repeatedly and detect interesting rules by their temporal behavior.

The idea of change mining or temporal mining respectively has been adapted for different applications. The study by [8] shows the applicability for customer segmentation in marketing. Further studies in this type of application can be found, whereby the underlying model is often cluster analysis with temporally changing parameters. In the field of patent analysis, the idea of identifying emerging patterns is used to detect trends. The use case of [21] involves learning association rules on the basis of several time slices of a patent database and determining the change in the resulting set of rules. This allows patent trends to be identified, giving business managers an advantage over their competitors. On Twitter, it is common to use hashtags that describe the content of a tweet and at the same time influence its visibility. To find suitable hashtags for a tweet, it is convenient to learn association rules based on existing tweets, which can suggest further hashtags for a given set of hashtags. Due to the large number of users and tweets and the constant expansion of the hashtag database, it is necessary to constantly update the rules. Using so-called temporal association rule mining, according to [1], not only can the rules be updated based on new data, but also the dynamics in the rules can be derived and, as a consequence, applied in a predictive manner.

In [17], a data mining framework for identifying unknown relationships within road accident data is presented. The focus of the paper lies on finding a suitable configuration for clustering the time series obtained from temporal frequent itemset mining. The authors later proposed to enhance the road accident data mining framework with a scoring procedure in order to automatically detect interesting relationships and derive road safety measures [18].

3 Data Mining Framework for Returns

In order to identify non-intuitive relationships within the returns data and especially changing relationships, we use frequent itemset mining (FIM). For the identified frequent itemsets, time series are generated in order to observe the relative frequencies of corresponding returns over time (step 1). The time series are then clustered by using time series clustering (step 2). For each cluster, a forecasting model can then be specified (step 3) that is suitable for all time series within the cluster and predicts the respective values of relative frequencies for the future. Due to the large number of predicted time series, an individual analysis by companies in the furniture industry is not possible. Therefore, a scoring procedure must be used to find the "most interesting" time series with non-intuitive relationships (step 4). The highest scoring time series can then be displayed in a dashboard (step 5). Figure 2 shows the implemented data mining framework for returns.

Fig. 2. Data Mining Framework for identifying relationships within returns data

Let us now take a closer look at the contents of the framework's steps: The **FIM algorithm** provides multiple itemsets, where an itemset $I = \{i_1, \ldots, i_m\}$ consists of $m \in \{1, \ldots, n\}$ elements; n is the number of features/items in the underlying data set. A possible itemset is, e.g., {LogisticType=Parcel, Country=DE} with $m = 2$. Each itemset has to be present in at least a certain minimal percentage of all returns (i.e., a minimum support $supp_{min}$ is given).

For obtaining only itemsets I that occur together with a certain probability, we set a lower bound on the all-confidence value as in the following Eq. (1) (cf. [19]):

$$\text{conf}_{\text{all}} = \frac{\text{supp}(\{i_1, \ldots, i_m\})}{\max\limits_{j=1,\ldots,m} \{\text{supp}(i_j)\}} \tag{1}$$

Please note that we cannot use the regular confidence measure introduced by [4], since we do not analyze association rules in our framework. Namely, the confidence gives the conditional probability of occurrence of the right-hand side of the association rule, given the items on the left-hand side of the rule. Using conf_{all}, we estimate the minimum confidence that any association rule generated from the considered itemset would have. In order to avoid that the number of itemsets to be analyzed is not reduced too much, the values of supp_{min} and conf_{all} have to be configured carefully for the dataset at hand.

Frequent itemsets are determined based on the entire data set to guarantee that the resulting feature combinations have a certain minimum frequency. Then, the relative frequencies (i. e., relative support) of the itemsets within each month are calculated. The use of relative values is particularly useful when considering that the numbers of returns (and also sales) in the furniture sector have increased significantly since the start of the Corona pandemic. By using relative values, it is still possible to see how one feature (or a combination of features) changes relative to all others over time. We generate a time series X^I for each itemset I, consisting of T timestamps, e. g., $T = 84$ for a time horizon of 7 years. For each month t with $t = 1, \ldots, T$ within the time series, x_t^I can take a value between 0 and 1. If the features represented by I are not present in any return in month t, x_t^I will be 0, while it will be 1 if all returns within this month support the itemset. At the end of the first step, we obtain a set of time series $\mathcal{X}$.

The first step of the framework generates a large number of time series for which we want to predict the temporal behavior. In order to determine the best forecasting model for each time series, we use **time series clustering** in the second step. For each cluster $k \in \mathcal{K}$, we then have to find a suitable forecasting model. Thus, the main goal of clustering is to achieve a good representation of the data by the individual cluster centroid, as we only examine centroid time series $X^{c,k}$ (cf Eq. (2)), when deciding on a forecasting model for cluster k. Typically, this results in a high degree of homogeneity within a cluster (i. e., compactness) and similar temporal behavior of all time series in a cluster.

A comprehensive overview of time series clustering methods is given in [3]. The authors indicate that several configurations to adjust the clustering of time series data may be taken into account, in particular, scaling (e. g., centering, normalizing, amplitude scaling), distance measure (e. g., Euclidean, dynamic time warping), clustering method (e. g., partitional, hierarchical with single or complete linkage), and number of clusters.

In order to determine the best configuration, various validation indices can be used to evaluate the results. Examples include indices such as Calinski-Harabasz, Gamma or Tau (see [9] for an overview). However, preliminary studies have shown that the goal of clustering to achieve high homogeneity can only be achieved with an adapted validation index. The developed ARIMA-based Mean Forecasting Error (AMFE) index shows how well a centroid is able to predict all time series of its cluster (the index is based on the work of [15]).

For every cluster $k \in \mathcal{K}$, the cluster's centroid time series $X^{c,k}$ is determined by first scaling each time series $(x^l)_{t=1,\ldots,T,l\in\mathcal{X}^k}$ in the set of time series $\mathcal{X}^k$ for cluster k. We obtain the scaled time series $(x'^l)_{t=1,\ldots,T,l\in\mathcal{X}^k}$ by applying the scaling method of the cluster configuration under investigation. It is important to note that when applying the AMFE validation index, we want to predict the last h timestamps and measure the corresponding accuracy. Hence, scaling only needs to be performed on the first $T - h$ timestamps for each time series. The centroid time series $X^{c,k}$ is then calculated as given in Eq. (2) with x'^l_t being the scaled (relative) support value of time series l at timestamp t.

$$
X^{c,k} = \left(\frac{1}{|\mathcal{X}^k|} \sum_{l\in\mathcal{X}^k} x'^l_t \right)_{t=1,\ldots,T-h} \qquad \forall k \in \mathcal{K} \qquad (2)
$$

As a predictive model, the AMFE index provides for the application of the Auto Regressive Integrated Moving Average (ARIMA) method. The model parameters are set automatically, according to the suggestion in [13]. The corresponding centroid time series $X^{c,k}$ for a cluster k is used as the training set and the monthly values are predicted for a forecast horizon of length h. Assuming that the predicted values $\hat{x}^l_t$ using the centroid time series for timestamps $T-h+1,\ldots,T$ are appropriate predicted values for all time series of cluster k, we can now measure the forecast accuracy for each time series using the Root Mean Square Error (RMSE). To obtain the AMFE index, we then sum the individual RMSE values over all time series and all clusters as given in Eq. (3).

$$
\text{AMFE} = \sum_{k\in\mathcal{K}} \sum_{l\in\mathcal{X}^k} \sqrt{\frac{1}{h} \sum_{t=T-h+1}^{T} (x^l_t - \hat{x}^l_t)^2} \qquad (3)
$$

The third step of the framework is to select the best **forecasting model** for each cluster. Here, *four* different *accuracy evaluations* are used to check different aspects of the forecasting models. We again separate $X^{c,k}$ into a training set and a test set. While the training set with timestamps $t = 1,\ldots,T - h$ is used to determine the parameters for individual forecasting models, the test set with timestamps $t = T - h + 1,\ldots,T$ is omitted. The *first evaluation* that can now be performed is to calculate the RMSE between the prediction $\hat{X}^{c,k}$ and the real values of the centroid $X^{c,k}$ for the prediction horizon of length h. The forecasting method that yields the smallest RMSE is appropriate. Only if two methods are equal in their test error, the training error (RMSE for $t = 1,\ldots,T - h$) is also included. As a *second* accuracy *evaluation*, we perform a one-step-ahead cross-validation for each centroid time series $X^{c,k}$ according to [12]. The procedure consists of a series of runs, where each test set includes only a single timestamp τ. The associated training set contains the timestamps smaller than τ. In each iteration, one more timestamp is added to the training set and the test set is rolled forward by one timestamp. The forecast accuracy is then calculated by averaging over the RMSE values of all test sets. The *third evaluation* is based on the Diebold-Mariano test (cf. [10]). This statistical test allows to accept or reject the null hypothesis H_0 of the forecasts of two models (models 1 and 2) being equally accurate. Therefore, we present the forecast results of every two models to the Diebold-Mariano test and reject the aforementioned H_0 in favor of the alternative H_1, stating that model 2 is significantly less accurate than model 1, if the corresponding $p < 0.05$. We count the number of times model 1 is determined more accurate to detect the statistically most accurate models. So far, the accuracy tests have been assessed on the basis of the centroid time series. Now, we want to estimate the predictive strength of the forecasting methods for the individual time series of a cluster. In the *fourth evaluation*, we therefore proceed similarly to the AMFE index. The accuracy of every method is identified when predicting the forecast horizon with the centroid time series $X^{c,k}$. The prediction is then compared to the real values of the time series $\mathcal{X}_k$. In this way, $|\mathcal{X}^k|$ RMSE values are obtained. A low average RMSE for a method is preferred as this indicates a good predictive strength of the centroid time series. Especially the fourth evaluation takes very long for a large number of time series. In order to reduce the execution time, we select the most promising forecasting methods with the first three evaluation procedures and apply the fourth evaluation only to this subset of methods.

Since not all predicted time series can be analyzed in detail, a **scoring procedure** is used in the fourth step of the framework to find the "most interesting" time series that reveals non-intuitive relationships. For example, an increasing trend could be identified with, e. g., noise components. The corresponding features occur with an accelerating percentage of returns and should therefore be investigated more closely. Another time series could show significant fluctuations, but not induced by natural variations. A third aspect is the forecast error caused by the centroid-based forecasting method. If the prediction is not reliable, it may be worthwhile to submit this time series to a person for review, as it may be assigned to an inappropriate cluster.

When the recurring behavior of the time series has changed between the last available data period (with T as the end timestamp) and a similar period in the forecast horizon h (starting at timestamp $T + 1$), then the first aspect, i. e., $\text{score}_{\text{fc\_change}} = \frac{1}{h} \sum_{t=T+1}^{T+h} |x_{t-h} - \hat{x}_t|$, shows a high value. With h, we also indicate the periodicity in the data (here, we assume $h = 12$, as we have monthly values with a yearly periodicity). As before, $\hat{x}_t$ is the predicted relative support value for timestamp t.

Some time series may be subject to large fluctuations, while others tend to be stable over time. Time series with a high complexity, i. e., the difference between values of consecutive months is large, are harder to predict. Therefore, these series get a higher score, i. e., $\text{score}_{\text{complexity}} = \sqrt{\sum_{t=2}^{T}(x_{t-1} - x_t)^2}$. The calculation is based on the complexity invariance distance by [5].

With $\text{score}_{\text{fc\_error}} = \sqrt{\frac{1}{h} \sum_{t=T-h+1}^{T}(x_t - \hat{x}_t)^2}$ we want to identify those time series that were not predicted well by the centroid-based forecasting (cf. [2]).

Those time series might be very different from the centroid and could have been assigned to the wrong cluster or show a very different behavior in recent months. A scoring procedure based on the three scores is used to identify "interesting" time series (and the corresponding combinations of features). The scores are summed up to one final score value by using adjustable weights $\gamma_1, \gamma_2, \gamma_3 \geq 0$, $\sum_{i=1}^{3} \gamma_i = 1$, to adapt their influence on the selection of interesting features.

$$\text{score}_{\text{final}} = \gamma_1 \cdot \text{score}_{\text{fc\_change}} + \gamma_2 \cdot \text{score}_{\text{complexity}} + \gamma_3 \cdot \text{score}_{\text{fc\_error}}$$

After determining the final score value for each time series, as in Eq. 3, the highest scoring time series are displayed in a **dashboard** in the last step of the framework. With this information, furniture retailing companies can then try to initiate reactive measures for efficient returns processing in a targeted manner.

4   Results and Discussion

In this section, we now consider the returns data of our cooperation partner in a case study. With about 300,000 returns from the years 2014 to 2020, we obtain 5,772 frequent itemsets with a respective set of $|\mathcal{X}| = 5,772$ time series with $T = 84$ timestamps each. As parameters for FIM in the first step of the framework, we chose $\text{supp}_{\text{min}} = 0.001$ to detect also very seldom occurring relationships, and $\text{conf}_{\text{all}} = 0.05$. Time series clustering in step 2 is performed with a configuration based on normalized data, Dynamic Time Warping [6] as distance measure, and hierarchical clustering with ward's linkage. With 5 clusters, we receive a good representation of the data structure, as shown in Fig. 3. The black, dotted line indicates the cluster centroid time series that is obtained after centering all time series within the cluster. Therefore, the centroid time series' mean is zero and negative values are present. The gray area represents the standard deviation.

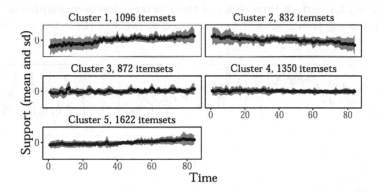

Fig. 3. Clusters' centroid time series and standard deviation based on centered data

For forecasting, we carefully select the following forecasting methods for each cluster (see [18] and [17]) using the selection method described for step 3 in

Sect. 3. Clusters 1 and 2 use *ARIMA* for depicting the increasing and decreasing trend. Here, exponential smoothing [12] would be an alternative method when only comparing the training and test error (first evaluation). In the cross-validation (second evaluation), it becomes obvious that ARIMA is superior to all other methods, which is also supported by the Diebold-Mariano test (third evaluation). For cluster 2, the exponential smoothing is deemed equal to ARIMA in the third evaluation, which is why the fourth evaluation is needed to clearly identify ARIMA as the best method for both clusters 1 and 2. For cluster 3, a *combined approach* of several forecasting methods (cf. [12]), is chosen with a clear best result in evaluations 1 and 2. Using the mean of forecasts from multiple forecasting methods (e. g., ARIMA, exponential smoothing, neural network, and TBATS) improves forecast accuracy. This is particularly useful, since there appears to be hidden seasonality in cluster 3 that a single forecasting method may not be able to capture. The *naïve method*, i. e., $\hat{x}_{t+1} = x_t$ is assumed, is appropriate for the rather stable time series in cluster 4. Cluster 5 shows a very slight increase and an unpredictable peak at the end of the third year. With a more sophisticated *neural network auto-regression approach* (cf. [12]), this behavior can best be captured, as all four evaluation methods show.

We first set the scoring weights in step 4 to $(\gamma_1, \gamma_2, \gamma_3) = (0.1, 0.6, 0.3)$ to emphasize the obvious fluctuations within the time series, which are observed in all clusters with varying intensity. Since the clusters all show a different behavior, it seems sensible to adjust the scoring weights according to the individual temporal progression. For clusters 1 and 2, special emphasis is given on selecting time series with a stronger trend well. Therefore, γ_1 is increased in favor of γ_2 and γ_3. Cluster 3 contains time series that seem to fluctuate without a clear trend. Consequently, γ_2 is increased. The most simple forecasting approach is used for cluster 4. In order to evaluate if this method leads to larger errors, γ_3 is highlighted here. The slightly larger standard deviation in the most recent months in cluster 5 indicate that the centroid-based forecasting might lead to higher errors for certain time series of the cluster. Moreover, emphasis is given to the increasing trend, so that γ_2 is reduced in favor of the other two weights.

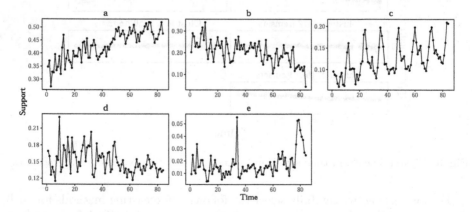

Fig. 4. Selected interesting time series from each cluster

In Fig. 4, a sample time series from each cluster selected by the scoring procedure with adjusted weights is shown. Table 2 demonstrates the scoring results of the three parts, the final score achieved, and the average support score of the itemset over all 96 months. The last column was added to help contextualize the RMSE value reflected in the $score_{fc\_error}$.

Table 2. Scoring results for selected itemset from each cluster

Itemset	Cluster	$score_{final}$	$score_{fc\_change}$	γ_1	$score_{fc\_complexity}$	γ_2	$score_{fc\_error}$	γ_3	avg. support
a	1	0.072	0.042	0.85	0.341	0.1	0.015	0.15	0.430
b	2	0.135	0.062	0.7	0.431	0.2	0.050	0.1	0.203
c	3	0.173	0.026	0.1	0.232	0.7	0.041	0.2	0.124
d	4	0.137	0.012	0.1	0.236	0.5	0.044	0.4	0.151
e	5	0.077	0.011	0.1	0.120	0.25	0.070	0.65	0.018

Itemset $\mathbf{a} = \{$ReturnQuantity $=$ Multiple Return, SendReplacement $= 0\}$ from cluster 1 shows a clear increase in the relative frequency of returns containing more than one product. Returns with multiple products lead to a higher workload and longer cycle times in the returns process than single-product returns, as the incoming packages must first be checked for completeness and the individual products may then need to be transported to different storage locations, provided they can be transferred back to stock. The growth in multiproduct returns must be carefully integrated into the planning of the returns process in the warehouse. In addition, there also appears to be a slight seasonal variation in this returns feature combination, whose precise prediction can further improve the returns process.

In contrast, a falling trend can be observed for itemset $\mathbf{b} = \{$DaysShippingAnd Return $= 0$–7, BackToStock $= 1$, ReturnReason $=$ Dislike$\}$ from cluster 2, which indicates that the proportion of returns initiated by the customer directly after delivery is decreasing. At the same time, the itemset includes the return reason of dislike which occurs less frequently in combination with short-term returns. In summary, it can be deduced from the temporal behavior of the itemset that customers generally keep products longer, return them for reasons other than disliking them, and that these often cannot be returned to stock either, as they have presumably suffered a loss of durability or become a warranty case. With this knowledge, the staff allocation in the returns warehouse can be matched with the shipping information, i.e., a return can nowadays be expected more than one week after the shipping.

From itemset $\mathbf{c} = \{$CommodityGroupSegm. $=$ Decoration$\}$ from cluster 3, the furniture retailer can learn that the returns of decoration products are subject to annual seasonal fluctuations and the share of these returns is increasing. If the share of decoration sales is increasing as well, the behavior is not surprising. For 2021, this commodity group has a return value, i.e., the net sales price of the returned products, of over 1 million Euro. The increasing trend in returns for this commodity group subsequently leads to a reduction in the expected revenue volume, so from an operational point of view it is sensible to track this commodity group in particular.

In cluster 4, we find itemset $\mathbf{d} = \{$CommodityGroupSegm. $=$ Kitchen&Table, BackToStock $= 1$, ReturnReason $=$ Dislike$\}$ which shows a time series with a flattening curve. The fluctuation within the time series has visibly decreased over time. This behavior can be explained with an increase in the quality of product descriptions and a higher marketing effort. For finding measures to enhance the returns management process, this time series is not as interesting as the others. Still, the non-intuitive relationship uncovered here can be used in the preventive returns management, as better product descriptions can obviously lead to fewer returns.

Finally, itemset $\mathbf{e} = \{$DaysOrderAndShipping $= 15$–179, Logistic $=$ Freight$\}$ from cluster 5 shows the effect of the Corona pandemic on the returns process. Products shipped by freight are usually bulky furniture, e. g., desks, sofas or cabinets. With the shortage of raw materials and an increasing demand for these goods due to extended stays at home and home office, the waiting times for these products became unusually long. The risk of customers buying the same product from a different retailer increases and, thus, the number of returns for the retailer with the longer waiting time. In the reactive returns management process, this knowledge can be used to schedule the returns warehouse staff accordingly, as the shipping date draws near.

5 Summary and Outlook

We presented a multi-step framework for analyzing returns data of a furniture online retailer. As a result, we obtained interesting and non-intuitive relationships between the returns features and could use them as indicators for possible improvements in the reactive returns management within a furniture company. Furthermore, we were able to quantify the monetary impact of the findings together with the company. The non-intuitive relationships revealed by the framework are particularly valuable here, as they might not have been transferred into measures. Moreover, a relationship is not denoted as interesting due to its overall frequency, but rather because of its progression over time. Based on the findings, existing reactive measures can be evaluated and, if necessary, adjusted considering this temporal aspect.

The results of our framework could also be used to optimize the preventive returns management. If it is found, e. g., that certain commodity groups seem to be more return prone in recent months, customers can be offered different prevention measures, such as higher discounts. The framework should then be adapted in the first step and use association rules instead of frequent itemsets in order to obtain rules that can easily be transferred into business decisions. Moreover, customer-based features should be included to target preventive measures more accurately. Also, product reviews and product descriptions could be analyzed using text mining approaches. The results can in turn be integrated in the data mining framework in order to estimate the effect of reviews or descriptions on the returns in the furniture retailing market. This could then explain relationships between product description, reviews, and returns with a possible indicator for the quality of the product description. Returns data from retailing sectors other than furniture can also be analyzed with the framework at hand if the attributes to be included are adapted to the retailer's needs.

References

1. Adedoyin-Olowe, M., Gaber, M.M., Stahl, F.: TRCM: a methodology for temporal analysis of evolving concepts in Twitter. In: Rutkowski, L., Korytkowski, M., Scherer, R., Tadeusiewicz, R., Zadeh, L.A., Zurada, J.M. (eds.) ICAISC 2013. LNCS (LNAI), vol. 7895, pp. 135–145. Springer, Heidelberg (2013). https://doi.org/10.1007/978-3-642-38610-7_13
2. Aggarwal, C.C.: Outlier Analysis. Springer, Cham (2017). https://doi.org/10.1007/978-3-319-47578-3
3. Aghabozorgi, S., Seyed Shirkhorshidi, A., Ying Wah, T.: Time-series clustering - a decade review. Inform. Syst. **53**, 16–38 (2015)
4. Agrawal, R., Imieliński, T., Swami, A.: Mining association rules between sets of items in large databases. ACM SIGMOD Rec. **22**(2), 207–216 (1993)
5. Batista, G.E., Wang, X., Keogh, E.J.: A complexity-invariant distance measure for time series. In: Liu, B., et al. (eds.) Proceedings of International Conference on Data Mining, pp. 699–710. SIAM (2011)
6. Berndt, D.J., Clifford, J.: Using dynamic time warping to find patterns in time series. In: Proceedings of International Conference on Knowledge Discovery Data Mining, pp. 359–370. AAAI Press (1994)
7. Böttcher, M., Höppner, F., Spiliopoulou, M.: On exploiting the power of time in data mining. ACM SIGKDD Explor. Newsl. **10**(2), 3–11 (2008)
8. Böttcher, M., Spott, M., Nauck, D., Kruse, R.: Mining changing customer segments in dynamic markets. Expert Syst. Appl. **36**(1), 155–164 (2009)
9. Charrad, M., Ghazzali, N., Boiteau, V., Niknafs, A.: NbClust : An R package for determining the relevant number of clusters in a data set. J. Stat. Softw. **61** (2014)
10. Diebold, F.X., Mariano, R.S.: Comparing predictive accuracy. J. Bus. Econ. Stat. **13** (1995)
11. eMarketer: Retail ecommerce sales worldwide (2021). https://www.emarketer.com/content/global-ecommerce-forecast-2021. Accessed 14 Dec 2021
12. Hyndman, R.J., Athanasopoulos, G.: Forecasting: Principles and Practice. OTexts, Melbourne, Australia (2021). OTexts.com/fpp3
13. Hyndman, R.J., Khandakar, Y.: Automatic time series forecasting: The forecast package for R. J. Stat. Softw. **27** (2008)
14. Infiniti Research Limited: Online furniture market by application and geography: forecast and analysis 2020–2024 (2021). https://www.technavio.com/report/online-furniture-market-industry-analysis. Accessed 14 Dec 2021
15. Laurinec, P., Lucká, M.: Clustering-based forecasting method for individual consumers electricity load using time series representations. Open Comput. Sci. **8**, 38–50 (2018)
16. Liu, B., Ma, Y., Lee, R.: Analyzing the interestingness of association rules from the temporal dimension. In: IEEE Internernational Conference on Data Mining, pp. 377–384 (2001)

17. Meißner, K., Rieck, J.: Data mining framework to derive measures for road safety. In: Perner, P. (ed.) Mach Learn Data Mining Pattern Recognition, vol. 2, pp. 625–639. ibai-publishing, Leipzig (2019)
18. Meißner, K., Rieck, J.: Decision support for road safety: development of key performance indicators for police analysts. Arch. Data Sci. Ser. A **6**(2) (2020)
19. Omiecinski, E.R.: Alternative interest measures for mining associations in databases. IEEE Trans. Knowl. Data Eng. **15**, 57–69 (2003)
20. Rogers, D.S., Lambert, D.M., Croxton, K.L., García-Dastugue, S.J.: The returns management process. Int. J. Logist. Manag. **13**(2), 1–18 (2002)
21. Shih, M.J., Liu, D.R., Hsu, M.L.: Discovering competitive intelligence by mining changes in patent trends. Expert Syst. Appl. **37**(4), 2882–2890 (2010)

DACE: Did I Catch You at a Good Time?

Anurag Modi$^{(\boxtimes)}$, Sailaja Rajanala, and Manish Singh

Department of Computer Science and Engineering, Indian Institute of Technology
Hyderabad, Kandi, India
{cs16mtech11003,cs15resch11009}@iith.ac.in, msingh@cse.iith.ac.in

Abstract. Social Information Seeking (SIS) is a platform for easy and
informal interaction among participants. This has been popularized by
many of the major prevailing Community Question Answering (CQA)
forums, such as Quora, Stackoverflow, etc. A user submits a question to
the forum that is later answered by one or more of the users in the forum.
These sites facilitate knowledge exchange between users through questions and answers. A large pool of knowledge has since been created.
Although hundreds of questions are posted every hour, many of them
remain unanswered due to lower quality, wrong choice of question tags,
bad routing of questions to experts, and dearth of proper answerers. In
this paper, we propose a solution to the problem of routing questions
to appropriate experts by utilizing the tag and time information of the
posted questions. We propose a recommendation model that uses a tag
network and temporal analysis to find the potential experts. Our experiments over a dataset from Stack Exchange show the effectiveness of our
approach over several baseline models.

Keywords: Community question answering · Expert
recommendation · Question routing · Expert finding

1 Introduction

The Internet is a large base for data, having an assortment of topics. Searches
over such a broad domain often give vague results. The CQA forums, which
operate only with dedicated communities by catering to individual domains,
are different. Here, users can post their questions, adding a set of tags, while
other users can answer these questions. Users can also vote on the answers to
highlight the most useful ones. Some of the popular CQA sites include Quora,
Stack Exchange, Yahoo! Answers, etc. To accommodate the huge flow of traffic,
owing to their popularity, these sites have further organized posts into categories
with the help of tags. Users can subscribe to tags and answer questions that
contain the tags. Tags also help accentuate the question's content.

In such a setting, in order to reach the potential answerers, the questions are
routed to all the users subscribed to that tag. A major drawback of this method
is that users may get bombarded with questions that they might not be interested
in answering, eventually losing interest in the site. Another problem is that any
user failing to adhere to proper tagging conventions will fail to grab the answerer's

© The Author(s), under exclusive license to Springer Nature Singapore Pte Ltd. 2022
E. Szczerbicki et al. (Eds.): ACIIDS 2022, CCIS 1716, pp. 313–326, 2022.
https://doi.org/10.1007/978-981-19-8234-7_25

attention to their questions. These questions may remain unanswered until some-one volunteers to re-tag or rephrase the question. This is evident from the fact that about 10% [11] of the questions remain unanswered, and our experiments showed that only 5% of the users answered a majority of the questions. For example, in the Software Engineering CQA site, 96.35% of the users have written less than 25 answers each, during their association with the forum.

[1] have analyzed a variety of reasons behind unanswered questions in CQA sites and found time to be one of the crucial factors. An aging post may get pushed down the furnace and eventually becomes invisible. Time also manifests into [6], changing user interests, evolving topic trends in the community, and addition/deletion of users and tags. One popular method to mitigate the problem of unanswered questions is to motivate the users to keep answering. This is done by offering incentives in the form of Badges and Reputation Scores [1]. The reputation score counts as the user's expertise, causing the system to route a bulk of questions to these 'experts.' Sadly, the experts are overburdened with all the questions being directed to them.

In this paper, along with the expertise and topical relevance of the answerer, we also consider the time of the post and the availability of the answerer before directing a question. This ensures that the question is directed to the answerers live at the moment while noting their experience in the topic. The topical aspect is incorporated using a tag network that resolves the mapping from question-topic to the answerer-topic. The subsequent sections show how we incorporate the tag and the temporal aspects for a better harvest.

The rest of the paper is organized as follows: Sect. 2 gives an insight into the related literature. Section 3 motivates the problem using data. Problem defini-tion is given in Sect. 4. Section 5 and Sect. 6 present the proposed models. The evaluation and results are presented in Sect. 7. Section 8 concludes the paper.

2   Related Work

The main goal of CQA systems is to provide the best answers to the recently asked questions. For the Software Engineering Dataset in Stack Exchange, we found that only 5% of users are involved in answering 96% of the questions. Question Routing to the potential answerers serves a twofold purpose: (a) Askers gets the question answered in a short time, and (b) We keep the experts involved with the site so that they do not lose their interest. In general, there are three popular approaches to solve this problem.

Graph Based Models: In graph-based methods, authors have modeled this prob-lem as a link analysis problem, thereby employing the algorithms such as PageR-ank and HITS for the same purpose. These works have done analyzed on the Yahoo! Answers [2,18,19]. In these methods, users are represented as nodes, and interaction between them is represented as the edge weight of their overall inter-action. The expertise score is generally measured as the node authority obtained by applying the algorithms such as HITS and PageRank on the graph. An inter-esting property of the graph is that shared interests and not social relationships usually bound users. Users come to the site to ask and answer questions related to their interests. An expertise calculation metric proposed in [18] found that Z-score based expertise measurement method worked better than HITS and gave a comparable performance to that of PageRank.

Topical Models: In topical models, authors have constructed user profiles based on user history, and then they build question profiles based on the text content present in the question [12,14,20]. They have used various machine learning classification models to find a match between the user profile and question profile. Language models [7] based on exact word matching fail to capture clear syntactic and semantics information. As a result of this limitation, latent topic models, such as Probabilistic Latent Semantic Analysis (PLSA) or Latent Dirichlet Allocation (LDA) [13,15], are used to feature both syntactic and semantic information.

Temporal Models: Temporal information has been used by [3] to predict the quality of the answer in order to find the best answer among a set of answers written for a particular question. Further, in order to solve the notion of user activeness, some work has been done in [4,17] to predict the user availability on a particular day. In [10], authors analyzed the evaluation of experts over time and showed that estimating expertise using temporal data outperforms the otherwise static approaches.

Temporal analysis shows that these systems are dynamic in nature in terms of the number of users and how many questions they choose to answer over an interval, users' experience as they answer questions, the relevance of the current set of active users to answer quality and the change of user interests. The present work is inspired by the need to address the constant drift in user interest and how user availability affects the answering pattern. Routing to the users who are no longer active inside the site or are answering the question's topic leads to unnecessary delays in receiving the answer.

3   Dataset Description

This work is done on the Software Engineering CQA site, part of the Stack Exchange community. We collected a dataset of 47K questions, 141K answers, and a total of 1639 tags. It has questions and answers from August 2008 till March 2018. Each question has three parts: title, body and tags. Each question may receive multiple answers. Users give answers to the question or even comment on the existing answers. If a comment helps solve the problem, it is awarded a score that is shown along with the comment. All the questions and answers receive upvotes or downvotes from other peer users, and the corresponding askers or answerers earn or lose reputation accordingly. If a question has received multiple answers, the asker can select one of the answers as the best answer. The chosen answer is called the Accepted Answer.

Figure 1 and 2 show some basic temporal analysis of the dataset. Figure 1 shows the concentration of the asked questions in a day and Fig. 2 throws light on the most active days of a week. Below are few observations that we made from the data.

– In Fig. 1, we can see that most of the posts in the site fall in the time interval of 16-20 hours (evening hours), i.e., at the end of the day. This might be an

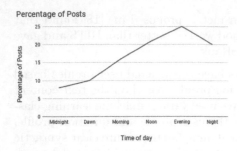

Fig. 1. Percentage of posts vs Time of the day

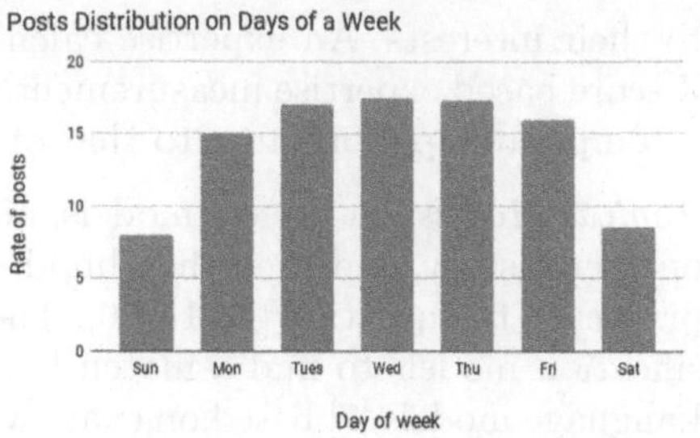

Fig. 2. Percentage of posts vs Days of a week

idle time for the asker and the answerer. Hence questions asked in this time interval tend to get a quicker reply than other time buckets.
- In Fig. 2, we observe that a majority of the posts are made during the working days, i.e., the weekdays.

We had also found that the most popular tags were mostly generic in nature. Either because the askers are unsure of the specific concern of their question or are not attentive enough to tag the question properly. A major concern is that, a small portion of the users answer a large portion of the posted questions. If a small number of experts are constantly bombarded with many generic questions that are not of their current interest, they may develop an unwillingness to answer more questions.

4   Problem Definition

In CQA services, the question-answering process is characterized by three crucial domain entities: Questions, Answers, and Users. A user can play two roles, namely an asker and an answerer. Every question has a set of tags associated with it, which help in identifying the topic of the question. Let $U = \{u_1, ..., u_n\}$ be the set of all users, $Q = \{q_1, ..., q_m\}$ be the set of all questions, and $T = \{t_1, ..., t_l\}$ be the set of all tags.

Problem Statement: *Given a question $q \in Q$ with tags $T_q \subset T$ asked at time τ, find a set of users $U_q \subset U$, who have high expertise with respect to the set of tags T_q and are active at time τ.*

While computing U_q, we consider only those users who were present in the CQA site before τ. Unlike existing work, we focus primarily on the tags and temporal information to find the experts in this paper. They use computationally expensive methods like topic modeling on the question and answer text to find the semantic relationships between users and questions. However, we exploit the tag information through a temporal analysis on the tag network to find experts who are semantically related to the question and are also currently active on the topics of the question.

Most of the existing work [18] is based on user participation in these sites. In Sect. 5.1, we discuss models based on user participation, which are our baseline models. We argue that user participation is not enough to compute user expertise effectively. In Sect. 5.2, we propose a model that takes into account the user's quality of participation. In Sect. 5.3, we further enhance the model discussed in Sect. 5.2, by considering the temporal information. Finally, in Sect. 6.2, we propose a model that banks on tag similarities tags to improve the overall performance.

5   Finding Topical Experts

In this section, we present our algorithms to find experts using the tags of a question. In Sect. 6, we will describe a method that uses network analysis on the tag network to expand the limited tag set of a question. Considering these extended tags greatly increases the accuracy of our expert finding algorithms.

5.1   Expertise Using Type of Participation

In CQA, a user has two primary roles: an asker and an answerer. One is considered an expert if one often acts as an answerer and rarely an asker. In general, it is assumed that asking many questions indicates a lack of expertise. If a user has asked and answered an equal number of questions, then his effective expertise is considered as zero. [10] has shown that the number of questions to answers ratio among the experts is around $1/15$.

The problem of identifying experts is similar to finding influential users or authorities in social network analysis. By modeling the CQA site as a social network, one can use popular link analysis algorithms, such as PageRank, Personalized PageRank, HITS, etc., to find experts. However, for CQA sites, it has been shown in [2,8,18] that even a simple Z-score metric, which uses only the number of questions asked and answered by each user, can find experts that are comparable to the experts obtained using the more computationally expensive link analysis algorithms mentioned above. The Z-score uses a directed network between users, where their asking and replying behavior relate to the users. The Z-score is defined as follows:

$$Z\text{-}Score(u_i) = \frac{\#ans_i - \#ask_i}{\sqrt{\#ans_i + \#ask_i}} \tag{1}$$

where $\#ans_i$ and $\#ask_i$ are the total number of answers given and the total number of questions asked by the user u_i. Z-score does not measure the expertise of a user with respect to a topic rather, it captures the global participation of the user. Therefore, we define topic sensitive Z-Score of a user u_i for a question q as:

$$TZ\text{-}Score(u_i, q) = \sum_{t_j \in T_q} \frac{\#ans_{ij} - \#ask_{ij}}{\sqrt{\#ans_{ij} + \#ask_{ij}}} \tag{2}$$

where $\#ans_{ij}$ and $\#ask_{ij}$ are the total number of answers given and the total number of questions asked by the user u_i on tag t_j. The topic-sensitive Z-Score is the aggregated Z-Score over all the tags of the given question q. For our problem, TZ-Score performed much better compared to simple Z-Score.

5.2 Expertise Using Community Perception

The models discussed in Sect. 5.1 account for the quantity rather than the quality of the answers for a given user. However, in this section, we present a model that considers the quality of answers. A user receives upvotes or downvotes based upon the acceptance of their contribution towards the community. The Z-Score metric can be easily gamed by giving low quality answers to a large number of questions. We hence introduce the concept of tag based quality assessment. To measure how the answers of a user on a given tag t is accepted by the community, we define tag expertise as follows:

$$AQual_t = \frac{\#v_t^+}{\#v_t^+ + \#v_t^-} \tag{3}$$

where $\#v_t^+$ and $\#v_t^-$ are the total number of upvotes and downvotes received by the user on the all the answers he had given to questions that have the tag t. The above expression has the limitation that it can not discriminate between tags on which the user has received fewer votes versus the tags for which the user has received a large number of votes. For both, the ratio of votes may be similar. We use Laplacian smoothing to give higher importance to tags with more votes thus the new tag expertise is:

$$AQual_t = \frac{\#v_t^+ + \beta}{\#v_t^+ + \#v_t^- + k * \beta} \tag{4}$$

here, the parameter β, which is a positive number, controls the level of smoothing, and k is the hyper-parameter used to control the effect of β. With this smoothing, if a tag has received few votes, then the expertise of the user on that tag will be close to the constant $\frac{1}{k}$. We have computed the expertise of a user with respect to an individual tag. Since a question can have multiple tags, the overall question expertise is:

$$TEV(u_i, q) = \sum_{t_j \in T_q} AQual_{ij} \tag{5}$$

where T_q denotes all the tags present in the question q, $AQual_{ij}$ denotes the community perception the user u_i's expertise on the tag t_j, and $TEV(u_i, q)$ denotes the topical expertise based on votes of the user u_i for the question q.

5.3 Expertise Using Temporal Participation

Due to the dynamic nature of CQA sites, we need to find experts taking into account their recent activity on the site [3]. [16] has shown that only 13% users are active and are responsible for 87% of answers. Accordingly, [10] has identified three different patterns among the users: (a) some users are consistently active in the community, (b) some users are initially very active but become passive over time, and (c) some users are initially passive but become very active over time. We consider two reasons as to why a user may not be answering: (a) The user has become inactive on the site, (b) The user's interest has shifted over time, hence is not replying to topics of previous interest. We try to capture both scenarios in our model. CQA sites do not provide the last login information of users; thus, to identify the user's last activity on the site, we use the last answer timestamp as the last login information. We take the difference between the posting time of a question and the user's last activity, measured in days. From experiments, we observed that the votes based model gives higher accuracy compared to Z-score based model. Hence we extend the votes based model with temporal information:

$$T\text{-}TEV(u_i, q, \tau) = \sum_{t_j \in T_q} \frac{AQual_{ij}}{1 + \kappa * \Delta\tau_j} \tag{6}$$

Here, $T\text{-}TEV(u_i, q, \tau)$ denotes the temporal topical expertise based on votes of user u_i on the question q, posted at time τ. $\Delta\tau_j$ is the difference of timestamp of the question and the timestamp of the last answer given by the user u_i on any question that had tag t_j.

6 Finding Extended Topical Experts

On a CQA site, users can only assign a limited number of tags to a question. Since the tag links are hidden from users, many questions with bad tags are not answered so well. In this section, we present our model that extends the temporal model discussed in Sect. 5.3 by looking at the nearby tags of tags given in the question with the help of a tag network structure.

6.1 Finding Related Tags Using Tag Network Analysis

Tag similarity can be inferred from their co-occurrence patterns. Tags co-occurring in a question convey similar concepts:

$$N(t_i, t_j) = \frac{\#(t_i, t_j)}{|Q|} \tag{7}$$

where $\#(t_i, t_j)$ is the number of questions containing the tags and $|Q|$ is the total number of questions. This score is normalized in the range between [0,1]. The limitation of this measure is that it only looks at the co-occurrence of tags. It will give high nearness score for tags that frequently co-occur. However, for infrequent tags, it will always give low scores. Moreover, it does not capture the directionality of the relationship between tags. For example, consider the two tag pairs (Java, JButton) and (Java, Android). Although the co-occurrence score of (Java, JButton) may be low due to the low frequency of JButton, we know that the tag JButton is highly likely to be followed by the tag Java. But vice versa is not guaranteed. On the other hand, if we consider the tag pair (Java, Android), then it is non-trivial to say which tag implies the other. Although they are both popular and have high co-occurrence values, we cannot easily determine which tag implies the other. To find the direction of the relationship, we use the following edge direction measure:

$$ED(t_i \rightarrow t_j) = \frac{\#(t_i, t_j)}{\#t_i} \qquad (8)$$

Using these two measures, we considered the following three types of tag graphs: undirected graph with edge weight as $N(t_i, t_j)$, directed graph with edge weights as $ED(t_i \rightarrow t_j)$, and weighted directed graph with $N(t_i, t_j)$ as edge weight and $ED(t_i \rightarrow t_j)$ to determine the edge directionality. For the last one, we put a directed edge only if $ED(t_i \rightarrow t_j)$ is greater than some threshold. For our dataset, we observed that the threshold of 0.02 gave the best result.

To find tags that are related to the tags given in the question, we perform community detection on the tag graph. Our third graph gave the best quality communities. Two tags are similar if they are in the same community. The distance between tag communities is used to draw an analogy between tags in distinct communities. In community detection, the weight and direction of edges in the input graph are very important in determining the communities.

6.2 Extended Topical Expertise

We consider two ways of expanding the seed set of tags: (a) Using the whole tag community, (b) Using the top-k neighboring tags within the community. Most of the good questions in CQA sites are tagged using a mix of generic and specific tags. For example, consider a question with tags: php, mysql, sql, security, and sql-injection. Here the generic tags are php, mysql and sql, and the specific tags are security and sql-injection. The specific tags tell what the question is about, and the generic tags give the surrounding context. Based on the size of the question domain, one has to use a different proportion of generic and specific tags. By performing community detection on the tag network of multiple CQA datasets, we observed that mostly specific tags form small communities and generic tags form big communities.

While expanding the seed set of tags, we need to consider whether the tag is specific or generic. The preference should be to expand the specific tags as they have a narrow scope and have precise information about what the question is about. On the other hand, expanding generic tags would lead to topic drift. We use the following to quantify tag specificity, where $|Q_t|$ is the number of questions with tag t and Q is the total number of questions:

$$ITF(t) = \log(\frac{|Q|}{|Q_t|}) \qquad (9)$$

If a question has multiple tags, it may belong to multiple tag communities. In our dataset, we observed that 94% of questions belonged to three communities at a time. We define the belongingness of a question q to a tag community C_k as:

$$B(q, C_k) = \sum_{t_j \in T_q \cap C_k} ITF(t_j) \tag{10}$$

where C_k is the kth tag community. We sum the ITF scores of all the tags that are present in the intersection of question tags T_q and the tag community C_k. The question will have a zero belongingness score to communities with empty tag intersections. The expert finding model T-TEV, introduced in Sect. 5.3 performs better than the other two models, but it only considers the recent contribution of a user on the tags given in the question. However, there are thousands of tags, and a question can have at most 4–5 tags. The question tags are not sufficient to determine user expertise. We need to look at the expertise of the user on tags that are closely related to the tags given in the question and also the most recent contribution the user has made to either the question tags or the tags related to question tags. For this we extend the T-TEV model discussed in Sect. 5.3 by considering the tag clusters as follows:

$$E\text{-}TEV(u_i, q, \tau) = \sum_{\forall C_{l_k}} \frac{AQual_{ik}}{1 + \kappa * \Delta C_k} * B(q, C_k) \tag{11}$$

E-$TEV(u_i, q, \tau)$ denotes the extended temporal topical expertise of user u_i on the question q asked at timestamp τ, Δc_k is the difference in days of the question timestamp and the timestamp of the last answer given by user u_i on any question that contained tags from cluster C_k, and $AQual_{ik}$ is the expertise of the user over all the tags in tag cluster C_k.

Because the user's activity and recent activity are computed with respect to the whole tag community, E-$TEV(u_i, q, \tau)$ gives higher weights to generic tags of the question since they are the popular tags within any community and will have high $AQual_{ik}$ values. But, these big communities can have a diverse set of topics, and the expertise we compute may not be relevant to the specific question. We propose a final model that considers only some top-m neighboring tags even within a community to address this problem. In this paper, we use $m = 5$. We can consider the small m neighboring tags within the big community as another small community, denoted as C'_k. Our improved model N-TEV that considers only neighboring tags within the community can be defined as:

$$N\text{-}TEV(u_i, q, \tau) = \sum_{\forall C'_k} \frac{AQual_{ik}}{1 + \kappa * \Delta C'_k} * B(q, C_k) \tag{12}$$

The question's belongingness to tag community $B(q, C_k)$ remains the same. The user's answer qualities to a community and the most recent contribution is computed with respect to the sub-community consisting of only the top-m neighboring tags. These neighboring tags together with the actual question tags are used in the expertise computation.

7   Evaluation

We start the section with data pre-processing since we had already explained the dataset in detail in Sect. 3. We follow it up with the evaluation measures and experimental results. The set of users in a CQA site keeps changing dynamically. Therefore, it is unlikely that we recommend future users who were not present at the time of posting. Hence, as a part of pre-processing, we weed out all those users who were not present at the time of the posting. Let R_q be the set of recommended users for a given question q, and U_q be the basic set of users who have answered the question. We remove from U_q the future users who joined the sites after the question was posted. We found that contributions from the future users in the answers were quite significant and amounted to almost 40% of the answers. Next, we state the evaluation measures and how we use them to evaluate the models. The evaluation section shows the comparison between the baseline models Z-Score, TZ-Score, TEV, T-TEV, and the proposed improvements E-TEV, N-TEV. During the experiments, we set $\kappa = 0.1$ in the Eqs. 6, 11 and 12.

Table 1. Evaluation results on the competing models

Measure		Model					
		Z-Score	TZ-Score	TEV	T-TEV	E-TEV	N-TEV
Precision@	5	0.018	0.026	0.046	0.052	**0.058**	**0.058**
	10	0.041	0.047	0.075	0.086	0.095	**0.099**
	20	0.072	0.076	0.112	0.135	0.150	**0.157**
	30	0.096	0.111	0.139	0.170	0.190	**0.202**
Recall@	5	0.038	0.039	0.066	0.074	0.082	**0.083**
	10	0.020	0.034	0.053	0.061	0.068	**0.071**
	20	0.017	0.028	0.040	0.047	0.054	**0.056**
	30	0.017	0.027	0.033	0.040	0.045	**0.048**
MSC@	5	0.139	0.178	0.280	0.311	0.348	**0.351**
	10	0.236	0.295	0.409	0.449	0.498	**0.516**
	20	0.407	0.433	0.543	0.601	0.663	**0.681**
	30	0.478	0.558	0.617	0.685	0.752	**0.773**

Result – We evaluate the proposed models using three popular information retrieval metrics: precision@n, recall@n and matching set count (msc@n) . These metrics have been used in the existing works [4,5,9] to evaluate expert finding algorithms in CQA sites. In general, for a given model, the scores follow *precision < recall < msc*. We have tabulated the results in Table 1.

Precision@n: Theoretically, precision@n is defined as the number of relevant predictions within the top-n recommendations and is given by:

$$precision@n = \sum_{q \in Q} \frac{|R_q \cap U_q|}{|R_q|}$$

Table 1 presents the results, and all the values were averaged over multiple test runs. From the table, the precision values seem to be falling into three ranges: low, medium, and high. Z-Score and TZ-Score methods depend on the number of answers, and hence they can be deceived by giving a large number of irrelevant answers. As a result, both Z-Score and TZ-Score fall under low precision values. TEV introduces the concept of quality through votes. Yet, it ignores the temporal and community relevance. We, therefore, find TEV in the medium range on the precision scale. T-TEV eliminates many inactive experts by introducing the temporal aspect and achieves higher precision than the classic TEV. Both E-TEV and N-TEV work on extended tag sets, and these models made the best recommendations. The reason for these best recommendations stems from the fact that these models localize both the expertise and availability to the specific tag communities. These localizations help in eliminating many time and topic irrelevant outliers from the recommendations. As seen in Table 1 although N-TEV promises to achieve better results by concentrating on the immediate neighborhood, it does not improve significantly over E-TEV. We observed that many questions were heavily tagged using only generic questions. This is why the *top-m* nearest tags also contained generic tags, and N-TEV failed to address the very specific tags. The performance of E-TEV and N-TEV are thus very close. Overall, T-TEV, E-TEV, and N-TEV achieve quite higher precision by recommending the most likely answerers.

Recall@n: Recall@n notes the fraction of the actual answerers who were present in the top-n predictions. Recall@n is given by the expression:

$$recall@n = \sum_{q \in Q} \frac{|R_q \cap U_q|}{|U_q|}$$

We have listed the recall values for the six competing models in Table 1. Similar to precision, recall also shows improvement with an increase in the value of n. When we compare the six methodologies in terms of their recall performance, we observe that many of the reasons that hold true for precision also hold for recall. In spite of that, we use both recall and precision to evaluate because recall is sometimes considered unreasonable as it expects that all of the relevant answerers be recommended ($|R_q \cap U_q| = |U_q|$). Precision is more appropriate because users do not generally require all of the answerers. It is enough to recommend at least a few of the relevant answerers within the top recommendations that are shown to the users.

Matching Set Count (MSC): Matching Set Count reports the number of times when, at least one actual user has been recommended correctly. This metric tells overall goodness of our model.

$$msc@n = \frac{1}{|Q|} \sum_{q \in Q} I_{[R_q \bigcap U_q]}$$

s.t

$$I_{[R_q \bigcap U_q]} = \begin{cases} 0, & \text{if } [R_q \bigcap U_q] = \emptyset \\ 1, & \text{otherwise} \end{cases} \tag{13}$$

where, $I_{[R_q \bigcap U_q]}$ is an indicator random variable. Ideally, MSC is expected to increase with the increase in the value of n. MSC is a much more relaxed metric and is mostly useful for performing a loose model inspection. We also compare our results with those of [17], the work reports MSC@10 on their two proposed variations of Z-Score. The first is the Z-Score with exponential discounting:

$$Z\text{-}Score_{exp}(u) = \sum_{i=1}^{Q} Z\text{-}Score_i(u) e^{-k\Delta_{t_i}} \tag{14}$$

The second is Z-Score with hyperbolic discounting:

$$Z\text{-}Score_{hyp}(u) = \sum_{i=1}^{Q} \frac{Z\text{-}Score_i(u)}{1 + k\Delta_{t_i}} \tag{15}$$

The work considers time Δ_{t_i} in the range of days to months. We only consider the day-level time slots. $Z\text{-}Score_{exp}(u)$ has an MSC@10 value of 0.3760 while $Z\text{-}Score_{hyp}(u)$ has an MSC@10 of 0.4400, both of them fall short of our proposed topic induced quality expertise models E-TEV and N-TEV that have an MSC@10 of 0.498 and 0.516 respectively. Finally, we note that MSC too follows the same trend in the scores that have been shown by recall and precision, and hence we carry forward the same arguments that we had given for recall and precision to MSC.

8   Conclusion

In this paper, we have proposed models that use limited information i.e. only tags and the user participation to recommend experts. We showed that computing the user expertise based on localized tags showed improvement over all the previous existing methods. We have also seen that these sites are dynamic, so considering models that takes into account the user recent activity performs better. Further, sometimes the localization can be too restrictive, so we have expanded the localized tags with the similar tags and proposed a community based user expertise estimation based on tags (E-TEV, N-TEV). The community based approaches showed the best performance over all the models we evaluated. Experimental results demonstrate the excellent performance of our methods E-TEV and N-TEV.

References

1. Asaduzzaman, M., Mashiyat, A.S., Roy, C.K., Schneider, K.A.: Answering questions about unanswered questions of stack overflow. In: Proceedings of the 10th Working Conference on Mining Software Repositories, pp. 97–100. IEEE Press (2013)
2. Bouguessa, M., Dumoulin, B., Wang, S.: Identifying authoritative actors in question-answering forums: the case of yahoo! answers. In: Proceedings of the 14th ACM SIGKDD International Conference on Knowledge Discovery and Data Mining, pp. 866–874. ACM (2008)
3. Cai, Y., Chakravarthy, S.: Predicting answer quality in q/a social networks: Using temporal features. Technical report, University of Texas at Arlington (2011)
4. Chang, S., Pal, A.: Routing questions for collaborative answering in community question answering. In: Proceedings of the 2013 IEEE/ACM International Conference on Advances in Social Networks Analysis and Mining, pp. 494–501. ACM (2013)
5. Choetkiertikul, M., Avery, D., Dam, H.K., Tran, T., Ghose, A.: Who will answer my question on stack overflow? In: Software Engineering Conference (ASWEC), 2015 24th Australasian, pp. 155–164. IEEE (2015)
6. Dror, G., Maarek, Y., Szpektor, I.: Will my question be answered? predicting "question answerability" in community question-answering sites. In: Blockeel, H., Kersting, K., Nijssen, S., Železný, F. (eds.) ECML PKDD 2013. LNCS (LNAI), vol. 8190, pp. 499–514. Springer, Heidelberg (2013). https://doi.org/10.1007/978-3-642-40994-3_32
7. Guo, J., Xu, S., Bao, S., Yu, Y.: Tapping on the potential of q&a community by recommending answer providers. In: Proceedings of the 17th ACM conference on Information and Knowledge Management, pp. 921–930. ACM (2008)
8. Lofgren, P., Banerjee, S., Goel, A.: Personalized pagerank estimation and search: a bidirectional approach. In: Proceedings of the Ninth ACM International Conference on Web Search and Data Mining, pp. 163–172 (2016)
9. Neshati, M., Fallahnejad, Z., Beigy, H.: On dynamicity of expert finding in community question answering. Inf. Process. Manage. **53**(5), 1026–1042 (2017)
10. Pal, A., Chang, S., Konstan, J.A.: Evolution of experts in question answering communities. In: ICWSM (2012)
11. Saha, R.K., Saha, A.K., Perry, D.E.: Toward understanding the causes of unanswered questions in software information sites: a case study of stack overflow. In: Proceedings of the 2013 9th Joint Meeting on Foundations of Software Engineering, pp. 663–666. ACM (2013)
12. Shah, C., Pomerantz, J.: Evaluating and predicting answer quality in community QA. In: Proceedings of the 33rd International ACM SIGIR Conference on Research and Development in Information Retrieval, pp. 411–418. ACM (2010)
13. Szpektor, I., Maarek, Y., Pelleg, D.: When relevance is not enough: promoting diversity and freshness in personalized question recommendation. In: Proceedings of the 22nd International conference on World Wide Web, pp. 1249–1260. ACM (2013)
14. Tian, Y., Kochhar, P.S., Lim, E.-P., Zhu, F., Lo, D.: Predicting best answerers for new questions: an approach leveraging topic modeling and collaborative voting. In: Nadamoto, A., Jatowt, A., Wierzbicki, A., Leidner, J.L. (eds.) SocInfo 2013. LNCS, vol. 8359, pp. 55–68. Springer, Heidelberg (2014). https://doi.org/10.1007/978-3-642-55285-4_5

15. Yang, B., Manandhar, S.: Exploring user expertise and descriptive ability in community question answering. In: Advances in Social Networks Analysis and Mining (ASONAM), 2014 IEEE/ACM International Conference on, pp. 320–327. IEEE (2014)

16. Yang, J., Tao, K., Bozzon, A., Houben, G.-J.: Sparrows and owls: characterisation of expert behaviour in stackoverflow. In: Dimitrova, V., Kuflik, T., Chin, D., Ricci, F., Dolog, P., Houben, G.-J. (eds.) UMAP 2014. LNCS, vol. 8538, pp. 266–277. Springer, Cham (2014). https://doi.org/10.1007/978-3-319-08786-3_23

17. Yeniterzi, R., Callan, J.: Moving from static to dynamic modeling of expertise for question routing in CQA sites. In: ICWSM, pp. 702–705 (2015)

18. Zhang, J., Ackerman, M.S., Adamic, L.: Expertise networks in online communities: structure and algorithms. In: Proceedings of the 16th International Conference on World Wide Web, pp. 221–230. ACM (2007)

19. Zhou, J., Zhang, Y., Cheng, J.: Preference-based mining of top-k influential nodes in social networks. Futur. Gener. Comput. Syst. **31**, 40–47 (2014)

20. Zhou, Z.M., Lan, M., Niu, Z.Y., Lu, Y.: Exploiting user profile information for answer ranking in CQA. In: Proceedings of the 21st International Conference on World Wide Web, pp. 767–774. ACM (2012)

Analysis of Dynamics of Emergence and Decline of Scientific Ideas Based on Optimistic and Pessimistic Fuzzy Aggregation Norms

Aleksandra Mrela[1]([✉]) [iD], Oleksandr Sokolov[2] [iD], Veslava Osinska[3] [iD],
and Wlodzislaw Duch[2] [iD]

[1] Institute of Informatics, Kazimierz Wielki University in Bydgoszcz,
Bydgoszcz, Poland
`a.mrela@ukw.edu.pl`
[2] Faculty of Physics, Astronomy and Informatics, Deparment of Informatics,
Nicolaus Copernicus University in Torun, Torun, Poland
`{osokolov,duch}@fizyka.umk.pl`
[3] Institute of Information and Communication Research, Nicolaus Copernicus
University in Torun, Torun, Poland
`wieo@umk.pl`
`https://ii.ukw.edu.pl/`

Abstract. Scientists develop new concepts, methods, and techniques to solve practical and theoretical problems. These ideas are disseminated among scientists representing the same discipline; some are known even among non-scientists (artificial intelligence, machine learning, or fractals). The spreading of new ideas in the scientific community is going with various intensities; some quickly emerge and die, and others exist for a long time. Scientists, like other people, would like to disseminate their concepts. They use different methods to spread them, such as publishing papers, writing books, giving lectures, taking part in conferences, being a member of interdisciplinary teams, and so on.

The paper presents the two different methods of analyzing the knowledge dissemination of scientific ideas based on fuzzy logic. One of these methods involves fuzzy aggregation norms and calculating and analyzing knowledge dissemination coefficients. The other considers the article's citations and extrapolates results to citations of papers consisting of the scientific field. Moreover, the multi-agent model of emergence and decline of scientific ideas among the scientific community is coded in Netlogo and presented to show the results of the multi-agent model of spreading the scientific concept.

Keywords: Knowledge dissemination · Multi-agent model · Fuzzy
aggregation norms · Citation · Journal databases

© The Author(s), under exclusive license to Springer Nature Singapore Pte Ltd. 2022
E. Szczerbicki et al. (Eds.): ACIIDS 2022, CCIS 1716, pp. 327–339, 2022.
https://doi.org/10.1007/978-981-19-8234-7_26

1   Introduction

Examining the whole science is almost impossible; however, some disciplines or research fields are relatively new and fast increasing as, for example, fuzzy set theory. To analyze its development, some scientometric measures, such as numbers of articles or citation rates, can be applied. Some researchers [1] strive to identify fundamental scientific knowledge development factors, design and improve predictive models. One of the fascinating topics is finding the algorithms for analyzing the dynamics of spreading news, for example, the twits on Twitter [2]. Hertling et al. [3], based on data from Wiki, created the consolidated knowledge graph from Wikis that they called DBkWik.

We propose the new knowledge dissemination and forgetting coefficient based on fuzzy logic and analyze its values to visualize the impact of citations of some papers on two research fields: fuzzy logic and Gestalt psychology. We use the simulation of the multi-agented model of knowledge and confidence dissemination. This model simplifies situations of receiving and spreading or forgetting some scientific ideas; however, changing parameters of knowledge dissemination and forgetting can observe scientific concepts' behaviors. Models based on fuzzy logic give many opportunities to simulate bibliometric measures.

2   Characteristics of Data Distribution

2.1   Fuzzy Logic

Fuzzy logic, as a form of multivalued logic, solves the problem of partial truths. In this concept, the level of estimated truth belongs to the interval [0,1], and 0 refers to false, 1 to whole truth as in classical Boolean logic. Here, the sentences can have a subjective value of truth like, for example, the sentence "The quality of the photo is high" has a different value of truth for various people. This idea was introduced by Lotfi Zadeh in 1965 when he initiated a fuzzy set theory [4]. The foundation of the fuzzy applications is the observation that while making decisions, people base on imprecise non-numerical knowledge [5].

Figure 1 (left) presents the graph of numbers of articles related to fuzzy logic published by journals indexed in Web of Science during 1990 and 2019. As can be noticed, the number of published articles is steadily increasing. The variable, called the number of citations per year, was calculated as the number of citations divided by the number of years between publication and the year 2019 (Fig. 1 (right)). In this case, we cannot observe that the variable is increasing what can be partly caused by the decreasing number of years when the articles are available to be read.

2.2   Gestalt Psychology

The second example is the scientific field, called Gestalt psychology, or gestaltism, a psychological concept created in the early 20th century in Austria and Germany. Works of M. Wertheimer, W. Köhler, and K. Koffka [6] were

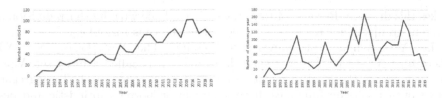

Fig. 1. Numbers of articles (left) and citations per year (right) related to fuzzy logic published by journals indexed in Web of Science during the 1990 and 2019 (left)

the foundation of this theory. Gestalt psychology indicates that living beings see the whole picture of reality as a pattern; they can recognize the configuration of items, not just as a set of individual items. This point of view represents the saying: "the whole is more than the sum of its parts" [7]. The principles of this theory are described with words: similarity, connection, closure; the usage of these terms shows how people see the reality of different objects.

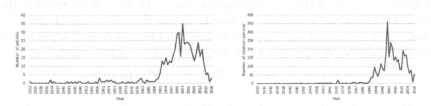

Fig. 2. Numbers of articles (left) and citations per year (right) related to (left) related to Gestalt psychology published by journals indexed in Web of Science during the 1922 and 2018

As observed (Fig. 2), only one or two papers were published in this scientific field for many years. Suddenly, in 1990, many articles were published, followed by their citations (this process of developing the scientific theories is sometimes called the Sleeping Beauty). The knowledge is disseminated in a non-determinant, unpredictable way. It is impossible to predict when there will be picks of articles.

It can be expected that the rest of the cases of knowledge dissemination that are brought by life are between these two extreme examples.

3   Methods

The articles increase and strengthen confidence in new ideas, methods, or techniques developed by researchers in scientific development. Due to the considered concept, published papers can be divided into groups: defining the new area, having a significant or some influence on the discipline development. The limits between these groups of articles are vague and depend on the person who makes this division. Because of that, the classical logic with its sharp division of different groups is not relevant, and the better choice is fuzzy logic.

Let X be a non-empty universe of discourse. The $A = \{(x, \mu_A), x \in X\}$, where $\mu_A : X \longrightarrow [0, 1]$ is a membership function, is called a fuzzy set. Value $\mu_A(x)$ describes the level of membership of element x to set A. To aggregate values of membership functions, fuzzy aggregation norms (optimistic and pessimistic) are applied [8]. Let $I = [0, 1]$. Then $S_o : I \times I \longrightarrow I$ is called an optimistic fuzzy aggregation norm if $S_o(0, 0) = 0$, and for each $x, y \in I$, we have $S_o(x, y) = S_o(y, x)$ and $S_o(x, y) \geq \max\{x, y\}$. Thus, the aggregation of two zeros is still zero. Moreover, the order of values does not matter during the calculations. Furthermore, the aggregation of two values is not smaller than any of the two aggregated values. In the paper, as an optimistic aggregation norm, the following function is chosen $S_o(x, y) = x + y - xy$, $x, y \in I$.

Function $S_p : I \times I \longrightarrow I$ is called a pessimistic fuzzy aggregation norm if $S_p(1, 1) = 1$, and for each $x, y \in I$, we have $S_p(x, y) = S_p(y, x)$ and $S_p(x, y) \leq \max\{x, y\}$. Hence, this aggregation of two ones, is still one. Moreover, the order of values does not matter and the result of pessimistic fuzzy aggregation is not be higher than any of the two aggregated values. Here, as a pessimistic fuzzy aggregation norm, the following function is chosen $S_p(x, y) = xy$, $x, y \in I$.

Let a denote the entity value. To iterate the fuzzy aggregation norm S the following formulae are applied. Thus, for $n = 1, 2, \ldots$ and $S = S_o$ or $S = S_p$,

$$S(0, a) = a \quad \text{and} \quad S^n(0, a) = S(S^{n-1}(0, a), a). \tag{1}$$

3.1   Knowledge Dissemination Coefficient

Let $\mathcal{A}$ denote the space of agents - articles published by the scientific community within the considered concept, method, or technique to disseminate knowledge. In the paper, the multi-agent model of knowledge dissemination is proposed. Let us distinguish in $\mathcal{A}$ the set of articles highly cited called Centers of Knowledge Dissemination (CKD).

Let $a = 0.001$ be an entity of knowledge dissemination and let each citation cases the knowledge coefficient increase. If there is no citation of the article in the previous year, then the knowledge dissemination of this article decreases with the forgetting entity $b = 0.9$. We apply the optimistic and pessimistic fuzzy aggregation norms to calculate the values of this coefficient in the following years. Thus, in the first year after the article publication with n citations, the knowledge dissemination and forgetting coefficient is equal to $coef_{kd} = coef_{kd}(1) = S^n(0, a)$.

Let $coef_{kd}(k)$ denote the considered coefficient calculated k years after the article publication. If n indicates the number of the citations, then, applying (1),

$$coef_{kd}(k + 1) = \begin{cases} S_p(coef_{kd}(k), b) & \text{if } n = 0 \\ S_o^n(coef_{kd}(k), a) & \text{if } n > 0 \end{cases} \tag{2}$$

3.2   Dynamic Behavior of Citations

Almost every idea or concept, particularly scientific, is featured by typical interest growth, and then it sooner or later vanishes. We assumed that, during the period when this paper influences the discipline development, the dynamic model of the paper's citation values is similar to the probability density function (pdf) of the normal distribution. Hence, using this model, we can try to predict the following numbers of citations. Therefore, after some time of growth, the time comes when the number of citations starts diminishing.

Accordingly, in the case of cited papers, there is a period when the number of citations increases, and it can be modeled like the left part of the pdf of the normal distribution. Of course, at the beginning of the process, citations increase, the mean and standard deviation are not known, and it requires some research to predict when there will be the maximum of this density function.

After we have done some research on the dynamics of papers' citations, we can extrapolate this idea to the development of scientific fields and even disciplines. The dynamics of their citations also follow the pdf of the normal distribution with, of course, higher means and standard deviations.

4 Analysis of the Dynamics of Citations of Influential Articles on Scientific Fields

Let us consider two pairs of scientific concepts in each of the two research fields: fuzzy logic and Gestalt psychology which will be represented by two essential articles, which introduced new directions in considered areas. The impact of papers on theory development is measured by the knowledge dissemination coefficients calculated on the foundation of citation numbers.

4.1 Knowledge Dissemination Coefficient

In the beginning, we consider two ideas from the scientific field of fuzzy logic.

Fuzzy Logic. Let us now consider two examples of fuzzy logic dissemination concepts:

- Zadeh, L.A.: Fuzzy logic = computing with words, [9]
- Mendel, J.M., John, R.I., Liu, F.: Interval Type-2 Fuzzy Logic Systems Made Simple, [10]

In [9], L. Zadeh introduced a methodology called word calculation (CW), in which he applied words rather than numbers in the process of inference. He claims that CW is a better choice when considered information is too imprecise, and the results have some tolerance for imprecision. The usage of inaccuracy tolerance is a central feature of the CW concept. In [10], the authors developed the idea of the interval type 2 fuzzy systems (IT2 FS) and prepared some innovative rules letting the IT2 FS be applied more easily and be more available and convenient to apply. These articles have the highest total number of citations ([9] − 1687 and [10] − 1026).

Zadeh's paper [9] was published in the year 1996, and the first citations were noted by Web of Science in 1997. Thus, the knowledge dissemination of Zadeh's concept is equal to 0, so $coef_{kd} = 0$. In the year 1997, the number of citations of this article was $n = 4$, so, by equation (2),

$$coef_{kd} = S^4 (0, 0.001) = S\left(S\left(S\left(S\left(0, 0.001\right), 0.001\right), 0.001\right), 0.001\right)$$
$$= S(S(S(0.001, 0.001), 0.001), 0.001) \;=\; 0.003994.$$

Table 1 presents steadily increasing knowledge dissemination and forgetting coefficients during the years 1997–2019.

Table 1. The knowledge dissemination and forgetting coefficients of Zadeh's article [9] during 1997–2019 and Mendel et al.'s publication [10] during 2007–2020

Year	1997	1998	1999	2000	2001	2002	2003	2004	2005	2006	2007	2008
$coef_{kd}$ [9]	0.004	0.021	0.047	0.088	0.150	0.203	0.238	0.275	0.311	0.361	0.417	0.454
$coef_{kd}$ [10]	-	-	-	-	-	-	-	-	-	-	0.018	0.054
Year	2009	2010	2011	2012	2013	2014	2015	2016	2017	2018	2019	
$coef_{kd}$ [9]	0.503	0.543	0.574	0.606	0.643	0.678	0.710	0.738	0.766	0.790	0.811	
$coef_{kd}$ [10]	0.086	0.121	0.158	0.202	0.256	0.328	0.407	0.475	0.534	0.584	0.597	

The graph of knowledge dissemination coefficients (Fig. 3) presents continuous increase of knowledge dissemination and forgetting coefficients in the case of both concepts Zadeh's [9] and Mendel et al.' [10] concepts in the fuzzy logic scientific field.

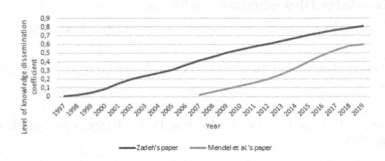

Fig. 3. The graph of levels of knowledge dissemination coefficient of the Zadeh's [9] 1997–2019 and Mendel et al.'s [10] papers during 1997–2020

Gestalt Psychology. To confirm our findings, we selected other topics regarding Gestalt psychology, and we chose two articles:

- Koffka, K.: Perception: an introduction to the Gestalt theorie, [11]
- Martin, D., Fowlkes, C., Tal, D., Malik, J.: A database of human segmented natural images and its application to evaluating segmentation algorithms and measuring ecological statistics, [12]

In [11], Koffka described three main features (sensation, association, and attention) based on Gestalt psychology in a different way than the other psychological theories. The "sensation" means that the world consists of elements that, after connecting, create stimuli in human lives. The "association" helps people choose which idea is better for individuals. The "attention" is responsible for the reaction to stimuli because if somebody does not notice them, they do not respond to them.

Figure 4 (left) presents the graph of knowledge dissemination and forgetting coefficients of Koffka's paper [11]. During years 1922–1954, a slow increase in the number of this article citations can be observed, then during the years 1954–2003 - slight decrease, and beginning in 2010, there is a higher increase in citations.

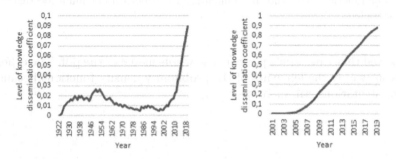

Fig. 4. The graph of knowledge dissemination coefficients of Koffka's paper [11] during 1922–2018 (left) and Martin et al.'s publications [12] during 2001–2019 (right)

Martin et al.'s article [12] presents a database that is created to contain segmentation of "ground truth" performed by humans for pictures of a wide range of natural scenes. They described a measure of error for quantifying consistency between these segmentations. As can be noticed (Fig. 4 (right)), the knowledge dissemination and forgetting coefficients are steadily increasing. These articles are the foundations of the development of this field because the following researchers read and cite them.

4.2   Estimation of Citation Dynamics

In this section, we analyze the dynamics of citations of the paper: Deng TQ, Heijmans HJAM (2002) Grey-scale morphology based on fuzzy logic [13] which frequencies and cumulative frequencies of citations are presented in Fig. 5.

Let X denote the number of citations of this article during the period 2013–2019. Based on these values, the probability distribution function of the normal distribution was experimentally found and is presented in Fig. 5 (left). Let $Y \sim N(9, 5^2)$ be a variable, which probability distribution function was experimentally found and is an approximation of X variable with the expected value $\mu = 9$ years and standard deviation $\sigma = 5$ years. Comparing the behavior of citations of this article and the other four articles (comp. Figs. 3 and 4), it can

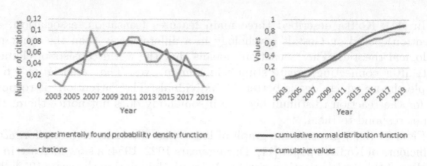

Fig. 5. Values of citations and experimentally found probability distribution function of the normal distribution between 2003 and 2019; the frequencies and probability distribution function (left) and the cumulative frequencies and cumulative distribution function (right)

be observed that this article presents the whole model of the pdf. The other four papers show only the left parts of the probability density functions because the number of citations still increases.

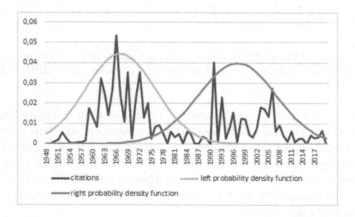

Fig. 6. Values of citations and experimentally found probability density functions of the normal distributions between 1948 and 2019 of scientific field "analog computers"

We have analyzed the citation dynamics of some research fields. In the case of the analog computers scientific field, it can be observed that the dynamics of citations cannot be modeled with one pdf of the normal distribution. After the period (1948–1978) of high citations, there is a period (1978–1989) of low citations, and then there is one more period (1989–2019) with high citations. Hence, we can model the dynamics of quotations with two probability density functions (Fig. 6).

5 Simulation of the Model of the Knowledge and Confidence Dissemination

This section presents the multi-agent simulation of development and aging/ disappearance of the scientific concept or discipline due to the NetLogo application. It involves agents because people solve problems, read books or articles, meet other people, take part in conferences and seminars, and so on. Hence, the foundation of the simulation is meeting with other agents to exchange knowledge about the concept (people) or citing other publications (articles).

To simulate the process of changing levels of knowledge and confidence, we apply the programmable modeling environment NetLogo and develop the application called Diss Fuzzy. One of the Diss Fuzzy realization scenes developed for simulation the process of the knowledge and confidence dissemination of the fuzzy logic concept is presented in Fig. 7 (left).

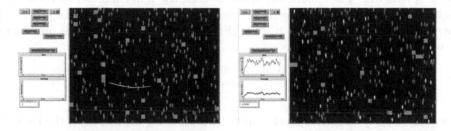

Fig. 7. The screenshots of Diss Fuzzy application for the simulation of the knowledge dissemination model in the fuzzy logic concept: the starting phase (left) and one of middle phases (right)

The simulation is based on the space of articles published in the fuzzy-logic discipline represented as gray symbols (turtles). The papers with high knowledge dissemination coefficients are called Knowledge Dissemination Centers (KDC - button "centers" sets the number of KDC and button "force" indicates the knowledge dissemination value) are expressed as green squares. The simulation follows the ant colony optimization algorithm (ACO) [14] that applied probability to solve computational problems for finding paths during walking through graphs.

The Diss Fuzzy application presents the simulation of a multi-agent model of knowledge dissemination, in which several KDCs influence the process of research. Agents, green turtles, look for published ideas, techniques, methods to solve their scientific problems. At the beginning, KDC's knowledge dissemination value (KDV) is equal to 0.9 and other agent's – 0. During this concept development process, researchers try to solve their problems and meet KDCs or other researchers. Meeting KDCs or other scientists causes the spread of knowledge, so the optimistic fuzzy aggregation norm is applied. However, when agents do not meet any KDC or other agents, the pessimistic fuzzy aggregation norm is applied, and the KDV decreases.

Let us assume that we set a number of agents during a period chosen for the stimulation (button "population" sets the number of gray symbols). During some time, agents meet the KDC (essential and frequently cited articles) or different agents, or stay alone for some time. Hence, after their knowledge dissemination calculations, the agents change their colors according to the following rules: stay gray (KDV$\leq$ 0.3), change color to yellow (0.3 <KDV$\leq$ 0.6), – to blue (0.6 <KDV$\leq$ 0.9) or – to red (KDV> 0.9).

This simulation presents the aggregated values of knowledge dissemination (graph "sum") and the mean value of knowledge dissemination (graph "mean"). Moreover, this simulation shows how agents behave according to their meeting the KDC articles, meeting each other, and staying alone. Changing the articles belonging to the KDC and forgetting coefficient ($b = 0.9$) shows the concept's chances of being well-known among the scientists related to this discipline or not being spread out. The simulation confirms that the fewer number of KDC, the higher likelihood the concept will decrease. All agents change color to gray, and even KDCs change their color to blue (Fig. 7 (right)), meaning fewer and fewer researchers quote this idea.

6 Discussion

Nowadays, many scientists develop more and more algorithms to be the basis of simulation and visualization methods of scientometric data [15–17].

Simulations based on fuzzy logic show how to use bibliometric data of different types (numbers of publications, citations, categories of publications according to disciplines) to model the shared space of scientific knowledge. The main goal of these simulations is to search for groups of researchers considering their scientific interests and achievements. Finding scientists whose areas of interest are similar may help solve problems faster.

Constructing different measures related to articles and their citations, we try to evaluate the scientific achievements of scientists, institutions, or disciplines. Based on these results, we simulate their scientific development.

One of the computer applications prepared for evaluation and visualization of scientists' achievements was the web interface ScienceFuzz. Sokolov et al. [18] developed the concept and measure of contribution to science of a researcher applying fuzzy logic methods. Based on this measure for different scientists, the visualization of their contribution was prepared and presented in Fig. 8 (left).

It is interesting to find measures for estimating the "distance" between one chosen article and the group of papers from the same or different disciplines. Considering common keywords and citations of a chosen group of articles, we can create the proximity space showing the "distance" between articles, where this chosen article is placed in the origin of the set of the axis (Fig. 8 (right)).

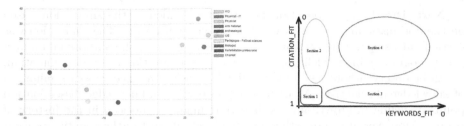

Fig. 8. Visualization of web interface ScienceFuzz prepared for the group of academics related to their contribution to science (left) Visualization of the proximity space of one article published in computer science discipline (right)

Modeling scientific knowledge space has many benefits for researchers, science managers, and science philosophers. These visualizations can help scientists search for researchers whose interests are similar or select the set of papers to read because they are similar or not in the proximity space of the previously studied one. So, we need appropriate applications, including visualization methods, to analyze how this space behaves depending on input data. By changing the data vector, we can simulate the predefined processes in the scientific ideas dissemination system. Therefore, specialist software developers should be equipped with large sets of data and proper computing methods that allow representing complex multi-parameterized knowledge.

7 Conclusions

The paper presents two methods of analyzing knowledge dissemination among the scientific community. One way uses the fuzzy logic based on scientometric data downloaded from the Web of Science, which enables us to look through the number of articles, and their importance measured by the number of citations per year. We apply the optimistic fuzzy aggregation norm to calculate the knowledge dissemination coefficient for each paper. The time range of the knowledge dissemination coefficient shows how vital the specified article might be for its concept of knowledge dissemination. The knowledge dissemination and forgetting coefficients calculated for selected articles with the highest citations within the period show the similarity to the cumulative normal distribution.

The second method involves on extrapolation of empirical data to the normal distribution and comparing their standard deviations. We observe that the citation numbers follow the probability density function of the normal distribution for selected papers. Moreover, we state that the results observed for articles can be extrapolated on the behavior of concepts, as scientific concepts and publications are developed for some time and based on citations. The lifetime of different scientific ideas varies and depends on many factors. For example, the concept of analog computers was trendy in the years 1960 - 1970 and then in the 1980s s was much less cited.

Next, Diss Fuzzy application is presented, which is the simulation based on the optimistic and pessimistic fuzzy aggregation norms. The simulation was carried out using a computer program written by one of the authors in a multi-agent programmable modeling environment, NetLogo. Based on this simulation, it can be observed how the individual KDC article influences the dissemination of knowledge of scientists. And, an aggregated value of knowledge dissemination point of cycling in growth and decline that might be noticed in the history of science. Moreover, it is interesting how the levels of trust in the scientific concept are spread out or being forgetting.

It can be expected that for every research field, there are articles that play the role of seeds of growth in this area. We show that these influential papers can be found by analyzing the citations (and knowledge dissemination coefficients). The impact of the predominant authors of the development of the considered field, like, for example, L. Zadeh, can be analyzed by considering the number of papers and the dynamics of their papers' citations. The appropriate authors can be classified as the founders or creators of considered fields.

In the future, we want to analyze the dynamics behavior of citations of different articles to predict citing range using proposed in the paper method, i.e., the fitting relationship between the pdf of the normal distribution and dynamics data. It will help predict when the citations of papers will start declining and then expect the emergence and decline of scientific concepts. Therefore, using our method, it is possible to predict new pivotal papers or scientific schools, which will be fundamental in field development.

By analyzing citation paths backward, it is possible to identify the most influential articles in the considered research area. Next, we can create a dynamics model by applying the proposed approach and, therefore, reveal when the fundamentals of scientific theories emerge and decline. The developed model will also help us to simulate future dynamical changes by use citation patterns.

References

1. Fortunato, S., et al.: Science of science, Science, March 2018 (2018). https://doi.org/10.1126/science.aao0185
2. Nugroho, R., Paris, C., Nepal, S., Yang, J., Zhao, W.: A survey of recent methods on deriving topics from Twitter: algorithm to evaluation. Knowl. Inf. Syst. **62**(7), 2485–2519 (2020). https://doi.org/10.1007/s10115-019-01429-z
3. Hertling, S., Paulheim, H.: DBkWik: extracting and integrating knowledge from thousands of Wikis. Knowl. Inf. Syst. **62**(6), 2169–2190 (2019). https://doi.org/10.1007/s10115-019-01415-5
4. Zadeh, L.A.: Fuzzy sets. Inf. Control **8**, 338–353 (1965). https://doi.org/10.1016/s0019-9958(65)90241-x
5. Novák, V., Perfilieva, I., Mockor, J.: Mathematical principles of fuzzy logic. Kluwer Academic, Dordrecht (1999). ISSN:978-0-7923-8595-0
6. Augustyn, A.,The Editors of Encyclopedia Brittanica: Gestalt psychology, Encyclopedia Brittanica (2020). https://www.britannica.com/science/Gestalt-psychology. Accessed 18 May 2020

7. Sternberg, R.J., Sternberg, K.: Cognitive Psychology: Cengage Learning, vol. 13, 6th edn. Belmont, California (2012). ISBN 978-1-133-31391-5
8. Sokolov, O., Osińska, W., Mreła, A., Duch, W.: Modeling of scientific publications disciplinary collocation based on optimistic fuzzy aggregation norms. In: Swiatek, J., Borzemski, L., Wilimowska, Z. (eds.) ISAT 2018. AISC, vol. 853, pp. 145–153. Springer, Cham (2019). https://doi.org/10.1007/978-3-319-99996-8_14
9. Zadeh, L.A.: Fuzzy logic = computing with words. IEEE Trans. Fuzzy Syst. **4**(2), 103–111 (1996). https://doi.org/10.1109/91.493904
10. Mendel, J.M., John, R.I., Liu, F.: Interval type-2 fuzzy logic systems made simple. IEEE Trans. Fuzzy Syst. **14**(6), 808–821 (2006). https://doi.org/10.1109/TFUZZ.2006.879986
11. Koffka, K.: Perception: an introduction to the Gestalt - theorie. Psychol. Bull. **19**, 531–585 (1922). https://doi.org/10.1037/h0072422
12. Martin, D., Fowlkes, C., Tal, D., Malik, J.: A database of human segmented natural images and its application to evaluating segmentation algorithms and measuring ecological statistics. In: Eight IEEE International Conference on Computer Vision, vol. II, Proceedings, pp. 416–423, (2001). https://doi.org/10.1109/iccv.2001.937655
13. Deng, T.Q., Heijmans, H.J.A.M.: Grey-scale morphology based on fuzzy logic. J. Math. Imaging Vision **16**, 155–171 (2002). https://doi.org/10.1023/A:1013999431844
14. Dorigo, M., Stutzle, T.: Ant Colony Optimization. MIT Press, Cambridge (2004). ISBN 0-262-04219-3, OCLC 57182707
15. Kang, Q., Li, H., Jing, Z.: Mapping and Visualization of Fuzzy Control Research: A Scientometric Analysis During 2010–2019, (2020). https://doi.org/10.1145/3421766.3421778
16. Darko, A., Chan, A.P.C., Adabre M.A., Edwards, D.J., Hosseini, M.R., Ameyaw, E.E.: Artificial intelligence in the AEC industry: scientometric analysis and visualization of research activities. Autom. Construct. **112**, 103081 (2020). https://doi.org/10.1016/j.autcon.2020.103081
17. Chen, C., Song, M.: Visualizing a field of research: a methodology of systematic scientometric reviews. PloS one. **14**(10), e0223994 (2019). https://doi.org/10.1371/journal.pone.0223994
18. Sokolov, O., Osińska, V., Mrela, A., Duch, W., Burak, M.: Scientists' contribution to science and methods of its visualization. In: Swiatek, J., Borzemski, L., Wilimowska, Z. (eds.) ISAT 2019. AISC, vol. 1051, pp. 159–168. Springer, Cham (2020). https://doi.org/10.1007/978-3-030-30604-5_14

Fusing Deep Learning with Support Vector Machines to Detect COVID-19 in X-Ray Images

Jakub Nalepa[✉][iD], Piotr Bosowski, Wojciech Dudzik[iD],
and Michal Kawulok[iD]

Faculty of Automatic Control, Electronics and Computer Science,
Silesian University of Technology, Gliwice, Poland
{jnalepa,michal.kawulok}@ieee.org

Abstract. Deep neural networks are powerful learning machines that have laid foundations for most of the recent advancements in data analysis. Their most important advantage lies in learning how to extract the features from raw data, and these deep features are later classified with fully-connected layers. Although there exist more effective classifiers, including support vector machines, their high computational complexity is a serious obstacle in using them for classifying highly-dimensional and often huge datasets of deep features. We introduce a new framework which allows us to classify the deep features with evolutionarily-optimized support vector machines and we apply it to a real-life problem of detecting COVID-19 from X-ray images. We demonstrate that the proposed approach is highly effective and it outperforms well-established transfer learning strategies, thus improving the potential of existing pre-trained deep models. It can be particularly beneficial in cases when the amount and quality of labeled data is insufficient for performing full training of a network, but still too large for training a regular support vector machine.

Keywords: Deep features · Support vector machines · Transfer learning · Memetic algorithm

1 Introduction

Deep learning has demonstrated enormous capabilities in data analysis and processing which allowed the researchers to achieve ground-breaking advancements that were recently reported in a variety of domains. Excellent performance of deep neural networks (DNNs) is a result of learning the data representation alongside the inference rules in a simultaneous manner from a training set. In the cases aimed at classifying the computer vision data, convolutional layers are employed at first to learn high-quality deep features from images presented during training. Such automatic feature learning allows for substituting a tedious

This work was supported by the National Science Centre under Grant DEC-2017/25/B/ST6/00474.

© The Author(s), under exclusive license to Springer Nature Singapore Pte Ltd. 2022
E. Szczerbicki et al. (Eds.): ACIIDS 2022, CCIS 1716, pp. 340–353, 2022.
https://doi.org/10.1007/978-981-19-8234-7_27

process of engineering hand-crafted features that are to be extracted from the raw input data. The convolutional layers are topped with fully-connected layers that perform the final classification—commonly, softmax regression or a multi-layered perceptron (MLP) are employed here. Although there are lots of practical real-world application of DNNs, in many cases their potential is limited due to high requirements concerned with the data that are to be used for training. It is not uncommon that the amount or quality of labeled data is insufficient, which makes it impossible to train the deep models or increases the risk of overfitting. This is inherent to many real-life cases concerned with medical imaging, where data availability is scarce and their labeling is quite costly.

1.1 Related Work

There have been many approaches developed to deal with the data scarcity, including unsupervised [36] and semi-supervised learning [26], as well as making the methods robust against weak labeling [24]. It is also common to augment the training data [3] by generating artificial samples that preserve the characteristics of the real data. However, it occurred that the transfer learning paradigm, proposed for manually-crafted machine learning pipelines [30], can be effectively exploited in deep learning. Basically, a model trained with a large-scale dataset [21] can be used as a baseline that is fine-tuned to deal with a specific new problem. Importantly, the amount of data necessary for such fine-tuning can be much smaller than for training a model from scratch—only the fully-connected layers are optimized, while the convolutional layers are frozen and not modified. Alternatively, a pre-trained model can be used and trained with the new data, allowing for modifying all the weights both in the convolutional and fully-connected layers. The performance of a network trained relying on transfer learning depends on how well the fully-connected layers classify the deep features extracted by the earlier-trained convolutional layers.

Although fully-connected neural networks (including MLPs) are not always the optimal choice for classifying highly-dimensional datasets with already extracted features [2], they can be trained using error backpropagation that is coherent with how the CNNs are trained. Support vector machines (SVMs) [13] are well-established classifiers, and they are known to be very efficient in solving challenging pattern recognition and computer vision classification tasks. However, it is rarely practised to exploit them to classify the deep features due to their high dimensionality and large amounts of the training samples. Even in the transfer learning approaches the data size may be too large for training SVMs due to high time $(O(|T|^3))$ and memory $(O(|T|^2))$ complexities of the training process, where $|T|$ is the cardinality of the training set (T). Moreover, SVMs are quite sensitive to their hyperparameters and without proper tuning they may not perform better than MLPs [2]. SVM training consists in finding the support vectors (S)—a small subset of T—that define a hyperplane separating the data from two classes. To deal with the cases that are not linearly-separable, kernel functions are used to indirectly map the data onto high-dimensional spaces in which the linear separability can be attained. Here, usually the radial basis functions (RBF) are exploited. There have been many attempts reported to enhance the SVM solvers [27], but efficient training of non-linear SVMs remains an open problem which is a serious obstacle in using them for large datasets.

There were just a few successful attempts to exploit SVMs with a linear kernel to classify deep features [31, 35]. This includes a famous R-CNN network for object detection [19], in which the features are extracted using convolutional layers, and classified using a linear SVM. Later, in fast R-CNN [18], the VGG16 network was exploited for extracting the features, and it was topped with a softmax classifier, reported to perform marginally better than a linear SVM.

Apart from enhancing the SVM solvers as such, there have been attempts to select the most valuable samples out of the whole dataset presented for training. This is underpinned with the fact that support vectors are a subset of T, hence removing the vectors that are unlikely to become the support vectors should not affect the final outcome. Existing approaches to SVM training set selection [29] can be categorized into those based on random sampling, active learning, local and global data geometry analysis, and evolutionary algorithms. There are also a few approaches that jointly optimize several aspects related with SVM training, including selecting the training set, features, as well as optimizing the SVM hyperparameters [1, 17]. Our Simultaneously-Evolved SVM (SE-SVM) [16] optimizes all of these three components in an evolutionary manner and it allows for training SVMs from large and difficult datasets. Even though the training set selection could help overcome the obstacles preventing the use of SVMs for classifying deep features, such approaches have not been reported so far.

We focus on improving the COVID-19 screening process, in particular regarding the diagnosis and assessing the severity of the disease in certain patients [28]—it has obviously been, together with modeling the COVID-19 epidemic [4, 34], attracting the research attention. X-ray is commonly performed as one of the initial investigations in COVID-19 [6, 37]. Although it renders lower sensitivity than computed tomography, it requires 30–70 times smaller radiation dose. As the process of X-ray image analysis is time-consuming for humans, machine learning algorithms are being developed here, including CNNs [9, 38].

1.2   Contribution

In the work reported here, we explore the possibilities of coupling evolutionarily-optimized SVMs with deep learning, and we validate our approach for a challenging real-life problem concerned with detecting COVID-19 cases based on X-ray images. Our contribution can be summarized in the following points:

- We introduce a new classification framework that combines the benefits of the SVMs with feature learning capabilities of convolutional neural nets.
- We demonstrate that our SE-SVM method that optimizes the SVM hyperparameters and selects the training samples along with the features can be successfully exploited to make SVMs suitable for classifying deep features.
- We show that our framework can be applied to classify deep features extracted using fully-trained models, as well as in transfer learning scenarios.
- We report the results of the extensive experimental study which indicate that our technique can be successfully applied to classify the real-life data.

2   Fusing Deep Learning with Support Vector Machines

To benefit from the advantages of automated representation learning which commonly allows us to capture deep features that would be difficult to extract (or even unknown) for humans with the advantages of well-established and widely-researched SVMs, we introduce an end-to-end engine presented in Fig. 1. The pipeline is independent from specific feature extractors—we can utilize the deep features elaborated at different levels of the underlying deep architectures, and feed them into the evolutionary approach which is aimed at selecting the subset of all features, training vectors (both will be used to train SVMs), and at optimizing the kernel and its hyperparameters. Once the evolutionary optimization has been concluded, we utilize the same feature extractor, followed with the feature selector over the test data that is classified using the evolved SVM.

We build upon SE-SVM—our recent evolutionary algorithm for selecting training sets, features, and the SVM model (being the kernel function alongside its hyperparameters). In SE-SVM (Fig. 2), each chromosome (individual) is composed of three parts $(\mathcal{M}, \mathcal{T}, \mathcal{F})$ which encode different aspects of the evolved SVMs (the SVM model hyperparameters, p selected training samples from T, and q selected features from F, respectively). To generate the initial population, we select an initial subset of features F' (out of all features F), according to the ranks obtained using a range of feature selection methods [33]. Here, each feature is assigned a single rank which corresponds to the probability of picking this feature in the roulette wheel selection, in which we sample $|F'|$ features to each individual, out of all $\alpha_F \cdot |F|$ most discriminative features (i.e., with the largest probabilities). For each chromosome, we randomly select $|T'|$ training vectors for the refined training sets—these sets are balanced, as we select the equal number of vectors from each class. Finally, each hyperparameter of the

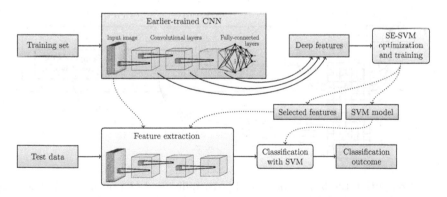

Fig. 1. Outline of the proposed solution. Deep features extracted using an earlier-trained CNN are fed to the SE-SVM engine which selects the features and generates the SVM model that is later used for classification. Blue blocks indicate the data, and the light orange blocks show the actions. The outcome of SE-SVM optimization procedure is shown with gray blocks. (Color figure online)

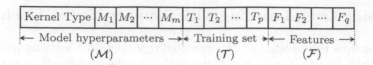

Fig. 2. A structure of the chromosome in SE-SVM. It is composed of three parts ($\mathcal{M}$, $\mathcal{T}$, $\mathcal{F}$) which encode the SVM model hyperparameters, p selected training samples from $\mathbf{T}$, and q selected features from $\mathbf{F}$, respectively.

SVM model ($\mathcal{M}$) is sampled randomly from the grid generated using a logarithmic step within the $[M_{\min}, M_{\max}]$ interval. Once the population is generated, the quality of each individual is quantified with its fitness, being the area under the receiver operating characteristic curve (AUC) obtained for the validation set $\mathbf{V}$ (Fig. 3). Here, an SVM is trained using $\mathbf{T}'$, $\mathbf{F}'$, and kernel hyperparameters which correspond to a given individual.

Once the population of N individuals is generated, it undergoes the evolutionary process (Fig. 4). For each parental pair, two children are elaborated in the crossover operation, where the kernel's hyperparameters become $x_{a+b} = x_a + \alpha \cdot (x_a - x_b)$, α is the random crossover weight, and $\alpha \in [-0.5, 1.5]$. For each child solution, we randomly select the refined training vector and feature subsets (containing $|\mathbf{T}'|$ and $|\mathbf{F}'|$ distinct vectors and features, respectively) from the intermediate sets containing all vectors and features inherited from the parents. To intensify the search in the most promising parts of the solution space, we capture the vectors that were annotated as SVs in the previous generation in the SV pool ($\mathcal{S}$). They are later used in the education operation for substituting up to $\min\{|\mathcal{S}|, S_e \cdot |\mathbf{T}'|\}$ random vectors from each offspring with probability P_{Te}. Analogously, we build the pool of the features ($\mathcal{F}$) that contains those fea-

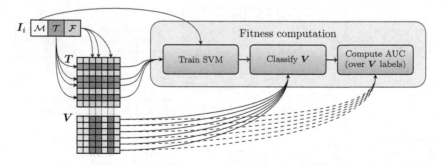

Fig. 3. Computing the fitness for a single i-th individual ($\mathbf{I}_i$) of SE-SVM. The chromosome is composed of three parts: $\mathcal{M}$ encodes the SVM model hyperparameters, $\mathcal{T}$ encodes the training subset $\mathbf{T}'$, and $\mathcal{F}$ encodes the selected features $\mathbf{F}'$. Feature selection is applied to both $\mathbf{T}$ and $\mathbf{V}$ (the columns in orange) and $\mathbf{T}'$ is a subset of $\mathbf{T}$ used for SVM training (rows marked in blue). The selected elements used for training ($\mathbf{T}' \times \mathbf{F}'$) and validation ($\mathbf{V} \times \mathbf{F}'$) are marked red. (Color figure online)

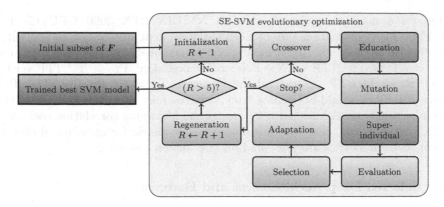

Fig. 4. Flowchart of the simultaneously-evolved SVM (SE-SVM). In orange, we annotate the steps that are executed only while selecting the refined training and feature sets (they are not utilized for optimizing the kernel's hyperparameters). (Color figure online)

tures that are included in the better-fitted part of the population (here, we sort all individuals according to their fitness values, and obtain two equinumerous subsets of better- and less-fitted individuals), and use it to perform education over the feature subsets (with the same parameterization as for T'). Each component of the child solution is finally mutated with probability P_m, P_t, and P_f ($\mathcal{M}$, T', and F', respectively). For the SVM model, we randomly select each hyperparameter value M_i from $M_i [M_i - u \cdot M_i, M_i + u \cdot M_i]$, where u is drawn from $[0.0, 0.1]$. For T' and F', we replace $f_t \cdot |T'|$ and $f_f \cdot |F'|$ random training vectors and features with those sampled from T and from the subset of all most informative features (half of all features according to the ranks extracted in the population's initialization step). To further exploit the information about the most promising parts of the solution space captured during the evolution, we generate *super individuals*, being the chromosomes containing random training vectors and features sampled from the SV and feature pools—it contains up to $\min\{|\mathcal{S}|, |T'|\}$ and $\min\{|\mathcal{F}|, |F'|\}$ vectors and features, respectively (for $\mathcal{M}$, we take the parameterization of the best solution in the population).

Once the intermediate population of child solutions is generated, we quantify their fitness over V, and N fittest chromosomes (out of the current population and the offspring solutions) survive to the next generation. Finally, we adaptively increase the size of the refined training and feature sets [25]. The evolution terminates after five re-generations, in which we re-initialize the population (while copying the best current individual)—the re-generations are triggered once the average fitness in the population has not been improved in two iterations.

3   Experimental Setup

In this work, we exploit our framework developed in [7], and implemented in Python 3.8.5 with the PyTorch 1.7 backend. The experiments were executed on a machine equipped with an NVIDIA RTX 3090 GPU (24 GB VRAM). The hyperparameters of SE-SVM were kept unchanged as suggested in [16]. To quantify the performance of the classifiers, we utilized accuracy: Acc $= (TP + TN)/(TP + TN + FN + FP)$, precision: Pr $= TP/(TP + FP)$, recall: Re $= TP/(TP + FN)$, and the F1 score: F1 $= (2 \cdot Pr \cdot Re)/(Pr + Re)$, where TP, FP, TN, and FN denote true positives, false positives, true negatives, and false negatives. Additionally, we report the Matthews correlation coefficient (MCC), since it was shown to be a more reliable metric for imbalanced classification [10]. All metrics are presented for the unseen test set Ψ.

3.1 Selected Deep Architectures and Features

Although our technique is architecture-agnostic, we focused on two families of the state-of-the-art deep learning models that have proved to be successful in various pattern recognition tasks. As feature extractors, we utilize the deep residual neural networks (ResNets) [20] with 50 and 101 layers (ResNet-50 and ResNet-101), together with the VGG networks [32] with 16 and 19 layers (VGG16 and VGG19; here, we exploit the classical models containing 3×3 convolutional kernels stacked in convolutional layers together with max pooling). For ResNets, we can observe that the number of layers may be substantially increased when compared to e.g., VGG networks, as skip connections allow us to perform efficient training in this context. For the ResNets, we extract the features after the final global pooling layer which constitute the input to its fully-connected part (2048 features), whereas for VGGs, we have 4096 features extracted analogously (i.e., those that are imputed to the classification part of the model).

Table 1. The datasets used for experiments. We present the number of COVID-19 and non-COVID-19 examples utilized from each set.

ID	Dataset	$\mathcal{C}$	COVID-19	non-COVID-19†
1	COVID-chestxray [12]	3	475	209
2	actualmed-COVID-chestxray [39]	2	58	127
3	figure1-COVID-chestxray [39]	3	33	5
4	bimcv-COVID-19-nega [22]	2	—	4535
5	padchest [8]	2	—	2589
6	bimcv-COVID-19-posi [22]	1	9171	—
7	tcia-COVID-19 [15]	1	251	—
8	COVID-19-radiography [11]	1	66	—
9	chexpert [23]	2	—	2589
		Total:	10054	10054

†For three-class sets, we merge healthy patients and those with other diseases.

3.2   COVID-19 Datasets

We approach the binary classification of COVID-19 and non-COVID-19 patients according to their X-ray images. There exist several image datasets in the literature that can be utilized for verifying the classification abilities of the supervised models in this context, and they are both two-class (COVID-19 vs. non-COVID-19 cases) and three-class (COVID-19, other diseases, and healthy patients) sets. Also, there are datasets that encompass COVID-19 X-ray images only. Overall, we include all of them in our experiments after the following pre-processing—we remove clearly incorrect X-ray images from each dataset, e.g., presenting different body areas, and group the scans according to their radiological view and negative/positive mode (the former were flipped to the positive mode) [7].

The three-class datasets are transformed into two-class ones by merging the non-COVID-19 and healthy classes into a single class. In Table 1, we gather the dataset characteristics after the merging step, and we also report the original number of classes ($\mathcal{C}$), together with the number of X-ray images after cleaning. In Fig. 5, in which we collect a set of example X-ray images, we can appreciate that the scans included in the corresponding datasets may not be trivial to interpret, even by a human reader [7], are of varying quality, and may include image artifacts that could influence the classification process. Finally, the images are split into the training T, validation V, and test Ψ sets (20%, 5%, and 75% images) with stratification, in order to keep the same contribution of each set across all subsets, and each experiment is repeated five times over the very same training/validation/test split. The images are normalized to fit the mean and standard deviation of ImageNet [14]. In this experimental study, we precisely follow the experimental procedure presented in our earlier work [7].

4   Experimental Results

In Table 2, we present the experimental results (over the test sets Ψ) obtained using all investigated deep architectures elaborated in the full training strategy, and following the transfer learning-based approach. In the former technique, the models were trained over the COVID-19 training data, and we kept either original classifier on top of the deep feature extractors, being the fully-connected (FC) model, or substituted it with our SE-SVM. In the transfer learning-based strategy, the feature extractors were pre-trained over ImageNet. Then, the FC classifier was fine-tuned over our T (in TL), or we utilize SE-SVM instead of it. We can observe that our evolutionary approach outperforms the FC (original) classifier in almost all metrics which indicates that the memetic algorithm effectively selects feature and training set subsets, ultimately allowing us to build well-generalizing classifiers in both full training and transfer learning-based approaches. Also, SE-SVM may offer significant reductions in the model's complexity. Although for ResNets the number of trainable parameters in the

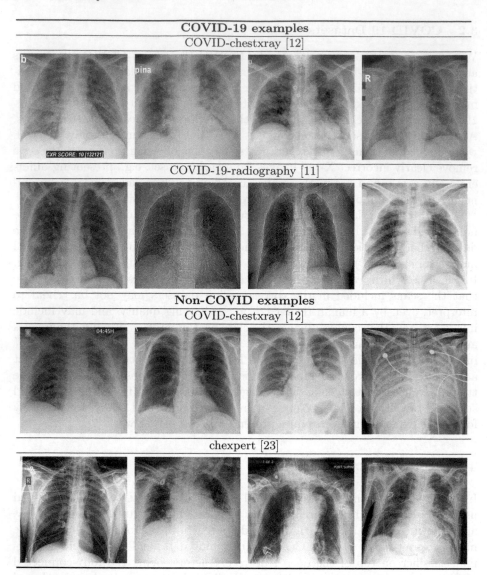

Fig. 5. Example X-ray images from the investigated datasets manifest high heterogeneity, are challenging to interpret, and are of varying quality (see e.g., visible textual artifacts in the first, third, and in the fourth rows).

classification part equals approx. $5 \cdot 10^3$ (these parameters are fine-tuned in the TL approach over the target COVID-19 training data), for VGGs we have up to $1.3 \cdot 10^6$ trainable parameters—the mean number of SVs for the evolved SVMs with the VGG backbones amounted to 3164.6 and 2876 for VGG16 and VGG19, respectively. This may open new doors for deploying such classification techniques in memory-constrained execution environments [5], especially given that the accuracy of the models were further improved. Note that we should confront the best model out of five evolved SVMs with the deep networks that underwent the end-to-end training in this context. In practical scenarios, we can execute multiple (perhaps parallel) evolutions to elaborate the final SVMs.

Table 2. The results (Acc, F1, MCC) obtained for each deep model trained in *i*) the **full training** strategy with the fully-connected classifier (FC), and with our simultaneously-evolved SVMs (mean and max), and *ii*) in the transfer learning-based (TL) approach. In the latter, we report the results obtained using the deep models pre-trained over ImageNet with their classification part fine-tuned over COVID-19 training data (TL), and obtained using the proposed fusing scheme, where SE-SVM is evolved on top of deep features extracted using the corresponding architectures trained over ImageNet (Fusion). The best results for both **full training** and **transfer learning-based approaches** are bold.

Full training			Transfer learning-based approach									
	Acc		Alg	Acc			F1			MCC		
Model	FC	Mean	Max		mean	Max	Std	Mean	Max	std	Mean	Max	Std
RN-50	**0.806**	0.803	0.804	TL	0.726	0.746	**0.014**	0.727	**0.760**	0.027	0.457	0.492	**0.024**
				SE-SVM	**0.742**	**0.770**	0.021	**0.731**	**0.760**	0.021	**0.486**	**0.542**	0.042
RN-101	0.792	0.800	**0.801**	TL	0.724	0.742	0.029	0.729	0.762	**0.022**	0.455	0.487	0.044
				SE-SVM	**0.761**	**0.773**	**0.019**	**0.751**	**0.767**	0.024	**0.523**	**0.547**	**0.037**
VGG16	0.791	0.796	**0.797**	TL	0.759	0.774	0.012	0.757	**0.788**	0.025	0.524	0.550	0.016
				SE-SVM	**0.772**	**0.782**	**0.006**	**0.764**	0.775	**0.009**	**0.545**	**0.566**	**0.011**
VGG19	0.779	0.794	**0.795**	TL	0.758	**0.776**	0.014	0.751	**0.789**	0.034	0.524	**0.553**	0.020
				SE-SVM	**0.765**	0.768	**0.002**	**0.758**	0.766	**0.007**	**0.532**	0.537	**0.004**

The pair-wise analysis of the precision-recall curves rendered in Fig. 6 indicates that fusing deep feature extractors with memetically-evolved SVMs virtually always leads to improving the mean and maximum precision of the classifier when compared to the TL approach (out of five independent executions). Although there are cases where recall was decreased for the proposed method (e.g., the mean recall for ResNet-50), the aggregated metrics in Table 2 show that TL fails to provide high-quality classification. Therefore, the simultaneously-evolved SVMs operating on the deep features extracted using ResNets and VGGs architectures not only allow us to reduce the complexity of the classification pipeline, but enable us to improve the classification performance of the originally-crafted deep learning models.

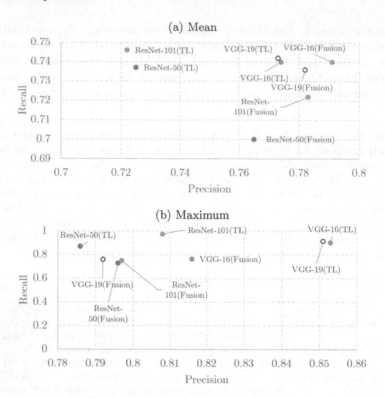

Fig. 6. The precision-recall curves for the (a) mean and (b) maximum precision-recall values obtained for each deep model trained in the transfer learning (TL) approach, and obtained using the proposed fusing scheme, where SE-SVM is evolved on top of deep features extracted using the corresponding architectures. The dots rendered in the same color correspond to the same deep learning architecture trained either in the TL strategy, or serving as a feature extraction backbone for the simultaneously-evolved SVMs. (Color figure online)

5   Conclusions and Future Work

In this work, we introduced a classification framework that combines deep learning feature extractors with evolutionarily-optimized SVMs, in order to benefit from the advantages of both approaches. Our technique is model-agnostic, and can be easily utilized to extract deep features using state-of-the-art architectures in both full training and transfer learning-based approaches. To verify the capabilities of the framework, and to confront it with the deep models trained in the end-to-end fashion and following the transfer learning approach, we tackled the problem of classifying X-ray images into the COVID-19 and non-COVID-19 cases. The experiments showed that our approach is able to outperform the models pre-trained over ImageNet, with their classification heads fine-tuned over target COVID-19 training data, and deliver significant decrease in the pipeline's complexity. Similarly, our algorithm delivered notable improvements in the hand-crafted state-of-the-art models topped with the fully-connected classifiers and learned in the end-to-end fashion over the COVID-19 training data.

Although we focused on extracting the deep features that are directly fed to the classification part of the models, the proposed technique can be used for elaborating deep features at different depths of the architecture. Utilizing such features constitutes an interesting research pathway that could be followed based on the insights of the work reported here. Finally, our current efforts are focused on deploying the pipeline for other "difficult" (i.e., highly-dimensional and not necessarily representative) data, especially for hyperspectral image analysis, and on investigating the generalization capabilities of the approach in such tasks.

References

1. Aladeemy, M., Tutun, S., Khasawneh, M.T.: A new hybrid approach for feature selection and support vector machine model selection based on self-adaptive cohort intelligence. Expert Syst. Appl. **88**, 118–131 (2017)
2. Amancio, D.R., et al.: A systematic comparison of supervised classifiers. PLoS ONE **9**(4), e94137 (2014)
3. Anaby-Tavor, A., et al.: Do not have enough data? Deep learning to the rescue! In: Proceedings of AAAI Conference on Artificial Intelligence, vol. 34, pp. 7383–7390 (2020)
4. Boccaletti, S., Ditto, W., Mindlin, G., Atangana, A.: Modeling and forecasting of epidemic spreading: the case of COVID-19 and beyond. Chaos, Solitons Fractals **135**, 109794 (2020)
5. Bolhasani, H., Mohseni, M., Rahmani, A.M.: Deep learning applications for IoT in healthcare: a systematic review. Inform. Med. Unlock. **23**, 100550 (2021)
6. Borakati, A., Perera, A., Johnson, J., Sood, T.: Diagnostic accuracy of X-ray versus CT in COVID-19: a propensity-matched database study. BMJ Open. **10**(11), e042946 (2020)
7. Bosowski, P., Bosowska, J., Nalepa, J.: Evolving deep ensembles for detecting COVID-19 In Chest X-Rays. In: Proceedings of IEEE ICIP, pp. 3772–3776 (2021)
8. Bustos, A., Pertusa, A., Salinas, J.M., de la Iglesia-Vayá, M.: PadChest: a large chest x-ray image dataset with multi-label annotated reports. Med. Image Anal. **66**, 101797 (2020)
9. Chandra, T.B., Verma, K., Singh, B.K., Jain, D., Netam, S.S.: Coronavirus disease (COVID-19) detection in Chest X-Ray images using majority voting based classifier ensemble. Expert Syst. Appl. **165**, 113909 (2021)
10. Chicco, D., Jurman, G.: The advantages of the Matthews correlation coefficient (MCC) over F1 score and accuracy in binary classification evaluation. BMC Genom. **21**(1), 6 (2020)
11. Chowdhury, M.E.H., et al.: Can AI help in screening viral and COVID-19 pneumonia? IEEE Access **8**, 132665–132676 (2020)
12. Cohen, J.P., Morrison, P., Dao, L., Roth, K., Duong, T.Q., Ghassemi, M.: COVID-19 Image Data Collection: Prospective Predictions Are the Future. arXiv 2006.11988 (2020). https://github.com/ieee8023/covid-chestxray-dataset
13. Cortes, C., Vapnik, V.: Support-vector networks. Mach. Learn. **20**(3), 273–297 (1995)
14. Deng, J., Dong, W., Socher, R., Li, L., Li, K., Fei-Fei, L.: ImageNet: a large-scale hierarchical image database. In: Proceedings of IEEE CVPR, pp. 248–255 (2009)

15. Desai, S., et al.: Chest imaging representing a COVID-19 positive rural U.S. population. Sci. Data. **7**(1), 414 (2020)
16. Dudzik, W., Kawulok, M., Nalepa, J.: Optimizing training data and hyperparameters of support vector machines using a memetic algorithm. In: Proceeding of ICMMI, pp. 229–238 (2019)
17. Dudzik, W., Nalepa, J., Kawulok, M.: Evolving data-adaptive support vector machines for binary classification. Knowl. Based Syst. **227**, 107221 (2021)
18. Girshick, R.: Fast R-CNN. In: Proceedings of IEEE ICCV, pp. 1440–1448 (2015)
19. Girshick, R., Donahue, J., Darrell, T., Malik, J.: Rich feature hierarchies for accurate object detection and semantic segmentation. In: Proceedings of IEEE CVPR, pp. 580–587 (2014)
20. He, K., Zhang, X., Ren, S., Sun, J.: Deep Residual Learning for Image Recognition. arXiv e-prints arXiv:1512.03385, December 2015
21. Huh, M., Agrawal, P., Efros, A.A.: What makes ImageNet good for transfer learning? arXiv preprint arXiv:1608.08614 (2016)
22. Iglesia la de Vayá, M., et al.: BIMCV COVID-19+: a large annotated dataset of RX and CT images from COVID-19 patients. arXiv e-prints arXiv:2006.01174 (2020)
23. Irvin, J., et al.: CheXpert: A Large Chest Radiograph Dataset with Uncertainty Labels and Expert Comparison. arXiv e-prints arXiv:1901.07031, January 2019
24. Kawulok, M., Nalepa, J.: Towards robust SVM training from weakly labeled large data sets. In: Proceedings of IAPR ACPR, pp. 464–468 (2015)
25. Kawulok, M., Nalepa, J.: Dynamically adaptive genetic algorithm to select training data for SVMs. In: Bazzan, A.L.C., Pichara, K. (eds.) IBERAMIA 2014. LNCS (LNAI), vol. 8864, pp. 242–254. Springer, Cham (2014). https://doi.org/10.1007/978-3-319-12027-0_20
26. Kiran, B.R., Thomas, D.M., Parakkal, R.: An overview of deep learning based methods for unsupervised and semi-supervised anomaly detection in videos. J. Imaging **4**(2), 36 (2018)
27. Le, Q.V., Sarlós, T., Smola, A.J.: FastFood: approximate kernel expansions in loglinear time. CoRR abs/1408.3060, pp. 1–8 (2014)
28. Melin, P., Monica, J.C., Sanchez, D., Castillo, O.: Multiple ensemble neural network models with fuzzy response aggregation for predicting COVID-19 time series: the case of Mexico. Healthcare **8**(2), 181 (2020)
29. Nalepa, J., Kawulok, M.: Selecting training sets for support vector machines: a review. Artif. Intell. Rev. **52**(2), 857–900 (2019)
30. Pan, S.J., Yang, Q.: A survey on transfer learning. IEEE Trans. Knowl. Data Eng. **22**(10), 1345–1359 (2009)
31. Ravi, A., Venugopal, H., Paul, S., Tizhoosh, H.R.: A dataset and preliminary results for umpire pose detection using SVM classification of deep features. In: Proceedings of IEEE SSCI, pp. 1396–1402. IEEE (2018)
32. Simonyan, K., Zisserman, A.: Very Deep Convolutional Networks for Large-Scale Image Recognition. arXiv e-prints arXiv:1409.1556, September 2014
33. Solorio-Fernández, S., Carrasco-Ochoa, J.A., Martínez-Trinidad, J.F.: A review of unsupervised feature selection methods. Artif. Intell. Rev. **53**(2), 907–948 (2020)
34. Sun, T., Wang, Y.: Modeling COVID-19 epidemic in Heilongjiang province, China. Chaos, Solitons Fractals **138**, 109949 (2020)
35. Tang, Y.: Deep learning using linear support vector machines. In: Proceedings of Workshop on Challenges in Representation Learning, ICML 2013 (2013)
36. Tulczyjew, L., Kawulok, M., Nalepa, J.: Unsupervised feature learning using recurrent neural nets for segmenting hyperspectral images. IEEE Geosci. Remote Sens. Lett. **18**(12), 2142–2146 (2021)

37. Varela-Santos, S., Melin, P.: A new approach for classifying coronavirus COVID-19 based on its manifestation on chest X-rays using texture features and neural networks. Inf. Sci. **545**, 403–414 (2021)
38. Wang, D., Mo, J., Zhou, G., Xu, L., Liu, Y.: An efficient mixture of deep and machine learning models for COVID-19 diagnosis in chest X-ray images. PLoS ONE **15**(11), 1–15 (2020)
39. Wang, L., Wong, A., Lin, Z.Q., McInnis, P., Chung, A., Gunraj, H.: Actualmed-COVID-chestxray-dataset. https://github.com/agchung

Image-Based Contextual Pill Recognition with Medical Knowledge Graph Assistance

Anh Duy Nguyen[1], Thuy Dung Nguyen[1], Huy Hieu Pham[2,3], Thanh Hung Nguyen[1], and Phi Le Nguyen[1(✉)]

[1] Hanoi University of Science and Technology, Hanoi, Vietnam
lenp@soict.hust.edu.vn
[2] College of Engineering and Computer Science, VinUniversity, Hanoi, Vietnam
[3] VinUni-Illinois Smart Health Center, VinUniversity, Hanoi, Vietnam

Abstract. In many healthcare applications, identifying pills given their captured images under various conditions and backgrounds has been becoming more and more essential. Several efforts have been devoted to utilizing the deep learning-based approach to tackle the pill recognition problem in the literature. However, due to the high similarity between pills' appearance, misrecognition often occurs, leaving pill recognition a challenge. To this end, in this paper, we introduce a novel approach named PIKA that leverages external knowledge to enhance pill recognition accuracy. Specifically, we address a practical scenario (which we call contextual pill recognition), aiming to identify pills in a picture of a patient's pill intake. Firstly, we propose a novel method for modeling the implicit association between pills in the presence of an external data source, in this case, prescriptions. Secondly, we present a walk-based graph embedding model that transforms from the graph space to vector space and extracts condensed relational features of the pills. Thirdly, a final framework is provided that leverages both image-based visual and graph-based relational features to accomplish the pill identification task. Within this framework, the visual representation of each pill is mapped to the graph embedding space, which is then used to execute *attention* over the graph representation, resulting in a semantically-rich context vector that aids in the final classification. To our knowledge, this is the first study to use external prescription data to establish associations between medicines and to classify them using this aiding information. The architecture of PIKA is lightweight and has the flexibility to incorporate into any recognition backbones. The experimental results show that by leveraging the external knowledge graph, PIKA can improve the recognition accuracy from 4.8% to 34.1% in terms of *F1*-score, compared to baselines.

Keywords: Pill recognition · Knowledge graph · Graph embedding

1 Introduction

Medicines are used to cure diseases and improve patients' health. Medication mistakes, however, may have serious consequences, including diminishing the efficacy of the treatment, causing adverse effects, or even leading to death. According

© The Author(s), under exclusive license to Springer Nature Singapore Pte Ltd. 2022
E. Szczerbicki et al. (Eds.): ACIIDS 2022, CCIS 1716, pp. 354–369, 2022.
https://doi.org/10.1007/978-981-19-8234-7_28

Groundtruth: Myonal_50mg   Ayale   Betaserc_16mg

Prediction: Betaserc_16mg Myonal_50mg   Ayale

Fig. 1. Ill-predicted medicines

to a WHO report, one-third of all mortality is caused by the misuse of drugs, not by disease [2]. Moreover, according to Yaniv *et al.* [20], medication errors claim the lives of about six to eight thousand people every year. To emphasize the significance of taking medication correctly, WHO has chosen the subject Medication Without Harm for World Patient Safety Day 2022 [1].

Medication errors may fall into many categories, one of which is incorrect pill intake, which occurs when the drugs taken differ from the prescription. This is due to the difficulty in manually distinguishing pills owing to the wide variety of drugs and similarities in pill colors and shapes. In such a context, many attempts have been made to assist users in identifying the pills automatically. In recent years, machine learning (ML) has emerged as a viable technique for tackling object classification problems. Many studies have employed machine learning in the pill recognition challenge [3,15,19]. Some common techniques such as convolutional neural networks (CNN) and Graph Neural Networks (GNN) are often used. For instance, in [19], the authors exploited Deep Convolution Network to identify pills. In [15], Enhanced Feature Pyramid Networks (EFPNs) and Global Convolution Network (GCN) are combined to enhance the pill localization accuracy. Besides, the authors leveraged the Xception network [4] to solve the pill recognition problem. The authors in [3] studied how to help visually impaired chronic patients in taking their medications correctly. To this end, they proposed a so-called MedGlasses system, which combines AI and IoT. MedGlasses comprises smart glasses capable of recognizing pills, a smartphone app capable of reading medication information from a QR code and reminding users to take the medication, and a server system to store user information. Furthermore, numerous efforts have strived to improve pill recognition accuracy by incorporating handcrafted features such as color, shape, and imprint. Ling et al. [9] investigated the problem of few-shot pill detection. The authors proposed a Multi-Stream (MS) deep learning model that combines information from four streams: RGB, Texture, Contour, and Imprinted Text. In addition, they offered a two-stage training technique to solve the data scarcity constraint; the first stage is to train with all samples, while the second concentrates only on the hard examples. In [12], the authors integrated three handcrafted features, namely shape, color, and imprinted text, to identify pills. Specifically, the authors first used statistical measurements from the pill's histogram to estimate the number of colors in the pill. The imprinted text on the pill was then extracted using text recognition tools. The author also used the decision tree technique to determine the pill shape. The color, shape, and imprinted text information are then used as input features to train the classification model.

Despite numerous efforts, pill recognition remains problematic. Especially, pill misidentification often occurs with tablets that look substantially similar. Figure 1 shows some of the misclassification results made by a deep learning model. To overcome the limitations of existing approaches, in this study, we propose a novel method that leverages external knowledge to increase the accuracy and, in particular, to tackle the misclassification of similar pills. Unlike the existing works, we focus on a practical application that recognizes pills in the patient's pill intake picture. The external knowledge we use is the information extracted from a given set of prescriptions. Our main idea is that by using such external knowledge, we can learn the relationship between the drugs, such as the co-occurrence likelihood of the pills. This knowledge will be utilized to improve the pill recognition model's accuracy.

To summarize, our main contributions are as follows:

- We are the first to address a so-called *contextual pill recognition* problem, which recognizes pills in a picture of a patient's pill intake.
- We build a dataset containing pill images taken in unconstraint conditions and a corresponding prescription collection.
- We propose a novel deep learning-based approach to solve the contextual pill recognition problem. Specifically, we design a method to construct a prescription-based knowledge graph representing the relationship between pills. We then present a graph embedding network to extract pills' relational features. Finally, we design a framework to fuse the graph-based relational information with the image-based visual features to make the final classification decision.
- We design loss functions and a training strategy to enhance the classification accuracy.
- We conduct thorough experiments on a dataset of drugs taken in real-world settings and compare the performance of the proposed solution to existing methods. The experimental findings indicate that our proposed model outperforms significantly the baselines.

The remainder of the paper is organized as follows. We introduce the related works in Sect. 2. Section 3 describes our proposed solution. We evaluate the effectiveness of the proposed approach in Sect. 4 and conclude the paper in Sect. 5. Our code and pre-trained deep learning models will be made publicly available on our project webpage (http://vaipe.io/) upon the publication of this paper.

2   Related Work

The contextual pill recognition can be treated as a traditional object identification problem. The conventional approach is to divide it into two stages. The first stage is responsible for segmenting each pill image, and the second one treats each pill box as a separate object and identifies it using an object recognition model. In [19], the authors employed Deep Convolution Network, Feature Pyramid Networks (EFPNs), combined with GCN for pill detection. They then used the Xception network to identify the pill. Ling et al. [9] studied the issue of pill identification with a limited number of samples. To improve identification accuracy, the author incorporated data from numerous sources, including RGB, Texture, Contour, and Imprinted Text. Hand-crafted features such as shape, color, and imprinted text were also used in the [12]. The shortcoming of these approaches is that they handle each pill in the picture separately, without taking use of the pill's interaction.

Contextual pill identification is analogous to the multi-label classification problem, which has drawn a lot of attention in recent years. Many research has employed external information to improve recognition accuracy in this problem. The most common strategy is to obtain the label co-occurrence relationship and use it in the recognition task. Label co-occurrence may be retrieved using a variety of approaches, including probabilistic models, neural networks, and graph networks. Li et al. employed conditional graphical Lasso model in [8] to statistically calculate the co-occurrence probability of the labels. Several works have adopted neural networks such as LSTM to simulate the interaction of labels to decrease the computation costs [16]. The author of [5] used the autoencoder Graph Isomorphism Network (GIN) to represent the label association. They also presented a collaborative training framework incorporating label semantic encoding and label-specific feature extraction. There are also several techniques to utilize relational information. Relational information, in particular, may be combined with visual characteristics in the final layers, as shown in [18]. It may also be injected into the middle CNN layers through lateral connections, as described in [17].

Contextual pill identification, on the other hand, differs from traditional multi-label classification in that the multi-label classification task tries to recognize the global information offered by the picture rather than finding and recognizing each item featured in the image. The second problem lies in modeling the label's relation. Indeed, traditional multi-label classification systems mainly construct label relationships based on the semantic meaning of the label's name. This strategy, however, does not work with medicine names since they often have no meaning. Furthermore, extracting correlations between medicine names from public data sources is difficult.

3   Proposed Approach

In this section we propose a novel pill recognition framework named PIKA (which stands for **P**ill **I**dentification with medical **K**nowledge gr**A**ph). We first present the main components of the PIKA framework (Sect. 3.1). We then describe how the prescription-based medical knowledge graph is built (Sect. 3.2) and explain how pill visual features are extracted (Sect. 3.3). Next, we combine the built medical knowledge graph and extracted visual features to enhance pill identification performance (Sect. 3.4). Finally, we introduce an auxiliary loss and a training strategy to improve the effectiveness of the proposed learning model (Sect. 3.5).

3.1 Overview

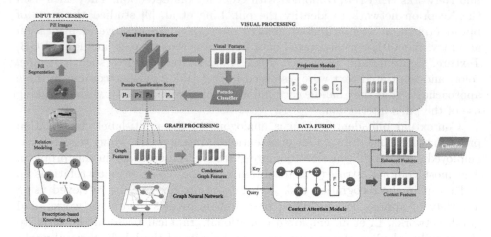

Fig. 2. Overview of the Proposed Framework. Firstly, the Input Processing Procedure is used to generate a non-directed Medical Knowledge Graph (MKG) $\mathcal{G} = <\mathcal{V}, \mathcal{E}, \mathcal{W}>$ from given prescriptions, and crop the input images into pill boxes. Secondly, the MKG is fed into a Graph embedding network to extract pills' relational features, while the cropped pill images are passed via a backbone network to retrieve its visual representations. At this stage, the graph-based relational features are combined with the pseudo-class scores produced by the visual backbone to make up its condensed version. Thirdly, the visual embedding get projected to the same hyper-plane as their counterparts in the graph space, with the aid of the Projection Module. Following, the projected visual features, coupled with graph-based relational information, are the input for the Context Attention Module to provide the context vector. Finally, the enriched visual features, which combine the context vector and the visual features, are fed into the final classifier to identify the pill.

As illustrated in Fig. 2, the proposed model comprises four major components: input processing, visual processing, graph processing, and information fusion. The first block, i.e., input processing, is in charge of locating and retrieving pill images and creating a graph modeling drug interactions. The visual processing block is used to extract visual features of the pills, while the graph processing module attempts to depict the relationship between the pills. The fusion layer then combines the visual characteristics of the pills with their graph-based relational features to generate the final classification decision. The overall flow is as follows.

- **Step 1**. The original image containing multiple pills is passed through an object localization model to identify and cut out bounding-box images of every pill. Note that we do not focus on the object detection problem in this work; thus, we can use any object detection model for this step.
- **Step 2**. We construct a graph from a given set of prescriptions, with nodes representing pills and edges reflecting drug linkages. We name this graph

the Prescription-based Medical Knowledge Graph or PMKG for short. The PMKG is then passed through a Graph Neural Network (GNN) to yield embedding vectors. Each embedding vector conveys information about a node and its relationship to the neighbors. The detailed algorithm is presented in Sect. 3.2.

- **Step 3**. The pills' images will then be put into the Visual processing module to extract the visual characteristic. On the one hand, these features will be fed into the data fusion block to make the classification decision. On the other hand, these features are put in a projection module. The objective of the projection module is to generate a representation similar to that of the graph processing block. The projected features are then utilized to learn the relationship between the pill images and the PMKG's nodes. The detail of the visual processing module will be described in Sect. 3.3.
- **Step 4**. The Graph embedding vector retrieved in Step 2 and the projected features acquired in Step 3 will be passed through an attention layer to generate a context vector. Finally, the context vector will be concatenated with the Visual feature before being fed into the final classifier, which will produce prediction results. The details of our losses functions are presented in Sect. 3.5.

3.2 Prescription-Based Medical Knowledge Graph

The key idea behind the proposed approach is to utilize the information on the relationship between pills via their corresponding prescriptions to enhance image-based pill recognition. To this end, a prescription-based medical knowledge graph is constructed. Our intuition is that all the medicines are prescribed to cure or alleviate some diseases or symptoms in actual pill captures. Hence, we can formulate that implicit relation through the direct relations between pills and diagnoses. This information contains in the prescriptions provided by pharmacists to their patients. This section covers our detailed methodology for knowledge graph modeling and our framework for embedding this graph.

Knowledge Graph Modelling. The Medical Knowledge Graph (MKG) is a weighted graph, denoted as $\mathcal{G} = <\mathcal{V}, \mathcal{E}, \mathcal{W}>$, whose vertices $\mathcal{V}$ represent pill classes, and the weights $\mathcal{W}$ indicate the relationship between the pills. With prescriptions as the initial data, two factors can be used to formulate graph edges $\mathcal{E}$, which are diagnoses and medications. As the relationship between pills is not explicitly presented in prescriptions, we model the relation representing the edge between two nodes (i.e., pill classes) C_i and C_j based on the following criteria.

- There is an edge between two pill classes C_i and C_j if and only if they have been prescribed for at least one shared diagnosis.
- The weight of an edge E_{ij} connecting pill classes C_i and C_j reflects the likelihood that these two medications will be given at the same time.

Instead of directly weighting the `Pill-Pill` edges, we determine the weights via `Diagnose-Pill` relation. In particular, we first define a so-called `Diagnose-Pill` impact factor, which reflects how important a pill is to a diagnosis or, in other words, how often a pill is prescribed to cure a diagnosis. Inspired by the Term Frequency (`tf`) – Inverse Dense Frequency (`idf`) often used in NLP domain, we define the impact factor of a pill P_j to a diagnose D_i (denoted as $\mathcal{I}(P_j, D_i)$) as follows.

$$\mathcal{I}(P_j, D_i) = \mathtt{tf}(D_j, P_i) \times \mathtt{idf}(P_i) = \frac{|\mathbb{S}(D_j, P_i)|}{|\mathbb{S}(D_j)|} \times \log \frac{|\mathbb{S}|}{|\mathbb{S}(P_i)|}, \tag{1}$$

where $\mathbb{S}$ represents the set of all prescriptions, $\mathbb{S}(D_j, P_i)$ depicts the collection of prescriptions containing both D_j and P_i, and $\mathbb{S}(D_j)$ illustrates the set of prescriptions containing D_j. After calculating the impact factors of the pills and diagnoses, we derive the weights between two pills by averaging their impact factors against all diagnoses, as shown below

$$\mathcal{W}(P_i, P_j) = \sum_{D \in \mathbb{D}} \mathcal{I}(P_i, D) + \mathcal{I}(P_j, D), \tag{2}$$

where $\mathcal{W}(P_i, P_j)$ depicts the weight between pills P_i, P_j, and $\mathbb{D}$ denotes the set of all diagnoses.

Knowledge Graph Embedding. As the MKG is sparse, we will not utilize it directly but pass it through a graph embedding module to extract the condensed meaningful information. Specifically, the graph embedding module helps project from the graph space into a vector space. Each vector corresponds to a node (i.e., a pill class) and conveys information about that node and its relationships with the neighbors. With the graph embedding module, we want to preserve the co-occurrence property of the pills, i.e., if two nodes V_i, V_j are neighbors in the original MKG, their corresponding presentations u_i and u_j should also have small distance in the vector space. To this end, we leverage the walk-based approach, which will train a graph embedding network using the skip-gram model with the following loss function

$$\mathcal{L}_g = -\sum_{i=1}^{n} \left[\sum_{u_j \in \mathbb{N}(u_i)} \sigma(u_i \cdot u_j) - \sum_{u_k \notin \mathbb{N}(u_i)} \log\left(e^{u_k \cdot u_i}\right) \right], \tag{3}$$

where n denotes the total number of nodes in the graph, u_i represents the embedding vector of node V_i, and $\mathbb{N}(u_i)$ depicts the set of V_i's 1-hop neighbors. By minimizing $\mathcal{L}_g$, we can reduce the distance between representations of neighboring nodes while increasing that of non-neighboring nodes.

3.3   Visual Processing Procedure

The Visual Processing block is responsible for retrieving two types of information. The former refers to the visual characteristics of individual pill images;

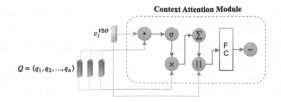

Fig. 3. Illustration of the Context Attention Module

meanwhile, the latter relates to the relational feature that represents the interaction between pills. We employ a conventional Convolutional neural networks such as VGG [14] or ResNet [6] to extract the visual features. Concerning the relational features, our idea is to distill knowledge from MKG into the representation of each pill using a projection layer. Besides, the Visual Processing block also contains a pseudo classifier module that helps to provide rough classification results. These results are then used to filter out condensed information from MKG (the details will be presented in Sect. 3.4).

V2G Projection Layer. The V2G projection layer obtains a pill's visual feature vector as the input. It passes through several layers to generate a representation with the same dimension as the MKG's node embedding vector. This layer can be mathematically represented as $v_i^{V2G} = \theta(v_i)$, where v_i and v_i^{V2G} are the representations in the visual and graph spaces, respectively; and $\theta(\cdot) : V \rightarrow U$ is a non-linear mapping. In the implementation, we formulate this mapping as a stack of Fully Connected (FC) layers, with $tanh$ as the middle activation function. Through the training processing, the $\theta(\cdot)$ will be optimized so that the probability distribution of the projected vectors is similar to that of the MKG's embedding vectors. This is accomplished by introducing the Linkage loss as described in Sect. 3.5.

Pseudo Classification Layer. The pseudo classifier produces temporary identification results. This rough classification result will be used as a filter layer responsible for extracting from the MKG only information related to the pills in the image (and omitting information from the nodes that are not associated with the pills in the picture). In our implementation, pseudo classification is currently implemented as a fully connected layer.

3.4 Data Fusion

In the Data Fusion block, we first extract the condensed information from the MKG and integrate it with the visual features using an attention mechanism to create the context feature. The context feature are then concatenated with the visual features before being fed into the final classification layer to make the final decision.

Condensed Relational Feature Extraction. The idea of the Condensed Feature Extraction module is to extract from the MKG only information related to the pills in the input image. Let N be the number of pill classes and M be the number of pills in the input image. Suppose $P = [p_{ij}]_{M \times N}$ is the matrix whose row vectors represent the logits produced by the pseudo classifier, and $U = [u_{kl}]_{N \times H}$ denotes the embedding matrix, whose each row represents a pill class' embedding vector. The condensed relational features, denoted as $\mathcal{R}$ is a set of M vectors, each depicts the condensed relational information of a pill (in the input image), extracted from the MKG. $\mathcal{R}$ is calculated by multiplying the softmax of P to U as follows.

$$\mathcal{R} = \sigma(P) \cdot U. \tag{4}$$

Here the symbol σ denotes the `Softmax` activation function. Intuitively, $\mathcal{R}$ is a matrix consisting of M rows. The i-th row of $\mathcal{R}$ is a weighted sum of all the MKG's node embeddings, whose weights are the classification probabilities corresponding to the i-th pill in the input image.

Attention Module. To avoid misclassification and improve the model's accuracy, besides the pure visual information extracted by the visual extractor described in Sect. 3.3, we leverage the attention mechanism to create a context vector that integrates both visual and relational features. The details of the attention module are illustrated in Fig. 3. Specifically, we use the projected features (i.e., produced by the Visual Projection module) as the key and value, and the graph embedding vectors as the query. The attention module first calculates the attention weights as the similarity of each projected feature to all the graph embedding vectors. The final context vector is then generated by taking the weighted sum of the projected features. The context vector is then fused with the visual features and passed to the final classifier.

3.5   Loss Functions

With additional modules for different purposes mentioned above, we also provide auxiliary losses for aiding the optimization process of the modules. This section is dedicated for presenting those losses.

Classification Loss. Our first objective function is the classification loss, which is composed of two terms. The first term's functionality is to bring the final output of PIKA's Classifier close to the actual result. The following one deal with the output of the Pseudo Classification layer. It is expected to produce the result that is best closed to ground truth also. Since we are dealing with multi-label problems, cross-entropy is used.

$$\mathcal{L}_c = -\frac{1}{N} \sum_{i=1}^{N} y_i \cdot \log(\tilde{y}_i) - \beta_{\text{loose}} * \frac{1}{N} \sum_{i=1}^{N} y_i \cdot \log(p_i), \tag{5}$$

where y_i denotes the one-hot vector - the ground truth of the i- pill, $\tilde{y}_i$ and p_i represent the Classifier's and the Pseudo Classifier's outputs, respectively. In the formula, there is an additional parameter β_{loose} ($0 \leq \beta_{\text{loose}} \leq 1$), which helps loosing the constraints for the Pseudo Classifier. The closer β_{loose} approaches 1, the more we expect that the output of Pseudo Classifier is similar to the main one. In our case, it is set as 0.1 for additional flexibility.

Linkage Loss. For the V2G projection layer, we propose an auxiliary loss called linkage loss, helping this module achieve its aim, i.e., mapping from the visual space $\mathcal{V}$ to the graph space $\mathcal{U}$. Let $\mathcal{V}^{V2G}$ be the vector spaces produced by the Projection layer; then, our objective is to bring $\mathcal{V}^{V2G}$ close to the graph space $\mathcal{U}$. To this end, we design the linkage loss as a type of probabilistic distance instead of a point-wise one. We believe it would loosen the constraint while also being robust enough to help the module converge. Let the distributions of $\mathcal{V}^{V2G}$ and $\mathcal{U}$ be modeled by two continuous random variables X, and G respectively. Firstly, we have to model the geometry of the distributions. A common way to accomplish this purpose is to investigate the pairwise interactions between sample points (with an ample number of data samples) [7,11] via the joint probability density of every two data samples. Let u_{ij} and v_{ij} be the joint density probability functions of the i-th and j-th data points of variable X and G, respectively; then u_{ij} and v_{ij} can be modeled using Kernel Density Estimation (KDE) [13] as follows.

$$u_{ij} = u_{i|j}u_j = \frac{1}{N}K\left(\mathbf{g}_i, \mathbf{g}_j; 2\sigma_{\mathcal{U}}^2\right); \quad v_{ij}^{V2G} = v_{i|j}^{V2G}v_j^{V2G} = \frac{1}{N}K\left(\mathbf{x}_i, \mathbf{x}_j; 2\sigma_{\mathcal{V}^{V2G}}^2\right),$$
$$(6)$$

in which $K\left(\cdot, \cdot; 2\sigma^2\right)$ denotes a symmetric kernel function with the width σ; $\mathbf{g}_i, \mathbf{g}_j$ are two data points sampled from the distribution of G, and $\mathbf{x}_i, \mathbf{x}_j$ are two data points sampled from the distribution of X; N is the number of samples. Ideally, we want to minimize the divergence of the joint density probability functions of U and V^{V2G}. However, learning a projection module that can accomplish this purpose is impossible. To alleviate this issue, we choose to replace the joint probability density function with the conditional probability distribution of the samples. Though the divergence of both two functions has the same convergence point (in case the kernel similarities are the same for both distributions), the use of conditional probability can better describe the local regions between data points [11] (expresses the probability of each sample to select each of its neighbors). The conditional probability distributions for the graph and projected visual spaces are defined as follows.

$$u_{i|j} = \frac{K\left(\mathbf{g}_i, \mathbf{g}_j; 2\sigma_{\mathcal{U}}^2\right)}{\sum_{k=1, k\neq j}^{N} K\left(\mathbf{g}_k, \mathbf{g}_j; 2\sigma_{\mathcal{U}}^2\right)}; \quad v_{i|j}^{V2G} = \frac{K\left(\mathbf{x}_i, \mathbf{x}_j; 2\sigma_{V^{V2G}}^2\right)}{\sum_{k=1, k\neq j}^{N} K\left(\mathbf{x}_k, \mathbf{x}_j; 2\sigma_{V^{V2G}}^2\right)}. \quad (7)$$

We use the Cosine Similarity as the kernel. Finally, the divergence metric we chose as our linkage loss function is the Jensen-Shannon (JS) Divergence:

$$\mathcal{L}_l = \frac{1}{2}\sum_{i=1}^{N}\sum_{j=1, i\neq j}^{N}\left[u_{j|i}\log\left(\frac{u_{j|i}}{v_{j|i}^{V2G}}\right) + v_{j|i}^{V2G}\log\left(\frac{v_{j|i}^{V2G}}{u_{j|i}}\right)\right]. \quad (8)$$

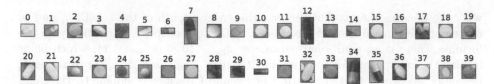

Fig. 4. The visualization of several representative examples from our customized pill dataset.

The total loss comprises of the Classification loss and Linkage loss as follows:

$$\mathcal{L} = \alpha \mathcal{L}_c + (1 - \alpha)\mathcal{L}_l, \text{with } \alpha \in (0, 1). \tag{9}$$

4   Performance Evaluation

In this section we evaluate the performance of our proposed model, PIKA. We perform several experiments on our custom pill images captured with mobile phones under unconstraint environments. Details about the dataset, together with our evaluation metrics and implementation details, would be covered in Subsect. 4.1. The numerical results are then presented in Sect. 4.2 and 4.3.

4.1   Experimental Setup

Dataset. To the best of our knowledge, the dataset of pill images and corresponding prescription set are not publicly available. That is our motivation to build our own dataset for this work. Table 1 describes some important statistics about it. In addition, the collecting and processing procedure is combined by the following steps.

Table 1. Dataset statistics

Images	Classes	Prescriptions	Train set	Test set
3,087	76	168	116 prescriptions 2,058 images	52 prescriptions 1,029 images

- We collect anonymous prescriptions of 168 patients from 4 hospitals in Vietnam. After processing the raw data, we converted them into JSON format for each prescriptions record; the pills are also indexed to form a dictionary, including 76 kinds of drugs.
- Since the process of collecting pills in accordance with prescriptions takes a great effort, time, and funding, in this current work, we have to collect images of 76 type of drugs which is not exactly the types in our collected prescriptions.

- Following, the collected pills are relabeled by our pill dictionary described above and grouped by prescriptions, with the number of images per prescription being 5. Figure 4 illustrates the appearances of collected pills with their mapped labels.
- Finally, we combine the retrieved sets of prescription photos into two sets, one for the training process and one for evaluation.

Evaluation Metrics. For assessing PIKA performance across all used backbones, as well as other testing scenarios, *Recall*, *Precision* and $F1$-score metrics are adopted altogether. The figures claimed in Sect. 4.2 and Sect. 4.3 are the averaged numbers achieved over all classes.

Implementation Details. In our PIKA implementation, the dimensions of the graph embeddings are set as 64. The Projection Module consists of 3 Fully Connected (FC) Layers, with middle *tanh* activation, and the output dimensions are 512, 256, 64 respectively. The optimizer used is AdamW [10], and the initial learning rate is 0.001. β_{loose} (Eq. 5) and α (Eq. 9) are set as 0.1 and 0.9 respectively. During the training process, the input images is resized to 224×224, with random rotation of $10°$ and horizontal flip for augmentation. The batch size is set as 32. For the backbones we fuse our framework with, all are kept the same as in the original papers [6,14], except the last classifier is adopted to output 76 scores in compliant with our 76 classes. All the implementation is performed with the help of *Pytorch* framework, and the training, as well as evaluation processes, are conducted with 2 NVIDIA GeForce RTX 3090 GPUs.

We use a two-step training approach for PIKA. We first train the graph module to convergence with its specified loss (Eq. 3). The converged model output is then utilized to train the rest of the PIKA framework. By doing so, we ensure that the graph embeddings are reliable enough and truly reflect our design intention of making them as references for projected visual vectors.

4.2   Comparison with Baselines

In this section, we will demonstrate the flexibility of PIKA by incorporating it with different backbones, including VGG and RESNET. We also investigate how significantly our proposed approach can improve the recognition accuracy compared to the baselines. The numerical results are presented in Table 2. As shown, PIKA, with all the backbones, enhances the performance by a large gap. Quantitatively, PIKA outperforms all compared SOTA significantly in terms of all metrics. Compared to VGG-16, PIKA improves the Precision, Recall, and $F1$-score by 5.36%, 11.44%, 9.49%, respectively. The performance gaps of PIKA to ResNet(s) are even more significant. Concerning all the settings of ResNet(s), PIKA improves the precision, recall, and $F1$-score by 45.83%, 58.67%, 58.11% on average, respectively. The most significant improvement can be found at ResNet-18, where PIKA improves the Precision, Recall, and $F1$-score by 48.41%, 68.18%, 66.20%, respectively.

Table 2. PIKA performace over different backbones. The best results are highlighted in **bold**.

Backbone		Precision	Recall	*F1*-score
VGG-16 [14]	Baseline	0.58967	0.47236	0.50121
	PIKA (ours)	**0.6213**	**0.5264**	**0.5488**
ResNet-18 [6]	Baseline	0.61020	0.49880	0.51570
	PIKA (ours)	**0.9056**	**0.8389**	**0.8571**
ResNet-34 [6]	Baseline	0.58200	0.49520	0.50870
	PIKA (ours)	**0.8832**	**0.8173**	**0.8315**
ResNet-50 [6]	Baseline	0.59612	0.51142	0.52146
	PIKA (ours)	**0.8664**	**0.7909**	**0.8101**
ResNet-101 [6]	Baseline	0.59120	0.50960	0.51620
	PIKA (ours)	**0.8148**	**0.7482**	**0.7609**

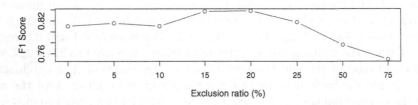

Fig. 5. *F1*-score of PIKA, given the Medical Knowledge Graph with different levels of edge cutting

4.3   Ablation Study

In this section, we first study the impacts of the Medical Knowledge Graph in Sect. 4.3. We then examine the impact of removing modules from the PIKA architecture on overall performance in Sect. 4.3 and 4.3.

Impacts of the Medical Knowledge Graph. When working with a graph, we should ensure that all the information from it is really beneficial for the model performance (containing no noise element). Since we built the Knowledge Graph by information from the set of prescriptions (Sect. 3.2), there are cases in which adding edges between some pills cause potential conflicts. We observe that while most edges have small weights, there are some with very large values. Those with small weights suggest they are potential noise that might hurt overall performance. With that in mind, we carry out an additional experiment for cutting edges and employ the *F1*-score for evaluation, which is plotted in Fig. 5. We first exclude 5% of edges with the lowest weights and increase the exclusion ratios up to 75%. The experiment results are shown in Fig. 5. As can be observed, some edges actually cause a negative impact on the overall result. The performance reaches its peak when excluding around 20% of edges with low weights and starts degrading afterward.

Table 3. PIKA performace with the Pseudo Classifier removal

Model	Precision	Recall	$F1$-score
ResNet-50 [6]	0.59612	0.51142	0.52146
PIKA	0.86640	0.79090	0.81010
PIKA Without Pseudo Classifier	0.67608	0.79778	0.69887

Impacts of the Pseudo Classification Layer. As declared in Subsect. 3.3, The Pseudo Classifier layer assists in removing redundant information from the MGK while retrieving condensed information about the pills in the input images. For this experiment, we use ResNet-50 as the backbone, and do training PIKA without Pseudo Classification Layer. The result is compared with the full version as well as our backbone. Specifically, employing the Pseudo Classifier improves the overall precision and $F1$-score by roughly 28% and 16%. The details of the result is presented in 3.

Impacts of the Projection Module, and Context Attention Module. Following, we study the performance of PIKA's when both Projection Moudule as well as Context Attention Module are removed. Instead of generating context vector c_i as the weighted sum of all condensed graph embeddings $q_i, i \in (0, \ldots, n)$, we directly take the mean over all q_i. For compliant with previous experiment, we also use ResNet-50 as our backbone as well as our baseline. As shown in Table 4, removing of the two modules leads to a degradation of 6% in the performance of PIKA.

Table 4. PIKA performace without Projection and Context Attention Modules.

Model	Precision	Recall	$F1$-score
ResNet-50 [6]	0.59612	0.51142	0.52146
PIKA	0.86640	0.79090	0.81010
PIKA w/o the Project and Attention Modules	0.82750	0.74700	0.76630

5   Conclusion and Future Work

In this study, we presented a novel approach to addressing challenges in image-based pill recognition. Specifically, we investigated a practical scenario aiming to identify pills from a patient's intake picture. The proposed method leverages additional information from prescriptions to improve pill recognition from photos. We first presented a method to construct a knowledge graph from prescriptions. We then designed a model to extract pills' relational information from the graph, and a framework to combine both the image-based visual and graph-based relational features for identifying pills. Extensive experiments on our real-world pill image dataset showed that the proposed framework outperforms the baselines by a significant margin, ranging from 4.8% to 34.1% in terms of $F1$-score. We also analyzed the effects of the prescription-based medical knowledge graph on pill recognition performance and discovered that the graph's accuracy is critical in boosting the overall system's performance. We are actively developing this study by gathering more pill and prescription datasets required to verify the suggested technique and prove its usefulness in different clinical settings. We believe that leveraging the external knowledge will improve the accuracy of pill identification significantly.

Acknowledgement. This work was funded by Vingroup Joint Stock Company (Vingroup JSC), Vingroup, and supported by Vingroup Innovation Foundation (VINIF) under project code VINIF.2021.DA00128.

References

1. World patient safety day (2022). https://www.who.int/news-room/events/detail/2022/09/17/default-calendar/world-patient-safety-day-2022. Accessed 14 Apr 2022
2. Chang, et al.: A deep learning-based intelligent medicine recognition system for chronic patients. IEEE Access **7**, 44441–44458 (2019). https://doi.org/10.1109/ACCESS.2019.2908843
3. Chang, et al.: Medglasses: a wearable smart-glasses-based drug pill recognition system using deep learning for visually impaired chronic patients. IEEE Access **8**, 17013–17024 (2020). https://doi.org/10.1109/ACCESS.2020.2967400
4. Chollet, et al.: Xception: deep learning with depthwise separable convolutions. In: Proceedings of the IEEE Conference on Computer vision and Pattern Recognition, pp. 1251–1258 (2017)
5. Hang, J.Y., Zhang, M.L.: Collaborative learning of label semantics and deep label-specific features for multi-label classification. IEEE Trans. Pattern Anal. Mach. Intell. **44**, 9860–9871 (2021). https://doi.org/10.1109/TPAMI.2021.3136592
6. He, et al.: Deep residual learning for image recognition. In: 2016 IEEE Conference on Computer Vision and Pattern Recognition (CVPR), pp. 770–778 (2016). https://doi.org/10.1109/CVPR.2016.90
7. Hinton, et al.: Stochastic neighbor embedding. In: Becker, S., Thrun, S., Obermayer, K. (eds.) Advances in Neural Information Processing Systems. vol. 15. MIT Press (2002). https://proceedings.neurips.cc/paper/2002/file/6150ccc6069bea6b5716254057a194ef-Paper.pdf
8. Li, Q., Qiao, M., Bian, W., Tao, D.: Conditional graphical lasso for multi-label image classification. In: Proceedings of the IEEE Conference on Computer Vision and Pattern Recognition (CVPR), June 2016
9. Ling, et al.: Few-shot pill recognition. In: Proceedings of the IEEE/CVF Conference on Computer Vision and Pattern Recognition (CVPR), June 2020
10. Loshchilov, I., et al.: Decoupled weight decay regularization. In: 7th International Conference on Learning Representations, ICLR 2019, New Orleans, LA, USA, May 6–9, 2019. OpenReview.net (2019), https://openreview.net/forum?id=Bkg6RiCqY7

11. van der Maaten, L., et al.: Visualizing data using t-SNE. J. Mach. Learn. Res. **9**(86), 2579–2605 (2008). http://jmlr.org/papers/v9/vandermaaten08a.html

12. Proma, et al.: Medicine recognition from colors and text. In: Proceedings of the 2019 3rd International Conference on Graphics and Signal Processing. ICGSP 2019, pp. 39–43., Association for Computing Machinery, New York, NY, USA (2019). https://doi.org/10.1145/3338472.3338484, https://doi.org/10.1145/3338472.3338484

13. Scott, et al.: Multivariate Density Estimation: Theory, Practice, and Visualization, 2nd edn., March 2015. https://doi.org/10.1002/9781118575574

14. Simonyan, K., et al.: Very deep convolutional networks for large-scale image recognition. In: Bengio, Y., LeCun, Y. (eds.) 3rd International Conference on Learning Representations, ICLR 2015, San Diego, CA, USA, 7–9 March 2015, Conference Track Proceedings (2015). http://arxiv.org/abs/1409.1556

15. Ting, H.W., et al.: A drug identification model developed using deep learning technologies: experience of a medical center in Taiwan. BMC Health Serv. Res. **20** (2020). https://doi.org/10.1186/s12913-020-05166-w, https://bmchealthservres.biomedcentral.com/articles/10.1186/s12913-020-05166-w#citeas

16. Wang, J., Yang, Y., Mao, J., Huang, Z., Huang, C., Xu, W.: CNN-RNN: a unified framework for multi-label image classification. In: Proceedings of the IEEE Conference on Computer Vision and Pattern Recognition (CVPR) , June 2016

17. Wang, Y., et al.: Multi-label classification with label graph superimposing. Proc. AAAI Conf. Artif. Intell. **34**(07), 12265–12272 (2020). https://doi.org/10.1609/aaai.v34i07.6909, https://ojs.aaai.org/index.php/AAAI/article/view/6909

18. Wang, Y., Xie, Y., Liu, Y., Zhou, K., Li, X.: Fast graph convolution network based multi-label image recognition via cross-modal fusion. In: Proceedings of the 29th ACM International Conference on Information & Knowledge Management, CIKM 2020, pp. 1575–1584. Association for Computing Machinery, New York, NY, USA (2020). https://doi.org/10.1145/3340531.3411880

19. Wong, Y.F., et al.: Development of fine-grained pill identification algorithm using deep convolutional network. J. Biomed. Inform. **74**, 130 136 (2017). https://doi.org/10.1016/j.jbi.2017.09.005, https://www.sciencedirect.com/science/article/pii/S1532046417302022

20. Yaniv, et al.: The national library of medicine pill image recognition challenge: an initial report. In: 2016 IEEE Applied Imagery Pattern Recognition Workshop (AIPR), pp. 1–9 (2016). https://doi.org/10.1109/AIPR.2016.8010584

A Legal Information Retrieval System for Statute Law

Chau Nguyen[✉][ID], Nguyen-Khang Le[ID], Dieu-Hien Nguyen[ID],
Phuong Nguyen[ID], and Le-Minh Nguyen[ID]

Japan Advanced Institute of Science and Technology, Nomi, Japan
{chau.nguyen,lnkhang,ndhien,phuongnm,nguyenml}@jaist.ac.jp

Abstract. The information retrieval task for statute law requires a
system to retrieve the relevant legal articles given a legal bar exam
query. The Transformer-based approaches have demonstrated robustness
over traditional machine learning and information retrieval methods for
legal documents. However, those approaches are mainly domain adaptation without attempting to tackle the challenges in the characteristics of the legal queries and the legal documents. This paper specifies
two challenges related to the characteristics of the two legal materials and proposes methods to tackle them effectively. Specifically, the
challenge of different language used (while the articles use abstract language, the queries may use the language to describe a specific scenario) is addressed by a specialized model. Besides, another specialized model can overcome the challenge of long articles and queries.
As shown in the experimental results, our proposed system achieved
a state-of-the-art F2 score of 76.87%, with an improvement of 3.85%
compared to the previous best system. The code will be available at
https://github.com/nguyenlab/statute_law_IR.

Keywords: Legal information retrieval system · Statute law · Statute
law information retrieval · COLIEE

1 Introduction

COLIEE (COmpetition on Legal Information Extraction/Entailment) is a
renowned international competition on legal text processing. It has been held
annually since 2014. In 2021, COLIEE included five tasks on case law and statute
law. Our work aims to address Task 3: information retrieval on statute law
(statute law is the written law that is passed by a body of legislature). Specifically, given a legal query, the system should return all relevant articles in the
corpus (see Table 1 for examples). In this paper, we describe our approach to the
information retrieval task for statute law on the English version of the Japanese
Civil Code corpus.

At the beginning of the competition, the traditional machine learning and
natural language processing approaches are popular for the information retrieval

© The Author(s), under exclusive license to Springer Nature Singapore Pte Ltd. 2022
E. Szczerbicki et al. (Eds.): ACIIDS 2022, CCIS 1716, pp. 370–382, 2022.
https://doi.org/10.1007/978-981-19-8234-7_29

task on statute law (COLIEE Task 3): support vector machines (SVMs) [6], BM25, TF-IDF, n-gram, Hidden Markov Model, Random Forests, etc. Years later, Deep Learning approaches were proposed, such as [7] employing long short-term memory (LSTM), SPABS [19] employing recurrent neural network (RNN) for text representation. Since the release of the BERT paper [4], because of its robustness, most of the participants employed BERT (and other Transformer-based models); some of them combined BERT's retrieval results with the retrieval results of well-known information retrieval methods (TF-IDF, BM25, Indri [17], or Word Movers' Distance [9]) to produce the final submission. It is undeniable that Transformer-based models have achieved significant improvement when applied to the legal domain in Task 3. However, the application is mainly domain adaptation, without observing the characteristics of the legal articles and legal queries, as well as an appropriate explanation for the choice of various pre-trained Transformer-based models for ensembling.

Table 1. Examples of training data for Task 3. Example 1 is about an abstract query and example 2 is about a specific-scenario query.

#	Query	Relevant Law Articles
1	Juristic act subject to a condition subsequent which is impossible shall be void	**Article 133** (1) A juridical act subject to an impossible condition precedent is void (2) A juridical act subject to an impossible condition subsequent is an unconditional juridical act
2	The family court appointed B as the administrator of the property of absentee A, as A went missing without appointing the one. In cases where A owns land X, B needs to obtain the permission of a family court in order to sell Land X as an agent of A	**Article 28** If an administrator needs to perform an act exceeding the authority provided for in Article 103, the administrator may perform that act after obtaining the permission of the family court. [...] **Article 103** An agent who has no specifically defined authority has the authority to perform the following acts only: (i) acts of preservation; [...]

Through our observation, we argue that there are two characteristics of the legal texts for the statute law information retrieval task that a system should take into consideration. While the legal articles has the abstract nature, a legal bar query may either be written in an abstract manner (example 1 in Table 1) or describe a very specific scenario (example 2 in Table 1). Hence, it is non-trivial for a sole model to generalize the relationship between the abstract legal articles and the legal bar queries. To address this issue, we propose to determine the specific-scenario queries, then employ a Transformer-based model to address only those queries, in addition to a Transformer-based model for addressing all queries. In the inference phase, we ensemble the retrieval results of the two models to acquire a retrieval result. The experimental results demonstrate an improvement up to 3.78% in the F2 score when applying this approach to a Transformer-based model. Besides, as shown in Fig. 1 and Fig. 2, a portion of legal articles as well as legal bar queries are relatively long. Hence, we propose to employ Longformer [1] to overcome the 512-token limitation of most off-the-shelf pre-trained Transformer-based models. This employment helps our system to further gain 1.28% F2 score. By combining the two proposed ideas, we achieve the state-of-the-art performance for COLIEE 2021's Task 3 with the F2 score of 76.87%, with an improvement of 3.85% compared to the previous best system [18].

In this paper, our contributions are three-fold:

- Propose to determine specific-scenario queries to facilitate Transformer-based models to better learn the specific relationship patterns between legal articles and legal bar queries.
- Propose to employ Longformer to address the long articles and long queries.
- Analyze comprehensively the contribution of the two proposed ideas for the system.

The remainder of the paper is organized as follows. Section 2 walks through related work. Section 3 describes the system. Section 4 presents the experimental results. Finally, Sect. 5 concludes our work.

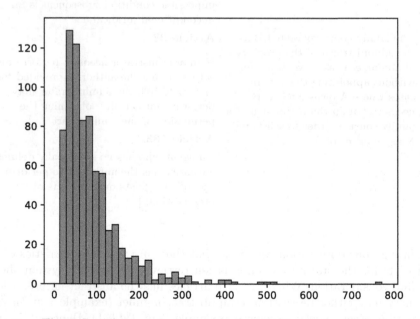

Fig. 1. Distribution of number of tokens of Civil Code articles

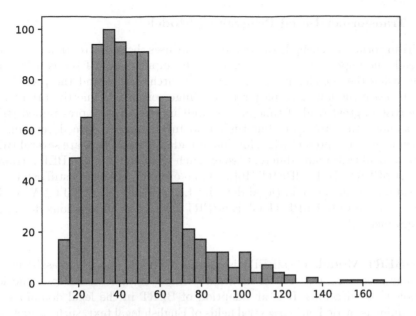

Fig. 2. Distribution of number of tokens of queries

2 Related Work

2.1 The COLIEE Competition

Five Tasks in COLIEE. In 2021, COLIEE included five tasks on case law and statute law. The case law component consisted of Task 1 (an information retrieval task on case law) and Task 2 (determining the entailment relation between the cases in the corpus and an unseen case). The statute law component consisted of Task 3 (an information retrieval task on statute law), Task 4 (determining the yes/no decision for a query based on the entailment relationship between the retrieved articles in Task 3 and the query), and Task 5 (the task of yes/no question answering without retrieved articles in Task 3).

Task 3 in COLIEE. The statute law retrieval task (Task 3 in COLIEE) aims to retrieve the relevant articles in a corpus that support the decision of a given legal bar exam query. The corpus data is the Japanese Civil Code (an English translation is also provided) which has 768 articles. The input for Task 3 is a legal bar exam query Q. The designed system should extract a subset of the Civil Code articles $A_{i|1 \leq i \leq n}$ which contains appropriate articles for determining the Yes/No decision for the query, i.e. Entails($A_{i|1 \leq i \leq n}$, Q) or Entails($A_{i|1 \leq i \leq n}$, not Q). For this retrieval task, the organizer favors recall over precision, so the F2 measure is used as the official evaluation measure (specifically, the macro average of F2: the average of evaluation values for each query over all the queries).

2.2   Transformer-Based Pre-trained Models

The Transformer is a deep learning model that uses the self-attention mechanism to weigh the importance of every part of the input data. BERT is a language model using the encoder in the Transformer architecture and the pre-training tasks to learn the language patterns over huge corpora. While the pre-training phase costs a great deal of time and computing resources, a pre-trained BERT model allows the process of fine-tuning on much smaller data, leveraging the learned language representation, for domain adaptation. There are several BERT variants to address many different issues, such as to enhance the BERT training phase (RoBERTa [12], AlBERT [10]), to make BERT lighter (DistilBERT [14]), to train on specific domain (legal domain: LegalBERT [2], BERTLAW[1] or biological domain: PubMedBERT [5], BioBERT [11]), or to address long documents (Longformer [1]).

LegalBERT Model. LegalBERT is a family of BERT models to assist natural language processing research in the legal domain, computational law, and legal technology applications. It is an adaption of BERT in the legal domain where pre-training is carried out on several fields of English legal text, such as contracts, court cases, and legislation. This particular BERT model has been performing better than the original version of BERT on legal domain-specific tasks.

Longformer Model. BERT and its variants fail to process long sequences of more than 512 tokens. Therefore, Longformer [1] was proposed by Beltagy et al. as a Transformer-based model with an attention mechanism that scales linearly with sequence length and can process documents of more than thousands of tokens. The ability to deal with long sequences of Longformer makes it a suitable candidate for the statute law retrieval task where the concatenation of a query and an article can be longer than 512 tokens.

3   Methodology

In this section, we describe the methods utilized in our system. First, we introduce our re-formulation of the retrieval task as a binary classification task. Second, we present the methods for tackling specific-scenario queries. Next, we mention our approach to addressing long legal texts. Last but not least, we present the mechanism for ensembling the retrieval results. Figure 3 shows the proposed system.

3.1   Fine-Tuning a Transformer-Based Model for Task 3

In this subsection, we describe the process of data preparation and fine-tuning for a Transformer-based model for the statute law retrieval task. This process

---

[1] https://huggingface.co/nguyenthanhasia/BERTLaw.

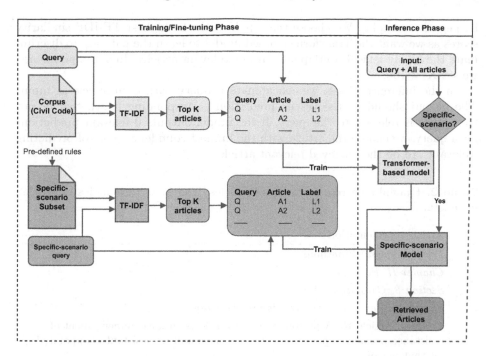

Fig. 3. The proposed system. We use 2 Transformer-based models which are Legal-BERT and Longformer in the experiments.

can be applied to any Transformer-based model. However, as we are considering legal documents, we utilize the pre-trained LegalBERT model as the base model because LegalBERT is specifically pre-trained on legal datasets. LegalBERT is also widely used in other legal processing tasks [3,16].

For this retrieval task, we need to determine the relevant articles for a given query. In other words, for each article in the corpus, we need to determine if there is an entailment relationship between a given query and the article. Therefore, we formulate the retrieval task as a sentence pair classification task, where the input is the pair of query and article, and the label is $1/0$, corresponding to whether or not there is an entailment relationship between the sentences. Specifically, the input is represented as *"[CLS]<tokens of query>[SEP]<tokens of artile>"* where *[CLS]* and *[SEP]* are two special tokens described in [4]. Following [18], we represent an article not only by its content but also with its structural metadata (see Table 2 for examples).

In the matter of preparing fine-tuning data, we need positive samples and negative samples. Positive samples are provided in the dataset where most queries have only 1 or 2 relevant articles. The maximum number of relevant articles in the dataset is six, but they rarely exist. To prepare negatives samples for a query, first, we represent the query and all articles in TF-IDF vectors and compute their similarity scores. After that, we consider the top K articles with the highest TF-IDF similarity scores, except for the articles labeled as relevant, to be negative samples. We choose the top K with the highest TF-IDF similarity scores as we want the Transformer-based model to learn the patterns to discriminate the highly-lexical-overlapped but not-relevant articles. In our experiments, we set $K = 100$.

In the inference phase, we concatenate a query with each article as input. The output should be the yes/no prediction corresponding to whether or not the article is relevant to the query. If the model outputs 0 relevant predictions for a query, we choose the article with the highest confidence score of predicting "relevant" to be the retrieved relevant article.

Table 2. Examples on representation of articles. The *italic texts* indicates article's metadata.

#	Article representation
1	*Part I. General Provisions*
	Chapter II. Persons
	Section 3. Capacity to Act
	Summary: Persons under Assistance; Assistants
	Content: Article 16. A person subject to a decision for commencement of assistance becomes a person under assistance, and an assistant is appointed for that person.
2	*Part III. Claims*
	Chapter V. Torts
	Summary: Capacity for Liability
	Content: Article 713. A person who has inflicted damage on another person while in a condition wherein the person lacked the capacity to appreciate their own liability for their acts due to a mental disability is not liable to compensate for this; provided, however, that this does not apply if the person has temporarily caused that condition, intentionally or negligently.

3.2 Determining Specific-Scenario Queries and Training Specific-Scenario Model

In general, the language used in written law has an abstract nature. In other words, the content of the law's articles is conceptual and abstract. This characteristic holds for the articles in the Civil Code. However, it is not the case for the legal bar queries: many of them are abstract queries, but many others describe a specific scenario in real life (see Table 1 for a comparison). The specific-scenario queries demand the examinee to have the ability to find the relevant abstract articles based on the understanding of the scenario. Generally, lexical-based approaches fail to handle specific-scenario queries because of the difference in the descriptive words used. For a Deep Learning-based approach, because of the robust generalization capability, the Deep Learning model may address specific-scenario queries besides the abstract queries. However, it is only possible if a sizable amount of data is provided. Task 3's data is relatively small, leading to a limitation in the generalization capacity of a Deep Learning-based model if it has to deal with all kinds of data simultaneously. Hence, we propose to filter the specific-scenario queries and manipulate them separately.

First, we determine the specific-scenario queries. As we observe on the legal bar queries, the specific-scenario queries consistently follow a template: to call the legal persons and objects by uppercase characters. For example, in example 2 of Table 1, the query is *"The family court appointed B as the administrator of the property of absentee A, as A went missing without appointing the one. In cases where A owns land X, B needs to obtain the permission of a family court in order to sell Land X as an agent of A. "*, which call the *the absentee* as A, call *the appointed administrator* as B, call *A's land* as X. Hence, we design rules to determine if the uppercase in a query implies a legal person or object. In our rules, we neglect the uppercase characters A and I because those characters may cause an inappropriate error in determining specific-scenario queries.

After that, we separately handle the specific-scenario queries and their relevant articles by a Transformer-based model. Following the procedure described in the previous subsection, we create fine-tuning data to fine-tune a model. We used the LegalBERT model fine-tuned on all Task 3's data, not the pre-trained LegalBERT model. The reason is that the pre-trained LegalBERT model only learned the legal language patterns during pre-training, but the LegalBERT model fine-tuned on the data of the statute law retrieval task further learns the patterns of the task. In other words, the fine-tuned LegalBERT model performs not only domain adaptation (for the legal domain) but also task adaptation (the statute law retrieval task on all kinds of queries), so it should be an appropriate initial setting for fine-tuning the specific-scenario data.

3.3   Addressing Long Articles and Queries

As a limitation of many pre-trained Transformer-based models in general (and LegalBERT in particular), there is a limitation of maximum tokens of the input, usually set to 512 tokens. However, a sizable proportion of the legal articles in the Civil Code are long, so when we concatenate a query and an article to be the input for LegalBERT, the latter part of the article will be truncated because of the problem of exceeding the maximum number of tokens (see Fig. 1 and 2 for the statistics on the number of tokens of queries and articles). As a result, the LegalBERT model is incapable of learning the patterns of relevant relationships between the query and the article in case the relevant part of the article is truncated. Furthermore, in this case, this positive sample becomes a noisy positive sample, which may even negatively affect the model's generalization capability.

For the reasons mentioned earlier, we propose to adopt Longformer as an additional model for capturing the patterns of the long inputs besides the normal-length inputs. The reason for Longformer adoption is straightforward: Longformer can handle the input length of up to 4,096 tokens. We follow the same procedure of fine-tuning LegalBERT to fine-tune the pre-trained Longformer model, including adding metadata to articles and preparing positive/negative samples.

3.4   Ensemble the Retrieval Results

A previous system [13] suggests that ensembling the retrieval results of multiple models should raise the system's recall, which often leads to an increase in the F2 score. We also employ this idea for our final retrieval results. Specifically, we ensemble the retrieval results of 4 models: the 2 LegalBERT models (fine-tuned on two cases: (1) all data and (2) only the data related to specific-scenario data) and the 2 Longformer models (fine-tuned on two cases). In short, the final retrieval results of our system are an ensemble of the retrieval results of 4 models to capture different data characteristics.

4   Experiments

4.1   Dataset

In the provided Civil Code in Task 3, there are 768 articles. Table 3 shows the information related to the number of queries and corresponding specific-scenario queries in the split training set, validation set, and test set.

Table 3. Number of queries and specific-scenario queries

Data	# queries	# specific-scenario queries
Training	748	103
Validation	58	16
Test	87	31

4.2   Experimental Results

Table 4 shows the performance of the models on Task 3's dataset. Our model outperforms the best system in the competition [18] by 3.85%. It can be seen that our model demonstrates superior recall (note that this retrieval task emphasizes recall) while achieving fair precision.

We conducted ablation studies to see how our approaches impact the retrieval results. As demonstrated in Table 5, when ensembling the predictions by the corresponding specific-scenario model, the F2 score always increases. Specifically, for LegalBERT, the F2 score increases by 3.78%, from 71.81% to 75.59%. For Longformer, the F2 score increases by 1.49%, from 70.00% to 71.49%. While the ensemble of LegalBERT and Longformer achieves 74.10% F2 score, further ensembling with their specific-scenario models raises the F2 score to 76.87%. In another view, in all cases, specific-scenario models contribute significantly to the recall score (5.56%, 3.09%, and 5.56% for LegalBERT, Longformer, and LegalBERT + Longformer, respectively) while remaining or minorly dropping the precision (0.88% in the worst case), which leads to the significant improvement in F2 score. Besides, with the support of the specific-scenario models, the number of retrieved relevant articles increases by 4 to 5, which helps significantly

Table 4. Performance of the systems. The first row indicates the proposed system. The following lines indicate the participants' systems in Task 3 (COLIEE 2021). **Bold texts** indicate highest results. Underlined texts indicate second-highest results.

System	F2 score (%)	Precision (%)	Recall (%)
Ours	**76.87**	65.80	**85.19**
OvGU_run1 [18]	73.02	67.49	77.78
JNLP.CrossLMultiLThreshold [13]	72.27	60.00	80.25
BM25.UA [8]	70.92	**75.31**	70.37
JNLP.CrossLBertJP [13]	70.90	62.41	77.16
R3.LLNTU	70.47	66.56	74.38
R2.LLNTU	70.39	67.70	73.15
R1.LLNTU	68.75	63.68	73.15
JNLP.CrossLBertJPC15030C15050 [13]	68.38	55.35	77.78
OvGU_run2 [18]	67.17	48.57	80.25
TFIDF.UA [8]	65.71	67.90	65.43
LM.UA [8]	54.60	56.79	54.32
TR_HB [15]	52.26	33.33	61.73
HUKB-3 [20]	52.24	29.01	69.75
HUKB-1 [20]	47.32	23.97	65.43
TR_AV1 [15]	35.99	26.22	51.23
TR_AV2 [15]	33.69	14.90	55.56
HUKB-2 [20]	32.58	32.72	32.72
OvGU_run3 [18]	30.16	15.70	70.06

Table 5. Ablation studies. *SS model* indicates whether or not to ensemble with corresponding specific-scenario models. *Return* indicates the number of relevant articles returned. *Retrieve* indicates the number of correct returned relevant articles. **Bold texts** indicate highest results.

Model	SS model?	F2 score	Precision	Recall	Return	Retrieve
LegalBERT		71.81	69.96	74.69	102	67
LegalBERT	✓	75.59	69.96	80.25	117	72
Longformer		70.00	**70.37**	71.60	95	64
Longformer	✓	71.49	69.49	74.69	110	68
LegalBERT + Longformer		74.10	66.15	79.63	128	73
LegalBERT + Longformer	✓	**76.87**	65.80	**85.19**	149	**78**

improve the macro average F2 score, especially when the specific-scenario model can retrieve relevant articles but the other model cannot retrieve any of them.

In Table 6, we give examples of the contribution of specific-scenario models to the base models. In other words, this table shows the cases where the base models (LegalBERT, Longformer, or LegalBERT + Longformer) cannot retrieve, but their corresponding specific-scenario models can retrieve the relevant articles.

Table 6. Examples on the contribution of specific-scenario (SS) models

---

LegalBERT and its SS model can retrieve but LegalBERT cannot

Query R02-8-E:

A took the jewelry that B had forgotten, believing without negligence that it belonged to A. In this case, A may not obtain the ownership of the jewelry by good faith acquisition

Retrieved article 192:

Part II Real Rights - Chapter II Possessory Rights - Sect. 2 Effect of Possessory Rights (Good Faith Acquisition)

Article 192 A person that commences the possession of movables peacefully and openly by a transactional act acquires the rights that are exercised with respect to the movables immediately if the person possesses it in good faith and without negligence

---

Longformer and its SS model can retrieve but Longformer cannot

---

Query R02-23-O:

If A delays in delivering X after the contract of sale stipulates that a third party (G) is to acquire the ownership of X and G manifests intention of availing of the benefit, B may not cancel the contract of sale without G's consent

Retrieved article 538:

Part III Claims - Chapter II Contracts - Sect. 1 General Provisions - Subsect. 2 Effect of Contracts

(Determination of Rights of the Third Party)

Article 538 (1) After rights of the third party have accrued pursuant to the provisions of the preceding Article, the parties may not modify or extinguish those rights

(2) If, after rights of the third party accrue pursuant to the provisions of the preceding Article, the obligor does not perform the obligation to the third party, the other party to the contract referred to in paragraph (1) of that Article may not cancel the contract without the consent of the third party

---

LegalBERT + Longformer and their SS models can retrieve but LegalBERT + Longformer cannot

---

Query R02-9-O:

A had owned land in an area of holiday homes. B, who owned neighboring land, began to construct a fence on A's land crossing the boundary without A's consent, and two years later the fence was completed. As of this time, A may not demand the removal of the fence against B by filing an action for maintenance of possession.

Retrieved article 201:

Part II Real Rights - Chapter II Possessory Rights - Sect.2 Effect of Possessory Rights (Periods of Time for Filing Possessory Actions)

Article 201 (1) An action for maintenance of possession must be filed during the obstruction or within one year after the obstruction stops; provided, however, that if the possessed thing has been damaged due to construction work and either one year has passed from the time when the construction was started or the construction has been completed, the action may not be filed

(2) An action for preservation of possession may be filed so long as the danger of obstruction exists. In this case, the provisions of the proviso to the preceding paragraph apply mutatis mutandis if the possessed thing is likely to be damaged by the construction work

(3) An action for recovery of possession must be filed within one year from the time when a possessor was forcibly dispossessed.

---

5   Conclusion

This paper specifies two challenges related to two characteristics of the legal bar exam queries and legal articles, which are neglected by previous approaches. The first challenge is that while the language used in legal articles is abstract, the language used in the legal bar exam queries may be either abstract or scenario-specific. We proposed to determine the specific-scenario queries and tackle them separately. The second challenge is that the long document may limit the performance of many available pre-trained models. We propose to leverage the capability of handling long documents of Longformer to tackle this challenge. By ensembling the retrieval results of the models, our system can achieve the best F2 score on the dataset of Task 3 (COLIEE 2021) with 76.87%, suggesting further research to observe and tackle particular characteristics of documents in the legal domain.

Acknowledgment. This work was supported by JSPS Kakenhi Grant Number 20H04295, 20K20406, and 20K20625.

References

1. Beltagy, I., Peters, M.E., Cohan, A.: Longformer: the long-document transformer. arXiv:2004.05150 (2020)
2. Chalkidis, I., Fergadiotis, M., Malakasiotis, P., Aletras, N., Androutsopoulos, I.: LEGAL-BERT: the muppets straight out of law school. In: Findings of the Association for Computational Linguistics: EMNLP 2020, pp. 2898–2904. Association for Computational Linguistics, Online, November 2020
3. Chalkidis, I., Fergadiotis, M., Manginas, N., Katakalou, E., Malakasiotis, P.: Regulatory compliance through doc2doc information retrieval: a case study in eu/uk legislation where text similarity has limitations. arXiv preprint arXiv:2101.10726 (2021)
4. Devlin, J., Chang, M.W., Lee, K., Toutanova, K.: BERT: pre-training of deep bidirectional transformers for language understanding. In: Proceedings of the 2019 Conference of the North American Chapter of the Association for Computational Linguistics: Human Language Technologies, Vol. 1 (Long and Short Papers), pp. 4171–4186. Association for Computational Linguistics, Minneapolis, Minnesota June 2019
5. Gu, Y., et al.: Domain-specific language model pretraining for biomedical natural language processing. ACM Trans. Comput. Healthcare **3**(1) (2021). https://doi.org/10.1145/3458754, https://doi.org/10.1145/3458754
6. Hearst, M., Dumais, S., Osuna, E., Platt, J., Scholkopf, B.: Support vector machines. IEEE Intell. Syst. Appl. **13**(4), 18–28 (1998). https://doi.org/10.1109/5254.708428
7. Kim, K., Hong, K., Rhim, Y.Y.: LSTM Based Legal Text Representation Learning (2017)
8. Kim, M.Y., Rabelo, J., Goebel., R.: Bm25 and transformer-based legal information extraction and entailment. In: Proceedings of the COLIEE Workshop in ICAIL (2021)

9. Kusner, M.J., Sun, Y., Kolkin, N.I., Weinberger, K.Q.: From word embeddings to document distances. In: Proceedings of the 32nd International Conference on International Conference on Machine Learning, ICM 2015, Vol. 37, pp. 957–966. JMLR.org (2015)

10. Lan, Z., Chen, M., Goodman, S., Gimpel, K., Sharma, P., Soricut, R.: Albert: a lite BERT for self-supervised learning of language representations. In: International Conference on Learning Representations (2020)

11. Lee, J., et al.: BioBERT: a pre-trained biomedical language representation model for biomedical text mining. Bioinformatics **36**(4), 1234–1240 (2019). https://doi.org/10.1093/bioinformatics/btz682, https://doi.org/10.1093/bioinformatics/btz682

12. Liu, Y., et al.: Roberta: a robustly optimized BERT pretraining approach. CoRR (2019)

13. Nguyen, H.T., et al.: JNLP team: deep learning approaches for legal processing tasks in COLIEE 2021. In: Proceedings of the COLIEE Workshop in ICAIL (2021)

14. Sanh, V., Debut, L., Chaumond, J., Wolf, T.: DistilBERT, a distilled version of BERT: smaller, faster, cheaper and lighter (2019). https://doi.org/10.48550/ARXIV.1910.01108, https://arxiv.org/abs/1910.01108

15. Schilder, F., Chinnappa, D., Madan, K., Harmouche, J., Vold, A., Bretz, H., Hudzina., J.: A pentapus grapples with legal reasoning. In: Proceedings of the COLIEE Workshop in ICAIL (2021)

16. Silveira, R., Fernandes, C., Neto, J.A.M., Furtado, V., Pimentel Filho, J.E.: Topic modelling of legal documents via legal-BERT. https://ceur-ws.org/. ISSN:1613-0073 (2021)

17. Strohman, T., Metzler, D., Turtle, H., Croft, W.: Indri: a language-model based search engine for complex queries. Information Retrieval-IR, January 2005

18. Wehnert, S., Sudhi, V., Dureja, S., Kutty, L., Shahania, S., De Luca, E.W.: Legal norm retrieval with variations of the BERT model combined with TF-IDF vectorization. In: Proceedings of the Eighteenth International Conference on Artificial Intelligence and Law, ICAIL 2021, pp. 285–294. Association for Computing Machinery, New York, NY, USA (2021). https://doi.org/10.1145/3462757.3466104, https://doi.org/10.1145/3462757.3466104

19. Yoshioka, M., Kano, Y., Kiyota, N., Satoh, K.: Overview of Japanese statute law retrieval and entailment task at COLIEE-2018. In: Twelfth international workshop on Juris-informatics (JURISIN 2018) (2018)

20. Yoshioka, M., et al.: BERT-based ensemble methods for information retrieval and legal textual entailment in COLIEE statute law task. In: Proceedings of the COLIEE Workshop in ICAIL (2021)

Exploring Retriever-Reader Approaches in Question-Answering on Scientific Documents

Dieu-Hien Nguyen[✉], Nguyen-Khang Le[✉], and Minh Le Nguyen[✉]

Japan Advanced Institute of Science and Technology, Nomi, Japan
{ndhien,lnkhang,nguyenml}@jaist.ac.jp
https://www.jaist.ac.jp

Abstract. As readers of scientific articles often read to answer specific questions, the task of Question-Answering (QA) in academic papers was proposed to evaluate the ability of intelligent systems to answer questions in long scientific documents. Due to the large contexts in the questions, this task poses many challenges to state-of-the-art QA models. This paper explores the retriever-reader approaches widely used in open-domain QA and their impact when adapting to QA on long scientific documents. By treating one scientific article as the corpus for retrieval, we propose a retriever-reader method to extract the answer from the relevant parts of the document and an effective sliding window technique that improves the pipeline by splitting the articles into disjoint text blocks of fixed size. Experiments on QASPER, a dataset for QA in Natural Language Processing papers, showed that our method outperforms all state-of-the-art models and establishes a new state-of-the-art in the extractive questions subset with 30.43% F1[1]The code and processed data are available at https://github.com/lekhang4497/qasper-retriever-reader.

Keywords: Question-answering · Retriever-reader · Long sequences

1 Introduction

Question-answering (QA) is one of the most important tasks in Natural Language Processing (NLP). Given a question and a context, a QA system is required to find the answer to the question from the context. Many datasets are proposed for the QA task [11,14,23,27,32]. Dasigi et al. [6] proposed QASPER, a dataset for QA on NLP papers. In QASPER, given an academic article and a question about the article, the QA system must find the answer to the question. QASPER is challenging to existing QA methods due to the long and complex contexts. QASPER introduced four types of answers: Extractive, Abstractive (free-form answer), Yes/No, and Unanswerable. This study focuses solely on the questions which have extractive answers.

D.-H. Nguyen and N.-K. Le—These authors contributed equally to this work.

© The Author(s), under exclusive license to Springer Nature Singapore Pte Ltd. 2022
E. Szczerbicki et al. (Eds.): ACIIDS 2022, CCIS 1716, pp. 383–395, 2022.
https://doi.org/10.1007/978-981-19-8234-7_30

One of the most significant properties of QASPER is that the contexts of the questions are significantly larger than that of other QA datasets. In specific, scientific papers are much longer than the typical 512 or 1024 token limit of most BERT-like models [5,7,15,17], which makes it difficult to apply these models on QASPER. Dasigi et al. [6] proposed a baseline model for QASPER called QASPER-LED which employs Longformer-Encoder-Decoder (LED) [2] to address the long context problem. QASPER-LED can process the sequence length of 16K tokens and encode 99% of the paper full texts in the QASPER dataset without truncation. However, by having to encode a large number of tokens, QASPER-LED may not efficiently capture the semantics of all the tokens compared to other BERT-like models [5,7,15,17] encoding a smaller number of tokens.

Aside from the standard QA task, the task of open-domain QA also gained much interest in the research community. In open-domain QA, only the questions are provided, and QA systems have to find information from a large corpus to answer the questions. Many methods were proposed for the task of open-domain QA. A typical approach to open-domain QA employs a retriever-reader pipeline that contains two main steps; the first step aims to retrieve relevant documents from a large corpus; the second step is a Machine Reading Comprehension (MRC) task that requires finding the answer in the relevant documents. Many approaches for the retriever component were proposed. Most common approaches can be categorized into Sparse Retriever and Dense Retriever. Sparse Retriever refers to techniques that find relevant documents using classical methods like TF-IDF, BM25. DrQA [4] is one of the first approaches to open-domain QA that combines these retrieval techniques and neural MRC models to answer open-domain questions. On the other hand, many Dense Retriever techniques were also proposed [12,16,24]. These techniques employ dual-encoders to encode the question and the document. In some regards, the problem of finding a piece of information from a long scientific paper in QASPER can resemble that of the open-domain QA task. Retrieval approaches in the first step of open-domain QA can help find relevant information in QASPER. However, to the best of our knowledge, no existing works explore the impact of open-domain QA retrieval methods on the QASPER dataset. This paper proposes a novel method that adapts open-domain QA's retriever-reader approaches to long scientific papers in QASPER by treating a single paper as a large corpus for retrieval.

Treating each scientific document as a corpus for retrieval enables us to utilize open-domain QA techniques and develop a retriever-reader pipeline that achieves the new state-of-the-art performance on QASPER. The main contributions in this paper are:

1. We propose a novel method that adapts retriever-reader approaches from Open-domain QA to the problem of QA in long scientific documents and established new state-of-the-art results in the QASPER dataset.
2. We conduct experiments on retriever and re-ranker to explore the impact of different passage splitting techniques on retrieval results in QASPER. We find that splitting articles using a sliding window improves the retrieval performance, and the window side of 150 produces the best result.

2 Related Work

2.1 Transformers Approaches for Long Documents

Most common Transformer-based models are unable to process long sequences because their self-attention operation scales quadratically with the sequence length. Therefore, architectures that address the long sequence problem were proposed. Longformer [2] was proposed by Beltagy et al. as a Transformer model with an attention mechanism that scales linearly with sequence length and can process documents of more than thousands of tokens. Ainslie et al. proposed Extended Transformer Construction (ETC) [1] which addresses the scaling input length and encoding structured inputs challenges of standard Transformer architectures. Zaheer et al. proposed BigBird [33], a Transformer architecture that extends ETC to more generic scenarios where prerequisite domain knowledge about structure present in the source data may be unavailable. However, because of the vast amount of information that these models have to process, their ability to capture semantics may not be as efficient as other Transformers models when dealing with shorter sequences.

2.2 Retriever-Reader Methods in Open-Domain QA

Retriever-Reader is one of the most common approaches in modern open-domain QA. A Retriever aims to retrieve relevant documents with regard to a given question, which can be considered as an Information Retrieval (IR) system, while a Reader, usually a neural Machine Reading Comprehension (MRC) model, aims at extracting the final answer from the retrieved documents. A document retriever plays an important role in identifying relevant documents for answer extraction. Traditional approaches such as DrQA implemented term-based passage retrievers (sparse retrievers) such as TF-IDF and BM25. Recently, deep learning has been employed to improve traditional passage retrievers. Dense retrievers have been proposed to represent both questions and documents as dense vectors using dual-encoders. Two major strategies in dual-encoders are using shared parameters across two encoders [19,24], and using two distinctly parameterized encoders [9,12,16,25]. Along with retrievers, Transformers-based re-rankers have also been applied to retrieval-based question answering [8,10,13,18,20,21,29,31]. Cross-encoder is one common approach for re-rankers. The Sentence-BERT (SBERT) [24] implementation of cross-encoder achieved competitive results on the IR corpus MS MARCO [3]. In a normal Open-domain QA setting, the corpus for retrieval is enormous (typically the whole Wikipedia corpus). Therefore, it is impractical for cross-encoder re-rankers to be applied to all passages in the corpus. However, in the setting of QA in long scientific documents, if we consider all passages in an article as the corpus for retrieval, it is feasible to apply cross-encoder re-rankers. Both term-based passage retrieving and cross-encoder re-ranking methods are explored in our experiments.

3   Method

To apply the retriever-reader approaches in open-domain QA, we formulate the task in QASPER as two separate problems: passage retrieval and answer extraction. In the passage retrieval problem, we consider an article A as the corpus for retrieval. A retriever is leveraged to retrieve m passages $P = [P_1, ..., P_i, ..., P_m]$ from an article A for a given question $Q = (q_1, ..., q_{|Q|})$, where $P_i = (p_i^1, p_i^2 ..., p_i^{|p_i|})$ is the i-th passage, $P_i \in A$, and $q_k \in Q$ and $p_i^j \in P_i$ are corresponding words. Following the work of [12,29], we split each article into multiple, disjoint text blocks of a fixed number of words. These text blocks are referred to as passages, and we consider these passages as our basic retrieval units. In the answer extraction problem, we only consider the questions in QASPER that have extractive answers. A reader is employed to extract the answer span from the relevant passages. Given a context passage $C = (c_1, c_2, ..., c_n)$ and a question $Q = (q_1, ..., q_{|Q|})$. The reader aims to find a text span $(c_i, c_{i+1}, ...c_j)$ from the context that answers the question Q. In our experiment, we only used one passage with the highest relevance score in the retrieval phase for the answer extraction phase. Figure 1 illustrates the proposed method.

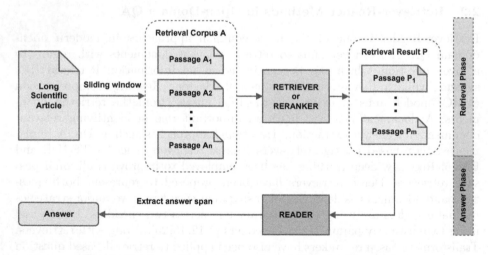

Fig. 1. Retriever-Reader approach on long scientific articles

Articles are pre-processed to form passages that are disjoint text blocks of W words. As dividing articles into non-overlapping passages may make answer spans near the boundary lose part of the contexts, we split articles into overlapping passages using a sliding window inspired by the work of Wang et al. [29]. For the sliding window, we use a stride $S = 50$ for all experiments. We conduct experiments with different values of W to select the best value.

We explore two types of approaches for the retriever component, namely retrieving and re-ranking. The retrieving approach employs TF-IDF to index passages of an article. The cosine similarity between the question and the passages is used to retrieve the top m most relevant passages. The re-ranking approach uses a Transformer cross-encoder model and outputs a score in $[0..1]$ for each question-passage pair that indicates the relevance of the passage regarding the question.

For the reader component, we employ Transformer-based readers. The retriever-reader approach enables the application of any state-of-the-art Transformer-based models in QA without the limitation of long sequences. As described previously, the reader aims to extract from the context $C = (c_1, c_2, ..., c_n)$ a text span $(c_i, c_{i+1}, ...c_j)$ that answers the question. Inspired by the success of Transformer models on many QA datasets, we employ a transfer learning approach and implement the reader using pre-trained Transformer models. We follow the implementation of Wolf et al. [30] and add a linear layer on top of the hidden-states output of the Transformer model to compute span start logits $Pstart_i$ and span end logits $Pend_i$ for each token c_i in the context. A score is calculated for each span $(c_i, c_{i+1}, ...c_j)$ using $Pstart_i$ and $Pend_j$; the span with the highest score is then chosen to be the answer for the question.

4 Experiments

4.1 Experimental Setup

Dataset. All experiments are conducted on the QASPER dataset [6], which consists of 5,049 questions over 1,585 NLP papers. The questions in QASPER are created by NLP practitioners who read only the title and abstract; a different set of NLP practitioners provides the answers. The dataset contains four subsets of questions, namely extractive, abstractive, yes/no questions, and unanswerable. In this study, we experiment with the subset of extractive questions, which account for 51.8% of the dataset.

Baselines. We compare our method with previous state-of-the-art models in QASPER, DocHopper [26] and QASPER-LED [6], and other competitive baselines. Sun et al. [26] proposed DocHopper as a model that iteratively attends to different parts of long, hierarchically structured documents to answer complex questions. QASPER-LED [6] is an encoder-decoder model based on Longformer [2]. As QASPER-LED can support sequence lengths up to about 16,000 tokens, 99% of the articles in the QASPER dataset can be processed without truncation [6]. We also compare our method with the ETC reader [1], one of the best models for processing long sequences, with a maximum of 4096 tokens capability. The result of the ETC reader on QASPER is taken from the work of Sun et al. [26] and is in two strategies. The first strategy is sequential reading, where ETC reads the article paragraph by paragraph and selects the most confident prediction. The second strategy is retrieval with a BM25 retriever and a fine-tuned

ETC reader. The performance is compared using the official QASPER evaluation metric F1 score. F1, Precision, and Recall estimate the average token-wise overlap between the predicted and gold answers. The F1 score is formulated as follows:

$$\text{Precision} = \frac{\text{Count of tokens predicted exactly}}{\text{Count of tokens predicted}}$$

$$\text{Recall} = \frac{\text{Count of tokens predicted exactly}}{\text{Count of gold standard tokens}}$$

$$\text{F1} = \frac{2 \, . \, \text{Precision} \, . \, \text{Recall}}{\text{Precision} + \text{Recall}}$$

Implementation Details. In the experiments, we choose TF-IDF as a sparse retriever and Transformer-based Cross-encoder as a re-ranker for comparisons. We use Scikit-learn [22] to implement the TF-IDF retriever. We implement the Cross-encoder re-ranker using SBERT [24] and Transformers [30] pre-trained model *cross-encoder/ms-marco-MiniLM-L-12-v2*, which is based on MiniLM [28] and fine-tuned on MSMARCO [3]. The readers are implemented using the Transformers library [30] and the pre-trained model RoBERTa [17], ELECTRA [5]. In some experiments, the *Oracle* setting is introduced as the upper-bound performance of the retrievers. In the *Oracle* setting, the input of the system is the passages containing the gold answers instead of a whole article. These passages are taken from the annotated evidences from QASPER. The results are measured using the official evaluation scripts of QASPER [6] and SQuAD 1.0 [23].

4.2   Experimental Results

Method Analysis. We conduct a series of experiments on QASPER development set to analyze different aspects of the proposed method.

The first set of experiments investigates the impact of different window sizes when applying a sliding window on the retrieval phase and the end-to-end QA pipeline. Figure 2 shows the impact of different window sizes and the number of retrieved passages on the retrieval accuracy. The retrieval accuracy is defined as the portion of the retrieval results that contains *at least* one gold answer. Figure 3 compares the performance of two Transformer-based readers RoBERTa [17] and ELECTRA [5], we use the large version of both models. RoBERTa and ELECTRA readers' performance peaks at window size $W = 150$ with F1 scores 28.66% and 30.43%, respectively. The performance of the retriever-reader pipeline is higher when applying the sliding window technique. This trend can be observed in both readers at all window sizes.

The second set of experiments investigates three different types of retrievers, namely Sparse Retriever, Dense Retriever, and Cross-encoder Re-ranker. Figure 4 compares the impact of these retrievers at different window sizes on the

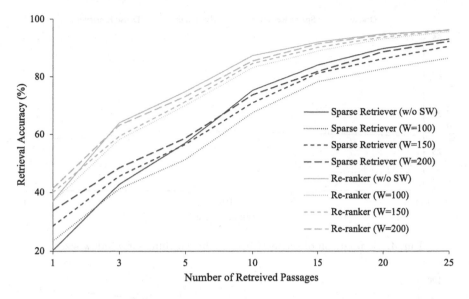

Fig. 2. Impact of the number of retrieved passages and window size on the Retrieval Accuracy. Comparison of the Sparse Retriever (TF-IDF) and the Cross-encoder Re-ranker (CE) with different window sizes $W \in \{100, 150, 200\}$

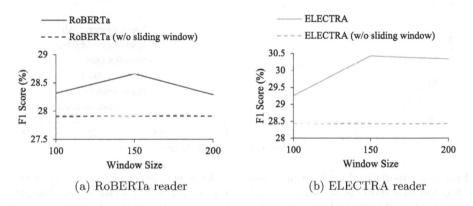

(a) RoBERTa reader   (b) ELECTRA reader

Fig. 3. Effect of a sliding window on end-to-end QA with different readers

end-to-end QA performance. An ELECTRA reader is used in all experiments to get the end-to-end answer. As mentioned in the implementation details, the *Oracle* represents the upper-bound performance of the retrievers. The result shows that Re-ranker performance consistently better than Sparse Retriever and Dense Retriever at all window sizes. The large gap between the Re-ranker and the *Oracle* indicates that there is room for improvement in the retrieval phase. Figure 5 compares retrieval accuracy of the three retrievers at different number

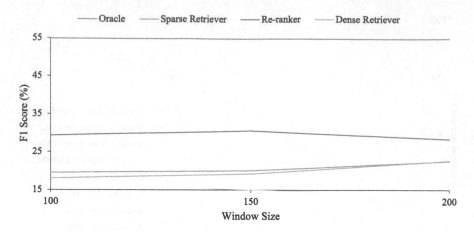

Fig. 4. Comparison of retriever approaches at different window sizes

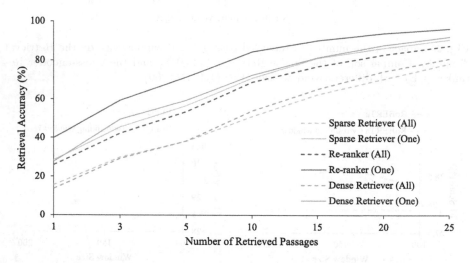

Fig. 5. Comparison of retriever approaches at different number of passages retrieved. The solid lines show the accuracy when the retrieved passages contain at least one gold answer (One). The dashed lines show the accuracy when the retrieved passages contain all gold answers (All)

of passages retrieved. The result shows that the Re-ranker approach consistently outperforms other two retrievers. The retrieval accuracy rises steadily when we increase the number of passages retrieved.

Comparison with State-of-the-Art Methods. We compare our method with state-of-the-art methods on QASPER development set (Table 1). Our method outperforms all state-of-the-art models including ETC [1], QASPER-LED [6], and DocHopper [26], which are designed for processing long sequences.

This indicates the efficiency of our retriever-reader approach and its ability to employ high-performance Transformer-based models such as RoBERTa, ELEC-TRA, without the limitation of long sequences.

Table 1. Comparison of the proposed method and state-of-the-art methods on QASPER development set (Extractive question subset)

Method	F1 Score
Retrieval + ETC	18.70
Sequential (ETC)	24.60
QASPER-LED	26.10
DocHopper	29.60
Proposed method - MiniLM Re-ranker - ELECTRA Reader - Sliding window (W=150)	**30.43**

Ablation Study. We perform an ablation study of different aspects of the proposed method to understand its relative importance. We focus on the following aspects: (1) impact of the sliding window technique, (2) similarity scores in Sparse Retriever and Dense Retriever, (3) different architectures in Dense Retrievers, (4) upper-bound performance of retrievers. The ablation study results are presented in Table 2. The first group is the standard-setting for comparison, which includes three retrievers (Sparse Retriever, Dense Retriever, Cross-encoder Re-ranker) and two readers (RoBERTa, ELECTRA). The second group shows the performance without applying a sliding window. A performance gain can be observed when applying a sliding window. The experiments in the third group use the dot product score instead of the cosine similarity score to compare the question and passage vectors in Sparse Retriever and Dense Retriever. There are minimal changes when applying a different similarity score. The fourth group is the evaluation of DPR [12], a dual-encoder architecture that uses two distinctly parameterized encoders instead of shared parameters across two encoders in the standard-setting. The result shows that DPR is comparable to MPNet Dense Retriever, and that the dot product score is more effective than cosine similarity in DPR. The last group is the *Oracle* setting, which represents the upper-bound performance of the retrievers.

Table 2. Ablation study of different aspect of the proposed method

Retriever	Reader	Sliding windows	Similarity score	F1 Score
Re-ranker (MiniLM)	RoBERTa	✓	-	28.66
	ELECTRA	✓	-	30.43
Sparse Retriever (TF-IDF)	RoBERTa	✓	Cosine	19.95
	ELECTRA	✓	Cosine	20.03
Dense Retriever (MPNet)	RoBERTa	✓	Cosine	18.78
	ELECTRA	✓	Cosine	19.16
Without sliding window				
Re-ranker (MiniLM)	RoBERTa	-	-	27.88
	ELECTRA	-	-	28.43
Sparse Retriever (TF-IDF)	RoBERTa	-	Cosine	18.34
	ELECTRA	-	Cosine	18.89
Dense Retriever (MPNet)	RoBERTa	-	Cosine	18.45
	ELECTRA	-	Cosine	18.53
Dot product similarity score				
Sparse Retriever (TF-IDF)	ELECTRA	✓	Dot product	20.03
	RoBERTa	✓	Dot product	19.95
Dense Retriever (MPNet)	RoBERTa	✓	Dot product	18.78
	ELECTRA	✓	Dot product	19.16
Dual-encoder				
DPR [12]	ELECTRA	v	Dot product	20.13
	ELECTRA	✓	Cosine	18.86
Oracle				
Re-ranker (MiniLM)	ELECTRA	✓	-	54.85
Sparse Retriever (TF-IDF)	ELECTRA	✓	Cosine	54.07
Dense Retriever (MPNet)	ELECTRA	✓	Cosine	53.29

5 Conclusions

We propose a method to adapt the retriever-reader approach in Open-domain QA to the problem of QA in long scientific documents. Our method allows us to employ efficient Transformer-based readers which overcome the previous limitations posed by long sequences. We also propose an effective sliding window technique that improves the performance of the retriever-reader pipeline by splitting the scientific articles into disjoint text blocks of fixed window size. Our analysis finds that Cross-encoder Re-rankers perform better than Sparse Retriever on scientific articles, and that a window size of 150 words produces the most effective results. The experimental results confirm that our method outperforms state-of-the-art models on the QASPER dataset. This study also paves the way for future research on efficient retrievers and readers to be applied in QA on long scientific documents without the obstacle of processing long sequences.

Acknowledgments. This work was supported by JSPS Kakenhi Grant Numbers 20H04295, 20K20406, and 20K20625.

References

1. Ainslie, J., et al.: ETC: encoding long and structured inputs in transformers. In: Proceedings of the 2020 Conference on Empirical Methods in Natural Language Processing (EMNLP), pp. 268–284. Association for Computational Linguistics, Online, November 2020
2. Beltagy, I., Peters, M.E., Cohan, A.: Longformer: the long-document transformer. CoRR (2020)
3. Campos, D.F.,et al.: Ms marco: a human generated machine reading comprehension dataset. ArXiv (2016)
4. Chen, D., Fisch, A., Weston, J., Bordes, A.: Reading Wikipedia to answer open-domain questions. In: Proceedings of the 55th Annual Meeting of the Association for Computational Linguistics. Association for Computational Linguistics (ACL) (2017)
5. Clark, K., Luong, M.T., Le, Q.V., Manning, C.D.: ELECTRA: pre-training text encoders as discriminators rather than generators. In: ICLR (2020)
6. Dasigi, P., Lo, K., Beltagy, I., Cohan, A., Smith, N.A., Gardner, M.: A dataset of information-seeking questions and answers anchored in research papers. In: Proceedings of the 2021 Conference of the North American Chapter of the Association for Computational Linguistics: Human Language Technologies, pp. 4599–4610. Association for Computational Linguistics, Online, June 2021
7. Devlin, J., Chang, M., Lee, K., Toutanova, K.: BERT: pre-training of deep bidirectional transformers for language understanding. In: Burstein, J., Doran, C., Solorio, T. (eds.) Proceedings of the 2019 Conference of the North American Chapter of the Association for Computational Linguistics: Human Language Technologies, NAACL-HLT 2019, Minneapolis, MN, USA, 2–7 June 2019, vol. 1 (Long and Short Papers), pp. 4171–4186. Association for Computational Linguistics (2019)
8. Gao, L., Dai, Z., Callan, J.: Modularized transformer-based ranking framework. In: Proceedings of the 2020 Conference on Empirical Methods in Natural Language Processing (EMNLP), pp. 4180–4190. Association for Computational Linguistics, Online, November 2020
9. Guu, K., Lee, K., Tung, Z., Pasupat, P., Chang, M.: REALM: retrieval-augmented language model pre-training. CoRR abs/2002.08909 (2020)
10. Iyer, S., Min, S., Mehdad, Y., Yih, W.: RECONSIDER: re-ranking using span-focused cross-attention for open domain question answering. CoRR (2020)
11. Joshi, M., Choi, E., Weld, D., Zettlemoyer, L.: TriviaQA: a large scale distantly supervised challenge dataset for reading comprehension. In: Proceedings of the 55th Annual Meeting of the Association for Computational Linguistics (Volume 1: Long Papers), pp. 1601–1611. Association for Computational Linguistics, Vancouver, Canada, July 2017. https://doi.org/10.18653/v1/P17-1147
12. Karpukhin, V., et al.: Dense passage retrieval for open-domain question answering. In: Proceedings of the 2020 Conference on Empirical Methods in Natural Language Processing (EMNLP), pp. 6769–6781. Association for Computational Linguistics, Online, November 2020
13. Khattab, O., Zaharia, M.: Colbert: Efficient and effective passage search via contextualized late interaction over BERT. CoRR (2020)

14. Kwiatkowski, T., et al.: Natural questions: a benchmark for question answering research. Trans. Assoc. Comput. Ling. (2019)
15. Lan, Z., Chen, M., Goodman, S., Gimpel, K., Sharma, P., Soricut, R.: Albert: a lite BERT for self-supervised learning of language representations. In: International Conference on Learning Representations (2020)
16. Lee, K., Chang, M.W., Toutanova, K.: Latent retrieval for weakly supervised open domain question answering. In: Proceedings of the 57th Annual Meeting of the Association for Computational Linguistics, pp. 6086–6096. Association for Computational Linguistics, Florence, Italy, July 2019. https://doi.org/10.18653/v1/P19-1612
17. Liu, Y., et al.: Roberta: a robustly optimized BERT pretraining approach. CoRR (2019)
18. Mao, Y., et al.: Reader-guided passage reranking for open-domain question answering. CoRR (2021)
19. Ni, J., et al.: Sentence-t5: scalable sentence encoders from pre-trained text-to-text models (2021). https://doi.org/10.48550/ARXIV.2108.08877, https://arxiv.org/abs/2108.08877
20. Nogueira, R., Cho, K.: Passage re-ranking with BERT. CoRR (2019)
21. Nogueira, R., Yang, W., Cho, K., Lin, J.: Multi-stage document ranking with BERT. CoRR (2019)
22. Pedregosa, F., et al.: Scikit-learn: machine learning in python. J. Mach. Learn. Res. **12**, 2825–2830 (2011)
23. Rajpurkar, P., Zhang, J., Lopyrev, K., Liang, P.: SQuAD: 100,000+ questions for machine comprehension of text. In: Proceedings of the 2016 Conference on Empirical Methods in Natural Language Processing. pp. 2383–2392. Association for Computational Linguistics, Austin, Texas, November 2016. https://doi.org/10.18653/v1/D16-1264
24. Reimers, N., Gurevych, I.: Sentence-BERT: sentence embeddings using Siamese BERT-networks. CoRR (2019)
25. Seo, M., Lee, J., Kwiatkowski, T., Parikh, A., Farhadi, A., Hajishirzi, H.: Real-time open-domain question answering with dense-sparse phrase index. In: Proceedings of the 57th Annual Meeting of the Association for Computational Linguistics, pp. 4430–4441. Association for Computational Linguistics, Florence, Italy, July 2019
26. Sun, H., Cohen, W.W., Salakhutdinov, R.: Iterative hierarchical attention for answering complex questions over long documents. In; ICLR (2021). https://doi.org/10.48550/ARXIV.2106.00200
27. Talmor, A., Berant, J.: The web as a knowledge-base for answering complex questions. In: Proceedings of the 2018 Conference of the North American Chapter of the Association for Computational Linguistics: Human Language Technologies, Volume 1 (Long Papers), pp. 641–651. Association for Computational Linguistics, New Orleans, Louisiana, June 2018. https://doi.org/10.18653/v1/N18-1059
28. Wang, W., Wei, F., Dong, L., Bao, H., Yang, N., Zhou, M.: Minilm: deep self-attention distillation for task-agnostic compression of pre-trained transformers. In: Proceedings of the 34th International Conference on Neural Information Processing Systems. NIPS 2020, Curran Associates Inc., Red Hook, NY, USA (2020)
29. Wang, Z., Ng, P., Ma, X., Nallapati, R., Xiang, B.: Multi-passage BERT: a globally normalized BERT model for open-domain question answering. In: EMNLP (2019)
30. Wolf, T., et al.: Transformers: State-of-the-art natural language processing. In: Proceedings of the 2020 Conference on Empirical Methods in Natural Language Processing: System Demonstrations, pp. 38–45. Association for Computational Linguistics, Online, October 2020

31. Yan, M., et al.: IDST at TREC 2019 deep learning track: deep cascade ranking with generation-based document expansion and pre-trained language modeling. In: Voorhees, E.M., Ellis, A. (eds.) Proceedings of the Twenty-Eighth Text REtrieval Conference, TREC 2019, Gaithersburg, Maryland, USA, 13–15 November 2019. NIST Special Publication, vol. 1250. National Institute of Standards and Technology (NIST) (2019)
32. Yang, Z., et al.: HotpotQA: a dataset for diverse, explainable multi-hop question answering. In: Proceedings of the 2018 Conference on Empirical Methods in Natural Language Processing, pp. 2369–2380. Association for Computational Linguistics, Brussels, Belgium, October–November 2018. https://doi.org/10.18653/v1/D18-1259
33. Zaheer, M., et al.: Big bird: transformers for longer sequences. In: 33th Proceeding Conference on Advances in Neural Information Processing Systems (2020)

P-FCloHUS: A Parallel Approach for Mining Frequent Closed High-Utility Sequences on Multi-core Processors

Hong-Phat Nguyen[1,2]([✉]) and Bac Le[1,2]

[1] Faculty of Information Technology, University of Science,
Ho Chi Minh City, Vietnam
lhbac@fit.hcmus.edu.vn
[2] Vietnam National University, Ho Chi Minh City, Vietnam
nhphat1997@gmail.com

Abstract. Frequent closed high-utility (FCHU) sequences are preferable to frequent closed sequences. Not only because of their utility-based nature that considerately contributes to taking decisive business actions, FCHU sequences also preserve necessary information for re-constructing frequent high-utility sequences. Despite of their vital role, mining FCHU sequences is a time consuming task when facing with large-scale datasets, or especially when the input thresholds are relatively small. To contend with these difficulties, this paper proposes a parallel algorithm named P-FCloHUS for fast mining FCHU sequences by making good use of multicore processors. By relying on a novel Single scan synchronization strategy that is facilitated by an efficiently Partitioned result space structure, P-FCloHUS successfully alleviates the communication cost between mining tasks and hence speeds up the parallel mining process. Experiments on both dense and sparse datasets show that P-FCloHUS outperforms the state-of-the-art FMaxCloHUSM in terms of runtime performance.

Keywords: Data mining · High-utility sequential pattern mining · Frequent closed sequence mining · Multi-core processors · Parallel mining

1 Introduction

FMaxCloHUSM [2] was introduced as the first algorithm for mining both FCHU [2] and FMaxHU [2] sequences separately, or simultaneously. Based on the relationship FMaxHU $\subseteq$ FCHU $\subseteq$ FHU, FMaxCloHUSM takes advantage of previously developed upper-bounds, early pruning strategies from state-of-the-art algorithms to achieve its outputs. Specifically, in order for a sequence α to become a member of a FCHU set, it first must be a frequent high-utility sequence. This means that the support measure, two upper-bounds LRU and RBU [5] can be used to filter out low-utility and/or infrequent sequences before performing any further checks. In addition to the SE [3] measure for early pruning non-closed sequences, the authors introduced the SLIP [5] measure.

© The Author(s), under exclusive license to Springer Nature Singapore Pte Ltd. 2022
E. Szczerbicki et al. (Eds.): ACIIDS 2022, CCIS 1716, pp. 396–408, 2022.
https://doi.org/10.1007/978-981-19-8234-7_31

Nonetheless, the runtime performance of FMaxCloHUSM is still high when the input thresholds, including *mu* (minimum utility) and *ms* (minimum support), are small. Or in a more practical situation where the dataset is huge containing a lot of sequences, FMaxCloHUSM takes rather long to obtain the result. And it could become inefficient if we perform FMaxCloHUSM on large datasets with small input threshold values. As a consequence, it is certainly necessary to develop a more scalable version of FMaxCloHUSM to deal with these situations.

In order to overcome the limitation of serial algorithms when facing large datasets or small input threshold values, researchers have applied the multi-core processor architecture to develop various parallel algorithms for mining frequent closed sequences [6], or high-utility sequences [4], and achieved comparatively good results. However, these proposals share the same disadvantages to their serial counterparts in that they do not take both the frequency and the utility of items into account at once. Additionally, each of these proposals has not completely been studied. Specifically, [4] mines high-utility sequences in an optimistic manner, [6] mines frequent closed sequences but it applies a parallel model named Melinda to maintain a shared memory space which creates another synchronization and thread communication overhead. The success of a parallel algorithm is a combination of efficiently breaking the original problem to individual tasks, maximizing the CPUs time and eventually optimizing the communication between tasks. Our work is the answer to this demand:

- We developed a pioneering algorithm for mining frequent closed high-utility sequences in parallel.
- We introduced a more efficient synchronization strategy named Single Scan Synchronization to speed up the communication between mining tasks.
- A novel data structure called Partitioned Result Space is devised to store intermediate candidates which facilitated the above synchronization strategy.
- Telling from the experimental results, our proposed algorithm outperforms FMaxCloHUSM in terms of runtime performance on both dense and sparse datasets.

The remaining sections of this paper are organized as follows. Section 2 contains preliminaries for mining frequent closed high-utility sequences. Section 3 describes Partitioned Result Space, Single Scan Synchronization strategy and our proposed P-FCHUS algorithm. Section 4 presents the experiment results. And Sect. 5 shows our conclusions as well as discussion of future work.

2   Preliminaries

Definition 1 (Quantitative Sequence Dataset). *Let* $I = \{i_1, i_2, ..., i_n\}$ *be a set of items that each* $i \in I$ *has an external utility representing its profit. A quantitative sequence* $S = E_1, E_2, ..., E_p$ *contains multiple quantitative itemsets* $(E_k | 1 \leq k \leq p)$ *where each one is a collection of quantitative items. A quantitative item is defined as a pair of* (i, q) *in that* $i \in I$, *and* $q \in R_+$ *which represents* *the quantity of i (or the internal utility of i) in this itemset. Also, all quantitative items in an itemset are organized in a lexicographical order $\succ$. The length and size of a quantitative sequence S is defined as the number of quantitative items(length(S) = $\sum_{k=1}^{p} |E_k|$), and the number of itemsets (size(S) = p) in S respectively. Consequently, we define a quantitative sequence dataset $\mathcal{D}$ as a collection of quantitative sequences.*

When an item is appended to the last itemset E_p of a sequence S such that the extension does not change the size of s, the extension is defined as an I-extension [8]. On the other hand, when an extension increases the size of s that is a S-extension [8].

Definition 2 (Sequence containment relation). *Given two sequences $S1 = E_1, E_2, ..., E_p$ and $S2 = F_1, F_2, ..., F_q$, S1 is said to be a supersequence of S2 ($S1 \sqsubseteq S2$), or S2 is a subsequence of S1 ($S2 \sqsupseteq S1$), when $E_{j_k} \subseteq F_k$ provided that $1 < j_1 < j_2 < ... < jq \leq p$ and $1 < k \leq q$.*

Definition 3 (Sequence utility measure). *The utility value of a pattern p in a quantitative dataset $\mathcal{D}$ is obtained by adding up utilities, computed in a pessimistic manner [5], of all occurrences of p in $\mathcal{D}$, or $\sum_{i=1}^{n} u(p, S_i)$ with n is the number of sequences. p is considered as a high-utility pattern when its utility value is not less than the minimum input utility threshold (mu).*

Definition 4 (Sequence support measure). *Given $\mathcal{D} = \{ S_1, S_2, ..., S_n \}$ is a dataset, in that n is the number of sequences, the support value of a pattern p is computed by counting the number of supersequences of p in $\mathcal{D}$, or $|S_i \in \mathcal{D}|p \sqsubseteq S_i|$. In fact, this support value is also referred to as the absolute support value of a pattern p. Apart of that, the relative support value is the result of the absolute support divided by the number of sequences in $\mathcal{D}$, or $\frac{|S_i \in \mathcal{D}|p \sqsubseteq S_i|}{n}$. p is considered as a frequent pattern when its support value is not less than the minimum input support threshold (ms).*

Definition 5 (Frequent closed high-utility sequences). *In order for a pattern p to be considered as a frequent closed high-utility pattern, p must be a frequent high-utility sequence in that neither of its utility nor support value is less than the corresponding minimum input threshold (mu or ms respectively). In addition to that, there does not exist any supersequence of p that shares the same support value to p.*

Consider an example quantitative dataset $\mathcal{D}$ with four quantitative sequences identified by sequence identities (SID), as presented in Table 2a, whose item external utilities are displayed in Table 2b correspondingly. Given a pair of input parameters with a minimum support = 3 and a minimum utility = 34, we can observe that both ac→a and b→a are frequent high-utility sequences. To be more specific, the former pattern appears in all sequences of $\mathcal{D}$ making it a frequent pattern with a support value = 4, and its utility value = 43. The latter appears in three sequences including S_2, S_3 and S_4 so its support value is 3 and its utility value is 35. However, only ac→a is eligible to become a frequent closed

Table 1. A sample dataset with sequences with internal item utilities (a) and external item utilities (b).

SID	Sequence
S_1	(a:2)(c:1)→(a:1)→(c:2)(d:4)
S_2	(b:2)→(a:2)(b:1)(c:3)→(b:3)(d:4)→(a:1)(b:2)
S_3	(a:3)(d:1)→(b:2)(c:4)(d:1)→(a:1)(b:1)(c:2)→(a:2)(d:1)
S_4	(a:1)(c:2)(d:3)→(a:2)(b:1)(c:1)→(a:3)(b:3)

(a)

Item	a	b	c	d
Utility	3	5	1	4

(b)

high-utility sequence because there does not exist any supersequence of ac→a that has an equal support value to ac→a. As opposed to that, the support value of b→ab is also 3 and it is a supersequence of b→a. As a result, b→a cannot be a frequent closed high-utility sequence.

3   Mining Frequent Closed High-Utility Sequences in Parallel

3.1   Multi-core Processors

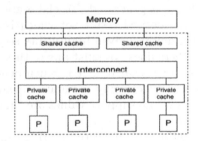

Fig. 1. A multi-core processor with private and shared caches

A multi-core processor is either homogeneous (where all cores of the processors are identical), or heterogeneous (where its cores do not share the same instruction set and/or performance) [1]. In this section, we discuss the former architecture of multi-core processor systems, and it is implicitly referred to as multi-core processors for the rest of this paper. Multiple parallel techniques, multithreaded programs and task-based programs can greatly benefit from a multi-core processor due to program instructions being separately executed by different computing units (or cores) at the same time. On top of that, each of these computing units might have a private cache which is for storing commonly used data and thus it considerably reduces the time needed for requesting data from the RAM. Also, a multi-core processor has a shared cache for data that is accessible to all its cores (or shared variables), and it maintains a cache-coherent memory system to keep a consistent view of these shared variables so that the latest globally updated data is available to all cores.

3.2   Partitioned Result Space Structure

As the mining process progresses, as in [2,6], it builds the search space, performs pruning unpromising candidates and updates the result set via a synchronization procedure. The synchronization begins whenever a new candidate sequence is generated. We observe that, there are two separate courses of action that need to be taken:

1. Perform a containment check to make sure that there are not any supersequence(s) whose support values are similar to the new candidate.
2. Eliminate previously reserved candidates if any. This occurs when the newly generated FCHU candidate shares the same support value to existing FCHU candidates, and this new FCHU candidate is a supersequence of those.

And each course of action requires a scan over a set where intermediate FCHU candidates are stored. Eventually these scanning procedures could cause a tremendous runtime penalty for the mining process when the number of intermediate candidates is huge in practice. Additionally, lengthy sequences make sequence containment check take longer to complete. Another observation is that we do not have to scan the whole set of existing FCHU candidate sequences when a new FCHU candidate is generated. To elaborate on this point, we need to take a closer look at the desired result set which is a collection of unique FHU sequences and in that any two given high-utility sequences α and β, whose support values are equal, there does not exist any of these containment relationships: $\alpha \sqsubseteq \beta$ or $\beta \sqsubseteq \alpha$. As a consequence, it is much beneficial to only perform a containment check between the newly generated candidate against existing FCHU candidate sequences whose support values are equal, not the whole set of FCHU candidate sequences.

To overcome this limitation, [6] suggested storing candidates that share the same support value and Sum-SIDs together as lists, then the above scanning procedures are only performed on one of those lists for each new candidate instead of the whole set of existing candidates. In a similar fashion, we devised a distinguishing structure called Partitioned Result Space to further reduce the cost of those scanning procedures. To be more specific, Partitioned Result Space only stores candidates by their support values and is a collection of lists in that each list maintains a *max_candidate_size* value representing the size of the largest candidate in that list. Putting candidates into Partitioned Result Space in this manner provides us with the following advantages:

- For those newly generated candidates whose sizes are larger than that of the *max_candidate_size* of a list, they meet the conditions to become members of the list without performing the first scanning procedure. Single Scan Synchronization technique relies on Partitioned Result Space, as presented in the next section.

– We only consider a subset of the exist FCHU candidate sequences that have an equal support value to the newly generated candidate, instead of the whole candidate set.

3.3   Single Scan Synchronization Strategy

Procedure Synchronize_FCHUS($p, FCHUS$)

.**Input**: A pattern p, FCHUS
.**Output**: FCHUS has been updated, $is\_s\_ext\_pruned$ and is_pruned

1: $is\_closed \leftarrow true$, $is\_s\_ext\_pruned \leftarrow false$, $is\_pruned \leftarrow false$
2: $corr\_list \leftarrow get\_corr\_list(FCHUS, supp(p))$
3: **if** $size(p) \leq corr\_list.max\_pattern\_size$ **then**
4:    **for** $\alpha \in corr\_list$ **and** is_closed **do**
5:       **if** $size(\alpha) \geq size(p)$ **and** $len(\alpha) \geq len(p)$ **then**
6:          **if** $p \sqsubset \alpha$ **then**
7:             $is\_closed \leftarrow false$
8:             **if** $SE(\alpha) = SE(p)$ **then**
9:                $is\_s\_ext\_pruned \leftarrow true$
10:                **if** $SLIP(\alpha) = SLIP(p)$ **then**
11:                   $is\_pruned \leftarrow true$
12:          **else**
13:             **if** $\alpha \sqsubset p$ **then**
14:                eliminate α from FCHUS
15:    **if** is_closed **then**
16:       $corr\_list \leftarrow corr\_list \cup p$
17:       $corr\_list.max\_pattern\_size \leftarrow size(p)$
18: **else**
19:    **for** $\alpha \in corr\_list$ **do**
20:       **if** $\alpha \sqsubset p$ **then**
21:          eliminate α from FCHUS
22:    $corr\_list \leftarrow corr\_list \cup p$
23:    $corr\_list.max\_pattern\_size \leftarrow size(p)$

Taking advantage of Partitioned Result Space is a clever way to minimize the number of candidates to examine in scanning procedures, but to make the most of it we designed a synchronization strategy where only one iteration is required. The rationale behind this strategy is to select which iteration to apply based on the result of comparing the size of newly generated candidates and the *max_candidate_size* value of their corresponding lists. There are two possible outcomes:

1. When the *max_candidate_size* of the corresponding list is smaller than the size of the currently considered candidate, that candidate is added to the list as a new FCHU and we update the *max_candidate_size* accordingly.

Besides, existing candidates must be examined and removed from the list if any of them becomes a non-FCHU by the candidate under consideration.

2. On the other hand (the size of the candidate is less than *max_candidate_size*), in this situation the corresponding list has candidates whose sizes are either greater (or equal to) or less than the newly generated candidate's. Therefore, we have to handle each group separately depending on their sizes. In addition, early pruning conditions SE [3] and SLIP [2] are also applied in this step.

As a consequence, we only need to execute one scanning process over the corresponding list, this enhancement partially contributes to speeding up the whole mining process. Details of the synchronization process is presented as the Synchronize_FCHUS procedure.

3.4   The Proposed P-FCloHUS Algorithm

Algorithm **P-FCloHUS**$(\mathcal{D}, ms, mu)$

.**Input**: QSDB $\mathcal{D}$, thresholds ms and mu
.**Output**: Partitioned result space FCHUS

1: $FCHUS \leftarrow \emptyset$
2: Scan $\mathcal{D}$ to construct SIDULs for all 1-item sequences
3: Remove all 1-item sequences whose $supp(sequence) < ms$ or $LRU(sequence) < mu$ from $\mathcal{D}$
4: $InitSet \leftarrow$ re-construct SIDULs from the updated $\mathcal{D}$
5: Initialize a team of threads equal to the number of available cores
6: **for** $p \in InitSet$ **do**
7:     Push **Mine_FCloHUS**$(p, InitSet, InitSet, ms, mu, FCHUS)$ into the task pool
8: Wait for all tasks to complete

This section describes the way we assembled previously presented structures, scanning strategies, early pruning conditions and the multi-core architecture to construct the proposed P-FCloHUS algorithm. The input of P-FCloHUS is comprised of a QSDB $\mathcal{D}$, two thresholds including a minimum support and a minimum utility, P-FCloHUS eventually returns a set of FCHUSs as its output. Briefly P-FCloHUS has two stages, namely **initial punning** and **recursive mining with parallelism** stage.

In the **initial punning** stage, for each of 1-item sequences P-FCloHUS scans $\mathcal{D}$ once to build a SIDUL [2] which is a handy representation for efficiently generating supersequences and quickly computing multiple measures including support, LRU, RBU, SE and SLIP down the road. Once all SIDULs are constructed, unpromising 1-item sequences are removed by either LRU or support, the remainders are considered as initial patterns and stored in an InitSet. Apart from that, FCHUS (a representative of the Partitioned Result Space) is initialized to be an empty set. Within the mining process, FCHUS is shared among all the tasks and subsequently gets updated in the synchronization step.

Procedure **MineFCloHUS**$(p, S, I, ms, mu, FCHUS)$

.Input: A pattern p, candidates for s/i-extentions (S/I) respectively, thresholds ms and mu, $FCHUS$
.Output: $FCHUS$ has been updated

1: $is\_s\_ext\_pruned \leftarrow false, is\_pruned \leftarrow false$
2: **if** $umin(p) \geq mu$ **then**
3:     $is\_s\_ext\_pruned, is\_pruned \leftarrow$ **Synchronize_FCHUS**$(p, FCHUS)$
4:     **if** is_pruned **then**
5:         return
6: **if** $RBU(p) < mu$ **then**
7:     return
8: $newS \leftarrow \emptyset, newI \leftarrow \emptyset$
9: **for** $i \in I$ **and** $i \succ lastItem(p)$ **do**
10:     **if** $LRU(p \diamond_i i) \geq mu$ **and** $supp(p \diamond_i i) \geq ms$ **then**
11:         $newI \leftarrow newI \cup i$
12:         $pi \leftarrow p \diamond_i i$
13:         **if** $SE(p) = SE(pi)$ **then**
14:             $is\_s\_ext\_pruned \leftarrow true$
15: **if** $\neg is\_s\_ext\_pruned$ **then**
16:     **for** $s \in S$ **do**
17:         **if** $LRU(p \diamond_s s) \geq mu$ **and** $supp(p \diamond_s s) \geq ms$ **then**
18:             $newS \leftarrow newS \cup i$
19:         **for** $s \in newS$ **do**
20:             Push **Mine_FCloHUS**$(p \diamond_s s, newS, newI, ms, mu, FCHUS)$ into the task pool
21: **else**
22:     $newS \leftarrow S$
23: **for** $s \in newI$ **do**
24:     Push **Mine_FCloHUS**$(p \diamond_i i, newS, newI, ms, mu, FCHUS)$ into the task pool
25: Wait for all tasks to complete

For the **recursive mining with parallelism** stage, P-FCloHUS creates as many tasks as the number of patterns in the InitSet. Each task is a unit of independent work which can be executed in parallel, and all tasks have their own data environment in that the data may hold either private variables (those are only visible to the task itself) or shared variables (those are accessible to other tasks, like FCHUS), or both. Once created tasks are executed immediately provided that there are idle threads around, otherwise tasks are deferred and placed into a conceptual pool. A unit of work, within the context of P-FCloHUS, is defined as a call to the Mine_FCloHUS procedure. As long as a pattern successfully made it to this point and its $umin(p)$ value satisfies the mu threshold, the pattern is eligible for proceeding with the synchronization as defined in the previous sections. Once the synchronization is complete, the pattern could be pruned, and its mining process is halted. Additionally, when the RBU(pattern) value is less than the mu threshold, the mining process of this branch is also stopped. Otherwise, i- and s-extensions of the pattern are constructed for each candidate item that meets the conditions of LRU and support. To fully take advantage of parallelism, the Mine_FCloHUS procedures creates tasks for all newly constructed extensions of the pattern, pushes them into the task pool and waits for them to finish. Finally, P-FCloHUS completes its mining process when there are no tasks left in the task pool and the all threads are idle.

4   Experimental Results

Experiments were carried out on five real-life datasets: BMS-Webview-1, BMS-Webview-2 [9], Online Retails [12], Foodmart [10] and Kosarak990K [11], detailed characteristics of each one are shown in Table 2. Items in Online Retails and Foodmart are integrated with their utility values. As opposed to that, BMS-Webview-1, BMS-Webview-2 and Kosarak990K are raw datasets without item utilities. Therefore, their item utilities are generated following the log-normal distribution. Regarding the experimental setup, we conducted experiments on an Intel Xeon Scalable Processors (Cascade Lake) 8-core CPU, with 3.6GHz and 16Gb RAM running Ubuntu 18.04 LTS.

Table 2. Datasets characteristics

Dataset	Sequences	Distinct items	Itemsets per sequence	Items per itemset
BMS-Webview-1	59,601	497	2.51	1
BMS-Webview-2	77,512	3340	4.62	1
Online Retails	4335	3928	4.24	20.99
Foodmart	8842	1559	6.59	4.63
Kosarak990K	990,000	41,270	8.14	1

To our best knowledge, P-FCloHUS is the first proposal for mining frequent closed high-utility patterns in a pessimistic approach on multi-core CPUs. FMax-CloHUSM is considered to be the serial counterpart of P-FCloHUS in that FMax-CloHUSM performs all mining tasks on a single core. Additionally, its original implementation was in Java 1.8. As a consequence, we re-implemented FMaxClo-HUSM from scratch using C++ to our best abilities and established a baseline, by mining only FCHU sequences, to which P-FCloHUS is compared.

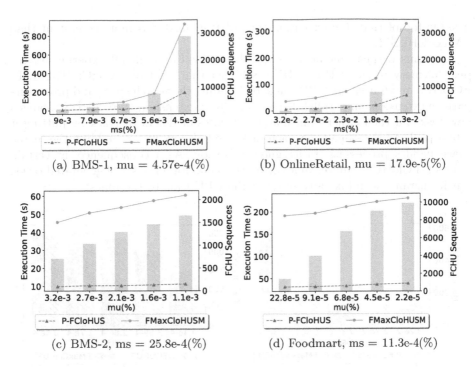

(a) BMS-1, mu = 4.57e-4(%)

(b) OnlineRetail, mu = 17.9e-5(%)

(c) BMS-2, ms = 25.8e-4(%)

(d) Foodmart, ms = 11.3e-4(%)

Fig. 2. Influence of minimum support (ms) and minimum utility (mu) values on runtime performance.

4.1 Influence of Input Thresholds on Runtime Performance and Memory Usage

In each experiment of this section, we keep the values of the minimum support (or the minimum utility parameter) unchanged while decreasing the values of the other one to capture the execution time and the peak memory usage. Also, the cardinality of FCHU sequences that are generated in each experiment is presented as bars in reference to the right axis. As comparing the execution time of P-FCloHUS with that of FMaxCloHUSM, shown by Figs. 2a and 2b, it is obvious that our proposed P-FCloHUS always yields better results regardless of the fluctuating values of the input thresholds. Also, it is shown that the smaller the minimum support is the larger the search space becomes and thus both P-FCloHUS and FMaxCloHUSM take longer to complete their mining process. In general, with the smallest values of the minimum support parameter, the runtime of P-FCloHUS is approximately 5 times less than that of FMaxCloHUSM in OnlineRetail and BMS-WebView-1. On the other hand, the changes in the minimum high utility parameter do not have that much of influence, in that the runtime does not vary as significantly as in the case of the minimum support parameter. Nonetheless, as shown by Figs. 2c and 2d, P-FCloHUS manages to get over 5.4 times faster than FMaxCloHUSM, given the smallest support values. On top of that, the execution time of P-FCloHUS is more consistent than FMaxCloHUSM.

In terms of peak memory usage, shown by Fig. 3, in all experiments the peak memory usage of P-FCloHUS is higher than that of FMaxCloHUSM. P-FCloHUS maximizes the CPU usage by building the search space and processing pattern extensions in parallel. For each pattern extension, P-FCloHUS creates a new task and then either immediately executes or defers the task by putting it into a pool. At the same time, each task itself also works on building the search space besides processing its assigned extension. As a consequence, at certain points P-FCloHUS requires more memory to maintain the set of generated tasks, but it guarantees to take advantage of the CPU time to the fullest.

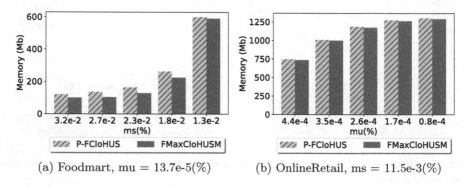

(a) Foodmart, mu = 13.7e-5(%)   (b) OnlineRetail, ms = 11.5e-3(%)

Fig. 3. Influence of minimum support (ms) and minimum utility (mu) values on memory usage

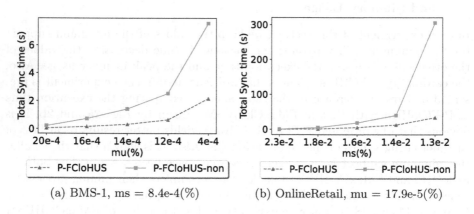

(a) BMS-1, ms = 8.4e-4(%)   (b) OnlineRetail, mu = 17.9e-5(%)

Fig. 4. Effectiveness of Single scan synchronization strategy

4.2   Effectiveness of the Single Scan Synchronization Strategy

As displayed in Fig. 4, the total number of seconds P-FCloHUS spends on the synchronization process is always lower than P-FCloHUS-non (without Single scan synchronization strategy). Even when the input thresholds become smaller, the synchronization time gap between the two implementations becomes more obvious in that P-FCloHUS is superior to P-FCloHUS-non. With the advantage of our proposal in the synchronization strategy, P-FCloHUS only performs a selective scan procedure and successfully shortens the required communication time between its mining tasks.

4.3   Scalability

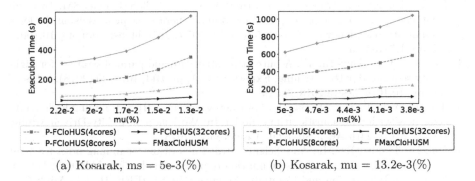

(a) Kosarak, ms = 5e-3(%)   (b) Kosarak, mu = 13.2e-3(%)

Fig. 5. Scalability on Kosarak990k

We performed more experiments using multiple CPU setups with various number of cores. When interpreting the results, we observed that the more cores we have the faster P-FCloHUS becomes. With that being said, as shown in Fig. 5 a 32-core CPU does not contribute as much to the runtime. Nevertheless, results on dense datasets are better than that of sparse datasets. In fact, we conducted experiments on Foodmart and with a 1×32-core CPU it takes only 6.4 s as compared to 16.4 s of a 1×16-core CPU which means up to 2.5 times faster, given mu=13.7–5(%) and ms =11.3e–4(%).

5   Conclusion and Future Work

In this work, by taking the advantage of multi-core processors we devised an efficient parallel solution for mining FCHU sequences. Also, a novel Single scan synchronization strategy was proposed to alleviate the communication cost between tasks and thus shorten the execution time in overall. Experiments carried out on both dense and spare datasets show that our proposed solution has made a notable improvement, in terms of runtime performance even when the input thresholds are very small.

In the future, we aim to work on a more scalable solution for mining FCHU sequences by applying the Single scan synchronization idea into distributed processing engines. These engines combine the computing power of multiple computers which open more opportunities to speed up the mining process.

References

1. Vajda, A.: Multi-core and Many-core Processor Architectures. In: Programming Many-Core Chips. Springer, Boston (2011)
2. Tin, T., Hai, D., Bac, L., Fournier-Viger, P.: FMaxCloHUSM: an efficient algorithm for mining frequent closed and maximal high utility sequences. Eng. Appli. Artif. Intell. **85**, 1–20 (2019). https://doi.org/10.1016/j.engappai.2019.05.010
3. Le, B., Duong, H., Truong, T., Fournier-Viger, P.: FCloSM, FGenSM: two efficient algorithms for mining frequent closed and generator sequences using the local pruning strategy. Knowl. Inf. Syst. **53**(1), 71–107 (2017). https://doi.org/10.1007/s10115-017-1032-6
4. Bac, L., Ut, H., Duy-Tai, D.: A pure array structure and parallel strategy for high-utility sequential pattern mining. Expert Syst. Appl. **104**, 107–120 (2018). https://doi.org/10.1016/j.eswa.2018.03.019
5. Tin, T., Anh, T., Hai, D., Bac, L., Fournier-Viger. P.: EHUSM: mining high utility sequences with a pessimistic utility model. In: Workshop on Utility-Driven Mining (UDM 2018), 24th ACM SIGKDD Conference (2018)
6. Hai, D., Tin, T., Bac, L.: An efficient parallel algorithm for mining both frequent closed and generator sequences on multi-core processors. In: 5th NAFOSTED Conference on Information and Computer Science (NICS). IEEE, Ho Chi Minh City (2018)
7. Yin, J., Zheng, Z., Cao, L.: Uspan: an efficient algorithm for mining high utility sequential patterns. In: Proceedings of the 18th ACM SIGKDD International Conference on Knowledge Discovery and Data Mining, pp. 660–668. ACM (2012)
8. Wang, J.-Z., Huang, J.-L., Chen, Y.-C.: On efficiently mining high utility sequential patterns. Knowl. Inf. Syst. **49**(2), 597–627 (2016). https://doi.org/10.1007/s10115-015-0914-8
9. Fournier-Viger, P., et al.: The SPMF open-source data mining library version 2. In: Berendt, B., et al. (eds.) ECML PKDD 2016. LNCS (LNAI), vol. 9853, pp. 36–40. Springer, Cham (2016). https://doi.org/10.1007/978-3-319-46131-1_8
10. Gorbach, I., Berger, A., Melomed, E.: Microsoft SQL Server 2008 Analysis Services Unleashed. Pearson Education, London (2008)
11. Repository, F.I.M.D.: Frequent itemset mining dataset repository. In: Workshop on Frequent Itemset Mining Implementations. http://fimi.ua.ac.be/data (2017)
12. Chen, D.D.: UCI machine learning repositories - Online retail dataset (2015)
13. Gan, W., Lin, J.C.-W., Fournier-Viger, P., Chao, H.-C., Yu, P.S.: A survey of parallel sequential pattern minin. In: ACM Transactions on Knowledge Discovery from DataVolume, vol. 13, no. 25, pp. 1–34 (2019). https://doi.org/10.1145/3314107
14. Truong-Chi, T., Fournier-Viger, P.: A survey of high utility sequential pattern mining. In: Fournier-Viger, P., Lin, J.C.-W., Nkambou, R., Vo, B., Tseng, V.S. (eds.) High-Utility Pattern Mining. SBD, vol. 51, pp. 97–129. Springer, Cham (2019). https://doi.org/10.1007/978-3-030-04921-8_4

dMITP-Miner: An Efficient Method for Mining Maximal Inter-transaction Patterns

Thanh-Ngo Nguyen[✉]

Department of Applied Informatics, Faculty of Information and Communication Technology,
Wrocław University of Science and Technology, Wrocław, Poland
thanh-ngo.nguyen@pwr.edu.pl

Abstract. In this paper, we propose an efficient algorithm, namely dMITP-Miner, for mining frequent maximal inter-transaction patterns (FMITPs). The proposed method uses diffset to store the information of patterns for efficiently mining FMITPs. In addition, we also proposed effective pruning strategies to help in reducing the search space to speed up the runtime and to cut down the memory usage. Experiments have been conducted to compare the effectiveness between the dMITP-Miner and the tMITP-Miner method in terms of runtime and memory usage.

Keywords: Pattern mining · Inter-transaction pattern mining · Maximal itemset mining · Frequent maximal inter-transaction pattern mining

1 Introduction

Frequent maximal pattern (FMP) mining is an interesting topic in data mining. Association rule mining (ARM) from a very large number of frequent patterns (FPs) would generate a lot of redundant association rules, which will make it harder for us to predict and make decisions. To solve this problem, condensed representations are used to not only reduce the overall size of frequent patterns collection, but also to obtain non-redundant association rules. One of the main types of condensed representation is frequent maximal patterns (FMPs). Although a set of FMPs is a subset of FPs, it still has the necessary properties for generating essential association rules and helps significantly reduce the search space, computation time, and memory usage. So far, many methods have been proposed for mining FMPs, consisting of MaxMiner [1], DepthProject [1], GenMax [2], dGenMax [2], MAFIA [3], TDM-MFI [4], and INLA-MFP [5].

So far, many algorithms have been proposed for mining frequent maximal patterns of items occurring within transactions, but there is no method for mining frequent maximal patterns (FMPs) across transactions in the database. In this study, we propose an efficient algorithm, namely dMITP-Miner, for mining frequent maximal inter-transaction patterns (FMITPs).

Our proposed algorithm has the following main contributions. We apply our proposed strategies presented in [6] and [7], which help fast pruning infrequent 1-patterns. Then, dMITP-Miner algorithm applies those strategies to reduce the search space in order to

© The Author(s), under exclusive license to Springer Nature Singapore Pte Ltd. 2022
E. Szczerbicki et al. (Eds.): ACIIDS 2022, CCIS 1716, pp. 409–422, 2022.
https://doi.org/10.1007/978-981-19-8234-7_32

quickly find all frequent inter-transaction patterns (FITPs) at the 1-pattern level with their tidsets. Next, the proposed algorithm uses DFS (Depth First Search) traversing to generate all FMITPs with their diffsets. The tidsets of FMPs are no longer used from the 2-pattern level onwards, diffsets are used to store the information of the patterns instead. Finally, experiments are conducted to prove the effectiveness between dMITP-Miner and tMITP-miner [8] algorithms in terms of runtime and memory usage.

The remainder of this article is structured as follows. Section 2 presents basic concepts and relevant works. Section 3 discusses the proposed algorithm (tMITP-Miner) for mining FMITPs. Experimental results are discussed in Sect. 4. Section 5 concludes the paper and shows future works.

2 Basic Concepts and Related Works

A transaction database D is defined as follows. A transaction database D consists of n transactions, $T = \{T_1, T_2, ..., T_n\}$, in which each transaction is defined as a subset of a set of distinct items, $I = \{i_1, i_2, ..., i_m\}$, where m is the number of items. A tidset is a subset of a set of transaction identifiers (tid) of D, tidset $\subseteq \{tid_1, tid_2, ..., tid_n\}$. Therefore, a D can be expressed as a set of tuples $\langle tid, T_{tid} \rangle$, where $T_{tid} \subseteq I$, and T_{tid} is a pattern occurring at tid transaction. The support of pattern X, denoted by support(X), is the number of transactions in D containing the pattern X. Assume that $\langle \alpha, T_\alpha \rangle$ and $\langle \beta, T_\beta \rangle$ are two transactions of D. The value of $(\alpha - \beta)$ is called relative distance between α and β, where $\alpha > \beta$, and β is called the reference point. With respect to β, an item i_k, where $k \in \{1, ..., m\}$ at α is called an extended item, denoted by $i_k(\alpha - \beta)$, where $(\alpha - \beta)$ is called the Span of the extended item. In the same way, with respect to the transaction at β, a transaction T_α at α is called an extended transaction and denoted as $T_\alpha(\alpha - \beta)$. Therefore, $T_\alpha(\alpha - \beta) = \{i_1(\alpha - \beta), ..., i_p(\alpha - \beta)\}$, where p is the number of items in T_α.

An example database consists of 6 transactions ($n = 6$) and $I = \{a, b, c, d\}$ is shown in Table 1. This database is also used to illustrate examples throughout this article. Therefore, with respect to the transaction at tid = 1 in the example database in Table 1, the extended transaction of the transaction at tid = 2 is $\{a(2–1), c(2–1), d(2–1)\} = \{a(1), c(1), d(1)\}$.

Suppose that $x_i(\omega_i)$ and $x_j(\omega_j)$ are two extended items that satisfy the following criteria: $x_i(\omega_i) < x_j(\omega_j)$ if $(\omega_i < \omega_j)$ or $(\omega_i = \omega_j$ and $x_i < x_j)$. In addition, $x_i(\omega_i) = x_j(\omega_j)$ if $\omega_i = \omega_j$ and $x_i = x_j$. For instance, $c(0) < c(1)$, $c(0) < d(0)$, and $c(1) = c(1)$. An inter-transaction pattern (ITP) is defined as a set of extended items, $\{x_1(\omega_1), x_2(\omega_2), ..., x_k(\omega_k)\}$, where $\omega_1 = 0$, $\omega_l \leq maxSpan$, maxSpan is a maximum Span given by user, $x_i(\omega_i) < x_j(\omega_j)$, and $1 \leq i < j \leq l$. A pattern is called a l-pattern, a pattern of length l, if it contains l extended items. For example, $\{a(0), b(0), a(1)\}$ is a 3-pattern. Let X be an inter-transaction pattern (ITP). X is called an FITP if support(X) $\geq$ minSup, where minSup is a minimum support given by user. An FITP X is called an FMITP if it does not have any superset. For instance, using the example in Table 1 with minSup = 50% and maxSpan = 1, we have only two FMITPs, $\{d(0), a(0), a(1)\}$ and $\{b(0), a(0), a(1), d(1)\}$.

There are many applications of FITP mining in the real life. Applications of FITP mining in predicting the movements of stock prices were presented by Lu et al. [9],

Table 1. A transaction database example

Tid	Items
1	$\{a, b\}$
2	$\{a, c, d\}$
3	$\{a\}$
4	$\{a, b, c, d\}$
5	$\{a, b, d\}$
6	$\{a, d\}$

and studying meteorological data has also been proposed by Li et al. [10]. Several other algorithms based on Apriori have also been proposed to mine FITP, such as E/EH-Apriori [11] and FITI [12]. Expanding the scope of the association rules mined from traditional one-way internal transaction association rules to multi-dimensional inter-transaction association rules was also introduced by Li et al. [13]. Lee et al. recently presented two algorithms ITP-Miner [14] and ICMiner [15] to mine FITPs and FCITPs. ITP-Miner is based on IT-Tree and DFS traversing to mine FITPs. While ICMiner, which is based on IT-Tree and CHARM properties, is used to mine all frequent closed inter-transaction patterns. Wang et al. proposed the PITP-Miner [16] algorithm, which relies on tree projection to mine entire sets of FITPs in a database. In addition, FITP mining has been applied to mine profit rules from stock databases by Hsieh et al., with approaches such as PRMiner [17], JCMiner and ATMiner [18]. The authors also presented ITR-Miner and NRIT [19] to mine redundant inter-union association rules. Nguyen et al. recently proposed two efficient methods, DITP-Miner [20] and FCITP [21], to effectively mine FITPs and FCITPs, respectively.

3 The Proposed Algorithm (DMITP-Miner) for Mining FMITPs

In this section, we propose an efficient algorithm, namely dMITP-Miner, for mining frequent maximal inter-transaction patterns (FMITPs). The proposed method uses diffset to store the information of patterns for efficiently mining FMITPs. In addition, we also proposed effective pruning strategies to help in reducing the search space to speed up the runtime and to cut down the memory usage. Experiments have been conducted to compare the effectiveness between the dMITP-Miner and the tMITP-Miner in terms of runtime and memory usage.

3.1 dMITP-Miner Algorithm

The dMITP-Miner consists of three subroutines, such as the main program of dMITP-Miner, the FIND-FMITPs procedure, and the SUBSET-CHECK procedure, which are shown in Figs. 1, 2, 3, respectively. Initially, the set of FMITPs is initialized to Ø, shown in Line 1.

Algorithm: dMITP-Miner $(D, minSup, maxSpan)$

Input: A transaction D, $minSup$, $maxSpan$.

Output: $FMITPs$, all frequent MITPs.

Begin

1    $FMITPs \leftarrow \varnothing$

2   Scan database D to generate FIT 1-pattern using *tidsets*

with $Span = 0$ and $Span \neq 0$, $0 \leq Span \leq maxSpan$. The proposed theorems are applied at this step to early prune infrequent patterns.

3   Add FIT 1-patterns with $Span = 0$ called $List_0$ into the root {} of the MITP-tree, sort $List_0$ in increasing order of *support*.

4   Add FIT 1-patterns with $Span > 0$ to $List_{sp}$, and sort $List_{sp}$ in increasing order according to $Span$.

5   **For** $i = 0$ to $List_0.count - 1$ **do**

6   Let $FIsNext \leftarrow \varnothing$

7   **For** $j = i + 1$ to $List_0.count - 1$ **do**

8                $chkdiffset = \{List_0[i].tidset\} \backslash \{List_0[j].tidset\}$

9                $support = List_0[i].support - chkdiffset$

10   **If** $support \geq minSup$ **then**

11   Creating $newNode \leftarrow \varnothing$

12                        $newNode.Add(List_0[i])$

13                        $newNode.Add(List_0[j])$

14                        $newNode.Add(support)$

15                        $newNode.Add(chkdiffset)$

16   Adding the $newNode$ to the $FIsNext$

17   **End for**

Fig. 1. The pseudo-code of the proposed algorithm, dMITP-Miner.

18   **For** $k = 0$ to $List_{sp}.count - 1$ **do**

19              $chkdiffset = \{List_0[i].tidset\}\backslash\{List_{sp}[k].tidset\}$

20              $support = List_0[i].support - chkdiffset$

21   **If** $support \geq minSup$ **then**

22   Creating $newNode \leftarrow \emptyset$

23                      $newNode.Add(List_0[i])$

24                      $newNode.Add\big(List_{sp}[k]\big)$

25                      $newNode.Add(support)$

26                      $newNode.Add(chkdiffset)$

27   Adding the $newNode$ to the $FIsNext$

28   **End for**

29   **If** $FIsNext \neq \emptyset$ **then**

            Sorting the $FIsNext$ in increasing order of *support*

30   **FIND-FMITPs(**$FIsNext$**)**

31   **If (SUBSET-CHECK(**$List_0[i]$**))** == false **then**

            FMITPs.Add($List_0[i]$)

32 **End for**

33 **End Algorithm**

Fig. 1. (*continued*)

Function **FIND-FMITPs(*FITs*)**

1    $Y \leftarrow \bigcup_{i=0}^{|FITs|-1} X_i$, where X_i is an element in the collection of *FITs*.

2   **If** $\exists M \in FMITPs$, such that $Y \subseteq M$ **then** return

3   **For** $i = 0$ to $|FITs|$ - 1 **do**

4   Let $FIsNext \leftarrow \emptyset$

5   **For** $j = i + 1$ to $|FITs|$ - 1 **do**

6      $diffset = \{FITs[j].diffset\} \backslash \{FITs[i].diffset\}$

7   *support* = *FITs[i].support* – *FITs$_{ij}$.diffset*

8   **If** (*support* ≥ *minSup*) **then**

9   *FITs$_{ij}$* = *FITs[i]* ∪ *FITs[j]*

10   *FITs$_{ij}$.support* = *support*

11   *FITs$_{ij}$.diffset* = *diffset*

12   *FIsNext* ← *FIsNext* ∪ *FITs$_{ij}$*

13   **End if**

14   **End for //** the For loop starts at Line 3

15   **If** *FIsNext* ≠ $\emptyset$ **then FIND-FMITPs(*FIsNext*)**

16   **Else If SUBSET-CHECK** (*FITs[i]*) == false **then**

17   Add *FITs[i]*) to *FMITPs*

18   **End If**

19   **End for**

Fig. 2. The procedure FIND-FMITPs of dMITP-Miner algorithm for recursively traversing the data to generate all FMITPs.

Function **SUBSET-CHECK(*fmitp*)**

1   **For each** *fmi* in *FMITPs* **do**

2   **If** *fmitp* ⊆ *fmi* **then**

3   **Return** *true*

4   **Return** *false*

Fig. 3. The pseudo-code of the procedure SUBSET-CHECK of dMITP-Miner.

Next, dMITP-Miner scans the database to find FIT 1-patterns using tidset with *Span* $= 0$ and *Span* > 0. In this step, the proposed theorems are applied to early prune infrequent 1-patterns, shown at Line 2.

Then, Lines 3–4 indicate that the FIT 1-patterns with *Span* $= 0$ and *Span* > 0 are added to *List*$_0$ and *List*$_{sp}$, respectively. *List*$_0$ and *List*$_{sp}$ are sorted in ascending order of *support* and *Span*, respectively.

Lines 5–28 indicate that dMITP-Miner utilizes Depth-First Search traversing to generate FIT 2-patterns, which are added to FIsNext. From the 2-pattern level onwards, diffset is used to determine patterns' support instead of using tidset as the previous level.

Line 29 indicates that dMITP-Miner checks whether FIsNext is null. If not, the FIT 2-patterns in the list FIsNext are resorted in ascending order of support.

In Line 30, the procedure FIND-FMITPs is recursively called on to find the FMITPs based on diffset with the list of FIT 2-patterns, called FIsNext, as input.

Figure 1 describes the performance of the dMITP-Miner algorithm that combines FITPs in the FIsNext to generate FMITPs. Initially, FIND-FMITPs checks whether the combination of all the elements of the list FITs is subsumed by any FMITP in the search set of FMITPs, shown in Lines 1–2 in Fig. 2. If so, the algorithm returns to the main program to continue executing the rest of the algorithm on the other branches. If not, dMITP-Miner combines 2-patterns to create FITPs for the next level (FIsNext), indicated in Lines 3–14 of Fig. 2.

At Line 15, dMITP-Miner checks if FIsNext is empty. If not, the FIND-FMITPs procedure is recursively called on, with FIsNext as input. If so, dMITP-Miner goes to Line 16 to run the SUBSET-CHECK. FIND-FMITPs is recursively executed until FIsNext is empty. And then FIND-FMITPs jumps to Line 16 to call the SUBSET-CHECK procedure to check if the largest pattern that has been created in the previous step is subsumed by any pattern in FMITPs. If not, dMITP-Miner adds the pattern to FMITPs. Then, the algorithm backtracks to the previous level to execute SUBSET-CHECK to find frequent MITPs until reaching the root node at the 2-pattern level.

Next, dMITP-Miner returns to the main program, and calls the SUBSET-CHECK procedure to check whether the FIT 1-pattern, *List*$_0$[i], is a frequent maximal ITP. If so, the algorithm adds this FIT 1-pattern to FMIITPs.

Likewise, all of the FMITPs are discovered by recursive performance of dMITP-Miner in the remaining branches until no FMITP is found. The algorithm dMITP-Miner terminates and returns the final search set, FMITPs.

3.2 Illustrative Example

We use the example database, shown in Table 1, with $minSup = 50\%$ and $maxSpan = 1$, to describe the execution of dMITP-Miner algorithm.

Initially, dMITP-Miner scans the database to generate FIT 1-patterns. In addition, our proposed theorems are applied in this step to reduce the research space and to quickly determine FIT 1-patterns. We obtain FIT 1-patterns with $Span = 0$, including $\{b(0)\}:3\langle 1, 4, 5\rangle$, $\{d(0)\}:4\langle 2, 4, 5, 6\rangle$, $\{a(0)\}:6\langle 1, 2, 3, 4, 5, 6\rangle$, which are added to the root$\{\}$ of the MITP-tree and sorted in ascending order of support. We also obtain FIT 1-patterns with $Span > 0$, in this case $Span = 1$, including $\{d(1)\}:4\langle 1, 3, 4, 5\rangle$, $\{a(1)\}:5\langle 1, 2, 3, 4, 5\rangle$, which are sorted in ascending order of support, and added to $List_{sp}$. $\{b(1)\}:2\langle 3, 4\rangle$ in which $support = 2$ is less than $minSup = 3$, and so it is pruned from $List_{sp}$.

The dMITP-Miner creates FMITPs by using the Depth-First Search manner. The proposed allgorithm uses diffset to quickly determine the support of patterns during the mining process.

For the branch at $[b(0)]$, dMITP-Miner generates FIT 2-patterns, which are $\{b(0)a(0)\}:3\langle\emptyset\rangle$, $\{b(0)a(1)\}:3\langle\emptyset\rangle$, and $\{b(0)d(1)\}:3\langle\emptyset\rangle$.

Next, dMITP-Miner algorithm calls on the procedure FIND-FMITPs with the collection of FIT 2-patterns, sorted in ascending order of support, as an input. FIND-FMITPs combines $\{b(0)a(0)\}:3\langle\emptyset\rangle$ and $b(0)a(1)\}:3\langle\emptyset\rangle$, $\{b(0)a(0)\}:3\langle\emptyset\rangle$ and $b(0)d(1)\}:3\langle\emptyset\rangle$ to create two 3-patterns, which are $\{b(0)a(0)a(1)\}:3\langle\emptyset\rangle$ and $\{b(0)a(0)d(1)\}:3\langle\emptyset\rangle$, respectively.

In the next step, the procedure FIND-FMITPs continues to be called to connect $\{b(0)a(0)a(1)\}:3\langle\emptyset\rangle$ and $\{b(0)a(0)d(1)\}:3\langle\emptyset\rangle$ to generate $\{b(0)a(0)a(1)d(1)\}:3\langle\emptyset\rangle$.

At this point, because the next level $FIsNext = \{\emptyset\}$, the procedure SUBSET-CHECK is called on to check whether $\{b(0)a(0)a(1)d(1)\}:3\langle\emptyset\rangle$ is subsumed by any FMITP in the set of FMITPs. Since $\{b(0)a(0)a(1)d(1)\}:3\langle\emptyset\rangle$ is not subsumed by any FMITP in the set of FMITPs, $\{b(0)a(0)a(1)d(1)\}:3\langle\emptyset\rangle$ is added to the set of FMITPs.

After that dMITP-Miner backtracks to $\{b(0)a(0)d(1)\}:3\langle\emptyset\rangle$, which is also a maximal candidate. However, since it is contained in $\{b(0)a(0)a(1)d(1)\}:3\langle\emptyset\rangle$, it is pruned.

The search backtracks to $\{b(0)a(1)\}:3\langle\emptyset\rangle$, and dMITP-Miner connects $\{b(0)a(1)\}:3\langle\emptyset\rangle$ and $\{b(0)d(1)\}:3\langle\emptyset\rangle$ to create $\{b(0)a(1)d(1)\}:3\langle\emptyset\rangle$. At this point, $\{b(0)a(1)d(1)\}:3\langle\emptyset\rangle$ is added to the set FMITPs because It has no other extensions, so that FMITPs $= \{\{b(0)a(1)d(1)\}:3\langle\emptyset\rangle\}$. And then, we backtrack to $\{b(0)a(1)d(1)\}:3\langle\emptyset\rangle$, which is also a candidate to be maximal. However, it is subsumed by $\{b(0)a(1)d(1)\}:3\langle\emptyset\rangle$ in the search set FMITPs, and so it is removed.

The proposed algorithm goes back to the main program to check whether $\{b(0)\}:3\langle\emptyset\rangle$ is a maximal pattern. It is pruned because it is contained in $\{b(0)a(1)d(1)\}:3\langle\emptyset\rangle$.

Likewise, for the branches at $[d(0)]$ and $[a(0)]$, dMITP-Miner generates all of the FMITPs, shown in Fig. 4, where the bold-border rectangles indicate that the patterns are maximal ones; the strikethrough lines indicate that the patterns are not maximal and should be removed by the SUBSET-CHECK procedure.

The final set that we need to find is FMITPs, including the two maximal patterns $\{b(0)a(0)a(1)d(1)\}:3\langle\emptyset\rangle$ and $\{d(0)a(0)a(1)\}:3\langle\emptyset\rangle$.

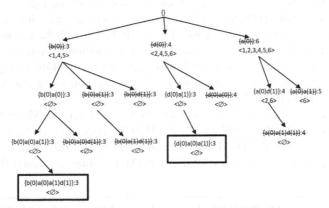

Fig. 4. An example of the performance of the dMITP-Miner algorithm on the example database with $minSup = 50\%$ and $maxSpan = 1$.

4 Experimental Results

The algorithms applied in the experiments were written using Visual C# 2019 and tested on a computer with the following specifications: CPU Intel(R) Core(TM) i7-8565U processor @ 1.80 GHz, 20 GB RAM, and running Windows 10. Experimental databases were downloaded from the Frequent Itemset Mining Dataset Repository (http://fimi.ua. ac.be/data), and their characteristics are presented in Table 2.

We compare the proposed algorithm, dMITP-Miner, with the tMITP-Miner algorithm, regarding the mining time and memory usage. Through the experimental evaluations, we varied the parameters such as *minSup*, and *maxSpan*, in order to accurately assess the effectiveness of the algorithms used in the tests.

Table 2. Characteristics of the databases used for experimentation

Dataset	#distinct items	#records	#Average length
Chess	76	3,196	37
Connect	129	67,557	43
T10I4D100K	870	100,000	10
T40I10D100K	942	100,000	40

4.1 Mining Time

In Figs. 5, 6, 7, 8, we compare the runtime of the tMITP-Miner and dMITP-Miner lgorithms for Chess, Connect, T10I4D100K, and T40I10D100K databases with various setting.

In Fig. 5 with the Chess database, on the left plot, we fix *maxSpan* = 1, and vary *minSup* in the range of {80%, 82%, 84%, 86%, 88%}; on the right plot, we fix minSup = 92%, and change *maxSpan* to a range of 0 to 3. In Fig. 6 with the Connect database, on the left plot, we fix *maxSpan* = 1, and vary *minSup* within a range of 91% to 94%; on the right plot, we fix *minSup* = 95%, and alter *maxSpan* within a range of 0 to 3. Analyzing experimental results shown in Figs. 5, 6 concerning dense databases, we can easily see that the runtime of dMITP-Miner is faster.

Likewise, Figs. 7, 8 report the running time of nMITP-Miner and tMITP-Miner for the sparse databases of T10I4D100K and T40I10D100K. Their experimental results show that the runtime of the dMITP-Miner is smaller than that of tMITP-Miner algorithm, although sometimes the runtimes of dMITP and tMITP-Miner are nearly the same.

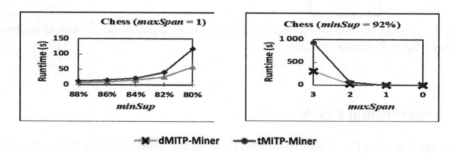

Fig. 5. Execution time varied *minSup, maxSpan* = 1; and varied *maxSpan, minSup* = 92%.

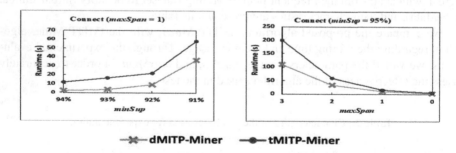

Fig. 6. Execution time varied *minSup, maxSpan* = 1; and varied *maxSpan, minSup* = 98%.

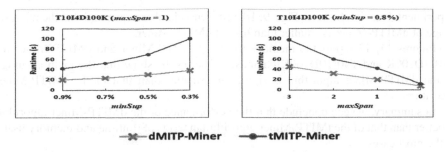

Fig. 7. Execution time varied *minSup, maxSpan* = 1; and varied *maxSpan, minSup* = 0.8%.

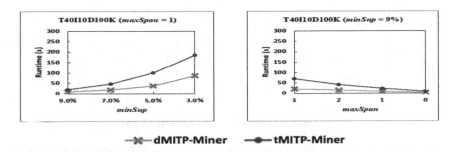

Fig. 8. Execution time varied *minSup, maxSpan* = 1; and varied *maxSpan, minSup* = 9%.

4.2 Memory Usage

Figures 9, 10, 11, 12 reports the memory usage of tMITP-Miner and dMITP-Miner algorithms for Chess, Connect, T10I4D100K, and T40I10D100K databases with various setting.

In Fig. 9 with the Chess database, on the left plot, we fix *maxSpan* = 1, and vary minSup in the range of {80%, 82%, 84%, 86%, 88%}; on the right plot, we fix minSup = 92%, and vary *maxSpan* in the range of 0 to 3. In Fig. 10 with the Connect database, on the left plot, we fix *maxSpan* = 1, and vary *minSup* in the range of 91% to 94%; on the right plot, we fix *minSup* = 95%, and vary *maxSpan* in the range of 0 to 3. Analyzing

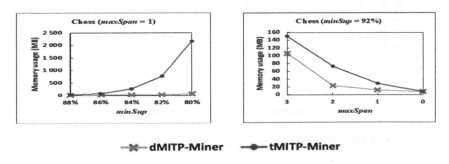

Fig. 9. Memory usage for varied *minSup, maxSpan* = 1; and varied *maxSpan, minSup* = 92%.

experimental results shown in Figs. 9, 10 with dense databases, we find that the memory usage of nMITP-Miner is smaller than that of dMITP-Miner.

Figures 11, 12 report the memory usage of tMITP-Miner and dMITP-Miner for T10I4D100K and T40I10D100K databases. The results show that the memory usage of the dMITP-Miner algorithm is significant smaller than that of the tMITP-Miner algorithm.

In summary, we can conclude that the performance of the dMITP-Miner algorithm is better than that of the tMITP-Miner algorithm in terms of runtime and memory usage in the most cases.

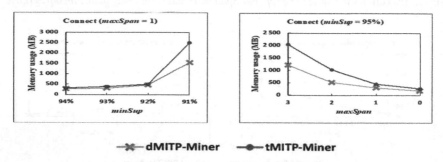

Fig. 10. Memory usage for varied *minSup*, *maxSpan* = 1; and varied *maxSpan*, *minSup* = 95%.

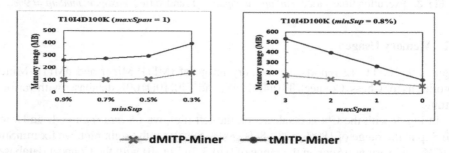

Fig. 11. Memory usage for varied *minSup*, *maxSpan* = 1; and varied *maxSpan*, *minSup* = 0.8%.

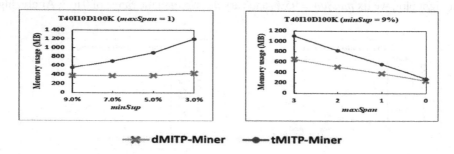

Fig. 12. Memory usage for varied *minSup*, *maxSpan* = 1; and varied *maxSpan*, *minSup* = 9%.

5   Conclusion and Future Works

In this paper, we proposed an efficient algorithm, dMITP-Miner, for mining frequent maximal inter-transaction patterns. The dMITP-Miner algorithm mines frequent maximal inter-transaction patterns based on the diffset to store mined patterns' information, for reducing computational cost and speeding up mining time.

In future works, we will develop efficient methods for mining FMITPs, and FCITPs as well as FITPs on incremental databases. Besides, it could be worth applying parallelism and cloud computing platform to these algorithms to make them feasible on the massive databases.

References

1. Agarwal, R.C., Aggarwal, C.C., Prasad, V.V.V.: Depth first generation of long patterns. In: Proceeding of the Sixth ACM SIGKDD International Conference on Knowledge Discovery and Data Mining, pp. 108–118 (2000). https://doi.org/10.1145/347090.347114
2. Gouda, K., Zaki, M.J.: GenMax: an efficient algorithm for mining maximal frequent itemsets. Data Min. Knowl. Discov. **11**(3), 223–242 (2005). https://doi.org/10.1007/s10618-005-0002-x
3. Burdick, D., Calimlim, M., Flannick, J., Gehrke, J., Yiu, T.: MAFIA: a maximal frequent itemset algorithm. IEEE Trans. Knowl. Data Eng. **17**(11), 1490–1504 (2005). https://doi.org/10.1109/TKDE.2005.183
4. Liu, X., Zhai, K., Pedrycz, W.: An improved association rules mining method. Expert Syst. Appl. **39**(1), 1362–1374 (2012). https://doi.org/10.1016/j.eswa.2011.08.018
5. Vo, B., Pham, S., Le, T., Deng, Z.H.: A novel approach for mining maximal frequent patterns. Expert Syst. Appl. (2017). https://doi.org/10.1016/j.eswa.2016.12.023
6. Nguyen, T.-N., Loan, N.T.T., Vo, B., Nguyen, N.-T.: An efficient algorithm for mining frequent closed inter-transaction patterns. In: Conference Proceedings - IEEE International Conference on Systems, Man and Cybernetics, vol. 2019-October (2019). https://doi.org/10.1109/SMC.2019.8914208
7. Nguyen, T.N., Nguyen, L.T.T., Vo, B., Nguyen, N.T., Nguyen, T.D.D.: An N-list-based approach for mining frequent inter-transaction patterns. IEEE Access **8**, 116840–116855 (2020). https://doi.org/10.1109/ACCESS.2020.3004530
8. Nguyen, T.-N., Nguyen, L.T.T., Vo, B., Kozierkiewicz, A.: Efficient method for mining maximal inter-transaction patterns. In: Nguyen, N.T., Hoang, B.H., Huynh, C.P., Hwang, D., Trawiński, B., Vossen, G. (eds.) ICCCI 2020. LNCS (LNAI), vol. 12496, pp. 316–327. Springer, Cham (2020). https://doi.org/10.1007/978-3-030-63007-2_25
9. Lu, H., Feng, L., Han, J.: Beyond intratransaction association analysis: mining multidimensional intertransaction association rules. ACM Trans. Inf. Syst. **18**, 423–454 (2000)
10. Feng, L., Dillon, T., Liu, J.: Inter-transactional association rules for multi-dimensional contexts for prediction and their application to studying meteorological data. Data Knowl. Eng. **37**(1), 85–115 (2001). https://doi.org/10.1016/S0169-023X(01)00003-9
11. Feng, L., Yu, J.X., Lu, H., Han, J.: A template model for multidimensional inter-transactional association rules. VLDB J. **11**(2), 153–175 (2002). https://doi.org/10.1007/s00778-002-0069-6
12. Tung, A.K.H., Lu, H., Han, J., Feng, L.: Efficient mining of intertransaction association rules. IEEE Trans. Knowl. Data Eng. **15**(1), 43–56 (2003). https://doi.org/10.1109/TKDE.2003.1161581

13. Li, Q., Feng, L., Wong, A.: From intra-transaction to generalized inter-transaction: landscaping multidimensional contexts in association rule mining. Inf. Sci. **172**(3–4), 361–395 (2005). https://doi.org/10.1016/j.ins.2004.07.006
14. Lee, A.J.T., Wang, C.S.: An efficient algorithm for mining frequent inter-transaction patterns. Inf. Sci. (2007). https://doi.org/10.1016/j.ins.2007.03.007
15. Lee, A.J.T., Wang, C.S., Weng, W.Y., Chen, Y.A., Wu, H.W.: An efficient algorithm for mining closed inter-transaction itemsets. Data Knowl. Eng. (2008). https://doi.org/10.1016/j.datak.2008.02.001
16. Wang, C.S., Chu, K.C.: Using a projection-based approach to mine frequent inter-transaction patterns. Expert Syst. Appl. **38**(9), 11024–11031 (2011). https://doi.org/10.1016/j.eswa.2011.02.146
17. Hsieh, Y.L., Yang, D.L., Wu, J.: Effective application of improved profit-mining algorithm for the interday trading model. Sci. World J. **2014** (2014) https://doi.org/10.1155/2014/874825
18. Hsieh, Y.L., Yang, D.L., Wu, J., Chen, Y.C.: Efficient mining of profit rules from closed inter-transaction itemsets. J. Inf. Sci. Eng. **32**(3), 575–595 (2016)
19. Wang, C.: Mining non-redundant inter-transaction rules. J. Inf. Sci. Eng. **31**(6), 1521–1536 (2015)
20. Nguyen, T.N., Nguyen, L.T.T., Nguyen, N.T.: An improved algorithm for mining frequent Inter-transaction patterns. In: Proceedings - 2017 IEEE International Conference on Innovations in Intelligent Systems and Applications, INISTA 2017, pp. 296–301 (2017). https://doi.org/10.1109/INISTA.2017.8001174
21. Nguyen, T.-N., Nguyen, L.T.T., Vo, B., Nguyen, N.T.: A fast algorithm for mining closed inter-transaction patterns. In: Fujita, H., Fournier-Viger, P., Ali, M., Sasaki, J. (eds.) IEA/AIE 2020. LNCS (LNAI), vol. 12144, pp. 820–831. Springer, Cham (2020). https://doi.org/10.1007/978-3-030-55789-8_70

ITCareerBot: A Personalized Career Counselling Chatbot

Duy Cuong Nguyen [1,2], Nguyen Hanh Dung Dinh [1,2], Cuong Pham-Nguyen[1,2](✉) (iD),
Thang Le Dinh[3] (iD), and Le Nguyen Hoai Nam[1,2]

[1] Faculty of Information Technology, University of Science, Ho Chi Minh City, Vietnam
pncuong@fit.hcmus.edu.vn
[2] Vietnam National University, Ho Chi Minh City, Vietnam
[3] School of Business, Université du Québec à Trois-Rivières, Québec City, Canada

Abstract. Nowadays, career counselling, which is a service designed to help people finding the right professional learning is emerging. In the information technology (IT) domain, this service is facing the challenge of changing very quickly in business environments, technologies and tools. Consequently, IT students and professionals often need additional knowledge and skills to fulfill market requirements and to target their professional goal in order to increase their opportunity for growth. This study aims at leveraging a specific type of chatbots to offer an intelligent and personalized advising learning services to job seekers as learners by providing information and recommendations of a learning path according to the market trends and learners' profile. Firstly, a chatbot framework is developed based on a context-aware knowledge model and a recommendation method. Thus, the context-aware knowledge base and its instance were built by analyzing different data sources collected from professional social networks and online education platforms. Furthermore, the recommendation method defines how the chatbot responds to user messages based on the matching between the current job seekers' skills and their career interest. Concerning research evaluation, the effectiveness of the proposed framework is validated by measuring the algorithms. Moreover, some efficient and satisfaction criteria were analyzed and evaluated based on the feedback from a survey.

Keywords: Career counselling · Personalized chatbot · Context-aware knowledge base

1 Introduction

The growth in amount and complexity of learning resources available online can lead to the information overload when spending time for searching and retrieving it. Professional learning needs vary from person to person depending on their goal and skills gap; therefore, there is no size that fits all solutions for success [1]. The key issue is that the job seekers as learners need access to learning resources based on their current context, which is defined based on their background, preferences, skills, and interest. Thus, technology-enhanced learning (TEL) systems must have the capability to reuse the

© The Author(s), under exclusive license to Springer Nature Singapore Pte Ltd. 2022
E. Szczerbicki et al. (Eds.): ACIIDS 2022, CCIS 1716, pp. 423–436, 2022.
https://doi.org/10.1007/978-981-19-8234-7_33

learning resources from large-scale repositories, to take into account the current context, and to allow dynamic adaptation to different learners [2]. Currently, personalized course recommender systems, one branch of the TEL systems, have proven to be useful supplements to traditional academic advising in helping students to select relevant courses for their specific goals [3, 4]. Besides, the recent advancement of conversational agents such as chatbots or digital assistants using artificial intelligence (AI) technology have provided promising opportunities in higher education [1]. The use of chatbots increases connectivity, efficiency, and reduces uncertainty in interactions [5]. Those services not only improve student engagement and support, but also lessen administrative workloads [6]. Indeed, chatbot technology is one of the most important approaches to enhancing and promoting a more personalized learning experience [5]. With regard to the career counselling domain, chatbots might be able to recommend courses to take, give career advice, and track students' progress [7]. However, how they can be used for personalized career counselling is still understudied and remains challenging research for the time being.

For this reason, this paper focuses on building a specific type of chatbots, called *ITCareerBot* for career counselling services. This system is specially designed for the learners where they can ask for different information such as for career-related courses to achieve a job, for skills gained after completing a course, for time to study a course, and for recommended resources of a specific course. In return, the system holds personalized conversations based on the acquired skills and learning path of the learners. The study includes several parts such as analyzing the data to identify requirements, designing data model and system architecture, implementing chatbot functionalities, and validating the approach by analyzing user surveys and performance testing.

The main contributions of the study are as follows: i) A context-aware knowledge base comprises an occupation and skills model, a course model, and a context model and its dataset. The models allow sharing and utilizing context-aware knowledge in a large range of applications thanks to the semantic web technology. The dataset is collected and analyzed from social IT professional networks and online education platforms, therefore it represents the job requirements of the IT industry; ii) A recommendation method, which is integrated in the response generation process, considers the learners' skills, occupation requirements and course model to provide the relevant advising learning path to the learners.

The paper is organized as follows. Section 2 introduces the related work. Section 3 conducts the motivation and research objective. Section 4 describes in detail the proposed approach, which is broken down into the general architecture, the proposition of the context-aware knowledge base and its instance, the user message analysis, the response generation, and the system implementation. Section 5 continues with the validation of the study. Section 6 highlights the main results and gives some perspectives.

2 Related Work

This section begins with context-aware and personalized chatbots, then discusses and highlights some recent approaches related to career counselling chatbots.

2.1 Context-Aware and Personalized Chatbots

Chatbot is an application that is designed to provide a convenient way for conversation with a human being by using natural language dialogues through textual or auditory methods [8]. Several studies are conducted to develop chatbot applications that capture and handle contextualization and personalized content in different fields such as education [9], healthcare [10], and business transactions [11]. In the higher education sector, the MOOCBuddy chatbot has found the best resources based on the user's social media profiles and interests [9]. In the healthcare sector, a chatbot was designed for controlling the level of asthma of pediatric asthmatic patients [10]. In the tourism sector, a chatbot was proposed to support tourists by recommending content and services according to the user profile [11]. In conclusion, these chatbots firstly, focus on extracting context information, then presenting them in two ways: using a knowledge model [9–11] or using a neural network model [12]. They use different methods to build an appropriate response such as machine learning model [11] or pattern matching [10]. Moreover, these chatbots can also use additional domain knowledge in order to enhance the significant user experience on a specific domain [10].

2.2 Career Counselling Chatbots

According to our observation, there are still few studies that have been proposed in recent years regarding career counselling chatbots. An intelligent career counselling bot was developed that supports the users' decision on their career [13]. In this system, users can ask questions about choosing a future career or providing the benefits of a career in industry using a chatbot system, which operates on a knowledge base to generate the answer. However, this research has two limitations: i) the responses are built for all users without considering their profiles and experiences, and ii) no evaluation was carried out to show whether the chatbot was effective in the education environment. Another study was conducted for designing Sammy, a chatbot that interviews students to investigate a need for the career counselling service in colleges [14]. This study is in progress and does not address any concrete technical solution. It collects student opinions about the service needed for career counselling, then analyzes and categorizes the findings.

There is a research gap concerning the personalized chatbots for career counselling services, which is the area that has not under-explored. The paper aims at filling this research gap by proposing an approach for building personalized chatbots for career counselling services that considers the learner profile and context to provide individualized responses. The following sections describe in detail the proposed approach in the IT domain, especially its application and validation.

3 Motivation

Career counselling is very important for everyone's career path, especially in the higher education sector. Since it helps students understanding what they have to do and what they need in each occupation, so students can make the decision to follow the job that they feel the most suitable for their personality, interests, abilities, and situation. The service motivates students to be willing to spend time and determination to pursue that choice. As a matter of fact, there are still some key issues. Firstly, the final year students do not have a right career orientation after graduation, struggled with choosing the right career path for their demands, not sure whether their chosen major is suitable for their desired future job [15]. Secondly, there is a lack of adaptation of the study program to each student's profile [16] that leads to a high dropout rate in universities because of losing motivation to learn [17].

According to our analysis of the data about the career counselling needs of the IT field, conducted in 2021 on the three social websites (Quora, Stack overflow, Stack exchange) with 2,860 questions raised by users shows that the need for asking a learning path of a specific occupation is absolutely dominant (83.4%), following by requesting skills required for an occupation (5.1%) and the training time to achieve an occupation (4.7%). Thus, career counselling services are becoming extremely urgent, especially a learning path of a specific occupation. In the context of such increasing demand, the use of career advice for IT professionals is not only inefficiency but also increases operational costs. Based on those analyses, the study aims at proposing a chatbot for providing career counselling services in the IT field. The chatbot can increase user satisfaction by speeding up response time, being available 24/7, handling multiple requests at once, and automating repetitive tasks. Current chatbot studies have a little focus on the learner information to effectively provide personalized feedback to each learner, which plays an important role in career counselling services. With such motivation, the main characteristic of the proposed chatbot is to be able to offer personalized career advice based on the learner's skills.

Concerning our previous studies, the FIT-EBot chatbot is proposed to support administrative and learning activities that showed the importance of engaging students in learning and reducing administrative workloads [6]. Moreover, an ontology-based knowledge model is implemented for representing IT Job postings, which consists of extracting and analyzing online job postings to build a knowledge model, and to serve a structured knowledge framework for representing job requirements [18]. In another study, a context-aware knowledge (CAK) model is developed to build the context-aware knowledge base for smart service systems [19].

To enhance the models proposed in our previous studies, this study introduces an integrated model, which organizes the domain and context-aware knowledge for context-aware smart service systems that integrate all the information and knowledge related to smart services. It refines the architecture for chatbots [6] and extends the knowledge representation models [18, 19] for a personalized career counselling service based on learner skills. The proposed system has the capability to provide smart services by considering the context and learners' skills and responding accordingly.

The main research question of this study is *"How to design and implement a personalized career counselling chatbot based on a context-aware knowledge model?"*. The exploratory research methodology is used to conduct the study to investigate the research question [20], which have not previously been studied in depth. The research process is as the followings. Firstly, a survey method and a review literature (Sect. 2 and 3) are used to identify the research problem and hypothesize the potential solution. Secondly, the case study is used to design and implement the proposed solution for the IT domain

(Sect. 4). Finally, another survey is used to collect and analyze the data to evaluate the solution (Sect. 5).

4   ITCareerBot - A Personalized Counselling Chatbot

This section presents the principles of the proposed approach for building the career counselling chatbot, called ITCareerBot. It includes the overall architecture that describes the system components and how they operate. Thus, the main process of collecting and analyzing data to build the context-aware knowledge base, the method for recommending responses and the system implementation are presented.

4.1   Architecture

The overall architecture for ITCareerBot consists of four key components (Fig. 1) as followings: User interface: through a web interface implemented with ReactJS, the ITCareerbot receives messages from users. Authentication: is responsible for handling login information and user registration. It is also a bridge to authenticate and communicate for other components that access to the knowledge base. Conversation handler: comprises of a user message analysis based on RASA's model trained by pre-labeled data, it is performed including user intent identification and entity extraction in order to provide personalized answers to each user. Knowledge base: all the above operations of the chatbot are served by a knowledge base, which is a context-aware ontology-based knowledge representing occupations and skills, courses, and context. Consequently, a knowledge base building process is proposed to populate data to the knowledge base. Response generator: a personalized counselling method is proposed for predicting the rating of an active user for each targeted learning path concerning a desired occupation. In particular, it provides a customized answer about the appropriate learning paths for each user as he/she provides the intended career in the future.

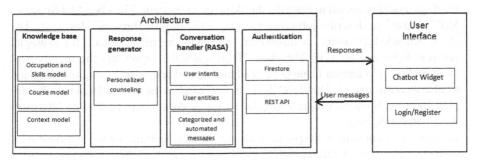

Fig. 1. Overall architecture of ITCareerBot

4.2   Context-Aware Knowledge Base

The knowledge base-building process consists of two steps: i) defining classes in the ontological model, and ii) populating the ontology with instances.

Defining Classes in the Ontological Model: Firstly, ontology modelling is selected to design the knowledge base because ontology represents shared understanding of the domain of interest, which enables the system and people to collaborate in a better way. Secondly, based on the discussion about the motivation in Sect. 3 and the observation from our collected data, a context-aware knowledge base is proposed for representing and organizing domain knowledge as well as user context. This context-aware knowledge base is an extension of our previous knowledge models, one from Job Posting model [18], which focuses on representing job-related knowledge about the labour market, and another from the CAK model [19], which organizes the domain and context knowledge for smart service systems.

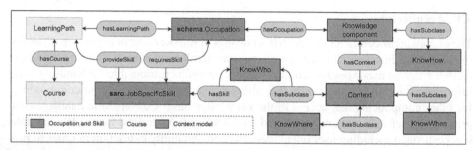

Fig. 2. High level of the context-aware knowledge base

Figure 2 provides a top-level view of the context-aware knowledge model, which mainly presents three sub-models:

- *Occupation and Skill model* represents concepts and relationships that are used to describe careers and their respective skills. The concept "JobSpecificSkill" from Job Postings model is reused to describe the skills in our system. The class "JobSpecific-Skill" is used to describe job-related skills, consisting of three subclasses: i) The class "Knowledge" defines a theoretical understanding of an object, for example, Android SDK and Java; ii) The class "TechnicalSkill" represents the requirement to be proficient in certain IT tasks such as mobile and responsive design, testing and troubleshooting; and iii) The class "Technology" handles the skills related to technologies, software, libraries, programming languages, and databases (including Microsoft Azure, ReactJS, etc.).
- *Course model* contains concepts for learning courses, learning paths, and their relationships. The class "LearningPath" describes a learning path built for a given career that has links to a set of courses required for a particular career. It has a relationship with the class "Occupation" via "hasLearningPath" and the class "JobSpecificSkill" via "provideSkill". The class "Course" represents learning courses and an estimated time to complete the learning.
- *Context model* represents user context describing the current situation of the users. The CAK model [19] is reused and refined by three classes: Context-Who, Context-Where and Context-When. *Context-Who* is the user representation element. Each

instance can be viewed as a user in the system. This class has a relationship with the class "JobSpecificSkill" to describe the technical skills of the user. *Context-Where* represents the context related to the learning method used in a learning path, for example, online or offline. *Context-When* represents the period to complete a learning path, e.g. three months, six months.

Moreover, other components from the CAK model are also extended to address other requirements: The component *"Know-How"* describes the actions through the use of the chatbot such as registration of a learning path. The component *"Know-Why"* can be viewed as reasons related to finding a learning path for a particular occupation, for example, why it is necessary to master certain skills to be able to do a job?

Populating Ontology with Instances: TO populate data to the ontology, the study prepared 65 different learning paths for seven occupations as shown in Table 1. These learning paths are automatically collected from the education platforms such as Coursera and Edx. A total of 183 associated skills are also collected and classified into three categories, which are knowledge (57.9%), technology (15.8%), and technical skill (26.3%). The dataset is accessible at https://bit.ly/ontology_dataset.

Table 1. Classes and their instances in the knowledge base

Class	Number of individuals	Class	Number of individuals
Occupation	7	Learning path	65
Knowledge	106	Course	196
TechnicalSkill	48	Context-Who	44
Technology	29	Context-Where	2

4.3 User Message Analysis

To be able to understand the user's text message and then to take appropriate actions, the ITCareerBot needs to perform the following language processing activities:

- *Intent Identification*: Intent is expressed through the text message that the user enters into the system. Chatbots need intent-aware to know how to respond to the user. Table 2 presents the intents defined in our Chatbot.
- *Entity Extraction*: For each intent identified, an entity associated with it is extracted on the user's text message.

For supporting these tasks, the Dual Intent Entity Transformer (DIET) [21], which is a multi-task architecture for intent classification and entity recognition, is used in this study. In particular, the architecture provides a list of possible intents for each income message by descending of intent similarity. Thus, the entity extraction task predicts entity labels by using Conditional Random Field [22]. Moreover, a dataset of 321 messages with their intents and entities collected from the social network forums.

Table 2. List of intents

User intent	Example	User intent	Example
ask_learning_path	How do I become a full stack developer with no experience?	ask_skill	Show me skill of course "Applied Machine Learning in Python"
view_course_detail	Could you show me the syllabus of course "Data Visualization with R"?	ask_course_url	How to access this course?
view_other_learning_path	What about other learning paths?	ask_duration	Let me know duration of course "Building Web Applications in Django"
view_other_course	I want to view another course	ask_personal_skill	I do not remember my skills

4.4   Response Generator - Personalized Counselling Method

This section presents a method of recommending suitable learning paths to users for their desired occupation. We predict the rating of an active user u for each targeted learning path lp concerning occupation o, denoted by $\hat{R}_{u,lp,o}$. The method is built based on the three combined factors:

Weight of skills covered in both the occupation o and the learning path lp, denoted by $occupation\_gain(lp, o)$.
Weight of skills covered in both the occupation o and the learning path lp, but have not yet acquired by the user u, denoted by $user\_gain(lp, o, u)$.
Weigh of additional skills not covered in the occupation o, denoted $additional\_gain(lp, o, u)$.

With such an analysis, we calculate $\hat{R}_{u,lp,o}$ as a weighted average of 3 factors over α, β, and γ, as follows:

$$\hat{R}_{u,lp,o} = \alpha \times occupation\_gain(lp, o) + \beta \times user\_gain(lp, u, o) + \gamma \times additional\_gain(lp, u, o)$$

$$(1)$$

To calculate the value of the three parameters ($\alpha\beta\gamma$), we collected user feedback about recommended learning paths for their demanding career, called H. The weights will be optimal when the ratings in set H ($R_{u,lp,o}$) are closest to their predicted ratings ($\widehat{R}_{u,lp,o}$). The objective function for this optimization is as follows:

$$\min_{\alpha,\beta,\gamma} \frac{1}{2} \cdot \sum_{(lp,o,u) \in H} \left(R_{u,lp,o} - \widehat{R}_{u,lp,o} \right)^2$$

$$\min_{\alpha,\beta,\gamma} \frac{1}{2} \cdot \sum_{(lp,o,u) \in H} \left(\begin{matrix} R_{u,lp,o} - \alpha \times occupation\_gain(lp, o) - \beta \times user\_gain(lp, u, o) \\ -\gamma \times additional\_gain(lp, u, o) \end{matrix} \right)^2 + \frac{\lambda}{2}(\alpha^2 + \beta^2 + \gamma^2)$$

$$(2)$$

where the last component, i.e., $\frac{\lambda}{2}(\alpha^2 + \beta^2 + \gamma^2)$, is used to avoid overfitting. The above optimization is solved by bridge regression. With the above method, we find that $\alpha = 0.47$, $\beta = 0.07$, and $\gamma = 0.54$ where the set H include 27 rating collected from 44 users. Finally, the top target learning paths with the highest predicted rating of active user u concerning occupation o will be selected for recommendation.

4.5 Implementation and Deployment

Regarding the proposed architecture for ITCareerBot, there are three main components for building this application:

- *Client*: a web application that allows users to interact with the chatbot. The application is built using ReactJS (https://reactjs.org/), which is a web framework that can create interactive applications. Moreover, it is implemented by using components from the material design library for better user experiences.
- *Server*: it includes a Python application for handling user requests. Flask (https://flask. palletsprojects.com/en/2.0.x/), a high-end framework built on the top of the Python programming language, enables building a faster application that can serve multiple users at the same time. For natural language processing, we choose Rasa (https://rasa. com/) because it is not only an open-source application, but also allows an integration with other platforms through API services to provide a flexible solution for chatbot development.
- *Knowledge base*: the knowledge base is implemented by using the Python library Owlready2 for importing, exporting and publishing the ontology.

The source code of the ITCareerBot application is published at https://bit.ly/it-car eer-bot. The chatbot service is available at: https://services.fit.hcmus.edu.vn:251/. An example is illustrated in Fig. 3 (a) where James asks the chatbot about the learning paths for a data scientist. Figure 3 (b) shows the skills that James acquired previously. Depending on James's skill and the required skills for a data scientist, the chatbot gave a list of three learning paths that are the best matched according to the weight calculated using the formula (1) (refer Fig. 4 (a)). In this situation, the chatbot suggested 3 top learning paths and the first one may be the best fit for James's progress because it provides new skills for his demand, which are Probability Theory and Statistical Inference. Figure 4 (b) shows more interactions from James on information about the learning path information, courses, course duration, and resources.

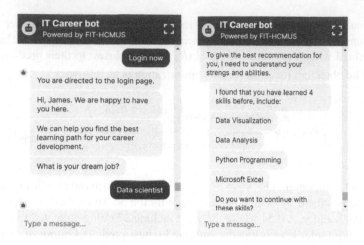

Fig. 3. Screenshots of interactive conversations

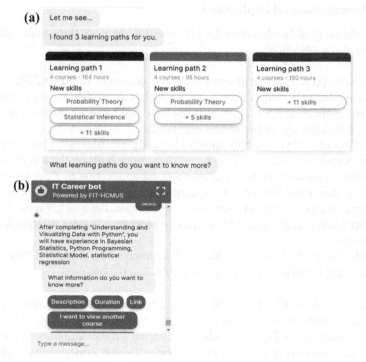

Fig. 4. (a) Illustration of top 3 learning paths recommended by the chatbot – (b) Conversations in detail information of a course

5 Experiments

In this section, experiments are conducted to evaluate our chatbot based on the three criteria: *Effectiveness, Efficiency* and *Satisfaction* [16].

5.1 Effectiveness

This criterion is related to the performance of the algorithms used in the chatbot, especially for user intent identification and entity extraction on user messages. *For Effectiveness* criterion, the test is performed in three times. For each time, the test set is randomly taken 20% and the remaining 80% is the training set. Precision, Recall, and F-score are used to evaluate the performance of our models which is shown in Table 3. It can be seen that our model always gives the average precision, recall and F1-score results greater than 85%.

Table 3. Intent classification and entity extraction results

	Measures	1st time	2nd time	3rd time	Average
Intent identification	Precision	0.891	0.931	0.832	0.884 ± 0.041
	Recall	0.921	0.953	0.874	0.916 ± 0.032
	F1-score	0.906	0.937	0.850	0.898 ± 0.036
Entity extraction	Precision	0.955	0.964	0.908	0.942 ± 0.025
	Recall	0.954	0.967	0.976	0.966 ± 0.009
	F1-score	0.954	0.964	0.940	0.953 ± 0.010

5.2 Efficiency and Satisfaction

The efficiency is judged through the relevance of the answer (i.e. how users find the right answer when using the chatbot). The satisfaction is related to the ease of use (i.e. whether the chatbots are easy to use), the ease of reading and understanding (i.e. how easy the users can hold and understand the responses). To have this done, a survey is

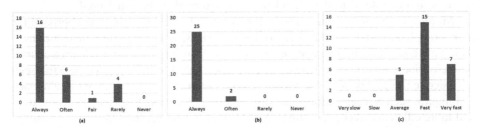

Fig. 5. (a) Efficiency - how frequency users get the relevant responses; (b) User satisfaction - the ease to understand and read the responses; (c) How long did users wait for the responses

conducted on 44 users in which 78% are students and 23% are employees. After using the chatbot, 27 users gave their feedback.

The survey shows a small-scale experiment indicating that the ITCareerBot basically provides the right answers. Figure 5 (a) presents the efficiency that the majority of users didn't or rarely found wrong answers from the chatbot (85.2%), and the answers match their expectation. Only some (14.8%) gave negative feedback that the responses are occasionally not relevant to their expectation. While Fig. 5 (b) shows the level of satisfaction of the consultation that was easily understood by all users and the conversations were easy to follow. It is also found that the satisfaction depends on other factors such as how quick the users can give a chat or the ability to shape the conversations. Therefore, the options were designed allowing users to ask questions by clicking on them instead of texting. The satisfaction is also represented by how quickly the system responds from the user perspective. The survey shown in Fig. 5 (c) is quite promising that all of them were satisfied with the response speed of the system. Of course, the response speed may vary depending on the amount of data loaded into the system as well. But it reflects the initial effectiveness when the proposed recommender algorithm is integrated into the system, which is acceptable.

6 Conclusion and Future Work

This study proposes an approach for building career counselling chatbots based on the context-aware knowledge model, called ITCareerBot approach. ITCareerBot is indeed an intelligent counselling chatbot to provide personalized career advising based on learning paths for a specific occupation. The proposed approach integrates a context-aware knowledge base and a recommendation method to generate the customized responses. The study refines and enhances the previous work of the authors to design the context-aware knowledge base for career counselling services that is based on the analysis of data collected from social and professional networks and then implemented the knowledge base using the ontology technology. The recommendation method considers the matching between the learners' skills, course model and occupation model to provide the conversations relevant to the learner's needs. The system evaluation is carried out based on three criteria: effectiveness, efficiency and satisfaction by both carrying out a user survey with small-scale and measuring NLU accuracy using F1-score. In the future work, this approach needs to be validated and experimented on a broader scale to prove their stability. Besides, the application of the approach for developing career counselling services for other domains than the IT domain also needs to be considered.

Moreover, one of our future research projects aims at enhancing the approach for more complicated and elaborated counselling services, such as refining the recommendation method to take into account other context dimensions (e.g. time to learn a course, online/offline, course fee, etc.) to improve the responses. Furthermore, it is also foreseen to integrate the context-aware knowledge model with the current artificial intelligence techniques, such as deep learning and reinforcement learning, to create new contextual and more efficient career counselling chatbots based on the current knowledge base.

Acknowledgments. This research is funded by the University of Science, VNU-HCM under grant number CNTT 2021–04.

References

1. Urdaneta-Ponte, M.C., Mendez-Zorrilla, A., Oleagordia-Ruiz, I.: Recommendation systems for education: systematic review. Electronics. **10**(14), 14, (2021). https://doi.org/10.3390/ele ctronics10141611
2. Pham-Nguyen, C., Garlatti, S., Lau, B., Barbry, B., Vantroys, T.: An adaptive and context-aware scenario model based on a web service architecture for pervasive learning systems. Int. J. Mob. Blend. Learn. (IJMBL) 2010, pp. 1159–1180 (2010). https://doi.org/10.4018/978-1-60566-982-3.ch062
3. Montuschi, P., Lamberti, F., Gatteschi, V., Demartini, C.: A semantic recommender system for adaptive learning. IT Professional **17**, 50–58 (2015). https://doi.org/10.1109/MITP.201 5.75
4. Khorasani, E.S., Zhenge, Z., Champaign, J.: A Markov chain collaborative filtering model for course enrollment recommendations. In: 2016 IEEE International Conference on Big Data (Big Data), pp. 3484–3490, December 2016. https://doi.org/10.1109/BigData.2016.7841011
5. Cunningham-Nelson, S., Boles, W., Trouton, L., Margerison, E: A review of chatbots in education: practical steps forward. In: 30th Annual Conference for the Australasian Association for Engineering Education (AAEE 2019): Educators Becoming Agents of Change: Innovate, Integrate, Motivate, Engineers Australia, Australia, pp. 299–306 (2019)
6. Hien, H., Pham-Nguyen, C.L., Nam, H.N., Le Dinh, T.: Intelligent Assistants in Higher-Education Environments: The FIT-EBot, a Chatbot for Administrative and Learning Support," SoICT 2018, pp. 69–76, December 2018. https://doi.org/10.1145/3287921.3287937
7. Lee, T., et al.: Intelligent career advisers in your pocket? A need assessment study of chatbots for student career advising. In: Twenty-fifth Americas Conference on Information Systems, Cancun 2019
8. Hussain, S., AmeriSianaki, O., Ababneh, N.: A survey on conversational agents/chatbots classification and design techniques. In: Barolli, L., Takizawa, M., Xhafa, F., Enokido, T. (eds.) Web, Artificial Intelligence and Network Applications. AISC, vol. 927, pp. 946–956. Springer, Cham (2019). https://doi.org/10.1007/978-3-030-15035-8_93
9. Holotescu, C.: MOOCBuddy: a Chatbot for personalized learning with MOOCs (2016)
10. Kadariya, D., Venkataramanan, R., Yip, H.Y., Kalra, M., Thirunarayanan, K., Sheth, A.: kBot: knowledge-enabled personalized chatbot for asthma self-management. Proc. Int. Conf. Smart Comput SMARTCOMP **2019**, 138–143 (2019). https://doi.org/10.1109/smartcomp. 2019.00043
11. Clarizia, F., Colace, F., De Santo, M., Lombardi, M., Pascale, F., Santaniello, D.: A Context-Aware Chatbot for Tourist Destinations, pp. 348–354, November 2019. https://doi.org/10. 1109/SITIS.2019.00063
12. Ma, Z., Dou, Z., Zhu, Y., Zhong, H., Wen, J.-R.: One Chatbot Per Person: Creating Personalized Chatbots based on Implicit User Profiles, pp. 555–564, July 2021. https://doi.org/10. 1145/3404835.3462828
13. Parab, A., Palkar, S., Maurya, S., Balpande, S.: An intelligent career counselling bot. IRJET. **04**(03), 6 (2017)
14. Zaidi, D., Raza, S., Sharma, L.: Artificial intelligence based career counselling chatbot a system for counselling. Ann. Roman. Soc. Cell Biol. **25**(6), 6 (2021)
15. Ellucian: Course correction: Helping students find and follow a path to success (2019). https:// www.ellucian.com/assets/en/2019-student-success-survey-results.pdf
16. Casas, J., Tricot, M.-O., Khaled, O.A., Mugellini, E., Cudré-Mauroux, P.: Trends & methods in chatbot evaluation. In: ICMI Companion (2020).https://doi.org/10.1145/3395035.3425319
17. Rostaminezhad, M, Mozayani, N., Norozi, D., Iziy, M.: Factors related to e-learner dropout: case study of IUST Elearning Center. Proc. Soc. Behav. Sci. **83**, (2013). https://doi.org/10. 1016/j.sbspro.2013.06.100

18. Thi, P., Diep, H., Nguyen Dinh, T., Pham-Nguyen, C., Le Dinh, T, Nam, L.: Towards an ontology-based knowledge base for job postings. In: 7th NAFOSTED NICS 2020, pp. 267–272, November 2020. https://doi.org/10.1109/NICS51282.2020.9335876
19. Le Dinh, T., Pham Thi, T.T., Pham-Nguyen, C., Nam, L.: A knowledge-based model for context-aware smart service systems. J. Inf. Telecommun. (2021). https://doi.org/10.1080/24751839.2021.1962105
20. Reiter, B.: Theory and Methodology of Exploratory Social Science Research (2017)
21. Bunk, T., Varshneya, D., Vlasov, V., Nichol, A.: DIET: Lightweight Language Understanding for Dialogue Systems (2020)
22. Lafferty, J., McCallum, A., Pereira, F.: Conditional random fields: probabilistic models for segmenting and labeling sequence data. In: Departmental Papers (CIS), June 2001

Scheduling Parallel Data Transfers in Multi-tiered Persistent Storage

Nan Noon Noon$^{(\boxtimes)}$ ⓘD, Janusz R. Getta ⓘD, and Tianbing Xia ⓘD

School of Computing and Information Technology, University of Wollongong,
Wollongong, Australia
nnn326@uowmail.edu.au, {jrg,txia}@uow.edu.au

Abstract. Multi-tiered persistent storage provides a logical view where all available storage is distributed over a number of levels of different speeds and capacities. Efficient scheduling of parallel data transfers in multi-tiered persistent storage is a significant problem for pipelined data processing. This work considers a class of database applications implemented as sequences of operations that transfer data between persistent storage tiers. We show how to partition the sets of data transfers to reduce the number of conflicts when data transfers are performed in parallel. The paper proposes the new rule-based algorithms for allocating parallel data transfer to the processors to minimize total processing time. The new algorithms evenly distribute the workload among the processors and reduce their idle times. We describe a number of experiments that validate the efficiency of parallel data transfer plans generated by the algorithms presented in the paper.

Keywords: Multi-tiered persistent storage · Scheduling · Parallel data processing · Performance tuning · Database management systems

1 Introduction

The promises created by the new data analysis techniques require high-capacity persistent storage devices to maintain the large amounts of data recorded during the activities of long-running organisations. The various types of persistent storage devices available on-site or in the clouds contribute to the global *multi-tiered view* of persistent storage [2,10]. In a multi-tiered view, data is distributed over many different persistent storage levels with different capacities and performance characteristics. Typically, the higher levels have shorter access times and lower capacities. Data processing in multi-tiered persistent storage is performed while data is transferred from level to level. Simultaneously running data processing applications compete for access to the highest levels where input/output operations performance is the best. The efficient resource allocation in multi-tiered persistent storage is a significant problem for efficient storage utilisation.

In this work, we look at a problem of efficient scheduling of parallel data transfers between the levels of multi-tiered persistent storage. We consider a

© The Author(s), under exclusive license to Springer Nature Singapore Pte Ltd. 2022
E. Szczerbicki et al. (Eds.): ACIIDS 2022, CCIS 1716, pp. 437–449, 2022.
https://doi.org/10.1007/978-981-19-8234-7_34

pipelined data processing model where the streams of data simultaneously pass through the processors located in the nodes of an acyclic directed graph. The processors read multiple data streams, perform operations on data and output data to the following processors in the pipelines. We assume that data can be simultaneously read and written from/to the different multi-tiered persistent storage. Thus, whenever it is possible, the processing of data is performed in parallel. On the other hand, the physical properties of multi-tiered persistent storage do not allow for two or more processors to simultaneously access the same level of storage in read or write modes. Such limitation contributes to the inevitable conflicts and delays when many applications are processed in parallel, and it requires appropriate scheduling of access to the levels of multi-tiered storage.

The scheduling algorithm presented in this work minimises the total parallel processing time for a given set of applications. It evenly balances the workload of the individual processors and reduces their idle times. The research contributions of the paper are the following:

1. We assume that database applications are implemented as sequences of operations on data. We show how to convert the sequences of operations into sets of data transfers between the levels of multi-tiered storage.
2. We show how to partition the sets of data transfers to reduce the total number of conflicts between the data transfers.
3. We propose the new rule-based algorithms for allocation of data transfer to the processors to minimize total processing time, evenly distributes the workload among the processors, and reduce the idle time of the processors.
4. We show how the pipelined data processing model can be efficiently implemented in a multi-tiered persistent storage model.

The paper is organised in the following way: an overview of the earlier research works in data transfer scheduling is presented in Sect. 2. Section 3 presents a model of multi-tiered persistent storage and explains the concepts later used in this work. The scheduling algorithms are presented in Sect. 4. The outcomes of the experiments are included in Sect. 5. Finally, Sect. 6 concludes the paper.

2   Previous Works

The scheduling algorithm is critical for better performance when processing the tasks/jobs on multicomputer systems. The rule-based scheduling methods have been already used for parallel manufacturing machines and parallel computing systems [3,12]. The priority scheduling rules algorithms proposed in [1] include FCFS, SPT, LPT Random, and the others. The same research also inestigates the distribution of resources over single and multiple processor systems. The solutions of the task scheduling problem under the LogP model presented in [11] included both theoretical and experimental results.

Many corporations are implementing massive relational databases to keep the organizations' operational and historical information. Parallel processing of large data is a common solution to solve performance problems. There are numerous kinds of research related to parallel data processing by partitioning the database automatically [5], cluster data for parallel database systems [4], using multi-dimension and allocating data for a parallel database system [9], and the others.

Our earlier research [6] contributed to the invention of automated performance tuning plans with materializations and indices over a single layer of multi-tiered persistent storage. We proposed a new resource allocation algorithm over multiple layers of multi-tiered persistent storage in [7,8]. Also in [7], we presented a new method for discovering the query processing plans for predicted workload using the new cost model. An extended Petri-net based model and optimization of query processing plans for multi-tiered persistent storage is presented in [8].

3 Basic Concepts

A list of storage tiers in multi-tiered persistent storage is denoted as a sequence of positive integer numbers $L = \langle l_0, \ldots, l_n \rangle$, where l_0 denotes the amounts of storage available at the lowest and slowest tier, and l_n denotes the amounts of storage available at the highest and fastest tier. An objective of this work is to find the best suboptimal parallel data processing plan for a given set of sequences of operations $\mathcal{E} = \{E_1, \ldots, E_n\}$, that transfer data between the tires of multi-tiered persistent storage. A set of sequences $\mathcal{E}$ is an optimal processing plan obtained from the algorithm published in [8]. Each $E_i \in \mathcal{E}$ is a sequence of operations $\langle e_1, \ldots, e_n \rangle$. An operation e_i is represented by a triple $\langle c_i : \{B_1, \ldots, B_m\}, \{B_{m+1}, \ldots, B_n\} \rangle$ where c_i is a code of an operation and $\{B_1, \ldots, B_m\}$ are the input data sets and $\{B_{m+1}, \ldots, B_n\}$ are the output data sets of an operation e_i. Each B_i is a set of pairs $\{\langle D_1, l_n \rangle, \ldots, \langle D_m, l_m \rangle\}$ where D_i for $i = 1, \ldots, m$ is the total number of data blocks, and l_j is a location of the data blocks at tier l_j. For example, a triple $\langle \pi : \{\langle 100, l_1 \rangle, \langle 250, l_2 \rangle\}, \{\langle 200, l_3 \rangle\} \rangle$ denotes a projection of 350 blocks of input data located at levels l_1 and l_2 into 200 blocks of output data located at a level l_3.

We assume that m processors $\{P_1, \ldots, P_m\}$ are available for parallel processing of a set of sequences of operations $\mathcal{E}$. The processors perform the bidirectional transfers of data between the tiers of persistent storage and transient data buffers and simultaneously process the operations on data. A characteristic of an atomic activity of a processor is described by a pair (t, l), where t is an estimated total number of time-units required to transfer the data blocks from/to l-th tier of persistent storage. In the future, a pair (t, l) is called a *transfer*. A *processing plan* is a sequence of transfers $\langle (t_i, l_x), \ldots, (t_j, l_y) \rangle$.

4   Parallel Processing Plans

4.1   An Overview

Allocation of data transfers to the processors is performed in the following steps. First, each sequence of operations $E_i \in \mathcal{E}$ implementing a data processing task is transformed into a *transfer plan* $Q_i = \langle (t_i, l_x), \ldots, (t_j, l_y) \rangle$ where t_i is the total number of time units spent on a transfer and l_i is a level in the multi-tiered storage involved. Section 4.2 explains the transformation process.

Next, a set of transfer plans $\{Q_1, \ldots Q_n\}$ obtained from the previous step is partitioned into a sequence of groups of transfer plans depending on the total number of transfers to/from a particular level in multi-tiered persistent storage. The transfer plans that contain data transfer to/from the most frequently used levels are included in the first group. An objective of this step is to implement the data transfers that may have a large number of conflicts first. If many transfers access the same level allocated at the end, the frequent conflicts will require idle time units allocated to the processors. Section 4.3 explains the partitioning process.

Next, we iterate over a sequence of groups of transfers and pick the *candidate transfers* from each group. A candidate data transfer is the first data transfer from each group that can be allocated to a processor. Thus, it does not conflict with a data transfer already allocated to a processor. If there are no *candidate transfers*, we move to the next group. If there are many *candidate transfers*, we apply a sequence of *scheduling rules* to reduce a set of *candidate transfers* to a single transfer. If there is only one *candidate transfer*, then it is allocated to a processor with the current lowest workload. Section 4.4 explains the application of the *scheduling rules*. Partitioning of a set of transfer plans is updated after a transfer is allocated to a processor, and a new set of candidate transfers is created. The complete scheduling algorithms are presented in Sect. 4.5.

4.2   Creating Transfer Plans

A set of sequences of operations $\mathcal{E} = \{E_1, \ldots, E_m\}$ and sequences of storage tiers in multi-tiered persistent storage $L = \langle l_0, \ldots, l_n \rangle$ are required to create the transfer plans. To create the data transfer plans we iterate over a set of sequences of operations $\mathcal{E}$. Let the current sequence be $E_i = \langle e_1, \ldots, e_n \rangle$. Then, for each operation $e_i \in E$, we get a set of the total number of read data blocks $\{B_1, \ldots, B_m\}$, and a set of the total number of write data blocks $\{B_{m+1}, \ldots, B_n\}$. Next, we compute transfers according to read/write data blocks. Due to the limited size of a data buffer, we cannot put an entire set of read/write data blocks into one transfer. Therefore, we have to get (D_i, l_j) from B and compute one transfer by one transfer. With a given (D_i, l_j), the estimated total time-units t_i required to read/write data blocks D_i at tier l_j is computed and a transfer (t_i, l_j) is created. Next, we append a transfer (t_i, l_j) to a transfer plan Q_i related to processing of an operation e_i. The same procedure is repeated for the next operation $e_{i+1} \in E$, and the next transfer (t_{i+1}, l_{i+1}) is appended to a transfer plans Q_i. When the transformation of the current E is completed, the algorithm takes the following sequence from $\mathcal{E}$ to create a transfer plans Q_{i+1}.

Q_1:	(5, l_0)				(4, l_1)			(3, l_2)		
Q_2:	(4, l_2)				(3, l_1)		(2, l_3)				
C:	1	2	3	4	5	6	7	8	9	10	11	12

Fig. 1. Visualization of the transfer plans obtained form query processing plans

For example, consider $\mathcal{E} = \{E_1, E_2\}$ where $E_1 = \langle e_1 \rangle$ and $E_2 = \langle e_2, e_3 \rangle$. Let $e_1 = \langle c1 : \{(10, l_0), (20, l_1)\}, \{(30, l_2)\} \rangle$. Assume that the capacity of the data buffer allows to read 30 data blocks from tiers l_0 and l_1 and to write 25 data blocks to tier l_2. Assume that the transmissions speed of data transfers to/from the tiers l_0, l_1, and l_2 are 2, 5, and 10 data blocks per time unit, respectively. Then, from the transmission speed, we find that 5-time units are needed to read 10 data blocks from l_0, 4-time units are needed to read 20 data blocks from l_1, and 3-time units are needed to write 30 data blocks from l_2. It provides the transfer plans $Q_1 = \langle (5, l_0), (4, l_1), (3, l_2) \rangle$. Assume that when we repeat the same procedure for E_2, then we get a transfer plans $Q_2 = \langle (4, l_2), (3, l_1), (2, l_3) \rangle$. The outcomes for this step are visualised in Fig. 1.

4.3 Partitioning of Transfer Plans

Before allocation of the transfers to the processors, a set of transfer plans $\{Q_1, \ldots, Q_n\}$ is partitioned to reduce the total number of conflicts. Partitioning starts by counting how many transfers access each level in the multitiered storage. The result is a set of pairs (l_i, c_i), where l_i is the level of the device, and c_i is a counter that counts how many transfers are accessing l_i. Next, the pairs with the same values of counters are placed into the same group. Then, the groups are arranged into a descending order of count value, i.e., $\langle \{(l_i, c_i), \ldots, (l_j, c_j)\}, \ldots, \{(l_m, 1), \ldots, (l_n, 1)\} \rangle$ where the value of $c_i = c_j$ and they are the highest counter value. Next, the procedure gets all the transfer plans such that their candidate transfers to access the same level from the first group of a sequence of pairs. Such a group of transfer plans forms a partition, and it is appended to a sequence of groups of transfer plans. All transfer plans that are not included in the first partition with transferred from/to levels a counter $n - 1$ are included in the second partition, and so on. The final result is denoted as a sequence of groups of transfer plans like $\langle Q_n, Q_{n-1}, \ldots, Q_1 \rangle$ where each Q_i is a set of transfer plans. Note that some of the partitions can be empty.

4.4 Applying Scheduling Rules

Two data transfers (t_i, l_i) and (t_j, l_j) allocated to the processors are in *conflict* if:

- both transfers attempt to access the same level of multi-tiered storage in the same time-unit and/or,
- both transfers belong to the same transfer plan, and their allocation to the processors violates their order in the transfer plan.

A data transfer (t_i, l_i) that belongs to a transfer plan Q_i is a *candidate transfer* for allocation to a processor if it is at the beginning of Q_i and it does not conflict with any other already allocated data transfers. An algorithm that finds a data transfer that can be allocated to a processor with the lowest current workload considers the first non-empty partition in a sequence of partitions $\langle Q_n, Q_{n-1}, \ldots, Q_1 \rangle$ obtained from the previous step and finds all *candidate transfers* from the partition. If no candidate transfers can be found, then an idle transfer in a single time unit is allocated to a processor until a set of *candidate transfers* is found again. If only one *candidate transfer* is found, then such a transfer is allocated to a processor with the current lowest workload. If more than one *candidate transfer* exists, the following *scheduling rules* are applied until a single transfer is found:

Rule 1: *From a set of candidate transfers, select the candidate transfers included in the longest transfer plans.*

The length of a sequence of transfers is measured as the total number of time units needed to be processed. The rule attempts to minimize the overall transfer time and to balance the current workload among many processors. For example, when a conflict over access to the same tier is found, the transfers included in the shorter sequences can be more efficiently allocated. The following rule is applied when Rule 1 finds more than one transfer:

Rule 2: *From a set of transfers returned by Rule 1 select the candidate transfers included in the transfer plans that consist of the largest number of transfers.*

An objective of this rule is to minimise the idle time of the processors. A sequence with many shorter transfers can easily fill up the gaps when a conflict happens. The following rule is applied when Rule 2 still cannot find a single transfer:

Rule 3: *If more than one transfer is found by Rule 2, then select the shortest candidate transfers.*

Rule 3 is justified by the observation that the smaller size of the candidate transfer can reduce waiting time for future allocation for other transfers. The benefit of this rule is the same as the benefit of Rule 2. A shorter transfer allows for a more efficient allocation of the remaining sequences of transfers. The following rule is applied when Rule 3 still cannot find a single transfer:

Rule 4: *If more than one transfer is found by Rule 3, then one of the transfers is randomly selected and assigned to a processor with the current lowest workload.*

The *scheduling rules* always provides a single candidate transfer that is allocated to a processor with the current lowest workload. After the allocation, a set of transfer plans is re-partitioned into a new sequence of partitions a sequence of partitions $\langle Q_n, Q_{n-1}, \ldots, Q_1 \rangle$ where each Q_i. Then, the next processor with the current lowest allocated workload is found, then a process described in the present section is repeated with a new set of *candidate transfers*. The process is formally described by the Algorithms included in the next section.

4.5   Generation of Parallel Processing Plans

An input to Algorithm 1 is a set of transfer plans $\{Q_1, \ldots, Q_m\}$ obtained from the transformation of query processing plans and a set of processors $\{P_1, \ldots, P_n\}$. The algorithm returns allocations of data transfers to the processor $P = \{P_1 : \langle Q_i : (t_i, l_i), \ldots, Q_j : (t_j, l_a) \rangle, \ldots, P_n : \langle Q_x : (t_x, l_y), \ldots, Q_a : (t_a, l_b) \rangle \}$.

Algorithm 1: Generate Allocation Plan.

– **Input:** A set of transfer plans $\{Q_1, \ldots, Q_m\}$ and a set of processors $\{P_1, \ldots, P_n\}$
– **Output:** A set of processors with allocated processing plans $P = \{P_1 : \langle Q_i : (t_i, l_i), \ldots, Q_j : (t_j, l_a) \rangle, \ldots, P_n : \langle Q_x : (t_x, l_y), \ldots, Q_a : (t_a, l_b) \rangle \}$.
  1. Copy a set of input transfer plans into $Temp_1 = \{Q_1, \ldots, Q_m\}$ and create empty sequences of groups of pairs $O = \langle \rangle$.
  2. While a set of sequences $Temp_1$ is not empty, perform the following actions:
     a. Get two sets of processors $\gamma = \{P_i, \ldots, P_j\}$ that have the lowest workload and a set of processors and $\alpha = \{P_x, \ldots, P_y\}$ that have the higher workload where $\{P_1, \ldots, P_n\} = \gamma \cup \alpha$. Let P_i be one of the processor in the lower workload processors where $P_i \in \gamma$.
     b. To initialise a set of sequences, use Algorithm 2 with two inputs $Temp_1$, and O, let the output from Algorithm 2 be $S = \langle Q_i, \ldots, Q_j \rangle$ and $O = \langle \{(l_i, c_i), \ldots, (l_j, c_j)\}, \ldots, \{(l_x, c_x), \ldots, (l_y, c_y)\} \rangle$.
     c. Iterate over S and let current set be $\mathcal{Q}_c = \{Q_i, \ldots, Q_j\}$.
       (i) To eliminate the conflicts, use Algorithm 3 with input $\mathcal{Q}_c$, let output result be $\mathcal{Q}_j = \{Q_x, \ldots, Q_y\}$ and number of Q in the $\mathcal{Q}_j$ be y.
       (ii) If $y = 0$ and $\mathcal{Q}_c$ is not the last set from S, then exit from the loop and go to 2.c.
       (iii) Else If $y > 1$, then use Algorithm 4 to choose the best sequence to allocate on P_i and update $\mathcal{Q}_j$ = the output from Algorithm 4 and update y = the number of Q in the $\mathcal{Q}_j$.
       (iv) If $y = 1$, then selected sequence from $\mathcal{Q}_j$ be Q_c.
          – Let the candidate transfer from Q_c be (t_i, l_j) and the currently available processor be P_i.
          – Next, update $P_i = P_i \cup Q_c : (t_i, l_j)$ and update $Q_c = Q_c \cap (t_i, l_j)$ from $Temp_1$, and Q_c removed from S, and P_i appended to α and removed from γ.
          – Get a pair (l_j, c_j) from O and decrease c_j by 1. Next, remove $((l_j, c_j)$ from the current set and append it into the other sets with the same counter value.
       (v) If y=0 and $\mathcal{Q}_c$ is the last set from S, then add one idle time unit on all processors in γ and repeat 2.b.

Algorithm 2: Initialise a Set of Sequences to Get the Partitioning of Transfer Plans.

- **Input:** A set of transfer plans $\{Q_1, \ldots, Q_m\}$ and a sequence of groups of pairs $O = \langle \{(l_i, c_i), \ldots, (l_j, c_j)\}, \ldots, \{(l_x, c_x), \ldots, (l_y, c_y)\} \rangle$.
- **Output:** A sequence of groups of transfer plans $\langle \mathcal{Q}_i, \ldots \mathcal{O}_j \rangle$ and updated O.
   1. If O is empty, then according to input, count how many transfers access the same level and record how many times appear like a pair (l_i, c_i) where l_i is the level of devices, and c_i is the integer count value.
      a. Next, sort those groups of pairs into descending order of count value and group all the same count values like $O = \{(l_i, c_i), \ldots, (l_j, c_j)\}$, $\ldots, \{(l_k, c_k), \ldots, (l_n, c_n)\}$ where c_i and c_j are the same values and c_k and c_n are the same values.
   3. Next, iterate over O and let current group be $\mathcal{O}_c = \{(l_i, c_i), \ldots, (l_j, c_j)\}$.
      a. Create empty a sequence of groups of transfer plans like $\mathcal{R} = \langle\{\}\rangle$.
      b. Next, get all the sequences that their candidate transfers' level $l_i \in$ levels from $\mathcal{O}_c$, then append all those transfer plans into a set like $\mathcal{Q}_c = \{Q_i, \ldots, Q_j\}$.
      c. Next, append it into $\mathcal{R}$.
      d. Iteration is stop when $\{Q_1, \ldots, Q_m\} \cap \mathcal{R} = \emptyset$.
   4. Return $\mathcal{R}$ and update O.

Algorithm 3: Eliminate the Conflict.

- **Input:** A set of sequences $\mathcal{Q}_c = \{Q_i, \ldots, Q_j\}$, and $\alpha = \{P_x, \ldots, P_y\}$.
- **Output:** Updated $\{Q_x, \ldots, Q_y\}$
   1. If α is empty, then no elimination, and no conflict and $\mathcal{R} = \mathcal{Q}_c$. Go to 3.
   2. Else copy input a set of sequences to $\mathcal{R} = \mathcal{Q}_c$.
      a. Next, remove all the sequences from $\mathcal{R}$ if their transfers come from the same sequences that are allocated at the end of each processor in α.
      c. Next, get all the levels $\mathcal{L} = \{l_i, \ldots, l_j\}$ from transfers that are allocated at the end of each processor in α.
      d. Next, remove all the sequences from $\mathcal{R}$ that the level of their candidate transfer is in $\mathcal{L}$.
   3. Return $\mathcal{R}$.

Algorithm 4: Choose the Best Sequences to Allocate Their Transfers over the Number of Available Processors.

- **Input:** A set of sequences of transfers $\mathcal{Q}_c = \{Q_i, \ldots, Q_j\}$.
- **Output:** $\mathcal{R} = \mathcal{Q}_c$.
   1. According to Rule 1, get the longest length of sequences from $\mathcal{Q}_c$ and place them into $\mathcal{Q}_i$, and the size of $\mathcal{Q}_i$ be s_i.
   2. If $s_i = 1$, then update $Result = \mathcal{Q}_i$ and go to 8.

3. Else, according to Rule 2, sort Q_i in descending order of the number of transfers.

    a. Next, pick all the sequences from Q_i with the largest number of transfers and copy those sequences into Q_j and let the size of Q_j be s_j.

4. If $s_j = 1$, then update $\mathcal{R} = Q_j$ and go to 8.

5. Else according to Rule 3, get sequences from Q_j that their first transfer size is the smallest size and copy those sequences into Q_k and let the size of Q_k be s_k.

6. If $s_k = 1$, then update $\mathcal{R} = Q_k$ and go to 8.

7. Else according to Rule 4, pick one sequence Q_c from Q_k and update $\mathcal{R} = Q_c$.

8. Return $\mathcal{R} = Q_c$.

Example. In this example we use 2 processors $\{P_1, P_2\}$ and three sequences Q_1, Q_2, Q_3 where $Q1 = \langle (5, l_0), (3, l_4), (2, l_0), (2, l_3), (5, l_0), (3, l_2) \rangle$ and $Q_2 = \langle (3, l_2), (2, l_1), (2, l_4), (2, l_3), (3, l_2), (3, l_4) \rangle$ and $Q_3 = \langle (2, l_1), (2, l_3), (2, l_4), (5, l_2), (4, l_1), (2, l_3) \rangle$.

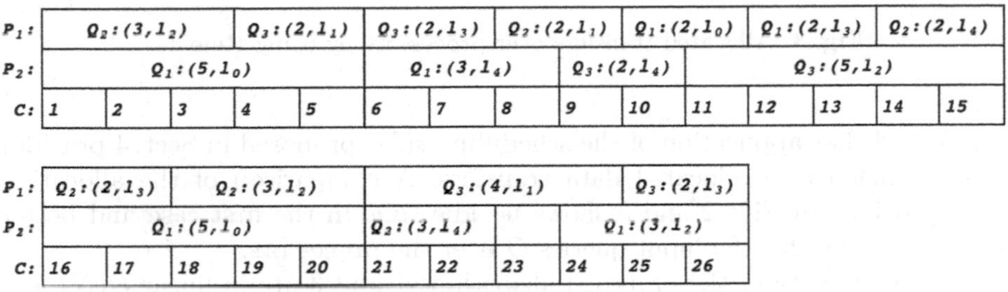

P_1:	Q_2:(3,l₂)			Q_3:(2,l₁)		Q_3:(2,l₃)		Q_2:(2,l₁)		Q_1:(2,l₀)		Q_1:(2,l₃)		Q_2:(2,l₄)	
P_2:	Q_1:(5,l₀)					Q_1:(3,l₄)			Q_3:(2,l₄)		Q_3:(5,l₂)				
C:	1	2	3	4	5	6	7	8	9	10	11	12	13	14	15

P_1:	Q_2:(2,l₃)		Q_2:(3,l₂)			Q_3:(4,l₁)				Q_3:(2,l₃)	
P_2:	Q_1:(5,l₀)					Q_2:(3,l₄)			Q_1:(3,l₂)		
C:	16	17	18	19	20	21	22	23	24	25	26

Fig. 2. Allocated data transfers to the processors through application of the scheduling rules proposed in Sect. 4.4.

Analysing Q_1, Q_2 and Q_3 by counting how many transfers are accessing the same level and grouping and counting them according to Algorithm 2. The output will be like $O = \langle \{(l_2, 4), (l_3, 4), (l_4, 4)\}, \{(l_0, 3), (l_1, 3)\} \rangle$. Next, we get two sets of sequences like $S = \langle Q_1, Q_2 \rangle$ where $Q_1 = \{Q_2\}$ and $Q_2 = \{Q_1, Q_3\}$. Q_2 is in the first group because of its current transfer accessing l_2. Q_1 is in the second group because its current transfer is accessing l_0. Q_3 is in the second group because its current transfer is accessing l_1. Next, we create two sets of processors, a group of higher workload processors $\alpha = \{\}$ and a group of lower workload processors $\gamma = \{P_1, P_2\}$. Next, pass Q_1 and α to Algorithm 3 to remove sequences that create conflict in the current stage. Because α is empty, a transfer plan Q_1 is not needed to eliminate in Algorithm 3. Next, pass Q_1 to Algorithm 1. Q_1 has only one transfer plans. Therefore, simply assign the candidate transfer from Q_2 to available processor $P_1 : \langle (Q_2 : (3, l_2)) \rangle$ and update $Q_2 = \langle (2, l_1), (2, l_4), (2, l_3), (3, l_2), (3, l_4) \rangle$. Update $\gamma = \{P_2\}$ and $\alpha = \{P_1\}$. Next, we pass Q_2 and α to Algorithm 3 to eliminate the conflict. Then, we find that the output from Algorithm 3 has more than one set. Therefore, we pass Q_2 into Algorithm 4 to apply schedule rules to get the best transfer to allocate in the available processor. According to the rule, we pick the candidate transfer from Q_1 to allocate at $P_2 : \langle Q_2 : (5, l_0) \rangle$. After all those iterations, Fig. 2 shows the output of Algorithm 2 with the best allocation plan. Next, we use the same data set from Example 1 but we only eliminate conflicts and we apply Rule 4 random transfers allocations. The results are presented in Fig. 3.

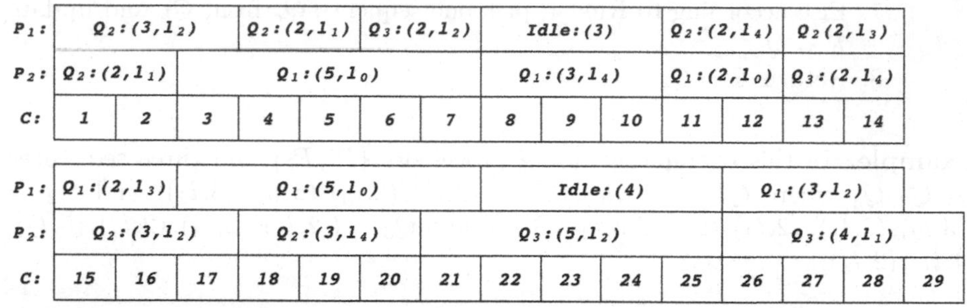

P_1:	Q_2:(3,1$_2$)			Q_2:(2,1$_1$)		Q_3:(2,1$_2$)		Idle:(3)			Q_2:(2,1$_4$)		Q_2(2,1$_3$)	
P_2:	Q_2:(2,1$_1$)		Q_1:(5,1$_0$)					Q_1:(3,1$_4$)			Q_1:(2,1$_0$)		Q_3:(2,1$_4$)	
C:	1	2	3	4	5	6	7	8	9	10	11	12	13	14

P_1:	Q_1:(2,1$_3$)		Q_1:(5,1$_0$)					Idle:(4)				Q_1:(3,1$_2$)			
P_2:	Q_2:(3,1$_2$)			Q_2:(3,1$_4$)			Q_3:(5,1$_2$)					Q_3:(4,1$_1$)			
C:	15	16	17	18	19	20	21	22	23	24	25	26	27	28	29

Fig. 3. Allocated transfers over processors by using Rule 4.

We find that application of the scheduling rules proposed in Sect. 4 provides a better balance of allocated data transfers. A comparison of the allocation plans provided in Figs. 2 and 3 shows no idle time in the first case and better compressed plan for the input queries Q over the processors.

The complexity of the proposed algorithms 1 and 3 are in linear $O(N)$ and algorithms 2 and 4 are in $O(N \log N)$ because those algorithms included sort and partitioning. All the algorithms pass the results from one algorithm to another, the last algorithm, *Algorithm 4* selects the transfer for the best allocation plan. Since the complexity is mixed with $O(N)$ and $O(N \log N)$, the processing time is directly related to the size/length of input data. The input data is a set of candidate transfers extracted from a set of queries Q. Therefore, the length/size of input data must be short/small to reduce the processing time. Thus, we applied several scheduling rules to candidate transfers and removed transfers that are not qualified in each rule.

5   Experiments

For the experiments, we created 12 testing datasets. To create a dataset, we found an optimal solution first, and then we reversed engineer an optimal solution to generate a set of queries and a set of sequences of transfers. The optimal solution was created by arranging several transfers on available processors such that the allocation is well-balanced on those processors and there are no idle times. Next, we applied several rules to each dataset and compare the result of the processing time for each dataset with a different scheduling method. We used the following scheduling rules to allocate transfers over processors for each dataset:

- *Shortest Processing Time (SPT)*: Select a transfer that has the shortest length and if more than one transfer is found, select the sequence with the smallest total time units.
- *First Come, First Served (FCFS)*: Select the transfer that belongs to the first sequence in the queue.
- *Combination of Scheduling Rules (CSR)*: Combination of scheduling rules proposed in this paper.
- *Random* scheduling *(R4)*: Select the transfer randomly chosen by the system.

Finally, we compared all solutions with the optimal solution denoted as the *Optimal Resource Allocation Plan (ORAP)*.

Table 1. Experiment plans

Dataset	Number of sequences	Total number of time-units	Experiments	Number of Processors
1	7	100	1, 2, and 3	4, 3, and 2
2	6	42	4, 5, and 6	4, 3, and 2
3	4	42	7 and 8	3 and 2
4	3	21	9	2
5	3	17	10	2
6	3	34	11	2
7	3	37	12	2

Table 1 aggregates information about datasets and processors used in each experiment. For example, in dataset 1, we have seven queries with hundred of time units. Experiment 1 uses this data set with four processors, experiment 2 uses this data set with three processors, and experiment 3 uses this data set with two processors. We use four different scheduling rules for each experiment and plug the execution time in Table 2. The processing time is measured by time unit because we use the measurement of each transfer in time unit too. Table 2 shows that even we use the same data set for experiments 1, 2, and 3, the results of time units are not the same because we use a different number of processors in each experiment. Finally, we apply four rules and experiment plans from Table 1 and compute 48 test cases, then plug the execution time unit into Table 2.

In summary, the total result of *CSR* is 256-time units, and by comparing with the *ORAP* result, it has six idle time units in experiments, which is better than the other three scheduling methods. As we can see in column *SPT*, the total result is 287-time units with 58 idle time units, and in column *FCFS*, the total result is 286, which has 57 idle time units when processing the 12 experiments. In the last rule, *R4*, the total processing time is 311, with 82 idle time units occurring in experiments.

Table 2. Experiment results

Experiment	$ORAP$	CSR	SPT	$FCFS$	$R4$
1	25	25	28	32	37
2	34	34	38	40	42
3	50	51	57	53	55
4	11	12	13	14	15
5	14	15	15	16	19
6	21	22	23	23	24
7	16	16	16	17	20
8	21	21	24	22	26
9	11	12	16	13	15
10	9	9	11	11	11
11	17	18	18	22	19
12	21	21	28	23	28
Total	229	256	287	286	311

We can see that column CSR achieve the optimal result. Although in some cases, like experiments 5, 7 and 11, the result of our algorithm in column CSR and the scheduling rule SPT achieve the optimal result, which means in some cases, our scheduling result is the same as other scheduling methods. However, CSR achieves better results in most experiments and sometimes even achieves optimal solutions. Overall, combinations of rules can achieve better results than less scheduling of rules. Although, more combinations of rules take more time for computation than one scheduling rule. Therefore, the proposed algorithms in this paper choose a few rules and build the best combination of rules to achieve a better resource allocation plan for parallel processing in a short time.

6   Summary and Conclusions

The paper presents new algorithms to create efficient processing plans for parallel data transfers between the levels of multi-tiered persistent storage. The optimisation of processing plans considers balancing workload among the processors and reduction of the idle time of the processors. First, we show how to transform the query processing plans into the sequences of data transfer plans between the levels of multi-tiered storage. Next, we present the main algorithm that transforms the sequences of data transfer plans into parallel data transfer plans. The main algorithm starts by analysing and partitioning of the original sequences of data transfer plans. The partitions are used to create an initial set of candidate data transfers to be allocated to one of the processors. Then, a collection of rules is applied to reduce a set of candidates to a single data transfer which is later on allocated to a processor with the current lowest workload. After re-partitioning the sequences of data transfer, a new set of candidate transfers is created, and its reduction is performed in the same way as before.

The algorithm presented in the paper does not always generate the optimal solution. Unfortunately, the generation of optimal plans takes too long to be used in practice. For example, in an extreme case, time spent on finding the optimal solution can be longer than the processing time of all tasks. Thus, the algorithm compromises the quality of the parallel data transfer plans and the time spent on generating such plans. Reduction of an initial collection of candidate data transfers through the application of the rules allows for flexibility in applying the algorithm. When more rules are applied, a solution is usually better at the expense of the extra time needed to process the rules. Fewer rules applied mean shorter processing time and possibly less optimal solution.

References

1. Blazewicz, J., Ecker, K.H., Pesh, E., Schmidt, G., Sterna, M., Weglarz, J.: Handbook on Scheduling From theory to Practice, 2nd edn. Springer, Cham (2019)
2. Data Storage Trends in 2020 and Beyond. https://www.spiceworks.com/marketing/-reports/storage-trends-in-2020-and-beyond/. Accessed 30 April 2021
3. Frachtenberg, E., Feitelson, D.G., Petrini, F., Fernandez, J.: Adaptive parallel job scheduling with flexible coscheduling. In: IEEE TPDS, vol. 16, no. 11, pp. 1066–1077 (2005)
4. Li, J., Naughton, J.F., Nehme, R.V.: Resource bricolage and resource selection for parallel database systems. VLDB J. **26**(1), 31–54 (2016). https://doi.org/10.1007/s00778-016-0435-4
5. Nehme, R., Bruno, N.: Automated partitioning design in parallel database systems. In: SIGMOD, Association for Computing Machinery, New York, NY, USA, pp. 1137–1148 (2011). https://doi.org/10.1145/1989323.1989444
6. Noon, N.N., Getta, J.R.: Automated performance tuning of data management systems with materializations and indices. J. Comput. Commun. **4**, 46–52 (2016). https://doi.org/10.4236/jcc.2016.45007
7. Noon, N.N., Getta, J.R.: Optimisation of query processing with multilevel storage. In: Nguyen, N.T., Trawiński, B., Fujita, H., Hong, T.-P. (eds.) ACIIDS 2016. LNCS (LNAI), vol. 9622, pp. 691 700. Springer, Heidelberg (2016). https://doi.org/10.1007/978-3-662-49390-8_67
8. Noon, N.N., Getta, J.R., Xia, T.: Optimization query processing for multi-tiered persistent storage. In: 2021 IEEE 4th International Conference on Computer and Communication Engineering Technology (CCET), pp. 131–135 (2021). https://doi.org/10.1109/CCET52649.2021.9544285
9. Stöhr, T., Märtens, H., Rahm, E.: Multi-dimensional database allocation for parallel data warehouses. In: Proceedings of the 26th International Conference on Very Large Databases, pp. 273–284 (2000)
10. Tiered Storage. https://searchstorage.techtarget.com/definition/tiered-storage Accessed 30 April 2021
11. Wang, K., Choi, S.H., Qin, H., Huang, Y.: A cluster-based scheduling model using SPT and SA for dynamic hybrid flow shop problems. Int. J. Adv. Manuf. Technol. **67**(9), 2243–2258 (2013). https://doi.org/10.1007/s00170-012-4645-7
12. Zhang, Y., Franke, H., Moreira, J., Sivasubramaniam, A.: An integrated approach to parallel scheduling using gang-scheduling, backfilling, and migration. IEEE Trans. Parallel Distrib. Syst. **14**(3), 23–247 (2003)

Fine-Tuning OCR Error Detection and Correction in a Polish Corpus of Scientific Abstracts

Maciej Ogrodniczuk[✉]

Institute of Computer Science, Polish Academy of Sciences, Warsaw, Poland
maciej.ogrodniczuk@ipipan.waw.pl

Abstract. The paper explores the idea of detecting and correcting post-OCR errors in a corpus of Polish scientific abstracts by first evaluating several available spellchecking approaches and then reusing one of the rule-based solutions to eliminate frequent errors most likely resulting from technical problems of the OCR process. The fine-tuning consisted in removing word breaks, rejecting corrections which change the case of the output, removing unnecessary spaces between word segments and restoring Polish letters replaced with spaces whenever the correction resulted in a valid Polish word. The obtained system proved competitive with language model-based solutions.

Keywords: OCR post-correction · POSMAC corpus · Polish

1 Introduction

The process of OCR may result in errors—that's a trivial observation. Lewandowski [4][1] mentions various factors contributing to unsatisfactory recognition rate of OCR, e.g. thinness of paper causing the contents of the back page to break through during scanning, imprecisions of print caused by the wear of the printing press or discontinuities in the letters, discolouration or damage caused during use. Various compensation mechanisms may be applied already at the stage of recognition but if the process is not supervised, many errors may remain.

This is also the case with The Polish Open Science Metadata Corpus (POSMAC) [6][2], a new source of scientific articles (abstract and full texts) acquired from the Polish Library of Science (LoS)[3]. The corpus contains over 142K files with over 55M words dated between 1934 and 2020 (with uneven distribution, see Fig. 1 for details), coming from over 900 Polish scientific journals and books, in most cases scanned and OCR-ed. The nature of the process influenced the content: the texts have been recognized in various periods, by heterogeneous teams and using methods varying from journal to journal so the spectrum of encountered errors can be wide.

---

[1] See also http://www.djvu.com.pl/galeria/UJ/Gazety_czasopisma.php.
[2] http://clip.ipipan.waw.pl/POSMAC.
[3] https://bibliotekanauki.pl/.

© The Author(s), under exclusive license to Springer Nature Singapore Pte Ltd. 2022
E. Szczerbicki et al. (Eds.): ACIIDS 2022, CCIS 1716, pp. 450–461, 2022.
https://doi.org/10.1007/978-981-19-8234-7_35

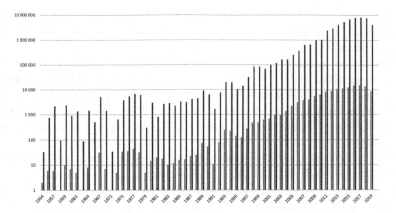

Fig. 1. Document and word count per year in POSMAC

POSMAC is currently being included in the set of CURLICAT[4] corpora [8] which motivates us to attempt to raise its quality by eliminating as many spelling errors as possible while trying not to introduce the new ones. This leads to our first conclusion that precision is what should matter most in the task while other measures such as recall are not that important (following the rule: "correct as much as you can but only when you are certain that the change will not result in an error"). Secondly, due to the large size of the corpus the corrections need to be applied in an automated manner.

These two requirements define our setup: we need to reuse or construct a precision-oriented non-interactive spellchecking tool for Polish which will be used to process the POSMAC corpus. To be able to select the tool we will be carrying out the small-scale evaluation on a manually corrected subset of the corpus.

2   Available Approaches

Since "most of the spelling approaches strongly depend on the specifics of the language and are hard to adapt to another language or a different application" [1], we decided to review several recent spellchecking initiatives specific to Polish and try to validate existing approaches before implementing a new one. Below we list the most available spellchecking tools reused in our experiment.

- LANGUAGETOOL is definitely the most popular error correction tool for Polish[5]. It is a multilingual grammar, style, and spell checker, recently made available in its non-interactive form as a CLARIN-PL service SPELLER[6].

---

[4] https://curlicat.eu/.
[5] https://languagetool.org/.
[6] https://ws.clarin-pl.eu/speller.

SPELLER also claims to use SPACY[7], a robust Python NLP library and AUTO-CORRECT[8], a spelling corrector in Python that currently supports 12 languages including Polish.

- SYMSPELL is another CLARIN-PL spellchecking service for Polish[9], using a fast symmetric delete spelling correction algorithm which provides single word and compound word-aware multi-word spelling correction as well as word segmentation of noisy text. The service integrates the original solution by Wolf Garbe[10] with the frequency dictionary generated from the KGR10 collection[11].

- ED 3 PL tool [13] has been developed for the most recent spellchecking task for Polish, i.e. PolEval 2021 Task 3: Post-correction of OCR results[12] [3]. The solution was based on a sequence-to-sequence model using T5 architecture [7] and a publicly available PLT5 LARGE language model for Polish[13]. ED 3 PL ranked second-best in the PolEval Task 3.

- Another group of tools worth testing are popular grammar and spellcheckers integrated with office applications such as Microsoft Word or Google Docs. They are not intended for non-interactive use and they do not have an auto-correct feature integrated into their regular interfaces but such behaviour can be simulated with macros replacing each detected problem with the first available suggestion (if there is any). For Microsoft Word, we used a Jay Freedman's macro[14] replacing spelling errors with the first suggestion while for Google Docs the first suggestion was selected manually (see Fig. 2).

```
Sub AcceptSpellingSuggestions()
    Dim er As Range
    For Each er In ActiveDocument.SpellingErrors
        If er.GetSpellingSuggestions.Count > 0 Then
            er.Text = er.GetSpellingSuggestions.Item(1).Name
        End If
    Next
End Sub
```

Fig. 2. Jay Freedman's macro for simulating non-interactive spelling correction in Microsoft Word

---

[7] https://spacy.io/.

[8] https://github.com/filyp/autocorrect.

[9] https://ws.clarin-pl.eu/symspell.

[10] https://github.com/wolfgarbe/SymSpell.

[11] https://huggingface.co/clarin-pl/fastText-kgr10.

[12] http://2021.poleval.pl/tasks/task3.

[13] https://huggingface.co/allegro/plt5-large.

[14] https://answers.microsoft.com/en-us/msoffice/forum/all/how-to-accept-all-autocorrect-suggestions-in/e8de0d2c-5429-4a48-8f0c-c62c0f69c717.

3   Evaluation of the Out-of-the-Box Solutions

Several metrics have been proposed for the evaluation of spellcheckers, e.g. word error rate (WER), used to rank the submissions in the PolEval 2021 Task 3 (see. e.g. [2] for review of different methods). Still, according to [1], "the most common evaluation metric is classification accuracy". The authors mention the fact that "only the best candidate from the suggestion list is considered, and order and count of the other proposed correction candidates are insignificant" as a disadvantage of this method and point out that "it is not suitable for evaluating an interactive system". Since our setup is non-interactive and best-candidate-only, we decided to select the classification-based method as our main ranking criterion and perform a detailed investigation of precision, recall and accuracy of the systems evaluated on a subset of POSMAC corpus.

Even though "it is virtually impossible to compare the performance of state-of-the-art spelling correction systems", as authors of [1] state, they report a range of results for various evaluation corpora and different languages. The best reported precision value is 97.8 for modern Greek, recall—99.2 for Arabic Newspaper Corpora and accuracy—95.72 for Chinese OCR Medical Records.

3.1   Development and Evaluation Sets

To prepare for the task, 1000 randomly selected sentences[15] from the POSMAC corpus were reviewed. This resulted in the development of an initial categorization of errors, used in further annotation. The error types mostly concern spelling; punctuation errors were not intended to be corrected[16].

For the evaluation, we randomly selected another set of sentences from the corpus and performed their manual correction. The annotator was instructed to mark error types with previously defined codes attached in square brackets to affected words. The process was supposed to finish after finding 500 errors which resulted in selecting 385 sentences. After carrying out the second pass to verify its results, several annotations were corrected (e.g. undetected missing diacritics in rare place names, missing error codes for corrections etc.) after consulting the PDF sources of articles from the Library of Science to resolve ambiguous interpretations. The final evaluation set eventually contains 10 871 words and 517 errors. Table 1 presents the categorization of errors with examples and counts of each error type.

After the first pass, the code set contained one more mark, [?], used to signal "other errors", unable to categorize by the annotator. There was only one instance marked, i.e. *Saw1g* which was resolved in the second pass to *Sawąg* (a typo in the name of the lake) by consulting the PDF source. Unclear cases, e.g. missing diacritics in proper names, as in *Damieckiej* (most likely *Damięckiej*), were intentionally kept consistent with the source.

---

[15] Detected automatically in the process of linguistic annotation with Concraft disambiguating tagger [9] which in some rare cases resulted in several true sentences treated as a single one.

[16] Compare e.g.   https://languagetool.org/development/api/org/languagetool/rules/Categories.html.

Table 1. Error categorization

Code	Explanation	Example	Correct form	Count
[D]	diacritic missing	sie	się	272
[-]	missing chracter	dziaania	działania	103
[+]	extra character	zajmniemy	zajmiemy	46
[S]	unnecessary space	oczyszczaln i	oczyszczalni	45
[T]	typo	zostaliWmy	zostaliśmy	20
[G]	words glued together	któryw	który	20
[C]	uppercase instead of lowercase or vice versa	zamoyskim	Zamoyskim	7
[P]	excessive punctuation	uniwersalne, narzędzie	uniwersalne narzędzie	2
[M]	metathesis, i.e replacement of two adjacent letters	szkalnych	szklanych	1
Any				**517**

3.2   Evaluation Method and Results

As stated before, standard classification notions and metrics were used:

	Words changed	Words left alone
words with incorrect spelling	*tp* (true positives: corrected errors)	*fn* (false negatives: errors but not corrected)
words spelt correctly	*fp* (false positives: not errors but corrected)	*tn* (true negatives: not errors and not corrected)

$$Precision = \tfrac{tp}{tp+fp} \qquad Accuracy = \tfrac{tp+tn}{tp+tn+fp+fn}$$

$$Recall = \tfrac{tp}{tp+fn} \qquad F_1 = \tfrac{2 \cdot tp}{2 \cdot tp+fp+fn}$$

The calculations were performed by applying the Merge algorithm[17] for three-way comparison of word-aligned ORIG (original sample), GOLD (manually corrected sample) and SYS (system output) files and interpreting its output by counting:

---

[17] https://metacpan.org/pod/Algorithm::Merge.

- *tp* when $ORIG \mathrel{!=} GOLD$ and $SYSTEM = GOLD$
- *fn* when $ORIG \mathrel{!=} GOLD$ and $SYSTEM \mathrel{!=} GOLD$
- *fp* when $ORIG = GOLD$ and $SYSTEM \mathrel{!=} GOLD$
- *tn* when $ORIG = GOLD$ and $SYSTEM = GOLD$

Table 2 presents the results of the evaluation. Even though the accuracy of most solutions seems sufficiently high, the precision is not satisfactory, most likely because of the scientific character of the texts. We will take a closer look at this issue in the next section. The low score of SYMSPELL must result from its improper configuration since even a simple rule correcting just one error in the set can reach higher overall accuracy.

Table 2. Error correction statistics for all investigated settings; bold means best

Tool name	tp	fp	P	R	F_1	A
SYMSPELL	85	1136	6.96	14.78	9.47	85.79
MICROSOFT	298	436	40.60	56.87	47.38	93.98
SPELLER	310	243	56.06	59.50	57.73	95.87
GOOGLE	403	**206**	**66.17**	68.19	67.17	96.42
ED 3 PL	**407**	214	65.54	**70.54**	**67.95**	**96.50**

4   Qualitative Error Analysis

The specificity of scientific data defines several requirements for the correction process. The ideal system should not attempt to correct citations including person names, foreign words and symbols. It needs to keep brackets, dashes and quotation marks in place and should not replace the word with its edit-distantly equivalent. All these problems were observed with the reviewed systems in varied intensity. We present the most characteristic features of each system and some interpretations below. Table 3 presents selected results for various error types which illustrate the differences between various approaches.

4.1   SYMSPELL

The particularly low score of the CLARIN-PL configuration of SYMSPELL results mostly from unnecessary spaces introduced around quotation marks and brackets, e.g. *(Kadrow 2010; Kadrow 2011a)* → *mężczyzn (Kadrow 2010; Kadrow 2011a)* or *"trojki"* → *"trojki"* but also in unexpected places such as date ranges, e.g. *330–347* → *330-3 47*. Since brackets are frequently used to mark citations in scientific texts, the number of such errors is high.

While the solution was most effective in removing word-break hyphens, at the same time, it was wrongly removing minus characters used as dashes or properly used hyphens in compound words, e.g. *bułgarsko-polskich* → *bułgarsko polskich* or symbols, e.g. *W(1-3)* → *W(13)*.

Table 3. Sample error correction results for categories from Table 1; bold values are correct

Error	Correct value	SPELLER	SYMSPELL
zamoyskim	**Zamoyskim**	**Zamoyskim**	zamoyskim
poary	**pożary**	pory	poary
sie	**się**	**się**	sie
któryw	**który w**	który	**który w**
oczyszczaln i	**oczyszczalni**	oczyszczalń i	**oczyszczalni**
zostaliWmy	**zostaliśmy**	**zostaliśmy**	zostali W my
zajmniemy	**zajmiemy**	**zajmiemy**	zajmniemy
dzia a	**działań**	dnia a	dzia a

Error	ED 3 PL	GOOGLE	MICROSOFT
zamoyskim	zamoyskim	zamoyskim	**Zamoyskim**
poary	poary	**pożary**	opary
sie	**się**	**się**	**się**
któryw	**który w**	**który w**	który
oczyszczaln i	oczyszczania i	**oczyszczalni**	oczyszczalń i
zostaliWmy	**zostaliśmy**	zostaliŚmy	**zostaliśmy**
zajmniemy	zajmniemy	**zajmiemy**	**zajmiemy**
dzia a	działania	dzia a	dziab a

SYMSPELL was also unnecessarily normalizing the case in acronyms, e.g. *MChAT-u → Mchatu* and was over creative in correcting proper names such as person names, again frequently used in citations, e.g. *Januszko-Szkiel → Janusz koszkiel.*

4.2 Microsoft Spellchecker

MICROSOFT spellchecker seems not to take into account any context information (beyond the word boundaries) which results in prioritizing existing words over other corrections, e.g. *wahan iami → wahań iłami.* This also concerns wrongly hyphenated words, e.g. changing *me-chanicznych → me-chemicznych* while just removing the hyphen would result in a perfectly correct word (which all other solutions discovered). This also concerns splitting unknown words into in-vocabulary segments as in *estymaty → estyma ty.*

The method is not frequency-based since *Krola* (EN: *the king* without a diacritic) is corrected to *Krolla* (a rare inflected proper name) instead of *Króla.*

4.3 SPELLER

Similarly to Microsoft spellchecker, the CLARIN-PL configuration of SPELLER consequently searches for Polish words to replace the foreign ones, e.g. *Polská*

Praha aneb Jak se z půlky stala polka → *Polská Praha Anek Jak se z pułku stała polka* and corrects out-of-vocabulary words by replacing them with in-vocabulary guesses, even in obvious cases e.g. *nawią zując* → *nawie żyjąc*. The model is capable of removing words, e.g. *okazały się być bardzo trwałe* → *okazały się bardzo trwałe*, usually resulting in errors.

4.4   Google Spellchecker

GOOGLE model is most likely trained on a large corpus without a dictionary which results in replacing less frequent (and thus missing from its limited vocabulary) and unknown words with their similar equivalents, e.g. *pielonych* (a valid rare form) → *zielonych*. Unfortunately, this also leads to acronym-unfriendly behaviour, i.e. changing *CMCU* → *MCU* (while other models keep it unchanged).

GOOGLE model also seems to take into account the local context which sometimes results in errors, e.g. changing proper singular forms to plural ones when a closer word is plural: *Okres$_{SG}$, gdy Bałabanow zrealizował swoje pierwsze filmy$_{PL}$, był$_{SG}$* (EN: *the period$_{SG}$ when Balabanow completed his first films$_{PL}$ was$_{SG}$*) → *Okres$_{PL}$, gdy Bałabanow zrealizował swoje pierwsze filmy$_{PL}$, były$_{PL}$* (EN: *the period$_{SG}$ when Balabanow completed his first films$_{PL}$ were$_{PL}$*).

4.5   ED 3 PL

ED 3 PL, based on transformer architecture, was very effective in replacing out-of-word hyphens (wrongly used to indicate pauses) with proper dashes or correcting HTML character entities: *Józef* → *Józef* (later removed from evaluation as an obvious conversion problem). The system (as the only one) could also effectively glue together words split into several segments, e.g. *pod ję tą* → *podjętą*.

The generative character of the system was sometimes creating unnecessary effects such as replacing correct words with their synonyms, e.g. *zaprezentowano* → *przedstawiono* (EN: *present*) but sometimes also fuzzynyms, e.g. *studenci* (EN: *students*) *to absolwenci* (*graduates*). In this first case, the behaviour of the system might not be perceived as invalid by a user while the second is obviously wrong. There were several similar cases of this type, e.g. *2002–2012* → *2002–12* which is another valid way of expressing the year range. At the same time the changes were often unpredictable and wrong, particularly concerning years in citations, e.g. *(Pękala 1984)* → *(Pękala 1983)*. Some changes were also corrupting valid words, e.g. *innowacyjności* → *innowacjości*.

5   Reuse and Recycle

The solution we propose intends to build on the results of SPELLER by making several adjustments to its corrections to eliminate false positives based on the character of our corpus. Taking into account the specifics of scientific texts (see Sect. 4) and its OCR provenance, we intend to:

1. remove word breaks (surprisingly, still present)
2. reject corrections which change the case of the output
3. remove unnecessary spaces between word segments
4. restore Polish letters which were replaced with spaces due to potential technical problems.

The two first methods are language-independent while the other two require a dictionary lookup to verify whether the proposed correction results in an existing word. For this purpose, we used the list of Polish inflected word forms made available by the creators of the morphological analyser Morfeusz[18] [10]. The dictionary comes in two flavours, based on PoliMorf [11] and The Grammatical Dictionary of Polish (SGJP) [12]. Each dictionary contains over 600K unique word forms absent from the other one (see Table 4) so a joint version was created to broaden the coverage.

Table 4. Counts of unique word forms in various dictionaries

Dictionary	Word form count
PoliMorf 2014	3 800 454
PoliMorf 2022	4 876 026
SGJP 2022	4 909 741
PoliMorf 2022 + SGJP 2022	5 336 228

5.1 Pre-processing

Since word breaks resulting from splitting the word between lines (e.g. *jakości*) still seem to appear in the SPELLER results and frequently result in changes applied to word segments independently, we decided to correct them in the pre-processing step.

Due to the high number of named entities in scientific texts (mostly person names in citations) it seemed worthwhile to test how keeping all words starting with an uppercase character would influence the results.

For cases when a word was split into two segments a mechanism glueing them together was applied when a resulting word was found in the joint dictionary of Polish word forms.

5.2 Adding Missing Polish Letters

Missing diacritics or in-word letters have already been added by existing rules of LANGUAGETOOL integrated with SPELLER. Still, there are cases when a Polish letter has been removed in the OCR process and space was output in its

---

[18] http://morfeusz.sgjp.pl/download/, version 20220410.

place, e.g. *wyznacza a* instead of *wyznaczała*. Again, as with broken words, for LANGUAGETOOL this means applying separate correction mechanisms to each segment individually rather than guessing the missing letter and concatenating it with the segments in the text.

The correction procedure subsequently investigated all Polish letters and attempted to join two-word segments with each of them. When a resulting word was found in the joint dictionary, the correction was applied. The operation was limited to in-word Polish letters, without adding them before or after the word which could also be the case of an error. This idea was not tested because it would by all means result in many errors since e.g. Polish ę or ł correspond to inflectional patterns, e.g. $robi_{\text{fin:sg:ter:imperf}}$ / $robię_{\text{fin:sg:pri:imperf}}$ / $robił_{\text{praet:sg:m1.m2.m3:ter:imperf}}$.

5.3   Evaluation of the Proposed Solution

The proposed solution was evaluated in stages; the results of this process are presented in Table 5. Since each step is independent of the others, the influence of the underlying method on the obtained scores can be easily calculated. Values of the three best original systems are given for reference.

Table 5. Four-step improvement of SPELLER results

Tool name	tp	fp	P	R	F_1	A
SPELLER	310	243	56.06	59.50	57.73	95.87
GOOGLE	403	206	66.17	68.19	67.17	96.42
ED 3 PL	**407**	214	65.54	70.54	67.95	96.50
SPELLER						
+ preprocessing	328	235	58.26	62.00	60.07	96.03
+ keep uppercase	325	179	64.48	60.63	62.50	96.45
+ glue words	345	**166**	67.51	63.19	65.28	96.66
+ add missing Polish letters	379	181	**67.68**	**72.05**	**69.80**	**97.01**

At the end of the day, the record number of hits still belongs to ED 3 PL system, but all other scores were subsequently raised by each next variant of the corrector. What is particularly important is the lowest number of false alarms raised, yet still far from making the tool usable without supervision.

6   Conclusions and Future Work

The presented solution shows how rule-based systems can still compete with language model-based solutions in a specialised setting to reduce the number of false positives and raise the precision of the system. Since the nature of errors detected by these two types of solutions varies, one of the next steps could be combining them in an ensemble or by creating a hybrid solution. But even with the current solution, several improvements can be made, e.g. detecting the language of the content to avoid correcting fragments in a foreign language or old Polish, paying attention to punctuation, dates and symbols.

What could also help analyse the results and fine-tune its subcomponents could be the calculation of our scores for each category of errors independently. Finer-grained categorization of errors could also be carried out, e.g. typos split into standard characters, Polish characters or frequent OCR errors such as confusing lowercase l with 1 and uppercase I or omitted characters into spaces vs. letters. In turn, standard measures could be calculated for each error subtype and the algorithm could be fine-tuned for different periods or scientific journals.

Acknowledgements. The work reported here was supported by the European Commission in the CEF Telecom Programme (Action No: 2019-EU-IA-0034, Grant Agreement No: INEA/CEF/ICT/A2019/1926831) and the Polish Ministry of Science and Higher Education: research project 5103/CEF/2020/2, funds for 2020-2022).

We would like to thank Krzysztof Wróbel for his language model-based error candidate detection experiment using the ED 3 pl tool and Stanisław Lorys for first-pass manual correction of the evaluation data and proposing the classification of spelling errors.

References

1. Hládek, D., Staš, J., Pleva, M.: Survey of automatic spelling correction. Electronics **9**(10) (2020). https://doi.org/10.3390/electronics9101670, https://www.mdpi.com/2079-9292/9/10/1670

2. van Huyssteen, G.B., Eiselen, E.R., Puttkammer, M.J.: Evaluating evaluation metrics for spelling checker evaluations. In: Proceedings of the First International Workshop on Proofing Tools and Language Technologies, pp. 91–99 (2004)

3. Kobyliński, Ł., Kieraś, W., Rynkun, S.: PolEval 2021 task 3: post-correction of OCR results. In: Ogrodniczuk and Kobyliński [5], pp. 85–91 (2021). http://poleval.pl/files/poleval2021.pdf

4. Lewandowski, R.: Społeczna korekta post-OCR w bibliotekach cyfrowych. In: Ilona Koutny, P.N. (ed.) Język, Komunikacja, Informacja, pp. 123–134. Sorus (2011). 5/2010-2011

5. Ogrodniczuk, M., Kobyliński, Ł. (eds.): Proceedings of the PolEval 2021 Workshop. Institute of Computer Science, Polish Academy of Sciences, Warsaw, Poland (2021). http://poleval.pl/files/poleval2021.pdf

6. Pęzik, P., Mikołajczyk, A., Wawrzyński, A., Nitoń, B., Ogrodniczuk, M.: Keyword extraction from short texts with a text-to-text transfer transformer. In: Szczerbicki, E. (ed.) ACIIDS 2022. CCIS, vol. 1716, pp. 530–542. Springer, Singapore (2022). https://doi.org/10.1007/978-981-19-8234-7_41

7. Raffel, C., et al.: Exploring the limits of transfer learning with a unified text-to-text transformer. J. Mach. Learn. Res. **21**(140), 1–67 (2020). http://jmlr.org/papers/v21/20-074.html

8. Váradi, T., et al.: Introducing the CURLICAT corpora: seven-language domain specific annotated corpora from curated sources. In: Calzolari, N., et al. (eds.) Proceedings of the Thirteenth International Conference on Language Resources and Evaluation (LREC 2022), pp. 100–108. European Language Resources Association (ELRA), Marseille (2022). http://www.lrec-conf.org/proceedings/lrec2022/pdf/2022.lrec-1.11.pdf

9. Waszczuk, J., Kieraś, W., Woliński, M.: Morphosyntactic disambiguation and segmentation for historical polish with graph-based conditional random fields. In: Sojka, P., Horák, A., Kopeček, I., Pala, K. (eds.) TSD 2018. LNCS (LNAI), vol. 11107, pp. 188–196. Springer, Cham (2018). https://doi.org/10.1007/978-3-030-00794-2_20

10. Woliński, M.: Morfeusz reloaded. In: Calzolari, N., et al. (eds.) Proceedings of the Ninth International Conference on Language Resources and Evaluation (LREC 2014), pp. 1106–1111. European Language Resources Association (ELRA), Reykjavík (2014). http://www.lrec-conf.org/proceedings/lrec2014/pdf/768_Paper.pdf

11. Woliński, M., Miłkowski, M., Ogrodniczuk, M., Przepiórkowski, A., Szałkiewicz: PoliMorf: a (not so) new open morphological dictionary for Polish. In: Calzolari, N., et al. (eds.) Proceedings of the Eighth International Conference on Language Resources and Evaluation (LREC 2012), pp. 860–864. European Language Resources Association (ELRA), Istanbul (2012). http://www.lrec-conf.org/proceedings/lrec2012/pdf/263_Paper.pdf

12. Woliński, M., Saloni, Z., Wołosz, R., Gruszczyński, W., Skowrońska, D., Bronk, Z.: Słownik gramatyczny języka polskiego (2020). http://sgjp.pl/. 4th edition

13. Wróbel, K.: OCR correction with encoder-decoder transformer. In: Ogrodniczuk and Kobyliński [5], pp. 97–102 (2021). http://poleval.pl/files/poleval2021.pdf

A Multi-label Classification Framework Using the Covering Based Decision Table

Thanh-Huyen Pham[1,2(✉)], Van-Tuan Phan[1], Thi-Ngan Pham[1,3], Thi-Hong Vuong[1], Tri-Thanh Nguyen[1], and Quang-Thuy Ha[1]

[1] Vietnam National University, Hanoi (VNU), VNU-University of Engineering and Technology (UET), No. 144, Xuan Thuy, Cau Giay, Hanoi, Vietnam
phamthanhhuyen@daihochalong.edu.vn, {hongvtn,ntthanh, thuyhq}@vnu.edu.vn
[2] Halong University, Quang Ninh, Vietnam
[3] The Vietnamese People's Police Academy, Hanoi, Vietnam

Abstract. Multi-label classification (MLC) has recently drawn much attention thanks to its usefulness and omnipresence in real-world applications, in which objects may be characterized by more than one labels. One of the challenges in MLC is to determine the relationship between the labels due to the fact that there is not any assumptions of the independence between labels, and there is not any information and knowledge about these relationships in a training dataset. Recently, many researches have focused on exploiting these label relationships to enhance the performance of the classification, however there have not many of them using the covering rough set. This paper propose a multi-label classification algorithm named CDTML, based on ML-KNN algorithm, using covering based decision table which exploits the relationship between labels to enhance the performance of the multi-label classifier. The experimental results on serveral dataset of Enron, Medical and a Vietnamese dataset of hotel reviews shown the effectiveness of the proposed algorithm.

Keywords: Multi-label classification · Covering based decision table · Rough set · Label relationship

1 Introduction

Multi-Label Classification is the task of assigning each of the given instances to a set of predefined labels/classes, in a domain where an instance can simultaneously belong to several classes. The multi-label classification has received increasingly attention and been applied to several domains, including web categorization, tag recommendation, gene function prediction, medical diagnosis and video indexing [1–6].

Let U be the input labeled instance collection, and a set L of q labels. The training dataset consists of $\{(u_1, L_1), (u_2, L_2), ..., (u_m, L_m)\}$, where $u_i \in U$ and $L_i \in L$ is a non empty subset labels, i.e., $L_i = \{l_{i1}, l_{i2}, \ldots, l_{i,l_i}\}$, $l_{ik} \in L(k = 1, 2, \ldots, l_i)$, where l_i is the number of labels in L_i.

© The Author(s), under exclusive license to Springer Nature Singapore Pte Ltd. 2022
E. Szczerbicki et al. (Eds.): ACIIDS 2022, CCIS 1716, pp. 462–476, 2022.
https://doi.org/10.1007/978-981-19-8234-7_36

The task of MLC is to construct the classification function $f : U \to 2^L$, so that, given a new unlabeled instance u, the function identifies a set of relevant labels $f(u) \subseteq L$. The performance of the classification function is evaluated on the testing dataset.

There are two main methods for tackling a multi-label classification problem: **problem transformation methods and algorithm adaptation methods**.

In the problem transformation approach, a multi-label classification task is transformed into a single-label one. After applying a certain single-label classification algorithm on domain data with different labels, a combination step of the classifiers' outputs is carried out to get the final results. Some popular algorithms, such as Binary Relevance, Classifier Chains, and Calibrated Label Ranking, belong to this approach. In the adaptation approach, popular learning techniques have been adapted directly for dealing with multi-label data. Some popular algorithms, such as ML-KNN, ML-DT, Rank-SVM, and CLM, follow this direction.

One of the challenges in MLC is to determine the label relationship due to the fact that there is not any assumptions of the independence between labels, and the there is not any information and knowledge about these relationships in training dataset. Recently, many researches have focused on exploiting these label connections [10, 11] to enhance the performance of the classification. According to our knowledge, there is not any work that applies the cover rough set technique to solve this problem. This paper propose the definition of covering based decision table, a special case of the cover lattice based decision table [12], and solutions to exploit the dependency between labels from the covering based decision table applying to the multi-label classification – ML-KNN. In original ML-KNN, the distance between instances is simply measured by Euclidean metric without considering the relationship between labels. In order to increase the effectiveness of the ML-KNN algorithm, our proposed method tries to find the nearest neighbours of an object based on the included cover from decision lattice including labels that have close correlation to the context of the object.

This paper's main contributions are (i) the definition of the covering based decision table, (ii) proposing a multi-label algorithm of CDTML-KNN based on ML-KNN exploiting the dependency between labels.

The remainder of this paper is organized as follows. Next section presents the definition of a covering based decision table and an example illustrating the covering decision table for the MLC. The proposed multi-label algorithm of CDTML-KNN based on ML-KNN and the multi-label classification framework using CDTML-KNN are presented in Sect. 3. The corresponding algorithms for solving these problems together with some analysis of the complexity of proposed algorithm are also discussed. Section 4 shows the experiments and some discussions on the results. The last section presents the conclusion of the paper.

2 Using Covering Based Decision Table in MLC

2.1 Problem of Determining Label Relationship in MLC Using Covering Based Decision Table

The proposed method applies the covering based rough set [12] on determining the relationships between labels as follows:

In the labeled instance collection $U, L = \{l_1, l_2, \ldots, l_k\}$ is the label set of all instances in U, in which $l(u) \subset L$ is the non-empty label set of the instance u.

For $\forall l \in L$: let $U_l = \{u \in U | l \in l(u)\}$ and $\forall l \in L : U_l \subset U$ let $C_L = \{U_l | l \in L\}$ be a cover of U.

For $\forall u \in U$, close neighbour set based on cover C_L of u is: $N_{C_L}(u) = \cap\{U_l \in C_L | u \in U_l\}$ showing the relationship between labels of instance u $\{l | u \in U_l\}$.

Due to label set L is the target variable in MLC, the cover $C_L = \{U_l | l \in L\}$ mentioned aboved belongs to decision attribute.

2.2 Definition of Covering Based Decision Table

Definition 1: Covering based decision table

The use of decision cover leads to the differences in covering based decision table definition from all other available definitions of covering based decision system such that: the covering based decision system $S = \langle U, \cup D\rangle$ [13] and the decision system $S = (U, C, \{d\})$ [15] have only one decision feature (D or $\{d\}$), another desision system λ-Pytago fuzzy cover [14] mentions about multiple decision features without mentioning the decision cover.

Definition 2: Positive region of covering based decision table.

Let $CDT = \langle U, CC, DC\rangle$ be a covering based decision table, and $Cov(CC) = \{N_{CC}(u) | u \in U\}$ be the included cover of decision cover. The positive region $POS_{CC}(DC)$ of decision cover DC based on condition cover CC is calculated as:

$POS_{CC}(DC) = \bigcup_{X \in Cov(DC)} \underline{CC}(X)$, where

$$\underline{CC}(X) = \bigcup \{N_{CC}(u) | N_{CC}(u) \subseteq X\} \tag{1}$$

Definition 3: The dependent level of covering based decision table

Let $CDT = \langle U, CC, DC\rangle$ be a covering based decision table. The dependent level of DC on CC, denoted $\rho(CC, DC)$, is calculated as:

$$\rho(CC, DC) = \frac{|POS_{CC}(DC)|}{|U|} \tag{2}$$

2.3 An Example of Covering Based Decision Table for the MLC

Let $U = \{u_1, u_2, \ldots, u_n\}$ be the universe set of n multi-label instances, $F = \{f_1, f_2, \ldots, f_m\}$ be the feature set of m binary $\{0, 1\}$ features, and $L = \{l_1, l_2, \ldots, l_k\}$ be the label set of k labels. The condition cover CC and decision cover DC in the covering based decision table $CDT = \langle U, CC, DC\rangle$ are defined as:

$$CC = \{FC_1, FC_2, \ldots, FC_m\} \tag{3}$$

$$DC = \{LC_1, LC_2, \ldots, LC_k\} \tag{4}$$

where

$$FC_i = \{u \in U \,|\, u(f_i) = 1\} \tag{5}$$

$$LC_i = \{u \in U \,|\, l_i(u) = 1\} \tag{6}$$

in which $l_i(u) = 1$ if l_i is a label of label set $l(u)$ of instance u

Note:

if $\bigcup_{i=1}^{m} FC_i \neq U$ we have $CC = \{FC_1, FC_2, \ldots, FC_m, FC_{m+1}\}$, where $FC_{m+1} = U \setminus \bigcup_{i=1}^{m} FC_i$.

if $\bigcup_{i=1}^{k} LC_i \neq U$ we have $DC = \{LC_1, LC_2, \ldots, LC_k, LC_{k+1}\}$, where $LC_{k+1} = U \setminus \bigcup_{i=1}^{k} LC_i$.

In the MLC on text document, U is a set of multi-labeled documents, each document u is represented based on the common features of text in form of vector space such as binary, term freqency, TFIDF features, etc. The feature set is denoted as $F = \{f_1, f_2, \ldots, f_m\}$. For the unlabeled document u, we have to predict potential labels in label set $L = \{l_1, l_2, \ldots, l_k\}$ correspond to u. Therefore, when $\bigcup_{i=1}^{m} FC_i \neq U$ or $\bigcup_{i=1}^{k} LC_i \neq U$ happens, more documents are needed.

When feature f_i is a continous value, using binning method or fuzzy method to transform the feature f_i into a finite set of binary features.

- According to [16–18], the minimum presentation of instance u based on condition cover and decision cover are:

$$Md_{CC}(u) = \{CC_i \in CC \,|\, u \in CC_i \wedge (\forall S \in CC \wedge u \in S \wedge S \subseteq CC_i \rightarrow CC_i = S)\}$$
$$Md_{DC}(u) = \{DC_i \in DC \,|\, u \in DC_i \wedge (\forall S \in DC \wedge u \in S \wedge S \subseteq DC_i \rightarrow DC_i = S)\}$$

- The close neighbours of u based on condition cover and decision cover are:

$$N_{CC}(u) = \cap\{CC_i \in CC \,|\, u \in CC_i\} = \bigcap_{CC_i \in Md_{CC}(u)} CC_i$$

$$N_{DC}(u) = \cap\{DC_i \in DC \,|\, u \in DC_i\} = \bigcap_{DC_i \in Md_{DC}(u)} DC_i$$

- Acording to [19], the included cover of condition cover and decision cover are:

$$Cov(CC) = \{N_{CC}(u) \,|\, u \in U\}$$
$$Cov(DC) = \{N_{DC}(u) \,|\, u \in U\}.$$

- Then the positive region and dependent level of covering based decision table are calculated according to the above definition 2 and 3.

3 The Multi-label Classification Framework Using the Covering Based Decision Table

3.1 The Proposed Algorithm CDTML-KNN for MLC Using Covering Based Decision Table

Let $D_{learn} = \{(u_1, Y_1), (u_2, Y_2), \ldots, (u_m, Y_m)\}$ be the training dataset of labeled instances and $U_{learn} = \{u_1, u_2, \ldots, u_m\}$ be the set of instances.

The covering based decision table $CDT = \langle U_{learn}, CC, DC \rangle$ is built according to the definition 1, 2, 3.

The proposed CDTML-KNN algorithm scheme is described in the Fig. 1 including two phases: CDTML-learner and CDTML-classifier. In the CDTML-learner phase, the task is to construct the multi-label classification model $CML = \{(u, L_u)|u \in U_{learn}, L_u \subseteq L\}$ where L_u is label set of u. (CDTML is an abbreviation of Cover Decision Multi-Label). The learning algorithm tries to exploit the relationship between labels [19] to directly predict potential labels for an unlabeled instance.

In the covering based decision table, label set of the close neighbour of u based on the included cover from decision cover includes labels that have close correlation to the context of u. In that label set, a label l with high reliability threshold is a potential label for u. Therefore, in the CDTML-classifier phase, the label set of an unlabeled instance is derived from the close neighbour set based on the included cover from decision cover based on the relationship between labels.

Procedure CDTML_learner $(D_{learn}, \mathbf{L}, \vec{y}_{u_i})$
(The CDTML_learner algorithm is a variant derived from the ML-KNN [7]).

Input:
    Let $D_{learn} = \{(u_1, L_{u_1}), (u_2, L_{u_2}), \ldots, (u_m, L_{u_m})\}$ be the training dataset of labeled instances, and $U_{learn} = \{u_1, u_2, \ldots, u_m\}$ be the learning dataset of instances which are

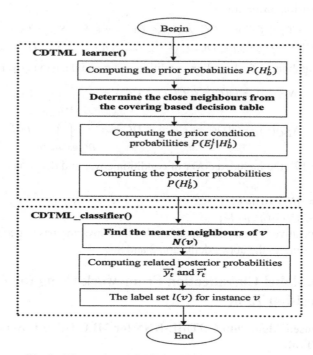

Fig. 1. The proposed CDTML-KNN algorithm scheme

presented in form of binary features. L_{u_i} is the label set of an instance u_i; $\forall u_i \in D_{learn}$ vector $|L|$ dimension $\vec{y}_{u_i}(l) = \begin{cases} 1 \, if \, l \in L_{u_i} \\ 0 \, if \, l \notin L_{u_i} \end{cases}$

Output:

The classifier:

$$CML = \left\{ \left(P\left(H_1^l\right), P\left(H_0^l\right), P\left(E_j^l | H_1^l\right), P\left(E_j^l | H_0^l\right) \right), l \in L, j = \{0, 1, \ldots, K\} \right\}$$

where $\left(P(H_1^l), P(H_0^l)\right)$ and $\left(P(H_1^l), P(H_0^l)\right)$ are the priori probability and posterior probability, respectively, as in ML-KNN algorithm [7]

Algorithm:

// Use ML-KNN to calculate the priori probabilities $P(H_b^l)$ ($l \in L, b \in \{0,1\}$)

1: **for** $l \in L$ **do**

2: $\qquad\qquad P(H_1^l) = \frac{\left(s + \sum_{i=1}^m \vec{y}_{u_i}(l)\right)}{(s \times 2 + m)}$; $P(H_0^l) = 1 - P(H_1^l)$;

// Determine the close neighbours from the covering based decision table

// for $\forall u \in U_{learn}$

3. Build the covering based decision table $CDT = \, < U_{learn}, CC, DC >$ on the learning dataset $U_{learn} = \{u_1, \ldots, u_m\}$;

4: Determine the included covers of condition cover $Cov(CC)$ and the included covers of decision cover $Cov(DC)$;

5: **for all** $u \in U_{learn}$ **do**

6: $\qquad\qquad N(u) \downarrow N_{Cov(CC)}(u) \supseteq N_{Cov(DC)}(u)$;

// $N(u)$ is non empty set because it contains at least an instance u

// Calculate the priori condition probabilities $P\left(E_j^l | H_b^l\right)$ ($l \in L, b \in \{0,1\}, j = 1, \ldots, K$)

7: **for** $l \in L$ **do begin**

8: $\qquad$ **for** $j \in \{0, 1, \ldots, K\}$ **do**

9: $\qquad\qquad c[j] = 0$; $c'[j] = 0$;

10: $\qquad$ **for** $i \in \{1, 2, \ldots, m\}$ **do**

11: $\qquad\qquad \delta = \vec{C}_{u_i}(l) = \sum_{a \in N_{u_i}} \vec{y}_a(l)$;

12: $\qquad\qquad$ if $\vec{y}_{u_i}(l) == 1$ then $c[\delta] = c[\delta] + 1$

13: $\qquad\qquad$ else $c'[\delta] = c'[\delta] + 1$;

14: $\qquad$ **for** $j \in \{1, 2, \ldots, K\}$ **do begin**

15: $\qquad\qquad P\left(E_j^l | H_1^l\right) = (s + c[j])/(s \times (K + 1) + \sum_{p=0}^K c[p])$;

16: $\qquad\qquad P\left(E_j^l | H_0^l\right) = (s + c'[j])/(s \times (K + 1) + \sum_{p=0}^K c'[p])$ **end**;

$\qquad$ **end**;

17: **CML_learner** $\downarrow \left\{ \left(P\left(E_j^l | H_1^l\right), P\left(E_j^l | H_0^l\right) \right), l \in L, j = \{0, 1, \ldots, K\} \right\}$

Procedure CDTML Classifier (CDTML_learner, α, U)

The algorithm bases on an assumption that there is an available similarity measure $m(u, v)$ or distance measure $d(u, v)$ of the two instances (u, v). Moreover, the computation time for $m(u, v)$ (or $d(u, v)$) is small (considered as unit of time).

Input:

$\quad$ **CML_learner** $\left\{ \left(P\left(E_j^l | H_1^l\right), P\left(E_j^l | H_0^l\right) \right) \right\}$, $l \in L, j = \{0, 1, \ldots, K\}$;

$\quad$ u: a new unlabeled instance

$\quad$ $0 < \alpha < 1$: a decision threshold to assign label for u.

Output:

$\quad$ The label set $l(u)$ for instance u.

Method:

$\quad$ // Find $N(u)$ which includes K elements $v \in U_{learn}$ which are the nearest neighbours of u; m: data sinilarity measure;

$\quad$ // calculate related posterior probabilities

1. $N(u) = \{v | m(v, u) = \max_K \{m(u, t) | t \in U_{learn}\}\}$;
2. **For** $l \in L$ **do begin.**
2. $\vec{C}_u(l) = \sum\limits_{a \in N(u)} \vec{y}_a(l)$;
3. $\vec{y}_u(l) = argmax_{b \in \{0,1\}} P(H_b^l) P\left(E_{\vec{C}_u(l)}^l | H_b^l\right)$;

4. $\vec{r}_u(l) = P\left(H_1^l | E_{\vec{C}_u(l)}^l\right) = \left(P(H_1^l) P\left(E_{\vec{C}_u(l)}^l | H_1^l\right)\right) / P\left(E_{\vec{C}_u(l)}^l\right)$

$\quad$ $\left(P(H_1^l) P\left(E_{\vec{C}_u(l)}^l | H_1^l\right)\right) / \left(\sum\limits_{b \in \{0,1\}} P(H_b^l) P\left(E_{\vec{C}_u(l)}^l | H_b^l\right)\right)$.

$\quad$ **end;**
5. $l_u = \left\{l \in L | \vec{y}_u(l) = 1 \wedge \vec{r}_u(l) \geq P(H_1^l) - \alpha\right\}$.

The Complexity of the Proposed Algoritm

The **CDTML_learner** algorithm: The process of building the induced cover of condition cover and decision cover (in step 2) has the computational complexity of 2-exponential level based on the size of set of instances U_{learn} and size of label set L. The process of predicting labels for each instance $u \in U_{learn}$ has the computational complexity is polynomial based on the size of set of instances U_{learn} and size of label set L. Therefore, the CDTML_learner algorithm computational complexity is polynomial. Due to the fact that the CDTML_learner is performed offline, these processes do not have bad affect on the whole process of classification.

$\quad$ The **CDTML_classifer** is quite simple and it has the computational complexity of linear level based on the size of U_{learn} and number of neighibour K. Therefore, this algorithm meets the requirement of time when it is performed online.

3.2 The Multi-Label Classification Framework using the Covering Based Decision Table

The proposed multi-label classification framework using the covering based decision table is described in the Fig. 2. Including two main phases.

The first phase prepares data for the next phase of performing classification algorithm. In this phase, the dataset will be checked whether it is presented in form of binary data or not. If the dataset is presented in real value features, such as TFIDF (a statistical measure that evaluates how relevant a word is to a document in a collection of documents), topic-document distributions of each document in the LDA model (an example of topic model used to classify text in a document to a particular topic), the dataset will be tranformed into binary features.

In our proposed framework as in Fig. 2, we use binning to discretize continuous values. Concretely, the continuous values are first sorted to be divided into a number of buckets or bins. In this work, we use two bins [min – median] and (median – max] to map the data in each bin to value of 0 and 1, respectively.

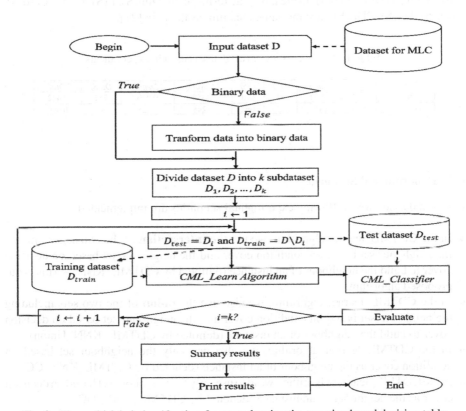

Fig. 2. The multi-label classification framework using the covering based decision table

In the next phase, we perform the proposed multi-label classification on the prepro-cessed dataset. And in order to evaluate the classifier, we use k-fold cross validation. This method divides the dataset randomly into k equal sized sub-datasets, called folds. Then k-1 of the folds are used as training data and the remaining one is used as testing set. The CDTML_learner is performed on the training data to produce multi-label classifier. Then the CDTML_classifier is run on the testing data to predict labels for the instances in testing data. The performance measure reported by k-fold cross-validation is then the average of the measures computed in the loop.

4 Experimental Results and Evaluation

4.1 The Datasets

We use two datasets for experiments, i.e., the fully public Enron dataset, Medical dataset [7] which are represented in form of binary features. These datasets have been used in several publications to make comparison of the effectiveness of proposed methods. Table 1 describes the characteristics of two datasets (*Enron* and *Medical* (http://mulan.source forge.net/datasets-mlc.html). In the table, the terms of |S|, Dim(S), L(S), F(S), LCard(S), Lden(S), DL(S), PDL(S) have the same meaning as those in [21].

Table 1. Characteristics of two datasets used in experiements

S	|S|	Dim(S)	L(S)	F(S)	LCard(S)	LDen(S)	DL(S)	PDL(S)
Enron	1702	1000	53	text	3658	0.070	753	0.442
Medical	978	1449	45	text	1245	0.028	94	0.096

4.2 Experimental Scenarios

For each dataset, four following experimental scenarios are implemented:

- In the CDTML_learner algorithm, we use the **intersection** of the two sets including the neighbour set based on condition cover and the neighbour set based on decision cover to build the neighbour of an instance (denoted by CDTML_KNN) – This is our proposed algorithm.
- In the CDTML_learner algorithm, we also use the **union** of the two sets including the neighbour set based on condition cover and the neighbour set based on decision cover to build the neighbour of an instance (denoted by CDTML_KNN_Union)
- In the CDTML_learner algorithm, we also use only the neighbour set based on condition cover as the neighbour of an instance (denoted by CDTML_KNN_CC)
- In the CDTML_learner algorithm, we also use only the neighbour set based on decision cover as the neighbour of an instance (denoted by CDTML_KNN_DC)

For each experiment, we configured different number of neighbours from 1 to 5.

We also performed the original ML-KNN as the base-line on two datasets to show the effectiveness of the proposed multi-label classification algorithm.

We used Precision (P), Recall (R) and F1-score to evaluate experimental results for each aspect (label), and for the general results of multiple classes, we used the averaged results of micro-averaged and macro-averaged measure [8] to give a view on the contribution of each aspect to the system. We performed the 5-cross validation for each dataset.

$L = \{l_j : j = 1..q\}$ is the set of all labels. Consider a binary evaluation measure $B(tp,$ $tn, fp, fn)$ that is calculated based on the number of true positives (tp), true negatives (tn), false positives (fp) and false negatives (fn). Let tp_i, tn_i, fp_i, and fn_i be the number of true positives, false positives, true negatives and false negatives after binary evaluation for a label l_i. The precision P, recall R, and F_1 is defined as where $P = TP_j/(TP_j + FP_j)$, $R = TP_j/(TP_j + FN_j)$, and $F_1 = \frac{P*R}{2(P+R)}$. Macro-average B_{macro} and micro-average B_{micro} can be computed as follows [20].

In other side, we also used the example-based metrics [4] which work by evaluating the performance of classification models on each test example separately and then returning the averaged value across the test set. These metrics include: Hamming loss (HL in short) - the fraction of instance-label pairs which have been misclassified; one-error - the fraction of examples whose top-ranked predicted label is not in the ground-truth relevant label set; coverage - the number of steps needed, on average, to move down the ranked label list of an example so as to cover all its relevant labels (CV in short); ranking loss (RL in short) - the average fraction of mis-ordered label pairs; average precision (AP in short) - the average fraction of relevant labels ranked higher than a particular label and accuracy (AC in short) - the proportion of the predicted correct labels to the total number of labels for that instance. Further- more, for average precision, the larger values the better performance; whereas, for the other four metrics, the smaller values the better performance.

For each kind of measures, the up and down arrows are put on the right side of each measure to indicate the higher/lower, the better performance.

4.3 Experimental Results and Discussions

The results of performing proposed algorithm on Enron dataset are shown in Table 2 and Table 4 and results of performing proposed algorithm on Medical dataset are shown in Table 3 and Table 5 using two kinds of evaluation measures.

Table 2 and Table 3 show the results of the proposed algoritm and its variants using the measures of Precision, Recall and F1-Score on the Enron and Medical dataset, respectively. The highest results of each scenario based on the number of neighbours are highlighted in bold and yellow colour. We also marked the second good results of each case in italic formatting style. In the Enron dataset, the best results belong to the proposed algorithm in case of using 1 and 2 nearest neighbours (the original ML-KNN also reaches the best result in case k = 1). In the remaining cases (k = 3,4,5) both the best results and the second good ones belong to the variants of our proposed algorithm. These results show the effectiveness of the proposed framework on this dataset. In the Medical dataset, the proposed algorithm and its variants are only better than the original ML-KNN in case of using 2-nearest neighbours to predicts labels for each instance of test dataset. In the remaining cases, the highest results of the proposed algorithm and its variants are little smaller than the result of the original ML-KNN.

In term of using measures: Hamming_Loss, Zero_one_loss, Coverage, Label_ranking, Average_Precision, Accuracy, the results of the proposed algorithm and its variants on the Enron and Medical dataset are shown in the Table 4 and Table 5, respectively. The best scores, the second good ones in each measure are highlighted in yellow with bold and italic formatting style too.

Table 2. The experimental results of proposed algorithm on the Enron dataset using measure of P (Precision), R (Recall), F1 (F1_Score).

	ML_KNN			CDTML_KNN			CDTML_KNN_Union			CDTML_KNN_DC			CDTML_KNN_CC		
	P↑	R↑	F1↑	P↑	R↑	F1↑	P↑	R↑	F1↑	P↑	R↑	F1↑	P↑	R↑	F1↑
1	39.80	26.20	**31.60**	39.80	26.20	**31.60**	53.80	18.80	28.00	52.40	19.20	28.00	41.40	25.80	31.80
2	41.40	30.60	35.00	35.40	35.40	**35.40**	49.40	25.80	33.80	49.20	26.00	34.00	37.20	33.80	*35.20*
3	47.80	23.40	31.60	33.20	40.80	36.60	49.40	29.80	*36.80*	46.80	31.40	**37.40**	34.40	35.60	34.80
4	52.00	22.80	31.80	29.80	41.80	34.80	47.00	32.40	*37.80*	45.60	34.60	**38.80**	32.60	37.40	34.80
5	51.40	23.80	32.20	27.80	43.60	34.20	46.00	34.60	*39.20*	44.80	36.20	**39.60**	30.20	36.60	32.60

Table 3. The experimental results of proposed algorithm on the Medical dataset using measure of P (Precision), R (Recall), F1 (F1_Score).

	ML_KNN			CDTML_KNN			CDTML_KNN_Union			CDTML_KNN_DC			CDTML_KNN_CC		
	P↑	R↑	F1↑	P↑	R↑	F1↑	P↑	R↑	F1↑	P↑	R↑	F1↑	P↑	R↑	F1↑
1	64.40	61.00	**62.80**	64.40	60.80	**62.80**	66.00	43.00	52.20	64.60	42.80	51.40	64.80	60.80	**62.80**
2	67.60	54.60	60.40	53.00	72.80	**61.00**	61.20	47.40	53.40	58.60	48.00	52.60	53.60	71.00	*60.80*
3	71.00	56.40	**62.60**	45.00	72.00	55.60	58.40	54.80	*56.00*	56.60	56.00	*56.00*	43.80	66.60	52.80
4	76.80	51.20	**61.00**	38.00	67.20	48.40	55.20	58.60	56.80	55.00	59.80	*57.20*	38.40	64.80	48.00
5	78.00	46.60	**58.40**	32.20	61.40	42.40	51.60	61.00	*56.00*	51.60	62.20	*56.00*	30.60	53.80	38.80

The results show that the proposed algorithm and its variants perform better the original ML-KNN in many of indexes on both Enron and Medical dataset. In the Enron dataset, the orginal ML-KNN reaches the best and seconde scores in Accuracy index (in case of using 3-nearest neighbours) and the best score in Zero_one_loss index (in case of using 1-nearest neighbours). However, the best and second scores in other indexes belong to the proposed algorithm and its variants. These results show that our proposed solution may get potential effect on some criteria such as Hamming_Loss, Coverage, Label_Ranking and Average_Precision. Especially in Medical dataset, all the best results belong to the proposed algorithm and its variants.

In comparison between the proposed algorithm of CDTML_KNN and its variants of CDTML_KNN_Union, CDTML_KNN_DC and CDTML_KNN_CC, the method of finding the neighbour set of an instance by intersection of the two sets of neighbours based on condition cover and decision cover often gets best results in case of small number of neighbours such as k = 1 and k = 2. This conclusion comes from the fact that with the small number of neighbours, the intersection of the two neighbour sets based on condition cover and decision cover leads to the high-quality neighbour set for each instance. In case of higher number of neighbours, the whole neighbour sets based on condition cover and decision cover and the union of the two sets may lead to the more effective options in finding neighbours for each instance. Therefore, the best results in those cases often belong to the variants of the proposed algorithm.

We also mention the results of performing several multi-label classification algorithms on the two datasets of Enron and Medical from the Giani et al. [9] in comparison with our results in the Table 6 based on measures of Haming loss (HL), Micro Precision (MicroP), Micro Recall (MicroR) and Accuracy (AC). The results show that our proposed algorithm gives little improvement in compared to the results in [9] espeacially according to the micro recall measure. In the Enron and dataset, our proposed algorithm gets much better results in term of micro recall. In the Medical dataset, our proposed

Table 4. The experimental results of proposed algorithm on the Enron dataset using measure of HL (Hamming_Loss), ZOL (Zero_one_loss), CV (Coverage), LR (Label_ranking), AP (Average_precision), AC (Accuracy)

K	HL↓	ZOL↓	CV↓	LR↓	AP↑	AC↑
			ML_KNN			
1	0.07259	**0.91882**	47.50647	0.70870	0.15138	*0.08118*
2	0.07151	0.97176	48.27059	0.69018	0.17184	0.02824
3	0.06507	0.91588	47.32824	0.73090	0.16195	**0.08412**
4	*0.06256*	0.96471	49.97059	0.77027	0.16872	0.03529
5	0.06293	0.97059	50.10647	0.76270	0.17103	0.02941
			CDTML_KNN			
1	0.07265	0.92220	47.59353	0.70965	0.15088	0.08000
2	0.08285	0.97706	45.13235	0.61452	0.16536	0.02294
3	0.09027	0.99353	**44.16588**	0.56939	0.17275	0.00647
4	0.10000	0.99647	*44.33882*	*0.56646*	0.16033	0.00353
5	0.10838	0.99824	44.40118	**0.55431**	0.15772	0.00176
			CDTML_KNN_Union			
1	**0.06240**	0.92824	48.60235	0.77072	0.15411	0.07176
2	0.06454	0.92765	46.61941	0.68866	0.17514	0.07235
3	0.06450	0.93176	46.40235	0.65728	0.19218	0.06824
4	0.06644	0.96824	45.83235	0.63476	0.19440	0.03176
5	0.06780	0.98941	45.74941	0.61442	*0.20027*	0.01059
			CDTML_KNN_DC			
1	0.06301	0.92765	48.57294	0.76885	0.15255	0.07235
2	0.06482	0.92765	46.59176	0.68555	0.17584	0.07235
3	0.06651	0.93118	45.87235	0.63708	0.19208	0.06882
4	0.06795	0.96765	45.48412	0.61133	0.19919	0.03235
5	0.06897	0.98941	45.23470	0.59937	**0.20336**	0.01059
			CDTML_KNN_CC			
1	0.07067	*0.92176*	47.73471	0.71192	0.15425	0.07824
2	0.07890	0.94059	45.72412	0.62765	0.16779	0.05941
3	0.08447	0.95353	46.89706	0.62457	0.16440	0.04647
4	0.08902	0.99647	46.89470	0.61951	0.16195	0.00353
5	0.09453	0.99765	47.40824	0.63638	0.15032	0.00235

algorithm also gets better result in term of micro recall and gets some second good result in term of Hamming_Loss and Accuracy. Recall measure shows the number of true positives divided by the total number of elements that actually belong to the positive class, averaged over all instances. The better of micro recall measure shows that the proposed algorithm gives the better prediction of the true labels for overall instances in general.

Table 5. The experimental results of proposed algorithm on the Medical dataset using measures of HL (Hamming_Loss), ZOL (Zero_one_loss), CV (Coverage), LR (Label_ranking), AP (Average_precision), AC (Accuracy)

K	HL↓	ZOL↓	CV↓	LR↓	AP↑	AC↑
			ML_KNN			
1	0.02015	0.52103	20.88718	0.37292	0.40404	0.47897
2	0.01992	0.58974	23.01128	0.42819	0.38109	0.41026
3	0.01860	0.56000	22.64513	0.42252	0.41111	0.44000
4	0.01800	0.58154	25.02462	0.47035	0.40448	0.41846
5	0.01844	0.60205	26.45333	0.51138	0.38226	0.39795
			CDTML_KNN			
1	0.02017	0.52103	20.88718	0.37326	0.40333	0.47900
2	0.02548	0.69026	15.49949	0.26807	0.39334	0.30974
3	0.03200	0.76410	15.80820	0.28437	0.33383	0.23590
4	0.03954	0.85026	18.07282	0.33232	0.26435	0.14974
5	0.04643	0.88923	21.01333	0.39903	0.20878	0.11077
			CDTML KNN Union			
1	0.02195	0.62564	28.05026	0.54404	0.30022	0.37436
2	0.02288	0.67385	26.29026	0.51874	0.30439	0.32615
3	0.02329	0.66462	22.92103	0.44589	0.33272	0.33528
4	0.02466	0.67692	21.42564	0.41058	0.33702	0.32308
5	0.02671	0.71282	20.19795	0.37814	0.32793	0.28718
			CDTML KNN DC			
1	0.02240	0.63077	28.18667	0.54665	0.29254	0.36923
2	0.02382	0.67590	25.89743	0.51020	0.29597	0.32410
3	0.02395	0.67692	22.41538	0.43571	0.33065	0.32308
4	0.02477	0.67282	20.85846	0.39951	0.34068	0.32718
5	0.02674	0.71077	19.80615	0.36906	0.33220	0.28923
			CML KNN CC			
1	0.01999	0.52205	20.93128	0.37428	0.40523	0.47795
2	0.02507	0.68410	16.32821	0.28843	0.38844	0.31590
3	0.03289	0.80718	18.48615	0.34882	0.30087	0.19282
4	0.03886	0.83897	19.13333	0.35720	0.25775	0.16103
5	0.04666	0.90462	24.46564	0.47292	0.17814	0.09538

Table 6. Comparing experimental results of the proposed algorithm to the results of M.U. Gandi and et al. [9] on the same datasets of Enron and medical using serveral multi-label classification algorithms according to measures of Haming loss (HL), precision minimum (Pmin), recall minimum (Rmin) and accuracy (AC)

Methods	MLKNN	BRKNN-a	BRKNN-b	RaKEL	AMLKNN	SMLKHH	ML-KNN	CDTMLKNN
				Enron dataset				
			M.U. Ghani et al., 2020 [10]				Ours (k=2)	
HL	0.014	0.021	0.024	0.011	0.024	0.015	0.0715	0.0829
MicroP	0.805	0.762	0.785	0.793	0.782	0.812	0.414	0.354
MicroR	0.092	0.061	0.077	0.081	0.027	0.051	0.306	0.354
AC	0.092	0.061	0.077	0.081	0.027	0.031	0.082	0.080
				Medical Dataset				
			M.U. Ghani et al., 2020 [10]				Ours (k=1)	
HL	0.019	0.226	0.312	0.020	0.021	0.022	0.0215	0.0202
MicroP	0.66	0.59	0.56	0.64	0.61	0.65	0.676	0.530
MicroR	0.512	0.431	0.431	0.381	0.410	0.432	0.546	0.728
AC	0.512	0.431	0.431	0.381	0.410	0.380	0.479	0.478,

5 Conclusions and Future Work

This paper proposes a solution to apply covering based rough set theory for multi-label classification. We define the covering decision table (CDT) and propose CDTML-KNN algorithm based on ML-KNN using the neighbours by CDT for calculating the priori condition probabilities. Experiments on two datasets Enron and Medical have been implemented and the results showed that CDTML-KNN has a performance-enhancing effect, especially in the degree of micro-average recall.

CDTML-KNN should be refined for more increasing the performance of multi-label classifier, in particular the degree of micro-average precision in future.

References

1. Elisseeff, A., Weston, J.: A kernel method for multi-labelled classification. NIPS **2001**, 681–687 (2001)
2. Rousu, J., Saunders, C., Szedmák, S., Shawe-Taylor, J.: Kernel-basedlearningofhierarchical multi-label classification models. J. Mach. Learn. Res. **7**, 1601–1626 (2006)
3. Silla, J.C.N., Freitas,A.A.:Asurveyofhierarchicalclassificationacrossdifferentapplication domains. Data Min. Knowl. Discov. (DATAMINE) 22(1–2), 31–72 (2011)
4. Tsoumakas, G., Katakis, I., Vlahavas, I.P.: Mining multi-label data. Data Min. Knowl. Discov. Handb. **2010**, 667–685 (2010)
5. Trohidis, K., Tsoumakas, G., Kalliris, G., Vlahavas, I.P.: Multi-label classification of music into emotions. ISMIR **2008**, 325–330 (2008)
6. Zhang, M.-L., Zhou, Z.-H.: ML-KNN: a lazy learning approach to multi-label learning. Pattern Recognit. (PR) **40**(7), 2038–2048 (2007)
7. http://mulan.sourceforge.net/datasets-mlc.html
8. Tsoumakas, G., Katakis, I., Vlahavas, I.P.: Mining multi-label data. In: Maimon, O., Rokach, L., (eds.) Data Mining and Knowledge Discovery Handbook, pp. 667–685, Heidelberg, Germany: Springer-Verlag, 2nd ed (2010)
9. Ghani, M.U., Rafi, M., Tahir, M.A.: Discriminative adaptive sets for multi-label classification. IEEE Access **8**, 227579–227595 (2020)
10. Liu, W., Shen, X., Wang, H., Tsang, I.W.: The Emerging Trends of Multi-Label Learning. CoRR abs/2011.11197 (2020)
11. Zhou, Z.H.: Exploiting label relationship in multi-label learning. In: UDM@IJCAI 2013, 1 (2013)
12. Pham, T.-H., Nguyen, T.-C.-V., Vuong, T.-H., Ho, T., Ha, Q.-T., Nguyen, T.-T.: A definition of covering based decision table and its sample applications. In: Kim, H., Kim, K.J., Park, S. (eds.) Information Science and Applications. LNEE, vol. 739, pp. 175–187. Springer, Singapore (2021). https://doi.org/10.1007/978-981-33-6385-4_17
13. Degang, C., Changzhong, W., Qinghua, H.: A new approach to attribute reduction of consistent and inconsistent covering decision systems with covering rough sets. Inf. Sci. **177**(17), 3500–3518 (2007)
14. Yan, C., Zhang, H.: Attribute reduction methods based on Pythagorean fuzzy covering information systems. IEEE Access, 1 (2020)
15. Zhang, B.-W., Min, F., Ciucci, D.: Representative-based classification through covering-based neighborhood rough sets. Appl. Intell. **43**(4), 840–854 (2015). https://doi.org/10.1007/s10489-015-0687-5
16. Bonikowski, Z., Bryniarski, E., Skardowska, U.W.: Extensions and intentions in the rough set theory. Inf. Sci. **107**(1–4), 149–167 (1998)

17. Pawlak, Z., Skowron, A.: Rudiments of rough sets. Inf. Sci. **177**(1), 3–27 (2007)
18. Zhan, J., Xu, W.: Two types of coverings based multigranulation rough fuzzy sets and applications to decision making. Artif. Intell. Rev. **53**(1), 167–198 (2018). https://doi.org/10.1007/s10462-018-9649-8
19. Pham, T.-N., Nguyen, V.-Q., Tran, V.-H., Nguyen, T.-T., Ha, Q.-T.: A semi-supervised multi-label classification framework with feature reduction and enrichment. J. Inf. Telecommun. **1**(2), 141–154 (2017)
20. Zhang, M.L., Zhou, Z.H.: A review on multi-label learning algorithms. IEEE Trans. Knowl. Data Eng. **26**(8), 1819–1837 (2014)
21. Zhang, M.-L., Lei, W.: LIFT: multi-label learning with label-specific features. IEEE Trans. Pattern Anal. Mach. Intell. **37**(1), 107–120 (2015)

En-SeqGAN: An Efficient Sequence Generation Model for Deceiving URL Classifiers

Tuan Dung Pham[1], Thi Thanh Thuy Pham[2](✉), and Viet Cuong Ta[1](✉)

[1] University of Engineering and Technology, VNU - Hanoi, Hanoi, Vietnam
cuongtv@vnu.edu.vn
[2] Faculty of Information Security, Academy of People Security, Hanoi, Vietnam
thanh-thuy.pham@mica.edu.vn

Abstract. Generative Adversarial Networks (GANs) are recently used to generate URL patterns to fool the phishing URL classifiers. Some of these works use Wasserstein GAN (WGAN) to generate domain samples for deceiving phishing URL detectors. However, WGAN-based models are designed to work mainly on continuous data and cannot capture the diverse set of patterns in a URL sequence. In order to overcome this issue, we propose En-SeqGAN which works on discrete data to generate full URL sequences. The proposed model is based on the standard SeqGAN with the addition of entropy regularization to encourage the model to produce diverse URL samples. Several intensive experiments are done to prove that the URL samples generated by the proposed model can evade the gray-box phishing detectors of LSTM and Random Forest. The efficiency of gray-box attack by En-SeqGAN on these URL classifiers outperforms both methods of SeqGAN and WGAN. Moreover, En-SeqGAN can generate well-structured URL samples with various URL sequence lengths.

Keywords: URL classfier · Text generation · Text diversity

1 Introduction

Malicious URLs caused 85% of detected web threats are according to Kaspersky [1]. These URLs are effective means of phishing attacks, with the two most common types being email spoofing, fake websites. Attackers create emails impersonating organizations, reputable units, relatives and then trick users into clicking on links and falling into traps. The emails from the spoofed addresses are very sophisticatedly disguised. They are similar to the original emails except for a few small details. Similarly, the design of a fake website is similar to the original website, but the link (URL) is just a little different without making the users notice it.

Some anti-phishing URL solutions are proposed, such as static and dynamic analysis of URLs, blacklist-based, heuristic-based approaches, and recently machine learning-based methods attract the most research attention and application. According to this approach, a classifier is trained on the URL datasets

© The Author(s), under exclusive license to Springer Nature Singapore Pte Ltd. 2022
E. Szczerbicki et al. (Eds.): ACIIDS 2022, CCIS 1716, pp. 477–489, 2022.
https://doi.org/10.1007/978-981-19-8234-7_37

to be able to classify malign or benign URL strings. With sufficiently large URL datasets, deep learning models can be applied to achieve better classification performance. In the context of information security, the classifiers can be considered as defenders. The attacker will try to find a way to bypass this defense mechanism by deceiving the classifiers. One of the recent popular methods of attackers is to use GAN networks to generate URL samples sophisticated enough to fool classifiers. Recent works try to generate some part of a URL string, such as its domain [3] or its feature [5]. Other works generate full URL strings [6] but the training data has to be put into different classes such as Video, Checkpoint or Window. The current problem of generating full URL sequences in recent works is that the generated URL strings might not have a standard structure of URL. One of the main reasons is the difficulty in balancing between the diversity of the generated patterns and the relation between each character in a URL string. In order to tackle this issue, in this work, an efficient discrete GAN model, named En-SeqGAN is proposed. It is the extension of SeqGAN [14] with additional entropy regularization in the objective function of the policy gradient training. This helps to encourage the model to generate more diverse and well-structured URL samples than the original one of SeqGAN.

The proposed model is tested on two scenarios of gray-box attack. The first one is set up with the script that the attacker (GAN model) knows phishing URLs in the training stage of classifiers. This means phishing URLs in classifier training are also used to train the GAN model. The second scenario is established with the constraint that the attacker do not know the labels of training data. The URL strings generated from our En-SeqGAN model are proven outperformed other GAN models of WGAN and SeqGAn in deceiving the classifiers of LSTM and Random Forest (RF).

The remain of this paper is organized as follows. Related works on GAN-based URL generation and fooling the classifiers by generated URL samples are presented in Sect. 2. Next, in Sect. 3, our proposed En-SeqGAN model is described in detail. Experiments and results are illustrated in Sect. 4. Finally, the conclusion and future works are discussed in Sect. 5.

2   Related Works

Machine learning (ML) or deep learning (DL) is now widely applied to solve the problems of information security. They are used not only to strengthen the security defense mechanism, but also used by hackers to enhance attacking performance. In the field of security defending by ML/DL, the classifiers are built to detect suspicious patterns, therefore they can be considered as the defenders. In the problem of detecting phishing URLs, the classifiers help to discover which testing URL string is malicious or clean. In some proposals, RF is used to classify URL strings based on their features [12]. Several works such as [13] and [2] employ different deep model architectures to classify phishing URLs. While the former uses the well-known LSTM architecture, the latter builds a deep convolution network which works on character and word components of the input URL.

In the field of attacking based on ML/DL, emerging today is evasion attack against ML/DL at the testing time. According to [7], there are three types of approach for this attack: white-box, black-box and gray-box attack. Recently, the rise of Generative Adversarial Networks (GANs), which are originally used for data enrichment in training DL models, has attracted the hacker world to make use of these to strengthen the attacking ability against the classifiers. GAN-based models have been proposed in several works to generate URL samples for deceiving the classifiers. Basically, GANs are used to generate (1) domain names in URL and (2) full URL strings. The models of DomainGAN [3], WGAN [11], DeepDGA [4], etc. are for domain name generation. Other works try to generate text string as a URL string [6,8], but the generated results do not present the standard structure of a URL string. Moreover, in these works, there is a lack of explicit evaluations of the quality of the generated URLs.

In order to efficiently apply GAN models for URL string generation, some improvements need to be done for current GANs. In this work, we apply SeqGAN [14] model and make a certain improvement to it. SeqGAN in origin uses Policy Gradient with REINFORCE [16] to train the generator while the discriminator is a classifier to discriminate real and generated text and provides reward signals for the generator updates. The samples generated by SeqGAN rely on an appropriate number of times for Monte Carlo search [17] to update the generator and maximize the expected end reward. But when SeqGAN focused on maximizing the reward, the framework might ignore the possibilities to explore more diverse samples. In order to apply SeqGAN to generate full and well-structured URL strings, entropy regularization is added to the objective function of SeqGAN. This improved SeqGAN helps to fool URL classifiers in an effective way, while maintaining the diversity of the character patterns in the URL string.

3   Proposed Method

3.1   The Overall Framework

The general pipeline of our framework is shown in Fig. 1. The attackers are GAN models that try to generate new URL strings from the original URL dataset. The classifiers trained on the original URL dataset will attempt to validate the generated URL data by GAN models. In this situation, the classifiers play the role of defenders.

The URL dataset includes two parts of clean and malicious URL strings. Each of these will be further divided into training and testing sets. The classifiers applied for experimental evaluations in this work are LSTM and RF. These classifiers are trained by the training set. They are then used to classify URL strings in the test set or the validation set (a set of URL strings generated by GAN models). In this work, other GAN models of WGAN and SeqGAN, together with our proposed En-SeqGAN model are applied to generate URL strings. To evaluate the efficiency of the GAN-generated URLs in deceiving the classifiers, two scenarios of gray-box attack are established: (1) There are only malicious URL strings in the original dataset that are brought into the GAN training phase to generate the new phishing URLs. The classifiers are then validated on these new URLs to show how they are evaded by GAN-generated URL strings. In this scenario, the attackers know about the phishing URLs and their labels; (2) All URL strings in the original dataset are used to train GAN models. However, GANs do not have any knowledge of their labels. The classifiers are then also validated on these GAN-generated URL strings.

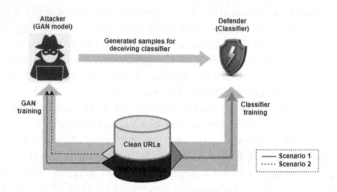

Fig. 1. The overall proposed framework.

3.2   En-SeqGAN Model

The original SeqGAN is trained on word-level embedding but we train En-SeqGAN using character-level embedding. En-SeqGAN will try to produce the generated URL sequence $y = (y_1, ..., y_t, ..., y_T)$ where $y_t \in \mathcal{Y}$ and $\mathcal{Y}$ is the character vocabulary. In order to generate the URL strings, En-SeqGAN considers the current output character $y_{1:t-1} = (y_1, y_2, ..., y_{t-1})$ as a state s. Borrowing the idea from reinforcement learning, the next character y_t can be chosen based on the current state s. With each action of choosing a character y_t, the Seq-GAN model would provide a corresponding reward to the generator. For a finite sequence of T characters, the end reward is computed as the sum of the reward from the beginning s_0 to the end state s_T. The objective of the generator is to maximize its expected end reward for completing a full sequence:

$$J(\theta) = \mathbb{E}[R_T | s_0, \theta] = \sum_{y1 \in \mathcal{Y}} G_\theta(y_1 | s_0) \cdot Q_{D_\phi}^{G_\theta}(s_0, y_1) \tag{1}$$

In the Eq. 1, R_T is the reward for complete the URL sequence. The generator G_θ is responsible for making the decision in choosing the next character while the discriminator D_ϕ acts as a guide for the generator. The discriminator provides the probability distributions of generated samples from the generator is sampled from the real URLs or the synthetic URLs. This output is used as the reward for the generator.

$$Q_{D_\phi}^{G_\theta}(s = Y_{1;T-1}, a = y_T) = D_\phi(Y_{1:T}) \qquad (2)$$

Equation 2 expresses the expected accumulative reward starting from state s, taking action s with policy G_θ. By using Monte-Carlo search [17] for N time, the appropriate character at timestep t could be predicted. Following [14], A N−time Monte Carlo is defined as:

$$\{Y_{1:T}^1, .., Y_{1:T}^N\} = MC^{G_\theta}(Y_{1:T}; N) \qquad (3)$$

The intermediate reward is then computed as follows:

$$Q_{D_\phi}^{G_\theta}(s = Y_{1:t-1}, a = y_t) = \begin{cases} \frac{1}{N}\sum_{n=1}^N D_\phi(Y_{1:T}^n), & t < T \\ D\phi(Y_{1:t}), & t = T \end{cases} \qquad (4)$$

where $Y_{1:T}^n \in MC^{G_\theta}(Y_{1:T}; N)$.

In the original SeqGAN implementation, the generator is updated using Monte Carlo searching for N times. If N is too small, the model may not have enough exploration for a better reward. In order to encourage the exploration of SeqGAN, we added an Entropy term to the objective function of SeqGAN. The entropy term is calculated based on the probability distribution of the action of choosing the next character. This could be calculated since the output probability for each action was computed then the action with the highest probability would be selected. Given the vocabulary $\mathcal{Y}$ has K different character, the entropy for each step would be calculated as Eq. 5.

$$H(G_\theta(a = y_t|s = Y_{1:t-1})) = \sum_{k=0}^K P(y_k)logP(y_k) \qquad (5)$$

When we have the entropy for each step, the final objective function can be presented as Eq. 6.

$$J(\theta) = \sum_{y_1 \in \mathcal{Y}} (G_\theta(y_1|s_0) \cdot Q_{D_\phi}^{G_\theta}(s_0, y_1) + \beta H(G_\theta(y_1|s_0))) \qquad (6)$$

where β denotes a constant hyperparameter for the entropy regularization.

Algorithm 1 shows full details of the proposed En-SeqGAN. At the beginning of the training stage, we use the maximum likelihood estimation (MLE) to pre-train G_θ. D_ϕ is then pre-trained via minimizing the cross-entropy loss. In the Policy Gradient training phase, G_θ is trained for g-step with Policy Gradient (PG). With each new action of choosing the character, we compute the entropy for that action, and then add the entropy into the objective function (Eq. 6). The detailed algorithm of this step is demonstrated in Algorithm 2. While the generator is improved with $g-step$ updates, the discriminator needs to be trained in $d - step$ period to keep pace with the generator.

Algorithm 1. En-SeqGAN Policy Gradient Training

1: MLE pretrain G_θ
2: Pretrain D_ϕ
3: **repeat**
4:     **for** g-steps **do**
5:         PG training G_θ
6:     **end for**
7:     **for** d-steps **do**
8:         Train the disciminator D_ϕ
9:     **end for**
10: **until** En-SeqGAN converge

Algorithm 2. En-SeqGAN Policy Gradient Training

1: **for** t from 1 to T **do**
2:     compute reward $Q_{D_\phi}^{G_\theta}(s = Y_{1:t-1}, a = y_t)$
3:     compute current entropy $H(G_\theta(y_t|Y_{1:t-1}))$
4: **end for**
5: compute the objective function $J(\theta)$ using Eq. 6
6: Update the parameters of G_θ

---

4   Experiments and Results

4.1   Experiment Setup

Data. We used the data from [21] to evaluate our proposed En-SeqGAN. The URLs in the data are crawled from Common Crawl website [19] and Phishtank [20] It resulted in 6 million legitimate URLs from Common Crawl and 1 million phish URLs from Phishtank. We follow the preprocessing procedure from [21] to remove the duplicate and invalid values. To evaluate our method in a consistent way, we randomly sample and then split the original data into 3 sets of small, medium and big sizes, named set A, B and C. The number of URL for set A, B and C is 30,000 (small), 150,000 (medium) and 300,000 (big), respectively. The phish/clean URL ratio in each set is 1:2 since the phish URLs are usually less than the clean URLs. We split each dataset with the train/test ratio of 7:3 while maintaining the phish/clean ratio of 1:2. The length of each URL is capped at 128 since the majority of the URL has less than 128 characters [21].

Classifier Setup. We choose LSTM and Random Forest (RF) as the classifiers for our pipeline. The settings for LSTM classifier include: The vocabulary size of 256 characters, which is set based on the observation that there are 256 unique characters in the experimental dataset; Embedding size of 128; Hidden size of 64; 5 epochs training with Adam optimizer and learning rate of 1e-3. With RF, we use entropy to measure the quality of RF's split. The maximum depth of the tree is 10. In order to train RF, we extract 9 features from an input URL string. The selected features are based on the works of [13] and [18], which are: *URL scheme, URL network location, hostname in URL, port number in URL,* *is dash in domain, is 'https' in domain, is '@' in URL, number of digit in URL* and *length of URL.*

GAN Setup. We train WGAN with a batch size of 64 for 3000 iterations. The number of critics is 10 and the lambda hyperparameter for gradient penalty is 10. For the optimizer of the Generator and the Discriminator, Adam algorithm is chosen with learning rate of 1e-4 and betas of 0.5 and 0.9. The generator of SeqGAN is pretrained using MLE for 20 epochs, while the disciminator is pretrained for 10 epochs. After completing the pretrained phase for both generator and discriminator, SeqGAN is trained using Policy gradient for 3 steps. In each step, the generator is trained first with Monte Carlo search for $N = 8$ times, then the discriminator is trained for 3 epochs. The batch size for SeqGAN training is 64. The dimension of embedding and hidden for generator is 32, and this for discriminator is 64.

Entropy Parameter in En-SeqGAN. In the case of En-SeqGAN, the entropy regularization in the objective function helps En-SeqGAN to explore more diverse samples. With each action of choosing the next character in a URL sequence, instead of always choosing the character with the highest probability, entropy term in the objective function enables the model to explore more choices of character while still maximizing the reward. The β parameter in the objective function controls how much exploration the model should have and. If we choose β too large, the model would focus on minimizing the entropy. Then, the probability of choosing each character in the vocabulary would be the same. This results in he distribution of the model would comes close to uniform distribution, eventually. Meanwhile, with too little exploration, the model would not discover other characters which could potentially maximize the reward. Therefore, choosing the optimal value for β is important.

Table 1 shows the performance of En-SeqGAN model with each value of the entropy parameter β. From our observation, $\beta = 2e-2$ has the best performance throughout most datasets and classifiers.

4.2   Classifier Fooling by Gray-Box Attack

In this work, two scenarios of gray-box attacks are made to evaluate the ability to fool the classifiers by GAN-generated URL strings. The classifiers of LSTM and RF are considered as the defenders. The attackers are GAN models of WGAN, SeqGAN and our proposal of En-SeqGAN. In addition, the evaluations on the testing set of the classifiers are also indicated to show the comparisons with the GAN models. We call this the Baseline evaluation.

Scenario 1 - Attacker Knows Phishing URLs in the Training Stage of Classifiers. It is assumed in this scenario that the attacker knows the phishing URL strings used in the training phase of the LSTM/RF classifiers. In order to perform the attack, GAN models are used to generate a number of malicious URL strings that are equal to the ones in the testing set of the classifiers. The defensibility of the classifiers will be then evaluated on phishing URLs generated by GANs. It is calculated by the number of correctly classified URLs over the total number of URLs. Table 1 shows the experimental results on the generated URLs by our En-SeqGAN and other GAN models. They are also compared with the Baseline experiments on the testing set at different data settings of A, B and C in the training phase of LSTM and RF classifiers.

Table 1. Number of samples in training set and classifier accuracy.

Model	β value	Set A (%)		Set B (%)		Set C (%)	
		LSTM	RF	LSTM	RF	LSTM	RF
Baseline	N/A	97.00	71.92	95.67	77.72	96.71	78.03
WGAN		85.64	99.99	87.53	99.99	95.74	99.99
SeqGAN		80.79	45.20	80.72	39.20	92.35	30.75
En-SeqGAN	$7e-3$	68.00	28.30	78.85	27.15	88.51	45.34
	$1e-2$	71.36	38.50	69.19	33.40	**84.96**	27.86
	2e−2	**60.63**	**16.83**	**83.12**	**20.52**	85.53	**25.76**

As shown in Table 1, our proposed method outperforms WGAN, SeqGAN and Baseline evaluations. For set A, with LSTM classifier, the detection accuracy of our proposed method is lower than other methods, from approximately 36% (compared to the Baseline method) to 25% (WGAN) or 20,16% (SeqGAN). The experimental results with RF are better than LSTM for all cases. The detection accuracy of our En-SeqGAN is only 16.83%, which is much lower than other methods. At settings of B and C, En-SeqGAN gains better results in comparison with other ones at both LSTM and RF classifiers, and the distinguishability of RF is much lower than LSTM classifier. Overall, the detection results gained from the proposed method tend to increase with the number of testing samples.

The experimental results in Table 1 prove that the ability to attack the classifiers obtained from the proposed GAN model is better than other models of WGAN and SeqGAN. This comes from the fact that (1) the distribution of the URL samples generated by WGAN or SeqGAN is different from that one in the training set than En-SeqGAN; (2) The structure of URL strings generated by these models (especially WGAN) is unstable in comparison with the URL standard structure. Therefore, they could be easily detected by the classifiers. The proof for these claims can be expressed as follows:

- For (1): This can be evaluated by Ngram analysis. In order to compare the generated and the original URL samples, bi-gram distributions of the first 30 bi-grams for each GAN model are calculated and analyzed. The bi-gram result for each method is shown in Fig. 2. It shows that WGAN bi-gram distribution is much different from the training set compared to the ones of SeqGAN and En-SeqGAN. En-SeqGAN has a more uniform bi-gram distribution than SeqGAN due to the entropy regularization. This encourages En-SeqGAN to generate more diverse URL strings. Therefore, it is easier to fool the classifiers of LSTM and RF than other ones.

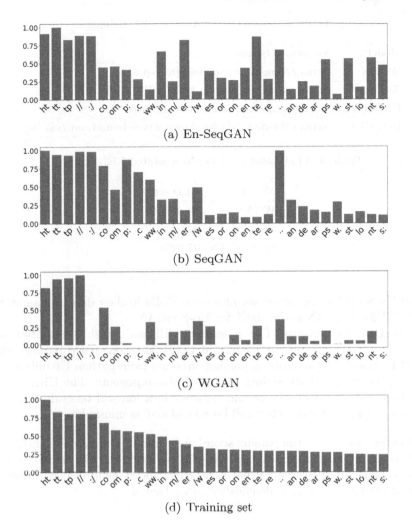

(a) En-SeqGAN

(b) SeqGAN

(c) WGAN

(d) Training set

Fig. 2. The bi-gram distributions of different GAN models compared to the training set.

- For (2): Some examples of the generated URL strings by GANs are demonstrated in Table 2.

  In this work, the GAN-generated URL strings are considered well-structured URLs if they meet the following criteria:

- Top-Level Domain (TLD): The generated URL samples should contain popular TLDs, otherwise they would be suspected as phishing URLs. The statistic of TLDs in URL strings generated by different GAN models is presented in Table 3. It can be seen that only 49.42% samples generated by WGAN have TLDs in their domain names. On the other hand, the majority of SeqGAN

Table 2. Generated samples of URL strings.

Model	Generated Samples
WGAN	https://cene-ronit.cla/setestntcogintore/%
SeqGAN	https://apsukwebar.co.uk/s/ApSH/VlinPLEP
En-SeqGAN	https://appoomorerum3uehmetrar.ru/
Real URL	https://kraditkartin-bankineg.server-bound.com/via-buy/

Table 3. TLD statistics in GAN-generated URL strings.

Model	TLD score
WGAN	49.42%
SeqGAN	92.22%
En-SeqGAN	97.09%

and En-SeqGAN-originated samples have TLDs in their domain names, with 92.22% for SeqGAN and 97.09% for En-SeqGAN.

- Basic URL components: The generated URL strings should contain some basic components, such as scheme, network location, path, params, query and fragment. In this work, a parsing function from python URLlib package is applied to split URL strings into several components. The URLs contain at least 2 elements of scheme and network location will be evaluated as the usable URLs, otherwise they will be considered as unusable.

In order to evaluate the parsing score, we generate a number of phish URLs equal to the number of real phish URLs in the test set. The parsing score is the percentage of URL samples that satisfy the above-mentioned criterion. The result of the parsing score is demonstrated in Table 4.

Table 4. The parsing score for GAN models.

Dataset	WGAN	SeqGAN	En-SeqGAN
Set A	78.56%	97.96%	97.36%
Set B	76.25%	98.43%	95.06%
Set C	80.01%	97.19%	98.18%
Average	78.27 ± 1.54%	97.86 ± 0.51%	96.86 ± 1.32%

It can be seen from Table 4 that the parsing scores of both SeqGAN and En-SeqGAN models are comparable and outperform the WGAN by a large margin. On the small and medium training sizes (set A and B), the adding entropy regularization has negative effects in modeling the URL structures which leads to our En-SeqGAN model having a lower parsing score than the standard SeqGAN model. On the large training (set C), our proposed model starts to learn the URL structures and has a better score than the standard one.

Scenario 2 - Attacker Does Not Know the Labels of the URL Strings Used in the Training Stage of the Classifiers. To further demonstrate the ability of our framework, the data set which includes both malign and benign URL strings in the training phase of the classifiers is also used by GAN models to generate the new URL samples. However, attackers (GAN models) are completely blind to the labels of this dataset. The result of this scenario is shown in Table 5. Our proposed method outperforms SeqGAN by 5.7%, 1.2%, and 1.8% in the case of LSTM classifier. These results are lower for RF classifier. In general, when testing with the increasing size of the dataset, the performance of LSTM classifier fooling will decrease, except for the case of set B. For RF and SeqGAN, the dataset size increases with fooling performance decrease. However, the ability to deceive RF classifier of En-SeqGAN is the opposite of SeqGAN, the increasing size of the dataset goes with the decrease in fooling performance.

Table 5. Number of samples in training set and classifier accuracy

Model	Set A (%)		Set B (%)		Set C (%)	
	LSTM	RF	LSTM	RF	LSTM	RF
SeqGAN	30.16	18.68	26.72	20.58	35.55	26.44
En-SeqGAN	26.83	22.76	22.53	21.54	32.94	16.42

4.3   Classifier Re-training with GAN-Generated URL Strings

Fig. 3. The retrain pipeline

A further experiment of the gray-box attack on the classifiers is done to evaluate the defensive ability of the classifiers when performing re-training them on the new URL strings generated by En-SeqGAN.

The experimental scenario in this case is indicated in Fig. 3. As in the scenario 1, phishing URL strings in the original dataset is used for training En-SeqGAN and LSTM/RF classifiers. Then, a new set of malign URL strings are generated by En-SeqGAN. This set is then divided into two subsets with ratio of 1:1, one is added to the previous training dataset for re-training the classifiers, and the other for testing the classifiers. The experimental results are shown in Table 6. The classifier's accuracy has been improved after the re-training process. For all experimental data settings of A, B and C, the LSTM classifier achieves more than 95% detection rate against phishing URL, while the accuracy of RF classifier is improved by a margin of 17.3%, 14.8% and 16.2% on set A, B and C.

Table 6. LSTM detection rate after retrain

Models	Set A	Set B	Set C
LSTM	71.36%	69.19%	84.96%
LSTM (Retrain)	96.20%	95.36%	98.54%
RF	38.50%	33.40%	27.86%
RF (Retrain)	55.83%	48.22%	44.15%

5   Conclusion

In this paper, we introduced En-SeqGAN, an URL generation method based on discrete text generation. Our proposed method is based on SeqGAN with an additional entropy regularization term in the objective function. The generated samples of En-SeqGAN show better performance in the task of gray-box attack compared to SeqGAN and WGAN. Compared to approaches based on continuous GAN such as WGAN, our model could balance between modeling the structural properties of an URL and improving the output sample diversities. From the results of our works, several directions could be further explored including extending the works to black-box and white-box attacks.

References

1. https://www.kaspersky.com/about/press-releases/2019_malware-variety-grows-by-137-in-2019-due-to-web-skimmers. Accessed 20 January 2020
2. Le, H., Pham, Q., Sahoo, D., Hoi, S.C.H.: URLNet: learning a URL representation with deep learning for malicious URL detection. arXiv preprint arXiv:1802.03162 (2018)
3. Corley, I., Lwowski, J., Hoffman, J.: Domaingan: generating adversarial examples to attack domain generation algorithm classifiers. arXiv preprint arXiv:1911.06285 (2019)
4. Anderson, H.S., Woodbridge, J., Filar, B.: DeepDGA: adversarially-tuned domain generation and detection. In: Proceedings of the 2016 ACM Workshop on Artificial Intelligence and Security, pp. 13–21 (2016)
5. AlEroud, A., Karabatis, G.: Bypassing detection of URL-based phishing attacks using generative adversarial deep neural networks. In: Proceedings of the Sixth International Workshop on Security and Privacy Analytics, pp. 53–60 (2020)

6. Trevisan, M., Drago, I.: Robust URL classification with generative adversarial networks. ACM SIGMETRICS Perform. Eval. Rev. **46**(3), 143–146 (2019)
7. Sabir, B., Babar, M.A., Gaire, R.: An evasion attack against ml-based phishing URL detectors. arXiv preprint arXiv:2005.08454 (2020)
8. Anand, A., Gorde, K., Moniz, J.R.A., Park, N., Chakraborty, T., Chu, B.-T.: Phishing URL detection with oversampling based on text generative adversarial networks. In: 2018 IEEE International Conference on Big Data (Big Data), pp. 1168–1177. IEEE (2018)
9. Goodfellow, I., et al.: Generative adversarial nets. Advances Neural Inf. Process. Syst. **27** (2014)
10. Goodfellow, I.: Generative adversarial networks for text. In: Conference on Neural Information Processing Systems (2016)
11. Gulrajani, I., Ahmed, F., Arjovsky, M., Dumoulin, V., Courville, A.: Improved training of wasserstein GANs. arXiv preprint arXiv:1704.00028 (2017)
12. Weedon, M., Tsaptsinos, D., Denholm-Price, J.: Random forest explorations for URL classification. In: 2017 International Conference on Cyber Situational Awareness, Data Analytics and Assessment (Cyber SA), pp. 1–4. IEEE (2017)
13. Bahnsen, A.C., Bohorquez, E.C., Villegas, S., Vargas, J., González, F.A.: Classifying phishing URLs using recurrent neural networks. In: 2017 APWG Symposium on Electronic Crime Research (eCrime), pp. 1–8. IEEE (2017)
14. Yu, L., Zhang, W., Wang, J., Yu, Y.: SeqGAN: sequence generative adversarial nets with policy gradient. In: Proceedings of the AAAI Conference on Artificial Intelligence, vol. 31, no. 1 (2017)
15. Xin, B., Yu, H., Qin, Y., Tang, Q., Zhu, Z.: Exploration entropy for reinforcement learning. Math. Probl. Eng. **2020** (2020)
16. Williams, R.J.: Simple statistical gradient-following algorithms for connectionist reinforcement learning. Mach. Learn. **8**(3), 229–256 (1992)
17. Browne, C.B., et al.: A survey of Monte Carlo tree search methods. IEEE Trans. Comput. Intell. AI Games **4**(1), 1–43 (2012)
18. Mohammad, R.M., Thabtah, F., McCluskey, L.: Phishing websites features. School of Computing and Engineering, University of Huddersfield (2015)
19. https://commoncrawl.org/
20. https://phishtank.org/
21. Pham, T.D., Pham, T.T.T., Hoang, S.T., Ta, V.C.: Exploring efficiency of GAN-based generated URLs for phishing URL detection. In: 2021 International Conference on Multimedia Analysis and Pattern Recognition (MAPR), pp. 1–6. IEEE (2021)

Towards Communication-Efficient Distributed Background Subtraction

Hung Ngoc Phan[1], Synh Viet-Uyen Ha[2], and Phuong Hoai Ha[1(✉)]

[1] UiT The Arctic University of Norway, Tromsø, Norway
{hung.n.phan,phuong.hoai.ha}@uit.no
[2] Ho Chi Minh International University, Vietnam National University,
Ho Chi Minh City, Vietnam
hvusynh@hcmiu.edu.vn

Abstract. Road traffic monitoring is one of the essential components in data analysis for urban air pollution prevention. In road traffic monitoring, background subtraction is a critical approach where moving objects are extracted via facilitating motion information of interest to static surroundings, known as backgrounds. To work with various contextual dynamics of nature scenes, supervised models of background subtraction aim to solve a gradient-based optimization problem on multi-modal sequences of videos by training a convolutional neural network. As video datasets are scaling up, distributing the model learning on multiple processing elements is a pivotal technique to leverage the computational power among various devices. However, one of major challenges in distributed machine learning is communication overhead.

This paper introduces a new communication-efficient distributed framework for background subtraction (CEDFrame), alleviating the communication overhead in distributed training with video data. The new framework utilizes event-triggered communication on a ring topology among workers and the Partitioned Globally Address Space (PGAS) paradigm for asynchronous computation. Through the new framework, we investigate how training a background subtraction tolerates the trade-offs between communication avoidance and accuracy in model learning. The experimental results on NVIDIA DGX-2 using the CDnet-2014 dataset show that the new framework can reduce the communication overhead by at least 94.71% while having a negligible decrement in testing accuracy (at most 2.68%).

Keywords: Traffic monitoring · Distributed machine learning · Asynchronous computation · Parallel computing · Background subtraction · Change detection

Supported by EEA grants (project HAPADS) and Research Council of Norway (projects eX3 and DAO). The evaluation was partly performed on resources provided by UNINETT Sigma2 (project NN9342K).

© The Author(s), under exclusive license to Springer Nature Singapore Pte Ltd. 2022
E. Szczerbicki et al. (Eds.): ACIIDS 2022, CCIS 1716, pp. 490–502, 2022.
https://doi.org/10.1007/978-981-19-8234-7_38

Fig. 1. Background subtraction with the *skating* sequence in CDnet-2014: (a) observed scene, (b) background image, (c) foreground.

1   Introduction

Road traffic is one of the primary sources contributing to urban air pollution. Therefore, road traffic monitoring is an appealing application in computer vision that concentrates on how to simulate high-level perception on data from real-world contexts to formulate visual understanding in the form of numerical representation and learning theories. With the rapid advancement of the field, background subtraction or change detection is a significant approach to motion analysis in video processing. The technique aims to segregate desired objects, called foregrounds, from the background scenes. The backgrounds are devoid of moving elements which are not of interest to the system (e.g., streets, houses, trees). Figure 1 shows an example of background subtraction. Since real-world situations have varying degrees of dynamics, such as lighting shifts, scene transformations, or bootstrapping, there are several approaches to subtract background scenes with context-specific adaptation [4].

The typical attention of background subtraction is to speculate underlying scenes' properties by presenting learning-based models that are basically grounded on learning towards collected data [5]. One of the most popular approaches to achieving the generalization of multi-modal data is to formulate background subtraction as probabilistic estimation for prediction in which an optimal model is obtained by performing the gradient-based method with a large-scale of training samples [16]. Besides concerns on accuracy due to the incompleteness of data, performing a model learning on a great deal of sampling data requires an appropriate scheme of resource usage that takes advantage of computational parallelism among leading-edge processing units to gain highly efficient model learning. As the scales of training datasets and model sizes increase dramatically, one of the popularly-used approaches is to decompose the mini-batch learning into multiple concurrent optimization pipelines [20,24]. In this context, data exchange between processing units potentially imposes a significant overhead, degrading the effectiveness of computing tasks.

Distributed machine learning has become a pivotal research field, in which communication-efficient algorithms are proposed to diminish communication overhead among parallel processing units and maintain a high ratio of the computation to communication. There are two typical strategies towards communication-efficient systems:

- *Asynchrony*: This approach aims to relax the synchronization among processing elements (PEs) [18]. In other words, message exchanges are reserved among distributed PEs at every iteration. However, instead of suspending aggregating the last updated model parameters sent by collaborating peers, PEs perform the model update with the most recently received values. This scheme allows model updates at PEs to be independent of each other, reducing the communication overhead. Moreover, this design addresses the straggler problems in large-scale training systems.
- *Communication-efficiency*: This approach aims to reduce communication among PEs while ensuring the accuracy of the target model [17]. By examining the staleness of model parameters, the scheme regulates the communication among PEs at every iteration, deciding whether it is necessary to communicate current states at every peer to aggregate the model updates. As the approach diminishes the amount of communication, the communication cost between PEs is significantly reduced.

In both theoretical analysis and applicable implementation, accommodating these two approaches simultaneously in distributed training of deep neural networks imposes a critical trade-off between model accuracy and communication-avoidance [22]. Background subtraction is a specific problem where we need to cope with a large scale of contextual dynamics encountered by moving objects on various camera scenes or video sequences. Communication efficiency in distributed training towards this research area is indispensable to achieving a scalable learning model.

To gain insights into the trade-offs, in this research, we propose a new asynchronous, server-free and communication-efficient framework for training a background subtraction model. Our framework uses event-triggered control to reduce communication among PEs in a ring topology, and employs asynchrony to eliminate synchronization overhead in model training. With this framework, we investigate the balance between accuracy and communication-avoidance for distributed background subtraction. In summary, our contributions are encapsulated as follows:

- First, we have developed a new framework named CEDFrame capable of transforming traditional *centralized* background subtraction models to communication efficient *distributed* schemes for investigating and optimizing the trade-off between accuracy and communication avoidance towards decentralized training (Sect. 3.1). The framework adopts an event-triggered scheme [9] to regulate the amount of message transmission across various control thresholds. We have leveraged the Partitioned Globally Address Space (PGAS) paradigm [2] for asynchronous computation while utilizing computational capability of GPUs to accelerate computation in model training. Delegating communication and computation to CPUs and GPUs respectively, we have tailored the design of the frameworks to utilize the computational capability and the memory of large training systems.
- Second, based on the new framework, we have introduced a new communication-efficient decentralized algorithm for background subtraction

named Distributed Motion Segmentation (D-MoSeg) (Sect. 3.2). We have employed the framework to train a background subtraction model to examine the generalization of the model across multi-contextual dynamics with respect to the effect of communication avoidance.
- Third, we have conducted experimental evaluation of the new algorithm on a state-of-the-art AI server NVIDIA DGX-2 (Sect. 4). Experimented on CDnet-2014 [23], a large-scale database of video sequences for background subtraction with various scenarios, the proposed framework can reduce the communication overhead by at least 94.71% while having a negligible decrement in testing accuracy (at most 2.68%).

The rest of our work is structured as follows: Sect. 2 encapsulates distributed machine learning techniques for data-driven models to avoid communication. Section 3 presents the proposed framework of communication-avoidance in distributed background subtraction. Section 4 extends our experimental investigation towards the distributed training of a background subtraction model over the accurate generalization in multi-modality. Section 5 concludes the work.

2   Related Work

As the scales of training datasets and model sizes grow substantially, distributed machine learning has emerged as a promising approach to reduce the training time by distributing computing tasks across multiple workers or processing elements (PEs). Recent research has demystified parallel stochastic gradient descent in neural networks with two conceptions: architecture-level and algorithm-level communication avoidance. Regarding architectural designs, distributed models are categorized into model parallelism and data parallelism. While model parallelism is proposed to cope with huge network design that does not fit in a single computational device [8], data parallelism is originated to compartmentalize a large dataset with replicated learning model throughout workers. In the data parallelism approach, model consistency, which defines how frequently workers exchange local model parameters with each other, not only affects the communication traffic but also interferes with the convergence and the performance of learning model during training. The model consistency can be classified into three categories: synchronous parallelism (SP), stale-synchronous parallelism (SSP) and asynchronous parallelism (ASP) [3].

Synchronous Parallelism (SP). In this scheme, at each iteration, all workers have to wait until parameter transmission completes at every worker before continuing the next iteration of training. Bulk synchronization parallelism [15] is a conventional synchronous parallel method. Synchronous parallelism is employed in two architectures: centralized parameter server (PS) and decentralized systems with collective communication (e.g., all-reduce). All workers are up-to-date with the same global model when gradient values are aggregated via the parameter server [19] or collective communication [3]. As the synchronous communication is compulsory at all workers, this scheme ensures the model convergence. However, great synchronization and communication cost limits the scalability and robustness of the synchronous parallelism scheme, especially with the presence of stragglers.

Stale-Synchronous Parallelism (SSP). The stale-synchronous parallelism [12] lets workers re-use stale values locally with a goal of reducing the communication and waiting time among workers. To ensure the model convergence, a threshold of staleness is introduced to ensure a bounded gap among workers with respect to their used values, forcing fast workers to wait for slow workers. Consequentially, stragglers may suspend the systems, degrading the effectiveness of the SSP scheme. To overcome this issue, Chen *et al.* [7] developed a novel model where the aggregation at the parameter server (PS) keeps updating only with a pre-defined number of early-coming workers, and then drops the slowest workers as they arrive. To release the communication burden at PS when multiple workers communicate simultaneously with PS, round-robin synchronization [6] coordinates workers in a sequence.

Asynchronous Parallelism (ASP). Eliminating the synchronization can be achieved with the asynchronous parallel (ASP) scheme. This scheme allows workers to *independently* transfers the local gradient values to the parameter server (PS) after the local training completes. The PS continuously updates the global model with received gradient values without waiting for other workers. The significant feature of the asynchronous design is to make large-scale systems faster, more robust, and immune to the failures of any workers. Grishchenko *et al.* exploited the sparsification of upward communications (i.e., from workers to master) in an asynchronous training system [10]. The authors simulated sparsification with a uniformly sampling of local update entries, which aims to make data communication more efficient. In general, without the synchronization among workers, asynchronous models usually end with a low degree of convergence in each iteration [7].

3   Communication-Efficient Distributed Training for Background Subtraction

3.1   Communication-Efficient Framework for Distributed Background Subtraction (CEDFrame)

Concerning a large-scale database of video sequences, we aim to decompose model learning of background subtraction into parallel convex optimization problems on a subset of visual data with smaller dimensional space. In our framework, parallel computing units (e.g., processes) are denoted as *workers* . Supposing N to be the size of the worker crew, we define $\Omega_k = \{\xi_{k_1}, \xi_{k_2}, ..., \xi_{k_T}\}$ as the set of data owned by worker $k \in [1, N]$ with a size of k_T. This is achieved via uniformly splitting the training data into N random sequences of video samples with different camera views. Each worker takes possession of a data segment, and their ownership keeps unchanged as the framework progresses. Since the optimization problem is spanned across multiple workers, we organize the processing group in a ring topology as illustrated in Fig. 2.

Algorithm 1. Communication-efficient framework for distributed background subtraction with N workers

```
 1: Input
 2:   D := {ξ₁, ξ₂, ..., ξ_T}: training data
 3:   F_θ (·): traditional centralized background subtraction
      model
 4:   θ: learnable parameters of F_θ
 5: procedure PROCESS
 6:   for all k ∈ [1...N] do in parallel
 7:     Ω_k ~ UniformSampling(D)
 8:     for t ∈ [1...nEpoch] do
 9:       for each ξ_i ~ UniformSampling(Ω_k) do
10:         Estimate ∇_θ F_{θ_k} (θ_t(k); ξ_i)
11:         if ‖θ_t^{send}(k_s, k_d)‖ - ‖θ_{t-1}^{send}(k_s, k_d)‖ ≥ δ
            then
12:           for each j ∈ Q_k do          ▷ Asynch.
              Comm.
13:             θ_{t'}^{recv}(j, k) ← θ_t^{send}(k, j)
14:             θ_t^{recv}(k, j) ← θ_{t''}^{send}(j, k)
15:           end for
16:         end if
17:         Update model via Eq. (2)
18:       end for
19:     end for
20:   end for
21: end procedure
22: Output
23:   F_{θ_{glob}} (·): distributed background subtraction model
24:   θ_{glob} ← (1/N) Σ_{k=1}^{N} θ_{nEpoch}(k): parameters of dis-
      tributed model
```

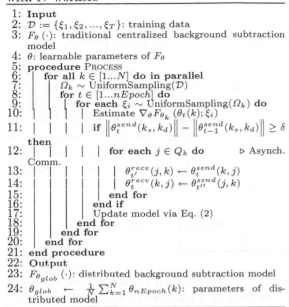

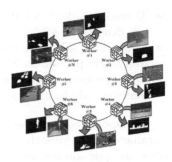

Fig. 2. Background subtraction with multi-contextual learning on a ring

Considering scene-specific learning at every worker, we formulate decentralized background subtraction as a distributed optimization problem. The decentralized stochastic gradient descent [17] resolves this issue by distributing optimization approach on a decentralized fashion:

$$\min_{\theta \in \mathbb{R}^D} f(\theta) = \frac{1}{N} \sum_{k=1}^{N} \underbrace{\mathbb{E}_{\xi_i \sim \Omega_k} F_k(\theta(k); \xi_i)}_{=:f_k(\theta(k))} \tag{1}$$

where $f_k(\theta(k))$ is the kth worker's local objective function that measures some sort of distances between model implication and segmentation labels over data samples ξ_i; and $\theta(k)$ represents learnable parameters in each client model.

The vanilla scheme requires each worker to communicate learnable parameters with neighbors in every epoch of model training, ensuring a parameter consistency across workers at every iteration. The decentralized parallel SGD is shown to achieve an equivalent computational complexity as well as convergence rate as centralized parallel SGD [8], but the efficiency of the decentralized approach is limited by the cost of synchronization. To relax the synchronization in data exchange, we facilitate the decentralized approach with asynchronous communication. With the ring arrangement, we define a communication channel for each worker by defining a list Q_k. Each element of the list, the index of collaborating peers of a worker, indicates the target worker that worker k communicates with during model synchronization. Regarding asynchronous communication, we present the exchanged model parameters in a couple of perspectives:

- At sending side: Learnable variables sent from worker k_s to worker k_d at step t, is denoted as $\theta_t^{send}(k_s, k_d)$.
- At receiving side: Parameters received at worker k_d from worker k_s at training step t, is expressed as $\theta_t^{recv}(k_d, k_s)$.
- The asynchronous communication between a sending side k_s at step t and a receiving side k_d at step t' is formalized as $\theta_{t'}^{recv}(k_d, k_s) := \theta_t^{send}(k_s, k_d)$.

In response to the asynchrony in data communication, workers transmit their parameters right after they complete the estimation of local gradients, which produces an approximate convergence rate as opposed to centralized parallel SGD in global evaluation [17]. Facilitating dense communication for every pair of workers may degrade the computation-communication ratio when the framework scales up. Instead, for each worker k, the parameter update is performed independently by aggregating and averaging the local value and received values from a smaller set of collaborating peers, which is explicitly expressed as:

$$\theta_{t+1}(k) = \underbrace{\frac{1}{|Q_k|+1}\left[\theta_t(k) + \sum_{j \in Q_k} \theta_t^{recv}(k,j)\right]}_{=:\bar{\theta}_t(k)} -\gamma\nabla_\theta F_{\theta_k}\left(\theta_t(k); \xi_i\right) \quad (2)$$

Although synchronous distributed SGD are shown to be a robust approach with the best speed-up [18], the method still has scalability issues on a slow network because of intensive communication. We tackle the issues by omitting unnecessary data exchange via employing a threshold scheme, EventGraD [9], in which each worker have to evaluate the changes in their local models. Specifically, when the normalized values of each model parameter amplifies up to a threshold δ as compared with the most recently communicated values in the previous iteration, the owning worker needs to communicate the new value to neighbours. Otherwise, the communication is neglected and the local model keeps updated with the last received values from collaborating peers. The formalism of this technique is expressed as:

$$\theta_t^{send}(k_s, k_d) := \begin{cases} \theta_t^{send}(k_s, k_d), & \text{if } \left\|\theta_t^{send}(k_s, k_d)\right\| - \left\|\theta_{t-1}^{send}(k_s, k_d)\right\| \geq \delta \\ \theta_{t-1}^{send}(k_s, k_d), & \text{otherwise} \end{cases} \quad (3)$$

The training ends up with a global model, which is concluded by averaging local models at all distributed workers. The Algorithm 1 encapsulates the parallel pipeline of our approach. In video analysis, background subtraction models cope with a variety of motion dynamics and contextual transformation across multiple scenes. In addition, training a model on a specific scene with a sufficient number of iterations may cause local fitting [1], which may significantly ruin the generalization of global model after we aggregate distributed models from all workers upon constantly changing views. To examine the trade-off between accuracy and communication-avoidance in the model using our framework, we incorporate our framework into a neural-network-based background subtraction in Sect. 3.2.

3.2 Communication-Efficient Distributed Motion Segmentation (D-MoSeg)

Background subtraction is a task to extract visual masks of moving objects in observed scenes. Employing a learning-based model on multiple workers is a straightforward approach to cope with large scale datasets of videos. In this context, we introduce a communication-efficient algorithm for Distributed Motion Segmentation (D-MoSeg). Distributed learning of the proposed framework is simulated with a compact convolutional auto-encoder for context-driven background subtraction, MEDAL-net [11]. The design of this architecture renders a light-weighted network of around 2,800 parameters via reducing the computational burden with depth-wise separable convolutions [13]. Furthermore, as the network is invariant with any dimensional requirements of input data, this background subtraction model makes our framework effortlessly applicable to distribute learning tasks across numerous workers without suffering restrictions on resource for model initialization. In addition, as the model concentrates on the representation of differences between observed images and their corresponding background scenes, we restrict the model behaviors and search direction towards subtracting backgrounds to examine the generalization on a plethora of contextual scenarios.

Considered on the T time steps, a time-series data of visual signal is given as $\chi_c^T = \{\mathbf{I}_1, \mathbf{I}_2, ..., \mathbf{I}_T | \mathbf{I}_i \in [0, 255]^{H \times W \times c}\}$, where $\mathbf{I}_i$ is a pixel map of a dimension of $H \times W$ described in a color space c. The motion segmentation of $\mathbf{I}_i$ is presented as a single-channel probability map $\hat{\mathbf{Y}}_i$, defined as:

$$\hat{\mathbf{Y}}_i = F_\theta(\mathbf{I}_i, BG(\mathbf{I}_i)) \sim P(\mathbf{I}_i|\theta) \tag{4}$$

where $BG(\mathbf{I}_i)$ is the background scene of $\mathbf{I}_i$, incorporating only static objects within the scene, which is structured with most frequently observed color intensities, and is estimated with statistical learning on Gaussian Mixture Model [21]; a set of non-linearity transformations, $F_\theta(\cdot)$, formulates a conditional formalism on high-dimensional parameters θ. From the continuous domain of a probabilistic space, the discrete foreground mask of $\mathbf{I}_i$ is obtained by applying a threshold scheme to eradicate noises and to facilitate for evaluation.

From this hypothesis, the capability of pattern recognition upon motion complexity is acquired from training on a large collections of sampling spectacles, where each sample, denoted as $\xi_i = \{\mathbf{I}_i, BG(\mathbf{I}_i), \hat{\mathbf{Y}}_i\}$, is a three-fold chronicle of an observed scene. The multi-contextal background subtraction in MEDAl-net is expressed as a binary prediction that is formulated as an optimization model on each of N workers:

$$\min_{\theta \in \mathbb{R}^D} f(\theta) = \frac{1}{N} \sum_{k=1}^N \underbrace{\mathbb{E}_{\xi_{k_i} \sim \Omega_k} F_\theta(\theta_k; \mathbf{I}_{k_i}, BG(\mathbf{I}_{k_i}), \hat{\mathbf{Y}}_{k_i})}_{=:f_k(\theta_k)} \tag{5}$$

where the training sample ξ_{k_i} at each worker k implies a probabilistic distribution of a client-partitioned dataset Ω_k; the target model is constructed with learnable parameters θ; and $F_\theta : \mathbb{R}^D \to \mathbb{R}$ presents the objective function of our optimization problem, which is explicitly penalized by a cross-entry estimation at every image point:

$$f = -\frac{1}{T} \sum_{i=1}^{T} \sum_{h=1}^{H} \sum_{w=1}^{W} [\mathbf{Y}_{i,h,w} \log(\hat{\mathbf{Y}}_{i,h,w}) \\ + (1 - \mathbf{Y}_{i,h,w}) \log(1 - \hat{\mathbf{Y}}_{i,h,w})] \tag{6}$$

where $\mathbf{Y}$ is the corresponding set of foreground binary masks for $\hat{\mathbf{Y}}$.

As the model is invariant to the dimension of input data, stochastic gradient descent is motivated with mini-batch learning to solve the objective function with iterative updates across various scenes with different resolutions at every worker:

$$\theta_{t+1}(k) = \bar{\theta}_t(k) - \gamma \nabla_\theta F_{\theta_k}\left(\theta_t(k); \mathbf{I}_i, BG(\mathbf{I}_i), \hat{\mathbf{Y}}_i\right) \tag{7}$$

where θ_{t+1} and $\bar{\theta}_t$ respectively represent the local parameters at time step $t+1$ and aggregated parameters from the distributed model at time step t. The model parameters are iteratively adjusted with a learning rate γ. Obviously, with a large-scale dataset, the iterative pipeline of training insists on a high ratio of the computation to communication to distribute stochastic model update among workers efficiently.

4 Experiments and Discussion

Recent research have demonstrated regular learning of background subtraction models to maximize the capability of scene-specific adaptation [1]. In this work, we employ our framework to accommodate a multi-modal background subtraction model and to train a compact neural network in a distributed fashion across various visual dynamics. Specifically, we perform the investigation on a NVIDIA DGX-2 server with two Intel Xeon Platinum 8168 CPUs (24-core, 2.7 GHz), 1.5 TB of memory and 16 NVIDIA Tesla V100 GPUs. The framework is implemented with UPC++ [2], a PGAS library, and PyTorch C++ API.

In order to formulate a multi-modal environment for the background subtraction model, we evaluate the training scheme with a large-scale database of videos for change detection, CDnet-2014 [23]. The dataset contains 53 camera views recorded at different visual resolutions describing 12 realistic situations of motion dynamics and conditions of noises as illustated in Fig. 3. This sequence is considered as one of the most challenging benchmarks for video analysis [14]. With around 160,000 annotated video frames, we distribute the network learning on a crew of workers to formulate a universal model for background subtraction. The learnable architecture in this context is a compact and scale-invariant auto-encoder MEDAL-net [11]. We extract the background scenes with a formalism of statistical learning using Gaussian Mixture Model [21] as a part of network input. Because of the fluctuation of actually observed data sequences when the

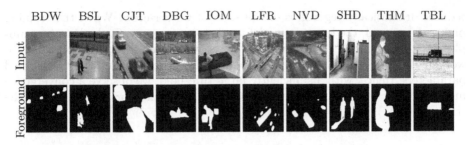

Fig. 3. The illustration of categories with visual dynamics in CDnet 2014, which are bad weather (*BDW*), baseline (*BSL*), camera jitter (*CJT*), dynamic background (*DBG*), intermittent object motion (*IOM*), low frame rate (*LFR*), night videos (*NVD*), shadow (*SHD*), thermal (*THM*), and turbulence (*TBL*).

Table 1. A comparison between the centralized approach MEDAL-net [11] and our new distributed approach D-MoSeg with $\delta = 0.005$ after 15 epochs.

#Workers	Threshold-free MEDAL-net [11]		Event-triggered D-MoSeg					
	Train. Acc.	Test. Acc.	% communication reduction	Train. Acc.	Δ Train. Acc.	Test. Acc.	Δ Test. Acc.	
2	96.58%	95.80%	94.71%	94.44%	−2.14%	93.12%	−2.68%	
4	96.07%	95.10%	98.43%	94.45%	−1.62%	93.12%	−1.98%	
8	95.78%	94.57%	97.45%	93.97%	−1.81%	92.57%	−2.00%	
16	95.07%	93.62%	94.96%	93.97%	−1.10%	92.57%	−1.04%	

recording camera rotates continuously in the collection PTZ of the dataset, we pass over this subdivision to sustainably model the underlying of given scenes.

With our framework, the data parallelism of the network training is simulated over a sets of concurrent workers, where visual scenarios of the dataset are randomly divided into equal compartments and is allocated on local storage. We evaluate the experiment with different sizes of the worker crew, including 2, 4, 8, and 16 workers (or PEs). Data-driven learning of the model is performed on each worker with a batch size of 16, and is supervised by Adam optimizer associating with a learning rate of 0.005. The experimental scheme is trained with 15 epochs.

To investigate the effect of communication avoidance in model learning, we examine the effect o communication reduction by the event-trigger framework on the accuracy of the background subtraction model. The percentage of data communication is measured with respect to different thresholds at every update step. The threshold is outlined with a range of 18 values, starting from 0 to 0.1. When the learning progress completes at every worker, the trained networks are then averaged across all workers to form a global model, and they are then acquired for evaluating the training accuracy and the testing accuracy on the whole dataset.

With each value of thresholds in event-trigger scheme, Fig. 4 summarizes the number of messages that are communicated during model training, and the accuracy of the network in training and testing with a various number of workers. In overall, as the threshold rises gradually, the amount of exchanged messages reduces dramatically regardless of the sizes of worker-crew. When the training processes proceed, the learning model tends to converge to fit the learning samples. At that moment, the difference of layer weights and bias is diminished; so workers do not perform unnecessary communicate to synchronize the learned parameters. Hence, with a sufficiently large threshold, we observe a convergence in the amount of transmitted messages within the framework at the end of the training.

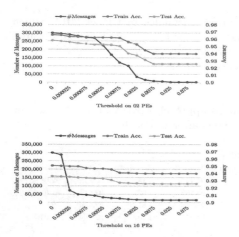

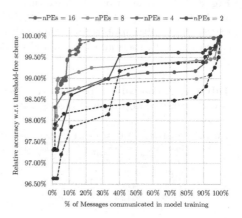

Fig. 4. The number of communicated messages and model accuracy versus different thresholds with 2 workers (PEs) and 16 workers (PEs) in the communication-aware model D-MoSeg.

Fig. 5. D-MoSeg relative accuracy versus the percentage of communicated messages in comparison to the communication-oblivious counterpart [11]. Solid lines depict accuracy in model training and dash lines indicate testing accuracy in evaluation.

To examine the effectiveness of the background subtraction model towards the communication reduction, we compare the accuracy of the communication-aware model D-MoSeg with the communication-oblivious counterpart MEDAL-net [11] Table 1 depicts the accuracy values of the trained model across different sizes of processing groups as the quantity of messages starts to converge at the threshold of $\delta = 0.005$. As we can see, the converge is reached with significance: the communication load is reduced by at least 94.71% compared to the regular threshold-free scheme, while the training accuracy and testing accuracy are reduced only by at most 2.14% and 2.68%, respectively (see the case of 2 workers in Table 1). The cut down in communicated messages restricts workers from knowing the contextual motion characteristics, which are exploited during model learning at other peers. However, this effect only results in a negligible decline in model accuracy when we evaluate global generalization. Figure 5 shows D-MoSeg relative accuracy with respect to the communication-oblivious counterpart (e.g., $\delta = 0$) versus the percentage of communicated messages. With 16 workers (PEs), the new communication-aware model D-MoSeg achieves relative training accuracy and testing accuracy of 98.84% and 98.88%, respectively, while using only 5.04% of messages communicated in the communication-oblivious counterpart.

5   Conclusion

Road traffic significantly contributes to urban air pollution, and therefore road traffic monitoring is a crucial component in air pollution prevention. This paper has introduced a communication-efficient distributed approach to road traffic monitoring based on background subtraction. Background subtraction is a specific problem where data-driven models cope with varying scenes for multi-contextual generalization. However, as training datasets scale up, communication overhead emerges as a bottleneck in distributed learning methods. This research has introduced a new framework CEDFrame to transform traditional centralized background subtraction models into communication-efficient distributed models. The framework utilizes an event-trigger method and asynchronous communication to reduce the communication overhead. We have developed the frameworks by adopting the computational capability of GPUs to accelerate computation in the model update. Using the new framework, we have developed a new communication-efficient decentralized algorithm for background subtraction D-MoSeg. The experimental investigation on a large-scale video dataset showed that our new framework could significantly reduce communication while having a negligible decrement in training and testing accuracy. For future work, examining the effect of stragglers and the staleness of model parameters during training is potential research.

References

1. Babaee, M., Dinh, D.T., Rigoll, G.: A deep convolutional neural network for video sequence background subtraction. Pattern Recogn. **76**, 635–649 (2018)
2. Bachan, J., et al.: UPC++: a high-performance communication framework for asynchronous computation. In: IEEE International Parallel and Distributed Processing Symposium (IPDPS), pp. 963–973 (2019)
3. Ben-Nun, T., Hoefler, T.: Demystifying parallel and distributed deep learning: an in-depth concurrency analysis. ACM Comput. Surv. **52**(4), 1–43 (2019)
4. Bouwmans, T.: Traditional and recent approaches in background modeling for foreground detection: An overview. Comput. Sci. Rev. **11–12**, 31–66 (2014)
5. Bouwmans, T., Javed, S., Sultana, M., Jung, S.K.: Deep neural network concepts for background subtraction: a systematic review and comparative evaluation. Neural Netw. **117**, 8–66 (2019)
6. Chen, C., Wang, W., Li, B.: Round-robin synchronization: mitigating communication bottlenecks in parameter servers. In: IEEE Conference on Computer Communications, pp. 532–540 (2019)
7. Chen, J., Monga, R., Bengio, S., Jozefowicz, R.: Revisiting distributed synchronous SGD. In: International Conference on Learning Representations Workshop Track (2016). https://arxiv.org/abs/1604.00981

8. Dean, J., et al.: Large scale distributed deep networks. In: Proceedings of the International Conference on Neural Information Processing Systems, pp. 1223–1231 (2012)
9. Ghosh, S., Gupta, V.: EventGraD: event-triggered communication in parallel stochastic gradient descent. In: 2020 IEEE/ACM Workshop on Machine Learning in High Performance Computing Environments (MLHPC), pp. 1–8 (2020)
10. Grishchenko, D., Iutzeler, F., Malick, J., Amini, M.: Distributed learning with sparse communications by identification. SIAM J. Math. Data Sci. **3**(2), 715–735 (2021)
11. Ha, S.V., Nguyen, C.T., Phan, H.N., Chung, N.M., Ha, P.H.: CDN-MEDAL: two-stage density and difference approximation framework for motion analysis. CoRR abs/2106.03776 (2021). https://arxiv.org/abs/2106.03776
12. Ho, Q., et al.: More effective distributed ml via a stale synchronous parallel parameter server. In: Proceedings of the International Conference on Neural Information Processing Systems, pp. 1223–1231 (2013)
13. Howard, A.G., et al.: MobileNets: efficient convolutional neural networks for mobile vision applications (2017)
14. Kalsotra, R., Arora, S.: A comprehensive survey of video datasets for background subtraction. IEEE Access **7**, 59143–59171 (2019)
15. Krizanc, R., Saarimaki, A.: Bulk synchronous parallel: practical experience with a model for parallel computing. In: Proceedings of the Conference on Parallel Architectures and Compilation Technique, pp. 208–217 (1996)
16. LeCun, Y., Chopra, S., Hadsell, R., Huang, F.J., et al.: A tutorial on energy-based learning. In: Predicting Structured Data. MIT Press (2006)
17. Lian, X., Zhang, C., Zhang, H., Hsieh, C.J., Zhang, W., Liu, J.: Can decentralized algorithms outperform centralized algorithms? A case study for decentralized parallel stochastic gradient descent. In: Proceedings of the International Conference on Neural Information Processing Systems, pp. 5336–5346 (2017)
18. Lian, X., Zhang, W., Zhang, C., Liu, J.: Asynchronous decentralized parallel stochastic gradient descent. In: Proceedings of the International Conference on Machine Learning, vol. 80, pp. 3043–3052 (2018)
19. Lin, Y., Han, S., Mao, H., Wang, Y., Dally, W.J.: Deep gradient compression: reducing the communication bandwidth for distributed training. In: The International Conference on Learning Representations (2018)
20. Shi, S., Wang, Q., Chu, X.: Performance modeling and evaluation of distributed deep learning frameworks on GPUs. In: 2018 IEEE 4th International Conference on Big Data Intelligence and Computing, pp. 949–957 (2018)
21. Stauffer, C., Grimson, W.: Adaptive background mixture models for real-time tracking. In: Proceedings of Conference on Computer Vision and Pattern Recognition, vol. 2, pp. 246–252 (1999)
22. Tang, Z., Shi, S., Chu, X., Wang, W., Li, B.: Communication-efficient distributed deep learning: a comprehensive survey. CoRR abs/2003.06307 (2020). https://arxiv.org/abs/2003.06307
23. Wang, Y., Jodoin, P.M., Porikli, F., Konrad, J., Benezeth, Y., Ishwar, P.: CDNet 2014: an expanded change detection benchmark dataset. In: IEEE Conference on Computer Vision and Pattern Recognition Workshops, pp. 393–400 (2014)
24. Zinkevich, M.A., Weimer, M., Smola, A., Li, L.: Parallelized stochastic gradient descent. In: Proceedings of the International Conference on Neural Information Processing Systems, pp. 2595–2603 (2010)

Critical Factors of Customers Loyalty in E-Commerce

Bartłomiej Pierański[1]($\boxtimes$) (iD), Arkadiusz Kawa[2] (iD), and Wojciech Zdrenka[1] (iD)

[1] Poznan University of Economics and Business, Poznan, Poland
bartlomiej.pieranski@ue.poznan.pl
[2] Poznan School of Logistics, Poznan, Poland
arkadiusz.kawa@wsl.com.pl

Abstract. The impact of customer loyalty on business performance seems indisputable. Having a loyal customer base comes with many advantages that directly contribute to increased profits. However, in the literature only a handful of studies dealt directly and comprehensively with customer loyalty to online retailers. For example, little consideration has been given to the complexity of the online retailer's operations, including the delivery of customer orders, a well-matched product range, complaint resolution, relationship building, etc. This study aimed at filling this gap. Therefore the aim of the article is to identify the factors that constitute customer loyalty of online retailers. Based on systematic literature review 85 items that may relate to loyalty were proposed. To extract factors out of proposed items exploratory factor analysis (EFA) was deployed. To acquire the required data the survey was carried out among Polish customers (N = 200) making purchase from an on line sellers. In order to assure the reliability of the research, the sample structure reflected the structure of the studied population. Based on the research 6 factors constituting customer loyalty have been extracted, that is: delivery conditions, convenience of shopping, social media presence, impressions of receiving the shipment, credibility and promotion.

Keywords: E-commerce · Customer loyalty · Exploratory factor analysis

1 Introduction

The advancement of e-commerce brings with it a number of benefits for individual customers. They have access to information about sellers and thus to their products at any time. They can easily find offers, compare them, read other users' opinions and buy cheaper. However, they have to wait for the product to be delivered. Apart from that, online shopping is connected with the risk of the seller being dishonest or making a mistake. This context makes building customer loyalty very difficult and long-lasting for online sellers. However, this does not mean that these vendors should stop their efforts to create a loyal customer base. The aim of the article is to identify the factors that constitute customer loyalty of online retailers. Consequently, the article is organized as follows. The second section contains a literature review on buyer loyalty and its role in buyer activity. The third section discusses the conducted research and its results. In

© The Author(s), under exclusive license to Springer Nature Singapore Pte Ltd. 2022
E. Szczerbicki et al. (Eds.): ACIIDS 2022, CCIS 1716, pp. 503–516, 2022.
https://doi.org/10.1007/978-981-19-8234-7_39

the fourth chapter describes the factors created on the basis of research that constitute buyer loyalty in e-commerce. The article ends with a summary chapter.

2 Literature Background

Loyalty is described as a sense of support or obligation to someone or something and loyalty to commitments or duties [1]. In management studies, customer loyalty is understood as a customer's willingness to purchase a particular brand's product or use a service again. Loyalty is an expression of the customer's trust in the company and manifests itself in the customer's emotional attachment to the company entity and the maintenance of a special type of bond [2].

Customer loyalty can be defined as the manifestation of psychological (attitude) and process (behavior) loyalty in a relationship between an agent and another entity, in the presence of alternative agents [2–4]. Loyalty leads to continued or repeated purchase of products or services from the same vendor, even when other vendors' offerings are more competitive [5].

Preserving the loyalty of current customers is considered as a strategy to maintain competitive advantage [6]. To retain a loyal customer costs less than to acquire a new one [7]. In addition, several positive benefits can result from retaining loyal customers: reduced search for alternatives [8], favorable reputation [9], greater stability regardless of competitors' actions [10], and greater tolerance for minor mistakes [11]. Avoiding customer churn should therefore motivate service providers to make greater efforts to retain existing customers.

Furthermore, the impact of customer loyalty on business performance seems indisputable. Having a loyal customer base comes with many advantages that directly contribute to increased profits. There are two main reasons why customer loyalty has a positive impact on company performance: increased sales and lower operating costs.

The positive effects of loyalty on sales include the fact that loyal customers spend more on chosen products and purchase more of them [12]. In addition, loyal customers are less sensitive to price changes, which makes it easier for them to accept price increases than for new customers. Loyal customers are more likely to use a wider range of products offered by the company to which they are loyal, which in the long term can affect not only a steady but also systematically growing sales revenue [13].

Customer loyalty also contributes to lowering the operating costs of the company. Having a loyal customer base leads to, among other things, lower costs in customer service, new customer acquisition, promotion and marketing, and handling returns and complaints [14].

To conclude, customer loyalty seems to be an critical element in the performance of any company. For this reason, many authors have tried to indicate what factors determine customer loyalty. It was researched that customer loyalty can be influenced by factors such as: image (of the product, brand, company), product quality [15], product customization [16], product innovation [17], advertising [18], flexibility of technical infrastructure and intangible resources [19], and even individual characteristics of customers [20].

However, most of the mentioned studies have not dealt directly and comprehensively with customer loyalty to online retailers. For example, little consideration has been given to the complexity of the online retailer's operations, including the delivery of customer orders, a well-matched product range, complaint resolution, relationship building, etc. In order to fill this gap, the authors proposed 85 variables that address buyer loyalty in a multifaceted way (see appendix 1). These variables are to be used to determine the factors that shape loyalty.

3 Method

3.1 Research Instrument and Sampling

The aim of this study was to identify the factors determining customers' loyalty towards on-line sellers. Based on systematic literature review 85 items that may related to loyalty were proposed. To extract factors out of proposed items exploratory factor analysis was deployed. Exploratory factor analysis allows the finding of an optimal number of latent variables that explain the interrelationships between observable variables [21]. The detection of an optimal group of main factors allows to explain the correlations between observable variables. The number of factors and factor loadings are determined during the analysis, and the interpretation of the obtained structure occurs only after the common factors are extracted. As a result of the exploratory factor analysis, it is possible to reduce the variables and detect the structure and general regularities between the variables. The purpose of the analysis is to reduce the number of variables studied to one that best explains the relationships and correlations that exist between the variables [22].

In order to achieve the aim of the study, data necessary for conducting the research were obtained by means of a questionnaire distributed via internet (CAWI - computer-assisted web interview). The questionnaire included introductory question, 85 research items (the 85 affirmative sentences presented in Appendix 1), as well as demographic questions. The aim of the introductory questions was to identify how many product (on average) each participant purchase on-line a month. Then the participants were asked to express their opinions on their attitude towards on-line sellers as well as their shopping behavior. Participants responded to each of the research item using a five-point Likert scale, where '1' meant strong disagreement with the statement, '5' full agreement. The choice of a five-point scale was based on the other study result that in Polish conditions this scale provides a high degree of internal consistency, as well as that is more suitable to cultural characteristics of Polish society.

The survey was carried out by market research agency among Polish customers making purchase from an on line sellers. In order to assure the reliability of the research, the sample structure reflected the structure of the studied population. The following items were used as variables: age, gender and education level. However, it must highlighted that these variables have not differentiate research results.

Before the main phase of data collection a pilot survey was conducted in order to assess understanding of the questions by respondents as well as participants fatigue related to the questionnaire length, etc. The pilot survey has not revealed any issues with completing the questionnaire by respondents, This result provide a basis to begin the main part of the research.

The sample size was set at the level of 200 respondents (N = 200). Each study had to meet the sample structure requirements. The data was collected by external market research agency. After obtaining 200 correctly completed questionnaires the data analysis could be provided.

3.2 Data Analysis

Based on the responses received in the survey, an exploratory factor analysis was conducted using the principal components method and varimax rotation.

First, the results were subjected to Bartlett's sphericity test and the KMO (Kaiser-Mayer-Olkin) measure was calculated [24]. Both the obtained measurements confirmed the basis for performing factor analysis: KMO = .839; Bartlett's sphericity test (X^2 = 12699.216, df = 3570, p = .000).

Six factors were then distinguished and factor rotation was performed. The purpose of factor rotation is to improve the explanation of a given factor solution [23]. A varimax rotation was used in the analysis. The result of the obtained rotation is presented in Table 1. To increase the readability of the matrix, values less than 0.6 were hidden in the matrix.

The following labels of the extracted factors have been proposed: delivery conditions, convenience of shopping, social media presence, impressions of receiving the shipment, credibility and promotion. All factors, together with items assigned to them are presented in Table 1.

Table 1. Results of EFA

Factor number/ Explained variance (%)	Factor label	Items	Rotated factor loading	Cronbach Alpha
F1/22.739	Delivery conditions	I buy from sellers who offer the lowest cost of product delivery	.632	.816
		I buy from sellers who offer courier delivery	.666	
		I buy from sellers who offer the option to choose delivery time	.725	
		I buy from sellers who inform about the status of my order	.734	

(*continued*)

Table 1. (*continued*)

Factor number/ Explained variance (%)	Factor label	Items	Rotated factor loading	Cronbach Alpha
		I buy from sellers who offer tracking	.771	
		I buy from sellers who collaborate with couriers that provide delivery time details	.665	
		I buy from sellers who collaborate with couriers who are flexible (e.g. on delivery time and place)	.629	
F2/10.687	Convenience of shopping	I buy from retailers that offer the ability to make purchases with mobile apps	.619	.852
		I buy from sellers who offer "off-the-shelf" products	.643	
		I buy from sellers who offer products available on request	.769	
		I buy from sellers who offer product delivery within 2 h	.669	
		I buy from sellers who offer same working day delivery	.713	
F3/5.687	Social media presence	I buy from sellers who run blogs on their websites	.600	.906

(*continued*)

Table 1. (*continued*)

Factor number/ Explained variance (%)	Factor label	Items	Rotated factor loading	Cronbach Alpha
		I buy products that are recommended by famous bloggers	.764	
		I buy from sellers that are recommended by famous bloggers	.857	
		I buy from sellers who have profiles on social media	.836	
F4/4.461	Impressions of receiving the shipment	I buy from sellers whose shipments are aesthetically wrapped	.605	.775
		I buy from sellers whose shipments are easy to open	.628	
		I buy from sellers who customize the package size to fit the product size	.610	
F5/3,579	Credibility	I buy from sellers who are positively reviewed by their customers	.605	.669
		I buy from sellers who have been in business for a long time	.689	
F6/2.966	Promotion	I buy from sellers I know from online advertising	.632	.875
		I buy products I know from conventional advertising (e.g. TV, radio)	.767	

(*continued*)

Table 1. (*continued*)

Factor number/ Explained variance (%)	Factor label	Items	Rotated factor loading	Cronbach Alpha
		I buy products I am familiar with from online advertising	.777	
		I buy from sellers whose advertising is tailored to my needs	.632	

Source: own compilation

In order to confirm the reliability of the scale of the obtained factors, and thus the internal consistency of the developed instrument, a Cronbach's alpha reliability analysis was carried out. For most of the factors, the obtained index is greater than 0.7 (see Table 1), which means that the obtained results are at a good level [25]. Only in the case of one factor was the value less than 0.7. However, some authors believe that any value higher than 0.6 is acceptable [24]. The six factors combined explain almost 53% of common variance.

4   Factors Shaping Customers' Loyalty in E-commerce

Delivery Conditions
In this factor, the highest factor loadings value was received by items related to shipment traceability. It is a consequence of the fact that after placing an order the customer has to wait for the goods to be delivered to the indicated place, it is important to keep the customer informed about the status of the order. From the customer's point of view, it is important to be kept informed about the delivery status of the order [26]. By staying informed about the delivery status, customers have the knowledge if the expected delivery date is compromised. Thus, they can better prepare to receive the shipment.

It is not only the mere fact of informing the customer about what stage their order is at, but also the timing of this communication itself that is important. Immediate order confirmation increases customer satisfaction (and as a result loyalty) compared to waiting a few hours or a few days for confirmation via email. This is especially important because, as research shows, customers currently check the status of their orders multiple times throughout the day [27].

Courier shipments are one of the most popular forms of delivery in e-commerce. Delivering your order directly to your home or work is a very convenient solution from the customers' perspective. The main problems of courier shipments include problems related to customers not being at the indicated address when the courier attempts to deliver the package. Therefore, the research indicates that flexibility, mainly related to the time of delivery, is one of the key factors constituting customer loyalty.

Convenience of Shopping

There were two main elements in this factor: availability of assortment (also available on request) and speed of delivery. The first element seems obvious and is related to the essence of commerce, i.e. maintaining constant availability of assortment and the possibility to order products that are not available for immediate purchase. The convenience of purchase is also influenced by the ability to order at any time and any place with the use of an application installed on a smartphone. In a highly competitive market, it is difficult to imagine building buyer loyalty without providing the basic service of assortment availability.

The second element, delivery speed, seems to be very interesting. Due to the lack of immediate access to products ordered online, the criterion of order delivery time is of great importance in building customer loyalty. Impatient customers prompt online retailers to offer services such as afternoon or evening delivery, Saturday and Sunday delivery in addition to standard courier services. One should note that this type of delivery is still relatively limited. However, given growing customer expectations, significantly shortening the delivery time of ordered products seems to be a direction that will be important for building customer loyalty.

Social Media Presence

This factor, next to another called 'promotion', is related to informing buyers about the company's offer and about the enterprise itself. In this case, the building of loyalty is largely influenced by activity on various social media platforms. The great importance of influencers is related to the great popularity they enjoy, especially among young buyers. Their recommendation of certain products and an online seller can lead to a so-called image transfer: the blogger's positive image is transferred to the image of the company and its products.

Impressions of Receiving the Shipment

In e-commerce the moment of purchase and delivery are separated in time. After ordering a product, customers do not receive it immediately, so they often wait impatiently for the delivery of the order. The feeling experienced when receiving the delivery and unboxing it is comparable to that of receiving a gift [28]. This involves an experience that involves customer's emotions. The experience is about the purchase process itself, but also about what came before and after the transaction. Studies have shown that the impression of the delivery is significantly influenced by the packaging. It also creates the first impression for the customer. What kind of materials the packaging is made of, how the product is protected for the time of shipment and whether it is easy to unpack the package can also have an impact on the customer's satisfaction with the purchase. Packaging is important as it is the first physical contact with the product. Therefore, it should be aesthetically pleasing to encourage customers to make further purchases. Additionally, the packaging must be easy and intuitive to open. Products packed in a way that is difficult to open may cause anger and frustration in customers due to the inability to open the package. In the literature, this phenomenon has even received its own term - wrap rage [29]. Studies have not indicated a significant role of couriers in influencing the impression of receiving products. This may be due to the increasing popularity of self-service forms of product pickup such as parcel lockers.

Credibility

A factor that relates to customer loyalty is the credibility of the online retailer. Research has shown that two elements are important in this case. One of them can be defined more quantitatively, i.e. number of years in business. It can be assumed that the credibility of the seller increases with the number of years of operation in the market. It should be noted that both loyalty building and credibility building are long-term processes. Therefore, only vendors with a relevant 'history' have a chance of achieving success in this area.

The second element is more qualitative. In building loyalty, it is not only the number of years of operation on the market that is important, but also the high assessment of this period by the clients of a specific online retailer. It is a manifestation of the so-called social proof of equity. It is expressed in the belief that since other buyers positively evaluate a given seller (and are even loyal to him), he is an entity with which it is worth to be associated with a longer term.

Promotion

This is another factor indicating that gaining buyers' loyalty requires constant communication with them. This time it is a more traditional and one-way communication (as opposed to (blogs) that is advertising. Advertising both in traditional media and online. In addition, advertising should include both the company and the products it offers. It is not a new or revealing concept. It seems that this factor can be described as necessary but not sufficient to gain loyal customers. Advertising the company and the products will not have much impact on buyer loyalty. On the other hand, lack of advertising may cause a dramatic decrease in loyalty.

5   Conclusions

The results of the conducted research indicate that in order to build buyer loyalty Internet sellers must take into account a wide spectrum of factors shaping loyalty. What is particularly important is that some of these factors are not under the direct control of the sellers. This is particularly true of the 'delivery conditions' and 'social media presence' factors. In both cases, online retailers have to rely on third parties. From a loyalty building point of view, relying on couriers to deliver packages is particularly dangerous. Their (inappropriate) behavior can damage online retailers' efforts to build buyer loyalty. It is also important to point out that loyalty is linked to positive emotions towards a company. Hence, building these emotions within the 'impressions from receiving the parcel' factor seems particularly important.

The research has a few limitations. First, it does not prioritize excreted factors in order of the criterion of impact on buyers' loyalty. Application of regression analysis would help to overcome this limitation. Secondly the research was conducted in Poland. It would be valuable to repeat them in at least other European countries, possibly on different continents. And thirdly, the research could be enriched to include elements undertaken by e-tailers that are related to environmental protection, sustainable logistics, etc.

Appendix 1

Items of EFA.

	Items
1	I buy from retailers offering one type of product (e.g. computers only)
2	I buy from retailers offering many different types of products (e.g. (e.g. computers, washing machines, refrigerators)
3	I buy from sellers offering well-known brand products
4	I buy from sellers offering private label products
5	I buy from sellers offering the possibility to design the product myself
6	I buy from sellers whose brand (name) is recognizable
7	I buy from sellers who have a positive reputation among customers
8	I buy products that have positive customer ratings
9	I buy from sellers who have been in business for a long time
10	I buy from sellers who also have stationary stores
11	I buy from sellers who offer the lowest price for a product
12	I buy from sellers who offer a discount
13	I buy from sellers who offer the lowest delivery cost
14	I buy from sellers who offer free delivery
15	I buy from sellers who offer payment on delivery
16	I buy from sellers who offer to pay by bank transfer
17	I am buying from sellers who offer modern payment methods (e.g. PayU, Przelewy24, Blik, PayPal)
18	I purchase from sellers who offer installment sales
19	I purchase from sellers, who offer deferred payment (e.g. within 30 days after the receipt of goods)
20	I buy from sellers I know from traditional advertising (e.g. TV, radio)
21	I buy from sellers I know from online advertising
22	I buy products that I know from traditional advertising (e.g. TV, radio)
23	I buy products that I know from online advertising
24	I buy from sellers whose advertising "follows" me on other websites
25	I buy from sellers whose advertising is tailored to my needs
26	I buy from sellers who send newsletters
27	I buy from retailers whose websites have tips on how to use their products

(continued)

(continued)

	Items
28	I buy from retailers who offer loyalty programs
29	I buy from retailers who run blogs on their websites
30	I buy products that are recommended by famous bloggers
31	I buy from sellers who are recommended by famous bloggers
32	I buy from sellers who have profiles in social networks
33	I buy products that are recommended by other people in social networks
34	I buy from sellers who allow me to give feedback on my purchases
35	I buy from retailers who are easy to contact (e.g. phone, email, form, chat)
36	I shop with sellers who have easy to understand terms and conditions of sale
37	I buy from sellers who make registering easy
38	I buy from sellers where I can buy without registering
39	I buy from sellers who allow me to compare products on offer
40	I buy from retailers whose website is easy to navigate
41	I buy from sellers who clearly display the products they offer
42	I buy from retailers whose websites adapt to the screen size of my device
43	I buy from retailers whose websites have an aesthetically pleasing design
44	I buy from retailers who have websites that remember my information
45	I buy from retailers who offer the option to make a purchase using a mobile app
46	I buy from retailers that allow me to see products in a store
47	I shop at retailers who offer "off-the-shelf" products
48	I buy from retailers who offer products that are available on request
49	I buy from retailers who offer 2 h delivery
50	I buy from retailers who offer same working day delivery
51	I buy from sellers who offer next working day delivery
52	I buy from sellers who offer delivery of products within 3 days or more
53	I buy from sellers who offer courier delivery
54	I buy from sellers offering mail order delivery
55	I buy from sellers offering delivery to self-service terminals (e.g. to a parcel locker)
56	I buy from sellers offering delivery to pick-up points (e.g. kiosks, petrol stations)
57	I buy from retailers who offer pickup in their stores
58	I buy from retailers who offer selectable delivery times
59	I buy from retailers who offer a delivery option on public holidays
60	I buy from sellers who provide information on the status of my order
61	I buy from sellers who offer tracking
62	I buy from sellers that cooperate with couriers who give delivery time information

(continued)

(*continued*)

	Items
63	I buy from sellers who cooperate with couriers who are on time
64	I buy from sellers who cooperate with couriers who care about their appearance
65	I buy from sellers cooperating with couriers who behave appropriately
66	I buy from retailers with couriers who are flexible (e.g. regarding delivery times and locations)
67	I buy from sellers whose shipments are nicely packaged
68	I buy from sellers who take care of the security of their shipments
69	I buy from sellers whose packages are easy to open
70	I buy from sellers who use environmentally friendly materials for packaging
71	I buy from retailers who match the size of the packaging to the size of the product
72	I buy from retailers who offer gift packaging
73	I buy from retailers whose packaging is easy to remove my personal information
74	I buy from retailers who offer free product returns
75	I buy from retailers who have an easy procedure for returning products
76	I buy from sellers who offer returnable packaging
77	I buy from sellers who offer to return used products
78	I buy from sellers who offer a possibility to return products for more than 14 days
79	I am satisfied with my purchase
80	I will again purchase from the same sellers in the near future
81	I have a feeling that sellers understand my needs
82	I will recommend my relatives or friends to make purchases from these sellers
83	I will continue to buy from the same sellers, even if the products offered by other sellers are more competitive
84	I will continue to buy from the same sellers, even if the product delivery offered by other sellers is more competitive
85	I will continue to buy from the same sellers, even if the payment methods for products offered by other sellers are more convenient

References

1. Cambridge University Press. Cambridge Dictionary. Access: 2021 (2021). https://dictionary.cambridge.org/
2. Olivier, R.I.: Whence consumer loyalty. J. Mark. **63**, 33–44 (1999)
3. Dick, A.I., Basu, K.: Customer royalty: toward an integrated conceptual framework. J. Acad. Mark. Sci. **22**(2) 99–113 (1994)
4. Melnyk, V., Osselaer, S.I., Bijmolt, T.: Are women more loyal customers than men? gender differences in loyalty to firms and individual service providers. J. Mark. **3**(4), 82–96 (2009)

5. Chiou, J.S., Pan, L.Y.: Antecedents of internet retailing loyalty: differences between heavy versus light shoppers. J. Bus. Psychol. **24**, 327–339 (2009)
6. Grönroos, C.: Marketing as promise management: regaining customer management. J. Bus. Ind. Mark **24**(5/6), 351–359 (2009)
7. Reichheld, F.: Loyalty Rules!: How Today's Leaders Build Lasting Relationships. Harvard Business Press, Boston, MA (2001)
8. Macintosh, G.: Perceived risk and outcome differences in multi-level service relationships. J. Serv. Mark. **16**(2), 143–157 (2002)
9. Reinartz, W.I., Kumar, V.: The mismanagement of customer loyalty. Harv. Bus. Rev. **80**(7), 4–12 (2002)
10. Bove, L.I., Johnson, L.: Does true personal or service loyalty last? a longitudinal study. J. Serv. Mark. **23**(3), strony 187–194 (2009)
11. Chen, S.C.: Customer value and customer loyalty: Is competition a missing link? J. Retail. Consum. Serv. **22**, 107–116 (2015)
12. Skowron, S.: Wpływ satysfakcji i lojalności klienta na wyniki finansowe przedsiębiorstw. W G. Rosa i A. Smalec, Marketing przyszłości – Trendy. Strategie. Instrumenty, pp. 377–390. Szczecin: Wydawnictwo Naukowe Uniwersytetu Szczecińskiego (2010)
13. Edvardsson, B., Michael, D., Gustafsson, A., Strandvik, T.: The effects of satisfaction and loyalty on profits and growth: Products versus services. Total Qual. Manag. **11**(7), 917–927 (2010)
14. Fredericks, J., Hurd, R., Ronald, R., Salter, J.: Connecting customer loyalty to financial results. Mark. Manag. **10**(1), 26–32 (2001)
15. Hallencreutz, J.I., Parmler, J.: Important drivers for customer satisfaction – from product focus to image and service quality. Total Qual. Manag. Bus. Excell. **32**(5–6), 501–510 (2021)
16. Du, X., Jiao, J., Tseng, M.: Understanding customer satisfaction in product customization. Int. J. Adv. Manufact. Technol. **31**, 396–406 (2006)
17. Stock, M., Zacharias, N.: Two sides of the same coin: how do different dimensions of product program innovativeness affect customer loyalty?: product program innovativeness and customer loyalty. J. Prod. Innov. Manag. **30**(3), 516–532 (2013)
18. Chih-Cheng, L., Ing-Long, W., Wei-Hung, H.: Developing customer product loyalty through mobile advertising: affective and cognitive perspectives. Int. J. Inf. Manag. **47**, 101-111 (2019)
19. Yu, J., Suburamanian, N., Ning, K., Edwards, D.: Product delivery service provider selection and customer satisfaction in the era of internet of things: a Chinese e-retailers' perspective. Int. J. Prod. Econ. **159**, 104–116 (2015)
20. Goncalves, H., Samaio, P., Ribeiro, S.: The customer satisfaction-customer loyalty relationship: Reassessing customer and relational characteristics moderating effects. Manag. Decis. **50**(9), 1509–1526 (2012)
21. Sagan, A.: Badania marketingowe. Podstawowe kierunki. Akademia Ekonomiczna w Krakowie, Kraków (2004)
22. Sztenberg-Lewandowska, M.: Analiza czynnikowa w badaniach marketingowych. Wydawnictwo Uniwersytetu Ekonomicznego we Wrocławiu: Wrocław (2008)
23. Tabachnick, B., Fidell, L.: Using Multivariate Statistics. Pearson Education Inc, Boston (2007)
24. Światowiec-Szczepańska, J.: Ryzyko partnerstwa strategicznego przedsiębiorstwa: ujęcie modelowe. Poznań: Wydawnictwo Uniwersytetu Ekonomicznego w Poznaniu (2012)
25. Hair, J., Black, W., Babin, B., Anderson, R., Tatham, R.: Multivariate Data Analysis (6th ed.). New Jersey: Pearson Educational Inc (2006)

26. Lu, Y., Guo, C., Lu, Y., Gupta, S.: The role of online communication in avoiding perceived restrictiveness of shopping websites: a social learning theory perspective. Nankai Bus. Rev. Int. **9**(2), 143–161 (2018)
27. Kalia, P., Kaur, N., Singh, T.: Consumer satisfaction in e-shopping: an overview. Indian J. Econ. Dev. **13**(2a), 569–576 (2017)
28. Kim, C., Self, J.A., Bae, J.: Exploring the first momentary unboxing experience with aesthetic interaction. Des. J. **21**(3), 417–438 (2018)
29. Anthony, K.H.: The problem with retail packaging, in a clam-shell. Toronto Star (Canada) 4 March 2017

An Efficient Multi-view Facial Expression Classifier Implementing on Edge Device

Muhamad Dwisnanto Putro[(✉)], Duy-Linh Nguyen, Adri Priadana,
and Kang-Hyun Jo

Department of Electrical, Electronic, and Computer Engineering, University of Ulsan,
Ulsan, Korea
{dputro,ndlinh301,priadana3202}@mail.ulsan.ac.kr, acejo@ulsan.ac.kr

Abstract. The robotic technology demands human-robot interaction to implement a real-time facial emotion detector. This system has a role in recognizing the expressions of the user. Therefore, this application is recommended to work quickly to support the robot's capabilities. It helps the robot to analyze the customer's face effectively. However, the previous methods weakly recognize non-frontal faces. It is caused by the facial pose variations only to show partial facial features. This paper proposes a multi-view real-time facial emotion detector based on a lightweight convolutional neural network. It offers a four-stage backbone as an efficient feature extractor that discriminates specific facial components. The convolution with Cross Stage Partial (CSP) approach was employed to reduce computations from convolution operations. The attention module is inserted into the CSP block. These modules also support the detector to work speedily on edge devices. The classification system learns the information about facial features from the KDEF dataset. As a result, facial emotion recognition achieves comparative performance to other methods with an accuracy of 97.10% on the KDEF, 73.95 on the FER-2013, and 84.91% on the RAFDB dataset. The integrated system using a face detector shows that the system obtains a data processing speed of 30 frames per second on the Jetson Nano.

1 Introduction

A robot is required to work automatically and has the capability of perception and action. Perception is the source of information, while the output is an action produced by the robot. Both components cooperate to achieve the goal. Besides, interaction with humans has a social purpose when the robot is implemented in a public area. Human-robot interaction (HRI) has a role in connecting and synchronizing information between robots and users. It implies a closer interaction and demands communication between the both. In addition, they share the workspace in terms of task achievement [19]. Therefore, the misunderstanding of perception will impact the mistake of robot action and incompatibility with the aim. Meanwhile, vision is an essential perceptual attribute to understanding the environment. Object information is the reference of decisions for the robot to do

© The Author(s), under exclusive license to Springer Nature Singapore Pte Ltd. 2022
E. Szczerbicki et al. (Eds.): ACIIDS 2022, CCIS 1716, pp. 517–529, 2022.
https://doi.org/10.1007/978-981-19-8234-7_40

something. Shape, texture, space, color, and value are the fundamental elements of visual information. It is used as simple knowledge and related to identifying an object.

Robotic vision has been widely implemented to support HRI. A service robot utilizes this technology to recognize user emotions. It is non-verbal communication that is useful for the robot to understand and evaluate the actions. Humans usually show certain expressions on purpose, but they may accidentally occur caused by feelings or emotions. There are six basic human expressions: fear, anger, disgust, surprise, sadness, and happiness [4]. Each emotion presents different feature textures and shapes. It has resulted from one or more movements of muscles in the face. Hence, facial features are the critical element in identifying human emotions. This attention focuses on the facial area [13]. Although gender affects the tendency to represent certain emotions, it has the same facial feature characteristic. The texture identification of facial features is closely related to the success of recognizing human emotions. Besides, this is also influenced by the relationship between facial components in each expression.

Computer vision employs feature extraction to discriminate specific features from the background. Then, it uses a classifier to predict the probability of each category. Several works have used conventional feature extraction [16–18], but this is not robust for non-frontal faces. This problem does not fully present the essential components of the face. Additionally, rotation-invariant decreases the classifier's performance and causes a classification system to produce high false positives. Convolutional Neural Network (CNN) is an excellent facial feature extraction [24]. It implements a weighted kernel to distinguish the important features of an object. Then, it employs back-propagation to update those weights. This approach delivers high performance for classification tasks. Therefore, several studies have applied it for facial expression recognition work [5,15,22]. Recently, various backbone architectures have been presented to distinguish distinctive object features clearly. However, the CNN model requires high GPU usage to work in real-time, while this accelerator is not cheap. On the other hand, computer vision methods are encouraged to be implemented in an edge device such as a Jetson Nano [12]. This device is compatible with sensors and actuators commonly used in robots.

Based on the previously mentioned problems, a real-time facial emotion detector is proposed to recognize multiple poses on basic human facial emotions. The main contributions of this work are as follows:

1. A new facial expression detector is offered to efficiently localize and identify the human facial emotion in different face profiles.
2. A CNN-based light architecture applies Cross Stage Partial (CSP) with an excitation module to reduce the computational operations and parameters.
3. The classification system achieves comparative performance to other methods and performs at a real-time processing speed of 30 FPS on a Jetson Nano.

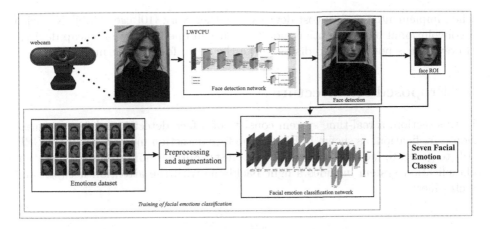

Fig. 1. The overview system of real-time facial emotions detector. It combines face detection and facial expression classification. LWFCPU is used as a face detector to quickly localize medium and large sized faces.

The rest of this paper is organized as follows: Sect. 2 discusses the general architecture and the proposed model. Section 3 explains implementation setup of the proposed model in the simulation. Section 4 presents the experimental results. Finally, conclusions and future work are discuss in Sect. 5.

2 Related Works

Several works have applied the CNN approach to classifying facial expressions. Webb et al. [22] have proposed a pre-trained of Deep Convolutional Neural Network (CNN) as a Stacked Convolutional Autoencoder (SCAE) to recognize human emotions that will be implemented in social robots. Transfer learning learns facial features in a greedy layer-wise unsupervised fashion more efficiently. On the other hand, the Multi-model network has obtained higher accuracy for classifying facial expressions in various illuminations and poses [15]. This residual CNN is used to extract specific facial features effectively. Combining 1×1 and 3×3 convolution allows the network to save the computation. In addition, a Squeeze-and-Excitation (SE) Module [7] is applied to the residual block to enhance interest features. Furthermore, Fareed et al. [5] implemented a face localization method at the beginning of the network using Dual Shot Face Detection (DSFD) to overcome the pose invariance. It uses a combination of Linear Discriminant Analysis (LDA) and Adaptive Boosting to re-extract the detected features. Although it obtains high performance, this backbone produces a lot of parameters and expensive computation. It requires a large amount of GPU memory when working in real-time. Multi-view facial expression classifier has been proposed by [1]. It uses a deep convolutional neural network with a transfer learning approach to discriminate the essential features. It applies DenseNet-161 architecture to extract the facial information, so this model tends to run slow when implemented on low-cost devices. Another work [10] uses MobileNet with a convolutional block attention module that can operate fast on cheap devices. However, it is not robust to discriminate the facial features for multi-profile.

3   Proposed Architecture

In this section, a real-time system consists of a face detector and facial expression classification, as shown in Fig. 1. The face detection method uses LWFCPU [14] to generate face ROI (Region of Interest). Furthermore, the facial emotion classification system includes a light backbone with the attention network and a classifier.

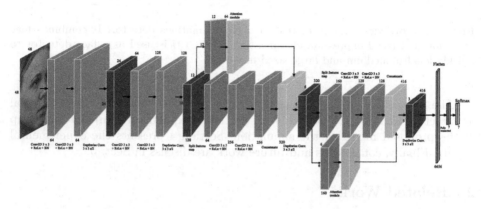

Fig. 2. The proposed architecture of real-time facial expression classification. It uses Cross Stage Partial (CSP) in two stages to reduce the number of operations on the convolutional layer.

3.1   Four-Stage Light Backbone

A CNN-based classification system relies upon the extractor features as an essential module to produce specific features. Each facial expression shows different facial organ information. It means that facial features are critical elements for recognizing each emotion. A four-stage light backbone was introduced using a sparse convolution operation. Figure 2 shows that this architecture consists of four stages using two 3 × 3 convolution layers. This block employs an effective filter to find the interest element for identifying the expression.

Furthermore, the proposed architecture applies a Cross Stage Partial (CSP) technique [21] that splits a feature map into two parts with the same number of channels. Then one chunk is transferred and aggregated to the end of the stage. It reduces the computation power of convolution operation without significantly degrading the extractor performance. Reducing the number of channels produces fewer computation costs than the normal process. It also saves the number of parameters. Additionally, the transfer layer avoids losing information caused by the splitting process, which cannot explore these interest elements at the next stage. Therefore, a CSP is only implemented in the third and fourth stages, containing medium and high-level features.

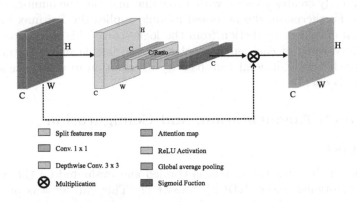

Fig. 3. A depthwise excitation module using weighted vector.

A superficial architecture is weak in discriminating facial features at a high-level frequency. Thus, the attention module enhances specific facial features related to each expression [20]. The proposed architecture develops a depthwise excitation module inserted at each skip connection of the CSP method. It highlights the intensity of the relationship between the facial components in a chunk map. A depthwise convolution is employed as a simple filter that keeps the number of channels of the filter equal to the input, as shown in Fig. 3. Then, Global Average Pooling (GAP) summarizes the intensity of the features as expressed as

$$s_i = W_{d2} \odot GAP(W_{d1} \odot x_i), \tag{1}$$

where $\odot$ is a linear operation of a depthwise convolution applied after and before pooling. It robustly extracted a representation of the essential features s_i. Furthermore, the output of the attention network can be illustrated as

$$At_i = x_i \cdot \sigma(W_{v2}ReLU(W_{v1}s_i)), \tag{2}$$

where σ is the sigmoid function on the sequential operations of the 1×1 convolutional and $ReLU$ activation. Finally, the input features are scaled with a weighted feature representation to update specific features. A depthwise excitation module combines a linear filter and the sequential weighted extraction. It enhances the quality that discriminates useful features and reduces the intensity of trivial features without significantly increasing computation.

3.2   Classifier Module

The backbone module generates a 3×3 feature map with 416 channels. The flatten method is applied to reshape tensors into raw vectors. This technique prevents information loss in the classification process. Instead of using the multi fully connected layers, it only uses a dense layer to compress the network parameters. It directly creates a vector with a size that matches the number of emotion categories. Furthermore, the proposed module applies the Softmax function to generate an output of prediction from the logit score. This activation produces a probability value of each emotion class in the last layer of the neural network. It predicts a multinomial probability distribution in which the sum of all predictions is one.

4   Dataset, Augmentation, and Configuration

4.1   Dataset

The proposed classification system is trained and evaluated on the Karolinska Directed Emotional Faces (KDEF) dataset [2]. This dataset was produced by Karolinska Institutet that consists of 4900 images of human facial expressions. It contains 70 individuals showing seven different emotional faces (neutral, happy, angry, fear, disgusted, sad, and surprised). The subjects are between 20 and 30 years of age. They did not wear earrings, eyeglasses, and makeup in the photo session and did not have beards and mustaches. It also provides five different angles (full left profile, half left profile, straight, half right profile, full right profile) with a 562×762 pixels resolution. On the other hand, the proposed model also evaluates on FER-2013 dataset [6] to comprehensively investigate its performance. This dataset provides 35,887 pictures with 48×48 pixels. The grayscale image covers seven emotions: anger, neutral, sad, fear, happy, surprise, and disgust. In addition, this database is a challenging dataset that inserts a few invalid labels. Additionally, it also utilizes the RAFDB [9] dataset to examine the proposed model. This dataset provides 30,000 facial images annotated. Our model uses basic emotion that contains 12,271 images for training and 3,068 images for testing.

4.2   Preprocessing and Augmentation

A face detector [14] is applied to the image dataset to generate the ROI of the face. It encourages the classification model to focus on facial areas. The training and evaluation process uses the RGB images with 48×48, resized from facial ROI. To expand the training dataset, this applies the augmentation method. Additionally, this technique also improves the performance and ability of the real-time detector. The first stage is manipulating various lighting using random contrast, brightness, saturation, and hue. Then, it implements multiple rotations to enrich the variety of facial poses. The last process is to apply a horizontal flip to the entire previous augmented image. In contrast, the augmentation technique is not utilized in the FER-2013 and RAFDB datasets.

4.3 Training Configuration

The training of the classification model uses several configurations and parameters. This setting helps optimize the training process. Categorical cross-entropy is used to calculate the loss of the prediction into the ground truth. Meanwhile, Adam (Adaptive Moment Estimation) is utilized to optimize this process with an epsilon of 10^{-7}. The KDEF dataset starts with the 10^{-4} learning rate. It then will be updated by multiplying 0.75 when the accuracy does not improve in 20 epochs. The proposed model was conducted in the Keras framework. The training uses a batch size of 128 with epochs of 50 on 10-fold. It uses K-fold cross-validation to split and evaluate the model. On the other hand, our model trained with on FER-2013 dataset that provides 3,589 images. It uses a 10^{-4} learning rate and 64 batch sizes in the 500 epochs. Besides, It sets 200 epochs, 32 batch sizes, and 10^{-4} learning rate for training configuration on the RAFDB dataset.

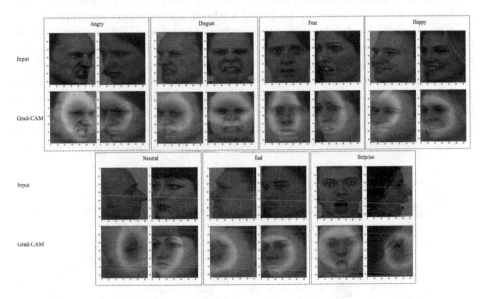

Fig. 4. Result of heat map attention for seven classes of emotions using GRAD-CAM approach.

5 Experiments and Results

5.1 Ablative Study

The proposed architecture consists of several modules that corporates to improve performance and efficiency. The ablation study is conducted to examine the effect of each module. The offered modules are applied one by one to analyze the

Table 1. Ablative result of proposed architecture on the FER-2013 dataset

Modules	Proposed model		
Four-stage backbone	✓	✓	✓
Cross stage partial		✓	✓
Depthwise excitation			✓
Parameters	2,353,223	1,996,903	**2,006,759**
Accuracy (%)	72.50	71.55	**73.95**

strength, as shown in Table 1. Firstly, the Fours-stages backbone is proposed as a shallow-layered feature extractor. This backbone obtains an accuracy of 72.50% and generates 2.36M parameters. Secondly, to reduce the training parameters by 0.35M, increasing the detector's efficiency, it applies the CSP approach without significantly decreasing the accuracy by 0.95%. Finally, the depthwise excitation module increases the accuracy by 2.40% without adding many parameters.

The attention module improves the quality of input features by strengthening the intensity of essential elements. Additionally, it also captures the relationship between these components that are related to each expression. Figure 4 shows that the proposed module concentrates and focuses on specific areas and organs of the face. The heat map indicates useful facial features to classify facial emotions. It can precisely localize the facial area of interest for the non-frontal face. Moreover, the proposed model pays attention to the eyes, eyebrows, nose, and cheeks. These elements are related to each other to generate certain emotions.

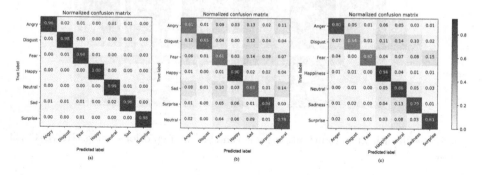

Fig. 5. Confusion matrix of evaluation at each emotion categories on KDEF (a), FER-2013 (b) and RAFDB (c) dataset.

5.2   Comparison on Datasets

This paper proposes the light backbone to distinguish essential features that can work in real-time. It uses a shallow layered convolution and the Cross Partial

Table 2. Evaluation of proposed architecture compared to other methods on KDEF, FER-2013 and RAFDB dataset

Method	Accuracy
KDEF dataset	
O-FER [3]	91.42
CCFN [23]	91.60
Multi-Xception	94.29
Resnet-19	94.49
Multi-C-Xception	94.63
DFSD-LDA-AdaBoost	95.06
Akhand et al. [1]	96.51
Proposed	97.10
FER-2013 dataset	
Multi-scale CNN	72.82
SNNs	73.00
Single MLCNN [11]	73.03
Ensemble MLCNNs [11]	74.09
AM-Net [8]	75.82
Proposed	73.95
RAFDB dataset	
MobileNetV1	81.62
PG-CNN	82.27
DLP-CNN	84.22
A-MobileNet [10]	84.49
Proposed	84.91

Stage to generate 1,996,903 parameters. The proposed classification system is trained and evaluated on the KDEF dataset. The evaluation results are also compared with previous methods. Table 2 shows that the proposed architecture achieves an accuracy of 97.10%. This result is superior to all facial expression methods that have been present in the KDEF dataset. The proposed model outperforms 1.59% of the Multi-fusion model incorporating a CNN-based residual and a Squeeze-and-Excitation (SE) module. As shown in Fig. 5(a), the prediction for each category is analyzed in the confusion matrix. The dark color indicates high accuracy obtained by each matrix element, and the bright color is vice versa. The proposed model performs best when it predicts "Happy". This emotion has a unique facial shape compared to other expressions. Meanwhile, "Fear" obtained the lowest score. Some instances are predicted "surprises" because both emotions show similar shapes and textures. Our model is also examined in realistic profile variation scenarios. As shown in Table 3, each profile is investigated that evaluated on the KDEF dataset. The proposed model is powerful in recognizing the center position that achieves the highest accuracy of 98.57%. In contrast, the full left pose obtains low accuracy of 95.59%.

Table 3. Evaluation of multi-profile facial expression

Face pose	Accuracy on KDEF (%)
Full left	95.59
Full right	95.72
Half left	98.23
Half right	98.27
Center	98.57

Table 4. Runtime efficiency compared to competitors on Jetson Nano

Method	Parameter	Accuracy (%)			Speed of integrated (FPS)
		KDEF	FER-2013	RAFDB	
Multi-model fusion [15]	1,206,279	93.42	–	–	26.38
AM-NET [8]	24,904,204	–	75.82	–	5.71
MLCNN [11]	20,787,783	–	73.03	–	10.89
Ensemble MLCNN [11]	92,825,543	–	74.09	–	Out of memory
Akhand et al. [1]	28,907,943	96.51	–	–	Out of memory
A-MobileNet [10]	3,321,513	–	–	84.49	20.35
Proposed detector	**2,006,759**	**97.10**	**73.95**	**84.91**	29.58

Furthermore, the proposed model examines difficult challenges using the FER-2013 dataset. It reached an accuracy of 73.95%, which is weaker than Ensemble MLCNN [11] and AM-NET [8]. However, it outperforms SSNs and single MLCNN [11], with a 1% difference. Our model is robust in recognizing the "Happy" category, as illustrated in Fig. 5(b) in contrast, it not powerful to classify "Angry" and "Fear" on this dataset. The proposed model also examines the performance using the RAFDB dataset, which shows that it is superior to other models. It higher 0.42% than [10], as shown in Table 3. Although the proposed model obtains low accuracy in recognizing "Disgust" emotion, It achieves accurate prediction in the "Happiness" category.

5.3   Real-Time Application

The practical application requires a vision-based detector to work in real-time. In addition, robotic technology implements it on edge devices, which are compatible with sensors and actuators. Hence, a real-time face emotion detector on the Jetson Nano with input from a webcam. It compares the proposed detector's speeds to a competitor integrated with a face detector [14], as shown in Fig. 1. Face detection produces facial ROI to avoid perturbation of background features. Table 4 shows that the Multi-model fusion has a small number of training parameters. However, the proposed detector achieves a more accurate performance on the classification system and requires a data processing speed of 29.58 FPS. Although AM-NET [8] and Ensemble MLCNN [11] achieve high accuracy, our

Fig. 6. Qualitative results in real-time application with multiple faces.

model is faster than the competitors. The proposed model is even faster than A-MobileNet [10] and Akhand et al. [1]. It proves that the proposed detector more efficiently works on an edge device. The two-stage detector sequentially employs face detection and a classification system to predict facial areas and classify them. Therefore, face detection is a mandatory process for generating facial patches. Then, the classification network estimates the emotion category. The effectiveness of the detector performance in real applications is shown in Fig. 6. It robustly detects and classifies the expression of multiple facial poses. This system is feasible to be implemented in robots to support human-robot interaction.

6   Conclusions

This paper proposes a real-time facial emotion detector to predict seven classes of multi-profile facial expressions implemented on an edge device. The integrated system can support the human-robot interaction system. The proposed architecture consists of a four-stage backbone to efficiently extract the specific features and a depthwise excitation module to increase the intensity of the useful features. The CSP approach improves the model's efficiency without significantly reducing the detector performance. In order to build a robust model implemented in real applications, a classification system is trained and evaluated on the KDEF and the FER-2013 dataset that provides multi-profile face instances. As a result, the proposed model achieves high accuracy, competitive with the previous methods. In addition, the integrated system achieves a data processing speed of 29.57 FPS when working on a Jetson Nano. Future work will explore the margin loss to improve accuracy by balancing true and false prediction losses.

Acknowledgment. This work was supported by the National Research Foundation of Korea (NRF) grant funded by the government (MSIT) (No. 2020R1A2C200897212).

References

1. Akhand, M.A.H., Roy, S., Siddique, N., Kamal, M.A.S., Shimamura, T.: Facial emotion recognition using transfer learning in the deep CNN. Electronics **10**(9), 1036 (2021)
2. Calvo, M., Lundqvist, D.: Facial expressions of emotion (KDEF): identification under different display-duration conditions. Behav. Res. Methods **40**, 109–115 (1998). http://www.kdef.se/
3. Dong, J., Zhang, L., Chen, Y., Jiang, W.: Occlusion expression recognition based on non-convex low-rank double dictionaries and occlusion error model. Signal Process.: Image Commun. **76**, 81–88 (2019)
4. Ekman, P.: Facial expressions of emotion: new findings, new questions. Psychol. Sci. **3**(1), 34–38 (1992)
5. Fareed, K., Sultan, F., Khan, K., Mahmood, Z.: A robust face recognition method for expression and pose variant images. In: 2020 14th International Conference on Open Source Systems and Technologies (ICOSST), pp. 1–6 (2020)
6. Goodfellow, I.J., et al.: Challenges in representation learning: a report on three machine learning contests. Neural Netw. **64**, 59–63 (2015). Special Issue on "Deep Learning of Representations"
7. Hu, J., Shen, L., Sun, G.: Squeeze-and-excitation networks. In: 2018 IEEE/CVF Conference on Computer Vision and Pattern Recognition, pp. 7132–7141 (2018)
8. Li, J., Jin, K., Zhou, D., Kubota, N., Ju, Z.: Attention mechanism-based CNN for facial expression recognition. Neurocomputing **411**, 340–350 (2020)
9. Li, S., Deng, W.: Reliable crowdsourcing and deep locality-preserving learning for unconstrained facial expression recognition. IEEE Trans. Image Process. **28**(1), 356–370 (2019)
10. Nan, Y., Ju, J., Hua, Q., Zhang, H., Wang, B.: A-mobilenet: an approach of facial expression recognition. Alex. Eng. J. **61**(6), 4435–4444 (2022). http://www.sciencedirect.com/science/article/pii/S1110016821006682
11. Nguyen, H.D., Kim, S.H., Lee, G.S., Yang, H.J., Na, I.S., Kim, S.H.: Facial expression recognition using a temporal ensemble of multi-level convolutional neural networks. IEEE Trans. Affect. Comput. **13**(1), 226–237 (2022)
12. Pathak, R., Singh, Y.: Real time baby facial expression recognition using deep learning and IoT edge computing. In: 2020 5th International Conference on Computing, Communication and Security (ICCCS), pp. 1–6 (2020)
13. Putro, M.D., Jo, K.: Real-time face tracking for human-robot interaction. In: Proceedings of the International Conference on Information and Communication Technology Robotics (ICT-ROBOT), pp. 1–4 (2018)

14. Putro, M.D., Nguyen, D., Jo, K.: Lightweight convolutional neural network for real-time face detector on CPU supporting interaction of service robot. In: 2020 13th International Conference on Human System Interaction (HSI), pp. 94–99 (2020)
15. Qi, A., Wei, J., Bai, B.: Research on deep learning expression recognition algorithm based on multi-model fusion. In: 2019 International Conference on Machine Learning, Big Data and Business Intelligence (MLBDBI), pp. 288–291 (2019)
16. Rao, Q., Qu, X., Mao, Q., Zhan, Y.: Multi-pose facial expression recognition based on SURF boosting. In: 2015 International Conference on Affective Computing and Intelligent Interaction (ACII), pp. 630–635 (2015)
17. Rujirakul, K., So-In, C.: Histogram equalized deep PCA with ELM classification for expressive face recognition. In: 2018 International Workshop on Advanced Image Technology (IWAIT), pp. 1–4 (2018)
18. Santra, B., Mukherjee, D.P.: Local saliency-inspired binary patterns for automatic recognition of multi-view facial expression. In: 2016 IEEE International Conference on Image Processing (ICIP), pp. 624–628 (2016)
19. Sirithunge, C., Ravindu, H.M., Bandara, T., Buddhika, A.G., Jayasekara, P., Chandima, D.P.: Situation awareness for proactive robots in HRI. In: 2019 IEEE/RSJ International Conference on Intelligent Robots and Systems (IROS), pp. 7813–7820 (2019)
20. Sun, W., Zhao, H., Jin, Z.: A visual attention based ROI detection method for facial expression recognition. Neurocomputing **296**, 12–22 (2018). http://www.sciencedirect.com/science/article/pii/S0925231218303266
21. Wang, C., Mark Liao, H., Wu, Y., Chen, P., Hsieh, J., Yeh, I.: CSPNet: a new backbone that can enhance learning capability of CNN. In: 2020 IEEE/CVF Conference on Computer Vision and Pattern Recognition Workshops (CVPRW), pp. 1571–1580 (2020)
22. Webb, N., Ruiz-Garcia, A., Elshaw, M., Palade, V.: Emotion recognition from face images in an unconstrained environment for usage on social robots. In: 2020 International Joint Conference on Neural Networks (IJCNN), pp. 1–8 (2020)
23. Ye, Y., Zhang, X., Lin, Y., Wang, H.: Facial expression recognition via region-based convolutional fusion network. J. Vis. Commun. Image Represent. **62**, 1–11 (2019)
24. Zeiler, M.D., Fergus, R.: Visualizing and understanding convolutional networks. In: Fleet, D., Pajdla, T., Schiele, B., Tuytelaars, T. (eds.) ECCV 2014. LNCS, vol. 8689, pp. 818–833. Springer, Cham (2014). https://doi.org/10.1007/978-3-319-10590-1_53

Keyword Extraction from Short Texts with a Text-to-Text Transfer Transformer

Piotr Pęzik[1,2](✉) (iD), Agnieszka Mikołajczyk[2](✉) (iD), Adam Wawrzyński[2](✉) (iD),
Bartłomiej Nitoń[3](✉) (iD), and Maciej Ogrodniczuk[3](✉) (iD)

[1] Faculty of Philology, University of Łódź, Łódź, Poland
piotr.pezik@gmail.com
[2] VoiceLab, NLP Lab, Gdańsk, Poland
agnieszka.mikolajczyk@voicelab.ai, adam.wawrzynski@voicelab.ai
[3] Institute of Computer Science, Polish Academy of Sciences, Warsaw, Poland
bartek.niton@gmail.com, maciej.ogrodniczuk@gmail.com

Abstract. The paper explores the relevance of the Text-To-Text Transfer Transformer language model (T5) for Polish (plT5) to the task of intrinsic and extrinsic keyword extraction from short text passages. The evaluation is carried out on the new Polish Open Science Metadata Corpus (POSMAC), which is released with this paper: a collection of 216,214 abstracts of scientific publications compiled in the CURLICAT project. We compare the results obtained by four different methods, i.e. plT5kw, extremeText, TermoPL, KeyBERT and conclude that the plT5kw model yields particularly promising results for both frequent and sparsely represented keywords. Furthermore, a plT5kw keyword generation model trained on the POSMAC also seems to produce highly useful results in cross-domain text labelling scenarios. We discuss the performance of the model on news stories and phone-based dialog transcripts which represent text genres and domains extrinsic to the dataset of scientific abstracts. Finally, we also attempt to characterize the challenges of evaluating a text-to-text model on both intrinsic and extrinsic keyword extraction.

Keywords: Keyword extraction · T5 language model · POSMAC · Polish

1 Keyword Extraction and Generation

The main NLP problem discussed in this paper can be described as keyword extraction or generation from short text passages. More specifically, given a span of text such as a concatenated title and abstract of a research paper, the task is to generate a small set of words or multiword phrases (usually nominal phrases) which succinctly describe its content. Approaches to this problem can be purely *extractive* or partly *abstractive*. In the former case, keywords are extracted and possibly normalized more or less directly from the text of the sample. Abstractive

© The Author(s), under exclusive license to Springer Nature Singapore Pte Ltd. 2022
E. Szczerbicki et al. (Eds.): ACIIDS 2022, CCIS 1716, pp. 530–542, 2022.
https://doi.org/10.1007/978-981-19-8234-7_41

methods can assign labels that may not have occurred in the original text sample or a restricted vocabulary of known keywords.

Despite the long tradition of keyword extraction as a distinct NLP task, "no single approach (...) effectively extracts keywords from different data sources" [5][1]. Extraction of keywords from longer texts can be approached similarly to term extraction and partly facilitated by considering word frequency distributions and identifying significantly frequent phrases as potential keywords. This paper focuses mostly on showcasing the applications of the T5 generative language model [13] and comparing its performance to text classification (extremeText/fastText) [10,17] and statistical terminology extraction (C/NC-values) [7] as baseline methods. Although the complementarity of statistical and transformer-based approaches to keyword extraction has been explored before [8], we are not aware of any published assessment of text-to-text generative models on this task.

From the point of view of model evaluation, it should be noted that the manual assignment of keywords to scientific articles, which are used as groundtruth annotations in our analysis, is far from deterministic and quite different from text classification or labelling based on a closed-set taxonomy. Authors usually draw a small set of terms from a largely uncontrolled vocabulary. Such descriptors may be terminological items used in the text of their paper, but they can also be more abstract or at least hyperonymic descriptors of its content. Synonyms, hyperonyms and abbreviated forms contribute to the apparent sparsity of the vocabulary, which over time tends to grow in a large collection of abstracts at a sublinear rate. This in turn has implications for building and evaluating automatic keyword extraction solutions. Firstly, the distribution of keywords as distinct class labels in many datasets is rather sparse, which means that the recall of rare keywords is unlikely to be high, at least in any supervised text classification scenario. Secondly, the evaluation of automatically assigned keywords is problematic as the 'ground truth' assignments are neither consistent nor exhaustive. The latter problem could be systematically addressed by measuring inter-rater agreement in datasets which are explicitly developed for NLP purposes. However, the corpus of scientific abstracts used in this study has been adapted from metadata sources which were not globally curated and checked for consistency.

Despite these methodological limitations, we believe that our evaluation of keyword generation approaches provides fresh insights into the transferability of a T5 model to loosely related topical domains and text genres. As shown in the last section of this paper, a model tuned on a high-quality corpus of scientific abstract extracts surprisingly accurate keywords from news stories and even spoken dialogue transcripts. Thus, the novelty of this paper consists in the fact that a) we test the relevance of text-to-text transfer transformers to the task of keyword generation and b) we evaluate and release a non-obvious dataset which shows significant potential of transferability to extrinsic domains and languages.

---

[1] This paper also offers an up-to-date review of keyword extraction methods.

2   The Polish Open Science Metadata Corpus

The source dataset used in this study was developed in CURLICAT[2], an international project aimed at delivering rich metadata monolingual corpora in seven EU languages, including Polish, and representing different topical domains and text genres. The Polish subset of CURLICAT (released for the first time with this paper) named Polish Open Science Metadata Corpus (POSMAC)[3]—contains a new source of valuable corpus data acquired from the Library of Science (LoS)[4], a platform providing open access to full texts of articles published in over 900 Polish scientific journals and full texts of selected scientific books together with extensive bibliographic metadata. More than 70% of the metadata records included in the resulting corpus contain keywords describing the content of the indexed articles. Since authors of the respective articles typically enter such keywords themselves, their selection is relatively uncontrolled. After lowercasing and ASCII-folding (i.e., removing Polish diacritics due to their inconsistent use), we found a total of 256 139 distinct keywords used in the corpus, with only 69 266 (ca. 27%) used more than once and 10 074 keywords assigned to 10 or more articles. Syntactically, the vast majority of keywords are lemmatized noun phrases whose length typically ranges from 1 to 3 words (mean = 2.39, sd = 1.22). A single article record is tagged with an average of 4.76 keywords (median = 4) (Table 1).

Table 1. Top 10 scientific domains represented in the POSMAC.

Domains	Documents	With keywords
Engineering and technical sciences	58 974	57 165
Social sciences	58 166	41 799
Agricultural sciences	29 811	15 492
Humanities	22 755	11 497
Exact and natural sciences	13 579	9 185
Humanities, Social sciences	12 809	7 063
Medical and health sciences	6 030	3 913
Medical and health sciences, Social sciences	828	571
Humanities, Medical and health sciences, Social sciences	601	455
Engineering and technical sciences, Humanities	312	312

---

[2] https://curlicat.eu/.
[3] http://clip.ipipan.waw.pl/POSMAC.
[4] https://bibliotekanauki.pl/.

3   Approaches

3.1   T5, PlT5 and PlT5kw

T5 stands for the Text-To-Text Transfer Transformer model proposed by [13]. In terms of its architecture, the model is based on the original encoder-decoder transformer implementation [16]. Unlike popular transformer-based language models used in classification tasks, T5 frames all NLP problems as text-to-text operations, where both the input and output are text strings. Although this approach may only seem natural for selected NLP problems such as question answering, translation or summarization, it has been demonstrated to apply to other tasks such as classification or regression tasks. In this study, the input to a T5 model is a concatenated title and abstract of a scientific paper and the text string output is a comma-separated list of lemmatized single- or multi-word 'keywords'[5]. In the case of morphologically rich languages such as Polish, such lemmatization may additionally involve number, case and gender agreement operations on the resulting multiword keywords. This requirement is particularly important for out-of-vocabulary (OOV) keywords which need to be lemmatized and formatted on demand.

For the extraction of Polish keywords, we used the plT5-base model [3][6] trained on six reference corpora of Polish. More specifically, we train the model to predict comma-separated keywords from article abstracts concatenated with titles. We used an Adam optimizer with 100 warm-up steps, linearly increasing the learning rate from zero to a target of $3e-5$. Additionally, we used a multiplicative scheduler that lowered the LR by 0.7 every epoch. We trained the model for ten epochs with a batch size of 8. The maximum input length was set to 512 tokens and the maximum target length was 128. We refer to the resulting keyword extraction model as **plT5kw**.

We experimented with `no_repeat_ngram_size` and `num_beams` parameters on *dev* subset of datasets to find out the best configuration. During evaluation on the test subset, we set `no_repeat_ngram_size` to 3 and `num_beams` to 4.

3.2   FastText and ExtremeText

FastText is a popular text classification library which uses vector representations of (sub)words as input to a relatively simple neural network [10]. Despite the obvious differences between supervised text classification and unsupervised keyword extraction, the assignment of keywords attested in a representative collection of tagged texts can be treated as a text labelling task. In the comparison described in this paper we used an extension of FastText called extremeText [17], which uses a Probabilistic Labels Tree loss function (PLT) to optimize the assignment of labels from very large taxonomies, such as the set of over 200 000 distinct keywords found in POSMAC. Using the PLT loss function, we trained

---

[5] We use the traditional term *keyword* to refer to potentially multiword phrases found in the *Keywords* section of a scientific abstract.

[6] https://huggingface.co/allegro/plt5-large.

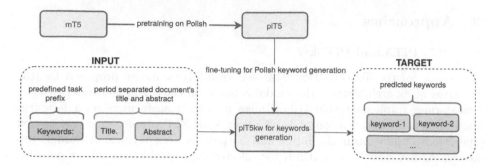

Fig. 1. Training procedure for our text-to-text transfer transformer model for keywords generation.

a keyword classifier with 300 dimensions in the hidden layer for 50 epochs to obtain the results reported below (Fig. 1).

3.3   TermoPL

TermoPL [11] is a statistical terminology extraction tool designed to identify recurrent words and multiword combinations in domain corpora of Polish. It identifies, lemmatizes and scores recurrent noun phrases as potential terminological items using a ranking function proposed by [7]. We include this approach to measure the upper bound of purely extractive keyword identification. In other words, we estimate the maximum recall of simply extracting and lemmatizing all noun phrases contained in any given abstract.

3.4   KeyBERT

KeyBERT [9] is a keyword extraction library utilizing BERT representations. For each document it creates a representation vector using a transformer-based language model. Next, word representations for each n-gram found in a given text are compared with the document vector using cosine vector distance scores. The most similar phrases are selected as those that represent the document content. Additionally, two methods are used to increase the diversity of the generated phrases: Maximum Sum Similarity and Maximal Marginal Relevance. We used KeyBERT with the *distiluse-base-multilingual-cased-v1* model from the Sentence Transformers library [14]. The filtering method used in the experiments was Maximal Margin Relevance, and the diversity factor was set to 0.7 with an n-gram range of (1, 2). The other parameters were used with their default values.

4   Intrinsic Evaluation

To evaluate the above-mentioned set of complementary keyword generation approaches intrinsically (i.e. on the original POSMAC dataset), abstracts annotated with keywords were split into a training and test set with a ratio of 70/30%.

To ensure consistent distribution of labels in the training and test set, we used an implementation of the iterative stratification algorithm[7] for multilabel data, originally proposed by [15]. The relevance and coverage of keyword assignments are evaluated in terms of micro- and macro- precision and recall values, as well as their harmonic means (F_1-scores) averaged over the documents in the test set. These scores are measured at several ranks (k = 1, 3, 5 and more) for each approach in two different scenarios: a) using the full set of keywords assigned in the training and test set and b) training and/or evaluating only on keywords which occur at least 10 times in the stratified dataset.

It should be noted that in addition to evaluating the four main approaches described in this paper, we also assessed several baseline keyword extraction approaches, including FirstPhrases and TopicRank [2], PositionRank [6], MultipartiteRank [1], TextRank [12], KPMiner [4] and TfIdf with some adjustments aimed at boosting their performance (such as lemmatizing input text). The results obtained for all of those methods were less than $0.025\,F_1$ on all ranks, which is why we excluded them from the detailed comparisons included below.

Table 2 compares the performance of extremeText and plT5kw on the task of extracting keywords from the full set of more than 200 000 items found in POSMAC. The highest average F_1 (harmonic mean of precision and recall) is obtained for both approaches at rank 5, although plT5kw clearly outperforms extremeText on this task both in terms of precision and recall at all the corresponding ranks. We include rank 10 for the extremeText classifier but not for plT5kw, because the former can be requested to produce a ranked list of keywords used in the training set of any length while the latter is implicitly trained to produce text strings with up to 4 commas on average. The results for Key-BERT for Polish keyword extraction are very poor both in terms of recall and precision, neither of which increases over 0.03 at any rank measured (see the qualitative explanations below). As signalled above, TermoPL is meant to be used on longer texts as it ranks terms by a score which is partly derived from their frequency in a sufficiently large corpus of texts. Nevertheless, looking at its recall when no rank limit is applied, it is interesting to observe that more than 33 percent of all keywords in our corpus are actually some form of nominal phrases found in the text of the abstracts.

The lower part of Table 2 shows the results of evaluating the four approaches on a set of 10,083 distinct keywords which were assigned to at least 10 different abstracts in the stratified dataset. As expected, the results for extremeText are slightly better in this run as they are not affected by very rare or unknown keywords in the test set. However, the tuned plT5kw is again significantly better in this scenario.

---

[7] See https://vict0rs.ch/2018/05/24/sample-multilabel-dataset/.

Table 2. Results of evaluation on the full set of POSMAC keywords. The upper part of the table presents the results for all keywords present in the dataset, while the lower part refers to experiments conducted with the rejection of keywords occurring less than 10 times.

Method	Rank	Micro			Macro		
		P	R	F_1	P	R	F_1
extremeText	1	0.175	0.038	0.063	0.007	0.004	0.005
	3	0.117	0.077	0.093	0.011	0.011	0.011
	5	0.090	0.099	0.094	0.013	0.016	0.015
	10	0.060	0.131	0.082	0.015	0.025	0.019
plT5kw	1	**0.345**	0.076	0.124	0.054	0.047	0.050
	3	0.328	0.212	0.257	0.133	0.127	0.129
	5	0.318	**0.237**	**0.271**	0.143	0.140	0.141
KeyBERT	1	0.030	0.007	0.011	0.004	0.003	0.003
	3	0.015	0.010	0.012	0.006	0.004	0.005
	5	0.011	0.012	0.011	0.006	0.005	0.005
TermoPL	1	0.118	0.026	0.043	0.004	0.003	0.003
	3	0.070	0.046	0.056	0.006	0.005	0.006
	5	0.051	0.056	0.053	0.007	0.007	0.007
	All	0.025	0.339	0.047	0.017	0.030	0.022
extremeText	1	0.210	0.077	0.112	0.037	0.017	0.023
	3	0.139	0.152	0.145	0.045	0.042	0.043
	5	0.107	0.196	0.139	0.049	0.063	0.055
	10	0.072	0.262	0.112	0.041	0.098	0.058
plT5kw	1	**0.377**	0.138	0.202	0.119	0.071	0.089
	3	0.361	0.301	0.328	0.185	0.147	0.164
	5	0.357	**0.316**	**0.335**	0.188	0.153	0.169
KeyBERT	1	0.018	0.007	0.010	0.003	0.001	0.001
	3	0.009	0.010	0.009	0.004	0.001	0.002
	5	0.007	0.012	0.009	0.004	0.001	0.002
TermoPL	1	0.076	0.028	0.041	0.002	0.001	0.001
	3	0.046	0.051	0.048	0.003	0.001	0.002
	5	0.033	0.061	0.043	0.003	0.001	0.002
	All	0.021	0.457	0.040	0.004	0.008	0.005

Table 3 reveals an interesting property of plT5kw. Its precision increases up to 0.425 at rank 1 when the predictions are limited to keywords found in the training set. The improvement in precision comes at the expense of recall which drops by nearly 10% points. This observation also means that unlike extremeText or any text classification model plT5kw is capable of assigning relevant keywords

Table 3. Evaluation of plT5kw on the set of keywords found in the training set.

Method	Rank	Micro			Macro		
		P	R	F_1	P	R	F_1
plT5kw	1	0.425	0.093	0.153	0.086	0.074	0.080
	3	0.415	0.212	0.281	0.165	0.158	0.161
	5	0.412	0.227	0.293	0.172	0.167	0.169

which were not seen in the training set. The transferability of plT5kw is further discussed in the next section of this paper.

5 Transfer to Other Domains

Although the results of intrinsic evaluation of keyword extraction from scientific abstract reported above may seem moderately useful, the plT5kw model trained on a rather narrowly defined source domain seems to produce surprisingly precise (although incomplete) keywords for samples of other topical domains and text genres. In this section, we explore the relevance of the plT5kw model trained on POSMAC to the domain of news stories and transcripts of conversational speech. We also compare the type of keywords produced by the four extraction approaches discussed above in more qualitative terms.

5.1 News Stories

Table 4 shows a set of shorthand English translations of headlines of recent news stories published in Polish web-based media outlets. The full text of each story is linked to the shorthand headline. The next four columns of the table show samples of keywords generated for the full text of each article by the four respective extraction methods described in this paper.

The overall quality of the extracted keywords can be considered from a number of perspectives. The **importance** of an extracted keyword (also known as **keyness**) refers to its potential to express the most important aspects of a text passage. Although all important keywords are also **relevant** (related to the content of the text sample), not all relevant keywords are equally important and usually some limit on the **complete** set of relevant keywords is required. The **abstraction** aspect of keywords pertains to the degree to which they can describe the content without necessarily relying on the verbatim word combinations used in a given text passage. The **transferability** of a keyword generation method refers to its ability to produce good quality keywords for texts from domains which are different from those of the originally labelled datasets. Finally, the **formatting** quality of a keyword refers to the correct lemmatization, true-casing or abbreviation of the extracted keywords.

The transferability of the keywords produced by **extremeText**, a closed-label set classifier is clearly limited. The predictions are far from complete and

Table 4. Comparison of keywords generated for 5 news stories.

#	Short title	plT5kw	KeyBERT	TermoPL	ExtremeText
1	Polish PM meets new German Chancellor	Niemcy, Polska, Unia Europejska, Nord Stream 2, bezpieczeństwo, kryzys migracyjny, polityka	premiera morawieckiego, migracyjne energetyczne, powiedzieli czego, będzie bardzo, serii spotkań	nowy kanclerz Niemiec, instrument szantażu, kwestia migracyjną, kanclerz Niemiec, Olaf Scholza, ... (237 in total)	rosja, polska, unia_europejska
2	Gas pipe explosion on Sicily	gaz, wybuch, Włochy	wybuchu gazociągu, czterech osób, miejscowości ravanusa, jak poinformowała, pomoże przeszukiwaniu	dziesiątek osób, miejsce wybuchu, wybuch gazociągu, włoska wyspa, ... (71 in total)	paleontologia, skamienialosci, fauna_kopalna
3	Person wounded in Kielce knife attack	Kielce, policja, rana, rynek	policji kielcach, rynku 31, wyjaśniają okoliczności, narzędziem przez, letni mężczyzna	kielecki rynek, poszukiwanie napastnika, ostre narzędzie, ... (44 in total)	bezpieczenstwo, kontrola, policja
4	Omicron coronavirus variant in UK	Covid, Omikron, Wielka Brytania, koronawirus, hospitalizacja	przypadki hospitalizacji, powiedzmy 50, minister edukacji, brytania pierwsze, liczba potwierdzonych	nowy wariant, wariant Omikron, wielka Brytania, ... (126 in total)	migracja, bezpieczenstwo, transport_kolejowy
5	Tatry National Park landmark vandalized	Tatry, wandalizm, szlak turystyczny	pomalowali granitowy, narodowy film, tatrzański park, morskiego oka, sprawę gdzie	morskie oko, tatrzański park narodowy, granitowy głaz, ... (88 in total)	historia, ochrona, bezpieczenstwo

they are only remotely relevant to the texts from the news domains in cases where some overlap exists between the original domain of scientific abstracts and a given news story. The labels are static, i.e. they are not dynamically reformatted or adjusted to the text samples.

The results produced by the **KeyBERT** model are probably the least convincing in this comparison. The model shows a clear preference for longer n-grams, which may not be syntactically complete nominal phrases or any regular phrases for that matter. The results are not lemmatized or properly cased, but their relevance is at least relatively easy to judge as they can be traced back to the exact span of text from which they were extracted.

As a terminology extraction solution **TermoPL** produces lemmatized although not always correctly cased noun phrases. Some of the results are clearly complementary to the keywords produced by plT5kw, but the choice of the most important items remains an issue as this solution requires a larger body of text to score its suggestions. The solution is domain-independent, but this also means that it does not transfer any knowledge about the desired keyword format or level of abstraction from other domains.

The keywords produced by **plT5kw** are mostly relevant and well abstracted although occasionally also too generic. For example the meeting of the Polish PM with the German Chancellor is tagged as *Poland* and *Germany* and the story about a gas explosion in Sicily gets the rather generic tag of *Italy*. The model does not seem to have a bias toward single- or multiword expressions. It produces correctly lemmatized, syntactically agreed and well-cased phrases. It seems to have transferred the skill of identifying, formatting and sometimes abstracting comma-separated nominal phrases without over-fitting excessively to the topics represented in the source domain. Needless to say, the recall of the model is far from perfect, but its precision is reliably stable.

5.2   Customer Support Dialogues

The promising results obtained on a sample corpus of news stories have led us to test plT5kw on the completely different domain of phone conversation transcripts which were sampled from the DiaBiz corpus.[8] The following excerpt from the DiaBiz corpus is a translation of a dialogue between a support agent informing a client about an outstanding electricity bill which has resulted in an energy supply disconnection. Our plT5kw model trained on scientific abstracts labels the following passage with two noun phrases: *loan* and *financial advisory* even though there is only a handful of abstracts with these keywords in the POSMAC:

> **Customer:** I can't imagine how I could live without electricity. I need to use my fridge and washing machine. I guess I have no... I don't even know where I could borrow some money. Is there any way I could pay my debt in some kind of installments. How should I go about it?
>
> **Agent:** It's alright. I understand and... I'm really sorry about your situation. Before we continue, however, we need to sort out a few formal issues. Can I ask you again to state your name and email address?

Table 5 shows frequencies of keywords assigned to a set of 50 DiaBiz transcripts representing scenarios from 6 different customer support domains. The recurrent keywords seem to accurately (if not exhaustively) summarize the underlying conversations. *Logistyka* (*logistics*) is the only potentially irrelevant keyword in this subset which may have resulted from some over-fitting of the model on the original domain of scientific abstracts.

---

[8] DiaBiz is a corpus developed in the CLARIN-Biz project. It contains some 4,000 phone-based customer support calls covering a range of topics and business processes.

Table 5. Frequent keywords generated by plT5kw for phone dialogues in different customer support domains and their English translations.

Domain	Keywords PL	Keywords EN
Medical	gastroskopia (4)	gastroscopy (4)
	diagnostyka medyczna (3)	medical diagnosis (3)
	numer PESEL (2)	National Identification Number (2)
	diagnostyka (2)	diagnosis (2)
	lekarz POZ (1)	GP (1)
Tourism	hotel (9)	hotel (9)
	turystyka (6)	tourism (6)
	Afryka (2)	Africa (2)
	Turcja (2)	Turkey (2)
	atrakcje (2)	attractions (2)
Insurance	naprawa (6)	repair (6)
	uszkodzenie (5)	damage (5)
	ekspres do kawy (3)	coffee machine (3)
	reklamacja (3)	complaints (3)
	ubezpieczenie (2)	insurance (2)
Banking	identyfikacja (6)	identification (6)
	bankowość internetowa (4)	online banking (4)
	logistyka (3)	logistics (3)
	Bank Narodowy S.A. (3)	National Bank S.A. (3)
	logowanie (2)	login (2)
Energy	licznik (6)	meter (6)
	zerwanie plomby (4)	seal break (4)
	plomba na liczniku (8)	seal on meter (8)
	PESEL (2)	National Identification Number (2)
	weryfikacja tożsamości (1)	identity verification (1)

6 Summary and Future Work

Our evaluation of a keyword extraction solution based on a text-to-text transformer shows that the fine-tuned model called plT5kw outperforms the other approaches when tested on the original dataset of scientific abstracts. Furthermore, a preliminary analysis of keywords assigned to text from very different domains (news stories and speech transcripts) shows that the proposed solution is capable of generating relevant, properly formatted and well-abstracted keywords on extrinsic text samples. One of the limitations of this study stems from the fact that manual keyword annotations are intrinsically biased against high recall evaluations as authors are artificially restricted to assign a limited number of terms to each text. Therefore, a more systematic quantitative evaluation on extrinsic domains would require manually annotated datasets verified for inter-rater agreement. We envisage further challenges which need to be addressed in future research on this problem. For example, it seems reasonable to assume that open-set keyword extraction could benefit from distributional vector-based techniques of normalizing semantically equivalent keywords. Also, there are potential benefits of zero- or few-shot fine-tuning of text-to-text keyword extraction models to the target domain, which need to be considered more systematically. Finally, the results obtained in this study may vary for different languages, which requires further evaluation, possibly on multilingual variants of the T5 model used.

Acknowledgements. The work reported here was supported by 1) the European Commission in the CEF Telecom Programme (Action No: 2019-EU-IA-0034, Grant Agreement No: INEA/CEF/ICT/A2019/1926831) and the Polish Ministry of Science and Higher Education: research project 5103/CEF/2020/2, funds for 2020-2022) and 2) the National Centre for Research and Development, research grant POIR.01.01.01-00-1237/19.

References

1. Boudin, F.: Unsupervised keyphrase extraction with multipartite graphs. In: Proceedings of the 2018 Conference of the North American Chapter of the Association for Computational Linguistics: Human Language Technologies, Volume 2 (Short Papers), pp. 667–672. Association for Computational Linguistics, New Orleans (2018). https://aclanthology.org/N18-2105
2. Bougouin, A., Boudin, F., Daille, B.: TopicRank: graph-based topic ranking for keyphrase extraction. In: Proceedings of the Sixth International Joint Conference on Natural Language Processing, pp. 543–551. Asian Federation of Natural Language Processing, Nagoya (2013). https://aclanthology.org/I13-1062
3. Chrabrowa, A., et al.: Evaluation of transfer learning for polish with a text-to-text model. In: Proceedings of the 13th Conference on Language Resources and Evaluation (LREC 2022), pp. 4374–4394. European Language Resources Association, Marseille (2022). https://www.lrec-conf.org/proceedings/lrec2022/pdf/2022.lrec-1.466.pdf
4. El-Beltagy, S.R., Rafea, A.: KP-miner: participation in SemEval-2. In: Proceedings of the 5th International Workshop on Semantic Evaluation, pp. 190–193. Association for Computational Linguistics, Uppsala (2010). https://aclanthology.org/S10-1041
5. Firoozeh, N., Nazarenko, A., Alizon, F., Daille, B.: Keyword extraction: issues and methods. Nat. Lang. Eng. **26**(3), 259–291 (2020)
6. Florescu, C., Caragea, C.: PositionRank: an unsupervised approach to keyphrase extraction from scholarly documents. In: Proceedings of the 55th Annual Meeting of the Association for Computational Linguistics (Volume 1: Long Papers), pp. 1105–1115. Association for Computational Linguistics, Vancouver (2017). https://aclanthology.org/P17-1102
7. Frantzi, K., Ananiadou, S., Mima, H.: Automatic recognition of multi-word terms: the C-value/NC-value method. Int. J. Digit. Libr. **3**(2), 115–130 (2000). https://doi.org/10.1007/s007999900023

8. Giarelis, N., Kanakaris, N., Karacapilidis, N.: A comparative assessment of state-of-the-art methods for multilingual unsupervised keyphrase extraction. In: Maglogiannis, I., Macintyre, J., Iliadis, L. (eds.) AIAI 2021. IAICT, vol. 627, pp. 635–645. Springer, Cham (2021). https://doi.org/10.1007/978-3-030-79150-6_50
9. Grootendorst, M.: KeyBERT: minimal keyword extraction with BERT (2020). https://doi.org/10.5281/zenodo.4461265
10. Joulin, A., Grave, E., Bojanowski, P., Mikolov, T.: Bag of tricks for efficient text classification. In: Proceedings of the 15th Conference of the European Chapter of the Association for Computational Linguistics: Volume 2, Short Papers, pp. 427–431. Association for Computational Linguistics, Valencia (2017). http://aclanthology.org/E17-2068
11. Marciniak, M., Mykowiecka, A., Rychlik, P.: TermoPL—a flexible tool for terminology extraction. In: Calzolari, N., et al. (eds.) Proceedings of the Tenth International Conference on Language Resources and Evaluation (LREC 2016), pp. 2278–2284. European Language Resources Association (2016). http://www.lrec-conf.org/proceedings/lrec2016/pdf/296_Paper.pdf
12. Mihalcea, R., Tarau, P.: TextRank: bringing order into text. In: Proceedings of the 2004 Conference on Empirical Methods in Natural Language Processing, pp. 404–411. Association for Computational Linguistics, Barcelona (2004). http://aclanthology.org/W04-3252
13. Raffel, C., et al.: Exploring the limits of transfer learning with a unified text-to-text transformer. J. Mach. Learn. Res. **21**(140), 1–67 (2020). http://jmlr.org/papers/v21/20-074.html
14. Reimers, N., Gurevych, I.: Making monolingual sentence embeddings multilingual using knowledge distillation. In: Proceedings of the 2020 Conference on Empirical Methods in Natural Language Processing (EMNLP), pp. 4512–4525. Association for Computational Linguistics (2020). http://aclanthology.org/2020.emnlp-main.365/
15. Sechidis, K., Tsoumakas, G., Vlahavas, I.: On the stratification of multi-label data. In: Gunopulos, D., Hofmann, T., Malerba, D., Vazirgiannis, M. (eds.) ECML PKDD 2011. LNCS (LNAI), vol. 6913, pp. 145–158. Springer, Heidelberg (2011). https://doi.org/10.1007/978-3-642-23808-6_10
16. Vaswani, A., et al.: Attention is all you need. In: Guyon, I., et al. (eds.) Advances in Neural Information Processing Systems 30: Proceedings of the Annual Conference on Neural Information Processing Systems (NeurIPS 2017), pp. 5998–6008 (2017). https://proceedings.neurips.cc/paper/2017/hash/3f5ee243547dee91fbd053c1c4a845aa-Abstract.html
17. Wydmuch, M., Jasinska, K., Kuznetsov, M., Busa-Fekete, R., Dembczyński, K.: A no-regret generalization of hierarchical softmax to extreme multi-label classification. In: Proceedings of the 32nd International Conference on Neural Information Processing Systems (NeurIPS 2018), pp. 6358–6368. Curran Associates Inc. (2018). https://proceedings.neurips.cc/paper/2018/hash/8b8388180314a337c9aa3c5aa8e2f37a-Abstract.html

Development Kazakh-Turkish Machine Translation on the Base of Complete Set of Endings Model

Aitan Qamet$^{(\boxtimes)}$ 🆔, Kamila Zhakypbayeva🆔, Aliya Turganbayeva🆔,
and Ualsher Tukeyev🆔

Al-Farabi Kazakh National University, Almaty, Kazakhstan
qametaitan@gmail.com, ualsher.tukeyev@gmail.com

Abstract. This article discusses Kazakh-Turkish machine translation based on the model of a complete set of endings. The morphological model CSE (Complete Set of Endings) is used for Kazakh-Turkish machine translation. To collect the necessary materials and implement the algorithm, a lot of research and careful work was carried out during the study. The main ones include creation of a set of suffixes in the Kazakh and Turkish languages; morphological analysis of endings and creation of corresponding morphological tables of two languages; create an appropriate list of Kazakh and Turkish stem dictionaries; create an appropriate list of Kazakh and Turkish stop-word dictionaries; develop Kazakh-Turkish machine translation algorithm based on the CSE model; create software based on this algorithm. The main part of the study consists of fragments of the collected material, as well as the main algorithms and results. Scientific contribution of the article: machine translation technology for Kazakh-Turkish translation is developed based on the CSE model. Experiment results shoes possibility of proposed technology of machine translation for Turkic languages.

Keywords: Machine translation · Morphological model · Complete set of endings · Algorithm · Suffixes

1 Introduction

Turkish languages, consisting of more than 40 languages, are the native language of more than 180 million people are the largest language group in the group of the Altai languages. Most Turkic languages have the similar phonology and syntax [1]. Despite the development of machine translation from Kazakh into various languages, there are still cases when some translation systems return the results of poor-quality translation. In addition to Turkish, many Turkic languages are among the languages with limited resources, and this factor may lead to a limitation of the scope of application of Turkic languages in the period of modern digitalization. This problem encourages researchers to consider various methods and algorithms and increase the number of resources needed. Nowadays, when information exchange is going on at a very fast pace, it is significant to develop Kazakh-Turkish machine translation and get high-quality results from it.

© The Author(s), under exclusive license to Springer Nature Singapore Pte Ltd. 2022
E. Szczerbicki et al. (Eds.): ACIIDS 2022, CCIS 1716, pp. 543–555, 2022.
https://doi.org/10.1007/978-981-19-8234-7_42

Kazakh and Turkish languages are close to each other languages belonging to the Turkic language group, and have a lot in common in terms of grammatical characteristics. This allows us to use the same model for both Kazakh and Turkish when using different treatments. To implement Kazakh-Turkish machine translation, the morphological model CSE (Complete Set of Endings) is taken as a basis. CSE (Complete Set of Endings) is a model of a complete set of endings, and the accumulation of all the connections in tables contributes to the implementation of various treatments [2].

The purpose of this article is to create a machine translation technology based on the CSE model and demonstrate its results. The results obtained in the experiment, when evaluated by the TER metric, show 0.56 of the text consisting of 630 words.

2 Related Works

Morphological analysis is one of the main directions of computational linguistics, especially in morphologically rich languages [3]. From pre-processing steps such as cleaning the hull and segmentation of the hull after that, the first and main stage of computer analysis of the text is morphological analysis, that is, the division of words into compound morphemes. The research in this article is an example for other languages that are agglutinative, like Turkish. In Turkish, one word contains 3 to 4 morphemes, and these morphemes can contain semantic and/or syntactic content. There can be not only a superficial form, but also a polymorphic structure. The article presents a morphological analyzer and presents its components, used codes and fragments of text resources. A feature of the analyzer allows considering the roots of words separately from morphemes, and simultaneously process large corpora. Morphology analyzer consists of five main components, namely vocabulary, end-state transformer, suffix rule engine, word structure model and only recently used cache.

The bare-forms in the lexicon consists of nouns, adjectives, verbs, adverbs, shortcuts, etc. Each bare-form appears the same in the lexicon, except verbs. Since the bare-forms of the verbs in Turkish do not have the infinitive affix 'mak', the lexicon includes all verbs without the infinitive affix. For instance, verbs 'abanmak' and 'abartmak' appear as 'aban' and 'abart' respectively. Since morphological analyzer must support all types of texts, the bare-forms with diacritics are included in two forms, with and without diacritics. For example, noun 'ruzg¨ar' appear both as ^'ruzg¨ar' and 'r^uzgar'. ¨ Special markers are included as bare-forms such as, etc. Some compound words are included in their affixed form. For instance, 'acemlalesi' appears as it is, but not as 'acemlale'. Foreign words, especially proper noun foreign words, are included, so that the system can easily recognize them as proper nouns. In the article, the authors show that they used the final state transducer (FST) to perform the work of the morphological analyzer. Depending on the number of initial states, the number of possible paths FST has sought, FST can output one or more possible morphological analyses [3]. Their analyzer successfully parsed generated tests cases with 99.36% accuracy. Performance experiments show that the authors' analyzer can analyse a big corpus with 37.2 million sentences in 24 min. Compared to the other analyzers, their tool's built-in cache mechanism leverages the memory efficiently, which leads to the reduction of the analysis times.

The following review is made in the dissertation work "Models and methods of Kazakh-Turkish machine translation" [4]. The peculiarity of this work is that for the first time, a statistical translation model was used for Kazakh-Turkish machine translation. During the study, an ontological model of the morphology of the Turkish and Kazakh languages and a mathematical model of the construction of sentences in Turkish, a parallel corpus of 213 thousand pairs of Kazakh-Turkish sentences were generalized. As a result of the work done, the analysis of the differences between the Kazakh and Turkish languages was carried out, the Kazakh-Turkish statistical machine translation was carried out, the program part and the results were presented. The results of this work can be used in the future when using various automated software applications for Kazakh-Turkish machine translation, when creating information search engines.

In our work is proposed alternative way for Kazakh-Turkish machine translation based on the new morphological model based on the complete set of endings (CSE).

3 Method

3.1 The Steps for Kazakh-Turkish Machine Translation Based on the CSE Model

In this work, we present a new solution for machine translation of the Kazakh-Turkish language. Although the development of machine translation is currently at a high level, the results of translation among Turkic languages and low-resource languages are not very high. Kazakh and Turkish have many common features, as they are Turkic languages. Kazakh and Turkish belong to the group of morphology rich languages, which provides us with excellent conditions for translation using the CSE morphological model [5].

After analyzing the basic methodology of Kazakh-Turkish translation, the next step is to determine the steps of machine translation.

The steps for Kazakh-Turkish machine translation based on the CSE model are as follows:

1. Development of a Complete Set of Endings for the Kazakh and Turkish Languages Using the Morphological Model CSE.
2. Creating of Morphological analysis of Kazakh and Turkish endings based on the complete set of endings.
3. Creating of correspondence table of the Kazakh and Turkish endings.
4. Creation a Corresponding List of Kazakh and Turkish Words Stem.
5. Creation a corresponding list of Kazakh and Turkish words Stop Word.
6. Development of an Algorithm for Machine Translation into Kazakh-Turkish Based on the CSE Model
7. Creating software based on the base of the machine translation algorithm.

A detailed description of the above steps is performed below.

3.2 Creating a Complete Set of Endings for the Kazakh and Turkish Languages Using the Morphological Model CSE

The morphological model CSE based on inferring of the complete set of endings for the Kazakh language [5]. The method of constructing the morphological model of CSE can be used in Turkish. The main features of the Turkish language are the law of consonance and agglutination, as well as the Kazakh language.

There are 4 suffixes type in Turkish that are connected to nominal bases (S): Plural affixes (K); Possessive affixes (T); Case affixes (C); Personal affixes (J).

Let's look at all the possible options for placing suffixes: from one type, from two different types, three different types and four different types. The number of placements in Turkish is defined by the placement formula [5].

The placement of one type of suffix (K, T, C, J) is a semantically valid definition. The two different suffixes types have 6 semantic convenient placements (KT, TC, CJ, KC, TJ, KJ). Placements with three different suffixes types have 4 semantic acceptable placements (KTC, KTJ, TCJ, KCJ). The four different suffixes types have one acceptable placement, KTCJ. We have considered suffixes in Turkish nouns (nouns, adjectives and nouns) and verb endings (verbs, participles, adjectives, adverbs). Example of inferring of endings for placement types KT, KC, KJ, KCJ presents in the Tables 1, 2, 3 and 4.

Complete set of Turkish endings: total – 3 247.

Table 1. Inferring of endings for placement type KT (Plural-possessive)

Turish	Suffixes type K	Suffixes type T		Number
		Singular	Plural	
Examples	lar- ler-	ım, im	ımız, imiz	2 * 5 = 10
		ın, in	ınız, iniz	
		ı, i	ı, i	
araba-	-lar-	ım, ın, ı	ımız, ınız	5
anne-	-ler-	im, in,i	imiz, iniz	5

Table 2. Inferring of endings for placement type KC (Plural-case)

	Suffixes type K	Suffixes type C		Number
Examples	lar- ler-	1. Nom 2. Acc 3. Dat 4. loc 5 abl 6 gen 7 instr	– ı, i, a, e da, de dan, den ın, in la, le	2 * 6 = 12
araba	-lar-	-ı, a, da, dan, ın, la		6
ev	-ler-	-i, e, de, den, in, le		6

Table 3. Inferring of endings for placement type KJ (Plural-personal)

	Suffixes type K	Suffixes type J	Number
Examples	lar- ler-	ım, ız im, iz sın, sınız sin, siniz	2 * 4 = 8
Araba	-lar-	-ım, ız, sın, sınız	4
Annt	-ler-	-im, iz, sin, siniz	4

Table 4. Inferring of endings for placement type KCJ (Plural-case-personal)

Suffixes type K	Suffixes type C	Suffixes type J		Number
		Singular	Plural	
lar	-a -da -dan -la	J1 - ım J2 -sın J3 -	-ız - sınız –	C3:8 C4:8 C5:8 C7:8
ler	-e -de -den -le	J1 - im J2 - sin J3 -	-iz -siniz –	Total:32
çocuk-lar	-dan-		-ız	
anne-ler	-den-	-sin		

3.3 Morphological Analysis of Turkish Endings

Examples of morphological analysis of the Turkish language for placement KT, KC, KJ in the Tables 5, 6, 7 and 8.

Table 5. Morphological analysis of Turkish KT endings

Turkish KT Endings	Morph analysis
lar-ım	NB*lar \<pl> *ım \<pos> \<sg> \<p1>
lar-ın	NB*lar \<pl> *ın \<pos> \<sg> \<p2>
lar-ı	NB*lar \<pl> *ı \<pos> \<sg> \<p3>
lar-ımız	NB*lar \<pl> *ımız \<pos> \<pl> \<p1>
lar-ınız	NB*lar \<pl> *ınız \<pos> \<pl > \<p2>

Table 6. Morphological analysis of Turkish KC endings

Turkish KC Endings	Morph analysis
lar-ı	NB*lar <pl> *ı <acc>
lar-a	NB*lar <pl> *a <dat>
lar -da	NB*lar <pl> *da <loc>
lar-dan	NB*lar <pl> *dan <abl>
lar-ın	NB*lar <pl> *ın <gen>
lar-la	NB*lar <pl> *la <instr>

Table 7. Morphological analysis of Turkish KJ endings

Turkish KJ Endings	Morph analysis
lar-ım	NB*lar <pl> *ım <p1>
lar-ız	NB*lar <pl> *ız <p1>
lar-sın	NB*lar <pl> *sın <p2>
lar-sınız	NB*lar <pl> *sınız <p2>
ler-im	NB*ler <pl> *im <p1>
ler-iz	NB*ler <pl> *iz <p1>
ler-sin	NB*ler <pl> *sin <p2>
ler-siniz	NB*ler <pl> *siniz <p2>
lar	NB*lar <pl> <p3>
ler	NB*ler <pl> <p3>

Table 8. Morphological analysis of Turkish KCJ endings

Turkish KCJ Endings	Morph analysis
lar-ı-yım	NB*lar <pl> *ı <acc> *yım <per> <sg> <p1>
lar-ı-yız	NB*lar <pl> *ı <acc> *yız <per> <pl> <p1>
lar-ı-sın	NB*lar <pl> *ı <acc> *sın <per> <sg > <p2>
lar-ı-sınız	NB*lar <pl> *ı <acc> *sınız <per> <pl> <p2>
lar-a-ım	NB*lar <pl> *a <dat> *ım <per> <sg> <p1>
lar-a-ız	NB*lar <pl> *a <dat> *ız <per> <pl> <p1>
lar-a-sın	NB*lar <pl> *a <dat> *sın <per> <sg> <p2>

(continued)

Table 8. (*continued*)

Turkish KCJ Endings	Morph analysis
lar-a-sınız	NB*lar <pl> *a <dat> *sınız <per> <pl> <p2>
lar-da-ım	NB*lar <pl> *da <loc> *ım <per> <sg> <pl>
lar-da-ız	NB*lar <pl> *da <loc> *ız <per> <pl> <pl>
lar-da-sın	NB*lar < pl> *da <loc> *sın <per> <sg> <p2 >
lar-da-sınız	NB*lar <pl> *da <loc> *sınız <per> < pl > < p2 >

3.4 Matching the Morphological Tables of the Kazakh and Turkish Endings

In this section, we identified Kazakh and Turkish endings by morphological features and created a correspondence table of Kazakh-Turkish endings and their morphological analysis (Table 9).

Table 9. Correspondence table of Kazakh-Turkish endings

Kazakh Endings	Kazakh Morph	Turkish Morph	Turkish Endings
dar	<NB> *dar <pl>	<NB> *lar < pl>	lar
m	<NB> *m <pos> <sg> <pl>	<NB> *m < pos> <sg> <pl>	m
ğa	<NB> *ğa <dat>	<NB> *a < dat>	a
myn	<NB> *myn <per> <sg> <pl>	<NB> * ım <per> <sg> <pl>	im
darym	<NB> *dar < pl > *ym < pos > < sg > < pl >	<NB> *lar < pl> *ım <pos> <sg> <pl>	larım
dardyŋ	<NB> *dar < pl > *dyŋ < gen>	<NB> *lar <pl > *ın <gen >	ların
darmyz	< NB *dar < p> *myz < per> <pl > < pl >	<NB> *dar <pl > *ım <per> <sg> <pl>	darım
mnyŋ	<NB> *m < pos> nyŋ <gen>	<NB> *ın <pos> <sg> *ın <gen>	mın
damyn	<NB> *da < loc> *myn <per> <sg > < pl>	<NB> *da <loc> *yım <per> <sg > <pl>	dayım
msyŋ	<NB> *m < pos > < pl> < sg> *syŋ <per> < sg> < p2>	<NB> *m <pos> <sg> <pl > *sın <per> <sg> <p2>	msın
darymnyŋ	<NB> *dar <pl> *ym <pos> <sg > <pl> *nyŋ < gen>	<NB> *lar <pl> *ım <pos> <sg> <pl> *ın <gen>	larımın
larymsyŋ	<NB > *dar <pl> *ym <pos> <sg > <pl> *syŋ <per> <sg> <p2>	<NB> *lar <pl> *ım <pos> <sg > <pl> *sın <per> <sg> <p2>	larımsın
larğamyn	<NB> *dar <pl> *ğa <dat> *myn <per> <sg> <pl>	<NB> *lar <pl> *a <dat> *ım <per> <sg> <pl>	laraım

In this way, a complete identification of the base of connections of each language was made. A total of 5368 connections were identified by morphological features. Based on the Kazakh language, the suffixes of the Turkish language were matched.

3.5 Create a Corresponding List of Kazakh and Turkish Stems

The prepared stem words in the Kazakh language were translated into Turkish using special dictionaries and an online translation system to create a mutually compatible list of the prepared Kazakh stem database and the Turkish language stem dictionary. Segment of corresponding list of Kazakh and Turkish Stems presents in Table 10.

Table 10. Kazakh-Turkish stem word table

Kazakh stem word	Turkish stem word
mınez	davranış
jol	yol
audan	alan
adamzat	insan
jer	jer
jaz	yaz
otyr	otur
jūmys	işü
radio	radyo
basta	başlat

3.6 Create a Matching List of Kazakh and Turkish Stop Words

Kazakh-Turkish Stop Words identification is not difficult. Because during practical work, we were able to make sure that there are not many stop words in each language.

The corresponding list of stop words of the Kazakh and Turkish languages is made of 503 lines. Segment of the corresponding list of stop words of the Kazakh and Turkish languages presents in the Table 11.

Table 11. Kazakh-Turkish stop word table (segment)

Kazakh stop word	Turkish stop word
mysaly	örneğin
kez	her
men	ile
üşın	için
siaqty	türü
jäne	ve

3.7 Development of an Algorithm for Machine Translation of Kazakh-Turkish Based on the CSE Model

An algorithm for machine translation from Kazakh into Turkic languages (Tatar, Turkish, Uzbek, etc.) bases on the model of a complete set of endings.

Here is a step-by-step description of this machine translation algorithm:

The given text or sentence is considered by words (Table 12).

1. Some word is given: w_i.
2. The given word w_i is compared with a dictionary of stop words. If the word w_i is in the stop-word dictionary, then it is considered a stop-word, and the stop-word in the target language corresponding to this word is taken as the translation of the word $(w_i^{TL} = stw_i^{TL})$. If no matches are found in the stop word dictionary, step 3 is performed.
3. The given word w_i is divided to the stem (s_i) and the ending (e_i) of using the stemming algorithm with stems-lexicon according to the CSE (Complete Set of Endings) morphology model [6, 7]: $w_i^{SL} = s_i^{SL} + e_i^{SL}$.
4. In the dictionary of stems in Kazakh and Turkic (it means Turkish) languages (corresponding to each other), the corresponding translation of the stems of the source language (SL) in the target language (TL) is searched. If the dictionary contains a stem s_i^{TL} corresponding to a stem s_i^{SL}, then s_i^{TL} is taken as a translation of the given s_i^{SL}. If not, the stem itself will be provided, i.e. s_i^{SL}.
5. The corresponding translation of the ending e_i of the source language (SL) in the target language (TL) is searched for in the table of morphological correspondence of Kazakh and Turkic languages. Find rows with ending e_i^{SL} in the Endings SL column of the table. The ending e_i^{TL} in the Endings TL column is taken as a translation, corresponding to the ending e_i^{SL} from the table. If there is more than one e_i^{TL}, the e_i^{TL} corresponding to the s_i^{TL} is chosen based on the rules of the language.
6. s_i^{TL} and e_i^{TL} will be combined and presented as a translation of the given word w_i. $s_i^{TL} + e_i^{TL} = w_i^{TL}$.
7. Concatenate (w_i^{TL}), $i = 0,..n$ for current sentence.

End.

Table 12. Implementation of the algorithm based on the example

Algorithm steps	By examples, Kazakh → Turkish
w_i	täsılderı
$w_i \neq stw_i$	–
$w_i^{SL} = s_i^{SL} + e_i^{SL}$	täsıl + derı
s_i^{TL} corresponding to s_i^{SL}	täsıl → yol
e_i^{TL} corresponding to e_i^{SL}	derı → ları
$s_i^{TL} + e_i^{TL} = w_i^{TL}$	yolları

3.8   Creating Software Based on the Algorithm

The algorithm is implemented in the Python programming language. The program accepts 4 documents at the entrance. They are:

- Morphological table of Kazakh-Turkish endings ("qaz-tr-tab.xlsx");
- Dictionary of Kazakh-Turkish systems ("qaz- tr -stems.xlsx");
- Kazakh-Turkish stop words ("qaz- tr -stopwords.xlsx");
- Text in the Kazakh language ("text-qaz.txt").

The result is a Turkish translation of the original Kazakh text or sentence.

4   Experiments and Results

In this paper, we have proposed a new way of Kazakh-Turkish machine translation using the morphological model CSE. The main advantage of the CSE model is the method of creating tables, which is usefully for linguists and propose to use for processing universal programs for different languages.

Due to the time constraints of scientific and technical work, a small translation model with 500 stems was created. The translation results are shown in the table below. Obviously, the higher the stem vocabulary, the higher the translation result.

In testing the operation of the machine translation algorithm based on the model of a complete set of Kazakh and Turkish endings, a case consisting of 45 parallel sentences in the Kazakh and Turkish languages was used.

Results for the Kazakh-Turkish language pair presents in the Table 13.

The metrics TER (Translation Error Rate), WER (Word Error Rate) and BLEU.

(Bilingual Evaluation Understudy) were used to evaluate the results of the machine. Translation.

The TER metric proposed by Snover in 2006 [8]. TER is defined as the minimum number of edits needed to change a hypothesis so that it exactly matches one of the references. The possible edits in TER include insertion, deletion, and substitution of single words, and an edit, which moves sequences of contiguous words.

WER allows measuring the distance between a machine translation and an exemplary translation in the same way as we measure the distance between a dictionary word and a word with a typo (counting whole words as characters, not letters). In fact, WER measures the minimum number of changes that need to be made to get a reference translation from the result of the MT's work [9, 10]. At the same time, WER can consider different variants of the reference translation with different word order.

The BLEU metric is currently the most popular in the modern assessment of MT. The BLEU metric allows considering not only the accuracy of the translation of individual words, but also chains of words (N-grams).

Table 13. Example of Kazakh-Turkish MT segment

Source text in Kazakh	Translated text by the our program	Correct translation of text
radiotehnika qazırgı kezde adamzat ömırınıŋ barlyq salasynda qoldanady mysaly, kez kelgen qaşyqtyqta radiotelefon bailanysyn ornatu, keskın, chertej, suret, gazet matrıcalaryn taratu, tez ärekettı telegraftyq radiobailanys jasau kosmos objektıları men jer, kosmos apparattarynyŋ öz arasynda tıkelei bailanys ornatylady alys qaşyqtyqtağy punkttermen radio, televizialyq bailanys jasau üşın paidalanatyn jerdıŋ jasandy serıkterı retranslacialyq stancia retınde bailanys liniasynyŋ qūramyna enıp otyr radiotehnika täsılderı avtomatty basqaru, rettelu jäne informaciany öŋdeu jüıelerınıŋ negızın qūraidy osyğan orai radiotehnika jetıstıkterı elektrondy esepteuış maşinalardy jetıldıruge mümkındık berdı mysaly, alğaşqy elektrondyq şamdarmen jūmys ıstese, odan keiıngı kezde maşinalar jartylai ötkızgıştı elementtermen, al soŋğy kezdegı maşinalar jartylai ötkızgıştı integralshema negızınde jūmys ısteitın boldy …	radioteknoloji şimdiki zamande insan hayatının hepsi alanında kullanacaklar örneğin, zaman gelenler mesafeda telsiztelefon iletişimı kurulum, görüntü, çizim, resim, gazete matrıslarıda dağıtım, hızlı oyunculuki telgraf radyoiletişim yapmak uzay nesneleri ile dünya, uzay araçlarıya kendi arasında doğrudan bir iletişim kurulacak uzun mesafeli noktalerle radyo, telekomünikasyon iletişim yapmak için kullanılanlar dünyain yapay uyduleri yenideniletim istasyon gibi iletişim hattının parçaıya nüfuzeta otur radioteknoloji teknikleri otomatik kontrol, düzenleme ve bilgiyi işleme sistemleriye temelini oluşturacaklar bu bağlamda radioteknoloji başarıleri elektronik sayaç makineları geliştirilmee izin veri örneğin, ilk elektronik lambalarla iş yapsa, ondan birsonraki zamande makinelar yarı iletken elemanlerle, son zamandaki makinelar yarı iletken entegredevre temelide iş yapenler oldu …	radyo teknolojisi şimdiki zamanda insan hayatının hepsi alanında kullanılmaktadır örneğin, herhangi bir mesafede telsiz telefon iletişiminin kurulması, görüntüler, çizimler, resimler, gazete matrislerinin dağıtımı, yüksek hızlı telgraf radyo iletişim yapmak uzay nesneleri ile dünya, uzay aracı kendi arasında doğrudan bir iletişim kurulacak uzun mesafeli noktalarla radyo, televizyon iletişim yapmak için kullanılan dünya'nın yapay uyduları yeniden iletim istasyonu gibi iletişim hattının parçaıya nüfuz ediyor radyo teknoloji teknikleri otomatik kontrol, düzenleme ve bilgiyi işleme sistemlerinin temelini oluşturur bu bağlamda, radyo teknoloji başarıları elektronik sayaç makinelerın geliştirilmesine izin verdi örneğin, ilk elektronik lambalarla iş yapsa, ondan bir sonraki zamanda makineler yarı iletken elemanlarla, son zamandaki makineler yarı iletken entegre devre temelinde iş yapmayı oldu …

A TER score is a value in the range of 0–1, but is frequently presented as a percentage, where lower is better. A high TER and WER score suggests that a translation will require more post-editing.

The results of experiments on WER, TER and BLEU metrics are presented in Table 14.

Table 14. Results of experiments

Language pair MT	TER	WER	BLEU
Kazakh-Turkish	0.56	0.56	20%

Although the results of a formal assessment of machine translation using the proposed technology show a high percentage of errors, the translation itself in meaning turned out to be very close to the translation template. This shows that the use of the proposed technology is possible. Moreover, the proposed machine translation technology does not need large volumes of parallel corpora for training.

5 Conclusion

Based on the CSE model of this research paper, a new way of machine translation of the Kazakh-Turkish language was made. The article describes the process of performing the steps necessary for the implementation of machine translation of the Kazakh-Turkish language based on the CSE model, provides fragments and examples of accumulated language resources. To implement machine translation, the necessary algorithm was created, its steps and formulas used are given. The algorithm is implemented in the Python programming language and the results are presented.

Scientific contribution of the article: a new machine translation technology created based on the CSE morphology model. This MT technology for agglutinative languages is not required big volume of parallel corpus for learning as neural machine translation. Further work: improve of quality of proposed machine translation technology, the creation of speech-to-speech technology based on the cascade model. To achieve this, we need to build a speech-to-text (STT) model, apply the technology developed in this article to the text-to-text (TTT) phase and build a text-to-speech (TTS) model.

References

1. Gutman, A., Avanzati, B.: The Languges Gulper. Turkish Languages [Electronic resource] (2013). http://www.languagesgulper.com/eng/Home.html
2. Tukeyev, U., Karibayeva, A., Zhumanov, Z.H.: Morphological segmentation method for turkic language neural machine translation. Cogent Eng. **7**(1), 1856500 (2020). https://doi.org/10.1080/23311916.2020.1856500
3. Yıldız, O.T., Avar, B., Ercan, G.: An open, extendible, and fast turkish morphological analyzer, ACL anthology. In: Proceedings of the International Conference on Recent Advances in Natural Language Processing (RANLP 2019), September, 2019, Varna, Bulgaria, INCOMA Ltd., pp. 1364–1372 (2019)
4. Zhetkenbay L.: Models and methods for the Kazakh-Turkish machine translation, PhD Dissertation (2021)

5. Tukeyev, U., Karibayeva, A.: Inferring the complete set of Kazakh endings as a language resource. In: Hernes, M., Wojtkiewicz, K., Szczerbicki, E. (eds.) ICCCI 2020. CCIS, vol. 1287, pp. 741–751. Springer, Cham (2020). https://doi.org/10.1007/978-3-030-63119-2_60
6. Tukeyev, U., Karibayeva, A., Turganbayeva, A., Amirova, D.: Universal programs for stemming, segmentation, morphological analysis of Turkic words. In: Nguyen, N.T., Iliadis, L., Maglogiannis, I., Trawiński, B. (eds.) ICCCI 2021. LNCS (LNAI), vol. 12876, pp. 643–654. Springer, Cham (2021). https://doi.org/10.1007/978-3-030-88081-1_48
7. NLP-KAZNU: https://github.com/NLP-KazNU/Stemming_algorithm_with_stems-lex icon_according_to_the_CSE_morphology_model
8. Snover, M., Dorr, B., Schwartz, R., Micciulla L., Makhoul, J.: A study of translation edit rate with targeted human annotation. In: Proceedings of the 7th Conference of the Association for Machine Translation of the Americas (AMTA 2006). Visions for the Future of Machine Translation, Cambridge, Massachusetts, USA, pp. 223–231 (2006)
9. Koehn, P.: Statistical Machine Translation. Cambridge, UK (2010)
10. Jurafsry, D., Martin, J.H.: Speech and Language Processing: Introduction to Natural Language Processing, Computational Linguistics and Speech Recognition. 2-ed (2008)

Gated 3D-CNN for Action Recognition

Labina Shrestha[1], Shikha Dubey[1], Farrukh Olimov[2], and Moongu Jeon[1(✉)]

[1] Gwangju Institute of Science and Technology, Gwangju, South Korea
{labinashr,shikha.d}@gm.gist.ac.kr, mgjeon@gist.ac.kr
[2] Threat Intelligence Team, Monitorapp, Seoul, South Korea
olimov.farrukh@gm.gist.ac.kr

Abstract. Human action recognition is an active field in computer vision tasks. It is mostly based on the extensively developed image recognition algorithm using convolutional neural networks(CNNs) or recurrent neural networks (RNNs). Action recognition is considered as a more challenging task than image recognition as a video consists of an image sequence that changes in every frame, and the model has to deal with both spatial and temporal information simultaneously. Recently proposed methods using the two-stream fusion technique show good performance in such tasks. However, these methods are computationally expensive and are complex to build for learning spatio-temporal dependencies of the action. This paper proposes a simple yet efficient deep neural network architecture, Gated 3D-CNN, consisting of 3D convolutional layers and gating modules to act as an LSTM model for learning spatial and temporal dependencies and give attention to essential features. The proposed method first learns spatial and temporal features of actions through 3D-CNN. Then, the sigmoid gated 3D convolution layers of local and global gating help to locate attention to the essential features of the action. The proposed architecture is comparatively simpler to implement and gives a competitive performance on the UFC-101 dataset.

Keywords: 3D-CNN · Attention mechanism · Action recognition · Gated 3D-CNN

1 Introduction

Action recognition has become a prevalent topic within the computer vision field in the last few years. Human action recognition is undoubtedly vital in computer vision applications, such as visual surveillance [21], behavior monitoring [12], human-robot interaction, human-computer interaction, and video understanding [4]. Action recognition architectures have achieved much good progress in recent years. However, many of these architectures are built on expensive and complex 3D spatiotemporal convolutions. For an architecture to perform well on videos, unlike image recognition, the action recognition method have to deal simultaneously with spatial and temporal data simultaneously. Recent action recognition methods mainly use options like 2D and 3DCNN for processing a video volume with a convolutional kernel.

© The Author(s), under exclusive license to Springer Nature Singapore Pte Ltd. 2022
E. Szczerbicki et al. (Eds.): ACIIDS 2022, CCIS 1716, pp. 556–565, 2022.
https://doi.org/10.1007/978-981-19-8234-7_43

Starting from CNN + LSTM [1], 2D CNNs have been used as two-stream ConvNets, assigning 2D CNN to learn spatial features and LSTM to learn temporal features. Two-Stream Convolutional Networks in [2] extract spatial and temporal features from RGB and stacked optical flow sequences. The most recent trend for action recognition is sifting to 3D CNNs, such as Inflated 3-dimensional convolutional network [3] and 3D Residual Network (3D ResNet) [5]. The 3D CNNs directly compute video volumes with spatiotemporal xyt kernels. These representative methods learn spatiotemporal features separately or in different stages. Learning spatiotemporal features simultaneously from videos will be more effective for video action recognition. However, in the previously proposed methods, they included an optical flow stream or LSTM to improve the performance. The previously proposed methods were expensive and complex to build as they needed extra streams or parameters to increase the performance.

In this paper, a simple yet efficient action recognition method is proposed based on 3-D convolution and sigmoid gated attention mechanism behaving like LSTM layer which helps to locate and give attention to essential features for spatial and temporal feature extraction. First, 3-D CNN extracts short-term spatiotemporal features from the input video. Later, convolutional layers followed by sigmoid activation are multiplied element-wise with the previous convolutional layer, which forms local and global gating. These gatings give attention to essential features for recognition and learning spatio-temporal dependencies.

The main contribution of the paper can be summarized as follows:

1. Simple deep neural architecture based on 3-D convolution and sigmoid gated attention mechanism proposed for action recognition.
2. Works efficiently without using any fine-tuning, transfer learning, and ensemble method.

The details of the paper are organized as follows: Sect. 2 reviews the related work of action recognition. Section 3 gives the details of the proposed method. Section 4 presents the experiments and implementation details. Section 5 presents the evaluation, and Sect. 6 gives the conclusion and future works.

2   Related Works

In this section, the related work of action recognition is reviewed. In the field of action recognition currently, there are primarily three fundamental approaches to extract spatiotemporal information: 2D CNNs, which includes two-stream ConvNets [6]; Temporal Segment Networks [7], and 3D CNNs, which includes C3D [22], I3D [3], 3D ResNets [5]; Slow-fast Network [14] and (2+1)D CNN which includes P3D [13], R(2+1)D [11].

2.1   Two-Stream Networks

There are various approaches using 2D CNNs to extract spatio-temporal information from the video [6–10]. Two-stream ConvNet [6] proposed an architecture based on two separate spatial and temporal recognition streams combined with late fusion. The method first decomposes video into spatial and temporal components using RGB and dense optical flow frames. These components are fed into separate deep ConvNet architectures to learn information about the appearance and movement of the object in a scene. Similarly, further experiments about how and where to fuse two separate domains, spatial and temporal, are performed for achieving an efficient model [7]. Temporal Segment Network(TSN) divides video frames into segments and extracts information from RGB and optical flow modalities for action recognition. LCRN [1] extracts feature from video frames using a 2DCNN and apply global temporal modeling using the LSTM layer.

2.2 3D CNN Networks

3D ConvNets is generally a natural and standard method for video action recognition as 3D CNN can learn spatial and temporal information simultaneously without any additional temporal stream. However, one issue of these models is that they have more parameters than 2D ConvNets because of additional temporal kernel dimensions, making them complex to train. Additionally, this prevents getting benefits from ImageNet pre-trained module. For the solution to this problem, I3D [3] was introduced. I3D adopts a two-stream configuration using 3D ConvNets along with the optical flow. While 3D ConvNets can directly learn about temporal patterns from the RGB stream, this paper states that their performance can still be significantly improved by including an optical-flow stream. Past 3D CNN models were relatively shallow, as mentioned in [5] ResNet model stating that kinetics-400 can be used for training very deep CNNs like Spatio-temporal 3D kernels. However, these methods were computationally heavy to train as they simultaneously require extra streams to extract spatial and temporal features.

2.3 (2+1)D CNN Networks

These methods show that factorizing the 3D convolutional filters into separate spatial and temporal components yields significant gains in accuracy. In the paper [13], $3 \times 3 \times 3$ convolutions are designed as $1 \times 3 \times 3$ convolutional filters on the spatial domain, equivalent to 2D CNN and $3 \times 1 \times 1$ convolutions to construct temporal connections on an adjacent feature. Similarly, bottleneck building blocks are built, which form a Pseudo-3D Residual Net. There were three different block implementations: spatial followed by temporal, spatial, and temporal in parallel, and spatial followed by temporal with skip connection from spatial convolution to the output of the block, respectively. This method utilizes 2D spatial convolution plus 1D temporal convolution, which helps perform significantly better than C3D, directly using 3D Spatio-temporal convolutions. Similarly, R(2+1)D [11], similar to P3D [13], uses a single type of spatiotemporal residual block homogeneously in all layers, but it does not include a bottleneck. Both of the methods show pretty good performance. However, while building a model, it needs to separate 3D convolutional filters into separate spatial and temporal components and divide bottleneck building blocks into three different blocks, making it complex to build.

2.4 Attention Mechanism

When humans view an action, they do not see the entire motion simultaneously, but they scan the global image to obtain the target region that needs to be focused. They give more attention to that region, giving more details of the desired target and suppressing the impact of other ineffective information on the current target. As inspired by the human visual attention mechanism, Xu et al. [15] introduced a soft attention mechanism for image captioning. This soft attention mechanism was then applied to video analysis tasks as well. Sharma et al. [16] proposed a soft attention LSTM model based on multi-layer recurrent neural networks. To improve the ability of the model to identify action in the video, it selectively focuses on some of the video frames in the video sequence. Yan et al. [17], Wang et al. [18] proposed a Hierarchical Attention Network. Authors [17] use the gradient estimation method for stochastic neurons to implement temporal boundary detectors and the stochastic hard attention mechanism. Whereas [18] combines the hidden state of the RGB modality LSTM with the hidden state of the optical flow modality LSTM as an input to the hierarchical attention mechanism. Yu et al. [19] proposed a joint spatial-temporal attention model. Inspired by ResNet, as the spatial model, they built a spatial convolution(2D) branch to obtain spatial attention guidance. Then, considering the temporal coherence in the short video clip, an extra-temporal convolution (1D) branch is constructed. The two branches are integrated into a spatial-temporal unit, and the softmax function obtains a spatial attention gate. At last, a two-level global attention branch is applied to get a better spatial attention guide. They use a bidirectional LSTM to build a temporal attention model. Then use the sigmoid and softmax functions to convert the hidden state of the bidirectional LSTM into a temporal attention score. However, these attention models are highly integrated with recurrent neural networks. The computational process is complicated, which brings the expensive computational cost to the training process of the network. To avoid the heavy computational burden, we proposed a simple yet efficient 3D ConvNets based on a sigmoid gated attention mechanism for the spatial-temporal information of the video action recognition.

3   Proposed Method

We propose a Gated 3D-CNN for video action recognition illustrated in Fig. 1. The architecture consists of 3D-CNN layers forming Local-Gate, Global-Gate, and Dense Neural Network layers for final prediction.

We begin by formalizing the operations performed by the network. At first, we split each video clip into 16 frames as input for 3D-CNN. As 3D-CNN uses a 5D tensor (batch size, channel, height, width, depth) as input, we have changed the number of frames accordingly. As shown in Fig. 1, the 3D-CNN of channel

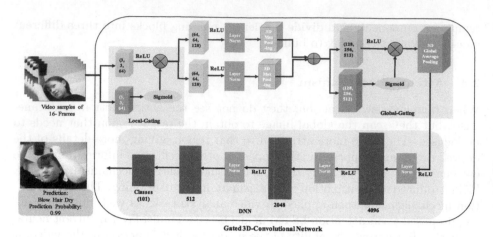

Fig. 1. The proposed architecture for video action recognition.

64, followed by the ReLU activation function, extracts spatial and temporal features from input frames. Simultaneously, the same input images are passed through the 3D-CNN of channel 64, followed by a sigmoid activation function. These extracted features from the output of respective layers are element-wise multiplied, forming a local gate.

The sigmoid activation function in our method is used to locate the essential features of the action. It gives the probability in the interval of [0 to 1]; it can be used for the models where we have to predict the probability as output between this range. With a sigmoid activation, our output is a single number between 0 and 1 which can be interpreted as the probability. Outputs with probability close to 0 can be predicted as less essential features, and those with output close to 1 can be predicted as essential features. We form a local gate by element-wise multiplication of output from ReLU activation function and sigmoid activation function, where the features with the highest probability will have high attention. The attention layer consists of output from the sigmoid activation function, which gives probability close to 1 for essential features, helping the model locate focus on more essential features for recognizing the action. The below equation explain the operations performed in a gated layer.

$$G = Sigmoid(F(I)) \otimes (F(I)) \tag{1}$$

where F stands for features extracted from an image I using 3D convolutional layer and G represents gated convolutional features.

The output obtained after element-wise multiplications are then used as input for the subsequent 3D-CNN layers, followed by ReLU, layer normalization, and 3D max pooling. These two 3D-CNN layers are then concatenated in dimension one to provide the same input for the following 3D-CNN layers. The extracted features are used again as input for the 3D-CNN layer with RelU activation function and 3D-CNN with sigmoid activation function layer separately. The extracted features from these layers are again element-wise multiplied with the output of the sigmoid activation layer to get essential features forming a gated layer. After the gated layer, a 3D global average pooling was utilized to give a single average value for each input channel forming a global-gate layer.

$$GA = \sum(Sigmoid(f(i)) \otimes f(i)) \tag{2}$$

Global attention (GA) can be achieved using the above equation. Where f stands for feature extraction using 3D convolution layer followed by layer normalization and max-pooling, and i stands for all the features extracted from previous layers. These extracted features are then passed through DNN layers, followed by ReLU activation and layer normalization. The dropout rate of 0.25 is used in between each DNN layer. At last, we have used the softmax layer, which predicts the action for the given video samples.

4 Experiments

In this section, we first introduce the dataset, followed by implementation details of our approach.

4.1 Dataset

We have used the UCF101 [20] dataset to train our model. UCF101 comprises realistic videos collected from YouTube. UCF gives the largest diversity in terms of actions and with the presence of significant variations in camera motion, object appearance and pose, object scale, viewpoint, cluttered background, illumination conditions, etc. It contains 101 action categories, with 13320 videos in total, and is grouped into 25 groups, where each group can consist of 4–7 videos of an action. These datasets were split into 8460 training, 2156 validation sets, and 2701 test sets.

4.2 Implementation Details

The model is built by using PyTorch 1.8 on a machine with NVidia GeForce RTX 2080 and RAM 8 GB. The model was trained for 100 epochs with an initial learning rate of 1e −4 and weight decay with the rate of 1e −4 after 4 steps followed by Adam optimizer.

As 3D-CNN takes input in 5D tensor along with height and width, we also feed the depth size. We split each video data into 16 frames. Then we have used spatially and temporally random cropping by resizing the video frame size to 128 × 1 71 pixels. We perform random horizontal flipping, random resize cropping

Table 1. Comparison of our proposed model with other models on UCF-101 test and val dataset

Method	Backbone	# of parameters(M)	Accuracy(%)
TSN [1]	CNN+LSTM	21.4	68.2
C3D [22]	VGG16-like	78.4	52.8
I3D [3]	ResNet50-like	33.2	69.5
Slow-Fast50 [14]	ResNet50	33.7	85.0
R(2+1)D [11]	ResNet50	33.2	88.0
Multiple gated layers with layer normalization and global average pooling(ours)	C3D-like	49.7	88.0

112×112 patch and random affine for data augmentation. For temporal cropping and temporal jittering, we have randomly selected the time index. The spatial crop is performed on the entire frame, so each frame is cropped on the exact location. The temporal jitter takes place via the selection of consecutive frames.

5 Evaluation

We have evaluated the model using a softmax classifier for the classes of UCF-101. The proposed deep architecture is designed from scratch. So, no additional mechanisms like pre-trained models on other datasets, fine-tuning, ensemble networks are used in our training. We have evaluated the test/validation datasets of UCF-101. Table 1 shows the comparison results with the previously published methods on the UCF-101 dataset. It shows that our proposed model, 3D-CNN with Sigmoid gating mechanism, outperforms 3D-CNN and other mentioned models. Figure 2 shows a qualitative analysis of our proposed model on the UCF-101 dataset. Figure 3 shows the comparison between the baseline model (C3D) and our model using the accuracy and loss graph for each epoch on a

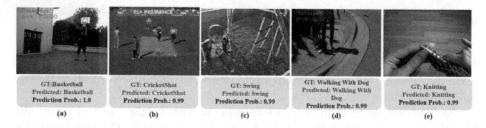

GT:Basketball Predicted: Basketball Prediction Prob.: 1.0 (a)

GT: CricketShot Predicted: CricketShot Prediction Prob.: 0.99 (b)

GT: Swing Predicted: Swing Prediction Prob.: 0.99 (c)

GT: Walking With Dog Predicted: Walking With Dog Prediction Prob.: 0.99 (d)

GT: Knitting Predicted: Knitting Prediction Prob.: 0.99 (e)

Fig. 2. Qualitative analysis of the proposed method on the UCF-101 dataset. In (a)-(e), the model predicts all the actions correctly with a higher probability. GT stands for ground truth.

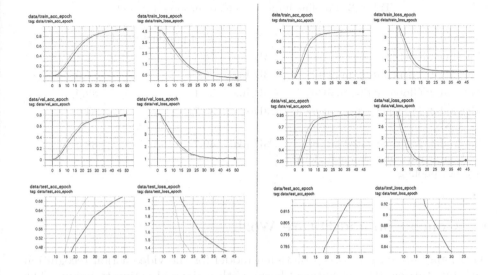

Fig. 3. Graphical comparison of accuracy and loss for each epoch in between 3D-CNN (Column 1) and 3D-CNN+Sigmoid-gated(Ours) (Column 2) models. The first, second, and third-row graphs are for train, validation, and test datasets, respectively.

train, validation, and test datasets. Table 2 consists of a baseline improvement of the proposed 3D-CNN gated method. We have used C3D as a baseline model.

To further improve our proposed idea, we have performed additional experiments by changing the layer size and the position of the Sigmoid gated layer. At first, Method-1: we have used two 3D-CNN layers where the first CNN layer uses a ReLU activation and the second CNN layer uses a Sigmoid activation function. Output from both layers is then element-wise multiplied to pay attention to essential features. Using two layers of 3D-CNN performs better than the baseline model. However, the model is computationally heavy as it uses four layers of dense neural networks. To further improve the performance, we have increased the size of 3D-CNN to four layers, Method-2: where sigmoid activation is included after the third convolutional layer and element-wise multiplication was performed between the third layer of 3D-CNN and sigmoid activation. We gain accuracy by 1%, whereas the number of parameters is reduced drastically. We further improved our model by adding six layers of the 3D-CNN layer, Method-3: where sigmoid activation is added after the first and fifth layers. Finally, we propose Method-4: where sigmoid activation is applied after the first and fifth layer from the final layer of 3D-CNN. It is passed through 3D global average pooling followed by layer normalization. Eventually, we have obtained our best result in Method-4.

Table 2. Baseline improvement of proposed model

Method	Backbone	# of parameters(M)	Accuracy(%)
Baseline Model [22]	C3D	78.4	52.8
Method-1: Local gating in 3D-CNN	C3D-like	209.3	81.0
Method-2: Global gating in 3D-CNN	C3D-like	38.1	82.0
Method-3: Multiple gated Layers in 3D-CNN	C3D-like	33.7	84.6
Method-4: Multiple gated layers with layer normalization and global average pooling	C3D-like	49.7	88.0

6   Conclusion and Future Work

This paper presents a 3D convolutional model for the video action recognition task by utilizing 3D convolutional layers with a sigmoid gating technique. The proposed architecture outperforms the other methods on the UCF-101 dataset without any additional modules like fusion streams, optical flow, or recurrent networks. Our proposed architecture is simple to implement and shows competitive performance compared to other recently proposed complex models without fine-tuning it with large-scale datasets. For future work, we will include transfer learning by training the model with large-scale datasets such as the Sports-1M datasets or Kinetic datasets in order to enhance the model's performance. Moreover, our future work will include studying various attention modules on the current proposed model.

Acknowledgment. This work was supported by the Ministry of Culture, Sports, and Tourism (MCST) and Korea Creative Content Agency(KOCCA) in the culture Technology (CT) Research Development Program (R20200600020) 2021.

References

1. Donahue, J., et al.: Long-term recurrent convolutional networks for visual recognition and description. IEEE Trans. Pattern Anal. Mach. Intel. (TPAMI) **39**(4), 677–691 (2017)
2. Simonyan, K., Zisserman, A.: Two-stream convolutional networks for action recognition in videos. In: Advances in Neural Information Processing Systems (NIPS), pp. 568–576 (2014)
3. Carreira, A., Zisserman, A.: Quo vadis, action recognition? a new model and the kinetics dataset. In: IEEE International Conference on Computer Vision and Pattern Recognition (CVPR), pp. 6299–6308 (2017)
4. Olimov, F., Dubey, S., Shrestha, L., Tin, T.T., Jeon, M.: Image captioning using multiple transformers for self-attention mechanism. Korea Software Congress, pp. 349–351 (2020)

5. Hara, K., Kataoka, H., Satoh, Y.: Can spatiotemporal 3D CNNs retrace the history of 2D CNNs and ImageNet?. In: IEEE International Conference on Computer Vision and Pattern Recognition (CVPR), pp. 6546–6555 (2018)
6. Simonyan, K., Zisserman, A.: Two-stream convolutional networks for action recognition in videos. In: Advances in Neural Information Processing Systems (NIPS) (2014)
7. Yorozu, Y., Hirano, M., Oka, K., Tagawa, Y.: Electron spectroscopy studies on magneto-optical media and plastic substrate interface. IEEE Transl. J. Magn. Japan 2, 740–741 (1987). [Digests 9th Annual Conference on Magnetics Japan, p. 301, 1982]
8. Feichtenhofer, C., Pinz, A., Zisserman, A.: Convolutional two-stream network fusion for video action recognition. In: IEEE Conference on Computer Vision and Pattern Recognition (CVPR) (2016)
9. Ji, S., Xu, W., Yang, M., Yu, K.: 3D convolutional neural networks for human action recognition. IEEE Trans. Pattern Anal. Mach. Intel. (TPAMI) 35(1), 221–231 (2013)
10. Karpathy, A., Toderici, G., Shetty, S., Leung, T., Sukthankar, R., Fei-Fei, L.: Large-scale video classification with convolutional neural networks. In: IEEE Conference on Computer Vision and Pattern Recognition (CVPR) (2014)
11. Tran, D., Wang, H., Torresani, L., Ray, J., LeCun, Y., Paluri, M.: A closer look at spatiotemporal convolutions for action recognition. In: IEEE International Conference on Computer Vision and Pattern Recognition (CVPR), pp. 6450–6459 (2018)
12. Dubey, S., Boragule, A., Jeon, M.: 3D ResNet with ranking loss function for abnormal activity detection in videos. In: IEEE International Conference on Control, Automation and Information Sciences (ICCAIS), pp. 1–6 (2019)
13. Qiu, Z., Yao, T., Mei, T.: Learning spatio-temporal representation with pseudo-3D residual networks. In: International Conference on Computer Vision (ICCV), pp. 5533–5541 (2017)
14. Feichtenhofer, C., et al.: SlowFast networks for video recognition. In: 2019 IEEE/CVF International Conference on Computer Vision (ICCV) (2019)
15. Xu, K., et al.: Show, attend and tell: neural image caption generation with visual attention. Comput. Sci. 2015, 2048–2057 (2015)
16. Sharma, S., Kiros, R., Salakhutdinov, R.: Action recognition using visual attentio. arXiv:1511.04119 (2015)
17. Yan, S., Smith, J.S., Lu, W., Zhang, B.: Hierarchical multi-scale attention networks for action recognition. Signal Process. Image Commun. 61, 73–84 (2018)
18. Wang, Y., Wang, S., Tang, J., O'Hare, N., Chang, Y., Li, B.: Hierarchical attention network for action recognition in videos. arXiv:1607.06416 (2016)
19. Yu, T., Guo, C., Wang, L., Gu, H., Xiang, S., Pan, C.: Joint spatial-temporal attention for action recognition. Pattern Recognit. Lett. 112, 226–233 (2018)
20. Soomro, K., Zamir A. R., Shah, M.: UCF101: a dataset of 101 human action classes from videos in the wild. CRCV-TR- 12–01 November 2012
21. Dubey, S., Boragule, A., Gwak, J., Jeon, M.: Anomalous Event Recognition in Videos Based on Joint Learning of Motion and Appearance with Multiple Ranking Measures. Appl. Sci. 11(3), 1344 (2021)
22. Tran, D., Bourdev, L., Fergus, R., Torresani, L., Paluri, M.: Learning spatiotemporal features with 3D convolutional networks. In: 2015 IEEE International Conference on Computer Vision (ICCV), pp. 4489–4497. IEEE (2015)

A Minimal Model of Cancer Growth, Metastasis and Treatment

Jaroslaw Smieja[1]($\boxtimes$) (iD), Andrzej Swierniak[1] (iD), and Marek Kimmel[2] (iD)

[1] Silesian University of Technology, Akademicka 16, 44-100 Gliwice, Poland
jaroslaw.smieja@polsl.pl
[2] Departments of Statistics and Bioengineering, Rice University, Houston, TX, USA

Abstract. The paper is concerned with modeling cancer growth, metastasis and response to anticancer treatment in a heterogeneous population of patients. Following a discussion of existing models, multicompartmental models are compared using Kaplan-Meier survival curves. Subsequently, different death conditions are analyzed, leading to the final conclusion that a simple, two-compartmental model describes primary and metastatic tumors well enough but death condition must fine-tuned to available clinical survival curves.

Keywords: Metastasis · Modeling of cancer growth · Kaplan-Meyer survival curves

1 Introduction

Lung cancer is one of the most commonly diagnosed cancer and is the leading cause of cancer-related deaths [1]. The most common histological subtype is non-small-cell lung carcinoma (NSCLC), accounting for 85% of all lung cancer cases [2]. Advanced NSCLC is more likely to metastasize, leading to severe symptoms and a decrease in overall survival. The presence of distant metastases is one of the most predictive factors of poor prognosis [3]. Mathematical models of cancer growth and treatment that take into account metastasis could therefore provide invaluable insight into at what time metastasis occurs in an individual patient and what is the treatment outcome prognosis for a specified treatment protocol. Thus, these models would facilitate identification of target groups for screening, determination of screening interval and risk-stratification [4, 5, 6] as well as choosing the most promising treatment modes [6]. This is needed, if precision oncology is to enter daily clinical practice.

Mathematical models have been used to analyze cancer growth and treatment outcome for quite a long time (see, e.g., [8, 9] and references therein). Three main approaches may be distinguished: ordinary differential equations (describing growth of tumor mass or cancer cell population in time), partial differential equations (taking into account spatial aspects of tumor growth or distributed parameters) or agent-based modeling (to take into account heterogeneity of cancer cell population and varying responses to treatment, stemming from it). Since this work is focused on the simplest model, paving the way for

© The Author(s), under exclusive license to Springer Nature Singapore Pte Ltd. 2022
E. Szczerbicki et al. (Eds.): ACIIDS 2022, CCIS 1716, pp. 566–577, 2022.
https://doi.org/10.1007/978-981-19-8234-7_44

future analytical approach to investigation of its properties, it employs the first family of models.

One of the most difficult tasks in modeling cancer treatment is model verification. Clinical data is usually available for a few time points only, which makes it impossible to estimate properly model parameter values. Identifying biomarkers that not only indicate patient state but whose measurement can be calibrated with tumor size (or size of population of cancer cells) would facilitate parametrization of model for individual patients. However, this is still not possible even for such well-known markers as PSA in a prostate cancer. Therefore, at the moment models should be kept as simple as possible and their quality should be checked against data which is the most prevalent in clinical practice, i.e. Kaplan-Meier survival curves [10], that provide information about treatment outcome prognosis.

The aim of this paper is to propose such model. It should satisfy partly contradictory requirements. On the one hand, it should contain the minimum number of compartments and parameters. On the other hand, it should allow to represent heterogeneous response to treatment in a population of patients and provide a good fit to clinical survival curves.

2   Modeling Metastasis – A Brief Literature Review

Initially, the tumor grows in a primary site and its cells do not have the ability to metastasize. They are usually assumed to be sensitive to chemo- and radiotherapy. After the primary tumor reaches certain size, the cells can spread to other organs, leading to appearance of a new cancer cell population in distant sites. The simplest case, which assumes only a single metastatic site, the system can be described by a two-compartmental model, with N_0 and N_1 compartments representing primary and metastatic tumor, respectively (Fig. 1). As it is assumed that radiotherapy $d(t)$ is administered locally, it does not affect the distant tumor. Chemotherapy, denoted by $v(t)$, may affect both primary and metastatic tumors. Gaining metastatic potential requires a series of mutations, which may also increase cells growth potential or their resistance to chemotherapeutic agents. Therefore, the chemotherapy is assumed to be less effective against the metastatic tumor, than against the primary one.

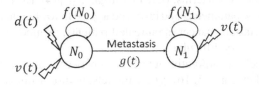

Fig. 1. The simplest, 2-compartmental model

It has been shown, however, that the number of such sites may range from one to several to more than twenty [11]. Such phenomenon was hypothesized before, and, to take that into account, a distributed-parameter model (without therapy) was developed in [12]. The primary tumor, whose size was denoted by $x_p(t)$, was assumed to grow according to the Gompertzian growth rate, i.e.

$$\frac{dx_p(t)}{dt} = g\big(x_p(t)\big), \tag{1}$$

where

$$g(x) = ax \log \frac{b}{x}. \tag{2}$$

The primary tumor has ability to metastasize into multiple distant sites. The colony size distribution of metastatic tumors with cell number x at time t, denoted by $\rho(x, t)$, is given by.

$$\frac{\partial \rho(x, t)}{\partial t} + \frac{\partial g(x)\rho(x, t)}{\partial x} = 0, \tag{3}$$

with the initial and boundary conditions.

$$\rho(x, 0) = 0, \tag{4}$$

$$g(1)\rho(1, t) = \int_1^\infty \beta(x)\rho(x, t)dx + \beta\big(x_p(t)\big), \tag{5}$$

where $\beta(x)$ represents the colonization rate

$$\beta(x) = mx^\alpha. \tag{6}$$

This model may be interpreted as allowing for infinite number of metastatic sites. Though neither this, nor direct interpretation of a continuous value of the number of metastatic sites model is biologically relevant at the first glance, it is a convenient mathematical approach to modeling that allows a concise description without an arbitrarily chosen number of metastatic sites which would prohibit generalization of analysis results. A similar approach might be found, e.g. in modeling of drug resistance of cancer cells [13]. Properties of a generalized model based on ideas introduced in [12], which allowed also for other growth terms, were investigated in [14]. However, while the model contains relatively few parameters and provided a good fit to clinical data as far as prediction of detecting metastatic cancer in untreated patients, its modification to incorporate anticancer therapy is very difficult.

Alternative models, incorporating interactions between cancer cells and immune system, were proposed in, e.g. [15, 16]. These models, in turn, while allowing for incorporation of various therapy modes, including immunotherapy, required many parameters. Therefore, in this paper, we return to simple compartmental model with the smallest number of compartments needed to provide good fit to clinical survival curves. Contrary to existing models that in most cases allow for metastasis at any moment, the proposed model is a switching one.

3 The Mathematical Model

Let us consider the model, presented in Fig. 2. Let us denote by $N_0(t)$ the population size of the primary tumor, with K_0 representing the so called carrying capacity for the primary tumor. If $d(t)$ and $c(t)$ denote radio- and chemotherapy, respectively, and we assume the standard linear-quadratic model of radiotherapy effect and Skipper hypothesis for chemotherapy, then the primary tumor growth before metastasis is given by the following ODE [17]:

$$\dot{N}_0 = -\rho_G N_0(t) ln\frac{N_0(t)}{K_0} - \gamma v(t)N_0(t) - \left(\alpha d(t) + \beta d(t)^2\right)N_0(t), \qquad (7)$$

where $v(t)$ represents chemotherapeutic drug effect given by

$$\dot{v}(t) = -\lambda v(t) + k_v c(t). \qquad (8)$$

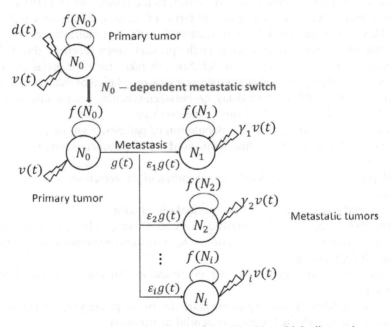

Fig. 2. Block diagram of a metastasis model with multiple distant sites

After the primary tumor gains metastatic property (in the model it is assumed to take place after it has reached a threshold size), the model structure switches into a compartmental one.

$$\dot{N}_0 = -\rho_G N_0(t) ln\frac{N_0(t)}{K_0} - \gamma v(t)N_0(t) - \left(\alpha d(t) + \beta d(t)^2\right)N_0(t) - g(t), \qquad (9)$$

where $g(t)$ represents the migration of cells from the primary to the metastatic sites. If $N_{i \geq 1}(t)$ denotes population sizes of a distant tumor at site i, with K_i representing their carrying capacities, then

$$\dot{N}_i = -\rho_i N_i(t) \ln\frac{N_1(t)}{K_i} + \varepsilon_i g(t) - \gamma_i v(t) N_i(t), \tag{10}$$

where ε_i denotes a fraction of metastatic cells from a primary site that effectively colonize the distant site and γ_i represent chemotherapy effectiveness on the $i-$ th distant tumor.

A hidden assumption in this model is that all distant tumors come from a single primary site. Actually, each metastatic tumor may be the source of new metastasis. This could be taken into account by modifying (10) in the following way:

$$\dot{N}_i = -\rho_i N_i(t) \ln\frac{N_1(t)}{K_i} + \varepsilon_i g(t) + \sum_{ij} \varepsilon_{ji} g_j(t) - \gamma_i v(t) N_i(t) - g_i(t). \tag{11}$$

However, this would result in having to estimate parameters ε_{ji} that describe a fraction of metastatic cells leaving the $j-$ th site and colonizing the $i-$ th site. In general, these parameters would not be identifiable. Moreover, as the results shown in the subsection show, one could obtain the same results in terms of survival curves for much simpler model. Therefore, in this work Eq. (10) is used to model metastatic cancer growth.

The metastatic switch is activated once the primary tumor reaches a threshold size, which is another parameter of the model. Since it takes time for metastatic cells to find an accommodating site and start growing a new population of cancer cells, another parameter has been added – time delay τ_{di} between reaching a metastatic size by the primary tumor and metastasis initiation in the $i-$ th site.

To account for heterogeneity in a population of patients, a virtual pool of patients has been created. For each individual in this pool model parameters have been sampled:

- initial primary tumor size $N_0(0)$ (at the moment of detection) – from a uniform distribution,
- tumor growth parameters ρ_i – from a normal distribution,
- parameters α, γ_i corresponding to radio- and chemotherapy efficacy – from a uniform distribution (parameter $\beta = \alpha/10$, , following a standard assumption in the LQ model of radiotherapy effects),
- parameters ε_i, corresponding to the colonization efficiency – from a uniform distribution,
- time delay τ_{di} between reaching a metastatic size by the primary tumor and metastasis initiation in the $i-$ th site – from exponential distribution.

These parameters have been used to simulate tumor growth and response to treatment of an individual patient. Reaching a threshold tumor size is equivalent to virtual patient death. The time of this event was recorded and subsequently used to create Kaplan-Meier survival curves.

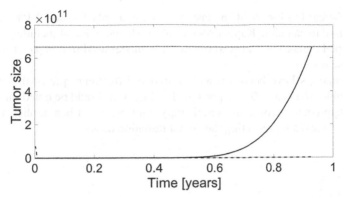

Fig. 3. Tumor growth and response to treatment in a single patient (a sample result): dashed and solid lines represent primary and metastatic tumor, respectively; dotted line represent tumor size threshold value used for death condition

4   Results and Analysis

A sample simulation result, showing an individual patient response to treatment is shown in Fig. 3. The plots show that initial decrease of the primary tumor is overshadowed by the growth of the metastatic tumor that leads to virtual patient death before one year after treatment. It should be noted that only standard treatment protocol, without chemotherapy aimed at the metastatic cancer, was applied here.

4.1   Sample Clinical Results

Recent data on NLSC patients from the Maria Skłodowska-Curie Institute – Oncology Centre (MSCI), branch in Gliwice, is presented in Fig. 4.

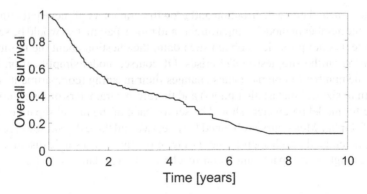

Fig. 4. Sample survival data for lung cancer patients

2-year overall survival (OS) is at about 50%, while 5-year OS and 10-year OS are at about 30% and 15%, respectively. On the other hand, recently published review shows

2-year and 5-year OS for NLSC metastatic patient at only 8% and 2.1%, respectively. Since data used to calculate Kaplan-Meier curves shown in Fig. 4 includes both patients who developed metastasis and who did not, the model used in this paper has not been fitted to these results.

All simulations have been run with a standard treatment protocol. The resulting control variables $d(t)$ and $c(t)$ are presented in Fig. 5. It should be noted that, following a standard approach, a constant radiotherapy equivalent has ben applied instead of a series of short spikes representing the actual radiation doses.

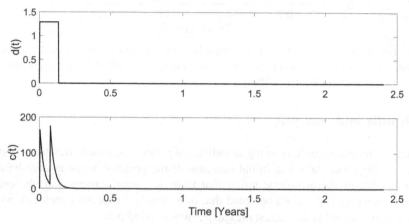

Fig. 5. Clinical treatment protocols – radiotherapy equivalent of a series of irradiations (top panel) and concentration of chemotherapeutic agent (bottom panel).

4.2 The Number of Compartments

If detailed clinical data on distribution and growth parameters of metastatic tumor were available, the number of model compartments and model parameters would be set accordingly. Since it is not possible to obtain such data, the question about the number of the compartments in the simplest model arises. Of course, model simplification based on reducing the number of compartments changes their meaning (compartments represent then a sum of sizes of metastatic tumors) and therefore parameters of distributions used to sample for model parameters should be set for each of the model separately. A comparison of Kaplan-Meier curves obtained for one, two and three distant sites are shown in Fig. 6. Apparently, through appropriate setting of parameters, a single distant metastatic tumor is enough to compare simulation results to clinical data, as all three curves are similar.

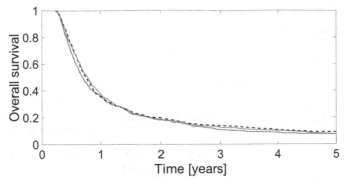

Fig. 6. Survival curves obtained for one (black dashed line), two (dotted line) and three (solid grey line) metastatic sites, with parameters tuned to obtain similar survival curves.

4.3 Death Condition

While setting up the death condition is relatively simple if only one tumor site is considered, the question about the threshold for multiple sites is not easy to answer. Even if only a single metastatic site is taken into account, at least two options arise, in which a virtual patients dies if:

- Either the primary or metastatic tumor reaches a given threshold value (with possible separate thresholds set for each of them),
- The weighted sum of primary and metastatic tumor sizes reaches a given threshold value.

The first option represents a situation, in which a single tumor, no matter if it is a primary or metastatic one, damages a vital organ, thus causing death. The second option takes into account possible negative effects of tumor growth, during which various substances released either by cancer cells or immune system lead to patient death. In both cases, choosing appropriate weighing factors, associated with primary and metastatic tumors, allow to account for different extent, to which each tumor affects the organism. A comparison of survival curves obtained for the same model parameters is shown in Fig. 5. If the metastatic cancer is more aggressive than the primary tumor but the death-threshold size is the same for both of them, survival curves almost overlap (black dotted and dashed grey lines). However, if the metastatic cancer causes death with a smaller size than the primary tumor, prognosis is worse (dashed black line). It should be noted that the same effects, concerning survival curve shape can be obtained either by setting separate threshold values for metastatic an primary tumors, or by appropriate setting weighing factors for a combined threshold value (Figs. 7 and 8).

The threshold sizes for death condition should also be a random parameter, however, sampled from a relatively narrow distribution as the mean value can be found in literature. For the second type of death condition, choice of weight factors for each tumor is a bigger problem, with large influence on final results. For example, depending on these weights, one-year survival could be either 30% or 70% (Fig. 6).

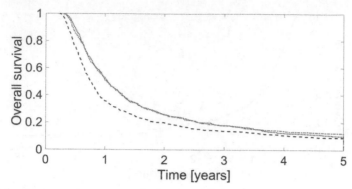

Fig. 7. Comparison of survival curves obtained for death condition of the first (solid grey) and second type (dashed and dotted black lines)

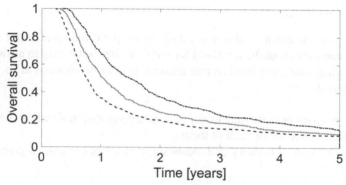

Fig. 8. The effects of changing parameters associated with the death condition, on survival curves

4.4 Taking into Account Negative Therapy Effects

Though, as indicated in Sect. 4.1., it is not the goal of this work to fit model to the sample survival curve shown in Fig. 4, the results shown in subsequent figures imply rather unrealistic 100% survival for the first few months following the beginning of treatment. It should be noted that, assuming that initially patients are metastasis-free, deaths in the first months cannot be due to metastatic cancer, as it needs time to develop. Therefore, one of the main reasons for this discrepancy is that all results, shown in the preceding sections do not take into account negative effects of therapy on healthy cells. These negative effects may lead to cancelling of therapy or may induce patient death regardless the tumor size.

The former effect could be incorporated in the model simply by creating a sub-population of virtual patients for whom the therapy has been cancelled after the first radio- or chemotherapy session. The latter effect has usually been taken into account indirectly in models used for therapy optimization by including an integral component in the minimized performance index hat represented cumulative negative therapy effects [8]. However, in the approach that is proposed in this paper, it is more convenient to introduce a separate, independent compartment that represents healthy cells. Therapy affects that compartment by decreasing the number of healthy cells. Falling below a certain percentage threshold results in patient death. Such approach has an additional advantage of making it possible to switching of therapy for patients whose healthy compartment was reduced below another threshold. Since these threshold values are chosen as fractions of initial compartment size, the initial number of cells does not correspond to any physical organ and can be assumed to take the value of 1.

Let us denote the negative therapy effects and their impact on healthy cells $x(t)$ and $y(t)$, respectively. The simplest, first order linear model of the negative therapy effects would then be given by n, its dynamics can be described by the following equations:

$$\dot{x} = k_d d(t) + k_v v(t) - k_x x, \tag{12}$$

$$\dot{y} = k_y \dot{x} - k_y y. \tag{13}$$

Then, assuming that the initial size of the healthy compartment is given by 1, its size at time t is given by

$$p(t) = 1 - y(t). \tag{14}$$

A sample illustration of the effects of a standard treatment protocol on the healthy cells compartment is shown in Fig. 9.

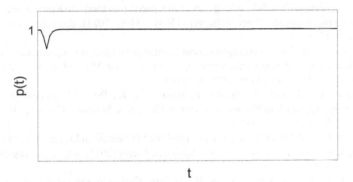

Fig. 9. Sample time course for healthy tissue

5 Conclusions

In the paper, we have proposed a minimal model of cancer growth with metastasis. We concluded that a two-compartmental model is sufficient to represent clinical data given by Kaplan-Meier survival curves and thus be useful in analysis of efficacy of various modes and protocols of treatment. Furthermore, it could also be utilized to predict the moment of detection of metastatic tumor, if reaching a given detection threshold by metastatic tumor, instead of death condition, was used in Kaplan-Meier curves.

Moreover, we addressed the problem of death condition for multicompartmental models, unfortunately, without unambiguous conclusions. There is no recommended type of death condition. Its type and parameters should be chosen in the procedure of fitting simulation-based survival curves to clinical data.

Acknowledgements. This work has been supported by the NCN grant DEC-2020/37/B/ST6/01959.

References

1. Dela Cruz, C.S., Tanoue, L.T., Matthay, R.A.: Lung cancer: epidemiology, etiology, and prevention. Clin. Chest Med. **32**(4), 605–644 (2011). https://doi.org/10.1016/j.ccm.2011.09.001
2. Inamura, K.: Lung cancer: understanding its molecular pathology and the 2015 WHO classification. Front. Oncol. **7**, 193 (2017). https://doi.org/10.3389/fonc.2017.00193
3. Popper, H.H.: Progression and metastasis of lung cancer. Cancer Metastasis Rev. **35**(1), 75–91 (2016). https://doi.org/10.1007/s10555-016-9618-0
4. Ten Haaf, K., van der Aalst, C.M., de Koning, H.J., Kaaks, R., Tammemägi, M.C.: Personalising lung cancer screening: an overview of risk-stratification opportunities and challenges. Int. J. Cancer, **149**(2): 250–263 (2021), doi:https://doi.org/10.1002/ijc.33578
5. Ten Haaf, K., et al.: Risk prediction models for selection of lung cancer screening candidates: a retrospective validation study. PLoS Med. **14**(4), e1002277 (2017). https://doi.org/10.1371/journal.pmed.1002277
6. Yeo, Y., et al.: Individual 5-Year lung cancer risk prediction model in Korea using a nationwide representative database. Cancers (Basel). **13**(14), 3496 (2021), doi:https://doi.org/10.3390/cancers13143496
7. Tufail, A.B., et al.: Deep learning in cancer diagnosis and prognosis prediction: a minireview on challenges, recent trends, and future directions. Comput Math Meth. Med. **2021**, 9025470 (2021). https://doi.org/10.1155/2021/9025470
8. Swierniak, A., Kimmel, M., Smieja, J., Puszynski, K., Psiuk-Maksymowicz, K.: System Engineering Approach to Planing Anticancer Therapies. Springer, Cham (2016). https://doi.org/10.1007/978-3-319-28095-0
9. Schaettler, H., Ledzewicz, U.: Optimal Control for Mathematical Models of Cancer Therapies. An Application of Geometric Methods, Springer, Cham (2015). https://doi.org/10.1007/978-1-4939-2972-6
10. Dudley, W.N., Wickham, R., Coombs, N.: An introduction to survival statistics: kaplan-meier analysis. J. Adv. Pract. Oncol. **7**(1), 91–100 (2016). https://doi.org/10.6004/jadpro.2016.7.1.8
11. Bilous, M., et al.: Quantitative mathematical modeling of clinical brain metastasis dynamics in non-small cell lung cancer. Sci. Rep. **9**(1), 13018 (2019). https://doi.org/10.1038/s41598-019-49407-3
12. Iwata, K., Kawasaki, K., Shigesada, N.: A dynamical model for the growth and size distribution of multiple metastatic tumors. J. Theor. Biol. **203**(2), 177–186 (2000). https://doi.org/10.1006/jtbi.2000.1075
13. Swierniak, A., Polanski, A., Smieja, J., Kimmel, M.: Modelling growth of drug resistant cancer populations as the system with positive feedback. Math. Comput. Model. **37**(11), 1245–1252 (2003). https://doi.org/10.1016/S0895-7177(03)00134-1
14. Hanin, L., Seidel, K., Stoevesandt, D.: A universal model of metastatic cancer, its parametric forms and their identification: what can be learned from site-specific volumes of metastases. J. Math. Biol. **72**(6), 1633–1662 (2015). https://doi.org/10.1007/s00285-015-0928-6

15. Serre, R., et al.: Mathematical Modeling of cancer immunotherapy and its synergy with radio-therapy. Cancer Res. **76**(17), 4931–4940 (2016). https://doi.org/10.1158/0008-5472.CAN-15-3567
16. Rhodes, A., Hillen, T.: A mathematical model for the immune-mediated theory of metastasis. J Theor Biol. **482**, 109999 (2019). https://doi.org/10.1016/j.jtbi.2019.109999
17. Smieja, J., Psiuk-Maksymowicz, K., Swierniak, A.: A framework for modeling and efficacy evaluation of treatment of cancer with metastasis. In: Pijanowska, D.G., Zieliński, K., Liebert, A., Kacprzyk, J. (eds.) Biocybernetics and Biomedical Engineering – Current Trends and Challenges. LNNS, vol. 293, pp. 88–97. Springer, Cham (2022). https://doi.org/10.1007/978-3-030-83704-4_9
18. Bar, J., et al.: Long-term survival of patients with metastatic non-small-cell lung cancer over five decades. J Oncol. **12**, 7836264 (2021). https://doi.org/10.1155/2021/7836264

Utility Driven Job Selection Problem on Road Networks

Mayank Singhal and Suman Banerjee$^{(\boxtimes)}$

Department of Computer Science and Engineering, Indian Institute of Technology
Jammu, Nagrota 181221, India
{2018ucs0064,suman.banerjee}@iitjammu.ac.in

Abstract. In this paper, we study the problem of UTILITY DRIVEN
JOB SELECTION on Road Networks for which the inputs are: a road
network with the vertices as the set of Point-Of-Interests (Henceforth
mentioned as POI) and the edges are road segments joining the POIs,
a set of jobs with their originating POI, starting time, duration, and
the utility. A worker can earn the utility associated with the job if (s)he
performs this. As the jobs are originating at different POIs, the worker
has to move from one POI to the other one to take up the job. Some
budget is available for this purpose. Any two jobs can be taken up by
the worker only if the finishing time of the first job plus traveling time
from the POI of the first job to the second one should be less than or
equal to the starting time of the second job. We call this constraint as the
temporal constraint. The goal of this problem is to choose a subset of the
jobs to maximize the earned utility such that the budget and temporal
constraints should not be violated. We present two solution approaches
with detailed analysis. First one of them works based on finding the
locally optimal job at the end of every job and we call this approach as the
Best First Search Approach. The other approach is based on the Nearest
Neighbor Search on road networks. We perform a set of experiments
with real-world trajectory datasets to demonstrate the efficiency and
effectiveness of the proposed solution approaches. We observe that the
proposed approaches lead to more utility compared to baseline methods.

Keywords: Point-of-interest · Road network · Spatial database

1 Introduction

In recent times, the study of road networks has been emerged in the area of data
management in general and spatial data management in particular [10]. Also, we
have witnessed a significant development of wireless internet and mobile devices.
Hence, for any moving person capturing their location information over time

The work of Suman Banerjee is supported by the Seed Grant (SGT-100047) provided
by the Indian Institute of Technology Jammu, India. Both the authors have contributed
equally in this work.

© The Author(s), under exclusive license to Springer Nature Singapore Pte Ltd. 2022
E. Szczerbicki et al. (Eds.): ACIIDS 2022, CCIS 1716, pp. 578–591, 2022.
https://doi.org/10.1007/978-981-19-8234-7_45

becomes easier. This leads to the availability of trajectory datasets in different repositories [14,18]. These datasets are effectively used for solving many decision making and recommendation problem that arise in day to day life including point-of-interest recommendation [16], group trip planning query [5], route recommendation [3,11], travel time prediction [7], finding most frequent paths [9], driving behavior prediction [8] and many more.

Among many one well studied problem in the context of road networks, is the Food Delivery Problem [15]. Now-a-days restaurants give the option to the customers for home delivery of the ordered food if the customer is ready to pay the delivery charge. Several startups have grown in this area, namely *Swiggy*[1], *Zomato*[2], etc. A delivery boy (mentioned as the 'worker' in this paper) can earn benefit by serving these jobs. In the literature, there exist some studies related to this problem. Yildiz et al. [15] studied the problem of meal delivery problem and they proposed a solution methodology with the assumption of the exact time of order. The objective of their study was to produce a solution that causes maximum number of order delivery. Reyes et al. [12] also studied the meal delivery problem and they developed optimization-based approaches tailored to solve the courier assignment problem and capacity management problem encountered in meal delivery problem. Ji et al. [6] studied the food delivery problem and solves only the batching problem but not the order carrier assignment problem and the routing problem. Zeng et al. [17] studied the problem of last mile delivery problem in a very generic setting but does not consider any time for food preparation. Dai et al. [2] studied the problem of managing the online placed but offline delivered orders by crowed sourced drivers for delivering the foods. In this paper, we formulate this problem as a discrete optimization problem and propose two solution approaches. In particular, we make the following contributions in this paper:

- We study the UTILITY DRIVEN JOB SELECTION Problem on Road Network where the goal is to select a subset of the jobs originated at different POIs to maximize the utility of the worker.
- We formulate this problem as a discrete optimization and propose two solution methodologies for this problem with detailed analysis and examples.
- Both the methodologies have been analyzed in detail to understand their time and space requirement.
- We conduct an extensive set of experiments with real-life trajectory datasets to show the effectiveness and efficiency of the proposed solution approaches.

The rest of the paper is organized as follows. Section 2 describes the background and defines the problem formally. Section 3 contains a detailed description of the proposed solution approaches. Section 4 describes the experimental evaluation, and finally, Sect. 5 concludes our study.

---

[1] https://www.swiggy.com/.
[2] https://www.zomato.com/.

2   Background and Problem Definition

In this section, we give the background and define the problem formally. Initially, we start by defining the road network.

Definition 1 (Road Network). *A road network is defined by a simple, weighted, undirected graph $\mathcal{G}(\mathcal{V}, \mathcal{E}, \omega)$ where the vertex set $\mathcal{V}(\mathcal{G}) = \{v_1, v_2, \ldots, v_n\}$ are the set of POIs of a city, and the edge set $\mathcal{E}(\mathcal{G}) = \{e_1, e_2, \ldots, e_m\}$ are the road segments joining the POIs and the edge weight function ω that assigns each edge to its corresponding distance; i.e.; $\omega : \mathcal{E}(\mathcal{G}) \longrightarrow \mathbb{R}^+$.*

We use standard graph-theoretic notations and terminologies from the book by Diestal [4]. As in this study, each vertex of $\mathcal{G}$ represents a POI, hence in the rest of the paper, we use the term 'vertex' and 'POI' interchangeably. We denote the number of vertices and edges of $\mathcal{G}$ by n and m, respectively. The weight of any edge $(v_i v_j) \in \mathcal{E}(\mathcal{G})$ is denoted by $\omega(v_i v_j)$. If the road network is connected then there must exist at least one path between every pair of vertices, and hence, there must exist a traveling cost as well. For any pair of non-adjacent pairs of POIs, i.e., $(v_i v_j) \notin \mathcal{E}(\mathcal{G})$, we define the travel cost as the minimum cost incurred among all possible paths reaching from v_i to v_j. We denote this by $\mathbb{C}(v_i v_j)$ and defined by the following equation:

$$\mathbb{C}(v_i v_j) = \begin{cases} \omega(v_i v_j), & \text{if } (v_i v_j) \in \mathcal{E}(\mathcal{G}) \\ \min_{p \in \mathbb{P}(v_i v_j)} \sum_{(uv) \in \mathcal{E}(p)} \omega(uv), & \text{otherwise} \end{cases}$$

Here, $\mathbb{P}(v_i v_j)$ is the set of all possible paths reaching from v_i to v_j and for any such path p, $\mathcal{E}(p)$ denotes the set of edges that constitute the path p. In this study, we consider that for any two POIs v_i and v_j, $\mathbb{C}(v_i v_j) = \mathbb{C}(v_j v_i)$. Here, a POI may refer to a hotel, restaurant, cafeteria, and so on. Now-a-days they provide an option of delivering the ordered foods to the residence of the customers and thus creates opportunities for people to earn revenue by serving the food delivery job. We formally define the notion of Job in Definition 2.

Definition 2 (Job). *Let, $\mathcal{J}$ be the set of jobs under consideration. Any job $j \in \mathcal{J}$ is defined by a corresponding quintuple $\mathbb{T}_J = (j_{id}, j_{p\_id}, j_u, t_{j^s}, j_d)$ and the meaning of each symbol is as follows:*

- j_{id}: *This attribute stores an id corresponding to each job such that each job can be identified uniquely in the job database.*
- j_{p_id}: *This attribute stores the POI_Id at which this job has been originated.*
- j_u: *This attribute stores the amount of utility to be paid to the worker after finishing this job.*
- t_{j^s}: *This attribute stores the starting time of the job.*
- j_d: *This attribute stores the duration of the job.*

It can be observed that in Definition 2 the fifth attribute can also be interpreted as the finishing time (denoted as t_{j^f}) also as this can be obtained by adding the duration of the job with the starting time. Also, it is natural to consider that for any job $j \in \mathcal{J}$, its finishing time must come after its starting time, and hence, $t_{j^f} > t_{j^s}$. We also have information about the travel time between any two POIs when the worker is traveling using the shortest path. For any two POIs v_i and v_j, we denote this quantity as $\mathcal{T}_{v_i, v_j}$. Suppose, $\mathcal{I} \subseteq \mathcal{J}$ be the set of jobs chosen by the worker. Then it is expected that these jobs should satisfy the following two constraints:

- **Temporal Constraint:** Consider any two subsequent jobs j_x and j_{x+1} originated at POI v_x and v_{x+1}, respectively. So, it is natural that if a worker wants to do the job $j \in \mathcal{J}$ originated at POI v_j and has the starting time t_{j^s} then the worker must be present at the POI v_j on or before t_{j^s}. So, assume that the worker finished his current assignment at POI v_x and at time t_x. Now, if he wishes to choose his next assignment at POI v_{x+1} having the starting time of the job as t_{x+1} then $t_{x+1} \geq t_x + \mathcal{T}_{x,x+1}$. We call this constraint as the temporal constraint.
- **Budget Constraint:** Once the worker finishes his job at POI v_x, and moves to the POI v_{x+1} then he needs to pay some price as travel cost. Assume that $j_1, j_2, \ldots, j_k$ is the set of sequenced jobs with their originated POIs at v_1, $v_2, \ldots, v_k$. Let, $\mathbb{C}(v_i, v_j)$ be the cost associated with traveling from v_i to v_j. The budget constraint signifies that the total cost for traveling should be less than the allocated budget; i.e.; $\sum_{i \in \{1,\ldots,k-1\}} \mathbb{C}(v_i, v_{i+1}) \leq B$.

We also assume that the information about the jobs is available before the worker starts his first job. Now, we state the notion of earned utility for any subset of jobs in Definition 3.

Definition 3 (Earned Utility). *For any subset of jobs $\mathcal{I} \subseteq \mathcal{J}$, we define the earned utility by the worker as the total utility that the worker can earn by performing the jobs in Set $\mathcal{I}$. We denote this by $\mathcal{B}(\mathcal{I})$ and define using Eq. 1.*

$$\mathcal{B}(\mathcal{I}) = \sum_{j \in \mathcal{I}} \mathcal{U}(j) \tag{1}$$

Here, $\mathcal{B}(.)$ is the earned utility function that maps each subset of the jobs to the total utility; i.e.; $\mathcal{B} : 2^{\mathcal{J}} \longrightarrow \mathbb{R}_0^+$, where $\mathcal{B}(\emptyset) = 0$. $\mathcal{U}(j)$ is the utility associated with the Job j.

Suppose, the worker has the budget B to spend for traveling while moving from one job to the next job. Now, the question is which jobs should be chosen by the worker to maximize the earned utility. We call this problem as the UTILITY DRIVEN JOB SELECTION Problem which is stated in Definition 4.

Definition 4 (Utility Driven Job Selection Problem). *Given a road network $\mathcal{G}(\mathcal{V}, \mathcal{E}, \omega)$ and a set of jobs $\mathcal{J}$ originated at different POIs, the goal of this problem is to select a subset of the jobs such that the earned utility is maximized within the allocated budget.*

From the computational point of view this problem can be posed as follows:

UTILITY DRIVEN JOB SELECTION Problem

Input: Road Network $\mathcal{G}(\mathcal{V}, \mathcal{E}, \omega)$, Set of Jobs $\mathcal{J}$ along with all the required information mentioned in Definition 2, Budget of the Worker B.

Problem Which jobs from the set $\mathcal{J}$ should be chosen by the worker such that the temporal constraint as well as the budget constraint is satisfied and the earned utility is maximized.

Output: A subset of the jobs $\mathcal{I} \subseteq \mathcal{J}$.

---

3   Proposed Solution Approaches

In this section, we describe the proposed solution approaches for the Utility Driven Job Selection Problem. The first one is the Best First Approach which is stated in the subsequent subsection.

3.1   Best First Search Approach

Assume that the worker w planned to work from time w^s till time w^f. In this approach first the jobs are sorted based on the starting time. The worker takes up the job that comes first in the time horizon after w^s. If there is a tie then the worker chooses one with the higher utility. From the second job onwards the process goes in the same way with one exception. Now, the worker chooses the 'Best' job applying the following criteria. Suppose, the worker is at the POI v_x and this is his i-th job that he has finished. Now, let j_{i+1}, j_{i+2}, ..., j_z are the set of jobs originated at the POIs v_{i+1}, v_{i+2}, ..., v_z respectively satisfies the temporal constraint. Now, the worker will try to choose the job $j \in \{j_{i+1}, j_{i+2}, \ldots, j_z\}$ originated at the POI v_y if $\mathcal{U}_J > \mathbb{C}(v_x, v_y)$. If there are more than one jobs that satisfies this criteria then the worker will choose one with the highest $(\mathcal{U}(j) - \mathbb{C}(v_x, v_j))$ value stated in

$$j^*_{i+1} = \underset{j \in \{j_i, j_{i+1}, \ldots, j_y\}}{argmax} \quad \mathcal{U}(j) - \mathbb{C}(v_x, v_j) \tag{2}$$

The worker will stop when either the budget of the worker is exhausted or the completion time of the worker is reached or both. This idea is described in Algorithm 1. For the simplicity, we also assume that the starting point of the worker is also a POI in the road network $\mathcal{G}$.

Description of Algorithm 1. We assume that the number of jobs in the database is k; i.e.; $|\mathcal{J}| = k$. $\mathcal{J}^w$ contains the subset of the jobs chosen for the worker and initially assigned to empty set. $\mathcal{U}^w$ denotes the utility earned by the worker w which is initialized to 0. v_c is the starting POI of the worker. As the worker starting from time w^s hence those jobs whose starting time is before w^s has no role to play. Hence, we delete all such jobs. Now, Line 6 to 15 Algorithm 1 is executed for selecting the first job. Even before that, we sort all the jobs based on the starting time. Until any one of the termination criteria is met we keep on scanning the jobs, we pick up the first job if it satisfies the temporal constraints. If a job does not obey this constraint then we delete this job as it can be done by the worker. As soon as one job is found, we exit from the while loop of Line 6. While exiting, we set the current time as the finishing time of the job selected as the first job. Also, the earned utility by the worker, the set of selected jobs, and the budget are updated accordingly. Subsequent jobs have been chosen and the selection process goes like this. Until one of the exiting criteria is met the remaining jobs are processed. Without loss of generality, we assume that the job in the i-th index (denoted as j_i) of the sorted list $\mathcal{J}$ and its originating time and finishing time are $t_{j_i^s}$. Now, we notice the jobs that have the same originating time as the $(i + 1)$-th job and we keep in the list $\mathcal{J}^z$. From these jobs we choose one that maximizes the difference between the utility earned by performing the job and the traveling cost inured is maximized. Once a job is selected accordingly all the parameters are updated. Finally, the set of selected jobs and the earned utility are returned.

Analysis of Algorithm 1. Now, we analyze Algorithm 1 to understand its time and space requirement. The statements mentioned from Line 1 to 3 are merely input statement and requires $\mathcal{O}(1)$ time. Line 4 can be implemented by just a single scan of the jobs and it takes $\mathcal{O}(k)$ time. Sorting the jobs require $\mathcal{O}(k \log k)$ time. Now, the running time of the remaining portion of the algorithm will depend on how many times the while loops in Line 6 and 15. Assume that $\mathbb{C}_{min}$ denotes the minimum traveling cost among all possible POI pairs; i.e.; $\mathbb{C}_{min} = \min\limits_{v_x, v_y \in \mathcal{V}(\mathcal{G})} \mathbb{C}(v_x, v_y)$. If the budget of the worker is B, then the maximum number of jobs that cannot be done by the worker $\frac{B}{\mathbb{C}_{min}}$. Consider the sorted list of jobs obtained after the execution of Line 5. Let, $t_{j_1^s}$ and $t_{j_k^s}$ denotes the originating time of the first and last job and this difference between $t_{j_k^s}$ and $t_{j_1^s}$ is denoted by Δ; i.e.; $\Delta = t_{j_k^s} - t_{j_1^s}$. Now, it is easy to observe that the both the while loops can run at most $min(\frac{B}{\mathbb{C}_{min}}, \Delta)$ times. We denote this quantity as r. Now, it is easy to observe that the for loop in Line 7 can runs at most $\mathcal{O}(k)$ times. Also, we can observe that the condition checking statements at Line 8 and other statements from Line 9 to 15 requires $\mathcal{O}(1)$ time. So, the running time from Line 6 to 15 requires $\mathcal{O}(r \cdot k)$ time. It is easy to observe that the statements of Line 16 and 17 requires $\mathcal{O}(1)$. Let, for any $t \in [t_{j_1^s}, t_{j_k^s}]$, $\mathcal{J}_t$ denotes the set of jobs with t as the Let, $\mathcal{J}_t^{max}$ denotes the maximum number of jobs at any particular time in the time interval $[t_{j_1^s}, t_{j_k^s}]$ as originating time; i.e.; $\mathcal{J}^{max} = \underset{t \in [t_{j_1^s}, t_{j_k^s}]}{argmax} \mathcal{J}_t$. It is easy to observe that the for loop in Line 18 can run at most $\mathcal{O}(\mathcal{J}^{max})$ many times. The condition checking statement of the if statement at Line 19 and statements in Line 20 and 22 will take $\mathcal{O}(1)$ time to execute. We can easily observe that the instruction in Line 23 can be implemented in $\mathcal{O}(\mathcal{J}_t)$ time. All the remaining

---

Algorithm 1: BEST FIRST APPROACH for the UTILITY DRIVEN POINT-OF-INTEREST SELECTION Problem

---

Input: A Road Network $\mathcal{G}(\mathcal{V}, \mathcal{E}, \omega)$, The Job Database $\mathcal{J}$, The Worker w with Its Initial Location, starting and ending time, Budget B.

Output: A Subset of the Jobs $\mathcal{J}^w \subseteq \mathcal{J}$.

1   $[w^s, w^f] \longleftarrow$ Working interval of the worker

2   $v_p \longleftarrow$ Starting location of the worker

3   $\mathcal{J}^w \longleftarrow \emptyset; \mathcal{U}^w \longleftarrow 0; t \longleftarrow w^s; i \longleftarrow 1$

4   $\mathcal{J} \longleftarrow \mathcal{J} \setminus \{j : t_{j^s} < w^s\}$

5   $\mathcal{J} \longleftarrow$ Sort the jobs based on the t_s value

6   **while** $B > 0$ *and* $t \leq t_{j_k^s}$ **do**

7   **for** $a = 1$ *to* k **do**

8   **if** $t + \mathcal{T}(v_x, v_a) \leq t_{j_a^s}$ *and* $\mathbb{C}(v_p, v_a) \leq B$ **then**

9              $\mathcal{J}^w \longleftarrow \mathcal{J}^w \cup \{j_a\}; \mathcal{U}^w \longleftarrow \mathcal{U}^w + \mathcal{U}(j_a)$

10              $t \longleftarrow t_{j_a^f}; B \longleftarrow B - \mathbb{C}(v_p, v_a)$

11   **break**

12   **else**

13              $\mathcal{J} \longleftarrow \mathcal{J} \setminus \{j_a\}$

14   **if** $|\mathcal{J}^w| == 1$ **then**

15   **break**

16   **while** $B > 0$ *and* $t \leq t_{j_k^s}$ **do**

17      $t_{j_{a+1}}^s \longleftarrow$ Starting time of the job j_{a+1}

18      $\mathcal{J}^z \longleftarrow j_{a+1}$

19   **for** $z = a + 2$ *to* k **do**

20   **if** $t_{j_{a+1}}^s == t_z^s$ **then**

21              $\mathcal{J}^z \longleftarrow \mathcal{J}^z \cup \{j_z\}$

22   **else**

23   **break**

24      $j^* \longleftarrow \underset{j \in \mathcal{J}^z \text{ and } t + \mathcal{T}(v_a, v_z) \leq t_j^s}{argmax} \mathcal{U}(j) - \mathbb{C}(j_a, j_z)$

25      $\mathcal{J}^w \longleftarrow \mathcal{J}^w \cup \{j^*\}; B \longleftarrow B - \mathbb{C}(j_a, j_z)$

26      $t \longleftarrow j_z^f; \mathcal{U}^w \longleftarrow \mathcal{U}^w + \mathcal{U}(j^*); a \longleftarrow z$

27 **return** $\mathcal{J}^w, \mathcal{U}^w$

---

instructions in Line 24 and 25 will take $\mathcal{O}(1)$ time. Hence, the time requirement from Line 15 to 25 requires $\mathcal{O}(r \cdot \mathcal{J}_t)$ time. Hence, the total time requirement of Algorithm 1 requires $\mathcal{O}(k + k \log k + r \cdot k + r \cdot \mathcal{J}_t) = \mathcal{O}(k \log k + r \cdot k + r \cdot \mathcal{J}_t)$. Other than the inputs extra space taken by Algorithm 1 is to store the lists $\mathcal{J}^w$ and $\mathcal{J}^z$ which requires $\mathcal{O}(k)$ space. All the remaining variables used in Algorithm 1 requires $\mathcal{O}(1)$ space. Hence, the space requirement of Algorithm 1 is of $\mathcal{O}(k)$. Note that in Algorithm 1 we consider that pairwise travel cost and time between is part of input itself. The final statement is mentioned in Theorem 1.

Theorem 1. *The running time and space requirement of Algorithm 1 is of* $\mathcal{O}(k \log k + r \cdot k + r \cdot \mathcal{J}_t)$ *and* $\mathcal{O}(k)$, *respectively.*

It is important to note that we are not considering the time requirement for computing the shortest path distance matrix as this can be computed offline.

3.2 Solution Approach Based on Nearest Neighbor Search

This method relies on computation of the nearest neighbor on road network. In this method, the nearest neighbor is searched based on the priority of the job which is stated in Definition 5. The priority function has been designed by observing the following facts:

- If the sum of traveling time for moving from current POI to the POI where the job has been originated and time requirement for performing the job is more then the priority of the job should be less.
- If the utility obtained by performing the job is higher then the priority of the job will also be more.

The priority can be recognized by a function $\mathbb{P}$ that maps every tuple of job and POI to its priority value which is a positive real number, i.e., $\mathbb{P} : \mathcal{J} \times \mathcal{V}(\mathcal{G}) \longrightarrow \mathbb{R}^+$.

Definition 5 (Priority of the Job). *For any job $j \in \mathcal{J}$ when the worker is at the POI v_i we denote its priority by $\mathbb{P}_i(j)$ and defined by Eq. 3.*

$$\mathbb{P}_i(j) = \frac{\mathcal{U}(j) - \mathbb{C}(v_i, v_j)}{\mathcal{T}(v_i, v_j) + (t_{j^f} - t_{j^s})} \tag{3}$$

From Definition 5 the following two points can be observed.

- From Eq. 3, it can be noticed that the priority function depends on the current POI of the worker.
- Secondly, for any particular POI the highest priority job will be one which has the higher utility and lower time requirement for completion of the job.

Description of Algorithm 2. Now, we state the working principle of Algorithm 2. First four lines of Algorithm 2 is same as Algorithm 1. Subsequently, we call the current location of the worker as previous because possibly the worker will move subsequently it will become the previous POI for him. Now, the job selection process starts. Until the budget of the worker is exhausted and the current time is less than the maximum working time of the worker the following steps are repeated. First, we take out the POIs where the Jobs in the database has been originated. Based on the current location of the worker we compute the priority of the jobs using Eq. 3. Next, the nearest neighbor is computed from the current location of the worker and the locations of the current jobs in $\mathcal{J}$. Here, we point out that the nearest neighbor is computed based on the previously computed priority values. Now, the job originated at the POI corresponding to the nearest POI based on the priority value. Next thing is to be checked whether this job satisfies the temporal constraint or not. If this constraint is satisfied then this job is taken up by the worker and the utility associated with this job is earned by the worker. The budget of the worker is reduced by the amount of traveling cost from the previous to next POI. The current time is updated as the finishing time of the job and *previous* POI has been updated by the next. If the job does not satisfy the temporal constraint then the job is removed from the job database. After exiting from the while loop we get the set of jobs along with the earned utility.

Algorithm 2: NEAREST NEIGHBOR SEARCH APPROACH for the UTILITY DRIVEN POINT-OF-INTEREST SELECTION Problem

---

Input: A Road Network $\mathcal{G}(\mathcal{V}, \mathcal{E}, \omega)$, The Job Database $\mathcal{J}$, The Worker w with Its Initial Location, starting and ending time, Budget B.

Output: A Subset of the Jobs $\mathcal{J}^w \subseteq \mathcal{J}$.

1 $[w^s, w^f] \longleftarrow$ Working interval of the worker
2 $v_p \longleftarrow$ Starting location of the worker
3 $\mathcal{J}^w \longleftarrow \emptyset; \mathcal{U}^w \longleftarrow 0; t \longleftarrow w^s;$
4 $\mathcal{J} \longleftarrow \mathcal{J} \setminus \{j : t_{j^s} < w^s\}$
5 $\mathcal{V}(\mathcal{G}) \longleftarrow \mathcal{V}(\mathcal{G}) \setminus \{v_p\}$
6 *previous* $\longleftarrow v_p$
7 **while** $B > 0$ *and* $t \leq t_{j_k^s}$ **do**
8     $V \longleftarrow$ POIs of the Jobs in $\mathcal{J}$
9     $\mathcal{P} \longleftarrow$ Calculate the Priority using Equation 3
10   *next* $\longleftarrow$ Nearest Neighbor Search (v_p, V) based on the Priority Value
11   **if** $\mathcal{T}(previous, next) + (t_{j_x^s} - t_{j_x^s}) \leq w^f$ **then**
12       $\mathcal{J}^w \longleftarrow \mathcal{J}^w \cup \{j_x\}$
13       $\mathcal{U}^w \longleftarrow \mathcal{U}^w + \mathcal{U}(v_j)$
14       $B \longleftarrow B - \mathbb{C}(previous, v_x)$
15       $t \longleftarrow t_{j_x^f};$ *previous* $\longleftarrow$ *next*
16   **else**
17       $\mathcal{J} \longleftarrow \mathcal{J} \setminus \{j_x\}$

18 **return** $\mathcal{J}^w, \mathcal{U}^w$

Analysis of Algorithm 2. Now, we proceed to analyze Algorithm 2. First three lines of Algorithm 2 is merely the inputs and as mentioned previously removing the jobs having the originating time before the starting time of the worker requires $\mathcal{O}(k)$ time. Line 6 requires $\mathcal{O}(1)$ time to execute. Like Algorithm 1, the running time of Algorithm 2 will also depends upon how many times the while loop at Line 7 is executing. As mentioned in Algorithm 1, the number of times the while loop is running is of $\mathcal{O}(r)$ where $r = min(\frac{B}{\mathbb{C}_{min}}, \Delta)$. Now, POIs corresponding to the jobs can be obtained by a single scan which requires $\mathcal{O}(k)$ time. From Eq. 3, it can be easily observed that for any particular job the computation of its priority requires $\mathcal{O}(1)$ time. Hence, for all the jobs computing the priority requires $\mathcal{O}(k)$ time. Subsequently, choosing the nearest neighbor will take $\mathcal{O}(k \log k)$ in the worst case. All the remaining statements of Algorithm 2 will take $\mathcal{O}(1)$ time. So, the total time requirement is of $\mathcal{O}(k \log k + r(k+))$ It is easy to observe that the space requirement of Algorithm 2 is of $\mathcal{O}(k)$ only. Hence, Theorem 2 holds.

Theorem 2. *The running time and space requirement of Algorithm 2 is of* $\mathcal{O}(k \log k)$ *and* $\mathcal{O}(k)$, *respectively.*

4 Experimental Details

In this section, we describe the experimental evaluations of the proposed solution approaches. Initially, we start by describing the datasets.

Description of the Datasets. In this study, we use three trajectory datasets, namely Europe Road Network (ERD), Minnesota Road Network (MNR), and Oldenburg Road Network (OBR) [13]. The first two have been downloaded from https://networkrepository.com/road.php and the third one has been downloaded from https://www.cs.utah.edu/~lifeifei/SpatialDataset.htm. Table 1 contains the basic statistics of the datasets.

Table 1. Basic statistics of the datasets

Dataset name	n	m	Density	Avg. degree
Europe Road Network	1.2K	1.4K	0.00205794	2
Minnesota Road Network	2.6K	3.3K	0.000946754	2
City of Oldenburg	6.1K	7K	0.000377	2.302

Algorithms in our Experiments. In this paper, we compare the performance of the proposed solution methodologies with the following two baseline methods:

- **Random (RANDOM):** In this method, the worker randomly picks up a job and checks its feasibility (both the budget constraint and temporal constraint). If they are satisfied then the job is taken up by the worker else the worker searches for another job until a suitable one is found.
- **Utility-Based Greedy (U-GREEDY):** In this method, the worker chooses the job that satisfies both the constraints and has the highest utility value. In this method, the objective is to become greedy with respect to the utility of the jobs.

Other than this we have the proposed solution methodologies: Best First Search(BFS) Approach, and Nearest Neighbor(NN) Approach. Additionally, For the second method, we create a variant of it where we consider that the underlying spatial database is indexed with $\mathcal{R}$-Tree. Due to space limitations, we can't discuss more on it. However, interested readers may look into [1].

Experimental Setup. We adopt the following experimental setup. In all three datasets, between every pair of vertices distance value is available. We assume that the travel time is proportional to the distance. We generate the travel time by multiplying 0.2 with the distance. We consider the time interval as [1, 5000] and we create 200, 400, and 800 jobs. For each job, we assign its utility from the interval $[9K, 12K]$. In our experiments, our goal is to check if we increase the number of jobs then how the number of performed jobs and the earned benefit is changing.

Experimental Results with Discussions. In this section, we describe the experimental results with detailed discussions. Figure 1 shows the plots of No. of Jobs Vs. Earned Utility and No. of Jobs Vs. No. of Performed Jobs for all the datasets. From the figure, we can observe that for all the datasets in most of the instances the proposed solution approaches lead to the more amount of earned utility compared to the baseline methods. Now, we explain the obtained results dataset wise. For the Europe Road network Dataset, we observe that among the proposed methodologies the jobs selected by the Best First Approach leads to more amount of earned utility. As an example when the number of jobs are 200, among the proposed methodologies the Best First Approach leads to the earned utility of 54362. However, among the baseline methods, the Utility-based Greedy approach leads to the earned utility of 47319, which is approximately 15% more compared to the baseline method. One important observation in this dataset is that the earned utility is not proportional to the number of available jobs. As an example, for the Best First Search method when the number of jobs has been increased from 200 to 400, the earned utility is decreased from 54362 to 23935. The reason behind this is that increasing the number of jobs does not ensure that it will increase the number of performed jobs and that is what has been reflected in our experiments (Fig. 1 (b), (d), (f)).

For the Minnesota Road Network dataset also the observations are quite similar. When the number of jobs are 200, the earned utility by the Nearest Neighbor Approach is 23986. However, among the baseline methods, the performance of the Random method is better than the Utility-based Greedy and the earned utility by the Random Method is 22219. This is approximately 8% more. In this dataset also, we observe when the number of jobs are increased from 200 to 400, the earned utility values are decreased for the Nearest Neighbor and Utility-based Greedy methods. For the Nearest Neighbor Method, the decrement is from 15059 to 7940 and the same for the Random Method drop down from 22219 to 7915. For the City of Oldenburg Road Network dataset also the observations are quite similar. Among the proposed methodologies, when the number of jobs are 200, the Best First Search Method leads to the maximum amount of earned utility and the amount is 53663 and the same for the Utility-based Greedy Method is 39330. This is approximately 35% more. Finally, from our experiments, we list out the following two key observations:

- The proposed solution approaches lead to more amount of earned benefit compared to baseline methods.
- Increase in number of jobs does not ensure the increase in the earned benefit.

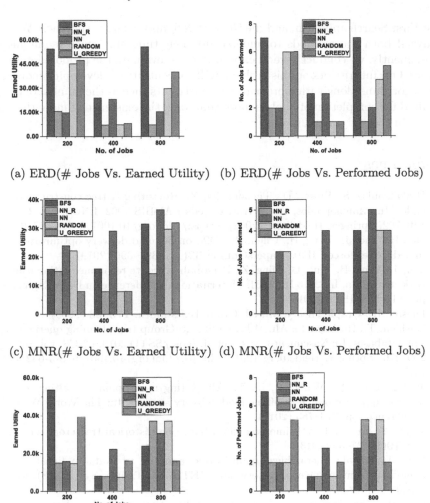

(a) ERD(# Jobs Vs. Earned Utility) (b) ERD(# Jobs Vs. Performed Jobs)

(c) MNR(# Jobs Vs. Earned Utility) (d) MNR(# Jobs Vs. Performed Jobs)

(e) OBR(# Jobs Vs. Earned Utility) (f) OBR(# Jobs Vs. Performed Jobs)

Fig. 1. No. of jobs vs. earned utility and no. of jobs vs. no. of performed jobs plots for three datasets

5 Conclusion and Future Research Directions

In this paper, we have studied the problem of Utility Driven Job Selection where the goal is to choose a subset of the jobs originated at different POIs of a road network such that the utility earned by performing the jobs is maximized and also the total cost for in-between travel cost by the worker is bounded by the given budget. For this problem, we develop two solution approaches namely the

Best First Search approach, and the Nearest Neighbor Search Approach. We have analyzed both the methods to understand their time and space requirements. Subsequently, we conduct several experiments to evaluate the proposed methodologies. Our future work on this problem will concentrate on developing more scalable algorithms along with more realistic constraints such as the number of people required for completion of a job is more than one, the existence of more than one worker in the system and so on.

References

1. Brakatsoulas, S., Pfoser, D., Theodoridis, Y.: Revisiting R-tree construction principles. In: Manolopoulos, Y., Návrat, P. (eds.) ADBIS 2002. LNCS, vol. 2435, pp. 149–162. Springer, Heidelberg (2002). https://doi.org/10.1007/3-540-45710-0_13
2. Dai, H., Tao, J., Jiang, H., Chen, W.: O2o on-demand delivery optimization with mixed driver forces. IFAC-PapersOnLine **52**(13), 391–396 (2019)
3. Dai, J., Yang, B., Guo, C., Ding, Z.: Personalized route recommendation using big trajectory data. In: 2015 IEEE 31st International Conference on Data Engineering, pp. 543–554. IEEE (2015)
4. Diestel, R.: Graph Theory, 3rd ed. Grad. Texts Math. **173**, 33 (2005)
5. Hashem, T., Hashem, T., Ali, M.E., Kulik, L.: Group trip planning queries in spatial databases. In: Nascimento, M.A., et al. (eds.) SSTD 2013. LNCS, vol. 8098, pp. 259–276. Springer, Heidelberg (2013). https://doi.org/10.1007/978-3-642-40235-7_15
6. Ji, S., Zheng, Y., Wang, Z., Li, T.: Alleviating users' pain of waiting: effective task grouping for online-to-offline food delivery services. In: The World Wide Web Conference, pp. 773–783 (2019)
7. Jiang, Y., Li, X.: Travel time prediction based on historical trajectory data. Ann. GIS **19**(1), 27–35 (2013)
8. Liao, L., et al.: Hierarchical quantitative analysis to evaluate unsafe driving behaviour from massive trajectory data. IET Intel. Transp. Syst. **14**(8), 849–856 (2020)
9. Luo, W., Tan, H., Chen, L., Ni, L.M.: Finding time period-based most frequent path in big trajectory data. In: Proceedings of the 2013 ACM SIGMOD International Conference on Management of Data, pp. 713–724 (2013)
10. Palanisamy, B., Ravichandran, S., Liu, L., Han, B., Lee, K., Pu, C.: Road network mix-zones for anonymous location based services. In: 2013 IEEE 29th International Conference on Data Engineering (ICDE), pp. 1300–1303. IEEE (2013)
11. Qu, B., Yang, W., Cui, G., Wang, X.: Profitable taxi travel route recommendation based on big taxi trajectory data. IEEE Trans. Intell. Transp. Syst. **21**(2), 653–668 (2019)
12. Reyes, D., Erera, A., Savelsbergh, M., Sahasrabudhe, S., O'Neil, R.: The meal delivery routing problem. Optim. Online, 6571 (2018)
13. Rossi, R.A., Ahmed, N.K.: The network data repository with interactive graph analytics and visualization. In: AAAI (2015). https://networkrepository.com
14. Wang, S., Bao, Z., Culpepper, J.S., Cong, G.: A survey on trajectory data management, analytics, and learning. ACM Comput. Surv. (CSUR) **54**(2), 1–36 (2021)
15. Yildiz, B., Savelsbergh, M.: Provably high-quality solutions for the meal delivery routing problem. Transp. Sci. **53**(5), 1372–1388 (2019)

16. Ying, J.J.C., Lu, E.H.C., Kuo, W.N., Tseng, V.S.: Urban point-of-interest recommendation by mining user check-in behaviors. In: Proceedings of the ACM SIGKDD International Workshop on Urban Computing, pp. 63–70 (2012)
17. Zeng, Y., Tong, Y., Chen, L.: Last-mile delivery made practical: an efficient route planning framework with theoretical guarantees. Proc. VLDB Endowment **13**(3), 320–333 (2019)
18. Zheng, Y.: Trajectory data mining: an overview. ACM Trans. Intell. Syst. Technol. (TIST) **6**(3), 1–41 (2015)

The Problem of Detecting Boxers
in the Boxing Ring

Piotr Stefański$^{(\boxtimes)}$ ⓘ, Jan Kozak$^{(\boxtimes)}$ ⓘ, and Tomasz Jach ⓘ

Department of Machine Learning, University of Economics in Katowice,
1 Maja, 40-287 Katowice, Poland
{piotr.stefanski,jan.kozak,tomasz.jach}@ue.katowice.pl

Abstract. Modern technology is strongly associated with sports. A perfect example of machine learning in sports is a support of detection of specific events or situations. Such a problem is present in boxing, where boxers' moves need to be precisely detected. However video analysis is labor intensive but may provide valuable information. The paper presents the problem of processing recordings of boxing boxers, in which the dynamics is at an extremely high level and some events last for fractions of seconds. Additionally, the competition is often watched by spectators blocking the view. The goal of this paper is to present accurate, precise and quick method of detecting the presence of pugilists in the ring. This will allow to evaluate and score the boxing fight later. To validate the experiment, relevant material had to be collected – the authors recorded real boxing bouts and prepared the complete training set. The proposed solution will be used to automatically filter-out uninteresting parts of footage, where boxers are not engaged in close-combats situation.

Keywords: Boxer detection · Video processing · Image processing · Dynamic sport analysis

1   Introduction

Nowadays, cameras recording videos can be found at every step, both outside and inside buildings belonging to the public and private infrastructure. Current science and technology allows to search for valuable information in recorded footage. For instance, machine learning solutions provide automatic car counting on highways, measurements of distance between people or verification of presence of facial masks.

Camera recordings are also used to analyse sports football games [13], tennis [15] and many other sports [2,7,14,16]. A similar problem is pursued in this work, as it is devoted to the use of camera images to detect boxers in a boxing ring and the preparation of a suitable test set.

There are a few publications on boxing analysis in current scientific resources, one of them [6] describes a system created for refereeing boxing bouts that was evaluated by boxers, coaches and a refereeing panel. It has been used during

© The Author(s), under exclusive license to Springer Nature Singapore Pte Ltd. 2022
E. Szczerbicki et al. (Eds.): ACIIDS 2022, CCIS 1716, pp. 592–603, 2022.
https://doi.org/10.1007/978-981-19-8234-7_46

boxing sparrings. Unfortunately, the system relied on sensors worn by the boxers. The authors of the publication [18] followed a similar path, where the boxer activity was analysed using sensors placed in gloves and on boxer's body. Due to specific regulations and general user experience, the boxing community prefers not to wear any extra equipment. This was the foundation of the new system which is being designed by the authors.

This paper is a preliminary work in building the complete automatic system of scoring boxer fights with no additional change to the boxers' outfits. As this is a brand new application of vision computing, we have decided to divide problems into smaller sub-problems. One of the first ones is to limit the amount of processing needed, thus – reducing the number of analysed frames. This is crucial for a fast and accurate training and overall quality of the solution. One might say that human silhouette identification is a well known method, but it has not been applied to situations where the information about physical contact occurring for less then 100 milliseconds is needed. Furthermore, for such a dynamic sport where fights are happening with spectators very closely to the fighters (which is not the case for instance in football), the standard solutions don't provide good results. Human detection silhouette systems exist, but none of them was applicable to the constrains stated in the paper (speed, performance, quality, lightning conditions, crowd detection, etc.). In another words, the vision computing methods are well known, but to apply them successfully to such a problem is a non-trivial task.

The purpose of this paper is to prepare a solution to correctly and quickly detect the boxers while ignoring other people outside the ring. This will allow for further work on boxing fight evaluation. For the purpose of this paper, the authors set up a recording environment and then recorded real boxing fights. A special type of equipment had to be considered, as boxing is a highly dynamic game. The detection will be based on micro-movements during close-combat, therefore high resolution and high frame rate is required. Better the quality, bigger the video files are which leads to increasing the computational complexity of the task. Only data collected in this way (in the form of recordings) could be used for further analysis, and finally for detecting boxers in the ring. As the bouts are quick (some of them are under 40 milliseconds), single static images provide no value for this task.

The remainder of the article is organised as follows. Section 1 contains an introduction to the topic of this article. Section 2 provides a description of the problems that arise during image preprocessing that need to be solved in order to detect boxers in a boxing ring. Section 3 presents a novel solution, proposed by the authors, which detects the boxers in the ring. Section 4 contains the results of the experiments performed along with accuracy metrics for the solution. In the last Sect. 5 authors summarise the work done and propose the direction of further works.

2   Detection of Boxers in the Boxing Ring

Currently, it is hard to find in public resources stable and good-quality recordings of boxing fights. To tackle the problem of detecting boxers in the ring, first the authors of this paper had to prepare actual recordings of boxing fights. In order to do this, it is necessary to select the appropriate equipment and decide how and where the cameras are to be placed. The inspiration for the placement can be found in the positions of the referees, who are located right in front of the ring on its three sides as shown in the Fig. 1. However, looking for a better solution than the current one (thanks to the use of computer vision), a serious problem is that the outside referees' view is blocked by the ropes, which are a real obstacle in seeing details during the fight.

When the recordings are ready, it is possible to proceed to the analysis. The process of video analysis can be understood as an iterative analysis over multiple individual frames. This is the preliminary step to find the periods of fight, where the boxers were in contact with each other. It turns out that individual frames take up much more storage space than one video file, which only confirms the effectiveness of data compression [17]. This is worth to keep in mind, because the data processing pipeline created must be prepared for such a volume of data.

Having single frames, one should start searching for boxers in the ring. This is a complex problem, because while recording the image of the ring, we also record everything that happens around it. Very frequently there are spectators outside the ring and other boxers preparing for the next fight. So it is necessary to ignore everything that happens outside the ring.

Boxer detection can start with a generic person detector. This has been a subject to multiple research [1,9], while confirming that the performance of machine learning models for character detection is at a high level. Novel meta-review has been conducted in [1]. The authors compare performance of several popular deep learning methods (Faster R-CNN [5,12], R-FCN [4], SSD [10] and YOLOv3 [11]), that have been applied to detecting people in urban traffic. For this purpose, the database "EuroCity Persons Dataset"[1] was used which contains 283200 tagged people in over 47300 images taken in 31 cities in 12 European countries. The authors found that the key aspect in person detection performance is the size of the data used when training the model. Diversity is also important because detection performance is affected by many factors including weather, lightning conditions and region of the world.

The existing people detectors provide a good performance when applied to counting or detecting individuals. However accurate, they do not differentiate who they detect - which is a major problem when using in detecting specific boxers in a boxing ring. The clothing of the boxers is also not fully regulated by the boxing rules. Only the boxer's helmet and gloves must be subordinated to the colour of the corner, which is blue or red respectively. Therefore, inferences based on colours must be made carefully because the colour of the jersey or

---

[1] https://eurocity-dataset.tudelft.nl/.

shorts that make up the majority of the clothing are not strictly defined and are subject to change.

It should also be noted that in the ring, in addition to the boxers, there is also a referee who is very close to the boxers. The referee has the task of separating the boxers when necessary, stopping and restarting the fight and drawing the attention of the boxers during infractions. The referee should therefore be ignored from the analysis. The problem is complex because since the COVID-19 pandemic, the referee also has a blue mask on his face. This may lead to further problems in distinguishing the blue-clad boxer from the referee.

3   Methodology

Due to the lack of publicly available stable and suitable for vision computing recordings of boxing fights, the solution to the problem of detecting boxers in the boxing ring had to start with the collection of such material. As noted before, the proper equipment is required for acquiring high quality footage. The authors had analysed multiple solutions and choose four GoPro Hero8 sport cameras along with tripods that were placed behind each corner of the boxing ring. The setup allowed boxing fights to be recorded from four different points. The placement of the cameras is shown in Fig. 1. In order to prepare a diverse train-set, the authors recorded fights with boxers of different age.

It is worth noting, that with this spacing of equipment, one of the cameras always has a good view of the boxers at any given time. If the boxers are covering each other for two of the cameras, the other two are placed in a good position for the boxers' profiles. Having four cameras placed like on Fig. 1, the blind-spots are minimised. The combined footage allows to observe the fight with more details than the three human referees can do on their own.

After collecting the necessary material, it is possible to solve the problem of detecting boxers in the ring. Due to the complexity of the problem (see Sect. 2), the Authors propose to divide it into several stages. The various steps are reflected in the Algorithm 1, which receives an image as input and returns a list of boxers and their positions as output. The algorithm starts from detecting all people in the picture, limiting the detections in the next step to people inside the ring. Finally, the referee is also excluded.

Algorithm 1: Proposed approach for detecting boxers in an image

---

    Input: *image* – one frame from video
    Output: *boxers* – list of coordinates of detected boxers
1 *persons* := find_persons_in_image(*image*);
2 *persons_on_ring* := get_only_persons_from_ring(*persons*);
3 *boxers* := get_only_boxers_from_ring(*persons_on_ring*);
4 **result** *boxers*;

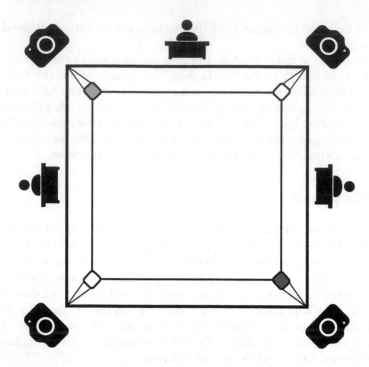

Fig. 1. Diagram of the location of cameras and referees around the boxing ring

While working on the approach, the authors have identified key success factors:

- filter out people who are outside the boxing ring;
- filter out boxers warming up outside the ring who are already wearing gloves and helmets;
- filter out the referee, who is constantly between the boxers;
- filter out the referee who is wearing a facial mask or standing against a red or blue corner;
- detecting obscured boxers' profiles.

At the very beginning, a data sample was selected to train the detection model. The footage was split into individual frames. Following that, the Algorithm 1 was started. The first stage, people detector, gave many false-positives, therefore the second phase commenced. After reducing the search area to the ring, vastly better results were achieved.

In order to filter out people who are outside the ring, the fact that the fight takes place on the ring mat on which the boxers move was used. Therefore, in order to reject individuals outside the ring, a cut-off line (visualised as a horizontal red line on Fig. 3) was used. By using the cut-off, only silhouettes located partially in the ring are analysed. As can be seen in the Fig. 3 the horizontal red line in the middle of a frame is at the height at which the camera registers the end of the mat of the farthest corner.

Another challenge stems from referee being present inside the ring. The referee is close to the boxers, which makes filtering them out complex. The cut-off line solution allowed us to reject many uninteresting characters, but it was not accurate enough and needed to be improved.

To solve the remaining problems, the fact that each boxers fighting in Olympic boxing is wearing a helmet and boxing gloves of a particular colour – red or blue – was used. Based on this, the hue, saturation, and brightness ranges in the HSV model [3,8] for blue and red were defined. This allowed us to create a filter that left only the colours of interest in the given image. The effect of changing the colour model from RGB [3,8] to HSV [3,8] and applying the said filter is shown in the Fig. 2. In this way, the boxers were detected and the referee, along with any people outside the ring, were automatically filtered out.

The solution has also been improved by filtering boxers who have already finished a fight, i.e. who are not directly participating in a duel. For this purpose, only the top 12.5% of a detected person is analysed. This area contains a head of the boxer. The solution allows to reject the boxers who are no longer wearing helmets (they take them off immediately after the fight in their corner).

The presented system detects the boxers and provides their relative coordinates, which enables further analysis and inference. Each detected boxer is placed in a rectangle – the upper left and bottom right corner coordinates are provided by the algorithm. Section 4 contains information about the accuracy of the proposed solution.

The Fig. 3 shows a summary of all previously described techniques, which finally lead to the detection of the boxers in the ring. Reviewing the images from left to right we first have a clean view where no technique has been used yet. The next image already shows all detected boxers in the image, then the third image already shows the cut-off line. The last image contains the final result, which shows only two boxers detected. Due to privacy concerns, the authors have blurred the faces of individuals.

4 Experiments

The proposed solution described in Sect. 3 relates to the detection of boxers in a boxing ring. In order to test the proposed approaches, experimental studies were conducted to evaluate the accuracy and coverage of each solution.

In order to achieve this goal, it was necessary to prepare an actual data set and then conduct the corresponding experiments. The accuracy was estimated from Eq. (1) and the coverage from Eq. (2), where according to the names: $number\_of\_correctly\_detected\_boxers$ represents the number of correctly detected boxers in the ring; $number\_of\_detected\_persons$ is the number of individuals detected per frame.

$$accuracy = \frac{number\_of\_correctly\_detected\_boxers}{number\_of\_detected\_persons} \qquad (1)$$

$$coverage = \frac{number\_of\_correctly\_detected\_boxers}{2} \cdot accuracy \qquad (2)$$

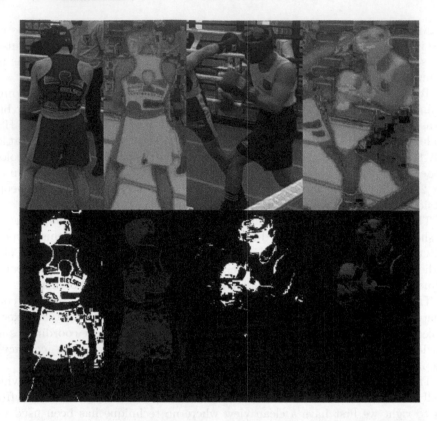

Fig. 2. Blue and red colour detection in search of boxers (Color figure online)

Fig. 3. Detecting boxers with the use of described techniques

4.1 Experimental Design and Data Set

Recorded boxing fights took place in Poland at the Silesian league games for juniors, cadets and seniors. The entire competition took four hours to complete, and as written in Sect. 3 the fights were recorded with four GoPro Hero8 cameras. The video was recorded in full HD resolution at 50 frames per second. The cameras were mounted behind each corner as shown in the Fig. 1, on 1.8 m high tripods. The cameras required connection to power banks and each had a 128 GB memory card. After four hours of recording, each memory card was nearly full, totaling just under 500 GB of recorded material.

The material was stored on a computer that had a 2TB hard drive, an 8-core processor with an Intel Core i7-2600 CPU @ 3.40 GHz and 16 GB of RAM. The experiments that have been described in this chapter were conducted on such configured hardware.

We tested three approaches during the experiments:

Approach 1 detect all persons on image.
Approach 2 from list of detected persons select who are in the ring.
Approach 3 from list of persons on the ring select only boxers.

Each of these approaches was reflected in the steps of the Algorithm 1 and tested on data from three time ranges: 30 s, 60 s for 120 s.

4.2 Results of Experiments

The results of the obtained experiments allow to evaluate the described approaches. Through this research, it is possible to confirm that it is possible to quickly identify the boxers in the ring while filtering out the other people. This is to be used for work related to the calculation of boxing fight statistics. In this section, representative results observed during the entire range of collected recordings are presented.

In Tables 1, 2 and 3 we present the results for all approaches and the three time ranges. It is important to note that each time period involves a different number of frames of film and so: 30 s using 50 fps equals to 1500 individual frames (observations). 60 s is 3000 and 120 s is 6000 observations respectively. Therefore, the results presented are average values. The processing of one frame for all the described approaches took about 0.065 s, which confirms the quickness of the proposed system.

As can be seen in Table 1, a 30 s video contains on average 3.90 people in any single frame; 1.89 are inside the ring and 1.12 are considered active boxers. This leads to a conclusion, that for the whole set of 1500 frames (30 s), 72% of detected individuals should not be evaluated during a combat. It should also be clarified that the 1.12 boxing detections are due to situations where one boxer covers up another boxer or the referee covers up a boxer. Reference to this problem will appear in further discussion. When the analysis is extended to 60 s (3000 observations), the situation is very similar, but the average number of boxers in the ring per frame decreases even more – to 0.81, and as many as 79% of individuals per observation are not boxers. The most difficult situation is for the 120-second analysis (6000 observations), as the average number of individuals per a single frame is 4.22, where the actual number of boxers is just 0.43 per frame. At that 1.85 people are in the ring – this is primarily due to the time when coaches are in the ring or boxers are being replaced. However, this shows the difficulty of the analysis because, on average, almost 90% of the people on one observation are not boxers involved in a fight.

Table 1. Average number of detected objects per time range

	Time range		
	30 s	60 s	120 s
Persons	3.8960	3.8157	4.2168
Persons on the ring	1.8853	1.7217	1.8513
Boxers	1.1193	0.8080	0.4363

In Tables 2 and 3 we present the classification accuracy and coverage depending on the tested approach (determined from Eqs. (1) and (2)). We analyse these results together, as this is the only way to reflect the actual performance of the method.

First, it can be noted that with one of the approaches we can get very high accuracy (Eq. (1)). Note that approach 1 obtains very low accuracy in each case – this is because it detects all individuals during each observation. Better results are already achieved with approach 2, but only for the time periods of 30 and 60 s. In these cases, detection of a boxer is already possible with about 50% accuracy. Approach 3 gives 100% accuracy, so detecting a boxer when using this approach makes it possible to conclude that it is a boxer (additionally involved in a fight).

However, it should be noted that each of these methods has low coverage (Eq. (2)) presented in Table 3. This is the result of boxer being covered by the referee or the other boxer. We will solve this problem in the future by trying to combine recordings from several cameras. However, at this stage it is necessary to present the results related to the analysis of only one of the cameras. In this case, it happens that only one boxer is detected, so the coverage, for the calculation of which the accuracy (see. Eqs.(1) and (2)) for the first approach is also used, decreases even below 10% (only for 1500 observations 16% is achieved). Approximately twice as good results are achieved with approach 2 (in each time range). In contrast, the best results were obtained for approach 3. Using all of the solutions presented in this paper, the coverage is 56% for 1500 observations, 40% for 3000 observations and 22% for 6000 observations (120 s). Given the fact, that this is a result for each camera individually, the authors find the results satisfying. Furthermore, if the video clips with identified boxers will be expanded to cover missing detections, the overall quality will provide sufficient data for further research.

Table 2. Accuracy of the analysed approaches

	Time range		
	30 s	60 s	120 s
Approach 1	0.2880	0.2118	0.1035
Approach 2	0.5937	0.4693	0.2357
Approach 3	1.0000	1.0000	1.0000

Table 3. Coverage of the analysed approaches

	Time range		
	30 s	60 s	120 s
Approach 1	0.1612	0.0856	0.0226
Approach 2	0.3323	0.1896	0.0514
Approach 3	0.5597	0.4040	0.2182

5 Conclusions

The purpose of this paper was to propose a system to detect boxers in a boxing ring. In order to do that, it is necessary to collect the data for training the classifiers and detectors. To do this, the authors recorded real boxing fights to prepare the training set for training the detectors.

The problem of detecting boxers in the ring is complex and was divided into three steps. First, all the people in the given image were detected, then the people outside the ring were filtered out using the elimination method, and in the next step the referee was filtered out. In this way, the proposed solution provides information about the number of boxers in the ring and the coordinates of their location.

The experiments confirm that the introduced solution allows for an improvement in the accuracy of detecting boxers in the ring. Starting from a simple approach that detected all people in a video frame, we were able to achieve an effect where only boxers in the ring were detected. In order to train any classifying system, the most time and resource consuming part, is the labelling of data. We have achieved the goal – that is to decrease the time spent by humans labelling each frame or video sequence only to the promising or relevant parts. Coverage values need further improvements, as not all boxers are always detected.

In the future, in addition to applying the current work to determine statistics related to boxing events, we also plan to address the problem where one boxer is not detected. To do this, we plan to synchronise the video from all cameras so that the system can detect each boxer based on 4 concurrent images. This should allow for improved coverage.

References

1. Braun, M., Krebs, S., Flohr, F., Gavrila, D.M.: Eurocity persons: a novel benchmark for person detection in traffic scenes. IEEE Trans. Pattern Anal. Mach. Intell. **41**(8), 1844–1861 (2019). https://doi.org/10.1109/TPAMI.2019.2897684
2. Burić, M., Pobar, M., Ivašić-Kos, M.: Object detection in sports videos. In: 2018 41st International Convention on Information and Communication Technology, Electronics and Microelectronics (MIPRO), pp. 1034–1039. IEEE (2018)
3. Chen, W., Shi, Y.Q., Xuan, G.: Identifying computer graphics using HSV color model and statistical moments of characteristic functions. In: 2007 IEEE International Conference on Multimedia and Expo, pp. 1123–1126. IEEE (2007)
4. Dai, J., Li, Y., He, K., Sun, J.: R-FCN: object detection via region-based fully convolutional networks. In: Advances in Neural Information Processing Systems, pp. 379–387 (2016)
5. Girshick, R., Donahue, J., Darrell, T., Malik, J.: Rich feature hierarchies for accurate object detection and semantic segmentation. In: Proceedings of the IEEE Conference on Computer Vision and Pattern Recognition, pp. 580–587 (2014)
6. Hahn, A., et al.: Development of an automated scoring system for amateur boxing. Procedia Eng. **2**(2), 3095–3101 (2010)
7. Jeffries, C.T.: Sports analytics with computer vision. The College of Wooster (2018)
8. Kolkur, S., Kalbande, D., Shimpi, P., Bapat, C., Jatakia, J.: Human skin detection using RGB, HSV and YCBCR color models. arXiv preprint arXiv:1708.02694 (2017)
9. Kundid Vasić, M., Papić, V.: Multimodel deep learning for person detection in aerial images. Electronics **9**(9), 1459 (2020)
10. Liu, W., et al.: SSD: single shot multibox detector. In: Leibe, B., Matas, J., Sebe, N., Welling, M. (eds.) ECCV 2016. LNCS, vol. 9905, pp. 21–37. Springer, Cham (2016). https://doi.org/10.1007/978-3-319-46448-0_2
11. Redmon, J., Farhadi, A.: Yolov3: an incremental improvement. arXiv preprint arXiv:1804.02767 (2018)
12. Ren, S., He, K., Girshick, R., Sun, J.: Faster R-CNN: towards real-time object detection with region proposal networks. Adv. Neural. Inf. Process. Syst. **28**, 91–99 (2015)
13. Setterwall, D.: Computerised video analysis of football-technical and commercial possibilities for football coaching. Unpublished Masters Thesis, Stockholms Universitet (2003)
14. Stein, M., et al.: Bring it to the pitch: combining video and movement data to enhance team sport analysis. IEEE Trans. Visual Comput. Graphics **24**(1), 13–22 (2017)
15. Sudhir, G., Lee, J.C.M., Jain, A.K.: Automatic classification of tennis video for high-level content-based retrieval. In: Proceedings 1998 IEEE International Workshop on Content-Based Access of Image and Video Database, pp. 81–90. IEEE (1998)
16. Thomas, G., Gade, R., Moeslund, T.B., Carr, P., Hilton, A.: Computer vision for sports: current applications and research topics. Comput. Vis. Image Underst. **159**, 3–18 (2017)

17. Wang, D.A., Strauss, C.M., Springer, J.M., Thresher, A., Pritchard, H., Kenyon, G.T.: Sparse mp4. In: 2020 IEEE Southwest Symposium on Image Analysis and Interpretation (SSIAI), pp. 99–103. IEEE (2020)
18. Worsey, M.T.O., Espinosa, H.G., Shepherd, J.B., Thiel, D.V.: An evaluation of wearable inertial sensor configuration and supervised machine learning models for automatic punch classification in boxing. IoT 1(2), 360–381 (2020)

Risk Assessment of Acute Kidney Disease and Chronic Kidney Disease for In-Hospital Patients with Acute Kidney Injury

Ja-Hwung Su[1], Terry Ting-Yu Chiou[2], Yi-Wen Liao[3,4(✉)], Yu-Siou Liao[1], Chien-Hsin Wu[2], and Wen-Yang Lin[1]

[1] Department of Computer Science and Information Engineering, National University of Kaohsiung, Kaohsiung, Taiwan
[2] Department of Diagnostic Radiology, Kaohsiung Chang Gung Memorial Hospital, Kaohsiung, Taiwan
[3] Department of Information Management, Cheng Shiu University, Kaohsiung, Taiwan
pinkwen923@gmail.com
[4] Department of Intelligent Commerce, National Kaohsiung University of Science and Technology, Kaohsiung, Taiwan

Abstract. Acute kidney injury (AKI) is a common and important complication in hospitalized patients. They may progress into acute kidney disease (AKD) or chronic kidney disease (CKD), and predispose to dialysis or death. These complications have become great burden on the society and National Health Insurance, Taiwan. Therefore, how to predict the risk for the kidney disease has been a hot topic over the past few decades. To tackle this issue, in this paper, we propose risk assessment methods that integrate techniques of data engineering and data mining to achieve high-fidelity prediction for AKD and CKD. Based on the real data from Kaohsiung Chang Gung Memorial Hospital, the factors are retrieved first. Next, the mining techniques of K-Nearest-Neighbors (KNN) and Support-Vector-Machine (SVM) are performed to classify the potential kidney disease. The experimental results reveal that, the precisions can reach around 75%. In the future, more precise models will be developed. Accordingly, the prediction models will be established and integrate into clinical practice to facilitate decision-making process for medical professionals.

Keywords: Risk assessment · Acute kidney disease · Chronic kidney disease · K-Nearest-Neighbors · Support-Vector-Machine

1 Introduction

Acute kidney injury (AKI) is an important and previously under-recognized complication with a tremendous impact on clinical outcomes and health care costs [4, 11, 12]. It has been shown that AKI occurs in 10–20% of patients in hospitals around the world. Our previous study based on 734,340 patients admitted to Chang Gung Memorial Hospitals in Taiwan from 2010 to 2014 showed the characteristics and an alarmingly high

© The Author(s), under exclusive license to Springer Nature Singapore Pte Ltd. 2022
E. Szczerbicki et al. (Eds.): ACIIDS 2022, CCIS 1716, pp. 604–614, 2022.
https://doi.org/10.1007/978-981-19-8234-7_47

mortality rate (30%) in AKI patients [5]. Furthermore, AKI patients are at increased risk of progressing to chronic kidney disease (CKD) and end-stage renal disease (ESRD), which impose extremely high burden on the health care system and the society [1, 9]. Recent expert consensus [2] had described the continuum of kidney disease from acute to chronic states as acute kidney injury (AKI), acute kidney disease (AKD) and CKD (shown in Fig. 1).

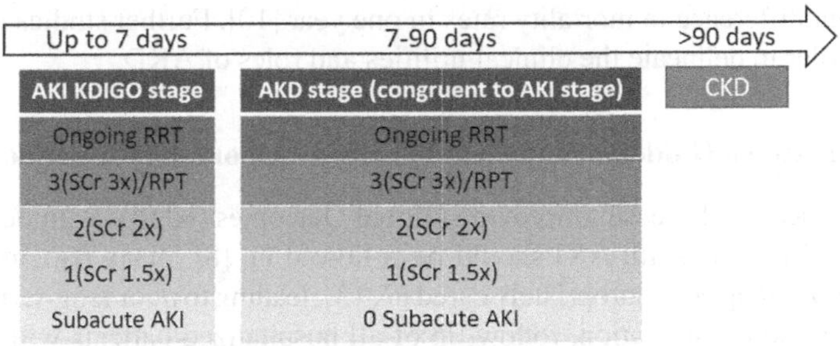

Fig. 1. Continuum and stages of kidney diseases: AKI, AKD and CKD. [2]

Potential risk factors of AKI, pertinent laboratory data, exams and subsequent major adverse kidney events (CKD, dialysis, death, etc) will be recorded. New biomarkers will also be tested. In recent years, Artificial Intelligence (AI) has been applied to industry, business, agriculture and medicine. AI in medicine refers to a set of machine learning methods discovering valuable information from a big data, eventually leading to innovations and improvements in clinical prediction and decision-aid. For this purpose, this paper presents risk assessment methods to predict the potential AKD and CKD in patients with in-Hospital Acute Kidney Injury. The major contribution can be described as follows.

I. From practical point of view, the proposed system can be applied to the existing clinic system for risk assessment of acute kidney injury. The doctor will obtain the assessment results just inputting a set of constraints. Or, the system will generate the potential assessments by diagnosis, treatments, biochemical tests, etc. With the assessments, a better treatment for a new patient will be recommended.
II. From technical point of view, the proposed method takes advantages of data engineering and data mining to extract the high-value features for automatically leveling the acute kidney injury. Moreover, the potential kidney injury will be shown to the doctors. These results will be important evidences for better treatments.

The evaluation results show that, the proposed methods achieve precisions around 75% in assessing the potential kidney diseases. The structure of this paper is presented as follows. A brief review of recent studies is shown in Sect. 2. In Sect. 3, the details of proposed methods for risk assessments are expressed. The experimental analysis is shown in Sect. 4 and the conclusion is conducted in Sect. 5.

2 Literature Review

2.1 Literature Gaps

Although AKI and CKD have been well characterized, AKD has been less well studied. A recent study from China demonstrated in hospitalized AKI patients that AKD was associated with increased 90-day mortality [14]. Another study from USA compared patients with AKD and those with early reversal of sepsis-associated AKI and found no significant difference in mortality rates in one year [10]. Further studies are urgently needed in order to delineate the clinical utilities and roles of AKD.

2.2 Gaps Between Guideline and Real Practice: Opportunity for Innovation

Although the Kidney Disease: Improving Global Outcomes (KDIGO) guideline recommends that all patients with AKI should be followed up [8], many patients with AKI were not followed up nor appropriately cared [7, 13], leading to poor long-term outcomes [3]. In real world consideration, follow-up of all hospitalized patients with AKI could impose high burden on health care system and may lead to unnecessary use of medical resources. Therefore, there is a great urgency in identifying the risk factors for AKD and future adverse kidney outcomes, including CKD and ESRD. This understanding is the key to stratifying AKD and non-AKD patients into different levels of future risks so that individualized management strategies can be designed with efficient utilization of health care resources. Our team recently developed a machine learning-generated risk score model to identify patients at risk of hospitalization after developing AKI in the community [6].

2.3 Biomarkers to Facilitate Risk Stratification in AKD

Current AKI classification criteria (shown in Fig. 2) rely on changes in serum creatinine (sCr) levels and/or urine output, but do not take into account the etiologies of AKI. Serum creatinine is a routine, but suboptimal marker of renal glomerular filtration function. For example, a patient's real GFR may decrease significantly with only minimal change on sCr. These limitations of sCr have prompted the search and development of new injury biomarkers for the recognition and diagnosis of AKI.

3 Proposed Method

As mentioned above, there actually exists a gap between the guideline and real practice for AKI care. Therefore, the goal of this paper is to narrow the gap by using biomarkers to facilitate risk stratification in AKD and CKD. To reach this goal (as shown in Fig. 3), we propose an approach that fuses techniques of data engineering and data mining to achieve higher quality of assessments of acute kidney injury. That is, the major intent behind the proposed methods is to discover the valuable knowledge from the in-hospital logs. After the doctor inputs a set of clinical parameters and constraints, the system will generate the potential assessments and predicted outcomes, from which more optimized management plans may be formulated.

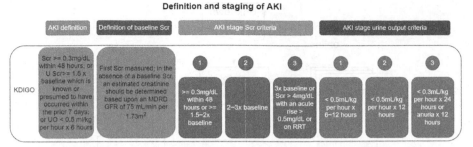

Fig. 2. Diagnosis and staging of acute kidney injury by KDIGO guideline 2012.

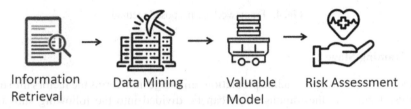

Information   Data Mining   Valuable   Risk Assessment
Retrieval   Model

Fig. 3. Scenario of proposed method.

3.1 Overview

The aim of disease risk assessment is to provide helpful information to prevent worsening of disease. Therefore, how to determine the valuable patterns and conduct useful pattern recognition have been challenging issues in the past few years. In principle, the disease risk assessment refers to a set of techniques mining patterns from big bioinformatics data. Although there have been numerous studies on this topic in the past, there remain the problems mentioned above. Hence, to attack such problems, we propose an intelligent method that integrates techniques of data engineering and data mining for more precise assessments. Overall, the framework can be divided into two stages, namely offline training and online prediction, as shown in Fig. 4.

I.   Data Cleaning: this is an important and foundation stage, including data filtering and feature selection. By these two operations, the data will be clean and pure.
II. Data Encoding: this stage is to code the selected features for training the assessment models.
III. Data Training: as the features are symbolized, the classification algorithms are performed to calculate the associations between the symbolic patterns and the kidney injury.
IV. Prediction: for an unknown report, it is recognized through operations of feature selection, feature encoding and classification. Finally, the resulting assessment is derived.

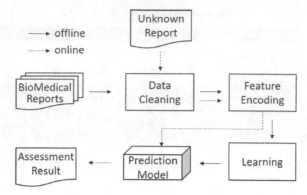

Fig. 4. Framework of proposed method.

3.2 Training Stage

To meet the requirement of online prediction, this stage transforms the factors into useful features. Therefore, the training stage can be divided into the following sub-stages, namely data cleaning, feature encoding and model construction.

A. *Data cleaning*

The data cleaning denotes a set of operations for data filtering and feature selection. Actually, in real applications, there exist three problems for online prediction. The first one indicates the data consists of irrelevant data collected from the hospital's autonomic alert system. The second one indicates a record/transaction consisting of useless attributes called features in this paper. The third one indicates that, the clinical report for a patient, in practical, contains numerical and semantic features. For example, it could contain useless records with missing values and unacceptable attribute values. Additionally, because there exist a number of redundant attributes, the dimensions need to be reduced by selecting the useful attributes. For the first and the second ones, it is processed by doctors in this paper. Accordingly, we obtain the pure transactions related to this topic. In the next sub-section, we will show how to deal with the third problem.

B. *Feature encoding*

In practical, the inconsistent feature format cannot be used in the training model. Hence, this problem is critical and needs to be coped with in this paper. After data cleaning, the remaining attributes are represented by two types, namely numerical and semantical attributes. For a semantical attribute, in this operation, we assign it a number code. For numerical attributes, we further fuzzlize it into several levels, including two types. One is the Potassium test and the other is the hospital-stay length. For the Potassium test, it is proposed by doctors, which can be divided into 4 levels defined as:

$\begin{cases} \text{Low, where the Potassium test} < 3.6, \\ \text{Normal, where } 3.6 < \text{the Potassium test} < 5.0, \\ \text{Somewhat high, where } 5.0 < \text{the Potassium test} < 6.0, \\ \text{High, where the Potassium test} > 3.6. \end{cases}$

For the hospital-stay length is divided into 3 levels according to the standard deviation, which is defined as:

$\begin{cases} \text{Low, where the length} < \text{a negative standard deviation,} \\ \text{Medium, where a negative standard deviation} < \text{the length} < \text{a positive standard deviation,} \\ \text{High, where the length} > \text{a positive standard deviation.} \end{cases}$

Then, levels of Potassium tests and hospital-stay lengths are encoded. Overall, in our data, there are 86 unique attributes, and each attribute is encoded into a number. Hence, a record can be defined as a set of attribute codes. Figure 5 is an example for data encoding. After encoding the attributes, the records are transformed into a set of codes which refer to the attributes. Figure 6 is an example of 10 encoding records where a record indicates a patient with several attribute numbers. Finally, each record is further transformed into a binary vector where a vector is represented by 86 binary values.

Attribute	Code
Aminoglycoside	20
NSAID/COXi	21
ACEi/ARB/Aliskiren	22
Calcineurin inhibitors	23
Colistin	24
Metformin	25

Fig. 5. Example of attribute encoding.

1	5	6	9	16	41	44	63
2	4	13	17	21	41	44	49
3	5	7	8	12	41	44	62
4	5	12	13	42	45	60	
5	4	6	9	15	44	46	61
6	5	9	13	43	47	51	
7	4	9	10	42	45	66	
8	5	9	10	19	41	44	68
9	4	13	42	45	57		
10	4	9	16	41	44	53	

Fig. 6. Example of encoding records.

C. *Model construction*

In this paper, two data mining algorithms are used as the classifiers, including KNN and SVM. Based on the encoding records, in this step, the leaning model will be constructed further.

3.3 Prediction Stage

Based on the constructed classifiers, the prediction can be performed online. In this stage, two well-known algorithms with respect to KNN and SVM serve as solutions for predicting an unknown record. In terms of SVM, the unknown record can be predicted as AKD or CKD. In terms of KNN, first, the most K relevant training instances will be determined by the similarity function, which is defined as:

$$sim(x, y) = \frac{\sum_{i=1}^{n} x_i * y_i}{\sqrt{\sum_{i=1}^{n} (x_i)^2} * \sqrt{\sum_{i=1}^{n} (y_i)^2}}, \tag{1}$$

where x and y denote two vectors, x_i and y_i denote the ith features and n is 86. Then the counts of AKD and CKD in K results will be accumulated individually. Finally, the larger one for counts of AKD and CKD is returned as the prediction result.

4 Experiments

To realize the effectiveness, in this paper, we made a number of experiments after materializing the methods, containing two main parts: 1) data analysis and 2) effectiveness evaluation. For the first part, what we want to show is the factor relations between non-AKD and AKD. For the second part, the main intent is to show the effectiveness of proposed methods, which can be further divided into three concepts: 1) experimental data settings 2) parameter settings and 3) effectiveness evaluations. The details are depicted in the following sub-sections.

4.1 Data Analysis

In Kaohsiung Chang Gung Memorial Hospital, an automatic AKI alert system has been conducted, which identifies AKI in hospitalized patients based on the KDIGO criteria (as soon as the confirmed serum creatinine data become available). Every year, the system detects ~1200 hospitalized patients who develop AKI during hospitalization. These patients are distributed throughout intensive care units (50%), and specialty wards (Internal Medicine subspecialties 30%; Surgical, Pediatric, gynecology combined 20%). The hospital mortality rate is about 30% and about 40% of AKI patients recovered renal function at discharge. We looked at the AKI patients from the internal medicine wards in 2019, and found that (shown in Table 1) AKI patients who subsequently developed AKD had lower SCr at baseline and at time of AKI, but higher SCr at time of discharge. Interestingly, there is a trend for AKD patients to have AKI occurring at a later hospital day (21 vs. 15 days). On the whole, there exist correlations between AKD and factors: SCr_Baseline, SCr (AKI), In-hospital length before occurring AKI and sCr at discharged.

Table 1. Comparison between AKD and non-AKD patients in AKI patients admitted to internal medicine specialty wards (2019).

	Non-AKD (108)		AKD (111)		p-value
	Mean	SD	Mean	SD	
Age	68	16	67	15	0.504
SCr_Baseline	1.24	1.03	0.93	0.73	<0.01
Increase in SCr levels	2.9	1.2	2.9	1.4	0.7
AKI stage	2	0	2	0	1
SCr (AKI)	3.36	2.51	2.55	1.94	<0.001
K (AKI)	4.3	0.8	4.2	1.0	0.3
In-hospital length before occurring AKI	15	19	21	31	0.073
sCr at discharged	1.50	1.65	2.92	3.48	<0.001

* Note: SD denotes standard deviation.

4.2 Experiments for Effectiveness

IN addition to data analysis above, the other issue to clarify is the effectiveness of proposed methods. In this sub-section, the experimental results are shown by concepts of data settings, parameter settings and effectiveness evaluations.

A. *Experimental data settings*

To carry out the experiments, we collected the data from Kaohsiung Chang Gung Memorial Hospital. This data is composed of 371 in-hospital patient records and 86 unique attributes. After the data encoding, each record is transformed into a binary vector. From the data, 70% of data was randomly selected for training, while 30% for testing. To make the experiment more solid, the evaluation was performed ten times by randomly splitting the data ten times also. The final demonstrated result is the average of precisions.

B. *Parameter settings*

This evaluation was made by KNN. The main intent is to clarify impacts of parameter K. Figure 7 shows the precisions of KNN for different K settings. In this experiment, the best performance appears as K is 10. The potential explanation is that, the fewer neighbors cannot provide sufficient information. In contrast, more neighbors contain noises that decrease the precision. However, the impact of K is not significant. Therefore, K is set as 10 in the following comparison with SVM.

C. *Effectiveness evaluations*

The final issue is to validate the effectiveness difference between KNN and SVM [15]. Figure 8 shows the comparison result, which delivers an aspect that KNN performs

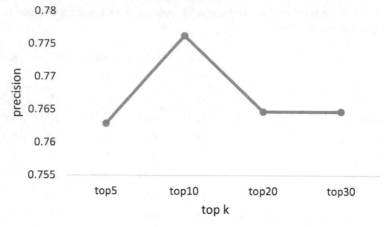

Fig. 7. Precisions of KNN under different K settings.

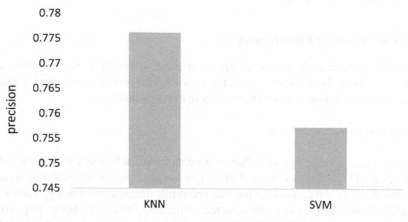

Fig. 8. Precisions of KNN and SVM.

slightly better than SVM. This result might be caused by the binary data format. However, the difference is not significant enough to identify SVM is not a good classifier.

5 Limitations

In this paper, there are several limitations to claim here. The data source comes from only patients in Kaohsiung Chang Gung Memorial Hospital, Taiwan. Second, the data size is 371. Third, the number of factors is 86. Fourth, the KNN is implemented by authors and SVM is downloaded in [15].

6 Conclusions

In recent years, health care has been paid much attention. In this field, AI plays a critical role for improving the care quality. In fact, there have been a lot of past studies made on this topic. Yet, few studies are proposed on the kidney injury care in Taiwan. Therefore, how to predict the potential kidney injury is an important issue, which can prevent the treatment delay. This inspires us to take a further step for proposing a predictor to estimate the potential kidney injury for an in-hospital patient. In this paper, we propose prediction methods which integrate techniques of data engineering and data mining. For data engineering, the data is cleaned by data filtering, feature selection and data transformation. For data mining, two classifiers including KNN and SVM are performed to predict the potential kidney injury. The experimental results reveal that, the precision can reach around 75%, which provides a baseline for further researches. Although the prediction methods for the potential kidney injury are proposed in this paper, there actually remain a set of future works to do. First, the data size will be enlarged to show the scalability. Second, more considerable factors will be added to increase the precision. Third, more powerful classifiers will be examined to investigate the prediction quality.

Acknowledgement. This research was supported by Ministry of Science and Technology, Taiwan, R.O.C. under grant no. 111-2410-H-230-003-MY2 and MOST 110-2221-E-390-015.

Institutional Review Board Statement. The data were approved by Kaohsiung Chang Gung Memorial Hospital, Taiwan, and all operations in this paper were executed according to the ethical standards of the Institutional Review Board, Taiwan.

References

1. Chawla, L.S., Eggers, P.W., Star, R.A., Kimmel, P.L.: Acute kidney injury and chronic kidney disease as interconnected syndromes. N. Engl. J. Med. **371**, 58–66 (2014)
2. Chawla, L.S., et al.: Acute kidney disease and renal recovery: consensus report of the Acute Disease Quality Initiative (ADQI) 16 Workgroup. Nat. Rev. Nephrol. **13**(4), 241–257 (2017)
3. Goldstein, S.L., Jaber, B.L., Faubel, S., Chawla, L.S.: Acute Kidney Injury Advisory Group of American Society of Nephrology, "AKI transition of care: a potential opportunity to detect and prevent CKD." Clin. J. Am. Soc. Nephrol. **8**(3), 476–483 (2013)
4. Hoste, E.A.J., et al.: Global epidemiology and outcomes of acute kidney injury. Nat. Rev. Nephrol. **14**(10), 607–625 (2018)
5. Hsu, C.N., et al.: Incidence, outcomes, and risk factors of community-acquired and hospital-acquired acute kidney injury: a retrospective cohort study. Medicine **95**(19), e3674 (2016)
6. Hsu, C.N., Liu, C.L., Tain, Y.L., Kuo, C.Y., Lin, Y.C.: Machine learning model for risk prediction of community-acquired acute kidney injury hospitalization from electronic health records: development and validation study. J. Med. Internet Res. **22**(8), e16903 (2020)
7. Harel, Z., et al.: Nephrologist follow-up improves all-cause mortality of severe acute kidney injury survivors. Kidney Int. **83**(5), 901–908 (2013)
8. Khwaja, A.: KDIGO clinical practice guidelines for acute kidney injury. Nephron Clin. Pract. **120**(4), c179–c184 (2012)
9. Li, P.K., Burdmann, E.A., Mehta, R.L.: Acute kidney injury: global health alert. Kidney Int. **83**(3), 372-6, 1–8 (2013)
10. Peerapornratana, S., et al.: Sepsis-ssociated acute kidney disease. Kidney Int. Rep. **5**(6), 839–850 (2020)
11. Riffaut, N., Moranne, O., Hertig, A., Hannedouche, T., Couchoud, C.: Outcomes of acute kidney injury depend on initial clinical features: a national French cohort study. Nephrol. Dial. Transplant. **33**(12), 2218–2227 (2018)

12. Silver, S.A., Long, J., Zheng, Y., Chertow, G.M.: Cost of acute kidney injury in hospitalized patients. J. Hosp. Med. **12**(2), 70–76 (2017)
13. Siew, E.D., et al.: Outpatient nephrology referral rates after acute kidney injury. J. Am. Soc. Nephrol. **23**(2), 305–312 (2012)
14. Xiao, Y.Q., et al.: Novel risk models to predict acute kidney disease and its outcomes in a Chinese hospitalized population with acute kidney injury. Sci Rep. **10**(1), 15636 (2020)
15. Support Vector Machine. http://www.csie.ntu.edu.tw/~cjlin/libsvm

Music Emotion Recognition Based on Term Frequency and Pattern Entropy

Ja-Hwung Su[1]([✉]), Yi-Wen Liao[2,3], and Liang-Yu Chen[1]

[1] Department of Computer Science and Information Engineering, National University of Kaohsiung, Kaohsiung, Taiwan
bb0820@ms22.hinet.net
[2] Department of Information Management, Cheng Shiu University, Kaohsiung, Taiwan
[3] Department of Intelligent Commerce, National Kaohsiung University of Science and Technology, Kaohsiung, Taiwan

Abstract. In fact, music emotion is a music preference factor because it can deliver the user's implicit emotions while listening to music. Therefore, a number of researches have been made on how to effectively recognize the music emotions over the past few decades. So called music emotion recognition refers a set of algorithms learning from the relations between low-level features and high-level emotions for predicting the music emotions. Although these forerunners have proposed effective methods, the emotion-to-acoustic diversity limits the advancement. To aim at this issue, in this paper, we present a method to increase the recognition quality by clarifying the diverse relations. In the proposed method, the music is represented by patterns. Next, the emotion frequencies and pattern entropies are calculated to show the distribution between concepts and music. Once the distribution is derived, the music emotion can be predicted more successfully. To reveal the effectiveness of proposed method, a comprehensive experiment is conducted and the results show the proposed method is more promising than the state-of-the-arts methods in emotion recognition.

Keywords: Music emotion · Music recognition · Entropy · Machine learning · Term frequency

1 Introduction

Music is life for some people who are always listening to music. Actually, music has been popular multimedia data in recent years because it can ease our daily life effectively. Therefore, a large need for music acquirements is booted and a number of online music websites exist then. To satisfy this need, music recommendation, music retrieval and music recognition are three hot research topics. For music retrieval, it allows the user to conduct a query by conceptual terms or content examples. In terms of a conceptual query, the user can submit an emotion terms by texting or detecting the emotion state. In terms of a content query, the user can submit an example with emotion features. Whatever the query type is, emotion is an important music preference factor for a user.

© The Author(s), under exclusive license to Springer Nature Singapore Pte Ltd. 2022
E. Szczerbicki et al. (Eds.): ACIIDS 2022, CCIS 1716, pp. 615–625, 2022.
https://doi.org/10.1007/978-981-19-8234-7_48

For example, people falling in love always listen to romantic music. Moreover, she/he in pain is willing to search sad music on music websites. This further incurs an issue for how to derive the music emotions to enrich listening experiences. For this issue, there are lots of past studies proposed using machine learning methods such as Support Vector Machine (SVM), Linear Discriminant Analysis (LDA) and so on. Although these forerunners are shown to be effective, there remains a problem called emotion-to-acoustic diversity that is not easy to deal with. So called emotion-to-acoustic diversity indicates the diverse relation existing between high-level emotions and low-level acoustic features. For example, an acoustic feature might be shared with different emotions, and in contrast, an emotion might exist in many acoustic features. Especially for multi-labeling, this problem heavily disrupts the machine recognition. To aim at this issue, in this paper, we propose a method that models the distribution between the emotions and features. In this method, the music with similar features is grouped into a cluster (pattern). Next, the pattern entropy and emotion frequency will be computed. According to the entropy and frequency, the emotion degrees for unknown music will be inferred effectively. The major contribution of this paper can be summarized in an aspect that, the relations between the music and concepts are derived by the music patterns. Therefore, the prediction quality is improved. To reveal the effectiveness of proposed method, a number of state-of-the-arts methods are compared by experiments. The experimental results show that, the proposed method results in better precisions than the compared methods.

The remaining of this paper is structured as follows. The related works are briefly reviewed in Sect. 2. In Sect. 3, the proposed method for music emotion recognition is presented in detail. The evaluation result is provided in Sect. 4. Finally, the conclusion and future works are made in Sect. 5.

2 Related Work

In fact, music recognition can be viewed as a basic technique that supports music retrieval and music recommendation. Further, music recognition can be divided into two categories, namely music classification and music multi-labeling. For music classification, it is a traditional topic classifying the music as a single genre. For music multi-labeling, music is labeled by multiple tags, such as emotions. In current music websites, the users are allowed to tag the music by conceptual terms. These terms are the bases of music search. Among the retrieval types, emotion-based music retrieval has been a rising paradigm that delivers the implicit music preference. Therefore, music emotion recognition is proposed for this need. Typically, music emotion recognition can be categorized into two sets, including general multi-labeling methods and deep learning methods. In the succeeding sub-sections, the related works are reviewed by categories.

2.1 General Multi-labeling Methods

In this type, methods can be further divided into two categories, namely multi-classification and multi-annotation. In terms of multi-classification, music emotion recognition is viewed as a classification problem that classifies music as several emotion tags. Hence, traditional classifiers such as k-Nearest-Neighbor (kNN) [10], SVM [7][16],

Linear Discriminant Analysis (LDA) [1], Random Forest (RF) [11], Naive Bayes [2], AdaBoost Decision Tree (ADT) [11], etc., are adopted as the recognizers. In addition to traditional classifiers, multi-annotation is another general multi-labeling type. Binary correlation (BR) [3] established a binary classifier for the emotions, but did not know the relationship between the emotion labels. Label Powerset (LP) [14] converts the label set into a new category, and then predicts the most possible set as the result. LP considered the correlation between the labels, but established too many classifiers. Random k labELsets (RAkEL) [15] randomly built a set of smaller label sets to reduce the number of label sets.

2.2 Deep Learning Methods

In addition to traditional multi-labeling methods above, in recent years, with the advancement of deep learning networks, music emotion tagging has been moved from music auditory methods to neural networks. Convolutional Neural Network is an effective method used for image recognition and VGG [13] is the popular one in the field of music recognition. The basic idea is to transform music into a Mel-Frequency spectrum image. Thereby, the music emotion recognition is regarded as an image recognition. Costa et al. [4] compared the deep learning method with the SVM method based on the spectrogram and the commonly used music auditory features, respectively. Ghosal et al. [6] discussed the effectiveness of various deep learning on music classification, including CNN Max Pooling, CNN Max Pooling LSTM, CNN Average Pooling and CNN Average Pooling LSTM. Oramas et al. [9] considered the characteristics of music audio and spectrum images at the same time. Nam et al. [8] discussed the evolution of musical characteristics learning. Dieleman et al. [5] recognized music using raw audio signals instead of spectrograms by CNN.

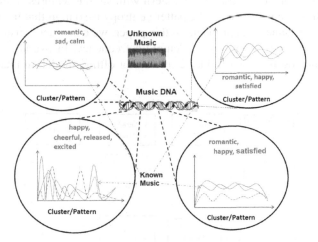

Fig. 1. Entropy scenario of proposed method.

3 Proposed Method

3.1 Core Idea

To touch the user emotion nearly, it needs an effective recognition method to represent the listening emotion. Although lots of methods are proposed on music emotion recognition using acoustic feature analysis, there remains an uncertain relation between acoustic features and emotions. To clarify the uncertain relation, the primary intent of this paper is to transform the recognition from feature space to pattern space [12]. The core idea relies on two major aspects: pattern entropy and emotion frequency. In terms of pattern entropy, it represents the diversity for a pattern. In the pattern space, each pattern is assigned a weight by calculating the entropy. A good pattern in this method can be identified as a pure cluster, that is, the related entropy is low. Besides pattern entropy, emotion frequency represents the emotion significance in a pattern. In summary, the fewer the emotions, the purer the pattern, the higher the discriminarity. From another viewpoint, the more frequent the emotion, the more representative the emotion. According to the patterns relevant to an unknown music piece, the emotions can be identified by pattern entropies and emotion frequencies. Based on these two aspects, for unknown music, the potential emotions in the relevant patterns will be inferred more precisely. On the whole, the entropy scenario can be shown in Fig. 1. In this example, known music with similar acoustic features is grouped into a set of clusters which are viewed as patterns. Each pattern is composed of numerous emotions. Further, the pattern entropy can be computed.

3.2 Framework

From above illustrations, we can know that, there really exists the problem of emotion-to-acoustic diversity. In the illustrations, a pattern with similar features contains a number of emotions. In some worse cases, the pattern entropy is so high that the relation is not easy to clarify. To attack this problem, in this paper, we construct a distribution model by computing the pattern entropy and emotion frequency. In overall, the framework of proposed method is shown in Fig. 2, including offline modeling phase and online prediction phase.

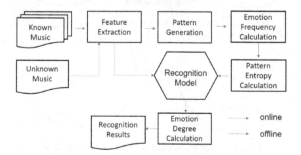

Fig. 2. Framework of proposed method.

I. Offline modeling phase: this is a fundamental phase that contains music feature extraction, pattern generation and recognition model construction. First, the music features are extracted from known music. Next, the known music is grouped into a set of clusters. Then, the pattern entropy and emotion frequency are calculated as a recognition model.

II. Online prediction phase: based on the recognition, the unknown music is also processed by feature extraction. Next, the related emotion degrees are calculated by using the pattern entropy and emotion frequency. Finally, the top-z emotions are returned.

3.3 Offline Modeling

The goal of this phase is to generate the emotion frequency and pattern entropy. Figure 3 depicts the workflow of offline modeling, including operations of feature extraction, feature normalization, clustering, emotion frequency calculation and pattern entropy calculation. In the constructed model, a cluster can be regarded as a pattern, which consists of several emotion terms. Hence, for each pattern, the emotion frequency and pattern entropy are calculated. Details of how it works are presented in the succeeding sub-sections.

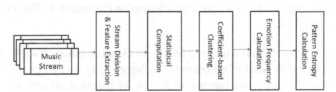

Fig. 3. Workflow of offline modeling.

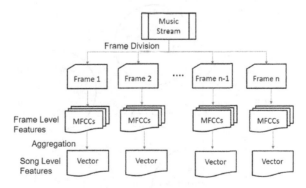

Fig. 4. Music feature structure.

A. Feature Extraction

Music feature has been studied for a long time. Until now, there have been a number of music features proposed for Music Information Retrieval, such as Modified Discrete Cosine Transform, Zero Crossing Rate, Spectral Centroid, Spectral Rolloff, Spectral Flux, Spectral Flatness Measure, Spectral Crest Factor, Linear Prediction Cepstral Coefficients, Chroma, Mel-scale Frequency Cepstral Coefficients. In this paper, Mel-scale Frequency Cepstral Coefficient (MFCC) is adopted as the acoustic feature. Figure 4 shows the music feature structure. In this structure, a music piece is divided into numerous frames and each frame is composed of a set of coefficients, which are called frame-level features in traditional. Next, the frame-level features are aggregated into one dimensional vector, which is called song-level feature. Finally, the song-level features are normalized as the basic features in the following operations.

B. Pattern Generation

In traditional Music Information Retrieval, music is represented as a song-level feature vector to recognize the music. However, it is not easy to identify the emotion-to-acoustic relation by the music feature. To aim at this issue, in this paper, the music will be further grouped into clusters also called patterns. In this method, k-means is the algorithm adopted for clustering music, and a pattern is defined in Definition 1. The related example is shown in Example 1.

Definition 1. Assume there is a training music set D and an emotion set E. In D, a music piece m_i is presented by a set of emotion terms, $m_i = \cup e_j$ where $e_j \in E$. Accordingly, the music in D is grouped into a pattern set $P \cup p_k$ by cosine similarity, and a pattern p_k is defined as $p_k = \{m_1, m_2, ..., m_q\}$ where $|p_k| = q$.

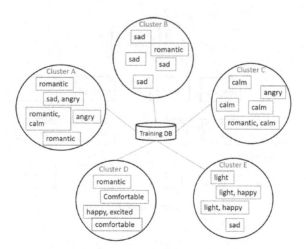

Fig. 5. Example of music patterns.

Example 1. Assume there are 8 unique emotions in D, with respect to {sad, calm, angry, romantic, comfortable, happy, light, excited}. Figure 5 is an example depicting that, 23 music pieces in D are grouped into 5 clusters {Cluster A, Cluster B, Cluster C, Cluster D, Cluster E}. In each cluster, numerous music pieces with several emotions are illustrated in rectangles. In this paper, the training music is annotated by experts.

C. *Emotion Frequency Calculation*

After the pattern generation, a pattern is composed of a music set. Because a music piece in a pattern contains an emotion set, a pattern can be further represented by an emotion set. Accordingly, the emotion frequencies in each pattern are calculated. In this paper, the jth emotion frequency in the kth pattern can be defined as f_j^k, which indicates the referred occurrence count in pattern k. Table 1 shows the emotion frequencies for each pattern.

Table 1. Example of emotion frequencies.

Emotion	Cluster A	Cluster B	Cluster C	Cluster D	Cluster E
Sad	1	4	0	0	1
Calm	1	0	4	0	0
Angry	2	0	1	0	0
Romantic	3	1	1	1	0
Comfortable	0	0	0	2	0
Happy	0	0	0	1	2
Light	0	0	0	0	3
Excited	0	0	0	1	0

D. *Pattern Entropy Calculation*

Based on the emotion frequency, the pattern entropy can be calculated thereupon. For the kth pattern, the related entropy is defined as:

$$Entropy_k = \sum_{x=1}^{|E|} \left(\frac{f_x^k}{\sum_{y=1}^{|E|} f_y^k} * log \frac{\sum_{y=1}^{|E|} f_y^k}{f_x^k} \right). \tag{1}$$

Table 2 shows the example of pattern entropies. In this example, pattern B is more discriminative than the other patterns, while pattern D is the worst for clarifying feature diversity.

Table 2. Example of pattern entropies.

Pattern	Entropy
Cluster A	3/7 * log(7/3) + 2/7 * log(7/2) + 1/7 * log(7/1) + 1/7 * log(7/1) = 0.555
Cluster B	4/5 * log(5/4) + 1/5 * log(5/1) = 0.217
Cluster C	4/6 * log(6/4) + 1/6 * log(6/1) + 1/6 * log(6/1) = 0.377
Cluster D	1/5 * log(5/1) + 2/5 * log(5/2) + 1/5 * log(5/1) + 1/5 * log(5/1) = 0.579
Cluster E	2/6 * log(6/2) + 3/6 * log(6/3) + 1/6 * log(6/1) = 0.439

Input: An unknown music piece m and a training model consisting of the emotion frequencies and pattern entropies;
Output: Top z emotions;
Algorithm: MERP (Music_Emotion_Recognition by Patterns)
1. **for** each cluster p_k in P **do**
2.   calculate the similarity between m and p_k;
3.   determine the most relevant cluster set S to m;
4. **for** each emotion in S **do**
5.   calculate the emotion degree by Eq. (2);
6.   rank the emotions by degrees;
7.   **return** top z emotions;

Fig. 6. Algorithm of MERP (Music_Emotion_Recognition by patterns).

Table 3. Example of prediction results.

Emotion	Degree
Sad	{(1/7) * (1/0.555)} + {(4/5) * (1/0.217)} + {(1/5) * (1/0.579)} = 4.297*
Calm	{(1/7) * (1/0.555)} + {(0/5) * (1/0.217)} + {(0/5) * (1/0.579)} = 0.257
Angry	{(2/7) * (1/0.555)} + {(0/5) * (1/0.217)} + {(0/5) * (1/0.579)} = 0.515
Romantic	{(3/7) * (1/0.555)} + {(1/5) * (1/0.217)} + {(0/5) * (1/0.579)} = 1.694*
Comfortable	{(0/7) * (1/0.555)} + {(0/5) * (1/0.217)} + {(2/5) * (1/0.579)} = 0.691
Happy	{(0/7) * (1/0.555)} + {(0/5) * (1/0.217)} + {(1/5) * (1/0.579)} = 0.354
Light	{(0/7) * (1/0.555)} + {(0/5) * (1/0.217)} + {(0/5) * (1/0.579)} = 0
Excited	{(0/7) * (1/0.555)} + {(0/5) * (1/0.217)} + {(1/5) * (1/0.579)} = 0.354

3.4 Online Prediction

Once the emotion frequency and pattern entropy are computed, the distribution between emotions and music is thereby constructed. In this distribution, the emotion frequency reveals how representative a pattern emotion is, while the pattern entropy reveals how discriminative a pattern is. The procedure can be shown in Fig. 6. For an unknown music piece m, first, the most relevant cluster set S is determined by the similarities between m and clusters. These relevant clusters are regarded as the patterns for m. Next, for each emotion e_j in S, the related degree d_j is computed, which can be defined as:

$$d_j = \sum_{x=1}^{|S|} \left(\frac{f_j^x}{\sum_{y=1}^{|E|} f_y^x} * \frac{1}{Entropy_x} \right). \tag{2}$$

Table 3 shows the example for the prediction result. In this example, assume the most 3 clusters are Clusters A, B and D. Then the degree for each emotion is calculated by Eq. (2). Finally, top 2 emotions {sad, romantic} are returned.

4   Experiment

4.1   Experimental Data

The experimental data called CAL500 came from Computer Audition Lab, which contains 436 music pieces and 18 emotions. Because the differences among 18 emotions are not significant, they were further simplified into 7 emotions with respect to {Sad, Romantic, Happy, Exciting, Light, Calm, Angry} in this paper. In the experiment, 70% of data was randomly selected for training and the others was adopted for testing. Furthermore, the music is grouped into 40 clusters and the most 5 clusters are determined in the prediction phase, that is, $k = 40$ and $|S| = 5$.

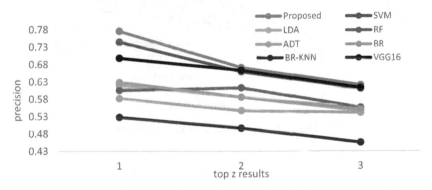

Fig. 7. Precisions of compared methods.

4.2   Experimental Results

To reveal the effectiveness of proposed idea, 7 methods were compared in the evaluation, including SVM, LDA, RF, ADT, BR, BRKNN and VGG16. Figures 7, 8 and 9 showing the precisions, recalls and F-measures of compared methods delivers some points. First, the precision gap of the proposed and compared methods is larger while $z = 1$. This is because the pattern entropy and emotion frequency are sensitive in top-1 emotion. Second, whatever for precision, recall and F-measure, the proposed method performs better than compared methods. Third, for VGG16, the music was transformed into a

Mel-Frequency Spectrogram. It performed slightly worse than SVM while $z = 1$, but very closely to SVM and the proposed method while $z = 2$ and 3. Fourth, the overall measure F-measure concludes an aspect that, the proposed method is more effective in tackling problem of emotion-to-acoustic diversity.

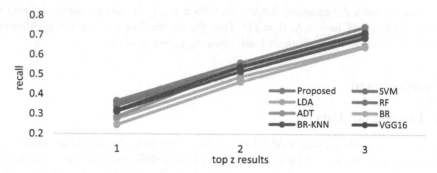

Fig. 8. Recalls of compared methods.

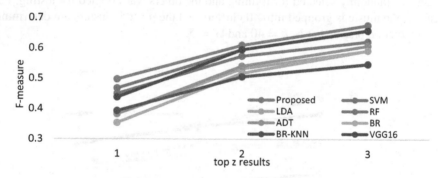

Fig. 9. F-measures of compared methods.

5 Conclusions

In the past few decades, music emotion recognition has been studied by a set of researches. Although the study focus has been moved from audio features to visual images, there remains a problem of emotion-to-acoustic diversity unsettled. This problem inspires us to propose a statistical solution that fuses Pattern-Recognition, Term-Frequency and Entropy. In terms of Pattern-Recognition, the original idea is to represent music by relevant patterns. In terms of Term-Frequency, it is oriented from Information Retrieval where the emotion frequency in a pattern represents the representativeness. In terms of Entropy, it says that, the pattern with a lower entropy is discriminative. Based on these ideas, the emotion is predicted more precisely. The evaluation result approves the contribution that, the proposed method works better than the state-of-the-arts methods in music recognition. In fact, this is just a beginning of proposed idea. In the future, our intent is to aggregate visual deep learning into this idea to achieve high-quality of music emotion recognition.

Acknowledgement. This research was supported by Ministry of Science and Technology, Taiwan, R.O.C. under grant no. 111-2410-H-230-003-MY2 and MOST 110-2221-E-390-015.

References

1. Alexandre-Cortizo, E., Rosa-Zurera, M., Lopes-Ferreras, F.: Application of fisher linear discriminant analysis to speech/music classification. In: Proceedings of the EUROCON International Conference on "Computer as a Tool" (2005)
2. Y. An, Sun, S., Wang, S.: Naive Bayes classifiers for music emotion classification based on lyrics. In: Proceedings of IEEE/ACIS 16th International Conference on Computer and Information Science (2017)
3. Boutell, M.R., Luo, J., Shen, X., Brown, C.M.: Learning multi-label scene classification. Pattern Recogn. **37**(9), 1757–1771 (2004)
4. Costa, U.M.G., Oliveira, L.S., Silla, C.N., Jr.: An evaluation of convolutional neural networks for music classification using spectrograms. Appl. Soft Comput. **52**, 28–38 (2017)
5. Dieleman, S., Schrauwen, B.: End-to-end learning for music audio. In: The 39th IEEE International Conference on Acoustics, Speech and Signal Processing (ICASSP), Florence, pp. 6964–6968 (2014)
6. Ghosal, D., Kolekar, M.H.: Music genre recognition using deep neural networks and transfer learning. In: Proceedings of Interspeech (2018)
7. Lidy, T., Rauber, A.: Evaluation of feature extractors and psycho-acoustic transformations for music genre classification. In: Proceedings of the International Conference of International Society for Music Information Retrieval (ISMIR) (2005)
8. Nam, J., Choi, K., Lee, J., Chou, S., Yang, Y.: Deep learning for audio-based music classification and tagging: teaching computers to distinguish rock from Bach. IEEE Signal Process. Mag. **36**(1), 41–51 (2019)
9. Oramas, S., Barbieri, F., Nieto, O., Serra, X.: Multimodal deep learning for music genre classification. Trans. Int. Soc. Music Inf. Retr. **1**(1), 4–21 (2018)
10. Pampalk, E., Flexer, A., Widmer, G.: Improvements of audio based music similarity and genre classification. In: Proceedings of the International Conference of International Society for Music Information Retrieval (ISMIR) (2005)
11. Santos, A.M., Canuto, A.M.P., Neto, A.F.: A Comparative analysis of classification methods to multi-label tasks in different application domains. Int. J. Comput. Inf. Syst. Ind. Manag. Appl. **3**, 218–227 (2011)
12. Su, J.-H., Chou, C.-L., Lin, C.-Y., Tseng, V.S.: Effective semantic annotation by image-to-concept distribution model. IEEE Trans. Multimedia (TMM) **13**(3), 530–538 (2011)
13. Simonyan, K., Zisserman, A.: Very deep convolutional networks for large-scale image recognition. arXiv preprint arXiv:1409.1556 (2014)
14. Tsoumakas, G., Katakis, I.: Multi-label classification: an overview. Int. J. Data Wareh. Min. **3**(3), 1–13 (2007)
15. Tsoumakas, G., Katakis, I., Vlahavas, I.: Random k-labelsets for multilabel classification. IEEE Trans. Knowl. Data Eng. **23**(7), 1079–1089 (2011)
16. Xu, C., Maddage, N.C., Shao, X., Cao, F., Tian, Q.: Musical genre classification using support vector machines, In: Proceedings of the IEEE International Conference on Acoustics, Speech, and Signal Processing (2003)

Hybrid Boustrophedon and Partition Tree Group Algorithm for Coverage Path Planning Problem with Energy Constraints

Tran Thi Cam Giang[1(✉)] and Huynh Thi Thanh Binh[2]

[1] ThuyLoi University, Hanoi, Vietnam
giangttc@tlu.edu.vn
[2] Hanoi University of Science and Technology, Hanoi, Vietnam
binhht@soict.hust.edu.vn

Abstract. Coverage path planning (CPP) finds the shortest feasible paths passing through all points of an environment while avoiding obstacles. Previous studies usually assume that a robot has infinite power and can fully cover the workspace with only one charge, but most mobile robots run under a limited energy budget. This study focuses on the CPP problem for a mobile robot with constrained energy power that satisfies two main optimization objectives: the total distance and the number of repeated cells. We propose a hybrid algorithm between the Boustrophedon and the partition tree group algorithms, namely B-WZone, for the CPP with energy constraints. The performance of this algorithm is compared with existing methods. The experimental results showed that the B-WZone algorithm helps the robot reduce energy consumption and traveling time in all the tested environments.

Keywords: Robotics · Coverage path planning · Energy constraints · Approximation · Boustrophedon decomposition

1 Introduction

The coverage path planning (CPP) is a fundamental problem in robotics with abundant real-world applications and many other potential applications, such as vacuum cleaning, painting, demining, and window cleaning robots [1,3]. The CPP problem is a study topic in robotics but is still considered an incompletely solved problem. The aim is to find paths that allow the robot to visit all points in the working environment.

The CPP is divided into two main versions based on the coverage range of the environment. The first version is OfflineCPP, where robot(s) have prior knowledge of the environment, including obstacles. The second version is OnlineCPP, where the robot does not know the environment's details and can accumulate knowledge of the environment during the coverage [1]. Many previous algorithms have been proposed to solve this CPP with simple assumptions, such as the environment is

© The Author(s), under exclusive license to Springer Nature Singapore Pte Ltd. 2022
E. Szczerbicki et al. (Eds.): ACIIDS 2022, CCIS 1716, pp. 626–640, 2022.
https://doi.org/10.1007/978-981-19-8234-7_49

a polygon, the robot is a unit point [3, 8, 9], and it can only move in four directions with an unlimited energy budget and visit all the accessible locations in an environment including obstacles by a unique single path. However, the assumption that robot(s) have an infinite power supply is not realistic. Robots have energy limitations and move by using batteries that run out after a certain time. A battery-powered robot must regularly return to the charging station to recharge before the battery runs out or to exchange batteries. Robots spend much more energy on some problematic missions, such as relief and rescue tasks or operating in rough environments, and they can not return to the charging station on time. Therefore, their mission might fail, or die on the way.

In recent years, studies have concentrated more on how to optimize the robot's energy. The coverage path planning problem with energy constraints is also considered and becomes more complex. Instead of a single path with unlimited energy power, we will plan multiple routes for the robot due to its inability to cover all the locations after one full recharge. These paths are limited to cycles. Besides, other recent papers have started mentioning more constraints such as optimizing the number of paths, restricting the repeated cells, etc. However, this OfflineCPP problem has not been completely solved. This paper has some significant contributions to achieving the maximum coverage and minimizing the coverage path in current CPP applications, as summarized below:

- Proposing the B-WZone coverage algorithm to obtain the maximum coverage in a known environment.
- Proposing a new approach dividing the working environment of the robot by split lines.
- Analyzing and evaluating the influence of factors such as the locations of the charging station and obstacles, and the energy of a robot on two criteria: total length and total number of paths.

The remaining part of this paper is split into five sections: definitions and formulations of the problem in Sect. 2, related work in the next section, and our proposed algorithms in the fourth section. In Sect. 5, we focus on exploiting the setups of our experiments, computational results on various test sets, and a performance comparison with other algorithms. Conclusions and discussions on future extensions are given in the last section.

2   Related Work

As mentioned previously, the classic OfflineCPP in which the robots have an unlimited energy budget for walking arbitrary long distances is no longer suitable for academics and industry. No robot can entirely cover a large environment by a single path. Moreover, the coverage problem for a robot without the energy constraints is considered a Traveling Salesperson Problem (TSP) [6]. For this reason, in the recent ten years, some algorithms have been proposed to solve the OfflineCPP with energy constraints. It becomes the Vehicle Routing Problem (VRP) [3,4] and the version of TSP closest to this CPP version is the Distance Vehicle Routing Problem (DVRP), where the energy consumption is proportional to the distance walked.

Since 2014, the coverage with energy constraints has started to receive much attention. Strimel et al. [10] in 2014 employed the boustrophedon cellular decomposition to cover the environment with a single charging station S, and before its battery runs out, the robot comes back to S. In 2016, Mishra et al. [11] constructed a coverage system for the problem of multiple robots by dividing the robots into two groups (workers and helpers). This model always covers the entire environment because when a worker's battery runs out, they must come back to recharge, and a helper will be sent to continue the work. In addition, Shnaps et al. [5] represented an online coverage method in a known environment by an approximation algorithm with a ratio ρ formulated by the longest distance and the energy budget.

In 2018, Wei et al. [6] revisited the model of Shnaps and Rimon [5] and then presented a constant-factor approximation algorithm for the energy-constrained OfflineCPP. The author introduced different travel strategies: first, visit the most distant cells, and then, the cells near the charging station. Their result is better than the algorithm of Shnaps and Rimon [5] according to two criteria: the number of paths and the total length of paths. However, the model of Wei has only been applied in contour-connected environments and has a lot of repeated cells during coverage.

In the same year 2018, Wei et al. reused the contour-connected method and the approximate cellular decomposition method [6,7], presenting a sweeping algorithm to partition a general environment into contour-connected subareas and ordering the partitioned subareas as a tree. Each node is a contour-connected subarea. Due to this method, their result reduced the number of paths returning to the charging station. However, there are some drawbacks of this algorithm: (1) robots are limited in linear motions, (2) the model solves the offline problem and does not consider any constraints other than the energy constraints, (3) the number of cells repeated is high, and finally, the obtained results can be reduced if the knowledge in advance of the robot is incomplete or invalid [12].

To remove the above limitations and to obtain the minimum as well as to complete coverage in a known environment, we propose the B-WZone coverage algorithm to solve a bigger cconstraints and two main objectives, including the number of paths and the total length of paths.

3   Problem Formulation

Input:	- An environment P is divided into cells
	- A robot with an energy budget B
	- A charging station S
	- A set of n static obstacles
Output:	Set of paths $\Pi=(\pi_1, \pi_2, \ldots, \pi_n)$
Constraints:	(1) Each path π_i starts and ends at S
	(2) Length of the path $\pi_i \leq B$
	(3) $\bigcup_{i=1}^n \pi_i = P$, paths of the set Π cover P
Objectives:	(1) $\Sigma_i^n \lvert \pi_i \rvert \longrightarrow Minimum$
	(2) $\lvert \Pi \rvert \longrightarrow Minimum$

The OfflineCPP problem has one robot with a limited energy B. An environment is set as a unit-grid (LxL size cell) laid out on a polygon P that contains a single charging station S. In order to calculate the traveling length, we will denote the cell's width as 1 unit distance. Obstacles have their shapes and locations, known in advance. A cell is white or free if an obstacle does not occupy it. Cells on the boundaries of the blocks may be partially occupied. The robot is represented as a cell that moves rectilinearly in P. We state this problem as above.

Initially, the robot stays at the charging station. It goes to work and must return to the charging station to recharge before the battery runs out. The robot's energy consumption is proportional to the distance moved, i.e., the energy budget of B permits the robot to walk B units distance (that is, $\lfloor B/L \rfloor$ cells). Hence, the number of cells in the environment P is at least $\lfloor B/L \rfloor + 1$ such that the robot cannot fully cover this environment by a single path. The robot can only walk at most B squares after a full charge, and it must be recharged at station S.

This paper concentrates on solving the above OfflineCPP with three constraints and two objectives using the B-WZone coverage algorithm. The algorithm will be shown in detail in the following sections.

4   B-WZone Coverage Algorithm

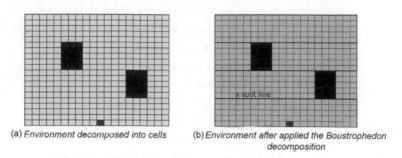

(a) *Environment decomposed into cells*   (b) *Environment after applied the Boustrophedon decomposition*

Fig. 1. Environment before and after decomposed

The B-WZone algorithm includes three key steps: (1) Environment Decomposition by the Boustrophedon method [1], (2) Grouping nodes of partition tree into working zone [6], and (3) Coverage by Boustrophedon Motions [1].

A working environment P for a robot consists of obstacles. Vertices of obstacles are gathered, then horizontal segments are extended both left and right of the vertex as presented in Fig. 1. These segments are called split lines $E = \{E_i | i = 1...n\}$. A coordinate system Oxy is set up in P where O is the position of the charging station S, Ox, and Oy parallel to the boundary of the environment, as shown in Fig. 2. A zone of cells, bounded by two split lines E_i and its neighbor E_{i+1}, is called node N_i. Our algorithm is shown in Algorithm 1.

Here, to clearly illustrate how to cover the workspace completely, we have a particular example (called Exp1). The environment consists of an environment P of size 20x20 that applied the approximate cellular decomposition method [7] (as shown in Fig. 1); a single robot with an energy $B = 80$; a single charging station S and two inner rectangular obstacles. Each cell has the same size as the robot and contains a number that represents the energy required from S to that cell, illustrated in Fig. 2.

The Boustrophedon decomposition algorithm was proposed in 1997 by Choset et al. [1,8,9] to overcome the trapezoidal decomposition limitations, in which the environment is divided into many cells that can be associated together to form bigger cells. The more cells are presented, the longer the final coverage path becomes. The Boustrophedon decomposition is proposed by using the main characteristic of the trapezoidal decomposition. Thus, it is quite similar to trapezoidal decomposition.

This paper benefits from the unique ability of the Boustrophedon to deal with cell over-generation since we only use vertices where a vertical line can go to both left and right of the vertex. These vertices are connected to create a "**split-line**".

The number of cells is reduced, and the absolute coverage path is shortened. For that reason, we use the Boustrophedon decomposition. The output is a set of minimal coverage paths $\Pi = \{\Pi_1, \Pi_2, ..., \Pi_n\}$, covering all cells in the working environment of the robot which satisfies all constraints and optimizes the two objectives above.

4.1   Boustrophedon Decomposition for the Work Environment P

Complete coverage is precisely a specific zigzag path through the adjacency zones related to the decomposition, as shown in Fig. 2 which illustrates how to decompose the robot's workspace by the Boustrophedon method. Figure 1 illustrates the decomposition in theory by using vertices that can extend above and below the vertex, along the vertical axis without cells' energy. In Fig. 2, the working space is partitioned into six subregions $N_i (i=1, ..., 6)$ by decomposing the environment into cells with the numbers presented in its energy unit. In particular, for the OfflineCPP with energy limitations, the environmental modeling depends on the position of the charging station S. It is divided into zones where robots can implement simple right-and-left motions quickly. Thus, we must calculate the order of the zones visited by using split lines to optimize the coverage path. This study uses the tree grouping algorithm to arrange the browsing order of Boustrophedon zones.

4.2   Grouping Nodes of Partition Tree

In this part, we reuse some keywords and definitions of contour-connected environments [6,7]. We introduce the grouping algorithm of zones to completely cover the workspace by Boustrophedon motions and build the partition tree T. Each node represents a subarea of the environment. The root node N_1 is the subarea containing the charging station S.

- If a subarea represented by the node N_i has a split-line that collides with the split-line of the other m subareas in which nothing is the parent node of N_i, the m nodes that denote those subareas will be the child nodes of N_i.
- If the split-lines of m different subareas (represented by m other nodes) collide together and collide with the split-line of a subarea N_j (not the parent node of these m subareas), then node N_j representing that subarea will be arbitrarily set as a child node of 1 of m nodes mentioned above.

Algorithm 1: Proposed B-WZone algorithm for the OfflineCPP

---

1 **Input:** A robot with an energy budget B, a charging station S, and a working environment including obstacles

2 **Output:** A set of the minimal coverage paths

3 **Initialize:** The set of the split lines E

4 **if** E_i *is one of the edges of obstacles* **then**

5 $\quad$ E_i is the split_line;   // Boustrophedon decomposition

6 $\quad$ The set of the nodes created by the split lines $N = \{N_i | i = 1..m\}$;

7 **if** $S \in N_j$ **then**

8 $\quad$ N_j is a root of tree T;

9 $\quad$ **if** N_p *and* N_q *have a common split_line* & N_q *is not parents of* N_p **then**

10 $\quad\quad$ N_q is the child nodes of N_p;

11 **if** N_k *has common split_lines with both* N_a *and* N_b *(which are not child nodes of* N_k*)* **then**

12 $\quad$ N_k is the child node of N_a or N_b;   // Partition tree

13 Grouping the nodes of the partition tree into a working zone $A = \{A_1, A_2, ..., A_n\}$ [7]

14 **for** u= *1 to r* **do**

15 $\quad$ Covering a sub-working zone A_u;   // Coverage by Boustrophedon motions

16 $\quad$ **for** v= *1 to s* **do**

17 $\quad\quad$ Recording Π_v;

18 $\quad\quad$ $c_0 \leftarrow$ Closet uncovered cell in A_u; Move to c_0;

19 $\quad\quad$ Coverage by Boustrophedon motions;

20 $\quad\quad$ **if** *remaining energy + number(cell) = B* & *number(next cell)* ¡ *number(cell)* **then**

21 $\quad\quad\quad$ continue covering;

22 $\quad\quad\quad$ **else** come back S;

We create the tree-like ordering of these partitioned subregions using the grouping algorithm. Each subregion represents a node. The tree is recursively built up. The root is the only subregion containing the charging station S, as shown in Fig. 4(a). Each node N_i on the tree has a set of children $\{N_i 1, ..., N_i p\}$. These subnodes are arranged to represent the subregions from the farthest split-line to the closest split-line to the charging station S.

Moreover, the robot has limited energy B which plays a significant role in the robot's survival. A subregion can be fully covered by a single path or not based on the available energy of the robot. The grouping algorithm is performed from the bottom upwards toward the top of the partition tree to create the working zone [6]. Each subzone is a set of grouped subregions. Let $\{A_1, ..., A_n\}$ be the subzones of the working zone A.

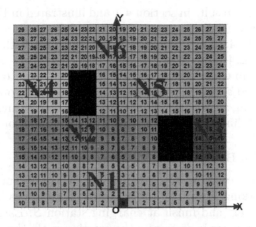

Fig. 2. Cells/subzones with energy units/colors (Color figure online)

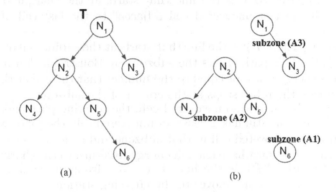

(a)

(b)

Fig. 3. (a) The corresponding partition tree (b) The working zone

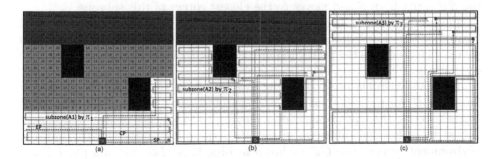

(a)

(b)

(c)

Fig. 4. (a) Three sequential parts of the blue path π_1 covering the subzone (A1), including the starting path (SP), the covering path (CP), and the ending path (EP) (b) Covering the second subzone by the yellow path π_2 (c) Finally, covering completely the working space with the red path π_3 (Color figure online)

From the example results in section 4.1 and illustrated in Fig. 2, the partition tree is built by applying the grouping algorithm. We obtain a working zone $A = \{A_1, A_2, A_3\}$ in Fig. 4. Zone A is divided into subzones with different numbers and colors, as in Fig. 4(c).

Therefore, we can easily split the entire environment into a working zone of grouped and ordered subregions by hybridizing the Boustrophedon decomposition and the grouping algorithm. Finally, we optimize the environment coverage path of robots with limited energy by Boustrophedon motions.

4.3   Coverage by Boustrophedon Motion

As identified above, covering the environment is equivalent to masking each subzone of the working zone. The robot covers all subzones by moving along a set of paths that start and finish at charging station S. Each path π_i consists of three consecutive parts in sequence: the starting path, the covering path, and the ending path:

- The starting path (SP): is the line that starts at the charging station and moves to the nearest uncovered cell adjacent to the last cell of the latest covering path.
- The covering path (CP): is the line that starts at the ending cell of the nearest starting path. This path covers the subzone by Boustrophedon motion until the robot's energy is less or equal to the number that the cell at that position brings. In case the robot stops at the corner of the subzone:
  - If the subzone has no uncovered cell, the covering path ends.
  - If the subzone still has at least an uncovered cell, the robot will move to the nearest uncovered cell in that subzone and continue covering. Notice that the robot must have enough energy to return to the charging station.
- The ending path (EP): is the line that starts from the ending cell of the nearest covering path and moves to the charging station.

The subzone A_1 containing S is the first to be covered. In A_1, if the charging station is one of the cells at the corner, the length of the SP is zero. Otherwise, the SP starts from S and moves to the closest corner of this subzone.

In other subzones $(A_2, ..., A_n)$, the first SP starts at S and walks to the cell located at the closest corner to S. Let $\{\Pi_1, \Pi_2, ..., \Pi_n\}$ be the set of solution paths. Thus, we have the path set Π and the length of the complete environment coverage is as $\sum_i^n \pi_i$.

Here, we continue illustrating the example in section 4.2, with the energy budget of 80 for the robot, as proposed in the paper of Wei et al. [6]. The robot starts covering the environment after moving to the corner of the environment closest to S. For the subregion in Fig. 4(a), the robot starts moving from the environment corner. The CP is shown in blue lines. The SP and the EP are described in black lines. For the subregion (2 and 3), the CP is in yellow and red lines. Two remaining paths are shown in black lines. The repeated path of the robot is a dotted line. After that, the first subzone is covered by path π_1, as presented in Fig. 4(b). Finally, the entire working zone is covered by the optimal paths as illustrated in Fig. 4(c).

5   Experiment and Result Analysis

5.1   Experimental Setup

This study considers the following objectives to evaluate the performance of the proposed B-WZone algorithm:

- Performances of the proposed algorithm are compared with those of the Log-algorithm coverage algorithm of Wei and Isler [7];
- Effect of obstacle density, the energy budget B, and the position of the charging station S on the complete coverage ability of the robot.

We design many different scenarios to benchmark our methods. Each scenario has approximately ten randomly generated instances and then this one randomly creates above ten different trials. Generally speaking, each scenario is experimented with approximately one hundred different trials. They are very diverse with different test environments, varied densities and shapes of obstacles, and the different positions of the charging station. Each trial is simulated 30 times on the same computer (Intel Core $i7 - 4790 - 3.60\,GHz, 16\,GBRAM$). In this paper, we introduce three main scenarios to show the performance of our algorithm as clearly presented in the next section. The number and the length of paths are two main measures that are applied to evaluate the performance of algorithms. In all scenarios, the unit of the path length is the cell's width on the map.

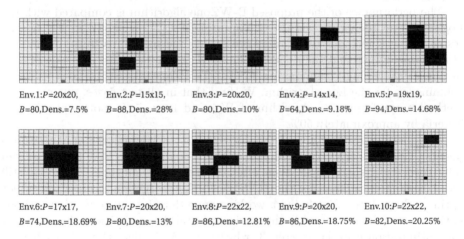

Env.1:P=20x20,   Env.2:P=15x15,   Env.3:P=20x20,   Env.4:P=14x14,   Env.5:P=19x19,
B=80,Dens.=7.5% B=88,Dens.=28% B=80,Dens.=10% B=64,Dens.=9.18% B=94,Dens.=14.68%

Env.6:P=17x17,   Env.7:P=20x20,   Env.8:P=22x22,   Env.9:P=20x20,   Env.10:P=22x22,
B=74,Dens.=18.69% B=80,Dens.=13% B=86,Dens.=12.81% B=86,Dens.=18.75% B=82,Dens.=20.25%

Fig. 5. Ten different working environments (denoted, Env.) with inter obstacles, different sizes of P, energy power B, and obstacle densities (denoted, Dens.)

5.2   Experimental Results

A. Evaluating the Performance of B-WZone. This scenario has ten different environments, shown in Fig. 5. The first environment is the same shape with

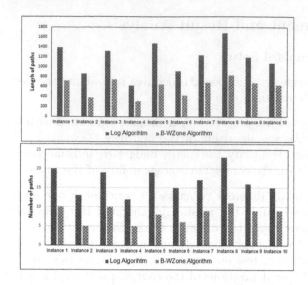

Fig. 6. Comparison between the Log-algorithm and our B-WZone algorithm

two inner obstacles in the experiment of Wei [7]. The remaining environments are randomly generated. The size of the workspace, the density, and the position of obstacles are different to compare the coverage capacity of B-WZone and the Log-algorithm.

The performance of the proposed B-WZone algorithm is compared with the Log-algorithm (denoted, LogAl.) of Wei and Isler [7], as shown in Fig. 6. The result in Fig. 6 includes two figures presenting the medium values of the sum of all paths' length and their corresponding paths' number for all trials of each instance. The orange columns are for the B-WZone algorithm, and the grey columns are for the Log-algorithm. We find that in all test cases, our proposed method outperforms the algorithm of Wei and Isler [7] in both optimization criteria by approximately 50%.

Our obtained result is completely better than the Log-algorithm in all experiments. This is clearly explained that if there is a subzone that the robot can fully cover by a single path, then after covering that subzone, the robot still has excess energy. Thus, for the "CPP with the energy constraints", it is not optimal. Steps 1 and 2, defining a working zone (forming subzones that a single path cannot fully cover) with any environmental decomposition, do not affect the optimization criteria. In step 3, which uses Wei's algorithm [7], each path consists of three sequential parts: from the charging station moving to the nearest uncovered cell, the covering motion, from the endpoint of the covering motion returning to the charging station. These three processes are equivalent to the three processes covering Boustrophedon motion. Moreover, the SP and EP of the two coverage algorithms are similar. Because the robot always consumes energy for the starting path equal to the number that the nearest uncovered cell brings, and the ending path always has a maximum value of $B/2$. About CP, the robot consumes 2 units of energy to visit one cell with Wei's coverage algorithm; meanwhile, the robot only consumes 1 unit of energy to visit one cell with the Boustrophedon coverage algorithm. Thus, in each coverage phase, with the same energy level, the number of cells covered by the Boustrophedon algorithm is always more than or equal to the number of cells covered by the algorithm of Wei. The total area of the environment $|P|$ is constant, so the number of paths required to visit all environment points with the Boustrophedon decomposition algorithm is always fewer than or equal to the number of paths needed to cover the environment by Wei's algorithm.

In addition, we exploit the influence of the obstacle density on the path's length in this scenario. We find that when the number of obstacles increases in the workspace, both the total length and the number of paths have no uptrend and no downtrend. Because these two measures still depend on the energy budget and the obstacle position to the charging station S.

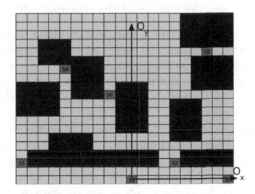

Fig. 7. Positions of the charging station S in 7 different test scenarios

B. Analyzing the Effect of the Energy Budget. B This scenario analyses the effect of the energy power B on the coverage capacity of the robot. The workspace of 20x20 and the positions and the shape of obstacles are fixed as in Fig. 7. The position of station S is S_1. We have ten dissimilar instances, and with each instance, we have ten different trials, by randomly seeding the power B according to a standard distribution from 80 to 120.

The result shown in Fig. 8 points out that when the robot's power increases, it is difficult to say that the length of the path Π significantly decreases, but there is a downtrend. The main reason is the difference in the repeated cells in the moving trajectory of the robot. Each path includes three parts (SP, CP, and EP). While the CP only needs to cover unvisited cells, SP has to lead the robot to the closet uncovered cells, and CP drives the robot back to S. Hence if the robot contains a power $B = B1$, and its stop point is almost on the axis Oy, both EP and SP would be short, the number of the repeated cells is dramatically small. In contrast, if the robot energy is $B = B2$ ($B2 > B1$ is

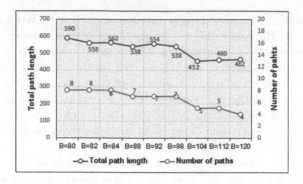

Fig. 8. Influence of the energy budget B

insignificant), and its stop point is distant from the axis Oy, then the length of EP and SP is longer, and the number of the repeated cells is bigger.

C. Analyzing the Effect of the Charging Station Position. S The last scenario, including seven different instances with ten dissimilar trials, considers the effect of the charging station S's position. The used environment is the same as in scenario 2 with $B = 80$. However, the position of the charging station S is changed in Fig. 7. The station S_1 is chosen as a center; then, the remaining stations are randomly generated.

Here, we consider the effect of the position of S on the performance of robot coverage. The results are represented in Fig. 9. The length and the number of paths depend on the location S in the workspace. From Fig. 7, these two measures are minimum when S is close to the center of the environment because the distance from S to the farthest cell is the smallest for all are cells in the workspace P.

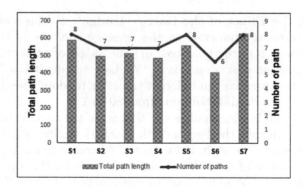

Fig. 9. Results of 7 test scenarios for different position of the station S.

6 Conclusion and Future Work

This paper proposed the B-WZone coverage algorithm that combines the Boustrophedon environmental decomposition and the tree grouping algorithm to solve the OfflineCPP with three constraints and two optimal objectives. The B-WZone algorithm keeps track of the remaining energy of the robot during the coverage process and designs the retreat path to the charging station; finally, after charging, it gives the advance path for the robot to a new waypoint to continue covering. This algorithm presented its actual performance: reducing the total number of paths, the length of the paths, and the number of repeating cells during the covering process. Our proposed B-WZone algorithm returns better results than the method introduced by Wei and Isler [6]. In the future, we will extend the recommended algorithm for the energy-constrained CPP problem in natural environments or multi-agent systems.

Acknowledgment. This research is funded by Hanoi University of Science and Technology (HUST) under project number T2022-PC-042.

References

1. Galceran, E., Carreras, M.: A survey on coverage path planning for robotics. Robot. Auton. Syst. **61**(12), 1258–1276 (2013)
2. Bormann, R., Jordan, F., Hampp, J., Hagele, M.: Indoor coverage path planning: survey, implementation, analysis. In: 2018 IEEE International Conference on Robotics and Automation (ICRA), pp. 1718–1725. IEEE (2018)
3. Sharma, G., Dutta, A., Kim, J. H.: Optimal online coverage path planning with energy constraints. In: Proceedings of the 18th International Conference on Autonomous Agents and MultiAgent Systems, pp. 1189–1197 (2019)
4. Laporte, G.: The vehicle routing problem: an overview of exact and approximate algorithms. Eur. J. Oper. Res. **59**, 3 (1992)
5. Shnaps, I., Rimon, E.: Online coverage of planar environments by a battery powered autonomous mobile robot. IEEE Trans. Autom. Sci. Eng. **13**(2), 425–436 (2016)
6. Wei, M., Isler, V.: Coverage path planning under the energy constraint. In: 2018 IEEE International Conference on Robotics and Automation (ICRA), pp. 368–373. IEEE (2018)
7. Wei, M., Isler, V.I.: A log-approximation for coverage path planning with the energy constraint. In: Proceedings International Conference on Automated Planning and Scheduling, ICAPS, vol. 2018, pp. 532–539
8. Choset, H., Pignon, P.: Coverage path planning: the boustrophedon cellular decomposition. In: Proceedings of International Conference on Field and Service Robotics (1997)
9. Choset, H., Acar, E., Rizzi, A.A., Luntz, J.: Exact cellular decompositions in terms of critical points of Morse functions. In: Proceedings IEEE International Conference Robotics and Automation ICRA2000, vol. 3, pp. 2270–2277 (2018)
10. Strimel, G.P., Veloso, M.M.: Coverage planning with finite resources. In: IEEE/RSJ International Conference on Intelligent Robots and Systems, IROS 2014, pp. 2950–2956. IEEE (2014)

11. Mishra, S., Rodriguez, S., Morales, M., Amato, N.M.: Battery-constrained coverage. In: IEEE International Conference on Automation Science and Engineering (CASE), pp. 695–700. IEEE (2016)
12. Shen, Z., Wilson, J.P., Gupta, S.: ϵ^*+: an Online coverage path planning algorithm for energy-constrained autonomous vehicles. In: Global Oceans 2020: Singapore-US Gulf Coast, pp. 1–6. IEEE (2020)

Predictive Modelling of Diseases Based on a Network and Machine Learning Approach

Tuan-Truong Quang[1,2], Nghia Le[2,3], and Bac Le[1,2(✉)]

[1] Faculty of Information Technology, University of Science,
Ho Chi Minh City, Vietnam
lhbac@fit.hcmus.edu.vn
[2] Vietnam National University, Ho Chi Minh City, Vietnam
nghialh@uit.edu.vn
[3] University of Information Technology, Ho Chi Minh City, Vietnam

Abstract. Chronic diseases have become the first prioritized concern of the health industry, so understanding the disease progression is necessary for predicting, planning and preparing resources to prevent and cure the diseases most effectively. Basing on patients' medical history, this research analyzes and builds disease network to exploit hidden information showing the disease relations and progressions, applys machine learning models to assess the risks of morbidity and predicts the risk of contracting cardiovascular diseases (CVD) in patients with type-2 diabetes (T2D). The research data includes 249,809 medical histories of 65,337 patients in Ho Chi Minh City, Vietnam. The accuracies of the four prediction models (SVM, DT, RF and KNN) range from 78% to 80%. The predicted data can be used promisingly as a reference for medical specialists to provide effective healthcare guidance to patients as well as for healthcare service providers to use their data effectively and enhance their service quality.

Keywords: Data mining · Network analysis · Graph database · Disease prediction · Non-communicable diseases · Machine learning

1 Introduction

Chronic diseases (non-communicable diseases) are diseases that have a long duration and are slow to progress. Four main types of chronic diseases are cardiovascular diseases, cancer, chronic respiratory diseases and diabetes. According the WHO, 77% of deaths and 70% of health costs are caused by them [11]. However, in Vietnam, they are often overlooked by the community. Especially, chronic diseases are also background diseases, an aggravating factor leading to death in current cases of infectious diseases or COVID-19 [25,27].

There have been many studies on the improvement of patients' health through prevention, early identification, and proper treatment. Disease prediction models developed by Davis et al. [5], K. Rajalakshmi and S.S. Dhenakaran

© The Author(s), under exclusive license to Springer Nature Singapore Pte Ltd. 2022
E. Szczerbicki et al. (Eds.): ACIIDS 2022, CCIS 1716, pp. 641–654, 2022.
https://doi.org/10.1007/978-981-19-8234-7_50

[9] analyzed data mining techniques in healthcare management systems. The cardiovascular disease prediction model of Chaitrali S. Dangare et al. [7] used popular classification models such as Decision Tree, Random Forest, Support Vector Machine, etc. Steinhaeuser and Chawla [3] developed a method to predict diseases by Collaborative Filtering. In addition, researchers have recently begun to include temporal information to study disease networks or incorporate disease time relationships into disease risk prediction models like the research by Mahdi Nasiri et al. [10], develop a disease network based on the administrative dataset by Folino et al. [4], apply the network approach to find useful hidden information to assess chronic disease morbidity risk by Arif Khan et al. [16,20].

However, most approaches have not shown the progression and association between diseases. They also have many limitations in accessing data because the patient's health data is often confidential, discrete, and not shared. Some regression models are not suitable because medical data has too many objects such as patients, diseases, doctors, drugs, etc. Therefore, model building is often complicated. Although machine learning methods are rich in techniques and tools, they do not show the necessary time and relationship factors in disease prediction. Models based on network analysis are often developed to find hidden patterns and relationships between objects. However, in the medical field, clinical diagnoses are often based on disease factors such as medical history, demographic information, vital signs, etc. These factors can also have a major influence on patient outcomes [21]. In most cases, this information has not been exploited.

This study proposes a new approach by extending and combining existing methods, with the overall goal of focusing on understanding the progression of chronic diseases through disease networks and identifying risks of other chronic diseases in the future by applying machine learning algorithms to develop disease prediction models. Network approaches can easily solve many problems in scientific field by modelling as networks and visualising as graphs. Moreover, these methods are suitable for understanding the complex relation between objects.

The structure of the study is presented as follows. The next section presents the research method, the dataset description, the details of the disease network construction and the way to analyze and exploit the disease network to extract the features. The third part presents analysis, results and experimental discussion of the proposed model. Part four concludes the study with a conclusion.

2   Material and Methods

2.1   Architecture Overview

This section goes into details about the disease prediction method. Data processing include selecting a cohort to study and build a disease network, extracting features, and finally applying four machine learning algorithms to build a disease prediction model (see Fig. 1). The input is the patients' medical history, and the output is the assessment of CVD risk in patients with T2D.

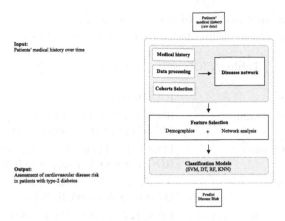

Fig. 1. Overview of prediction framework

2.2 Dataset Description

The data in this study was collected and extracted from medical history data of both inpatients and outpatients at hospitals in Ho Chi Minh City, including 65,337 patients, 249,809 medical history and 469,093 diagnostic results. Sample data information is shown in Table 1.

Table 1. Extract the research dataset

ID	Year of Birth	Gender	Medical examination date	Discharge date	ICD-10 Codes
50312	1965	Female	9/10/2018	9/14/2018	D68; I50; I48; I05
156116	1972	Male	9/13/2018	9/19/2018	I42; I10; E78.4
373674	1962	Male	7/2/2020	7/6/2020	I25; I10; E11; E78
371138	1974	Female	5/31/2020	6/1/2020	I10; I49; F41

To ensure that the dataset is suitable, the study has introduced several data processing like cleaning and filtering data to show the relationship between the patients' medical visits such as (1) Remove duplicate data, or data that lack basic information such as year of birth, or gender. (2) Only take information of patients with at least one hospitalization. (3) Take only valid ICD-10 codes (the 10th revision of the International Statistical Classification of Diseases and Related Health Problems [19]) included in the Elixhauser Comorbidities index [2].

With the 10th edition containing over 70,000 codes, considering all the codes individually can make analysis, modeling, and visualization more difficult and complex. Therefore, the classification codes will be grouped together. The study applied the Elixhauser Comorbidities index [2], including 31 comorbidities. However, when selecting the cohort, the study identified 5 cardiovascular diseases and 2 diabetes-related diseases (diabetes-uncomplicated, diabetes-complicated), so these 7 diseases were eliminated, leaving 24 comorbidities.

Table 2. ICD codes for CVD and T2D [2]

Comorbidities	ICD-10 codes
Congestive heart failure	I09.9, I11.0, I13.0, I13.2, I25.5, I42.0, I42.5-I42.9, I43.x, I50.x, P29.0
Cardiac arrhythmias	I44.1-I44.3, I45.6, I45.9, I47.x-I49.x, ROO.O, ROO.1, ROO.8, T82.1, Z45.0, Z95.0
Valvular disease	A52.0, I05.x-I08.x, I09.1, I09.8, I34.x-I39.x, Q23.O- Q23.3, Z95.2, Z95.4
Pulmonary circulation disorders	I26.x, I27.x, I28.0, I28.8, I28.9
Peripheral vascular disorders	I70.x, I71.x, I73.1, I73.8, I73.9, I77.1, I79.0, I79.2, K55.1, K55.8, K55.9, Z95.8, Z95.9
Type 2 diabetes	E11.0, E11.1, E11.2-E11.9

To find the risk of CVD in patients with T2D, it is necessary to find the cause or the risk factors associated with the disease, so the two cohorts selected for this study are: The group of patients with only T2D and the group with both T2D and CVD. Patients in the $Cohort_{T2D}$ are ones whose entire medical history contains one or more of the T2D codes and does not have any heart disease classification codes. Patients in the $Cohort_{T2D\_CVD}$ are ones who have disease classification codes for both T2D and CVD (see Table 2).

2.3 Building Disease Network

The study applied graph theory of Khan et al. [16]. Risk factors, time factor and data scalability lead to increased complexity of system design, requiring a more flexible system than a relational database management system (RDBMS). Using a graph database can solve this. The symptoms of each disease and the relationship between diseases can be clearly displayed and the ability to query is very efficient. In this study, Neo4j [22] is used to build and exploit networks.

Chronic disease network is aggregated from two base comorbidity networks of two cohorts, namely patients with T2D only and patients with both T2D and CVD. They are aggregated from the individual networks with the respective diseases, and the individual network represents a patient's health trajectory.

Individual Disease Network. This network shows a patient's health trajectory, indicating disease progression by different hospitalizations. In Fig. 2, each node represents a disease and the edge represents the progression of the disease.

Base Comorbidity Network. This network shows the health trajectory of a group of subjects with some common condition. Based on $Cohort_{T2D}$ and $Cohort_{T2D\_CVD}$, two corresponding networks are developed (see Fig. 3).

Fig. 2. Illustration of the process of building an individual disease network

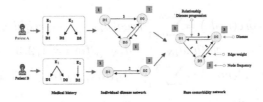

Fig. 3. Illustration of the process of building a base comorbidity network

Chronic Disease Network. After creating two base comorbidity networks for two cohorts, the study proceeds to synthesize and normalize them into a final network. The process is based on the study of Khan et al. [13]. (see Fig. 4).

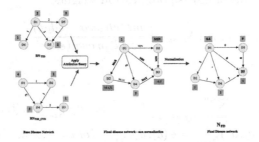

Fig. 4. Illustration of the process of synthesizing chronic disease network

2.4 Analysis of Disease Network Exploitation

Three factors are considered to assess if test patients have a risk of CVD. First, do their medical histories include diseases that have a high frequency in the network? Second, do their disease patterns match the network? Finally, do patients belong to a cluster of diseases that are at high risk of CVD? The study extracted five features from two categories including demographics and disease network. Feature extraction method is based on the study of Md Ekramul Hossain [26].

Network Features F_{node}:
The value is calculated by comparing the individual network of the test patient N_{test} with the final network N_{FD} in terms of disease frequency. A high value

means the patient has a diagnosed disease already existing in the N_{FD} network and is in the value domain from 0 to 1. F_{node} is defined as follows:

$$F_{node}(N_{test}) = \frac{match\_score(node)}{total\_preval(node)} \tag{1}$$

where:

$$match\_score(node) = \sum_{i=1}^{n} freq(d_{iN_{test}}) \times freq(d_{iN_{FD}})$$
$$, with : d_{iN_{test}} = d_{iN_{FD}} \ for \ i = 1, 2, 3, ...n$$
$$total\_preval(node) = \sum_{i=1}^{m} freq(d_{iN_{test}}) \ for \ i = 1, 2, 3, ...m$$

where d_i is the ith network node, n is the total number of common nodes of the two disease networks N_{test} and N_{FD} and m is the total number of nodes of the disease network N_{test}, $match\_score(node)$ is calculated as the product of the total number of common nodes then added together, and finally $total\_preval(node)$ is the total number of nodes in the disease network N_{test}.

F_{edge}: Similarly, the value of edge feature is calculated by comparing the individual disease network of the test patients N_{test} with the final aggregate disease network N_{FD} in terms of disease progression weights.

$$F_{edge}(N_{test}) = \frac{match\_score(edge)}{total\_preval(edge)} \tag{2}$$

where:

$$match\_score(edge) = \sum_{i=1,j=1,i \neq j}^{n} freq(e\,(d_i, d_j)_{N_{test}}) \times freq(e\,(d_i, d_j)_{N_{FD}})$$
$$, with : e\,(d_i, d_j)_{N_{test}} = e\,(d_i, d_j)_{N_{FD}} \ for \ i = 1, 2, 3, ...n$$
$$total\_preval(edge) = \sum_{i=1,j=1,i \neq j}^{k} freq(e\,(d_i, d_j)_{N_{test}}) \ for \ i = 1, 2, 3, ...k$$

where $e\,(d_i, d_j)$ is the edge of the disease network and k is the total number of edges of the disease network N_{test}.

$F_{cluster}$: Comorbidities have common risk factors, so they tend to form clusters. Therefore, the disease network is divided into clusters by applying Louvain algorithm [28]. If two nodes of an edge of the test individual disease network N_{test} belong to the same cluster in the disease network N_{FD}, they will be counted. The study calculates the total number of matched edges and divides it by the total number of edges of the disease network N_{FD}. $F_{cluster}$ is defined as follows:

$$F_{cluster}(N_{test}) = \frac{count\_match(edges)}{number\,of\,total\,edges\,in\,N_{FD}} \tag{3}$$

with:

$$count\_match(edges) = Count\,of\,edges\,in\,N_{test}\,have\,same\,cluster\,in\,N_{FD}$$

Demographics Features

F_{age}: The value of age feature lies in the value domain from *0* to *1*. To calculate this value, the study divides the age of test patients by the distance between the maximum and minimum ages in the research dataset.

$$F_{age}(N_{test}) = \frac{Age\,of\,N_{test}}{Max\,age_{cohort} - Min\,age_{cohort}} \tag{4}$$

F_{gender}: The value of a gender feature belongs to one of two values. If the gender is *male*, the value is *1* and if *female*, then the value is *0*.

$$F_{gender}(N_{test}) = \begin{cases} 1, if\,N_{test}\,is\,Male \\ 0, if\,N_{test}\,is\,Female \end{cases} \tag{5}$$

2.5   Developing Risk Prediction Model

Apply Machine Learning Algorithms. There are many models applied in disease prediction [17,18]. In this study, four machine learning algorithms are used: Support Vector Machine, Decision Tree, Random Forest and K-Nearest Neighbour to develop risk prediction models of CVD in T2D patients.

Model Validation. 65% of patients in each cohort were randomly selected to build the network. The remaining 35% was divided into the training dataset and the test dataset. *10-fold cross-validation* was used to train and test the model to evaluate the performance of the models (see Fig. 5).

Fig. 5. Way to divide research dataset

The study used a confusion matrix to calculate the common measures such as accuracy, precision, recall, F_1 score and ROC curve to evaluate the efficiency.

3   Result and Discussions

From 249,809 medical histories of 65,337 patients, after identifying two cohorts with 6,212 patients, the study grouped the diseases according to the Elixhauser Comorbidities index [2], so The remaining study patients were 4,470 patients.

648   T.-T. Quang et al.

3.1   Disease Network Exploitation

To build and visualize the disease network, the study uses a graph database management system (Neo4j) [22]. Table 3 below shows the total number of nodes and edges in the three disease networks.

Table 3. The number of properties of the three disease networks

Property	BN_{T2D}	BN_{T2D_CVD}	N_{FD}
Number of nodes	18	19	19
Number of edges	54	61	65

The final disease network was created from two base comorbidity networks of the two cohorts (BN_{T2D} and BN_{T2D_CVD}). Therefore, the frequency of the node will represent the prevalence of the disease (see Table 4). In the study, these diseases were risk factors for the progression of CVD in T2D patients.

Table 4. Most common diseases of the two cohorts

BN_{T2D}	Frequency	BN_{T2D_CVD}	Frequency
Hypertension Uncomplicated	22298	Hypertension Uncomplicated	8177
Renal Failure	1138	Renal Failure	662
Chronic Pulmonary Disease	168	Chronic Pulmonary Disease	146
Hypertension Complicated	102	Hypothyroidism	60
Hypothyroidism	81	Other Neurological Disorders	19
Obesity	36	Solid Tumor Without Metastasis	13
Liver Disease	29	Hypertension Complicated	10

Based on the two base comorbidity networks, the final disease network (N_{FD}) is generated by aggregating the nodes and edges of the two base networks. This disease network represents characteristics unique to the progression of CVD in T2D patients. In the N_{FD} disease network, the node frequency and edge weight are normalized to range from 0 to 1. Table 5 shows the five most common models representing cardiovascular disease progression in patients with T2D.

Table 5. Most common disease progression models

Original disease	Progressed disease	Weight
Lymphoma	Renal Failure	1.0
Other Neurological Disorders	Renal Failure	1.0
Depression	Chronic Pulmonary Disease	1.0
Renal Failure	Liver Disease	1.0
Chronic Pulmonary Disease	Hypothyroidism	1.0

Within the scope of research, the study applies the Louvain algorithm [28] to cluster in the final disease network N_{FD}, in order to find the groups of diseases in which the diseases tend to occur together. The study used *'Graph Data Science'* [28] in Neo4j to cluster and found five clusters of diseases. The list of diseases in each cluster is shown in Table 6 below.

Table 6. Clustering using the louvain algorithm

Cluster 1	Renal Failure, Other Neurological Disorders, Lymphoma, Deficiency Anemia, Fluid And Electrolyte Disorders
Cluster 2	Hypertension Uncomplicated, Hypertension Complicated, Peptic Ulcer Disease Excluding Bleeding, AIDS HIV, Weight Loss, Rheumatoid Arthritis Collagen, Blood Loss Anemia
Cluster 3	Solid Tumor Without Metastasis, Liver Disease, Obesity
Cluster 4	Hypothyroidism, Alcohol Abuse
Cluster 5	Chronic Pulmonary Disease, Depression

As can be seen from cluster one, diseases that leads to CVD like renal failure, fluid and electrolyte disorders, lymphoma fall into the same group [13]. Furthermore, these diseases may be potential risk factors for the progression of CVD in patients with T2D.

After normalization, the disease network is visualized as shown in Fig. 6 below, where nodes represent chronic comorbidities including 19 chronic diseases, and edges represent disease progression.

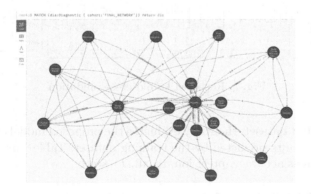

Fig. 6. Disease network visualization

3.2   Developing Disease Prediction Model

Within the scope of the research, four disease prediction models were developed: SVM, DT, RF and KNN. After dividing the research dataset into two cohorts, the study decided to split the dataset into two parts. Next, the study builds and compares the individual disease network with the training dataset and the test dataset with the final disease network to extract three features related to the disease network: Nodes, edges, and clusters. The remaining two features, age and gender, were extracted from the dataset, without going through the disease network. Finally, the study used *10-fold cross-validation* method to train and test the model with the the training dataset; and the test dataset is used to measure the performance of each model. Table 7 below shows that the proposed models have good results in predicting the risk of CVD in patients with T2D.

Table 7. The performance of models based on training

Model	Accuracy (%)	Variance
SVM	80.02	0.003
DT	79.12	0.004
RF	78.75	0.003
KNN	78.67	0.004

Overall, the accuracies of the four models are almost similar. However, the study found that the predictive model based on SVM had the best accuracy of 80.02%, followed by the DT with an accuracy of 79.12%. Figure 7 shows the results of the proposed models through *repeated 10-fold cross-validation.*

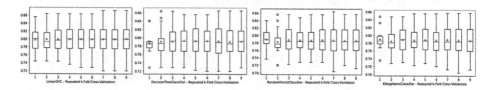

Fig. 7. Repeated k-Fold cross-validation

With the test dataset, the study evaluates the proposed models to avoid deviations in the results predicted by the training dataset. Table 8 presents popular measures such as accuracy, precision, recall, F_1 score.

Table 8. The performance of models based on test dataset

Model	Accuracy (%)	Precision (%)	Recall (%)	F1 score (%)
SVM	79.90	77.00	80.00	72.00
DT	80.00	72.00	76.00	70.00
RF	79.20	74.00	77.00	69.00
KNN	81.00	70.00	76.00	66.00

In addition, in predicting disease diagnoses, the ROC curve is used to find the cut off points of the quantitative variables that have the best value for discriminating two states (e.g. ill/not ill). Figure 8 shows the ROC curve and the AUC index for the four models used in this study. To predict CVD in patients with T2D, the DT model had the highest classification index with AUC of 0.78, followed by the RF model with AUC index of 0.77. The AUC of the models are all greater than 0.60 [8] as shown in Fig. 8. This suggests that the proposed models are able to effectively predict the risk of CVD in patients with T2D.

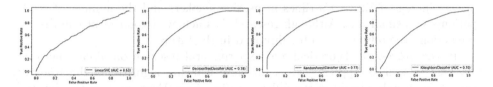

Fig. 8. ROC curves for the four proposed models

3.3 Discussion

There are many complications of chronic comorbidities between CVD and T2D because of their complex relationship. These chronic comorbidities are often due to the progression of one or both of the above diseases. Since comorbidities often share common risk factors, early identification of patients with these chronic conditions can help prevent its complications. This is important for planning and preparing resources for disease prevention and treatment. The study proposed a model to predict the risk of CVD in patients with T2D because among the complications caused by diabetes, cardiovascular complications are the most common [23]. Table 9 below summarizes and compares several related disease prediction modeling studies. Although, the approach is to use only the disease classification code combined with some other basic features (age and gender) but it gives quite good accuracy. Therefore, this is expected to be a new development direction in the current context of very little and sparse medical data.

Table 9. Comparing some disease prediction models

Disease	Method	Accuracy (%)	Author
T2D leading to CVD	Logistic regression	76% – 81%	Young et al. (2018) [14]
T2D leading to CVD	Cox proportional hazards model	70%	Kengne et al. (2011) [6]
T2D leading to CVD	Network analysis and machine learning	78% – 80%	Proposed model

Despite the good and promising results, this proposed method also has some limitations. First, the dataset used in the study is collected from actual data. However, with the local information technology infrastructure in medical examination and treatment facilities, there is a lack of data linkage among facilities. In addition, the fact that many different versions of the ICD codes are being used in hospitals and other medical facilities is also a challenge. Therefore, data collection is also a limitation in this study. Second, other important risk factors such as smoking and alcohol use were not mentioned in this study. In fact, smoking increases the risk of cardiovascular disease. The risk of cardiovascular disease increased 1.2 to 1.6 times in passive smokers and the number of study patients was small [11]. Although research has achieved good results in disease prediction, it surely needs to be improved in the future.

In the process of theoretical and experimental research on disease network analysis as well as applying some machine learning algorithms, the research can be further developed in the following directions. First, expand the dataset. The study is only based on the history of medical examination in a hospital, so the study will continue to integrate new datasets later. Especially, Vietnam is promoting the implementation of electronic medical records at all medical examination facilities, which will bring great development opportunities in the future. Second, expand the research scope. The study now can only predict CVD risk in T2D patients, so the research is aiming to develop a more general model which can make prediction for a variety of diseases in the future.

4   Conclusion

Disease prediction is a research topic that plays an important role in the health industry and especially in preventive medicine. In the context of the rapid increase of chronic diseases, especially in low- or middle-income countries, and the increasing burden of disease due to population aging in many parts of the world, the results of disease prediction models are important inputs for planning and preparing resources for effective disease prevention. Therefore, this study focuses on understanding the progression of chronic diseases to build disease risk prediction models. To develop the models, the study has extracted five features, three of which are from the disease network and the other two are from demographic information. These features were then used to develop four models to predict CVD in T2D patients. The accuracies of the four prediction models range from 78% to 80%. The results show that with the approach using only international disease classification codes, gender, and age, this is a highly anticipated approach in the current context of very little, sparse, and asynchronous medical data.

References

1. Cox, D.R.: Regression models and life-tables. J. Royal Statist. Soc. Ser. B (Methodol.) **34**(2), 187–202 (1972)
2. Quan, H., et al.: Coding algorithms for defining comorbidities in ICD-9-CM and ICD-10 administrative data (2005)
3. Steinhaeuser, K., Chawla, N.V.: A network-based approach to understanding and predicting diseases. In: Social Computing and Behavioral Modeling (2009)
4. Folino, F., Pizzuti, C., Ventura, M.: A comorbidity network approach to predict disease risk. In: Khuri, S., Lhotská, L., Pisanti, N. (eds.) ITBAM 2010. LNCS, vol. 6266, pp. 102–109. Springer, Heidelberg (2010). https://doi.org/10.1007/978-3-642-15020-3_10
5. Davis, D.A., Chawla, N.V., Christakis, N.A., Barabási, A.-L.: Time to CARE: a collaborative engine for practical disease prediction. In: Data Mining and Knowledge Discovery, pp, 388–415 (2010)
6. Kengne, A.P., Patel, A., Marre, M., Travert, F., Lievre: contemporary model for cardiovascular risk prediction in people with type 2 diabetes (2011)
7. Dangare, C.S., Apte, S.S.: Improved study of heart disease prediction system using data mining classification techniques (2012)
8. Application of ROC curve in medical research. https://bvag.com.vn/wp-content/uploads/2013/01/k2_attachments_UNG-DUNG-DUONG-CONG-ROC.pdf. Accessed 15 Apr 2022
9. Rajalakshmi, K., Dhenakaran, S.S., Roobin, N.: Comparative analysis of K-means algorithm in disease prediction (2015)
10. Nasiri, M., Minaei, B., Kiani, A.: Dynamic recommendation: disease prediction and prevention using recommender system. Int. J. Basic Sci. Med. **1**(1), 13–17 (2016)
11. Ministry Of Health Of VietNam. https://vncdc.gov.vn/files/document/2016/4/chien-luoc-quoc-gia-phong-chong-benh-khong-lay-nhiem.pdf. Accessed 15 Apr 2022
12. Khan, A., Uddin, S., Srinivasan, U.: Adapting graph theory and social network measures on healthcare data - a new framework to understand chronic disease progression (2016)
13. Khan, A., Uddin, S., Srinivasan, U.: Understanding chronic disease comorbidities from Baseline Networks - knowledge discovery utilising administrative healthcare data (2017)
14. Young, J.B., Gauthier-Loiselle, M., Bailey, R.A., Manceur: development of predictive risk models for major adverse cardiovascular events among patients with type 2 diabetes mellitus using health insurance claims data (2018)
15. Memarzadeh, H., Ghadiri, N.: A graph database approach for temporal modeling of disease progression, Sara Parikhah Zarmehr (2018)
16. Khana, A., Uddina, S., Srinivasan, U.: Comorbidity network for chronic disease: a novel approach to understand type 2 diabetes progression (2018)
17. Dahiwade, D., Patle, G., Meshram, E.: Designing disease prediction model using machine learning approach (2019)
18. Hossain, E., Khan, A., Moni, M.A., Uddin, S.: Use of electronic health data for disease prediction: a comprehensive literature review (2019)
19. World Health Organization: World Health Organisation. International Classifications of Diseases (2020)
20. Hossain, E., Uddin, S., Khan, A., Moni, M.A.: a framework to understand the progression of cardiovascular disease for type 2 diabetes mellitus patients using a network approach (2020)

21. Primary prevention of cardiovascular disease. https://emohbackup.moh.gov.vn/publish/home?documentId=8165. Accessed 15 Apr 2022
22. Estelle Scifo: Hands-on graph analytics with Neo4j. Packt (2020)
23. Trang, N.N., Vu, N.A., Van Chi, L.: Heart failure in diabetic patients: from mechanism of pathogenesis to update treatment (2021)
24. Santhi, P., Ajayb, R., Harshini, D., Sri, S.S.J.: A survey on heart attack prediction using machine learning (2021)
25. Fekadu, G., Bekele, F., Tolossa, T.: Impact of COVID-19 pandemic on chronic diseases care follow-up and current perspectives in low resource settings: a narrative review (2021)
26. Hossain, E., Uddin, S., Khan, A.: Impact of COVID-19 pandemic on chronic diseases care follow-up and current perspectives in low resource settings: a narrative review (2021)
27. Karen, A., Richardson, L., Wright, J., Petersen, R.: Covid-19 and chronic disease: the impact now and in the future (2021)
28. Stamile, C., Marzullo, A.: Graph machine learning. Packt, Enrico Deusebio (2021)

DeepDream Algorithm for Data Augmentation in a Neural Network Ensemble Applied to Multiclass Image Classification

Dmitrii Viaktin[1,2]($\boxtimes$) (iD), Begonya Garcia-Zapirain[1] (iD), and Amaia Mendez Zorrilla[1] (iD)

[1] University of Deusto, Unibertsitate Etorb., 24, 48007 Bilbo, Bizkaia, Spain
{dmitrii.viatkin,mbgarciazapi,amaia.mendez}@deusto.es
[2] Northern (Arctic) Federal University, Severnaya Dvina Embankment, 17, Arkhangelsk, Arkhangelsk Region, Russia

Abstract. This paper presents the application of Deep-Dream algorithm for data augmentation applied to images. This algorithm analyzes the image by a trained neural network and hides main features of the image. Importance and place of the features is estimated based on neural network layers output values. The new neural network trained on the processed data are forced to search and train a new set of features in the data, since the known features have been hidden. Trained on original and processed data neural networks are used in an ensemble. Experiments were conducted with a balanced images dataset with 5000 images in 10 classes. Experiment was conducted with a neural network based on InceptionV3 architecture in two variations: with non pretrained weights and with pretrained weights. The neural network received a 256 × 256 pixel image as input. Training was conducted using categorical cross entropy loss function, accuracy metric, Adam optimizer with a learning rate of 0.0001. The improvements of the algorithm are almost insignificant when classifying an ensemble of neural network models for a small number of classes, but the impact of the algorithm increases as the number of classes increases. For binary classification there may be no improvement in ensemble accuracy, but when the number of classes increases and becomes more than 5, the influence of the algorithm on the accuracy of the final ensemble increases. The improvement in ensemble accuracy can be 0.5–4%, depending on the initial training conditions without the use of other types of data processing and augmentation.

Keywords: Neural network · Augmentation · DeepDream · Ensemble · Algorithm

1 Introduction

Neural networks are trained to find and analyze sets of features in the data during training. Data augmentation allows making small changes to the data and allows neural networks to find the most stable feature sets in the data and improve the values of the loss function and target metrics of the neural network [1–4]. Depending on the staring conditions,

© The Author(s), under exclusive license to Springer Nature Singapore Pte Ltd. 2022
E. Szczerbicki et al. (Eds.): ACIIDS 2022, CCIS 1716, pp. 655–667, 2022.
https://doi.org/10.1007/978-981-19-8234-7_51

hyperparameters, and training data structure, each neural network finds a unique set of features for analyzed data [1, 4, 5]. These feature sets for trained neural networks are similar for the same data and for the same task, but not absolutely repeated. This difference makes it possible to combine neural networks into ensembles to improve the values of target metrics and loss function [6, 7].

The neural networks in the ensemble must be pretrained on similar tasks. But if the feature sets detected by the neural networks are very similar, there will not be much benefit from combining them into an ensemble. Otherwise, if neural networks are trained for similar tasks, but detect different sets of features, their combining into ensemble will significantly improve the final neural network model [6–8].

The improvement of loss functions and target metrics values for the ensemble of neural networks increase when the difference between the detected feature sets of pretrained neural networks in this ensemble increases [6, 7]. However, unless preventive measures are taken to find different feature sets, the models will detect similar feature sets and the benefit of using these neural networks in ensembles will be low [7, 8]. Using data augmentation to train neural networks in different ways to analyze the data can help find the most diverse sets of features in the data [1, 3].

Classical image augmentation techniques such as geometric transformations, noise [2] and the use of generative neural networks [5] expand the number of detectable main features in the data. But hidden combinations of secondary features can be missed in the training process because the main features have a much greater influence on the loss function and target metrics than the secondary features.

This paper describes an image augmentation algorithm based on the DeepDream [9] algorithm. The developed algorithm can process images and hide the main features of the image based on output layer values of trained neural network. As it becomes difficult for the neural network to detect the main features on processed images, the neural network is trained to analyze combinations of secondary features that are ignored when training on the source unprocessed data. As a result, a neural network trained on the processed data usually has worse performance than the model trained on the original source data. However, combining a model trained on processed images and a model trained on source images into an ensemble improves the performance of the final ensemble more than just combining the two neural network models because neural networks are trained to detect different feature sets.

2 Materials

This research used a dataset for classification tasks with images of animals. The images are separated into 10 classes: dog, horse, cat, elephant, butterfly, chicken, cow, sheep, squirrel, and spider. The dataset is available in the open access [10].

The original dataset contains an unbalanced number of classes. For example, class "dog" has 4863 images, but class "cat" has 1668 images. To remove heterogeneity of the dataset, the number of images in each class is reduced to 500, in the whole dataset to 5000. Neural network is trained independently with a different number of classes from 2 to 10 classes based on this dataset. The images from the training dataset part are processed by the developed data augmentation algorithm based on output layers values of trained neural network. After that step processed images are used for a new neural network with the same architecture and new weights training.

3 Methods

In this subsection, the details about the neural networks used in this research are described. The order of application of the methods used is shown below (see Fig. 1).

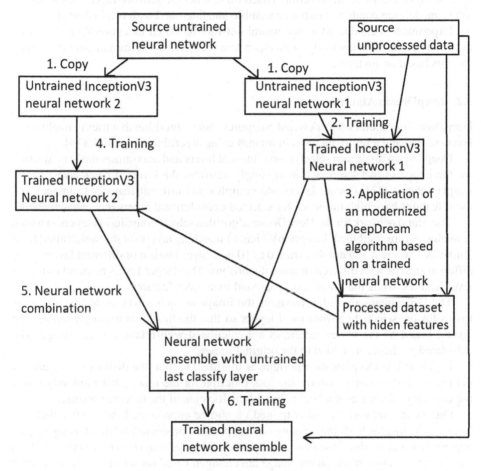

Fig. 1. Order of application of the methods.

3.1 InceptionV3 Neural Network Architecture

Inceptionv3 is Google's convolutional neural network to assist in image analysis and object detection [11]. Inceptionv3 was structured to keep the advantages of deep neural networks while keeping the number of parameters from growing too large. The model given has less than 25 million parameters [11].

Neural network with InceptionV3 architecture is trained on a balanced dataset [10]. The neural network was implemented using the TensorFlow library.

This network architecture was chosen because it is suitable for the DeepDream algorithm since it has many combined convolutional layers.

In this paper, two InceptionV3 based neural network models are created: one model is trained on source unprocessed data, the second model is trained on images processed by a modified DeepDream algorithm based on first neural network layer output values. These models are combined into an ensemble and finetuned with original images.

Experiment is conducted with a neural network based on InceptionV3 architecture in two variations independently: with clean non pretrained weights and with pretrained weights based on ImageNet.

3.2 DeepDream Algorithm

DeepDream is a neural network based computer vision algorithm that uses convolutional layers to find and amplify patterns in images using algorithmic pareidolia [9].

Deep Dream algorithm selects convolutional layers and maximizes the loss function for the image so that the image increasingly activates the layers. Lower layers create simple patterns [12]. Deeper layers add complex and difficult features to images and these features have high influence for selected convolutional layers that can activate it.

The neural network for the DeepDream algorithm selects convolution layers in which convolutions are combined. InceptionV3 has 11 matching layers for this task, called from "mixedX", where X is a number from 0 to 10 inclusive. The use of different layers gives different images with different feature distortions. The deeper layers respond to higher level features, while the lower layers respond to simpler features.

The DeepDream algorithm modifies the image in such a way as to maximize the losses for the selected convolutional layers so that the image increasingly excites the layers. Based on the losses, gradients are calculated with relation to the image. The calculated gradients are added to the original image.

In this article DeepDream algorithm is modified to hide the distinctive features of the image. It does not maximize the loss function for the image, but randomly either increases it or decreases gradient values at the location of the detected feature.

One neural network model is trained on source unprocessed data. After that features on the images from the training dataset part are processed by the developed data augmentation algorithm based on output layers values of trained neural network. Pixel values in the feature place on the image are changed based on selected neural network convolutional layer output values.

The stronger the selected convolutional layer reacts to and activates on a pixel in the image, the stronger its change in the original image will be. Loss value is calculated based on comparison between image and selected layers output values. Gradient values are calculated based on layers output values and loss value. The gradient values are randomly assigned a positive sign with a 50% probability or a negative sign with a 50% probability to hide features rather than maximize them. The resulting gradient values are added to the pixel values in the image, which distorts the feature, lowers the response of the convolutional layer to it, and reduces the probability of detection. This operation can be performed several times on the image.

An example of applying this algorithm to an image is shown below (see Fig. 2).

Fig. 2. Source and processed by developed algorithm images.

Looking on the image we see that the left part of Fig. 2 shows the original image, and the right part shows the image processed by the upgraded DeepDream algorithm in 30 iterations. The environmental features that do not affect the classification result were almost unchanged. The features that have a great influence on the classification result have been significantly distorted and the probability of their detection in the training of the neural network has become small. Minor environmental features that partially overlap important features and are at the boundary with the object were subjected to more distortions than features distant from the object, but much less than the main features of the object. This effect can be observed in Fig. 2, drawing attention to the grass.

Second neural network was trained on the processed images. Usually, this neural network has worse performance than the model trained on the original source data. However, these neural networks detect different feature sets. Combining a model trained on processed images and a model trained on source images into an ensemble improves the performance of the final ensemble.

The DeepDream algorithm modifies the image to maximize the features in the image for the neural network. The main difference of the algorithm described in this paper is that it aims at hiding such features.

3.3 Ensemble Neural Networks

Neural networks are flexible and scalable algorithms that can adapt to the data used in training. However, they are trained with a stochastic learning algorithm and adapt to the features of the trained data during training. Therefore, even neural networks of the same architecture trained on the same data set, but started training with different parameters of weights, can find different variants of the optimal set of weights in each training, which in turn leads to different predictions. To improve training results and reduce overtraining, an approach is used that is based on training on the same data and then combining multiple neural networks with different architectures [13]. This is called ensemble learning and not only reduces the variance of the predictions but can also lead to predictions that are better than any single model.

In this paper, two InceptionV3 based neural network models are combined into an ensemble. Combination of these models significantly improves loss function and metric values because each model has been trained for the different feature sets detection.

4   Process of Algorithm Development and Training of Neural Network Model

A neural network for the classification problem is developed. Since the basic DeepDream algorithm was implemented based on the InceptionV3 architecture, the InceptionV3 neural network architecture was chosen as the basic architecture for testing. The input image size was chosen to be 256×256 pixel. This architecture is upgraded to solve the problem of image classification and is shown below (see Fig. 3).

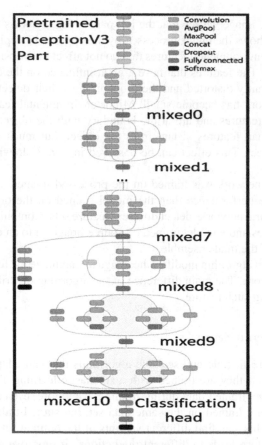

Fig. 3. InceptionV3 based architecture for the neural network [11].

Two copies of the neural network with the same initial values of weights are created and saved. This is done to eliminate the effect of random initialization of the weights of the neural network. These neural network models will be trained independently of each other before combining into an ensemble. Once combined into an ensemble, the neural networks will be finetuned.

The first neural network is trained on a training set of original unprocessed images with the following parameters: input image size - 256×256 pixels, number of epochs - 60, batches size - 25 images, optimizer – Adam, learning rate 0.0001, loss function - categorical cross entropy, target metric - accuracy. The choice of a learning rate of 0.0001 for the Adam optimizer is based on the experimental results that at this learning rate the model with InceptionV3 architecture successfully learns both with pretrained weights and with random weights. The dynamic learning rate was not used, as it could affect the final results of the modified DeepDream algorithm. On average, with the specified learning rate for the Adam optimizer, the model reaches the minimum value of cross entropy at 20–40 epochs. 60 epochs allow to make sure the best loss function result was achieved. Every epoch the training result is tested on validation data. The neural network whose weights correspond to the minimal value of categorical cross entropy on the validation set is saved.

At the end of training, the neural network model with the best categorical cross entropy scores is restored from the saved file. The images from the training dataset are processed by the feature hiding algorithm developed in this paper based on the DeepDream algorithm. During image processing, a previously trained neural network is used for feature extraction.

For this DeepDream based algorithm work it is necessary to choose the layers that will be analyzed when the algorithm works. It is recommended to choose the middle layers of the model. In this work layers mixed4, mixed5, mixed6, mixed7 are chosen. These layers are in the center of the model and its features are not combined into high level descriptions of objects based on their features, as in last convolutional layers. Also, these layers do not describe geometric primitives like the first convolutional layers.

Based on the output values of the selected layers, the loss function value for a given image is calculated. Based on the calculated loss function value, gradient values are calculated. The application of gradient values to the original image by DeepDream algorithm will amplify the features to which the convolution layers have reacted and make the features more visible. The effect on the main detected features of the objects in the image will be much higher than the effect on the background features of the image.

The DeepDream algorithm aims at amplifying the detected features by the algorithm described above. In this paper, it is modified. Gradients with a probability of 50% can change the sign. Changing the sign of the gradient will hide these features. But if you constantly invert the sign of the gradient, the image will be subjected to serious distortions. It will remove not only the object's features, but all other features as well. Changing the gradient sign with a 50% probability will significantly distort only the main detected object features. The unlikely features detected in the background of the image will be distorted minimally. After several iterations of the modified algorithm, the detected object features will change significantly, and the background will remain almost unchanged. An example of the processed image at different stages of processing by the developed algorithm is shown below (see Fig. 4).

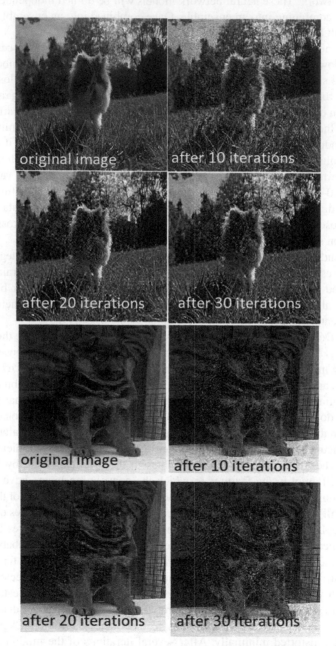

Fig. 4. Example of image processing by developed algorithm.

Figure 4 showed that with increasing number of iterations passed, the main features of the image become stronger, while the secondary features, detection of which the neural network is not trained, remain almost unchanged after several operations. Even in the case of random distortion of background features, as shown in Fig. 4 in the 10th iteration of processing, the background features will recover due to the features of the algorithm.

The training images are processed by a modified DeepDream feature hiding algorithm. This processed training dataset is used to train the second created copy of the neural network created at the beginning of the experiment.

The second neural network is trained on a processed training set of images with hidden features with the following parameters: input image size - 256×256 pixels, number of epochs - 60, batches size - 25 images, optimizer – Adam, learning rate 0.0001, loss function - categorical cross entropy, target metric - accuracy. Every epoch the training result is tested on validation data. The neural network whose weights correspond to the minimal value of categorical cross entropy on the validation set is saved. At the end of training, the neural network model with the best categorical cross entropy scores is restored from the saved file.

The accuracy value of the second neural network model trained on the processed images is lower than the accuracy value of the first neural network model trained on the raw images.

The categorical cross entropy value of the second neural network model trained on the processed images is higher than the categorical cross entropy value of the first neural network model trained on the raw images.

The second model cannot find the main features in the images because they have been hidden. The second model is trained on a different set of features than the first model.

The neural network models are combined into an ensemble. In both models the last classification layer is removed, the penultimate layers are merged, a new classification layer is created. Trainable parameter of models is disabled and the last classification layer of the ensemble is finetuned.

The final neural network ensemble is trained on a processed training set of original unprocessed images with the following parameters: input image size - 256×256 pixels, number of epochs - 10, batches size - 25 images, optimizer – Adam, learning rate 0.00001, loss function - categorical cross entropy, target metric - accuracy. Every epoch the training result is tested on validation data. The ensemble whose weights correspond to the minimal value of categorical cross entropy on the validation set is saved. At the end of training, the ensemble with the best categorical cross entropy scores is restored from the saved file.

The results of ensemble training show an improvement in results compared to the original neural networks. The result is especially noticeable when the number of classes for classification is increased.

The experiments were conducted for two variants of neural network weights: for neural networks that are based on the pretrained by ImageNet data version of the InceptionV3 architecture, and for neural networks with random weights trained from zero. In both cases, the neural network head, including the classification layer, was trained from zero.

For each of the variants we tested the algorithm for neural networks trained on the number of classes from 2 to 10.

Trained neural networks were tested in ensembles in combinations: trained on original images and trained on original images, trained on original images and trained on processed images, trained on processed images and trained on processed images.

Finally, a total of 36 neural networks and 54 ensembles of neural networks were trained.

All training conditions, except the number of classes and the initialization option for the weights in the neural networks remain constant for all experiments.

The obtained categorical cross entropy value and accuracy value for neural networks and its ensembles on validation dataset are shown in Table 1.

Table 1. Obtained categorical cross entropy value and accuracy value for neural networks and its ensembles.

Number of classes	Trained on original images	Trained on processed images	Ensemble original/processed	Ensemble original/original	Ensemble processedl/processed
Accuracy value. Pretrained weights					
10	0.957	0.958	0.963	0.954	0.959
9	0.957	0.953	0.965	0.956	0.952
8	0.947	0.948	0.964	0.955	0.950
7	0.968	0.965	0.975	0.966	0.967
6	0.975	0.975	0.959	0.945	0.949
5	0.976	0.961	0.971	0.972	0.980
4	0.969	0.978	0.971	0.962	0.965
3	0.978	0.975	0.952	0.928	0.989
2	0.957	0.951	0.963	0.954	0.959
Categorical cross entropy value. Pretrained weights					
10	0.124	0.173	0.119	0.156	0.147
9	0.143	0.200	0.118	0.151	0.192
8	0.160	0.170	0.120	0.156	0.171
7	0.099	0.129	0.087	0.122	0.087
6	0.085	0.113	0.152	0.226	0.168
5	0.096	0.144	0.112	0.147	0.032

(continued)

Table 1. (*continued*)

Number of classes	Trained on original images	Trained on processed images	Ensemble original/processed	Ensemble original/original	Ensemble processedl/processed
4	0.103	0.081	0.093	0.166	0.133
3	0.065	0.069	0.152	0.214	0.071
2	0.163	0.173	0.155	0.217	0.200
Accuracy value. Random start weights					
10	0.501	0.526	0.583	0.548	0.516
9	0.551	0.526	0.597	0.564	0.559
8	0.551	0.557	0.578	0.581	0.586
7	0.630	0.603	0.632	0.621	0.629
6	0.642	0.566	0.657	0.641	0.651
5	0.647	0.673	0.704	0.697	0.666
4	0.715	0.760	0.776	0.769	0.713
3	0.803	0.720	0.818	0.618	0.811
2	0.891	0.880	0.829	0.818	0.760
Categorical cross entropy value. Random start weights					
10	1.639	1.590	1.346	2.160	2.623
9	1.514	1.590	1.664	1.581	1.651
8	1.274	1.397	1.843	1.585	1.464
7	1.112	1.489	1.325	1.575	1.245
6	1.190	1.194	1.312	1.098	1.272
5	1.006	1.166	1.141	0.992	1.155
4	1.289	0.880	1.516	0.876	1.008
3	1.224	1.028	0.856	0.859	1.699
2	0.322	0.348	1.052	0.756	0.856

The test results in Table 1 show the image classification accuracy and categorical cross entropy value for trained neural networks and their ensembles. Neural networks were trained the number of classes from 2 to 10. The number of classes on which the neural network was trained is shown in first column. The second column shows the results of neural network training on unprocessed images. The third column shows the results of neural network training on the processed by neural network from column 2 images.

Neural networks were combined into ensembles. The neural network from columns 2 and 3 is shown in column 4. The union of two neural networks from column 2 is shown in column 5. The union of two neural networks from column 3 is shown in column 6.

Ensembles of neural networks consisting of a neural network trained on the original raw images and a neural network trained on the processed images show better accuracy compared to other ensemble variants. The value of categorical entropy in the same ensemble types decreases.

The effect of using the modified DeepDream algorithm for hiding features in an image increases with the number of classes. However, when the number of classes is small, it is hardly visible. This effect is most visible for the training neural networks with random initialization of start weights, training from zero.

Pretrained networks are already trained on large datasets and already contain information about the features of the data. With a large amount of data, it is easier for neural networks to find different features and they are already trained to find them.

The effect of the DeepDream algorithm is most pronounced when training neural networks from zero, with an increasing number of classes. On a small number of classes, it is difficult to find a large number of the features and differences between classes. However, as the number of classes grows, the number of features and differences between classes grows according to the quadratic law. Hiding the features that describe these differences forces neural networks to concentrate on learning to work with implicit features.

Accuracy increases by 0.5–1.5% for ensembles based on pretrained neural networks and by 4–5% for neural networks with random initialization of initial weights.

5   Conclusions

This paper considers a new ensemble model for multiclass image classification using data augmentation. DeepDream algorithm [9] has been used for data augmentation and was adjusted to modify images based on the output values of layers of a pretrained neural network InceptionV3. These modified images can be used to retrain the neural network with a set of features other than those detected by the original pretrained neural network. Neural networks trained on the data augmented dataset, when combined in an ensemble with neural networks trained on the original data, improve the performance of the final ensemble more than other combinations of neural networks in the ensemble. This effect is because the neural network cannot find simple feature sets in the images during training because these features have been hidden by the developed algorithm. The neural network is trained to find and analyze secondary feature sets that have not been modified.

As a result of applying this algorithm in the neural networks training and combining these neural networks into an ensemble, the ensemble accuracy increases up to 0.5–1% for ensembles based on pretrained neural networks and up to 5% for neural networks with random initialization of initial weights.

The improvements of the neural networks ensemble trained on images processed by modified DeepDream algorithm are insignificant for a small number of classes, but the impact of the algorithm application increases as the number of classes increases. For binary classification there may be no improvement in ensemble accuracy, but when the number of classes increases and becomes more than 5, the influence of the algorithm on the accuracy of the final ensemble increases.

The article [1] describes a method of image augmentation, based on the principle of combining images, which allows to obtain an improvement in accuracy for GAN by 5–7%. Traditional approaches to image augmentation, based on the geometric transformations, can improve model accuracy from 1% to 7%, depending on the used algorithms [2].

Combining different approaches to image augmentation, based on different principles, can further improve the values of target metrics of the model [2].

In the future, we plan to upgrade the algorithm not only for two dimensional convolutional layers, but also for different types of neural network layers.

References

1. Luis, P., Jason, W.: The effectiveness of data augmentation in image classification using deep learning
2. Shorten, C., Khoshgoftaar, T.M.: A survey on image data augmentation for deep learning. J. Big Data **6**(1), 1–48 (2019). https://doi.org/10.1186/s40537-019-0197-0
3. Ilya, K., Denis, Y., Rob, F.: Image augmentation is all you need: regularizing deep reinforcement learning from pixels. arXiv preprint arXiv:2004.13649
4. Han, D., Liu, Q., Fan, W.: A new image classification method using CNN transfer learning and web data augmentation. Expert Syst. Appl. **95**, 43–56 (2018)
5. Shin, H.-C., et al.: Medical image synthesis for data augmentation and anonymization using generative adversarial networks. In: Gooya, A., Goksel, O., Oguz, I., Burgos, N. (eds.) SASHIMI 2018. LNCS, vol. 11037, pp. 1–11. Springer, Cham (2018). https://doi.org/10.1007/978-3-030-00536-8_1
6. Koitka, S., Friedrich, C.M.: Optimized convolutional neural network ensembles for medical subfigure classification. In: Jones, G.J.F., et al. (eds.) CLEF 2017. LNCS, vol. 10456, pp. 57–68. Springer, Cham (2017). https://doi.org/10.1007/978-3-319-65813-1_5
7. Li, H., Wang, X., Ding, S.: Research and development of neural network ensembles: a survey. Artif. Intell. Rev. **49**(4), 455–479 (2017). https://doi.org/10.1007/s10462-016-9535-1
8. William, B., Tim, G., Andreas, N., Jan, K.: The power of ensembles for active learning in image classification. In: Proceedings of the IEEE Conference on Computer Vision and Pattern Recognition (CVPR), pp. 9368–9377 (2018)
9. Mordvintsev, A., Olah, C., Tyka, M.: DeepDream - a code example for visualizing Neural Networks. Google Research (2015)
10. Alessio, C.: Animals-10 dataset. Kaggle (2019). https://www.kaggle.com/alessiocorrado99/animals10
11. Christian S., Vincent V., Sergey I., Jonathon S., Wojna Z.: Rethinking the inception architecture for computer vision. arXiv preprint arXiv:1512.00567v3
12. Gregory, C.: Deep dream. SubStance **45**(2), 61–77 (2016)
13. Alam, K.M.R., Siddique, N., Adeli, H.: A dynamic ensemble learning algorithm for neural networks. Neural Comput. Appl. **32**(12), 8675–8690 (2019). https://doi.org/10.1007/s00521-019-04359-7

Auto Machine Learning-Based Approach for Source Printer Identification

Phu-Qui Vo[1,2] , Nhan Tam Dang[1,2] , Q. Phu Nguyen[1,2(✉)] ,
An Mai[1,2(✉)] , Loan T. T. Nguyen[1,2] , Quoc-Thông Nguyen[3] ,
and Ngoc-Thanh Nguyen[4]

[1] School of Computer Science and Engineering, International University,
Ho Chi Minh City, Vietnam
[2] Vietnam National University, Ho Chi Minh City, Vietnam
{dtnhan,nqphu,mhban,nttloan}@hcmiu.edu.vn
[3] Sofft Industries, Lyon, France
quoc-thong.nguyen@sofft.fr
[4] Department of Applied Informatics, Wroclaw University of Science and Technology,
Wrocław, Poland
Ngoc-Thanh.Nguyen@pwr.edu.pl

Abstract. This study investigates the applicability of the Auto Machine Learning-based approach (AutoML) for analyzing microscopic printed document images to attribute that document to its source printer. In this perspective, AutoML, a new rising star of machine learning in practice, has shone brightly as it can satisfy the demand of Machine Learning practitioner communities. In this work, three candidates from popular Machine Learning models and two representatives from AutoML are nominated for a competition. The challenges of traditional methods and the merits of applying AutoML are highlighted through the experiments. Especially the power of ensemble methods to achieve the best possible model for our experimental dataset. Furthermore, the learnability of AutoML to the different levels of uncertainties of printed patterns is also recognized.

Keywords: Machine learning · Source printer identification ·
AutoML · Microscopic images

1 Introduction

Digital transformation impels the dominion of digital documents, but the transformation of printed documents to their digital version encounters many issues such as transition cost, workforce acceptability, and security. Besides, many financial and administrative transactions rely on printed documents (e.g., agreements, contracts, and records). Thus, printed and digital documents are like two sides of the same coin nowadays. However, the advantages of technology make the process of reproducing and counterfeiting printed documents with malicious intent simplified without many resources. It leads to many issues in almost all

© The Author(s), under exclusive license to Springer Nature Singapore Pte Ltd. 2022
E. Szczerbicki et al. (Eds.): ACIIDS 2022, CCIS 1716, pp. 668–680, 2022.
https://doi.org/10.1007/978-981-19-8234-7_52

business fields. For example, for those working on financial service, we all know the importance of financial reports, and imagine that if these reports were modified and re-printed, then the performance metrics were recorded to input to the backtesting system. It aims to fool the system to provide good trading performance, thus mislead the investors, and the aftermath is extremely terrible [1, 2]. Based on a survey from International Data Corporation (IDC), 2.8 trillion pages were printed in 2020 [3]. Such widespread use of printed documents raises significant challenges and makes printed documents verification an urgent task that requires fast and accurate digital systems to predict their origin and integrity. Indications referring to the model, type, or brand of the printer can yield proper knowledge about a printed document's origin and integrity [4]. The issue of matching a printed document to its source printer using digital approaches is drawing the extensive attention of researchers in the literature [5, 6].

Source printer identification can be classified into two main approaches in general: intrinsic and extrinsic. The former approach exploits the remaining traces established by the combination of various printers' electro-mechanical parts [7], while the latter one relies on inserting artifacts into the printed document [8]. Aside from being intricate and cost-intensive, extrinsic methods depend on the printer's authentication before the printing processes begin, which may not be achievable since integrating such methods into their products is not a legal constraint to the fabricator. By contrast, intrinsic methods are only based on investigating documents that were printed from questioned printers and also be able to apply to examine documents printed in the past.

For the intrinsic approach, exploiting paper's physical properties and ink's fluid properties are often used in traditional methods. Some examples that can be mentioned are the comparison of the difference between distinct sets of banding frequencies given by halftones' distance together with ink density [9] or focusing on printed materials which will be analyzed through chemical assays tool [10]. The drawback of these methods is also expensive because of the requirement of equipment. In addition, chemical analyses can cause unintended consequences or destroy the evidence of committing a crime. In another approach, the authors in [11] focused on the thorough analysis of noises derived from the printed documents to perform a hypothesis testing problem to compute different confident levels of source identification via a general formulation.

With the booming of artificial intelligence, the thorough exploitation of texture features combined with machine learning for printer source attribution is becoming prominent. [12] is one of the recent works that apply this method by combining niching genetic search and characteristics of the letter'WOO' to select the good enough reduced feature set for K-Nearest Neighbors (KNN) classification. [13] applied Support Vector Machine (SVM) and Random Forest (RF) machine learning models on five extracted features of microscopic printed images analyzing eight patterns printed on two kinds of paper with three different printers. The authors of this study show that they can manually apply a selected machine learning model to the indicated pattern to get the best classification performance. From the shared private dataset of them, [14] is our previous work that applies the features selection approach to reduce the number of training features while keeping the same classification performance. In that study, we apply some machine learning models to manually selected features to achieve our best result.

Obviously, we can see that the manual tasks of selecting models, patterns, and features to achieve high-performance results in printer classification are labor-intensive. Hence, this study will apply two AutoML representatives to extracted features of microscopic printed images dataset in the previous studies [13,14], to explore the potential of the AutoML-based approach in omitting manual tasks for the source printer identification problem.

2   Data and Features Description

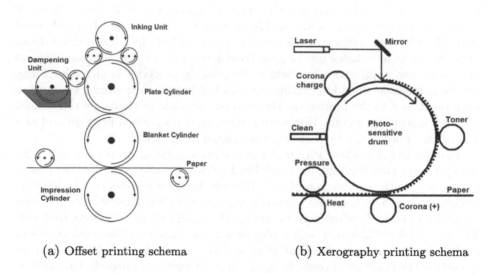

(a) Offset printing schema   (b) Xerography printing schema

Fig. 1. Printing technologies

Similar to our previous studies [13,14], the goal of this paper is to incorporate the mutual interactions of printing process and patterns, the ink drop distributions and the randomness in the paper's surface to intendedly generate more uncertainty in the original printed documents in the attempt to add more adversarial noises into the counterfeit printed ones that can help to detect better the counterfeit source printers. Based on this goal, we generated the dataset of printed documents from three types of printing technologies, two types of papers and different patterns. This examined dataset was achieved with numerous labor hours following these steps:

Firstly, two ubiquitous printing processes, Offset and Xerography, were used to print on two types of substrate: (1) natural uncoated paper and (2) paper coated with one or several layers. Offset printing is a lithographic technique in which the inked image is transferred (or "offset") from a printing plate (which contains the pattern image) to a rubber blanket and then to the printing surface [15]. Figure 1a demonstrates the schema of offset printing. Two universal techniques of offset printing process were used in this work are: (1) Conventional Offset Printing wherein water and additives dampen the image-carrier plate and (2) Waterless Offset Printing in which a highly ink-repellent silicone overlays the ink-free areas of the printing plate. Xerography (also named laser printer) is a dry photocopying technique in which the laser beam will electrostatically charge the photoconductor to collect the particular inks, powder, or liquid toners that have the opposite charge with the photoconductor surface. After that, an elevated temperature will fix the transferred ink to the substrate [15]. The schema of Xerography is illustrated in Fig. 1b.

Fig. 2. The eight investigated patterns

Secondly, eight different selected patterns in Fig. 2 were printed with the aforementioned setups. Those patterns were created with a selection from the appraisal of microscopic observation. In the sample collection procedure, the samples are collected using an optical Zeiss Microscope with an AxioCam camera. Figure 3 and Fig. 4 show the results after this step.

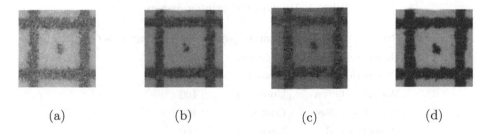

(a)   (b)   (c)   (d)

Fig. 3. The uncoated (a, c) and coated (b, d) papers with conventional (a, b) and waterless (c, d) offset printing technologies

Lastly, the study on the single dot was carried out under the micro-scale [16,17]. The printed parts are the main concern in the experiment. Thus, for each printed pattern sample, the shape descriptor indexes [18] are computed. Shape descriptor indexes are obtained from the printed segments by computing their area, perimeter, and convex area, where $A(px^2)$ is the area, $A_c(px^2)$ is the convex area, $P(px)$ is the perimeter, and $P_c(px)$ is the convex perimeter. The unit "px" means "pixel", but as long as the measuring unit is the same

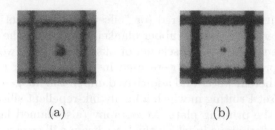

(a)   (b)

Fig. 4. The uncoated (a) and coated (b) papers with xerography printing technology

for all indexes, it contributes nothing to machine learning models building. For each printed pattern sample, a vector of five features (area, perimeter, solidity, convexity, and circularity) is collected to build the dataset that was used to train on various machine learning models in this study. The proposed experiment is supervised on two kinds of printing paper with three printing technologies. Therefore, we have six printing sources in total that were detailed in Table 1.

$$Solidity = \frac{A}{A_c} \tag{1}$$

$$Convexity = \frac{P_c}{P} \tag{2}$$

$$Circularity = \sqrt{\frac{4\pi A}{P^2}} \tag{3}$$

Table 1. Printers and printing papers

Label	Printing technology	Printing paper	No. of samples per pattern
1	Conventional Offset	Uncoated	100
2	Conventional Offset	Coated	100
3	Waterless Offset	Uncoated	100
4	Waterless Offset	Coated	100
5	HP-600 M620	Uncoated	100
6	HP-600 M620	Coated	100

3   Proposed Method

Our work on source printing documents using a Machine Learning life cycle is as followed. After extracting crucial information which are: area, perimeter, solidity, convexity, and circularity. We proceed to select the appropriate algorithm and train our model. To guide the model to have a better search space in the domain for better results, fine-tuning with hyperparameter optimization cannot be omitted. The model evaluation phase combined with two previous steps forms an infinite loop until we can find the best model for our problem or until the deadline is reached.

The whole life cycle is displayed in full as shown in Fig. 5. Every step in the whole process here is all handled manually and as such, the problem consumes a lot of our time and effort to tackle.

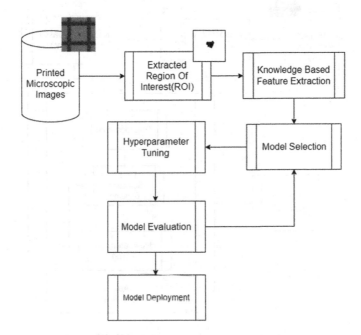

Fig. 5. Our approach using ML life cycle

However, the Machine Learning pipeline does not just stop at training, evaluating, and deploying the model. There is a huge amount of works needed to be done, which is more crucial than training the model itself. Data cleaning to fix any anomalies or inconsistencies in calculated information from the collected image. Preprocessing to make the model less susceptible to bias, and overfitting, or easier to discover any underlying information for training. There is still a heap of processes to be considered yet we have barely touched only just the tip of the iceberg. If we press on solving the problem using the previous approach, there is no telling just how much time and effort we have to invest until a better pipeline was found. Machine Learning can achieve an impressive result, though, heavily relies on the Machine Learning and domain expert performing mentioned tasks. Working in a non-automatic manner becomes the bottleneck as the complexity of these tasks just keep piling up until it is beyond the scope of a Machine Learning practitioner.

674   P.-Q. Vo et al.

The rapid growth of Machine Learning demands the methods that citizen Machine Learning practitioners can still achieve and deploy efficient models without any prior knowledge or experience. Such a research area that aims at progressive automation in Machine Learning is called AutoML. Figure 6 shows our life cycle embracing the AutoML approach.

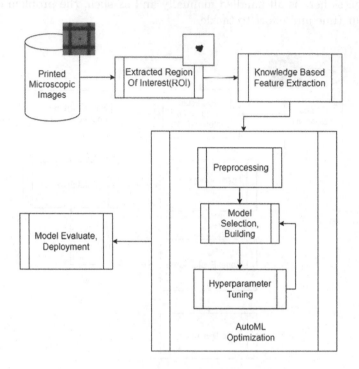

Fig. 6. Our approach using AutoML life cycle

4   Experiments and Discussion

We perform experiments using three most common singular Machine Learning models: SVM, Decision Tree, Random Forest; compared to two AutoML representatives: AutoSkLearn and TPOT. We summarized and made a comparison between five approaches based on a confusion matrix, classification report, and accuracy score.

According to the previous work [13], the authors have stated that only the last pattern of the printed microscopic images contributes the most promising information for the Machine Learning model to perform the classification task. The authors perform various experiments using SVM with the default pipeline to find out the golden pattern manually. The author directed the preprocessing phase to make the model more robust and boosted in accuracy. However, the authors stop only at the step of filtering out which feature is useful for the model. We continue the experiments using all patterns of the printed microscopic images to validate the power of the AutoML. In the first experiment, we are using SVM to reproduce the results the authors have stated in the work [13]. The classification report of the experiment is recorded in Table 2.

Table 2. SVM classification

	Precision	Recall	F1-score	Support
1	0.5	0.56	0.53	320
2	0.69	0.86	0.77	320
3	0.52	0.47	0.50	320
4	0.84	0.99	0.91	320
5	0.66	0.68	0.67	320
6	0.70	0.38	0.49	320
Accuracy			0.66	1920
Macro average	0.65	0.66	0.64	1920
Weighted average	0.65	0.66	0.64	1920

The results are just what the authors have performed previously in their work [13]. SVM is a simple algorithm that every expert should have in his/her arsenal. The appealing point of SVM is that it can achieve mind-blowing results while using small computational power. SVM algorithm first maps our knowledge-based extract feature into high dimension space. Then it will proceed to find the most optimal separator (boundary) to group data into the corresponding class. However, the results in Table 2 might hint to us that the feature space of all patterns are overlap or is closely tight to each other, and thus, the algorithm has trouble finding the correct boundary to our dataset.

The next experiment we perform is using the Decision Tree algorithm. A tree has many analogies in real life and it even widely influences the Machine Learning field. As the name goes, the algorithm uses a tree-like model to visually and explicitly represent the decisions and decision makings. For our case, the model will use information from five knowledge-based features namely area, perimeter, circularity, convexity, and solidity. The decision tree is represented in an upside-down manner, the visualization is more of the actual root of the tree. To make a decision, we need certain conditions, and based on such criteria, we will split further into different branches. Such conditions are called internal nodes and the first condition is root. The end of the branch that is not split anymore is the decision or the leaf node. Having features from domain experts with diversity value, we hope the model will give much better results from SVM. The classification report of the model is recorded in Table 3.

Table 3. Decision tree classification

	Precision	Recall	F1-score	Support
1	0.68	0.70	0.69	320
2	0.78	0.78	0.78	320
3	0.67	0.66	0.66	320
4	0.95	0.96	0.95	320
5	0.64	0.64	0.64	320
6	0.65	0.65	0.65	320
Accuracy			0.66	1920
Macro average	0.73	0.73	0.73	1920
Weighted average	0.73	0.73	0.73	1920

The results are much better than SVM, however, in general still not adequately high. Just like the feature space mapping in SVM, the value of five attributes make the decision-making conditions not clear enough for the model to clarify six corresponding classes. The deliberate singular Machine Learning model may not be sufficient to achieve a higher statistical value.

Then we embrace the ensemble theory which indicates using multiple learning algorithms could obtain better predictive performance than any of the constituent models alone. Thus, our candidate is the Random Forest algorithm as it is one of the most prominent single machine learning models among ensemble approach for learning diverse patterns data via different trees [19]. Each tree of the forest predicts an outcome and the most votes outcome will be the final result of the model. The principle behind Random Forest in particular and ensemble methods, in general, is simple yet powerful - the wisdom of the crowd. However, this is only good if each individual in the crowd does not have the error in the same direction. The results of the model are recorded in Table 4, which is impressive since the F1-score goes up from 0.73 in the case of the Decision Tree algorithm to 0.79.

Table 4. Random Forest classification

	Precision	Recall	F1-score	Support
1	0.79	0.74	0.76	320
2	0.82	0.86	0.84	320
3	0.73	0.76	0.74	320
4	0.95	0.97	0.96	320
5	0.72	0.71	0.71	320
6	0.74	0.72	0.73	320
Accuracy			0.66	1920
Macro average	0.79	0.79	0.79	1920
Weighted average	0.79	0.79	0.79	1920

Keep in mind, that all the experiments so far are default pipelines, we have not yet touched anything related to preprocessing or hyperparameter tuning phase. These two phases will be performed automatically and fully optimized by AutoML. The two AutoML we used are AutoSKLearn and TPOT. The outcomes of AutoSKLearn [20] and TPOT [21] are recorded correspondingly in Table 5 and Table 6.

Table 5. AutoSKLearn classification

	Precision	Recall	F1-score	Support
1	0.8	0.76	0.78	320
2	0.83	0.85	0.84	320
3	0.75	0.77	0.76	320
4	0.93	0.98	0.95	320
5	0.71	0.70	0.70	320
6	0.73	0.72	0.72	320
Accuracy			0.79	1920
Macro average	0.79	0.79	0.79	1920
Weighted average	0.79	0.79	0.79	1920

Table 6. TPOT classification

	Precision	Recall	F1-score	Support
1	0.81	0.76	0.79	320
2	0.83	0.85	0.84	320
3	0.74	0.78	0.76	320
4	0.94	0.97	0.96	320
5	0.72	0.72	0.72	320
6	0.75	0.71	0.73	320
Accuracy			0.8	1920
Macro average	0.8	0.8	0.8	1920
Weighted average	0.8	0.8	0.8	1920

The results are just to firm our belief in the optimization merits of AutoML. Even though the pattern range extracted manually contributes the most to the model, the boost from AutoML is worth mentioning. Especially since we do not require any specific deep domain knowledge and just let AutoML do the best jobs they are designed to do (Fig. 7).

Accuracy Score

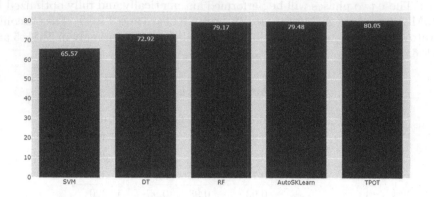

Fig. 7. Comparison of accuracy score

5   Conclusion and Future Work

We have proposed a method borrowing the computational power of AutoML to produce the best possible model for printed microscopic images source identification. Our thorough experiments have shown that the AutoML approach is superior to three well-known traditional single Machine Learning models when we took into account all the patterns. This approach is helpful in the sense that we do not need to rely on expert knowledge of selecting the best pattern for achieving sufficiently good performance. Therefore, it emphasizes a significant advantage of AutoML which can learn the uncertainties of many different patterns for identification problem, and of course, this is extremely useful in industrial applications.

In our future works, we will extend our discussion in this paper by considering more learnable models and testing them against different patterns or sub-patterns to validate which contribute the most to the task of source printed microscopic images classification under the viewpoint of AutoML.

Acknowledgement. This research is supported by a project with the International University, Ho Chi Minh City, Vietnam (contract No. T2020-01-IT/HĐ-ĐHQT-QLKH, dated 01/02/2021).

References

1. Bailey, D.H., Borwein, J., Lopez de Prado, M., Zhu, Q.J.: The probability of back-test overfitting. J. Comput. Financ. (2016, forthcoming)

2. Tran, T., Nguyen, N., Nguyen, T., Mai, A.: Voting shrinkage algorithm for covariance matrix estimation and its application to portfolio selection. In: 2020 RIVF International Conference on Computing and Communication Technologies (RIVF), pp. 1–6. IEEE (2020)

3. IDC Forecasts Worldwide Page Volumes to Rebound in 2021, But Will Not Reach Pre-covid-19 Levels. https://www.idc.com/getdoc.jsp?containerId=prUS48126321. Accessed Oct 2021

4. Oliver, J., Chen, J.: Use of signature analysis to discriminate digital printing technologies. In: NIP & Digital Fabrication Conference. Society for Imaging Science and Technology, vol. 1, pp. 218–222 (2002)

5. Chiang, P.-J., et al.: Printer and scanner forensics: models and methods. In: Sencar, H.T., Velastin, S., Nikolaidis, N., Lian, S. (eds.) Intelligent Multimedia Analysis for Security Applications, vol. 282, pp. 145–187. Springer, Heidelberg (2010). https://doi.org/10.1007/978-3-642-11756-5_7

6. Ferreira, A., Navarro, L.C., Pinheiro, G., dos Santos, J.A., Rocha, A.: Laser printer attribution: exploring new features and beyond. Forensic Sci. Int. **247**, 105–125 (2015)

7. Khanna, N., Delp, E.J.: Intrinsic signatures for scanned documents forensics: effect of font shape and size. In: Proceedings of 2010 IEEE International Symposium on Circuits and Systems, pp. 3060–3063. IEEE (2010)

8. Chiang, P.-J., Allebach, J.P., Chiu, G.T.-C.: Extrinsic signature embedding and detection in electrophotographic halftoned images through exposure modulation. IEEE Trans. Inf. Forensics Secur. **6**(3), 946–959 (2011)

9. Mikkilineni, A.K., Ali, G.N., Chiang, P.-J., Chiu, G.T., Allebach, J.P., Delp, E.J.: Signature-embedding in printed documents for security and forensic applications. In: Security, Steganography, and Watermarking of Multimedia Contents VI, vol. 5306. International Society for Optics and Photonics, pp. 455–466 (2004)

10. LaPorte, G.M.: Chemical analysis for the scientific examination of questioned documents. Forensic Chem.: Fundam. Appl. 318–353 (2015)

11. Mai, B.A.H., Sawaya, W., Bas, P.: Image model and printed document authentication: a theoretical analysis. In: IEEE International Conference on Image Processing. IEEE-ICIP (2014)

12. Darwish, S.M., ELgohary, H.M.: Building an expert system for printer forensics: a new printer identification model based on niching genetic algorithm. Expert Syst. **38**(2), e12624 (2021)

13. Nguyen, Q.-T., Mai, A., Chagas, L., Reverdy-Bruas, N.: Microscopic printing analysis and application for classification of source printer. Comput. Secur. **108**, 102320 (2021)

14. Nguyen, Q.P., Dang, N.T., Mai, A., Nguyen, V.S.: Features selection in microscopic printing analysis for source printer identification with machine learning. In: Dang, T.K., Küng, J., Chung, T.M., Takizawa, M. (eds.) FDSE 2021. CCIS, vol. 1500, pp. 210–223. Springer, Singapore (2021). https://doi.org/10.1007/978-981-16-8062-5_14

15. Kipphan, H.: Handbook of Print Media: Technologies and Production Methods. Springer, Heidelberg (2001)

16. Nguyen, T.Q., Delignon, Y., Chagas, L., Septier, F.: Printer identification from micro-metric scale printing. In: 2014 IEEE International Conference on Acoustics, Speech and Signal Processing (ICASSP), pp. 6236–6239. IEEE (2014)

17. Nguyen, Q.T., Delignon, Y., Septier, F., Phan-Ho, A.T.: Probabilistic modelling of printed dots at the microscopic scale. Signal Process.: Image Commun. **62**, 129–138 (2018)

18. Olson, E., et al.: Particle shape factors and their use in image analysis part 1: theory. J. GXP Compliance **15**(3), 85 (2011)
19. Tran, T., Tran, L., Mai, A.: K-segments under bagging approach: an experimental study on extremely imbalanced data classification. In: 19th International Symposium on Communications and Information Technologies (ISCIT), pp. 492–495. IEEE (2019)
20. Feurer, M., Klein, A., Eggensperger, K., Springenberg, J., Blum, M., Hutter, F.: Efficient and robust automated machine learning. In: Advances in Neural Information Processing Systems, vol. 28, pp. 2962–2970 (2015)
21. Olson, R.S., Bartley, N., Urbanowicz, R.J., Moore, J.H.: Evaluation of a tree-based pipeline optimization tool for automating data science. In: Proceedings of the Genetic and Evolutionary Computation Conference 2016, ser. GECCO 2016, pp. 485–492. ACM, New York (2016). http://doi.acm.org/10.1145/2908812.2908918

EfficientRec: An Unlimited User Scale Recommendation System Based on Clustering and User's Interaction Embedding Profile

Vu Hong Quan[1]($\boxtimes$), Le Hoang Ngan[1], Le Minh Duc[1],
Nguyen Tran Ngoc Linh[1], and Hoang Quynh-Le[2]

[1] Data Analytics Center, Viettel Telecom, Viettel Group, Hanoi, Vietnam
{quanvh8,nganlh,duclm29,linhntn3}@viettel.com.vn
[2] University of Engineering and Technology, Vietnam National University,
Hanoi, Vietnam
lhquynh@vnu.edu.vn

Abstract. Recommendation systems are highly interested in technology companies nowadays. The businesses are constantly growing users and products, causing the number of users and items to continuously increase over time, to very large numbers. Traditional recommendation algorithms with complexity dependent on the number of users and items make them difficult to adapt to the industrial environment. In this paper, we introduce a new method applying graph neural networks with a contrastive learning framework in extracting user preferences. We incorporate a soft clustering architecture that significantly reduces the computational cost of the inference process. Experiments show that the model is able to learn user preferences with low computational cost in both training and prediction phases. At the same time, the model gives a very good accuracy. We call this architecture EfficientRec (Our source code available at: https://github.com/quanvu0996/EfficientRec) with the implication of model compactness and the ability to scale to unlimited users and products.

Keywords: Recommendation system · Graph neural networks · Contrastive learning · Soft clustering networks

1 Introduction

Personalization is the topic of investment with high returns in recent years. Two typical collaborative filtering (CF) algorithms for the recommendation problem are matrix factorization [6] and two-head DNNs [3,4]. While recent studies focus on the accuracy of the recommendation system in the lab and achieve positive results such as BiVAE [1], VASP [2],... We find these methods facing difficulties in deploying on the production environment because:

First, the architecture of these models is not optimized. These models use user_id embedding as part of the model. This leads to the calculation complexity and size of the model depending on the number of users. When the number

© The Author(s), under exclusive license to Springer Nature Singapore Pte Ltd. 2022
E. Szczerbicki et al. (Eds.): ACIIDS 2022, CCIS 1716, pp. 681–696, 2022.
https://doi.org/10.1007/978-981-19-8234-7_53

of users increases, it is forced to re-train a new model, the model cannot recommend for new users. When the number of users is large, the size and calculation complexity of the model become very large [7,8]. These limitations in reality are very common in businesses when the number of users is large and constantly increasing.

Second, the item selection process of these models is not optimal. Models deployed in the lab often try to predict the entire utility matrix. The reason is to evaluate a model's performance in the laboratory, we must rely on its predictions for a few items that have been rated in the test set. If a user is recommended items that the user has not rated, we do not know whether the recommendation is correct or not. Predicting the entire utility matrix is very expensive, for each user we have to calculate for both items that are liked and not liked. Unlike the lab, the production recommendations will be evaluated on A/B Testing. A product that has not been rated in the past if it is recommended, users can interact and show their level of favor. The production recommendation is to search for the items that the user liked.

Some papers try to solve the first problem by using online learning [9] or parallel [10,11] matrix factorization. More recently, [12] proposed a distributed alternative stochastic gradient distribution solver for an LFA-based recommendation based on a distribution mechanism including efficient data partitioning. Clustering is a potential idea to solve both problems [15–17]. Clustering could improve recommendation accuracy [13], increase the diversity of lists of recommendations [14],... Although these methods help the model become trainable on a large scale, the model size and cold start problems still remain.

In this paper, we try to solve these two non-optimal points, and propose a new architecture that can effectively be implemented in the production environment. Our main contributions include:

- Building recommendation system with complexity independent of the number of users. It does not use user_id so it can scale unlimited with the number of users without affecting the performance of the model. At the same time, the model can operate with new users without having to build and retrain the model.
- Proposing the algorithm of clustering item selection to help prune a large number of unnecessary parts of the utility matrix, making the personalization problem become search items that users liked.
- Application of contrastive learning architecture to extract the user's preference effectively.

2   Related Works

2.1   Graph Neural Network in Recommend System

In recent years, studies on the application of GNN to recommendation systems have been proposed. The most intuitive reason is that GNN techniques have demonstrated to power representational learning for graph data in a variety of domains. User-item interaction prediction is one of classic problems in recommendation, then, user-item interaction data can be represented by a bipartite graph, the edges corresponding to the interaction of the user-item. Van Den Berg et al. [18] first applied GNN with GC-MC model on user-item rating graph to learn embedded representation of user and item. In fact, the recommended dataset can be up to billions of nodes and edges, where each node contains many features, it is difficult to apply traditional GNN models due to large memory usage and long training time. To deal with the large-scale graphs, one of the classic ways is to apply graph sampling. GraphSAGE [19] randomly samples a fixed number of neighbors, and PinSage [20] employs the random walk strategy for sampling. However, sampling will lose more or less part of the information, and few studies focus on how to design an effective sampling strategy to balance the effectiveness and scalability.

2.2 Self-supervised Learning

Self-supervised learning (SSL) as a technique to learn with unlabeled data, recently applied to recommendation for mitigating the data sparsity issue. The basic idea is to augment the training data with various data augmentation, and supervised tasks to predict or reconstitute the original examples as auxiliary tasks. SSL has been widely applied in many fields, such as data augmentation methods in image processing or masked language tasks in BERT [24] model applied in natural language processing. Inspired by the success of SSL in other fields, recent studies have applied SSL to recommendation systems and have achieved remarkable achievements. Kun Zhou et al. [21] introduced the $S^3 - Rec$ model, the main idea is to utilize the intrinsic data correlation to derive self-supervision signals and enhance the data representations via pre-training methods for improving sequential recommendation. Tiansheng Yao et al. [22] introduced a multi-task self-supervised learning (SSL) framework for large-scale item recommendations by adding regularization to improve generalization. More recently, in [23], the authors explored self-supervised learning on user-item graph, so as to improve the accuracy and robustness of GCNs for recommendation.

3 Proposal Model

3.1 Architecture

We propose a recommended system architecture consisting of two parts: clustering model and item selection model. The clustering model learns and extracts the characteristics of the user's behavior, and then assigns clusters for them. The clusters identify users with similar preferences. Given the items catalog $T = \{t_1, t_2, ..., t_p\}$ with p items. For a sample user u_i with demographic information vector d_i, we have a set of interacted items $S_i = \{t_{i1}, t_{i2}, t_{i3}, ..., t_{iq}; t_{ij} \in T, q \leqslant p\}$. Items in S_i are known the rating value corresponding to the rating

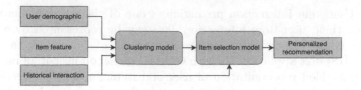

Fig. 1. Overall architecture

vector $r_i = \{r_{i1}, r_{i2}, r_{i3}, ..., r_{iq}\}$. Clustering model H will perform interaction embedding and combine with user demographic d_i to build a vector z_i:

$$z_i \leftarrow H(s_i, r_i, d_i)$$

z_i is a vector that expresses the user's preference. Using the z_i vector, we identify the top of the most outstanding features of the user behavior and assign clusters by them. With the item selection model, each user cluster that has been identified from the clustering model will be used to select a set of favorite items. For each user, he/she's clusters will vote to choose the best appropriate items and recommend them for the user (Fig. 1).

3.2 Interaction Embedding

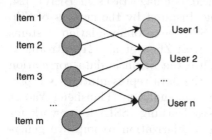

Fig. 2. Interactions are considered as a directional graph

Similar to [18], we consider the interaction data of users and items as a directional graph. In which nodes are users, items and the edges indicate interactive relationships. The magnitude of the edges are rating values. The rating value needs to be normalized in the range of $[-1, 1]$. The positive rating values indicate the user's liking; the negative rating indicates the dislike of the user with the item (Fig. 2).

Consider the user u_i, each interacted item t_{ij} in S_i has two information: feature vector v_{ij} and id of the item id_{ij}. The feature vector v_k contains content information of the item such as description, duration, genre, price,... Thus, for the item set S_i, we have a matrix of the item features $V_i = \{v_{i1}, v_{i2}, v_{i3}, ..., v_{iq}\}$. The id_{ij} contains hidden information of the item and forms the collaborative filtering properties for the model. We use an embedding layer EM to convert id_{ij} into a representative vector e_{ij}: $e_{ij} \leftarrow EM(id_{ij})$

Combine e_{ij} with v_{ij}, we obtained a characteristic vector including both hidden and visible information of the item t_{ij}: $f_{ij} = concat(v_{ij}, e_{ij})$. Similar to a graph network (GNN), we calculate the f_{ij} for each item in the interactive set S_i and then add them together to obtain the user embedding vector x_i. To produce the magnitude of liking/ dislike, we use the rating of each item as an attention module:

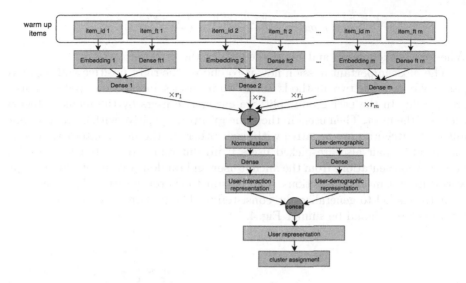

Fig. 3. Interaction embedding model.

$$x_i \leftarrow \frac{1}{q} \sum_{j=1}^{q} (r_{ij} \times f_{ij})$$

We combine x_i with demographic information d_i to obtain the characteristic vector of each user. This vector will go through fully connected layers F to learn and form the preference vector z_i as mentioned in 3.1: $z_i - F(concat(x_i, d_i))$.

The architecture of the preference extracting model shows as Fig. 3.

3.3 Contrastive Training

Clustering model H learn a preference vector $z_i \leftarrow H(s_i, r_i, d_i)$ for each user u_i. Also, z_i plays the cluster assignment layer. We expect the cluster assignment layer to express the user's preference. Each cluster corresponds to a feature of preference and has a meaningful implication, for example a cluster of action movies, a cluster of long duration movies, a cluster of Jackie Chan's movies,... or some hidden characteristics that do not exist in feature vector v_{ij} of each item. We expect the following properties of z_i:

- Consistency: Embedding vectors show the preference of a user or very similar users should be close to each other.
- Distinguishing: Between different users, the embedding vector tends to be different. The more different in user's preferences, the more distance between embedding vectors.

We use a triplet contrastive learning architecture [16] to achieve these goals. For three embedding vector z_i, z_i^p which is similar to z_i, and z_i^n which is difference with z_i, the loss function is define as:

$$L = max(m + \frac{\|z_i - z_i^p\|}{l} - \frac{\|z_i - z_i^n\|}{l}, 0)$$

Where m is the margin and l is the length of the preference vector.

The most important mission now is to choose the right positive and negative pairs. We propose two methods to do that: user's interaction split and user group split. In the user group split, we categorize users by the movie category they like the most. Then users in the same group are positive with each other and different categories are negative with each other. In the user's interaction split, the negative pair also are picked users from different groups, but the positive pair are representations from the anchor user and randomly split into two groups: warm up and mask interactions. The reason to choose positive that way is we want the model to generalize the consistency. The preference vectors extracted from one user should be similar Fig. 4.

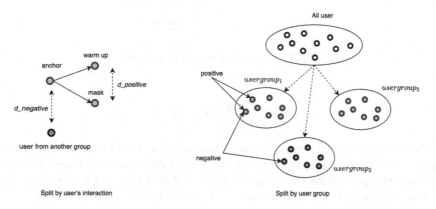

Fig. 4. Split strategies to get positive and negative representation pairs for triplet contrastive training. This splittings ensure the model leans consistency and distinguishing properties

3.4   Item Selection Pipeline

Soft Clustering vs Hard Clustering

While traditional clustering algorithms try to classify each user (data point) into a cluster such as Kmeans, DBSCAN, ... In a recommender model, this classification have a number of weaknesses:

- Sparsity: some users are classified alone or are divided into a cluster with very few users. For example, user 7 and user 4 in the Fig. 5 are classified into clusters 4A and 3A. This makes the number of interactions in the cluster too sparse and does not guarantee the reliability of recommendation.
- Hard split margin: with points near the classification boundary, although they are very close to each other, they can be classified into 2 completely different clusters. For example, user 5 and user 7, though very close, are divided into 2 cluster clusters 2a, cluster 4a.

These weaknesses could lead to low efficiency when deploying the recommendation system. We argue that using a soft clustering architecture, in which each data point is allowed to be classified in more than one cluster, would bring better performance in the recommendation field. If a user is divided into a cluster with very few users, then there is still the probability that the user is divided into another cluster with more users. Two users which are close to each other but be splitted into two clusters, can be classified into the same another cluster and thus can still effectively collaborate with each other.

To implement soft clustering, we use the user profile vector to be the cluster assignment layer. We use the sigmoid activation function to allow each user to be classified into many different clusters.

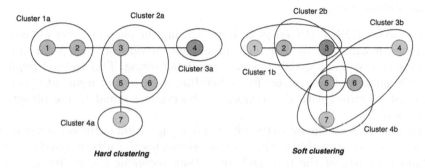

Fig. 5. Soft clustering compared to hard clustering, for a sparsity dataset, soft clustering lead to more comprehensive view

Implementation of Soft Clustering

In order to build a set of recommendations effectively and save computation costs, we will only consider the favorite items. Considering user u_i, the preference vector has been calculated as $z_i = H(S_i) = [rc_{i1}, rc_{i2}, rc_{i3}..rc_{ib}]$, b is the number of clusters. Consider the top k cluster of the user $CL = \arg\max(z_i, \text{top\_k}) = [gr_1, gr_2, gr_3, ...gr_k]$ is the top k cluster id best score in z_i corresponding to the confident vector $\zeta \subset z_i$. Considering the user u_i, the favorite set of item is $S_i^f = [t_{f1}, t_{f2}, ...t_{f\kappa}]$, $S_i^f \subset S_i$, corresponding to rating $r_i^f = [r_{f1}, ...r_{f\kappa}]$, in which the t_{fj} items are favorited by u_i, then $r_{fj} > 0$.

We build a shortlist of items by clusters. The shortlist contains the favorite item in accordance with that cluster, the level of confident to determine how the item g is suitable for the cluster f to be determined by:

$$\Im_{gf} = \frac{\sum_{i=1}^{N}(r_{ig} * \zeta_{if})}{\sum_{i=1}^{N}(\zeta_{if})}$$

Where N is total number of user, r_{ig} is rating of user u_i with item g, ζ_{if} is confident score of user u_i to be classified to the cluster f. In recommendation phase, for each user, we look up their clusters and let clusters vote for the best suitable items.

4 Offline Experiment

4.1 Experiment Setting

Dataset

We use Movielen 20M (ML20M) [26], a relatively large and popular data set in the research field to test our proposed architecture performance. In addition, because ML20M is the dataset without user's demographic information, we use the Book-crossing dataset (BC) [27] to examine the effectiveness of embedding demographic information.

Baseline Methods

We use 2 methods that represent two methodologies of implementing the recommendation system:

- Two-tower DNN (2DNNs) [3,4]: Representing the deep learning models that embed information of user and embed information of item, then multiply these two vectors together to create predicted rating. This method requires a large amount of parameters for embedding user_id and item_id. Then, the model is trained with the number of observations equal to the observation ratings.
- Alternating least square (ALS) [6]: A classic algorithm in the branch of matrix factorization algorithms. This method separates the utility matrix into the hidden matrix of the user and item, then recreates the utility matrix by multiplying these two hidden matrices together.

Metrics

As presented at 3, our architecture will only focus on recommending liked items and ignore unliked items. Therefore, the ranking metrics for such as NDCG, MAP are not suitable to evaluate the recommendation performance. In this study we use precision@50 to evaluate the model performance. The model is considered effective when recommending the products that users like.

$$precision@k = \frac{|\Re_i^k \cap S_i^f|}{|\Re_i^k \cap S_i|}$$

4.2 Experiment Results

Training ER model, the loss function tends to decrease after each epoch, proving that the architecture is convergent, the model can learn the characteristics of users based on their interactive history Fig. 7a. Figure 6a shows the vector preference of some users. After training, the ER model has built a user profile which shows the user's preference and distinguishes the preference of different users. Some users have similar vector profiles and are identified as people who share the same cluster. Figure 6b show the embedding vectors by user group. It proves that the contrastive learning has learned the preference of users and can distinguish users with different preferences while pulling users with similar preference to close each other. In addition, the model discovered that users who prefer thriller movies tend to be similar to users who prefer action movies; users that prefer romance movies tend to be close with users that like comedy movies while far from users that like action movies. That discovery makes sense even though no semantic relation between movie categories is provided for the model, then proves the efficiency of the contrastive training.

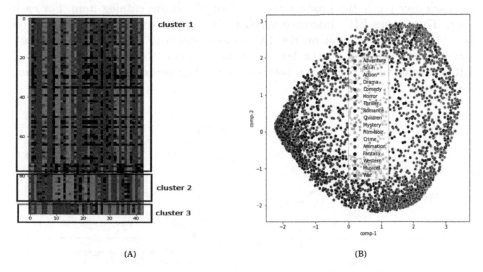

(A)   (B)

Fig. 6. (A) Spectrogram of user's preference vectors in hard split cluster. Each row is a preference vector of a user. The lighter pixel corresponds with a higher value of the user fitted to the cluster; (B) PCA plots show embedding vectors of user preferences. Labels are the category that users favorite the most. Users with the same first category seem close to each other.

Table 1. Training time comparition

Method	ML20M	BC
ALS	6383	5189
2DNNs	4703	4221
ER interaction split	443	382
ER user group split	425	367

Table 2. Inference time comparition

Method	ML20M	BC
2DNNs	21810	392584
ALS	23555	474780
ER interaction split	516	432
ER user group split	933	839

The ER model has a significantly lower number of parameters 2DNNs, in addition to 2DNNs and ALS models will have to train with data scores corresponding to the ratings, while the ER training model with the number of data points is corresponding to the user number. In the ML20M data set, the number of users is 145 times less than the number of ratings; in the BC data set, the number of users is 4 times less than the number of user. Combining these two factors helps the ER model training significantly faster 2DNNs. During the training, the ER model runs 12 times faster than 2DNNs with the ML20M data set and is 6 times faster with the BC. While ALS learn linearly correlation of users and items so it has a quite low training time and even quicker than our ER model (Tables 1 and 2).

In the inference process, while ER only needs to scan and choose on a very limited number of items in the shortlists, the ALS or 2DNNs models must predict for each user pair - the product then sort on the entire catalog item. For each user. This causes ER's inference speed to be 42 times faster than 2DNNs on the ML20M dataset, and on the BC dataset which is a very sparse dataset, ER's Inference speed is even 908 times faster than 2DNNs. These results of ER compared to ALS are even better because ALS gives the computation time longer than 2DNNs.

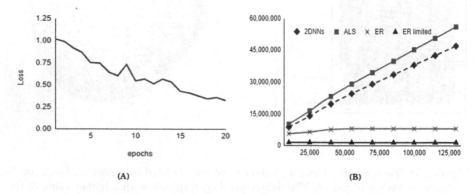

(A)   (B)

Fig. 7. (A) Loss of user embedding vector model is convergent; (B) Compare models parameters, ER has number of parameter which independent with use's number and smaller than other models. ER model with limited item catalog has much smaller than full item catalog model

Table 3. Precision@50 comparition between models

Method	ML20M	BC
2DNNs	0.9721	0.7622
ALS	0.9582	0.7272
ER interaction split	0.9732	0.7736
ER user group split	0.9752	0.7621

Both 2DNNs and ER models are the hybrid of content-based and collaborative filtering while ALS is a pure collaborative filtering model. This gives 2DNNs and ER an advantage compared to ALS at cold start users and sparsity dataset. The test results show that ER for the accuracy of the small-scale recommendation ($k = 50$ items) is better than the 2DNNs and ALS methods. Especially in the sparse BC dataset ALS gives significantly poor efficiency than ER (Table 3).

5   Online Experiments

Since this research is for efficient deployment in industry environment, we conduct an online testing on practical services to evaluate the effectiveness of the model. In the production environment, the data are mainly implicit ratings, observed through the user interactions and sequentially over time.

Dataset: We use TV360 service, with 2 product groups: movies, videos. Movie data has 7000 series of movies, is a relatively dense dataset, while the video product with 200,000 videos is a very sparse data set. With 2 million active users, the scale makes traditional methods extremely expensive. Table 4 compare some statistics of 2 datasets, in which $sparseratio = rating\_num/(user\_num \times item\_num)$.

Table 4. Statistics of online datasets

Dataset info	TV360's films	TV360's videos
Active user	1,875,642	732,514
Number of item	7,251	185,324
Number of rating	5,347,897	3,040,837
Sparse ratio	0.0393%	0.0022%
Liked ratings (implicit)	92.01%	94.09%
Disliked ratings (implicit)	7.99%	5.91%

Metric: We perform A/B testing, by randomly dividing the user volumes into the same 3 sets with the same number of users, homogeneous by stratified sampling. Then we compare the average view number per user (ACPU) and the average watched duration (at second) per user (ADPU).

Results: Experimental results show that, for the unbalanced dataset (most interactions are liked) in the industrial environment, the ER model has a significantly better performance than the 2DNNs and ALS models (Table 5).

Table 5. Results of the online experiments

Methods	TV360's films		TV360's videos	
	ACPU	ADPU	ACPU	ADPU
2DNNs	0.0152	13.896	0.0322	10.526
ALS	0.0121	12.190	0.0160	4.277
ER interaction split	0.0186	15.018	0.0421	12.290
ER user group split	0.0176	14.272	0.0381	13.155

6   Conclusion

Models that their complexity depend on the number of users and items, are extremely expensive in the computation cost, causing great challenges in deploying on the production environment. In this paper, we presented a framework that allows training and inference effectively with low calculation costs and high accuracy. By using interaction embedding, we do not need to use user_id and allow the model scale to an infinite number of users without affecting the model performance. The calculated data points are each user instead of each rating that help accelerate training significantly, especially for large interactive datasets. Proposals on recommendations according to clustering and shortlist memory gives good effect in recommending and reducing a significant amount of inference costs, especially in sparse dataset. However, clustering recommendations are still an idea that needs more studies to increase accuracy. We expect researchers to continue developing this idea and put it into application in a super -large recommendation system.

Appendix A   Online Sequencial Split

In the online experiment, the ER user interaction split, we divide the data into the corresponding data segments: warm up, mask, target similar to offline experiments, but they are divided sequentially in the sequence of time. Users' interactions show the user's preference, we assume that with movie and video services, this preference is unchanged for less than 6 months. Therefore, the preference vectors of the same user extracted from the warm up, mask set tend to be the same, although different timeframes, the vectors still tend to be similar than preference vectors extracted from different users. Then, we still apply the contrastive learning architecture to train the model. Implicit rating is defined based on the user's viewing time. Because most interactions are reflected when users like the product, to detect the disliked products, we select the products that have been recommended for many times but not be interacted with (Fig. 8).

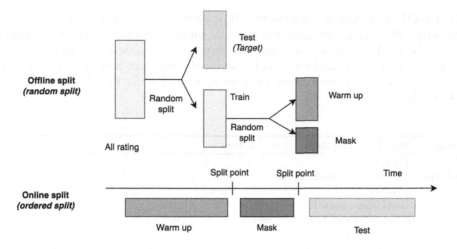

Fig. 8. Sequencial warm up - mask split versus random split

Appendix B   Item Selection Pseudocode

We propose a pseudo code to identify shortlist as Algorithm 1. Algorithm 1 runs independently between users and can be distributed among computers performed

---

Algorithm 1. Form shortlist for clusters

Input: $H, user\_list, S, r$
Output: shortlist $\Im$
   Initialisation :
   $\Im = $ dict{ cluster_id: dict{item : score}} ;
   // *Accumulated rating and counter* :
   $\Im^{rating} = $ dict{ cluster_id: dict{item:score}};
   $\Im^{count} = $ dict{ cluster_id: dict{item: count}};
   for user_i in user_list **do**
      $z_i = H(S_i)$
      $S_i^f = S_i[\text{where rating} > 0] = [t_{f1}, t_{f2}, ...t_{f\kappa}]$
      $r_i^f = r_i[\text{where rating} > 0] = [r_{f1}, r_{f2}, ...r_{f\kappa}]$
      $CL = \arg\max(z_i, \text{top\_k}) = [gr_1, gr_2, ..., gr_k]$
      $\zeta = z_i[\text{where index in } CL] = [rc_{gr1}, rc_{gr2}, ..., rc_{grk}]$
      for cluster in CL **do**
         for item in S_i^f **do**
            $\Im^{rating}[\text{cluster}][\text{item}]+ = r_i^f[\text{item}] * \zeta[\text{cluster}]$
            $\Im^{count}[\text{cluster}][\text{item}]+ = \zeta[\text{cluster}]$
         end for
      end for
   end for
   $\Im[i][j] = \Im^{rating}[i][j] / \Im^{count}[i][j]$
   return $\Im$

---

in parallel, then summarizing the final $\Im$ according to Map-Reduce methodology. Shortlist $\Im$ is relatively small because the number of clusters is much smaller than the number of users and items. However, in case of desire to reduce storage capacity, we can sort and retain only the most prominent items for each cluster.

Pseudo code to recommend for user u_i after having the shortlist show as Algorithm 2.

Algorithm 2. Recommend item for user

Input: $H, u_i, S_i, \Im$
Output: recommendation list $\Re$
    Initialisation :
    $\Re_i$ = dict{item : score} ;
    // *Accumulated rating and counter* :
    $\Re^{rating}$ = dict{item:score};
    $\Re^{count}$ = dict{item: count};
    $z_i = H(S_i)$
    CL =argmax(z_i, top k) = $[gr1, gr2, ...grk]$
    $\zeta = z_i$[index in CL] = $[rc_{gr1}, ..., rc_{grk}]$
    for cluster in CL **do**
        for item in $\Im$[cluster] **do**
            $\Re_i^{rating}$ [item] +=$\Im$ [cluster][item]*ζ[cluster]
            $\Re_i^{count}$ [item] += ζ[cluster]
        end for
    end for
    $\Re[j] = \Re^{rating}$ [j] / $\Re^{count}$[j]
    return $\Re$

References

1. Truong, Q.-T., Salah, A., Lauw, H.: Bilateral variational autoencoder for collaborative filtering, pp. 292–300 (2021). https://doi.org/10.1145/3437963.3441759
2. Vančura, V., Kordík, P.: Deep variational autoencoder with shallow parallel path for top-N recommendation (VASP). In: Farkaš, I., Masulli, P., Otte, S., Wermter, S. (eds.) ICANN 2021. LNCS, vol. 12895, pp. 138–149. Springer, Cham (2021). https://doi.org/10.1007/978-3-030-86383-8_11
3. Krichene, W., et al.: Efficient training on very large corpora via Gramian estimation. In: ICLR 2019 (2019)
4. Mehrotra, R., Lalmas, M., Kenney, D., Lim-Meng, T., Hashemian, G.: Jointly leveraging intent and interaction signals to predict user satisfaction with slate recommendations. In: WWW 2019 (2019)
5. Koren, Y., Bell, R., Volinsky, C.: Matrix factorization techniques for recommender systems. Computer **42**(8), 30–37 (2009). https://doi.org/10.1109/MC.2009.263
6. Hu, Y., Koren, Y., Volinsky, C.: Collaborative filtering for implicit feedback datasets. In: Eighth IEEE International Conference on Data Mining, pp. 263–272 (2008). https://doi.org/10.1109/ICDM.2008.22

7. Schafer, J.B., Frankowski, D., Herlocker, J., Sen, S.: Collaborative filtering recommender systems. In: Brusilovsky, P., Kobsa, A., Nejdl, W. (eds.) The Adaptive Web. LNCS, vol. 4321, pp. 291–324. Springer, Heidelberg (2007). https://doi.org/10.1007/978-3-540-72079-9_9

8. Adomavicius, G., Tuzhilin, A.: Toward the next generation of recommender systems: a survey of the state-of-the-art and possible extensions. IEEE Trans. Knowl. Data Eng. **17**, 734–749 (2005)

9. Sarwar, B., Karypis, G., Konstan, J., Riedl, J.: Incremental singular value decomposition algorithms for highly scalable recommender systems. In: Proceedings of the 5th International Conference in Computers and Information Technology (2002)

10. Yu, H.-F., Hsieh, C.-J., Si, S., Dhillon, I.S.: Scalable coordinate descent approaches to parallel matrix factorization for recommender systems. In: Proceedings of the IEEE International Conference Data Mining, pp. 765–774 (2012)

11. Yu, H.F., Hsieh, C.J., Si, S., et al.: Parallel matrix factorization for recommender systems. Knowl Inf Syst. **41**, 793–819 (2014). https://doi.org/10.1007/s10115-013-0682-2

12. Shi, X., He, Q., Luo, X., Bai, Y., Shang, M.: Large-scale and scalable latent factor analysis via distributed alternative stochastic gradient descent for recommender systems. IEEE Trans. Big Data **8**(2), 420–431 (2022). https://doi.org/10.1109/TBDATA.2020.2973141

13. Nilashi, M., Ibrahim, O., Bagherifard, K.: A recommender system based on collaborative filtering using ontology and dimensionality reduction techniques. Expert Syst. Appl. **92**, 507–520 (2018)

14. Aytekin, T., Karakaya, M.Ö.: Clustering-based diversity improvement in top-N recommendation. J. Intel. Inf. Syst. **42**(1), 1–18 (2014)

15. Zhang, J.: Robust collaborative filtering based on multiple clustering. In: 2019 IEEE 7th International Conference on Computer Science and Network Technology (ICCSNT), pp. 174–178. IEEE (2019)

16. O'Mahony, M.P., Hurley, N.J., Silvestre, G.C.M.: Promoting recommendations: an attack on collaborative filtering. In: Hameurlain, A., Cicchetti, R., Traunmüller, R. (eds.) DEXA 2002. LNCS, vol. 2453, pp. 494–503. Springer, Heidelberg (2002). https://doi.org/10.1007/3-540-46146-9_49

17. Mobasher, B., Burke, R.D., Bhaumik, R., Williams, C.: Towards trustworthy recommender systems: an analysis of attack models and algorithm robustness. ACM TOIT **7**(4), Article no. 23 (2007)

18. van den Berg, R., Kipf, T.N., Welling, M.: Graph convolutional matrix completion. arXiv preprint arXiv:1706.02263 (2017)

19. Hamilton, W.L., Ying, R., Leskovec, J.: Inductive representation learning on large graphs. In: NeurIPS, pp. 1025–1035 (2017)

20. Ying, R., He, R., Chen, K., Eksombatchai, P., Hamilton, W.L., Leskovec, J.: Graph convolutional neural networks for web-scale recommender systems. In: SIGKDD, pp. 974–983 (2018)

21. Zhou, K., et al.: S3-Rec: self-supervised learning for sequential recommendation with mutual information maximization. In: CIKM, pp. 1893–1902 (2020)

22. Yao, T., et al.: Self-supervised learning for large-scale item recommendations. In: CIKM (2021)

23. Wu, J., et al.: Self-supervised graph learning for recommendation. In: SIGIR, pp. 726–735 (2021)

24. Devlin, J., Chang, M., Lee, K., Toutanova, K.: BERT: pre-training of deep bidirectional transformers for language understanding. arXiv, abs/1810.04805 (2019)

25. Schroff, F., Kalenichenko, D., Philbin, J.: FaceNet: a unified embedding for face recognition and clustering. In: IEEE Conference on Computer Vision and Pattern Recognition (CVPR), pp. 815–823 (2015). https://doi.org/10.1109/CVPR.2015.7298682
26. Maxwell Harper, F., Konstan, J.A.: The MovieLens datasets: history and context. ACM Trans. Interact. Intell. Syst. (TiiS) 5(4), 19, Article 19 (2015). https://doi.org/10.1145/2827872
27. Ziegler, C.-N., McNee, S.M., Konstan, J.A., Lausen, G.: Improving recommendation lists through topic diversification. In: Proceedings of the 14th International World Wide Web Conference (WWW 2005), Chiba, Japan, 10–14 May 2005 (2005)

Agent Based Model of Elementary School Group Learning

Barbara Wedrychowicz[1]($\boxtimes$), Marcin Maleszka[1] (ID), and Nguyen Van Sinh[2,3]

[1] Wroclaw University of Science and Technology, st. Wyspianskiego 27,
50-370 Wroclaw, Poland
227994@student.pwr.edu.pl, marcin.maleszka@pwr.edu.pl
[2] School of Computer Science and Engineering International University,
Ho Chi Minh City, Vietnam
nvsinh@hcmiu.edu.vn
[3] Vietnam National University, Ho Chi Minh City, Vietnam

Abstract. The paper describes an agent model built to simulate the behavior of primary school students during group work. The model is focused on predicting the change of student knowledge due to cooperation, compared to individual learning. The model takes into account students learning on their own and from others, as well as their ease of learning, communicativeness, and others. We conducted extensive observation studies of real students in a primary school in Poland. This data was analysed to prepare a basic regression model of real students. We compared this real data model with data gathered during simulation. Some preliminary findings on how to improve learning during groupwork are currently being tested with the same group of real students.

Keywords: Agent based modeling · Teaching model · Group modeling · Multi-agent simulation

1 Introduction

Working in groups is a common tool in education. There is an implicit assumption that some combination of students in a group could increase the quality and speed of their work, following common practices in management. Teachers may assume that it will also help students learn faster. Due to the lack of research on the topic, groups are often selected at random, or teachers allow students to create groups on their own. This motivated us to develop a model to simulate these groups and optimize their composition.

This research was intended to verify the thesis that on the basis of theoretical modeling and observation of real groups, it is possible to develop a model of students working in a group, complete with emergent behaviours that sometimes occur during their cooperation. The aim was to use this model to improve the methods of teaching students by groupwork. We first observed how real students behave in class during both individual and group work. We observed

© The Author(s), under exclusive license to Springer Nature Singapore Pte Ltd. 2022
E. Szczerbicki et al. (Eds.): ACIIDS 2022, CCIS 1716, pp. 697–710, 2022.
https://doi.org/10.1007/978-981-19-8234-7_54

primary school students in Poland over the period of one school semester. We gathered data on their attributes and the change of knowledge in different scenarios. With such a dataset, we conducted a general analysis of this behavior, considering which student attributes are important during learning. We used these observations, together with suggestions from the literature, to develop an agent model of students during groupwork. The model reflects the behavior of real students, including initially unintended emergent behaviors, e.g., refusal to work in the same group.

This paper is structured as follows: the next section gives a brief overview of related work about using groupwork for students. Section 3 describes the agent model of the situation. Section 4 describes both the dataset and the analysis of observations of real groups of students, as well as the simulations of the group with the agent model. Finally, Sect. 5 contains the final results and possible directions for teachers.

2   Related Works

One of the classical approaches [2] states that the more active and the more participating the student is, the more effective is his learning. Other works [2, 7,10] discuss that interaction between students leads to higher grades, faster memorization, higher satisfaction, and higher chances of continuing education in the next tier. A group of students always has a leader, who coordinates the work of the team and motivates them. When considering *the product*, it is more efficient for one of the students to be a member of the group, instead of the role staying with the teacher [1]. On the other hand, a group with an external leader has increased internal communication and leads to a better understanding of topics. Initially leaderless groups of students usually determine an internal leader at some point, in order to coordinate better. Additionally, the leader may focus either on the individuals of the group, or on the group as a whole. This impacts the behavior of the group as a whole. Some experiments have shown that too much focus on an individual decreases not only the efficiency of groupwork, but also of individuals [11].

Some researchers [3] have found out that grouping students based on their abilities has usually a weak, but positive impact on the quality of cooperation and the increase of their knowledge. The impact is much lower than many other factors, e.g. audio-visual stimulation. Sometimes an incorrect group formation may even lead to a decrease in learning quality. When basing on abilities, the group may be formed on the basis of current knowledge or previous achievements. It may be also done randomly, or by allowing students to group themselves. In the latter case, the basis for group formation is usually mutual sympathy, ease of cooperation, and similarity in work ethics. On the other hand, it was determined that students are more patient than adults when working with less knowledgeable partners [4].

Other researchers [5] point out that the full potential of the group can only be achieved when taking into account positive interactions, personal and group responsibility, a will and an ability to cooperate, and the openness of students. Different levels of these attributes in different students lead to different approaches to groupwork, and selecting students by these parameters could be a basis for group formation.

A four perspective model [8] poses that it is not necessary for the group aim and individual aims to be similar, and even that the ability to cooperate is not a hard requirement for groups to succeed. However, even in this model, if these options are present, they are a positive factor on student learning.

Other works posit that the most important knowledge requires time to transfer between group members [6], with some students being faster to acquire it. Group members require time to determine what is the important knowledge and how to best learn it. Additionally, while determining the most knowledgeable student in a group may be fast, learning from them may not be the easiest. Students may also individually learn from others, independent of the cooperation inside the group. Again, a person searches for the one with the most knowledge to learn from them. At the same time, their high interest in the topic may lead to spreading their own knowledge to other, less knowledgeable students.

3   Observations and the Proposed Model

The model developed in our research is based on a real group of students in grades four through eight, working in groups on small projects during ICT classes in one school in Wroclaw, Poland, between September 2021 and January 2022. The students were divided into groups by random draw, with teacher criteria (similar knowledge level; different knowledge level; good students with bad students; students interested in a topic together), or selected groups on their own. The initial observations of the groups have shown the following points that the model would need to represent:

- Good students preferred to select group partners based on their positive relations.
- The best students tried to not be put in the same group.
- Bad students preferred to select groups, where most other students were good (more knowledgeable).
- Some students did not want to cooperate – they enforced their ideas on the entire group, even if their own knowledge was insufficient.
- Some students only wanted to work in previously selected groups of a determined size and did not want to work in other groups (e.g., with a 3-person group instead of their preselected 4-person group).
- Some groups lacked any cooperation – each student worked independently on his own part.

In terms of group leaders, the abovementioned literature described leaderless groups as being more conductive to knowledge increase, but also more prone to internal conflicts. Taking into account the specifics of schoolwork, the teacher took the role of the external leader for every group.

The students were described mostly by subjective attributes:

- Age – an objective measure used for making comparisons in the same tiers.
- Group (G) – the code of student's group used to show which students worked together in each observation).
- KnowledgeBeforeTeacher (KBT) – a teacher rating of student knowledge after a theoretical introduction to the topic, but before groupwork; range $[0-10]$.
- KnowledgeBeforeStudent (KBS) – student rating of his own knowledge after a theoretical introduction to the topic, but before groupwork; range $[0-10]$.
- KnowledgeAfterTeacher (KAT) – a teacher rating of student knowledge after groupwork; range $[0-10]$.
- KnowledgeAfterStudent (KAS) – a student rating of his own knowledge after groupwork; range $[0-10]$.
- Communicativeness (C) – a teacher's subjective rating on how easy it is for a student to communicate knowledge to others, including correctness and clarity of messages; range $[0-5$.
- LeaderPotential (L) – a teacher's subjective rating on how good a student is at leading the group in some tasks; range $[0-5]$.
- Interest (I) – a rating of student interest in the topic, determined by teacher rating (care in solving tasks, ease of asking questions, volunteering to solve all problems) and student rating (interest in the topic, preparedness); range $[0-5]$.
- Ease (E) – a teacher's subjective rating of student's ease of learning for the specific topic; range $[0-5]$.

An example of several students described with those attributes are shown in Table 1. Rows depict specific students, e.g. the first row is a ten year old (4th grade), who after introduction to the topic rates himself 2, but the teacher rates him 3. After the groupwork is finished, both of them give rating 3 (the teacher sees improvement, but the student does not).

Table 1. Selected examples of observed real students during 3–4 person groupwork.

	Age	G	KBT	KBS	KAT	KAS	C	L	I	E
1	10	a3	2	3	3	3	5	2	2	4
2	11	a2	3	3	3	3	4	3	1	3
3	10	a1	1	3	5	6	3	4	3	3
4	9	a3	2	5	8	8	5	5	4	5
5	14	b1	2	7	8	9	4	3	5	5

Following the analysis of real students, we developed a multiagent model of students working in a group. A single agent is represented by parameters similar to those describing a real student:

- Leadership potential (in experiments selected randomly in range $[0, 5]$).

- Outgoing, ease of communication with others (selected randomly in range $[0, 5)$).
- Interest in the topic (selected randomly in range $[0, 5)$).
- Ease of learning (selected randomly in range $[0, 5)$).

Every agent has also some initial value of their knowledge_level:

$$knowledge\_level = max\_kowledge\_level \cdot \frac{easy\_learning}{max\_range} \cdot \frac{interest}{max\_range}$$

where:

- max_knowledg_level = 10, similarly to the maximum of the range used for real students.
- max_range = 10 is the sum of the values of this agent and any other interacting agent possible maximum value of "easy of learning" attribute.

There are two important agent actions that we describe in the model: learning (on their own) and teaching (others). Based on the observations of real groups of students, we also added forgetting behavior as a third possible action. Learning and forgetting are conducted by the agent on its own, while teaching occurs during interaction. In this initial research, we assume that all agent attributes influence learning new knowledge at the same rate.

During the groupwork each agent learns individually at the following rate:

$$knowledge\_level = knowledge\_level + \frac{easy\_learning}{max\_range} \cdot \frac{interest}{max\_range}$$

Additionally, as with real students, some agents may increase their interest in the topic, which in turn increases the knowledge acquisition rate.

$$interest = interest + \frac{knowledge\_level}{max\_knowledge\_level} \cdot \frac{interest}{max\_range}$$

Forgetting knowledge happens between simulations and is inversely proportional to the agent's interest. As this paper only discusses singular simulations and not entire cycles of learning (i.e., a school semester), it will not be further considered.

Teaching is determined by additional learning from other, neighbouring (i.e. in the same group) agents:

$$extra\_knowledge = knowledge\_level \cdot \left(\frac{interest}{max\_range} + \frac{outgoing}{max\_range}\right)$$

The model has been implemented in GAMA agent environment and was evaluated in simulational experiments. With GAMA it was possible to add the grouping behaviour of agents as a variant of agent movement. Initial localization in an abstract space is random, and the agents move randomly through it. Once they find an agent that they should group with (e.g., a random one, a similar one, etc.), they stop moving and create a group. More agents may join that group later, if the same conditions are met.

4   Evaluation of the Model

Evaluation of the model was conducted by comparing it with the observations of
a real group of students. Some initial information about the observed attributes
of students was provided in the previous section, as the basis for developing the
agent model. Before building the agent model, we also analised real students'
groupwork, based on the data gathered.

4.1   Dataset: A Real Group of Students

Students were observed during their activities in normal ICT class activities.
The observations were done in Primary School in Wroclaw, Poland, in grades 4,
5, 7, and 8, for a period of 5 months (September 2021 to January 2022). During
some classes student attributes were estimated, and during others groupwork was
conducted. During groupwork students were doing task intended for increasing
their knowledge or for repetition (better remembering) of said knowledge. With
the teacher functioning as the external leader, groups were divided at random,
by personal preference, and by explicit teacher selection.

For initial analysis of students, before groupwork, we considered them in
two cohorts: younger (grade 4 and 5) and older (grade 7 and 8). This allowed to
eliminate some of the problems when comparing students of different ages, which
could arise due to different level of mental development. Additionally, different
behaviors in each group could be observed. This paper presents the results of
the older cohort.

Currently, we are also processing the full data into an anonymized open-data
format. The overall dataset contains data as shown in Table 5 for more than
100 students, each described in at least 10 rows (10 different learning scenarios
during the observation period).

4.2   Analysis of Dataset

The observed attributes of students were analysed in terms of their relation to
initial (pre-groupwork) knowledge. We used multiple regression analysis in Analysis ToolPak for MS Excel. The calculated regression statistics are as follows:

- Multiple R: 0.917143862
- R-Squared: 0.841152864
- Adjusted R Squared: 0.818460416
- Standard error: 0.989074069
- Observations: 33

The R-squared value shows that the model (knowledge level) fits the data
(student attributes) at almost 85%. With a standard error of ca. 75%, none of
the observed values were eliminated from further analysis.

Table 2 shows the strongest correlation of initial knowledge with E (ease of
learning) and I (interest in topic), the remaining two are much less important.

Table 2. Correlation between the initial student knowledge and independent variables – student attributes.

	KBT	C	L	I	E
KBT	1.000				
C	0.046	1.000			
L	−0.333	0.000	1.000		
I	0.591	0.166	−0.043	1.000	
E	0.658	−0.199	−0.251	−0.042	1.000

Table 3. Descriptive statistics.

Attributes	Standard error	t	Stat	p-value	Lower 95%	Upper 95%
Intersection	−0.415	0.521	−0.796	0.433	−1.482	0.652
C	0.084	0.083	1.015	0.319	−0.086	0.253
L	−0.130	0.072	−1.799	0.083	−0.279	0.018
I	0.588	0.075	7.844	1.521E−08	0.435	0.742
E	0.712	0.085	8.342	4.474E−09	0.537	0.887

The attributes are also not interrelated, therefore all were used in the later parts of analysis.

Analysis shown in Table 3 shows that attributes C (communicativeness) and L (leadership) are statistically insignificant, therefore we did not use them for the model of initial knowledge. After removing those two attributes, the descriptive statistics change to those shown in Table 4.

Table 4. Descriptive statistics.

Attributes	Standard error	t	Stat	p-value	Lower 95%	Upper 95%
Intersection	−0.657	0.325	−2.020	0.052	−1.320	0.007
I	0.608	0.077	7.908	0.000	0.451	0.765
E	0.734	0.084	8.725	0.000	0.562	0.906

Figures 1 and 2 show graphically how ease of learning and student interest influence the initial knowledge in the model.

Based on the above analysis, with statistical significance for $\alpha = 0.05$, we determined that the initial knowledge of the student could be estimated with the equation:

$$knowledge\_level = -0.675 + 0.608 \cdot easy_l earning + 0.734 \cdot interest$$

The negative bias is the knowledge that students *forget* during learning, while only their ease of learning and their interest in the topic influence their results.

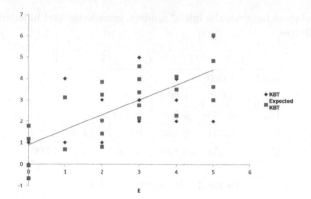

Fig. 1. Regression for ease of learning (E) and initial knowledge.

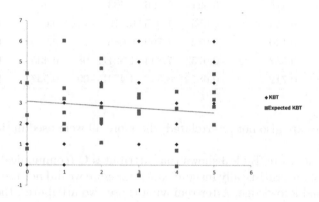

Fig. 2. Regression for student interest (I) and initial knowledge.

We conducted a similar analysis for the observed final knowledge of students (after groupwork), which due to the paper length limitation we will not describe here. In this case, it can be estimated with the equation:

$$knowledge\_level = 0.866 \cdot easy_l earning + 1.096 \cdot interest$$

Next, a similar analysis was conducted for observation of students working in pairs. Table 5 contains selected rows and all attributes (columns) that were observed. First columns describe the observed student, while columns labeled with 2 (e.g., KBT2) describe his partner during groupwork. The column δK provides the calculated increase of knowledge in comparison to students learning outside the group (based on previously calculated equations).

For the pairwork of students we also conducted the multiple regression analysis. Initial step is shown in Tables 6 and allows to determine the highest correlation between δK to be Communicativeness of both students. Additionally,

Table 5. Observation data on real students in grade 7 and grade 8 during groupwork (pairs).

Group	KBT	KBS	KAS	KAT	C	L	I	E	KBT2	C2	L2	I2	E2	δK
a1	5	8	8	4	0	5	0	5	1	0	5	3	0	−2.39
a1	1	3	5	1	0	5	3	0	5	0	5	0	5	−1.152
a2	5	5	9	5	1	2	2	4	2	1	2	4	2	−1.88
a2	2	3	5	3	1	2	4	2	5	1	2	2	4	−1.092
a3	3	4	8	4	2	2	1	3	2	2	2	2	3	−0.218
a3	2	1	7	4	2	2	2	3	3	2	2	1	3	0.398
a4	3	3	7	5	2	3	3	3	5	2	4	2	3	0.014
a4	5	5	10	7	2	4	2	3	3	2	3	3	3	0.398
a5	5	6	10	8	2	5	2	3	3	2	5	5	1	1.398
a5	3	6	9	4	2	5	5	1	5	2	5	2	3	−1.198
b1	6	7	10	8	3	0	3	4	5	3	0	3	5	−0.264
b1	5	6	10	7	3	0	3	5	6	3	0	3	4	−0.542
b2	3	3	4	5	3	1	1	2	1	3	3	2	2	1.06
b2	1	2	10	6	3	3	2	2	3	3	1	1	2	3.676
b3	5	3	9	7	3	4	0	4	3	3	4	2	3	0.888
b3	3	3	10	5	3	4	2	3	5	3	4	0	4	0.398
b4	5	5	9	8	3	5	2	4	6	4	0	2	4	1.12
b4	6	10	10	8	4	0	2	4	5	3	5	2	4	0.12
b5	5	7	10	10	4	0	3	3	6	4	1	4	2	3.014
b5	6	9	10	9	4	1	4	2	5	4	0	3	3	0.908
b6	2	2	7	3	4	2	0	2	3	4	3	2	3	0.444
b6	3	3	9	7	4	3	2	3	2	4	2	0	2	2.398
b7	7	7	10	10	4	3	5	5	4	4	4	1	5	−0.31
b7	4	7	8	10	4	4	1	5	7	4	3	5	5	4.226
b8	4	4	8	8	4	5	1	3	0	5	3	4	0	2.782
b8	0	3	5	3	5	3	4	0	4	4	5	1	3	1.464
c1	4	6	10	9	5	3	5	3	1	5	4	0	0	2.246
c1	1	4	5	5	5	4	0	0	4	5	3	5	3	4
c2	0	3	7	6	5	4	1	1	4	5	4	4	3	5.338
c2	4	5	7	9	5	4	4	3	0	5	4	1	1	2.63
c3	3	3	10	9	5	5	1	0	5	5	5	5	3	5.616
c3	4	5	9	9	5	5	5	2	4	5	5	5	2	2.524
c3	5	7	10	9	5	5	5	3	3	5	5	1	0	1.246

Interest of the other student, Ease of learning of the observed student, and the initial knowledge of the observed student are important. Only those were further analysed, as shown in Table 7.

Table 6. Correlation between the initial student knowledge and independent variables during work in pairs.

	KBT	C	L	I	E	KBT2	C2	L2	I2	E2	δK
KBT	1.000										
C	−0.036	1.000									
L	−0.211	0.000	1.000								
I	0.207	0.166	−0.043	1.000							
E	0.744	−0.199	−0.251	−0.042	1.000						
KBT2	0.035	−0.001	−0.180	0.153	−0.039	1.000					
C2	−0.001	0.971	0.088	0.127	−0.156	−0.036	1.000				
L2	−0.180	0.088	0.585	0.084	−0.289	−0.211	0.000	1.000			
I2	0.153	0.127	0.084	−0.328	−0.016	0.207	0.166	−0.043	1.000		
E2	−0.039	−0.156	−0.289	−0.016	0.008	0.744	−0.199	−0.251	−0.042	1.000	
δK	−0.317	0.746	0.228	−0.186	−0.355	0.035	0.770	0.047	0.358	−0.159	1.000

Table 7. Descriptive statistics.

Attributes	Standard error	t	Stat	p-value	Lower 95%	Upper 95%
Intersection	−1.470	0.646	−2.274	0.031	−2.796	−0.144
KBT	−0.461	0.156	−2.960	0.006	−0.781	−0.142
C	−0.085	0.529	−0.160	0.874	−1.170	1.001
E	0.099	0.194	0.508	0.615	−0.300	0.497
C2	1.062	0.527	2.014	0.054	−0.020	2.144
I2	0.371	0.118	3.138	0.004	0.128	0.613

The analysis shows that both C (communicativeness) and E (ease of learning) of the observed student are statistically insignificant, therefore we repeated the analysis with the remaining parameters, as shown in Table 8.

Finally, we can determine the equation describing the learning of a student from his group partner as follows:

$$extra\_knowledge = -1.375 - 0.398 \cdot knowledge\_level+$$

$$+0.966 \cdot Communicativeness\_Other + 1.096 \cdot Interest\_Other$$

Table 8. Descriptive statistics.

Attributes	Standard error	t	Stat	p-value	Lower 95%	Upper 95%
Intersection	−1.375	0.568	−2.423	0.022	−2.536	−0.214
KBT	−0.398	0.098	−4.061	0.001	−0.599	−0.198
C2	0.966	0.119	8.084	0.001	0.722	1.210
I2	0.363	0.112	3.251	0.003	0.135	0.592

4.3   Agent Simulation

We developed a multiagent model of students during groupwork, based on the observations and analysis presented in the previous subsection. The GAMA [9] agent environment was used. It provided not only numerical results, but also a visual representation of the simulations (examples are shown in Fig. 3 and Fig. 4). Agents were implemented according to the model outlined in Sect. 3.

Fig. 3. Simulation of groupwork with emergent behavior – agents grouping incorrectly.

A numerical overview of the simulation of pairwork is presented in Table 9. Initially, the agents (representing students) are not grouped and have some random parameters. The simulation is run and observed by discrete simulations, each representing one minute of class time (full class takes 45 min at this educational level in Poland). In observations, we have determined that after theoretical introduction the groupwork starts between 15th and 20th minute of class. Previous to that, the students are creating groups, or discussing cooperation. Thus, we observe the simulated group of agents after 10th and 20th iteration – as Table 9 shows only some groups have been formed at the first point. At the latter point, all groups are formed and groupwork starts. The agents learn on their own and from others, according to the model described in Sect. 3. We observe them at half of their groupwork time (iteration 32) and at the end of it (iteration 45). As with real groups, the knowledge increase is not linear but increases over time. Knowledge level at the end of the simulation (end of class) varies, but very rarely there is none, which also fits the observational data.

Fig. 4. Simulation of groupwork with similar agents. Green: agents attained full knowledge (9 or 10). Yellow: agents with large increase of knowledge (final knowledge 6–9). Orange: agents that learned at least some knowledge (final knowledge 3–6). (Color figure online)

Table 9. Learning in pairs, each row represents one agent (student). Columns are: Group ID, Agent found group in (1) iteration, Communicativeness, Leadership potential, Interest in topic, Ease of Learning, Knowledge in (1) iteration, Agent found group in (10) iterations, Knowledge in (10) iterations, Agent found group in (32) iterations, Knowledge in (32) iterations, Knowledge in (45) iterations. Each iteration represents 1 min of real time for students in class (45 min lessons).

g_id	Groups (1)	C	L	I	E	K (1)	Groups (10)	K (1)	Groups (32)	K (32)	K (45)
1	False	0	5	0	5	2.365	True	2.365	True	2.54	6.36
1	False	0	5	3	0	1.527	True	1.527	True	1.65	4.11
2	False	1	2	2	4	3.225	False	3.225	True	3.51	8.71
2	False	1	2	4	2	3.477	False	3.477	True	3.79	9.41
3	False	2	2	1	3	1.883	True	1.883	True	2.06	5.11
3	False	2	2	2	3	2.617	True	2.617	True	2.88	7.11
4	False	2	3	3	3	3.351	False	3.351	True	3.71	9.12
4	False	2	4	2	3	2.617	False	2.617	True	2.92	7.14
5	False	2	5	2	3	2.617	True	2.617	True	2.95	7.15
5	False	2	5	5	1	3.603	True	3.603	True	4.05	9.87

Similar simulations have been conducted for larger (3 or 4 agents) groups. The groups are formed between 17th and 24th iteration (17th and 24th minute of class) and at the end of simulation the knowledge level varies. The difference is that the learning is much more varied: most agents attain a high level of knowledge, but some learn almost nothing. Agents with low interest and less communicative learn much slower in larger groups, as with real groups of students. This is visualised in Fig. 4.

We compared the agent simulation to real observations of student learning. Specifically, we compared the sets of differences between initial and final knowledge in the observations, and the set of differences between initial and learned knowledge after 45 iterations in the agent model, for different sizes of groups. For initial knowledge the standard error is 0.99 and for the final knowledge it is 1.07. The agent model does not increase the difference significantly.

The agent model we developed exhibited several emergent behaviours in simulation. These reflect the real behavior of students in class:

- Some agents (students) are reluctant to learn at all.
- Some agents (students) are reluctant to work in groups.
- Sometimes only one agent (student) works and learns in the group.
- The groups that form are not as in the planned division.

5   Conclusions

This paper describes the key elements of our research on developing a model of a group of students learning during groupwork. We conducted long-term observations of students of a primary school in Poland. We considered students' initial knowledge, communicativeness, their interest in the topic, leadership potential, ease of learning; and various sizes of group. Based on the observations, we build a basic multiple regression model of students, as well as an agent-based model. Some emergent behaviors occurred during the agent simulation, which were not intended, but which reflect real student behaviors during classes.

The aim of the overall research is to improve student learning by changing parameters that depend on the teacher. While the student's interest in the topic is independent of the teacher, the group size or method of division could be modified to speed up knowledge acquisition. Even from this initial research, the following methods to improve learning may be proposed:

- During work in pairs students should be joined based on different initial knowledge level, but similar communicativeness.
- Increasing time for groupwork (initially the knowledge increases slowly, but speeds up over time).
- During work in groups of any size, students should have similar communicativeness and interest in the topic.
- Work in pairs is the best approach to bring all students to similar level of knowledge (when bad students are paired with good students; and very bad ones with knowledgeable students that are also communicative).

These initial results are currently being tested in a real classroom environment, while we work to improve the model. Even working with a small number of student attributes gives a very good representation of a real group, and we want to add more descriptors as necessary.

References

1. Barge, J.K.: Leadership as medium: a leaderless group discussion model. Commun. Q. **37**(4), 237–247 (1989)
2. Burke, A.: Group work: how to use groups effectively. J. Effective Teach. **11**(2), 87–95 (2011)
3. Dolata, R.: Czy segregacja uczniow ze wzgledu na uprzednie osiagniecia szkolne zwieksza efektywnosc nauczania mierzona metoda EWD. XIV Konferencja Diagnostyki Edukacyjnej, Opole (2008)
4. Ehly, S.W., Larsen, S.C.: Peer tutoring to individualize instruction. Elem. Sch. J. **76**(8), 475–480 (1976)
5. Johnson, D.W., Johnson, R.T.: Cooperation and Competition: Theory and Research. Interaction Book Company (1989)
6. Luttmer, E.G.: Four models of knowledge diffusion and growth. Federal Reserve Bank of Minneapolis, Research Department (2015)
7. Cotton, K.: School improvement research series. School wide and Classroom Discipline (2001)
8. Slavin, R.E.: Cooperative Learning and Academic Achievement: Why Does Groupwork Work? [Aprendizaje cooperativo y rendimiento académico:¿ por qué funciona el trabajo en grupo?]. Anales de psicología/Ann. Psychol. **30**(3), 785–791 (2014)
9. Taillandier, P., et al.: Building, composing and experimenting complex spatial models with the GAMA platform. GeoInformatica **23**(2), 299–322 (2019)

710   B. Wedrychowicz et al.

10. Wasley, P.: Underrepresented students benefit most from 'engagement'. Chron. High. Educ. **53**(13), A39 (2006)
11. Wu, J.B., Tsui, A.S., Kinicki, A.J.: Consequences of differentiated leadership in groups. Acad. Manag. J. **53**(1), 90–106 (2010)

Clinically-relevant Summarisation of Cataract Surgery Videos Using Deep Learning

Jesse Whitten[1], James McKelvie[2], and Michael Mayo[1(✉)]

[1] Department of Computer Science, University of Waikato, Hamilton, New Zealand
michael.mayo@waikato.ac.nz
[2] Department of Ophthalmology, University of Auckland, Auckland, New Zealand

Abstract. Cataract surgery is one of the most frequently performed medical procedures worldwide, an estimated 20 million such surgeries occurring annually. However, the training required to become a competent cataract surgeon takes years due to its challenging technical nature. This limits the supply of capable surgeons. One aspect of modern cataract surgery is that video recordings are routinely taken using microscope cameras, and these recordings can be used to review errors and improve technique throughout surgical training. However, reviewing raw surgery video footage is tedious and may not lead to actionable insights improving surgeon performance. To tackle this issue, a novel artificial intelligence (AI)-based framework for the extraction of detailed surgery video summary statistics directly from the raw surgery footage is proposed. The input to the system is a video of a cataract surgery procedures and the output is a summary report. The approach uses deep learning models (ResNet-50, ResNet-152 and InceptionV3 were tested) to identify and time surgical instrument activity. Additionally, a unique dataset consisting of 57,422 hand-labelled frames extracted from a new locally-sourced video dataset of 29 retrospective cataract surgery recordings was created. Testing these predictive models with 4-fold cross validation across ten different surgical instruments resulted in a best mean testing prediction area under the ROC curve of 97.6%, and a mean testing sensitivity of 96.6%. Given these high levels of accuracy, the reports generated by our system are high quality and could be used to provide actionable insight into surgical technique during surgical training.

Keywords: Cataract surgery videos · Deep learning · Video summarisation · Surgeon training

1 Introduction

Patients with cataracts who undergo cataracts removal surgery usually gain significant improvements in visual acuity and quality of life. Cataracts are caused by opacification of the natural lens of the eye, and when they are removed, they are replaced by a synthetic lens called an intraocular lens. Without surgery, the

© The Author(s), under exclusive license to Springer Nature Singapore Pte Ltd. 2022
E. Szczerbicki et al. (Eds.): ACIIDS 2022, CCIS 1716, pp. 711–723, 2022.
https://doi.org/10.1007/978-981-19-8234-7_55

risk of permanent blindness is significantly increased for patients with cataracts. The replacement procedure typically lasts 15–30 min and makes use of a number of advanced medical techniques and technologies including microscope cameras that provide extremely high definition digital views of the pupil during the surgery. Figure 1 depicts examples of several of these tools in action during a cataract surgery. Usually, ten or so different surgical tools are used during a cataract removal procedure, and these are the focus of this paper.

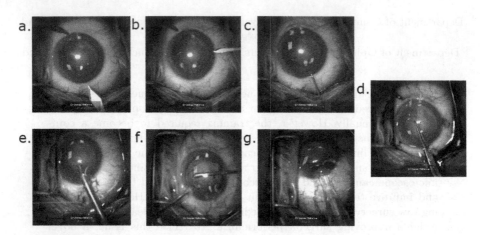

Fig. 1. Common cataract surgery instruments in current use. **Key: a.** (top) Forceps, (bottom) 2.4 mm Keratome Blade; **b.** (top) Forceps, (right) 1.1 mm Paracentesis Blade; **c.** Rycroft Cannula; **d.** Rhexis Forceps; **e.** (bottom left) Chopper, (center) Phacoemulsification Probe; **f.** Irrigation/Aspiration Probes; **g.** Lens Cartridge Injector.

A significant issue with cataract surgery is the current shortage of trained cataract surgeons. Training a surgeon takes five-seven years following a period of time as a junior doctor. A significant component of the training concerns surgical techniques, and feedback on technique is given either live as a surgery happens or after the fact as video footage is reviewed. However, given that the video footage is raw and the surgery has a non-trivial duration, manual review can be time consuming and involve a number of fast forward/rewind operations in order to find specific points in the surgery where feedback can be focused. Furthermore, there is no overall summary of the surgery that can be used to obtain general insight, e.g. pauses between surgical phases may be too long, which is difficult to discern from the raw video footage without a full review while noting down timing manually. Figure 2 illustrates the full complexity of a typical modern cataract surgery process.

This paper proposes a novel deep learning-based framework for the summarisation of cataract surgery videos. Our focus is detecting and summarising the duration and patterns of surgical instrument use, along with periods of idle time in which no surgical tools are in use. In our proposal, recognition and tracking instruments during surgery is performed using deep learning models; surgery

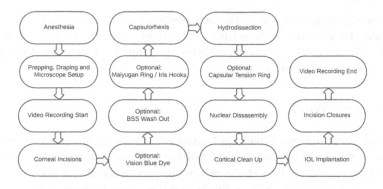

Fig. 2. Steps in a cataract surgery operation.

summaries are then presented after labelling the video footage in the form of visual instrument sequence charts and detailed tabular summaries of instrument usage statistics. Such a process compresses a typically long and unedited video into a concise, representative clinical analysis report that would take no more than a couple of pages, making it useful for cataract surgeon training and other types of quantitative analysis. The primary time saving benefit for surgeons and trainees is that viewing the entirety of the surgery videos is not needed.

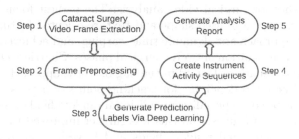

Fig. 3. Report generation pipeline.

Figure 3 shows the proposed framework from a high level: in step one frames are extracted from a cataract surgery video at a specified frame rate and are then preprocessed in step two. In step three, the time series of preprocessed frames is labelled using a deep learning model, which generates a corresponding multivariate time series of label predictions. These prediction time series are then post-processed in step four to tidy up errors and smooth out any noise, and then lastly, in step five, the prediction vector is processed into instrument activity sequences that are presented as clinically relevant summary reports. The reports concisely show the occurrences, duration, and proportions of time that the operating surgeon spent with each instrument, including idle time during instrument transitions. Such details can provide metrics for quality improvement and highlight timeline abnormalities or segments of the operation that are challenging or could be improved.

2   Related Work

In general, there are two broad applications in the literature for the analysis of cataract surgical videos: *phase identification* and *surgical tool identification*. A phase refers to a particular stage in the surgery, such one of the steps shown in Fig. 2. Phase detection from a single frame or even a sequence of consecutive frames is difficult because the same surgical tools could be used in different phases; accurate phase detection therefore requires a holistic analysis of the entire surgery. Surgical tool identification, on the other hand, is used to accurately determine which tool or tools are in use in each localised portion of the video, a problem more related to traditional object detection. Surgical tool detection can either be viewed as a standalone problem by itself (the approach taken here), or as an additional input to a phase detection process. Phase detection, however, does not necessarily require surgical tool recognition and has been performed without it.

Prior to the deep learning revolution, a handful of research works starting circa 2011 considered traditional computer vision handcrafted features and statistical approaches for surgical video analysis. The earliest focus was on phase detection. For example, [8] used shape and texture-oriented features with a bag of visual words approach and dynamic time warping, and achieved a respectable 94% accuracy for recognition of twelve surgical phases. Charriere et al. [4] worked on improving the visual words used in the bag of words approach, proposing the use of "space-time interest points" for tracking points of interest across frames. [11] proposed the use of a specialised conditional random field classifier that took as input a sequence of frames, and this was further improved by [5] in followup work combining conditional random fields and Bayesian networks. This work achieved 98% phase classification accuracy. However, these successful pre-deep learning approaches were not further developed.

Into the deep learning era, it was quickly realised that deep learning approaches tended to struggle with phase classification, mainly due to the high number of phases. Deep learning-related research therefore turned to instrument recognition as opposed to phase detection, and a seminal publication by Al Hajj et al. [1] is an early example involving deep learning models to detect ten different surgical instruments which demonstrated area under the ROC (AUC) curve accuracy in the range $(0.953, 0.987)$, a promising result. The input to the deep learning systems described here was a series of 16 frames, representing 0.64 s of video.

The problem of instrument classification was then extended out to the wider research community with the CATARACTS challenge [2]. This challenge provided a dataset containing over nine hours of cataract surgery video recordings, annotated by a panel of two expert surgeons, and is multi-labeled with 21 individual surgical instrument indicators. The dataset contains surgeries performed on 50 patients and all videos have a resolution of 1920×1080 pixels, with a frame rate of 30 frames per second. Fourteen teams and the challenge organisers each contributed one or more deep learning models to best classify the test data, competing to maximise the mean AUC over each instrument class. The top ranked teams achieved a predictive testing mean AUC over all instrument classes of 0.9812–0.9971, again a very respectable range of scores. However, a distinct disadvantage of the challenge was that the larger problem of phase classification was not tackled.

Deep learning approaches for cataract surgery phase classification have just recently been revisited. As mentioned, this is the more difficult challenge because the wider context of the entire overall surgery must be taken into account. To illustrate the challenge, [14] proposes two phase classification deep learning approaches based on recurrent neural networks, and obtained accuracies in the range of 68–78% depending on approach. The higher accuracies were always achieved when surgical tool classification was performed firstly, with tool predictions being provided as additional binary inputs to the phase classifier. Similarly, [9] explored the use of convolutional neural networks for phase classification and obtained sensitivities of 0.67 and 0.72 respectively. While it is difficult to compare the phase classification models proposed in both [9,14] due to differing performance metrics and datasets, they both provided arguably low results for phase classification

The following year in 2019 a critical question was posed by the review paper [13], can cataract surgical phases be sufficiently detected through deep learning techniques? To answer this question, five algorithms with differing input data were compared: (1) a support vector machine input with cross-sectional instrument annotation data; (2) a recurrent neural network with a time series of instrument annotations as input; (3) a convolutional neural network with cross-sectional image data as input; (4) a convolutional/recurrent hybrid network with a time series of images as input; and (5) a convolutional/recurrent hybrid network with a time series of images and instrument annotations as input. Each algorithm was trained and evaluated using five-fold cross-validation on a dataset of 100 surgery videos labelled with ten surgical phases. Like previous work, the authors found that the use of instrument annotations as input features led to better performance than video images alone, and that temporal modelling of instrument annotations led to more accurate models than analyzing cross-sectional snapshots of instruments.

In summary, while traditional statistical methods have proven effective at phase classification, deep learning approaches are effective at instrument recognition, and only effective for classifying phases when instrument-level annotations are provided.

A general critique that can be levelled at the field is that there is no standardized benchmarks for comparing different methods. Different authors use different data and different metrics for assessing predictive performance. This is compounded by the rapid advance of technology in this area: earlier videos, for example, can be considered rather low quality and "grainy" compared to footage obtained with modern microscopic cameras. Some reported improvements in accuracies may therefore be due to improved data quality rather than better algorithms.

Furthermore, technology and techniques advance rapidly and new tools or phases may appear. This is plainly evident in the research literature where there appears to be no agreement on the phases or tools. Each approach must therefore evaluated locally. To address some of these issues, we compare convolutional-based approaches on a more modern New Zealand dataset of cataract surgery videos. As far as the authors are aware, no AI techniques for surgical tool or phase recognition have been applied to New Zealand data. One of our research questions, therefore (in addition to the clinical relevance of the summary reports), is how accurate deep approaches to surgical tool recognition will be on this data.

3   Cataract Surgery Video Dataset Description

Our local New Zealand cataract surgery video dataset comprises recordings of surgeries performed on 29 eyes the same number of different patients. All surgeries were performed by an expert surgeon. The videos range in length from 5.70 to 21.56 min in duration, with a mean of 11.46 min, and were recorded using a modern Zeiss Lumera 700 surgical microscope. This camera records at a rate of 25 frames per second (FPS) and each surgery therefore consists of 17,193 frames on average.

To obtain a representative sample of frames for model training and evaluation, frames were sampled at a rate of 6 FPS, skipping sequential duplicate frames. Initially the dataset was labelled with a single binary class indicating if an instrument was engaged/in contact with the eye or not. This allowed for the separation of frames in the dataset into active and idle stages. Following this, the frames in the active stage were further labelled by nine binary indicators, each indicator denoting the presence or absence of one of the instruments. The final full labelled dataset has ten labels per frame (i.e. one idle label and nine instrument labels), and for the non-idle frames, the frame may have multiple positive labels if more than one tool in is use for that frame. Thus, the dataset is set up as a multi-label image classification problem.

A total of 57,422 labelled and preprocessed frames from the 29 unique videos were labelled in total. Table 1 shows the label frequencies by frame (noting that a frame could have one or more labels, so the total number of labels exceeds the total number of frames). It is also important to note that the blade classes and the lens cartridge injector class all occur with significantly less frequency than the other classes, potentially leading to training difficulties due to label imbalance/rarity. This is essentially due to the nature of the incision phase; the Keratome instruments are only engaged with the eye for a short duration, similarly with the Lens Cartridge Injector.

Table 1. Dataset label distributions.

Instrument name	Frequency
Idle (No instrument)	16,826
Forceps	2,750
2.4 mm Keratome le	234
1.1 mm Paracentesis blade	270
Rycroft Cannula	8,355
Chopper	14,899
Phacoemulsification probes	15,219
Irrigation and aspiration probe	12,157
Rhexis forceps	3,342
Lens cartridge injector	750

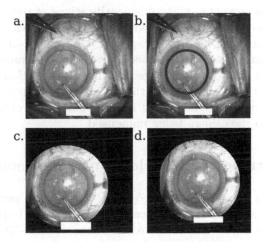

Fig. 4. Preprocessed frames with identifying information removed.

All sampled frames were preprocessed to eliminate parts of the image outside of the pupil area. The preprocessing essentially followed a technique derived from those used in several related papers [4,8], where the pupil is first segmented and isolated (in order to discard irrelevant surrounding visual information), then translated to the center of image, which reduces the confounding impact of rapid involuntary eye movements.

The effects of these steps can be seen in Fig. 4, where Fig. 4(a) shows the original frame, Fig. 4(b) depicts the effect of applying the Hough circle transform algorithm [3] for segmentation, Fig. 4(c) illustrates masking out of surrounding information, and Fig. 4(d) shows the final translated image. The frames are also cropped to a square, then resized to a uniform shape that depends on the deep learning model (e.g. 224×224 for the resnet models).

The Hough circle transform was used to identify and segment the pupil similar to how images were preprocessed in earlier works [4,5,10]. However, this approach presented several difficulties which were not reported in those works. For example, a number of patients had insufficiently circular pupils, or they had distinct vein patterns that would be sometimes misidentified as circles. The limbus of the eye (the outside edge of the iris) was also problematic, as being circular it was also often misidentified as the pupil.

Several techniques were employed to improve the basic Hough transform and make it more effective, including the requirement that the outer edge of a bounding circle (pupil outer edge) be darker than the inside edge, and that only circles within a certain realistic size range could be identified [4]. A "sliding window" system was then applied to frames in temporal order to ensure that new bounding circle locations were close to the average bounding circle locations detected in the previous several frames, on the grounds that the pupil is unlikely to move far between two consecutive frames.

While this idea prevented many misidentifications of the pupil in single isolated frames, it also potentially introduces delays to the tracking of the bounding circle if the patient abruptly moves their eye. However, using these techniques produced a satisfactory segmentation accuracy for 99% of frames, which was sufficient for the next deep learning stage. Further investigation of the remaining pupil misidentification cases revealed that these were often at the beginning or end of the operation, where the patient may have been out of frame or the video was blurred due to the camera being unfocused.

4 Deep Learning Model Selection Experiments

Developing a deep learning model to extract instrument activity information from surgical videos is a key component of the proposed framework. We built and compared three different CNN architectures: ResNet-50 and -152 [7] and InceptionV3 [12]. We utilised transfer learning in all cases, initialising the models with weights from previous training on the ImageNet database [6], but replacing the final ImageNet classification dense layer with a new classification layer with ten outputs. Each base model was trained on our novel dataset four times in a four-fold cross validation experiment, each with an incremental number of frozen layers: 0%, 50%, 75% and 100%. This was to assess whether or not features and weights obtained from ImageNet were directly applicable to this problem. Therefore, in summary, given three different model architectures and four degrees of frozen layers, a total of twelve different predictive models configurations were evaluated.

Next, we divided the surgical videos into four mutually exclusive and exhaustive subsets. Four subsets were chosen because some instruments were used so rarely that they only appear in four surgery videos; thus four was the maximum number of subsets that could be used while having a video with each instrument occurring at least once in each subset. A four-fold cross validation approach was then used to evaluate the twelve model configurations described above: each model was trained on three of the subsets and tested on the fourth subset, and this was repeated three more times, using a different test subset each time. Our test accuracies are therefore averages over the four folds.

Each model was trained using the same optimiser, batch size and learning rate as the instrument classification model proposed in [14], as these were previously found to be effective choices. Models were each trained for 20 epochs, and real time data augmentation was used to generate minibatches for training: preprocessed frames were rotated randomly between 0 and 30 °C, a random 0–20% shift and shear range was applied, frames were randomly horizontally flipped, and a random 0–20% zoom range was applied.

Table 2. Predictive model testing AUC results.

Instrument name	ResNet-50	ResNet-152	InceptionV3
Idle (No Instrument)	**0.974**	**0.974**	0.971
Forceps	0.979	0.980	**0.984**
2.4 mm Keratome blade	0.947	0.960	**0.988**
1.1 mm Paracentesis blade	0.931	0.873	**0.937**
Rycroft Cannula	**0.950**	0.925	0.944
Chopper	0.995	**0.996**	0.995
Phacoemulsificationl probe	**0.997**	**0.997**	0.994
Irrigation/Aspiration probe	**0.990**	0.989	**0.990**
Rhexis forceps	**0.993**	**0.993**	0.990
Lens cartridge injector	0.935	**0.966**	0.963
Mean AUC	0.969	0.960	**0.976**

Table 3. Predictive model sensitivity and specificity results.

	ResNet-50	ResNet-152	InceptionV3
Sensitivity	**0.966**	0.947	0.959
Specificity	**0.998**	0.997	0.997

In terms of results, it was found that the models with 0% frozen layers were significantly more accurate than models with differing proportions of frozen layers, measured by both sensitivity and AUC, with the one exception of the ResNet-152 model, where the 50% frozen model performed slightly better than its 0% frozen counterpart. The accuracy metrics for the top performing models for each deep architecture are presented in Tables 2 and 3.

In more detail, Table 2 shows that all three best models perform very similarly. Notably, however, the InceptionV3 model performs well on the 2.4 mm and 1.1 mm Keratome instruments, the Forceps and the Lens Cartridge Injector, which all had a much lower distribution of instances in the dataset. InceptionV3 also achieved the highest mean testing prediction AUC of 0.976. Table 3 shows that the ResNet-50 model has higher testing sensitivity of 96.6% ResNet-152 tends to perform slightly poorer than the other models by most metrics. Based on these results, InceptionV3 was selected as the preferential model for labelling the frames, due to its superior predictive performance especially on the less well-balanced classes.

5   Clinical Analysis of Predicted Annotations

After labelling the cataract surgery video frames using the InceptionV3 model, our system next generates a clinically relevant summary of the surgery. Key advantages of this report are that surgeons can easily find key sections of the video to revisit, and the traces of instrument activity such as the proportions of idle time throughout surgery and the length of time taken using particular tools can be easily seen visually at a glance. Particularly, these details allow a surgeon to immediately see which surgical steps were most difficult and required increased time; which patterns in instrument usage were abnormal and may indicate technical difficulties requiring feedback; and where efficiency can be improved by reducing idle time.

Instrument activity sequences are defined as a continuous sequence of frames containing the presence of a particular instrument. To smooth out noise in the predicted label sequences and make them more readable, a two second smoothing window was applied to the predictions: if a tool was in use for less than two seconds surrounded by periods of non-use, that sequence of predictions was removed; conversely, if a tool was in use for more than two seconds, but had a two second gap in the predictions where its use was not detected, then the gap was removed and it was assumed that the tool was in use but simply not detected. This approach effectively reduced false negative instrument predictions and eliminated short pauses within the surgery, simplifying the tool usage charts by finding longer and fewer sequences. However, a disadvantage of this approach is that tools which are generally not is use very frequently such as the blade instruments can inadvertently be pruned from the chart. Further research is therefore needed to improve the postprocessing in this respect.

The sequence data is then presented in a two primary ways: visually as a Gantt chart-like plot, with tool (on the y axis) vs time (on x), and in a set of tabular summaries, one per tool.

Figure 5 shows an example of a visual instrument sequence chart. "Reading" the diagram would, to an expert surgeon, reveal the progression of phases. For example, in the sample chart, firstly Keratome instruments are used to perform the incisions, then the Rhexis Forceps are used for capsulorhexis, and this is followed by the Phacoemulsification probe and the Chopper instrument used in conjunction for the nuclear disassembly stage. Next, the chart shows usage of the Irrigation/Aspiration probes for cortical cleanup, and finally the Lens Cartridge Injector is used for the intraocular lens implantation.

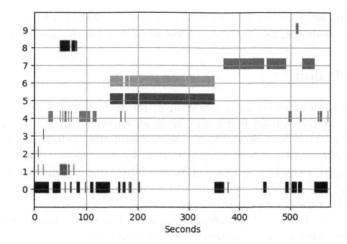

Fig. 5. Instrument sequence chart representation. Key: **(0)** Idle Class, **(1)** Forceps, **(2)** 2.4 mm Keratome Blade, **(3)** 1.1 mm Paracentesis Blade, **(4)** Rycroft Cannula, **(5)** Chopper, **(6)** Phacoemulsification Probe, **(7)** Irrigation/Aspiration Probe, **(8)** Rhexis Forceps, **(9)** Lens Cartridge Injector.

Throughout the chart concurrent usage of multiple instruments across multiple phases, e.g. the Forceps and the Rycroft Cannula, is also shown. Idle time is included and typically marks the transition periods between phases. To summarise, the instrument sequence chart is a succint summary of cateract surgery video.

Table 4. Instrument statistical results for the Irrigation and Aspiration instrument, as seen in Fig. 5.

Use:	Start time:	End time:	Duration:
Use 1	06:09 (mm:ss)	07:28 (mm:ss)	01:18 (mm:ss)
Use 2	07:33 (mm:ss)	08:11 (mm:ss)	00:38 (mm:ss)
Use 3	08:43 (mm:ss)	09:07 (mm:ss)	00:23 (mm:ss)
Proportion of video:	24.2%	**Total duration:**	02:20 (mm:ss)

A more thorough statistical summary is also provided with the generated report. An example of part of this summary for the same example video is shown in Table 4. The report contains a breakdown of the individual uses of each instrument, complete with video annotations and usage proportions. The timing data enables a surgeon to rapidly locate points in the video where each an instrument is used. Each instrument also has the full time duration calculated and returned as a proportion of the surgery, which can be useful to compare against "standard" or average surgery times.

Initial informal evaluations with several senior ophthalmologists resulted in enthusiastic feedback, and we are continuing evaluation in this area.

6   Conclusion

This paper has described an exploration of the use of deep learning for surgical instrument recognition in modern cataract surgery videos obtained from a local hospital. Few prior works have gone beyond the evaluation of models in terms of accuracy in order to generate clinically-relevant reports. Our reports were developed with the assistance of an specialist cataract surgeon (the second author), and our prototype is end-to-end with the input being a raw video and the output being the surgical summary.

Our research has also highlighted a number of areas for future work by and large are not considered in the literature. These include:

- The surgery segmentation problem – often surgeries are recorded back to back with little downtime due to throughput pressures. The video recorder may not be stopped at the end of one surgery and restarted at the beginning of the next. Can the start of a surgery be automatically detected?
- Blurry frame detection – an out of focus camera will not have any instruments clearly visible. Can these frames be detected and eliminated? Likewise for frames where the pupil is not present.
- The label imbalance problem – given that some tools are used far less frequently than others, can better frame sampling and/or augmentation techniques be developed specifically for cataract surgery models?
- Domain generalisation – existing deep approaches train monolithic models recognising all types of instruments in the training data. However, medical technology evolves quickly and new instruments frequently arrive while older instruments may be phased out. Can we develop a more modular approach allowing new instruments to be added while not needing to retrain the model on the current instruments?
- Real time complications detection – rapid hand movements and/or pupil movements are known to be predictors of surgical complication. Can this and other indicators of complications be detected in real time so alerts can be generated?

All of these topics represent valid avenues for future research.

References

1. Al Hajj, H., Lamard, M., Charrière, K., Cochener, B., Quellec, G.: Surgical tool detection in cataract surgery videos through multi-image fusion inside a convolutional neural network. In: 2017 39th Annual International Conference of the IEEE Engineering in Medicine and Biology Society (EMBC), pp. 2002–2005 (2017). https://doi.org/10.1109/EMBC.2017.8037244

2. Al Hajj, H., et al.: Cataracts challenge on automatic tool annotation for cataract surgery. Med. Image Anal. **52**, 24–41 (2019). https://doi.org/10.1016/j.media.2018.11.008
3. Ballard, D.: Generalizing the hough transform to detect arbitrary shapes. Pattern Recogn. **13**(2), 111–122 (1981)
4. Charriere, K., Quellec, G., Lamard, M., Coatrieux, G., Cochener, B., Cazuguel, G.: Automated surgical step recognition in normalized cataract surgery videos. In: 36th Annual International Conference of the IEEE Engineering in Medicine and Biology Society, EMBC 2014, pp. 4647–4650 (2014). https://doi.org/10.1109/EMBC.2014.6944660
5. Charrière, K., et al.: Real-time analysis of cataract surgery videos using statistical models (2017). https://doi.org/10.1007/s11042-017-4793-8
6. Deng, J., Dong, W., Socher, R., Li, L., Kai Li, Li Fei-Fei: Imagenet: a large-scale hierarchical image database. In: 2009 IEEE Conference on Computer Vision and Pattern Recognition, pp. 248–255 (2009)
7. He, K., Zhang, X., Ren, S., Sun, J.: Deep residual learning for image recognition. In: 2016 IEEE Conference on Computer Vision and Pattern Recognition (CVPR), pp. 770–778 (2016)
8. Lalys, F., Riffaud, L., Bouget, D., Jannin, P.: A framework for the recognition of high-level surgical tasks from video images for cataract surgeries. IEEE Trans. Bio-med. Eng. **59**, 966–976 (2011). https://doi.org/10.1109/TBME.2011.2181168
9. Primus, M.J., et al.: Frame-based classification of operation phases in cataract surgery videos. In: Schoeffmann, K., et al. (eds.) MMM 2018. LNCS, vol. 10704, pp. 241–253. Springer, Cham (2018). https://doi.org/10.1007/978-3-319-73603-7_20
10. Quellec, G., Charriere, K., Lamard, M., Cochener, B., Cazuguel, G.: Normalizing videos of anterior eye segment surgeries. In: 2014 36th Annual International Conference of the IEEE Engineering in Medicine and Biology Society, EMBC 2014, pp. 122–125 (2014). https://doi.org/10.1109/EMBC.2014.6943544
11. Quellec, G., Lamard, M., Cochener, B., Cazuguel, G.: Real-time segmentation and recognition of surgical tasks in cataract surgery videos. IEEE Trans. Med. Imaging **33**, 2352–2360 (2014). https://doi.org/10.1109/TMI.2014.2340473
12. Szegedy, C., Vanhoucke, V., Ioffe, S., Shlens, J., Wojna, Z.: Rethinking the inception architecture for computer vision. In: 2016 IEEE Conference on Computer Vision and Pattern Recognition (CVPR), pp. 2818–2826 (2016)
13. Yu, F., et al.: Assessment of automated identification of phases in videos of cataract surgery using machine learning and deep learning techniques. JAMA Netw. Open **2**(4), e191860–e191860 (2019). https://doi.org/10.1001/jamanetworkopen.2019.1860
14. Zisimopoulos, O., et al.: Deepphase: surgical phase recognition in cataracts videos. ArXiv abs/1807.10565 (2018)

An Empirical Comparison of Steganography and Steganalysis Solutions

Wera Wiecek[1], Piotr Jozwiak[1], Ireneusz Jozwiak[2],
and Michal Kedziora[1(✉)]

[1] Wroclaw University of Science and Technology, Wroclaw, Poland
michal.kedziora@pwr.edu.pl
[2] Military University of Land Forces, Wroclaw, Poland

Abstract. Steganography is a discipline of hiding secret data in the media that is the carrier, in such a way that outsiders do not know of its presence. The most common way to hide information is to replace the least significant bits of the image pixels with bits of the embedded message. In this work, digital images of different formats were used as media to determine the effect of the image format on the final value of pixels in the altered image. Available steganography solutions that allow embedding of files that are images or text files were used to hide information in images. The purpose of carrying out tests was to determine the different ways of embedding data in the images and the effect of the size of the hidden payload on the amount of change in the pixels intensities.

Keywords: Steganography · Steganalysis · LSB

1 Introduction

Communication is an everyday activity that allows achieving many different goals. Nevertheless, there are cases when the fact of communication taking place between the parties is expected to remain a secret. In such situations steganography is used. It ensures complete discretion of the information transfer. The information to be transmitted is concealed in the chosen carrier which is then sent to the recipient. Reading the embedded message is only possible if the person knows how and where to find the hidden information. Steganography can only be used if the fact that the communication that has taken place between the parties is kept secret. Meeting this condition makes it possible to transmit secret data in a medium that is public for others. The most common way to hide information in digital image is to replace the least significant bits (LSB) of the image pixels with bits of the embedded message.

In this paper, research was conducted to test the effectiveness of a method for detecting the presence of steganography use. The work focuses on the use of digital image as an information carrier. A self-created database of stego images was analyzed in order to reach relevant conclusions. The results were analyzed

© The Author(s), under exclusive license to Springer Nature Singapore Pte Ltd. 2022
E. Szczerbicki et al. (Eds.): ACIIDS 2022, CCIS 1716, pp. 724–736, 2022.
https://doi.org/10.1007/978-981-19-8234-7_56

in order to determine how selected steganographic solutions hide information in images and how the size of the hidden file affects the extent of changes made to the image after embedding a secret message in it.

The remainder of this paper is structured as follows. In related work chapter we present survey of similar papers involving steganography techiniques and its comparison. In next chapter we present methodology and assumptions set for the research performed in the paper. Next we present the results of analysis of ways of hiding information in images by given solutions and the influence of the size of hidden payloads on the number of pixels used to embed them. The section also contains performance comparisons for programs using the same method of payload embedding. The final section contains conclusions about the work as a whole. How the obtained results relate to the generally established assumptions related to the embedding of information is also described. For example, it is shown how the results obtained for images of different format depend on their structure.

2 Related Work

In most cases, the found studies focused on a general presentation of steganalysis and steganography technologies using media of different formats [1,2,4,11,12, 18]. They also presented a variety of tools that can be used to embed information into the media [9,12]. In this paper, the scope of research is limited to steganalysis and steganography using a digital image as an information carrier, so the base of related work was narrowed to those whose study focuses on image steganography.

The steganographic solutions are divided according to whether the algorithm belongs to the spatial domain or the transformation domain. Depending on the author, related articles focused on presenting the algorithms used in each domain and the image formats compatible with them [3,6,7,9,10,13,15,17]. Moreover, the following were addressed: image structure, color depth, and the effect that compression has on embedded payload [13,15]. The difference between steganography and cryptography was described in articles [11,13]. The theoretical part of this paper was written based on selected information featured in these articles.

Many publications have focused their attention mainly on the architecture and performance of the tools used to hide information in an image [5,7,16]. An attempt to recover data embedded in a stego image using a given tool has been performed in those articles to examine, whether the used algorithm is effective. An example can be a solution that hides payload bits in the least significant bits of clusters of pixels that was presented in article [8].The authors used Edge Detection Filter to determine a group of 8 pixels with a dark shade. If such a cluster of pixels was located, it was taken as a single byte and a binary version of the embedded text was hidden in their least significant bits. The changes associated with such payload insertion were more imperceptible, because to the human eye, a single pixel of a different color stands out more against a uniform background than several located in close proximity.

3   Methodology

Analysis and comparisons were performed on all images included in the established database. The results obtained for stego images based on one of the cover image were presented for each of eight steganographic solutions. The included Figures show the combined results for stego images with three different sizes of payload. It is always incremental and presented from left to right.

CounterSteg software was used in this paper to analyze the obtained stego images. The main source for the description of the program's functionality was an article by M. Pelosi and C. Easttom [14]. The article contains a description of the tool itself as well as several tests of its effectiveness in analyzing images of PNG format.

Figure 1 shows that Geocaching Toolbox uses only the LSB bit plane of pixels to embed the payload bits. In all cases less than 1 percent of the total available pixels were changed. This indicates that the information is most likely compressed before the hiding process is performed. Slice of each image has been further zoomed in to allow the changes to be seen more accurately. The payload bits are embedded in a thin strip at the bottom of the image. Thickness of the strip becomes larger as the size of the hidden TXT file increases. The differences in the amount of pixels used to hide the payload are small between all stego images. All of them stay under 1 percent. Since consecutive pixels are picked to embed the payload, selecting pixels in single-color areas of the image will not be avoided in this solution.

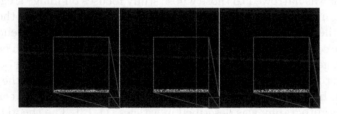

Fig. 1. LSB bit planes of comparisons performed for cover image and stego images that were obtained from Geocaching Toolbox.

Manytools Steganography solution uses the last two bit planes of pixels to embed a payload into an image. Strip of consecutive pixels located on the left side of the image is used in last and second to last bit plane. Those strips for stego images with different sizes of payload can be seen on Fig. 2. The solution overwrites all subsequent pixels and does not avoid embedding payload bits in single-color areas. Pixels used for embedding are selected equally in both bit planes.

The payload is hidden by the Mobilefish software in a strip of pixels at the top of the image in the LSB bit plane. Pixels are selected sequentially in rows starting from the top of the image, which was show on Fig. 3. Thus, this solution is similar

Fig. 2. LSB bit planes of comparisons performed for cover image and stego images that were obtained from Manytools Steganography

to Geocaching Toolbox and Manytools Steganography but it allows hiding only payloads of small sizes. The payload is also most likely compressed before it is embedded, but to a lesser extent than for the aforementioned Geocaching Toolbox solution, since no additional approximation of the result for LSB bit plane analysis is required to notice changes. This software does not skip selecting pixels in the areas representing a single color.

Fig. 3. LSB bit planes of comparisons performed for cover image and stego images that were obtained from Mobilefish

The Steganografie solution accepts JPG-format images as cover images and returns a PNG-format stego image. Because the image is converted from one format to another, distortions are introduced into the stego image, which are detected when comparing it with the original cover image. This solution also does not provide a way to hide larger files. The number of changed pixels for all bit planes except the LSB bit plane are the same for all stego images. Differences between LSB bit planes of comparison of stego images containing payloads of various sizes was presented in Fig. 4. The changes that were made to the image are clearly visible. Steganografie embeds the payload bits in the pixels selected sequentially from the top of the image.

The changes are also visible in the LSB bit plane of the stego image analysis (Fig. 5). The black area in the first two images depicts a white bird in the original cover image. The solution does not avoid embedding data in such single-colored areas, as can be seen in the result on the right side of this Figure. This area has been completely overwritten. Although Steganografie selects pixels from the top of the image, just like the Mobilefish solution does, the amount of pixels used

Fig. 4. LSB bit planes of comparisons performed for cover image and stego images that were obtained from Steganografie

is much larger. This shows that the software in question does not use payload compression before its embedding.

Fig. 5. LSB bit planes of analysis of stego images that were obtained from Steganografie

The Steganography Online solution uses only LSB bit plane to embed information. A change of such a large number of pixels is easy to detect even by non-complex steganalysis systems. LSB bit plane values of comparison of all stego images do not provide a way to determine on what basis the pixels were selected. Images of pixel changes in those bit planes look like noise. More can be deduced by analyzing the LSB bit plane of the stego image itself (Fig. 6). Implemented changes can be seen very accurately. The black area in the results represents the zero intensity value of a each pixel contained in this space. This means that the LSB bit plane is zeroed by Steganography Online before the information is embedded.

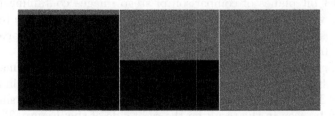

Fig. 6. LSB bit planes of comparisons performed for cover image and stego images that were obtained from Steganography Online

The pixels used for embedding are selected sequentially starting from the top of the image. It is most prominent in Fig. 6. A huge difference in the area occupied by pixels which were changed to hide information can also be seen between stego images with different payloads. Steganography Online software does not compress the file before hiding it. Embedding it in the single-colored areas is also not avoided. This is not done because the LSB bit plane is zeroed anyway.

In SteganPEG software all bit planes of the image are used to embed information. The biggest number of pixels are selected in LSB bit plane and their number decreases as we approach most significant bit (MSB) plane. Number of pixels used in each of the bit planes is different between the results for the three stego images, therefore is not related to the format of the image used as in Steganografie. After analyzing the LSB bit plane zoom of all stego images (Fig. 7), it is apparent that the pixels are not chosen randomly. They are selected in such a way as to ensure that pixels in large areas of one color are not altered. Solution used by SteganPEG is more advanced compared to the other introduced software, but it requires much more pixels to achieve full embedding of the payload.

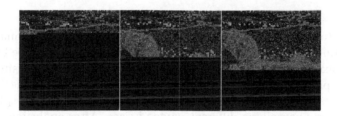

Fig. 7. LSB bit planes of comparisons performed for cover image and stego images that were obtained from SteganPEG.

OpenPuff was able to produce stego images with different output formats. In PNG images, only the LSB bit of the image plane is used as the embedding location for the payload bits. For stego images with different hidden payload sizes, always 13 percent of all available pixels was used, and the difference between used amount is very small. A surprising result was that the fewest pixels were changed when embedding the file with the largest size. Compared to most of approaches presented earlier, the amount of pixels used is significantly larger. Figure 8 shows the LSB bit plane of comparison performed for two images and of one stego image analysis. Their analysis shows that the OpenPuff program selects pixels across the entire LSB bit plane and ensures that pixels are not changed in areas where their intensity level is high. A black area visible in upper right corner of Fig. 8 illustrates the lack of differences between the cover image and the stego image pixel values in this area. In the original cover image, it is an area of highly saturated sky, the pixel value of which has been pulled up to pure white. The presence of black values means that OpenPuff does not change the pixels in this area to avoid making changes that are strongly visible to the human eye. Results obtained for BMP format images were similar to those for PNG images. When a JPG image is used as the cover image, OpenPuff uses a different approach to hiding information than with other formats (Fig. 9). The LSB bit plane has the most changes and the MSB bit plane has the least. Each successive bit plane starting from LSB has a decreasing number of changed pixels. Despite the different way of hiding information, avoidance of using pixels located in saturated areas is maintained.

Fig. 8. LSB bit planes of analysis of PNG stego image that was obtained from OpenPuff (left side) and its comparison with PNG cover image (right side)

Thanks to SilentEye software it is possible to obtain stego images in two different formats: JPG and BMP. Data is embedded in the last three bit planes of the image pixels. By choosing the pixels over several bit planes, a small number of changed pixels can be achieved. For SilentEye this amount is less than 1 percent for each bit plane. Figure 10 shows close-ups of LSB bit plane zooms for stego images containing different payload sizes. After analyzing the Fig. 10, it can be determined that information is embedded in pixels by rows, where the distance between pixels is defined by the amount of data required to be embedded. Selected pixels form a repetitive pattern that is different for each stego image with different sizes of hidden payloads.

Fig. 9. Bit planes with numbers (from left to right) 6, 4, 2, 0 that were the outcome of comparison of JPG cover image and stego image obtained from OpenPuff

When it comes to JPG images all bit planes of the image are used to embed the payload. Most of these changes are made in the LSB bit plane and with each more significant bit plane the amount of changes decreases by about a half.

When the file size exceeds a certain value the pixels are not selected over the whole image but starting from the top (Fig. 11). High values achieved for JPG images by SilentEye steganography program are easy to detect.

4   Comparison of Steganalysis Solutions

A variety of approaches to hiding data were presented. No pair of solutions used exactly the same approach and implementation. In five of eight used solutions, only LSB bit plane is used to embed information. However, each of them use a different method of pixel selection itself. The Geocaching Toolbox and Mobilefish solutions both use a similar strategy, but the difference is in the location of the pixel strip. Both solutions most likely use payload compression before hiding it, as the numbers of changed pixels for these two solutions is low.

Fig. 10. LSB bit planes of comparisons performed for BMP cover image and stego images that were obtained from SilentEye.

The method of embedding information that is the easiest to detect among solutions that use only LSB bit plane as a location of hidden bits is used in Steganography Online. Selecting a strip of pixels at the top of the image is not different from Mobilefish's. The difference between the two solutions is that in Steganography Online the LSB plane is zeroed before embedding the information. This solution also doesn't provide data compression. Zeroing of LSB bit plane before embedding and the lack of compression makes the achieved number of used pixels almost the highest of all solutions.

The Steganografie solution also uses only the last bit plane to embed text files. The number of bits used is one of the higher ones. It is not only due to the fact that no data compression is being performed before the embedding, but also because of the additional noise introduced during processing of the cover images that are JPG. With the help of CounterSteg, it has been determined that because of this extra data being introduced when creating the stego image, the differences between the stego image and the cover image are large. They are not related to the embedded payload itself.

The OpenPuff, for PNG and BMP images, also uses the last bit plane to hide information. Of five mentioned solutions, this approach is the most advanced, because it avoids hiding data in solid color areas and selects pixels randomly.

Its downside, however, is the number of pixels that must be changed to embed the payload. Compared to solutions such as Geocaching Toolbox or Manytools Steganography, this amount is significantly higher. Manytools Steganography and SilentEye programs use more than one bit plane to embed the payload but at the same time they avoid using all the available bit planes. For both of them the number of pixels used reaches the lowest values out of all other solutions. Manytools Steganography chooses a simpler approach to selecting the pixels themselves, since it takes a strip of them that is located on the left side of an image. In contrast, a more interesting solution is used by SilentEye. The pixels are selected based on the corresponding pattern, which is dependent on the size of the payload that is to be hidden.

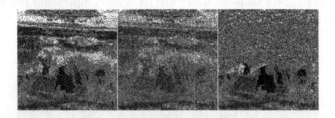

Fig. 11. LSB bit planes of comparisons performed for JPG cover image and stego images that were obtained from SilentEye

When the cover image is in JPG format, OpenPuff and SilentEye solutions use all bit planes to hide information. SteganPEG also uses all bit planes, but only JPG images can be processed by this software. For all three solutions, the number of pixels changed during payload embedding is very high. Values are so high most probably because of usage of cover images in JPG format which is a lossy compression format. When using this format, some additional noise is added during the image embedding. OpenPuff and SilentEye solutions, when using a different format image as a cover image, use far less bit planes to embed the information. For JPG format images, the same method and location of hiding bits of information is used as for the other formats, but aforementioned additional noise is also detected by CounterSteg.

None of the presented examples is completely undetectable. Most solutions hide information in a strip of pixels next to each other, which is very easy to detect even with bit analysis of the image itself. SteganPEG and OpenPuff do not use pixels located in the areas of high pixel intensity, which is recommended because human vision picks up such changes easier. However, both solutions require a large number of pixels to achieve this.

5   Results for Hiding Payload of Different Sizes

In this section, a comparison for hiding payloads of different sizes that are text files will be presented. Results for each solution are held in the tables included below. The data contained in tables were obtained from the analysis of the comparison executed using CounterSteg for "Elephant" as a cover image. Figure 1 contains results for programs that made it possible to hide the payloads equal in size to Payload10.txt and larger than that. Figure 2 contains results for software that allowed hiding payloads of the size equal to Payload10.txt and smaller. Data for the software Steganography and SilentEye was divided between the two tables.

Table 1. Results of embedding payloads with bigger sizes

Software	Image format	Hidden payload	Amount of pixels used to embed payload
Geocaching Toolbox		Payload10.txt	5 491
	PNG	Payload100.txt	6 326
		Payload200.txt	6 322
Manytools Steganography		Payload10.txt	3 313
	PNG	Payload100.txt	6 322
		Payload200.txt	9 267
Steganografie	JPG>PNG	Payload10.txt	514 461
		Payload100.txt	1 104 286
Steganography Online		Payload10.txt	1 501 467
	PNG	Payload100.txt	1 500 327
		Payload200.txt	1 501 093
SteganPEG		Payload10.txt	125 618
	JPG	Payload100.txt	297 046
		Payload200.txt	462 420
SilentEye		Payload10.txt	2 479
	BMP	Payload100.txt	4 781
		Payload200.txt	7 183

After analyzing the results in Table 1, distinctive approaches for embedding larger file sizes can be identified. Obtained results are not fully uniform, because the programs use images of different formats. The largest amount of changes was made when embedding the image by the Steganography Online solution. For each size of the embedded file, the amount of pixels used is very similar. This is caused by zeroing the LSB bit plane before embedding the information into the image. The two solutions included in the table, which also achieved a fairly high pixel count, use JPG formatted images as the cover image. These solutions are Steganografie and SteganPEG. When using the first software it was not possible to embed the bigges payload and difference between amounts of used pixels for smaller files is high compared to other results. SteganPEG also uses a lot of pixels, but the difference in amounts for individual files is much smaller. SilentEye has shown a small amount of altered pixels when using BMP format images as a cover image. The amount increases slowly with the size of embedded files getting bigger. However, the smallest difference between the number of bits is seen for Geocaching Toolbox. This solution uses the highest data compression ratio among all solutions that implement it. Consequently, its use requires the least amount of pixels to embed large files. Based on the values obtained for the Manytools Steganography solution, it was concluded that it ranks between the two previously mentioned solutions. The amount of pixels used is low for smaller payload sizes, but also increases more rapidly than in the case of Geocaching Toolbox.

Table 2. Results of embedding payloads with smaller sizes

Software	Image format	Hidden payload	Amount of pixels used to embed payload
Mobilefish	PNG	PayloadStanza.txt	1 266
		Payload1.txt	4 751
		Payload10.txt	5 568
Steganografie	PNG	Payload1.txt	446 591
		Payload10.txt	514 461
OpenPuff	PNG	PayloadStanza.txt	406 620
		Payload1.txt	406 515
		Payload10.txt	406 573
	BMP	PayloadStanza.txt	405 934
		Payload1.txt	406 092
		Payload10.txt	406 238
	JPG	PayloadStanza.txt	125 088
SilentEye	JPG	PayloadStanza.txt	2 462 031
		Payload1.txt	2 533 681
		Payload10.txt	2 569 016

Values shown in Table 2 were obtained from programs that have lower maximum size values of hidden files than those presented in Table 1. Most of them use large number of pixels to hide payloads of small size. The least amount is used by Mobilefish. For this software the amount of pixels used for embedding Payload10.txt file is similar to the results obtained for the Geocaching Toolbox. The increase in number of pixels used to hide payloads of different sizes for this software is not that drastic. The OpenPuff and the SilentEye software are the only solutions that allow choosing which format the stego image is going to be. Thanks to them it is possible to show that one program can use different ways of hiding information depending the format of the input cover image. Despite using a small number of pixels when hiding large payloads in BMP images, SilentEye achieves large values when hiding small payloads in JPG images. The size that can be hidden is related to the compression of the used images. JPG images have significantly less hiding capacity than images in BMP format, which has been proven using the SilentEye solution. This is also visible for the OpenPuff solution. When using PNG and BMP format images as carriers, this software was able to hide larger files such as Payload10.txt, while only PayloadStanza.txt, which is the smallest of the hidden TXT files, was embedded in JPG image. The difference between OpenPuff and SilentEye, however, lies in the number of pixels used for images with different formats. In SilentEye, several hundred times more pixels are used when embedding in JPG format images than with other formats. For OpenPuff, the correlation is reversed - the number of used pixels when embedding in JPG images is over 3 times smaller compared to the hiding payloads in images of other formats. For both solutions the amount of the altered pixels is relatively high. Steganografie uses a large number of pixels when embedding smaller file sizes. This number is not as high as that achieved by SilentEye for JPG images, but when compared to the Mobilefish results it is a large value. After analyzing data from both tables, it was concluded that some solutions perform better at hiding information of different sizes than others. The format of an image in which the information is being hidden is also important. As an example, SilentEye embeds large payloads well in BMP and small payload values in JPG images rather poorly.

6   Conclusion

A total of eight steganographic solutions were used to obtain the stego image database. All of them allowed hidding TXT files with different sizes inside digital images. Analysis of all stego images obtained from different software were performed. By analyzing the output of CounterSteg, it was possible to determine how each solution hides information. The obtained results confirmed that the most commonly used method for embedding text files in images is the substitution of LSB bit plane of pixels. In the investigated solutions, the strips of pixels on one side of the image were most often selected for substitution. There were solutions that were exceptions to both rules, such as SteganPEG and SilentEye.

An analysis of the effect of the image format on the robustness and effectiveness of the method used was also conducted. The programs that used the JPG format images gave the highest results of number of pixel changes. This is related to the compression of JPG images. These are lossy image formats, which means that the stego images with this format are very susceptible to any changes made to them. This was confirmed by the results that showed large changes visible in images, which were not related to the input process itself. The PNG and BMP are therefore better formats to use for steganography. They provide good hiding capacity and high robustness of the obtained stego images.

The effect of the size of the hidden data has also been studied. It was found that some solutions perform better than others at hiding large sized information in an image. When embedding the text files of different sizes, the pixel selection method was preserved and only the number of used pixels changed. The exception was the use of a JPG image by the SilentEye solution. When a specific payload size was reached, the embedding method changed. The size of the text file that could be hidden in the image by the software depended on whether its compression was implemented. It was determined that the Geocaching Toolbox software uses data compression before file embedding. This can be seen by looking at how little the amounts of changed pixels vary after embedding files of different sizes. Among the solutions for hiding text files, SilentEye showed the greatest robustness and imperceptibility. However, this is true only when the format used is BMP. For this format, low amounts of altered pixels and a unique way of selecting pixel locations in the last three bits are achieved. On the other hand, when this program uses the JPG format the highest amounts of used pixels are reached. The probability of detecting such changes by the steganalysis tool is very high.

References

1. Altaay, A.A.J., Sahib, S.B., Zamani, M.: An introduction to image steganography techniques. In: 2012 International Conference on Advanced Computer Science Applications and Technologies (ACSAT), pp. 122–126. IEEE (2012)
2. Bennett, K.: Linguistic steganography: survey, analysis, and robustness concerns for hiding information in text. CERIAS Tech Report (2004)
3. Cheddad, A., Condell, J., Curran, K., Mc Kevitt, P.: Digital image steganography: survey and analysis of current methods. Signal Process. **90**(3), 727–752 (2010)
4. Garbarczuk, W., Kopniak, P.: Steganografia: wspolczesne metody ochrony informacji (przeglad). Pomiary Automatyka Kontrola **51**(3), 21–25 (2005)
5. Gupta, L.K., Singh, A., Yadav, V.K., Srivastava, A.: Performance analysis of open puff steganography tool using various image formats. In: International Conference on Innovative Advancement in Engineering and Technology (2020)
6. Hamid, N., Yahya, A., Ahmad, R.B., Al-Qershi, O.M.: Image steganography techniques: an overview. Int. J. Comput. Sci. Secur. (IJCSS) **6**(3), 168–187 (2012)
7. Hosmer, C.: Discovering hidden evidence. J. Dig. Forens. Pract. **1**(1), 47–56 (2006)
8. Jain, N., Meshram, S., Dubey, S.: Image steganography using LSB and edge - detection technique. Int. J. Soft Comput. Eng. **2**(3), 217–222 (2012)
9. Johnson, N.F., Jajodia, S.: Exploring steganography: seeing the unseen. Computer **31**(2), 26–34 (1998)
10. Krishna, V., Kumbharana, C.K.: An analysis of different image formats for steganography. Int. J. Emerg. Technol. Innov. Res. (JETIR) **8**(10), 299–307 (2021)
11. Kumar, A., Pooja, K.: Steganography-A data Hiding Technique. Int. J. Comput. Appl. **9**(7), 19–23 (2010)
12. Mazur, H., Mazur, Z., Mendyk-Krajewska, T.: Zastosowanie steganografii w sieciach komputerowych. Ekonomiczne Problemy Usług **117**, 697–706 (2015)
13. Morkel, T., Eloff, J.H., Olivier, M.S.: An overview of image steganography. In: ISSA, vol. 1, pp. 1–11 (2005)
14. Pelosi, M., Easttom, C.: Identification of LSB image steganography using cover image comparisons. J. Dig. Forens. Secur. Law **15**(2), 6 (2021)
15. Poornima, R., Iswarya, R.: An overview of digital image steganography. Int. J. Comput. Sci. Eng. Surv. **4**(1), 23 (2013)
16. Swain, G.: Steganography in digital images using maximum difference of neighboring pixel values. Int. J. Secur. Appl. **7**(6), 285–294 (2013)
17. Swain, G., Lenka, S.K.: Classification of image steganography techniques in spatial domain: a study. J. Comput. Sci. Eng. Technol. (IJCSET) **5**(03), 219–232 (2014)
18. Zaidoon, K., Zaidan, A., Zaidan, B., Alanazi, H.: Overview: main fundamentals for steganography. J. Comput. **2**(3), 158–165 (2010)

Cost-Oriented Candidate Screening Using Machine Learning Algorithms

Shachar Wild[(✉)] and Mark Last

Department of Software and Information Systems Engineering,
Ben-Gurion University of the Negev, Beersheba, Israel
{wildsha,mlast}@post.bgu.ac.il

Abstract. Choosing the right candidates for any kind of position, whether it is for academic studies or for a professional job, is not an easy task, since each candidate has multiple traits, which may impact her or his success probability in a different way. Furthermore, admitting inappropriate candidates and leaving out the right ones may incur significant costs to the screening organization. Therefore, such a candidate selection process requires a lot of time and resources. In this paper, we treat this task as a cost optimization problem and use machine learning methods to predict the most cost-effective number of candidates to admit, given a ranked list of all candidates and a cost function. This is a general problem, which applies to various domains, such as: job candidate screening, student admission, document retrieval, and diagnostic testing. We conduct comprehensive experiments on two real-world case studies that demonstrate the effectiveness of the proposed method in finding the optimal number of admitted candidates.

Keywords: Candidate screening · Candidate list truncation · Prediction models · Constrained optimization · Asymmetric error costs

1 Introduction

There are various methods for ranking the available candidates for academic studies, job positions, military training courses, diagnostic tests, etc. However, the problem of determining how many of top-ranking candidates to admit still remains open. Furthermore, the False Negative (FN) error of rejecting a successful candidate may be far more costly than the False Positive (FP) error of admitting a failing one. In such cases, the main goal is to admit as few candidates as possible, while losing (rejecting) a minimal (if any) amount of good candidates. For example, the cost of rejecting good students by the university is losing them forever, as they will turn to studies in other institutions, whereas the admitted weak students will most probably dropout before graduating. This is demonstrated by a study, which dealt with dropout rates in higher education institutions in Europe [26].

In the information retrieval field, when using a document search engine [23], the documents are ranked and presented to the user by their relevancy to a

© The Author(s), under exclusive license to Springer Nature Singapore Pte Ltd. 2022
E. Szczerbicki et al. (Eds.): ACIIDS 2022, CCIS 1716, pp. 737–750, 2022.
https://doi.org/10.1007/978-981-19-8234-7_57

query's terms. Like in the previous case study, the *FN* error (not retrieving a highly relevant document) is more severe than the *FP* error (retrieving an irrelevant document). Hence, a search engine aims at retrieving a minimal list of top-ranking documents, without missing any relevant ones.

When performing diagnostic testing, we would usually attempt to avoid unnecessary tests in order to save resources. This can be demonstrated by examining the COVID-19 testing problem [12]. While identifying all infected people is crucial for stopping the spread of the virus, testing a person who is not infected would not do a great damage. In other words, similar to the previous two cases, the *FN* error (not testing an infected person) is far more severe than the *FP* error (testing a healthy person).

Several past studies [5,7,18] emphasised the importance of identifying the optimal number of candidates, and proposed efficient methods to truncate ranked lists, with the aim of optimizing a specific statistical measure, such as F-Score [25] and Discounted Cumulative Gain [15]. While these methods do manage to efficiently achieve their task, they do not examine whether the found threshold's value minimizes the total cost of *FP* and *FN* cases. Furthermore, when trying to find the cut-off point, which maximizes a specific measure, the selected threshold may be too high and there are cases in which several cut-off points have the same measure value. Following this, a tie-breaker is needed in order to choose the preferred cut-off value, which in our case, is the one that results in the minimal cost of *FP* and *FN* errors.

Therefore, the problem which we examine in our research is finding an optimal truncation threshold, which given a candidates ranked list and a cost function, will retrieve a sub-list of admitted candidates resulting in a minimal overall cost. Our algorithm will incorporate both *FN* and *FP* costs. The proposed solution will be generic and thus it can be applied to any of the case studies which were mentioned above, and to others as well. In other words, a candidate may refer to a document, a potentially infected person, applicant to an academic institution and so on. To predict the optimal truncation threshold, we are using machine learning algorithms.

Our paper is organized as follows: In Sect. 2, we provide a brief overview of related work on candidate screening methods; in Sect. 3, we formally define the candidate list truncation problem; in Sect. 4, we describe the proposed methodology that was used in this work; in Sect. 5, we describe the datasets and evaluation methods used in our evaluation experiments; in Sect. 6, we present and discuss the obtained results; Finally, Sect. 7 presents the conclusions of our study and outlines future research directions.

2   Related Work

The candidate list truncation problem is encountered in various fields. For instance, the study presented in [5] addresses the problem of truncating a ranked list of retrieved documents. To minimize the risk of retrieving an irrelevant document, it proposes to use the Expectation Maximization algorithm [19] for estimating the list truncation position that will optimize a given IR measure. The authors achieved significant performance improvements in F1-score. However, their study relies on a distribution assumption, which, as the authors themselves admit, does not always hold.

The work presented in a later study [18] attempted to improve the performance of the list truncation task, without assuming any score distribution of the ranked lists. It does assume, however, that the ranked list is given beforehand. It does so by proposing an innovative model, called BiCut, implemented using an LSTM-based approach. In general, it partitions a given ordered list, while minimizing a predefined cost function of a specific user need. In other words, this study reviews the dynamic truncation problem, which is aimed at maximizing an external metric at a given truncation position. It is noteworthy, however, that this algorithm may suffer from several drawbacks: First, it is not computationally efficient, since the cutoff value k for each ranker is found using brute force search methods. Secondly, it makes use of BiLSTM algorithms, which are slow and non-parallelizable.

Finally, a recent work [7] proposes a new method, called CHOPPY, which focuses on designing more effective models for accurate and dynamic truncation of ranked lists, while overcoming the limitations of the BiCut model. Given any user-selected metric, this method is aimed at minimizing the expected training loss over various cut positions. Not only that the authors managed to improve the predictive performance on this task, but also managed to improve the algorithm's speed significantly, which was a major drawback of the BiCut algorithm.

However, none of the above studies considered the problem of predicting the optimal truncation point with respect to the FP and the FN costs incurred by the admission decisions.

3   Problem Statement

In our research, we represent the ranked lists truncation problem as predicting the best truncation position, which minimizes the total error cost. Formally, for a ranked candidates list:

- N - Size of the ranked list (fixed).
- k - Truncation threshold, where: $0 \le k \le N$.
  * This is our decision variable. All top k candidates are admitted, whereas the rest are rejected.
- i - Ranking of candidate, where: $1 \le i \le N$.
  * Assumed to be based on some ranking algorithm.
- O_i - Actual outcome of candidate i, where $O_i \in \{0, 1\}$.
  * 0 - failed, 1 - succeeded.
  * Unknown at the admission time.
- TN - Number of accepted candidates who succeed.
- FP - Number of accepted candidates who fail.
- FN - Number of rejected candidates who would succeed.
- C_{FP} - Cost of making one FP error (accepting one failed candidate).

– C_{FN} - Cost of making one FN error (rejecting one successful candidate).

Where:

$$TN = \sum_{i=0}^{k} O_i \tag{1}$$

$$FP = \sum_{i=0}^{k} (1 - O_i) \tag{2}$$

$$FN = \sum_{i=k+1}^{N} O_i \tag{3}$$

$$Cost(k) = \frac{C_{FP} \cdot \sum_{i=0}^{k}(1 - O_i) + C_{FN} \cdot \sum_{i=k+1}^{N} O_i}{C_{FN} \cdot N} \tag{4}$$

where $C_{FN} \cdot N$ represents the cost of truncating the entire list, which consists of only successful candidates. As mentioned earlier, since we assume that FN errors are more costly than the FP ones, C_{FN} will be higher than C_{FP} and thus this scenario represents the highest possible cost. Accordingly, dividing the calculated cost by this value is done in the purpose of transforming and normalizing the cost into the [0;1] range. The outcome of the overall cost function will vary depending on the selected truncation point k. Therefore, given the FP, FN costs ratio, this problem can be defined as finding the minimum possible cost by predicting k_{opt}, such that:

$$k_{opt} = \arg\min_{k} Cost(k) \tag{5}$$

$$\text{s.t.} \quad 0 \le k \le N$$

Using this minimum function, we assume that the admission decisions are taken solely according to the candidate ranking without any exceptions. This problem applies to various case studies, specifically to the three mentioned above, as follows: In the "Candidate Screening" case study, N refers to the number of initial candidates applied to a certain position or course, C_{FP} represents the cost of wasting resources on admitting a failed candidate and C_{FN} is the cost of losing a successful candidate. As for the "Diagnostic Testing" case study, N represents the number of people who are susceptible to an infectious disease (not immune), where C_{FP} is the cost of a wasted diagnostic test (coming out negative) and C_{FN} is the cost of not testing an infected person, who will not be isolated and as a result may transmit the disease to other people. Finally, in the "Document Retrieval" case study, N refers to the total number of documents matching a certain query, C_{FP} represents the cost of retrieving an irrelevant document and C_{FN} is the cost of missing a relevant document.

4   Methodology

Following this, we propose an algorithm which, given a ranked list and FP and FN costs ratio, will predict the optimal cut-off point. This problem can be seen as a regression task, since the value of the predicted truncation point k is a number. The algorithm steps are described below.

During the training step, we fit a regression model which, given the ranking score of each candidate, predicts the optimal truncation threshold k. First, we obtain the FP to FN costs ratio for a given case study. Afterwards, the training algorithm receives candidate groups with known outcomes (whether succeeded or failed). Using a ranking procedure, each candidate in every group is ranked. Then we identify the optimal k for each group of ranked candidates using the cost function described in Eq. 5 and the actual outcomes. Finally, we train a k-prediction model, which obtains the optimal k value for each group as output and the candidate ranking scores as input.

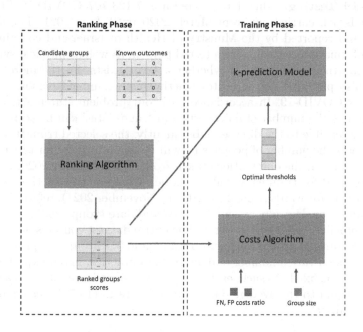

Fig. 1. Proposed training pipeline for all candidate groups.

For each group of ranked candidates, we predict the optimal truncation threshold k using the trained model introduced in Fig. 1.

The real outcome of each candidate can be obtained by accepting all candidates in the group and following them up until their outcome (success or failure) becomes available. Then we can calculate the actual cost incurred by the selected threshold k and compare it to the optimal, minimal cost using the Eq. 5.

5   Evaluation

Our evaluation experiments are conducted to answer the following research questions: (1) Can we identify group-specific truncation thresholds, which result in a lower total cost than a fixed cut-off point baseline? (2) Will the predicted truncation points result in significantly shorter candidate lists than the initial number of candidates? In this section, we describe the experimental plan we used to evaluate our models and explore these questions in depth.

5.1   Experimental Settings

We based our experiments on two publicly available datasets which were obtained from the following sources: Ministry of Health of Israel [2,3], Kaggle Data Science Community [4].

COVID-19 Testing. This dataset contains 7,123,707 COVID-19 PCR tests results in Israel, carried out from March 2020 until June 2021. The data was gathered and reported by the Ministry of Health of Israel and contains demographic information regarding each tested person, as well as physical symptoms, such as: shortness of breath, or whether a fever exists. Furthermore, the test result is also provided and indicates whether the examined person was found positive for COVID-19. In accordance with our problem statement, a 'group' can be seen as the number of daily tests and 'candidates' can be seen as people who are susceptible to the disease. Subsequently, the selected truncation threshold represents the number of people who will be recommended for testing. As for the data partition, the observations taken from April and May 2020, referred as train1, are used for training a ranking model. Complementary, the tests which were observed afterwards (from June 2020 to November 2021), referred as train2, are kept for chronologically assembling the candidate groups and are used in the proposed pipeline, described in Fig. 1. The entire dataset contains 542 candidate groups, including 24 groups assigned to train1 and 518 groups assigned to train2. Despite having a varied number of daily tests in practice, in our experiments, we assumed it to be fixed. As such, each group was assigned a number of candidates, which was equal to the average daily number of tests (13,751 - calculated from the train2 subset).

Credit Card Fraud Detection. This dataset [1] contains 284,807 credit card transactions, made in September 2013 by European cardholders, and it is aimed to help credit card companies in recognizing fraudulent credit card transactions. In accordance with our problem statement, candidates can be seen as credit card transactions. The chosen truncation threshold represents the number of most suspicious transactions, which will be recommended for manual screening. The candidates are randomly sampled, using bootstrap re-sampling technique [13] with a random seed value, and split into 1,000 groups of 500 transactions each, where each group contains 35 % of malicious transactions, while the rest are

Table 1. General overview of the used data.

Dataset	Source	#Features	#Instances	#Candidates Train1-Train2	#Groups	Group size (N)
COVID-19 tests	Israeli ministry of health	9	7,530,647	338,195 7,123,707	542	13,752
Credit card fraud detection	Kaggle	31	284,807	100,000 400,000	1,000	500

legitimate. Following this, train1 is composed of 20 % of the groups and is used to train the examined ranking model, while train2 consists of the rest of the groups and it is used for the main pipeline, described in Fig. 1.

Method Implementation. We implemented the proposed method using Python 3.8 and Jupyter Notebook Integrated Development Environment. Experiments were conducted on a computer with an Intel i5-5200U processor running at 2.20 GHz, using 8 GB of RAM, on Windows 10.

Baseline Method. We compare our models with the following method for determining a truncation cut-off point for each given candidate group: For all possible truncation thresholds, a fixed cut-off point is applied. Following this, the selected threshold is the one which results in the lowest average cost, across all examined groups in the training set.

Candidate Scoring Algorithms. For each given candidate group, an algorithm is used to rank the candidates based on their estimated likelihood of a successful outcome. In order to rank each candidate, we examine the following classification algorithms: Random Forest [10] and Logistic Regression [22]. We use the default parameter settings for training each corresponding algorithm.

k-Prediction Algorithms. In order to predict the optimal truncation threshold k, the following regression algorithms are used: Support Vector Regression [6], Bayesian Regression [9], Ridge Regression [20], Random Forest Regressor [16], Neural Networks [21].

5.2   Evaluation Methods and Metrics

Each ranking algorithm is trained on the first set of candidate groups, while the second set is used for the threshold prediction framework described in Fig. 1. For the first set, 10-fold cross validation [14], F-Score [25] and Average Precision [27] are used to evaluate the ranking model.

As for the second set of candidate groups, each one is ranked using the validated ranking model described above. In addition, general statistical measures - Mean, Standard Deviation, Median and Skewness [17] - of each group are calculated and treated as additional features, along with the ranking scores of each individual candidate. We conducted all our experiments using 5-fold cross validation. Out of the data selected for training each fold, 10% was reserved for validation and all results are shown as the average of the test results of each fold. We compare the performance of the models by the average total cost across all groups, which is derived by the truncation thresholds identified by Eq. 5. It is noteworthy that the predicted truncation cut-off is not fixed and thus may differ across groups. We address this metric formally as follows:

$$Average\ Cost = \frac{\sum_{i=0}^{G} C_{i,k_i}}{G} \tag{6}$$

where G is the number of candidate groups and C_{i,k_i} represents the total cost of group i, resulting from the predicted truncation threshold k_i and the actual candidate outcomes.

Additionally, we introduce another metric, which calculates the difference between the costs of the predicted truncation points and the ones obtained from the optimal thresholds (i.e. the ones that result in the minimum costs). The metric is defined as follows:

$$Cost\ Error = \frac{\sum_{i=0}^{G}(C_{i,k_i} - C_{i,k_i^*})}{\sum_{i=0}^{G} C_{i,k_i^*}} \tag{7}$$

Such that:

$$\sum_{i=0}^{G} C_{i,k_i} \geq \sum_{i=0}^{G} C_{i,k_i^*}$$

where, for group indexed i: k_i represents its predicted truncation threshold k, whereas k_i^* represents its optimal threshold.

Finally, in the aim to compare our machine learning based method to the baseline method, we use paired t-test [24] to determine if there is a significant difference between the means of the corresponding average costs. Since, as shown in Table 1, there are more than 25 observations and no extreme outliers in both examined datasets, the t-test should work well, even for moderately skewed distributions [11]. Moreover, Pearson correlation [8] is calculated to validate the similar trends between different truncation point values. As for hyper-parameter optimization, we use grid search, along with 3-fold cross validation, to find the best setting for each examined regression model.

5.3   Cost Ratios

As mentioned above, we assume that making a *FN* error is more harmful than having a *FP* error, and thus its resulting cost should be higher: Not identifying a COVID-19 positive case can further spread the virus and therefore may be considered as more severe than a test wasted on a negative result. Also, an undetected credit card fraud may cause more damage to its owner and to the credit card company than performing an extra checkup of a legitimate transaction. As such, for both datasets, mentioned in Table 1, our experiments are conducted using the cost ratios of 1:2, 1:4, and 1:6, respectively, to examine the impact of this error's severity on the predicted truncation thresholds, and accordingly on its incurred average costs.

6 Results and Discussion

COVID-19 Testing. As shown in Fig. 2 for the costs ratio of 1:4 and candidate ranking by the Random Forest algorithm, the models, which utilize the proposed machine learning framework, can achieve a significant improvement over the baseline fixed-threshold method.

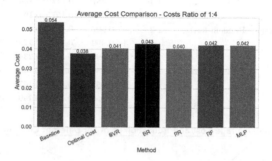

Fig. 2. Average costs comparison across each method, using Random Forest ranking algorithm and costs ratio of 1:4 (*FP* and *FN* costs respectively) - COVID-19 Tests data.

To explore it in more depth, in Table 2 we examine the impact of the costs ratio and the ranking algorithm on the cost error performance. It is noteworthy that the machine learning models achieve a significant improvement over the baseline fixed-threshold method for all three examined costs ratios and for both ranking algorithms. This improvement arises from the proposed framework's ability to identify a flexible truncation point, which minimizes the error cost for each individual group.

Furthermore, we also see in Fig. 3 that different values of the cost ratio result in varying optimal truncation points and average costs. More specifically, having higher *FN* cost, compared to the *FP* cost, results in a higher optimal truncation average cutoff point but at a lower average optimal cost. This trade-off suggests that the more severe is the error from not testing an infected person, the more tests are needed to avoid potential infections and also to provide medical treatment accordingly. Alternatively, when this error is not considered very harmful, based on the proposed approach, we will recommend to perform less diagnostic tests and consequently reduce the average cost incurred by this process.

Table 2. Cost results for each experiment. Costs Ratio refers to the costs of *FP* and *FN* respectively and [†] marks a statistically significant difference against the baseline method ($p < 0.05$ for paired t-test) for each cost. For each configuration, the best result is shown in bold. The examined regression models: Support Vector Regression (SVR), Bayesian Regression (BR), Ridge Regression (RR), Random Forest Regressor (RFR) and Multilayer Perceptron (MLP).

Data set	Ranking algorithm	Cost ratio	Oracle					
			Baseline	SVR	BR	RR	RFR	MLP
COVID-19 testing	Random forest	1:2	0.404	0.141[†]	0.142[†]	**0.121[†]**	0.162[†]	0.143[†]
		1:4	0.420	0.071[†]	0.132	**0.067[†]**	0.128[†]	0.099[†]
		1:6	0.410	0.101[†]	0.172	**0.098[†]**	0.172	0.182
	Logistic regression	1:2	0.386	0.192[†]	**0.162[†]**	**0.162[†]**	0.178[†]	0.194[†]
		1:4	0.387	0.117[†]	0.166	**0.105[†]**	0.153	0.200[†]
		1:6	0.373	0.151[†]	0.197	**0.139[†]**	0.186	0.270
Credit card fraud detection	Random forest	1:2	0.997	0.126[†]	0.119[†]	0.175[†]	0.30[†]3	**0.116[†]**
		1:4	0.999	0.163[†]	0.174[†]	**0.159[†]**	0.422[†]	0.174[†]
		1:6	0.999	0.251[†]	0.234[†]	0.232[†]	0.444[†]	**0.224[†]**
	Logistic regression	1:2	0.180	0.103[†]	**0.098[†]**	0.102[†]	0.104[†]	0.100[†]
		1:4	0.158	0.150	0.147	0.153	**0.144**	0.149
		1:6	0.150	**0.138**	0.140	**0.138**	0.142	0.139

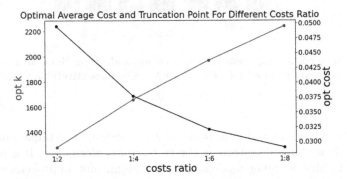

Fig. 3. Optimal average truncation cutoff and cost for different costs ratio (*FP* and *FN* costs respectively), using Random Forest ranking. A clear trade-off is evident - COVID-19 Tests data.

Finally, viewing Fig. 4, across the examined time period, the optimal and real truncation points share a relatively similar trend, with Pearson correlation of 0.75. Moreover, the predicted truncation points result in smaller costs, when compared to the costs incurred by the real ones. The differences are statistically significant using paired t-test, with $p < 0.05$. In other words, it is evident that using the proposed cost function, not only that the number of people to be recommended for COVID-19 testing would be better correlated with the real number of people infected with the virus on the corresponding day, but the overall costs incurred from our recommendations would be significantly lower.

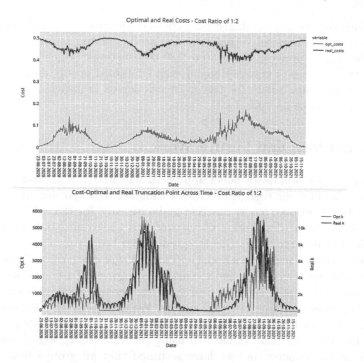

Fig. 4. Top: Real and optimal truncation costs. Bottom: Real and optimal truncation points. Both obtained using Logistic Regression ranking algorithm and costs ratio of 1:2 (*FP* and *FN* costs respectively).

Credit Card Fraud Detection. It is evident from Fig. 5 that the machine learning models predict cutoff points with similar distribution to the optimal ones. That is to say, for each examined group, the number of recommended transactions to be checked against frauds is very close to the optimal amount of

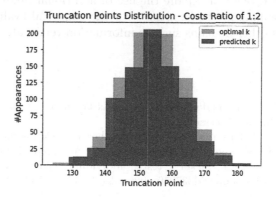

Fig. 5. Distribution of predicted and optimal truncation points, using Random Forest ranking algorithm, Ridge Regression model and costs ratio of 1:2 (*FP* and *FN* costs respectively) - Credit Card Fraud Detection data.

transactions to be checked. Hence the expected incurred costs will be relatively low. Likewise, it is noticeable that both the predicted and optimal cutoff points are ranging from approximately 130 to 180 transactions, which is less than half of the initial number of transactions in each examined group, described earlier. Performing checkups solely for the most suspicious transactions may further assist in saving time and efforts.

7 Conclusions and Future Work

In this paper, we propose a novel approach, which treats a candidate screening process as an error cost problem and thus attempts to minimize this cost. Accordingly, we propose a cost function and a pipeline for ranked list truncation that learns the score distribution of relevant and irrelevant candidates and uses a machine learning model to directly predict the best truncation cut-off point for a given group of candidates and a specific *FP:FN* costs ratio. This approach is generic and thus can be applied to various categories of a candidate screening process. We show that it achieves nearly optimal error-cost performance for two case studies using various prediction models. We then perform a sensitivity analysis of the proposed pipeline settings, showing a strong and stable performance across a range of cost ratio values and using several ranking algorithms.

While in our experiments we have assumed that all groups have the same number of candidates, the future work could address the issue of dealing with candidate lists of variable size. Moreover, as there exist screening processes, which involve incremental admission decisions, identifying the cost-optimal number of accepted candidates at each admission step may be needed. Potential future work may also improve the efficiency of the training procedure, which currently iterates over all possible truncation thresholds to find the optimal cost of each group. In addition to that, since threshold finding is important topic in Machine Learning Community, the proposed method can be compared to various threshold selection techniques from literature, such as the ones presented in [5,7,18]. Finally, one can explore the use of additional prediction algorithms and candidate ranking methods, along with the empirical evaluation on candidate screening in other domains such as information retrieval.

References

1. Kaggle - credit card fraud detection data set (2017). https://www.kaggle.com/mlg-ulb/creditcardfraud. Accessed 22 July 2021
2. Israel COVID-19 data tracker - daily number of sick people (2021). https://datadashboard.health.gov.il/COVID-19/general. Accessed 21 July 2021
3. Israel COVID-19 data tracker - tested individuals (2021). https://data.gov.il/dataset/covid-19/resource/d337959a-020a-4ed3-84f7-fca182292308. Accessed 21 July 2021
4. The world's largest data science community with powerful tools and resources (2021). https://www.kaggle.com. Accessed 19 July 2021

5. Arampatzis, A., Kamps, J., Robertson, S.: Where to stop reading a ranked list? Threshold optimization using truncated score distributions. In: Proceedings of the 32nd International ACM SIGIR Conference on Research and Development in Information Retrieval, pp. 524–531 (2009)
6. Awad, M., Khanna, R.: Support vector regression. In: Awad, M., Khanna, R. (eds.) Efficient Learning Machines, pp. 67–80. Springer, Cham (2015). https://doi.org/10.1007/978-1-4302-5990-9_4
7. Bahri, D., Tay, Y., Zheng, C., Metzler, D., Tomkins, A.: Choppy: cut transformer for ranked list truncation. In: Proceedings of the 43rd International ACM SIGIR Conference on Research and Development in Information Retrieval, pp. 1513–1516 (2020)
8. Benesty, J., Chen, J., Huang, Y., Cohen, I.: Pearson correlation coefficient. In: Cohen, I., Huang, Y., Chen, J., Benesty, J. (eds.) Noise Reduction in Speech Processing, pp. 1–4. Springer, Heidelberg (2009). https://doi.org/10.1007/978-3-642-00296-0_5
9. Bishop, C.M., Tipping, M.E.: Bayesian regression and classification. NATO Sci. Ser. sub Ser. III Comput. Syst. Sci. **190**, 267–288 (2003)
10. Breiman, L.: Random forests. Mach. Learn. **45**(1), 5–32 (2001). https://doi.org/10.1023/a:1010933404324
11. le Cessie, S., Goeman, J.J., Dekkers, O.M.: Who is afraid of non-normal data? Choosing between parametric and non-parametric tests. Eur. J. Endocrinol. **182**(2), E1–E3 (2020)
12. Cucinotta, D., Vanelli, M.: WHO declares COVID-19 a pandemic. Acta Bio Medica: Atenei Parmensis **91**(1), 157 (2020)
13. Dixon, P.M.: Bootstrap resampling. In: Encyclopedia of Environmetrics, vol. 1 (2006)
14. Friedman, J., Hastie, T., Tibshirani, R., et al.: The Elements of Statistical Learning. Springer Series in Statistics, vol. 1. Springer, New York (2001). https://doi.org/10.1007/978-0-387-21606-5
15. Järvelin, K., Kekäläinen, J.: Cumulated gain-based evaluation of IR techniques. ACM Trans. Inf. Syst. (TOIS) **20**(4), 422–446 (2002)
16. Korstanje, J.: The random forest. In: Korstanje, J. (ed.) Advanced Forecasting with Python, pp. 179–191. Springer, Cham (2021). https://doi.org/10.1007/978-1-4842-7150-6_14
17. Lee, Y.G., Kim, S.Y.: Introduction to Statistics, pp. 342–351. Yulgokbooks, Korea (2008)
18. Lien, Y.C., Cohen, D., Croft, W.B.: An assumption-free approach to the dynamic truncation of ranked lists. In: Proceedings of the 2019 ACM SIGIR International Conference on Theory of Information Retrieval, pp. 79–82 (2019)
19. Manmatha, R., Rath, T., Feng, F.: Modeling score distributions for combining the outputs of search engines. In: Proceedings of the 24th Annual International ACM SIGIR Conference on Research and Development in Information Retrieval, pp. 267–275 (2001)
20. Marquardt, D.W., Snee, R.D.: Ridge regression in practice. Am. Stat. **29**(1), 3–20 (1975)
21. Müller, B., Reinhardt, J., Strickland, M.T.: Neural Networks: An Introduction. Springer, Heidelberg (2012)
22. Peng, C.Y.J., Lee, K.L., Ingersoll, G.M.: An introduction to logistic regression analysis and reporting. J. Educ. Res. **96**(1), 3–14 (2002)
23. Ryan, G.J., Ryan, S.W., Ryan, C.M., Munro, W.A., Robinson, D.: Search engine, US Patent 6,421,675, 16 July 2002

24. Skaik, Y.A.: The bread and butter of statistical analysis "t-test": uses and misuses (2015)
25. Sokolova, M., Japkowicz, N., Szpakowicz, S.: Beyond accuracy, F-score and ROC: a family of discriminant measures for performance evaluation. In: Sattar, A., Kang, B. (eds.) AI 2006. LNCS (LNAI), vol. 4304, pp. 1015–1021. Springer, Heidelberg (2006). https://doi.org/10.1007/11941439_114
26. Stiburek, S., Vlk, A., Švec, V.: Study of the success and dropout in the higher education policy in Europe and V4 countries. Hung. Educ. Res. J. **7**(1), 43–56 (2017)
27. Zhang, E., Zhang, Y.: Average precision. In: Liu, L., Özsu, M.T. (eds.) Encyclopedia of Database Systems, pp. 192–193. Springer, Boston (2009). https://doi.org/10.1007/978-0-387-39940-9_482

Design of IoT Based Patient Health Monitoring System

Yerlan Zaitin[1]($\boxtimes$) (iD), Octavian Postolache[2] (iD), and Madina Mansurova[1] (iD)

[1] Al-Farabi Kazakh National University, Almaty, Kazakhstan
yzaitin@gmail.com
[2] ISCTE-Instituto Universitário de Lisboa, Lisbon, Portugal
Octavian.Adrian.Postolache@iscte-iul.pt

Abstract. Internet of Things allows health care providers to break out of traditional clinical settings. Home monitoring systems allow to monitor the health of patients when they are not in the doctor's office. Many years of research have shown that remote monitoring of patients is one of the most effective treatments for chronic diseases such as diabetes, heart failure and chronic obstructive pulmonary disease (COPD), but also increases patient participation and reduces emergency admissions. Assisted and individually adapted environments will be possible through the introduction of technologies that provide individual medical care to anyone living in an environment of their choice. In this article, we consider several requirements for the development of such systems, in particular sensors for automatic detection of physiological parameters of the patient's health data which will be send to the cloud where in real time artificial intelligence will process the data and present it to the doctor in the form of infographics that can be easily analyzed, the mobile app where a patient can see own health parameters and contact with a doctor and the website where the doctor, based on real-time data, can examine the patient and, in an emergency, contact with a patient and warn against future diseases.

Keywords: Component · Health monitoring · Internet of Things · Physiological signs monitoring · Ambient assisted living · Telemedicine

1 Introduction

The Internet of Things provides a continuous platform for facilitating interaction between people and various physical and virtual entities, including individual healthcare domains. The lack of access to medical resources, the growing number of older people with chronic diseases and their need for remote monitoring, rising medical costs and the desire for telemedicine in developing countries make IoT an interesting topic in healthcare. In addition to providing specialized medical services to improve the quality of life, IoT can reduce the burden on the sanitation system [1]. The integration of traditional urban infrastructure is the most important and will be made possible using the smart city concept and IoT technology. IoT technology uses city sensors for social and economic

© The Author(s), under exclusive license to Springer Nature Singapore Pte Ltd. 2022
E. Szczerbicki et al. (Eds.): ACIIDS 2022, CCIS 1716, pp. 751–762, 2022.
https://doi.org/10.1007/978-981-19-8234-7_58

development to develop smart cities and their services. Therefore, the system governance structure requires collaboration between the public and private sectors for smart city infrastructure. In addition to engaging the information technology (IT) sector, he has made it very efficient with the concept of smart cities. When we mention smart city concepts, many definitions can be photographed because the definition of smart cities is inherently unclear and pre-defined definitions are not enough. With the advent of information and communication technologies (ICT), cities need to invest in human capital to improve their lives, using education, as well as quality of life, rational organization of health care, open and strategic management, effective scientific mobilization, and high sustainability. The safety of residents as well as their high level of privacy are known as smart cities. The need for smart cities has attracted the attention of industry and scientists. This can be demonstrated by considering the investment scenarios of companies such as Siemens, Intel and IBM and further expansion of their investments in the future [2].

Telemedicine has great potential to change the healthcare system by reducing the number of patients in medical institutions and moving many consultations and examinations to a virtual environment. There, medical staff can provide all the necessary assistance and information for many patients through a single control center, regardless of location. The fields of telemedicine have different goals to ensure maximum effectiveness in today's healthcare system. Thus, patients with rare diseases can receive qualified advice from a specialist in another region of the country. This is important because a medical diagnosis obtained directly from the patient at home significantly reduces hospital costs and allows for more effective treatment tailored to the patient. Real-time monitoring is indicated for heart failure, asthma attacks, etc. can be used to prevent many emergency conditions, such as. In a hospital where there is a shortage of specialists in the intensive care unit, there may be several specialists who can remotely monitor patients and report to a specialist who can care for patients [3].

Ambient Assisted Life (AAL) builds on top of these smart home services and requires the reuse of better technology and monitoring tools. These systems are visible through an ecosystem of wearable and non-wearable medical sensors, wireless sensors and drive networks (WSANs) and software applications that, when interconnected, provide a complete view of the patient's health status for specific environmental conditions and provide the necessary medical services.. That is, the AAL system is based on the architecture of the IoT system, which is aimed at healthcare. The information received from the sensor network is sent to the coordinate node/gateway, and then to the cloud centers, where the data is processed by data analysis algorithms [4].

Over the past decade, various types of AAL-based smart home designs have been published in the literature. Many projects offer effective solutions to increase human independence in the living environment by monitoring daily life activity or physiological state in real time using wearable smart sensors. However, few are considering implementing wearable smart sensors for patient monitoring solutions. Patients may not be comfortable wearing smart sensors and will not wear smart sensors for long periods of time. For this reason, it is important to monitor patients with sensors that collect patient data without their presence.

This work aims to consider the components required to create a system that collects physiological data from patients without the involvement of the healthcare system. This study aims to discuss the solutions for remote patient monitoring presented in the literature describing vital sign monitoring systems and identifying the most important physiological parameters that need to be considered to ensure a viable diagnosis of health status, and create a prototype of a long- acting system and the methods for detecting early changes in patients' health parameters, which could help to provide measures for disease prevention. The novel diagnostic system will help to implement a relatively simple and inexpensive health control of a patient over a long period.

This paper is organized as follows: after this introductory section, Sect. 2 addresses related works of the monitoring systems and considers the most important vital signs that should be monitored in order to give an appropriate assessment of an individual's health conditions; Sect. 3 refers to the architecture of the monitoring system; Sect. 4 Provides information about the devices required to implement the monitoring system; Sect. 5 concludes the paper.

2 Related Work

Up to now, several researchers have considered several ways and methods of remote monitoring of patients. Online monitoring systems, which have a capability of real-time monitoring and classification of patient behavior and health status, have been proposed by several authors [5, 6]. The paper [2] describes various types of sensors that measure physiological parameters. However, a large number of existing studies in the broader literature have examined hand-held or wearable sensors. Patients may not wear such sensors for long periods of time. Another disadvantage of these sensors is that the battery does not last long. The paper [11] provides a review of various existing solutions for monitoring systems by using low-power consumption and low cost sensor nodes.

Blood pressure monitoring (BPT) is a telemedicine strategy that allows patients to remotely send blood pressure data and additional health information from home or public places to a doctor's office or hospital. Several randomized controlled trials provide compelling evidence that regular and long-term use of BPT in combination with teleconsultation and control of controlled patients is associated with a significant reduction in blood pressure compared to conventional treatment, especially in high-risk patients. Parati G. et al. [15] demonstrated the following modern devices for remote measurement of blood pressure, for example: automated devices (wired or wireless); multi- parameter monitoring devices (e.g. single-channel ECG, pulse oximetry, body temperature, blood glucose, drug treatment reception), also known as "medical tights"; wireless smartphone applications (paired with an external phone) wireless blood pressure monitor or smartphone cuff device); wearable monitors for long-term monitoring (e.g. wrist) tonometers or digital plethysmographs.

Mobile health (mHealth) technologies play a key role in epidemiological situations such as the ongoing COVID-19 epidemic, allowing citizens to take control of their health at home and at home. Despite the quarantine, the patient is in constant contact with doctors. Particular attention should be paid to self-control vital parameters such as blood oxygen saturation (SpO2). Abnormal values are warning signs of possible infection

COVID-19. Casalino G. [16] proposed a method of non-contact measurement of oxygen saturation in the blood, based on a combination of signal processing and computer vision techniques. This method developed a method of measuring SpO2 by capturing short videos of the patient's face and monitoring the changes in the cardiovascular tissue in some areas of the face.

The method introduced by Cosoli G. et al. [7] has the advantage of monitoring the cardiological parameters of patients using capacitive electrodes and conductive fabrics in the bathroom, in the toilet or embedded in armchairs. These solutions for remote monitoring (employing sensing electrodes distributed on the living environment furniture) attempt to reduce the healthcare costs, with a pivotal role played by wireless communication systems enabling data transfer to the hospital/the healthcare server or, more generally, to a specific base station or to a smartphone application;

The field of smart clothing is experiencing rapid development both in clinical and sport applications. Coosemans et al. [12] implemented an intracorporeal ECG monitoring system for children at high risk of sudden infant death syndrome (SIDS). Stainless steel electrodes are woven and woven into an elastic band; circuit inductively (132 kHz) through two coils (also used for data transfer): the receiver embedded in a large external and flexible circuit to overcome inconsistencies with movements (connected to electrodes with buttons) to the sensor interface. Sampling rate: 300 Hz), includes all electronics for data processing and wireless transmission (16.5 kbps, distance from external coil up to 18 cm). Le et al. [13] also used coils to inductively power a wireless ECG monitoring system.

With the advent of information and communication technologies (ICT), the use of knowledge and quality of life of urban residents to invest in human capital to improve their lives, rational organization of health care, open and strategic management, effective mobilization, high stability, security… residents and their privacy with a high degree of privacy, known as smart cities, is explained in Zhang Hui's work on smart city and IoT system communication [26].

This technology is gradually introduced in our cities. For example, capital of Kazakhstan Nur-Sultan where is the branching of Smart City 'healthcare' emerging. What we cannot say about other cities making the project promising in the field of healthcare described in SIST conference [27] and in a journal article [28].

We identify that such a system should be able to allow patients to stay at home during remote check-up and reassurance thanks to physiological measurements taken twice an hour and remotely evaluated by healthcare professionals at least three times a day. This will reduce the number of patients that need to go to the clinics and increase the commitment of the patients with their rehabilitation process. Such a system was designed to allow the rural population to remotely monitor and analyze their health with the help of highly qualified specialists.

3   Architecture of IoT Monitoring System

The IoT diagnostic system architecture is described in Fig. 1. It is described by a combination of a three-tier architecture with reception, network and application applications, as well as a cloud architecture. In the architecture of the IoT diagnostic system, cloud computing seems convenient, as it provides flexibility and scalability for users and developers [17]. Users can access services such as servers, databases, data processing and storage tools. Developers can work and use the necessary data generation, artificial intelligence and visualization tools through the cloud. The design of the IoT diagnostic system depends on the system functionality, power consumption, durability, cost, etc., which contributes to the trade-off between them [18–21].

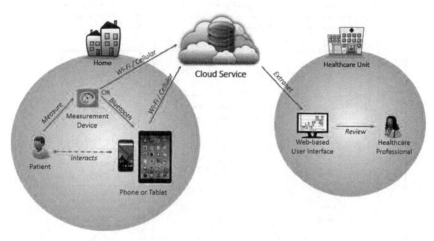

Fig. 1. IoT monitoring system architecture

System flowcharts are a way of showing how data is transferred in a system and how decisions are made to manage events. Symbols are used to indicate this. They are interconnected to show what happens to the data and where it goes. The a) - flowchart of the monitoring system on Fig. 2 is flow chart from patient side. Shows how mobile application works. Checking connection, reading data from sensors and sending to the cloud. Where it will be processing and warn back as AI monitoring or doctor's feedback. It works still Bluetooth works. The b) flowchart on Fig. 2 – flow chart from doctor's side. Shows how site works. After checking connection with internet takes data from cloud and after processing analyze it. And sends feedback to patients. Works still monitoring works. The c) flowchart on Fig. 2 – flow charts from the system administrator shows how monitoring system works. After connection from patient's and doctor's side takes data from server and starts processing. Where data will go through several stages 1. Digitization of analog data. 2. Rounding (some data). 3. Distribution. After what it will be sending to Doctor and AI monitoring system where after analyzing data comes back to patient. Works in real time while doctor or patient stops.

A data flow diagram (DFD) shows the information flow of the system we are implementing. The Fig. 3 below shows the DFD level 0 of the monitoring system. PSMS –Patient Smart Monitoring System based on two entities and their mutual communication. DFD has two additional databases. One for patient information and health data and second for doctor's information. System has many processes described as one (SPMS). Main purpose of SPMS process is connection and processing data. DFD has two main data flowing between entity and database. They are Patient health and Patient's/Doctor's

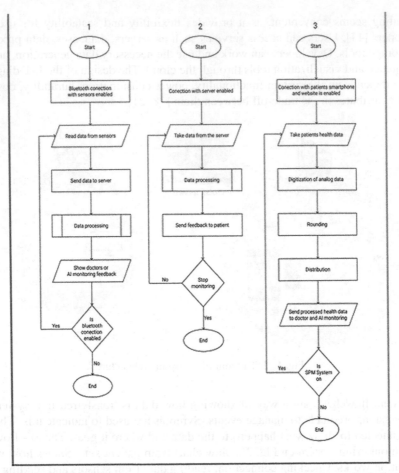

Fig. 2. Flowchart of the monitoring system a) patient side flowchart, b) medical doctor side flowchart, c) system administrator side flowchart

info. PSMS process using "PatientDB" to warn data about patient health (Heart rate, saturation, temp…) and information (Full name, phone number, adress, e-mail), also taking data about doctor info (Full name, position, address…) from "DoctorDB" to warn to patient.

The Fig. 4 below shows the DFD level 1 of the monitoring system. This DFD shows more detailed process work in PSM System. There one more entity as "Ambulance service" and divided PSMS process as "AI monitoring" and "Data processing". System still works as described in DFD level 0 but because of adding new entity became the reason for the appearance of three data flows as "Call" and "Notification" to inform "Ambulance service" and "Help" to illustrate work of ambulance. PSMS is 'doctor' and 'AI monitoring' which takes data after processing and warning as feedback from doctor or as simple data of health by AI monitoring with some recommendation.

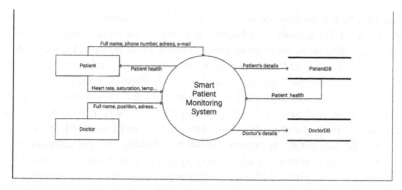

Fig. 3. Data flow diagram level 0 of the PSMS

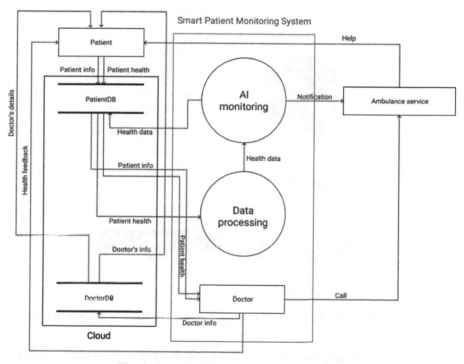

Fig. 4. Data flow diagram level 1 of the PSMS

4   Implementation and Results

In this work we designed and developed the mobile APP because of its ability of connecting to the microcontrollers and to the cloud services with Bluetooth and wi-fi where a patient can see own health parameters, send his/her data in real-time to the doctor and contact with a doctor. 1st page – Welcome page where user (Patient) takes main information. Right here user will be given a choice to Sign Up if he is recently downloaded or to Sign In if he has an account already. There he can change the language (example: Russian, Kazakh). By default, it is English language. 2nd page – Sign Up page where new user for creating an account input 3 information about himself. First is Name (username), second is E-mail address and third Create password (and confirm it). After that he needs to agree with the "Terms of Service" and "Privacy Policy" by radio button. Also, he will have a chance to go back or if it does not need to continue by clicking right bottom button (Fig. 5, 6 and 7). 3rd page is Sign In page where user who has already account can Log In by entering his Name (username) and Password. If he will forget his password, he can always restore password by clicking 'Forgot password?' button. Also, there is a 'Remember me' radio button by clicking user can only once log in and after that enter to the system without authorization. Also, there are 'language change' and 'go back' buttons.

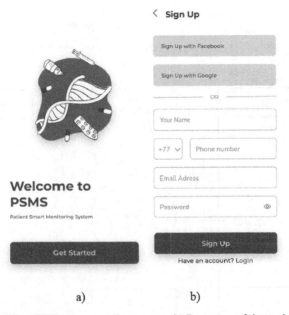

a)   b)

Fig. 5. a) Mobile APP Prototype welcome page b) Prototype of the registration page.

In this work we designed and developed the website where the doctor, based on real-time data, can examine the patient and, in an emergency, contact with a patient and warn against future diseases. Login page. It consists of 2 text boxes, where users will be able to input their email and password (Fig. 8).

A utility model has been created for this project, with the help of which the patient will collect analyzes, after that all the results will be sent to a database, from where, using a website or a mobile application, the doctor will be able to monitor Patient physiological parameters.

To create this device, we decided to use the ESP8266 NodeMCU v3 microcontroller, since ESP8266 is already installed in this board, which will allow us to send information via the Internet. In addition, one of the advantages of this board is the presence of an I2C

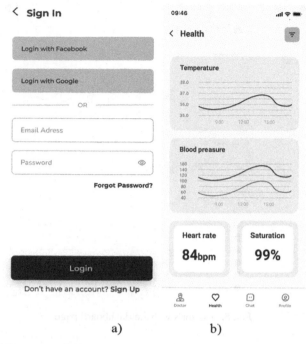

a)   b)

Fig. 6. a) Prototype of the sign in page b) Prototype of Patient Health Status page

Fig. 7. Prototype of the main menu

bus, which allows us to connect useful and accurate sensors, such as the MAX30102 sensor, which can accurately determine the heartbeat and blood saturation. Another sensor that also uses the I2C bus for connecting to NodeMCU v3 is the MAX30205. It can measure a person's temperature and does it with an accuracy of 0.1 C [22–25]. In order to record data using these sensors, the patient simply needs to fix all the sensors on his arm, and then press the button, which will be located on the body of the utility model. After that, all the necessary data will be collected within a minute and sent to the database. We decided to use FireBase for the database, since its API is very convenient to use for all the tasks that we need, which include sending and reading data from a mobile application, a website and a microcontroller [26].

Fig. 8. Doctor's website dashboard page

5   Discussion and Conclusion

In the first stage of our research, we created architecture of the Monitoring system based on the IoT method and includes a three-tier architecture with perception, network, application layers, and cloud-based architecture. This work examines and analyzes the requirements for remote patient monitoring. The flow of data in the system is represented by a DFD diagram. The mobile application and the website were designed and developed. Through the mobile application, patients can see their physiological condition and information about the doctor. They can also consult a doctor. With the help of the Web application, the doctor can monitor the patient's health and receive a notification when the patient's health deteriorates. The devices needed to collect physiological data from patients were identified. The NodeMCU V3 ESP8266 microcontroller does not require much energy and allows you to connect additional sensors. Sensors such as MAX30102 and DHT22 (AM2302) allow simple and easy retrieval of important physiological data from patients.

At the next stage, in coordination with health care organizations, the system will be tested and experimented with remote monitoring of the health of volunteer patients. Data will be collected and analyzed to see how effective the developed patient monitoring system is.

Acknowledgment. This work was funded by Committee of Science of Republic of Kazakhstan AP09260767 «Development of an intellectual information and analytical system for assessing the health status of students in Kazakhstan» (2021–2023).

References

1. Kashani, M.H., et al.: A systematic review of IoT in healthcare: applications, techniques, and trends. J. Netw. Comput. Appl. **192**, 103164 (2021)
2. Poongodi, M., Sharma, A., Hamdi, M., Maode, M., Chilamkurti, N.: Smart healthcare in smart cities: wireless patient monitoring system using IoT. J. Supercomput. **77**(11), 12230–12255 (2021). https://doi.org/10.1007/s11227-021-03765-w
3. Romanovs, A., Sultanovs, E., Buss, E., Merkuryev, Y., Majore, G.: Challenges and solutions for resilient telemedicine services. In: 2020 IEEE 8th Workshop on Advances in Information, Electronic and Electrical Engineering (AIEEE), pp. 1–7. IEEE, April 2021
4. Jacob, R.M., Postolache, O., Cercas, F.: Physiological and behavior monitoring systems for smart healthcare environments: a review. Sensors **20**(8), 2186 (2020)
5. Baig, M.M., Hosseini, H.G., Lindén, M.: Machine learning-based clinical decision support system for early diagnosis from real-time physiological data. In: 2016 IEEE Region 10 Conference (TENCON), pp. 2943–2946. IEEE (2016)
6. Zhang, K., Ling, W.: Health monitoring of human multiple physiological parameters based on wireless remote medical system. IEEE Access **8**, 71146–71159 (2020)
7. Cosoli, G., et al.: Wireless ECG and cardiac monitoring systems: state of the art, available commercial devices and useful electronic components. Measurement **177**, 109243 (2021)
8. Angelucci, A., et al.: Smart textiles and sensorized garments for physiological monitoring: a review of available solutions and techniques. Sensors **21**(3), 814 (2021)
9. Tamura, T.: Home geriatric physiological measurements. Physiol. Meas. **33**(10), R47 (2012)
10. Souri, A., et al.: A new machine learning-based healthcare monitoring model for student's condition diagnosis in Internet of Things environment. Soft Comput. **24**, 17111–17121 (2020)
11. Sharma, B., Koundal, D.: Cattle health monitoring system using wireless sensor network: a survey from innovation perspective. Inst. Eng. Technol. IET Wirel. Sens. Syst. **8**(4), 143–151 (2018)
12. Coosemans, J., Hermans, B., Puers, R.: Integrating wireless ECG monitoring in textiles. Sens. Actuators A Phys. **130–131**, 48–53 (2006). https://doi.org/10.1016/j.sna.2005.10.052
13. Le, T., Huerta, M., Moravec, A., Cao, H.: Wireless passive monitoring of electrocardiogram in firefighters, in: IMBioc 2018 - 2018 IEEE/MTT-S International Microwave Biomedical Conference, pp. 121–123 (2018). https://doi.org/10.1109/IMBIOC.2018.8428884
14. https://www.lucidchart.com/pages/er-diagrams/#section_0
15. Parati, G., et al.: Home blood pressure telemonitoring in the 21st century. J. Clin. Hypertens. **20**(7), 1128–1132 (2018)
16. Casalino, G., Castellano, G., Zaza, G.: A mHealth solution for contact-less self-monitoring of blood oxygen saturation. In: 2020 IEEE Symposium on Computers and Communications (ISCC), pp. 1–7. IEEE (2020)
17. Mansurova, M., Barakhnin, V., Khibatkhanuly, Y., Pastushkov, I.: Named entity extraction from semi-structured data using machine learning algorithms. In: Nguyen, N.T., Chbeir, R., Exposito, E., Aniorté, P., Trawiński, B. (eds.) ICCCI 2019. LNCS (LNAI), vol. 11684, pp. 58–69. Springer, Cham (2019). https://doi.org/10.1007/978-3-030-28374-2_6
18. Mansurova, M., Alimzhanov, E., Dadykina, E.: Parallel algorithm of RDF data compression and decompression based on MapReduce Hadoop technology
19. Kuņicina, N., Zabašta, A., Bruzgiene, R., Čaiko, J., Patļins, A.: The resilience of automatic wireless meters reading for distribution networks in smart city model. In: 2018 IEEE 59th International Scientific Conference on Power and Electrical Engineering of Riga Technical University (RTUCON 2018): Conference Proceedings, Latvia, Riga, Piscataway, 12–14 November 2018, pp. 1–6. IEEE (2018). ISBN 978-1-5386-6904-4. e-ISBN 978-1-5386-6903-7. https://doi.org/10.1109/RTUCON.2018.8659889

20. Zabašta, A., Kuņicina, N., Kondratjevs, K., Patļins, A., Čaiko, J.: Development of sensor system for legacy and smart municipal systems infrastructure control. In: Proceeding of EPE'18 ECCE Europe, Latvia, Riga, 18–20 September 2018, pp. 1–6 (2018). ISBN 9789075815290
21. Ribickis, L., et al.: Sensor network technology applications in the water supply and transport systems
22. Zabašta, A., Šeļmanovs-Plešs, V., Kuņicina, N., Ribickis, L.: Wireless sensor networks for optimumisation of district heating. In: Proceedings of 15th International Power Electronics and MotionControl Conference (EPE PEMC 2012 ECCE), Serbia, Novi Sad, 4–6 September 2012, pp. 1–5. IEEE, Piscataway (2012). ISBN 978-1-4673-1970-6. e-ISBN 978-1-4673-1971-3. https://doi.org/10.1109/EPEPEMC.2012.6397233
23. Kondratjevs, K., Zabašta, A., Kuņicina, N., Ribickis, L. development of pseudo autonomous wireless sensor monitoring system for water distribution network. In: IEEE 23rd International Symposium on Industrial Electronics (ISIE 2014): Proceedings, Turkey, Istanbul, 1–4 June 2014, pp. 1454–1458. IEEE, Piscataway (2014). ISBN 978-1-4799-2399-1. ISSN 2163-5145. https://doi.org/10.1109/ISIE.2014.6864828
24. Kuņicina, N., Zabašta, A., Bruzgiene, R., Čaiko, J., Patļins, A.: The resilience of automatic wireless meters reading for distribution networks in smart city model. In: 2018 IEEE 59th International Scientific Conference on Power and Electrical Engineering of Riga Technical University (RTUCON2018): Conference Proceedings, Latvia, Riga, 12–14 November 2018, pp. 1–6.. IEEE, Piscataway (2018). ISBN 978-1-5386-6904-4. e-ISBN 978-1-5386-6903-7. https://doi.org/10.1109/RTUCON.2018.8659889
25. Moroney, L.: The firebase realtime database. In: The Definitive Guide to Firebase, pp. 51–71. Apress, Berkeley (2017)
26. Zhang, H., et al.: SafeCity: Toward safe and secured data management design for IoT-enabled smart city planning. IEEE Access 8, 145256–145267 (2020)
27. Dubirova, Z., Mendybayev, B.: Managing the transformation of relations between the state, the city and citizens on the example of iKomek109-digital service model of Nur-Sultan City. In: 2021 IEEE International Conference on Smart Information Systems and Technologies (SIST). IEEE (2021)
28. Zholdas, N., Mansurova, M., Postolache, O., Kalimoldayev, M., Sarsembayeva, T.: A personalized mHealth monitoring system for children and adolescents with T1 diabetes by utilizing IoT sensors and assessing physical activities. Int. J. Comput. Commun. Control 17(3), 4558 (2022). https://doi.org/10.15837/ijccc.2022.3.4558

Author Index

Printed in the United States
by Baker & Taylor Publisher Services